INTERNATIONAL MOVEMENT OF CHILDREN

OF CHILDREN

LAW PRACTICE AND PROCEDURE

Nigel Lowe, Professor of Law, Cardiff University Law School, Wales

Mark Everall QC, 1 Hare Court, Temple

Michael Nicholls, 1 Hare Court, Temple

ƒ Family Law

2004

Published by
Jordan Publishing Limited
21 St Thomas Street
Bristol BS1 6JS

British Library Cataloguing-in-Publication Data
A catalogue record for this book is available from the British Library.

ISBN 0 85308 725 3

Typeset by Jordan Publishing Limited
Printed by MPG Books Ltd, Bodmin, Cornwall

FOREWORD

When the relationship between parents deteriorates to the point where they separate or are about to separate, children may become particularly vulnerable, even in purely domestic situations. When, in addition, the separation involves the crossing of borders, the vulnerability of children may be significantly compounded by issues of what is known as 'private international law'. With globalisation and regional integration on the rise, ever more children and their parents are likely to be caught in the intricacies of conflicts of jurisdiction and judgments relating to the long-term welfare of children, and of different laws applicable to parental responsibility.

International co-operation has, therefore, become indispensable, in two respects: first, to resolve these issues of conflicts of jurisdiction, applicable law and recognition and enforcement of foreign judgments; secondly, to provide a framework for close co-operation between courts and other authorities in order to discover the whereabouts of children, provide information about the child's current situation and background to foreign courts or authorities seeking to protect the child, as well as facilitate agreed solutions.

While on the European continent a tradition of over a century exists of resolving the former issues through international Conventions – until recently, without too much attention being paid to issues of close judicial and administrative co-operation – the United Kingdom and other common law countries have long relied on their, often similar, domestic legislation. The United Kingdom chose not to join the 1902 and 1961 Hague Conventions on the Protection of Children, and became only relatively recently engaged in the international legislative process – to find itself now confronted with an almost overwhelming variety of world-wide and European legal instruments. On the other hand, the United Kingdom and other common law countries have been strong and successful advocates for the inclusion in these new instruments of frameworks for judicial and administrative co-operation. Also, courts and Central Authorities in the United Kingdom have been singularly bold and effective in ensuring the taking of measures to protect children in cross-border situations.

This book gives a full picture of the issues and available legal solutions concerning the international movement of children, in particular from and towards the United Kingdom, notably England and Wales. It deals with four central themes: jurisdiction; the lawful cross-border movement of children; their unlawful movement; and international access. It analyses, for each theme, the relevant legal sources: national, bilateral, European (Council of Europe and European Union), and world-wide (United Nations and Hague Conference on Private International Law), as well as the inter-relationships between these sources. Moreover, it provides insightful background material on, and parallels in, other jurisdictions (including the United States and other common law jurisdictions).

It is written with meticulous precision and reflects a remarkable effort to take into account the latest developments. Throughout this book the reader will sense the authors' deep drive to penetrate into the real practical problems children and their parents face; consistent with this approach, the authors also suggest solutions where the available legal sources are silent or ambiguous. This work is an exceptional testimony of many years of dedication by all three writers to the cause of combating international child abduction and of promoting the fundamental right of children to maintain personal relations and direct contact with both parents.

This book needs no recommendation: it is indispensable for legal practitioners – both in and outside the United Kingdom – who may be called upon to help children and their parents when they move across international frontiers.

Hans van Loon
Secretary General of the Hague Conference on Private International Law

PREFACE

This book has had a lengthy gestation period. We originally envisaged a book on international child abduction. But as time went by we realised that the lives of an increasing number of children and their parents were being profoundly affected not only by abduction, but also simply because they were separated (or wanted to be separated) by an international frontier, and that their problems were becoming more, rather than less, complicated as more international bodies tried to solve them. We became concerned at the proliferation of international instruments governing children's cases, so that even apparently straightforward issues were beginning to be complicated by the need to decide which Convention or Regulation should be applied.

So it became apparent to us that, as well as abduction, matters such as jurisdiction, recognition, enforcement and relocation were becoming increasingly important to more than just a few specialists, and that there was no comprehensive, readily available source of information and advice, especially practical advice, about how to deal with them.

We have endeavoured to cover what we think are now the essential topics as best we can, although the need to keep this book to manageable proportions has meant that we have confined ourselves to what is essentially private international law, and have made no attempt to cover immigration, asylum, refugees or international adoption.

We mention the proliferation of international instruments because, until recently, those dealing with the movement of children really had to consider only the 1980 Hague Abduction Convention and, to a lesser extent in England and Wales, the Council of Europe's 1980 Custody Convention. Those Conventions are still important, and the extent to which the international movement of children, particularly unlawful movement, has attracted increasing public attention can be seen by the fact that, at the time of publication, the 1980 Hague Abduction Convention, which is widely and rightly regarded as being a most successful international instrument for the protection of children, now has 74 Contracting States. But it is the newer instruments, their application and their relationship with the older Conventions and with each other which are now becoming the focus of attention – 'conflict of Conventions' is replacing 'conflict of laws'.

Of the newer instruments, the Hague Conference on Private International Law has revisited international protection of children with its 1996 Hague Convention on Jurisdiction, Applicable Law, Recognition, Enforcement and Co-operation in Respect of Parental Responsibility and Measures for the Protection of Children, which came into force in 2002, and which has now been signed by all 15 Member States of the European Union. The Council of Europe has for some time been working towards the harmonisation of family law within its Member States, primarily by promoting common principles and good practice. Those relating to contact are reflected in its latest Convention on Contact Concerning Children, adopted by the Committee of Ministers on 3 May 2002 and opened for signature on 3 May 2003, which sets out the principles to be applied to contact orders and fixes safeguards for the return of children after visiting a parent in another State. But the work of the Council of Europe in the field of family law is being overtaken by an even newer entrant into the arena, the European Union, whose interest in family law is said to be justified by the supposed fetter on free movement and the internal market caused by the lack of a uniform code ascribing jurisdiction in matrimonial causes or commonly held principles of recognition and enforcement of matrimonial orders and orders relating to the children of the spouses.[1] The EU is a particularly powerful player in the field because of its ability to impose its wishes by making regulations which have direct effect in Member States and consequently to prevent them from acting independently. So far as children are concerned, the key Regulation is known as 'Brussels II',[2] which began life as a Convention extending what were the Brussels and Lugano Conventions to matrimonial matters and the children of both spouses involved. But the pace of change is such that Brussels II has now been revised and will come into force on 1 March 2005. The revised Regulation will apply to all children and deals with recognition and enforcement of orders relating to children including child abduction within the Member States.

This increased level of international activity has led to a noticeable and welcome increase in judicial co-operation. In the past judges might have been reticent about speaking to a judge in another State, for fear that it might not be regarded as proper, or might be a breach of due process, but there has been a realisation that children's cases need bold and incisive action to ensure that decisions are made with a minimum of delay and uncertainty. Judicial conferences have been very valuable in bringing judges together to discuss approaches to common problems and to reinforce mutual understanding. Meetings between the judges of the United Kingdom and Germany took place at Dartington in May 1997, at Wüstrau in September 1998, at Edinburgh in September 2000 and Trier in September 2002, and there was a meeting between Francophone judges and the judges of the United Kingdom in Dartington in June 2001. The conclusions (*inter alios* on the importance of holding international conferences for judges, academics and practitioners, the need for effective international judicial co-operation and the desirability of concentrating jurisdiction in a limited number of courts and/or tribunals) at a meeting in De Ruwenberg in June 2000 were affirmed in Washington in September 2000. Both ministers and judges attended the fourth meeting of the Special Commission in March 1991 held at The Hague to discuss the operation of the 1980 Hague Abduction Convention, the judges for the first

---

[1]   Viz under Art 65 EC. But note that the proposed replacement of this provision by draft Arts 111–170 of the proposed Constitution would seem to vest even more wide-ranging powers in the EU to harmonise the laws of Member States.

[2]   Council Regulation (EC) No 1347/2000.

time in their judicial capacities. The necessity for judicial and administrative co-operation will be increased by the general movement away from the principle of courts having continuing jurisdiction to vary their own orders, which is being replaced by the concept of jurisdiction following habitual residence, as provided for in Brussels II and the 1996 Hague Convention.

Children's cases in England and Wales have been affected by domestic, as well as international, changes including the Human Rights Act 1998, although the impact of that Act has not, perhaps, been as great in this area of the law as some might have believed (or wished). Administratively, the creation of CAFCASS to replace the service previously provided by the court welfare officers, guardians ad litem and the Official Solicitor has not been a conspicuous success, one of the first tasks the new management having to face being a judicial review of their employment policy.

Despite the apparent multiplicity of statutes, Conventions and Regulations, the co-operation and the good intentions, some real problems remain unsolved. Current international instruments still do not deal very effectively with access, and there are still conflicts of jurisdiction and conflicts of orders. Furthermore, they do not apply to Islamic States. Continuing to differentiate, as the EU has done in Brussels II, between the children of spouses, step-children and children born out of wedlock will still lead, for the time being, to the prospect of partial recognition of orders and continuing injustice for some unmarried fathers who have failed to obtain parental responsibility. It is also questionable whether the dogged loyalty paid to the 1980 Hague Abduction Convention by courts, especially the English courts, in returning children after an abduction is always truly in their best interests. Nearly three-quarters of 'abductors' are mothers who are the primary carers of their children. A significant number are trying to escape from violence or exploitation, or have husbands or partners involved in organised crime or corruption,[3] from which even the most sophisticated States are unable to guarantee protection. So proceeding on the footing that all removals are axiomatically harmful, and all returns beneficial, in the face of all evidence and experience to the contrary, is not calculated to enhance public confidence. The other deficiencies of the 1980 Hague Abduction Convention, which have been mentioned by many commentators, include its inability to deal with access, and some of the more creative parenting arrangements involving a child living in different countries for appreciable periods of time (known as 'shuttle custody orders').

Other issues which we think need to be addressed in England include the inability of the courts to recognise orders other than those made by other courts in the United Kingdom or States Parties to the 1980 European Custody Convention or the EU Member States, and their inability, at least in theory, to make orders in advance of the arrival of a child, which means that the courts

---

[3] See, in particular, 'The Hague Child Abduction Convention Turns Twenty: Gender Politics and Other Issues', Silberman, *New York University Journal of International Law and Politics*, Vol 33 (Fall 2000), No 1, and 'The Outcomes for Children Returned Following an Abduction' (Reunite Research Unit, September 2003).

of England and Wales are not able to provide the comfort of a 'mirror' or 'back-to-back' order which they themselves might require as a precondition to permitting a child to leave the jurisdiction.

We owe a great debt of gratitude for the help that we have received from a number of people in writing this book. In particular, we would like to thank Sarah Armstrong of the Permanent Bureau of the Hague Conference who wrote the first draft of Chapter 23; The Hon Justice JV Kay, judge of the Family Court of Australia, who wrote the first draft of the section on international relocation under Australian law in Chapter 8 and Professor Robert Spector, Glen R Watson Centennial Professor of Law, University of Oklahoma Law Center, who wrote the first draft of Chapter 5. We are also grateful for the help received from Emily Atkinson, formerly of Cardiff Law School; Sheila Barker of Morton Fraser Solicitors, Edinburgh; The Hon Justice Rod Burr, judge of the Family Court of Australia; Margaret Casey, barrister, New Zealand; Sue Cheesly, Acting Deputy High Court Tipstaff; Dr Anthony Dickey, QC, Western Australia; Monika Ekström of the European Commission; Robert Emery, High Court Tipstaff; Kim Finnis, solicitor, Guildford; Stephen Gocke, Department of Constitutional Affairs; Ananda Hall, Family Division Lawyer (Chambers of the President of the Family Division); Mike Hinchliffe, CAFCASS Legal; Paul King of the English Child Abduction Unit; Paula Lavery of the Northern Ireland Central Authority; Sally Nicholes, solicitor, Middletons, Melbourne; Oliver Parker, Department of Constitutional Affairs; Sarah Parsons of the Consular Division of the Foreign and Commonwealth Office, Head of that Division's Child Abduction Unit; Duncan Ranton, solicitor, solicitor and barrister (Victoria), Kingsley Napley, London; Barbara Schuck of the German Central Authority; Andrea Schulz, First Secretary to the Permanent Bureau of the Hague Conference; Professor Eric Smithburn, University of Notre Dame, Indiana; Professor Brenda Sufrin, University of Bristol; Debbie Taylor, barrister, London; David Truex, solicitor, barrister and solicitor (Australia), International Family Law Chambers, London; and James Young of Cardiff Law School.

We also owe a considerable debt of thanks to Jordan Publishing for their forbearance in waiting for the manuscript and for undertaking numerous last-minute changes. Finally we thank Sharon Willicombe of Cardiff Law School for typing (and re-typing) much of the manuscript.

We have endeavoured to state the law as we understand it to be as at August 2003.

Nigel Lowe
Mark Everall
Michael Nicholls
Autumnal Equinox 2003

CONTENTS

PART I – JURISDICTION

PART III – THE UNLAWFUL MOVEMENT OF CHILDREN

Chapter 21 – INTERNATIONAL ABDUCTIONS: PRACTICE AND PROCEDURE IN ENGLAND AND WALES 463

Chapter 22 – INTERNATIONAL ABDUCTIONS: PRACTICE AND PROCEDURE FOR DEALING WITH INCOMING APPLICATIONS FOR RETURN IN SELECTED OTHER JURISDICTIONS

PART IV – INTERNATIONAL ACCESS

APPENDICES

TABLE OF CASES

References are to paragraph numbers.

TABLE OF STATUTES

References are to paragraph numbers.

TABLE OF STATUTORY INSTRUMENTS AND GUIDANCE

References are to paragraph numbers.

TABLE OF INTERNATIONAL MATERIALS

References are to paragraph numbers.

International Movement of Children

TABLE OF LEGISLATION OF OTHER JURISDICTIONS

References are to paragraph numbers.

PART I

JURISDICTION

Chapter 1

INTRODUCTION AND GENERAL JURISDICTIONAL CONCEPTS

DEFINING JURISDICTION

1.1 'Jurisdiction' is often used to describe a territorial area subject to one system of law, such as England and Wales, Scotland, Northern Ireland or a State in the United States of America, but in the strict sense it means the ability of a court to hear and determine disputes and make valid and enforceable orders. A power which enables a court to make substantive orders, such as an order under s 8 of the Children Act 1989 or a return order under the Hague Convention on the Civil Aspects of International Child Abduction ('the 1980 Hague Abduction Convention') is sometimes referred to as a rule of 'original' or 'direct' jurisdiction. A more limited power, such as the ability to modify existing orders or the ability to fix the conditions for the implementation and exercise of rights of access conferred by Art 11(2) of the 1980 European Convention[1] on Recognition and Enforcement of Decisions concerning Custody of Children ('the 1980 European Custody Convention') is referred to as a rule of 'indirect' jurisdiction. Original jurisdiction is founded upon some connection ('nexus') between the litigants or subject-matter of the litigation and the territory in which the court is situated. In family matters, this nexus may be the nationality, domicile, habitual residence or presence of one or more of the parties or the children in question, which are referred to as 'jurisdictional bases'.

---

[1]   Sometimes known as the Luxembourg Convention, see **19.2**.

LIMITS ON THE ABILITY TO HEAR DISPUTES

1.2 Courts may be constrained in the ability conferred upon them by the various national and international instruments to exercise jurisdiction to hear disputes not only by the requirement for the appropriate jurisdictional base to be satisfied, but also by the existence of other proceedings, or a better claim to exercise jurisdiction, so that the court may not be able to hear the case, or if it does, it may only exercise limited powers. For example, once notice of wrongful removal or retention has been received, Art 16 of the 1980 Hague Abduction Convention prevents the judicial or administrative authorities of a Contracting State from making a decision on the 'merits of rights of custody' until it has been determined that a child will not be returned,[2] and s 16 of the Child Abduction and Custody Act 1985 prevents a court from registering a custody decision under the 1980 European Custody Convention whilst an application under the 1980 Hague Abduction Convention is pending. Modern international instruments dealing with jurisdiction in family matters tend to include a 'protective measures' provision enabling courts to take provisional protective measures even if they do not have jurisdiction over the substance of the matter.[3]

FORUM NON CONVENIENS: LIS ALIBI PENDENS

1.3 The fact that a court has jurisdiction to entertain an application does not necessarily mean that it will do so. The courts of some countries may be obliged to hear and determine proceedings properly brought before them, but others may have the ability to decide not to entertain the proceedings either because there are proceedings in respect of the same issue in progress elsewhere (*lis (alibi) pendens*), or because a court or other body elsewhere is better placed to determine the issue (*forum conveniens*). Courts may also place a limit on the issues they are prepared to entertain. The English High Court has an inherent jurisdiction, supported by statute, to stay or strike out proceedings whenever necessary to prevent injustice.[4] It has also put a voluntary limit on its

---

2   Child Abduction and Custody Act 1985, ss 9 and 20.

3   See, for example, Art 12 of the Council Regulation (EC) No 1347/2000 of 29 May 2000 on jurisdiction and the recognition and enforcement of judgments in matrimonial matters and in matters of parental responsibility for the children of both spouses (sometimes referred to as 'Brussels II') (see OJ L160/19, 30 June 2000) and Art 11 of the 1996 Hague Convention on Jurisdiction, Applicable Law, Recognition, Enforcement and Co-operation in respect of Parental Responsibility and Measures for the Protection of Children.

4   Supreme Court Act 1982, s 49(3); Family Law Act 1986, s 5; *Spiliada Maritime Corp v Cansulex Ltd* [1987] AC 460; *Connelly v RTZ Corp plc* [1998] AC 854; *H v H (Minors) (Forum Conveniens) Nos 1 and 2)* [1993] 1 FLR 958; *Re S (Residence Order: Forum Conveniens)* [1995] 1 FLR 314. A stay will not be granted unless it can be shown that a more appropriate forum is available, but factors in determining a forum issue have been described as 'legion'. In children's cases they include: the child's welfare (an important, but not paramount, consideration); his habitual residence; the efficiency, expedition and economy of the proceedings; the

powers, so that although its inherent, *parens patriae*, jurisdiction (which in the past was usually exercised by making the child concerned a ward of court, but more recently has been exercised without conferring that status),[5] is theoretically limitless, it has declined to exercise its powers to interfere where children are involved in matters concerning immigration, criminal investigations or military discipline.[6]

LIMITS ON THE ABILITY TO MAKE VALID AND ENFORCEABLE ORDERS

1.4 'Jurisdiction' not only describes the limits of a court's power to hear disputes, but also the limits on its power to make orders which require persons to act or refrain from acting in a particular way in relation to others. Put in human rights terms, 'jurisdiction' in the context of family law limits the scope of the State's ability to intervene to protect the right to family life. So, however socially desirable it might be, and however much in the welfare interests of a child, there is no power in court to resolve a dispute by requiring the child's parents to live together, or to see him or her or to prevent a person in whose favour a contact order has been made from leaving the country.

APPLICABLE LAW

1.5 The question of jurisdiction is closely connected with the question of which law the court will apply. This has not caused the courts of England and Wales much difficulty in the past, because if they have jurisdiction in matters relating to the welfare of children, they will apply the *lexi fori*, ie the law of England and Wales, regardless of the nationality, residence or domicile of the child concerned. However, when the United Kingdom ratifies the 1996 Hague Convention on Jurisdiction, Applicable Law, Recognition, Enforcement and Co-operation in respect of Parental Responsibility and Measures for the Protection of Children ('the 1996 Hague Convention'),[7] its courts may, exceptionally, apply or take into consideration the law of another State 'with which the situation has a substantial connection'.[8]

---

availability and cost of legal representation and the availability of legal aid; the availability of witnesses and the cost of travel; the ability of the court to ascertain the wishes and feelings of the child; and the availability of independent reporting facilities – see **3.41**.

[5] *Re Z (A Minor) (Freedom of Publication)* [1997] Fam 1, [1996] 1 FLR 191, CA.

[6] See *Rayden and Jackson on Divorce and Family Matters*, 17th edn (Butterworths, 1997), para 42.7.

[7] On which see **24.56–24.57**.

[8] 1996 Hague Convention, Art 15(2), discussed at **24.30**.

Chapter 2

THE BACKGROUND TO THE FAMILY LAW ACT 1986 AND THE COUNCIL REGULATION

THE BACKGROUND TO THE FAMILY LAW ACT 1986

2.1 Jurisdiction in its strict sense has, until relatively recently, not attracted much attention in children's cases in the United Kingdom, although before the Family Law Act 1986 came into force the rules were diverse and complicated. The different parts of the United Kingdom had different jurisdictional rules. In England and Wales there were different rules of jurisdiction for each of the various proceedings in which disputes about the care and welfare of children could be resolved. Wardship was based on the duty of allegiance and the reciprocal right of protection, so that a child could be made a ward on the basis of British nationality,[1] ordinary residence within England and Wales or mere presence.[2] Custody orders made in matrimonial proceedings depended on the domicile or habitual residence of one of the spouses, and proceedings before magistrates' courts depended on one of the parties or the child residing within the district or area of the court. In Scotland the Court of Session regarded the court of the child's domicile as having pre-eminent jurisdiction. This diversity and complexity sometimes led to uncertainty as to whether an order was validly made, even if the parties had agreed that the court should hear and determine their case, because jurisdiction is something which cannot

---

[1] See *Re P (GE) (An Infant)* [1965] Ch 568 and Lowe and White, *Wards of Court*, 2nd edn (Barry Rose, 1986). But note the remarks of Thorpe LJ about the undesirability of founding jurisdiction solely on nationality in *Al Habtoor v Fotheringham* [2001] EWCA Civ 186, [2001] 1 FLR 951 at [42].

[2] Because aliens within the realm owe a temporary duty of allegiance.

be conferred by consent. There was also the problem that, in England and Wales, orders made in another part of the United Kingdom were treated no differently from an order made in any other part of the world: they were neither recognised nor enforceable.

2.2 The result of this confusion and lack of reciprocity was that there could be, and were, cases where competing orders were made in respect of the same child. No case illustrates this better than *Babington v Babington*,[3] in which the wife, a Scottish domiciliary, left the matrimonial home in Scotland to live in England. She made her 11-year-old daughter, who attended a boarding school in England but who hitherto had spent her holidays with the wife's parents in Scotland, a ward of court.[4] The effect of wardship was to prevent the child going to Scotland without the English court's consent.[5] Meanwhile the husband, also a Scottish domiciliary, petitioned the Scottish Court of Session for what was then known as custody and access. Taking the view that as the court of domicile it had pre-eminent jurisdiction, the Court of Session granted access to the husband. The husband then applied to the English court for leave to take the children out of the jurisdiction. The wife opposed the application, and herself sought leave to take the child to Switzerland for a holiday. Notwithstanding the Scottish order, the English court refused the husband's application and granted the wife's instead. As the English and Scottish Law Commissions subsequently commented:[6]

> 'The English court disregarded the order of the Scottish court and the Scottish court disregarded the fact that the child was an English ward of court. The English court's order prevailed merely because it could be enforced, although the child had stronger connections with Scotland where she was domiciled, had her home, and normally spent her holidays.'

2.3 Although *Babington* caused deep resentment in Scotland, where it was called 'legal kidnapping', it was by no means unknown for an English court order to be frustrated by the Scottish Court of Session. Indeed, at one time it was not uncommon for English wards of court to seek to evade an order restraining their marriage by crossing what was sometimes referred to as the 'tartan curtain'.[7] In *Hoy v Hoy*,[8] a mother obtained an order in English wardship proceedings restraining her 16-year-old daughter, who was domiciled in England but resident in Scotland, from marrying a domiciled Scotsman then resident in Scotland. The Court of Session refused to enforce the order, holding that while it looked upon a High Court order with respect it was

---

3   1955 SC 115.
4   The full effects of wardship are discussed at **6.13** *et seq*.
5   Note that now under Family Law Act 1986, s 38 (discussed at **6.14**) wardship no longer automatically prevents a child going to another part of the United Kingdom in which he or she is habitually resident.
6   Law Com Working Paper No 68/Scot Law Com Memorandum No 23, *Custody of Children – Jurisdiction and Enforcement within the United Kingdom* (1976), para 3.12.
7   See eg (1958) 108 LJ 17.
8   1968 SLT 413.

nevertheless not bound by its decision, and in this particular case since neither the child or the man in question were present in England, the order was 'clearly one which the Court of Chancery had no jurisdiction to pronounce'.[9]

2.4   Although there had been signs of a more conciliatory line,[10] clearly, the potential clashes of jurisdiction and the general lack of recognition and enforcement powers were unsatisfactory. Reform, however, was a long time coming. In 1959, the Hodson Committee produced a report,[11] which included recommendations that primary jurisdiction should be afforded to the country within the United Kingdom in which the child was 'ordinarily resident' and that there should be automatic recognition of orders made within the United Kingdom. However, the recommendations were never implemented,[12] probably because of a strong dissenting note.[13]

2.5   In 1972, the English and Scottish Law Commissions were asked to review the basis of jurisdiction of courts in the British Isles to make custody and wardship orders, and their recognition and enforcement.[14] The work was limited to the United Kingdom, and so did not include Jersey, Guernsey or the Isle of Man and nor did it address the question of international cases. Nevertheless, the outcome proved successful (although only after protracted discussion),[15] and the Family Law Act 1986, which came into force in 1988,[16] was a great improvement on what had gone before. It provided for the first time uniform definitions and identical rules of jurisdiction, recognition and enforcement throughout the United Kingdom and the Isle of Man,[17] with some very useful miscellaneous provisions. The Law Commissions[18] hoped that the jurisdictional rules would minimise the risks of concurrent assumptions of jurisdiction by courts within the United Kingdom, while the recognition and enforcement rules would provide a simple procedure for the

---

9   Until 1971 the Court of Chancery exercised the wardship jurisdiction.

10   See eg *Re G (An Infant)* [1969] 2 All ER 1135, [1969] 1 WLR 1001 and *Re S (M) (An Infant)* [1971] Ch 621, [1971] 1 All ER 459.

11   *Report of the Committee on Conflicts of Jurisdiction Affecting Children*, Cmnd 842 (1959).

12   *Ibid.* And see Lowe and White, *Wards of Court*, 1st edn (Butterworths, 1979).

13   By Michael Albery QC. See also the criticisms of O Kahn-Freund (1960) 23 MLR 64 and Gareth Jones (1960) 14 ICLQ 15.

14   See Law Com Working Paper No 68/Scot Law Com Memorandum No 23 *Custody of Children – Jurisdiction and Enforcement within the United Kingdom* (1976).

15   It took 9 years to produce the final report, viz *Custody of Children: Jurisdiction and Enforcement within the United Kingdom*, Law Com No 138/Scot Law Com No 91, in 1985, following the working paper published in 1976.

16   4 April 1988 (SI 1988/375).

17   Section 42(1) applies the Act to England and Wales, Scotland and Northern Ireland, and the Family Law Act 1986 (Dependent Territories) Order 1991, SI 1991/1723, made pursuant to s 43 (which defines 'dependent territory') extends it to the Isle of Man.

18   Law Com No 138/Scot Law Com No 91, paras 1.6 and 1.9.

mutual recognition and enforcement of orders. The result is that the Act, if properly applied, considerably reduces, but does not eliminate, conflicts of jurisdiction within the United Kingdom and the Isle of Man.

The shortcomings of the Family Law Act 1986

2.6 Despite being an improvement on the previous position, the 1986 Act is limited in scope and, worse, it is notoriously difficult to interpret.[19] Geographically, although it has been extended to the Isle of Man, it has not been extended to the Channel Islands, although it could be. Procedurally, it has not entirely avoided concurrent assumption of jurisdiction; first, because of the precedence, whenever instituted, of matrimonial proceedings and the possibility of instituting concurrent matrimonial proceedings in the different parts of the United Kingdom or the Isle of Man; and secondly, because proceedings based on the child's habitual residence will supersede those based on his presence. There is also the problem that the apparently straightforward rules relating to superseding orders have been complicated by the case-law.[20]

2.7 The Act does not deal with jurisdiction in respect of public law (care) proceedings, guardianship, parental responsibility orders and those orders made within the wardship or inherent jurisdiction which do not give the care of a child to a person or provide for contact or education,[21] for all of which there appear to be no statutory rules. It provides a system for the recognition and enforcement throughout the United Kingdom and the Isle of Man of orders made in any one part of the kingdom or dependent territory, but there is nothing equivalent to recognising and enforcing 'rights of custody' as there is under the 1980 Hague Abduction Convention, and the procedure for mutual recognition and enforcement is unnecessarily complicated. The Act also makes no mention of international cases, although it has a direct effect upon them.

2.8 The lack of any provision for an international element in the Family Law Act 1986 is surprising, because two international Conventions, the 1980 Hague Abduction Convention and the 1980 European Custody Convention, were both incorporated into English law on 1 August 1986 by the Child Abduction and Custody Act 1985,[22] which restricts the jurisdiction of the courts to make orders while applications under the two Conventions are pending. Adopting these two Conventions and the 1965 Hague Convention on Jurisdiction, Applicable Law and Recognition of Decrees relating to Adoptions[23] was the English response to problem of conflicts of international jurisdiction. However, Part I of the Family Law Act 1986 also regulates jurisdiction in

---

[19] See Lowe 'The Family Law Act 1986 – A Critique' [2002] Fam Law 39.

[20] See **3.25**.

[21] Family Law Act 1986, s 1(1)(d).

[22] SI 1986/1048.

[23] Adoption Act 1976, s 17. Intercountry adoption is now the subject of the 1993 Hague Convention on Protection of Children and Co-operation in respect of Intercountry Adoption which the United Kingdom ratified in June 2003.

international cases.[24] Therefore if the effect of the Family Law Act 1986 was to simplify the rules of jurisdiction within the United Kingdom in private law cases, they have again been made complicated by the Council Regulation, often referred to as 'Brussels II', which came into force with direct effect on 1 March 2001 and which ascribes jurisdiction over matrimonial proceedings and matters relating to parental responsibility over the children of both of the divorcing spouses within the EU (with the exception of Denmark).

THE BACKGROUND TO THE COUNCIL REGULATION

2.9 Council Regulation (EC) No 1347/2000 on jurisdiction and the recognition and enforcement of judgments in matrimonial matters and in matters of parental responsibility for children of both spouses ('the Council Regulation') essentially extends what was formerly the 1968 EC Convention on Jurisdiction and Enforcement of Judgments in Civil and Commercial Matters (known as 'Brussels I')[25] to matrimonial matters and parental responsibility for children of the spouses. Its justification, as expressed in its preamble, is the restraints that the jurisdictional and enforcement differences between the Member States of the EU place on the free movement of persons and the operation of the internal market. Its purpose is to unify the rules of conflict of jurisdiction in matrimonial matters and matters relating to parental responsibility 'so as to simplify the formalities for rapid and automatic recognition and enforcement of judgments'.[26] It is also intended to deter international child abduction by maintaining the lawful habitual residence of the child as 'the grounds of jurisdiction'.[27]

2.10 At the time of Brussels I, what was then the EEC had no wish to regulate family matters,[28] but as the internal market progressed the EU widened its area of concern and, with the establishment of what was then

---

[24] See *Re S (Residence Order: Forum Conveniens)* [1995] 1 FLR 314 at 321, per Thorpe LJ.

[25] Brussels I and its extensions and the 1988 Lugano Convention (which is modelled closely on Brussels I) between the EC and the EFTA States were incorporated into English law by the Civil Jurisdiction and Judgments Act 1982. Brussels I, now replaced, as between Member States other than Denmark, by Council Regulation (EC) No 44/2001, is of some relevance to family law because, although it expressly excludes judgments relating to status (eg divorce and nullity) and rights of property arising from marriage, it can be used to enforce orders or judgments in matrimonial maintenance claims (but not in relation to 'rights in property arising out of a matrimonial relationship') – see Hodson, 'Disclosure, Adverse Inferences and Conduct – Al Khatib v Masry' [2002] Fam Law 444 at 447.

[26] Preamble, Recital (4).

[27] Preamble, Recital (13).

[28] Indeed, the Jenard Report on the Convention of 27 September 1968 (on Jurisdiction and the Enforcement of Judgments in Civil and Commercial Matters (1979) OJ (C59) 1) had pointed out the difficulties of including family matters.

Art K.3 of the Treaty of European Union, it became, in some people's view,[29] inevitable that matters of status would have to be revisited. A formal proposal was made by Germany in 1992, arising from a longstanding difficulty with France over recognition and enforcement in relation to divorce and legal separation.[30] The German proposal was confined to divorce, separation and annulment, but in 1995 Spain and France proposed the inclusion of questions relating to children and, despite objections that it would impinge on the revision of the 1961 Hague Convention on the Protection of Minors,[31] the Council of Ministers gave instructions to proceed in September 1995. A Convention, modelled on Brussels I (which itself has now been made into Council Regulation (EC) No 44/2001 of 22 December 2000),[32] was prepared and presented to the Council of Ministers for signature in May 1998, but the Treaty of Amsterdam had conferred a right of initiative on the Commission under what is now Title IV of the new Treaty of the European Community, which led to a Commission proposal for a Regulation based on the text of the Convention. The Regulation was adopted by the Council on 29 May 2000 and came into force on 1 March 2001[33] with direct effect. It applies to civil proceedings relating to divorce, separation or annulment within the EU instituted after that date and to those instituted before, if they comply with its jurisdictional requirements.[34] It binds all Member States except Denmark.[35]

---

[29]   See eg Peter Beaton, 'The Brussels II Regulation' – a paper given at the UK–German Conference on Family Law held in Edinburgh, September 2000.

[30]   Article 14 of the French Civil Code gave a French citizen the right to sue and be sued in the French courts, and the French refused to recognise the validity of proceedings elsewhere other than by choice of the French spouse. The British view was that the problem was adequately addressed by the 1970 Hague Convention on Recognition of Divorces and Legal Separations, but neither France nor Germany felt able to ratify that Convention, and felt that extending Brussels I would be a proper solution. See Ian Karsten QC (now Judge Karsten QC), 'Brussels II – An English Perspective' [1998] IFL 75 and Shannon and Kennedy, 'Jurisdiction and Recognition and Enforcement Issues in Proceedings Concerning Parental Responsibility under the Brussels II Convention' [2000] IFL 111 (but note that these articles were written about the proposed Convention, not the Regulation).

[31]   The United Kingdom is not a party to this Convention. The revision of the 1961 Hague Convention on the Protection of Minors led to the 1996 Hague Convention on Jurisdiction, Applicable Law, Recognition, Enforcement and Co-operation in Respect of Parental Responsibility and Measures for the Protection of Children (19 October 1996), on which see Chapter 24, and Lowe, 'New International Conventions Affecting the Law Relating to Children – a Cause for Concern' [2001] IFL 171; Clive, 'The New Hague Convention on Children' (1993) 3 *Juridical Law Review* 169; Nygh, 'The New Hague Child Protection Convention' (1997) 11 Int Jo of Law, Policy and the Family; Silberman, 'The 1996 Hague Convention on the Protection of Children: Should the United States Join?' (2000) 34 *Family Law Quarterly* 239, and Lowe, 'The 1996 Convention on the Protection of Children – a Fresh Appraisal' [2002] CFLQ 191.

[32]   OJ L 012, 16 January 2001.

[33]   Article 46.

[34]   Article 42.

[35]   Article 1(3) and Preamble, Recital (25).

Interpretation of the Council Regulation

2.11 When considering and interpreting the Council Regulation, it has to be remembered that EU Regulations are directly effective. Direct effect means that domestic legislation has to be read alongside (rather than instead of) a Regulation and will not, so far as is possible, repeat its provisions. The Council Regulation was originally in the form of a draft Convention known as 'Brussels II' because Brussels I was seen as a general Convention and the proposed Brussels II Convention as a *lex specialis*, following its principles as far as possible.[36] So, as the Borras Report (the Explanatory Report on the proposed Brussels II Convention)[37] explains, identical terms in Brussels I (now Council Regulation (EC) No 44/2001) and the Council Regulation must be given the same meaning. Concepts like habitual residence and the service of documents will therefore be defined by the jurisprudence of Brussels I, not domestic law, although in the Council Regulation 'domicile' has the same meaning as it has under the law of the United Kingdom and Ireland.[38] The ECJ case-law on the meaning of Articles, words and phrases in Brussels I will have to be taken into account, because they will have the same meaning in the Council Regulation. It may also be necessary to have regard to the text of Brussels I (and now Council Regulation (EC) No 44/2001), the Jenard Report[39] on Brussels I and material relating to the Council Regulation itself, including the Borras Report.

2.12 The effect of the Council Regulation coming into force is that there are now three jurisdictional schemes within the United Kingdom relating to private law disputes about children: one in which jurisdiction is conferred because their parents are involved in matrimonial proceedings under the Council Regulation; one dealing with children whose parents are involved in matrimonial proceedings other than by way of the Council Regulation and one dealing with those whose parents are not involved in matrimonial proceedings at all.[40]

---

[36] Shannon with Kennedy, 'Jurisdictional and Recognition and Enforcement Issues in Proceedings Concerning Parental Responsibility under the Brussels II Convention' [2000] IFL 111, at n 11. And see Barker and Smith, 'A Response to Brussels II – A View from Scotland' [2002] IFL 44.

[37] (1998) OJ C221/27, at para 6.

[38] Article 2(2).

[39] (1979) OJ (C59) 1.

[40] It is important to realise that in cases in which an English court is entertaining an application relating to 'parental responsibility' where there are proceedings in England and Wales for divorce or nullity as a result of the jurisdiction conferred by the Council Regulation, it is exercising jurisdiction over them by virtue of the Council Regulation, and that the rules for recognition and enforcement within the EU apply to the judgment (see **4.9** *et seq*).

THE FUTURE

The European Union

2.13   In the future, there are likely to be further complications. The EU is continuing to take an interest in family law as part of its general objective of harmonising (unifying) jurisdiction, recognition and enforcement within its area. It has embarked on an ambitious programme of mutual recognition, with the aim of extending the areas of the existing Community instruments and the progressive abolition of the *exequatur* process in civil and commercial matters. As part of this, there was a proposal made by the Commission on 3 May 2002 to replace the Council Regulation with a new regulation concerning jurisdiction and the recognition of judgments in matters relating to parental responsibility and amending Council Regulation (EC) No 44/2001 in respect of maintenance.

2.14   This May 2002 proposal arose from a French initiative of 3 July 2000 on the mutual enforcement of judgments on rights of access to children, including the abolition of the *exequatur* procedure and automatic return of children unlawfully retained after access,[41] and from a decision of the Justice and Home Affairs Council in November 2000 to adopt a programme to abolish the *exequatur* procedure in civil and commercial cases, including extending the Council Regulation to all children and abolishing the *exequatur* in access cases. A decision was made to pursue the French initiative in parallel with extending the scope of the Council Regulation, so as to allow equality of treatment for all children, and the proposed instrument became known as 'Brussels II bis'.[42]

2.15   The May 2002 proposal is a continuation of 'Brussels II bis' and is a single and all-embracing EU instrument applying to jurisdiction and recognition of judgments in matrimonial matters, and jurisdiction, recognition and enforcement of all judgments in all civil proceedings relating to parental responsibility, when ancillary to parental responsibility proceedings.[43] The revision of Brussels II, which was finally agreed upon in late 2003, is discussed in Chapter 18.

The 1996 Hague Convention on the Protection of Children

2.16   There is also strong support for the EU, and therefore the United Kingdom, to become a party to the 1996 Hague Convention on the Protection

---

[41]   The French initiative, sometimes referred to as 'Brussels IIa' or 'II bis', was linked to the Council Regulation and so was confined to access orders made in matrimonial proceedings in respect of the children of both spouses.

[42]   The text of the proposal and the Explanatory Memorandum are to be found at [2002] IFL 23 *et seq*. Note also the discussion of whether to add a protocol to the 1980 Hague Abduction Convention on trans-frontier contact: see further **25.40–25.41**.

[43]   See Everall and Nicholls, 'Brussels I and II – The Impact on Family Law' [2002] Fam Law 674.

of Children,[44] which is intended to 'eliminate in principle all competition between the authorities of different States in taking measures of protection for the person or the property of the child',[45] as well as providing rules relating to applicable law and the recognition and enforcement of orders made in Contracting States. This Convention is discussed in Chapter 24.

Council of Europe

2.17   The Council of Europe has completed a new Convention on Contact Concerning Children, adopted by the Committee of Ministers on 3 May 2002 and opened for signature in May 2003. At the time of writing, the UK Government is seeking views on whether to ratify. This Convention is discussed in Chapter 25.[46]

---

[44]   See **24.57**.
[45]   Explanatory Report (Professor Lagarde), para 6.
[46]   Discussed at **25.83** *et seq*.

Chapter 3

THE FAMILY LAW ACT 1986

INTRODUCTION

3.1 Prior to 1 March 2001 when the Council Regulation[1] came into force, the Family Law Act 1986 conferred primary jurisdiction to make orders under Part I of that Act on the court in that part of the United Kingdom or specified dependent territory in which matrimonial proceedings in respect of the marriage of the parents of the child were continuing. Although intended to deal with conflicts of jurisdiction within the United Kingdom, the 1986 Act

---

[1] Viz Regulation (EC) No 1347/2000, discussed at **2.9** *et seq* and **4.9** *et seq*.

nevertheless had extraterritorial effect, so that a spouse who returned to England and Wales and instituted matrimonial proceedings thereby conferred on the English court jurisdiction to entertain applications about the children of both spouses. That provision has been superseded by the Council Regulation, under which the existence of matrimonial proceedings between the parents confers primary jurisdiction over disputes about parental responsibility on the courts of the country within the EU seized of the matrimonial proceedings, provided that the children are habitually resident there.[2]

THE APPLICATION OF THE FAMILY LAW ACT 1986

3.2	Part I of the 1986 Act is confined to the jurisdiction to make, and the subsequent recognition and enforcement of, 'Part I orders'. So far as England and Wales is concerned, 'Part I orders' are defined by s 1(1)(a) to mean s 8 orders under the Children Act 1989[3] (excluding variations or discharges)[4] and by s 1(1)(d) to mean orders made under the High Court's inherent jurisdiction giving care of the child to any person or providing for contact with or the education of the child, excluding variations or revocations of such orders[5] (but not orders that simply protect the child).[6] Similar definitions, s 1(1)(c) and (e), apply in Northern Ireland, to orders made under Art 8 of the Children (Northern Ireland) Order 1995 and to those made under the Northern Ireland High Court's inherent jurisdiction, giving care of the child to any person or providing for contact with or the education of the child, but again, in each case excluding variations or discharges.[7] The provision applying to Scotland, s 1(1)(b), is more elaborate but basically comprises orders with respect to residence, custody, care and control, contact or access,

---

[2]	Or they are habitually resident in one of the Member States, one of the spouses has parental responsibility for them, both spouses accept the jurisdiction and it is in the best interests of the children: Art 3 (see **4.17**).

[3]	By reason of s 1(3)(a) 'Part I orders' also includes existing custody orders made before the implementation of the Children Act 1989, viz those made under Guardianship of Minors Act 1971, ss 9(1), 10(1)(a), 11(a), or 14A(2); Guardianship Act 1973, s 2(4)(b) or (5); Matrimonial Causes Act 1973, s 42(1) or (2); Children Act 1975, s 33(1) (the former custodianship orders) and Domestic Proceedings and Magistrates' Courts Act 1978, s 8(2) or s 19(1)(ii).

[4]	The reason for excluding variations and discharges was the belief (see Law Com No 138/Scot Law Com No 91, para 4.30) that 'once a court has made a custodial order any power which it has to vary that order should remain exercisable notwithstanding that the original basis of jurisdiction to make a custody order no longer exists', which was in any event thought to reflect the then law in all three UK jurisdictions; but note the difference now in Scotland under the 1986 Act: see below.

[5]	It also includes any existing order vesting care and control or access.

[6]	It does not, for example, apply to collection and location orders: see **10.28**.

[7]	By reason of s 1(3)(a) it also includes former 'custody orders' made before implementation of the Children (Northern Ireland) Order 1995, viz Guardianship of Infants Act 1886, s 5 and Domestic Proceedings (Northern Ireland) Order 1980, Arts 19(2), 20(1)(ii).

education and upbringing but, for reasons that are not clear, does not expressly exclude variations or discharges of such orders.

3.3 Although all 'Part I orders' relate to children, the definition of a 'child' varies according to the context. Hence, a 'child' for the general purposes of jurisdiction means, in England and Wales and Northern Ireland, a person under the age of 18 but, in Scotland, a person under the age of 16.[8] However, for the purposes of recognition and enforcement, in all cases a 'child' means a person under the age of 16.[9]

NON-INCLUSION OF THE CHANNEL ISLANDS

3.4 Although there is power under s 43(2)(b) to extend the application of the 1986 Act to the Channel Islands, no such extension has yet been made. This means that orders made in one part of the United Kingdom or in the Isle of Man are neither recognisable nor enforceable in the Channel Islands[10], nor vice versa, although no doubt they would be treated with the greatest respect. Because the Channel Islands are regarded as part of the United Kingdom for the purposes of the 1980 Hague Abduction Convention and the 1980 European Custody Convention, abductions to and from there must be dealt with as if they were between non-Convention countries. This is an unsatisfactory position which clearly needs to be attended to in any review of the operation of the 1986 Act.

INTER-RELATIONSHIP WITH THE COUNCIL REGULATION

3.5 An added complication to the operation of the Family Law Act 1986 is the application of the Council Regulation, which provides a common set of jurisdictional rules to be applied in matrimonial proceedings and certain issues relating to children[11] throughout Member States of the European Union (except Denmark)[12] and for the consequent recognition and enforcement of judgments made in those proceedings. So far as children are concerned, the Council Regulation has a more limited application than the 1986 Act, being

---

8   Family Law Act 1986, ss 7(a) (England and Wales), 24 (Northern Ireland) and 18(1) (Scotland).
9   *Ibid*, ss 25(1) and 27(5). Note also that the special rules relating to a child's habitual residence under s 41 (discussed below) only apply to children under the age of 16.
10 See, for example, *F v H* [2002] Fam Law 10, Royal Court of Jersey (Samedi Division).
11 See **3.6** below.
12 Article 1(3). For a full list of Member States to which the Regulation applies, see the definition of 'Contracting State' provided by Domicile and Matrimonial Proceedings Act 1973, ss 5(1A)(a), as amended (England and Wales); 12(5)(b), as amended (Scotland); and Matrimonial Causes (Northern Ireland) Order 1978, Art 49(8)(a), as amended (Northern Ireland).

confined to matters relating to parental responsibility[13] over a child of *both* spouses involved in matrimonial proceedings.[14] Where the Council Regulation has no application, ie where there are no matrimonial proceedings in a Member State (including the United Kingdom), or where there are, but the court is not exercising jurisdiction by virtue of the Council Regulation or the child concerned is not a child of both spouses or, *a fortiori,* where the parents of the child concerned are not married to each other, then the 1986 Act is fully operative. However, the difficulty is that when the Council Regulation does apply, the 1986 Act is not ousted for all purposes. But its precise application is, perhaps, open to some debate.

HOW THE 1986 ACT OPERATES IN CONJUNCTION WITH THE COUNCIL REGULATION

3.6 The Council Regulation takes precedence over domestic legislation, which means that in deciding whether to hear an application domestic courts should *first* apply the Council Regulation to determine whether they have or, equally importantly, do not have jurisdiction. It has to be said that this is not immediately apparent from the consequential amendments made to the 1986 Act,[15] which seem to provide that jurisdiction may be taken either on the basis of the Council Regulation *or* the 1986 Act.[16] The amendments also imply that jurisdiction to entertain matrimonial proceedings under the Council Regulation is of itself sufficient to found jurisdiction to make an order, no mention being made of the provisions of Art 3. Section 2 of the 1986 Act, as amended, reads:

'**2 Jurisdiction: general**

(1) A court in England and Wales shall not have jurisdiction to make a section 1(1)(a) order with respect to a child in or in connection with matrimonial proceedings in England and Wales unless –

(a)   the child concerned is a child of both parties to the matrimonial proceedings and the court has jurisdiction to entertain those proceedings by virtue of the Council Regulation, or[17]

(b)   the condition in section 2A of this Act is satisfied.'

---

13   Parental responsibility is not defined in the Regulation.

14   See Art 3.

15   Sections 2(1) (England), 15(1) (Scotland) and 19(1) (Northern Ireland), made respectively by the European Communities (Matrimonial Jurisdiction and Judgments) Regulations 2001, SI 2001/310, the European Communities (Matrimonial Jurisdiction and Judgments) (Scotland) Regulations 2001, SSI 2001/36, and the European Communities (Matrimonial Jurisdiction and Judgments) (Northern Ireland) Regulations 2001, SI 2001/660.

16   Which leads one to ask if the amendments have been correctly worded.

17   Inserted by European Communities (Matrimonial Jurisdiction and Judgments) Regulations 2001, SI 2001/310, reg 6.

3.7 If, applying the Council Regulation, the court of another relevant Member State is already seized of the same cause of action in relation to the child, then proceedings *must* be declined.[18] Similarly, where a court is seized of a case over which it has no jurisdiction under the Council Regulation but over which a court in another Member State has jurisdiction, then it shall declare of its own motion that it has no jurisdiction.[19] Even if no other Member State court is seized of the case, domestic courts must, in the first instance, still apply the Council Regulation's rules on jurisdiction, since by Art 8 it is only where *no* court of a Member State has jurisdiction under the Council Regulation that States are free to apply their own rules, although not to the extent of entertaining proceedings against a spouse who is habitually resident in, or a national of (or in the case of the United Kingdom and Ireland, a domiciliary of) another Member State, who may only be 'sued' in accordance with Arts 2 to 6.[20] What this seems to mean is that where an issue relating to parental responsibility of a child of both spouses involved in matrimonial proceedings is sought to be litigated, the courts must first determine whether there is jurisdiction under the Council Regulation to hear the matrimonial proceedings[21] and, if so, must then determine whether there is jurisdiction under the Council Regulation to hear the child-related issue. Since the basic connecting factor governing jurisdiction under the Council Regulation in matrimonial cases is both spouses' habitual residence[22] and in the case of the child-related issue, the child's habitual residence,[23] it follows that in so-called purely 'domestic' cases, jurisdiction must now be taken under the Council Regulation. However, this will not prevent the order concerning the child being a 'Part I order' for the purposes of the Family Law Act 1986. Accordingly, since it is clear that the Council Regulation has no application to the recognition and enforcement of a judgment *within* a single Member State,[24] if it is subsequently sought to enforce that order in another part of the United Kingdom or in the Isle of Man, one must still apply the 1986 Act.

3.8 So far as jurisdictional conflicts within the United Kingdom and the Isle of Man are concerned, it seems reasonably clear that the Council Regulation has no application, since it does not govern such conflicts within a single Member State. Although Art 41, when dealing with Member States with two or

---

18 Article 11(3). See *Wermuth v Wermuth (No 1)* [2002] EWHC 3049 (Fam), [2003] 1 FLR 1022 and *A v L (Jurisdiction: Brussels II)* [2002] 1 FLR 1042.

19 Article 9. But note that, unlike under the 1986 Act (see **3.14** and **3.15** below) jurisdiction under Art 3 is strictly limited in time and ends upon the final determination of the matrimonial proceedings, or if at that stage a determination on parental responsibility is still pending, upon a final judgment on that issue – see Art 3(3).

20 Article 7.

21 See Domicile and Matrimonial Proceedings Act 1973, s 5(2), as amended.

22 See Art 2(1)(a).

23 See Art 3(1).

24 See Arts 14 and 21, which respectively refer to the recognition and enforcement in one Member State of orders which have been made in *another* Member State.

more legal systems, provides for the application of concepts such as habitual residence and (in the case of the United Kingdom) domicile to each territorial unit – which might suggest that the Council Regulation consequently governs jurisdictional priority between the different parts of the United Kingdom and the Isle of Man – both Arts 9 and 11 require the court to decline jurisdiction only if a court of another Member State is or could be properly seized of the case, so it seems that internal priority of jurisdiction remains subject to the 1986 Act.

THE COMMON JURISDICTIONAL RULES CREATED BY THE 1986 ACT

3.9   To ensure that only one court in the United Kingdom or the Isle of Man has jurisdiction to make a 'Part I order' over a child, except in emergencies, the 1986 Act created common jurisdictional rules in the form of a tripartite scheme of priorities. Although its principal aim was to resolve conflicts of jurisdiction within the United Kingdom, in fact the rules laid down have a more general application and, subject to the Council Regulation, apply to all applications for Part I orders whether or not there is an internal (UK) or international issue. The jurisdictional scheme is as follows:[25]

(1)   primary jurisdiction over the children of both spouses[26] is vested in the court in which matrimonial (that is, divorce, nullity or judicial separation or, in Scotland, separation) proceedings are 'continuing'.[27] They take precedence, whether instituted under the Council Regulation or otherwise, whenever instituted (but note that divorce or nullity proceedings take precedence over judicial separation proceedings);

(2)   if there are no such proceedings, that is, in what the Act refers to as 'non-matrimonial' proceedings, jurisdiction is vested in the court of the place in which, on the relevant date,[28] the child is habitually resident; but

(3)   where neither (1) or (2) applies, jurisdiction is vested in the court of the place where, on the relevant date, the child is physically present; but in any event

---

[25]   Family Law Act 1986, ss 2, 2A and 3 (England and Wales); ss 8–11 and 13 (Scotland); and ss 19, 19A and 20 (Northern Ireland). NB: there is a lacuna in the 1986 Act inasmuch as s 2(3)(a) states that the English High Court's jurisdiction to make a s 1(1)(d) order is subject to the condition set out in s 3 being satisfied, but s 3(1) refers only to s 2(2) and not, as is clearly intended, to s 2(3) as well. There is no lacuna in ss 19 and 20 in respect of the High Court of Northern Ireland's jurisdiction to make an order under s 1(1)(e).

[26]   See **3.13** and **3.21** below.

[27]   For the meaning of 'continuing', see **3.14**.

[28]   Ie on the date on which application for the order is made or, in the event of there being no application, on the date of the order: FLA 1986, s 7(c) (England and Wales), for the application of which see *Re J (Abduction: Declaration of Wrongful Removal)* [1999] 2 FLR 653 at 657–658, per Hale J, and s 20(6) (Northern Ireland). The definition is different in Scotland: see s 18(2).

(4) notwithstanding (1) or (2), in cases of emergency, ie where the court considers that the exercise of its powers is necessary for the child's protection, jurisdiction can also be taken on the basis of the child's physical presence.[29]

3.10 It will be apparent that, under this scheme, in the absence of matrimonial proceedings, if the child is neither habitually resident nor physically present, there is no jurisdiction to make a Part I order.[30] This is a serious disadvantage in international cases because not only is there no mechanism for the recognition and enforcement of foreign orders other than under the 1980 European Custody Convention, but also the courts of the United Kingdom have no power to make orders to protect a child in advance of arrival.[31] So an American parent whose child is about to come to England under the terms of an (American) order providing him with visitation (contact) cannot either enforce the American order or insist that an order is made in similar terms in England in advance of the child's arrival. Any enforcement of the American order would have to be by way of proceedings under the Children Act 1989 once the child had arrived in England.[32]

3.11 Even if a court has jurisdiction upon one of the foregoing bases, it has a discretion either to refuse to make an order on the ground that the issue has already been determined in another jurisdiction or to grant a stay (or in Scotland, a sist) on the basis that there are proceedings continuing elsewhere and that it would be more appropriate for matters to be determined in proceedings to be taken elsewhere.[33]

3.12 Although in general terms the basic rules seem straightforward, in practice their application has proved problematic at times and not all conflicts have been avoided. Indeed, some conflicts seem to be inherent within the general scheme. Three areas in particular have caused difficulty: namely, the complicated inter-relationship with the matrimonial jurisdiction, the uncertainty of the application of the concept of habitual residence and

---

[29] Sections 2(3)(b) (England and Wales), 12 (Scotland) and 19(3)(b) (Northern Ireland).

[30] See eg *Re M (Abduction: Habitual Residence)* [1996] 1 FLR 887, CA. But cf *Re P (A Child: Mirror Orders)* [2000] 1 FLR 435, discussed further below at **3.43**. Note also that Ward J's decision in *F v S (Wardship: Jurisdiction)* [1991] 2 FLR 349 that the absence of jurisdiction under the 1986 Act did not preclude him having jurisdiction in wardship proceedings, based on the child's allegiance, to make an order requiring disclosure of the child's whereabouts since that fell outside the definition of a 'Part I order', although not commented upon in the subsequent appeal before the Court of Appeal (see [1993] 2 FLR 684), has since been disapproved in *Al Habtoor v Fotheringham* [2001] EWCA Civ 186, [2001] 1 FLR 951, CA.

[31] At any rate in theory, but see *Re P (A Child: Mirror Orders)* (above), discussed at **3.43**.

[32] See **4.6**.

[33] Family Law Act 1986, ss 5 (England and Wales), 14 (Scotland) and 22 (Northern Ireland), discussed further below at **3.35** *et seq*.

the application of the provisions[34] allowing orders in one jurisdiction to supersede earlier orders made in another jurisdiction.

The primacy of matrimonial proceedings

Divorce and nullity proceedings take precedence over separation proceedings

3.13 Under the general scheme, as stated above, primary jurisdiction over the children of both spouses is vested in the court in which matrimonial, that is divorce, nullity or judicial separation (or, in Scotland, separation) proceedings are 'continuing'. However, divorce and nullity proceedings take precedence over the separation proceedings. Accordingly, there is no jurisdiction to make a Part I order in separation proceedings if, after the grant of the decree, divorce or nullity proceedings are 'continuing' in another part of the United Kingdom or the Isle of Man.[35]

Meaning of 'continuing' proceedings

3.14 Proceedings are 'continuing' for the purposes of the 1986 Act from the time the petition is filed until the child reaches the age of 18 in England and Wales, Northern Ireland and the Isle of Man, or 16 in Scotland, unless those proceedings have been dismissed.[36] In other words, the prohibition on taking jurisdiction extends beyond the court hearing and lasts for the potential life of the child-related order, as illustrated by *B v B (Scottish Contact Order: Jurisdiction To Vary)*.[37] The mother and two daughters left the matrimonial home in Scotland to live in Wales. The husband remained in Scotland. In 1993, the Scottish Court of Session granted a divorce and awarded custody to the mother and staying access to the father in Scotland. In 1994, however, the mother stopped contact, alleging that her daughters had complained about their treatment by the father. Her subsequent application to the Court of Session to discharge or reduce contact was refused. Instead, the court made an order for staying contact with the father. Upon the mother's subsequent refusal to comply with this order, the father registered it in the High Court of England and Wales and then sought to enforce it.[38] Meanwhile, in 1995, the mother brought proceedings in England and Wales for reduced contact under both the High Court's inherent jurisdiction and the Children Act 1989. Connell J dismissed the mother's application for want of jurisdiction because, as the Scottish orders for the children (who were aged 7 and 5) made in the

---

[34] Viz ss 6 (England and Wales), 15 (Scotland) and 23 (Northern Ireland).

[35] Sections 2A(2) (England and Wales), 13(3) (Scotland) and 19A(2) (Northern Ireland).

[36] Section 42(2), (3). But note that, notwithstanding a dismissal, certain Part I orders can still be made provided they are made forthwith or, where an application has been made, on or before the dismissal: ss 2A(1)(c) (England and Wales – power confined to s 8 orders under the Children Act 1989), 13(2) (Scotland), and 19A(1)(c) (Northern Ireland – power confined to art 8 orders under the Children (Northern Ireland) Order 1995).

[37] [1996] 1 WLR 231, [1996] 1 FLR 688.

[38] See Chapter 11, for discussion of registration and enforcement of orders from one part of the United Kingdom to another.

divorce proceedings were 'continuing', exclusive jurisdiction remained in the Scottish Court.[39]

3.15 The retention of 'continuing' matrimonial proceedings as a jurisdictional base seems to give rise to a potential conflict between the 1986 Act and the Council Regulation, which provides that jurisdiction over matters relating to parental responsibility for a child of both spouses ceases as soon as the judgment allowing or refusing the application for divorce, legal separation or annulment has become final or, if at that time there were proceedings relating to parental responsibility pending, as soon as the judgment in those proceedings becomes final. It might seem, therefore, as if a court entertaining matrimonial proceedings under the Council Regulation, but unable to deal with the children because, perhaps, they were not habitually resident in a Member State, would nevertheless be able to claim jurisdiction over them on the basis that the matrimonial proceedings were 'continuing' and the condition in s 2A was satisfied.

Matrimonial proceedings take precedence whenever instituted

3.16 The apparent simplicity of the prioritising scheme of the 1986 Act is flawed to the extent that matrimonial proceedings take precedence *whenever* they are instituted. Consequently, while, in the absence of matrimonial proceedings, jurisdiction can properly be taken on the basis of the child's habitual residence, such proceedings are liable to be overtaken or 'trumped' by subsequent matrimonial proceedings. Moreover, since jurisdiction in matrimonial proceedings is founded upon either spouse's (ie not the child's) habitual residence or domicile (provided no court of a Contracting State has jurisdiction under the Council Regulation),[40] it is possible for non-matrimonial proceedings to be properly instituted on the basis of the child's habitual residence (say, in England and Wales) only to be superseded by divorce proceedings subsequently brought (say, in Scotland).[41] In other words, notwithstanding the aim of the 1986 Act to minimise the taking of concurrent proceedings over a child, two sets of proceedings can quite properly be brought in different parts of the United Kingdom or the Isle of Man.

The position where two sets of matrimonial proceedings are brought

3.17 Since matrimonial proceedings can be founded upon *either* spouse's habitual residence or, if the Council Regulation does not apply, domicile, it is possible for each party to institute separate proceedings in different parts of

---

[39] He rejected the contention that in respect of the inherent jurisdiction application he should make an order on the basis of the children's presence and their need for immediate protection. See further **3.24**.

[40] See Domicile and Matrimonial Proceedings Act 1973, s 5(2), (3), as amended by SI 2001/310 (England and Wales); s 7, as amended by SSI 2001/36 (Scotland); and Matrimonial Causes (Northern Ireland) Order 1978, art 49, as amended by SI 2001/660 (Northern Ireland).

[41] See eg *A v A (Forum Conveniens)* [1999] 1 FLR 1.

the United Kingdom or the Isle of Man. In such cases, as Hughes J observed in *A v A (Forum Conveniens),*[42] there are no reciprocal statutory provisions (equivalent to those under the Family Law Act 1986) excluding jurisdiction of one court or the other. Instead, one has to look to the Domicile and Matrimonial Proceedings Act 1973[43] to determine which set of proceedings has priority. That Act makes a distinction between cases where proceedings have been instituted in a 'related jurisdiction' (ie jurisdictions in other parts of the United Kingdom, the Isle of Man or the Channel Islands)[44] in which the parties were habitually resident for one year when they last lived together, and cases in which proceedings are continuing in 'another jurisdiction'. In the former case, provision is made for mandatory stays,[45] whereas in the latter case, the court has a discretion whether or not to stay proceedings.[46] An example of a case falling under the former head is *M v M (Abduction: England and Scotland)*[47] in which, after the husband left the army in 1994, he and his family went to live in Scotland. The family obtained local authority accommodation, the children went to school and both husband and wife obtained jobs. In 1996, however, without her husband's knowledge, the wife and children left Scotland for England, from where she obtained an ex parte residence order and a prohibited steps order preventing her husband from removing the children from England. Two days later, the wife instituted divorce proceedings. Shortly afterwards, the husband issued children proceedings in Scotland, but these were adjourned pending the outcome of the English proceedings.

3.18 The husband himself would have issued divorce proceedings in Scotland, but the first instance judge in England had expressly forbidden him to do so. The judge based his decision on his finding that the children were not habitually resident anywhere and that their welfare required them to remain in England. On appeal, the Court of Appeal held that the judge had been wrong about habitual residence,[48] and about applying the welfare principle to the question of the husband's institution of divorce proceedings in Scotland. On this latter point, it was held that the judge should have applied the 1973 Act and in particular Sch 1, para 8, instead of the welfare principle. Had the judge done so, the Court of Appeal held that, far from granting an

---

42   [1999] 1 FLR 1 at 4.
43   In Northern Ireland the equivalent statute is the Matrimonial Causes (Northern Ireland) Order 1978.
44   See Domicile and Matrimonial Proceedings Act 1973, Sch 1, para 3(2) (England and Wales); Sch 3, para 3(2) (Scotland); Matrimonial Causes (Northern Ireland) Order 1978, Sch 1, para 3(2) (Northern Ireland).
45   See Domicile and Matrimonial Proceedings Act 1973, Sch 1, para 8 (England and Wales); Sch 3, para 8 (Scotland). The equivalent provision in Northern Ireland is Matrimonial Causes (Northern Ireland) Order 1978, Sch 1, para 8.
46   See Sch 1, para 9 (England and Wales); Sch 3, para 9 (Scotland) to the 1973 Act; and Sch 1, para 9 (Northern Ireland) to the 1978 Order.
47   [1997] 2 FLR 263, CA. See also *T v T (Custody: Jurisdiction)* [1992] 1 FLR 43.
48   This aspect of the decision is discussed at **4.57** below.

injunction to prevent the husband from bringing divorce proceedings in Scotland, the English proceedings should have been stayed to allow him to do so. Accordingly, the injunction was discharged, and the English proceedings were stayed until they were brought to an end by the filing of the Scottish divorce proceedings.

3.19 In contrast, in *A v A (Forum Conveniens)*,[49] Welsh parents and their three children moved to Scotland following the husband's RAF posting there but, within 8 weeks, the mother left him and the children and returned to Wales. For the next 8 months the mother enjoyed regular staying contact with her children, but at the end of one such visit she refused to return them as agreed. The eldest child, however, returned to her father in Scotland of her own volition. The husband filed for divorce in Scotland and sought residence orders in respect of all three children. After being served with notice of these proceedings, the mother applied in Wales for residence orders in respect of the two youngest children and for contact with the eldest. The Scottish court, having received a letter from the mother's solicitors challenging its jurisdiction, made an interim ex parte residence order in favour of the husband and ordered the mother to deliver up the children. The mother responded by filing divorce proceedings in Wales in which she sought residence orders. These proceedings were transferred to the High Court, the county court judge having in the meantime made a residence order in the mother's favour but giving the husband liberty to apply to discharge the order. Since the husband had not been habitually resident in Scotland for one year at the time of the ending of the parties' cohabitation there was therefore a discretion to stay proceedings. Applying the test established in *The Spiliada*,[50] namely, which is the more suitable or appropriate tribunal to resolve the question between the parties, Hughes J considered that the Scottish court was the appropriate court. He reached this conclusion for the following reasons: the connections of the parties with the respective jurisdictions; the fact that the children were habitually resident in Scotland; the physical presence of the eldest child in Scotland (where she would be likely to continue to live); the wrongful retention by the mother of the younger children in Wales; and the convenience of having a welfare report prepared by a locally based officer.

3.20 Although no doubt Hughes J's decision was sensible and certainly avoided any embarrassing conflict, the obvious danger inherent in a discretionary power is that the courts will not necessarily defer to one another.

Jurisdiction in non-matrimonial proceedings – habitual residence and presence

3.21 In the absence of matrimonial proceedings in respect of the marriage of the parents of the child concerned, ie in 'non-matrimonial' cases, as the

---

[49] [1999] 1 FLR 1.
[50] *Spiliada Maritime Corporation v Cansulex: The Spiliada* [1987] AC 460, [1986] All ER 843, HL, discussed further at **3.41**.

1986 Act refers to them,[51] primary jurisdiction is vested in the court of the child's habitual residence.[52] The principal difficulty of applying this jurisdictional criterion is determining in any particular case where, if anywhere, the child is habitually resident.[53]

3.22 When the child is not habitually resident anywhere in the United Kingdom or the Isle of Man, jurisdiction can be taken on the basis of the child's presence in England and Wales on the 'relevant date'[54] (the 'residual presence'[55] basis of jurisdiction).[56]

The emergency jurisdiction

3.23 In cases of emergency, irrespective of whether there are continuing matrimonial proceedings, or whether the child is habitually resident, in another part of the United Kingdom or the Isle of Man, jurisdiction can be taken on the basis of the child's presence[57] whenever the court 'considers that the immediate exercise of its powers is necessary for [the child's] protection'.[58] So far as England and Wales and Northern Ireland are concerned, this emergency jurisdiction can be exercised only by the High Court, and within their respective inherent jurisdictions with respect to children,[59] but in Scotland both the Court of Session and the Sheriff Court can act.[60]

3.24 Although making provision for emergencies was bound to create some potential conflict, some provision is clearly necessary and in any event it is intended only to be used as a temporary expedient. Accordingly, the exercise of the emergency jurisdiction does not preclude a court with primary

---

51 See s 2(2). In England and Wales this encompasses proceedings for 'Part I' orders either made in 'freestanding' proceedings concerning children or ancillary to applications for financial relief or protection from domestic violence. In Scotland these proceedings are referred to as 'independent proceedings', see s 8.

52 Family Law Act 1986, ss 2(2), (3), 3(1)(a) (England and Wales), 8, 9 (Scotland) and 19 and 20(1)(a) (Northern Ireland).

53 See **4.24** *et seq* and **4.44**.

54 The date of the application or, if there is no application, the date on which the court is considering whether to make an order – s 7.

55 Law Com Working Paper No 68/Scot Law Com Memorandum No 23, *Custody of Children – Jurisdiction and Enforcement within the United Kingdom* (1976), para 4.23.

56 Family Law Act 1986, ss 2(2), (3), 3(1)(b) (England and Wales), 8, 10 (Scotland) and 19 and 20(1)(b) (Northern Ireland).

57 So far as England and Wales and Northern Ireland are concerned, either at the date of application, where application is made for an order, or at the date of the order where no such application is made (eg where the court acts of its own motion, see Law Com No 138/Scot Law Com No 91, para 4.28): ss 7(c) (England and Wales) and 24(c) (Northern Ireland). In Scotland the child must be present at the date of application: s 18(2).

58 Sections 2(3) (England and Wales), 12 (Scotland) and 19(3) (Northern Ireland).

59 See s 2(3)(b) which confines the emergency power in England and Wales to the court that can make s 1(1)(d) orders, ie the High Court, and s 19(3), which confines the emergency power in Northern Ireland to the court that can make s 1(1)(e) orders, ie the Northern Ireland High Court.

60 Section 12.

jurisdiction from dealing with the matter, nor indeed from coming to a different conclusion, at a later stage. Furthermore, it was never intended that this emergency jurisdiction should be frequently invoked. As the Law Commissions emphasised,[61] it is designed to be used only where immediate intervention is necessary for the protection of the child. In *B v B (Scottish Contact Order: Jurisdiction to Vary)*,[62] which has been the only reported case to discuss its exercise, Connell J refused to exercise the emergency jurisdiction notwithstanding allegations about mistreatment of his daughters by the father during contact. As he observed, the mother was not in any event contesting even staying contact in principle, and the last contact occasion (albeit that it was supervised) had been a success. In his view there was no situation of urgency to justify the invocation of the emergency jurisdiction.

Superseding orders

3.25   An additional complicating factor concerning the application of the jurisdictional rules under the 1986 Act is the power to make a superseding order. So far as England and Wales is concerned the relevant provision is s 6(1) which provides:

> 'If a Part I order made by a court in Scotland, Northern Ireland or a specified dependent territory (or a variation of such an order) comes into force with respect to a child at a time when a Part I order made by a court in England and Wales has effect with respect to him, the latter order shall cease to have effect so far as it makes provision for any matter for which the same or different provision is made by (or by the variation of) the order made by the court in Scotland, Northern Ireland or the territory.'

3.26   For Northern Ireland the equivalent provision is s 23(1) which is identical to s 6(1). In Scotland, however, the relevant provision, s 15(1), while of similar effect, is phrased differently[63] including, crucially, referring to the later Part I order as being 'competently' made. In Hale J's view in *D v D (Custody: Jurisdiction)*,[64] however, it must have been the intention of Parliament to limit the ambit of s 6(1) (and, *pari passu*, s 23(1)) to later orders 'competently made'[65] and the provision should now presumably be read to that effect.

3.27   The Law Commissions' intention in recommending that a later validly made order should supersede an earlier one was simply to overcome the second court's obvious inability to revoke the previous order made by a court

---

61   Law Com No 138/Scot Law Com No 91 at para 4.19.

62   [1996] 1 WLR 231, [1996] 1 FLR 688.

63   Eg, s 15(1)(a) includes an order relating to the parental responsibilities or parental rights in relation to that child which is made outside the United Kingdom or the Isle of Man and recognised in Scotland by virtue of s 26.

64   [1996] 1 FLR 574 at 582.

65   Hale J cited in support, the Law Commissions' explanatory notes to clause 6(1) of their Draft Bill: Law Com No 138/Scot Law Com No 91 at p 159.

of another jurisdiction.[66] In this way they hoped to ensure that there could only be one valid Part I order in respect of the same child at any one time within the United Kingdom or the Isle of Man. What the Commissions specifically had in mind was the case where a court in one part of the United Kingdom makes an order on the basis of the child's habitual residence but a later order is made in another part in the course of divorce proceedings. But a similar result would also follow where the first order is based on the child's presence and the later order is based on the child's habitual residence. In other words, the superseding power is simply the inevitable corollary of having a hierarchy of jurisdictional bases.[67] The resulting case-law, however, has not proved straightforward, in part, it must be said, because the rules have been applied erroneously.

3.28 In *T v T (Custody: Jurisdiction)*[68] a father removed his child from the Scottish matrimonial home without the mother's knowledge or consent and took him to his parents' home in England. The mother quickly obtained an interim custody order from the Scottish Court of Session. The father responded by instituting divorce proceedings in England. Subsequent to this, the Scottish order was duly registered at the English High Court but soon after that the father obtained, upon an ex parte application, inter alia, an interim custody order made by the local county court in England. The mother then applied to the English High Court, also ex parte, effectively to enforce the original Scottish decision.[69] Douglas Brown J ordered that all the relevant proceedings to be transferred to the High Court and stayed[70] but, in the meantime, the child should be handed over to the mother. On the day of the final determination of the proceeding before the High Court, the mother filed for divorce in Scotland.

3.29 Insofar as the mother was seeking to enforce the initial Scottish order, the matter was disposed of by reference to s 15(1). It was held that, since the interim custody order made by the local county court in England was competently made under the divorce jurisdiction (it was accepted that the father was domiciled in England and Wales) then, under the terms of s 15(1), the initial Scottish order ceased to have effect. Accordingly, the application to enforce the order was misconceived as there was no order to enforce.

3.30 That, however, was not the end of the matter, because the mother's subsequent institution of divorce proceedings in Scotland brought into play the previously discussed mandatory staying provisions under Sch 1, para 8 to the Domicile and Matrimonial Proceedings Act 1973. Accordingly, the English

---

[66] See Law Com No 138/Scot Law Com No 91, para 4.115.

[67] Although note that it equally means that an order competently made under the emergency jurisdiction supersedes any earlier Part I order.

[68] [1992] 1 FLR 43.

[69] The system of registration and enforcement is discussed below in Chapter 11.

[70] Indeed, his Lordship recommended that all proceedings involving other UK jurisdictions should be transferred to the High Court; see further below at **3.50**.

proceedings were stayed in favour of the Scottish divorce proceedings. Hence, by this tortuous route, as Douglas Brown J was able to conclude:[71]

> 'the correct result has been achieved, namely, that a boy habitually resident in Scotland, who should not have been taken from Scotland, will have his future decided there.'

3.31 A less satisfactory result was achieved in *S v S (Custody: Jurisdiction)*[72] which purportedly followed *T v T*. In this case, Scottish parents married and lived in Scotland where they had one child. After their separation in 1989 they continued to live in Scotland, the child remaining with his mother but with the father having regular contact. In 1992, however, the father assumed the care of the child and issued custody proceedings in Scotland. The mother also sought custody in these proceedings but, in December 1992, without the father's knowledge, she removed the child to England. The father was immediately granted interim custody with full custody being granted some months later (ie in June 1993) by the Scottish court. These orders, however, could not be enforced as the mother's whereabouts were unknown. She was eventually traced to England in February 1994. In that month she applied, inter alia, for a residence order in an English county court. In March 1994, the Scottish order was duly registered but, shortly after that, the county court made an ex parte 'interim' residence order in favour of the mother. In June 1994, the father sought to enforce the duly registered Scottish order in the High Court.

3.32 The mother argued that, as a result of s 15(1), the ex parte interim residence order made by the English county court 'trumped' the Scottish order so that there was nothing left to be enforced. The father counter-argued that s 15(1) did not apply to so-called 'interim residence orders'. Bracewell J, however, rejected the father's argument saying that, although it had become 'common parlance to speak of "interim residence orders" ... in fact there is no such creature within the Children Act 1989'. In other words, residence orders of even the shortest duration have exactly the same effect as a so-called 'full' residence order. Accordingly, in her Ladyship's view, s 15(1) did apply in this case with the consequential result that the English order superseded the Scottish order so that there was nothing to enforce. In reaching this decision, Bracewell J took the view that s 15(1) fettered her discretion, pursuant to s 5 (discussed below), to dismiss or stay the mother's application. The father's application was therefore dismissed.

3.33 Although it can be fairly questioned whether, as a matter of policy, it is right that an interim order that, for example, a child reside with a named person for one week should have what one commentator has described as[73] an absurdly disproportionate effect in superseding an earlier order made in

---

71 [1992] 1 FLR 43 at 50. See also the comments in this case by Douglas at [1992] Fam Law 195 who surely correctly argued that the county court judge should not have made the interim orders in the first place.

72 [1995] 1 FLR 155.

73 Cretney, [1995] Fam Law 120 at 121.

another part of the United Kingdom or the Isle of Man, it is submitted that Bracewell J was right in law on that point.[74] Indeed in *A v A (Forum Conveniens)*[75] Hughes J expressly warned that the effect of s 15:

> 'is something which should no doubt be borne in mind by practitioners and courts when an application is made for an *interim residence order* and there is already in existence a Scottish order.' [Emphasis added.]

3.34   However, the correctness of the decision can be attacked on two other grounds.[76] First, there seemed to have been no enquiry as to whether the English order was 'competently made'.[77] Given that the Scottish court must have taken jurisdiction on the child's habitual residence, that surely prevented the English court from asserting jurisdiction.[78] Secondly, even if there was jurisdiction to make an order, Bracewell J wrongly considered that s 15(1) removed her discretion to stay the mother's application.[79]

The discretion to refuse or stay applications

3.35   As intimated earlier, one further complication is the fact that, notwithstanding that a court may have jurisdiction under any of the bases already discussed, it is always nevertheless vested with a discretion either to refuse to make a Part I order or to stay (or, in Scotland, sist) an application.

3.36   So far as England and Wales is concerned,[80] s 5(1) of the Family Law Act 1986 provides:

> 'A court in England and Wales which has jurisdiction to make a Part I order may refuse an application for the order in any case where the matter in question has already been determined in proceedings outside England and Wales.'

It is to be noted that the power under s 5(1) is not confined to cases where orders have been made elsewhere in the United Kingdom or the Isle of Man.

---

[74]   There is general agreement among commentators that the 1989 Act does not distinguish so-called 'interim' residence orders from 'final' orders, see eg White, Carr and Lowe, *The Children Act in Practice*, 3rd edn (Butterworths, 2002) at **5.20**, Lowe and Douglas, *Bromley's Family Law*, 9th edn (Butterworths, 1998) at 415, and Hershman and McFarlane, *Children, Law and Practice* (Family Law, looseleaf) at **C[257]**.

[75]   [1999] 1 FLR 1 at 7. Note also Hale J's comments in *D v D (Custody: Jurisdiction)* [1996] 1 FLR 574 at 583, that if an ex parte interim order made in England supersedes an earlier Scottish order, 'the same should apply in reverse, and even an interim ex parte order in Scotland should supersede an earlier inter partes order in England'.

[76]   For an excellent critique of the decision, see Cretney's comments at [1995] Fam Law 120–121.

[77]   As Hale J diplomatically observed in *D v D (Custody: Jurisdiction)* [1996] 1 FLR 574 at 583: 'Bracewell J did not spell out the basis of the English court's jurisdiction in that case'.

[78]   See the arguments of Cretney, *op cit*, n 73, at 121.

[79]   See **3.40** below.

[80]   For the equivalent provisions for Scotland and Northern Ireland, see respectively ss 14(2) and 22(1).

3.37 As the Law Commissions explained when recommending this provision,[81] it enables the court to refuse to allow the Part I order issue to be reopened, even where it has jurisdiction, if it considers that the issue has already been fully explored and there has been no change of circumstances justifying a rehearing. Clearly, it will be highly relevant to the exercise of this discretion as to how thoroughly the issue was argued in the earlier case. For example, an ex parte hearing is unlikely to be considered to constitute a sufficient investigation for these purposes.[82] Another factor is how recent the original order is.

3.38 In addition to s 5(1), there is a power in matrimonial proceedings, under s 2A(4),[83] to direct that no s 8 order under the Children Act 1989 be made by any court in, or in connection with, these proceedings where it considers 'that it would be more appropriate for Part I matters relating to the child to be determined outside England and Wales'. This power, which is confined to matrimonial proceedings, overlaps with the more general power under s 5(1) but, as the Law Commissions explained,[84] the distinction is that, unlike s 5(1), s 2A(4) enables the court 'to waive its potential jurisdiction without first having to have a [Part I] application before it'.

3.39 Section 5(2) vests, 'at any stage of the proceedings', a general power in an English court to which an application for or to vary a Part I order is made, to stay proceedings where it appears either:

'(a)   that proceedings with respect to the matters to which the application relates are continuing outside England and Wales, or

(b)   that it would be more appropriate for those matters to be determined in proceedings to be taken outside England and Wales.'[85]

Section 5(2) vests a wide discretion to grant stays. Like s 5(1), it is not confined to cases arising solely within the United Kingdom or the Isle of Man and, as s 5(2)(a) and (b) make clear, it can be exercised either where there are relevant continuing proceedings elsewhere or where there are no other proceedings. It seems established[86] that the court has power to act of its own motion to decide

---

81   See Law Com No 138/Scot Law Com No 91 at p 155.

82   Although it may be an excellent reason for granting a stay: see further **3.39** below.

83   For the equivalent provisions in Scotland and Northern Ireland, see respectively ss 13(6)(b) and 19A(4). For an example of the court exercising its discretion under s 2A(4) in favour of the matter being decided in Scotland, see *Re S (Jurisdiction To Stay Application)* [1995] 1 FLR 1093, per Thorpe J.

84   Law Com No 138/Scot Law Com No 91 at p 155. The power was briefly discussed in *M v M (Abduction: England and Scotland)* [1997] FLR 263, CA, although it was coupled with a consideration of the power to stay under s 5(2).

85   For the equivalent power in Northern Ireland, see s 22(2). In Scotland the equivalent power to sist proceedings is governed by s 14(2), on which see *B v B* 1998 SLT 1245, *Calleja v Calleja* 1997 SLT 579 and *Hill v Hill* 1991 SLT 189.

86   See *Re S (Residence Order: Forum Conveniens)* [1995] 1 FLR 314, per Thorpe J, followed in *H v H (A Minor) (No 2) (Forum Conveniens)* [1997] 1 FCR 603, per Bracewell J.

the appropriate forum. In other words, the court can order a stay whether or not such an application has been made.

3.40   Given s 5(2)(b), it seems clear that Bracewell J was wrong in *S v S (Custody: Jurisdiction)*[87] to consider that the superseding of an earlier order by a later one in any way fettered the discretion to grant a stay. On the other hand, notwithstanding the generality of the discretion, it is well established[88] that in the context of matrimonial proceedings the staying provisions provided by Sch 1, paras 8 and 9 to the Domicile and Matrimonial Proceedings Act 1973 should be applied in preference.

3.41   In *Re S (A Minor) (Stay of Proceedings)*[89] the Court of Appeal accepted that the principles upon which the discretion under s 5 should be exercised are those established by *Spiliada Maritime Corporation v Cansulex Ltd*[90] and *de Dampierre v de Dampierre*.[91] Broadly, this test, now commonly referred to as the '*Spiliada* test', involves determining which is the more suitable or appropriate tribunal to resolve the question between the parties. If the respondent satisfies the court that such a forum exists a stay will be granted unless the applicant can show that there are circumstances (viz substantial injustice) which require that a stay should nevertheless not be granted. There is a conflict of views as to whether, in applying this test, the court should consider the child's welfare to be the paramount consideration[92] but, in any event, it is clearly an important consideration. Equally, the child's habitual residence is important.[93] Other factors include the relative ease or difficulty of

---

[87]   [1995] 1 FLR 155, discussed above at **3.31–3.32**.

[88]   See *M v M (Abduction: England and Scotland)* [1997] 2 FLR 263, CA, *T v T (Custody: Jurisdiction)* [1992] 1 FLR 43 and *A v A (Forum Conveniens)* [1999] 1 FLR 1. In any event, s 5(4) states that nothing in the section 'shall affect any power exercisable apart from this section to refuse an application to grant or resolve a stay'. Section 22(4) is in similar terms for Northern Ireland but there is no equivalent provision in Scotland.

[89]   [1993] 2 FLR 912 at 914 per Lloyd LJ. See also the historical analysis by Thorpe J in *Re S (Residence Order: Forum Conveniens)* [1995] 1 FLR 314 at 322–323.

[90]   [1987] AC 460, [1986] 3 All ER 843, HL.

[91]   [1998] AC 92, [1987] 2 All ER 1, [1987] 2 FLR 300, HL.

[92]   See, on the one hand, *H v H (Minors) (Forum Conveniens) (Nos 1 and 2)* [1993] 1 FLR 958, in which Waite J thought the child's welfare was paramount, which was followed by Bracewell J in *H v H (A Minor) (No 2) (Forum Conveniens)* [1997] 1 FCR 603. On the other hand, in *Re S (Residence Order: Forum Conveniens)*[1995] 1 FLR 314, Thorpe J thought that the child's welfare was not paramount. In the Scottish decision, *B v B* 1998 SLT 1245 at 1246, Lord Maclean agreed with Thorpe J's analysis.

[93]   See eg *H v H (A Minor) (No 2) (Forum Conveniens)* (above) per Bracewell J; *Re M (Jurisdiction: Forums Conveniens)* [1995] 2 FLR 224, CA – jurisdiction declined in respect of children habitually resident in Malta; and *Re F (Residence Order: Jurisdiction)* [1995] 2 FLR 518 – cogent reasons needed to justify an English court hearing in a case where a child is habitually resident in another Contracting State under the 1980 Hague Abduction Convention or the 1980 European Custody Convention – per Singer J.

obtaining evidence through, for example, welfare reports, and the convenience of the adult parties involved.[94]

3.42   If proceedings are stayed, the stay covers *all* aspects of the proceedings, including, for example, enforcing or varying any undertakings.[95] On the other hand, stays are not necessarily permanent. Indeed under s 5(3)[96] stays can be removed:

> 'if it appears to the court that there has been unreasonable delay in the taking or prosecution of the other proceeding … or that these proceedings are stayed, sisted or concluded.'

In part this provision is intended to guard against the use of stays as a delaying tactic but it also covers the case where, for whatever reasons, the court in another part of the United Kingdom or the Isle of Man subsequently relinquishes jurisdiction.[97]

The difficulty of accommodating mirror orders

3.43   Although the principal purpose of the 1986 Act was to create common jurisdictional rules within the United Kingdom, it is evident that the Act operates more generally and that, subject now to the application of the Council Regulation, it applies to all cases in which a Part I order is sought even where the child is associated with jurisdictions outside the United Kingdom and the Isle of Man. Whether this was intended may be debated,[98] but the effect of the 1986 Act is that, on the face of it, in the absence of matrimonial proceedings, if the child is neither habitually resident nor physically present there is no jurisdiction to make a Part I order.[99] However, such a rigid interpretation would mean that courts would be powerless to make a 'mirror' or 'back to back' order at the request of a foreign court to protect a child as when he or she arrives here. This was the dilemma facing Singer J in *Re P (A Child: Mirror Orders)*.[100] That case concerned an Iranian national father who resided in England and a mother who had both British and American nationality but who resided in the United States to which she had taken the

---

[94]   See *Re S (A Minor) (Stay of Proceedings)* [1993] 2 FLR 912. Presumably, where the court raises the issue of its own motion, it must satisfy itself that another tribunal is more suitable. See also *W and W v H (Child Abduction: Surrogacy) No 2* [2002] 2 FLR 252.

[95]   *Re S (A Minor) (Stay of Proceedings)* (above).

[96]   Section 22(3) provides the equivalent provision in Northern Ireland, but in Scotland there is no equivalent provision – s 13(7) simply vests a general power of recall.

[97]   See the explanation at Law Com No 138/Scot Law Com No 91, para 4.103.

[98]   See Thorpe J in *Re S (Residence Order: Forum Conveniens)* [1995] 1 FLR 314 at 321 and note also Singer J's observation in *Re P (A Child: Mirror Orders)* [2000] 1 FLR 435 at 437 that the Preamble to the 1986 Act does not on its face contemplate the legislation having effect outside the confines of the United Kingdom. However, it does refer to 'the effect and enforcement of restrictions on the removal of children from the United Kingdom'.

[99]   See eg *Re M (Abduction: Habitual Residence)* [1996] 1 FLR 887, CA.

[100] [2000] 1 FLR 435. On which see the excellent note by Beevers, '*Re P (A Child: Mirror Orders)* Jurisdiction to grant a mirror order' [2000] CFLQ 413.

child sometime earlier. The father's application for a return order under the 1980 Hague Abduction Convention was refused but instead the American judge granted him some staying contact in England. However, before that contact could take place, the American judge required the English High Court to put in place an order mirroring the American contact order and preventing any unauthorised removal of the child from England during the contact period. The problem for Singer J was that, given that the child was neither habitually resident nor present in England or Wales, there was no apparent jurisdiction to make the required order no matter how much it was in the child's interests to do so. However, considering it to be 'a matter of common sense, of comity and ... of public policy' that the English court accommodate the wish of a foreign court that there should be an order in England mirroring the foreign order so that contact could take place there and in the confident expectation that, had it contemplated the problem, 'Parliament would not have wished to restrict or to frustrate such a potentially beneficial procedure', Singer J, whilst acknowledging the 'substantial difficulties about entertaining this application' resolved to make the order upon the basis that it would only take effect each time the child came to the jurisdiction for the purpose of contact thereby regulated and would cease to have effect each time the child left the jurisdiction.

3.44   Although it is clearly desirable that the English court should be able to assist the smooth functioning of a foreign order, in this case, for access taking place in England, it must be doubted whether in fact it was right to hold that there was jurisdiction.[101] Ironically, Singer J declined to accept what might have been the better argument, namely, that he was being asked to make an order that fell outside Part I[102] and that he was therefore free to exercise his inherent powers[103] according to common law rules.[104] Patently, the position

---

[101]   The meaning of Family Law Act 1986, s 7(c) is plain and, with respect, precluded the assumption of jurisdiction under s 2 where the child was neither habitually resident nor present in England and Wales at the 'relevant date'.

[102]   The argument being that a mirror order was supportive of a foreign order and being ancillary or auxiliary was therefore outside the definition of a Part I order.

[103]   Singer J rejected this (see [2000] 1 FLR 435 at 442) on the ground that s 1(1)(d) was all-embracing and must be taken to have removed all other inherent powers. Cf *F v S (Wardship: Jurisdiction)* [1991] 2 FLR 349, in which Ward J held that the absence of jurisdiction under the 1986 Act did not preclude him having jurisdiction in wardship proceedings, based on the child's allegiance, to make an order requiring disclosure of the child's whereabouts since that fell outside the definition of a Part I order. This aspect of the decision was not commented upon in the subsequent appeal before the Court of Appeal: see [1993] 2 FLR 686 (and see **3.10** above).

[104]   According to which, in theory, jurisdiction can be based on allegiance (but cf *Al Habtoor v Fotheringham* [2001] EWCA Civ 186, [2001] 1 FLR 951, CA, in which Thorpe LJ ruled that the inherent jurisdiction should no longer be based on British nationality). As Beevers, *op cit*, n 100, at 416, points out, the child in this case probably did have British nationality. (Note also her other arguments based on Art 8 of the European Convention on Human Rights.) Interestingly, it has since been held in Jersey that there is an inherent power to make a mirror order, in that case, in respect of English children: see *F v H* (unreported) 27 July 2001, Royal Court of Jersey (Samedi Division).

needs to be clarified and courts clearly empowered to make mirror orders in the type of circumstances involved in *Re P*.[105]

COMMENTARY – THE NEED FOR REFORM

3.45 Although the Family Law Act 1986 represented an enormous stride forward for dealing with children's cases within the United Kingdom and the Isle of Man (it must not be forgotten how hard the English and Scottish Law Commissions had to work to reach an agreement) it cannot now be said that resulting law is satisfactory.

3.46 The contrary seems to be the case. Whilst the provisions dealing with jurisdiction are difficult and complicated (now exacerbated by the implementation of the Council Regulation) and, moreover, do not prevent conflicting decisions concerning the same child being made in different jurisdictions within the United Kingdom, at the same time the rules for recognition and enforcement are over-elaborate, slow and expensive and, not surprisingly, rather infrequently invoked. There are also an irritating number of drafting deficiencies that need to be attended to.[106] There is urgent need to reform the rules so as clearly to allow the courts to make mirror orders and finally any resulting, hopefully more coherent and understandable, scheme should be applied to the Channel Islands.

3.47 As just intimated, there are three major concerns about the current rules governing jurisdiction, namely their complexity (as Thorpe J said in *Re S (Residence Order: Forum Conveniens)*:[107] 'Part I of the Family Law Act 1986 is not easy to understand either in its layout or its language'), their inability to prevent conflicts arising within the United Kingdom and their inadequacy to permit the making of mirror orders.

3.48 With regard to the inability to prevent conflicts continuing to arise it should be acknowledged that, to some extent, these conflicts have resulted either from factual ignorance, that is, where orders are made in one jurisdiction without knowledge of an existing order in another, or from a misapplication of the Family Law Act 1986.

Procedural improvements

3.49 So far as factual ignorance is concerned, while acknowledging that the scope for investigation is obviously limited in cases of ex parte applications,

---

[105] See, for example, in Australia, where s 69E of the Family Law Act 1975 (Cth) provides: '(1) Proceedings may be instituted under this Act in relation to a child only if … (e) it would be in accordance with a treaty or arrangement in force between Australia and an overseas jurisdiction, or the common law rules, for the court to exercise jurisdiction in the proceedings'.

[106] Eg the failure to cross-reference ss 2(3) and 3(1).

[107] [1995] 1 FLR 314 at 320.

attention should nevertheless be drawn to the requirement in divorce proceedings in Appendix 2 to the Family Proceedings Rules 1991 to state in the petition whether there are or have been 'any other proceedings in any court in England and Wales or elsewhere with reference to ... any child of the family'[108] and to the less explicit requirement upon the applicant in Children Act 1989 proceedings in Form C1 (para 11) to state 'whether, to your knowledge, the adult has been involved in a court case concerning a child'. In other words, the court might well be furnished with sufficient information to be put on notice that there are or have been proceedings elsewhere in the United Kingdom. It should certainly be a standard question that a court puts to the applicant as to whether, to the applicant's knowledge, there have been other proceedings about the child. It should also be added that under s 33 of the 1986 Act, in any proceedings for a Part I order in which there is inadequate information about the child's whereabouts, the court has power to 'order any person who it has reason to believe may have relevant information to disclose it to the court'.

3.50   Once it becomes apparent that there are, or may be, proceedings elsewhere in the United Kingdom or the Isle of Man it should surely be standard practice to transfer proceedings to the High Court if they are not brought there in the first place. Douglas Brown J recommended as such in *T v T (Custody: Jurisdiction)*[109] and indeed referred to the Official Solicitor's 'helpful suggestion' that the then Practice Direction[110] be amended to make explicit reference to orders made in a Scottish court which are or may be intended to be recognised and enforced in England and Wales. It is time that the practicality of this suggestion be investigated.[111]

Substantive law reform

3.51   Helpful though the foregoing suggested procedural improvements may be, they cannot hide the need for substantive law reform. As a matter of priority, attention needs to be paid to the issue of superseding orders. First, it should be made clear that only orders 'competently' made can have this effect at all. This is an explicit requirement under s 15(1) so far as Scottish orders are concerned and Hale J was surely right when she said in *D v D (Custody: Jurisdiction)*[112] that it is implicit in s 6(1) so far as English orders are concerned (and by parity of reasoning in s 24(1) so far as Northern Ireland orders are

---

[108]   Para 1(i). Note also the requirements concerning the petitioner's habitual residence in para 1(a).

[109]   [1992] 1 FLR 43 at 47–48.

[110]   Ie *President's Direction: Distribution and Transfer between the High Court and County Courts of Family Business and Family Proceedings* [1988] 1 FLR 540. The transfer provisions are now contained in the Children (Allocation of Proceedings) Order 1991, SI 1991/1677.

[111]   One possible argument against requiring such cases to be heard in the High Court is the lack of a High Court Registry north of Preston on the North West Circuit. But there is no evidence that cross-border issues are a particular problem for this region.

[112]   [1996] 1 FLR 574 at 562, discussed at **3.26**.

concerned). Ideally, however, the Act should be amended to reflect this. Secondly, although it is right to say that the Children Act 1989 knows of no such creature as an 'interim residence order', nevertheless, as one leading commentator has said,[113] it surely cannot be right that an ex parte residence order, made for a limited duration, should have the disproportionate effect of superseding an earlier final inter partes order made in another jurisdiction. It is still open to the Court of Appeal to hold that for the purpose of the superseding provision of the 1986 Act, an 'order' does not include a holding or interim order. In the absence of such a ruling, legislative reform might again be necessary.

3.52 Whether it is necessary to have so many jurisdictional bases is debatable. In particular it might be questioned whether it is right to give priority to matrimonial proceedings. The thinking behind this has always been that it is sensible to have all the relevant proceedings before a single court. While there is obvious merit in this, it has not remained an unchallenged proposition, particularly since jurisdiction is taken on the basis of the adults' domicile or habitual residence. It is to be observed that the automatic priority of matrimonial proceedings was not accepted in the 1996 Hague Convention on the Protection of Children, although jurisdiction on that basis is preserved provided all the parties consent.[114] Were the 1986 Act to be revisited, consideration would have to be given as to whether it should be amended along the lines of the 1996 Convention. But even if no amendments are recommended, it is by no means clear why there should be separate and different provisions governing stays.[115] Quite apart from being confusing to have separate provisions, why is it that, in the case of matrimonial proceedings, there are provisions for compulsory stays even when involving children[116] but not in non-matrimonial proceedings? It is suggested that there should be uniform provisions governing stays.

---

[113] Cretney [1995] Fam Law 120 at 121.

[114] See Art 10 of the 1996 Convention, discussed at **24.21–24.22** and on which see Clive, 'The New Hague Convention on Children' (1998) 3 *Juridical Review* 169 at 175–177 and Nygh, 'The New Hague Child Protection Convention' (1997) 11 *Int Jo of the Law, Policy and the Family* 344 at 350–351.

[115] Viz, in the case of matrimonial proceedings, those provided by Sch 1 to the Domicile and Matrimonial Proceedings Act 1973 and those applicable to non-matrimonial proceedings in ss 2A(4) and 5 of the Family Law Act 1986, discussed above at **3.35** *et seq*.

[116] Viz under Sch 1, para 8 to the 1973 Act, see **3.17** above.

Chapter 4

THE CURRENT BASES OF JURISDICTION IN ENGLAND AND WALES

INTRODUCTION

4.1 Proceedings involving questions of legal status or legal relationships require a more substantial connection between the jurisdiction (in the sense of England and Wales as a territorial area governed by one system of law) and the litigants or the child than proceedings which have less far-reaching consequences. Jurisdiction in adoption proceedings is based on a combination of the age, marital status and domicile within the United Kingdom, the Channel Islands or the Isle of Man of the prospective adoptive parents.[1] The jurisdictional bases for making parental orders in favour of gamete donors under s 30 of the Human Fertilisation and Embryology Act 1990 are the age and domicile of the applicants, coupled with requirements that they must be married and that the application for the order must be made within 6 months of the birth of the child, who must have his home with them at the time of both the application and the making of the order.[2]

4.2 There are no statutory provisions governing jurisdiction to appoint guardians under s 5 of the Children Act 1989, or the acquisition of parental responsibility by a father under s 4, although in *Re S (Parental Responsibility: Jurisdiction)*[3] Butler-Sloss LJ said:

> 'For my part, I am satisfied from the wording of the Family Law Act 1986 and the Children Act 1989 that there is jurisdiction for the court to exercise, if it is

---

[1]   Adoption Act 1976, ss 14, 15. In the case of a Convention adoption (that is, an adoption made under the 1965 Hague Convention on Jurisdiction, Applicable Law and Recognition of Decrees Relating to Adoption, which was ratified by the United Kingdom on 24 August 1978 and came into force on 23 October 1978 as between the United Kingdom, Austria and Switzerland, see the Convention Adoption (Austria and Switzerland) Order 1978, SI 1978/1431), jurisdiction was based on habitual residence. Prospectively, jurisdiction to make domestic adoption orders will be governed by s 49 of the Adoption and Children Act 2002. By s 50, an unmarried couple will be able to apply for a joint adoption. Intercountry adoptions are now subject to the 1993 Hague Convention on Protection of Children and Co-operation in respect of Intercountry Adoption, which the United Kingdom ratified in June 2003. The United Kingdom, together with Austria and Switzerland, intends to denounce the 1965 Convention. For a discussion of the new law on intercountry adoption, see Bridge and Swindells, *Adoption – The Modern Law* (Family Law, 2003), ch 14.

[2]   Human Fertilisation and Embryology Act 1990, s 30.

[3]   [1998] 2 FLR 921. Presumably, this ruling applies to making parental responsibility agreements as well.

proper to do so, in respect of a child who is permanently out of the jurisdiction, even if born out of the jurisdiction, under s 4, an application for a parental responsibility order which is an order which is different in kind from the s 8 orders.'

4.3 It is difficult to discern from this judgment the jurisdictional base for the exercise of the power to confer parental responsibility upon a father, although one assumes that at least one of the parents must have some real and substantial connection with England and Wales. However, this lack of an obvious juridical connecting factor does give rise to concern as to whether the order would be recognised, especially by the State of the child's domicile, which under English law would be that of the mother.[4]

4.4 Jurisdiction in public law proceedings is based on either the habitual (or 'ordinary') residence or the presence of the child within England and Wales at the time the application is made. The 'presence' basis of jurisdiction is unaffected by the child being habitually resident in another part of the United Kingdom or elsewhere, although the English courts may decline to exercise jurisdiction on the basis that another jurisdiction is a more appropriate forum.[5]

Wardship and the inherent jurisdiction

4.5 Although it may not be strictly accurate historically, for modern purposes, wardship is probably best regarded as a status which may be, but does not have to be, imposed by the High Court in the exercise of its inherent (prerogative) jurisdiction over children.[6] The significant difference is that by imposing the status of ward, the child's legal custody is in the court, so no important step may be taken in his life without the court's permission.[7] In theory, the jurisdiction to confer the status of ward is based on allegiance to the Crown and the reciprocal duty of protection, but in no modern case has nationality alone been a sufficient foundation upon which to make an order, whether or not imposing the status of ward.[8] The ability to exercise the inherent jurisdiction has been constrained by the Family Law Act 1986, the Children Act 1989[9] and by the judges, who have declined to exercise the jurisdiction when the matter in question has been covered by statute, or where the issue falls within the competence of another prerogative jurisdiction, such as military discipline, or where Parliament has entrusted the exercise of a

---

4   See **4.22** below.
5   *London Borough of Southwark v B* [1993] 2 FLR 559; *Re R (Care Orders: Jurisdiction)* [1995] 1 FLR 712; *Re M (Minor) (Care Order: Jurisdiction)* [1997] Fam 67. See also **11.44** and *Rayden and Jackson on Divorce and Family Matters,* 17th edn (Butterworths, 1997), para 37.19.
6   *Re Z (A Minor) (Freedom of Publication)* [1997] Fam 1, [1996] 1 FLR 191. And see Seymour, 'Parens Patriae and Wardship Powers: Their Nature and Origins', (1994) 14 *Oxford Journal of Legal Studies* 159.
7   *Re S (Infants)* [1967] 1 All ER 202.
8   Lowe and White, *Wards of Court*, 2nd edn (Barry Rose, 1986). See also *Al Habtoor v Fotheringham* [2000] EWCA Civ 186, [2001] 1 FLR 951.
9   Sections 9(5) and 100.

discretionary power to another body, such as a local authority, immigration authorities or another court.[10]

4.6 The question of whether the High Court could exercise its inherent jurisdiction to make orders when there is no power to make a substantive order under Part I of the Family Law Act 1986 was considered by Ward J in *F v S (Wardship: Jurisdiction)*.[11] He held that that the absence of jurisdiction under the 1986 Act did not preclude him having jurisdiction in wardship proceedings, based on the child's allegiance, to make an order requiring disclosure of the child's whereabouts,[12] since that fell outside the definition of a 'Part I order'. Although this aspect of the decision was not commented upon in the subsequent appeal before the Court of Appeal,[13] it has since been disapproved in *Al Habtoor v Fotheringham*.[14]

4.7 The most common area by far in which issues relating to jurisdiction arise is when the proceedings relate to the exercise of parental responsibility, whether by way of applications for orders under s 8 of the Children Act 1989 or for orders under the inherent jurisdiction of the High Court with respect to children which involve the care of a child, contact with a child or the education or upbringing of a child. Such orders are referred to as 'Part I orders'[15] because original jurisdiction[16] to make them is conferred on the courts of the United Kingdom and specified dependent territories by Part I of the Family Law Act 1986, as amended to accommodate the Council Regulation on jurisdiction and the recognition of judgments in matrimonial matters and in matters of parental responsibility for children of both spouses ('the Council Regulation').[17]

THE JURISDICTIONAL CONNECTING FACTORS – MATRIMONIAL PROCEEDINGS, DOMICILE AND HABITUAL RESIDENCE

Matrimonial proceedings

4.8 The ability of courts in England and Wales to entertain matrimonial proceedings is provided for in the Domicile and Matrimonial Proceedings

---

10   *Re Z (A Minor) (Freedom of Publication)* [1997] Fam 1, [1996] 1 FLR 191.

11   [1991] 2 FLR 349.

12   An order under s 33 of the Family Law Act 1986 requiring a person to disclose information relevant to a child's whereabouts can only be made '... *in proceedings for or relating to a Part I order* ...' (emphasis added).

13   [1993] 2 FLR 684.

14   [2001] EWCA Civ 186, [2001] 1 FLR 951.

15   Family Law Act 1986, s 1(1).

16   The jurisdictional rules set out in the Part I of the Family Law Act 1986 do not apply to applications to vary or discharge an order – see s 1(1).

17   Council Regulation (EC) No 1347/2000 of 29 May 2000, often referred to as 'Brussels II'.

Act 1973, as amended to accommodate the Council Regulation.[18] Section 5(2) provides:

> 'The court shall have jurisdiction to entertain proceedings for divorce or judicial separation if (and only if) –
>
> (a)   the court has jurisdiction under the Council Regulation; or
> (b)   no court of a Contracting State has jurisdiction under the Council Regulation and either of the parties to the marriage is domiciled in England and Wales on the date when the proceedings are begun.'

MATRIMONIAL JURISDICTION UNDER THE COUNCIL REGULATION

4.9   Historically, there have always been two approaches to jurisdiction in private law disputes about children. One approach has been that primary jurisdiction should go to the court seized of any matrimonial proceedings between the parents, so that it can be satisfied before the marriage is dissolved that proper arrangements are in place for the children;[19] the other is that decisions relating to the care and welfare of children are best made in the country of their habitual residence.[20] The Council Regulation tries to reconcile the tension between two different approaches by providing that jurisdiction is based on a combination of both.

Scope of the Council Regulation

4.10   The Council Regulation applies to civil proceedings relating to divorce, legal separation or marriage annulment, and to civil proceedings relating to parental responsibility for the children of both spouses on the occasion of such matrimonial proceedings. 'Civil' proceedings excludes religious proceedings.

Children affected by the Council Regulation

4.11   The Council Regulation applies to matters relating to parental responsibility for the 'children of both spouses' involved in matrimonial proceedings. 'Children of both spouses' does not mean children of the family. It probably includes adopted children, but step-children and children born out of wedlock are excluded. It is not clear whether children born to the spouses by artificial or assisted methods of conception are included.

---

[18]   By the European Communities (Matrimonial Jurisdiction and Judgments) Regulations 2001, SI 2001/310, reg 3.

[19]   Eg the Family Law Act 1986.

[20]   Eg the 1996 Hague Convention on jurisdiction, applicable law, recognition, enforcement and co-operation in respect of parental responsibility and measures for the protection of children (the 1996 Hague Convention on the Protection of Children).

4.12   By limiting its scope to the children of both spouses, the Council Regulation complicates the international rules of jurisdiction relating to children by creating a class of children to which special rules apply, although it has to be said that the position is no different *within* the United Kingdom because jurisdiction to make a 'Part I order' under the Family Law Act 1986[21] in or in connection with matrimonial proceedings also extends only to children of both spouses.[22]

'Parental responsibility'

4.13   'Parental responsibility' is not defined in the Council Regulation, and it is not clear how far it would extend beyond the issues of with whom the child is to live or with whom the child shall have contact. It may well extend to disputes about schooling, but does it extend to prohibiting the publication of information by persons other than parents? Section 8 of the Children Act 1989 defines prohibited steps and specific issue orders in terms of parental responsibility. Such orders can be made in respect of persons other than parents.[23]

Jurisdiction

4.14   Article 2 sets out the rules of direct jurisdiction for matrimonial proceedings, giving a choice of jurisdictional connecting factors based on habitual residence or nationality (or, in the case of the United Kingdom and Ireland, 'domicile') with no hierarchy. Those connecting factors are:

(i)   both spouses' habitual residence;
(ii)   the last habitual residence of both spouses, one spouse still being habitually resident there;
(iii) the respondent spouse's habitual residence;
(iv)   in cases of a joint application, either spouse's habitual residence;
(v)   the applicant's habitual residence based on 12 months' residence immediately before the application;
(vi)   the applicant's habitual residence based on 6 months' residence immediately before the application coupled with nationality or (in the case of the United Kingdom and Ireland) domicile;
(vii) the nationality of both spouses or, in the case of the United Kingdom and Ireland, their domicile.

If no Member State has jurisdiction under (i)–(vii) above, jurisdiction is determined according to the laws of each State.[24]

---

[21]   See **3.2** above.
[22]   Family Law Act 1986, s 2A, discussed at **3.6** above.
[23]   See eg the discussion in White, Carr and Lowe, *The Children Act in Practice*, 3rd edn (Butterworths, 2002) at **5.70** *et seq*.
[24]   Article 8.

4.15 The non-hierarchical structure of the connecting factors means that courts may have concurrent jurisdiction, but in such a case, courts must defer to the court first seized of the case,[25] unless there is a need to take urgent protective measures.[26] A court is deemed to be seized of a case when 'the document instituting the proceedings or an equivalent document is lodged with the court', provided that steps are taken to serve it; or, when it must be served before being lodged, when it is received by the authority responsible for service.[27]

4.16 A court must, if the court of another Member State has jurisdiction, declare of its own motion that it has no jurisdiction if it is seized of a case over which it has no jurisdiction under the Regulation.[28] There is no power to decline jurisdiction in favour of more appropriate forum.

4.17 Jurisdiction over matters 'relating to parental responsibility for the children of both spouses' follows jurisdiction over the matrimonial proceedings, but is not automatic. Article 3 provides that a court[29] of a Member State, having established jurisdiction over the matrimonial proceedings, can then deal with the children provided that they are either habitually resident in that Member State or are habitually resident in another Member State and at least one spouse has parental responsibility in relation to them and the jurisdiction of the court is accepted by both spouses and is in the best interests of the children. The Council Regulation does not provide for continuing, exclusive jurisdiction, even in the sense of the power to vary a previous order. Jurisdiction continues only until either the decision relating to the matrimonial proceedings becomes final or comes to an end for another reason or, if they are then still pending, the decision in the proceedings relating to parental responsibility becomes final or comes to an end for another reason (Art 3), when presumably jurisdiction becomes at large according to the laws of the Member States (Art 7).

4.18 The exercise of jurisdiction is also subject to Arts 3 and 16 of the 1980 Hague Abduction Convention.[30] In other words, the 1980 Hague Abduction Convention takes precedence over the Council Regulation.

---

[25] Article 11. See **3.7** above.

[26] Article 12. See *A v L (Jurisdiction: Brussels II)* [2002] 1 FLR 1042 and *Wermuth v Wermuth* [2002] EWCA Civ 50, [2003] 1 WLR 942, sub nom *Wermuth v Wermuth (No 2)* [2003] 1 FLR 1029.

[27] Article 11(4).

[28] Article 9.

[29] 'Court' includes all authorities, judicial or otherwise, with jurisdiction over matrimonial matters and civil proceedings relating to parental responsibility – Preamble, Recital (9) and Art 1(2).

[30] Article 4. Article 3 of the 1980 Hague Abduction Convention defines a wrongful removal or retention, Art 16 restrains State Parties from making decisions on the 'merits of rights of custody' until it has been determined that the child shall not be returned under the Convention – see s 9 of the Child Abduction and Custody Act 1985.

MATRIMONIAL JURISDICTION OTHER THAN UNDER THE COUNCIL REGULATION

4.19   If no court of a Contracting State has jurisdiction under the Council Regulation, then the courts of England and Wales can entertain matrimonial proceedings if, on the date when they are begun, either of the spouses is domiciled in England and Wales.[31]

Domicile[32]

4.20   When we are born, we become members of both a political and a civil society. The political society determines our nationality. The civil society determines our civil status, and also the law which attaches to us – our personal law. That attachment to a civil society is our domicile, and the personal law, which remains attached to us wherever we are until we become members of another civil society, is the law of our domicile. If we change our domicile by choice and become members of another civil society, it is the law of that society that becomes attached to us.

4.21   Domicile is therefore the legal, and often the factual, relationship between a person and a territorial area subject to one system of law, which may be a State, such as France; a part of a State, such as England and Wales; a state in the United States of America; or a territory.[33] The relationship may arise from being, like a child, legally dependent upon someone else, or from residence coupled with an intention of making the place a permanent home.

> 'By domicile we mean home, the permanent home; and if you do not understand your permanent home I am afraid that no illustration drawn from foreign writers or foreign languages will be very much help to you.'[34]

Everybody has a domicile at all times, regardless of their having no home or residence,[35] and no one can have more than one domicile at any one time.[36]

---

31   Domicile and Matrimonial Proceedings Act 1973, s 5 (see **4.8** above). Note that habitual residence in the jurisdiction for 12 months preceding the presentation of the petition is no longer a ground of jurisdiction in cases other than under the Council Regulation.

32   See Dicey & Morris, *The Conflict of Laws*, 13th edn (Sweet & Maxwell), vol 1, chapter 6.

33   But see Arts 2(1)(a) and 41 of the Council Regulation, which appear to suggest that, for the purpose of the Council Regulation, one can be domiciled in the United Kingdom.

34   *Wicker v Hume* (1858) 7 HLC 124 at 160. The difficulty of defining domicile is discussed in *Forbes v Forbes* (1854) Kay 341; and *Lord v Colvin* (1859) 4 Drew 366, 28 LJ Ch 361: 'I would venture to suggest that the definition of an acquired domicile might stand thus: "That place is properly the domicile of a person in which he has voluntarily fixed the habitation of himself and his family, not for a mere special and temporary purpose, but with a present intention of making it his permanent home, unless and until something (which is unexpected or the happening of which is uncertain) shall occur to induce him to adopt some other permanent home)"', per Sir Richard Kindersley V-C.

35   *Re Craignish* [1892] 3 Ch 180 at 192: 'A man may in fact be homeless, but he cannot in law be without a domicile' per Chitty J.

The domicile of children[37]

4.22 The domicile of children who are to be the subject of proceedings is not a basis of jurisdiction, but it may sometimes be necessary to apply the rules of domicile in relation to children to identify an adult's domicile of origin if that were relevant to jurisdiction in relation to that adult. A child's domicile does, however, identify their personal law. This is important because it is our personal law which determines our capacity to enter into legal relationships. So, for example, the ability of an English girl of 16 to have a termination of her pregnancy in Italy depends partly on Italian domestic law and partly on English law. Italian law will determine whether in her personal circumstances an abortion is permitted, but her capacity to consent to it is a matter of English law.[38]

4.23 In the law of England and Wales and Northern Ireland, the domicile of children is derived from that of their parents, and they do not acquire a capacity to change their domicile until they reach the age of 16 years.[39] The domicile of legitimate children (children born in wedlock) is that of their father. So that if mother, father and children are all living together, or if the mother and father are living apart but share the arrangements for the care of their children, the children will take the domicile of their father. If, however, the parents are living apart and the children have a home with their mother and no home with their father, they will take the domicile of their mother.[40] In those circumstances, they will continue to take their mother's domicile even if they stop living with her, provided that they do not have a home with their father.[41] If they do, their domicile will change to that of their father. The domicile of children born out of wedlock is that of their mother, but whether their domicile changes with that of their mother depends on the circumstances.[42]

HABITUAL RESIDENCE

4.24 By far the most important connecting factor in family matters is now habitual residence. For some time there has been wide international acceptance that the State of a child's habitual residence is, in all but exceptional

---

36 *Garthwaite v Garthwaite* [1964] P 356 at 379, [1964] 2 All ER 233 at 236, CA: 'It is not possible to have more than one domicile at one and the same time' per Willmer LJ. The expression 'de facto domicile' is a contradiction in terms: domicile is something which every person acquires by operation of law.

37 See Dicey & Morris, *The Conflict of Laws, op cit* at n 32, chapter 6, p 139.

38 As a 16-year-old, she can give a valid consent by virtue of s 8 of the Family Law Reform Act 1969.

39 Domicile and Matrimonial Proceedings Act 1973, s 3.

40 *Ibid*, s 4.

41 Domicile and Matrimonial Proceedings Act 1973, s 4.

42 See Dicey & Morris *The Conflict of Laws, op cit* at n 32, chapter 6, p 140.

circumstances, the most appropriate forum for deciding what is in his welfare interests.[43] More recently, habitual residence has become the predominant factor in determining which State within the EU has jurisdiction over matrimonial proceedings and whether that court also has jurisdiction over the children of both spouses in matters relating to parental responsibility.[44] Habitual residence has for some time been an important factor in determining jurisdiction in internal law. In the United Kingdom it is one of the bases of jurisdiction on which the courts can make a wide range of orders in family matters, including orders about the upbringing of children,[45] the return of children wrongfully removed from the United Kingdom[46] or wrongfully removed or retained away from their State of habitual residence,[47] as well as declarations relating to status,[48] and orders in matrimonial proceedings, including financial provision, maintenance assessments and recovering maintenance abroad.[49] In the United States, habitual residence is the basis for determining jurisdiction in the American Uniform Child Custody Jurisdiction Act and its successor, the Uniform Child Custody Jurisdiction and Enforcement Act.[50]

4.25 The adoption of habitual residence as an international juridical connecting factor had its origins in the desire to move away from nationality and particularly domicile, with its varying interpretations in different States and its concept of dependency, and to make it clear that what was envisaged was the child's actual residence.[51] However, unlike domicile, habitual residence is an ephemeral concept.[52] Not only can it be lost in a single day, it is also possible to have more than one. It is also possible to have no habitual residence, because an habitual residence might have been lost, but a new one not yet acquired,[53] an important point in the context of proceedings under the

---

[43] See Law Com No 138/Scot Law Com No 91, paras 4.12 *et seq*. And see *Al Habtoor v Fotheringham* [2001] EWCA Civ 186, [2001] 1 FLR 951; 1980 European Custody Convention, Art 10; 1996 Hague Convention on the Protection of Children, Art 5.

[44] Council Regulation, Art 2. See **4.17** above.

[45] Family Law Act 1986, ss 2 and 3. See **3.9** above.

[46] *Ibid*, s 41. See **4.74**.

[47] Child Abduction and Custody Act 1985. See **14.4** *et seq*.

[48] Family Law Act 1986, ss 55–57.

[49] See, respectively: Family Law Act 1986; Child Abduction and Custody Act 1985; Adoption Act 1976; Domicile and Matrimonial Proceedings Act 1973; Matrimonial and Family Proceedings Act 1984; Matrimonial Causes Act 1973; Child Support Act 1991 and Civil Jurisdiction and Judgments Act 1982. And see Adoption Act 1976, s 13(4), inserted by s 11 of the Adoption (Intercountry Aspects) Act 1999.

[50] Discussed at **5.3** *et seq*.

[51] See Schuz, 'Habitual residence of children under the Hague Child Abduction Convention – theory and practice' [2001] CFLQ 1. For the background to the emergence of habitual residence as a juridical connecting factor in Europe, see LI de Winter, 'Nationality or Domicile?' *Hague de Receuil* 349 at 419 *et seq*.

[52] Per Waite LJ in *Re K (Abduction: Consent: Forum Conveniens)* [1995] 2 FLR 211.

[53] See *Al Habtoor v Fotheringham* [2001] EWCA Civ 186, [2001] 1 FLR 951.

1980 Hague Abduction Convention which only applies to children habitually resident in a Contracting State immediately before any breach of custody or access rights.[54] Habitual residence is said on eminent authority to be a question of fact,[55] but plainly, in the case of children that cannot be the case. The proposition that one joint holder of parental responsibility cannot unilaterally change a child's habitual residence must be rule of law. So it must be a mixed question of fact and law.[56]

4.26　Although the authors know of no authority on the question of whether children of an age to be the subject of proceedings about their upbringing are capable of determining for themselves their habitual residence, the conclusion of the Third Meeting of the Special Commission to discuss the operation of the 1980 Hague Abduction Convention[57] was of the view that they were. It could be, therefore, that a competent, wrongfully retained 15-year-old could claim to have changed his habitual residence to avoid a return order.[58]

Habitual residence and ordinary residence[59]

4.27　Although there is authority to the effect that there is no difference between habitual residence and ordinary residence,[60] in the leading case of *Nessa v Chief Adjudication Officer*,[61] the House of Lords left undecided whether

---

54　Article 4.

55　See **4.31** below.

56　The US Court of Appeals for the 3rd, 8th and 9th Circuits has held that it raises mixed questions of fact and law and is thus subject to review on appeal – see *Feder v Evans-Feder* 866 F Supp 860; *Silverman v Silverman*, 8th Cir, No 02-2496 (5 August 2003, US Court of Appeals for the 8th Circuit, sitting *en banc*).

57　In March 1997.

58　There seems to be nothing in the 1980 Hague Abduction Convention to say specifically that the concept of 'Gillick' competency is disapplied (*Gillick v West Norfolk and Wisbech Area Health Authority and Department of Health and Social Security* [1986] AC 112). However, Lord Denning MR in *Re P (GE) (An Infant)* [1965] Ch 568, [1965] 2 WLR 1 said 'what is the ordinary residence of a child of tender years who cannot decide for himself where to live, let us say under the age of 16?'

59　'Ordinary residence' determines the responsibility of local authorities under the Children Act 1989 and also appears in the legislation relating to taxation (Taxation and Chargeable Gains Act 1992), recovery of maintenance (Maintenance Enforcement Act 1991), nationality (British Nationality Act 1981) and care in the community (National Assistance Act 1948).

60　In *Gateshead Metropolitan Borough Council v L* [1996] 3 WLR 426 at 429, Wilson J said that, since *Shah*, 'ordinary residence and habitual residence have been synonymous'. A similar view was expressed by Bush J in *Kapur v Kapur* [1984] FLR 920, Butler-Sloss LJ in *M v M (Abduction: England and Scotland)* [1997] 2 FLR 263 at 267 and Dame Elizabeth Butler-Sloss P in *Armstrong v Armstrong* [2003] EWHC 777 (Fam), [2003] 2 FLR 375 at [12], and, in another context (claiming income support), it was also accepted by Thorpe LJ in *Nessa v Chief Adjudication Officer* [1998] 1 FLR 879, CA. And see *Rydder v Rydder* 49 F 3d 369 (8th Cir 1995).

61　[1999] 1 WLR 1937, [1999] 2 FLR 1116, [1999] 4 All ER 677, HL.

'ordinary residence' and 'habitual residence' were always synonymous.[62] Nevertheless, in *Ikimi v Ikimi*,[63] Thorpe LJ said:

> 'It seems to me that, having traced the origins of the shift in language from "ordinarily" to "habitually", precisely the same meaning must be given to each in determining the bounds of this court's divorce jurisdiction. In his speech in the case of *Nessa v Chief Adjudication Officer* [1999] 2 FLR 1116, [1999] 1 WLR 1937, at 1120A and 1941E respectively, Lord Slynn of Hadley left open the question as to whether the two adverbs are always synonymous. But it seems to me plain that they must be so in this field.'

The meaning of 'habitual residence'

4.28 Despite the importance of 'habitual residence' in areas of the law as diverse as the recovery of abducted children and entitlement to State benefits, it is not defined in any convention, statute or statutory instrument. It is generally thought to have the same meaning wherever it is found, but some caution is necessary. In *Ikimi v Ikimi*[64] Thorpe LJ said:

> 'I am further of the opinion that it is essential that the same meaning be given to "habitually" wherever it appears in family law statutes. I would not, however, necessarily make the same extension to the Hague Convention on the Civil Aspects of International Child Abduction 1980, which is an international instrument, the construction of which is settled and developed within the wider field of international jurisprudence.'

So there is the possibility that 'habitually' may not have quite the same meaning in the 1980 Hague Abduction Convention as in a domestic statute.[65] And the interpretation of the concept for the purposes of the Council Regulation[66] will be a matter for the European Court of Justice, so it might be that, for example, one could have two habitual residences for some purposes, but not others. There is already a divergence in England, insofar as it seems that an adult can have more than one concurrent habitual residence for the purposes of divorce proceedings,[67] but a child can only have one habitual

---

[62] 'I am not satisfied, but it is unnecessary to decide, that they are always synonymous. Each may take a shade of meaning from the context and the object and purpose of the legislation. But there is a core of common meaning which makes it relevant to consider what has been said in cases dealing with both ordinary and habitual residence' per Lord Slynn.

[63] [2001] EWCA Civ 873, [2002] Fam 72, [2001] 2 FLR 1288, at [31].

[64] *Ibid.*

[65] Questions of habitual residence in relation to applications for return orders under the 1980 Hague Abduction Convention are a matter for the requested State, which will apply its own law: see *Re P (Abduction: Declaration)* [1995] 1 FLR 831. See also 'Case Digest, Habitual Residence' [2002] IFL 187.

[66] Viz Council Regulation (EC) No 1347/2000 (Brussels II).

[67] *Ikimi v Ikimi* [2001] EWCA Civ 873, [2002] Fam 72, [2001] 2 FLR 1288; see **4.38**.

residence at any point in time for the purposes of the 1980 Hague Abduction Convention.[68]

4.29 For a concept which is said not to be a term of art or an artificial legal construct,[69] but simply based on fact, habitual residence has attracted a considerable amount of judicial attention and not a little difficulty. One difficulty stems from the leading English authorities, on which other jurisdictions have placed reliance, not being family cases,[70] and another is that a number of the leading cases deal with the loss, rather than the acquisition, of habitual residence.[71] In children's cases this leads to a tension arising between the understandable desire to see a person spending some appreciable time in a place before it can be described as being his 'habitual' residence, and the wish to ascribe an habitual residence to a child very quickly to avoid the possibility that, by not having an habitual residence, he might be denied the benefits afforded by the various national and international instruments for the protection of children.[72]

4.30 Despite its universality of application, habitual residence has become a somewhat slippery concept,[73] in which words such as 'appreciable' take on a meaning beyond the immediately apparent, and in which decisions may differ depending upon whether one is looking just at a specific date, or back over a period of time to a specific date.[74] It is also a concept which is subject to sudden, radical, changes to achieve what the court perceives to be a just result. Until very recently one could have said with certainty that one could not be

---

[68] *Re V (Abduction: Habitual Residence)* [1995] 2 FLR 992; see **4.39**.

[69] Per Millett LJ in *Re M (Abduction: Habitual Residence)* [1996] 1 FLR 887 at 895G–H.

[70] *Akbarali v Brent London Borough Council; Abdullah v Shropshire County Council; Shabpar v Barnet London Borough Council; Jitendra Shah v Barnet London Borough Council; Barnet London Borough Council v Nilish Shah* (hereafter referred to as *Shah*) [1983] 2 AC 309, [1983] 2 WLR 16, HL; *Nessa v Chief Adjudication Officer* [1999] 1 WLR 1937, [1999] 2 FLR 1116. In *Ikimi v Ikimi* (above) Thorpe LJ said that 'However the difficulty of the judicial task stems from the unusual facts of the case and a wealth of authority on similar or identical statutory language in other fields of litigation including bankruptcy, tax, immigration and state benefits.'

[71] See, for example, *Re J (A Minor) (Abduction: Custody Rights)* [1990] 2 AC 562, sub nom *C v S (A Minor) (Abduction)* [1990] 2 FLR 442 and *Re M (Minor) (Residence Order: Jurisdiction)* [1993] 1 FLR 495. In *Rydder v Rydder* 49 Fed 3d 369 at 373, courts were enjoined not to apply the term 'habitual residence' restrictively.

[72] See **4.60**.

[73] *Nunc te videt, nunc ne videt*: one of the reasons for choosing habitual residence as a basis of jurisdiction rather than domicile was said to be the difficulty of determining domicile, which depends upon a person's intention as to where he or she is permanently to reside (see above). In the case of children, it would be necessary first to determine the domicile of the parents, and then apply the rules relating to the domicile of the children (see Domicile and Family Proceedings Act 1973). Both habitual residence and domicile are regarded as being less artificial as bases of jurisdiction than nationality. For a discussion about the various bases of jurisdiction, see Thue, 'Connecting Factors in International Law' in Lowe and Douglas (eds), *Families Across Frontiers* (Kluwer, 1996) at p 53.

[74] See *Nessa v Chief Adjudication Officer* [1998] 1 FLR 879 at 882H–883B, CA.

habitually resident in a jurisdiction without ever having been there.[75] However, in *B v H (Habitual Residence: Wardship)*[76] Charles J decided otherwise in relation to a baby born outside the country of habitual residence of either of his parents.

4.31 The modern meaning of habitual residence is to be found in the House of Lords' decision in *Shah*,[77] a case about the meaning of 'ordinarily resident' in a statute relating to the entitlement of overseas students to maintenance grants. Essentially, habitual residence refers to a person's abode in a particular place or country which he has adopted voluntarily and for settled purposes as part of the regular order of his life for the time being, whether of long or short duration.[78] It is based on fact, and so is not a term of art,[79] and is to be understood according to its ordinary and natural meaning, decided by reference to all the circumstances of the particular case.[80]

Acquiring an habitual residence

An 'appreciable period of time' and a 'settled intention'

4.32 No mention was made of it being necessary to spend any particular period of time in a State before acquiring an habitual residence there until in 1992 the House of Lords considered the removal by the mother of a child from Western Australia where, at the time, unmarried fathers did not have rights of custody. In *Re J (A Minor) (Abduction: Custody Rights)*[81] Lord Brandon said:

> 'In considering this issue it seems to me to be helpful to deal first with a number of preliminary points. The first point is that the expression "habitually resident", as used in Art 3 of the Convention, is nowhere defined. It follows, I think, that the expression is not be to treated as a term of art with some special meaning, but is rather to be understood according to the ordinary and natural meaning of the two words which it contains. The second point is that the question whether a person is or is not habitually resident in a specified country is a question of fact to be decided by reference to all the circumstances of any particular case. The third point is that there is a significant difference between a person ceasing to be habitually resident in country A, and his subsequently becoming habitually resident in country B. A person may cease to be habitually resident in country A

---

[75] *Nessa v Chief Adjudication Officer* [1999] 1 WLR 1937 at 1942F–H, [1999] 2 FLR 1116 at 1121A–D.

[76] [2002] 1 FLR 388. See **4.47**.

[77] [1983] 2 AC 309, [1983] 2 WLR 16, HL.

[78] Per Lord Scarman in *Shah* [1983] 2 AC 309 at 343, [1983] 2 WLR 16 at 26H. This formulation has been relied on by many courts in many countries, including the United States, Australia, Canada and Israel.

[79] *Re M (Abduction: Habitual Residence)* [1996] 1 FLR 887.

[80] *Re J (A Minor) (Abduction: Custody Rights)* [1990] 2 AC 562 at 578, sub nom *C v S (A Minor) (Abduction)* [1990] 2 FLR 442 at 454.

[81] *Re J (A Minor) (Abduction: Custody Rights)* [1990] 2 AC 562 at 578F–579B, sub nom *C v S (A Minor) (Abduction)* [1990] 2 FLR 442 at 454A–D.

in a single day if he or she leaves it with a settled intention not to return to it but to take up long-term residence in country B instead. Such a person cannot, however, become habitually resident in country B in a single day. An appreciable period of time and a settled intention will be necessary to enable him or her to become so. During that appreciable period of time the person will have ceased to be habitually resident in country A but not yet have become habitually resident in country B. The fourth point is that, where a child of J's age is in the sole lawful custody of the mother, his situation with regard to habitual residence will necessarily be the same as hers.'

4.33 The requirement to spend an 'appreciable period of time' in the new State was clearly a departure from the previous position, when the period could be of long or short duration, provided that the new abode was adopted voluntarily and for a settled purpose.[82] However, the necessity for spending an appreciable period of time in the new State was authoritatively stated in what is now the leading case on the acquisition of habitual residence, *Nessa v Chief Adjudication Officer*.[83] The following propositions were set out by Lord Slynn:

(i) Lord Brandon's speech in *Re J (A Minor) (Abduction: Custody Rights)*[84] was approved and followed: to establish habitual residence an appreciable period of time and a settled intention is necessary; the person needs to have taken up residence and lived there for some time.[85]

(ii) '[R]esidence for an appreciable period' as meant by Lord Brandon is a question of fact to be decided on the date where the determination has to be made on the circumstances of each case whether and when that habitual residence had been established:

'Bringing possessions, doing everything necessary to establish residence before coming, having a right of abode, seeking to bring family, "durable ties" with the country of residence or intended residence, and many other factors have to be taken into account. The requisite period is not a fixed period. It may be longer where there are doubts. It may be short (as the House accepted in *Re S (A Minor) (Custody: Habitual Residence)* [1998] AC 750, at 763A [Lord Slynn], and *Re F (A Minor) (Child Abduction)* [1992] 1 FLR 548, 555, where Butler-Sloss LJ said "A month can be … an appreciable period of time").'[86]

(iii) However:

'There may indeed be special cases where the person concerned is not coming here for the first time, but is resuming an habitual residence previously had: *Lewis v Lewis* [1956] 1 WLR 200; *Swaddling v Adjudication Officer* (Case C-90/97) [1999] 2

---

82 *Shah* (above) at 343H and 26H respectively.
83 [1999] 1 WLR 1937, [1999] 2 FLR 1116, HL. This is also a case about entitlement to financial benefits from the State.
84 [1990] 2 AC 562, sub nom *C v S (A Minor) (Abduction)* [1990] 2 FLR 442. In the Court of Appeal decision in *Nessa v Chief Adjudication Officer*, Thorpe LJ had pointed out that these remarks were *obiter*: [1998] 1 FLR 879 at 885.
85 [1999] 1 WLR 1937 at 1942E–G, [1999] 2 FLR 116 at 1121A–D.
86 At 1942H–1943A and 1121D–F respectively.

FLR 184, ECJ. On such facts, the adjudication officer may or of course may not be satisfied that the previous habitual residence has been resumed. This position is quite different from that of someone coming to the United Kingdom for the first time.'[87]

(iv) It was said (without deciding) that there may be cases where, for the purposes of making particular legislation effective (as for founding jurisdiction), it is necessary that a person should be habitually or ordinarily resident in some State at any one time.[88]

The 'settled intention' or 'settled purpose'

4.34 Lord Brandon's reformulation of the principles in *Shah* referred to a 'settled intention', rather than a 'settled purpose'. This has caused some confusion in the examination of the content of the purpose or intention. In *A v A (Child Abduction)*,[89] Rattee J said that the intention must be to take up long-term residence. However, that is not consistent with *Shah*, in which a residence of short duration was considered to be adequate, provided it was for a settled purpose. It has now been authoritatively stated in *Al Habtoor v Fotheringham*[90] that the purpose may be of long or short-term duration. The purpose may be associated with education, as in the *Shah* case, business or employment (including a military posting)[91] or joining a family. It seems to be enough that the purpose is associated with residence, so that in *Re B (Minors) (Abduction) (No 2)*[92] Waite J was able to find that providing a base for reconciliation and for planning a fresh start was a settled purpose which continued for a period which could readily be described as appreciable, despite the father's impatience at its failure and private resolve to bring it to an end. However, in *Re B (Child Abduction: Habitual Residence)*[93] Ewbank J found that a mother who had spent 2 months in Canada trying to effect a reconciliation with the father had not been there long enough to form the necessary settled intention, and consequently the child, who was in her sole custody, had not acquired an habitual residence there. Note should also be taken of Waite J's comment in *Re B (Minors) (Abduction) (No 2)*[94] that 'A settled purpose is not

---

[87] At 1943A–B and 1121F–G respectively.
[88] At 1942E–F and 1121A–B respectively.
[89] [1993] 2 FLR 225.
[90] [2001] EWCA Civ 186, [2001] 1 FLR 951, at [37].
[91] *Re A (Abduction: Habitual Residence)* [1996] 1 FLR 1: children of a US serviceman posted to Iceland and who had lived there with the requisite degree of continuity and settled purpose were habitually resident there.
[92] [1993] 1 FLR 993.
[93] [1994] 2 FLR 915.
[94] [1993] 1 FLR 993 at 998. See also the remarks of Bennett J in *Breuning v Breuning* [2002] EWHC 236 (Fam), [2002] 1 FLR 888, to the effect that when habitual residence was at issue, simplicity of inquiry should be encouraged and discursive evidence about the history or background involving long periods of time should be discouraged.

something to be searched for under a microscope. If it is there at all it will stand out clearly as a matter of general impression'.

Involuntary or unlawful presence

4.35 An involuntary or unlawful presence cannot found an habitual residence.[95] It is for this reason that it is said that, although habitual residence is a question of fact, a child who has been wrongfully removed to another jurisdiction cannot acquire an habitual residence there.[96]

Limited right to remain

4.36 That a person has only a limited right to remain in a State does not prevent him from being habitually resident there. In *Kapur v Kapur*[97] a husband who had a restricted right, renewed annually, to remain in the United Kingdom for the settled purpose of education was held to have been habitually resident for a year for preceding the presentation of a petition for divorce.

More than one habitual residence

4.37 Although there are old authorities from taxation and other fields which show that someone can have an ordinary residence in more than one country at the same time,[98] it might seem, from what has been said above that, at least for the purposes of jurisdiction in family cases, a person ought to have one habitual residence or none. The reality is that affluent people often have homes in different parts of the world, moving between them as frequently or infrequently as the demands of family and business require, and the vagaries of international politics permit.

4.38 In *Ikimi v Ikimi*,[99] a Nigerian couple had residences in both Nigeria and England since 1978. The four children, the three eldest of whom held British and Nigerian citizenship, were all born and almost entirely educated in England. Between November 1995 and July 1998 the couple had been unable to enter England because of EU sanctions. When the sanctions lifted in 1998 the wife came to England and shortly afterwards the husband petitioned for divorce in Nigeria. Almost a year later, the wife petitioned for divorce in England and a preliminary issue arose as to whether she had been habitually resident there for one year preceding her petition because she had only spent 161 days of that year in England. Thorpe LJ held that a person could be 'habitually resident in England and Wales' for the whole one-year period required to found jurisdiction in matrimonial proceedings[100] even though they

---

95   *Shah* [1983] 2 AC 309 at 344B–C, [1983] 2 WLR 16 at 27B–C.
96   But see **4.59** below.
97   [1984] FLR 920.
98   *Cooper (Surveyor of Taxes) v Cadwallader* [1904] 5 TC 101; *Re Norris (ex parte Reynolds)* (1888) 4 TLR 452; and *Pittar v Richardson* (1917) 87 LJKB 59.
99   [2001] EWCA Civ 873, [2002] Fam 72, [2001] 2 FLR 1288. See also *Armstrong v Armstrong* [2003] EWHC 777 (Fam), [2003] 2 FLR 375.
100 Under s 5(2) of the Domicile and Matrimonial Proceedings Act 1973 as it was then.

were also habitually resident in another country. A person may be ordinarily resident in two countries at the same time, but would still have to have spent an appreciable part of the relevant year within the English jurisdiction to establish habitual residence there.

4.39 The present state of the law seems to be that it is possible to have two or more concurrent habitual residences for the purposes of matrimonial proceedings, although to engage the English courts one would have to spend an appreciable part of the relevant year within this jurisdiction.[101] There is authority for the proposition that, for the purposes of the 1980 Hague Abduction Convention, a person can have two habitual residences, although not concurrently.[102]

Temporary absence

4.40 Habitual residence in a jurisdiction does not necessarily come to an end because of short or temporary absence.[103]

Losing an habitual residence

4.41 An habitual residence can be lost in a single day if a person leaves it with a settled intention not to return.[104] The formulation of the intention is sufficient to found the loss, so that if during a temporary presence in another State, one forms the intention of settling there, one would lose one's previous habitual residence, although it may take some time for the residence in the new State to become 'habitual'. In *Re F (Minors) (Abduction: Habitual Residence)*[105] the parents, while on holiday in England, decided to stay permanently. They left the children with the grandparents and went back briefly to Ontario before returning England. The marriage failed and the father went back to Ontario and sought the return of the children, but his application failed on the basis that they had become habitually resident in England once he and the mother had agreed to settle there.

4.42 However, it is not clear whether the formulation of the intention when one is within one's State of habitual residence is sufficient to found the loss of that habitual residence, or whether one must actually leave that country. As habitual residence is said to be a matter of fact, it would seem that forming the intent alone is not enough.

4.43 Short of an intention to leave permanently, it is difficult to say how long an absence must be before it is enough to lose an habitual residence. In

---

[101] *Ikimi v Ikimi* (above), at [35]. And see *Breuning v Breuning* [2001] EWHC 236 (Fam), [2003] 1 FLR 888.

[102] *Re V (Abduction: Habitual Residence)* [1995] 2 FLR 992; see **4.69**.

[103] *Re M (Minors) (Residence Order: Jurisdiction)* [1993] 1 FLR 495 at 501, citing *Rellis v Hart* [1992] GWD 1456; *Re M (Minors) (Abduction: Habitual Residence)* [1996] 1 FLR 887.

[104] *Re J (A Minor) (Abduction: Custody Rights)* [1990] 2 AC 562 at 578H, sub nom *C v S (A Minor) (Abduction)* [1990] 2 FLR 442 at 454C, HL.

[105] [1992] 2 FCR 595.

Re B-M (Wardship: Jurisdiction)[106] a German mother with sole custody left England and took her child to Germany. The next day the father made an ex parte application in wardship, and Eastham J, having heard evidence to the effect that the mother had recently extended a lease, accepted jurisdiction on the basis that she was still habitually resident in England.

THE HABITUAL RESIDENCE OF CHILDREN

4.44   Despite the gallant attempts of appellate courts to make it simple, determining the habitual residence of children is often far from easy. So much depends on their circumstances and the intentions of their parents, very often at a variance with each other, that it is all but impossible in many cases just to apply a simple factual test, especially when, as is so often the case, the question to be addressed is whether the child concerned has lost or acquired an habitual residence. There is also the difficulty, hardly acknowledged, that there is no uniform approach to determining the habitual residence of children.[107] The following tests have been used.

The dependency test

4.45   The earliest approach, understandably, was to say that the habitual residence of children was dependent, rather like domicile, upon that of their parents. So Lord Denning MR in *Re P (GE) (An Infant)*[108] was able to say that where the parents lived together in the matrimonial home, their child's ordinary residence would be there, regardless of where he was being educated. In *Re A (Minors) (Abduction: Habitual Residence)*[109] Cazalet J held that a child's habitual residence was 'necessarily' that of its parents, and in *Re A (Wardship: Jurisdiction)*[110] Hale J said:[111]

> 'It is obvious common sense that where both parents have equal responsibility, as they have here, and both are habitually resident here, a strong burden is placed upon anyone who wishes to show that their child's habitual residence for these purposes is different from theirs. I do not doubt that it is open to them to agree to change their child's habitual residence without changing their own but an agreement to send their child abroad to a boarding-school would undoubtedly not suffice. No authorities directly relevant to this point have been cited to me

---

[106]   [1993] 1 FLR 979. This decision has been heavily criticised, not least in Germany. See Lowe and Nicholls, 'Child Abduction: The Wardship Jurisdiction and the Hague Convention' [1994] Fam Law 191. It has, however, been approved, inter alia by the House of Lords in *Re S (A Minor) (Custody: Habitual Residence)* [1998] AC 750, [1998] 1 FLR 122.

[107]   See Schuz, 'Habitual residence of children under the Hague Child Abduction Convention – theory and practice' [2001] CFLQ 1, cited in *Re G (Abduction: Rights of Custody)* [2002] 2 FLR 703, per Sumner J.

[108]   [1965] Ch 568, [1965] 2 WLR 1.

[109]   [1996] 1 WLR 25 at 29.

[110]   [1995] 1 FLR 767.

[111]   *Ibid* at 772.

but one may, in passing, refer to s 72(1)(a) of the Adoption Act 1976. This provides that in determining where a child has his home there is to be disregarded absence in hospital or boarding-school or any other temporary absence. The concept of a home, although not necessarily identical to, must be very like that of habitual residence. Similar provision is made as to the definition of "ordinary residence" in s 105(6) of the Children Act 1989.'

4.46 This 'dependency' approach is necessarily legalistic, rather than factual.[112] It has the advantage of solving the problem of separated parents by ascribing to the child (on a factual basis) the habitual residence of the parent in whose care it is. In the case of a young child being looked after by a parent, it undoubtedly reflects the reality of the situation.[113] However, the 'dependency' approach does have its drawbacks. It looks strained and artificial when a child spends a considerable amount of time, for example at a school, in another jurisdiction. It might be thought to favour abductors,[114] although this concern has tended to be resolved by the long-standing rule of law[115] to the effect that one holder of parental rights (responsibility) cannot unilaterally change a child's habitual residence.[116] It denies to competent children the capacity or legal ability to form the requisite voluntary settled intention or purpose to acquire an habitual residence and it underestimates the almost infinite variety of arrangements which parents make for the care of their children in the modern world, which often leads to difficulty in identifying a child's 'home'. Where a child has his 'home' is a question not always easy to answer. Clearly, it must involve more than mere presence in a parent's home, otherwise every time a child went from one parent to stay with the other he would change his home and his habitual residence. There must be an element of settlement, and the many other qualities which make a home different to a transitory residence, however welcoming, which means that 'home' must include elements of intention or purpose. Even so, children no less than adults may have more than one home, spending time equally settled and happy with both of their separated parents. Perhaps the solution is to look at the date in question, and

---

[112] And as a consequence has been rejected as a model for standardisation: see Resolution 72(1) of the Committee of Ministers of the Council of Europe of 18 January 1972 in 'Standardisation of the legal concepts of "domicile" and "residence", r 11: "A person's residence or habitual residence" does not depend upon that of another person'. See further Beaumont and McEleavy, *The Hague Convention on International Child Abduction* (Oxford University Press, 1999).

[113] In *Re F (A Minor) (Child Abduction)* [1992] 1 FLR 548, Butler-Sloss LJ said that 'A young child cannot acquire habitual residence in isolation from those who care for him. While "A" lived with both parents, he shared their common habitual residence or lack of it' (at 551).

[114] In *Nunez-Escudero v Tice-Menly* 58 F 3d 374, the Court of Appeal for the 8th Circuit rejected a mother's contention that the child's habitual residence followed hers.

[115] See *Re P (GE) (An Infant)* [1965] Ch 568 [1965] 2 WLR 1.

[116] See **4.57** below.

attribute the child's habitual residence to the home he is occupying at the time.[117]

4.47 Finally, applied in its most extreme form, as was done in respect of a newly born baby in *B v H (Habitual Residence: Wardship)*,[118] it ascribes an habitual residence to a child even if he himself could not satisfy the most commonly accepted criteria for being habitually resident in that country, one of which is having been there. *B v H (Habitual Residence: Wardship)* was considered in *W and B v H (Child Abduction: Surrogacy)*,[119] an unusual case in which a Californian couple brought proceedings under the 1980 Hague Abduction Convention to secure the return of twins born to a surrogate mother. The surrogate mother had become pregnant in California, but, following a disagreement, had returned to England for the birth. The applicants had to prove that the children were habitually resident in California immediately before the alleged retention and sought to argue, relying on *B v H (Habitual Residence: Wardship)*, that, since in California legal rights and responsibilities in respect of the children attached only to W, they should be regarded as being habitually resident there. Hedley J said that, while he would not assert that as a matter of fact no child can have an habitual residence where he has never been, and casting no doubt on the factual conclusion in *B v H (Habitual Residence: Wardship)*, he remained hesitant, because it seemed to him that, if taken out of the context of the case, Charles J's propositions ran the risk against which the Court of Appeal had repeatedly warned of confusing a legal and a factual position. If Charles J was asserting that as a matter of law a baby takes the habitual residence of his parents, then that was to confuse domicile with habitual residence, with which Hedley J disagreed. If, however, he was asserting a proposition of fact, it could not be good for all cases, each of which must stand alone.[120]

The parental rights test

4.48 Another approach to determining the habitual residence of children is to say that it depends on the wish of the parent who has the right to determine where the child will live, regardless of where the child is actually living. It has been suggested that this 'parental rights' model is the foundation for the operation of the 1980 Hague Abduction Convention, because the concept of a 'wrongful' removal is based in particular on the breach of a right to determine the child's place of residence,[121] rather than the factual position. It might seem as if the English courts adopted this as an approach in the early cases, because

---

[117] See **4.30** and **4.51**.
[118] [2002] 1 FLR 388. See **4.30** and **4.65**.
[119] [2002] 1 FLR 1008.
[120] *Ibid* at [23].
[121] Article 5.

in *Re J (A Minor) (Abduction: Custody Rights)*[122] Lord Donaldson MR said, in the
Court of Appeal, that:

> 'in the ordinary case of a married couple, in my judgment, it would not be
> possible for one parent unilaterally to terminate the habitual residence of the
> child by removing the child from the jurisdiction wrongfully and in breach of
> the other parent's rights.'

4.49   Later, in the House of Lords, Lord Brandon said 'where a child of J's
age is in the sole lawful custody of the mother, his situation with regard to
habitual residence will necessarily be the same as hers'.[123] These remarks have
been interpreted as bringing to an end an habitual residence acquired by a child
with the consent of both parents when one of them revoked that consent. In
Re A (Wardship: Jurisdiction)[124] Hale J said:

> 'Although it is not strictly necessary for me to do so, I would further accept the
> argument of the Official Solicitor that, even if there had been such an agreement
> as would change the child's habitual residence for the time being, it would have
> required the continued agreement of both parents to make that situation
> continue. Despite the normal principle that each parent can act unilaterally it
> must be possible for either parent in that position, and in the absence of a court
> order, to revoke their agreement to their child being habitually resident abroad,
> so as to have the dispute between them resolved in their own home country
> where they both are.'

However, as we shall see, the parental rights model has been decisively rejected
by the English Court of Appeal.

The child-centered test

4.50   This test is closely aligned with the fact-based test (see below), because
it looks at the nature and quality of the child's residence in a particular country,
rather than any intention or connexion on the part of the parents. In
Re P (GE) (An Infant)[125] Pearson and Russell LJJ indicated that even if the
father had formed an intention to remain in Israel, the child's residence there
was insecure and unsettled, and so he remained ordinarily resident in England.
In *Re Bates*,[126] a case not reported in England but often cited in the United
States,[127] it was held that the residence whose habituality had to be established
was that of the child, not the mother. Justice Boggs in *Friederich v Friederich*,[128] a
seminal American case under the 1980 Hague Abduction Convention, stressed

---

[122] [1990] 2 AC 562 at 572B–C, sub nom *C v S (A Minor) (Abduction)* [1990] 2 FLR 442 at 449H.
[123] *Ibid*, at 579A–B and 454D respectively.
[124] [1995] 1 FLR 767.
[125] [1965] Ch 568, [1965] 2 WLR 1.
[126] 22 February 1989, unreported. Cited in *V v B (A Minor) (Abduction)* [1991] 1 FLR 266.
[127] Eg *Armiliato v Zaric-armiliato*, S.D.N.Y, No 01 Civ 0136, 3 May 2001. The *Bates* case can be
       found   on   the   website   of   Mr   William   Hilton   at   http://www.hiltonhouse.
       com.cases.Bates_uk.txt.
[128] US Court of Appeals; 983 F Supp 2d 1396.

that it was the habitual residence of the child which had to be determined, looking backwards in time and not forwards, and that '[H]abitual residence can be "altered" only by change in geography and the passage of time, not by changes in parental affection and responsibility'. This independent, child-centered approach has been influential and has been followed both in the United States and in other Contracting States, but as one commentator has pointed out, judges in most cases are still looking at the intentions of the parents when determining a child's habitual residence,[129] especially if what has to be determined is whether there has been a change. In *Mozes v Mozes*[130] the US Appeals Court for the 9th Circuit held that the acquisition of an habitual residence requires a settled intent, which in the case of a child is that of his parents. So a child's habitual residence will not change unless there is agreement between the parents. In *Re N (Abduction: Habitual Residence)*[131] Black J relied heavily on the 'conditional nature of the enterprise undertaken by the mother' in finding that the children had not become habitually resident in Spain, to which they had gone from England with both their mother and their father with the intention, at least on the part of the father, of starting a new life. She rejected the suggestion that, if faced with a conflict of habitual residences of parents, one should look at the objective evidence and ask: if the children were asked where they lived, what would they say?[132]

The fact-based test

4.51 The authority for the fact-based test is so eminent, arising as it does from the speeches of the House of Lords in *R v Barnet London Borough Council, ex parte Shah*[133] and the speech of Lord Brandon in *Re J (A Minor) (Abduction: Custody Rights)*,[134] that one could say almost with certainty that the state of English law is that habitual residence is a question of fact. In *W and B v H*[135] Hedley J said, rather plaintively:

> 'Once again I was taken to series of authorities the tenor of which was that habitual residence (unlike domicile) was a question of fact in each case. I wondered, if that were so, why we were going through many authorities.'[136]

---

[129] See Schuz, 'Habitual residence of children under the Hague Child Abduction Convention – theory and practice' [2001] CFLQ 1.

[130] 9th Cir, No 98–56505, 9 January 2001.

[131] [2000] 2 FLR 899.

[132] At 908G. And see **4.64**.

[133] [1983] 2 AC 309, [1983] 2 WLR 16. And see *Silverman v Silverman*, 8th Cir, No 02-2496 (5 August 2003, US Court of Appeals for the 8th Circuit, sitting *en banc*) (habitual residence under the 1980 Hague Abduction Convention is a fact-based enquiry to be analysed on a case-by-case basis).

[134] [1990] 2 AC 562 at 578F–579B, sub nom *C v S (A Minor) (Abduction)* [1990] 2 FLR 442 at 454A–C.

[135] [2002] 1 FLR 1008.

[136] *Ibid* at [16].

The answer must be, almost, but not quite, because of the tendency of the judges to regard changes in a child's habitual residence as being dependent on the intentions of the parents.[137]

4.52 In *Re J (A Minor) (Abduction: Custody Rights)* a child had been removed from Western Australia by his mother. After the removal the father, who had no parental rights at the time,[138] obtained an order vesting sole custodial rights in him and declaring the child's removal to be wrongful. To obtain a return order under the 1980 Hague Abduction Convention the father had to show that the child was habitually resident in Western Australia at the time of removal.[139] He argued that the child had remained habitually resident in Western Australia despite his removal to, and retention in, England by his mother. However, on the basis that:

> '… the question of whether a person is or is not habitually resident in a specified country is a question of fact to be decided by reference to all the circumstances of a particular case and that "… where a child of J's age is in the sole lawful custody of the mother, his situation with regard to habitual residence will necessarily be the same as hers",'[140]

it was held that J ceased to be habitually resident in Western Australia when he left for England with his mother, who had a settled intention that neither she nor J should continue to be habitually resident there.

4.53 In the context of the 1980 Hague Abduction Convention, the Pérez-Vera Report makes it clear that habitual residence is a 'well established concept in the Hague Conference, which regards it as a question of pure fact, differing in that respect from domicile'.[141]

4.54 The fact-based test has been applied at an appellate level to disapprove decisions which have been based on dependency. *Re M (Minor) (Residence Order: Jurisdiction)*[142] involved a jurisdictional dispute between England and Scotland. The mother, the sole holder of parental responsibility, had agreed that her three children would live with their grandparents in Scotland, but when they came to stay with her in England she refused to return them. The grandparents got an ex parte custody order in Scotland, but on the day it was served on her the mother applied for a residence order. The grandparents appealed the English judge's decision that he had jurisdiction to determine the mother's applications. It was held that the children had been habitually resident in Scotland, but that habitual residence had ceased when the mother decided not

---

137 See *Re N (Abduction: Habitual Residence)* [2000] 2 FLR 899.
138 The law in Western Australia changed as a result of the case of *Re B (A Minor) (Abduction)* [1994] 2 FLR 249, and parental rights were conferred on unmarried fathers: see Family Court Act 1997 (WA), s 69(1).
139 See **12.21**.
140 [1990] 2 AC 562 at 579A–B, [1990] 2 FLR 442 at 45L.
141 Paragraph 66.
142 [1993] 1 FLR 495 at 499G.

to return them. Drawing on the speech of Lord Brandon in *Re J*, Balcombe LJ said:

> 'There is no statutory definition of habitual residence. However the following propositions may be deduced from the authorities:
>
> ...
>
> (2) Habitual residence is primarily a question of fact to be decided by reference to all the circumstances of any particular case – *Re J (A Minor) (Abduction: Custody Rights)* [1990] 2 AC 562 at p 578, sub nom *C v S (A Minor) (Abduction)* [1990] 2 FLR 442 at p 454.
>
> ...
>
> (4) Where the habitual residence of a young child is in question, the element of volition will usually be that of the person or persons who has or have parental responsibility for that child. Where a young child is in the physical care of its mother and where, as here, she alone has parental responsibility for the child, then the child's situation with regard to habitual residence will necessarily be the same as hers.
>
> "The fourth point is that, where a child of J's age is in the sole lawful custody of the mother, his situation with regard to habitual residence will necessarily be the same as hers ... " (per Lord Brandon of Oakbrook in *Re J* (above) at pp 479 and 454 respectively; see also *Re S (A Minor) (Abduction)* [1991] 2 FLR 1 at pp 16–17).
>
> The judge appeared to accept a submission on behalf of the mother, based on the passage from Lord Brandon's speech in *Re J* which I have cited above, that in the present case the children's habitual residence remained throughout in England and Wales, because the mother remained habitually resident in Oxford, and that their habitual residence necessarily followed that the mother, who alone had parental responsibility for them. This appears to me to be a misinterpretation of Lord Brandon's fourth point. Where he refers to the child being in the "sole lawful custody" of the mother he was clearly using custody in the sense of physical possession or care, as was the fact in that case. I do not read his words as intending to suggest that the habitual residence of a child is necessarily the same as that of the parent who alone has parental responsibility, notwithstanding that the child may have been living apart from that parent for a period which may have lasted for several years. That would be inconsistent with his second point that habitual residence is a question of fact. All he was saying was that where a young child is in the physical care of a mother who alone has parental responsibility for the child, then normally the child's habitual residence will be the same as hers, since it is her will that determines the element of volition involved in the concept of habitual residence.'

4.55 Balcombe LJ was not prepared to say that the children had acquired an habitual residence in England, but Hoffmann LJ said that, had it been necessary for the decision, he would have less difficulty in finding that they had become habitually resident in England.[143]

---

[143] [1993] 1 FLR 495 at 503.

4.56   Having disapproved of the dependency test in *Re M (Minors) (Residence Order: Jurisdiction)*, Balcombe LJ later applied the same reasoning in *Re M (Abduction: Habitual Residence)*,[144] a case in which parents had sent their child to live in India with the paternal grandparents. The mother changed her mind, but that did not mean that the child became habitually resident in England again; in all probability he was still habitually resident in India.[145] Although approving of Hale J's finding in *Re A (Wardship: Jurisdiction)*[146] that to send children to Pakistan for the temporary purpose of education was not of itself sufficient to change their habitual residence because it must depend upon the circumstances of the case, he disapproved of her accepting the proposition that if an agreement to send a child abroad failed it could not be a settled agreement, because habitual residence is a question of fact, and not to be determined 'by concepts of that nature'.[147]

Children losing and acquiring an habitual residence

4.57   There is one common rule; a wrongful removal or retention must not be allowed to change a child's habitual residence. In *Re P (GE) (An Infant)*[148] Lord Denning said:

> 'I do not see that a child's ordinary residence, so found, can be changed by kidnapping him and taking him from his home, even if one of his parents is the kidnapper.'[149]

4.58   More recently, in *Re S (A Minor) (Custody: Habitual Residence)*[150] the mother, who was the sole holder of parental rights and was habitually resident in England, died. The maternal grandmother and aunt took the child to Ireland, but that move could not change the child's habitual residence. As Lord Slynn said:[151]

> 'Neither appellant had parental rights over the child, who was too young to form any intention as to his own future residence, and two days with the appellants in Ireland is not sufficient of itself to result in his existing habitual residence being lost and a new one gained.'

In the context of the 1980 Hague Abduction Convention, Hale J said:[152]

---

144   [1996] 1 FLR 887.
145   At 895E–F.
146   [1995] 1 FLR 767.
147   At 894B–C.
148   [1965] Ch 568 at 586, [1965] 2 WLR 1 at 10.
149   And see Lord Donaldson MR in *Re J (A Minor) (Abduction: Custody Rights)* [1990] 2 AC 562, sub nom *C v S (A Minor) (Abduction)* [1990] 2 FLR 442.
150   [1998] AC 750, [1998] 1 FLR 122, HL.
151   [1998] AC 750 at 762, [1998] 1 FLR 122 at 127.
152   *Re A (Wardship: Jurisdiction)* [1995] 1 FLR 767.

'It stands to reason that that Convention could not operate were one parent to be able, unilaterally, to change the habitual residence of the child because the whole purpose of the Convention is to stop parents doing just that.'

4.59 It is now generally accepted that this rule of law must at some point give way to the facts, and so after an indefinable period of time a child who has been wrongfully removed or retained will acquire a new habitual residence, a point implicitly recognised in both s 41 of the Family Law Act 1986[153] and Art 7(1) of the 1996 Hague Convention on the Protection of Children.[154]

An 'appreciable period of time' for a child

The 'quality of connection'

4.60 The proposition that it may take an appreciable period of time to acquire an habitual residence has been the cause of some concern to family lawyers, and one addressed by Thorpe LJ in his dissenting judgment in the Court of Appeal[155] in *Nessa v Chief Adjudication Officer*. He pointed out that it is:

'... particularly undesirable that there should be a vacuum between habitual residences for children who would be temporarily deprived of rights, protection, or benefits.'[156]

He went on to say:

'For the family lawyer perhaps the adjective "habitual" does not in this context carry its literal sense so much as the sense of the quality of the connection of the individual to the relevant society for the purpose of the Convention or legislation to be applied. The adjective ensures that that connection is not transitory or temporary but enduring and the necessary durability can be judged prospectively in exceptional cases.'

4.61 The difficulty is that on the authorities there must be enough time for the residence to be described as 'habitual', but Thorpe LJ was surely right when he pointed to the quality of the connection as the decisive factor in children's cases, rather than simply time itself.[157] With the appropriate quality of connection, the actual time needed to acquire a new habitual residence might be quite short. As Lord Slynn pointed out in *Re S (Custody: Habitual Residence)*,[158] if a mother with parental rights on whom the child's habitual residence depended left one country to go to another with the established intention of settling permanently, 'her habitual residence and that of the child may change very quickly'.[159] Two months in Australia was held to be

---

[153] Discussed at **4.74** below.
[154] Discussed at **24.23** below.
[155] [1998] 1 FLR 879, [1998] 2 All ER 728, CA.
[156] [1998] 1 FLR 879 at 889.
[157] In *Cruse v Chittum* [1974] 2 All ER 940, Lane J referred to the quality, rather than the length of the period of residence.
[158] [1998] AC 750, [1998] 1 FLR 122, HL.
[159] [1998] AC 750 at 762F–763B, [1998] 1 FLR 122 at 126H–127C.

adequate to demonstrate that 'a sufficient degree of continuity of residence' had been established in *V v B (A Minor) (Abduction)*[160] and, as we have seen,[161] Butler-Sloss LJ has expressed the view that, with a settled intention to emigrate from the United Kingdom and settle in Australia, a month can be an appreciable period of time.[162] It was the quality of connection which enabled Hoffmann LJ to say that if a child comes into the home of a parent which is the undoubted habitual residence of that parent and where the child is to remain, 'I do not see why the child's residence should not forthwith be treated as habitual'.[163]

4.62   But without the requisite quality of connection, a period of time which might otherwise be enough to describe a person's residence as being habitual may not be enough. In *Re S (Minors) (Abduction; Wrongful Retention)*,[164] Wall J held that children who had come to England from Israel with parents who had been offered scholarships and had agreed to stay for at least a year (described by Balcombe LJ as 'clearly a temporary purpose'[165]) were still habitually resident in Israel when, 8 months after their arrival, their mother obtained an ex parte interim residence and prohibited steps order in the English court because she said she feared that the father would remove the children and return with them to Israel.[166] This decision has been criticised, with some justification, because the parents were in England for a settled purpose for an appreciable period of time.[167] However, the courts in the United States, which have also looked at the quality of the child's connection with the State said to be his habitual residence, would probably support it. The court in *Mozes v Mozes*,[168] holding that a 15-month stay in California did not establish an habitual residence on the part of the child, said that the academic year abroad was a familiar phenomenon, and that the children involved were expected to form close cultural and personal ties in the countries they visit, but the ordinary expectation is that at the end they will resume residence in their home

---

160   [1991] 1 FLR 266.

161   See **4.33** above.

162   *Re F (A Minor) (Child Abduction)* [1992] 1 FLR 548 at 555. And see *Re A (Abduction: Habitual Residence)* in which it was held that the child had acquired an habitual residence in Iceland after 2 years of the father's 3-year posting.

163   *Re M (Minors) (Residence Order: Jurisdiction)* [1993] 1 FLR 495 at 503A–E, following *Re S (A Minor) (Abduction)* [1991] 2 FLR 1.

164   [1994] 1 FLR 82.

165   In *Re M (Abduction: Habitual Residence)* [1996] 1 FLR 887.

166   The father had issued proceedings under the 1980 Hague Abduction Convention because the mother had said that she would not return the children at any time in the future and therefore, irrespective of the original agreement, and the fact that the act of retention took place within the agreed period, she could no longer rely on the father's agreement to the limited period of removal or retention as protecting her under either Art 3 or Art 13.

167   See Beaumont and McEleavy, *The Hague Convention on International Child Abduction* (OUP, 1999), p 107, n 121 and Schuz, 'Habitual residence of children under the Hague Child Abduction Convention – theory and practice' [2001] CFLQ 1.

168   9th Cir, No 98–56505, 9 January 2001.

country. For a change of habitual residence, a change in geography was required, with the passage of an appreciable period of time for 'acclimatization'. Simple consent on the part of one parent to the child being in another country would not be enough. In *Paz v Paz*,[169] a case under the 1980 Hague Abduction Convention in which a father sought the return of his daughter to New Zealand, the judge noted that in determining habitual residence the courts had given considerable weight to the evidence that a child had become 'acclimated' to her surrounds in the alleged country of residence. In dismissing the application, the judge said that the child had changed her country of residence on numerous occasions, and had only become 'settled' in New Zealand during her 10-month stay there to the same extent that she had been 'settled' in any previous location.

4.63 Quality of connection has been linked with parental intentions, so that in *Isaac v Rice*,[170] a re-abduction case, it was held that, despite having been in Israel for 11 years after being abducted by his father, the child had not become habitually resident there because his mother did not intend him to live there.

Common settled intention

4.64 For a child to acquire an habitual residence, it seems that a settled intention or purpose has to be shared by the holders of parental responsibility. In *Mozes v Mozes*[171] the court found that the trial judge had given insufficient weight to the importance of shared parental intent under the 1980 Hague Abduction Convention. So a limited stay while parents are at cross-purposes, even if not communicated, might not be enough. In *Re N (Abduction: Habitual Residence)*[172] Black J said:

> 'In my view, it is important to recognise that what the father seeks to establish is that the children's place of habitual residence has changed. I have concluded that this cannot happen where he alone of the parents with whom they are living has lost the habitual residence that he shared with the mother and the children and become habitually resident elsewhere. It is argued on behalf of the father that the mother's endorsement of the move to Spain, albeit with reservations, should be taken as agreement to or acquiescence in the children's habitual residence changing to Spain once their father became habitually resident there. I do not consider that the conditional enterprise undertaken by this mother had this effect, and in particular not where the father had been told expressly about the conditional nature of the move, where the marriage had not improved whilst the parties were in Spain, and in the light of the paucity and lateness of arrangements made in Spain for the family and the period over which the stay in Spain lasted. Accordingly, I have concluded that the children did not lose their habitual residence in England or become habitually resident in Spain at any time before they left that country with their mother on 15 February 2000. It follows

---

[169] S.D.N.Y. No 01 Civ 6463, 29 October 2001.
[170] 1998 US Dist Lexis 12602.
[171] Above.
[172] [2000] 2 FLR 899.

that the mother's removal of the children was not wrongful and the father's application for their return to Spain fails.'

Newly born babies

4.65   In *B v H (Habitual Residence: Wardship)*[173] the father and the mother (who was pregnant at the time) and their three children went to Bangladesh after a reconciliation, for what the mother believed to be a visit of 4 or 5 weeks. However, the father refused to return to England or allow the mother and children to do so, so that her baby was born in Bangladesh. There was then a violent incident, and the mother left the father, got a divorce and her passport, and returned to England, but had to leave all four children behind. In England the mother applied to make all four children wards, with care and control to her and orders requiring the father to return them to the England. Holding that the habitual residence of the three oldest children remained in England,[174] Charles J decided that at birth the habitual residence of a baby was that of the people who had parental responsibility for him. Therefore, the mere fact of being born abroad did not deprive a child of an habitual residence. In effect, Charles J applied the 'dependency' test[175] to ascertain the baby's habitual residence.[176]

Temporary leave to remove and 'shuttle' custody orders

4.66   Giving a parent permission to take a child temporarily out of the country for a short, defined stay in another jurisdiction causes few problems. The proposed stay is clearly temporary, and lacks the elements of appreciable time and settled intention to acquire a new habitual residence. In the case of children who are very young, and who are to spend some time in a foreign country before returning to their home to start their primary education, there is usually no difficulty. Older children may, however, may express a wish to stay, and that may lead to problems, although a refusal to return a child would usually be met with a prompt application for a return order. Some States, however, notably the United States of America, sometimes give permission either to remove a child for a substantial period of time, 1 or 2 years, or provide for a child to spend appreciable periods of time with each parent (known as 'shuttle custody orders'). In terms of determining the child's habitual residence, these cases can be problematic. In the absence of any rules

---

[173]   [2002] 1 FLR 388.

[174]   Because: the trip to Bangladesh had been presented to the mother as a temporary visit; one of two holders of parental responsibility cannot unilaterally change a child's habitual residence; and the mother never formed any intention of living permanently in Bangladesh.

[175]   See **4.45**.

[176]   But see *W and B v H (Child Abduction: Surrogacy)* [2002] 1 FLR 1007, in which Hedley J said that '[i]f Charles J is asserting as a matter of law that a baby takes the habitual residence of his parents then that is to confuse domicile with habitual residence and I would have respectfully to disagree. If what he asserts is a proposition of fact, then, by definition, it cannot be good for all cases. Each one must stand alone'.

of recognition or mechanism for the enforcement of foreign orders, other than under the limited provisions of the 1980 European Custody Convention, the English courts have experienced some difficulty when these orders have been breached. The more cynical might think that the well-advised ask for a limited leave to remove, wait for a suitable period of time in excess of a year, and then make an application for a residence (custody) order and to modify the contact (visitation) provisions of the order giving leave to remove. An obvious difficulty facing the aggrieved parent is that the child might be found to have acquired a new habitual residence. His only salvation is the proposition that parents must have a common intention to change a child's habitual residence. But when a child has been living in a country for 2 years, that begins to look like a triumph of legalism over common sense. In *Watson v Jamieson*[177] two children left New Zealand to spend 2 years with their father in Scotland. Shortly before the 2-year period expired, he said that he was not going to return them. The mother's application for a return order, on the basis that the children's permanent home was in New Zealand and the time in Scotland a temporary interruption, was dismissed on the basis that it would be 'unrealistic' to say that the children were still habitually resident in New Zealand, and that they had acquired an habitual residence in Scotland.

4.67 Subject only to the rule of law which requires both parents to agree to a change of habitual residence, it appears that orders giving leave to remove for periods of more than 6 months and orders alternating custody or physical care are not susceptible to policing by the 1980 Hague Abduction Convention. So aggrieved parents will have to resort to domestic proceedings, because even attempts by more far-sighted (or experienced) courts to establish exclusive, continuing jurisdiction to ensure that their intentions are carried out have not met with a great deal of success. In the *Johnson* case,[178] a 'shuttle custody order' was agreed between the parents and approved by an American court. The child would spend 2 years in Sweden, and then 2 years in the United States, the American court would have continuing exclusive jurisdiction over custody matters (the Commonwealth of Virginia remaining the child's place of residence for that purpose) and the parents held themselves bound by the 1980 Hague Abduction Convention. However, when the mother refused to comply with the order and send the child from Sweden to America after the first 2 years, the Swedish courts held that she was habitually resident in Sweden.

4.68 In the future these problems may be less acute if States adopt the 1996 Hague Convention on the Protection of Children, which contains extensive recognition and enforcement provisions.[179]

---

[177] 1998 SLT 180.

[178] Transcript, Supreme Administrative Court, Sweden, 9 May 1996; *Johnson v Johnson*, 26 Va App 135, 493 S.E. 2d 668 (1997).

[179] See Chapter 24.

Children with more than one habitual residence

4.69 In *Re V (Abduction; Habitual Residence)*[180] a family lived in Corfu in the summer and London in the winter. After the father had left London for Corfu, the mother refused to join him and started divorce and Children Act 1989 proceedings. The father applied for a stay and the return of the children to Greece under the 1980 Hague Abduction Convention, contending that the habitual residence of the family was Corfu and that the London house was not a family home but an investment property, so that the refusal of the mother to follow him to Corfu with the children was a wrongful retention. Alternatively, he contended that, assuming the children had been habitually resident in England in the winter, his consent to the mother and children not accompanying him when he had left for Corfu had been vitiated by her deceit, so that the habitual residence of the family should be taken as reverting to Corfu. The mother's case was that the parents and children were habitually resident in both Corfu and England concurrently, a situation that could not fit into the framework of the Convention, or alternatively that their habitual residence was consecutive, changing as the family moved from one country to the other according to the season, and had been England on the relevant date. Douglas Brown J held that the family could be regarded as habitually resident in both London and Corfu, but that they could not be habitually resident in more than one place at the same time. Concurrent habitual residence was a concept that could not fit in with the aims of the Convention and the children were habitually resident in England at the moment the mother failed to return them. Accordingly, the father failed to show that the children were habitually resident in Corfu on the relevant date and his application under the Convention failed.

4.70 It remains to be seen whether concurrent habitual residence will continue to be regarded as being inimical to the operation of the 1980 Hague Abduction Convention, but if habitual residence is a question of fact, there is no reason why such a finding should not be made. If it were, it would not necessarily be fatal to the operation of the Convention. A removal from one habitual residence to another, or a retention in one of two habitual residences could still be 'wrongful', because the child's connection with the State to which he is taken to, or retained in, is only relevant to the extent that the child settled there.[181]

Children with no habitual residence

4.71 On any test, factual or otherwise, it is possible for a child to have no habitual residence. He may have been lawfully removed from and lost an habitual residence, but his parent or parents may not have been in a new State

---

180   [1995] 2 FLR 992.
181   Article 12. Note that it is not a requirement of the 1980 Hague Abduction Convention that the child is returned to the State from which he has been removed. See **16.5**.

long enough for his residence there to be described as 'habitual', or they may have no shared, settled intention of remaining in the new State or anywhere. This lack of a habitual residence would exclude the child from the scope of the 1980 Hague Abduction Convention. Mention has already been made of the concern of family lawyers that children should not be deprived of protection; in particular, the dissenting speech of Thorpe LJ in *Nessa*,[182] and in the earlier case of *Re F (A Minor) (Child Abduction)*[183] Butler-Sloss LJ said that 'we should not strain to find a lack of habitual residence where, on a broad canvas, the child has settled in a particular country'.

Children in hiding

4.72   If children are hidden away, it seems to be accepted that they cannot acquire an habitual residence. This may be because their presence is unlawful, or because the purpose or intention of the parent who is hiding them cannot properly be described as being 'settled'.[184] In *Re L (Abduction; Pending Criminal Proceedings)*,[185] a Danish mother wrongfully removed the children from Florida to Denmark and then, after their American father had succeeded in obtaining an order for their return under the 1980 Hague Abduction Convention, brought them to England and hid them for a year before they were found and the father instituted proceedings there. Wilson J said, in response to the argument that the children had become settled in England, that:

> 'The mother might or might not have demonstrated that the children were now settled in their new environment. The proposition is harder to demonstrate than at first appears. In *Re S (A Minor) (Abduction)* [1991] 2 FLR 1, 24C, Purchas LJ described what was required as a long-term settled position; and in *Re N (Minors) (Abduction)* [1991] 1 FLR 413, 418C, Bracewell J observed that the position had to be as permanent as anything in life could be said to be permanent. Whether a Danish mother who has been present with the children in England for a year only because it has been a good hiding-place and who faces likely extradition proceedings could demonstrate the children's settlement in England within the meaning of those authorities is doubtful.'

4.73   But even if a child is hidden, there must come a point at which he becomes habitually resident in the new State, when his quality of connection with it becomes enduring. Much may depend on the circumstances of the concealment and the attitude of the judicial authorities, the United States, for

---

[182]   See **4.60**.

[183]   [1992] 1 FLR 548. For an American decision holding that a child had no habitual residence, see *Delvoye v Lee*, 3rd Cir, No 02-3943 (20 May 2003).

[184]   In American jurisprudence, the concept of discounting time in hiding is called 'tolling': see *Belay v Getachew*, D Md No AW-03-761 (8 July 2003) (child well settled in new environment, but one-year period until father discovered the child's whereabouts was 'tolled' and the child returned).

[185]   [1999] 1 FLR 433.

example disregarding or 'tolling' the time a child spends in concealment for the purposes of Art 12.[186]

Deemed habitual residence – Family Law Act 1986, s 41

4.74 Section 41 of the Family Law Act 1986 is a deeming provision which applies only to Part I of the Family Law Act 1986 and has no application to removals from the United Kingdom to a foreign jurisdiction.[187] It provides that a child under the age of 16 who has been wrongfully removed from or retained outside a part of the United Kingdom or the Isle of Man in which he was habitually resident will be deemed for the purposes of Part I of the Family Law Act 1986 to continue, for one year after the removal or retention, to be habitually resident in that part of the United Kingdom or the Isle of Man, notwithstanding that he or she has become habitually resident in another part.

4.75 A removal to or a retention in another jurisdiction within the United Kingdom is 'wrongful' if it is without the consent of all the persons having a right to determine where he is to reside or in contravention of a court order.[188] Hence, it will not be wrongful for an unmarried mother, with sole parental responsibility, to remove her child without the father's consent.[189] Under s 41(3) such deemed habitual residence ceases if the child becomes 16 or becomes habitually resident in another part of the United Kingdom with the consent of all those having the right to determine where the child is to reside and not in contravention of a court order.

4.76 What s 41 is intended to do is to ensure that the courts of the part of the United Kingdom or the Isle of Man in which the child was habitually resident immediately before the removal or retention will retain jurisdiction for one year.[190] Read literally, however, s 41(1) requires the child to be habitually resident in the part of the United Kingdom or the Isle of Man to which he or she has wrongfully been taken or retained. It accordingly has no application to children who, having been wrongfully removed or retained, have lost their original habitual residence but have not required a new one. In other words, jurisdiction will *solely* be vested in the place where the child is present. While such an interpretation is unlikely to be adopted, it provides yet another example of the deficiencies of the 1986 Act's provisions. Furthermore, even

---

[186] Eg *Hemard v Hemard* (ND Texas, 1995, civil action file no 7-94-CV-110X), and see Garbolino, *International Child Abduction; Guide to Handling Hague Convention Cases in US Courts*, 3rd edn (The National Judicial College, 2000), p 150.

[187] See *Re S (A Child: Abduction)* [2002] EWCA Civ 1941, [2003] 1 FLR 1008.

[188] Section 41(2).

[189] Cf *Re M (Minors) (Residence Order: Jurisdiction)* [1993] 1 FLR 495, CA. *Aliter* if the parents are married or where the unmarried father has parental responsibility by a formal agreement or court order. For an example of where s 41 was held to operate to prevent the English court having jurisdiction following a married mother's unilateral removal of her children from Scotland, see *D v D (Custody: Jurisdiction)* [1996] 1 FLR 574.

[190] See Law Com No 138/Scot Law Com No 91, the Explanatory Notes to clause 40(1) at 251.

without this complication, s 41 has been criticised[191] for being 'too rigid and, in any event, too long a period to be ignored in the case of young children', although it has to be said that a similar restriction has since been adopted in the international sphere by Art 7 of the 1996 Hague Convention on the Protection of Children.

SUMMARY OF THE LAW

4.77 An examination of the authorities shows that the preponderance of opinion is that whether a person is habitually resident in a particular country depends on two elements; residence for an appreciable period of time and a settled intention. As a matter of law, habitual residence is a question of fact to be determined by all the circumstances of the case. However, in the case of children it is in practice dealt with as a mixture of fact and law. It is, however, very difficult to be precise about the relative weight of fact and law. Where no question of loss or acquisition of an habitual residence arises, fact plays the dominant role. But when questions arise about whether a child has lost or acquired an habitual residence, a strong element of dependency arises, and the status of the children becomes dependent on the intentions which parents have for their children.[192] That dependency is reflected in the rule of law that no unilateral action by one parent can change a child's habitual residence[193] and that parents must have a common, shared intention. This rule is determinative until at some point in time it must give way to fact. When that will be depends entirely upon the opinion of the court. As we have seen, some courts have taken the view that it would be a very long time indeed,[194] others that 2 years would be enough.[195]

4.78 However, in the ordinary course of events, the habitual residence of children whose parents are married is that of the parents, one of whom cannot change the children's habitual residence except with the agreement of, tacit consent of,[196] or acquiescence over a period of time of, the other, or an order of a court.[197] Where a young child is in the physical care of his mother, who has sole parental responsibility, 'his situation with regard to habitual residence will necessarily be the same as hers'[198] and, unless there is some restraint in place, a parent with sole parental responsibility can change a child's habitual

---

[191] By Lowe and White, *Wards of Court*, 2nd edn (Barry Rose, 1986), paras 17–59.
[192] Eg *Re N (Abduction: Habitual Residence)* [2000] 2 FLR 899.
[193] *Re P (GE) (An Infant)* [1965] Ch 568 at 586, [1965] 2 WLR 1 at 10.
[194] *Isaac v Rice* 1998 US Dist Lexis 12602; see **4.63**.
[195] *Watson v Jamieson; Johnson v Johnson* 1998 SLT 180; see **4.69**.
[196] *Re B (Minors) (Abduction) (No 2)* [1993] 1 FLR 993.
[197] *Re S (Minors) (Child Abduction)* [1994] Fam 70 at 82A.
[198] In *Re J (A Minor) (Abduction: Custody Rights)* [1990] 2 AC 562 at 579A–B, sub nom *C v S (A Minor) (Abduction)* [1990] 2 FLR 442 at 454.

residence at any time.[199] No action by a person who does not hold parental responsibility can change a child's habitual residence without the consent of all holders of parental responsibility or their acquiescence over a period of time.[200]

4.79　In the light of this, some of the remarks in the earlier cases should be treated with caution. It is no longer right to say that sending a child to a foreign boarding school will not change his habitual residence.[201] Much will depend on the quality of his connection both with his 'home' State and with the State in which he is being educated. But if his connection with the State in which he is being educated is not transitory or temporary, there is no reason why it should not be habitual.[202] To say otherwise would mean that a child abducted from a foreign boarding school would not be protected by the 1980 Hague Abduction Convention.

A SHORT GUIDE TO JURISDICTION IN PRIVATE LAW CHILDREN'S CASES IN ENGLAND AND WALES

4.80　The private law orders subject to statutory jurisdictional rules are original orders under Children Act 1989, s 8, and orders made within the High Court's inherent jurisdiction with respect to children insofar as they give the care of a child to a person or provide for contact with, or the education of, a child.[203] Only original orders, and not variations of previous orders, are 'Part I orders' and subject to the jurisdictional rules in the Council Regulation and Part I of 1986 Act.[204]

4.81　For jurisdictional purposes, children's cases are divided into four classes:

(1) where both of the parents are involved in matrimonial proceedings in England and Wales relating to their marriage;

(2) where both of the parents are involved in matrimonial proceedings elsewhere in the United Kingdom relating to their marriage;

(3) where both of the parents are involved in matrimonial proceedings elsewhere in the EU (with the exception of Denmark) relating to their marriage; and

(4) all other cases, including those in which only one of the parents is involved in matrimonial proceedings, whether in England and Wales or elsewhere in the UK or the EU, cases in which one or both parents are involved in matrimonial proceedings in Denmark or outside the EU, and

---

[199]　*Ibid*, at 579B–D and 454, respectively.

[200]　*Re S (A Minor) (Custody: Habitual Residence)* [1998] AC 750, [1998] 1 FLR 122, HL.

[201]　*Re P (GE) (An Infant)* [1965] Ch 568, [1965] 2 WLR 1.

[202]　See *Re M (Abduction: Habitual Residence)* [1996] 1 FLR 887, see **4.56**.

[203]　Family Law Act 1986, s 1(1)(a) and (d). See **3.2**.

[204]　*Ibid*, ss 1(1)(a), (d) and 2. See **3.2** and *Re S (Residence Order: Forum Conveniens)* [1995] 1 FLR 314.

cases in which the parents are not involved in matrimonial proceedings at all.

In the first case, the English courts can exercise jurisdiction either:

(i) under the provisions of the Council Regulation, provided that the children are habitually resident in England and Wales or are habitually resident in another Member State, one of the parents has parental responsibility for them and the jurisdiction of the court is accepted by both parents and is in the best interests of the children[205] or, if the Council Regulation does not apply;[206]

(ii) under the 1986 Act on the basis that there are matrimonial proceedings 'continuing' in England and Wales in respect of the marriage of the parents of the child concerned.[207]

The significant differences are that:

(a) the jurisdiction conferred by the Council Regulation over the children comes to an end when the decree nisi is made absolute or, if the application in relation to the children is still pending, when that application is determined,[208] whereas the jurisdiction under the 1986 Act continues until the children reach the age of 18;[209]

(b) only an order made under the Council Regulation will fall within its rules for recognition and enforcement. Orders made other than under the Council Regulation can only be recognised and enforced under the 1980 European Custody Convention.[210]

4.82 Where there are matrimonial proceedings between the parents in progress elsewhere in the United Kingdom, the English courts may not entertain an application for a (Children Act 1989) s 8 order[211] unless the court in which the matrimonial proceedings are continuing considers that it would be appropriate for it to do so,[212] but if the children are present within England and Wales the High Court can exercise its inherent jurisdiction for their immediate protection.[213]

4.83 If there are matrimonial proceedings between the parents in progress elsewhere in the EU (with the exception of Denmark) before a court which has

---

[205] Article 3. See **4.17**.

[206] See **4.19** *et seq.* Note that a spouse who is habitually resident in a Member State or is a national of a Member State (or in the case of the United Kingdom and Ireland is domiciled there) can *only* be sued in accordance with Arts 2–6: see **3.7**.

[207] Family Law Act 1986, s 2A. See **3.6** and **3.21**.

[208] Article 3(3). See **3.14**.

[209] Family Law Act 1986, s 42(2). See **3.14**.

[210] See Chapter 19.

[211] Family Law Act 1986, s 3(2).

[212] *Ibid*, ss 13(6) and 19A(4). See **3.13**.

[213] *Ibid*, ss 1(1)(d) and 2(3)(b). See **3.23**.

jurisdiction over the children, the English courts must decline jurisdiction[214] unless they intend to take only provisional, including protective, measures.[215]

Protective measures

4.84   Article 12 of the Council Regulation permits courts of a Member State which do not otherwise have jurisdiction nevertheless to take 'such provisional, including protective, measures in respect of persons or assets in that State as may be available under the law of that Member State …'.[216]

4.85   In the cases where only one of the parents is involved in matrimonial proceedings in England and Wales or elsewhere in the United Kingdom or the EU, or cases in which one or both parents are involved in matrimonial proceedings in Denmark or outside the EU, and cases in which the parents are not involved in matrimonial proceedings at all, the English courts can exercise jurisdiction under the 1986 Act on the basis of the children being either habitually resident or present within England and Wales on the 'relevant date'.[217] If the children are present within England and Wales, but are habitually resident elsewhere in the United Kingdom, only the High Court can exercise its inherent jurisdiction for their immediate protection.[218] If the children are present within England and Wales, but are habitually resident somewhere other than in the United Kingdom, the court may stay the proceedings on the basis that it would be more appropriate for the matter to be determined elsewhere.[219]

---

[214]   Articles 7, 9 and 11. See **3.7**.

[215]   Article 12.

[216]   The scope of Art 12 has been considered in *Wermuth v Wermuth* [2002] EWCA Civ 50, [2003] 1 WLR 942, sub nom *Wermuth v Wermuth (No 2)* [2003] 1 FLR 1029. See also *A v L (Jurisdiction: Brussels II)* [2002] 1 FLR 1042.

[217]   Family Law Act 1986, s 7(c). See **3.21**.

[218]   *Ibid*, ss 1(1)(d) and 2(3)(b).

[219]   *Ibid*, s 5(2).

Chapter 5

INTERNATIONAL CHILD CUSTODY JURISDICTION IN THE UNITED STATES[1]

INTRODUCTION

5.1 In the United States, the problems of domestic relations, including the subjects of marriage, divorce or dissolution of marriage, maintenance, division of marital property, custody and access to children, as well as other areas of parental responsibility, are almost exclusively within the control of the individual states. Since each individual state is solely competent to decide cases involving problems of domestic relations, such as custody and visitation issues, they relate to each other in the same way as independent countries. It therefore became necessary to develop some method to determine which state has jurisdiction to decide issues involving custody of and access to children.

5.2 The first major attempt to provide uniform rules of jurisdiction in cases involving custody of children occurred with promulgation of the Uniform Child Custody Jurisdiction Act (UCCJA). This Act was revised in 1997 with the promulgation of the Uniform Child Custody Jurisdiction and Enforcement Act (UCCJEA) which has been adopted in approximately half of the states.

---

[1] This chapter is written by Robert G Spector, Glenn R Watson Centennial Professor of Law, University of Oklahoma Law Center and Reporter for the Uniform Child Custody Jurisdiction and Enforcement.

THE INTERNATIONAL CASE: THE UCCJA[2]

5.3   The UCCJA authorised states to take jurisdiction of a child custody determination when one of four circumstances existed: the state was the home state of the child or had been the home state of the child within 6 months of the commencement of the custody proceeding if a parent or person acting as a parent continued to reside in the state; the child or the child and one parent had substantial connections with the state and there existed in the state substantial evidence concerning the child's future care; there was an emergency; no other state would have jurisdiction to make a custody determination. States were also required to enforce custody determinations made consistently with the jurisdictional principles of the UCCJA and were not to modify custody determination made by other states unless the other state no longer had jurisdiction under the UCCJA and the state which sought to modify the determination did have jurisdiction under that Act. States were required to decline jurisdiction if another state had assumed jurisdiction in accordance with the UCCJA. States were also authorised to decline jurisdiction if another state would be a more convenient forum and, in certain circumstances, where the petitioner had engaged in reprehensible conduct.

5.4   Section 23 of the UCCJA provided that the general policies of the Act applied to foreign custody determinations. Foreign custody determinations were to be recognised and enforced if they were made consistently with the UCCJA and there was reasonable notice and opportunity to be heard. There were two types of issues that arose under this section. The first was whether a US court would defer to a foreign tribunal when that tribunal would have jurisdiction under the UCCJA and the case was filed first in that tribunal. The second issue was whether the a state of the United States would recognise, under this section, a custody determination made by a foreign tribunal.

5.5   On the first issue, the UCCJA was ambiguous and only required application of the 'general policies' of the Act. Frequently, courts in the United States would apply the same jurisdictional principles to international cases that they would apply in interstate cases. However, not all states followed the same practice. Most American states enforced foreign custody orders if made consistently with the jurisdictional standards of the UCCJA and reasonable notice and opportunity to be heard were afforded all participants. However, four states refused to enact s 23 of the UCCJA and thus were able to undermine the UCCJA principles of recognition and enforcement of custody determinations by countries with appropriate jurisdiction.

---

[2]   For a full discussion of international child custody jurisdiction, see RG Spector, 'International Child Custody Jurisdiction and the Uniform Child Custody Jurisdiction and Enforcement Act' (2000) 33 NYUJ of Int Law and Politics 251. Information on the UCCJEA and other uniform acts can be found on the website of the National Commissioners on Uniform State Laws at http://www.nccusl.org.

THE INTERNATIONAL CASE: THE UCCJEA

5.6 Section 105 of the UCCJEA provides that a court of the United States shall treat a court of a foreign country as if it was a state of the United States for the purposes of applying the jurisdiction and co-operation sections of the Act. It further provides that a court of the United States shall enforce a foreign custody determination if it was made under factual circumstances in substantial conformity with the jurisdictional provisions of Art 2 of the UCCJEA. However, a court need not apply this section if the foreign custody law would violate fundamental principles of human rights. Thus the United States will follow the same principles of jurisdiction in international cases as it would follow in cases between states of the United States. Those jurisdictional principles are as follows.

Child custody jurisdiction under the UCCJEA

Original jurisdiction: home state

5.7 Jurisdiction to make a child custody determination as an original matter is governed by s 201 of the UCCJEA. That section provides for one primary jurisdiction and a number of subsidiary jurisdictions. Primary jurisdiction resides in the child's home state. 'Home state' is defined in s 102(7) as the state in which a child has lived with a parent or a person acting as a parent for at least 6 consecutive months immediately before the commencement of a child custody proceeding. In the case of a child less than 6 months of age, the term means the state in which the child lived from birth with any of the persons mentioned. A period of temporary absence of any of the mentioned persons is part of the period.

5.8 Section 201 of the UCCJEA gives exclusive jurisdiction to the state that is the home state of the child. It also provides that this 'home state' jurisdiction extends to cases where the state was the home state of the child within 6 months before the commencement of the proceeding and the child is absent from the state but a parent or person acting as a parent continues to live in the state.

Significant connection jurisdiction

5.9 If there is no home state, then a state where the child and the child's parents, or the child and at least one parent or a person acting as a parent, have a significant connection, other than mere physical presence, and there is available in that state substantial evidence concerning the child's care, protection, training, and personal relationships, may assume jurisdiction.

Exclusive continuing jurisdiction

5.10 One of the most significant sections of the UCCJEA provides that the state which made the original custody determination continues to retain jurisdiction over all aspects of that determination until the occurrence of one of two events: first, this continuing jurisdiction is lost when a court of the state that made the original custody determination finds that neither the child, the child and one parent, nor the child and a person acting as a parent have a significant connection with it and that substantial evidence is no longer available in that state concerning the child's care, protection, training, and personal relationships. In other words, even if the child has acquired a new home state, the original decree state retains exclusive, continuing jurisdiction, so long as the general requisites of the 'substantial connection' jurisdiction provisions of s 201 are met. If the relationship between the child and the person remaining in the state with exclusive, continuing jurisdiction becomes so attenuated that the court could no longer find significant connections and substantial evidence, jurisdiction would no longer exist. As long as one parent, or person acting as a parent, remains in the original decree state, that state is the sole determinant of whether jurisdiction continues. A party seeking to modify a custody determination must obtain an order from the original decree state stating that it no longer has jurisdiction.

5.11   Secondly, jurisdiction is lost when a court of any state determines that the child, the child's parents, and any person acting as a parent do not presently reside in the original state. If the child, the parents, and all persons acting as parents have all left the state which made the custody determination prior to the commencement of the modification proceeding, considerations of waste of resources dictate that a court in another state, as well as a court in original decree state, can decide that the original state has lost exclusive, continuing jurisdiction.

Temporary emergency jurisdiction

5.12   The UCCJEA provides for one temporary concurrent basis of jurisdiction to deal with emergencies. An emergency occurs when a child is abandoned in the state or when the child, a sibling of the child, or parent of the child is threatened with mistreatment or abuse. The concurrent nature of the jurisdiction means that a court may take cognisance of the case to protect the child even though it can claim neither home state nor significant connection jurisdiction. The duties of states to recognise, enforce and not modify a custody determination of another state do not take precedence over the need to enter a temporary emergency order to protect the child. However, a custody determination made under the emergency jurisdiction provisions must be a temporary order. The purpose of the emergency temporary order is to protect the child until the state that appropriately has jurisdiction under the original jurisdiction provisions or the continuing jurisdiction provisions is able to enter an order to resolve the emergency.

Abstention from jurisdiction

5.13   Three sections of the UCCJEA speak to the question of when a state which has jurisdiction should refrain from exercising it:

(a)   Simultaneous proceedings or lis pendis

5.14   There is one situation where concurrent jurisdiction is possible under the UCCJEA. It occurs when there is no state that can exercise home state jurisdiction, or no state with exclusive continuing jurisdiction, and more than one state that can exercise significant connection jurisdiction. For those cases, the UCCJEA, in s 206, retains the 'first in time' rule of the UCCJA. This section requires that before a court may proceed with a custody determination, it must find out from the pleadings and other documents that have been submitted whether a custody proceeding has already begun. If one has been commenced in a state that would otherwise have jurisdiction under the UCCJEA, it must communicate with that court. If the court that would otherwise have jurisdiction under the UCCJEA refuses to decline in favour of the forum, then that forum must dismiss the case.

(b)   Forum non conveniens

5.15   The doctrine of *forum non conveniens* is firmly established in American jurisprudence. Simply put, if a state that would otherwise have jurisdiction determines that some other state would be a more appropriate forum to decide the case, it may decline jurisdiction in favour of that forum. This principle is a significant part of the UCCJEA jurisdictional provisions. Both the sections on home state jurisdiction and exclusive continuing jurisdiction authorise the courts of those states to decide if another state would be a more appropriate forum, and if so, to decline jurisdiction in favour of that state.

(c)   Declining jurisdiction because of unreasonable conduct

5.16   Section 208 of the UCCJEA applies to those situations where jurisdiction exists because of the unjustified conduct of the person seeking to invoke it. The focus in this section is on the unjustified conduct of the person who invokes the jurisdiction of the court. A technical illegality or wrong is insufficient to trigger its applicability. This section also authorises the court to fashion an appropriate remedy for the safety of the child and to prevent a repetition of the unjustified conduct.

Communication and co-operation between tribunals

5.17   The UCCJEA contains specific provisions providing for communication and co-operation between tribunals of different states. Section 110 authorises courts in the United States to communicate with another court concerning any child custody proceeding. This includes international tribunals.[3] The court may allow the parties to participate in the communication. If they are not able to participate, the parties must be given an opportunity to present facts and legal arguments before a decision on jurisdiction is made. In any event, a record of the communication must be made and the parties must be given access to the record.

---

3   See *Stock v Stock*, 677 So 2d 1341 (Fla Ct App 1996); *Ivaldi v Ivaldi*, 685 A.2d 1319 (NJ 1996).

5.18   Section 111 authorises a court to offer testimony of witnesses who are located in another state by any means allowable in the state for such testimony to be presented. It may also allow an individual in another state to be deposed or to testify by telephone, audio visual or other electronic means before a designated court or at another location in that state. Documentary evidence may be transmitted from one state to another by technological means that do not produce an original writing.

5.19   Section 112 allows a court in the United States to co-operate with tribunals in other states to hold an evidentiary hearing, order the production of evidence, order a custody evaluation, forward a transcript of a prior proceeding or any other information in the court's possession and order a person to appear in a proceeding with the child. The section also provides that any expenses associated with the co-operation process can be assessed against the parties in accordance with local law.

5.20   These provisions also apply in international child custody cases which should make the resolution of these cases much easier.

PART II

THE LAWFUL MOVEMENT OF CHILDREN

Introduction to Part II

THE LAWFUL MOVEMENT OF CHILDREN

The movement of children inside or across national or jurisdictional boundaries is, like many other aspects of children's lives, largely controlled by those who have parental responsibility for them. Unless there is something specifically preventing them from doing so, a sole holder of parental responsibility can take a child anywhere in England and Wales or abroad, temporarily or permanently, and joint holders of parental responsibility can agree between themselves to do so.[1] When making such a decision, those holders of parental responsibility are under no obligation to consider the child's welfare,[2] or the ties of affection which he might have with his wider family, his friends, his school and all those who do not have parental responsibility.

Fathers whose children are born out of wedlock are therefore in a particularly vulnerable position if they have not acquired parental responsibility,[3] because English law, unlike some other jurisdictions, does not fetter the choice of a custodial parent as to where they will live. There is no equivalent to the provisions in, for example, New York, which restrain a custodial parent from moving so as to frustrate visitation rights, and no right on the part of those not having parental responsibility to be consulted about any proposed change of residence. The proposition of Sachs LJ in *Poel v Poel*[4] that 'The way in which the parent who properly has custody of a child may choose in a reasonable manner to order his or her way of life is one of those things which the parent

---

[1] In such circumstances, no offence under the Child Abduction Act 1984 would be committed: see Chapter 10.

[2] The paramountcy of the child's welfare only applies in the context of litigation, and then only when a court is determining a question with respect to the upbringing of a child or the administration of his property or the application of any income arising from it: Children Act 1989, s 1, and see the discussion in White, Carr and Lowe, *Children Act in Practice*, 3rd edn (Butterworths, 2002) at **2.2** *et seq*.

[3] *Re W (Minors) (Abduction: Father's Rights), Re B (Minor) (Abduction: Father's Rights)* [1999] Fam 1, sub nom *Re W; Re B (Child Abduction: Unmarried Father)* [1998] 2 FLR 146, Hale J (a father without parental responsibility does not have rights of custody for the purposes of the 1980 Hague Abduction Convention, and a mother is entitled as a matter of English domestic law to remove a child from the jurisdiction unless there is in force an order prohibiting removal or there are proceedings pending either for an order prohibiting removal or for an order which would give the father parental responsibility). And see *Re J (Abduction: Declaration of Wrongful Removal)* [1999] 2 FLR 653.

[4] [1970] 1 WLR 1469.

who has not been given custody may well have to bear …' is still broadly correct today, even after the reforms in family relationships, particularly the sharing of parental responsibility, brought about by the Children Act 1989.[5]

So, if a father has a contact order, but not parental responsibility, there is nothing to stop the mother moving to a remote part of the United Kingdom[6] or, subject to the possibility that the father or someone else might have 'inchoate' rights of custody for the purposes of the 1980 Hague Abduction Convention,[7] taking the child away from the jurisdiction permanently. Those advising fathers who do not have parental responsibility for their children should give serious consideration to making an application for a prohibited steps order if there is any possibility that the mother might remove the child from the jurisdiction.[8] Notwithstanding the 'no order' principle,[9] an order should be sought and made even if the mother is prepared to give an assurance or undertaking not to remove, because only then will there be 'rights of custody' in the court for the purposes of the 1980 Hague Abduction Convention,[10] and only then can the court be given a measure of assurance that the child will remain in the jurisdiction, or be returned to it in the event that he is taken to a country which is a signatory to either the 1980 Hague Abduction Convention or the 1980 European Custody Convention, so that he can be protected from the harmful effects of an abduction and so that questions about his future care and welfare can be determined in the country of his habitual residence, and not in a forum chosen by the mother.

---

5 See the judgment of Butler-Sloss LJ in *Re E (Residence: Imposition of Conditions)* [1997] 2 FLR 638.

6 See *Re S (A Child) (Residence Order: Conditions)* [2001] EWCA Civ 847, [2001] 3 FCR 154 at [15]; and *Re H (Children) (Residence Order: Condition)* [2001] EWCA Civ 1338, [2001] 2 FLR 1277.

7 See **14.49** *et seq.*

8 *Re J (Abduction: Declaration of Wrongful Removal)* [1999] 2 FLR 653.

9 Children Act 1989, s 1(5). And see *Dawson v Wearmouth* [1999] 2 AC 308, [1999] 1 FLR 1167, HL, as to the meaning and effect of s 1(5), and *Re X and Y (Leave to Remove from Jurisdiction: No Order Principle)* [2001] 1 FLR 118 (disapproved in the context of relocation cases in *Re H (Children) (Residence Order: Condition)* (above) at [19]).

10 See **14.23**.

Chapter 6

RESTRAINTS ON REMOVAL

JOINT HOLDERS OF PARENTAL RESPONSIBILITY

6.1   Despite s 2(7) of the Children Act 1989 providing that each person with parental responsibility for a child may 'act alone and without the other (or others) in meeting that responsibility', if there are joint holders of parental responsibility one of them cannot remove the child from the United Kingdom[1] without the consent of the other or others, or the leave of a court. To do so would breach their 'rights of custody' within the meaning of Arts 3 and 5 of the Hague Convention[2] and may also cause them to be guilty of an offence under s 1 of the Child Abduction Act 1984[3] or the common law offence of kidnapping.[4]

---

[1]   The United Kingdom is defined as Great Britain, viz England and Wales, and Scotland and Northern Ireland: Interpretation Act 1978, s 5, Sch 1.

[2]   See **14.23** *et seq.*

[3]   Discussed at **9.4** *et seq.*

[4]   Discussed at **9.11** *et seq.*

RESIDENCE ORDERS

Movement within the United Kingdom

6.2   There is no statutory requirement of consent or leave of the court in respect of moving a child anywhere within the United Kingdom.[5] Prior to the Children Act 1989: 'to my knowledge, residence restrictions were not attached to custody orders and only rarely to an order in wardship which did not involve a public law element. An order granting custody to a parent who was to live within the jurisdiction gave the custodial parent the right to decide where to live and with whom. If the plans were unsuitable it might be a reason not to make the custody order in favour of that parent'.[6]

6.3   The position has not changed with the introduction of shared parental responsibility and the substitution of residence orders for custody orders. A primary carer may, however, be faced with an application for a prohibited steps order or the imposition of conditions on a residence order,[7] but the court will not in private law proceedings, other than in an exceptional case, seek to dictate the primary carer's place of residence within the United Kingdom, because to do so would be an unsustainable restriction on adult liberties and likely to have an adverse effect on the welfare of the child by denying the primary carer reasonable freedom of choice.[8] In *Re E (Residence: Imposition of Conditions)*[9] the judge at first instance found that the mother was the more suitable carer, but (intending that the father should maintain contact with the children) he decided the issue of with whom the children should live separately from the question of where they should live. The court welfare officer felt strongly that the children should not move from London because, being of mixed race, they fitted more easily into the multiracial and multicultural life style of London. The judge made residence orders in respect of the children in favour of the mother and imposed a requirement under s 11(7) of the Children Act 1989 that the children continue to reside at a named address unless otherwise ordered or agreed by the father. The mother's appeal against that requirement was upheld, the Court of Appeal saying that although the wording of s 11(7) was wide enough to enable courts to make orders with restrictions on residence to specified places within the United Kingdom, a restriction on the right of the carer of the child to choose where to live sat uneasily with the general understanding of a residence order. A general imposition of requirements (subject to exceptional cases) on residence orders was not contemplated by the legislature, and where a parent was

---

5   *Re E (Residence: Imposition of Conditions)* [1997] 2 FLR 638 at 641, CA. See also Art 2 of Protocol 4 to the European Convention of Human Rights, discussed at **7.20**.
6   Per Butler-Sloss LJ in *Re E (Minors) (Residence: Imposition of Conditions)* (above).
7   *Re H (Children) (Residence Order: Condition)* [2001] EWCA Civ 1338, [2001] 2 FLR 1277 at [19].
8   *Re S (A Child) (Residence Order: Condition)* [2001] EWCA Civ 847, [2001] 3 FCR 154.
9   [1997] 2 FLR 638, CA.

entirely suitable and the court intends to make a residence order in his or her favour, a condition of residence was an unwarranted imposition upon the right to choose where to live within the United Kingdom or with whom.[10]

6.4 The correct approach, therefore, is to look at the issue of where the children will live as one of the relevant factors in the context of the cross-applications for residence and not as a separate issue divorced from the question of residence. If the case is finely balanced between the respective advantages and disadvantages of the parents, the proposals put forward by each parent will assume considerable importance. If one parent's plan is to remove the children against their wishes to a part of the country less suitable for them, it is an important factor to be taken into account by the court and might persuade the court in some cases to make a residence order in favour of the other parent.[11]

Exceptional cases

6.5 An exceptional case might be where the court has concerns about the ability of the parent to be granted a residence order to be a satisfactory carer, but there is no better solution than to place the child with that parent. Then the court might consider it necessary to keep some control over the parent by way of conditions which include a condition of residence.[12] In *Re S (A Child) (Residence Order: Condition)*[13] the judge thought that the case, involving a child with Down's Syndrome whose mother intended to move to Cornwall from Croydon, was exceptional, the expert evidence being that the child would find it difficult to adjust to reduced contact with her father, and would be unsettled by losing contact with her paternal family and moving school. Although the father finally did not seek to pursue his applications for a residence order or a prohibited steps order preventing his daughter's removal from the Croydon area, the judge decided to make a residence order (which the mother had not sought) and imposed a condition that 'the child continue to reside within the Borough of Croydon unless otherwise ordered ...', alternatively that she '... should not be removed from the area without the leave of the court'. In his judgment, Thorpe LJ said that since the Children Act 1989[14] sought only to prohibit the removal of children from the United Kingdom and not, as formerly was sometimes the case, from the jurisdiction, it was implicit that the

---

[10] This latter remark reflected the judgment of the Court of Appeal in *Re D (Residence: Imposition of Conditions)* [1996] 2 FLR 281, which the court adopted. In that case, a mother had originally agreed that she would not bring the children into contact with the man with whom she had been living. On her subsequent application to discharge that condition the court held that a s 11(7) condition could not exclude another person from the mother's home, thereby interfering with her right to live with whom she liked. Ward LJ said: 'The court was not in a position to overrule her decision to live her life as she chose. What was before the court was the issue of whether she should have the children living with her.'

[11] *Re E (Residence: Imposition of Conditions)* [1997] 2 FLR 638 at 642.

[12] Per Butler-Sloss LJ in *Re E (Residence: Imposition of Conditions)* (above) at 642.

[13] [2001] EWCA Civ 847, [2001] 3 FCR 154.

[14] See s 13, discussed below at **6.7**.

court would not ordinarily seek to dictate the primary carer's place of residence. Restrictions were often contrary to good sense and were likely to have an adverse effect on the welfare of the children indirectly through the emotional and psychological disturbance caused to the primary carer by denial of the freedom to exercise reasonable choice.[15] Referring extensively to *Re E (Residence: Imposition of Conditions)*, Thorpe LJ said that he was in no doubt that Butler-Sloss LJ was 'guarding against the danger of never saying never in family law litigation' and that she was giving the clearest guide that it would be highly exceptional that the imposition of a condition would be justified, and probably restricted to a case 'as yet unforeseen and may be difficult to foresee', in which the ability of the primary carer to perform to a satisfactory level required the buttress of a s 11(7) order. He went on to say that the judgment of Butler-Sloss LJ was not to be interpreted as giving a general latitude to strive for some sort of ideal above the rival proposals of the available primary carers, which could lead to quite unsustainable restrictions on ordinary adult liberties, extending even to the secondary carers' chosen way of life. Subsequently, however, the case returned to the Court of Appeal, where it was held that the circumstances in *Re S* were truly exceptional and the mother was prevented from taking the child to live in Cornwall.[16]

Public law cases

6.6 In *Re E (Residence: Imposition of Conditions)*[17] Butler-Sloss LJ remarked that in public law cases involving local authorities, where a residence order may be made by the court in preference to a care order, s 11(7) conditions might be applied in somewhat different circumstances to those in private law cases.

Automatic restrictions on international movement – section 13 of the Children Act 1989

6.7 Section 13 of the Children Act 1989 imposes a restraint on the international movement of children if there is a residence order in force and there is more than one holder of parental responsibility, except to the extent that the holder of the residence order can take the child out of the jurisdiction for periods of up to a month at a time, on an unlimited number of occasions. Section 13 does not impose a restraint on movement within the United Kingdom.[18]

6.8 Section 13 provides:

　'(1) Where a residence order is in force with respect to a child, no person may:

---

15 [2001] EWCA Civ 847, [2001] 3 FCR 154 at [16].
16 *Re S (A Child) (Residence Order: Condition) (No 2)* [2002] EWCA Civ 1795, [2003] 1 FCR 138.
17 [1997] 2 FLR 638 at 642.
18 *Payne v Payne* [2001] EWCA Civ 116, [2001] 1 FLR 1052 at [36]; *Re H (Children) (Residence Order: Condition)* [2001] EWCA Civ 1338, [2001] 2 FLR 1277 at [16]; *Re S (A Child) (Residence: Condition)* (above).

(b)   remove him from the United Kingdom;

without either the written consent of every person who has parental responsibility for the child or the leave of the court.

(2)   Subsection (1)(b) does not prevent the removal of a child, for a period of less than one month, by the person in whose favour the residence order is made.

(3)   In making a residence order with respect to a child the court may grant the leave required by subsection (1)(b), either generally or for specified purposes.'[19]

6.9   However, there are real difficulties over the enforcement of the prohibitions in s 13 because it provides no direct penalty or sanction[20] for removing a child without the written consent of everyone who has parental responsibility for the child or the leave of the court, although breach might result either in an offence being committed under s 1 of the Child Abduction Act 1984 or in common law kidnapping.

6.10   Where there is a residence order in force, but no other holder of parental responsibility, there is no obligation on the holder of parental responsibility to make an application to the court for leave to remove, even if there are those, including a father without parental responsibility, who would object to the removal if they were given the opportunity to do so.[21]

6.11   If the residence order ceases to have effect because the parents live together for a continuous period of 6 months, any order giving leave to remove also ceases to have effect.[22]

PENDING PROCEEDINGS

6.12   The mere fact that proceedings relating to a child are pending does not, under English domestic law, in itself create a restraint on removal.[23] However, the existence of pending proceedings, provided that they raise a question of custody within the meaning of the 1980 Hague Abduction Convention, may

---

[19]   Note that by the Children Act 1989, s 14C(3), prospectively inserted by s 115 of the Adoption and Children Act 2002, special guardians will be permitted to take children outside the United Kingdom for a period of up to 3 months without the need for consent.

[20]   See *Re S (A Child: Abduction)* [2002] EWCA Civ 1941, [2003] 1 FLR 1008 at [40], per Thorpe LJ. Furthermore, it may not be possible to attach a penal notice to a s 13 direction so as to be able to invoke sanctions for contempt of court: see *Re P (Minors) (Custody Order: Penal Notice)* [1990] 1 WLR 613, CA.

[21]   *Re W (Minors) (Abduction: Father's Rights), Re B (Minor) (Abduction: Father's Rights)* [1999] Fam 1, [1998] 2 FLR 146.

[22]   Children Act 1989, s 11(5) and *Re P (Abduction: Declaration)* [1995] 1 FLR 831.

[23]   There are implied prohibitions on removal during pending proceedings in other jurisdictions. As an example, see *C v C (Minors) (Child Abduction)* [1992] 1 FLR 163, in which it was held that removal of a child from New York state in breach of an implied prohibition on removal constituted a wrongful removal for the purposes of the 1980 Hague Abduction Convention.

confer on the court a 'right of custody' for the purposes of that Convention, and thus make a removal of the child 'wrongful'.[24]

WARDS OF COURT

6.13 The status of ward has always carried with it an automatic prohibition on the removal of the ward from the jurisdiction of England and Wales,[25] a prohibition imposed immediately the child becomes a ward on the issuing of the originating summons.[26] Removal of the child without the leave of the court constitutes a contempt and a breach of rights of custody in the wardship court.[27]

6.14 That general rule is modified[28] if the ward's parents are involved in divorce, nullity or judicial separation proceedings relating to their marriage elsewhere in the United Kingdom or in a specified dependent territory (ie the Isle of Man), or if the ward is habitually resident in another part of the United Kingdom or a specified dependent territory. In such a case, unless the ward has attained the age of 16 and the other part of the United Kingdom is Scotland, he may be removed:

(i) without the consent of any court, to that part of the United Kingdom or specified dependent territory in which the proceedings relating to his parent's marriage are taking place, or in which he is habitually resident;[29]

(ii) to any other place with the leave of the appropriate court in that part of the United Kingdom or specified dependent territory in which the proceedings relating to his parent's marriage are taking place.[30]

CHILDREN IN CARE

6.15 It is an offence[31] to take a child away from, keep a child away from, or to induce, assist or incite a child to run away from or stay away from, a person ('the responsible person')[32] who has the care of him by virtue of a care order or an emergency protection order or by virtue of the child having been taken

---

24 See **14.67** *et seq*.

25 Family Law Act 1986, s 38(1). See also the discussion in Lowe and White, *Wards of Court*, 2nd edn (Barry Rose, 1986) at 5.2 and 8.4.

26 See Supreme Court Act 1981, s 41(2) and Family Proceedings Rules 1991, r 5.3.

27 *Re J (A Minor) (Abduction: Ward of Court)* [1989] Fam 85; *Re S (A Minor) (Custody: Habitual Residence)* [1997] 3 WLR 597.

28 By s 38 of the Family Law Act 1986.

29 Family Law Act 1986, s 38(3)(a).

30 *Ibid*, s 38(3)(b).

31 Children Act 1989, s 49, discussed further at **9.17**.

32 *Ibid*, s 49(2).

into police protection.[33] The court has power to make a 'recovery order' in respect of a child who has been unlawfully taken or kept away from, or who has run away from, the responsible person, or who is missing.[34]

REMOVAL OF CHILDREN FOR ADOPTION ABROAD

6.16 Section 56(1) of the Adoption Act 1976 imposes an absolute prohibition on taking or sending a child who is a British subject or a citizen of the Republic of Ireland out of Great Britain to anywhere out of the British Islands[35] with a view to his adoption by anyone not a parent, guardian or relative,[36] except pursuant to an order made under s 55 of the Adoption Act 1976 or with the approval of the court given under Sch 2, para 19(6) to the Children Act 1989.[37] Any person, including any director, manager, member of the committee, secretary or other officer of a corporate body (provided that they consented to or connived at the commission of the offence or if it was attributable to their neglect) who takes or sends a child out of Great Britain to any place in breach of the provisions of s 56(1), or makes or takes part in any arrangements for placing a child with any person for that purpose, commits a criminal offence.[38] A person is deemed to take part in placing a child with a person for the purpose of s 56(1) if he facilitates the placing of the child with that person, or initiates or takes part in any negotiations of which the purpose or effect is the conclusion of any agreement or the making of any arrangement therefor, and if he causes another person to do so.[39]

6.17 The words 'with a view to his adoption' are broad and comprehensive, and cover even intermediate steps in the process, so that when a married couple who were domiciled and resident in Denmark wanted to adopt an

---

33 Children Act 1989, s 46(2).

34 *Ibid*, s 50.

35 The British Islands are the United Kingdom, the Channel Islands, the Isle of Man and the Republic of Ireland: Interpretation Act 1978, ss 5, 22(1), Sch 1, Sch 2, para 4(2) (*Halsbury's Statutes* (4th edn), vol 41, 899).

36 'Guardian' and 'relative' are defined by Adoption Act 1976, s 72(1), as amended by Children Act 1989, Sch 10, para 30; see also *Re C (Minors) (Adoption by Relative)* [1989] 1 WLR 61, CA (a great-uncle is not a 'relative' for the purposes of the Adoption Act 1976).

37 See *Re W (Care: Leave to Place outside Jurisdiction)* [1994] 2 FLR 1087 and *Re S (Freeing For Adoption)* [2002] EWCA Civ 798, [2002] 2 FLR 681.

38 And is liable on summary conviction to imprisonment for a term not exceeding 3 months or a fine not exceeding level 5 on the standard scale or both (s 56(1)).

39 Adoption Act 1976, s 56(3). Note that from 30 April 2001 anyone habitually resident in the British Islands other than a parent, relative or guardian who brings a child habitually resident outside the British Islands into the United Kingdom for the purpose of adoption without complying with the requirements of the regulations made by the Secretary of State commits an offence: Adoption Act 1976, s 56A, inserted by Adoption (Intercountry Aspects) Act 1999, s 14, and SI 2000/1279. Note also that the restrictions imposed by Adoption Act 1976, s 56 are prospectively to be replaced by s 85 of the Adoption and Children Act 2002, discussed by Bridge and Swindells in *Adoption: The Modern Law* (Family Law, 2003) at **16.28**.

illegitimate English child and, having made her a ward, applied for leave to remove her for 6 months before returning and applying for a provisional adoption order, the application was refused under the equivalent provision then in force, s 52 of the Adoption Act 1958.[40]

___

40   *Re M (An Infant)* [1973] Fam 66.

Chapter 7

INTERNATIONAL RELOCATION: APPLICATIONS FOR LEAVE TO REMOVE FROM ENGLAND AND WALES

THE PRINCIPLES ON WHICH PERMANENT LEAVE TO REMOVE WILL BE GRANTED

7.1   In February 2001, in what is now the leading authority, *Payne v Payne*,[1] Thorpe LJ pointed out that the applicant in a relocation case is invariably the mother and primary carer, that her motivation for moving generally arises from her remarriage or urge to return home, and that the father's opposition is commonly founded on a resultant reduction in his contact with, and influence on, the children.[2] He identified the consistent application of two propositions for the last 30 years: the welfare of the child is the paramount consideration; and refusing the primary carer's reasonable proposals for the relocation of her family life is likely to impact detrimentally on the welfare of her dependent children.[3] Therefore, a mother's application to relocate will be granted unless the court concludes that it is incompatible with the welfare of the children.[4]

---

1   [2001] EWCA Civ 166, [2001] Fam 473, [2001] 1 FLR 1052. Although decided in 1970, the modern principles on which a court will grant leave for a child to be removed permanently from the jurisdiction are set out in *Poel v Poel* [1970] 1 WLR 1469, and it was said in *Re H (Application to Remove from Jurisdiction)* [1998] 1 FLR 848 that the later cases have added little to the jurisprudence, and not a lot is to be gained by seeking support from past decisions, however superficially similar the factual matrix may appear to be. In *Re H (Children) (Residence Order: Condition)* [2001] EWCA Civ 1332, [2001] 2 FLR 1277 at [19], Thorpe LJ said: 'Trial judges should direct themselves only to the decision of this court in *Payne v Payne*'.

2   *Payne v Payne* (above) at [27].

3   *Ibid* at [26]. The question to be addressed was expressed as whether the proposed move is a reasonable one from the point of view of the adults involved. If so, it is likely to be consistent with the welfare of the child, and leave should be refused only if it is clearly shown beyond any doubt that the interests of the children and the custodial parent are incompatible: see *Chamberlain v de la Mare* (1983) 4 FLR 434, cited with approval in *Re H (Application to Remove from Jurisdiction)* [1998] 1 FLR 848. See also *Re B (Removal from Jurisdiction); Re S (Removal from Jurisdiction)* [2003] EWCA Civ 1149, [2003] 2 FLR 1043.

4   *Ibid*. 'So the approach of the court is to sanction the realistic proposal of the custodial parent, unless that proposal is inconsistent with the child's welfare', per Thorpe J in *Re K (A Minor) (Removal from Jurisdiction)* [1992] 2 FLR 98. See also *Re K (Application to Remove from Jurisdiction)* [1998] 2 FLR 1006; *Re W (Minors) (Removal from Jurisdiction)* [1994] 1 FCR 93: '… and I am perfectly satisfied in this case that the mother's proposal to return to Pittsburgh with the two children should be granted since it has not been clearly shown that the move would be against the children's interests', per Thorpe J; and *Re F (A Ward) (Leave to Remove a Ward out of the Jurisdiction)* [1988] 2 FLR 116, CA, in which it was held that an application should always be considered on the premise that it was reasonable, but the reasonableness of proposals cannot be judged without taking into account the effect a refusal would have. Both have to be considered together. In *Re S (A Child) (Residence Order: Condition)* [2001] EWCA Civ 847, [2001] 3 FCR 154, Clarke LJ said at [37] that: 'The principal carer will ordinarily be entitled to move to wherever he or she wishes. However, in the *Payne v Payne* class of case the application will ordinarily be granted unless the court concludes that it is incompatible with the welfare of the child' (approved by Dame Elizabeth Butler-Sloss P in *Re S (A Child) (Residence Order: Condition) (No 2)* [2002] EWCA Civ 1795, [2003] 1 FCR 138, at [21]).

Payne v Payne – the modern approach to relocation

7.2   However, there is no presumption of law that favours the reasonable proposals of a caring parent.[5] To avoid the risk of infringing the respondent's right to family life and a fair trial,[6] the court should ask itself whether the mother's application is genuine (in the sense that it is not motivated by some selfish desire to exclude the father) and realistic, being founded on well-researched and investigated proposals. If it fails either of those tests, it will inevitably be refused. If the mother's application passes those tests, then the father's position should be examined to find out if he is motivated by a genuine concern for the children's welfare or some ulterior motive. The court should then examine the extent of the detriment to the father and his relationship with the children if the application were granted, and the extent to which it would be offset by extension of the child's relationships with the maternal family and homeland, and the impact on the mother (either as single parent or new wife) of refusing her realistic proposals. Then:[7]

> 'The outcome of the second and third appraisals must then be brought into an overriding review of the child's welfare as the paramount consideration, directed by the statutory checklist insofar as appropriate.'

7.3   But in carrying into effect this discipline, the importance which the court has consistently attached to the emotional and psychological well being of the primary carer should not be diminished. In any evaluation of the welfare of the child as the paramount consideration, great weight must be given to this factor, because the most crucial assessment and finding for the judge is likely to be the effect of refusing the application on the mother's future psychological and emotional stability.[8]

Explaining *Payne v Payne*

7.4   In *Re C (Permission to Remove from Jurisdiction),*[9] Charles J considered, explained and applied the principles set out in *Payne v Payne* to an application by a mother to return to her home in Singapore with the two children after the failure of her marriage to an Englishman. He thought that the most important point was that the existence of a genuine and reasonable wish of the custodial parent to move outside the United Kingdom does not create a presumption in

---

[5]   [2001] EWCA Civ 166, [2001] Fam 473, [2001] 1 FLR 1052 at [25].

[6]   European Convention for the Protection of Human Rights and Fundamental Freedoms (ECHR), Arts 8 and 6.

[7]   *Payne v Payne* (above) at [40]. And see the judgment of Dame Elizabeth Butler-Sloss P at [85], in which she sets out considerations which should be in the forefront of the judge's mind when trying one of these difficult cases.

[8]   *Ibid* at [32]. And see *L v L (Leave to Remove Children from Jurisdiction: Effect on Children* [2002] EWHC 2577 (Fam), [2003] 1 FLR 900. See also *Re B (Removal from Jurisdiction); Re S (Removal from Jurisdiction)* [2003] EWCA Civ 1149, [2003] 2 FLR 1043.

[9]   [2003] EWHC 596 (Fam), [2003] 1 FLR 1066.

favour of permission for such a move being given.[10] Other important matters[11] were that the application should not be decided by reference to the class or sub-class of case in which it could be said to fall, but by considering the facts and competing considerations; and that showing that the application was (a) genuine and (b) practical created in effect conditions or hurdles which the applicant had to cross to get to the next stage of the assessment, which was whether granting the application would best promote the welfare of the child. Further, the reasonableness of the proposal should be considered from the viewpoints of the children and adults involved, and the guidance in *Payne v Payne* was not limited to directing the court to the factors it should consider, but also indicated the weight to be given to them and thus to the reasons for their relevance and importance in determining what would best promote the welfare of the child in the circumstances of the case.

The reasonable proposals of the applicant

7.5   The reason for giving great weight to the reasonable proposal of an applicant who is a primary carer is the desirability of promoting happiness and stability in the home and the likely detrimental impact on the primary carer, and thus the children, if the proposal cannot be implemented. So if the court concludes that a refusal of the application will be likely to have a detrimental impact on the care that the primary carer will give, that harm will usually outweigh the likelihood of harm flowing from other effects of the proposed move, based as it is on the importance of stability and happiness in the home.

Reduction in contact

7.6   Usually the harm that is likely to flow from a reduction in contact will not found the conclusion that the welfare of the child would be best promoted by refusing the application, but *Payne v Payne* is only giving guidance, and the competing considerations between a reasonable proposal for a move and a reasonable objection must be carefully considered and weighed, assessing the available possibilities and in particular considering the manner in which the competing welfare factors, such as promoting stability in the home and promoting contact, apply.[12]

Residence in issue

7.7   The approach to relocation set out above is on the basis that the question of which parent should be the child's residential parent is not in issue. If there is real dispute as to which parent the children should live with, and the

---

10   [2003] EWHC 596 (Fam), [2003] 1 FLR 1066 at [19].

11   *Ibid* at [24].

12   Further factors are likely to include the circumstances in which the child or children came to be living with one parent rather than the other, the ages of the children, their connection with the countries involved, and the ability of the family to maintain contact after a move (*ibid* at [24]).

decision is finely balanced, then the future plans of each parent are clearly relevant, but if the decision as to residence is clear, then the plans for removal from the jurisdiction are not likely to be significant in the decision about residence.[13]

The plans for the future

7.8   An applicant for leave to remove does not have to give the precise details of, or guarantee the success of, his or her plans for the future,[14] but applications have been refused because of the unsatisfactory nature of the applicant's plans. In *M v A (Wardship: Removal from Jurisdiction)*[15] the mother's plans to move to Canada were ill thought-out, little researched and did not accommodate the needs of the children who loved both homes and did not want the status quo changed.

Adverse or different living conditions

7.9   The fact that adverse, or significantly different, living conditions exist in the country to which the children would be taken is a relevant factor; but the central and crucial point is – what course would better promote the medium- to long-term welfare of the children? In *Re K (Application to Remove from Jurisdiction)*[16] leave was granted to a mother to take the children to Nigeria, despite the differences between the general living conditions, environment and culture in the United Kingdom and Nigeria, and the adverse conditions existing in Nigeria at the time. The medium- to long-term welfare of the children was held to be best promoted by their living in Nigeria with their mother, who had been their primary carer and whose wish to live there was genuine.

Relocation and the 'no order' principle

7.10   The court will make an order on the application. These cases are often fiercely contested, with cross-applications for residence orders or a counter-application for a prohibited steps order. As Thorpe LJ expressed it in *Re H (Children) (Residence Order: Condition)*,[17] when dealing with the test

---

13   [2003] EWHC 596 (Fam), [2003] 1 FLR 1066 at [86].
14   See *Re W (Minors) (Removal from Jurisdiction)* [1994] 1 FCR 842, in which the allegation of ill thought-out plans failed: Thorpe J held that the applicant was not required to guarantee the precise details of the future life but merely had to establish the interest, capacity and capability to pursue the plans. Cf *Re M (Leave to Remove Child from Jurisdiction)* [1999] 2 FLR 334, in which leave to remove was granted in advance of detailed plans.
15   [1993] 2 FLR 715.
16   [1998] 2 FLR 1006. And see *A v A (Child: Removal from Jurisdiction)* (1980) 1 FLR 380, in which the court asked the question in respect of the custodial mother: 'where is she going to have the best chance of bringing up this child reasonably well?'.
17   [2001] EWCA Civ 1332, [2001] 2 FLR 1277 at [19].

propounded by Munby J in *Re X and Y (Leave to Remove from the Jurisdiction: No Order Principle)*,[18] 'No order is simply not an option'.

Unsuccessful applications

7.11   Although the general approach of the courts has been that, provided the request is bona fide, leave will be granted unless it can be shown to be against the child's interests, such applications are by no means bound to succeed.[19] They are always difficult cases which require very profound investigation and judgment.[20]

7.12   Applications have been refused because of the disruption that the relocation would cause to the relationship between the children and their father. In *Tyler v Tyler*[21] there was a joint custody order with reasonable access to the father, which had worked well, even after the mother moved away, and the father obtained a defined access order. On the mother's application for leave to remove the children to Australia, the judge, upheld by the Court of Appeal, found that her desire to go was reasonable and sensible, but that there was a strong bond between the father and his sons, and that 'for all practical purposes real access and real contact between the boys and their father would come to an end if the boys went to Australia now'. Recognising that the mother would feel bitterness and frustration in having her application refused, the judge nevertheless felt that she would be able to cope and not let it damage the boys' relationship with their father.

7.13   Another case in which the child's relationship with his father outweighed his mother's reasonable wishes to relocate was *MH v GP (Child: Emigration)*.[22] The mother had inherited money and wanted to go to New Zealand, expressing a preference for an open, healthy life in a healthy environment and for the value of Rudolf Steiner education. The father

---

[18]   [2001] 2 FLR 118. In *Re H (Children) (Residence Order: Condition)* [2001] EWCA Civ 1332, [2001] 2 FLR 1277, in which Munby J held that *Dawson v Wearmouth* [1999] 2 AC 308, [1999] 1 FLR 1167, HL, provided authoritative guidance on the proper meaning and effect of s 1(5) of the Children Act 1989, namely, that it placed the burden on the party applying for an order to make out a positive case that, on the balance of probabilities, it was in the interests of the child that the order should be made, Thorpe LJ said that *Re X and Y* should not be followed.

[19]   *Re H (Application to Remove from the Jurisdiction)* [1998] 1 FLR 848 at 850C.

[20]   *Ibid* at 853D. And see *M v M (Minors) (Removal from Jurisdiction)* [1992] 2 FLR 303, in which the Court of Appeal remitted a case for hearing by a judge of the Family Division because the judge failed to take into account the serious and harmful consequences to the children of the very successful indoctrination by the mother against the father and of the likely withering away and ultimate cessation of their relationship with him.

[21]   [1989] 2 FLR 158. The Court of Appeal noted that no prior application by a custodial parent seemed to have been refused, and that if a custodial parent had genuine and reasonable desire to emigrate then the court should hesitate long before refusing permission to take the children. In this case, the court found that the mother was motivated by bitterness and hostility towards the father.

[22]   [1995] 2 FLR 106.

believed that the development of the child's relationship with him and his family was of particular importance in view of the mother's strong commitment to a philosophy of education very distinct from the norm. Applying the principles of *Poel v Poel*,[23] Thorpe J (as he was then) said that the welfare of the child was the first and paramount consideration,[24] but that leave should not be withheld unless the interests of the children and those of the custodial parent were clearly shown to be incompatible, thus creating a presumption[25] in favour of a reasonable application by a caring parent. However, although the mother had everything to offer the child as a single parent committed to his primary care, her individuality and idealism were areas of vulnerability, which could be compensated and safeguarded by the development of his relationship with his much more ordinary, much more grounded father. Accordingly, Thorpe J said that he had 'reached the clear and unhesitating conclusion that the maintenance and development of the relationship between D and his father is of such importance to his future welfare that the reasonable proposals of his mother as the primary carer are quite incompatible with welfare'. The mother's application accordingly failed.

7.14   In October 1999, a split Court of Appeal (Morritt and Chadwick LJJ; Thorpe LJ dissenting) in *Re C (Leave to Remove from Jurisdiction)*[26] dismissed a mother's appeal against refusal of leave to take her 6-year-old daughter to Singapore where her husband (who came from there) intended to practise medicine. The judge at first instance, who approached the case by way of the statutory checklist in s 1(3) of the Children Act 1989, described the step-father as a thoughtful and caring man, but it seemed clear that if leave was refused, he would return to Singapore, where his roots were and his future lay. The mother, a French national whose family were all in France, had lived in England since she was 19. The father, who at the time had contact every third weekend and shared the school holidays, opposed the move and sought prohibited steps and residence orders. Although the mother's position at one stage was that if leave were refused, she would leave the child in England and go to Singapore, during the hearing she made it clear that she would not in any

---

[23]   'So in approaching the first question, whether or not there should be leave for permanent removal, I apply the principles which have stood largely unchanged since the decision of the Court of Appeal in *Poel v Poel* [1970] 1 WLR 1469. In the later case of *Chamberlain v de la Mare* (1983) 4 FLR 434, a strong Court of Appeal stated that, in considering whether to give leave, the welfare of the child was the first and paramount consideration, but that leave should not be withheld unless the interests of the children and those of the custodial parent were clearly shown to be incompatible. That statement of principle creates a presumption in favour of the reasonable application of the custodial parent, but in weighing whether the reasonable application is or is not incompatible with the welfare of D, I have to assess the importance of the relationship between D and his father', per Thorpe J.

[24]   The reference to 'first and paramount' reflects the then governing statute, the Guardianship of Minors Act 1971, s 1.

[25]   It is no longer correct to say that there is a presumption. See *Payne v Payne* [2001] EWCA Civ 166, [2001] Fam 473, [2001] 1 FLR 1052 at [25], and **7.2** above.

[26]   [2000] 2 FLR 457.

circumstances leave the child, and that if her application were refused she would stay in England and her new husband would go to for Singapore on his own. On appeal, the mother contended that the judge had failed to give appropriate weight to the risk of emotional harm to the child as a result of the break-up of her new family and the emotional impact on the mother of being forced to stay in a country not her country of origin and being separated from her husband.

7.15   In the judgment of Chadwick LJ, the trial judge could not be said to have failed to have directed himself as to the correct approach to the very difficult decision which he had to make. In particular, he had in mind the effect that his ruling would have on the mother, the step-father and the child. In those circumstances, it was important, therefore:

> '... to keep in mind the proper role of an appellate court. Where a judge has directed himself correctly in law, an appellate court should not interfere with his exercise of a discretionary jurisdiction unless satisfied that he has failed to take into account some matter which he should have taken into account, has taken into account some matter which he should have left out of account, or, for some other reason, has reached a decision which is plainly wrong.'[27]

7.16   In his dissenting judgment, Thorpe LJ said[28] that, in order to weigh the mother's submission, he:

> 'would stand back from the judgment and suggest that the essential balance that had to be carried out in this case was to identify the obvious consequences of granting the mother leave against the obvious consequences of refusing leave. Those consequences having been identified, a balance then had to be struck to determine whether or not the resulting risk of harm to S was such as to outweigh the presumption that reasonable proposals from the custodial parent should receive the endorsement of the court.'

7.17   In Thorpe LJ's view, if the judge was going to approach his decision through the stairway of the checklist, he should have done so by considering each category, then asking what the consequence for S might be if the application were refused, as well as if it were granted, and then striking a balance as to which threatened to be more harmful to the child. The judge

---

27   [2000] 2 FLR 457 at 464F–H. Note the cases cited there on the proper role of an appellate court, and in particular the extract from the speech of Lord Hoffmann in *Piglowska v Piglowski* [1999] 1 WLR 1360, [1999] 2 FLR 763, quoting what he said in *Biogen Inc v Medeva plc* [1997] RPC 1: 'The need for appellate caution in reversing the judge's evaluation of the facts is based upon much more solid grounds than professional courtesy. It is because specific findings of fact, even by the most meticulous judge, are inherently an incomplete statement of the impression which was made upon him by the primary evidence. His expressed findings are always surrounded by a penumbra of imprecision as to emphasis, relative weight, minor qualification and nuance ... of which time and language do not permit exact description, but which may play an important part in the judge's overall evaluation'. See also *Re B (A Minor) (Adoption: Natural Parent)* [2001] UKHL 70, [2002] 1 WLR 258, [2002] 1 FLR 196, per Lord Nicholls at [17].

28   [2000] 2 FLR 457 at 459D–F. Cf *Re C (Permission to Remove from Jurisdiction)* [2003] EWHC 596 (Fam), [2003] 1 FLR 1066, discussed at **7.4**.

failed to identify a most important consideration, and failed to deal with it explicitly in his judgment so as to demonstrate that he had given it the weight it demanded before reaching the conclusion that the father's opposition was to succeed.

Cross-applications for residence orders

7.18   In those cases in which the parent opposing the move has also sought a residence order, it has been held that mothers who were generally competent mothers should not risk losing primary care of their children by making an unsuccessful attempt to remove them from the jurisdiction.[29] In *Payne v Payne*,[30] Thorpe LJ dealt with cross-applications for residence orders, many of which he referred to as being 'largely tactical' because they enable:

'... the strategist to cross-examine along the lines of: what will you do if your application is refused? If the mother responds by saying that she will remain with the child then the cross-examiner feels that he has demonstrated that the impact of refusal upon the mother would not be that significant. If on the other hand she says that she herself will go nevertheless then the cross-examiner feels that he has demonstrated that the mother is shallow, or uncaring or self-centred. But experienced family judges are well used to tactics and will readily distinguish between the cross-application that has some pre-existing foundation and one that is purely tactical. There are probably dangers in compartmentalising the two applications. As far as possible they should be tried and decided together. The judge in the end must evaluate comparatively each option for the child, one against another. Often that will mean evaluating a home with mother in this jurisdiction, against a home with mother wherever she seeks to go, against a home in this jurisdiction with father. Then in explaining his first choice the judge will inevitably be delivering judgment on both applications.'

Relocation and human rights

7.19   The Human Rights Act 1998, which came into force on 2 October 2000,[31] inevitably raised the question of whether the right to family life enshrined in Art 8 would necessitate a different, perhaps more stringent, approach to applications for leave to remove. In the context of permanent leave to remove, on 29 February 2000 the Court of Appeal in *Re A (Permission to Remove Child from Jurisdiction: Human Rights)*[32] considered an appeal by a father against an order giving leave to the mother to take their 10-month-old daughter to New York on the basis of the mother's undertakings to litigate all questions relating to contact in the courts of England and Wales, and offering contact at least twice a year in England, and more if she was in the country, contact in New York and to keep him informed by e-mail and letter.

[29]   *Re T (Removal from Jurisdiction)* [1996] 2 FLR 352. And see *M v A (Wardship: Removal from Jurisdiction)* [1993] 2 FLR 715.
[30]   [2001] EWCA Civ 166, [2001] 1 FLR 1052 at [42].
[31]   SI 2000/1851.
[32]   [2000] 2 FLR 225.

The mother's reasons for going to New York were that it was there that she had been trained as a musician, and where she had recently been offered work. The father, who appealed in person, said that the right to family life of both himself and his daughter had been insufficiently weighed in the balance, and that the consequence of the limited contact that he was to have would be insufficient to establish a meaningful relationship with his daughter, the likely reality being that he would increasingly fade from her life. The Court of Appeal took the view that the judge had directed himself on proper lines; that is to say, 'in essence, that, if the custodian parent takes a reasonable decision, then the court ordinarily will not interfere with that unless there is some compelling reason in the child's best interests to the contrary'.[33] Article 8(2) required the right of the father and child to family life under Art 8(1) to be balanced against the mother's right to live her private life as she wished and her freedom to work where she reasonably chose to do so. Ward LJ said that for his part he could see no prospect of the Court of Appeal interfering with the established line of authority which bound them at the moment, and which the judge applied. He also said that he doubted that it would be different when the Convention came into force of law.[34] Buxton LJ, dismissing the appeal for the same reasons, added that he thought it doubtful whether balancing a right to contact to a child against the rights to family life of the mother and child herself fell within the purview of the Convention at all.[35] In these observations, Buxton LJ drew attention to the debate, in the context of family law, on the 'horizontal' and 'vertical' effects of the ECHR in private law proceedings.[36]

7.20 However, appreciation of the part that the ECHR has to play in family proceedings evolved quite rapidly, and by February 2001 Thorpe LJ was able to say in *Payne v Payne*[37] that the view that it had no place in this area of litigation was unsustainable in the light of *Glaser v United Kingdom*[38] and *Douglas,*

---

[33] [2000] 2 FLR 225 at (4).

[34] *Ibid* at (5).

[35] *Ibid* at (16).

[36] The case-law of the ECHR makes it clear that it has a role in regulating actions between private individuals (known as the 'horizontal effect') as well as between individuals and the State (known as the 'vertical effect'): see Human Rights Act 1998, s 6 and *Marckx v Belgium* Series A, No 31, (1979) 2 EHRR 330, ECtHR; *X and Y v The Netherlands* Series A No 91, (1995) 8 EHRR 235, ECtHR; *Hokkanen v Finland* Series A, No 299–A, (1994) 19 EHRR 139, [1996] 1 FLR 289, ECtHR. And see Horowitz, Kingscote and Nicholls, *The Human Rights Act 1998 – A Special Bulletin for Family Lawyers* (Butterworths, 1999), pp 12 and 24, and *Rayden & Jackson on Divorce and Family Matters*, 17th edn (Butterworths), para 57.14.

[37] [2001] EWCA Civ 166, [2001] 1 FLR 1052 at [34] *et seq*.

[38] Case No 32346/96, [2001] 1 FLR 153, ECtHR. Delay in enforcing an English contact order did not amount to a violation of the father's human rights. It was not disputed that his alleged inability to secure contact with his children concerned 'family life' within the meaning of Art 8 of the ECHR.

Zeta-Jones, Northern and Shell plc v Hello![39] He went on to draw attention to the right of freedom of movement in Art 2 of Protocol 4, which provides that:

'(1)   Everyone lawfully within the territory of a state shall, within that territory, have the right to liberty of movement and freedom to choose his residence.

(2)   Everybody shall be free to leave any country, including his own.

(3)   No restrictions shall be placed on the exercise of these rights other than such as are in accordance with law and are necessary in a democratic society in the interests of national security or public safety, for the maintenance of public order, for the prevention of crime, for the protection of health and morals, or for the protection of the rights and freedom of others.'

7.21   This Article, although not ratified by the United Kingdom, lent force, in Thorpe LJ's view, to the argument that failure or refusal to recognise a right of mobility beyond a 'somewhat fortuitous jurisdictional boundary represents a stance of disproportionate parochialism', and was illustrative of the general proposition that each member of the family had rights to assert, and in balancing them the court had to adhere to the paramountcy of the welfare principle.

7.22   Shortly afterwards, in April 2001, Hogg J considered the question of human rights in an application for temporary leave to remove, although *Payne v Payne* was not cited to her. In *Re S (Leave to Remove from Jurisdiction: Securing Return from Holiday)*[40] a mother sought leave to take two boys aged 5 and 8 on holiday to India. The application was opposed by the father, because he thought that the boys were likely to be treated harshly by the maternal family and that the mother and her family were planning for her to stay in India with them. In relation to human rights, Hogg J said:[41]

'I have considered what their rights are. They have rights under the European Convention for the Protection of Human Rights and Fundamental Freedoms 1950, and their rights are to be citizens of this country, to be educated here, to know and love both sides of their family and to be full members of the State here.'

But she went on to say that she had to consider other matters, the welfare issues, on a more immediate basis.

7.23   It now seems clear that in human rights terms, applications for leave to remove are interferences with family life and must be determined 'in accordance with the law' and be justified in terms of Art 8(2). Being private law proceedings, the ECHR has 'horizontal effect', protecting the rights of individuals in disputes between them,[42] and that at present the judiciary are

---

[39]   [2001] 1 FLR 982, cited in relation to the 'horizontal' effect of the ECHR (see [79]–[86], [128]–[135]).

[40]   [2001] 2 FLR 507.

[41]   *Ibid* at 512H–513B.

[42]   *Hoffmann v Austria* Series A, No 255–C, (1993) 17 EHRR 293, ECtHR. And see *Hokkanen v Finland* Series A, No 299–A, (1994) 19 EHRR 139, [1996] 1 FLR 289. As to the procedure for relying on any provision or right arising from the Human Rights Act 1998, see FPR

satisfied that the duty to carry out the balancing exercise in Art 8(2) is discharged if the current approach to relocation cases is adopted.

Summary

7.24   In summary, a successful application for permanent leave to remove must be well researched and well prepared, with the circumstances and conditions in the country to which the applicant aspires to relocate being thoroughly explored.[43] The proposals must not be opposed by children who have reached the age at which their views should be taken into account. They must be practical and reasonable so that the application is founded on realistic plans for the future, including reliable proposals for contact with the left-behind parent, supported, if at all possible, by orders in like terms in the new country.

7.25   However, the Court of Appeal's decision in *Re C (Leave to Remove from Jurisdiction)*[44] must strike a note of warning that it is by no means a foregone conclusion that a court will support reasonable plans, and that an appellate court will be very slow to interfere with a refusal of leave, even if they or another judge might have granted the application.

PRACTICE ON APPLICATIONS FOR LEAVE TO REMOVE

Forum

7.26   Applications for permanent leave to remove should be made to the High Court or the county court, depending on the complexity or difficulty of the case.[45] An application for permanent leave to remove likely to involve consideration of foreign law or a foreign legal system, and which may require mirror orders to be put in place, should be heard in the High Court,[46] as should an application for temporary leave to remove likely to require such safeguards to secure the safe return of the child.[47]

1991, r 10.26. See also *Practice Direction: Human Rights Act 1998* reported at [2000] 2 FLR 429 (citation of authorities and allocation to judges).

43   *Re S (A Child) (Residence Order: Condition)* [2001] EWCA Civ 847, [2001] 3 FCR 154 at [18].

44   [2000] 2 FLR 457, discussed at **7.14**.

45   Although an application for leave to remove a child from the jurisdiction can be made to any court, the magistrates' court is not a suitable forum, and any application for permanent leave to remove instituted there should be transferred either to the county court or the High Court, depending on its complexity – see *MH v GP (Child: Emigration)* [1995] 2 FLR 106.

46   *Re K (Removal from Jurisdiction: Practice)* [1999] 2 FLR 1084.

47   *Ibid.*

The form of the proceedings

7.27   An application for leave to remove a ward should be made by way of an application within the wardship proceedings. An application in respect of a child who is the subject of a residence order should be by way of an application under s 13(1) of the Children Act 1989.[48] All other applications for leave to remove may be made by way of an application for a specific issue order, a residence order with leave to remove, or a contact order with leave to remove for a holiday or holidays abroad.

7.28   Oral evidence is necessary to enable the judge to evaluate how much trust to put in the applicant. Not only has the magnitude of the risk of retention to be assessed, but also the risk attaching to the consequences of retention. An impeccable record as a caring parent is of no relevance to assessing the magnitude of the consequences of a retention in breach of the terms of an order.[49] What is needed is proper evidence about the nature of the legal system in the State to which the child is to be taken and the availability and effectiveness of mechanisms for ensuring return.

7.29   Trial judges should direct themselves only by reference to the decision of the Court of Appeal in *Payne v Payne*.[50] The first questions to be addressed are whether the application is genuine, and not motivated by a selfish desire to exclude the other parent from the child's life, and whether the plans are realistic, founded upon practical proposals which are well researched and investigated. If those matters are satisfied, then the position of the other parent must be examined to see if it is motivated by a genuine concern for the child's welfare or driven by an ulterior motive, the extent to which granting the application would be detrimental to the relationship with the child, and (if applicable) the extent to which the detriment would be offset by the extension of the child's relationships with the applicant's family in his or her homeland.

Children's wishes and feelings; the views of the children and family reporter

7.30   The wishes and feelings of children who are able to express them should be taken into account – in *M v M (Minors) (Removal from Jurisdiction)*[51] it was held by the Court of Appeal that failure to take into account the wishes and feelings of intelligent and articulate children aged 10 and 11 years and the views of the welfare officer vitiated the judge's decision.

---

[48]   See **7.39**.
[49]   *Re K (Removal from Jurisdiction: Practice)* [1999] 2 FLR 1084.
[50]   Per Thorpe LJ in *Re H (Children) (Residence Order: Condition)* [2001] EWCA Civ 1338, [2001] 2 FLR 1277 at [19]. See *Payne v Payne* [2001] EWCA Civ 166, [2001] Fam 473, [2001] 1 FLR 1052 at [40], [41] and [85].
[51]   [1992] 2 FLR 303, CA.

The welfare checklist

7.31   The welfare checklist in s 1(3) of the Children Act 1989 applies to applications for residence or contact orders with leave to remove[52] or for leave to remove by way of an application for a specific issue order or within wardship. Reference to the checklist is not mandatory in applications under s 13 of Children Act 1989, but it is a useful aide-mémoire.[53]

Conditions on permanent leave to remove

7.32   Leave to remove has sometimes been given subject to conditions. In *Re S (Removal from Jurisdiction)*[54] a Chilean mother sought leave to remove her 6-year-old son to Chile, where her family lived and she had an offer of employment. The boy's father, who had parental responsibility and contact orders, originally consented to removal, but then withdrew his consent because he had problems with contact which led him to believe that the mother would not abide by a contact order, which would be difficult to enforce in Chile. There were also concerns about whether the mother would ensure that the child went to school regularly. In holding that the child's future lay with the mother, and hers in Chile, her proposals being both reasonable and realistic, Richard Anelay QC gave leave to remove conditional upon the mother obtaining at her own expense authentication of the contact order in the Chilean Supreme Court. Since it would not be in the child's interests to delay departure, the mother was required to deposit £135,000 in an account in the name of the father's solicitors, pending notification of the authentication being implemented. Once the court had proof of the deposit of the funds, the mother was to be given leave to remove, and the money would be returned to her when the authentication was completed.

7.33   At a time when it is becoming generally accepted that decisions about the care and welfare of children should be made in the country with which they have the closest connection, usually that of their habitual residence,[55] it is no longer appropriate to make an order giving leave for the permanent

---

52   *H v H (Residence Order: Leave to Remove from Jurisdiction)* [1995] 1 FLR 529.

53   *Re B (Minors) (Change of Surname)* [1996]1 FLR 791. But note that Hale J's comments in *Re M (Leave to Remove Child from Jurisdiction)* [1999] 2 FLR 334 at 341, questioning this distinction.

54   [1999] 1 FLR 850.

55   The modern concept that jurisdiction follows habitual residence is reflected in the Preamble to the 1980 Hague Abduction Convention, the 1996 Hague Convention on the Protection of Children and Council Regulation (EC) No 1347/200: see **4.24** above. Previously, it was widely held that courts should always retain jurisdiction to vary their own orders so that, for example, an application for a variation is not a 'Part I order' for the purposes of the jurisdictional rules in Part I of the Family Law Act 1986 (see **3.2**).

removal to be subject to a condition that the applicant will return the child to the jurisdiction if called upon to do so.[56]

Temporary removals and removals for contact – ensuring return

7.34 Parliament has provided that the holder of a residence order may take the child out of the jurisdiction for up to a month at a time, with no limit on the number of occasions, without the need to seek the consent of the other holders of parental responsibility or the leave of the court.[57]

7.35 If the removal of the child becomes an issue, however, the court will have to balance the benefit to the child of the proposed visit, very often to see relatives and gain some knowledge of the life and culture of one of his parents, against the risk that he might not be returned. So courts will inevitably be cautious in giving leave for a child to be taken to another jurisdiction, even where the removal is said to be for a limited period, particularly if the State to which the child is to be taken is not a Contracting State to either the 1980 Hague Abduction Convention or the 1980 European Custody Convention. It has long been the practice of the courts, despite their faith in the concept of comity, to put in place mechanisms to ensure the return of the child at the end of the period for which leave has been given. Those mechanisms might include the deposit of money by way of a bond or security,[58] a charge on property or a requirement that an order in like terms to the order of the English court is made in the State to which the child is to go – known as a 'mirror' or 'back-to-back' order.

7.36 Although given in the context of an application to remove a child from the jurisdiction for a holiday, the judgment of the Court of Appeal in *Re K (A Minor) (Removal from Jurisdiction: Practice)*[59] is also helpful in illustrating how seriously the courts regard all cases involving leave to remove. The father, who was the child's primary carer, was born in Bangladesh[60] and wanted to take the child there for a holiday. The mother's contact order provided that her written consent was necessary, which she refused. At first instance, the judge allowed the father's application on the basis that he could be trusted to bring the child back at the end of the visit. On the mother's appeal it was held that such applications should be heard by a judge of the Family Division, and should be thoroughly prepared. The judge should assess both the magnitude of the risk

---

[56] *Re S (Residence Order: Forum Conveniens)* [1995] 1 FLR 314. Note that, according to *Re S*, an undertaking to return is not of itself enough to confer jurisdiction under Part I of the Family Law Act 1986.

[57] Children Act 1989, s 13(2). Note that, under Children Act 1989, s 14C(3), prospectively inserted by s 115 of the Adoption and Children Act 2002, special guardians will be permitted to take children outside the United Kingdom for a period of up to 3 months without the need for anyone else's consent.

[58] *Poel v Poel* [1970] 1 WLR 1469.

[59] [1999] 2 FLR 1084.

[60] Bangladesh is not a party to the 1980 Hague Abduction Convention.

of breach of the contact order and the magnitude of the consequences of any such breach. In those cases in which the consequences would be irretrievable separation of the child from his previous roots, the court should build in all practical safeguards. If there is to be an evaluation of the applicant's trust, there should be oral evidence to enable the judge to assess credibility and reliability from exposure in the witness-box. Where there is a possibility of competitive litigation in two systems of law reflecting different traditions and cultures, it is desirable to confine the risk by putting in place, wherever possible, whatever buttresses can be devised for the primary adjudication in England and Wales, including notarised agreements, mirror orders and financial bonds; trusting in the applicant or requiring undertakings was not sufficient. There should be expert evidence about the practicalities of implementing the proposed safeguards.

7.37　In *Re S (Leave to Remove from Jurisdiction: Securing Return from Holiday)*,[61] Hogg J was faced with trying to put in place safeguards for the return of two boys from India in a very short space of time. Mirror orders were impractical in the time available and monetary security was not offered. The children were made wards, and a declaration made to the effect that their habitual residence was in England and Wales and that they were British citizens. Signed undertakings were required from the mother that she would return the children to the jurisdiction by a specified date and not thereafter return them to India without the father's written permission or an order of the court, that on return she would deposit the children's passports with her solicitors, to be held by them and not released without the leave of the court or the written consent of the father, and that she was to provide the father with legible copies of the airline tickets, showing the date and time of the return flight, a copy of the application to the Indian High Commission for visas for the children and copies of the visas themselves, and a full itinerary. An order was made restraining the mother from surrendering the children's current passports before expiry and from doing so in India, and from seeking Indian passports or citizenship for the children while in India and requiring her to seek only a short tourist visa and not to extend that visa while in India. The order was to be served on the Indian High Commission and on the Foreign and Commonwealth Office (FCO), for onward transmission to the British High Commission in Delhi and such consulates in India as the FCO might think appropriate.

7.38　Guidance as to the form of safeguards and orders which might be made where the system of family in the friendly foreign jurisdiction State has its roots in Islam is to be found in *Note: Re T (Staying Contact in Non-Convention Country)*.[62] In that case, after it had been decided that the child, a girl aged 6 years, should live with her mother in England, the court decided that she should remain a ward and that she should have contact, including holiday

---

[61]　[2001] 2 FLR 507.
[62]　[1999] 1 FLR 262.

staying contact, in Egypt with her father. However, before contact took place in Egypt:

(1)　the father, the paternal grandmother and the mother should enter into a notarised agreement to include provisions:
    (a)　that the child would live with the mother in England;
    (b)　that the child would leave Egypt after any contact in that country and the father would place no obstacle in the way; and
(2)　the parties should apply for a 'mirror order' in the Cairo court, confirming:
    (a)　the child's residence with the mother in London;
    (b)　that the child would be returned to England at the end of any periods of contact there.

In addition, except for the purposes of obtaining the 'mirror order', jurisdiction in relation to the child should be with the Family Division of the English High Court. In due course, the notarised agreement was made and the court in Cairo made an order in substantially the same terms as the notarised agreement. The father also, in effect, entered into a £50,000 bond to guarantee the child's return after the first period of staying contact in Egypt. In August 1998 the child spent a period of 3 weeks with the father in Egypt and was returned to England at the end of the visit. In *Re L (Removal from Jurisdiction: Holiday)*[63] the mother of a 3-year-old boy wanted to take him to Sharjah for a 28-day holiday at a time when she and the father were involved in litigation relating both to the child and to ancillary relief. The father opposed the application. Connell J, guided in particular by s 1(1) and (3) of the Children Act 1989, identified the likely effect of any change of circumstances and the risk of harm as being the most important factors, and assessed the risks. He asked whether the mother was bona fide in putting her applications to the court, whether she genuinely wished to go to Sharjar for a holiday, and whether she would, as she had promised him, return at the end of the holiday. Having reached the conclusion that the mother had a genuine intention to return, and that it was in the child's interest to see the members of his broader family, especially his grandmother, who was in delicate health, he addressed the magnitude of the consequences of the child not being returned and the safeguards which could be put in place, as required by *Re K (Removal from Jurisdiction: Practice)*.[64] Mirror orders were not, he held, a fundamental prerequisite to leave being granted, but the court had to insist on preconditions for leave, which were a deposit of £50,000 with the court by way of a bond or security, and an undertaking by the mother to return the child by a certain date. Referring to *Re A (Security for Return to Jurisdiction) (Note)*[65] (in which Wall J gave a mother leave to take her child to Saudi Arabia for a month's holiday conditional upon the swearing of solemn declarations on

---

[63]　[2001] 1 FLR 241.
[64]　[1999] 2 FLR 1084.
[65]　[1999] 2 FLR 1, discussed at **9.40**.

the *Koran* before a Sharià judge that the child would be returned), he also required declarations on the *Koran* to be made by the mother and her family guaranteeing the child's safe return. In addition, the mother was to provide the father with full details of her travel plans: when she was leaving; when she was returning; which airline she was travelling on, together with copies of the tickets.

SPECIAL CIRCUMSTANCES

Applications for leave to remove under section 13 of the Children Act 1989

7.39 Applications for leave to remove under the provisions of s 13 are made by way of a free-standing application, not under s 8.[66] The respondents to the application and those to whom notice must be given are the same as for an application for a s 8 order and are set out in Appendix 3 to the Family Proceedings Rules 1991. Although the child's welfare is the paramount consideration,[67] reference to the checklist in s 1(3) of the Children Act 1989 is not mandatory because the court is required only to 'have regard in particular' to those matters when considering whether to make, vary or discharge a s 8 order in the face of opposition by a party or when considering whether to make, vary or discharge an order under Part IV (see s 1(4)); nevertheless, it provides a useful aide-mémoire.[68] The order is drawn in form C44.[69]

When the primary carer has not been identified

7.40 In almost all relocation cases, the applicant is the mother and primary carer of the child, and the motivation for the move arises from her remarriage or urge to return home, and the father's opposition is commonly founded on the resultant reduction in contact and loss of influence over his child.[70] However, there are cases in which the primary carer has not been identified, and the approach of the court must be to examine the competing proposals and decide which is better calculated to serve the welfare interests of the child.[71]

---

[66] FPR 1991, r 4.1(2)(c). *Re B (Minors) (Change of Surname)* [1996] 1 FLR 791; *Dawson v Wearmouth* [1999] 2 AC 308, [1999] 1 FLR 1167; *Re H (Children) (Residence Order: Condition)* [2001] EWCA Civ 1338, [2001] 2 FLR 1277. But note Hale J's comments in *Re M (Leave to Remove Child from Jurisdiction)* [1999] 2 FLR 334 at 341, questioning this distinction.

[67] *Re L (Removal from Jurisdiction: Holiday)* [2001] 1 FLR 1241.

[68] *Re B (Minors) (Change of Surname)* [1996] 1 FLR 791 at 793A; *Dawson v Wearmouth* (above).

[69] FPR 1991, r 4.21(5) and Sch 1.

[70] *Payne v Payne* [2001] EWCA Civ 166, [2001] 1 FLR 1052 at [27].

[71] See the remarks about cross-applications for residence orders by Thorpe LJ in *Payne v Payne* (above) and the Australian approach to relocation cases (discussed at **8.18** *et seq*).

Local authorities arranging for children to live abroad

7.41 If the child is being looked after, the local authority may arrange for or assist in arranging for, the child to live outside England and Wales with the approval of every person with parental responsibility,[72] but while a care order is in force, no one may remove the child from the United Kingdom without either the written consent of every person with parental responsibility or the leave of the court.[73] However, the local authority in whose care the child is may remove him from the United Kingdom for a period of less than one month[74] and may, with the approval of the court, arrange for him to live outside England and Wales.[75] However, when dealing with an application by a local authority, a court may simply make a residence order instead to dispense with any unnecessary procedural difficulties to arrive at what the judge thinks to be the best interests of the child.[76]

7.42 Applications for the approval of the court must be instituted in the magistrates' court.[77] Approval will not be given unless it is in the child's best interests, suitable arrangements have been, or will be, made for his reception and welfare in the country in which he will live, and the child and every person with parental responsibility has consented, although the child's consent can be dispensed with if the court considers that he does not have sufficient understanding to give or withhold it.[78] If a person whose consent is required fails to give it, the court can nevertheless give its approval if it is satisfied that he cannot be found, is incapable of consenting or is withholding his consent unreasonably,[79] but may order that its decision is not to have effect during the appeal period.[80]

Wards of court

7.43 An application for leave to remove a ward should be made by summons within the wardship proceedings, and should be heard by a judge, unless the application is unopposed or is for a temporary removal (unless opposed on the ground that the child might not be returned), when it should be heard by a

---

72 Children Act 1989, Sch 2, para 19(2).
73 *Ibid* s 33(7). See Chapter 11 on children abducted within the British Isles.
74 *Ibid*, s 33(8)(a).
75 *Ibid*, Sch 2, para 19(1). Note that this may be for adoption – s 56 of the Adoption Act 1976 is disapplied when the child goes abroad with the approval of the court given under these provisions (above).
76 *Re G (Leave to Appeal: Jurisdiction)* [1999] 1 FLR 771.
77 Children (Allocation of Proceedings) Order 1991, art 3 – but note the exceptions in this article and in art 4, and the remarks in *MH v GP (Child: Emigration)* [1995] 2 FLR 106 about the suitability of the magistrates' court as a forum.
78 Children Act 1989, Sch 2, para 19(3) and (4). See *Re J (Freeing for Adoption)* [2000] 2 FLR 58 at 67 for the degree of understanding necessary on the part of the child.
79 *Ibid*, Sch 2, para 19(5), on which see *Re W (Care: Leave To Place Outside Jurisdiction)* [1994] 2 FLR 1087 and *Re G (Minors) (Care: Leave To Place Outside Jurisdiction)* [1994] 2 FLR 301.
80 *Ibid*, Sch 2, para 19(7) and (8).

district judge. The district judge can make such order as he sees fit, or refer the
matter to a judge.[81]

---

[81] *Practice Direction: Wardship and Guardianship: Removal of Children out of England and Wales* [1984]
1 WLR 855, [1984] FLR 502. Note that *Practice Direction: Family Division: Wards of Court* [1989]
2 FLR 310, which enables local authorities to arrange for wards who are in their care to go
abroad for holidays and educational journeys without the necessity of obtaining specific
authority from the court, will have been superseded by the provisions of s 91(4) of the
Children Act 1989 (the making of a care order in respect of a ward brings the wardship to
an end). Note also the *Registrar's Direction* of 15 May 1987 about the precautions to be put in
place if the child is living with foster-parents whose identity should be kept confidential.

Chapter 8

INTERNATIONAL RELOCATION: THE POSITION IN SOME OTHER JURISDICTIONS

INTRODUCTION

8.1 The ease of international travel has facilitated an increasing opportunity for the development of relationships between citizens of different countries.[1] Globalisation of economies has witnessed the development of associated enterprises and has opened the way for many people to cross international borders in the pursuit of a career or a livelihood. As a result, these situations have led to considerable difficulties when parties with children separate, and the residential parent wishes to relocate, especially to another country. Such a move will frequently bring about a significant change in the relationship between the left-behind parent and the child. A court-imposed restraint on any such move not only may anger the restrained parent but may also lead to an inability on his or her behalf to function fully as an effective parent. The consequent effects upon the welfare of the child are well documented.

8.2 In *Payne v Payne*,[2] Thorpe LJ referred to the clear interaction between the approach of courts in abduction cases and relocation cases, pointing out that if courts adopt a chauvinistic approach to applications to relocate, there is a risk that parents will resort to flight, whereas recognition of the respect due to a primary carer's reasonable proposals for relocation encourages applications. Accordingly, it is desirable that there should be uniformity within the international community. Thorpe LJ went on to say that he thought there was

---

[1] 'It only takes a half a day to be a thousand miles away': Oscar Hammerstein II, *Carmen Jones*.
[2] [2001] EWCA Civ 166, [2001] Fam 473, [2001] 1 FLR 1052 at [28].

some prospect of standardisation at a point close to the approach adopted in England.

8.3 At the international common law conference held in Washington in September 2000, it was apparent that for all the jurisdictions represented, Australia, Canada, Ireland, New Zealand, the United Kingdom and the United States of America, the welfare of the child was the paramount consideration, although some afforded greater weight than others to the harm that the refusal of the primary carer's reasonable proposal to relocate was likely to cause the children. At the conclusion of the Washington conference, the delegates proposed a number of 'Best Practices' which they hoped would improve the operation of the 1980 Hague Abduction Convention.[3] One proposal dealt with relocation cases:

> '9. Courts take significantly different approaches to relocation cases, which are occurring with a frequency not contemplated in 1980 when the Hague Child Abduction Convention was drafted. Courts should be aware that highly restrictive approaches to relocation can adversely affect the operation of the Hague Child Abduction Convention.'

8.4 Three approaches to relocation cases were identified by Ann M Driscoll in an article entitled 'In Search of a Standard: Resolving the Relocation Problem in New York'.[4]

> 'In theory, there are three approaches to resolving a relocation problem: the court will either favor the custodian, favor the non-custodian, or advocate a "neutral" approach whereby, in theory, neither parent is favored. A state will adhere to one of these general approaches by means of either a presumption or through an allocation of the burden of proof. The laws of some states contain outright presumptions that clearly favor either the custodial or the non-custodial parent. Other states create presumptions through the interpretation of laws and precedents. Similarly, the burden of proof can be directly or indirectly allocated to favor either the custodial or non-custodial parent. The result can be either a light burden on the favored parent (indirectly placing the real burden of proof on the adverse party), or a burden that directly falls on the unfavored parent.

> The "neutral" approach to resolving relocation problems, in theory, requires a court only to consider the welfare of the child involved. As a matter of policy, all courts hearing custody disputes look to the child's best interests, and some even make claims of neutrality. However, the child's interests do not exist in a vacuum, but rather, are naturally interwoven with the interests of both parents. Thus, in actuality, one parent will be favored under the guise of the best interests of the child.'

---

[3] The 'Best Practices' adopted at the conclusion of the Washington Common Law Judicial Conference in September 2000 were parallel to the resolutions adopted at the Judicial Seminar on the International Protection of Children held at De Ruwenberg in June 2000 (both are set out in Appendix 1). Materials from the Washington conference can be found on the website of the US Department of State's Office of Children's Issues at www.travel.state.gov/children's_issues.html.

[4] (1997) 26 (No 1) *Hofstra Law Review* 205.

THE UNITED STATES OF AMERICA

8.5   In recent years there have been numerous relocation cases in the United States. Family law being a matter for the individual states, and not the Federal Government, it is impossible to say that there are any general principles which can be applied to parental relocation cases:[5]

> 'We note that our research has failed to reveal a consistent, universally accepted approach to the question of when a custodial parent may relocate out-of-state over the objection of the non-custodial parent. In fact, the opposite is true. Across the country, applicable standards remain distressingly disparate.'

Accordingly, the first question to be addressed, as in so many legal matters involving the United States, is where the application is to be made.

8.6   In some states, the state legislature has provided guidelines, while in others it is the courts which have determined the principles to be applied.[6] The result is a range of decisions from the restrictive to the liberal. Where the legislature has provided guidelines, and the burden has been placed on the parent seeking removal to prove that it is the child's best interests,[7] attempts to ameliorate the position have been struck down as being contrary to the policy of the legislation.[8]

8.7   In Minnesota a more liberal approach has been evolved from a legislative provision to the effect that the court should retain the custodian established by prior order unless:[9]

> '(iii) the child's present environment endangers his physical or emotional health or impairs his emotional development and the harm likely to be caused by the change of environment is outweighed by the advantage of change to the child.'

The court held that the provision should be construed as 'establishing an implicit presumption that removal will be permitted, subject to the non-custodial parent's ability to establish that removal is not in the best interests of the child',[10] thus placing the burden on the non-custodial parent to prove that the move is not in the child's best interests.

8.8   Of the decisions made without legislative assistance, *D'Onofrio v D'Onofrio*[11] was, until the decision in *Burgess v Burgess*,[12] the case most frequently

---

5   *Gruber v Gruber* 583 A 2d 434, 437 (Pa 1990) (Pennsylvania).
6   This position has led one author to entitle his paper 'A Toss of the Dice … The Gamble with Post-Divorce Relocation Laws' ((1989) 18 *Hofstra Law Review* 127, 128, n 10).
7   Eg in Ilinois – Ill Rev Stat Ch 40, ¶ 609 (1985).
8   See *In re Eckert* 518 N.E. 2d at 1045, reversing the intermediate appellate court (518 N.E. 2d 1041).
9   Minn Stat § 518.18(d) (1982).
10   *Auge v Auge* 334 N.W. 2d 393 Minn (1993).
11   365 A 2d 27 (NJ 1976) (New Jersey).
12   913 P 2d 473 (Cal 1996).

cited throughout the United States. In *D'Onofrio*, the court adopted a two-stage process. First, the parent seeking to remove the child had to establish that it would be a real advantage to both parent and child, and secondly, the court would go on to weigh several factors to accommodate the competing interests of the other family members. Those factors included improvement in the quality of life of both parent and child resulting from the move, the motives of the parents in seeking and opposing removal, the realistic opportunity for visitation with the non-custodial parent, and the likelihood of the custodial parent complying with any altered visitation requirements arising from the move.[13]

8.9 The inconsistent decisions of the appellate courts of California[14] were resolved by the California Supreme Court in *Burgess v Burgess*,[15] which held that the custodial parent may change the child's residence if the child's rights or welfare are not prejudiced.

8.10 Joint legal and physical custody has posed additional problems. In New Mexico it was held in *Murphy v Jaramillo*[16] that in such circumstances the ordinary rule – that states that the parent with physical custody may determine where the child shall live unless it can be shown that the move is not in his best interests – does not apply, and removal by one or both custodians may constitute a 'sufficient change of circumstances justifying a modification of the original'.[17] Both parents having sought to relocate with the child, the court declined to put the burden of proof on either and required each parent to demonstrate that the proposed move was in the child's best interests, so that they were on an equal footing before the court.

8.11 American cases have shown a clear trend towards permitting the proposed relocation, and the more recent have adopted a shifting burden of proof. The parent proposing relocation must show that the move is not motivated from spite, after which the burden shifts to the parent opposing the move. What that parent has to prove varies from state to state.

8.12 Currently, the most liberal state in terms of freedom of movement is Oklahoma. In *Kaiser v Kaiser*,[18] the court found that the constitutional protection of the family from unwarranted state interference required that the

---

[13] The court said that it 'should not insist that the advantages of the move be sacrificed and the opportunity for a better and more comfortable lifestyle for the mother and children be forfeited solely to maintain weekly visitation by the father where reasonable alternative visitation is available': *ibid* at 30.

[14] *In re Marriage of McGinnis* 91 Cal Rptr 2d 182 (1992) and *In re Marriage of Roe* 18 Cal App 4th 1485 (1993). These cases held that the burden of proof was on the parent seeking to remove the child to show that the move was 'essential', 'expedient' or 'imperative', or necessary, not detrimental to the non-custodial parent and in the best interests of the child.

[15] Above.

[16] 795 P 2d 1028 (NM App, 1990).

[17] *Ibid* at 1031–1032.

[18] 23 P 3d 278 (Oklahoma, 2001).

custodial parent should be allowed to move unless there was a threat of harm to the child arising from the proposed place of relocation. That finding is, however, the subject of a proposed change by the state legislature.[19]

CANADA

8.13 Although the guiding principle in matters of custody and access is the best interests of the child, there was until recently some uncertainty as to how this principle was to be applied to relocation cases. The custodial parent having been identified, was it part of his or her responsibilities to decide on the child's place of residence, so that the non-custodial parent had to show that the proposed move was not in the child's best interests, and did any attempt to restrict that choice infringe on the freedom of the custodial parent to decide where to live – the 'mobility right'? Alternatively, once a material change of circumstances had been established, were both parents in the same position, with no presumptions as to the decision? The dilemma was resolved by the Supreme Court of Canada in *Gordon v Goertz*,[20] in which the majority decided that there were two stages to a relocation application: first, the applicant must show a material change in the circumstances of the child; and secondly, provided that the first stage is satisfied, the judge must consider the merits and make an order which best reflects the interests of the child in the new circumstances. Not every move by a custodial parent will constitute a 'material change' not considered when the custody order was made. The move might, for example, have been in contemplation when the original order was made, or the parent with access rights may not have exercised those rights. In considering the merits, the judge must look at the matter afresh, and apply the best interests test, which precludes consideration of past conduct by a parent unless it is relevant to his or her ability to act as a parent,[21] and includes the 'maximum contact' principle, which, although not absolute, does suggest that the legislature indicated that maximum contact with both parents was generally in a child's best interests.[22]

---

[19] It remains to be seen whether the court will sanction the change or find it to be unconstitutional.

[20] (1996) 134 DLR (4th) 321, on which see Barton, 'When did you next see your father?' [1997] CFLQ 73.

[21] Divorce Act RSC 1985 (as amended), s 16(9).

[22] *Ibid*, s 16(10).

AUSTRALIA[23]

8.14   There are many similarities in the way in which the English and Australian courts deal with children's cases, but there are also differences. The recent reform of the Australian law relating to children[24] was informed in part by the Children Act 1989, but the Australian courts are in some ways both more robust and more progressive than those of England. They are more willing to support fathers as caring parents in disputes over residence and to support a child's right to contact with his or her father by being more ready to change residence in the father's favour if the mother proves unwilling to abide by a contact order. The importance that the Australian courts attach to contact is reflected in their approach to relocation cases.

8.15   Like the courts of the United States, those of Australia have to deal with both interstate and international relocations. However, unlike the United States, the Family Court of Australia has a uniformity of approach to relocation cases, despite the federal nature of the State and the geographical size of its jurisdiction.

8.16   That approach has in the past been very similar to that of the English courts, whose decisions the Australian courts considered. As examples, leave to relocate has been granted where refusal would cause too great a hardship to the applicant mother and therefore undue suffering for the child,[25] and where there was a potential for sexual abuse of the children and harassment of the mother by the father.[26] Limits have sometimes been put on the time that the caring parent has been permitted to take the child abroad[27] and also sureties for return have been required.[28] Leave has been refused where the

---

[23]   Written in collaboration with Justice JV Kay, Judge of the Appeal Division, Family Court of Australia. For a summary of current Australian relocation cases, see *Australian Family Law and Practice*, Vol 1, para 16–510.

[24]   The Family Law Act 1975 was amended by the Family Law Reform Act 1995 (in force 11 June 1996) (see *B v B: Family Law Reform Act 1995* (1997) FLC 92–755, and **8.21**). The reforms include, for example, more extensive provisions than in the Children Act 1989 for determining the best interests of the child, the need to maintain a connection with the lifestyle, culture and traditions of Aboriginal peoples, and the ability of grandparents and any other person concerned with the care, welfare or development of the child to institute proceedings without the need for the leave of the court (Family Law Act 1975, Division 10).

[25]   *Fragomeli v Fragomeli* (1993) FLC 92–393 (see **8.19**).

[26]   *I v I* (1995) FLC 92–604 (see **8.19**).

[27]   *Kuebler v Kuebler* (1978) FLC 90–434. The care-giving mother was about to marry a geneticist who had a job in the Galapagos Islands. The court balanced the effect on the father–child relationship and the right of the mother to control her destiny provided she appreciated the child's welfare needs, and gave her leave to remove for 12 months on paying a surety into court. Also considered were the length of the proposed stay out of the jurisdiction, the bona fides of the application, the effect on the child of being deprived of access, the welfare threats of the new environment, and the degree to which the court could be satisfied that the promise to return would be honoured (the mother's new husband was Australian, which increased the probability of return).

[28]   *Ibid.*

court and other parent have been misled[29] and where the plans for relocation were too uncertain.[30] However, there has more recently been a divergence of approach, as Australian decisions have had to be considered in the light of both changes to the domestic law made by the Family Law Reform Act 1995 and the effect of international instruments. However, despite a perception that the earlier cases leaned in favour of the custodian's freedom of movement,[31] it has been held that, notwithstanding the recent legislative changes,[32] it never was the case that a parent's right to relocate usurped the best interests of the child.[33]

The Australian and English approach to international relocation

8.17   More recently, the Australian and the English courts appear to have adopted different approaches to resolving relocation disputes. It would seem from the judgment of the English Court of Appeal in *Payne v Payne*[34] that the English position favours the custodian. The child's welfare is seen as being intricately interwoven with that of the primary caregiver. A happy parent equates to a happy child. The enquiry at court is to see whether the motivation behind the move is bona fide. If so, then unless the evidence clearly demonstrates that the child's welfare will be more detrimentally affected if the move takes place than if the custodial parent is prevented from relocating, the move will be permitted.

---

[29] *Fryda v Johnson* (1979) FLC 90–634. The mother misled the court at the time of the original custody decision, saying that she intended to live in the former matrimonial home, but shortly after she was awarded custody, she applied to take the children to Japan with the American naval officer she wanted to marry. That application was refused and the father was awarded custody with access to the mother.

[30] *R v R* (1984) FLC 91–571. At first instance, upheld on appeal, the judge found the mother to have both a negative attitude to ongoing access with the father, and an ability to provide access which was dependent on very uncertain events. Factors which have prominence in overseas, as opposed to domestic, relocation cases include whether the children will adjust to cultural and racial differences, the relationship with the non-custodial parent and the differences in the legal systems with regard to children. The observation of Fogerty J in *Crossley* (22 December 1980, unreported) to the effect that, although the court may choose a person as custodian, the welfare of the child might require restraints to be placed upon them, was noted.

[31] See, for example, the cases cited in *Holmes v Holmes* (1998) FLC 91–918 at 76,661–76,664.

[32] The amendment of the Family Law Act 1975 by the Family Law Reform Act 1995.

[33] Said in response to the Attorney-General's argument as intervenor in *B v B: Family Law Reform Act 1995* (1997) FLC 92–755 that the new Part VII, especially s 60B, inserted into the Family Law Act 1975 by the Family Law Reform Act 1995 made it unsafe to rely on earlier decisions on relocation (and see *Holmes* (above) at 76,663). The Attorney-General's objections to reliance by the other parties on the United Nations Convention on the Rights of the Child (UNCROC) and the International Covenant on Civil and Political Rights and the Convention on Elimination of All Forms of Discrimination Against Women on the basis that the statute was comprehensive and stood alone were also dismissed. However, s 60B(2)(b), the right of regular contact, was described as 'critical'. It was also said that UNCROC had almost universal acceptance (*Teoh's case*).

[34] [2001] EWCA Civ 166, [2001] Fam 473, [2001] 1 FLR 1052.

The Australian position

8.18   The major cases on relocation that have been considered by Australian courts have mainly involved a domestic move rather than an international one, whereas the major English cases have all dealt with international relocation. This may be the result of the respective sizes of the countries, as a move within Australia would involve the same distance and difficulties as a move to a separate country from England. In *AMS v AIF; AIF v AMS*,[35] the mother wanted to move from Perth to Darwin, about the same distance as between London and Cairo, and involving a 4-hour flight. Kirby J sitting in the High Court of Australia referred to the difference that distance makes:

> '147 ... a more relaxed attitude should be adopted to relocation within Australia then relocation overseas ... . But even where the proposal is made to remove the child to another country, courts will not necessarily restrain such moves, despite the inevitable implications they will have for the child's contact with, and access to, the other parent. Proof that the custodial (or residence) parent has remarried and wishes to join a new spouse overseas, wishes to return to a supportive family in the land of origin, or has a well thought out and reasonable plan of migration may suffice to convince the court having jurisdiction over the child, that the best interests of the child favour continuance of the custodial (or residence) arrangement in another jurisdiction but with different orders as to access and contact.'

8.19   In *Fragomeli v Fragomeli*[36] and *I v I*[37] the Full Court of the Family Court of Australia emphasised that the approach to be taken in relocation cases was based firmly upon the principle that the paramount consideration was to be the welfare of the child. A custodial parent should be free to order his or her

---

[35]   (1999) 199 CLR 160.

[36]   (1993) FLC 92–393. The mother remarried a Petty Officer in the US Navy and applied to relocate to Hawaii. Although she had misled the court, her appeal against a restriction on removal from Western Australia was allowed. The welfare of the child was paramount, but the main object of the Family Law Act 1975 was to allow parties to a marriage which had broken down to make a new life for themselves, provided that the custodian did what was reasonably to be expected for the child in all the circumstances, because children may be adversely effected if their custodian is not permitted to relocate. To prevent the mother from joining her new husband was unjust and unreasonable because it made her role as custodian unduly onerous (decision in *Holmes v Holmes* (1998) FLC 91–918 applied).

[37]   (1995) FLC 92–604. The mother, born in the United Kingdom, wanted to return home from Perth, WA. Supervised access was granted to the father because of his inappropriate, sexualised behaviour with the children. On appeal, the restriction on the mother removing the children from Australia was lifted. The approach in *Fragomeli* (above) was approved; subject to welfare, a custodian, particularly one with sole guardianship, was free to order his or her life without the interference of the court. Requiring the mother to stay in Australia, to her a foreign country, with no means of support and subject to harassment and abuse from the father, would place an unreasonable strain upon her and may seriously impair her parenting ability and affect the children's welfare (note that there was psychiatric evidence recommending that mother move interstate or some distance away to avoid a high risk of physical violence from the father).

own life without undue interference from the other parent or the court; but conditions may be placed upon a custodial parent concerning where he or she may live, according to what is in the best interests of the child.

8.20 Thereafter, there were significant and extensive alterations to the family law statutory regime in Australia in 1995. Many of the ideas incorporated in the English Children Act 1989 were enacted, especially the change in language. Article 9 of the United Nations Convention on the Rights of the Child (UNCROC) was enacted in s 60B of the Family Law Act 1975 in the following form (emphasis added):

'(1) The object of this Part is to ensure that children receive adequate and proper parenting to help them achieve their full potential, and to ensure that parents fulfil their duties, and meet their responsibilities, concerning the care, welfare and development of their children.

(2) The principles underlying these objects are that, *except when it is or would be contrary to a child's best interests*:

(a)   *children have the right to know and be cared for by both their parents,* regardless of whether their parents are married, separated, have never married or have never lived together; and

(b)   *children have a right of contact, on a regular basis, with both their parents* and with other people significant to their care, welfare and development; and

(c)   parents share duties and responsibilities concerning the care, welfare and development of their children; and

(d)   parents should agree about the future parenting of their children.'

8.21 The principle that relocation decisions are made on the basis of the best interests of the child was reinforced by the decision of the Full Court of the Family Court of Australia in *B v B: Family Law Reform Act 1995*,[38] an interstate relocation case in which the mother sought to move from Cairns, Queensland to Bendigo, Victoria with her fiancé. *B v B* is the modern reference point and foundation of recent decisions. That case, with its comprehensive analysis of the law, including that of the United Kingdom and Canada, identified the important question as that of weighing the child staying with the relocating parent against the changes to the child's environment and the loss or reduction of contact with the other parent resulting from relocation.[39] Nicholson CJ,

---

[38]   (1997) FLC 92–755. Applied in *Markowski and Hughes* (judgment 15 December 1998) Australian Family Lawyer, Vol 13, No 4, Winter 1999 – dismissal of an appeal by father against order permitting relocation of 5-year-old child with mother and mother's fiancé who had been offered promotion in Singapore. There had been frequent contact between father and child since the separation of the mother and father, and it was common ground that they had an excellent relationship. Factors considered by the trial judge (who expressed sympathy with the father and commented on the complexities of adjudicating evenly-balanced relocation cases) included economic advantages of the promotion, disadvantages to the child of reduced contact with the father at such a young age and the negativity which might result from being denied the opportunity of promotion, and the possible effects of any such negativity on the quality of the mother's parenting.

[39]   Paragraph 9.62.

Fogarty J and Lindenmayer J wrote what was intended to be an omnibus judgment on the operation of the major amendments. The Full Court said:

> '7.2 ... relocation cases are not a separate category within the Family Law Act, to be determined by their own principles and rules ...

> 7.11 Obviously where the contemplated relocation is interstate or overseas the issue of maintaining contact becomes more acute, but the basic principles remain the same. The difference is that the consequences are greater and the court is required to factor that in as a significant circumstance in determining the ultimate questions – whether to permit relocation and on what terms.'

8.22 Ultimately, that question is determined by reference to the interests of the child, but considerations likely to have relevance are: the degree and quality of the relationship between the child and parent with whom he is living; the degree and quality of contact with the other parent; the reason for relocating; and the distance and permanence of the proposed change. Other matters might include the dislocation of the child from his environment, his age and wishes, the feasibility and costs of travel for contact and of other forms of contact. As to the reasons for relocation, these may be both economic and personal, and if improvements will occur in either of these areas, it is likely to impact directly on the best interests of the child.

8.23 Despite this, the Full Court in *B v B* accepted the rather specific test set out in *Holmes v Holmes*,[40] a case in which an American mother wanted to return to the United States, as a guide to determining whether to permit relocation:

> '(1) Is the application to remove the children from their previous environment made bona fide? [the so-called "compelling reasons" test] ...

> (2) If it is bona fide, can the Court be reasonably satisfied that the custodian will comply with orders for access and other orders made to ensure the continuance of the relationship between the children and the non-custodian? ...

> (3) The general effect upon the welfare of the children in granting or refusing the application ... '

8.24 This latter consideration might include reference to the effect on the child of deprivation or diminution of access and general association with the non-custodian and his family, and any disadvantages to the welfare of the child in the proposed new environment in isolation or comparison with the previous environment, in the context of which the genuine wishes of an unchallenged custodian were an important consideration.

8.25 The court also said that refusing to allow a relocation might seem to be too great an imposition on the freedom of movement of the caring parent, but the ultimate issue under Part VII of the Family Law Act 1975 (of which relocation proceedings are but a particular example) is the best interests of the

---

[40] (1998) FLC 91–918, at 76,663.

child, which override the parent's freedom of movement when they are in conflict. This test seems to resemble closely that set out by Thorpe LJ in *Payne v Payne*[41] rather than the broader principles referred to in *I v I*.[42]

8.26 A change to the *Holmes* test was signalled by the High Court in *AMS v AIF; AIF v AMS*,[43] a case in which various constitutional and jurisdictional matters involving Western Australian and federal legislation were considered within the context of a proposed relocation. Kirby J held (and the majority of other judges agreed) that:

> '191 ... to impose upon a custodial (or residence) parent the obligation to demonstrate "compelling reasons" to justify relocation of that parent's residence, with consequent relocation of the residence of the child, is not warranted either by the statutory instructions to regard as paramount the welfare of the child or by the practicalities affecting parents ... At least in the case of a proposed relocation within Australia, the need to demonstrate "compelling reasons" imposes on a custodial parent an unreasonable inhibition. It effectively ties that parent to an obligation of physical proximity to a person with whom, by definition, the personal relationship which gave rise to the birth of the child has finished or at least significantly altered.'

8.27 Kirby J sets out in his judgment[44] the general principles relating to relocation: each case depends on the application of legislation which is constantly being amended and re-expressed, but unless legislation otherwise provides, no single factor can determine the issues concerning the residence of a child when relocation is proposed. The statutory instruction to treat the welfare or best interests of the child as a paramount consideration does not mean that the legitimate interests or desires of the parents ought to be ignored, the legislation being enacted in a society which attaches a very high importance to freedom of movement and the right of adults to decide where to live. Kirby J also suggested that a more relaxed attitude should be adopted to relocation within Australia than overseas,[45] and that just as conditions can be imposed on a custodial parent as to where the child can live, so the fact of disturbing a child can be taken into account when proposals for change are made. There is no justification for requiring the parent proposing relocation to show compelling reasons, but it has to be shown that the proposed change is for the welfare of, or in the best interests of, the child.[46] As to the appeal (which was upheld on the ground that the judge erred in holding that reasons

---

[41] [2001] EWCA Civ 166, [2001] Fam 473, [2001] 1 FLR 1052.

[42] (1995) FLC 92–393.

[43] (1999) 199 CLR 160.

[44] At para 141.

[45] And see *Holmes v Holmes* (1998) FLC 91–918 at 76,664.

[46] On this point, see *Martin v Matruglio* (1999) FLC 92–876, in which a mother's appeal against a refusal to allow her to relocate from Canberra to Sydney was allowed, the judge having erred in requiring 'imperative' reasons for moving, and failing to give sufficient weight to the general effect of his decision on the welfare of the children and the mother having tried to increase their contact with the father.

for relocation needed to be compelling), appellate courts reviewing the exercise of a discretion at first instance will avoid being overly critical,[47] given the large element of judgement, discretion and intuition involved.

8.28   As to the approach to be adopted when dealing with a relocation case, the Full Court held in *Paskandy v Paskandy*[48] that the decision in *AMS v AIF; AIF v AMS* made it clear that a court dealing with a relocation case cannot proceed in a way which separates the issues of relocation from residence and the best interests of the child. They rejected the approach of dissecting the case into discrete issues: a primary issue as to who should have residence and a further, separate, issue as to whether relocation should be 'permitted'. The Full Court found that the proper approach was to identify the competing proposals, and then to identify which of the proposals was preferable, with the child's welfare being the paramount consideration. Accordingly, there is no obligation on the applicant parent to demonstrate 'compelling reasons' to justify the proposed relocation. The first step is to identify the competing proposals, the next to determine which is preferable (the child's welfare being the paramount consideration), following the legislative directions and relocation factors in *B v B: Family Law Reform Act 1995* and *AMS v AIF; AIF v AMS*, particularly the need not to impose an impediment on freedom of movement greater than that reasonably required.

8.29   In the subsequent case of *A v A: Relocation Approach*[49] the Full Court held that the reasons for the proposed relocation as they bear upon the child's best interests are to be weighed with the other matters that are raised in the case, rather than treated as a separate issue. Their Honours said that the statement in *B v B* (above):

> '9.63 … it is important for the court to consider whether the reasons to relocate are genuine, whether they are optional or whether they are seen as important or essential for the orderly life of that parent. The three-tiered test in relation to this referred to in *Holmes* … remains a valid guide to these aspects',

was no longer considered as good law.

8.30   This rejection by Australian courts of the 'compelling reasons' approach and the move away from a dissection of the case into discrete issues appears to represent a dramatic shift from the way English courts have dealt with relocation. Whereas English decisions have emphasised bona fides and the wishes of the residential parent, recent Australian decisions have moved towards identifying competing proposals, with an emphasis on the child's best interests.

---

47   Or pernickety.
48   (1999) FLC 92–878 (Hungarian mother wanting to return home).
49   (2000) 26 Fam LR 382 (mother wanted to relocate to Portugal to be with her other child of a previous relationship).

8.31　That the Australian courts place considerable weight on proper contact with the non-caregiving parent can be seen from the judgment of the Full Court in *R v R*,[50] which dismissed an appeal by a mother who, unhappy in Australia, had been refused leave to take the four children back to Scotland, from where she and the father had emigrated and where she said that there was extended family support available to her, employment to go to and secure housing available. The two eldest children said they wanted to go and had had no significant contact with the father for some time. The father opposed the application and the trial judge, applying *B v B: Family Law Reform Act 1995*,[51] said that he was not prepared to take an 'unacceptable risk' in relation to the welfare of the younger children in respect of contact with their father in the short and long term in order to meet the concerns of the mother and give effect to the wishes of the two elder children, which in his view were not satisfactorily based.[52] As to the mother's disappointment, the evidence fell far short of establishing that she would be unable to function as a parent if she were not permitted to return to Scotland.

8.32　The importance of contact with the father was further emphasised in *H v E*,[53] in which a mother, her husband and the children had relocated from Melbourne to Brisbane without informing the father and in breach of orders restraining movement. The judge balanced the competing considerations for allowing the mother and child in question to remain in Brisbane and requiring their return and, reaching the conclusion that frequent and regular contact with the father was in the interests of the child, ordered the mother to live in Melbourne. Dismissing the mother's appeal and remarking that the relocation had taken place in circumstances which were neither necessary nor desirable, the Full Court said that the approach to relocation cases was to be found in *B v B: Family Law Reform Act 1995*.[54] Although a good relationship between father and child had developed and could be maintained on limited contact, the judge had applied the correct principles and properly balanced the competing considerations.

---

[50]　(1998) FLC 92–820, an appeal from Fogarty J.

[51]　(1997) FLC 92–755: 'Whilst the right of a residence parent to live his or her own life, including where and under what circumstances, is an important matter, it is subservient to and must give way to the best interests of the children involved in that case to the extent that they are inconsistent or in conflict', per Fogarty J.

[52]　The judge concluded that the essential reasons for their wishes were to support their mother and the allure of travel. It is important to note that the judge took the view that the fact that the children were in accord with the mother's views removed what would otherwise be a considerable impediment, but could not be used by itself as a significant, independent reason for reaching a conclusion favourable to her.

[53]　(1999) FLC 92–45.

[54]　(1997) FLC 92–755. In *H v E* the mother, father and child had never, apart from 3 weeks after the child's birth, lived together as a family, and the relocation to Brisbane had been perpetrated by a deception on the part of the step-father.

Conclusion

8.33 The attitude of the Australian courts towards international relocation has moved away from the English test as expressed in *Payne v Payne*[55] and towards a broader test that such considerations are but one factor to be considered in the ultimate determination of what is in the best interests of the child. However, both English and Australian courts have stressed that parents have a right to freedom of movement, and that preventing relocation may impinge on the happiness of the resident parent and thus affect the welfare of the child.

8.34 But it is to be firmly remembered that looks can be deceiving. In all of the reported Australian international cases except *Skeates-Udy v Skeates*,[56] the outcome has been that the custodial mother has been allowed to move, or at least an order prohibiting such a move has led to a retrial. Even in *Lourie v Perlstein*,[57] the only reported case involving a custodial father, he was allowed to move after 12 months of access to strengthen the mother's ties with the children. Therefore, hidden under the guise of 'best interests', the facts tend to dictate the outcome. A firmly entrenched custodial parent (with a good reason to go) is likely to be permitted to relocate, be she (or occasionally he) Australian or English, despite the different approaches of the English and Australian courts.

---

55 [2001] EWCA Civ 166, [2001] Fam 473, [2001] 1 FLR 1052.
56 (1995) FLC 92–626 (peripatetic mother wishing to travel to Oregon, USA, to further alternative medicine studies).
57 (1993) FLC 92–405 (custodial father had a lifelong ambition to settle in Israel).

PART III

THE UNLAWFUL MOVEMENT
OF CHILDREN

Chapter 9

PREVENTING CHILD ABDUCTION

INTRODUCTION

9.1 This chapter deals with the steps available to prevent or deter the unlawful removal or retention ('abduction') of a child away from his home or, often with more profound consequences, away from England and Wales. Once a child is taken out of the jurisdiction it is harder both to find and to recover the child. Thus it is vital to prevent removal in the first place. Practitioners must consider whether to use civil proceedings (ie to obtain specific orders restricting a child's removal from the jurisdiction) or to rely upon the criminal sanctions imposed primarily under the Child Abduction Act 1984.[1] The criminal law and in particular the power to arrest a person attempting to abduct or in the act of committing an offence by abducting the child may be of assistance if sensitively employed,[2] although the role of the criminal law is limited in abductions within the United Kingdom.[3]

9.2 Where the threatened abduction would be an offence under the Child Abduction Act 1984, there is now no requirement to obtain a civil court order in order to obtain police assistance[4] (including a Port Alert).[5]

9.3 Although a court order may not be a necessary preliminary to police action nor necessary to make a removal or retention unlawful, it may nevertheless be advantageous to obtain an order if it can be done speedily, since:

(i)   it establishes a person's bona fides which may help to convince the police to assist;

(ii) it will enable the applicant to enlist the help of government agencies to trace the child;[6]

(iii) it is usually required before the Passport Agency will refuse to issue a passport[7] or the court will order the surrender of a British, or on occasion a foreign, passport;[8]

(iv) an order is required if it becomes necessary to invoke the Brussels II Council Regulation[9] or the 1980 European Custody Convention;[10]

---

[1] Note, however, that the Child Abduction Act 1984 only criminalises the wrongful removal of children (under the age of 16) by their parents when the child is removed from the United Kingdom, viz England and Wales, Scotland and Northern Ireland: see **9.4** below.

[2] See **9.20** and Home Office Circular No 75/1984 (Child Abduction Act 1984). See also the need for sensitivity in deciding whether to bring charges after a child has been abducted. See also Chapter 10.

[3] See **9.4**.

[4] As the Home Office Guidance makes clear, the police have authority to act at any stage of an attempted abduction: Home Office Circular No 75/1984 (Child Abduction Act 1984).

[5] See **9.55**.

[6] See **10.23**.

[7] See **9.52**.

[8] See **9.48**.

[9] See Chapter 18.

[10] Signed at Luxembourg on 20 May 1980; see Chapter 19.

(v)   an order is helpful if it is sought to recover the child from another part of the United Kingdom or the Isle of Man;[11]

(vi)   an order may be required by the authorities of the State to which a child has been removed or in which he is retained;[12]

(vii) an order or a recital to an order can establish the habitual residence of a child or can record an agreement as to which court should have jurisdiction;[13] and

(viii) above all, an order removes any doubt as to the prohibition on removal in the minds of the potential abductor and official bodies.

CRIMINAL LAW

Child Abduction Act 1984: abductions from the United Kingdom by parents and other persons connected with the child

9.4   The Child Abduction Act 1984 replaced the offence of child stealing under the Offences Against the Person Act 1861, s 56, with two new offences. One deals with the taking or sending of a child under the age of 16 out of the United Kingdom (viz England and Wales, Scotland and Northern Ireland)[14] by 'a person connected with the child' without 'the appropriate consent'.[15] Accordingly, an abduction by a parent or other person connected with the child is not a criminal offence where the removal is to another part of the United Kingdom, unless it is contrary to the common law or the child is in local authority care.[16] A person is connected with a child for the purposes of the section if he is a parent of the child, or, in the case of a child whose parents were not married to each other at the time of his birth, where there are reasonable grounds for believing that he is the father of the child, or he is the guardian of the child or he is a person in whose favour a residence order is in force with respect to the child or he has custody of the child.[17]

---

11   See Chapter 11.

12   Local advice should be sought if there is a risk of abduction to a specific State which is not a party to the 1980 Hague Abduction Convention or another international instrument. See generally **20.73** *et seq*.

13   See **9.36** and **9.41**.

14   Interpretation Act 1978, Sch 1.

15   Child Abduction Act 1984, s 1(1) establishes this offence under the law of England and Wales. As to 'taking' and 'sending', see s 3, and R *v* C *(Kidnapping: Abduction)* [1991] 2 FLR 252, CA. There is a similar offence under the law of Scotland under s 6 of the Child Abduction Act 1984 and in Northern Ireland under the Child Abduction (Northern Ireland) Order 1985, SI 1985/1638 (N1 17).

16   If the child is in local authority care, an offence under s 49 of the Children Act 1989 would be committed. See **6.15** and **9.17**.

17   Child Abduction Act 1984, s 1(2), as substituted by Children Act 1989, Sch 12, para 37(2). As to guardianship and residence orders, see respectively Children Act 1989, ss 5 and 6, and s 8 *et seq*. As from a date to be appointed, a connected person will include a special guardian (appointed under Children Act 1989, ss 14A–14G): see Child Abduction Act 1984, s 1(2)(ca), as inserted by Adoption and Children Act 2002, s 139 and Sch 3.

9.5 Defences to a charge under s 1(1) are available under s 1(5), so that an offence is not committed if the person removing the child believes that the person from whom consent is required has consented or would consent if he was aware of all the relevant circumstances; or he has taken all reasonable steps to communicate with the other person but has been unable to communicate with him; or the other person has unreasonably refused to consent unless that person has a residence order or custody order in his favour. Furthermore, where proceedings are brought under s 1(1) and there is evidence raising a defence under s 1(5), it is for the prosecution to prove that the defence is not made out.[18] Prosecution in such circumstances may not be unproblematic.

9.6 The 'appropriate consent' means the consent (which can be oral or written) of each of the following: the child's mother; the child's father, if he has parental responsibility for him; any guardian of the child; any person in whose favour a residence order is in force with respect to the child; or any person who has custody of the child.[19] The term also includes leave of the court granted under Part II of the Children Act 1989 or, if any person has custody of the child, the leave of the court which awarded custody to him.[20] Therefore, in the absence of a residence order, it is an offence for one parent to remove a child from the United Kingdom without the consent of the other if that other has parental responsibility. However, a person does not commit an offence under the section by taking or sending a child out of the United Kingdom without obtaining the appropriate consent if he is a person in whose favour there is a residence order in force with respect to the child and he takes or sends the child out of the jurisdiction for a period of less than one month and the removal is not in breach of an order (such as a prohibited steps order) made under Part II of the Children Act 1989.[21] It should be noted that, where a parent has sole parental responsibility as, for example, the unmarried mother where the father has not acquired parental responsibility by court order or

18 Child Abduction Act 1984, s 1(6).
19 *Ibid* s 1(3)(a) as substituted by Children Act 1989, Sch 12, para 37(2). In certain circumstances, an offence is not committed notwithstanding the absence of consent: see Child Abduction Act 1984, s 1(5). However, it is no defence that the child has consented, see *R v A (Child Abduction)* [2000] 1 WLR 1879, [2000] 2 All ER 177, CA, and see further n 27 below. As to parental responsibility, see Children Act 1989, s 3. As to the meaning of 'custody' under Child Abduction Act 1984, s 1, see s 1(7)(b). As from a date to be appointed, appropriate consent may be given to the special guardian (appointed under Children Act 1989, ss 14A–14G): see Child Abduction Act 1984, s 1(3)(a)(iiia), as inserted by Adoption and Children Act 2002, s 139 and Sch 3.
20 *Ibid*, s 1(3)(b),(c), as substituted by Children Act 1989, Sch 12, para 37(2).
21 *Ibid*, s 1(4), (4A), as substituted by Children Act 1989, Sch 12, para 37(2). A person will also not commit an offence if he is a special guardian (appointed under Children Act 1989, ss 14A–14G) and he takes the child out of the United Kingdom for less than 3 months: see Child Abduction Act 1984, s 1(4)(a), (b), as inserted by Adoption and Children Act 2002, s 139 and Sch 3 from a date to be appointed.

agreement,[22] or where the married parent is the sole living parent, then no consent for the child's removal is required.

9.7 The appropriate consent is required from the local authority where the child is in care, from the adoption agency where the child is subject to an order freeing him for adoption,[23] from the court in which an application for a freeing order or adoption order is pending and from the court in which an application for an order under s 55 of the Adoption Act 1976 is pending or has been made.[24]

9.8 The Child Abduction Act 1984 also enables one parent to try to stop the other from abducting since it is an offence to attempt to take a child out of the United Kingdom.[25] The police can arrest without a warrant anyone they reasonably suspect of attempting to take a child out of the United Kingdom.[26]

Child Abduction Act 1984: abduction by other persons

9.9 Section 2 of the 1984 Act deals with the offence of abduction of a child by other persons: an offence is committed if a person without lawful authority or excuse takes or detains a child under the age of 16 so as to remove him from the lawful control of any person having lawful control of the child or so as to keep him out of the lawful control of any person entitled to lawful control of the child.[27] This offence is not one of strict liability and the accused

---

[22]   As emphasised by Hale J in *Re W, Re B (Abduction: Father's Rights)* [1999] Fam 1, [1998] 3 WLR 1372, [1998] 2 FLR 146.

[23]   As to freeing for adoption, see Adoption Act 1976, s 18.

[24]   Section 1(8) of and the Schedule to the Child Abduction Act 1984. As to the circumstances in which it is a criminal offence to take or send a child abroad for adoption, see **6.16**.

[25]   For a successful prosecution for an attempted abduction, see *R v Griffin* [1993] Crim LR 515, CA.

[26]   For guidance, see Home Office Circular No 75/1984.

[27]   Child Abduction Act 1984, s 2. 'Lawful control' is not to be equated with legal custody: *O v Governor of Holloway Prison and Government of the USA* [2000] 1 FLR 147, Div Ct. As to 'detaining', see *ibid*, s 3. As to 'taking', see *ibid*, s 3 and *R v A* [2000] 1 WLR 1874, [2000] 2 All ER 177, sub nom *Re Owens* [2000] 1 Cr App R 418, CA (for the purposes of ss 2(1)(b) and 3(a), the defendant's acts did not need to be the sole cause of the child accompanying him; it was sufficient that those acts were an effective cause of the child accompanying him and it was immaterial that there were also other causes, such as the child's state of mind). As to the absence of consent, see *R v D* [1984] AC 778 at 806, [1984] 2 All ER 449 at 457, HL, per Lord Brandon:

'That third ingredient, as I formulated it earlier, consists of the absence of consent on the part of the person taken or carried away. I see no good reason why, in relation to the kidnapping of a child, it should not in all cases be the absence of the child's consent which is material, whatever its age may be. In the case of a very young child, it would not have the understanding or the intelligence to give its consent, so that absence of consent would be a necessary inference from its age. In the case of an older child, however, it must, I think, be a question of fact for a jury whether the child concerned has sufficient understanding and intelligence to give its consent; if, but only if, the jury considers that a child has these qualities, it must then go on to consider whether it has been proved that the child did not give its consent. While the matter will always be for the jury alone to decide, I should not

must have the necessary *mens rea*.[28] Furthermore, the offence cannot be committed by the parents if married at the time of the birth or by the mother if not married to the father or by other persons with parental responsibility. On the other hand, this offence is committed regardless of whether the abduction leads to the removal of the child from England or Wales. Where the parents were not married to one another at the time of the birth, it is a defence if the abductor believes that the child is over 16 or that he is the father or, at the time of the offence, on reasonable grounds he believed that he was the father.[29]

9.10 Any person providing a refuge for a child under the provisions of s 51 of the Children Act 1989 does not commit an offence under s 2 of the Child Abduction Act 1984.[30]

Common law offences: kidnapping and false imprisonment

9.11 Following the House of Lords' decision in *R v D*,[31] it is now clear that parents who abduct their unmarried children under the age of 18 can be guilty of the common law crime of kidnapping.[32] In that case an estranged father forced his way, uninvited, into the mother's flat together with two accomplices, both of whom had knives or other sharp instruments and one of whom wore a stocking mask. The father removed his 5-year-old daughter (who had been made a ward of court specifically to prevent her removal) from the understandably terrified mother. Furthermore, one accomplice stayed behind threatening to use an alleged 'gas bomb' to prevent the mother informing the police before the father made good his escape. In fact the mother, having pursued the father to New Zealand, recovered her daughter

---

expect a jury to find at all frequently that a child under fourteen had sufficient understanding and intelligence to give its consent.

I should add that, while the absence of the consent of the person having custody or care and control of a child is not material to what I have stated to be the third ingredient of the common law offence of kidnapping, the giving of consent by such a person may be very relevant to the fourth ingredient, in that, depending on all the circumstances, it might well support a defence of lawful excuse.'

See also the discussion in *Gillick v West Norfolk and Wisbech Area Health Authority* [1986] AC 112, [1986] 1 FLR 224, HL. As to control, see *R v Leather* [1993] 2 FLR 770, CA (the section does not contemplate the geographical removal; the offence is committed if the child is deflected by some action of the accused from that which he would otherwise have been doing with the consent of his parents into some action induced by the accused).

28 *O v Governor of Holloway Prison and Government of the USA* [2000] 1 FLR 147. Cf *R v Mousir* [1987] Crim LR 562.

29 Child Abduction Act 1984, s 2(3).

30 Children Act 1989, s 51.

31 [1984] AC, 778 [1984] 2 All ER 449, on which see the detailed analysis by Lowe at (1984) 134 NLJ 995.

32 Although note the more cautious approach of Lord Bridge who, alone among their Lordships, preferred to leave open whether the offence was wider than acting in contravention of a court order restricting the father's parental rights.

only for the father later, forcibly, to remove the child for a second time, on this occasion to Ireland.

9.12 On these facts, the House of Lords, overruling the Court of Appeal, upheld the father's conviction of common law kidnapping. In their view, five elements have to be satisfied for a successful prosecution, namely:

(1) the taking or carrying away of the child by the parent;
(2) by force or by fraud;[33]
(3) without the consent of the child so taken or carried away;[34]
(4) without lawful excuse; and
(5) that the 'conduct of the parent is so bad that an ordinary right thinking person would immediately and without hesitation regard it as criminal in nature'.

9.13 With regard to the fourth requirement, the House of Lords specifically rejected the father's argument that at common law he had absolute authority over his child, and on the facts, he was found to have no lawful excuse for his actions. No doubt mothers are in a similar position, and it is certainly possible to envisage situations in which parents acting in unison could be guilty as, for example, by drugging their 15-year-old child to overcome his or her refusal to emigrate with them.[35]

9.14 The fifth element is an important limitation. The House of Lords were concerned that civil, rather than criminal, remedies should normally be used to combat abductions, and they certainly did not want one parent bringing a private prosecution. In this respect it is to be noted that, following Lord Scarman's recommendation in *R v D*, Child Abduction Act 1984, s 5 requires the consent of the Director of Public Prosecutions to instituting any prosecution for an offence of kidnapping. It has also since been established[36] that, insofar as they overlap, prosecutions under the Child Abduction Act 1984 should be brought in preference to prosecuting the common law offence.

9.15 Following *R v D* there have been few reported instances of common law prosecutions against parents. However, soon after the House of Lords' decision, in *R v Rahman*[37] a father was convicted of the common law offence

---

[33] See *R v Cort* [2003] TLR 429, CA (fraud negatived consent).

[34] With regard to the third requirement, although it is the absence of the *child's* consent that is essential to the commission of the offence, Lord Brandon intimated that he 'would not expect a jury to find at all frequently that a child under 14 had sufficient understanding and intelligence to give its consent'; see n 27 above.

[35] Cf *Re KR (Abduction: Forcible Removal By Parents)* [1999] 2 FLR 542 at 543, where Singer J commented: 'Child abduction is still child abduction when both parents are the abductors and the child is very nearly an adult'.

[36] *R v C (Kidnapping: Abduction)* [1991] 2 FLR 252, CA.

[37] (1985) 81 Cr App Rep 349, CA, commented upon by Khan at [1986] Fam Law 69.

of falsely imprisoning his teenaged daughter by forcibly pushing her into a car and telling her falsely that he was taking her to Bangladesh to visit her sick grandmother, when in reality, he wanted her to return to her land of birth.[38]

9.16   There is also the offence of abduction of unmarried girls contrary to ss 19 and 20 of the Sexual Offences Act 1956.

Abduction of children in care

9.17   Section 49 of the Children Act 1989 makes it an offence for any person, including a parent or other person with parental responsibility, to abduct from the person responsible for him a child who is in care or is the subject of an emergency protection order or is in police protection.[39] It is also an offence for a person, knowingly and without lawful authority or reasonable excuse, to take or to keep such child away from the responsible person or to induce, assist or incite such a child to run away or stay away from the responsible person.[40] 'Responsible person' means any person who for the time being has care of the child by virtue of the care order or the emergency protection order, or where the child is in police protection. In *Re R (Recovery Orders)*[41] it was held that, by virtue of ss 33(3) and 49 of the 1989 Act, it is for the local authority alone to specify who the responsible person should be at any given time. This offence needs to be considered alongside the power to make recovery orders under s 50 of the Children Act 1989.[42] Indeed, where a parent is thought to have abducted a child out of care and is elsewhere in the United Kingdom, seeking a recovery order would seem to be the more effective remedy.

9.18   However, a person who provides a refuge to child under s 50 of the Children Act 1989 does not commit an offence under either that Act or the Child Abduction Act 1984.[43]

Powers of arrest and the use of the criminal law

9.19   Any person, including a parent, may arrest without warrant anyone who is in the act of committing, or whom he has reasonable grounds for suspecting to be committing, an offence under s 1 or s 2 of the Child Abduction Act 1984 or anyone who is guilty of such offence or whom he has reasonable

---

[38]   Following a struggle, the father was arrested and passports and tickets to Bangladesh were found on him.

[39]   Children Act 1989, s 49(2). For 'child' and 'child who is in care', see s 105(1); for 'emergency protection order', see s 44(4); for 'in police protection', see s 46(2).

[40]   *Ibid*, s 49(1). A person guilty of such an offence is liable on summary conviction to imprisonment for a term not exceeding 6 months, or to a fine not exceeding level 5 on the standard scale, or to both: s 49(3).

[41]   [1998] 2 FLR 401.

[42]   See **6.15** and **11.48**.

[43]   Children Act 1989, s 50(5).

grounds for suspecting to be guilty of such offence.[44] A police constable who has reasonable grounds for suspecting that such offence has been committed may arrest anyone whom he has reasonable grounds for suspecting to be guilty of the offence; further, he may arrest anyone who is about to commit such offence or anyone whom he has reasonable grounds for suspecting to be about to commit such offence.[45] Importantly, these powers of arrest also apply where the offence is the attempt to commit an offence under s 1 or s 2 of the Child Abduction Act 1984.[46]

9.20 These powers of arrest are of particular use in preventing abduction. However, as discussed at the Third Meeting of the Special Commission to Review the Operation of the Hague Abduction Convention, the criminal law needs to be used sensitively; criminal proceedings may deter a person from returning to the State from which the child has been removed and may deter an amicable resolution.[47] It may also cause a court to hesitate before ordering the return of a child if the child's primary carer is likely to be imprisoned if he or she returns with the child. Accordingly, the English High Court frequently accepts from a person seeking the return of a child from England to its home State an undertaking not to institute or voluntarily to support any proceedings for the punishment or committal of the abductor in respect of any crime or contempt arising from the wrongful removal.[48] However, in *Re L (Abduction: Pending Criminal Proceedings)*,[49] Wilson J ordered the return of the children to Florida under the Hague Abduction Convention despite an outstanding warrant for their mother's arrest; he found that there was no reason to think that the Florida state prosecutor, in considering whether to continue with the prosecution of the mother for the abduction, and the Florida criminal court, in deciding whether to grant bail, or in the event of a conviction in deciding

---

44 Police and Criminal Evidence Act 1984, s 24(4), (5). See Home Office Circular No 75/1984 (Child Abduction Act 1984). The number of reported offences of child abduction (under ss 1 and 2) between April 1997 and March 1998 was 390 (which may have involved more than one child), and between April 1998 and March 1999 was 490 involving 502 children; there were 77 prosecutions in 1997 and 104 prosecutions in 1998 (Source: Home Office Criminal Justice Unit England and Wales).

45 Police and Criminal Evidence Act 1984, s 24(6), (7).

46 *Ibid*, s 24(3). For a successful prosecution of an attempted abduction, see *R v Griffin* [1993] Crim LR 515, CA. As to the proper role of the police, see **10.49**.

47 Checklist of Issues to be Considered at the Third Meeting of the Special Commission to Review the Operation of the Hague Convention on the Civil Aspects of International Child Abduction drawn by Adair Dyer, Deputy Secretary General of the Permanent Bureau of the Conference, January 1997, Question 2. At the meeting of the Special Commission in September 2002, the Conference formally sanctioned the Permanent Bureau to continue to gather information about preventative measures taken by Contracting States: see Recommendation 1(b).

48 *C v C (Minor: Abduction: Rights of Custody Abroad)* [1989] 2 All ER 465, [1989] 1 WLR 654, CA; *Re G (A Minor) (Abduction)* [1989] 2 FLR 475, CA. As to the use of undertakings in child abduction proceedings in England and Wales, see **17.123**.

49 [1999] 1 FLR 843. See also *Re C (Abduction: Grave Risk of Psychological Harm)* [1999] 1 FLR 1145, CA, and the discussion at **17.104**.

whether to sentence the mother to a term of imprisonment, would fail to pay significant regard to the children's interests. A different course was taken in *Re M and J (Abduction) (International Judicial Collaboration)*,[50] where Singer J liaised directly with the Californian criminal court judge who recalled and suspended the warrant of imprisonment of the abductor until child issues had been resolved in California.

9.21   After an abduction, Interpol will act on a criminal complaint or a missing persons report.[51] In *Re L (Abduction: Pending Criminal Proceedings)*[52] the issue in Florida of a warrant for arrest triggered the international police activity which led to the mother and children being found in England.

CIVIL REMEDIES: PREVENTING THE CHILD'S REMOVAL OR RETENTION

Orders expressly prohibiting the child's removal or retention

9.22   A person may obtain a prohibited steps order expressly forbidding the removal of the child from the United Kingdom or any specified part of the United Kingdom or from the care of the person with whom he is living.[53] An order in similar terms can be made by way of an injunction ancillary to a residence order[54] or under the inherent jurisdiction.[55] Either order may be applied for ex parte (ie without notice) where the circumstances justify it, for example in cases of urgency.[56]

9.23   Where removal would be otherwise unlawful, it is not necessary to obtain an order to make the removal wrongful.[57] Nevertheless, there are

---

[50]   [2000] 1 FLR 803.

[51]   Checklist of Issues to be Considered at the Third Meeting of the Special Commission to Review the Operation of the Hague Convention on the Civil Aspects of International Child Abduction drawn by Adair Dyer, Deputy Secretary General of the Permanent Bureau of the Conference, January 1997, Question 5.

[52]   [1999] 1 FLR 843.

[53]   *Re D (A Minor) (Child Removal from Jurisdiction)* [1992] 1 WLR 315, [1992] 1 All ER 892, CA. As to prohibited steps orders, see *Rayden and Jackson on Divorce and Family Matters*, 17th edn (Butterworths), para 40.46. An order is generally effective from the first moment of the day upon which it is made: *Re S (A Minor) (Custody: Habitual Residence)* [1998] AC 750, [1998] 1 FLR 122, HL.

[54]   *M v M (Residence Order: Ancillary Injunction)* [1994] Fam Law 440; *C v K (Inherent Powers: Exclusion Order)* [1996] 2 FLR 506.

[55]   As to the automatic prohibition on removal of a ward of court and other advantages of making a child a ward of court, see **6.13**.

[56]   *Re D (A Minor) (Child Removal from Jurisdiction)* (above) (the mother would probably not attend an inter partes hearing and could be protected by having liberty to apply to vary or set aside the order); *Re S (A Minor) (Custody: Habitual Residence)* (above) (court correct to deal with an application where the child was habitually resident in England despite foreign court's order made ex parte half an hour earlier which reached a different view of the facts).

[57]   See **9.3**.

significant advantages in having an order as has already been discussed. Furthermore, in cases where the person seeking to prevent the removal does not have parental responsibility and does not otherwise have the right to determine a child's habitual residence, it is essential that there is in existence, before the removal from England and Wales, an order which either expressly prohibits removal or gives the person parental responsibility or in some other way confers on that person the right to determine the child's habitual residence. Otherwise, the person removing the child will act lawfully. Moreover, the English court may not have jurisdiction to make an order after the child has been removed in circumstances where the child's English habitual residence has ended on removal; if the person removing the child has sole parental responsibility, it is possible for the child's habitual residence to cease as a result of that person's unilateral act.[58] As the circumstances in the two cases of *Re W (Minors) (Abduction: Father's Rights)*, *Re B (A Minor) (Abduction: Father's Rights)*[59] make clear, this is particularly relevant in respect of an unmarried father.

9.24   After a removal, an order is sometimes essential before seeking a return and, even if not a prerequisite, is usually advisable.[60]

9.25   Where the court fears that the parent with whom a child lives may remove the child unlawfully and irretrievably from the United Kingdom, the court may order that the child reside with the other parent, as happened in *Re K (Residence Order: Securing Contact)*.[61] In that case, there was 'a very serious danger' that the mother, whose application for leave to remove had been refused, would nevertheless remove the child from England, and other preventative measures were inadequate.

Effect throughout the United Kingdom of orders restricting removal

9.26   The position of children abducted within the British Isles is discussed in Chapter 11. However, the effect of s 36 of the Family Law Act 1986 should be noted. It applies to any order made by a court in the United Kingdom or the Isle of Man; but it does not apply to an order made in the Channel Islands.[62] To come within s 36, the order must prohibit the removal of a child under the age of 16 from the United Kingdom or from any specified part of it or from any such territory. Section 36 ceases to apply to the order when the

---

[58] *F v S (Wardship Jurisdiction)* [1991] 2 FLR 349, overruled on the facts *F v S (Wardship: Jurisdiction)* [1993] 2 FLR 686, CA; *Re B-M (Wardship: Jurisdiction)* [1993] 1 FLR 979; *Re S (A Minor) (Custody: Habitual Residence)* [1998] AC 750, [1997] 4 All ER 251, HL. As to jurisdiction in children cases, see Chapters 1 to 5.

[59] [1999] Fam 1, [1998] 2 FLR 146, Hale J.

[60] See **9.3**.

[61] [1999] 1 FLR 583, CA.

[62] The Isle of Man is a 'specified dependent territory': Family Law Act 1986 (Dependent Territories) Order 1991, SI 1991/1723. As to specified dependent territory, see Family Law Act 1986, s 43. The power to extend the provisions of Part I of the Family Law Act 1986 has been exercised in respect of the Isle of Man, but not in respect of the Channel Islands.

child attains the age of 16.[63] An order which comes within s 36 has effect in each part of the United Kingdom other than the part in which it was made (a) as if it had been made by the appropriate court in the other part, and (b) in the case of an order which has the effect of prohibiting the child's removal to that other part, as if it had included a prohibition on his further removal to any place except one to which he could be removed consistently with the order.[64]

Automatic prohibitions on removal

9.27 A person may prevent the lawful removal of a child by obtaining an order which carries with it an automatic prohibition on removal of the child from the jurisdiction.[65]

Parental responsibility

9.28 Where there is no residence order (made under the Children Act 1989) in force, no person may remove a child permanently from England and Wales unless all those with parental responsibility agree or the leave of the court is obtained.[66] As Hale J authoritatively demonstrated in *Re W (Minors) (Abduction: Father's Rights), Re B (Minors) (Abduction: Father's Rights)*,[67] the key concept in this field is parental responsibility, which in English law means 'all the rights, duties, powers, responsibilities and authority which by law a parent of a child has in relation to the child and his property';[68] as the Court of Appeal in *Re M (Minors) (Residence Orders: Jurisdiction)*[69] made clear, it includes the right to determine where a child shall live. The importance of parental responsibility in this context is reinforced by s 1 of the Child Abduction Act 1984. As we have seen above, s 1(1) makes it an offence for a parent to take or send a child out of the United Kingdom without 'the appropriate consent' which, in effect, is the consent of all those with parental responsibility; in this way, an important limitation is placed on the power under s 2(7) of the Children Act 1989 of each of those with parental responsibility to 'act alone and without the other (or others) in meeting that responsibility'. We have already referred to the relevance for the unmarried father who does not automatically acquire parental responsibility.[70]

---

63 Family Law Act 1986, s 36(4).
64 *Ibid*, s 36(1), (2). The references to prohibitions on a child's removal include references to prohibitions subject to exceptions; and in a case where removal is prohibited except with the consent of the court, nothing is to be construed as affecting the identity of the court whose consent is required; see s 36(3). See generally Chapter 11.
65 See generally Chapter 6.
66 *Re W (Minors) (Abduction: Father's Rights), Re B (A Minor) (Abduction: Father's Rights)* [1999] Fam 1, [1998] 2 FLR 146, CA.
67 [1999] Fam 1, Hale J.
68 Children Act 1989, s 3(1).
69 [1993] 1 FLR 495 at 499E.
70 Children Act 1989, s 2(2). However, as from a date to be appointed, s 4 of the Children Act 1989 is amended to provided that an unmarried father registered on the birth certificate

Residence order

9.29   Where a residence order is in force with respect to a child, no person may remove him from the United Kingdom without the written consent of every person who has parental responsibility for him or the leave of the court.[71] For these purposes, the United Kingdom means England and Wales, Scotland and Northern Ireland; neither the Channel Islands nor the Isle of Man is within the United Kingdom.[72] The restriction does not apply to prevent the removal of the child for a period of less than one month by the person in whose favour the residence order is made;[73] the Child Abduction Act 1984 was amended to bring it into line with the Children Act 1989, and s 1(4) and (4A) of the 1984 Act reflects this rule. When making the residence order, the court may grant the necessary leave to remove the child either generally or for specified purposes.[74] The requisite consents or leave of the court are no longer necessary to remove a child from England and Wales to another part of the United Kingdom.

Wardship

9.30   'The origins of wardship are buried deep in the murky history of feudal times.'[75] Since at least the seventeenth century, a ward of court may not be removed from England and Wales except with the leave of the High Court;[76] no order of the court is necessary.[77] This rule of law is modified by the Family

---

after the amendment is brought into force thereby acquires parental responsibility: see Adoption and Children Act 2002, s 111.

[71]   Children Act 1989, s 13(1)(b). As to parental responsibility, see s 3, and *Rayden and Jackson on Divorce and Family Matters*, 17th edn (Butterworths), para 39.6 *et seq*.

As from a date to be appointed, Children Act 1989 is amended by the insertion of new sections, ss 14A–14G, which give the court power to appoint a 'special guardian' for the child: Adoption and Children Act 2002, s 115. Where a special guardianship order is in force, no person may remove the child from the United Kingdom without either the written consent of every person with parental responsibility or the leave of the court; however, this does not prevent the removal for a period of less than 3 months by the special guardian: Children Act 1989, s 14C.

[72]   United Kingdom is defined as Great Britain and Northern Ireland; Great Britain means England, Scotland and Wales: Interpretation Act 1978, s 5, Sch 1. Neither the Channel Islands nor the Isle of Man is within the United Kingdom; however, some sections of the Family Law Act 1986 are extended to the Isle of Man: see Family Law Act 1986 (Dependent Territories) Order 1991, SI 1991/1723.

[73]   Children Act 1989, s 13(2).

[74]   *Ibid*, s 13(3).

[75]   *Re Z (A Minor) (Freedom of Publication)* [1997] Fam 1 at 12, [1996] 1 FLR 191 at 196, per Ward LJ. See also **4.5**, and Lowe and White, *Wards of Court*, 2nd edn (Barry Rose, 1986). It might be noted that in Scotland there is no wardship jurisdiction.

[76]   *Foster v Denny* (1677) 2 Cas 237; *Mountstuart v Mountstuart* (1801) 6 Ves 363; *De Manneville v De Manneville* (1804) 10 Ves 52 at 56; *Campbell v Mackay* (1837) 2 My & Cr 31; *Re Thomas* (1853) 22 LJ 1075; *Rochford v Hackman* (1854) Kay 308; *Dawson v Jay, Re Dawson* (1854) 3 De GM & G 764; *Hope v Hope* (1854) 4 De GM & G 328. As to obtaining leave to remove a child permanently from the jurisdiction, see Chapter 7 above.

[77]   Family Law Act 1986, s 38(1).

Law Act 1986 to the effect that if a child is habitually resident in another part of the United Kingdom or specified dependent territory[78] or divorce, nullity or judicial separation proceedings are continuing there, the child can freely move there.[79]

9.31 In 1993, in *Re T (A Minor) (Wardship: Representation)*,[80] a case not involving international issues, the Court of Appeal gave guidance that wardship should be invoked only where the particular circumstances indicate that a question concerning a child cannot be as effectively resolved under the Children Act 1989, which had come into force in October 1991. Wardship has an important continuing role to curb abduction, particularly, as Thorpe LJ pointed out in *Re H (Abduction: Rights of Custody)*,[81] where one of the jurisdictions concerned is not a signatory to the 1980 Hague Abduction Convention. Because of the speed with which a child may be made a ward of court,[82] it is advantageous to invoke the wardship jurisdiction where no other proceedings exist. This was done successfully in *Re S (A Minor) (Custody: Habitual Residence)*.[83] Furthermore, unlike the automatic restriction where a residence order is in force, removal from the jurisdiction of a ward without court leave is a contempt of court;[84] and the court can then deploy its enforcement powers, such as sequestration. Unless other court proceedings are already in existence, it is normally quicker to make the child a ward of court – at least in the first instance. Nevertheless, the disadvantage of wardship should not be overlooked: namely that it is unlikely that more than a few jurisdictions will be familiar with the concept, procedures and remedies associated with wardship.

Pending proceedings

9.32 In English law, there is no general provision prohibiting the removal of a child who is the subject of pending proceedings before a court.[85] This

---

[78] Family Law Act 1986, s 43; only the Isle of Man has been so specific: see **6.13**.

[79] *Ibid*, s 38: see **6.14**.

[80] [1994] Fam 49, [1993] 2 FLR 278.

[81] The decision in the Court of Appeal is reported at [2000] 1 FLR 201; this aspect of the judgment of Thorpe LJ was not disapproved in the House of Lords: [2000] AC 291, [2000] 1 FLR 374.

[82] A minor becomes a ward of the High Court automatically on the issuing of the application (by originating summons) unless he is the subject of a care order (see Supreme Court Act 1981, s 41), although the wardship will lapse in due course unless confirmed by an order (see FPR 1991, r 5.3). A judge can order that a child become a ward, and in an emergency such an order can be made ex parte (ie without notice): see Supreme Court Act 1981, s 41.

[83] [1998] AC 750, [1998] 1 FLR 122, HL.

[84] *Hockly v Lukin* (1762) 1 Dick 353; *Lord Wellesley's Case* (1831) 2 Russ & M 639; *Harrison v Goodall* (1852) Kay 310; *Re J (An Infant)* (1913) 108 LT 554; cf *Re P (Minors) (Custody Orders: Penal Notice)* [1990] 1 WLR 613, CA; *D v D (Access: Contempt: Committal)* [1991] 2 FLR 34, CA.

[85] *Re W (Minors) (Abduction: Father's Rights), Re B (Minors) (Abduction: Father's Rights)* [1999] Fam 1, Hale J.

contrasts with the law in some other jurisdictions: for example, in Australia, s 65Z of the Family Law Act 1975 (Cth) makes it an offence for any party to pending proceedings about the future of a child to take that child abroad without the consent of all the other parties to the proceedings or a court order made since the proceedings began. The circumstances in which pending proceedings can invest a court with rights of custody for the purposes of Art 3 of the 1980 Hague Abduction Convention are discussed in Chapter 14.

Orders, mirror orders and other measures to ensure return where temporary removal permitted

9.33   Where contact is to take place outside England and Wales, there may be a risk that the child will not be returned at the end of the contact period. In *Re R (Child Abduction: Acquiescence)*,[86] Hale J pointed out that one of the purposes of the 1980 Hague Abduction Convention is that it enables the custodial parent to agree to contact outside the jurisdiction:

> 'when parents separate and they live in different countries, it is in the highest degree important for the welfare of the children generally that the custodial parent in one country ... can send the children for visitation access or contact ... to the non-custodial parent in the confident belief that at the end of that period the children will be returned pursuant to any agreement or order of the court that already exists ... [If] a custodial parent fears that a child may not be returned ... [he] will be reluctant to send the children for access and that must be to the detriment of children generally.'

9.34   While the risk of a failure to return is less if the 1980 Hague Abduction Convention or 1980 European Custody Convention[87] are available to enforce a return, even a return from a Hague or European Convention country may not be without difficulty and cost. The safeguards discussed here should be considered in the light of the practical experience of the operation of the Conventions in the country concerned.

Orders as to return and residence

9.35   To meet the risk of a failure to return, it is prudent to include in the contact order an order that the child be returned to England and Wales at the end of any period of contact;[88] alternatively, the English court may be willing to accept an undertaking to the court in the same terms,[89] as was given in *F v F (Minors) (Custody: Foreign Order)*[90] in connection with contact in France. However, the courts of a foreign country may not understand the status and effect of an undertaking given to the English court, and an express order is

---

[86]   [1995] 1 FLR 716 at 731.

[87]   Or the Brussels II Council Regulation (or any replacement): see Chapter 18.

[88]   As to contact orders generally, see *Rayden and Jackson on Divorce and Family Matters*, 17th edn (Butterworths), para 40.41.

[89]   As to undertakings and safe harbour orders in the context of the 1980 Hague Abduction Convention, see **17.123** *et seq*.

[90]   [1989] Fam 1 at 16, [1988] 3 WLR 959, sub nom *Re F (Minors: Foreign Order)* [1989] 1 FLR 335.

therefore often preferable. The 2003 Council of Europe Convention on Contact Concerning Children[91] includes, among suggested mechanisms to safeguard the child at the end of a cross-border contact visit, the giving of undertakings or stipulations.

9.36 Consideration should also be given to whether there should be an order making it plain that the child's home is in England with the primary carer. Although the Children Act 1989 gives prominence to the so-called 'no order' principle,[92] this would provide a good reason to make a residence order, even though there may be ostensible agreement about the child's residence. In this connection, it is important to bear in mind that the English order must appear unambiguous to the foreign court as to the requirements to return the child after contact and to the child residing in England.

9.37 Following the guidance given by the Court of Appeal in 1999 in *Re K (A Minor) (Removal from Jurisdiction: Practice)*[93] the trial court (and advisers) should consider not only the risk of the child not being returned after a period of contact, but also the magnitude of the consequence of the failure to comply with the obligation to return the child at the end of contact. Where the consequence would have a major impact on the well-being of the child, for example a prolonged period away from home with his or her education disrupted or an irretrievable separation of the child from his or her previous roots, advisers, and if necessary the court, should seek to achieve what security they can for the child by building in all practical safeguards.

Mirror orders

9.38 In addition to the express orders already referred to, advisers and the court should explore the practicalities of registering the English order in the foreign country or of obtaining an order in the foreign country to similar effect to that made by the English court. These latter orders are often referred to as 'mirror orders'. In *F v F (Minors) (Custody: Foreign Order)*[94] Booth J directed that no access take place in France until such time as either the English order was registered and enforceable in France under the 1980 European Custody Convention or an order in the same terms as to custody and access was made and was enforceable in France. In *Re S (Removal from Jurisdiction)*,[95] permission to remove a child from England to live in Chile was made conditional upon the mother obtaining the authentication of the English order giving contact to the father, a procedure known as *exequator*, in the Chilean Supreme Court. In *Re T (Staying Contact in Non-Convention Country) (Note)*,[96] the father gave an undertaking to make a notarised agreement with

---

91   See Chapter 25. The text is set out in Appendix 1 in Part V below. The United Kingdom has not ratified the 2003 Convention.
92   Section 1(5).
93   [1999] 2 FLR 1084, CA.
94   [1989] Fam 1 at 16, sub nom *Re F (Minors) (Custody: Foreign Order)* [1989] 1 FLR 335 at 348.
95   [1999] 1 FLR 850.
96   [1999] 1 FLR 262.

the mother and other relations to provide that an application would be made to obtain a mirror order in Egypt where the staying contact as ordered by the English court was to take place.

Registering orders

9.39   Legislation in the State in which the cross-border access is to take place may provide for the registration of the original access order thereby creating another avenue for mirror orders to be established by registration. The 1980 European Custody Convention[97] provides for the recognition of orders for custody and access. Similarly, the so-called Brussels II Council Regulation provides for recognition of certain custody and access orders.[98] In England and Wales, an incoming order under these instruments is registered (subject to defences) and can be enforced as if it is a domestic order. In Australia, there is provision for the registration of child orders (but not interim or ex parte orders) from certain countries[99] and, if registered, the order is enforceable as a domestic order. However, in respect of registration in Australia, the United Kingdom is not, perhaps surprisingly, a 'prescribed overseas jurisdiction'.

Other measures

9.40   There may, however, be practical difficulties in registering English orders or obtaining mirror orders. In *Re HB (Abduction: Children's Objections to Return)*[100] the English Court of Appeal had suggested that once the primary jurisdiction had been established, mirror orders in Denmark and England might prove useful for the future; yet at the subsequent hearing in England, it emerged that there might be difficulties in obtaining in Denmark an order to mirror the English order and that questions of access were normally dealt with by an administrative authority rather than a court.[101] Therefore, other measures should be explored. Measures include notarised agreements enforceable in the foreign country (giving effect to the English residence and contact orders) or the swearing by those having contact (or indeed by third parties) of a binding oath before the appropriate foreign court that the child will be permitted to return at the end of contact, as was required in *Re T (Staying Contact in Non-Convention Country) (Note)*.[102] In *Re A (Security for Return to Jurisdiction) (Note)*[103] permission was granted for a holiday in Saudi Arabia but the order included provision for sworn declarations on the *Koran* before a Sharià Court by the maternal grandfather and uncle who were not parties to the contact application.

---

[97]   See Chapter 19.
[98]   See Council Regulation (EC) No 1347/2000: see Chapter 18.
[99]   Family Law Act 1975 (Cth) and Sch 1A to the Family Law Regulations 1984.
[100] [1998] 1 FLR 422, CA.
[101] *Re HB (Abduction: Children's Objections) (No 2)* [1999] 1 FLR 564 at 568, per Hale J.
[102] [1999] 1 FLR 262. See also *Re L (Removal from the Jurisdiction: Holiday)* [2001] 1 FLR 241.
[103] [1999] 2 FLR 1.

9.41   The Court of Appeal in *Re K (A Minor) (Removal from the Jurisdiction: Practice)*[104] stressed the desirability of including provision in orders that the primary jurisdiction for the resolution of disputes concerning the child will be England; the aim is to preclude the possibility of competitive litigation in two jurisdictions which may reflect different traditions and cultures. Thus in *Re T (Staying Contact in Non-Convention Country) (Note)*,[105] provision was made for the obtaining of an order in Egypt to ensure that the primary jurisdiction should be exercised by the English court.

9.42   In England, it has been said that these matters should be decided by a judge with appropriate experience, who will usually be a judge of the Family Division; and that the court should hear oral evidence, including expert evidence.[106]

9.43   The court's power to impose a condition upon a contact or other order made under the Children Act 1989 is found either in the express power given by s 11(7) to impose conditions on a section 8 order or in the traditional use of the court's inherent power to attach conditions to its orders; the 1989 Act has not reduced the flexible range of powers available to the court.[107]

Jurisdiction to make a mirror order

9.44   The existence of a jurisdiction in England and Wales to make mirror orders is problematic. It is discussed in Chapter 3.[108]

Requiring a bond or security to ensure a child's return

9.45   Where the court has power to give leave to remove a child from the jurisdiction,[109] there is power in wardship proceedings and in other High Court proceedings[110] to require the person given leave to provide a bond or other security to ensure that the child will be returned. Guidance was given in 1987 by the Family Division Sub-Committee of the Supreme Court Procedure Committee.[111] It is set out below:

> 'Guidance by Family Division Sub-Committee of the Supreme Court Procedure Committee, with the concurrence of the President, as to forms of security where temporary leave to remove from the jurisdiction is sought. In proper cases one or more of the following safeguards can be adopted by the court:

---

[104]   [1999] 2 FLR 1084. See also **7.38**.

[105]   [1999] 1 FLR 262.

[106]   *Re K (A Minor) (Removal from the Jurisdiction: Practice)* (above) (a judge of the Family Division should deal with a case which involves consideration of the legal system of a foreign country and which may require mirror orders).

[107]   *Re M (Leave to Remove from the Jurisdiction)* [1999] 2 FLR 334. For a discussion of s 11(7), see White, Carr and Lowe, *Children Act in Practice*, 3rd edn (Butterworths, 2002), at 5.48 *et seq*.

[108]   See **3.43–3.44**.

[109]   As to applications for leave to remove, see Chapter 7.

[110]   There appears to be no reason why this power cannot be exercised in other High Court proceedings.

[111]   [1987] Fam Law 263.

(1) An undertaking by the removing parent to enter into a bond with the registrar [now District Judge] of the court in an appropriate sum to secure compliance with the order. If the condition of the bond is broken, the court can consider an application along the lines envisaged by s 135(4) of the Supreme Court Act 1981 to assign the bond to the injured parent to provide a fund to cover the cost of recovering the child from the foreign jurisdiction. As yet, no rules have been made under s 135.

(2) An undertaking to procure a surety (or sureties) to be similarly bound. This surety could be a bank or other financial institution or some other person acceptable to the court.

(3) The provision of further security for the due performance of the bond by way of a deposit of money or a charge on some property, for example the applicant's shares or his home. The problem is that charging land may not always be possible or practicable. It may be easy enough to charge unregistered, unencumbered land by deposit of the title deeds with the applicant's solicitors who can, in turn, undertake, without leave of the court, not to release the deeds until satisfied that the child has returned. If the property is jointly owned or encumbered, then the consent of those interested parties must be obtained. The proper inquiries must also be made of those in actual occupation of land to which they claim to be beneficially entitled. If completely effective protection is to be achieved, then the charge must be registered.

In view of the cost and delay in providing the full panoply of protection, the committee emphasises that all of these steps may only be required when it is considered that there is a real danger that the child may not be returned. Nothing in this Guidance is intended to lead to the imposition of these safeguards as a matter of course and to create as the rule what is intended to apply to the exceptional case only. The court will continue to hold the delicate balance between, on the one hand, having the power to insist on solid security to ensure compliance with its orders and, on the other hand, not so regularly imposing onerous obligations that a well-intentioned applicant may be discouraged from applying at all or a vindictive parent may abuse the process by unnecessarily seeking security simply out of spite.

Where a bond is required, an appropriate form of deed would be as follows:

"We AB of and CD of are jointly and severally bound to the [District Judge] of [the court] in the sum of [   ] for the payment of which we bind ourselves and each of us and our [executors and administrators] [successors]. The condition of this obligation is that if XY (the removing parent) complies with the order dated and returns the child(ren) VY and WY to the jurisdiction as required by the said order, then this obligation shall be void and of no effect, but shall otherwise remain in full force and effect.

Signed, sealed and delivered, etc.'"

9.46 In the event of the condition of the bond being broken, the court may assign the bond to the injured party to provide a fund to cover the cost of recovering the child. Such a bond or security should be required only where there is a real danger that the child may not be returned. The normal practice is for the bond or other security to be imposed by consent and as a condition precedent to the grant of leave to remove and not by way of a direct order imposing it.[112] In *Re T (Staying Contact in Non-Convention Country) (Note)*,[113] a further measure to ensure the return of the child following contact in Egypt was the giving of a bond by the father. In *Re L (Removal from Jurisdiction: Holiday)*,[114] the parent seeking contact out of England was required to deposit £50,000 with the court by way of a bond or security. The 2003 Council of Europe Convention on Contact Concerning Children[115] includes, among suggested mechanisms to safeguard the child at the end of a cross-border contact visit, the giving of financial guarantees and charges over property.

9.47   Where there has been an earlier contempt of the English court, there is power to take security for good behaviour.[116]

Passports: ordering surrender and preventing reissue

Ordering surrender of passports: statutory power

9.48   Under the provisions of s 37 of the Family Law Act 1986, where there is in force an order prohibiting or otherwise restricting the removal of a child from the United Kingdom or any specified part of it or the Isle of Man,[117] the court by which the order was in fact made (or by which it is treated under s 36 of the Family Law Act 1986[118] as having been made) may require any person to surrender any UK passport[119] which has been issued to, or contains particulars of, the child. This provision therefore applies to abductions or threatened abductions within the United Kingdom and from the United Kingdom. However, it will be noted that the provisions relate only to current passports issued by the Government of the United Kingdom.[120] To prevent reissue of a UK passport, the court notifies the Passport Agency in every case where such surrender has been ordered;[121] but it should be noted that the court does not notify the Passport Agency when only an order restricting removal from the jurisdiction is made. It may be prudent for the

---

[112]   *Re H (Minors) (Wardship: Surety)* [1991] 1 FLR 40, CA.

[113]   [1999] 1 FLR 262, discussed at **9.40**.

[114]   [2001] 1 FLR 241.

[115]   See Chapter 25. The text is set out in Appendix 1 in Part V. The United Kingdom has not yet ratified the 2003 Convention.

[116]   RSC Ord 52, r 9, which continues to apply to family proceedings: see FPR 1991, r 1.3 and CPR 1998, r 2.1; *Skipworth's and the Defendant's Case* (1873) LR 9 QB 230 at 241.

[117]   The Isle of Man is a specified dependent territory: Family Law Act 1986 (Dependent Territories) Order 1991, SI 1991/1723.

[118]   See **11.5**.

[119]   Family Law Act 1986, s 37(2).

[120]   *Ibid*, s 37(1). Since 5 October 1998 it is no longer possible to apply to put children on the passport of an adult. Instead, applications have to be made for children to be issued with their own passports, although adults' passports with their children's names already on them remain valid, see **9.54**.

[121]   *Practice Direction* [1983] 1 WLR 558, [1983] 2 All ER 253.

person fearing abduction to notify the Passport Agency of any orders restricting the issue, or requiring the surrender, of passports; and, if that person has parental responsibility, of his or her objection to the issue of a passport.

Ordering surrender of passports: inherent power

9.49 The inherent power of the High Court is wider than the statutory power. The High Court has an inherent power to order the surrender of a passport held by a person whom the court fears might remove the child, whether or not it contains particulars of the child and whether or not it is a UK passport.[122] When, for example, a child is brought to England unlawfully and a parent seeks the peremptory return of the child to the country of origin, it is normal to order at the outset that, until the hearing, the defendant, whether or not he or she holds a British passport or a passport of another country, does not leave England and surrenders his or her passport and the passport of the child. Such an order is made either under s 5 or under s 19 of the Child Abduction and Custody Act 1985, if applicable,[123] or pursuant to the court's inherent power.[124] Another example is where a foreign parent or a British parent with foreign connections, who might be disposed to misuse a period of contact in England in order to remove the child overseas, is ordered in the exercise of the inherent power to surrender his or her passport. In *Re A-K (Foreign Passport: Jurisdiction)*,[125] the Court of Appeal dismissed an appeal by a father from the making of an order that, for the purposes of the contact in England, the father surrender his Iranian passport, to be held by his solicitors on their undertaking to the court not to release it except with the agreement of mother's solicitors or the permission of the court; the complaint that such an order was not necessary and restricted his freedom of movement was rejected.

9.50 The court may also order the surrender of a passport pending compliance with an order to return a child to England and Wales. In *Re A (Return of Passport)*[126] a father was held to be in contempt for failing to comply with an order to return the children from Bangladesh; Hale J ordered the father to surrender his passport to be held until further order; Johnson J at a later hearing ordered the release of the passport to the father to enable him to go to Bangladesh to collect the children, but the Court of Appeal reversed this order.

---

[122] As to the power to restrain a person from leaving the jurisdiction, see **9.60**. As to the powers of the High Court in cases under the 1980 Hague Abduction Convention and the 1980 European Custody Convention, see Chapters 12–17 and 19 respectively.

[123] See Chapters 12–17 and 19 respectively.

[124] *B v B (Injunction: Jurisdiction)* [1998] 1 WLR 329, sub nom *B v B (Injunction: Restraint on Leaving Jurisdiction)* [1997] 2 FLR 148, approved in *Gough v Chief Constable of the Derbyshire Constabulary* [2002] 2 All ER 985 at [53], [57], CA.

[125] [1997] 2 FLR 569.

[126] [1997] 2 FLR 137, CA

9.51   On surrender, the passport may be held by the court, but one of the parties' solicitors usually agrees to hold the passport to the order of the court. In such circumstances, the Court of Appeal has emphasised in *Al-Khandri v JR Brown & Co*[127] that the solicitor owes not only a duty to the court but a duty of care to the party for whose protection the passport is held.

Preventing the issue or reissue of passports

9.52   The United Kingdom Passport Agency has published guidance on the circumstances in which it will not grant passport facilities to children following the lodging of objections by parents or others or where a child is a ward of court.[128] Otherwise passport facilities are normally granted to children with the consent of either parent (or person acting in *loco parentis* or with parental responsibility); where parents are not married to each other, the mother's consent is required unless the father has parental responsibility.[129] Where the child is entitled to passport facilities from a country other than the United Kingdom, contact should be made with the relevant embassy or consulate; however, under English law, the consulate or embassy is not required to comply with any request made to it not to issue a passport. Furthermore, the English court cannot order a foreign embassy or consulate to comply with such a request.[130]

9.53   The court can grant an injunction[131] or make a prohibited steps order[132] prohibiting a person from applying for a passport for a child. In *Re S (Leave to Remove from Jurisdiction: Securing Return from Holiday)*[133] the mother was ordered not to surrender the children's British passports while in India on holiday, nor to apply for Indian passports or citizenship;[134] and, furthermore, the order was required to be served on the Indian High Commission in London and the British High Commission in Delhi.

9.54   Since 5 October 1998 it has no longer been possible to apply to put children on the passport of an adult. Instead, applications have to be made for children to be issued with their own passports. Children already included in parents' passports can continue to travel on these passports until they reach the age of 16 or the passport expires or is amended.

All Ports Warning system

9.55   Where there is a real and imminent threat that a child is about to be removed from the United Kingdom, the applicant or his solicitor may contact

---

127   [1988] QB 665, [1988] 2 WLR 671, CA.
128   [1994] Fam Law 651. The guidance is set out below in Appendix 3.
129   As to parental responsibility, see **9.28**.
130   Diplomatic Privileges Act 1964 and State Immunity Act 1978. See also **21.35**.
131   As to injunctions, see *Rayden and Jackson on Divorce and Family Matters*, 17th edn (Butterworths), paras 32.71 and 39.2, note 17.
132   Children Act 1989, s 8.
133   [2001] 2 FLR 507.
134   She was also ordered to apply only for 3-month visitor visas to India.

a police station and request a Port Alert. The procedure is set out in a Practice Direction[135] and in the Home Office Circular 21/1986. A request should not be sought merely by way of insurance. The request should normally be to the applicant's local police station, but in urgent cases, contact may be made with any police station. If it is considered appropriate by the police, they will institute the Port Alert system to try to prevent removal from the jurisdiction. They will circulate information about the child, the person likely to remove him and to whom he should be returned if intercepted to police at all sea ports and airports in the United Kingdom and to the Police National Ports Office via the police national computer. The Police National Ports Office transmits a daily summary (known as 'the child warning list') of all such circulations to all police units at all sea ports and airports, who pass it to the Immigration Service and in appropriate circumstances to HM Customs. For an effective application, the request should contain as much of the information set out in the Practice Direction as possible.[136] The child's name will remain on the stop list under the Port Alert for 4 weeks. After that time it will be removed automatically unless a further request for a Port Alert is made.

9.56 It is not necessary first to obtain a court order in respect of a child under 16 years before a request is made. If an order has been made, it should be produced to the police. Where the child is aged between 16 and 18 years, it is a prerequisite that there is an order restricting the child's removal from the United Kingdom. Where the child is a ward of court, evidence of this must be produced to the police.

9.57 In cases where the threat of removal may not easily be apparent but is in fact real and imminent, the applicant can ask the court to include in the order being made a request by the court for a Port Alert. On very rare occasions, when no one else is able to institute a Port Alert, it may be necessary for the High Court or the Court of Appeal to direct that the National Ports Office institute a Port Alert.[137]

9.58 In practice, the Port Alert system operates to identify children or adults connected with them coming into the United Kingdom as well as those attempting to leave the United Kingdom. Where a Port Alert has been instituted but the need for it has passed, the police should be informed in

---

[135] *Registrar's Direction (Children: Removal from Jurisdiction)* [1986] 1 WLR 475, [1986] 2 FLR 89.
[136] Including:
   Name, sex, date of birth, description and passport number of child;
   Name, sex, description, nationality and passport number of the abductor;
   Their relationship;
   Whether the child will assist in the removal;
   Name, relationship, nationality, and telephone number of the applicant;
   Solicitor's name and telephone number;
   Likely time of arrival, port of embarkation and port of destination.
[137] Recent guidance on the out-of-hours procedure and a model order provided by the Child Abduction Unit of the Lord Chancellor's Department are set out in Appendix 3 below.

order that their records can be amended and, if the Port Alert is still current, an unnecessary stop avoided.

9.59 With the ending of routine embarkation controls in 1998 the effectiveness of this preventative measure is dependant on the liaison between the police at individual air and sea ports and the security staff at those ports. However, it remains available in conjunction with other preventative measures to deter potential abductors; in 1999, the details of 774 children were circulated on the Child Abduction Warning List.[138] The Immigration Service's Border Agencies Working Group carried out an Embarkation Control Review at the request of the Home Secretary and reported to the Home Secretary in 1999; among other recommendations, it recommended improved awareness training for airport security staff in handling the child warning list. The effectiveness of the Port Alert system is likely to be increased with improvements in technology at points of departure from and entry to the United Kingdom. The ending of the system of placing a child on a parent's passport has added to its effectiveness.[139]

Restraining a person from leaving the jurisdiction

9.60 When it is feared that a child may be abducted from England or from the United Kingdom, the court has power to restrain a person from leaving the jurisdiction. Thus when, for example, a child is brought to England unlawfully and a parent seeks the peremptory return of the child to the country of origin under the 1980 Hague Abduction Convention or under the inherent jurisdiction, it is normal to order[140] at the outset that, until the hearing, the defendant do not leave England and do surrender his or her passports and the passports of the child. Such an order is made either under s 5 or s 19 of the Child Abduction and Custody Act 1985, if applicable, or pursuant to the court's inherent power.[141] The High Court's jurisdiction to make orders restraining a person from leaving the jurisdiction if it is necessary in order to protect the welfare of the child in the proceedings before it is well established. In *Re J (A Minor) (Wardship)*,[142] in 1987, an order was made ex parte (and continued inter partes)[143] restraining a mother from leaving the jurisdiction before a blood test to establish the ward's parentage had been carried out; the power was available to assist the court in providing for the welfare and future upbringing of the child. As was stressed in *Re J*, the order is

---

[138] Source: National Ports Office; the figure for 1997 was 704 and for 1998 was 700.

[139] See **9.54**.

[140] For the various orders which may be made, see Chapter 21 where passport orders, location orders and collection orders are discussed.

[141] *B v B (Injunction: Jurisdiction)* [1998] 1 WLR 329, sub nom *B v B (Injunction: Restraint on Leaving Jurisdiction)* [1997] 3 All ER 258, [1997] 2 FLR 148, approved in *Gough v Chief Constable of the Derbyshire Constabulary* [2002] 2 All ER 985 at [53], [57], CA.

[142] [1988] 1 FLR 65.

[143] *Re I (A Minor)* (1987) *The Times*, 22 May.

an interference with the freedom of the individual, so the period of the order should be no longer than is necessary for the purpose it is intended to serve.[144]

The future: judicial co-operation

9.61   Considerations of comity have long played a part in the approach of the English and other common law jurisdictions. In English law in the nineteenth century, the foreign order was generally determinative of the decision in England relating to a foreign child, as in *Nugent v Vetzera*.[145] Since the paramountcy given to the welfare of the child, comity has remained a material consideration: thus, in the Judicial Committee of the Privy Council in 1951 in *McKee v McKee*[146] Lord Simmonds stated that, although the Ontario court should give independent judgment to the merits of the child's welfare, reasons of comity demanded that the Californian order be given grave consideration by the Ontario court. International Conventions may lessen the problems of competing jurisdictions in children cases.[147] Closer co-operation internationally between the courts of different States has an important part to play and is to be welcomed as a contribution to preventing abduction, to preventing the abductor from benefiting from his unwise actions and generally to securing the best interests of the child. In *Re HB (Abduction: Children's Objections)*,[148] Thorpe LJ suggested that:

> '... it is important ... that the court systems in each jurisdiction should equally act in concert. Once the primary jurisdiction is established then mirror orders in the other and the effective use of the Convention gives the opportunity for collaborative judicial function. The Danish judge and the English judge should in any future proceedings if possible be in direct communication.'

9.62   This spirit of judicial collaboration was enthusiastically put into practice between England and California in *Re M and J (Abduction: International Judicial Collaboration)*;[149] the judge of the Family Division of the English High Court liaised directly: first with the criminal court judge in California, who recalled and suspended the abductor's warrant of imprisonment until the child issues had been resolved in California; and secondly, with the Californian family court judge, who arranged for an early listing of the children case in California; the English judge also requested Official Solicitor to investigate and report on the children's circumstances in England, to which they had been abducted, and the report was sent to Californian judge who would hear the children case

---

[144]   See further *Gough v Chief Constable of the Derbyshire Constabulary* [2002] 2 All ER 985, CA.

[145]   (1866) LR 2 Eq 704 at 714. *Aliter* if the child was a British subject: see *Dawson v Jay* (1854) 3 De G M&G 764.

[146]   [1951] AC 352.

[147]   For example, the 1996 Hague Convention on Jurisdiction, Applicable Law, Recognition, Enforcement and Co-operation in Respect of Parental Responsibility and Measures for the Protection of Children (discussed in Chapter 24 below) or the 2003 Council of Europe Convention on Contact Concerning Children (discussed in Chapter 25 below). See also the Brussels II Council Regulation discussed in Chapter 18.

[148]   [1998] 1 FLR 422.

[149]   [2000] 1 FLR 803.

if an order for return under the Hague Abduction Convention were made. It is important where a judge hearing a case proposes to communicate with a judge in another jurisdiction that the consent of the parties is obtained; alternatively, that the judge should make known his intentions and invite submissions from the parties on the point. Equally importantly, the content of the communication should be made known to the parties.[150]

9.63   International judicial conferences in the field of child abduction are becoming more common. Four UK–German judicial conferences have been held in recent years; in September 2000, a common law judicial conference was held in Washington DC with participation by the judiciary of the United States, the United Kingdom, Australia, New Zealand, Canada and Eire. In some jurisdictions, such as England and Wales,[151] international liaison judges have been appointed. Bilateral arrangements between States often make provision for judicial co-operation.[152]

---

[150]   As to the provisions in the United States for communication between courts of different States, including courts in foreign countries, see **5.17**. See also the observations of Hong Kong SAR Court of Appeal in *D v G* (4 December 2001, CACV 3646/2001) at [24]–[25].

[151]   New Zealand, Australia, California and Quebec are among some of the other jurisdictions with liaison judges.

[152]   See generally Chapter 18.

Chapter 10

TRACING AN ABDUCTED CHILD

INTRODUCTION

10.1 This chapter deals with the steps which can be taken to trace the whereabouts of a child after his abduction from his home in England and Wales or after his abduction from another part of the United Kingdom or from a country outside the United Kingdom. The choice of remedy once the child has been found will depend on where he is and is considered in elsewhere in this book.

(i)   If the child has been abducted to or from another part of the United Kingdom, the steps to obtain his recovery are dealt with in Chapter 11.

(ii) If the child has been abducted to or from a country which is a party to either the 1980 Hague Abduction Convention or the 1980 European Custody Convention, the steps to be taken to obtain his recovery are dealt with in Chapters 12–17 and 19.

(iii) If the child has been abducted to or from a Member State of the European Union, the steps to be taken to obtain his recovery are dealt with in Chapter 18.

(iv) If the child has been abducted to or from a country outside the United Kingdom which is not a party to the Hague or European Conventions, the steps to be taken to obtain his recovery are dealt with in Chapter 20.

POWER TO ORDER DISCLOSURE OF CHILD'S WHEREABOUTS: STATUTORY POWERS

Section 33 of Family Law Act 1986

10.2 Section 33 of the Family Law Act 1986 confers a general power on all courts in proceedings for, or relating to, a Part I order, as defined for the purposes of that statute, to require disclosure of the child's whereabouts.[1] This statutory power is given to courts in England and Wales, Scotland and Northern Ireland and also, by the Family Law Act 1986 (Dependent Territories) Order 1991,[2] to courts in the Isle of Man.

10.3 Part I proceedings are proceedings for a 'Part I order', which is defined by s 1(1)(a) to mean a s 8 order made under the Children Act 1989[3] (but not variations or discharges) and by s 1(1)(d) to mean an order[4] made under the

---

[1]   References to Part I proceedings in respect of a child are references to any proceedings for a Part I order: Family Law Act 1986, s 42(7). As to the meaning of a 'Part I order', see **3.2** and **10.3**.

[2]   SI 1991/1732, and Family Law Act 1986, s 43, which define 'dependent territory' for the purposes of the 1986 Act. Note that the 1986 Act has not yet been extended to the Channel Islands.

[3]   It also includes any order which would have been a 'custody order' by virtue of Family Law Act 1986, s 1 before amendment by the Children Act 1989: see Family Law Act 1986, s 1(3).

[4]   *Ibid.*

High Court's inherent jurisdiction with respect to children, giving care of the child to any person or providing for contact with or the education of the child, excluding variations or discharges of such orders. Orders that simply protect the child, such as collection and location orders (formerly known as seek and find orders), are therefore not Part I orders. 'Part I order' is given an extended meaning for the purposes of s 33 to include existing orders under pre-Children Act 1989 statutes.[5]

10.4 Proceedings under the 1980 Hague Abduction Convention and the 1980 European Custody Convention are not Part I proceedings, but proceedings taken following a non-Convention abduction may well be Part I proceedings. However, under either of the aforementioned Conventions, the Central Authorities may be able to play a role in locating the child.[6]

10.5 Where, in proceedings for, or relating to, a Part I order as extended, adequate information as to the child's whereabouts is not available, the court may order any person it has reason to believe may have relevant information to disclose it to the court.[7] The Court of Appeal, in *S v S (Chief Constable of West Yorkshire Police Intervening)*,[8] drew attention to the words of the section, which make plain that the order should require disclosure to the court, not to the party or his or her lawyers.

The requirement to disclose: self-incrimination

10.6 A person is not excused from complying with such an order by reason that to do so may incriminate him or his spouse of an offence; but a statement or admission made in compliance with such an order is not admissible in evidence against either of them in proceedings for any offence other than perjury.[9] This provision is analogous to s 98 of the Children Act 1989.[10] As was pointed out in the leading case, *Re C (A Minor) (Care Proceedings: Disclosure)*,[11] the protection given by s 98 gives protection only against statements being used in evidence in criminal proceedings and does not

---

[5] Reference should be made to the precise terms of Family Law Act 1986, ss 40(1) and 32. The extended meaning applies to the recognition and enforcement provisions and the supplementary provisions of the 1986 Act.

[6] See respectively **13.24–13.26** and **19.19**.

[7] Family Law Act 1986, s 33(1). Similar provisions are enacted in relation to courts in Scotland: see s 33(3).

[8] [1998] 1 WLR 1716, [1999] 1 All ER 281, sub nom *Chief Constable of West Yorkshire Police v S* [1998] 2 FLR 973, CA.

[9] Family Law Act 1986, s 33(2).

[10] As to Children Act 1989, s 98, see *Rayden and Jackson on Divorce and Family Matters*, 17th edn (Butterworths), para 38.28 and White, Carr and Lowe, *Children Act in Practice*, 3rd edn (Butterworths, 2002), 11.64 *et seq*.

[11] [1997] Fam 76, [1997] 2 WLR 322, sub nom *Re EC (Disclosure of Material)* [1996] 2 FLR 725, CA.

prohibit disclosure of a statement or admission to the police to enable them to shape their enquiries. The court or legal advisers may wish to point this out to a person required to comply with an order under s 33.[12]

10.7 Client's legal professional privilege is overridden to the extent that the solicitor is obliged to disclose all relevant information, including communications from his client which may assist in locating the child, but it is not overridden in any other respect.[13]

10.8 As was discovered when the child was eventually found after many months in *Re D (A Minor) (Child Abduction)*,[14] a case heard early in the life of this new statutory power, whereas the court has power to require witnesses to attend to give information as to the abducted child's whereabouts, there is no power to order a person to give evidence after the child has been found and has been surrendered to the court: the power cannot be used to discover what has been happening in the child's life or to discover who has been involved in the abduction. This limitation has drawbacks when the court is having to assess future risk, but the limitation on the power appropriately reflects the privilege against self-incrimination.

10.9 In proceedings under Part II of the Child Abduction and Custody Act 1985 (ie under the 1980 European Custody Convention), there is power under the Family Proceedings Rules 1991 (FPR 1991) to order any person with relevant information about the child who is the subject of the proceedings to disclose that information and for that purpose to order the person to file an affidavit;[15] but this power does not override the right against self-incrimination.

Orders directed to the police

10.10 It is not routine for the court to direct the police to disclose an address. Indeed, wider considerations of public policy (for example, the need for confidentiality in order to encourage disclosure of information to the police and otherwise to avoid the police becoming unpaid enquiry agents) dictate that such orders should be made only in exceptional circumstances.[16] It was suggested in *S v S (Chief Constable of West Yorkshire Police Intervening)* that if the child is at risk, it may be preferable that the police inform the social

---

[12] *Re C (A Minor) (Care Proceedings: Disclosure)* [1997] Fam 76, [1997] 2 WLR 322, sub nom *Re EC (Disclosure of Material)* [1996] 2 FLR 725, CA, per Swinton Thomas LJ.

[13] *Re B (Abduction: Disclosure)* [1995] 1 FLR 774, CA. See also the discussion at **10.17** below. As to when a solicitor is required voluntarily to disclose information relating to child abuse or child abduction in breach of legal professional privilege, see *Rayden and Jackson on Divorce and Family Matters*, 17th edn (Butterworths), paras 38.24 and 38.27.

[14] [1989] 1 FLR 97.

[15] FPR 1991, r 6.16. As to practice and procedure generally, see Chapter 21.

[16] *S v S (Chief Constable of West Yorkshire Police Intervening)* [1998] 1 WLR 1716, [1999] 1 All ER 281, sub nom *Chief Constable of West Yorkshire Police v S* [1998] 2 FLR 973, CA.

services department or that a seek and find order is made under s 34.[17] Nevertheless, the police cannot give a categorical assurance that the identity of those giving information about a child's whereabouts will remain confidential.[18]

10.11 Arrangements whereby government departments will disclose information are dealt with below.[19]

The order under section 33

10.12 An application under s 33 may be made ex parte (ie without notice).[20] Where it is desirable that the abductor should not be alerted to the existence of an order made under s 33 (or under the inherent jurisdiction as discussed below), the s 33 order should be drawn as a separate order and should include a provision that the existence of the order is not to be disclosed to the abductor.[21] This is particularly appropriate in orders ordering disclosure of information by third parties such as telephone companies, banks, credit card companies and the like, both to assist in the search for the child and to protect the third party. However, it has been said not to be appropriate when the order is directed to a person's solicitor.[22]

The 1980 Hague Abduction Convention and the 1980 European Custody Convention

10.13 We have noted that proceedings under the 1980 Hague Abduction Convention and the 1980 European Custody Convention are not Part I proceedings. Therefore, a power in the same terms as those of a s 33 order is given to the court in proceedings brought under the Child Abduction and Custody Act 1985 in reliance on the Hague and European Conventions.[23]

Child in care

10.14 Where a child is in care or subject to an emergency protection order or in police protection and is unlawfully taken away or kept away from the

---

[17] See **10.36**.

[18] *S v S (Chief Constable of West Yorkshire Police Intervening)* (above).

[19] See **10.23**.

[20] FPR 1991, r 6.17(4). As to the procedure for applying for an order in the High Court or the county court and the form of order, see FPR 1991, r 6.17. For draft orders, see Appendix 4. Breach of the order is a contempt. As to procedure for applying for an order in the magistrates' court, see Family Proceedings Courts (Children Act 1989) Rules 1991 (FPC(CA)R 1991), r 31A; breach of the order is enforced under Magistrates' Courts Act 1980, s 63(3): Children Act 1989, s 14(1).

[21] *Re H (Child Abduction: Whereabouts Order to Solicitors)* [2000] 1 FLR 766 (an order directed to third parties (but not solicitors) may include a term restraining the third party from disclosing to the abductor the fact that an order has been made).

[22] *Ibid*, discussed at **10.18** below.

[23] Child Abduction and Custody Act 1985, s 24A, as inserted by Family Law Act 1986, s 67(4).

responsible person,[24] a recovery order may be made.[25] *Re R (A Minor) (Recovery Order)*[26] confirmed that, in deciding whether to make a recovery order, the child's welfare is the court's paramount consideration. The recovery order operates, *inter alia*, as a direction to any person who is in a position to do so to produce the child on request of an authorised person.[27] A recovery order made in England and Wales has effect in Scotland;[28] separate provisions govern the enforcement of recovery orders in the other parts of the United Kingdom.[29]

POWER TO ORDER DISCLOSURE OF CHILD'S WHEREABOUTS: THE INHERENT JURISDICTION

Wardship and the exercise of the inherent power

10.15 In wardship proceedings, the parties are required to state the whereabouts of the ward and keep the court informed of any changes in the child's whereabouts.[30]

10.16 The High Court has long had, and exercised summarily, a wide power to order, the attendance of any person thought to be in a position to give information as to the whereabouts of a ward or of a child in respect of whom the court is exercising its inherent jurisdiction.[31] These powers are used frequently in cases involving abductions under the 1980 Hague Abduction Convention and 1980 European Custody Convention and also in non-Convention abductions. Failure to disclose information as to the whereabouts of such a child constitutes a serious contempt of court.[32]

Legal professional privilege

10.17 A solicitor can be required to disclose to the court any information which may lead to the whereabouts of such a child even though the information has been communicated to him in the course of his professional retainer;[33] and to that extent, as was pointed out in *Re B (Abduction: Disclosure)*,[34]

---

24 That is the person who for the time being has care of the child by virtue of a care order, emergency protection order or police protection order: Children Act 1989, ss 50(2), 49(2)(c).
25 Children Act 1989, s 50.
26 [1998] 2 FLR 401.
27 Children Act 1989, s 50(3).
28 *Ibid*, s 50(13). See also **11.49**.
29 Children (Prescribed Orders – Northern Ireland, Guernsey and Isle of Man) Regulations 1991, SI 1991/2032. See also **11.47**.
30 FPR 1991, r 5.1(7), (8), (9).
31 *Hockly v Lukin* (1762) 1 Dick 353; *Rosenberg v Lindo* (1883) 48 LT 478; *N v N* (1969) 113 Sol Jo 999.
32 *Mustafa v Mustafa* (1967) *The Times*, 11, 13 September, O'Connor J.
33 *Ramsbotham v Senior* (1869) LR 8 Eq 575; *Burton v Earl of Darnley* (1869) LR 8 Eq 576n; *Re B (Abduction: Disclosure)* [1995] 1 FLR 774, CA.
34 [1995] 1 FLR 774, CA.

privilege does not exist. However, as the Court of Appeal emphasised in *Re B (Abduction: Disclosure)* and as we discussed above[35] in relation to the statutory power to order disclosure, a client's legal professional privilege is overridden to the extent that the solicitor is entitled and obliged to disclose all relevant information, including communications from his client which may assist in locating the child, but it is not overridden in any other respect. Under an order that the solicitor disclose all documents relevant to the child's whereabouts, the solicitor is entitled and obliged to disclose any information or communications from his client which may assist in ascertaining the child's or the client's present whereabouts; it is usually sufficient to leave the solicitor to use his honest professional judgment as to how those principles are to be applied to the documents and information in his possession.[36]

10.18   However, Butler-Sloss and Hoffmann LJJ in *Re B (Abduction: Disclosure)* stated that it is wrong in principle to require a solicitor to mislead his client. Thus the judge was right to refuse to order the solicitor not to disclose to his client the fact that he had been ordered to disclose any information which may come to his knowledge as to the child's whereabouts. Butler-Sloss LJ added that the solicitor need not officiously seek to tell his client what is going on and can wait for the client to ask. In some, if not many, cases, this advice may be a difficult and uncomfortable course for a solicitor to follow. In *Re H (Child Abduction: Whereabouts Order to Solicitors)*[37] Hughes J gave the following guidance: it is likely to be inappropriate to make an order which has the effect of requiring a solicitor to mislead his client or of disabling a solicitor from giving advice to his client. However, when an order for disclosure by a solicitor of the whereabouts of a child is sought it may be appropriate, in addition to the principal order, to make an order barring the solicitor for a brief period (for example, a period sufficient to enable the Tipstaff to act upon any information disclosed by the solicitor) from disclosing to the client the fact that the order has been served and complied with.

10.19   Care needs to be taken in drafting the terms of the order sought against a solicitor. In *Re H (Child Abduction: Whereabouts Order to Solicitors)* the solicitors succeeded in their application to discharge the order requiring them not to disclose to their client the fact that an order had been made ordering the solicitors to disclose all information held by them as to the whereabouts of a child abducted by the client; costs were ordered to follow the event and the solicitors obtained an order for their costs although no criticism could be made of the party seeking the order.

---

[35]   See **10.6**.
[36]   *Re B (Abduction: Disclosure)* (above) per Hoffmann LJ.
[37]   [2000] 1 FLR 766.

Voluntary disclosure by solicitors

10.20   In *Essex County Council v R (Note)*[38] Thorpe J said:

'For my part, I would wish to see case-law go yet further and to make it plain that the legal representatives in possession of such material relevant to determination but contrary to the interests of their client, not only are unable to resist disclosure by reliance on legal professional privilege, but have a positive duty to disclose to the other parties and to the court.'

The House of Lords in *Re L (A Minor) (Police Investigation: Privilege)*[39] left open whether the duty favoured in *Essex County Council v R* exists and, if so, how far it extends. Professional guidance as to a solicitor's duty is to be found in the Law Society's *Guide to the Professional Conduct of Solicitors* (7th and 8th edns); and also in the 5th edition of the Solicitors Family Law Association *Guide to Good Practice for Solicitors Acting for Children* (May 2000).[40]

Information from airlines

10.21   Where a person seeks an order for the return to him of a child about to arrive by air in England and he desires information to enable him to meet the aeroplane, the court may direct that the airline operating the flight and, if he has the information, the immigration officer, should disclose the information to the applicant.[41]

Assistance by telephone companies

10.22   The location of children can sometimes be aided by information given by the two major providers of telephone services within the United Kingdom, namely, British Telecommunications plc and Mercury Communications Limited, in order to trace telephone calls made to and from numbers in the United Kingdom and to identify the names and addresses of callers.[42] Generally, such information cannot be disclosed without the written consent of a customer or a court order;[43] but these restrictions do not apply to any disclosure for the purposes of prevention or detection of crime or for the purposes of criminal proceedings. Practitioners who think that the monitoring of telephone calls could assist them in tracing missing children should contact

---

[38]   [1994] Fam 167 at 168H; [1993] 2 FLR 826 at 828. These observations were repeated by Wall J in *Re DH (A Minor) (Child Abuse)* [1994] 1 FLR 679. See also the discussion in *Vernon v Bosley (No 2)* [1999] QB 18, [1997] 1 All ER 614, CA.

[39]   [1997] AC 16, [1996] 1 FLR 731, HL.

[40]   See also the Protocol for the Working Relationship between Children Panel Solicitors and Guardians ad litem (Law Society, 2000).

[41]   *Practice Direction (Arrival of Child in England by Air)* [1980] 1 WLR 73, [1980] 1 All ER 288.

[42]   See Atkinson and Nicholls, 'Tracing and Recording Telephone Calls' [1996] Fam Law 104 and Atkinson [1996] Fam Law 491.

[43]   See Telecommunications Act 1984, s 45 (as amended by Interception of Telecommunications Act 1985, Sch 2).

BT's Network Special Investigation unit before applying to the court, since that unit has considerable experience of dealing with such problems as confidentiality and can save the enquirer much time and expense.

INFORMATION FROM GOVERNMENT DEPARTMENTS

10.23 The formal arrangements whereby government departments will disclose addresses to enable a child to be traced are set out in a Practice Direction.[44] The arrangements cover:

(a) tracing the address of a person in proceedings against whom another person is seeking to enforce an order for financial provision either for himself or for the child of the former marriage; and

(b) tracing the whereabouts of a child, or a person with whom the child is said to be, in proceedings under the Child Abduction and Custody Act 1985 or in which a s 8 order[45] or an order under the inherent jurisdiction giving care of a child to any person or making provisions for the education of or contact with a child is being sought or enforced.

The request should give the information specified by the Practice Direction for the particular department and should certify the matters required by it.

10.24 The arrangements apply to all government departments, but the Department of Work and Pensions, the Office of National Statistics, the National Health Service Agency Central Register, the Passport Office, the Ministry of Defence and the Child Support Agency are likely to be of most use.[46] In *Re C (A Minor) (Child Support Agency: Disclosure)*[47] it was held that the court has no power under s 50(6) of the Child Support Act 1991 to give leave to or to direct the Secretary of State for Social Security to disclose information held by the Agency.[48] However, under the Child Support (Information, Evidence and Disclosure) Regulations 1992,[49] the Secretary of State or the child support officer may disclose information to a court where the court has exercised any power to make, vary or revive a maintenance order or vary a

---

[44] *Practice Direction (Disclosure of Addresses)* [1989] 1 WLR 219, [1989] 1 All ER 765, as amended by *Practice Direction* [1995] 2 FLR 813.

[45] Ie residence orders, contact orders, prohibited steps orders and specific issue orders under ss 8 and 10 of the Children Act 1989.

[46] As to the position of the police, see **10.10** above.

[47] [1995] 1 FLR 201.

[48] However, the Secretary of State conceded that, on an application for a s 8 order, the court could request the Secretary of State to disclose to the applicant the address of the child's absent parent in accordance with *Practice Direction (Disclosure of Addresses)* (above) and a request was made by the court; but note the Comment at [1995] Fam Law 183.

[49] SI 1992/1812, as amended by the Child Support (Information, Evidence and Disclosure and Maintenance Arrangements and Jurisdiction) (Amendment) Regulations 2000, SI 2001/161.

maintenance agreement, and the disclosure is made for the purposes of proceedings before the court in relation to that order or agreement.

10.25 In the High Court and county court, the request is usually made by the district judge to whom application is made.

10.26 When the department is able to supply the address to the court, it is passed on to the applicant or his solicitor on the understanding that it is to be used only for the purpose of the proceedings.

PUBLICITY

10.27 The court may expressly authorise publicity to assist in finding a missing child and thereby prevent such publicity from breaching the prohibition found in s 12(1) of the Administration of Justice Act 1960 on the publication of information relating to proceedings in private which covers proceedings under the inherent jurisdiction with respect to children (including wardship) or under the Children Act 1989 or which relate wholly or mainly to the maintenance or upbringing of a child.[50] For this purpose, the proceedings may be adjourned for a short period to enable the representatives of the press to attend; however, it may be more convenient to give the information to the press after the hearing. It may also be sensible to prepare a statement to be released to the press, bearing in mind the need of the press for a story.[51] In this respect, the guidance suggested by the Court of Appeal in *Re G (Celebrities: Publicity)*[52] can be adapted: the statement can be agreed between those parties before the court and approved by the court. Where the Tipstaff or the Child Abduction Unit is involved, it is prudent to liaise with them, particularly over the timing of publicity; for example, it may be preferable to delay publicity in order to avoid alerting an abductor to the fact that steps are being taken to trace the child.

HIGH COURT ORDERS

Collection orders and location orders

10.28 Under its inherent jurisdiction, the High Court may make a collection order or a location order.[53] Each order is in two parts. In respect of a collection order, the first part, which is the collection order proper, orders that

---

[50] Administration of Justice Act 1960, s 12 (as amended). As to the extent of the confidentiality attaching to proceedings relating to abducted children, see **21.97–21.99**.

[51] See the helpful advice given by Pearson (of the Press Association) in 'Publicity in Children Cases' [1991] Fam Law 402 and in 'Media – The Last Resort' [1990] *The Lawyer* 11.

[52] [1999] 1 FLR 409, CA.

[53] Before 11 February 2002, collection orders were known as search and find orders or find and return orders, and location orders were known as seek and locate orders. See generally **21.47**.

the child must be placed into the temporary care of the plaintiff (or some other named person)[54] until a further hearing of the court, which must take place within 3 working days of the child being placed in the plaintiff's care; and that the defendant (or some other named person) and any other person who is in a position to do so, deliver the child into the charge of the Tipstaff. If the person is not in a position to do so, he is required to inform the Tipstaff of the child's whereabouts or, failing that, inform him of all matters within his knowledge or understanding which might reasonably assist in locating the child; he is also required to hand to the Tipstaff (for safekeeping until the court makes a further order) passports and travel documents relating to the defendant and the child.[55] The second part of the order is directed to the Tipstaff and usually includes a bench warrant. The order directs the Tipstaff to take charge of the child and to place the child into the care of a named person; and, where a bench warrant is included in the order, the Tipstaff is empowered to arrest and detain anyone whom he has reasonable cause to believe has disobeyed the order and to bring that person before the court as soon as practicable and in any event no later than the working day immediately following arrest.[56] Collection orders are frequently made in cases under the 1980 Hague Abduction Convention and the 1980 European Custody Convention.

10.29 A location order requires the defendant (or some other named person) and any person served with the order to inform the Tipstaff of the child's whereabouts or inform him of all matters within his knowledge or understanding which might reasonably assist in locating the child; it also requires the defendant or other person to hand to the Tipstaff (for safekeeping until the court makes a further order) passports and travel documents relating to the defendant and the child. The second part of the location order, as with a collection order, is directed to the Tipstaff and directs him to locate the child. It is similar to the second part of the collection order.

Arrest and detention

10.30 As explained in *Re B (Child Abduction: Wardship: Power to Detain)*,[57] the power to arrest, detain and bring before the court is in aid of the civil

---

54 Where the left-behind parent or carer is overseas and therefore may not immediately be available, it is the practice of the High Court to direct the Tipstaff to arrange for the child to be accommodated by the relevant local authority social services department. See Children Act 1989, s 20(1).

55 See also the discussion at **21.47**.

56 *Re B (Child Abduction: Wardship: Power to Detain)* [1994] 2 FLR 479, CA. See also FPR 1991, r 5.2 for the circumstances in which the Tipstaff may execute an order or warrant issued in proceedings in the Principal Registry of the Family Division which are treated as pending in a county court, see FPR 1991, r 7.2(3), (3A), (4). The role of the Tipstaff in tracing a child is discussed further at **10.34**.

57 [1994] 2 FLR 479, CA.

proceedings before it and is ancillary to other orders made by the court.[58] The person arrested and brought before the court may be found to be in contempt, but the exercise of the jurisdiction is not based upon contempt of court but upon ensuring compliance with the directions of the court. Once the detained person has complied with the order, for example by providing all the information he has as to whereabouts of a child or by returning or causing the child to be returned to the jurisdiction, there is nothing further that the court can require him to do; he may not be further detained.[59] The court is entitled to refuse to release the arrested person until it is satisfied that he has provided the court with all the information which it requires and which the person is able to provide; further, the court may make specific orders requiring the person to do such things within his power as the court considers would assist in procuring compliance with the order of the court.[60] Only if the court is satisfied that the person is in contempt may he thereafter be deprived further of his liberty. In *Re B (Child Abduction: Wardship: Power to Detain)*, it was said that if the person is *prima facie* in contempt and the proceedings are part heard and are continuing and the court is satisfied that the person will not attend voluntarily the hearing the next day, the person may be detained until the conclusion of the hearing in order to ensure his attendance. However, the court may not detain a party or witness at the end of the hearing in order to compel another person to comply with an order.

10.31   The Court of Appeal drew attention to the absence of a power to compel a person who is in England and Wales, but who is not himself in contempt, to bring back to the jurisdiction a child who has been removed or retained therefrom; the order in *Re B (Child Abduction: Wardship: Power to Detain)* that the father be detained by the Tipstaff until the children were taken to the British Embassy in Algiers was made without jurisdiction.

Forms of order

10.32   The prescribed forms for location and collection orders can be adapted to the requirements of the individual case. However, the wording of these new forms of order has been drafted to ensure compliance with the ECHR; it follows that any adaptation must be similarly compliant. The prescribed forms are set out in full in Appendix 4. To avoid misunderstanding, an applicant should familiarise himself with the prescribed wording and identify to the judge any provisions which he invites the court to vary in the circumstances of the case.[61]

---

[58]   This is recognised by FPR 1991, r 5.2.

[59]   *Re B (Child Abduction: Wardship: Power to Detain)* [1994] 2 FLR 479, CA.

[60]   *Ibid.*

[61]   For example, whether the Tipstaff is directed merely to locate the child and take possession of the travel documents of the abductor or whether the Tipstaff is directed to take the child into his possession and deliver the child into the care of the applicant or some other safe person.

10.33   The power of the High Court to secure compliance with any direction relating to a ward of court may be exercised by an order addressed to the Tipstaff.[62] Location and collection orders are usually exercised through wardship but can be exercised by the High Court outside wardship.[63]

Function of the Tipstaff

10.34   The Tipstaff is the enforcement officer of the High Court at the Royal Courts of Justice. He has a deputy and assistants and can authorise police officers to act on his behalf. Any obligation to give information to the Tipstaff or to hand over a child to the Tipstaff includes an obligation to do so to his deputy or assistant or a police officer acting on his behalf.

10.35   The function of the Tipstaff is to execute orders of the High Court and he does not fulfil the role of an enquiry agent. Accordingly, while he will always act upon relevant information given to him, he does not have the resources, nor is it his function, to set up independent lines of enquiry of his own. It is, therefore, very important that solicitors and those applying for a collection or location orders should pursue their own lines of enquiry and provide the Tipstaff with all available information to enable him to execute the order. He usually acts with the assistance of the police, whom he authorises to act on his behalf.

ABDUCTION WITHIN THE UNITED KINGDOM: STATUTORY POWER TO ORDER RECOVERY AND DELIVERY OF A CHILD

10.36   Section 34 of the Family Law Act 1986 confers powers of recovery and delivery of a child on all courts in England and Wales in relation to Part I proceedings.[64] We have already discussed 'Part I orders' and 'Part I proceedings' in connection with s 33 of the Family Law Act 1986.[65] Proceedings under the 1980 Hague Abduction Convention and 1980 European Custody Convention are not Part I proceedings, and the inherent jurisdiction of the High Court has to be used. Proceedings taken following a non-Convention abduction may well be Part I proceedings.

---

[62]   FPR 1991, r 5.2.
[63]   Wardship is often invoked in cases of abduction.
[64]   As to Part I proceedings, see **3.2** and **10.3**.
[65]   See for more detail, **10.2–10.4**.

10.37   Where:

(a)   a person is required by a Part I order,[66] or an order for the enforcement of a Part I order,[67] to give up a child to another person ('the person concerned'); and

(b)   the court which made the order imposing the requirement is satisfied that the child has not been given up in accordance with the order,

the court may make an order authorising an officer of the court (who in the High Court is the Tipstaff, and in the county court is the bailiff) or a constable to take charge of the child and deliver him to the person concerned.[68] As was made clear in *R v Chief Constable of Cheshire ex parte K*,[69] the section authorises the police to act; it imposes no absolute duty to act. The order gives authority only to officers of the court and police officers in England and Wales. If the child is thought to be in another part of the United Kingdom, the court in Scotland, Northern Ireland or the Isle of Man being asked to enforce the English Part I order should be asked to make a recovery order under the powers it has under the Family Law Act 1986.[70]

10.38   The authority conferred by such an order includes authority to enter and search any premises where the person acting in pursuance of the order has reason to believe the child may be found and to use such force as may be necessary to give effect to the purpose of the order.[71] An application under s 34 may be made ex parte (ie without notice).[72] The procedure for applying for a s 34 order and the form of order are set out in FPR 1991, r 6.17.[73]

10.39   The power under s 34 is without prejudice to any power conferred on a court by or under any other enactment or rule of law;[74] thus the inherent jurisdiction of the High Court is preserved.[75]

---

[66]   'Part I order' is defined in Family Law Act 1986, s 1 and includes a s 8 order and orders under the inherent jurisdiction giving care and control to any person or making provision for the education of or for contact with a child, and also includes orders within the meaning of s 40. As to the meaning of a 'Part I order', see also **10.3**.

[67]   As to the enforcement of Part I orders, see Chapter 11.

[68]   Family Law Act 1986, s 34(1).

[69]   [1990] 1 FLR 70. However, see *Osman v United Kingdom* [1999] 1 FLR 193, ECtHR.

[70]   See Chapter 11.

[71]   Family Law Act 1986, s 34(2).

[72]   FPR 1991, r 6.17(4).

[73]   A draft order is set out in Appendix 4. As to procedure for applying for an order in the magistrates' court, see FPC(CA)R 1991, r 31A; breach of the order is enforced under Magistrates' Courts Act 1980, s 63(3): Children Act 1989, s 14(1).

[74]   Family Law Act 1986, s 34(4).

[75]   See **10.28**.

THE CRIMINAL LAW: EXTRADITION

10.40 Where an offence has been committed, it may be possible to apply to extradite the offender from the country to which he has gone in order that he may be tried for the offence in England and Wales. However, extradition is only possible in respect of those countries with which there is a treaty having effect under the Extradition Act 1989.[76] Extradition obtains the return of the abductor, not the child; however, the abductor may in some circumstances have no practicable alternative but to return with the child. Nevertheless, as we pointed out earlier, the criminal law should be used sensitively and care taken that the situation is not worsened by bringing criminal proceedings.[77]

ACQUIRING THE FINANCIAL RESOURCES TO SECURE RETURN

Sequestration

10.41 Where a person required by an order to do an act within a specified time fails to do it within that time or a person disobeys an order requiring him to abstain from doing an act, the order may be enforced, with leave of the court, by a writ of sequestration against the property of that person.[78] An order made under the 1980 Hague Abduction Convention that the child 'be returned to [the State of his habitual residence] forthwith', has been held to be sufficiently clear as to what is required to be done that it can be enforced by writ of sequestration.[79] It is available against the property of those who assist in the abduction of children: the court will give leave for the issue of a writ of sequestration against the property of third parties if it is sure, on the criminal standard of proof, that the third party knew of the order and deliberately frustrated it or aided and abetted the principal contemnor in avoiding compliance.[80] In *Re S (Abduction: Sequestration)*,[81] following the failure of the mother to return the child to Israel in accordance with an order made pursuant to Art 12 of the 1980 Hague Abduction Convention, the court ordered that a writ of sequestration be issued against the property of the mother's male friend who was not a party to the original proceedings, who was not named in the order and who had not been served with the order. The judge was satisfied that the man knew of the order, knew what it required and had deliberately

---

[76] For a list of the treaties currently in force, see 18 *Halsbury's Laws* (4th edn), para 208 and the Cumulative Supplement thereto.

[77] See **9.20**.

[78] RSC Ord 45, r 5 which continues to apply to family proceedings as defined in Matrimonial and Family Proceedings Act 1984, s 32.

[79] *Re S (Abduction: Sequestration)* [1995] 1 FLR 858.

[80] *Ibid.*

[81] [1995] 1 FLR 858.

conducted himself so as to frustrate the order or aided and abetted the mother in so doing.

10.42 The importance of complying properly with the procedural requirements of sequestration[82] was stressed in *Re S (Abduction: Sequestration)*. The remedy is only available in the High Court and, if necessary, the proceedings should be transferred to the High Court in order to take advantage of sequestration. The removal of a child in breach of an order prohibiting such removal or a failure to return a child by a specified time would be a contempt. A penal notice should be attached to the order.[83]

10.43 The writ gives the sequestrators power to seize the contemnor's real and personal estate and to hold it until the order is complied with. The court may give leave to the sequestrators to sell assets to enable any sum payable under the order or any fine to be paid. The court may also give leave to the sequestrators to let the real property or to raise money by way of a loan secured on the property to enable the wronged party to finance proceedings in a foreign court to secure compliance with the order. In *Richardson v Richardson*,[84] the mother refused to comply with an access order and removed the children to Ireland; sequestrators were given leave to raise money against her property to enable the father to take proceedings in Ireland to enforce the access order.

10.44 The costs of sequestration are high and, before embarking on sequestration, a careful assessment should always be made as to whether the costs are justified.

Preserving the property for the purposes of sequestration

10.45 The court can make an order restraining the contemnor from dealing with or disposing of his or her real or personal estate pending the issuing of an application for leave for a writ of sequestration.[85]

Forfeiture of a bond or security

10.46 Where an order has not been complied with, any bond or other security may be forfeited.[86]

---

[82] Reference can be made eg to *Rayden and Jackson on Divorce and Family Matters*, 17th edn (Butterworths), paras 34.51 *et seq*, *Arlidge, Eady and Smith on Contempt*, 2nd edn (Sweet and Maxwell, 2000) at 14.83, and Borrie and Lowe, *The Laws of Contempt*, 3rd edn (Butterworths, 1996) at 606.

[83] A copy of a s 8 order may be endorsed with a penal notice in the county court only on the direction of a judge or district judge: FPR 1991, r 4.21A.

[84] [1989] Fam 95, [1989] 3 WLR 865. In *Mir v Mir* [1992] Fam 79, [1992] 2 WLR 225, sequestrators were given leave to sell the property for a similar purpose.

[85] *Richardson v Richardson* [1989] Fam 95 at 97F, [1989] 3 WLR 865 at 867C–D.

[86] As to bonds and security for good behaviour, see **9.45**.

Costs

10.47 Where a child has been abducted, the English court is very likely[87] to order that the abductor pay the costs of English proceedings to trace and recover the child: the irresponsibility and harm involved in the abduction take such cases outside the type of child case in which there is usually no order as to costs. The question of costs is discussed in Chapter 21.

Fighting fund

10.48 In *Al Khatib v Masry*,[88] Munby J held that abduction of children by the husband denying them any contact with their mother was conduct which it was inequitable to disregard when considering, under s 25 of the Matrimonial Causes Act 1973, what ancillary relief order to make on the occasion of divorce; and he held that such conduct justified a war chest or fighting fund above the lump sum otherwise awarded to enable the mother to fund future proceedings to recover the children; whatever was left of the fund could be returned to the husband as soon as the children were returned to the mother or to England and Wales.

ASSISTANCE: PROCEDURAL AND PRACTICAL ADVICE

10.49 We set out below some agencies which provide procedural and practical advice.

(1) **The Lord Chancellor's Child Abduction Unit:** The Child Abduction Unit is part of the Department of Constitutional Affairs (formerly the Lord Chancellor's Department) and is attached to the Official Solicitor's Office.[89] It can provide information and practical and procedural advice about tracing children and the steps to take to recover children in all abductions from England and Wales. In relation to abductions to and from Contracting States, both to the 1980 Hague Abduction Convention and the 1980 European Custody Convention, the Child Abduction Unit discharges the functions of the Lord Chancellor as Central Authority for England and Wales.

(2) **The Central Authority for Scotland and the Central Authority for Northern Ireland.**[90]

(3) **The Consular Directorate of the Foreign and Commonwealth Office.**[91]

---

[87]   Subject to the financial means and, where relevant, the legal aid status of the abductor.

[88]   [2002] EWHC 108 (Fam), [2002] 1 FLR 1053.

[89]   See generally **13.10**.

[90]   See **13.9**.

[91]   See the discussion at **20.75** *et seq.*

(4) **Reunite**: National Council for Abducted Children.[92]
(5) **Police**:   As seen above, police assistance may be available if a criminal offence has been committed or is threatened,[93] or to prevent a breach of the peace,[94] or where a child may need to be taken into police protection,[95] or where a person is reported missing.[96] In *Re J (Minors) (Ex Parte Orders)*,[97] Hale J gave guidance after consultation with Sir Stephen Brown P; the police should always be clear as to their role in the particular case, be it to effect a recovery order, to take a child into police protection or to prevent an apprehended breach of the peace; if they attend to prevent a breach of the peace, they should take care to understand what the order requires. It should be borne in mind that the intervention of a public authority may worsen a domestic situation as well as ameliorate it.[98]
(6) **Interpol**:   Interpol is a police-to-police organisation. Contact with Interpol may be made through the British police. Interpol will act on a criminal complaint or a missing persons report.[99]
(7) **Foreign embassies**:   Foreign embassies may assist in putting a parent of an abducted child in touch with the appropriate authorities in the foreign State to which a child has been abducted.

---

[92] See generally **20.75**.
[93] See generally **9.4–9.21**.
[94] See, for example, *Re J (Minors) (Ex Parte Orders)* [1997] 1 FLR 606, Hale J (judgment given after consultation with Sir Stephen Brown P).
[95] Children Act 1989, s 46.
[96] See, for example, *Re J (Minors) (Ex Parte Orders)* (above).
[97] [1997] 1 FLR 606.
[98] *R v Chief Constable of Cheshire ex parte K* [1990] 1 FLR 70.
[99] Checklist of Issues to be Considered at the Third Meeting of the Special Commission to Review the Operation of the Hague Convention on the Civil Aspects of International Child Abduction drawn by Adair Dyer, Deputy Secretary General of the Permanent Bureau of the Conference, January 1997, Question 5. See also **20.84**.

Chapter 11

CHILDREN ABDUCTED WITHIN THE BRITISH ISLES

INTRODUCTION

11.1 Although child abduction is more immediately associated with the wrongful movement of children across international frontiers, their wrongful removal to, or retention within, different parts of the British Isles[1] can be equally, if not more, problematic. Notwithstanding that England and Wales, Scotland, Northern Ireland, the Isle of Man and the Channel Islands constitute separate legal jurisdictions, for the purposes of both the 1980 Hague Abduction Convention and the 1980 European Custody Convention, the British Isles is treated as a single Contracting State. Consequently, neither

---

[1] The term 'British Isles' is used to comprise England and Wales, Scotland, Northern Ireland, the Isle of Man and the Channel Islands.

Convention applies to abductions within the British Isles.[2] Accordingly, one must look to the domestic law for any remedy which, as will be seen, principally means applying the Family Law Act 1986.[3]

11.2   In the context of abductions within the British Isles, the criminal law has limited application, since the Child Abduction Act 1984[4] only criminalises the wrongful removal of children (under the age of 16) by their parents out of the United Kingdom (viz England and Wales, Scotland and Northern Ireland).[5] Accordingly, parental child abductions from one part of the United Kingdom to another can constitute a crime only if caught by the common law or, if the child is in local authority care in England and Wales, under s 49 of the Children Act 1989.[6] One consequence of the general inapplicability of the Child Abduction Act 1984 is that the police have no power to prevent removals of children from one part of the United Kingdom to another.

THE CIVIL LAW – THE APPLICATION OF THE FAMILY LAW ACT 1986

Background to the 1986 Act

11.3   Before implementation of the Family Law Act 1986, orders made in another part of the United Kingdom were treated no differently from an order made in any other part of the world: they were neither recognised nor enforceable.[7] To overcome these difficulties, Chapter V of the 1986 Act makes provision both for the recognition and for the enforcement of 'Part I orders'. By 'Part I order' is meant any order as defined by s 1(3) of the Act[8] – save and insofar as it 'includes provision as to the means by which rights conferred by the order are to be enforced'.[9] It also includes orders made before

---

2   Note, however, that while the United Kingdom ratified the Hague Abduction Convention and European Custody Convention on behalf of England and Wales, Scotland and Northern Ireland and subsequently extended the Conventions to the Isle of Man, *no* extension has been made in respect of the Channel Islands. Accordingly, abductions to or from the Channel Islands can never be caught by either Convention even if children have been brought to or from a Contracting State other than the United Kingdom.

3   For a discussion of the jurisdictional rules under the Family Law Act 1986, see Chapter 3.

4   Discussed at **9.4** *et seq*.

5   Interpretation Act 1978, Sch 1. Note therefore that wrongful removals to the Channel Islands or the Isle of Man are caught by the 1984 Act.

6   Or, in Northern Ireland, under Art 68 of the Children (Northern Ireland) Order 1995.

7   See eg *Babington v Babington* 1955 SC 115, 1955 SLT 170 and the other cases cited at **2.2–2.4** above.

8   See s 32(1), and note the extended definition in s 32(2) so far as recognition is concerned in Scotland. Section 1(3) is discussed above at **3.2**.

9   Family Law Act 1986, s 25(2), and see *Re K (A Minor) (Wardship: Jurisdiction: Interim Order)* [1991] 2 FLR 104, CA, in which it was accepted that an injunction that a child be returned to the mother within 48 hours of her launching of a custody application could not be enforced under the 1986 Act.

implementation of the 1986 Act provided, had the Act been in force, they could properly have been made and would not have ceased to have effect by reason of being superseded by a later order.[10]

Recognition

11.4   Under s 25 of the 1986 Act, any 'Part I order' made by a court in any part of the United Kingdom or the Isle of Man, and in force in respect of a child under the age of 16, shall be recognised in any other part of the United Kingdom or the Isle of Man 'as having the same effect ... as if it had been made by the appropriate court ... and as if that court had had jurisdiction to make it'.

11.5   As the Law Commissions observed,[11] there are clear advantages in having statutory provision for recognition. For example, it clarifies the position particularly for third parties; it protects those who act on the basis of an order made in another part of the United Kingdom or the Isle of Man, and reduces, if not eliminates, the need to bring fresh legal proceedings merely to safeguard rights conferred by a court order in another part. So, for example, it can be assumed that those with a residence order in their favour can exercise parental responsibility in any other part of the United Kingdom or the Isle of Man. Similarly, any restraint of publicity order made under s 8 of the Children Act 1989 in England and Wales,[12] for example, should be enough to ban publicity throughout the United Kingdom and the Isle of Man. Another example, commonly cited,[13] is that a prohibition against a child's removal from any part of the United Kingdom will be effective throughout the United Kingdom. However, express provision is made by s 36 not merely for such

---

[10]   Section 32(1) and (3). This could still be relevant in the case of 'continuing' custody or access orders originally made in respect of babies but where the children subject to these orders are still not yet 18 (England and Wales and Northern Ireland) or 16 (Scotland). For the meaning of 'continuing' see **3.14**. The effect of superseding orders under ss 6, 15 and 23 is discussed above at **3.25** *et seq*. Note also s 26 which makes special provision for Scotland to ensure that recognition of orders relating to parental responsibilities or parental rights made outside the United Kingdom applies to orders made in the country of the child's habitual residence and not domicile as formerly, see Law Com No 138/Scot Law Com No 91 at paras 5.11 *et seq*.

[11]   See Law Com No 138/Scot Law Com No 91, at para 5.9.

[12]   Although not one made under the High Court's inherent jurisdiction since that would fall outside the definition of a 'Part I order' under the terms of s 1(1)(d), discussed at **3.2**. For an example of a restraint of publicity order being made under s 8 of the Children Act 1989, see *Re Z (A Minor) (Identification: Restrictions on Publication)* [1997] Fam 1, sub nom *Re Z (A Minor) (Freedom of Publication)* [1996] 1 FLR 191, CA, for an analysis of which see *Kelly v BBC* [2001] Fam 59 at 81–83, [2001] 1 FLR 197 at 224–227, per Munby J.

[13]   Indeed, that was the example cited by the Law Commissions in their Working Paper, Law Com Working Paper No 68/Scot Law Com Memorandum No 23, at paras 4.12, 6.19 and 6.50(2).

orders to be effective throughout the United Kingdom but for them to be enforceable as if they were made by the appropriate court in any part.[14]

11.6 Important though the principle of recognition is, its significance is limited in that it does not of itself imply enforceability. Indeed, s 25(3) expressly states that:

> 'A court in a part of the United Kingdom[15] in which a Part I order is recognised ... shall not enforce the order unless it has been registered in that part of the United Kingdom ... and proceedings for enforcement are taken in accordance with ... this Act.'

This position is based on the Law Commissions' view[16] that, given the relative independence of each legal system, it was not practical to have a scheme for automatic enforcement. In other words, as the Law Commissions put it,[17] the effect of recognition of a Part I order is to 'authorise, but not to require, compliance with the order'.

Enforcement

Stage 1 of the process – applying to register the order

11.7 The first stage in the enforcement process is to register the order, the 1986 Act having introduced a registration system similar to that for the registration of maintenance orders. For this purpose, application must be made to the court that made the original order for it to be registered in another part of the United Kingdom or the Isle of Man.

11.8 Under s 27(1), any person on whom rights have been conferred by a Part I order may apply for that order to be registered in another part of the United Kingdom or the Isle of Man. Such applications must be made in the prescribed manner, containing the prescribed information and be accompanied by the prescribed documents.[18] Upon receiving the application, the court must, unless it appears that the order is no longer in force, or that the child has attained the age of 16,[19] cause the following documents to be

---

[14]   This is an important exception to the general rule under the Act that recognition does not itself imply enforceability. See further **11.6** below.

[15]   It will be noted that no reference is made in this sub-section to 'dependent territory'. But this is surely an oversight. Accordingly, it must be assumed that an order made in one part of the United Kingdom is not immediately enforceable in the Isle of Man, or vice versa.

[16]   See Law Com No 138/Scot Law Com No 91, at para 5.10.

[17]   *Ibid*, at para 5.10.

[18]   Family Law Act 1986, s 27(2). So far as England and Wales is concerned, applications to register High Court or county court orders must be made in accordance with FPR 1991, rr 7.7–7.15 and the Magistrates' Courts (Family Law Act 1986) Rules 1988 (MC(FLA)R 1988).

[19]   See, in England and Wales, FPR 1991, r 7.8(6) and MC(FLA)R 1988, r 3(4). In such cases, the proper officer or clerk must give the applicant notice and reasons for their refusal. In the case of applications to the High Court or county court, this must be done within 14 days of the decision. No time is specified in the rules governing applications to magistrates' courts.

sent to the 'appropriate court' (that is, the Supreme Court of the relevant jurisdiction, ie the English High Court, the Northern Ireland High Court, the Scottish Court of Session or the Manx High Court)[20] in the part of the United Kingdom or the Isle of Man specified in the application, namely:

(a) a certified copy of the order,

(b) prescribed particulars of any amending order, and

(c) a copy of the application and accompanying documents.[21]

11.9 So far as England and Wales is concerned, an application for the registration of a Part I order made by the High Court or a county court must be made in accordance with FPR 1991, r 7.8. This provides an administrative process in which the applicant is required, in the case of a High Court order, to lodge in the principal registry or the district registry, as the case may be, or in the case of a county court order, to file in that court, a certified copy of the order and of any order varying it, and an affidavit in support of the application, together with a copy thereof. The affidavit must state, *inter alia*: the name and address of the applicant and his interest under the order, and of any other person who has an interest in the order; the name, date of birth and whereabouts or suspected whereabouts of the child; and in which of the jurisdictions of Scotland, Northern Ireland or the Isle of Man the order is to be registered. The proper officer, having sent the documents to the appropriate court, will keep the original affidavit, record the fact of transmission in the court records and file a copy of the documents. When he receives notice of the registration, he must also record the fact in the court records. If the proper officer of the court which made the order refuses to send the documents to the appropriate court,[22] the applicant may apply to the judge in chambers for an order that the documents be sent.[23]

11.10 An application for the registration of a Part I order made by a magistrates' court must be made in accordance with the MC(FLA)R 1988. It should be made in writing in Form 1 of the Schedule and be accompanied by a certified copy of the order and of any variation and of any other document relevant to the application. Provided the application complies with these requirements, then unless the order is no longer in force, or the child has attained the age of 16 years, the court must cause the clerk to send the prescribed documents to the appropriate court.

11.11 Where the prescribed officer of the appropriate court receives a certified copy of a Part I order, he is required forthwith to cause the order,

---

20 See Family Law Act 1986, s 32(1).

21 *Ibid*, s 27(3). A 'certified copy' in relation to an order of any court means a copy certified by the prescribed officer of the court to be a true copy of the order or of the official record of the order: s 42(1).

22 He must refuse to send the documents if it appears to him that the child has attained the age of 16: FPR 1991, r 7.8(6).

23 *Ibid*, r 7.8(7).

together with particulars of any variation, to be registered in that court in the prescribed manner.[24] So far as England and Wales is concerned, the registration in the High Court of Part I orders made in Scotland, Northern Ireland or the Isle of Man is carried out in accordance with FPR 1991, r 7.9.[25]

11.12   An order in respect of a child who has attained the age of 16 cannot be registered, and the registration of an order ceases to have effect on the attainment by the child of that age.[26]

11.13   There is no scrutiny as to why it is sought to register the order, ie there is no need to show that a removal is imminent. It can therefore be invoked as an insurance, for example, where the parties come from different jurisdictions and it is felt that one party might be tempted to return home.

(a)   The number of registrations[27]

11.14   The number of registrations is small. Indeed, as the chart opposite shows, not only is the number of registrations small but it seems to be declining. Predictably, most registrations are between England and Wales and Scotland, with the majority being of registrations of English orders in Scotland. Overall, out of a total of 149 orders registered since 1998, 110 were from England and Wales, 31 from Scotland, 5 from Northern Ireland and 3 from the Isle of Man.

(b)   Cancellation and variation of registration

11.15   There is a detailed procedure both for cancelling and for varying registration. A court which revokes (or in Scotland, recalls) or varies an order registered under s 27 of the Family Law Act 1986 shall cause notice of the revocation, recall or variation to be given in the prescribed manner to the prescribed officer of the court in which it is registered.[28]

---

[24]   Family Law Act 1986, s 27(4).

[25]   The applicant for the registration of a Part I order, any person who satisfies the district judge that he has an interest under the Part I order, and any person who obtains the leave of a district judge, may inspect and bespeak copies of any entry in the register: FPR 1991, r 7.15.

[26]   Family Law Act 1986, s 27(5).

[27]   We are extremely grateful to Ruth Ewen, Support Branch Manager for the Family Proceedings Department in the Principal Registry of the Family Division, who supplied the English statistics, Pam McFarlane, Depute in Charge of the Offices of the Court of Session, who supplied the Scottish statistics, Fiona McKernan, Administrative Officer, Northern Ireland Court Services, who supplied the Northern Irish statistics, and Jane Williams, Clerk to the Second Deemster, Isle of Man Courts of Justice, who supplied the Manx statistics.

[28]   Family Law Act 1986, s 28(1). 'Prescribed' means prescribed by rules of court: see s 42(1). As to the procedure to be followed where the Part I order is varied or revoked by the High Court or any county court and the varied or revoked order is to be sent to the appropriate court, see FPR 1991, r 7.10. As to the procedure to be followed where the Part I order is varied or revoked by a magistrates' court and the varied or revoked order is to be sent to the appropriate court, see MC(FLA)R 1988, r 4.

The number of registrations under the Family Law Act 1986

YEAR	England and Wales	Scotland	Northern Ireland	Isle of Man	Total
1998	10 (8 from Scotland, 2 from Northern Ireland)	33 (31 from England and Wales, 2 from Northern Ireland)	7 (6 from England and Wales, 1 from Scotland)	0	50
1999	11 (10 from Scotland, 1 from Isle of Man)	11 (All from England and Wales)	5 (All from England and Wales)	0	27
2000	8 (6 from Scotland, 1 from Northern Ireland, 1 from Isle of Man)	22 (All from England and Wales)	4 (All from England and Wales)	2 (Both from England and Wales)	36
2001	1 (From Scotland)	18 (All from England and Wales)	7 (5 from England and Wales, 1 from Scotland, 1 from Isle of Man)	1 (From England and Wales)	27
2002 (Until 30 June)	4 (All from Scotland)	5 (All from England and Wales)	0	0	9
Total Number of Registrations since inception of scheme	Total Number since 1988: 153	Total Number since 1988: 335	Total Number since 1990: 37	Total Number since 1991: 11	536

11.16   On receiving the notice, the prescribed officer:

(a)   in the case of the revocation or recall of the order, shall cancel the registration; and

(b)   in the case of the variation of the order, shall cause particulars of the variation to be registered in the prescribed manner.[29]

11.17   Where:

(a)   an order registered under s 27 of the 1986 Act ceases (in whole or in part) to have effect in the part of the United Kingdom in which it was made,[30] otherwise than because of its revocation, recall or variation, or

(b)   an order registered under s 27 in Scotland ceases (in whole or in part) to have effect there as a result of the making of an order in proceedings outside the United Kingdom,

the court in which the order is registered may, of its own motion or on the application of any person who appears to the court to have any interest in the matter, cancel the registration (or, if the order has ceased to have effect in part, cancel the registration so far as it relates to the provisions which have ceased to have effect).[31]

11.18   The procedure on an application to the High Court to cancel the registration in England and Wales of a Part I order made in Scotland, Northern Ireland or the Isle of Man is governed by FPR 1991, r 7.11; the applicant for the Part I order must be a party to the application.[32]

Stage 2 – applying to enforce the order

11.19   Under s 29(1), once a Part I order has been registered in accordance with s 27, the registering court has the same enforcement powers as it would have had if it had itself made the order and had jurisdiction to make it. Even so, an application to enforce the order[33] is still required.

11.20   Where enforcement proceedings are brought, the court must either enforce the order or stay (or in Scotland, sist) or dismiss the application. However, at any time pending the outcome of an enforcement application, the court may give such interim directions as it thinks fit for the purpose of securing the welfare of the child or of preventing changes in the circumstances

---

[29]   Family Law Act 1986, s 28(1)(a) and (b). As to the procedure to be followed where the Part I order made in Scotland, Northern Ireland or the Isle of Man is varied, recalled or revoked, and the varied, revoked, or recalled order is sent to the High Court, see FPR 1991, r 7.11.

[30]   One example is where a later, competently made order in another jurisdiction supersedes the one sought to be enforced, see the discussion above at **3.25** *et seq.*

[31]   Family Law Act 1986, s 28(2). Note also the powers under s 31 to cancel a registration following the dismissal of enforcement proceedings, discussed below at **11.31**.

[32]   FPR 1991, r 7.11(3).

[33]   That can take the form of seeking to attach a penal notice to the original order, see eg *B v B Scottish Contact Order: Jurisdiction to Vary)* [1996] 1 WLR 231, [1996] 1 FLR 688.

relevant to the determination of the application.[34] So far as the English High Court is concerned, applications for interim directions may be heard and determined by a district judge,[35] and the parties to the enforcement proceedings and, if he is not a party thereto, the applicant for the Part I order should be made parties to the application.[36]

11.21 Where, in accordance with s 29, proceedings are taken in any court for the enforcement of an order registered in that court, any person who appears to the court to have an interest in the matter may apply either for the proceedings to be stayed or for the proceedings to be dismissed.[37] So far as proceedings in England and Wales are concerned, applications for stays or dismissals may be heard and determined by a district judge and, as for interim direction applications, parties to the enforcement proceedings, and, if he is not a party already, the applicant for the Part I order must be made parties to these proceedings.[38]

(a) Staying or sisting

11.22 Under s 30(1), applications for stays or sists may be made on the ground that the applicant has taken or intends to take other proceedings (in the United Kingdom or elsewhere) as a result of which the order may cease to have effect, or may have a different effect, in the part of the United Kingdom, or the Isle of Man, in which it is registered. In recommending this power, the Law Commissions had in mind[39] applications based on (i) a claim that the original order was made without jurisdiction and which should therefore be revoked in the jurisdiction in which it was made, or (ii) a claim that, because of a change of circumstances since it was made, the original order should be varied or revoked.

11.23 Section 30(4) additionally provides that:

'Nothing in this section shall affect any power exercisable apart from this section to grant ... a stay or sist.'

This latter provision is intended to preserve the registering court's residual jurisdiction to grant a stay or sist over and above the more specific power under s 30(1). The Law Commissions thought[40] this power could be useful in rare cases such as where the child is undergoing medical treatment or is taking an important school examination, where immediate enforcement would be inappropriate. It was not intended thereby to confer a general power on the registering court to review the merits of the original order.

---

[34] Family Law Act 1986, s 29(2).
[35] FPR 1991, r 7.12(1).
[36] *Ibid*, r 7.12(2).
[37] *Ibid*, r 7.13(1).
[38] *Ibid*, r 7.13(2).
[39] See Law Com No 138/Scot Law Com No 91, paras 5.33–5.37 and the Explanatory Notes to the draft Bill at p 233.
[40] Law Com No 138/Scot Law Com No 91 at para 5.37.

(I)   APPLYING SECTION 30 – THE ENGLISH POSITION

11.24   The limited power under s 30 was emphasised by the Court of Appeal in *Re M (Minors) (Custody: Jurisdiction)*.[41] There, it was accepted[42] that when considering an enforcement application the court should have regard to the principle of comity and should not purport to act as a court of appeal from the court that originally made the order in question. Consequently, the judge should not question the correctness of the procedures and orders of the other UK (or Manx) court. In other words, in the absence of wholly unusual circumstances, the normal procedure is to order enforcement. In *Re M* itself, the court upheld Bracewell J's refusal to order a stay of a duly registered Scottish interim custody order due to expire in 3 months' time, so as to enable the children to remain in England. Sir Stephen Brown P commented that Bracewell J:

> '… was quite right not to be drawn into hearing what should have amounted to an interim custody application, and which would in effect have sought to vary the effective order of the Scottish court.'

(II)   APPLYING SECTION 30 – THE SCOTTISH POSITION

11.25   At one stage, it seemed that a different attitude was taken in Scotland, following the Court of Session's decision in *Woodcock v Woodcock*.[43] In that case a mother left the matrimonial home in England and took her young son to Scotland. The father obtained an ex parte order from the English High Court that the child become a ward of court, remain in the father's interim care and control and that the mother hand over the child to him. Having duly registered the order in the Court of Session, the father then petitioned for its enforcement. The court refused to enforce the order, taking the view that the proceedings should be sisted to allow the mother to contest custody in divorce proceedings in England, subsequently instituted by the father. It was further held that, in pursuance of its power to make interim directions under s 29(2), the court was entitled to make its own judgment of the child's welfare. It accordingly refused to enforce the English order and ordered instead that the child should, for the time being, stay with his mother. The court concluded:[44]

> '… while the Act has laid down the procedure for enforcement of custody orders made by a foreign court, it has not elided the limited protective jurisdiction of the Court of Session to refuse to give effect to the custody order of a foreign court … which the Court of Session may always exercise if it is satisfied that enforcement of the foreign decree would result in physical or moral injury to the child.'

---

41   [1992] 2 FLR 382.
42   *Ibid* at 386–387, per Sir Stephen Brown P.
43   1990 SLT 848.
44   *Ibid* at 853.

11.26 *Woodcock* has rightly been criticised.[45] As one commentary has said,[46] if its interpretation of s 29(2) is correct then, in direct contrast to Sir Stephen Brown P's entreaties in *Re M*, the enforcement proceedings will amount to an appeal from the court whose decision has been registered under s 27. Such an approach surely frustrates the clear object of the 1986 Act to facilitate the simple and speedy cross-jurisdiction enforcement of Part I orders within the United Kingdom and the Isle of Man.

11.27 Although it has since been said that s 30 'appears to give a broad discretion' to sist proceedings,[47] a quite different stance since has been taken by the Court of Session in *Cook v Blackley*.[48] In this case, the father of a child who was the subject of an English residence order which had been registered in the Court of Session sought to enforce it under s 29 by ordering the mother, who had failed to return the child after residential contact, to deliver the child to the father. Opposing the application, the mother moved the court to sist the proceedings to enable her to seek a variation of the original English residence order. The court rejected the mother's application, and, having expressly referred approvingly to the decision in *Re M (Minors) (Custody: Jurisdiction)*,[49] Lord Sutherland (delivering the opinion of court) rejected the Lord Ordinary's opinion that he had an open-ended discretion to grant a sist, commenting:[50]

> 'The underlying purpose of the provisions in the Act is to ensure that orders made in one part of the United Kingdom are fully recognised and enforced in all other parts. While the provisions in s 30 are designed to permit a sist of a petition for enforcement, it does not appear to us that the intention of this section is to allow an open ended discretion to sist if the sort of criteria exist which would be relevant to an application for interim custody or for variation of an existing custody order.'

His Lordship added:

> 'Nothing in s 30 should prevent the court from recognising its residual jurisdiction, to protect the child from psychological or physical harm, but that is not a matter which arises in the present case. Where, however, all that can be said is that proceedings are contemplated or have been raised which, in the fullness of time, might or might not lead to a variation, the court should be slow to refuse enforcement of the order by granting a sist, particularly as the sisting of the cause allows the parent holding the child to proceed with his or her contemplated proceedings at a leisurely pace.'

---

[45] See Edwards 'A Domestic Muddle: Custody Orders in the United Kingdom' (1992) 41 ICLQ 444 and Young at [1993] Fam Law 61.

[46] Edwards, *op cit* (above), at 448.

[47] Per Lord Coulsfield in *Rellis v Hart* 1993 SLT 738 at 741.

[48] 1997 SLT 853.

[49] [1992] 2 FLR 382. Ironically, no reference was made to *Woodcock v Woodcock*.

[50] 1997 SLT 853 at 855–6.

Accordingly, English and Scottish law are now *ad idem* in restrictively interpreting their powers to order stays or sists.

11.28   The power to grant a stay or sist is a discretionary one and may be refused even if the objector has made out a *prima facie* case.[51] However, if after considering such an application the court considers that the proceedings for enforcement should be stayed or sisted in order that other proceedings may be taken or concluded, it shall stay or sist the proceedings for enforcement accordingly.[52]

11.29   Under s 30(3), the court may remove a stay or recall a sist so granted if it appears to the court:

(1)   that there has been unreasonable delay in the taking or prosecution of the other proceedings referred to above; or
(2)   that those other proceedings are concluded and that the registered order, or a relevant part of it, is still in force.

The purpose of this provision is to preserve the registering court's control over objections so as to be able to avoid attempts to delay enforcement indefinitely and to allow any stay or sist to be removed if the decision in the original court is adverse to the objector's claim.[53]

(b)   Dismissals

11.30   In contrast to stays (or sists), which are primarily intended as temporary holding measures in the one court so as to allow full investigation to be conducted in another court, dismissals are intended to be more permanent in the sense of putting an end to the proceedings. In the Law Commissions' view,[54] this more drastic power is justified where it is clear that the order sought to be enforced has ceased to have effect. Implementing the Commissions' recommendations, s 31(1) provides that an interested person may apply in any enforcement proceedings to have the proceedings dismissed upon the sole ground[55] that the order in question has (in whole or in part) ceased to have effect in the part of the United Kingdom or the Isle of Man in which it was made. Under s 31(3), if, after considering an application for the dismissal of enforcement proceedings, the court is satisfied that the registered order has ceased to have effect, it must dismiss the proceedings for enforcement or, if it is satisfied that the order has ceased to have effect in part,

---

[51]   See the Law Commissions' comments on their Draft Bill: Law Com No 138/Scot Law Com No 91 at p 223.
[52]   Family Law Act 1986, s 30(2).
[53]   See the Law Commissions' comments, *op cit*, n 51, at p 223.
[54]   *Ibid*, at para 5.32.
[55]   Note that s 31(2) provides a special ground in Scotland, namely, in enforcement proceedings before the Court of Session, an interested person may apply for these proceedings to be dismissed on the ground that the order has (in whole or in part) ceased to have effect in Scotland as a result of the making of an order in proceedings outside the United Kingdom. See further Law Com No 138/Scot Law No 91, at para 5.32, n 564.

it must dismiss the proceedings insofar as they relate to the enforcement of provisions which have ceased to have effect.

11.31 The dismissal of the enforcement proceedings will also entitle the court to cancel the registration pursuant to the power under s 28 and, indeed, the Law Commissions envisaged cancellation to be the normal consequence.[56] As the Commissions also observed,[57] the normal reason that an order ceases to have effect in relation to a child under the age of 16 is where it has been superseded by a later order, either within the jurisdiction, or by a court in another part of the United Kingdom or the Isle of Man.[58] It is to be noted that under this provision the decision whether the order sought to be enforced has ceased to have effect is taken by the court of registration.

Commentary – rethinking the enforcement process

11.32 Although the Family Law Act 1986 represented an enormous stride forward for dealing with children's cases within the United Kingdom and the Isle of Man (nor must it be forgotten how hard the English and Scottish Law Commissions had to work to reach an agreement) it cannot now be said that resulting law is satisfactory. Indeed to the contrary, the rules for recognition and enforcement are over-elaborate, slow and expensive and, not surprisingly, rather infrequently invoked. It is submitted that the time has come to think again about the enforcement process under the 1986 Act.

11.33 As under the 1980 European Custody Convention,[59] a prior court order is an essential pre-requisite but, unlike that under Convention, there is no administrative body either to help applicants or generally to administer the system (indeed, given the low numbers of registrations, it would not greatly add to the burden of Central Authorities set up to administer the 1980 Hague Abduction and European Custody Conventions if they were given a similar role in relation to UK applications). Furthermore, the costs of enforcement fall upon the parties themselves.

11.34 The separate need first to register the order (which itself involves a cumbersome two-stage process of having to apply to the court that made the original order for that court to send the necessary documents to the registering court and for that latter court then to register the order) and then to bring separate enforcement proceedings is surely unnecessarily complicated. Even if it remains the case, as the Law Commissions explained when making their recommendations,[60] that the independence of the legal systems of the United Kingdom make it impracticable 'to envisage a scheme of automatic enforcement', it ought to be possible to cut out at least the registration stage.

---

[56] *Ibid* at para 5.32.
[57] *Ibid* at p 227.
[58] Superseding orders are discussed above at **3.25** *et seq*.
[59] See Chapter 19.
[60] See Law Com No 138/Scot Law Com No 91 at para 5.10.

In other words, applicants ought simply to be empowered to bring enforcement proceedings, albeit that proof will be needed of the original order.[61]

11.35   But is a straightforward mandatory scheme of automatic mutual recognition and enforcement too much to ask for? It is hard to justify why an order made in Truro or Pembroke is automatically enforceable in Newcastle, yet an order made in Morpeth is not similarly enforceable in Leith. Indeed, one might have thought, given that the United Kingdom is treated as a single State for the purpose of the ECHR, that an unduly elaborate system (as arguably the 1986 Act is) could fall foul of Art 6 in preventing the determination of civil rights within a reasonable time or, possibly, Art 8 as interfering with the right to respect for family life. However, in *Glaser v United Kingdom*,[62] the European Court of Human Rights considered that the 1986 Act provides a coherent mechanism for enforcement and that, given the complexity of the proceedings, notwithstanding that they had taken 3 years, the case had not exceeded a reasonable time so that Art 6 had not been violated. Although this decision has spared the United Kingdom the embarrassment of forcibly having to reform the 1986 Act,[63] it is suggested nevertheless that radical improvements are needed. In any event, the EU policy of abolishing *exequatur* powers as stated in the Preamble to the revised Brussels II might eventually force further changes.[64]

THE CIVIL LAW – CASES FALLING OUTSIDE THE FAMILY LAW ACT 1986

11.36   The Family Law Act 1986 does not deal with all child abduction issues arising within the British Isles. It does not apply to abductions within a single jurisdiction nor does it apply to abductions to or from the Channel Islands. Furthermore, abductions of children over the age of 16 and abductions of children who are in the care or supervision of local authorities also fall outside the scope of the 1986 Act.

Abduction within a single jurisdiction

11.37   Child abduction is by no means exclusively an international or cross-border phenomenon. It can and does arise purely domestically. Where such an issue comes before the court, the better view is that, while abduction is certainly a factor, there are no pre-set rules determining who should have a

---

[61]   This could be done administratively.

[62]   [2001] 1 FLR 253, ECtHR.

[63]   Ie under Art 53 of the ECHR, States are obliged to change their domestic law if it is found to be in breach of the Convention.

[64]   See **2.13** above.

residence order since that is governed solely by reference to the paramountcy principle.

11.38   Early case-law, notably *W v D (Interim Custody Order)*,[65] seemed to suggest that, in cases of what was then referred to as 'child snatching', there was a strong presumption in favour of restoring the child to the left-behind parent. However, the Court of Appeal has since resiled from this position. In *Re J (A Minor) (Interim Custody: Appeal)*,[66] in which an unmarried father retained the child beyond the terms of an access visit and made serious allegations regarding the mother's care of the child, the Court of Appeal upheld the first instance decision granting the father interim custody. In reaching this decision, the court emphasised that while 'child snatching' was a powerful factor when considering that child's future, the paramount consideration was the child's welfare. There was no principle requiring the automatic return of the child pending the full hearing.

11.39   It is submitted that, as an expression of principle, *Re J* should be regarded as the leading case, although the earlier decisions might well be justified on their particular facts,[67] and in any event preserving the *status quo ante* is often likely to prove the decisive factor.

Abductions to or from the Channel Islands

11.40   As previously stated,[68] although there is power to extend the Family Law Act 1986 to the Channel Islands,[69] it has not yet been exercised. Accordingly, since the Channel Islands are nevertheless regarded as part of the United Kingdom for the purposes of both the 1980 Hague Abduction Convention and the 1980 European Custody Convention,[70] abductions to and from there must be dealt with as if they were non-Convention countries.[71] In other words, orders made in one part of the United Kingdom or the Isle of Man are not recognisable or enforceable in the Channel Islands nor vice versa, although no doubt they would be treated with the greatest of respect.

---

[65]   (1979) 1 FLR 393, sub nom *Witter v Drummond* (1979) 10 Fam Law 149, CA. See also *Jenkins v Jenkins* (1978) 1 FLR 148, CA. See further the discussion in *Butterworths Family Law Service* at **3A [6607]**.

[66]   [1989] 2 FLR 304, CA, which expressly approved an earlier first instance decision, *Re R (Minors) (Interim Custody Order)* (1980) 2 FLR 316. See also *Harvey v Beavis* [1993] CLY 2788, CA, discussed in *Butterworths Family Law Service* at **3A [6607]**.

[67]   Both *W v D* and *Re J* were referred to by Douglas Brown J in *T v T (Custody: Jurisdiction)* [1992] 1 FLR 43 at 50, who considered the case before him to be factually closer to the former than the latter.

[68]   See n 2 above.

[69]   Viz under s 43(2) of the Family Law Act 1986.

[70]   See Chapters 12 and 19 respectively.

[71]   See Chapter 20.

Abductions of children over the age of 16

11.41 The recognition and enforcement provisions of the Family Law Act 1986 do not apply to children aged 16 or over.[72] Accordingly, in the perhaps unlikely event of recourse being had to the civil law[73] to enforce orders in respect of such older children made elsewhere in the United Kingdom or the Isle of Man, applications will have to be dealt with under the common law, although no doubt along the lines developed in the so-called 'non-Convention' cases.[74]

Children in local authority care, etc

11.42 Care orders, and indeed all other types of public law orders concerning children, fall outside the definition of 'Part I orders' in the Family Law Act 1986. Accordingly, that Act has no direct application. In fact, there appears to be no statute governing the jurisdiction to make public law orders in the first place, although, once they have been made, there are elaborate provisions governing the transfer of public orders within the United Kingdom, the Isle of Man and the Channel Islands. There are also both civil and criminal law provisions dealing with children abducted from care.

Jurisdiction

11.43 The first reported case to consider the issue of jurisdiction to make a care order was *Re R (Care Orders: Jurisdiction)*,[75] which concerned a mother and child who had come to England from Jamaica. They had only limited permission to remain and both were liable to be deported. Following the alleged mistreatment of the child by the mother, the local authority applied for a care order, and the question of jurisdiction was raised. Singer J held that while the Family Law Act 1986 had no direct application to public law proceedings it should nevertheless be applied by analogy. Accordingly, in his Lordship's view, there was jurisdiction to hear care order applications on the basis of either the child's habitual residence or presence.

11.44 Taking Singer J's approach to its logical conclusion,[76] if the 1986 Act does apply by analogy then, if the child was habitually resident elsewhere in the United Kingdom or the Isle of Man, there would be no jurisdiction to make public law orders, save on an emergency basis when an order would be made on the basis of the child's presence. It was precisely this issue that arose in

---

[72] See **11.4**.

[73] One might suppose that in the case of older children the criminal law, if at all, is more likely to be relevant, but it is not unknown for civil actions to be relevant, cf *Re KR (Abduction: Forcible Removal By Parents)* [1999] 2 FLR 542.

[74] See Chapter 20.

[75] [1995] 1 FLR 711.

[76] Although note that Hale J, in *Re M (A Minor) (Care Order: Jurisdiction)* [1997] Fam 67, [1997] 1 FLR 456, considered that the ratio of *Re R* was simply that jurisdiction would be taken upon the basis of the child's presence.

Re M (A Minor) (Care Order: Jurisdiction).[77] In that case the child in question was born in Scotland to parents habitually resident there. The family came to England and, very shortly after their arrival, social services became involved following an alleged assault on the child by the father. An emergency protection order was made followed by interim care orders. Both parents returned to Scotland. The child was placed with the paternal grandparents, and the care plan was that he should be placed with them and have contact with his parents. Subsequently, a question was raised as to jurisdiction. Hale J ruled that the 1986 Act had no application at all. As she pointed out,[78] public law orders were deliberately excluded by the Law Commissions[79] when making their recommendations that led to the passing of the 1986 Act. In her Ladyship's view, the child's presence alone was sufficient to found jurisdiction irrespective of where the child's habitual residence was. As she said, if a local authority:

'... have reason to believe that a child in their area is suffering or is likely to suffer significant harm unless action is taken to protect him, they should be free to seek that protection without having to consider complicated issues of where the child may be habitually resident.'

Implicitly acknowledging the application of the principle of *forum conveniens*, Hale J rejected the argument that in this case England was not the convenient forum, not least because the incident that led to proceedings being brought had taken place in England.

11.45 One result of Hale J's decision is that there could be concurrent proceedings within the United Kingdom. However, her Ladyship expressed the hope that, in such circumstances, 'the authorities in each county would try to act in harmony rather than in competition with one another'. She did point out that, whereas in private law proceedings the same parties were involved, in public proceedings they were not. Accordingly, there could be no guarantee that if proceedings were not taken in the one jurisdiction they would be brought in the other.

The transfer of public law orders to other parts of the United Kingdom, etc

11.46 The powers to place outside the jurisdiction those children in local authority care in England and Wales are laid down by Sch 2, para 19 to the Children Act 1989. Paragraph 19(1) specifies that such placements require court approval which, under para 19(3), can be given only if the court is satisfied that such arrangements are in the child's best interests and that suitable arrangements have been, or will be, made in the county in which he will live. This general power is further supplemented by specific regulations

---

[77] [1997] Fam 67, [1997] 1 FLR 456.
[78] *Ibid* at 70 and 459 respectively.
[79] See Law Com No 138/Scot Law Com No 91, at paras 1.28, 3.4–3.6.

permitting the formal transfer of care orders to other parts of the United Kingdom, Isle of Man and Guernsey (but note, not Jersey).[80]

11.47 So far as Scotland is concerned, the relevant Regulations are the Children (Reciprocal Enforcement of Prescribed Orders, etc (England and Wales and Northern Ireland)) (Scotland) Regulations 1996.[81] These provide for the reciprocal transfer of care, supervision and educational supervision orders between England and Wales and Scotland, and between Northern Ireland and Scotland. So far as other parts of the British Isles are concerned, provided a full care order has been made,[82] under the Children (Prescribed Orders – Northern Ireland, Guernsey and the Isle of Man) Regulations 1991,[83] responsibility for the child may be transferred to Northern Ireland, the Isle of Man or Guernsey (but note, not Jersey). In each case, once the transfer has been effected the order made in England and Wales ceases to have effect.

Recovery of children abducted out of care

11.48 As Hale J observed in *Re M (Care Orders: Committals)*,[84] one of the reasons for the Law Commissions not having to consider care orders when considering jurisdiction and enforcement of orders concerning children was that machinery already existed for recovery of children in care taken to other parts of the United Kingdom. Currently, so far as England and Wales is concerned,[85] that machinery is provided by the Children Act 1989, principally s 50.[86] Under s 50(1), where it appears to the court that a child who is in local authority care, is the subject of an emergency protection order or is in police protection has been unlawfully taken away or is being unlawfully kept away from the responsible person,[87] then the court can make a recovery order. A recovery order operates, *inter alia*, as a direction to any person who is in a position to do so to produce the child on request to an authorised person.[88]

11.49 Under s 50(13), a recovery order made in England and Wales has the effect in Scotland as if it had been made by the Court of Session and as if that court had had jurisdiction to make it.

---

[80] *Sed quaere?*

[81] SI 1996/3267, which came into force on 1 April 1997.

[82] But not an interim care order, see *Re P (Minors) (Interim Order)* [1993] 2 FLR 742.

[83] SI 1991/2032, issued pursuant to the powers provided for by s 101 of the Children Act 1989.

[84] [1997] Fam 67 at 70, [1997] 1 FLR 45 at 459.

[85] The equivalent power in Northern Ireland is provided by Art 69 of the Children (Northern Ireland) Order 1995.

[86] Although note that, under s 49, it is an offence to remove, without lawful authority or excuse, a child from a 'responsible person' for a child in care, see **9.17**. For a detailed discussion of recovery orders, see *Butterworths Family Law Service* at **3A [3927]** *et seq*.

[87] Ie the person who for the time being has care of the child by virtue of the care order, emergency protection order or police protection order: ss 50(2), 49(2)(c).

[88] Children Act 1989, s 50(3). Under s 50(9) it is an offence intentionally to obstruct the removal of the child by an authorised person.

Chapter 12

INTERNATIONAL ABDUCTIONS: HAGUE ABDUCTION CONVENTION: INTRODUCTION AND HISTORY

ORIGINS OF THE CONVENTION[1]

12.1 The proposal to have an international treaty specifically dealing with abduction of children by one of the parents was first made by the Canadian expert, T Bradbrooke Smith, at a Special Commission held in The Hague in January 1976 to consider what subjects should be included on the Conference's future work agenda. That proposal led the then Deputy Secretary-General of the Conference, Georges Droz, to prepare a preliminary study of the subject which was presented to the Thirteenth Session of the Conference held in October 1976.[2] Notwithstanding that similar work was also being undertaken by the Council of Europe,[3] the Thirteenth Session warmly supported the Recommendation that the Conference undertake the topic. Further impetus for the initiative was later given by the Commonwealth Law Ministers' decision at their Barbados meeting in May 1980[4] that the Commonwealth Secretariat should follow the discussions at The Hague.[5]

12.2 Following the green light given by the Thirteenth Session, the Permanent Bureau initiated a study of both the legal and the social aspects of

---

[1] See generally Adair Dyer, 'Report on international child abduction by one parent ("legal kidnapping")', Preliminary Document No 1 of 1978, Acts and Documents of the Fourteenth Session, vol 3 at 12 (hereafter 'the Dyer Report'); Anton, 'The Hague Convention on International Child Abduction' (1981) 30 ICLQ 537; and *Thomson v Thomson* (1995) 119 DLR (4th) 253, at 270–272, per La Forest J (Can Sup Ct).

[2] See 'Note on Legal Kidnapping', Preliminary Document No 9 of September 1976, Acts and Documents of the Thirteenth Session, vol 1 at 121.

[3] See Chapter 19.

[4] Made at the suggestion of John Eekelaar, who had prepared for the Barbados meeting a valuable study of the problem in Commonwealth legal systems, since contained in his article 'International Child Abduction By Parents' (1982) 33 *University of Toronto LJ* 281.

[5] In due course, the Secretariat was represented during the final discussions of the draft Convention.

international child abduction. This study was conducted by Adair Dyer, the then First Secretary to the Conference, whose thorough comparative and analytical Report[6] together with a Questionnaire was submitted to Governments in the summer of 1978. Following the replies to this questionnaire (which gave overwhelming support to increased co-operation to deal with the problem) a Special Commission was convened in March 1979,[7] the object of which was to find agreement on the basis upon which a future Convention could be founded. There then followed a meeting convened by Georges Droz, comprising himself and Professors Anton and Pérez-Vera and Adair Dyer, held in September in 1979[8] at which compromises were arrived at and which then formed the fundamental basis of the 'Sketch of a Preliminary Draft of a Convention on International Child Abduction by One Parent'.[9] This draft sketch was presented to and discussed by a further meeting of the Special Commission held in November 1979, which eventually adopted it.

12.3   The draft Convention, as adopted by the November 1979 meeting, together with a valuable commentary upon it by Professor Pérez-Vera,[10] was circulated to Governments for their comments. Both the draft and the commentary drew largely favourable comments and formed the basis of the discussions of the Fourteenth Session of the Hague Conference held 6–25 October 1980. It was at this meeting that the final version was agreed upon. As Pérez-Vera's Explanatory Report explains,[11] the Convention was formally adopted on 24 October 1980 by the Fourteenth Session in Plenary Session and by the unanimous vote of the States that were present.[12] On the following day, delegates signed the Final Act of the Fourteenth Session containing both the text of the Convention and a Recommendation containing the model form intended for use in return applications in respect of children wrongfully abducted or retained. However, contrary to the usual practice of the Hague Conference, the Convention was made available for formal

---

6   Viz the Dyer Report, *op cit*, at n 1.

7   This Commission was chaired by Professor Anton (UK) with Dean Leal (Canada) as Vice-Chairman. Professor Elisa Pérez-Vera (Spain) was appointed as the Reporter.

8   See the Report of the Special Commission (prepared by Pérez-Vera) at para 15. This report is not to be confused with the later Explanatory Report of the final Convention also prepared by Pérez-Vera and to which extensive reference will be made.

9   Working Document No 11 of the November 1979 Special Commission.

10   Viz the report referred to in n 8.

11   Elisa Pérez-Vera, *Explanatory Report on the Hague Convention of 25 October 1980 on the Civil Aspects of International Child Abduction* (hereafter 'the Pérez-Vera Report'), para 1.

12   Viz Australia, Austria, Belgium, Canada, Czechoslovakia, Denmark, Finland, France, Germany, Greece, Ireland, Japan, Luxembourg, the Netherlands, Norway, Portugal, Spain, Sweden, Switzerland, the United Kingdom, the United States, Venezuela and Yugoslavia. Egypt, Israel and Italy did not participate in the vote, despite their active role in the First Commission's proceedings. It might also be noted that not all Member States attended the meetings. Those that did not were Argentina, Turkey and Surinam.

signature immediately after the Closing Session. Four States, Canada, France, Greece and Switzerland, formally signed, which is why the Convention bears the date 25 October 1980.[13]

AIMS AND OBJECTIVES OF THE CONVENTION

Securing prompt returns and respect for rights of access

12.4 One of the beauties of the Hague Abduction Convention is the simplicity of its objectives, which are set out in Art 1 (not specifically enacted by the United Kingdom),[14] namely:

'(a) to secure the prompt return of children wrongfully removed to or retained in any Contracting State; and

(b) to ensure that rights of custody and of access under the law of one Contracting State are respected in other Contracting States.'

12.5 In turn, these objectives are based, as the Preamble (not specifically enacted by the United Kingdom)[15] explains, upon the firm conviction 'that the interests of children are of paramount importance in matters relating to their custody' and upon the desire 'to protect children internationally from the harmful effects of their wrongful removal or retention and to establish procedures to ensure their prompt return to the State of their habitual residence, as well as to secure protection for rights of access'.

12.6 As Art 1 indicates, different remedies are given for breach of rights of custody and breach of rights of access. The former are protected under Art 12 by the remedy of the child's speedy return; the latter are protected under Art 21 by remedies to organise and secure the effective exercise of access. As a matter of fact, in relation to return orders, as was observed at the third meeting to review the operation of the Convention,[16] there is a difference of wording between the Preamble and the text of the Convention. Whereas the Preamble refers to the return of children to the State of their habitual residence, the text merely refers to a return without specifying that it should be

---

[13] Ironically not all of these States were the first to ratify. In fact, the first three States to ratify the Convention were Canada, France and Portugal. Those ratifications took effect on 1 December 1983. Switzerland ratified on 1 January 1984 while the Greek ratification only took effect in June 1993. For further discussion of ratifications, see **12.37** *et seq*.

[14] The Convention, as enacted by the United Kingdom, is contained in Sch 1 to the Child Abduction and Custody Act 1985: see further **12.55**. Notwithstanding its non-incorporation, both Art 1 and the Preamble have nevertheless been referred to 'as useful to recall' by Lord Slynn in *Re S (A Minor) (Custody: Habitual Residence)* [1998] AC 750 at 766, sub nom *Re S (Custody: Habitual Residence)* [1998] 1 FLR 122 at 130. For other references, see eg *Re M (Abduction: Psychological Harm)* [1997] 2 FLR 690 at 694, in turn citing *Re A (A Minor) (Abduction)* [1988] 1 FLR 365 at 367 (per Nourse LJ).

[15] See n 14 above.

[16] See the Report of the Third Meeting of the Special Commission (17–21 March 1997, at The Hague).

to the State of habitual residence. This difference, as will be seen,[17] has led to different interpretations among Contracting States as to whether the return should be to the applicant parent or to the Central Authority of the Requesting State.

12.7   Although, as one judge has observed, there is 'a sharp distinction'[18] between protecting rights of custody and rights of access there is no formal hierarchy of objectives under the Convention.[19] Nevertheless the vast majority of applications (83% according to the statistical survey of all applications made in 1999)[20] are for return and it is this aspect that generally receives more attention. We concentrate on return applications in this chapter and discuss access in Chapter 25.

The relevance of the child's welfare

12.8   Although the Preamble refers to the 'paramount' importance of the interests of the children in matters relating to their custody, this should not be taken to mean that an individual child's welfare is paramount in a Hague return application. As La Forest J points out in the Canadian Supreme Court decision, *Thomson v Thomson*,[21] the Preamble 'speaks of the "interests of children" generally, not the interest of the particular child before the court'. Furthermore, Art 16 expressly forbids the court of the requested State from deciding on the merits of the rights of custody until it has been determined that the child is not to be returned under the Convention.[22] In summary, the Convention is predicated upon the premise that children's interests are

---

[17]   See **16.5** *et seq*.

[18]   Ward LJ in *Re V-B (Abduction Custody Rights)* [1999] 2 FLR 192 at 198.

[19]   See the Pérez-Vera Report at para 18, but cf La Forest J who in *Thomson v Thomson* (1995) 119 DLR (4th) 253 commented that it was clear 'that the primary object of the Convention is the enforcement of custody rights'.

[20]   See Lowe, Armstrong and Mathias, 'A Statistical Analysis of Applications made in 1999 under the Hague Convention of 25 October 1980 on the Civil Aspects of International Child Abduction', Preliminary Document No 3 (Revised Version, November 2001) available on the Hague Conference website at http://www.hcch.net/e/conventions/reports28e.html (hereinafter referred to as 'the 1999 Statistical Survey').

[21]   (1995) 119 DLR (4th) 253 at 273. See also eg *Re M (A Minor) (Child Abduction)* [1994] 1 FCR 390 at 392–393, per Butler-Sloss LJ; *De Lewinski v Director General, NSW Department of Community Services* (1996) 70 ALJR 932 at 941; *Clarkson v Carson* [1996] 1 NZLR 349, and *Currier v Currier* 845F Supp 916 at 920 (1996). Note that the English courts take the view that even where an exception to the obligation to return has been established the child's welfare is still not paramount in deciding whether to order a return: see **17.4**. This has been questioned by Nygh in 'The international abduction of children', in Doek, van Loon and Vlaardingerbroek (eds), *Children on the Move* (Martinus Nijhoff, 1996), p 29 at p 36. For a critical examination of the application of the welfare principle under the Convention, see Schuz, 'The Hague Child Abduction Convention: Family Law and Private International Law' (1995) 44 ICLQ 771.

[22]   Discussed further at **21.39**. See also Art 19 which provides that a decision to return the child under the Convention 'shall not be taken to be a determination on the merits of any custody issue'.

generally best served in cases of wrongful removal or retention by promptly returning them to the State of their habitual residence. As the Pérez-Vera Report says:[23]

> 'the Convention rests implicitly upon the principle that any debate on the merits of the question, ie of custody rights, should take place before the competent authorities in the State where the child had its habitual residence prior to its removal.'

12.9   The fact that an individual child's interests are not the paramount consideration when determining a return application prompts the question as to the Hague Abduction Convention's compatibility with the requirement under Art 3 of the UN Convention on the Rights of the Child 1989 (UNCROC 1989) that in all actions concerning children 'whether undertaken by public or private social welfare institutions, courts of law, administrative authorities or legislative bodies, the best interests of the child shall be a primary consideration'. Indeed, this very question was raised in the Australian case, *In the Marriage of Murray and Tam*,[24] in which it was argued that Art 3 required that no decision to return a child should be taken without the child's welfare being treated as the primary consideration. The argument was rejected on the basis that, unlike the Hague Convention, the UN Convention, though ratified by Australia, had not been implemented by legislation and that, in any event, Art 11 of UNCROC 1989 entreats States 'to take measures to combat the illicit transfer and non-return of children abroad'.

12.10   With respect to the Full Court of the Family Court of Australia, the second reason is stronger than the first and, moreover, is further bolstered by Art 35 which entreats States to 'take all appropriate national, bilateral and multilateral measures to prevent the abduction of children for any purpose or in any form'. Perhaps the answer to the application of Art 3 is that, by providing admittedly limited exceptions to the obligation to return, the Hague Convention does pay sufficient regard to the interests of each child, especially as it is not determining the merits of any custody dispute but rather the forum in which that dispute must be determined. At any rate, it was this line of argument that led the German Constitutional Court to rule that the Hague Abduction Convention was compatible with the UN Convention.[25]

12.11   Whether re-abduction is a special case can perhaps be debated. Certainly the German Constitutional Court thought so in the *Tiemann* case.[26] As one commentator has put it,[27] in a situation where 'a return order is still pending concerning the first abduction, the court may not presume that the

---

23   At para 19.

24   (1993) 16 Fam LR 982, discussed by Nygh, *op cit*, n 21, at pp 40–41. See also *McCall and the State of the Central Authority* (1994) 18 Fam LR 307.

25   *G and G v Decision of OLG Hamm* 18 January 1995, 35 ILM 529 (1996).

26   BVerfGE 99, 145 (FRG).

27   Coester-Waltjen, 'The Future of the Convention: The Rise of Domestic and International Tension – The European Perspective' (2000) 33 NY Int Jo of Int Law and Politics 59 at 72.

best interests of the child requires its immediate return (to the abductor), rather it must consider the facts of the case more carefully to avoid "to and fro orders". Otherwise, the court would jeopardize the child's best interests and the fundamental rights of the child'. With this in mind, the court ruled that because both parents seemed to have disqualified themselves as agents of the child's best interests, the child had to be represented by a third person and be heard by the court. Although there is a clear logic in this approach, the danger is that it provides some encouragement to re-abduct. In the event, however, in this case the children were returned to the mother in France notwithstanding her original abduction from Germany.

12.12 It is unlikely that a return order made under the Hague Abduction Convention will be thought to be in breach of Art 8 of the ECHR on interfering with the right to respect for family life.[28] To the contrary, there have been three important rulings, namely, *Ignaccola-Zenide v Romania*,[29] *Sylvester v Austria*[30] and *Maire v Portugal*,[31] in which the failure of the domestic authorities to take adequate measures to enforce a return order has been held to be a breach of Art 8 on the basis of a failure to meet the positive obligation on States to ensure effective respect for family life by taking measures to enforce a parent's right to be reunited with his or her child.

AN INTRODUCTORY OVERVIEW OF THE CONVENTION

The basic scheme

Protecting rights of custody

12.13 Applicants seeking a child's return must first establish that the removal or retention is 'wrongful' as defined by Art 3, namely, that:

'(a) it is in breach of rights of custody … under the law of the State in which the child was habitually resident immediately before the removal or retention; and

(b) at the time of removal or retention those rights were actually exercised … or would have been so exercised but for the removal or retention.'

---

[28] Cf *Re F (Abduction: Child Right to Family Life)* [1999] Fam Law 806, in which custody of two girls had been shared between the unmarried Portuguese parents. However, the mother, who had subsequently come to England with one daughter and wrongfully detained the other, unsuccessfully argued that by splitting the two siblings a return order would be in breach of Art 8 of the ECHR. As Cazalet J pointed out, the mother's own actions had disrupted the previous settled arrangements sanctioned by the Portuguese court.

[29] Application No 3169/96 (2001) 31 EHRR 7, ECtHR.

[30] Application Nos 36812/97 and 40104/98 [2003] 2 FLR 210, ECtHR.

[31] Application No 48206/99, ECtHR.

For these purposes, such rights of custody can arise 'by operation of law, or by reason of a judicial or administrative decision, or by reason of an agreement having legal effect under the law of that State'.

12.14 We discuss the concepts of wrongful removal and wrongful retention in Chapter 14. Suffice to say here that establishing a breach of rights of custody for the purposes of proving wrongful removal or retention does not necessarily depend upon there being a breach of a court order, but can instead be established by reference to the applicant's rights under the law of the habitual residence. This innovative and more sophisticated approach[32] is quite different from that of the 1980 European Custody Convention, which is confined more traditionally to the recognition and enforcement of custody judgments,[33] and is simpler to operate.

12.15 Although it is not necessary to have a court order, under Art 15, judicial or administrative authorities of the requested State can request the applicant to obtain from the authorities of the State of the child's habitual residence, a decision or determination that a removal or retention was 'wrongful' within the meaning of Art 3. Unlike the 1980 European Custody Convention under which a post-abduction order (or 'chasing order' as such orders are commonly known) will be essential if there is no pre-existing order,[34] an Art 15 declaration is intended to assist in the authority's adjudication.[35] As the Pérez-Vera Report makes clear,[36] such a request is voluntary in that the return of the child 'cannot be made conditional upon such decision or other determination being provided'. We consider declarations in detail in Chapter 15.

12.16 Provided the hurdle of establishing a wrongful removal or retention is overcome, and provided the application is made within one year, then under Art 12 the authorities of the requested State must 'order the return of the child forthwith'. Returns may be effected voluntarily (under Art 10, Central Authorities are under an obligation to take all appropriate measures to secure voluntary returns)[37] or by court order. In either event, under Art 11 it is incumbent upon the authorities to 'act expeditiously' and an applicant has a right to request the reasons for delay if no decision has been reached within 6 weeks from the date of the commencement of proceedings. According to

---

[32] See the excellent analysis by Bruch, 'How to Draft a Successful Family Law Convention: Lessons from the Child Abduction Conventions' in *Children on the Move, op cit*, n 21, at 49 *et seq.*

[33] See Chapter 19.

[34] Discussed at **19.8** and **19.59** *et seq.*

[35] Note the English practice of granting declarations (pursuant to s 8 of the Child Abduction and Custody Act 1985) at the behest of the applicant whether or not a request has been made by the requested State: see eg *Re P (Abduction: Declaration)* [1995] 1 FLR 831 and *Re G (Abduction: Rights of Custody)* [2002] 2 FLR 703, discussed at **15.1** *et seq.*

[36] At para 120.

[37] See **13.31**.

the 1999 Statistical Survey,[38] globally, 18% of applications ended in a voluntary return as against 32% in which there was a judicial order for return. Limited exceptions to this obligation to return are provided for by Arts 13 and 20. Where an application is brought more than one year after the wrongful removal or retention then, under Art 12, there is still an obligation to return unless the child is 'now settled in its new environment'. These exceptions to the obligation to order a return are discussed in detail in Chapter 17.

Protecting rights of access

12.17   The scheme for protecting rights of access is less clear than that for protecting rights of custody. Unlike for the latter it is not necessary to establish a wrongful removal or retention but, pursuant to Art 4,[39] applicants must prove a breach of their access rights. Provided this hurdle can be overcome then applicants can look to the Central Authorities 'to make arrangements for organising or securing the effective exercise of rights of access',[40] but the Convention appears to place no obligation upon the courts to enforce access.[41] However, as we discuss in Chapter 25, there is some disagreement about this, with some States permitting access to be resolved under the Convention and others leaving applicants to invoke domestic law.

When the Convention applies

12.18   Article 4 provides:

> 'The Convention shall apply to any child who was habitually resident in a Contracting State immediately before any breach of custody or access rights. The Convention shall cease to apply when the child attains the age of 16 years.'

No application to children aged 16 or over

12.19   The Convention has no application to children once they have attained 16. As the Pérez-Vera Report observes,[42] this age limit is more restrictive than that accepted by other Hague Conventions.[43] According to the Report, this is because 'a person of more than 16 years of age generally has a mind of his own which cannot easily be ignored either by one or other of his parents, or by a judicial or administrative authority'. On the other hand, opting

---

[38] *Op cit*, n 20.
[39] Discussed below at **12.18** *et seq*.
[40] See Art 7f.
[41] See Art 21.
[42] At para 77.
[43] The Report itself refers, *inter alia*, to the 1956 and 1958 Maintenance Conventions and to the 1961 Protection of Minors Convention, but it may be noted that both the 1993 Intercountry Adoption Convention and, more importantly, the 1996 Protection of Children Convention both apply to children up to the age of 18. But a similar age restriction applies under the 1980 European Custody Convention: see Chapter 19.

for a simple cut-off at 16 means that the Convention *prima facie* applies to children under that age even if by the law of their habitual residence they have the right to choose their own place of residence.

12.20 According to the English decision, *Re H (Abduction: Child of 16)*,[44] Art 4 is to be interpreted strictly inasmuch as the Convention should be regarded as ceasing to apply to a child once he reaches 16 even where he was under that age when the application was made and notwithstanding that the Convention would continue to apply to a younger sibling.[45]

Child must be habitually resident in a Contracting State before breach

12.21 As Art 4 makes clear, for the Convention to apply, the child must have been habitually resident in a Contracting State before there was any breach of custody or access rights. It seems, however, that in this respect a distinction is to be drawn between return applications and those for access. In the former cases, regard has also to be had to Art 3 (which, as we have seen, defines 'wrongful removal or retention') which makes it clear that the Convention protects rights of custody under the law of the Contracting State in which the child is habitually resident.[46] However, as Hoffmann LJ said in *Re G (A Minor) (Enforcement of Access Abroad)*,[47] that does not in itself require a narrow interpretation of Art 4. He consequently held that in access applications, provided the child is habitually resident in *a* Contracting State, it is not necessary to show that the child was habitually resident in *the* State in which the access rights originally accrued.

12.22 'Habitual residence' is not defined in the Convention and has been the subject of considerable litigation. The concept is discussed in Chapter 4.

Who can invoke the Convention?

Applications for return

12.23 Article 8 provides that 'any person, institution or other body claiming that a child has been removed or retained in breach of custody rights' may apply for the child's return. Commonly, applicants are left-behind parents, but it is clear from Art 8 that any person, institution or body may seek a return

---

44   [2000] 2 FLR 51, per Bracewell J.
45   The application of the Convention to siblings was identified at the Second Meeting of the Special Commission to Review the Convention (January 1993) as the one problem of having a strict cut-off age limit under Art 4. Cf the discussion by Garbolino, *International Child Custody Cases: Handling Hague Convention Cases in US Courts*, 3rd edn (The National Judicial College, 2000), at s 4.2. It is submitted that the strict interpretation applied in *Re H* is to be preferred. According to the 1999 Statistical Survey, one application concerned a child aged 16 or over.
46   See eg *Re S (A Minor) (Abduction)* [1991] 2 FLR 1, CA, and *Re F (A Minor) (Child Abduction)* [1992] 1 FLR 548, CA, in which it was held that it is the child's residence immediately before the wrongful removal or retention that is relevant.
47   [1993] Fam 216, [1993] 2 WLR 824, [1993] 1 FLR 669, CA, discussed at **25.11**.

provided it can be shown that the child's removal or retention is 'wrongful' within the meaning of Art 3. On the face of it, this means that any person (eg grandparents or other relatives)[48] or institution or body (eg courts, local authorities or other public bodies)[49] whose rights of custody have been broken can apply. However, in *Ontario Court v M and M (Abduction: Children's Objections)*[50] Hollis J questioned the standing of a foreign court to make an application, pointing out that it was not competent to be sued in civil litigation nor could it be ordered to pay costs. It is perhaps a nice point whether the applicant must have the rights of custody claimed to have been broken. At the Third Review, for example, it was speculated whether a child of sufficient maturity would have locus standi to apply. The English courts, at least, take the view, at any rate in the context of applications by parents, that it is not necessary for the applicant to have the rights claimed to have been broken in cases where the court's right of custody has been broken.[51]

Applications for access

12.24   The Convention does not deal directly with who can apply for access. Instead Art 21 simply says that applications can be presented to Central Authorities 'in the same way as an application for the return of the child'. Whether this means that an applicant need not have the rights of access claimed to be broken is perhaps an open point, although given the nature of the remedy sought there would seem less scope for arguing that they need not.

How the Convention may be invoked

Applying for a return

12.25   Under Art 8 an applicant 'claiming that a child has been removed or retained in breach of custody rights may apply either to the Central Authority of the child's habitual residence or to the Central Authority of any other Contracting State for assistance in securing the return of the child'. However, pursuant to Art 29, this right is without prejudice to an applicant's right to apply 'directly to the judicial or administrative authorities of a Contracting State, whether or not under the provisions of this Convention'.

12.26   Although Art 8 leaves the applicant free to apply to whichever Central Authority he considers most appropriate, in practice it is easiest, and normally most efficient, to apply to the home Authority which will then transmit the

---

48   See eg *Re R (Abduction: Hague and European Conventions)* [1997] 1 FLR 663, CA, although note Hale J's doubts at first instance.

49   Including licensed adoption agencies: see eg *Re JS (Private International Adoption)* [2000] 2 FLR 638.

50   [1997] 1 FLR 475 at 476. See further **14.79**.

51   See eg *Re J (Abduction: Ward of Court)* [1989] Fam 85, sub nom *Re J (A Minor) (Abduction)* [1990] 1 FLR 276 and *Re H (Abduction: Rights of Custody)* [2000] 2 AC 291, [2000] 1 FLR 374, HL. Cf the view taken by the Massachusetts Supreme Court in *Viragh v Foldes* 415 Mass 96, 612 NE 2d 241 (1993 Mass).

application to the Central Authority of the State to which the child is said to have been taken or retained.[52] Nevertheless the Pérez-Vera Report makes the point[53] that the text of the Convention expressly mentions the Central Authority of the child's habitual residence 'for reasons of efficiency' and should not therefore 'be understood as signifying that applications directed to her Central Authorities are to be regarded as exceptional'.

12.27   The freedom, preserved by Art 29, to apply directly to the court where the child is located is to be noted. As Pérez-Vera Report says,[54] applicants using this method are *prima facie* put to the choice of whether or not to submit their application under the Convention. While they would normally be advised to do so since it is likely to increase the chances of obtaining a return order, the Pérez-Vera Report makes the important point that the authorities are not obliged to apply 'the provisions of the Convention, unless the State has incorporated them into its internal law, in terms of Art 2 of the Convention'. This means that applicants will need to check the relevant internal law. Given the general difficulties of making applications in foreign courts, applicants will normally be advised to apply for returns via the Central Authority, although on occasion it could be quicker to make a direct application. There are no statistics on how often this option is used in practice.

Applying for access

12.28   Article 21 provides that applications for organising or securing the effective exercise of rights of access may be presented to the Central Authorities of the Contracting States in the same way as an application for a return. Article 29 similarly preserves the right to apply for access directly to the court where the child is located. Although Central Authorities can play a significant role in securing access, given that many States, including England and Wales,[55] do not consider that the Convention imposes any duties on courts to deal with access issues, there may be some point in directly applying to a foreign court under its domestic law.

The role of Central Authorities and of the Permanent Bureau

12.29   We discuss in detail the role of Central Authorities in Chapter 13. Suffice to say here that they are administrative bodies or offices which each Contracting State is obliged to establish. They are concerned with the day-to-day operation of the Convention, their principal duty being to make and receive and process individual applications. In contrast, the Permanent Bureau of the Hague Conference, which is situated in The Hague, is more concerned with the overall operation of the Convention. The Bureau is the administrative

---

52   The role of Central Authorities is considered in detail in Chapter 13.
53   At para 99.
54   At para 139.
55   See *Re G (A Minor) (Enforcement of Access Abroad)* [1993] Fam 216, [1993] 2 WLR 824, [1993] 1 FLR 669, CA, discussed at **25.20** *et seq*.

office of the Conference and is charged with overseeing the operation of all the Hague Conventions including the 1980 Abduction Convention as well as spearheading new initiatives. So far as the 1980 Abduction Convention is concerned, as the *Guide to Good Practice: Part II – Implementing Measures*[56] explains, the Permanent Bureau:

> 'provides technical assistance and gives policy advice to States on the implementation of the Convention; monitors the operation of the Convention and facilitates its review by providing a forum to interested States and other international governmental and non-governmental organisations; encourages consistent interpretation and application of the Convention by attending and analysing case law, current practice and statistics; and maintains information concerning the status of the Convention and the Central and other national Authorities appointed to carry the duties under the Convention.'

Importantly, it organises periodic Special Commissions to review the operation of the Convention.[57] The Bureau maintains a website[58] containing a range of information about the Convention.

Interpreting the Convention

The application of the Vienna Convention on the Law of Treaties

12.30   Article 31 of the 1969 Vienna Convention on the Law of Treaties, which came into force on 27 January 1980, requires:

> '1.   A treaty shall be interpreted in good faith in accordance with the ordinary meaning to be given to the terms of the treaty in their context and in the light of its object and purpose.
> 2.   The context for the purpose of the interpretation of a treaty shall comprise, in addition to the text, including its preamble and annexes:
>   (a)   any agreement relating to the treaty which was made between all the parties in connexion with the conclusion of the treaty; ...'

Article 32 further provides:

> 'Recourse may be had to supplementary means of interpretation, including the preparatory work of the treaty and the circumstances of its inclusion, in order to confirm the meaning resulting from the application of Art 32, or to determine the meaning when the interpretation according to Art 31:
>
> (a)   leaves the meaning ambiguous or obscure; or
> (b)   leads to a result which is manifestly absurd or unreasonable.'

---

[56]   At 10.2. The Guide was produced by the Permanent Bureau of the Hague Conference of Private International Law and published by Family Law in 2003, and is also available on the Hague Conference website (see n 58 below).

[57]   To date there have been four Special Commissions to review the general operation of the Convention called in 1989, 1993, 1997 and 2001. In addition, a further Special Commission was held in 2002 to consider good practice and access.

[58]   At http://www.hcch.net.

Finally, as one English judge has put it,[59] '[m]aking it abundantly clear that a consensus view is desirable', Art 31(3)(b) requires that account be taken of:

'any subsequent practice in the application of the Treaty which establishes the agreement of the parties regarding its interpretation.'

12.31 In summary, what the Vienna Convention requires is that the Convention be interpreted purposively and in a manner accepted internationally without therefore attributing to any of its terms a specialist meaning which it may have acquired under domestic law. The desired approach is well summed up by the second conclusion of the Report of the second meeting of the Special Commission to review the operation of the Convention in January 1993, namely:

'The key concepts which determine the scope of the Convention are not dependent for their meaning on any single legal system. Thus the expression "rights of custody", for example, does not coincide with any particular concept of custody in a domestic law, but draws its meaning from the definitive structure and purposes of the Convention.'[60]

Important aids to interpretation

12.32 As La Forest J said in the Canadian decision, *Thomson v Thomson*,[61] pursuant to Art 31(2) of the Vienna Convention, it is permissible when interpreting the Convention to consult to the *travaux préparatoires* to the Hague Convention which are conveniently found in vol 3 of the Acts and Documents of the Fourteenth Session. The most extensively cited document is the Explanatory Report prepared by Professor Elisa Pérez-Vera (although it has been pointed out that this Report was prepared after the Fourteenth Session of the Hague Conference and was not therefore approved by it).[62] Other important sources both as to what was intended by the Convention and how it is being generally interpreted are the Special Commission meetings to review the operation of the Convention, the conclusions and recommendations of which can be found on the Hague Conference website.[63]

12.33 An important aid to international interpretation of the Convention is provided in the key judgments of the different jurisdictions. Access to these

---

[59] Ward LJ in *Re V-B (Abduction: Custody Right)* [1999] 2 FLR 192 at 197. The Vienna Convention was also expressly referred to by Hale J in *Re W, Re B (Child Abduction: Unmarried Father)* [1998] 2 FLR 146 at 158 and by La Forest J in the Canadian Supreme Court decision, *Thomson v Thomson* (1995) 119 DLR (4th) 253 at 272.

[60] Cited by Ward LJ in *Re V-B* (above) at 196. See also the similar comments in the Pérez-Vera Report, at para 85, and in relation to the interpretation of Art 13, see *Re H (Minors) (Abduction: Acquiescence)* [1998] AC 72, 87F, [1997] 1 FLR 872 at 881H, per Lord Browne-Wilkinson.

[61] (1995) 119 DLR (4th) 253 at 272–273.

[62] See *S v S* 2003 SLT 344 at [14], per Lord Clarke, and note also Stuart White J's comments in *R v R (Residence Order: Child Abduction)* [1995] Fam 209 at 215, [1995] 2 FLR 625 at 630.

[63] See n 58.

judgments has been immeasurably aided by the creation of the International Child Abduction Database, known as INCADAT. This database, which was set up following the recommendation of the third meeting of the Special Commission to review the operation of the Convention, and which is maintained by the Bureau on behalf of the Conference, is structured around the summaries of leading cases from different Contracting States. It can be accessed directly at http://www.incadat.com or via the Hague Conference website.[64]

Good practice

12.34 Although the need for uniform judicial interpretation of the Convention has long been recognised it has taken longer for there to be acceptance of the need for more uniform practice. The need for a paper on what was described as 'best practices' was recognised by the First International Forum hosted by the National Center for Missing and Exploited Children (NCMEC), held in Washington DC in 1998. Subsequently, judicial conferences in Du Ruwenberg in June 2000,[65] and Washington DC in September 2000[66] and at the Second International Forum held in November 2000[67] recommended that 'best practice' be discussed at the fourth Special Commission meeting.

12.35 Best practice was included on the Fourth Special Commission's agenda, although after discussion it was determined to adapt the vocabulary and focus on 'good' rather than 'best' practice. Although the idea of producing a paper on good practice was generally welcomed, the precise ambit and status generated considerable discussion. In the event, the following recommendation was adopted:[68]

> 'Contracting States to the Convention should co-operate with each other and with the Permanent Bureau to develop a good practice guide which expands on Art 7 of the Convention. This guide would be a practical, "how-to" guide, to implement the Convention. It would concentrate on operational issues and be targeted particularly at new Contracting States. It would not be binding nor infringe upon the independence on the judiciary. The methodology should be left to the Permanent Bureau.'

---

[64] See n 58.

[65] Judicial Seminar on the International Protection of the Child, De Ruwenberg, 3–6 June 2000.

[66] Common Law Judicial Conference on International Child Custody, Washington DC, 17–21 September 2000.

[67] Held in Alexandria, Virginia, USA, in November 2000.

[68] Viz Recommendation 1.16 of the Conclusions and Recommendations of the Fourth Meeting of the Special Commission to Review the Operation of the Hague Convention of 25 October 1980 on the Civil Aspects of International Child Abduction (22–28 March 2001), drawn up by the Permanent Bureau (hereinafter referred to as 'Conclusions and Recommendations of the Fourth Meeting of the Special Commission').

12.36   Following this remit, the Permanent Bureau, in part aided by a Good Practice Report prepared by NCMEC,[69] prepared an extensive document entitled 'Guide to Good Practice' which was subsequently adopted at a Special Commission meeting held in September 2002 and finally published in 2003.[70] Although it covers many aspects of practice concerning implementing measures and Central Authority practice, it is not concerned with judicial interpretation nor with issues such as prevention and enforcement. However, at its September 2002 meeting, the Special Commission recommended that further guidance on prevention and enforcement be prepared by the Bureau.[71]

THE CONTRACTING STATES

The distinction between ratifications and accessions

12.37   In common with other Hague Conventions, the 1980 Abduction Convention makes a distinction between ratifications and accessions inasmuch as all Contracting States, both present and future, are obliged to accept all ratifying States but have a choice as to whether to accept an acceding State. Ratifications and accessions are dealt with by Arts 37 and 38, which were not drafted by the Special Commissions, as all draft Conventions constructed during a Session of the Conference are subject to uniform treatment with regard to the final clauses. The Special Commission did, however, favour the idea that any State should have the 'opportunity to accede to the Convention, but the accession will take effect only in the relations between the acceding State and the Contracting States that have raised no objections to it within a certain period of time'. This was considered to be a 'balance between the desire for universality and the conviction that a system of co-operation is only effective when there is between the parties a sufficient degree of mutual trust'.[72] This construct was not, however, adopted for Conventions arising out of the Fourteenth Session as, under Art 38, 'accession[s] will have effect only as regards the relations between the acceding State and such Contracting States as will have declared their acceptance of the accession'. In other words, Contracting States must formally accept accessions in order for the Convention to enter into force between the newly acceding State and the existing Contracting State. Merely not objecting to the accession is not sufficient to bring the Convention into force between the two States. This

---

[69]   Viz Lowe and Armstrong, *Good Practice in Handling Hague Abduction Convention Return Applications* (NCMEC, 2002), which was based on the practice in some of the busiest jurisdictions under the Convention, namely, Australia, Canada, France, Germany, Mexico, the United Kingdom and the United States. Separate 'Country Reports' on each of these jurisdictions, and on Ireland too, have also been published by NCMEC.

[70]   *Op cit*, n 56.

[71]   See Recommendations 1(b) and 1(c) of the Conclusions and Recommendations of the Special Commission of September–October 2002 on the Hague Child Abduction Convention.

[72]   See the Report of the Special Commission (prepared by Pérez-Vera), at para 49.

construct differs from other Hague Conventions concerning children, which require a positive veto.[73]

Which States can ratify?

12.38 Article 37 of the Convention declares that it 'shall be open for signature by the States which were Member States of the Hague Conference on Private International Law at the time of its Fourteenth Session' which was the time the Convention was negotiated. In other words, all countries which were Member States at this time are entitled to ratify. Conversely, as Art 38 provides, all States which were not Member States of the Hague Conference at the time of the Fourteenth Session are entitled to accede to the Convention. In fact, membership at the relevant time has been complicated by the subsequent break-up of both Czechoslovakia and Yugoslavia, and the handing back to China of Hong Kong and Macao. In the former cases, the new countries, the Czech Republic, Slovakia, Croatia, Slovenia, Bosnia and Herzegovina, and the Former Republic of Macedonia, have each been permitted to ratify, while the ratifications made on behalf of Hong Kong and Macao, by the United Kingdom and Portugal respectively, remain in force notwithstanding that those territories are now part of China. As of August 2003, only Egypt, Japan and Surinam are still entitled to ratify. All the other Member States at the time of the Fourteenth Session have already done so.

The number of Contracting States

12.39 After a relatively slow start – only 12 States had ratified and 2 States acceded by the end of 1989 – by the end of the 1990s the number of Contracting States had expanded to 57, and as of August 2003 there were 74 Contracting States. After UNCROC 1989, the 1980 Hague Abduction Convention is the most widely accepted international Convention dealing with children.[74]

12.40 The fact that existing Contracting States, be they acceding or ratifying States, have positively to accept newly acceding States may cause confusion since, although as of August 2003 there were 74 Contracting States, the Convention is not in force between all 74 States, since many have not accepted certain accessions. Indeed, policy on accepting accessions varies considerably from one State to another. Australia, Canada and the Netherlands, for

---

[73] Cf the Hague Convention on Protection of Children and Co-operation in respect of Intercountry Adoption 1993, (the 1993 Hague Intercountry Adoption Convention) and the Hague Convention on Jurisdiction, Applicable Law, Recognition, Enforcement and Co-operation in respect of Parental Responsibility and Measures for the Protection of Children 1996 under which accessions enter into force automatically between States, provided an objection has not been formally entered within a specified period of time.

[74] As of August 2003 there were 53 Contracting States to the 1993 Hague Intercountry Adoption Convention and 31 to the 1980 European Custody Convention.

example, seem ready to accept most accessions,[75] whereas France and the United States have been more reluctant to do so.[76] So far as the United Kingdom is concerned, accessions were accepted as a matter of course until May 1998 when it accepted that of Turkmenistan. However, save for Malta, which accession was accepted in March 2002, no further accessions were accepted until September 2003 when a further 7 States were accepted.[77] As of September 2003, the Convention was in force between 61 States and the United Kingdom.[78] The Hague Conference website keeps a record of the current status of the Convention, which is useful for Central Authorities and individuals to see if the Convention is in force between themselves and the relevant foreign State.

12.41 Whether a more homogeneous response to accepting accessions will be adopted following the establishment of a standard questionnaire (adopted at the fourth meeting of the Special Commission to review the operation of the 1980 Convention)[79] to be completed by nearly acceding States, remains to be seen.

How and when ratifications, accessions and declarations take effect

12.42 To effect a ratification or accession, the relevant instruments have to be deposited with the Ministry of Foreign Affairs of the Kingdom of the Netherlands.[80] In each case, the Convention enters into force on the first day of the third calendar month after the deposit of the relevant instrument.[81] A similar procedure must be followed with regard to declarations of acceptance of accessions by existing Contracting States, although in this case the Duty Ministry of Foreign Affairs must forward, through diplomatic channels, a certified copy of the declaration to each of the Contracting States. Declarations take effect on the first day of the third calendar month after the deposit of the declaration.[82]

---

[75] As of August 2003, the Convention was in force between 69 States and Australia, and 71 States and the Netherlands. As of November 2003 the Convention was in force between 66 States and Canada.

[76] As of August 2003 the Convention was in force between only 44 States and France, and 53 States and the United States.

[77] Viz Belarus, Estonia, Fiji, Latvia, Peru, Uruguay and Uzbekistan: see the Child Abduction and Custody (Parties to Conventions) (Amendment) Order 2003, SI 2003/1518.

[78] For a discussion of the issue of accepting accessions, see Lowe and Armstrong, *Good Practice Report* (NCMEC, 2002) at 2.3.

[79] 22–28 March 2001, Recommendation Part II.

[80] See Arts 37 and 38.

[81] Article 43(1), which repeats the provision made for accessions in Art 38.

[82] Article 38.

Convention not retrospective

12.43 The date on which ratifications, accessions and declarations take effect is important, since Art 35 provides that the Convention 'shall apply as between Contracting States only to wrongful removals or retentions occurring after its entry into force in those States'.[83] In other words, in respect of return applications,[84] at least, the Convention does not operate retrospectively.

The territorial extent of ratifications etc

12.44 Articles 39 and 40 deal with the territorial extent of Contracting States' ratifications and accessions. Whereas Art 39 is concerned with the application of the Convention to territories for the international relations of which a Contracting State is responsible, Art 40 deals with the situation where the Contracting State itself (as in the case of the United Kingdom) comprises two or more territorial units with different systems of law. In each case, the State, when signing or depositing its instrument of ratification etc, may specify the territory (or territories) or territorial unit (or units) to which the Convention will apply.[85] States are also permitted subsequently to extend the application of the Convention to other territories or units[86] or to withdraw previously declared extensions or applications.[87]

12.45 Exercising these powers, Australia has limited the ratification to its States and mainland Territories, Denmark has excluded the Faroe Islands and Greenland, and the Netherlands has confined its ratification to its Kingdom in Europe. On the other hand, France's ratification extends both to the mainland (*France Métropolitaine*) and to its Overseas Departments (*Départments d'Outre-Mer*), namely, Martinique, Guyane, Guadeloupe, Réunion and Saint-Pierre-et-Miquelon, and its Overseas Territories (*Territoires d'Outre Mer*), namely Nouvelle-Calédonie, Wall et Futana and Polynésie Francaise.[88] The United Kingdom, having initially ratified the Convention on behalf of England and Wales, Scotland and Northern Ireland, has since extended its ratification to the

---

[83] Note that, although the United Kingdom has not directly implemented Art 35, the same provision is made in s 2 of the Child Abduction and Custody Act 1985. For a discussion of the position in the United Kingdom, see **12.58**.

[84] *Aliter* for access, see **25.9** *et seq*.

[85] Such declarations must be notified to the Dutch Ministry of Foreign Affairs.

[86] Such extensions take effect on the first day of the third calendar month after due notification to the Dutch Ministry of Foreign Affairs: see Art 43(2).

[87] See Art 44. Such 'denunciations' (see **12.48**) must be notified to the Dutch Ministry of Foreign Affairs at least 6 months before the expiry of the 5-year period of the official ratification or accession or its renewal.

[88] Note that in each case the responsibility for handling applications lies with the French Central Authority situated in Paris.

Isle of Man, the Cayman Islands, the Falkland Islands, Montserrat and Bermuda.[89]

12.46 A curiosity of the Convention is Art 41 which provides that neither ratifications or accessions nor the application of the Convention to different territorial units carry any 'implication as to the internal distribution of powers within that State'. As the Pérez-Vera Report explains,[90] although this may seem self-evident,[91] it was inserted 'largely to satisfy the Australian delegation, for which the absence of such a provision would apparently have created constitutional difficulties'.

Duration of ratifications and accessions and denunciations

12.47 Under Art 44, ratifications and accessions remain in force for 5 years but in the absence of a denunciation are tacitly renewed every 5 years. In other words, ratifications and accessions can only be brought to an end by the *positive* act of denunciation by the State concerned.

12.48 Any Contracting State can denounce its ratification or accession either totally or for certain of its territories or territorial units. Denunciations must be notified to the Dutch Ministry of Foreign Affairs at least 6 months before the expiry of the 5-year period.[92] To date there have been no denunciations.

RESERVATIONS

12.49 By Art 42 the only reservations that are permitted are those provided for in Arts 24 and 26 (discussed below). These reservations should be made not later than the time of ratification or accession or upon the making of a declaration extending the operation of the Convention to other territories or territorial units. Any reservation can be subsequently withdrawn. Such withdrawals must be formally notified to the Dutch Ministry of Foreign Affairs and will take effect on the first day of the third calendar month following due notification.

12.50 The key reservation is that permitted under Art 26, namely, that a Contracting State 'shall not be bound to assume any costs ... resulting from the participation of legal counsel or advisers or from court proceedings, except insofar as those costs may be covered by its system of legal aid and advice'. This reservation is in derogation of the obligation of Central Authorities and public services not to require the applicant to pay towards the costs of legal

---

[89] It will be noted that the ratification does not extend to the Channel Islands (*sed quaere?*) (on which see n 103 below) and that, unlike France, each of the units and territories has its own separate Central Authority.

[90] At para 149.

[91] Indeed the Canadian delegation considered the provision to be unnecessary.

[92] See Art 44.

proceedings.[93] As the Pérez-Vera Report says,[94] permitting this reservation was the only way of resolving one of the most controversial matters dealt with by the Fourteenth Session.

12.51 It is not uncommon for States to take this reservation, which means that, where it is available, applicants wishing to instruct lawyers to take proceedings will have to rely on the requested State's legal aid system.[95] Given the absence of a comprehensive system of legal aid in the United States, that country's reservation has been subjected to much criticism.[96] In response to this criticism, the Department of Justice in association with the US Central Authority agreed in 1985 to fund the creation of a network of lawyers willing and able to provide *pro bono* or reduced fee assistance in Convention cases, known as the International Child Abduction Attorney Network (ICAAN).[97] Ironically, the United Kingdom also made a reservation under Art 26 but in fact generously gives applicants for return free legal representation regardless of means.[98] Among the countries which have not made a reservation on Art 26 are Australia and Ireland.

12.52 The only other reservation permitted under the Convention is that under Art 24 by which Central Authorities can refuse to accept applications, communications and documentation either in English or in French but not both. Exercising this right, the United States has made a reservation stating that all applications must be accompanied by a translation into English. The French reservation states that all applications must be in French or accompanied by a translation into French. Neither State offers funding to pay for translations.[99]

12.53 A complete list of reservations made by each Contracting State can be found on the Hague Conference website.[100]

---

[93] Ie it cannot derogate from the obligation of each Central Authority to bear its own costs: see further **13.13**.

[94] At para 135.

[95] In some countries, eg France, notwithstanding its reservation, applications solely taken by the *Procureur* are free, although applicants are often advised to appoint their own lawyers: see Lowe, Armstrong, Mathias and Navarro, *Country Report: France* (NCMEC, 2002).

[96] For a summary of which, see the National Report for the USA – Common Law Judicial Conference on International Parental Child Abduction, Washington DC, September 2000.

[97] See the discussion by Lowe, Armstrong and Mathias, *Country Report: United States* (NCMEC, 2002) at 3.4.

[98] For a discussion of public funding in the United Kingdom, see **21.15**.

[99] For further details see Lowe, Armstrong and Mathias, *Country Report: United States* (above) and Lowe, Armstrong, Mathias and Navarro, *Country Report: France* (above), and for a discussion of translation issues generally see Lowe and Armstrong, *Good Practice Report* (NCMEC, 2002) at 5.2.4.

[100] See n 58.

IMPLEMENTATION BY THE UNITED KINGDOM

12.54 Exercising its right as a Member State of the Hague Conference, the United Kingdom ratified the Convention with effect from 1 August 1986. The United Kingdom was the fifth Contracting State to the Convention.[101] The ratification was initially made on behalf of England and Wales, Scotland and Northern Ireland but has since been extended to include the Isle of Man, the Cayman Islands, the Falkland Islands, Montserrat and Bermuda.[102] It is to be noted that ratification does not extend to the Channel Islands.[103]

12.55 The United Kingdom implemented the Hague Convention through Part I of the Child Abduction and Custody Act 1985, and Sch 1 to that Act sets out the Articles of the Convention as directly incorporated into UK law. It is to be noted that Sch 1 by no means reproduces the Convention in its entirety. Neither the Preamble nor Arts 1 or 2, for example, are included. Other notably absent provisions include Arts 20 and 35.[104] Some absences are more understandable than others. It is easy to see, for example, why all the final clauses continued in Chapter VI are omitted since they are more in the form of internal regulation of the mechanisms and effects of ratifications.[105] Article 35's absence is explained by the fact that its substance is contained in s 2(2) of the 1985 Act.[106] More questionable is the non-incorporation of Art 20, which we discuss in Chapter 17,[107] and there seems little to justify the exclusion of the Preamble and the two opening Articles.

12.56 So far as England and Wales are concerned, domestic rules of practice and procedure under the 1985 Act are provided by Part VI of the Family Proceedings Rules 1991 (FPR 1991). Those for Scotland are provided by Rules 70.1–70.8 of the Rules of the Court of Session, and those for Northern Ireland are provided by Part III of Ord 90 of the Rules of the Supreme Court (NI) 1980.

---

[101] Canada, France, Portugal and Switzerland had previously ratified the Convention.

[102] See respectively the Child Abduction and Custody Act 1985 (Isle of Man) Order 1994, SI 1994/2799; the Child Abduction and Custody (Falkland Islands) Order 1996, SI 1996/3156; and the Child Abduction and Custody (Cayman Islands) Order 1997, SI 1997/2574. To date there is no statutory instrument recognising the extensions to Bermuda and Montserrat. According to the Convention website operated by the Permanent Bureau of the Hague Conference, the Convention entered into force for both these territories on 1 March 1999: see http://www.hcch.net/e/status.abdshte.html.

[103] As explained in Chapter 11, n 2, abductions to and from the Channel Islands must be dealt with as if they were non-Convention territories. Non-Convention cases are discussed in Chapter 20.

[104] Other provisions not specifically enacted are Arts 23, 25, 33 and 34.

[105] Although note the reference to Arts 39 and 40 in s 2(3) of the 1985 Act.

[106] Discussed at **12.58**.

[107] See **17.186** *et seq*.

The Contracting States to which the Convention applies

12.57 Among the provisions of the 1985 Act are those dealing respectively with Contracting States and judicial authorities. With regard to the former, s 2(1) provides that the States within which the Convention operates, so far as the United Kingdom is concerned, are those specified by Order in Council. The relevant Order is the Child Abduction and Custody (Parties to Conventions) Order 1986,[108] Sch 1 to which contains the list of the Contracting States which are binding upon or accepted by the United Kingdom. Although the list is regularly amended, it is not always up to date. For example, notwithstanding its ratification (which the United Kingdom had therefore to accept) in August 2000, Turkey was not included in the list until December 2001.[109] This was a serious omission since domestic law was not therefore in conformity with international obligations.[110]

Convention not retrospective

12.58 Mention has previously been made of Art 35[111] which is enacted in terms of s 2(2) of the 1985 Act, by providing, *inter alia*, that unless otherwise provided by Order in Council:

> 'the Convention shall apply as between the United Kingdom and that State only in relation to wrongful removals or retentions occurring on or after that date [ie the date specifying the coming into force of the Convention for that State as specified by Order in Council].'

Applying this section, it has been held by the House of Lords in *Re H (Minors) (Abduction: Custody Rights); Re S (Minors) (Abduction: Custody Rights)*[112] that, with regard to return applications,[113] the Convention has no retrospective effect.

Reservation

12.59 As previously mentioned[114] the only reservation made by the United Kingdom is on the question of costs under Art 26. Section 11 of the 1985 Act spells out this reservation by providing that costs of litigation are not borne by any Minister or other authority but rather by the Legal Services Commission (in England and Wales) or the legal aid authorities in Scotland and Northern

---

[108] SI 1986/1159.

[109] Ie when the Child Abduction and Custody (Parties to Conventions) (Amendment) Order 2001, SI 2001/3923, was issued. This instrument also included Slovakia for the first time, even though it had ratified on 1 February 2001.

[110] A similar problem remains in relation to Sch 2 which contains the relevant list of States for the purposes of the 1980 European Custody Convention. See **19.29**, n 45.

[111] See **12.55**.

[112] [1991] 2 AC 476, [1991] 2 FLR 262. A similar conclusion had been reached in *Kilgour v Kilgour* 1987 SLT 568, per Lord Prosser.

[113] The position is different with respect to access applications: see **25.8** *et seq*.

[114] See **12.51**.

Ireland. In fact, the United Kingdom treats applicants generously by affording legal representation free of charge regardless of the party's means.[115]

Judicial authorities

12.60 Section 4 of the 1985 Act confines jurisdiction to entertain applications under the Hague Convention to the High Court in England and Wales and in Northern Ireland, and to the Court of Session in Scotland. By concentrating jurisdiction at this level, the judiciary have developed a high degree of expertise in dealing with these cases. Indeed, the UK practice in this respect is a model one, and one of recommendations of the fourth meeting of the Special Commission to review the operation of the Convention specifically[116] 'calls upon Contracting States to bear in mind the considerable advantages to be gained by a concentration of jurisdiction to deal with Hague Convention cases within a limited number of courts'.

Priority over the 1980 European Custody Convention

12.61 Another important provision contained in the 1985 Act is s 16(4)(c) which in effect provides that Hague Convention applications have priority over those made under the 1980 European Custody Convention.[117]

Inter-relationship with Brussels II

12.62 The inter-relationship between the 1980 Hague Abduction Convention and the so-called Brussels II Regulation is discussed in Chapter 18.[118]

THE USE MADE OF THE CONVENTION

12.63 At the time that the Convention was being negotiated there were no comprehensive statistics, although it was assumed that the phenomenon of parental child abduction was a growing one, and that abductors were commonly non-custodial fathers.[119] Although it remains the case that there are

---

[115] See **21.15**.

[116] See Recommendation 3.1.

[117] But note the discussion at **19.70**.

[118] See **18.26** *et seq*.

[119] See the analysis by the Dyer Report, at pp 18–21. In the questionnaire sent with the Dyer Report (see **12.2**), governments were asked to supply available statistics, but as Anton, *op cit*, n 1, observed, only a few countries submitted figures, namely: Australia (10); Belgium (15); Denmark (8); and France (75) (1977) and (130) (1978). The American response stated: 'while no official statistics were available, published estimates of parental abductors (inter state and international) range from 25,000 to 100,000 per annum' (but see the later study by Helzick, 'Returning United States Children Abducted to Foreign Countries: The Need to Implement The Hague Convention on the Civil Aspects of International Child Abduction' (1987) 5 BU Int'l LJ 119, in which the author refers to 276 cases in the United States in 1986). See also Agopian's study of 91 families known to the Los Angeles County in which he found 71% of abductors to be fathers: Agopian, 'Parental Child Stealing: Participants and the Victimisation

no reliable global statistics for non-Convention abductions,[120] there have been a number of studies into use made of the 1980 Abduction Convention.[121] The most comprehensive of these studies is that prepared for the Bureau by Cardiff Law School for the fourth meeting of the Special Commission to review the operation of the Convention.[122] This latter work, which has since been updated, and is available on the Hague Conference website,[123] analysed applications made under the Convention in 1999. Information, as supplied by Central Authorities,[124] was collected on the gender and nationality of the abductor,[125] the number, age and gender of the children, outcomes up to 30 June 2001,[126] the speed of outcomes and on whether the application was concluded after an appeal. The Report is in two parts comprising a global survey and a detailed analysis by country.

The number of applications

12.64 The survey calculated that there was a maximum of 1280 applications (it had information on 1268), comprising 1060 return applications (83%) and 220 access applications (17%) involving an estimated total of 2030 children (it had information on 2015).[127] Since this was a survey of applications handled by Central Authorities, it is possible that there were some additional applications made directly to courts that were not recorded by Central Authorities.

Process' (1980) 2-4 *Victimology: An Int J* 5, and *Parental Child-stealing* (1981); Janvier, McCormick and Donaldson's survey of 65 parents who sought help in locating their children from missing children's organisations, who found fathers to constitute 76% of abductors: Janvier et al, 'Parental Kidnapping: A Survey of Left-Behind Parents' (1990) *Juvenile and Family Court Journal* 41; and Finkelhar et al's 1986 national telephone survey which found fathers to constitute 75% of the abductors: see Finkelhar, Hotaling and Sedlak, 'Children Abducted by Family Members: a National Household Survey of Incidence and Episode Characteristics' (1991) 53 *Journal of Marriage and the Family* 805.

120 See Chapter 20.

121 Notably Chiancone and Girdner, *Issues in Resolving Cases of International Child Abduction, Final Report to the Office of Juvenile Justice and Delinquency Prosecution* (ABA Center on Children and the Law, 2000) and Lowe and Perry, 'International Child Abduction – The English Experience' (1999) 48 ICLQ 127. Other important studies include: Hatcher, Barton and Brooks, *Families of Missing Children: Psychological Consequences* (1992); Greif and Hegar, *When Parents Kidnap* (Free Press, New York, 1993); Girdner and Hoff (eds), *Obstacles to the Recovery and Return of Parentally Abducted Children: Final Report* (1992); and Fisher, *Missing Children Research Project: Vol 1 Findings of the Study* (1989).

122 Viz the statistical survey drawn up by Lowe, Armstrong and Mathias, *op cit*, n 20. The project had been generously funded by the Nuffield Foundation.

123 At http://www.hcch.net/e/conventions/reports28e.html.

124 The information is based on detailed responses by the Central Authorities of 34 Contracting States and on numbers provided by four other States.

125 Referred to in the Report as the 'taking person'.

126 Ie 18 months after the last possible application in 1999 could have been received.

127 Given that the survey included information on outgoing as well as incoming applications handled by Central Authorities, the only cases not captured by the survey were those between Contracting States for which it had no information.

12.65   A fifth of all the estimated applications were made to the United States,[128] with England and Wales receiving the second greatest number of applications (amounting to 14% of the estimated total).[129] Applications to England and Wales were nearly double those received by Germany which handled the third highest number.[130] Several Central Authorities handled no applications in 1999.[131]

About the abductors

12.66   So far as return applications are concerned, 69% of abductions were found to be by females, virtually all of whom were likely to be mothers,[132] 30% by males, and 1% by both. Although this finding is in line with other studies, notably by Lowe and Perry,[133] and shows that abductions, at any rate those dealt with under the Hague Convention, are not, if they ever were, predominantly about fathers taking the children, it masks some interesting regional differences. For example, between 88% and 100% of applications received by Scandinavian countries were made by females, and whereas in applications to England and Wales from the United States 85% of abductors were female, only 58% were females in applications to the United States from England and Wales.[134] One can only speculate on the reasons for these differences.

12.67   Just over half of the abductors (52%) were found to have the same nationality as the requested State and could therefore be presumed to be going home.[135] But again there were some interesting regional differences, notably that in applications to Australia, only 22% of the abductors were Australian

---

128   Amounting to 254 applications overall (comprising 210 return and 44 access applications). This comprised 22% of the Authorities surveyed.

129   Totalling 174 applications (comprising 149 return and 25 access applications).

130   Viz 94 applications (comprising 70 return and 24 access applications). Australia handled 78 applications (64 return and 14 access applications), with France receiving the fifth highest number, viz 42 return and 15 access applications.

131   Viz Belarus, Macao, Bermuda, the Falkland Islands, the Isle of Man, Montserrat, Uzbekistan and the Canadian Provinces of New Brunswick, Newfoundland, Prince Edward Island, Nanavut, Northwest Territories and Yukon.

132   The questionnaire asked about gender rather than the relationship but information gained from the United States returns confirmed that in almost all applications females and males correspond to mothers and fathers. In their study of cases handled by England and Wales, Lowe and Perry, *op cit*, n 121, found that only 3% of abductions were not by one or other of the child's parents.

133   *Op cit*, n 121, at 132–133, who found, in their analysis of cases handled by the English Child Abduction Unit, that between 1987 and 1996 there had been a considerable shift in the ratio of mother to father abductors from about 1:1 in 1987 to more than 2.5:1 in 1996.

134   The Anglo-American pattern was first highlighted by Lowe, 'The 1980 Hague Convention on the Civil Aspects of International Child Abduction: An English Viewpoint' (2000) 33 NYU Jo of International Law and Politics 179 at 184–185.

135   This was the assumption made by Lowe and Perry, *op cit*, n 121. But note that in some cases the abductors will have dual nationality.

nationals.[136] There was little difference in the overall pattern between male and female abductors, with 53% of the former and 52% of the latter being nationals of the requested State.[137]

12.68 Whether these findings have significance for the Convention's future has been debated. Indeed, at the third meeting of the Special Commission to review the operation of the Convention[138] some discussion focused on the apparently changing nature of international child abduction and in particular upon the fact (which cannot be substantiated by the 1999 study) that increasing numbers of abductions appear to be by primary care-giving mothers attempting to escape domestic violence by going home. However, the finding that abducting fathers are just as likely to be 'going home' as mothers must act as something of a counter-balance to any idea of disapplying the Convention in these circumstances, and in any event, irrespective of the reasons, the fact remains that all abductions involve disrupting the child's home and that is the 'evil' that the Convention is basically designed to avoid.

About the children

12.69 The 1999 Statistical Survey found that 63% of return applications involved a single child and 30% two children. One application involved a sibling group of six children. 38% of the children were under the age of 5; 42% aged between 5 and 9; and 21% aged between 10 and 16.

Outcomes

12.70 So far as outcome is concerned, the survey found that half of all the applications ended either in a voluntary return (18%) or a judicial order for return (32%). While this return rate might seem relatively low, it needs to be considered alongside the finding that 11% of applications were rejected either because of location difficulties or because they fell outside the Convention criteria.[139] Furthermore 14% of applications were withdrawn,[140] and 9% were

---

[136] In contrast, all eight abductors in applications to Hungary were Hungarian.

[137] Cf Lowe and Perry, *op cit*, n 121, who found that 61% of males and 69% of females had the same nationality as the requested State.

[138] Held at The Hague, 17–21 March 1997.

[139] If rejected applications are excluded the overall 'return rate' rises to 56%. In addition, in a further 20 applications, access was either ordered or agreed. If this latter outcome is 'factored in', 58% ended in what might considered to be a 'positive' outcome.

[140] A small study of applications made to and from England and Wales (see the 1999 Statistical Survey, Global Report, at para 17) found a variety of reasons for withdrawing, including the cessation of communication between the applicant and the lawyer or Central Authority, legal aid problems, private agreements between the parties, and an application for access being made instead. In other words, some applications may be withdrawn because of 'positive' reasons, such as access being agreed, while others are withdrawn for more 'negative' reasons, perhaps to do with the system itself. If both rejected and withdrawn applications are excluded, the 'return rate' rises to 67%.

still pending even by 30 June 2001.[141] Of those applications resulting in the child's return, 64% were the result of judicial orders and 36% of voluntary agreements. Of the cases that went to court, 74% ended in a judicial return order and 26% in a refusal (judicial refusals accounted for 11% of all applications). Of all applications made to court, 14% were found to have been appealed and of these 72% were found to have upheld the first instance decision with an overall 56% resulting in a return and 44% in a refusal.

Speed of outcome

12.71 So far as speed of outcome is concerned it was found that globally voluntary returns took an average 84 days, judicial returns, 107 days, and judicial refusals, 147 days, but these figures mask enormous variations and both median, minimum and maximum figures are also included in the report. Some cases were resolved extremely quickly, with the quickest judicial return being made within one day of the application, and the fastest judicial refusal taking just 5 days. Conversely, other cases were resolved extremely slowly with the slowest judicial return taking 718 days (just over 2 years) and the slowest judicial refusal taking 606 days (just over 18 months). Some countries did rather better than others. Cases taking a long time to be resolved raise the question as to whether a return is indeed the right solution. As the *Guide to Good Practice: Part I – Central Authority Practice* emphasises, speed is essential to the successful operation of the Convention.[142]

Access

12.72 A similarly detailed analysis was made of access applications made in 1999. There were some interesting differences from return applications. For example, 86% of respondents were female (compared with 69% in return applications). Only 40% (as against 52%) were of the same nationality as the requested State. Applications were slightly more likely to concern single children – 69% as against 63% of return applications. In all, 43% of applications concluded with the applicant gaining access either as a result of a voluntary agreement or court order. This compares with the 50% of return applications ending with a voluntary or judicial return. Paradoxically, of the applications that reached court, exactly the same proportion as in return applications, 74%, were granted. A higher proportion of access applications, 13%, were still pending as of 30 June 2001 as against 9% of return applications, and considerably more applications were withdrawn – 26% as against 14%. On the other hand, rather fewer access applications were rejected, 5% as against 9% of return applications, principally because it seems that less difficulty is experienced in locating the child. Access applications were

---

[141] A significant proportion (33%) of these applications were to Mexico.

[142] *Op cit*, n 56, at 15.1. Speed is further underscored by the revised Brussels II Regulation, under which, as between Member States, a court will be required, save in exceptional circumstances, to issue its judgment 'no later than six weeks after the application is lodged'.

found to be much slower in reaching a conclusion than return applications, with barely 5% being judicially resolved within 6 weeks (compared with 26% of return applications) and 71% taking over 6 months (compared with 19% of return applications). Voluntary settlements were also slower with 18% being reached within 6 weeks (compared with 50% of return settlements) and 42% taking longer than 6 months (compared with 14% of return settlements).

12.73   Taken as a whole, the findings support the generally held view that access provisions are not working as well as the return provisions, although perhaps not as badly as some had feared.

Chapter 13

INTERNATIONAL ABDUCTIONS: HAGUE ABDUCTION CONVENTION: CENTRAL AUTHORITIES

INTRODUCTION AND BACKGROUND[1]

13.1 Forming an integral part of the Hague Convention machinery and one which has been instrumental in its success are the Central Authorities which each Contracting State is obliged to establish.[2] In essence, Central Authorities are administrative bodies or offices through which applications can be made and received[3] and which are generally charged to co-operate with one another so as to ensure that the Convention's objects are achieved.[4]

---

[1] For an excellent discussion of the history and role of Central Authorities, see Bruch, 'The Central Authority's Role Under the Hague Child Abduction Convention: A Friend in Deed' (1994) 28 Family LQ 35.

[2] See Art 6, discussed further at **13.4**.

[3] But applicants are not obliged to use Central Authorities: see Art 29, discussed at **12.25–12.27**.

[4] See Art 7, discussed further below at **13.15**.

13.2 Although the idea of Central Authorities conducting day-to-day treaty obligations in specific cases was not a novelty of this Convention (earlier models can be found, for example, in the 1956 United Nations Maintenance Convention, the 1965 Hague Convention on the Service Abroad of Judicial and Extra Judicial Documents in Civil or Commercial Matters and the 1970 Hague Convention on the Taking of Evidence Abroad in Civil or Commercial Matters), the 1980 Abduction Convention did break new ground by making them centralised 'two-way' authorities charged with both initiating and receiving requests.[5]

13.3 As the Pérez-Vera Report explains,[6] a convention such as the 1980 Abduction Convention which is based on co-operation:

'... can in theory impose direct co-operation among competent internal authorities ... or it can act through the creation of Central Authorities in each Contracting State, so as to co-ordinate and "channel" the desired co-operation.'

Although the Special Commission quickly agreed on the desirability of the second alternative (with the result that 'the Convention is built for the most part around the intervention and the powers of the Central Authorities'),[7] there was a conflict of view between 'delegations which wanted strong Central Authorities with wide-ranging powers of action and initiative' and 'those which saw these Authorities as straight-forward administrative mechanisms for promoting action by the parties'. To accommodate this conflict, the framework of the Convention is deliberately flexible. For example, whilst it obliges Contracting States to establish a Central Authority, it does not prescribe how this should be done. Similarly, 'although the Convention clearly sets out the principal obligations laid upon Central Authorities, it lets each Contracting State decide upon the appropriate means for discharging them'.[8] Furthermore, States are free to undertake further duties compatible with the Convention, if they so choose. In the result, as one commentator contemporaneously observed,[9] 'the extent of the role of the central authorities will vary from State to State, but the fact of their existence should itself be a deterrent to potential abductors'.

---

[5] See Bruch, *op cit*, n 1, at 38.
[6] At para 42.
[7] See the Special Commission Report of 1979, at para 26.
[8] Pérez-Vera Report, at para 88.
[9] Anton, 'The Hague Convention on International Child Abduction' (1981) 30 ICLQ 537 at 547.

THE OBLIGATION TO ESTABLISH CENTRAL AUTHORITIES[10]

13.4 The creation of a Central Authority to facilitate the operation of the Convention is mandatory, Art 6(1) providing that Contracting States:

> '... *shall* designate a Central Authority to discharge the duties which are imposed by the Convention upon such authorities' (emphasis added).

However, following the long-established tradition of the Hague Conference, Art 6(2) provides that Contracting States which are 'Federal States, States with more than one system of law or States having autonomous territorial organizations' are permitted to 'appoint more than one Central Authority and specify the territorial extent of their powers'.

13.5 Article 6(2) is permissive in the sense that States are not obliged to establish more than one Authority (although if they do so they are obliged to 'designate the Central Authority to which applications may be addressed for transmission to the appropriate Central Authority within that State'[11]), and by no means all Contracting States comprising multiple jurisdictions have designated more than one Central Authority. The United States, Germany and Mexico, for example, have each designated a single Central Authority, although in the case of the United States, the functions are split between the State Department, which deals with outgoing cases, and the National Center for Missing and Exploited Children (NCMEC), which deals with incoming applications.[12] Among the States that have established more than one Central Authority are the United Kingdom, Australia and Canada.[13] In point of fact, most Contracting States have a single Central Authority.

13.6 Because of its key importance, the Central Authority (or Authorities) should be designated at the time of State ratification or accession and be ready to function when the Convention formally enters into force.[14] For most States the creation and establishment of a Central Authority will need to be done via implementing legislation (in the United Kingdom, for example, it was done by the Child Abduction and Custody Act 1985), but in some (for example,

---

[10] See generally Lowe and Armstrong, *Good Practice Report* (NCMEC, 2002), Chapter 3, and the Hague Conference on Private International Law Permanent Bureau, *Guide to Good Practice: Part II – Implementing Measures* (Family Law, 2003), Part 4.

[11] See Art 6(2). This obligation is not always strictly observed. But see the recommendations by Lowe and Armstrong, *Good Practice Report, op cit*, n 10 at 3.5.

[12] See **21.160**.

[13] For discussion of the position in the United Kingdom, see further at **13.9**. For discussion of the position in selected other jurisdictions, namely, Australia, Canada, France, Germany, Ireland and the United States, see Chapter 22. For more detailed discussion, see Lowe and Armstrong et al's *Country Reports* respectively for Australia, Canada, France, Germany, Ireland, Mexico, the United Kingdom and the United States (NCMEC, 2002).

[14] This is one of the recommendations in the Permanent Bureau's *Guide to Good Practice: Part II – Implementing Measures, op cit*, n 10, at 4.1.

France) the establishment can be purely an administrative process. In the past, not all States have set up a Central Authority, even when the Convention has come into force,[15] but in future, accessions are not likely to be accepted unless existing States are satisfied that an effective Central Authority has been established.[16]

LOCATION AND STRUCTURE OF CENTRAL AUTHORITIES

General overview

13.7   Although it is mandatory to establish a Central Authority, neither its location nor its structure is dictated by the Convention. This was deliberate as it was recognised[17] when drafting the instrument that given that the internal organisation of States differed greatly it would be beneficial to leave undefined the structure and capacity of Central Authorities. In the result, there is considerable diversity in location, structure, personnel who work in them and resources with which they work. Furthermore, States are free to determine whether the obligations imposed, *inter alia*, by Art 7 are discharged by the Central Authority itself or by what are described as 'intermediaries'. Consequently, the very role played by Central Authorities varies enormously. In Australia, for example, the Central Authorities act as the applicant in any court case,[18] whereas in the United Kingdom[19] and Ireland[20] the Central Authorities have a strictly administrative role. In States which have more than one Central Authority, the Federal Central Authority's function can also vary. In Canada, for example, its role is confined to providing information and tracing and does not deal directly with individual applications. In contrast, all applications to and from Australia have to be channelled via the Commonwealth Central Authority, and the regional Central Authorities essentially act on its behalf.

---

[15]   Spain, for example, did not initially have the necessary implementing measures in place and more recently both Fiji and Mauritius brought the Convention into force without having a Central Authority.

[16]   The fourth meeting of the Special Commission to review the operation of the Convention approved a questionnaire to be addressed to newly acceding States in which they are asked for the designation and contact details of their Central Authority. See Part II of the Final Report (The Hague, 22–28 March 2001). It is a specific recommendation of the *Guide to Good Practice: Part II – Implementing Measures, op cit*, n 10, at 4.1.1, that the Central Authority is established before the entry into force or ratification of the Convention and that details are notified to the depository and to the Permanent Bureau.

[17]   See the Pérez-Vera Report at para 45.

[18]   See further **22.5**.

[19]   See further **13.10**.

[20]   See further **22.32**.

13.8 It is not uncommon for Central Authorities to be located[21] in the Ministry of Justice,[22] but other locations include Ministries of Foreign Affairs[23] and Social Affairs,[24] community services departments,[25] the federal prosecutor's office[26] and police departments.[27] Research undertaken by the American Bar Association in 1995[28] found that Central Authorities at that time were generally small, comprising about three persons who spent less than half their time on Convention applications. However, there are considerable variations, with larger well-resourced offices and full-time staff, as in Germany and the United States at one end of the spectrum, compared with one individual who works part-time on applications, as in the Cayman Islands, for example, on the other. Clearly, staffing and resources are related to workload. According to the 1999 Statistical Survey,[29] individual offices handled between 329 and 0 new applications.[30] However, regardless of personnel, the key point is that Central Authorities should be properly established and sufficiently resourced to fulfil their obligations.[31]

The position in the United Kingdom

13.9 As the United Kingdom[32] comprises three distinct jurisdictions, namely England and Wales, Northern Ireland and Scotland, it is therefore a Contracting State operating 'more than one system of law' for the purposes of Art 6(2) and thus entitled to designate more than one Central Authority.

---

[21] The following information is taken from Bruch, *op cit*, n 1, at notes 12 and 17, and *Guide to Good Practice: Part II – Implementing Measures, op cit*, n 10, at 4.1.2.

[22] Eg Austria, Canada (except Prince Edward Island), Denmark, Finland, France, Greece, Hungary, Iceland, Ireland, Israel, Luxembourg, the Netherlands, Norway, Poland, Romania, South Africa, Spain, Sri Lanka, Switzerland and Turkey.

[23] Eg Ecuador, Mexico, Sweden and the United States.

[24] Eg Belize, Burkina Faso and Croatia.

[25] Eg in the Australian States or Territories of the Australian Capital Territory, the Northern Territory, Queensland, Tasmania and Victoria.

[26] Eg Germany.

[27] Eg South Australia and Western Australia.

[28] Chiancone and Girdner, *Issues in Resolving Cases of International Child Abduction, Final Report to the Office of Juvenile Justice and Delinquency Prevention, Washington DC* (American Bar Association Center on Children and the Law, 2000).

[29] Lowe, Armstrong and Mathias, 'A Statistical Analysis of Applications made in 1999 under the Hague Convention of 25 October 1980 on the Civil Aspects of International Child Abduction', Preliminary Document No 3 (Revised Version, November 2001) available on the Hague Conference website at http://www.hcch.net/e/conventions/reports28e.html (hereinafter referred to as 'the 1999 Statistical Survey').

[30] The most applications, 329, handled by a single office was by England and Wales. Although the United States had overall the most applications in total, 466 in 1999, they were split between the State Department and NCMEC. Several Central Authorities handled no new applications in 1999.

[31] See *Guide to Good Practice: Part II – Implementing Measures, op cit*, n 10, at 1.1.

[32] As defined by Interpretation Act 1978, Sch 1, para 5. It should be noted that neither the Channel Islands nor the Isle of Man are part of the United Kingdom.

Exercising this right, the implementing legislation, the Child Abduction and Custody Act 1985, provides that the Lord Chancellor is the Central Authority both for England and Wales and for Northern Ireland,[33] although in each jurisdiction a separate administrative body (see below) actually undertakes the Central Authority functions, and the Minister of Justice, in Scotland.[34] In addition, the United Kingdom has extended its ratification to certain Dependent Territories, namely Bermuda, the Cayman Islands, the Falkland Islands, the Isle of Man and Montserrat, each of which has a separate Central Authority.[35]

13.10   In England and Wales, the functions of the Central Authority are discharged on the Lord Chancellor's behalf by the Official Solicitor through the Child Abduction Unit, which is situated in London.[36] The Unit is headed by a lawyer and comprises a divisional manager and two full-time administrative staff who work solely on abduction, under both the 1980 Hague Abduction Convention and the 1980 European Custody Convention. They do not, however, deal with abductions involving non-Convention States, which are dealt with by the Foreign and Commonwealth Office. The lawyer is on hand to vet problematic cases, but as a general rule the Central Authority has a limited administrative function.[37] In fact, the Central Authority for England and Wales has the smallest staff in proportion to the number of cases it handles, compared with any other Central Authority. However, as it deals solely with abduction cases, and has no other responsibilities, it is able to act efficiently and expeditiously. The Unit has a small budget, only £205,000 in the financial year ending April 2000.[38] Much of this budget is spent on translation, which the Central Authority undertakes in all cases where it is needed.[39] The Unit has produced a booklet containing advice for parents, an updated version of which is online.[40] The Central Authority for England and Wales is designated as the Central Authority to which all applications may be sent for

---

[33]   See s 3(1)(a). In fact, any application to the United Kingdom can be made via the Lord Chancellor's Child Abduction Unit: see further **21.10**. Note that the UK Government has stated its intention to abolish the post of Lord Chancellor. Presumably, his functions will in due course be transferred to the Secretary of State for Constitutional Affairs.

[34]   Note that, although s 3(1)(b) of the 1985 Act refers to the Scottish Central Authority as the 'Secretary of State', in fact, by reason of Scotland Act 1998, s 53, the Minister of Justice is the Central Authority.

[35]   See **12.45**.

[36]   Viz at 81 Chancery Lane, London WC2A 1DD, tel: +44 (0)207 9117047/7045; fax: +44 (0)207 9117248.

[37]   See **21.14**.

[38]   See *National Report of the Delegation of England and Wales, Overview of Procedural and Substantive Law Regarding International Child Custody and the Hague Abduction Convention*, presented at the Common Law Judicial Conference held in Washington DC, September 2000 (hereafter referred to as 'National Report for England and Wales').

[39]   The Central Translators in London charge £25 per page.

[40]   *Child Abduction – Advice to Parents* (1996). For the website, see www.offsol.demon.co.uk.

transmission to the relevant Central Authority within the United Kingdom.[41] However, in practice, applications are sent directly to the Central Authority of the relevant jurisdiction.

13.11 In Scotland, the duties of the Central Authority are discharged by the Scottish Central Authority, which is situated in the Civil Justice and International Division of the Scottish Executive Justice Department based in Edinburgh.[42] Each Branch within the International Division is headed by a practising solicitor, and overall responsibility lies with the head of the Division, who is also a practising solicitor. The Scottish Central Authority comprises one full-time member of administrative staff and one quarter of the time of a policy adviser. It has produced a helpful booklet[43] which at the time of writing is under review, the plan being to also make it available in electronic form.[44]

13.12 The Northern Ireland Court Services undertakes the duties of the Central Authority in Northern Ireland.[45] There are no dedicated resources, and the relevant functions are discharged by an administrator and a lawyer (requiring one quarter and one fifth of their respective time). At the time of writing, a website is anticipated to be online in autumn 2003 and a booklet is being prepared.

OBLIGATIONS, POWERS AND FUNCTIONS

The overall scheme

13.13 The Convention sets out a number of obligations, powers and functions of Central Authorities. This is done principally, but not exclusively, by Art 7. That Article is structured in two paragraphs, the first of which sets out the general duty of co-operation, while the second lists some[46] of the principal functions that Central Authorities have 'either directly or through an intermediary' to discharge at the different stages of intervention in the typical

---

[41] See Child Abduction and Custody Act 1985, s 3(2), (3).

[42] Viz at Central Authority for Scotland, Scottish Executive, Justice Department, Civil Justice and International Division, St Andrews' House, Regent Road, Edinburgh EH1 3DG, tel: +44 (0)131 2444827/4829; fax: +44 (0)131 2444848.

[43] *Child Abduction from Scotland* (Scottish Courts Administration, 1996). Note also *Practical Police Guidance on the Unlawful Removal of Children Abroad* (Association of Chief Police Officers in Scotland, 2001).

[44] The Authority also intends to attach papers to the Scottish Executive website including detailed information on child abduction and copies of the application form which could be downloaded.

[45] Its address is Northern Ireland Court Services, Civil and Family Branch, 21st Floor, Windsor House, 9–15 Bedford Street, Belfast BT2 7LT, tel: +44 (0)28 9032 8594; fax: +44 (0)28 9031 4854.

[46] Ie this list is not intended to be exhaustive. This is made clear by the words 'in particular' in the second paragraph to Art 7 when describing the obligation to 'take all appropriate measures'. See also the Pérez-Vera Report, at para 90.

case of a child removal.[47] But these functions have to be understood in the context of the important obligation both to receive and to transmit applications, pursuant to Arts 8 and 9. Additional duties include assistance 'so far as practicable' in obtaining a determination that a removal or retention was 'wrongful' for the purposes of the Convention,[48] and the monitoring of delays in the processing of return applications.[49] Importantly, in applying the Convention, each Central Authority must bear its own costs.[50]

13.14   While the first paragraph of Art 7 squarely places the duty of co-operation upon Central Authorities, the second paragraph refers to the discharge of the listed functions either by the Authorities directly or through an intermediary (which can be a public or private agency). This was done so as to permit each Contracting State to decide upon the appropriate means for discharging these functions and thus to be able to work within the context of the respective internal laws.[51] Flexibility is further promoted by the requirement that the functions should be discharged only where it is 'appropriate'. According to Singer J in *Re M and J (Abduction: International Judicial Collaboration)*[52] it is within the scope of Art 7 as a whole for a judge hearing a 1980 Hague Abduction Convention application to make direct contact with a foreign judge.

The duty to promote co-operation

13.15   The opening paragraph of Art 7 provides:

> 'Central Authorities shall co-operate with each other and promote co-operation amongst the competent authorities in their respective State to secure the prompt return of children and to achieve the other objects of this Convention.'

13.16   As the Pérez-Vera Report says,[53] co-operation has to develop on two levels, namely, as between Central Authorities and amongst competent authorities within the State.[54] So far as the former is concerned the experience

---

[47]   See the Pérez-Vera Report, at paras 88 and 90. But note the obligation in Art 7(f) *inter alia* 'to make arrangements for organizing or securing the effective exercise of rights of access', discussed in Chapter 25.

[48]   Viz under Art 15, discussed in Chapter 19.

[49]   See Art 11, which provides that a Central Authority may enquire as to the reasons for delay if no decision on a return application has been made by the judicial or administrative authority within 6 weeks of commencement of proceedings. Article 11 also provides that 'If a reply is received by the Central Authority of the requested State, that Authority shall transmit the reply to the Central Authority of the requesting State, or to the applicant, as the case may be'.

[50]   See Art 26.

[51]   See the Pérez-Vera Report, at para 88, and the Special Commission Report (1979), at para 27.

[52]   [2000] 1 FLR 803. For judicial communication, see also **9.62**.

[53]   At para 89.

[54]   As the Canadian Delegation remarked in its comments to Preliminary Document No 6 in Acts and Documents of the Fourteenth Session, vol III, at 227, it is not intended by this

has been that co-operation has developed through regular communication at the operational level of handling individual cases. But it has also been enhanced by the periodic formal reviews of the Convention held by the Permanent Bureau, which provide an opportunity for Central Authority staff to meet each other and to discuss problems of mutual interest. At the fourth meeting to review the Convention, it was specifically recommended[55] that Central Authorities be 'encouraged, in addressing any practical problems concerning the proper functioning of the Convention, to engage in dialogue with one another. Where a group of Central Authorities share a common problem, consideration should be given to joint meetings which might in some cases be facilitated by the Hague Conference'. It also recommended[56] that Authorities explore ways of sharing their expertise and experiences with other Central Authorities when requested to do so.

Receiving and transmitting applications

13.17   Pursuant to the right conferred by Art 8[57] on individuals seeking to invoke the Convention to apply to any Central Authority, Art 9 provides:

> 'If the Central Authority which receives an application referred to in Art 8 has reason to believe that the child is in another Contracting State, it shall directly and without delay transmit the application to the Central Authority if that State and inform the requesting Central Authority, or the applicant, as the case may be.'

13.18   Essentially, Art 9 operates in two separate circumstances, namely, where a Central Authority receives an application from the applicant, usually in the State of child's habitual residence, and is thus operating as the requesting State, and where it receives an application from the requesting Central Authority but then discovers that the child is located in a third State. In each case the Authority should transmit the application to the Authority of the State where the child is thought to be located. In the latter case, there is an obligation to inform the requesting Central Authority of the onward transmission.[58]

---

provision to obligate direct co-operation, which it considers its counterpart in Art 3(2) of the 1980 European Custody Convention to require.

55   See Conclusions and Recommendations of the Fourth Meeting of the Special Commission to Review the Operation of the Hague Convention of 25 October 1980 on the Civil Aspects of International Child Abduction (22–28 March 2001) (hereinafter referred to as 'Conclusions and Recommendations of the Fourth Meeting of the Special Commission'), para 2.9.

56   *Ibid* at para 2.7.

57   Discussed at **12.25–12.26**. This right is without prejudice to the right of individuals to apply directly to the relevant court; see Art 29, discussed at **12.25** and **12.27**.

58   Cf the Pérez-Vera Report, at para 102, which comments that Art 9 'has not been very artfully drafted', since there would appear to be no obligation upon the Central Authority of the requested State to inform the Authority of the requesting State unless a second Authority is involved. However, this surely confuses the obligation to inform the requesting

13.19 In general, a Central Authority is bound to receive applications made under the Convention.[59] The only exception is, pursuant to Art 27, 'where it is manifest that the requirements of the Convention are not fulfilled or that the application is otherwise not well founded'. In such cases, 'the Central Authority shall forthwith inform the applicant or the Central Authority through which the application was submitted, as the case may be, of its reasons'. Article 27 permits both the Central Authority initially seized of the application and the Authority which receives an application from another Authority, to reject it.

13.20 Although, as the Pérez-Vera Report says,[60] '[c]ommon sense would indicate that Central Authorities cannot be obliged to accept applications which belong outside the scope of the Convention, or are manifestly without foundation', it is clearly a significant decision that should not be taken lightly. According to the 1999 Statistical Survey,[61] 11% of return applications made in 1999[62] were rejected by Authorities of requested States,[63] although over half (59%) were because the child was either located in another State[64] or not located at all. Other reasons for rejection included the child being over the age of 16, the applicant not having rights of custody, and the Convention not being in force between the requesting and requested States.

Locating the child

13.21 By Art 7(a), Central Authorities are enjoined either directly or through intermediaries to take all appropriate measures 'to discover the whereabouts of a child who has been wrongfully removed or retained'.

Central Authority of onward transmission which is what Art 9 is about, with the duty to acknowledge the receipt of the application which falls outside the Article but within that of general co-operation under Art 7. In any event, it is standard practice to acknowledge the receipt of an application, although this has been underscored by the recommendation of the fourth meeting of the Special Commission that 'Central Authorities should acknowledge receipt of an application immediately' (Conclusions and Recommendations of the Fourth Meeting of the Special Commission, at para 1.3). This has now been incorporated into *Guide to Good Practice: Part II – Implementing Measures*, op cit, n 10, at 4.4.

[59] See Anton, 'The Hague Convention on International Child Abduction' (1981) 30 ICLQ 537 at 548.

[60] At para 137.

[61] *Op cit*, n 29.

[62] That is, 102 out of 952 applications. Only 5% of access applications were rejected. It is surmised that that was because there were less difficulties in locating the children. In terms of numbers, England and Wales rejected the most applications, 22 out of 149 return applications, amounting to 15%.

[63] It is not known how many were rejected by the requesting States.

[64] Of course some of these cases will have resulted in further applications in the appropriate State.

13.22 At the time when the Convention was concluded, the location of the child was envisaged to be one of the most pressing problems[65] and, although this view was based upon the stereotypical image of abductions by non-primary caregiving fathers, location can still be problematic. Indeed, according to the 1999 Statistical Survey, in over one quarter (26%) of applications rejected by requested States the reason was because the child could not be found.[66] In addition, applications particularly in Mexico and the United States are often left open for lengthy periods because of location difficulties.[67]

13.23 In many cases, the applicant will know where the child is, so that location will be a simple task. Indeed, Art 8 requires that applications contain 'all available information relating to the whereabouts of the child and the identity of the person with whom the child is presumed to be', a point underscored by the Conclusions and Recommendations of the Fourth Meeting of the Special Commission, which stated[68] that applications should contain 'detailed information on location of the child'. Where the applicant or the requesting Central Authority is aware of information relating to the location of the child, this information must be transmitted to the requested Central Authority without delay.

13.24 Where location is an issue, Central Authorities can make use of authorities and organisations in their State which have experience of locating missing persons. In many States the police are called upon to help locate children, although it has been suggested that, in States where parental abduction is not a crime, the police may not act with urgency given that they have many other duties competing for their time.[69] Indeed, the French Central Authority has commented that on occasions the French authorities will advise the left-behind parent to bring a criminal claim as this gives greater investigative powers to the police to locate a child than they have in civil cases.[70] Similarly, in Canada, criminal charges can be helpful with regard to locating children. Often criminal charges will be dropped once a child has been located, and the civil Convention remedy will be pursued. If criminal charges

---

[65] See Anton, 'The Hague Convention on International Child Abduction' (1981) 30 ICLQ 537 at 547, who commented 'The *main problem* for the person from whom the child has been abducted ... is the practical role of tracing the child' (emphasis added).

[66] See the 1999 Statistical Survey, which recorded 27 such cases.

[67] See Lowe and Armstrong, *Good Practice Report* (NCMEC, 2002) at p 35. According to Bruch, 'The Central Authority's Role Under the Hague Child Abduction Convention: A Friend in Deed' (1994) 28 Family LQ 35 at 61, n 45, during the first 3 years of the Convention's operation in the United States, location was an issue in 60 out of 335 cases.

[68] At para 1.6.

[69] At the Second International Forum on Parental Child Abduction held in Alexandria, USA, in November 2000, in a presentation entitled 'Should International Child Abduction be treated as a Felony?', Anne-Marie Hutchinson proposed that Contracting States should set up a scheme to use powers of police and Interpol for all Hague abduction cases, whether or not an offence has been committed.

[70] See Lowe and Armstrong, *Good Practice Report, op cit*, n 67, at p 35.

have been issued in the United States, the local police can contact Interpol who can assist in locating the child. In such cases, NCMEC acts as a liaison with Interpol.

13.25 Many Contracting States utilise bodies specialised in dealing with locating missing children. In the United States, for example, there are 50 State Clearinghouses plus a clearinghouse in the District of Columbia which operate as missing children's registries. Moreover, NCMEC, which acts as the Central Authority for incoming applications, is itself a specialist missing children's organisation. In Canada, the Royal Canadian Mounted Police operates a Missing Children's Registry, which is useful for helping to locate children.

13.26 The fourth meeting of the Special Commission commented[71] that 'Central Authorities, in seeking to locate children, should be able to obtain information from other governmental agencies and authorities and to communicate such information to interested authorities'. It further stated that '[w]here possible their enquiries should be exempted from legislation or regulations concerning the confidentiality of such information'. In many States, Central Authorities are able to access government records in order to trace abducted children. In the United Kingdom, for example, various government agencies can be ordered to assist in tracing a missing child.[72] Similarly in Australia, the Federal and State police, the Department of Immigration, the Secretary of Foreign Affairs and Trade and the relevant Embassies or High Commissions may be required to assist in enquiries concerning the location of a missing child. A warrant can also be issued to the Federal and/or State police for the possession of the child. Where such a warrant has been issued, the court may overrule any secrecy regulations on government documentation which may hold information on the whereabouts of the child. In the United States, the International Child Abduction Remedies Act (ICARA) of 1988, which implements the Convention, gives the American Central Authority power of access to certain American records which may have information regarding the location of the child or the abductor.[73] In Germany, legislation known as the BKAGesetz empowers the Central Authority to obtain information to aid the location of a missing child from the Federal Criminal Police Office (Interpol Germany) or from local police stations.

13.27 Domestic legislation can also be of assistance in locating children. In the United Kingdom, for example, the court can order any person to reveal the child's location.[74] Failure to comply with such an order is punishable as contempt, which includes possible imprisonment. The police are also entitled

---

[71] At para 1.9.
[72] *Practice Direction (Disclosure of Addresses)* [1989] 1 WLR 219, [1989] 1 All ER 765, as amended by *Practice Direction* [1995] 2 FLR 813.
[73] See ICARA § 11608(a).
[74] Family Law Act 1986, s 33: see **10.3** and **10.15**.

to search property and recover children.[75] In Australia, the Commonwealth Central Authority can apply to the court for a location order[76] requiring a person to give to the court information about the whereabouts of the child which he may have or which he may obtain. When a child is located, a recovery order[77] will enable authorities to recover and return the child to the person seeking recovery.

13.28 The fourth meeting of the Special Commission recommended that each Central Authority should provide a website or brochure, which could detail 'means by which a missing child may be located'.[78] In the questionnaire approved by the Special Commission for newly acceding States, States are asked to 'indicate the agencies involved and the processes available for the location of missing children'.[79] In this regard, the Central Authority websites in Australia, Canada, England and Wales, and the United States contain information on how to search for a missing child as well as links to non-governmental organisations which may be able to assist in the search and provide support to the applicant parent.[80] It is a point of good practice that Central Authorities have adequate links with authorities and organisations able to assist in locating missing children within their State.

Providing interim protection

13.29 Article 7(b) enjoins Central Authorities either directly or through intermediaries to take all appropriate measures 'to prevent further harm to the child or prejudice to interested parties by taking or causing to be taken provisional measures'.

13.30 As the Pérez-Vera Report says,[81] the provisional measures envisaged are basically those designed to prevent another removal of the child. The ability of the Central Authority itself to put in place protective measures will vary according to the relevant internal laws,[82] but the key point is that the Authority should promote the taking of such measures. In the United Kingdom, once an application has been made to court, relevant directions may be given 'for the purpose of securing the welfare of the child concerned in

---

[75] Family Law Act 1986, s 34, and for application to Scotland, see s 40(2).

[76] See Family Law Act 1975 (Cth), ss 67J, 67K, 67L, 67M, 67N, 67P.

[77] *Ibid*, ss 67Q, 67R, 67S, 67T, 67U, 67V, 67W, 67X, 67Y.

[78] Conclusions and Recommendations of the Fourth Meeting of the Special Commission, para 1.8, and see *Guide to Good Practice: Part II – Implementing Measures*, *op cit*, n 10, at 4.10.

[79] At para 2.3 II.

[80] See Australia: http://www.law.gov.au/childabduction/inforforparents.html; Canada: http://www.missingchildren.ca; http://www.mcsc.ca; USA: http://www.missingkids.com; UK – England and Wales: http://www.offsol.demon.co.uk.

[81] At para 91.

[82] In Alberta, Canada, once the Central Authority takes charge of the child, a designated director may provide for the child's care and maintenance: International Child Abduction Act, SA 1986, s 5.

preventing changes in the circumstances relevant to the determination of the application'.[83] Exercising this power, it has been held[84] appropriate to authorise the Tipstaff to collect the child and return him to the applicant, even before the child's arrival in the jurisdiction.

Voluntary return

13.31   An important obligation is that under Art 7(c), namely that Central Authorities either directly or through intermediaries take all appropriate steps 'to secure the voluntary return of the child or to bring about an amicable resolution of the issues'. This obligation is reinforced by Art 10 which, in the context of return applications, directs the Central Authority of the State where the child is 'to take or cause to be taken all appropriate measures in order to obtain the voluntary return of the child'. According to the Pérez-Vera Report,[85] the inclusion of Art 10 giving preferential treatment to Art 7(c) 'highlights the interest of the Convention in seeing parties have recourse to this way of proceeding'.[86] The importance of seeking voluntary resolution was further emphasised by the Fourth Special Commission which stated that, 'Central Authorities should encourage voluntary return where possible'.[87] However, the international judicial seminar at De Ruwenberg[88] (October 2001) stated in its conclusions and recommendations:

> 'Measures employed to assist in securing the voluntary return of the child or to bring about an amicable resolution of the issues are encouraged but should not result in any undue delay in return proceedings.'

According to the 1999 Statistical Survey,[89] 18% of return applications ended in a voluntary return, as against 32% which ended in a judicial return.

13.32   Although the method and means of seeking a voluntary resolution are not prescribed by the Convention, the Pérez-Vera Report comments[90] that:

---

83   Child Abduction and Custody Act 1985, s 5.
84   See *Re N (Child Abduction: Jurisdiction)* [1995] Fam 96, [1995] 2 WLR 233, sub nom *A v A (Abduction: Jurisdiction)* [1995] 1 FLR 341.
85   At para 103.
86   Note also *Re H (Minors) (Abduction: Acquiescence)* [1998] AC 72, [1997] 2 WLR 563, [1997] 1 FLR 872 (discussed at **17.78**), in which the House of Lords suggested that judges should be slow to infer an intention to acquiesce for the purpose of Art 13(a) from attempts by a wronged parent to effect a reconciliation or reach an amicable agreement.
87   See Conclusions and Recommendations of the Fourth Meeting of the Special Commission, para 1.10. A Working Document produced by International Social Services also emphasised the importance of voluntary resolution, stating that extra-judicial solutions are usually preferable to court proceedings: see Working Document No 8 submitted to the fourth meeting of the Special Commission.
88   Facilitated by the Hague Conference on Private International Law and attended by judges from England and Wales, France, Germany, the Netherlands, Scotland, Sweden and the United States.
89   *Op cit*, n 29. This does not include voluntary arrangements such as access being agreed.
90   At para 92.

'it is the Central Authorities which, in those stages, preceding the possible judicial or administrative proceedings, will direct the development of the problem; it is therefore for them to decide when the attempts to secure the "voluntary return" of the child or to bring about an "amicable resolution" have failed.'

Nevertheless, as Art 7(c) expressly permits, Central Authorities can also act through intermediaries. As the fourth meeting of the Special Commission concluded:[91]

'Central Authorities should as a matter of practice seek to achieve voluntary return, as intended by Art 7(c) of the Convention, where possible and appropriate by instructing to this end legal agents involved, whether state attorneys or private practitioners, or by referral of parties to a specialist organisation providing an appropriate mediation service. The role played by the courts in this regard is also recognised.'

13.33   The lack of prescription concerning the means and methods of seeking voluntary resolution has led to considerable diversity in interpreting these provisions. In Australia, Germany, the Netherlands, Scotland, the United States and some Canadian jurisdictions, the Central Authority is involved, to some degree, in negotiating a voluntary resolution.[92] In Australia, the implementing Regulations initially required the Central Authority to seek an amicable resolution and a voluntary return.[93] In the Canadian Provinces of British Columbia and Manitoba, the Central Authorities will make a request for a voluntary return if it is considered appropriate. In some other Canadian jurisdictions and in Ireland, Central Authorities initiate contact with bodies such as the police who may be involved in bringing about voluntary resolutions. Several Central Authorities (for example, those of Scotland, the United States and several of the Canadian authorities) initiate suggestion of voluntary resolution by sending a letter to the abductor requesting that the abductor return the child within a certain period of time. In some jurisdictions, so as not to create delay, court proceedings are initiated simultaneously with the attempts to seek a voluntary resolution, in case negotiations fail. Since reforms introduced in October 2000 this has been the procedure adopted in Germany. In contrast, in other jurisdictions, notably Austria, Israel, New Zealand, England and Wales, and Northern Ireland, judicial proceedings are commenced immediately although concurrent attempts to bring about a voluntary resolution might be made. However, in England and Wales in 2002, Reunite proposed a mediation pilot scheme, limited initially to England and

---

91   Conclusions and Recommendations of the Fourth Meeting of the Special Commission, at para 1.10, and now incorporated into *Guide to Good Practice: Part II – Implementing Measures, op cit*, n 10, at 4.12.

92   See Lowe and Armstrong, *Good Practice Report* (NCMEC, 2002), at pp 39 *et seq*, and the Report of the Third Meeting of the Special Commission (17–21 March 1997) at para 43.

93   Viz Family Law (Child Abduction Convention) Regulations 1986, reg 13(4), but this has since been amended so as to give the Central Authority a discretion.

Wales, Ireland and France.[94] Mediation will take place during a court-endorsed adjournment of the Hague proceedings; public funding will be available and the costs of travel and accommodation will be met by the scheme.[95]

13.34 As one commentator has ably demonstrated,[96] the difference of approach is well reflected in statistics. Analysing States that immediately undertook to secure voluntary returns, namely, France, Germany, Scotland and the Netherlands, as against those which immediately began court proceedings, namely, Austria, Israel, New Zealand, and England and Wales, she found that in 1999, 'between 46% and 10% of applications to the former States ended up in court, while between 78% and 58% of applications to the latter States went to court. Conversely, between 80% and 16% of applications to the former States resulted in a voluntary return, while in no State where voluntary resolution was not primarily sought was there a voluntary return rate above 15%'. In England and Wales the proportion of voluntary returns, at 5% in 1999,[97] is particularly low, and the practice[98] of immediately forwarding incoming applications to a lawyer within 24 hours of its receipt has been criticised[99] as giving too little attention to the need to consider an amicable solution. The desirability of amicable solutions cannot be denied. Indeed, the UK delegation itself recognised this in a Working Document presented to the fourth meeting of the Special Commission,[100] which commented:

> '[t]he disruption to the child is minimal; the polarisation of parties, attitudes which so often results from court action is avoided and so the chance of a satisfactory long term solution is greater.'

Nevertheless, it has to be recognised that this solution is not always appropriate, for example, in situations where it may cause or allow the abductor to flee with the child.

---

[94] See the discussion of mediation in Freeman, Hutchinson and Setright, 'Child Abduction – A Role for Mediation' [2002] IFL 104. In the event, France will not be part of initial scheme. Instead, the scheme will extend to Sweden.

[95] *Ibid.* The pilot scheme can only come into operation when endorsed by the Hague Secretariat, the English Central Authority and the Central Authorities of the other project States. It will run initially for 12 months. It is hoped that the scheme will become operational before the end of 2003.

[96] Armstrong, 'Is the Jurisdiction of England and Wales Correctly Applying the 1980 Hague Convention on the Civil Aspects of International Child Abduction?' (2002) 51 ICLQ 427 at 431.

[97] See the 1999 Statistical Survey. See also Lowe and Perry, 'International Child Abduction – The English Experience' (1999) 48 ICLQ 127, who found that, in 1996, 8% of incoming applications to England and Wales resulted in a voluntary return compared with 22% of outgoing applications.

[98] See **21.14**.

[99] By Armstrong, *op cit*, n 96.

[100] Viz Working Document No 9 Revised, which highlights the Scottish system in which the Central Authority sends a letter to the lawyer assigned to the case encouraging the lawyer first to seek a voluntary resolution. Eight out of ten return applications made in 1999 to Scotland were resolved by a voluntary return.

The provision of information

13.35 There are a number of provisions concerned with the provision of information either with regard to the particular case or more generally. In former case, Art 7(d) and Art 7(e) respectively enjoin Central Authorities either directly or through an intermediary to take all appropriate steps:

'to exchange, where desirable, information relating to the social background of the child;'

and

'to provide information of a general character as to the law of their State in connection with the application of the Convention.'

13.36 With regard to Art 7(d), the Pérez-Vera Report makes the point[101] that the words 'where desirable' have been included to avoid imposing an inflexible burden and in any event that it was important not to create a provision which could be used as a delaying tactic. So far as the United Kingdom is concerned, s 6 of the Child Abduction and Custody Act 1985 provides that, where a request is made under Art 7(d), the Central Authority on behalf of the Lord Chancellor or Minister of Justice in Scotland can require a local authority or CAFCASS officer to make a report for, and any court to which a written report relating to the child has been made to send a copy to, the Central Authority.

13.37 With regard to Art 7(e), the Pérez-Vera Report explains[102] that it is envisaged both to operate where a removal occurs before any decision concerning custody has been made (in which case the Authority of the child's habitual residence should produce a certificate on the relevant law) and to explain to individuals how the Convention works. Article 7(e) does not oblige Central Authorities to give legal advice about the particular case.

13.38 With regard to providing information of a more general nature, Art 7(i) provides that Central Authorities should either directly or through intermediaries take all appropriate steps:

'to keep each other informed with respect to the operation of this Convention and, as far as possible, to eliminate any obstacles to its application.'

According to the Pérez-Vera Report,[103] this obligation operates at two complementary levels, namely, at the level of bilateral relations and at the multilateral level through participating in Commissions organised by the Permanent Bureau. The fourth meeting of the Special Commission

---

[101] At para 93.
[102] At para 94.
[103] At para 98.

recommended[104] that established Central Authorities should be 'encouraged to explore ways of sharing their expertise and experience with other Central Authorities when requested to do so'. The Commission[105] also recommended that Authorities be 'encouraged to maintain accurate statistics concerning the cases dealt with them' and that they should make annual returns to the Permanent Bureau.

Instituting proceedings and securing legal aid and legal representation

13.39   A key obligation is that under Art 7(f) namely:

> 'to initiate or facilitate the institution of judicial or administrative proceedings with a view to obtaining the return of the child and, in a proper case, to make arrangements for organizing or securing the effective exercise of rights of access.'

In most States, proceedings must be instituted before judicial authorities rather than administrative authorities.[106] This obligation is discharged in different ways. In some States, for example those in Australia, the Central Authority itself acts as the applicant, but in most States, proceedings are brought by lawyers on behalf of applicants. The practice in the United Kingdom, for example, with regard to incoming return applications, is to ask a private firm of solicitors to represent the applicant.[107] The papers are normally passed on within 24 hours of their receipt.

13.40   In cases where the Central Authority is not able to apply directly to the courts, Art 7(g) provides that Central Authorities, either directly or through intermediaries, take all appropriate measures:

> 'where the circumstances so require, to provide or facilitate the provision of legal aid and advice, including the participation of legal counsel and advisers.'

13.41   The Pérez-Vera Report explains[108] that the phrase 'where the circumstances so require' is intended to refer to the applicant's lack of economic means as determined by the criteria laid down by the law of the State in which aid is being sought. It does not refer to 'abstract considerations as to the convenience or otherwise of granting legal aid'. As we discuss in Chapter 21, the availability of legal aid is determined by internal law and is therefore outside the Central Authorities' control. Some States, such as Australia and the United Kingdom, are remarkably generous. Others, notably the United States, have no legal aid, although strenuous efforts have been

---

[104] See Conclusions and Recommendations of the Fourth Meeting of the Special Commission, para 1.13, now incorporated into *Guide to Good Practice: Part II – Implementing Measures, op cit*, n 10, at 6.1.

[105] Conclusions and Recommendations of the Fourth Meeting of the Special Commission, at para 2.7.

[106] Although in Denmark, for instance, administrative authorities are called upon to deal with access cases.

[107] For further detail, see Chapter 21.

[108] At para 96.

made by NCMEC to establish a pool of attorneys who are able to offer a reduced fee or to act *pro bono* for Convention applications.

Securing the child's safe return

13.42   Article 7(h) entreats Central Authorities, either directly or through intermediaries, to take all appropriate measures:

> 'to provide such administrative arrangements as may be necessary and appropriate to secure the safe return of the child.'

13.43   The application of this provision has been the subject of some debate.[109] At the third meeting to review the operation of the Convention in 1997,[110] the Australian Delegation formally proposed that Art 7(h) be regarded as imposing a duty upon Central Authorities to protect the welfare of children upon their return.[111] Although this proposal drew substantial support, because of the extra commitment and costs involved, no clear-cut recommendation was made, although it was recognised to be 'essential to the integrity of the Convention to ensure the safety of children on their return to their country of habitual residence'. The fourth meeting of the Special Commission concluded:[112]

> 'To the extent permitted by the powers of their Central Authority and by the legal and social welfare systems of their country, Contracting States accept that Central Authorities have an obligation under Art 7(h) to ensure appropriate child protection bodies are alerted so they may act to protect the welfare of children upon return in certain cases where their safety is at issue until the jurisdiction of the appropriate court has been effectively invoked.
>
> It is recognised that, in most cases, a consideration of the child's best interests requires that both parents have the opportunity to participate and be heard in custody proceedings. Central Authorities should therefore co-operate to the fullest extent possible to provide information in respect of legal, financial, protection and other resources in the requesting State, and facilitate timely contact with these bodies in appropriate cases.
>
> The measures which may be taken in fulfilment of the obligation under Art 7(h) to take or cause to be taken an action to protect the welfare of children may include, for example:

---

[109]   See generally Sandor, 'Review of the Hague Child Abduction Convention: protecting both children and adults until and upon return?' (2001) 15 *Australian Journal of Family Law* 1.

[110]   See Report of the Third Meeting of the Special Commission to Review the Operation of the Hague Convention on the Civil Aspects of International Child Abduction (17–21 March 1997).

[111]   In the Australian decision *Cooper v Casey* (1995) FLC 920575, Nicholson CJ took the view that Art 7 did impose such an obligation. This is supported by the NZ Court of Appeal decision in *A v Central Authority for New Zealand* [1996] 2 NZLR 517.

[112]   Conclusions and Recommendations of the Fourth Meeting of the Special Commission, at para 1.13, now incorporated into *Guide to Good Practice: Part II – Implementing Measures, op cit*, n 10, at 3.18.

(a)   alerting the appropriate protection agencies or judicial authorities in the requesting State of the return of a child who may be in danger;
(b)   advising the requested State, upon request, of the protective measures and services available in the requesting State to secure the safe return of a particular child;
(c)   encouraging the use of Art 21 of the Convention to secure the effective exercise of access or visitation rights.

It is recognised that the protection of the child may also sometimes require steps to be taken to protect an accompanying parent.'

13.44   Whether States will be prepared at future meetings of the Special Commission to go further and squarely place the obligation to ensure the safety of returned children upon Central Authorities remains to be seen. It should be noted, however, that there are other techniques for seeking to protect children, including accepting undertakings, and making mirror or safe harbour orders.[113] Furthermore, as we discuss in Chapter 24, the 1996 Hague Convention on the Protection of Children also contains some useful provisions to protect children.[114]

---

[113] See **17.123** *et seq.*
[114] Viz Arts 11 and 12, discussed at **24.16–24.17**.

Chapter 14

INTERNATIONAL ABDUCTIONS: HAGUE ABDUCTION CONVENTION: CONVENTION CONCEPTS

INTRODUCTION

14.1 In the same way that proceedings under the 1980 Hague Abduction Convention are *sui generis,* being neither adversarial nor inquisitorial,[1] some of the concepts in the 1980 Hague Abduction Convention have their own particular meaning within the jurisprudence of the Convention. The second meeting of the Special Commission to review the operation of the Convention in January 1993 said in its conclusions that:

> 'The key concepts which determine the scope of the Convention are not dependent for their meaning on any single legal system. Thus the expression "rights of custody", for example, does not coincide with any particular concept of custody in a domestic law, but draws its meaning from the definitions, structure and purposes of the Convention.'

In setting out its conclusions and recommendations, the fourth meeting of the Special Commission[2] said that the Convention should be interpreted having regard to its autonomous nature and in the light of its objects, and emphasised the continuing importance of the Pérez-Vera Report as an aid to the interpretation and understanding.[3]

---

[1] *Re N (Child Abduction: Habitual Residence)* [1993] 2 FLR 124.

[2] At The Hague, 22–28 March 2001.

[3] Conclusions and Recommendations of the Fourth Meeting of the Special Commission to Review the Operation of the Hague Convention of 25 October 1980 on the Civil Aspects of International Child Abduction (22–28 March 2001) (hereinafter 'Conclusions and Recommendations of the Fourth Meeting of the Special Commission), paras 4.1 and 4.2. And note Art 31 of the 1969 Vienna Convention on the Law of Treaties, discussed at **12.30** and **12.31**, to which the Pérez-Vera Report (at para 84) refers '… a classic rule of

THE NECESSITY FOR UNIFORM INTERPRETATION AMONGST CONTRACTING STATES

14.2 The necessity for uniform interpretation of the Convention was explained by Lord Browne-Wilkinson, in *Re H (Abduction: Acquiescence)*,[4] who said:

'An international Convention, expressed in different languages and intended to apply to a wide range of differing legal systems, cannot be construed differently in different jurisdictions. The Convention must have the same meaning and effect under the laws of all Contracting States. I would therefore reject any construction of Art 13 which reflects purely English law rules as to the meaning of the word "acquiescence". I would also deplore attempts to introduce special rules of law applicable in England alone ... which are not to be found in the Convention itself or in the general law of all developed nations.'

As we shall see as we examine the concept of 'rights of custody', there has, with one or two exceptions, been a remarkable unanimity of interpretation amongst Contracting States, with frequent references by the courts to decisions made in other jurisdictions.[5]

THE OBJECTS OF THE CONVENTION – A BROAD AND PURPOSIVE CONSTRUCTION

14.3 When reading what follows, it has to be borne in mind that the courts, especially the English courts, strive to achieve what they perceive to be the objectives of the Convention,[6] and take the view that:[7]

'It is the duty of the court to construe the Convention in a purposive way and to make the Convention work. It is repugnant to the philosophy of the Convention for one parent unilaterally, secretly and with full knowledge that it is against the wishes of the other parent who possesses "rights of custody", to remove the child from the jurisdiction of the child's habitual residence.'

In pursuing this policy, the English courts have adopted a broad, liberal and purposive approach to interpretation, so that 'habitually' may not have quite

---

treaty law requires that a treaty's terms be interpreted in their context and by taking into account the objective and end sought by the treaty'.

4   [1998] AC 72 at 87F, [1997] 1 FLR 872 at 881H.

5   The most notable exceptions are the concept of 'inchoate' rights of custody (see **14.49** *et seq*) and a divergence of opinion as to whether a restriction on removal in support of an access order constitutes a right of custody (see **14.44**).

6   See **12.4** *et seq*.

7   Per Butler-Sloss LJ in *Re F (A Minor) (Abduction: Custody Rights Abroad)* [1995] Fam 224, sub nom *Re F (Child Abduction: Risk if Returned)* [1995] 2 FLR 31, at 229E–H and 34H respectively.

the same meaning within the Convention as in a domestic statute,[8] and 'wrongful', 'retention' and 'rights of custody' are wider concepts than they might appear at first sight. As Waite LJ said:[9]

> 'The purposes of the Hague Convention were, in part at least, humanitarian. The objective is to spare children already suffering the effects of breakdown in their parents' relationship the further disruption which is suffered when they are taken arbitrarily by one parent from their settled environment and moved to another country for the sake of finding there a supposedly more sympathetic forum or a more congenial base. The expression "rights of custody" when used in the Convention therefore needs to be construed in the sense that will best accord with that objective. In most cases, that will involve giving the term the widest sense possible.'

WRONGFUL REMOVALS AND RETENTIONS

14.4   The Convention works not by recognising and enforcing court orders, but by returning children who have been 'wrongfully' removed or retained away from their State of habitual residence. So, although it is not necessary to have a court order before invoking the Convention, it has to be shown that the removal was 'wrongful' in Convention terms.

The Convention definition of 'wrongful'

14.5   Article 3 provides that:

> 'The removal or retention of a child[[10]] is to be considered wrongful where—
>
> (a)   it is in breach of rights of custody attributed to a person, an institution or any other body, either jointly or alone, under the law of the State in which

---

8   In *Ikimi v Ikimi* [2001] EWCA Civ 873, [2002] Fam 72, [2001] 2 FLR 1288, a case involving the English court's jurisdiction to entertain divorce proceedings, Thorpe LJ said of 'habitual residence': 'I am further of the opinion that it is essential that the same meaning be given to "habitually" wherever it appears in family law statutes. I would not however necessarily make the same extension to the Hague Convention on the Civil Aspects of International Child Abduction 1980 which is an international instrument, the construction of which is settled and developed within the wider field of international jurisprudence'. As to the meaning of 'habitual residence' for the purposes of the Convention, see **4.24** *et seq*.

9   *Re B (A Minor) (Abduction)* [1994] 2 FLR 249 at 260.

10   It has not been determined whether, for Convention purposes, 'child' includes a foetus. In *B v H (Habitual Residence: Wardship)* [2002] 1 FLR 388, Charles J, referring to *Attorney-General's Reference (No 3 of 1994)* [1998] AC 245, expressed the view (at [138]) that the approach of the House of Lords in treating a foetus as a 'unique organism' might enable a father who would not acquire parental responsibility on birth to issue proceedings to give him (or possibly, we might add, the court) rights of custody before the pregnant mother left the jurisdiction. However, the decisions in *Re F (In Utero)* [1988] Fam 122, [1988] 2 FLR 307 (no jurisdiction to make an unborn child a ward of court, even to protect it from damage likely to be caused by the mother), *C v S* [1988] QB 135 (a father may not apply for an injunction to prevent an abortion), *Paton v British Pregnancy Advisory Service Trustees* [1979] QB 276, and *Paton v United Kingdom* (1980) 3 EHRR 408 seem to present serious obstacles to this proposition.

the child was habitually resident immediately before the removal or retention; and

(b)   at the time of removal or retention those rights were actually exercised, either jointly or alone, or would have been so exercised but for the removal or retention.

The rights of custody mentioned in sub-paragraph (a) above may arise in particular by operation of law or by reason of a judicial or administrative decision, or by reason of an agreement having legal effect under the law of that State.'

Article 3 involves a number of concepts, each of which has proved to be problematic in one way or another. We consider those concepts and their difficulties below, but in doing so it should be borne in mind that the burden of proving that a removal or retention was wrongful lies with the applicant for the return order, and failure to discharge that burden will cause the application to fail, as happened in *Re M (Abduction: Acquiescence)*[11] when the experts disagreed as to whether a provisional custody order made by a Greek court had the effect of restricting the mother's right to determine the child's place of residence.

A removal must be across an international frontier

14.6   The Convention is concerned only with international abduction, so removal and retention must be away from the jurisdiction of the courts of the State of the child's habitual residence, not just away from the care of a person, body or institution with rights of custody.[12] A removal for Convention purposes occurs only when the child is taken out of – that is, across the frontier of – his State of habitual residence. He may have been unlawfully removed within his State of habitual residence, but that does not constitute a 'wrongful removal'. Lord Brandon made this clear in *Re H; Re S (Abduction: Custody Rights)*,[13] saying that:

'The preamble of the Convention shows that it is aimed at the protection of children *internationally* (my emphasis) from wrongful removal or retention. Article 1(a) shows that the first object of the Convention is to secure the prompt return to the State of their habitual residence (that State being a Contracting State) of children in two categories: (1) children who have been wrongfully removed from the State of their habitual residence to another Contracting State; and (2) children who have been wrongfully retained in a Contracting State other than the State of their habitual residence, instead of being returned to the latter State. The Convention is not concerned with children who have been wrongfully removed or retained within the borders of the State of their habitual residence.

So far as category (1) is concerned, it appears to me that a child only comes within it if it is wrongfully taken out, ie across the frontier, of the State of its habitual residence. Until that happens, although the child may already have been

---

[11]   [1996] 1 FLR 315.

[12]   *Re H; Re S (Abduction: Custody Rights)* [1991] 2 AC 476 at 500, [1991] 2 FLR 262 at 272.

[13]   *Ibid* at 498 and 270, respectively.

wrongfully removed within the borders of the State of its habitual residence, it will not have been wrongfully removed for the purposes of the Convention.'

Retention must be away from the State of habitual residence

14.7   Similarly, a child who is wrongfully retained inside the State of his habitual residence is not protected by the Convention. A wrongful retention occurs in Convention terms when a child is lawfully removed from his State of habitual residence and is subsequently retained contrary to, for example, a court order or an agreement between the parents, instead of being returned to his State of habitual residence. Lord Brandon, considering wrongful retentions, said:[14]

'So far as category (2) is concerned, it appears to me that a child can only come within it if it has first been removed rightfully (for example, under a court order or an agreement between its two parents) out of the State of its habitual residence, and subsequently retained wrongfully (for example, contrary to a court order or an agreement between its two parents), instead of being returned to the State of its habitual residence. The wrongful retention of a child in one place in the State of its habitual residence, instead of its being returned to another place within the same State, would not be a wrongful retention for the purposes of the Convention. The typical (but not necessarily the only) case of a child within category (2) is that of a child who is rightfully taken out of the State of its habitual residence to another contracting State for a specified period of staying access with its non-custodial parent, and wrongfully not returned to the State of its habitual residence at the expiry of that period.'

Removal and retention are mutually exclusive

14.8   Removal and retention are mutually exclusive concepts, both of which occur on a specific occasion – a retention is not a continuing state of affairs. Again, this was made clear by Lord Brandon in *Re H; Re S (Abduction: Custody Rights)*[15] when he referred to Art 12 and said:

'The period of one year referred to in this article is a period measured from the date of the wrongful removal or retention. That appears to me to show clearly that, for the purposes of the Convention, both removal and retention are events occurring on a specific occasion, for otherwise it would be impossible to measure a period of one year from their occurrence. It was submitted by Mr Munby that, in the case of retention, the date from which the period of one year was to be measured was the date of the inception of the retention and that, if Art 12 was interpreted in that way, it was not inconsistent with retention being a continuing state of affairs. I find myself unable to accept that submission. To interpret Art 12 in that way involves inserting into it words which are not there and, if intended to apply, could readily have been put in. I consider that Art 12 leads inevitably to the conclusion that retention, like removal, is an event occurring on a specific occasion.

---

[14]   *Re H; Re S (Abduction: Custody Rights)* [1991] 2 AC 476 at 499, [1991] 2 FLR 262 at 271.
[15]   At 499–500 and 271–272, respectively.

With regard to the second point, whether removal and retention are mutually exclusive concepts, it appears to me that, once it is accepted that retention is not a continuing state of affairs, but an event occurring on a specific occasion, it necessarily follows that removal and retention are mutually exclusive concepts. For the purposes of the Convention, removal occurs when a child, which has previously been in the State of its habitual residence, is taken away across the frontier of that State; whereas retention occurs where a child, which has previously been for a limited period of time outside the State of its habitual residence, is not returned to that State on the expiry of such limited period. That being so, it seems to me that removal and retention are basically different concepts, so that it is impossible either for them to overlap each other or for either to follow upon the other.'

The exclusivity does not mean, however, that a child cannot be both wrongfully removed and wrongfully retained: 'Even though the two are separate and mutually exclusive both can occur on the facts in relation to the same child at different times'.[16]

Removals and retentions are 'wrongful', not unlawful

14.9 For a removal or a retention to be 'wrongful' within the meaning of the Convention terms does not necessarily mean that it has to be unlawful in terms of the domestic law of the State of the child's habitual residence. All that is necessary is that the requirements of the Convention are fulfilled. There will be occasions when applying a Convention interpretation to circumstances will produce a different result than if domestic law were applied. A removal which is entirely proper under the law of the State of the child's habitual residence may nevertheless be regarded as 'wrongful' in Convention terms. So, where parents have an equal right to make decisions about their child, and the law of the State of the child's habitual residence provides no restraint on international movement, removing the child without the knowledge or consent of the other parent may nevertheless be 'wrongful'. In *Re F (A Minor) (Abduction: Custody Rights Abroad)*,[17] the mother's removal of the child from Colorado, although not in breach of the law of Colorado, was held by the Court of Appeal to have rendered 'nugatory' the equal and separate rights that the father enjoyed, and in particular that the child should reside in the United States, and therefore constituted a breach of his rights of custody. Even if domestic law appears to confer 'sole custody' on a parent, a secretive removal may be held to be wrongful, so that in *Re D (Abduction: Custody Rights)*[18] a provision in Zimbabwean law dating from 1961 which provided that '[w]here either of the parents of a minor leaves the other and such parents commence to live apart, the mother of that minor child shall have sole custody of that

---

[16] Per Lord Slynn in *Re S (Custody: Habitual Residence)* [1998] AC 750 at 767, [1998] 1 FLR 122 at 131.

[17] [1995] Fam 224, sub nom *Re F (Child Abduction: Risk if Returned)* [1995] 2 FLR 31.

[18] [1999] 2 FLR 626.

minor until an order regulating the custody of that minor is made under section four of this section or by a superior court' was held not to deprive the father of his 'rights of custody' for Convention purposes.

Good faith and acting on legal advice

14.10   This, of course, has worrying implications for those advising parents, because for the purposes of the Convention it is irrelevant that the removal was carried out in good faith acting upon legal advice. In *Re F (A Minor) (Child Abduction)*,[19] Butler-Sloss LJ said of the removal of a child from Australia to England by the father:

> 'The removal of A from New South Wales to England by the father was, in my view, entirely wrong and contrary to the welfare of this child. Any legal advice or advice from the Australian immigration authorities as to his right to remove the child does not change a unilateral and unjustified act of taking a child from one country to another, without either the knowledge or consent of the other parent. That, however, is not the issue in this case. The question is whether the removal of A from Australia contravenes the Hague Convention.'

14.11   Another example of an apparently lawful removal effected on advice and apparently supported by an order of a court is *K v K*,[20] in which a mother had been advised by her Swiss lawyers that she would not be breaking any law by leaving Switzerland with the child, although they strongly advised her against telling the father about her plans. The mother and father then reached an agreement about the arrangements for the child, which was subsequently made into an order by consent which, although not entirely clear, appeared to give the mother custody ('*garde*') and directed that parental authority over the child would be exercised by the mother and father in common. When that order was made the father still did not know about the mother's plans to go to England. When the father applied for the return of the child, Bodey J was placed in the position of having two irreconcilable approaches by Swiss courts. One, by denying the father a declaration under Art 15, implied that he did not have 'rights of custody', and another said in terms or by necessary implication that he did. Bodey J held that the father had 'rights of custody' and ordered the return of the child on the basis that:

> '... the preferred approach of Swiss law is, or would be, or should be, that the father did have (and should have been accorded) the right not only to be consulted but also to agree or disagree as to which country J should be brought up in; this being as a consequence of his right to exercise parental authority in common with the mother pursuant to the consent order of 26 January 2001.'[21]

---

[19]   [1992] 1 FLR 548.

[20]   Unreported transcript, 16 August 2001.

[21]   He also ordered the child's return to Switzerland under the inherent jurisdiction, on the basis that it would be in his best interests.

When does a child become 'wrongfully retained'?

14.12   The decision of the House of Lords in *Re H; Re S (Minors) (Abduction: Custody Rights)*[22] makes it clear that to establish that the child has been wrongfully retained within the meaning of Art 3, the complaining parent must prove an event occurring on the specific occasion which constitutes the act of wrongful retention.[23] Wrongful retention under the Convention not being a continuing state of affairs,[24] if a child is wrongfully removed but then returned (even for a very short period of time) to his State of habitual residence, any subsequent removal is a new 'wrongful removal', and time for the purposes of Art 12 starts to run from the date of that new removal.[25]

14.13   A wrongful retention usually occurs when a child is not returned at the end of a period of time which it has been agreed he will spend abroad. But it can also occur when, after a lawful removal, there is a refusal to comply with a request to return the child made by a person who has acquired rights of custody subsequent to the removal, or by a subsequent order of a court (a 'chasing order').[26]

14.14   In the first instance, Lord Brandon's speech in *Re H; Re S (Minors) (Abduction: Custody Rights)*[27] seems to imply that a wrongful retention might not start until the end of the period of time which the child can lawfully spend in the other Contracting State. However, in *Re S (Minors) (Abduction: Wrongful Retention)*,[28] a case involving two Israeli scientists who had agreed to come to England with their children for at least a year, Wall J held that when, before the expiry of the agreed period, the mother announced her intention not to return the children to Israel, it amounted to a wrongful retention because she could no longer rely on the father's agreement to the limited period of removal or retention as protecting her either under Art 3 or under Art 13(a). 'As Mr Turner puts it, she cannot have the benefit of the agreement without the burden.'[29] It is not necessary for the period of time that the child is to spend

---

[22]   [1991] 2 AC 476, [1992] 2 FLR 262.

[23]   And see *Re S (A Minor) (Custody: Habitual Residence)* [1998] AC 750, [1998] 1 FLR 122, in which Lord Slynn said (at 767 and 131–132, respectively): 'It must, however, be necessary to point specifically to the event which constitutes the removal or the retention. This is necessarily so because of the provision of Art 12 that for an order for the return of the child to be made at the date of commencement of the proceedings, a period of less than one year has elapsed "from the date" of the wrongful removal or retention'.

[24]   See **14.8**. And see *Re H; Re S (Abduction: Custody Rights)* (above) and *Re S (Minors) (Abduction: Wrongful Retention)* [1994] Fam 70, sub nom *Re S (Minors) (Child Abduction: Wrongful Retention)* [1994] 1 FLR 82, in which Wall J said: 'Thus in the instant case the father must point to a specific event at a specific point in time which constitutes the act of wrongful retention'.

[25]   *Re S (Child Abduction: Delay)* [1998] 1 FLR 651. As to Art 12, see Chapter 16.

[26]   *Re S (A Minor) (Custody: Habitual Residence)* [1998] AC 750 at 768, [1998] 1 FLR 122 at 132. See **14.12**.

[27]   [1991] 2 AC 476, [1991] 2 FLR 262.

[28]   [1994] Fam 70, sub nom *Re S (Minors) (Child Abduction:Wrongful Retention)* [1994] 1 FLR 82.

[29]   *Ibid* at 81 and 93, respectively.

away from his habitual residence to be defined for a refusal to return to constitute a wrongful retention, provided that his habitual residence has not changed.[30]

Chasing orders

14.15   A lawful removal can become a wrongful retention if an order requiring the child's return is disobeyed. In *Re S (A Minor) (Custody: Habitual Residence)*[31] a child whose mother had died was taken by his grandmother and aunt from England to Ireland without the knowledge or consent of the father, who did not have parental responsibility. That removal was not 'wrongful' in Convention terms, because the father had no rights of custody. But when an order made by the English High Court in the exercise of its wardship jurisdiction requiring the child's return was disobeyed, there was a wrongful retention.[32] In its *Practice Note (Hague Convention: Applications by Fathers without Parental Responsibility)*,[33] the Central Authority for England and Wales took the view that a refusal to return in breach of an order made after removal could constitute a wrongful retention only if at the time the order was made the child was still habitually resident in the requesting State.[34]

Retention by court order

14.16   'Retention', construed, as it is, purposively and not semantically, includes not only physical retention by an abductor, but also 'juridical orders obtained on his initiative which have the effect of frustrating a child's return to the jurisdiction of its habitual residence'.[35] It follows that a court order designed only to ensure the continued presence of a child in accordance with an agreement between the parents would not constitute a wrongful retention.[36]

---

[30]   See *H v H (Child Abduction: Stay of Domestic Proceedings)* [1994] 1 FLR 530. And see *Re H (Abduction: Habitual Residence: Consent)* [2000] 2 FLR 294. At some point during a period of lawful residence in the requested State, the child's habitual residence may well change. In *Menachem v Frydman-Menachem*, D Md, No AW-02-1921, (US District Court for the District of Maryland, 14 January 2003) two sisters who had spent 2½ years in Maryland since their parents had arrived there from Israel were found to be habitually resident there when, after the parents could not agree whether or not to return to Israel, the father issued Convention proceedings. As to 'habitual residence', see **4.24** *et seq*.

[31]   [1998] AC 750, [1998] 1 FLR 122. As to wardship, see **14.75**.

[32]   *Ibid* at 768 and 132, respectively.

[33]   [1998] 1 FLR 491.

[34]   In *Re S (A Minor) (Custody: Habitual Residence)* [1998] AC 750, [1998] 1 FLR 122, neither the grandmother nor the aunt had power to change the child's habitual residence, and so the English courts retained jurisdiction to make orders notwithstanding the removal of the child (who was an Irish national) to Ireland. As to changing a child's habitual residence, see **4.57** *et seq*.

[35]   Per Waite J in *Re B (Minors) (Abduction) (No. 2)* [1993] 1 FLR 993 at 999.

[36]   'Thus, if the mother in the instant case applied for prohibited steps and residence orders for the sole purpose of protecting the presence of the children within the jurisdiction until 1 September 1993, I would find it difficult to find that an act of wrongful retention …',

Does the decision not to return have to be communicated?

14.17   It is not entirely clear whether a wrongful retention starts when the decision is made not to return the child, or when that decision is communicated to the other parent. In reaching his decision in *Re S (Minors) (Abduction: Wrongful Retention)*, Wall J relied on *Re AZ (A Minor) (Abduction: Acquiescence)*[37] in which Booth J had found that the child had been wrongfully retained at two points in time: first, when the mother decided not to return the child to Germany in breach of the father's rights; and secondly, when the child's aunt made an ex parte (without notice) application for residence and prohibited steps orders. The Court of Appeal, however, had reservations and said that an uncommunicated decision not to return a child in the future, from which the mother could later resile, could hardly constitute a wrongful retention.[38] But Wall J held that 'equally, as an issue of fact, it seems to me that the decision which precedes the announcement, even if not communicated to the father, must be capable itself of constituting an act of wrongful retention', and from the evidence in the case he was able to fix the time at which the mother formed the intention not to return.

14.18   We think that the answer is to be found in the facts of each case, so that an application made to a court without notice to the other parent for an order intended to keep the child permanently away from his State of habitual residence would constitute an act of wrongful retention, whereas a private, uncommunicated intention would not, if only because unscrupulous parents might otherwise try to claim that the date of the wrongful retention was more than 12 months prior to the date of the commencement of the proceedings for the return order, to take advantage of the provisions in the second paragraph of Art 12.[39]

Whose rights have to be breached?

14.19   Article 8 provides that 'any person, institution or other body claiming that a child has been removed or retained in breach of custody rights may apply …'. In the ordinary case, the applicant for a return order relies on the removal or retention as having breached his or her rights. But if even if the applicant has no 'rights of custody' he may be able to make an application, because the English courts have held that not only can an applicant for a return order rely on a breach of someone else's rights, but also that a person can be in breach of his own rights.

---

per Wall J in *Re S (Minors) (Abduction: Wrongful Retention)* [1994] Fam 70 at 81D–F, sub nom *Re S (Minors) (Child Abduction: Wrongful Retention)* [1994] 1 FLR 82 at 93.

[37]   [1993] 1 FLR 682.

[38]   At 689.

[39]   See **17.5** *et seq*.

14.20   An applicant who has no rights usually relies on rights held by a body or institution, often a court,[40] but it might be that the abductor's rights are in some way qualified, so that removal constitutes a breach of those rights. In *Re H (A Minor) (Abduction)*[41] it was held that there was nothing in Art 3 which indicated that the 'breach of rights of custody' had to be a breach of rights belonging to some other person and, accordingly, the mother was in breach of her own rights of custody when she brought the child to England from Canada in breach of the terms of an interim custody order which conferred those rights upon her, but which also included a restriction on removal.

Who determines whether rights have been breached?

14.21   It is for the courts of the requested State to determine whether or not the removal or retention of a child has breached rights of custody. A determination on this point, or a declaration made under Art 15, made in the requesting State is persuasive only.[42]

Consent to removal does not preclude a return order

14.22   It might be thought that if a holder of rights of custody had, in the exercise of those rights, consented to the removal of the child, that removal must necessarily be lawful, and so could not possibly be described as 'wrongful' in Convention terms. However, such is not the case, because consent is dealt with in Art 13(a) and falls to be considered as an exception to the obligation to return, which if proved, opens up a discretion in the court as to whether or not to order the return of the child.[43]

RIGHTS OF CUSTODY

14.23   The concept of 'rights of custody', although fundamental to the operation of the Convention, is not easy to define. It has always been the case that '"rights of custody" within the Convention are broader than an order of the court and parents have rights in respect of their children without the need to have them declared by the court or defined by court order'.[44] But when the

---

[40]   See **14.67** *et seq*.

[41]   [1990] 2 FLR 439.

[42]   See *In re F (A Minor) (Abduction: Custody Rights Abroad)* [1995] Fam 224, sub nom *Re F (Child Abduction: Risk if Returned)* [1995] 2 FLR 31. As to declarations, see Chapter 15.

[43]   See *Re C (Abduction: Consent)* [1996] 1 FLR 414; *Re O (Abduction: Consent and Acquiescence)* [1997] 1 FLR 924; *T v T (Abduction: Consent)* [1999] 2 FLR 912. As to Art 13(a), see **17.41** *et seq*.

[44]   Per Butler-Sloss LJ in *Re F (A Minor) (Abduction: Custody Rights Abroad)* [1995] Fam 224, sub nom *Re F (Child Abduction: Risk if Returned)* [1995] 2 FLR 31. It was not intended to imply that being a parent was of itself enough to confer rights of custody for Convention purposes. The clearest example of a class of parents who may well not have rights of custody are unmarried fathers (see **14.49** *et seq*). A recent example of an unmarried father

Convention was drafted it was, generally speaking, plain who had custody of a child (even if that custody was shared), and on separation and divorce there was usually a clear distinction between the custodial and the non-custodial parent. Since then, States have increasingly moved away from having such a clear distinction to more complicated ways of ascribing responsibility for children after the breakdown of a marriage or a relationship, so that it is now quite possible for a holder of 'rights of custody' not only to have no entitlement to the actual care of the child, but not even the right to see the child. In some of the cases we have seen, it has been difficult to see how the 'rights' which have been held to be 'rights of custody' could have had any meaningful impact on the child's life.

14.24 We have also noticed that, in their desire to deter international child abduction and help parents and others whom they believe to have been wronged by the clandestine removal of children for whom they have been caring, the courts of the various Contracting States have ascribed the status of 'rights of custody' to situations which would hardly be recognised as a custody right outside the technical world of the Convention.[45] An example of this is to be found in the cases involving unmarried fathers without parental rights. Perceiving these applicants to have been treated unjustly in the past, the English courts have attempted to improve their position by extending the concept of rights of custody to include 'inchoate' rights.[46]

14.25 The result of this is that sometimes it has been difficult know whether the courts of another State will hold that a 'right of custody' exists or not, and this has led to people being wrongly or incompletely advised when they have sought help about taking their child to live in another country.[47] One matter is clear, however: before 'rights of custody' can exist in relation to a child, the child concerned must have been habitually resident in a Contracting State immediately before any breach of those rights.[48]

Who determines 'rights of custody'?

14.26 Article 3(a) provides that rights of custody are 'attributed ... under the law of the State in which the child was habitually resident immediately before the removal or retention'. A plain reading of Art 13(a) might imply that whether a person, institution or body had rights of custody for the purposes of the Convention was a matter for the law of the requesting State.[49] However, it

---

being found to have no rights of custody is in *In re Vernor*, Tex Ct App, No 03-02-00580-CV (26 November 2002).

[45] See, for example, **14.49** on 'inchoate' rights of custody and **14.67** on rights of custody in a court.

[46] See **14.49**.

[47] Note that whether or not the removal is lawful under the domestic law of the requesting State may be irrelevant: see **14.9**.

[48] Article 4.

[49] And see the Pérez-Vera Report, at paras 64–67.

is clear in England that this is not the case. In 1988 in *Re C (A Minor) (Abduction)*[50] Lord Donaldson MR said in the Court of Appeal:

'We are necessarily concerned with Australian law because we are bidden by Art 3 to decide whether the removal of the child was in breach of "rights of custody" attributed to the father either jointly or alone under that law, but it matters not in the least how those rights are described in Australian law. What matters is whether those rights fall within the Convention definition of "rights of custody". Equally, it matters not in the least whether those rights would be regarded as rights of custody under English law, if they fall within the definition.'

14.27   So what rights someone has in relation to the child in question is a matter for the law of the State of the child's habitual residence, but whether those rights amount to 'rights of custody' for Convention purposes is a question for the courts of the requesting State.[51]

Rights of custody and the time of the wrongful removal or retention

14.28   Rights of custody must be in existence[52] and actually being exercised[53] at the time of the removal or retention.

The sources of rights of custody – the scope of Article 3, *renvoi* and applicable law

14.29   The word 'may' in Art 3 indicates that what follows are examples only, and are not to be regarded as an exhaustive list. It is this freedom, coupled with a purposive interpretation, which has expanded the sources of rights of custody.[54]

14.30   The law of the State in which the child was habitually resident immediately before the removal or retention referred to in Art 3(a) includes its

---

50   [1989] 1 FLR 403 at 412.

51   *Re F (A Minor) (Abduction: Custody Rights Abroad)* [1995] Fam 224, sub nom *Re F (Child Abduction: Risk if Returned)* [1995] 2 FLR 31. It is for this reason that a declaration, whether granted under Art 15 or otherwise, is persuasive only: see **15.9** (and see *Re V-B (Abduction: Custody Rights)* [1999] 2 FLR 192). Note that Australia, having abandoned the concepts of 'custody' and 'access' in 1996, specifies in its domestic legislation when a person has custody rights or access rights for the purposes of the Convention: see Family Law Act 1975, s 111B (see also Nicholes, 'The Family Law Reform Act and the Hague Convention', *Law Institute Journal*, Special Issue, September 1996, p 35).

52   Because they must breached by the removal or retention: see Art 3. So an order conferring rights after removal cannot make the *removal* wrongful (see *Re J (A Minor) (Abduction: Custody Rights)* [1990] 2 AC 562, sub nom *C v S (A Minor) (Abduction)* [1990] 2 FLR 442), although a retention in breach of a subsequent order, provided that the child's habitual residence has not changed, may be a wrongful retention (see *Re S (Custody: Habitual Residence)* [1998] 1 FLR 122).

53   Either jointly or alone, 'or would have been so exercised but for the removal or retention': see **14.81–14.83**.

54   See *Re O (Child Abduction: Custody Rights)* [1997] 2 FLR 702 at 708–709. As to the development of 'inchoate' rights of custody, see **14.49**.

law relating to conflicts.[55] This was a departure for the Hague Conference, which had previously specified that the applicable law would be the internal law of a State party. The omission of 'internal' is understood to mean incorporation of a State's rules of private international law as well as its internal law so, in resolving the question of whether a person has rights of custody in the State of the child's habitual residence, regard might have to be paid to the law of another State.

14.31   An example of this might be found in rights of custody conferred by an order of a court. When Art 3 provides that rights of custody '… may arise in particular by operation of law or by reason of a judicial or administrative decision, or by reason of an agreement having legal effect under the law of that State …',[56] it is not necessary for the order or decision which confers rights of custody to have been made in the State of the child's habitual residence immediately before the wrongful removal or retention, provided that it is recognised there.[57]

14.32   Article 31(b) provides that if a Contracting State, such as the United Kingdom or the United States, has different systems of law which apply in different territorial units of that State, references to the law of the State of habitual residence are construed as referring to the law of the territorial unit where the child habitually resides.

The Convention definition of 'rights of custody'

14.33   Article 5 of the Convention provides:

'For the purposes of this Convention—

(a)   "rights of custody" shall include rights relating to the care of the person of the child and, in particular, the right to determine the child's place of residence.'

The Pérez-Vera Report on rights of custody

14.34   The Pérez-Vera Report begins by concentrating on readily identifiable legal rights protected by the law of the State of the child's habitual residence:[58]

'The juridical element

As for what could be termed the juridical element present in these situations, the Convention is intended to defend those relationships which are already protected, at any rate by virtue of an apparent right to custody in the State of the child's habitual residence, ie by virtue of the law of the State where the child's relationships developed prior to its removal.'

---

[55]   See the Pérez-Vera Report, at para 66.
[56]   Ie the law of the State in which the child was habitually resident immediately before the removal or retention.
[57]   See **14.15**.
[58]   Paragraph 65.

14.35 But later the Report explains that the scope of the protection includes not only extant legal rights, but situations which could give rise to a 'claim':[59]

> 'The foregoing considerations show that the law of the child's habitual residence is invoked in the widest possible sense. Likewise, the sources from which the custody rights which it is sought to protect derive, are all those upon which a claim can be based within the context of the legal system concerned. In this regard, paragraph 2 of Article 3 takes into consideration some – no doubt the most important – of those sources, while emphasising that the list is not exhaustive.
>
> This paragraph provides that "the rights of custody mentioned in subparagraph (a) above may arise in particular", thus underlining the fact that other sorts of rights may exist which are not contained within the text itself. Now, as we shall see in the following paragraphs, these sources cover a vast juridical area, and the fact that they are not exhaustively set out must be understood as favouring a flexible interpretation of the terms used, which allows the greatest possible number of cases to be brought into consideration.'

Rights of custody and rights of access

14.36 Although the drafters of the Convention favoured a broad and purposive interpretation of the concept of 'rights of custody', it is clear that the Convention differentiates sharply between rights of custody and rights of access, and that this distinction should be preserved.[60]

Beyond legal and domestic rights

14.37 It is clear that what matters is the nature and quality of the rights in the State of the child's habitual residence, rather than how those rights are described or labelled. In 1988 it seemed as if the Court of Appeal in *Re C (A Minor) (Abduction)*[61] went further by endorsing a wider interpretation of 'rights of custody' which extended beyond those purely legal rights which would be protected in the requesting State. Butler Sloss LJ said:[62]

> 'The words of Art 5 must, in my view, be read into Art 3 and may in certain circumstances extend the concept of custody beyond the ordinarily understood domestic approach.'

---

[59] Paragraph 67.

[60] *Re V-B (Abduction: Custody Rights)* [1999] 2 FLR 192, *S v H (Abduction: Access Rights)* [1998] Fam 49, [1997] 1 FLR 971, and *Re W (Minors) (Abduction: Father's Rights)*, *Re B (A Minor) (Abduction: Father's Rights)* [1999] Fam 1, sub nom *Re W; Re B (Child Abduction: Unmarried Father)* [1998] 2 FLR 146, in which Hale J said (at 13 and 157, respectively): 'Thus a deliberate distinction is drawn between rights of custody and rights of access ... . Rights of custody are protected under Art 12 by the remedy of speedy return to the country where the children were habitually resident before they were removed. Rights of access are protected under Art 21 by remedies to organise and secure their effective exercise in the country where the children are now living'. See also *Re H (Child Abduction) (Unmarried Father: Rights of Custody)* [2003] EWHC 492 (Fam), [2003] 2 FLR 153.

[61] [1989] 1 FLR 403.

[62] At 407.

14.38   But in 1990 in *Re J (A Minor) (Abduction: Custody Rights)*,[63] both the Court of Appeal and the House of Lords appeared to take the more restrictive view that the Convention protected only established, legal rights[64] and not *de facto* custody. Lord Brandon, with whom the other Lords of Appeal agreed, said:

> 'So far as legal rights of custody are concerned, however, these belonged to the mother alone, and included in those rights was the right to decide where J should reside. It follows, in my opinion, that the removal of J by the mother was not wrongful within the meaning of Art 3 of the Convention.'

14.39   However, as the jurisprudence of the Convention developed, Contracting States have moved away from this somewhat absolutist position, although in England and Wales the enthusiasm for applying a broad and purposive definition has not been at all easy to reconcile with the binding authority of *Re J*.[65] Perhaps the best known of the later formulations was by Waite LJ in 1994 in *Re B (A Minor) (Abduction)*[66] in which he accepted the submissions of counsel to the effect that the earlier authorities[67] established that:

> 'The Convention is to be construed broadly as an international agreement according to its general tenor and purpose, without attributing to any of its terms a specialist meaning which the word or words in question may have acquired under the domestic law of England',

and that:

> '"Rights of custody" is a term which, when so construed, enlarges upon, and is not necessarily synonymous with, the simple connotations of "custody" when that word is used alone ...'

14.40   In Australia, the Full Court of the Family Court of Australia has made it clear that the concept of 'rights of custody' under the Convention is

---

63   [1990] 2 AC 562, sub nom *C v S (A Minor) (Abduction)* [1990] 2 FLR 442 at 453.

64   *Ibid* at 570C–E and 572B–D (Lord Donaldson), and 577F–H (Lord Brandon).

65   See **14.49** *et seq* on 'inchoate' rights of custody; the Practice Note issued by the Central Authority for England, *Practice Note (Hague Convention: Applications by Fathers without Parental Responsibility)* [1998] 1 FLR 491; *Re W (Minors) (Abduction: Father's Rights), Re B (A Minor) (Abduction: Father's Rights)* [1999] Fam 1, sub nom *Re W; Re B (Child Abduction: Unmarried Father)* [1998] 2 FLR 146; *Re C (Child Abduction) (Unmarried Father: Rights of Custody)* [2002] EWCA 2219 (Fam), [2003] 1 FLR 252; and *Re H (Child Abduction) (Unmarried Father: Rights of Custody)* [2003] EWHC 492 (Fam), [2003] 2 FLR 153.

66   [1994] 2 FLR 249 at 257.

67   *C v C (Abduction: Rights of Custody)* [1989] 1 WLR 654, sub nom *Re C (A Minor) (Abduction)* [1989] 1 FLR 403. See also *Re F (A Minor) (Abduction: Custody Rights Abroad)* [1995] Fam 224, sub nom *Re F (Child Abduction: Risk if Returned)* [1995] 2 FLR 31; *Re D (Abduction: Custody Rights)* [1999] 2 FLR 626.

sui generis and has no necessary connection with rights of custody under Australian domestic law.[68]

Identifying 'rights of custody'

14.41 We cannot say that there is any essential feature in the rights in the requesting State which must be present to bring them within 'rights of custody'. We say this because, as the jurisprudence has developed, there has been some consideration of whether, whatever else they might consist of, there is some essential element which must be present in the rights under consideration to bring them within 'rights of custody'. One suggestion was that the words 'shall include' in Art 5 means that the rights *must* include a right to determine (including a right to determine by veto) a child's place of residence.[69] However, so far as English law is concerned, Hale J dismissed this in *Re W; Re B (Minors) (Abduction: Father's Rights)*,[70] holding, by reference to the French text which simply reads 'le "droit de garde" comprend ...', that 'shall include' is equally capable of meaning 'includes' and that:[71]

> 'Furthermore, the words "shall include" must equally apply to the reference to "rights relating to the care of the person of the child": if it had been mandatory to include these, it would not have been permissible to extend the concept to a bare right to veto travel abroad possessed by people who have no rights relating to the care of the child.'

The right to determine the child's place of residence

14.42 However, it is clear that if the rights in question do include a right to determine a child's place of residence, they will amount to 'rights of custody' for the purposes of the Convention:[72]

> '"Custody", as a matter of non-technical English, means "safekeeping, protection, charge, care, guardianship" (I take that from the *Shorter Oxford English Dictionary*); but "rights of custody" as defined in the Convention includes a much more precise meaning which will, I apprehend, usually be decisive of most applications under the Convention. This is "the right to determine the child's place of residence".'

Restrictions on removal

14.43 The view generally held amongst Contracting States is that a court order or administrative decision does not have to confer 'custody' in the sense of daily care and control. Provided that it meets the criteria of Art 5, it will

---

68   *McCall and McCall; State Central Authority (Applicant); Attorney-General (Cth) (Intervener)* (1995) FLC ¶ 92–551 at 81,515–81,517.
69   Dr Anthony Dickey in *Child Abduction in Family Law* (CCH Australia Ltd, 1999), at para 317 says that this interpretation of rights of custody had not been adopted in any reported case, but may be implicit in the decision in *State Central Authority v Ayob* (1997) FLC ¶ 92–746.
70   [1999] Fam 1, sub nom *Re W; Re B (Child Abduction: Unmarried Father)* [1998] 2 FLR 146.
71   *Ibid* at 9 and 153. respectively.
72   Per Lord Donaldson in *Re C (A Minor) (Abduction)* [1989] 1 FLR 403 at 413.

confer rights of custody. So an order made by a court prohibiting removal without the consent of the other parent, or, indeed, anybody, would amount to a right of custody for the purposes of the Convention, because such an order would confer upon the person empowered to give or withhold consent a right to determine the child's place of residence as described by Art 5.[73]

Restrictions on removal in support of rights of access

14.44   Despite the sharp distinction which the Convention draws between rights of custody and rights of access,[74] rights of custody are usually held to arise from such an order even if the restraint on removal was in support of rights of access, rather than of custody. At the third meeting of the Special Commission to review the operation of the Convention, this approach was commonly, but not uniformly, held amongst Contracting States, but as recently as November 2002, an American court felt able to say that no clear consensus had emerged.[75]

14.45   The contrary view has been held in the United States by the US Court of Appeals for the Second Circuit in *Croll v Croll*,[76] which was followed in *Gonzalez v Gutierrez*.[77] In *Croll* a District Court in Hong Kong had granted the mother custody, care and control and the father reasonable access, and restrained the removal of the child without the leave of the court or the consent of the other parent. The US Court of Appeals took the view[78] that the:

> '... ne exeat clause does not transmute access rights into rights of custody under the Convention. Ne exeat or not, Mr Croll's rights include none of the powers (or burdens) of a custodial parent, and are therefore properly classified as rights of access.'[79]

14.46   In *Gonzalez*, which involved the removal of children from Mexico to California, contrary to a *ne exeat* clause in the parents' divorce agreement, the US Court of Appeals for the 9th Circuit also rejected the view that a 'right' granted under a *ne exeat* clause amounted to a right to determine the child's place of residence. It was at most a veto power serving 'only to allow a parent

---

73   *Re C (A Minor) (Abduction)* [1989] 1 FLR 403 at 413. Note also *Re H (Child Abduction) (Unmarried Father: Rights of Custody)* [2003] EWHC 492 (Fam), [2003] 2 FLR 153, in which Holman J held that a letter written by the mother's solicitors to the father confirming that she was not leaving the jurisdiction was sufficient to confer, for the purposes of Art 5, rights of custody on the unmarried father.

74   See **14.36**.

75   *Gonzalez v Gutierrez* 9th Cir, No 02–55079 (20 November 2002).

76   229 F 3d 133 (2d Cir 2000) (binding in New York and Vermont).

77   9th Cir, No 02–55079 (20 November 2002).

78   With one judge dissenting.

79   For a criticism of the *Croll* case, see Weiner, 'Navigating the Road Between Uniformity and Progress: The Need for Purposive Analysis of The Hague Convention on the Civil Aspects of International Child Abduction', *Columbia Human Rights Law Review*, vol 33, no 2 (Spring 2002).

with access rights to impose a limitation on the custodial parent's right to expatriate his child'. There was no right to direct where the children should live either in Mexico or elsewhere, so it 'hardly amounts to a right of custody, in the plainest sense of the term'. It was a condition designed to protect access rights, and no more. And the Supreme Court of Canada has twice expressed doubts as to whether, once a final custody order has been made, a right of veto which merely protects another person's rights of access would amount to 'rights of custody'.[80]

Implied restrictions on removal

14.47   A restriction on the removal of a child does not have to be imposed by a court order – an implied restriction is enough to constitute a 'right of custody'. In *C v C (Minors) (Child Abduction)*[81] it was held that there is no distinction in law between an express prohibition contained in an order and an implicit prohibition derived from settled case-law to the effect that a custodial parent is not entitled to frustrate visitation rights by removing the children to a distant locality.

Rights to be consulted and to oversee education and living conditions

14.48   Whilst a meaningful, decision-making role in a child's life amounts to a right of custody,[82] a right merely to be consulted or informed about residence, or any other issue, without an associated right to object, does not amount to a right of custody. While consultation is of considerable importance, it has little legal effect and does not amount to a veto on removal.[83] Similarly, a right to

---

[80]   *Thomson v Thomson* (1995) 119 DLR (4th) 253, para 67, and *DS v VW and JS and Rodrigue Blais* [1996] 2 SCR 108. And see the *Overall Conclusions of the Special Commission on the Operation of the Convention* (October 1989), paras 9 and 10, and the Report of the Second Special Commission (January 1993), p 28, summarised in *S v H (Abduction: Access Rights)* [1998] Fam 49 at 56, [1997] 3 WLR 1086 at 1092, [1997] 1 FLR 971 at 977. See also Silberman, 'The Hague Child Abduction Convention Turns Twenty: Gender Politics and Other Issues', *New York University Journal of International Law and Politics*, vol 33 (Fall 2000), No 1, p 226.

[81]   [1992] 1 FLR 163. See *Re H (Child Abduction) (Unmarried Father: Rights of Custody)* [2003] EWHC 492 (Fam), [2003] 2 FLR 153 (letters exchanged between solicitors confirming that the mother was not moving to Spain had the effect of attributing to the father a right of custody within the meaning of Art 5. The father had the right to apply to the court for an order prohibiting the removal of the child and it was likely that, for a period at least, such an order would have been made).

[82]   *Whallon v Lynn,* 1st Cir, No 00–2041 (27 October 2000) – *patria potestas* conferred by Mexican law on an unmarried father is independent of mere visitation rights and amounts to a right of custody (disapproved in *Gonzalez v Gutierrez,* 9th Cir, No 02–55079 (20 November 2002), on a parent given access rights from a custody agreement). And see *Gil v Rodriguez* 184 F Supp 2d 1221 Cir, No 20–55079 (20 November 2002) to the extent that the *patria potestas* cannot confer rights of custody (MD Fla 2002) (doctrine of *patria potestas* in Venezuelan law gave father a right of custody).

[83]   *Re V-B (Abduction: Custody Rights)* [1999] 2 FLR 192.

watch over a child's education and living conditions does not amount to a right of custody.[84]

Extending rights of custody – inchoate rights of custody

The origin of 'inchoate rights of custody'

14.49 The concept of 'inchoate rights of custody' first arose as an extension of the definition of 'rights of custody' in the decision of the Court of Appeal in *Re B (A Minor) (Abduction)*,[85] a case in which the removal of a child from Australia was perpetrated by the mother by a deception upon the father who, not being married to the mother, had no rights of custody under the law of Western Australia as it then was.[86] Waite LJ said:[87]

> 'The difficulty lies in fixing the limits of the concept of "rights". Is it to be confined to what lawyers would instantly recognise as established rights – that is to say those which are propounded by law or conferred by court order: or is it capable of being applied in a Convention context to describe the inchoate rights of those who are carrying out duties and enjoying privileges of a custodial or parental character which, though not yet formally recognised or granted by law, a court would nevertheless be likely to uphold in the interests of the child concerned?
>
> The answer to that question must, in my judgment, depend upon the circumstances of each case. If, before the child's abduction, the aggrieved parent was exercising functions in the requesting State of a parental or custodial nature without the benefit of any court order or official custodial status, it must in every case be a question for the courts of the requested State to determine whether those functions fall to be regarded as "rights of custody" within the terms of the Convention. At one end of the scale is (for example) a transient cohabitee of the sole legal custodian whose status and functions would be unlikely to be regarded as qualifying for recognition as carrying Convention rights. The opposite would be true, at the other end of the scale, of a relative or friend who has assumed the role of a substitute parent in place of the legal custodian.
>
> When that approach is applied to the particular circumstances of the present case, the answer reached by the judge was in my judgment unimpeachable. The father who saw off this young boy at Perth airport on 25 August 1993 was the child's primary carer, sharing his upbringing with the maternal grandmother as his secondary carer. It was a settled status which the absent mother, as the only parent with official custodial rights, had at first tacitly and later (by her acceptance of the father's right to insist on her signature of the minutes) expressly approved. I accept Mr Holman's submission that it was a status which any court, including the FCWA, would be bound to uphold; at least to the point

---

84 *S v H (Abduction: Access Rights)* [1998] Fam 49, [1997] 3 WLR 1086, [1997] 1 FLR 971.

85 [1994] 2 FLR 249, CA.

86 It was as a result of this case that the law in Western Australia was changed to confer parental responsibility on each parent of a child, which has effect 'despite any changes in the nature of the relationships of the child's parents. It is not affected, for example, by the parents becoming separated or by either or both of them marrying or re-marrying': see Family Court Act 1997, s 69 (WA) (FCA), repealing Family Court Act 1975 (WA).

87 At 261.

of refusing to allow it to be disturbed – abruptly or without due opportunity of a consideration of the claims of the child's welfare – merely at the dictate of a sudden reassertion by the mother of her official rights. It was a status which falls properly to be regarded as carrying rights. It was a status which falls properly to be regarded as carrying with it rights in the Convention sense, breach of which by unauthorised removal would be rendered wrongful within the terms of Arts 3 and 5.'

14.50   So it appears that the Court of Appeal envisaged that inchoate rights could be held by not only by a parent, but also by 'a relative or friend who has assumed the role of a substitute parent in place of the legal custodian'.

'Inchoate rights of custody' after Re B

14.51   In *Re O (Child Abduction: Custody Rights)*,[88] Cazalet J held that German grandparents had inchoate rights of custody in respect of their granddaughter, who had been placed with them by her mother in August 1995. She was taken away by her mother in October 1995, but came to live with them again in May 1996 when the mother was injured in a road accident. Later, when the mother told the grandparents she was moving to England, they started custody proceedings. Those proceedings were not served, but the mother brought the child to England. In examining the law, Cazalet J said:[89]

'Against Mr Hollow's submission as to the limiting effect of the last paragraph of Art 3, it is important, in addition to what I have said, to bear in mind that the word "may" is used. The paragraph starts, "The rights of custody mentioned in sub-paragraph (a) above may arise …". Accordingly, rights of custody, in my view, are not confined solely to the specific situations set out in the Article; the court may step beyond them, as the court did in *Re B* (above). I turn to consider – and I believe this to be the correct approach – whether there was an agreement, following the passage in Waite LJ's judgment, whereby either the mother can properly be said to have agreed to J making her home with the grandmother, or alternatively, whether some situation arose whereby the grandparents were carrying out duties and enjoying the privileges of a custodial or parental character which the court would be likely to uphold in the interests of the child concerned.'

Later[90] he said that:

'Mr Setright invites me to say that an agreement can be spelled out from the conduct of the parties or the exchanges that have taken place between them to the effect that the grandparents should have full custodial rights. Whilst I have reservations as to whether any such agreement came into being, I have no hesitation in coming to the conclusion that the grandparents held joint custodial rights within the provisions of Waite LJ's definition. In the circumstances to which I have already made detailed reference, they carried out full parental responsibilities over a substantial period of time, and accordingly must be taken to have established their joint rights of custody within Art 3.'

---

[88]   [1997] 2 FLR 702 (judgment given 5 March 1997)
[89]   At 708.
[90]   At 710.

14.52   In an attempt to reconcile the apparent divergence between the decision of the House of Lords in *Re J (A Minor) (Abduction: Custody Rights)*[91]and the decision in *Re B*, the Lord Chancellor's Child Abduction Unit in its *Practice Note (Hague Convention: Applications by Fathers without Parental Responsibility)*,[92] said:

> 'Two reported English decisions appear to have expanded the concept of rights of custody to include more than strictly legal rights. It would seem from those decisions that if a father does not have parental responsibility, but immediately prior to the removal or retention was exercising parental functions over a substantial period of time, he may have "inchoate" rights of custody which constitute "rights of custody" within the meaning of the Convention. These are "the inchoate rights of those who are carrying out duties and enjoying privileges of a custodial or parental character which, though not yet formally recognised or granted by law, a court would nevertheless be likely to uphold in the interests of the child concerned" – see *Re B (A Minor) (Abduction)* [1994] 2 FLR 249, 261A–B, per Waite LJ, followed in *Re O (Child Abduction: Custody Rights)* [1997] 2 FLR 702. It is not easy to reconcile these decisions with the decision of the House of Lords in the case of *Re J (A Minor) (Abduction: Custody Rights)* [1990] 2 AC 562 sub nom *C v S (A Minor) (Abduction)* [1990] 2 FLR 442, but distinguishing features were that the persons whose rights of custody were held to have been breached were exercising their responsibilities either alone or with someone who did not have custodial rights, and also that in the one case an agreement relating to custody was about to be perfected and in the other custody proceedings were pending. It would seem from *Re J* that de facto joint custody is not enough.'

14.53   Those propositions were examined by Hale J in *Re W; Re B (Minors) (Abduction: Father's Rights)*,[93] a case in which two unmarried fathers sought declarations in respect of the removal of their children. She said of *Re B*:

> 'He [Waite LJ] concluded that it depended upon the circumstances of each case and must be a question for the courts of the requested (rather than the requesting) State. He envisaged a scale at the top end of which was "a relative or friend who has assumed the role of a substitute parent in place of a legal custodian". He appears, at 262, to have distinguished the facts from *Re J* on the basis that the father's consent had been obtained by a deceit which was cruel both to the father and to the child, who would suffer if his expectation of returning to the only country he had ever known and "the only parent who had given him continuous and consistent care" was destroyed. He continued (at 262B): "Nor is there any principle to be deduced from the decision in that case which would require the father in the present case to be treated, notwithstanding his very different circumstances, as a party who had been merely exercising what Lord Brandon described as 'de facto custody'".
>
> Peter Gibson LJ gave a dissenting judgment, which is all the stronger for his obvious regret in reaching the conclusion that he did. He did so on the basis of the decision in the House of Lords in *Re J* ... that "the rights in question must be

---

[91]   [1990] 2 AC 562, sub nom *C v S (A Minor) (Abduction)* [1990] 2 FLR 442.
[92]   14 October 1997, reported at [1998] 1 FLR 491.
[93]   [1999] Fam 1 at 11, sub nom *Re W; Re B (Child Abduction: Unmarried Father)* [1998] 2 FLR 146 at 155.

more than de facto rights". As the father had no legal rights until the agreement had been approved by the court he had no rights of custody under the Convention. I must confess to having the same difficulty as he did in reconciling the majority decision with that in *Re J* even though I recognise that the merits in *Re B* ... were all on the father's side.'

14.54 So by 1998 English law had recognised a right of custody for the purposes of the Convention in fathers and grandparents, and possibly other relatives or friends, who had the primary care of the child, to the exclusion of the holder or holders of parental responsibility, immediately before the removal.

14.55 Since then, the question of inchoate rights has been considered by Sumner J in *Re G (Abduction: Rights of Custody)*,[94] by Munby J in *Re C (Child Abduction) (Unmarried Father: Rights of Custody)*,[95] and by the President of the Family Division, Dame Elizabeth Butler-Sloss in *Re F (Abduction: Unmarried Father: Sole Carer)*.[96] In *Re G (Abduction: Rights of Custody)*, a child's mother, the sole holder of parental rights, was persuaded by the father's family to bring her daughter to England from South Africa, where the mother had been considering placing her for adoption. On 12 December 2000, shortly after her arrival in England, the child, D, went to live with her paternal grandmother, Mrs M, who was later joined by the father. The mother lived separately in London. On 30 June 2000 the child went to her mother again when the father's family went on a boating holiday. During that holiday the mother took the child to South Africa and placed her for adoption. In reaching his conclusions, Sumner J said:[97]

'It is fundamental to a proper analysis of Mrs M's rights of custody, if any, to consider three particular elements. They are the circumstances in which D was placed in her care, the mother's intention at the time, and the length of time and manner in which Mrs M exercised that care. Those matters chiefly determine whether Mrs M was by the end of June 2001 exercising "functions of a parental or custodial nature".'

And later:[98]

'I am satisfied that by the end of June 2001 Mrs M had rights of custody. D had been placed with her with the mother's agreement. Whether that agreement arose because it was the mother's wish or because there was little realistic alternative does not in my judgment matter. It was not a situation to which the mother was objecting.'

---

[94]　[2002] 2 FLR 703 (judgment given 18 March 2002).
[95]　[2002] EWHC 2219 (Fam), [2003] 1 FLR 252.
[96]　[2002] EWHC 2896 (Fam), [2003] 1 FLR 839.
[97]　[2002] 2 FLR 703 at [102].
[98]　*Ibid* at [107].

14.56 In *Re C (Child Abduction) (Unmarried Father: Rights of Custody)*,[99] Munby J, dealing with an unmarried father whose child had been taken to Ireland by the mother, summarised the previous authorities, and said that *Re B* and *Re G* showed that there can be circumstances in which an unmarried father will acquire rights of custody, even if he is not the sole primary carer of his child, and even if he is sharing care with another – at least if that other is someone other than the child's mother. But that is as far as the authorities go, and to go any further would be inconsistent with what the House of Lords said in *Re J*.[100] So an unmarried father who shares the care of his child in the way that mothers and fathers living under the same roof commonly do, does not have rights of custody.[101]

14.57 The question of whether inchoate rights of custody could extend to persons other than fathers or grandparents was considered by the President in *Re F (Abduction: Unmarried Father: Sole Carer)*,[102] in which a child, who had been left by the mother in the care of the plaintiff (who believed himself to be the child's father), was taken from England to the mother in Australia without his knowledge or consent. In the declaratory proceedings, the mother raised the issue of paternity, and directions were given for DNA testing. However, on the day of the mother's application to set aside earlier orders made without notice requiring the child's return and a declaration that his removal was 'wrongful' with the terms of the Convention, the results were not available. But the President held that the issue was irrelevant, saying that:

> 'In my judgment, I come to the conclusion that there are circumstances in which a person who is not related by blood to the child who has been in his care may nonetheless be found to have inchoate rights of custody. It starts, in my view, in the situation as to what is the purpose of the Convention. The purpose of the Convention is, as Waite LJ said, not to allow children to be removed arbitrarily from one jurisdiction to another; secondly, that the underlying principle of the *Re B (A Minor) (Abduction)* case and the judgment of Waite LJ is not the blood relationship of parent or grandparent who does not have parental responsibility but the situation of the exclusivity of the care of the child.'

In moving on from the position of the carer to the nature of inchoate rights, the President took the view that a right to go to court and seek an injunction was only a starting point – there had to be a reasonable prospect of success of the inchoate rights being perfected, which in this case meant an application for a residence order. On the facts of the case, she felt that if the plaintiff had made an application for a residence order he had good prospects of success, so his inchoate rights were capable of being perfected.[103]

---

99   [2002] EWHC 2219 (Fam), [2003] 1 FLR 252.
100   *Ibid* at [37].
101   *Ibid* at [43]
102   [2002] EWHC 2896 (Fam), [2003] 1 FLR 839.
103   In subsequent proceedings in Australia, an order was made by consent for the return of the child to the United Kingdom.

Summary of inchoate rights in English law

14.58   English law recognises a 'right of custody' for the purposes of the Convention for those who have the care of the child to the exclusion of holders of parental responsibility, although it appears not to be necessary to be exercising that exclusive care immediately before the removal. However, whether any particular plaintiff has inchoate rights depends on the facts of the case. The test seems to be not whether the plaintiff could apply for an injunction, but whether there is a reasonable prospect of the inchoate rights being perfected – that is, a whether the plaintiff has a reasonable prospect of getting a residence order or its equivalent.

Inchoate rights in other jurisdictions

14.59   Although approved in New Zealand,[104] the concept of inchoate rights of custody has not attracted universal support. It was rejected by a majority of four to one in the Supreme Court of Ireland in *HI v MG (Child Abduction: Wrongful Removal)*,[105] in which an Egyptian father and British mother had married in an Islamic ceremony in New York which had no legal effect. The child lived for the first 5½ years of his life with his mother and father as a family, and then the parents parted. When the mother left the United States and went to Ireland, the father sought the return of the child and the mother argued that he had no rights of custody. There was conflicting evidence before the trial judge; one expert contending that the father had rights of custody under the law of New York State, the other that he did not. The trial judge found that the father had no legal rights of custody in New York, but accepted that he had inchoate rights which 'would almost inevitably have crystallised into established rights by court approval of the acknowledgement of paternity'.[106] The mother appealed, and in the Supreme Court, Keane J, having reviewed and approved the law relating to rights of custody in a court as being purposive and flexible construction of the Convention, went on to say:

> 'It is going significantly further to say, however, that there exists, in addition, an undefined hinterland of "inchoate" rights of custody not attributed in any sense by the law of the requesting state to the party asserting them or to the court itself, but regarded by the court of the requested state as being capable of protection under the terms of the Hague Convention. I am satisfied that the decision of the majority of the English Court of Appeal in *Re B (A Minor) (Abduction)* [1994] 2 FLR 249 to that effect should not be followed.'

---

[104]   *Anderson v Paterson* [2002] NZFLR 641, in which Judge Bisphan held that the crucial issue was the existence of an interest or expectation which was enforceable. The unmarried father had a right to apply for custody and access orders pursuant to Guradianship Act 1968, ss 11 and 15 which was sufficient to qualify as a 'right of custody' under the Convention, being a right which could be effectively exercised and, ultimately, enforced.

[105]   [2000] IR 110.

[106]   At 120. The judge also held that there were no rights of custody in the court in New York.

Problems with inchoate rights of custody

14.60   Some of the earlier uncertainties about inchoate rights of custody have been resolved by the decision of the President in *Re F (Abduction: Unmarried Father: Sole Carer).*[107] It is now clear that it is the quality of care that matters, not the person or persons providing it, and the test as to whether they would have a reasonable prospect of having their inchoate rights perfected by an order of a court seems to us to be something on which any competent family lawyer could advise. So it seems that a range of people may acquire these inchoate rights, including foster-carers and those in private fostering arrangements,[108] and that such rights are not lost when the holders of parental responsibility resume the care of the child, but rather at the time when any application on their part to perfect their inchoate rights is unlikely to succeed. However, there are still some problems. It is not clear the extent to which the acquisition of these inchoate rights depends on the willingness of the holder of legal rights to agree to care being exercised (even if there was no realistic alternative), or on there being no active objection, and to what extent these 'rights' reach beyond the narrow scope of the Convention. We say this because, in English law, holders of parental responsibility are empowered by statute to arrange for some or all of that responsibility to be met by one or more persons acting on their behalf.[109] The Children Act 1989 Guidance[110] suggested:

> 'Thus the Act recognises the right of parents to delegate responsibility for their child on a temporary basis, for example to a babysitter or for a school trip, but it will still be the parent's duty to ensure that the arrangements made for temporary care of the child are satisfactory',

but there is nothing in the statute to suggest that the delegation should be of a very limited duration, or that the person to whom the delegation is made acquires any rights.

Inchoate rights and habitual residence

14.61   In particular, there is nothing to suggest that a sole holder of parental responsibility, by asking others to look after the child, might lose the right to determine the child's habitual residence. Indeed, to the contrary, it is established[111] that *de facto* carers cannot change a child's habitual residence by taking him or her out of the jurisdiction. The law is that, unless there is some restraint in place, a parent with sole parental responsibility can change a child's

---

[107]   [2002] EWHC 2896 (Fam), [2003] 1 FLR 839.

[108]   See *Re F (Abduction: Unmarried Father: Sole Carer)* (above).

[109]   Children Act 1989, s 2(9).

[110]   *The Children Act 1989 Guidance and Regulations* (HMSO, 1991), vol 1, para 2.10.

[111]   See *Re S (A Minor) (Custody: Habitual Residence)* [1998] AC 750, [1998] 1 FLR 122, per Lord Slynn.

habitual residence at any time.[112] In *Re M (Minors) (Residence Order: Jurisdiction)*[113] a mother had decided not to return her children to the grandparents' home in Scotland, where they had been staying. Balcombe LJ said:

> 'Their Scottish residence was brought to an end when the mother who, as I once again stress, alone had parental responsibility for the children and alone could determine where they should live, had decided – as is evidenced by her applications to the Oxford County Court as well as her previous communications to the father and grandparents – that they should no longer reside with the grandparents in Scotland.'

14.62 The question of whether an inchoate right under the Convention amounts to a restraint on this aspect of parental responsibility was not directly addressed by the Court of Appeal in *Re B (A Minor) (Abduction)*[114] or any of the later cases, but if it does, it could lead to quite serious difficulties in determining questions of jurisdiction. We think that the better view is that the concept of inchoate rights of custody is confined to the operation of the Convention, and is limited to conferring what might be described as 'Convention rights', because it is not necessary for the operation of the Convention to consider whether the removal changed the child's habitual residence.

To whom can rights of custody be attributed?

14.63 The words 'a person, an institution or any other body' in Art 3(a) envisage a very wide range of holders of rights of custody. It is not necessary that the rights should be solely vested in one person, institution or other body, and nor is it necessary for joint holders to have equal rights:[115]

> 'This right may be in the court, the mother, the father, some caretaking institution, such as a local authority, or it may, as in this case, be a divided right, insofar as the child is to reside in Australia, the right being that of the mother; but, insofar as any question arises as to the child residing outside Australia, it being a joint right subject always, of course, to the overriding rights of the court.'

Rights of custody in a person, institution or other body

14.64 There does not appear to have been any difficulty in the operation of the Convention in the concept of a person or persons having rights of custody. Our experience has been that the domestic law of the various Contracting States has been clear in ascribing rights to persons. The question usually raised is whether they amount to 'rights of custody' for Convention

---

[112] *Re J (A Minor) (Abduction: Custody Rights)* [1990] 2 AC 562 at 579B–D, sub nom *C v S (Minor) (Abduction)* [1990] 2 FLR 442 at 454E–F.

[113] [1993] 1 FLR 495, CA.

[114] [1994] 2 FLR 249.

[115] Per Lord Donaldson MR in *C v C (Abduction: Rights of Custody)* [1989] 1 WLR 654 at 663H, sub nom *Re C (A Minor) (Abduction)* [1989] 1 FLR 403 at 413.

purposes. Persons are probably the only class within Art 3 who can have 'inchoate' rights of custody.[116]

14.65 In English law, every person who has parental responsibility for a child, whether by operation of law, court order or agreement between the parents, has 'rights of custody' for Convention purposes.[117]

14.66 Equally, institutions or other bodies do not seem to have posed much difficulty – in *Re JS (Private International Adoption)*,[118] an adoption agency in the United States was held to have rights of custody, which were breached when the prospective adoptive parents refused to comply with a request to return the child, a request which had been made after the adoption agency had been notified by an English local authority of concerns about the proposed adoptive parents' ability to provide a safe home.

Rights of custody in a court

14.67 Since Lord Donaldson MR mentioned in *Re C (A Minor) (Abduction)*[119] the possibility that a court might have rights of custody, a number of jurisdictions, including England and Wales, Scotland, Australia, New Zealand and Canada, have accepted that pending proceedings could give rise to a right of custody in the court seised of them.[120] A pending custody application might well confer rights of custody on a court but, because the Convention clearly differentiates between custody and access, a pending contact[121] application would not do so.[122]

---

[116] 'I do not believe that courts can have inchoate rights of custody ...', per Dame Elizabeth Butler-Sloss P in *Re F (Abduction: Unmarried Father: Sole Carer)* [2002] EWHC 2896 (Fam), [2003] 1 FLR 839.

[117] See Children Act 1989, ss 2, 3 4, 12 and 33. Married parents and unmarried mothers automatically have parental responsibility; unmarried fathers can acquire it by agreement with the mother (a parental responsibility agreement) or by obtaining a parental responsibility order. Holders of a residence order have parental responsibility, as do local authorities with a care order.

[118] [2000] 2 FLR 638.

[119] [1989] 1 FLR 403.

[120] *Re H (A Minor) (Abduction: Rights of Custody)* [2000] 2 AC 291, [2000] 1 FLR 374, HL. In Ireland, see *HI v MG (Child Abduction: Wrongful Removal)* [2000] IR 110; in Australia, see *Seroka v Bellah* 1995 SLT 204, *Secretary, A-G's Department v TS* [2000] Fam CA 1692, at para 54 *et seq* (Nicholson CJ approving Thorpe LJ in *Re H (Abduction: Rights of Custody)* [2000] 1 FLR 201), *Brooke and Director-General, Community Services* [2002] Fam CA 258; in New Zealand, see *Re Olson v Olson*, Family Court of New Zealand, 1994 FP 37/94; and in Canada, see *Thomson v Thomson* [1994] 3 SCR 551, (1995) 119 DLR (4th) 253.

[121] Or access or visitation.

[122] *Re V-B (Abduction: Custody Rights)* [1999] 2 FLR 192 at 203B–D and *Re H (Abduction: Rights of Custody)* [2000] 1 FLR 201 at 207C–E and 211H–212B. And see the decisions of the Supreme Court of Canada in *Thomson v Thomson* [1994] 3 SCR 551, (1995) 119 DLR (4th) 253, and *W(V) v S(D)* (1996) 134 DLR (4th) 481. Note, however, that if there was some express or implied prohibition on removal during the pendency of the proceedings, breach of that provision would be a breach of rights of custody, and that if a contact order were to be made which included a prohibition, express or implied, on removal from the State of the

Pending custody applications

14.68   In *B v B (Child Abduction: Custody Rights)*,[123] the English Court of Appeal held that a foreign court seised of an application which gave it the right to determine the child's place of residence had rights of custody which were breached by the mother when she removed the child from his habitual residence. In that case, the foreign court had embarked upon the exercise of its rights of custody by adjourning the matter, by giving directions as to how it should be dealt with and by making an interim custody order. This view was supported by the Canadian Supreme Court in *Thomson v Thomson*[124] in which La Forest J said:

> 'It seems to me that when a court has before it an issue of who shall be accorded custody of a child, and awards interim custody to one of the parents in the course of dealing with that issue, it has rights relating to the care and control of the child and, in particular, the right to determine the child's place of residence. It has long been established that a court may be a body or institution capable of caring for the person of a child.'

14.69   The leading English authority on the question of a court's rights of custody arising from pending proceedings is now *Re H (A Minor) (Abduction: Rights of Custody)*,[125] which involved the removal of a child from the Republic of Ireland to England by her mother during the pendency of her father's application for his appointment as her guardian and to specify the access he should have to her.[126] The matter came before the court in Ireland inter partes, when it was adjourned by consent, with access to the father being agreed. Access took place in accordance with the agreement until the mother left Ireland without the father's knowledge or consent. In the absence of the mother, the Irish court appointed the father guardian of his child and granted him defined access. Having located his daughter in England, the father instituted proceedings for her return to the Republic of Ireland under the 1980 Hague Abduction Convention. The mother denied that either the father or the Irish court had 'rights of custody', or that the removal breached such rights, or that the father could rely on rights that were not his own. At first instance, the father's application was refused on the basis that neither the father nor the Irish court had rights of custody but, on appeal,[127] the Court of Appeal held that whether an application before a court was such as to give the court rights of custody depended on the particular circumstances of the case. An application which in substance sought only the determination, definition or

---

child's habitual residence without the leave of the court, that order would create a right of custody: see **14.42** *et seq*.

[123] [1993] Fam 32, at 38C, 42G, sub nom *B v B (Abduction)* [1993] 1 FLR 238, at 243A, 247F. And see *Thorn v Dryden-Hall* [1997] 28 RFL(4) 297 (British Columbia Court of Appeal).

[124] [1994] 3 SCR 351, (1995) 119 DLR (4th) 253.

[125] [2000] 2 AC 291, [2000] 1 FLR 374, HL.

[126] In an earlier application in the same proceedings, a custody order had been made, by consent, in favour of the mother with defined access to the father.

[127] *Re H (Abduction: Rights of Custody)* [2000] 1 FLR 201.

qualification of contact could not vest a right of custody, but an application which in substance sought the determination of issues of physical care, parental responsibility or the jurisdiction in which the responsibility of physical care would be exercised may or may not suffice to vest rights of custody in the court of issue. To determine whether rights are vested it is necessary to scrutinise the nature of the application, its merits and the applicant's commitment to its pursuit. The mere issue of a hopeless or insincere application would vest nothing in the court, being at that stage no more than 'the tool of the applicant's manipulation'. Equally, the issue of an arguably meritorious application may be offset if thereafter by inactivity or inconsistent statement the applicant belies his seeming intention to obtain judgment. 'In the end each case must call for its own evaluation always giving the Article its wide and purposive construction.'[128]

14.70 In the House of Lords, Lord Mackay, approaching the various questions on the basis that the Convention is to be applied under a variety of systems of law and should therefore be given a purposive construction to make as effective as possible the machinery set up under it, reached the following conclusions:

(i) a court may be an 'other body' for the purposes of Art 8,[129] particularly since the phraseology chosen in the Convention was deliberately wide;

(ii) a court may have 'rights of custody' as defined by Art 5. Many of the matters relating to the care of the person of the child will consist in duties and powers rather than rights in the narrow sense, and the characterisation in the Convention of the right to determine a child's place of residence as a 'right' underlines the width to be given to the word 'rights' in the Convention;

(iii) the application to the court must raise a question of custody within the meaning of the Convention, which will require in every case a consideration of the terms of the application;

(iv) the time at which the application confers rights of custody on the court is at the latest the date of service;

(v) unless the application is stayed or some equivalent action is taken, the court's jurisdiction is continuously invoked until the application is disposed of;

---

[128] Per Thorpe LJ at 212. In his judgment, Thorpe LJ examined the development of the law relating to rights of custody in a court, including the cases of *Re C (A Minor) (Abduction)* [1989] 1 FLR 403, *B v B (Child Abduction: Custody Rights)* [1993] Fam 32, sub nom *B v B (Abduction)* [1993] 1 FLR 238, *Re B (A Minor) (Abduction)* [1994] 2 FLR 249, *Re W (Minors) (Abduction: Father's Rights)* [1999] Fam 1, sub nom *Re W; Re B (Child Abduction: Unmarried Father)* [1998] 2 FLR 146, *Re J (Abduction: Declaration of Wrongful Removal)* [1999] 2 FLR 653, and *Re C (Abduction: Wrongful Removal)* [1999] 2 FLR 859.

[129] Article 8 reads 'Any person, institution, or other body claiming that a child has been removed or retained in breach of custody rights may apply …'.

(vi) questions about the merits of the application, or the good faith of the applicant, are matters for the court of the child's habitual residence to deal with;

(vii) a person who has invoked the jurisdiction of a court as a result of which the court has rights of custody in respect of a child should be entitled to apply to the courts of the country to which that child has been wrongfully removed for the restoration of the child to the jurisdiction of his or her habitual residence, because to hold otherwise would be an unnecessary obstacle to the smooth working of the Convention.

14.71 In this case, the application for guardianship under the Irish Guardianship of Infants Act 1964 was held to amount to an application raising a question of custody within the meaning of the Convention despite the award of custody to the mother by consent, because it was implied in that consent, as appeared from the terms relating to access, that the day-to-day care of the child would be exercised at the mother's address. Once the father was appointed guardian, he had an equal right with the mother to determine where the child should live and in particular whether she should be removed from Ireland,[130] and in default of agreement the matter would have to be referred to the court.[131]

Rights of custody in an English court

14.72 Accordingly, if a person with sole parental responsibility removes a child from the United Kingdom while proceedings relating to the child are pending, the removal is likely to be wrongful within the meaning of Art 3 if, before the date of removal, an application which raises matters of custody within the meaning of the Convention has been served. The mere issue of proceedings will not usually be sufficient[132] to invest a court with rights

---

[130] 'I do not regard the award of custody by consent in proceedings which were still pending and in which active consideration of an application for guardianship by the father was taking place at the time of the removal as destructive of the court's power to decide the child's place of residence', per Lord Mackay.

[131] Contrast the position of the father in the case of *Re V-B (Abduction: Custody Rights)* [1999] 2 FLR 192, CA, who had a Dutch order which conferred upon him a right to be consulted on questions of residence and other issues, but no right to object.

[132] *Re B (Abduction: Rights of Custody)* [1997] 2 FLR 594 at 599E–600H; *Re W (Minors) (Abduction: Father's Rights)* [1999] Fam 1 at 19B–D, sub nom *Re W; Re B (Child Abduction: Unmarried Father)* [1998] 2 FLR 146 at 162H–163B; *Re H (A Child) (Abduction: Rights of Custody)* [2000] 2 AC 291 at 304D–H, [2000] 1 FLR 374 at 380. The complaint of the father in *Re B (Abduction: Rights of Custody)* to the ECtHR that unmarried fathers were discriminated against in the protection of their relationships with their children was declared inadmissible (14 September 1999) on the basis that there was an objective and reasonable justification for the difference in treatment between married and unmarried fathers with regard to the automatic acquisition of parental rights, relating to the range of possible relationships between them and their children – see *B v UK* [2000] 1 FLR 1, in which the ECtHR said that it found the High Court's view that the 'mere institution of proceedings' was insufficient to confer rights of custody on a court 'convincing'.

of custody, but if before service the court has made directions or interim orders, that is likely to suffice,[133] and special cases may arise.[134]

Proceedings which may give rise to a right of custody in an English court

14.73 Proceedings which may give rise to a right of custody in an English court include an application for a residence order (which invokes the court's powers to determine the child's place of residence, and therefore necessarily involves the exercise of the court's rights of custody within the meaning of the Hague Convention),[135] an application for an order restraining the removal of a child from the jurisdiction,[136] and an application for a parental responsibility order, the effect of which is equivalent to an order prohibiting removal.[137]

14.74 In addition, any proceedings in which there is an issue as to whether or not a child should be taken abroad will also confer rights of custody on the court.[138] Further, if a court has jurisdiction to make an order requiring the return of a child to the jurisdiction, it assumes rights of custody when it makes such an order.[139] However, pending proceedings under the Convention itself do not give rise to a right of custody.[140]

Wardship proceedings

14.75 There is no doubt that, where a child is a ward of court, the court is 'a person, an institution or any other body' within the meaning of Arts 3 and 8 and has 'rights of custody'.[141] Wardship proceedings might, however, be thought to fall into a special category because the status of ward of court (and

---

133 *Re H (A Minor) (Abduction: Rights of Custody)* [2000] 2 AC 291 at 304F–H, [2000] 1 FLR 374 at 380.

134 *Ibid.*

135 *Re H (Abduction: Rights of Custody)* [2000] 1 FLR 201, approving *Re W (Minors) (Abduction: Father's Rights)* [1999] Fam 1, sub nom *Re W; Re B (Child Abduction: Unmarried Father)* [1998] 2 FLR 146, *Re J (Abduction: Declaration of Wrongful Removal)* [1999] 2 FLR 653 and *Re C (Abduction: Wrongful Removal)* [1999] 2 FLR 859.

136 *Re J (Abduction: Declaration of Wrongful Removal)* (above).

137 *Re C (Abduction: Wrongful Removal)* (above), in which the view expressed by the Central Authority for England and Wales in its *Practice Note (Hague Convention: Applications by Fathers Without Parental Responsibility)* (14 October 1997) [1998] 1 FLR 491 to the effect that pending proceedings for a parental responsibility order did not create a right of custody in the court was rejected by Hale J.

138 *Re J (Abduction: Declaration of Wrongful Removal)* (above) at 657C–E.

139 *Ibid* at 657E–658D. If a court has jurisdiction to make an order under s 8 of the Children Act 1989 (see Part I of the Family Law Act 1986 discussed in Chapter 3), it may make an order different in terms to that sought in the application which founded the jurisdiction, and so require the return of a child removed during the pendency of the proceedings and by so doing acquire rights of custody for 1980 Hague Abduction Convention purposes. Failure to comply with the return order would constitute a wrongful retention: see *Re S (A Minor) (Custody: Habitual Residence)* [1998] AC 750, [1998] 1 FLR 122, HL.

140 *Re L (Abduction: Pending Criminal Proceedings)* [1999] 1 FLR 433.

141 *Re J (Abduction: Ward of Court)* [1989] Fam 85, sub nom *Re J (A Minor) (Abduction)* [1990] 1 FLR 276.

therefore the automatic prohibition on removal from the jurisdiction)[142] is imposed on immediately on the issue of an originating summons.[143]

14.76 However, it is clear that, since the implementation of the Children Act 1989 in October 1991, wardship has diminished in importance (except, perhaps, in non-Convention abduction cases),[144] and there has been a disinclination to ascribe to it any special status or importance.[145] The proceedings in *Re H (A Minor) (Abduction: Rights of Custody)* were wardship proceedings, but although Lord Mackay acknowledged[146] that the issue of the application made the child a ward, he considered that, generally speaking, there was much force in using service of the application as the time when the court's jurisdiction is invoked (although interim orders may be made before service, and special cases may arise).

14.77 So, unless the court makes orders before service or special circumstances arise, the originating summons in wardship would have to have been served prior to the removal to confer 'rights of custody' on the High Court for the purposes of the Convention.

Can a court really have and enforce rights?

14.78 Whether or not a court can have rights of custody is a settled question as far as English law is concerned, but it is not without its difficulties or its critics. In *Seroka v Bellah*,[147] Lord Prosser, sitting at first instance in the Scottish Court of Session, expressed misgiving at the concept of a court having 'rights' or actually exercising them at a specified time, or whether they would have been exercised but for a removal or retention. In his view, courts have power to attribute rights, rather than exercise them, although he conceded that a court may 'determine' a child's place of residence when exercising its powers in that connection. And Chadwick LJ in *Re H (Abduction: Rights of Custody)*[148] said

---

[142] Subject to the provisions of Family Law Act 1986, s 38, which permit the removal of the ward to another part of the United Kingdom if he is habitually resident there or there are matrimonial proceedings in respect of the marriage of his parents in progress there, unless he has attained the age of 16 and the other part of the United Kingdom is Scotland: see **6.14**.

[143] Supreme Court Act 1981, s 41(2); Family Proceedings Rules 1991, r 5.3; Family Law Act 1986, s 38.

[144] For non-Convention cases, see Chapter 20.

[145] 'Today I would not give greater status to an application issued in wardship proceedings in the absence of exceptional circumstances. Wardship has an important continuing role to curb or retrieve abduction where one of the jurisdictions is not a signatory to the 1980 Convention, but where a case is either within or without the Art 5 definition I do not consider that the issue of wardship proceedings should ordinarily be judged to have strengthened the applicant's hand': per Thorpe LJ in *Re H (Abduction: Rights of Custody)* [2000] 1 FLR 201 at 212. And see his observations about the use of wardship in *Al Habtoor v Fotheringham* [2001] EWCA Civ 186, [2001] 1 FLR 951.

[146] [2000] 2 AC 291 at 304, [2000] 1 FLR 374 at 380.

[147] 1995 SLT 204.

[148] [2000] 1 FLR 201.

that if the law had not developed as it had, he would have taken the view that Lord Donaldson's observations in *Re C (A Minor) (Abduction)*[149] were not reflected by the other members of the court, were not necessary to his decision and not binding on the Court of Appeal in subsequent cases, and that, were it not for the decision in *B v B*, he might have been able to give effect to his own misgivings, well expressed by Lord Prosser.

14.79 Other than to those familiar with the wardship jurisdiction,[150] courts do seem unlikely holders of rights of custody and less likely litigants. Unlike other bodies or institutions, they can neither sue nor be sued, and cannot be ordered to pay costs.[151]

14.80 Notwithstanding the decision of the House of Lords in *Re H*,[152] the jurisprudence about rights of custody and pending proceedings is still to some extent evolving, and it would be prudent, if acting for a litigant whose rights of custody seem questionable, to apply at the outset of any proceedings for an order restraining the removal of the child without either the leave of the court or the consent of the applicant in writing, and to make sure that the application is served.

Actual exercise of rights of custody[153]

14.81 Article 3(b) requires that at the time of the removal or retention, the custody rights of the custodial parent 'were actually exercised, either jointly or alone, or would have been so exercised but for the removal or retention'. In *Re H; Re S (Abduction: Custody Rights)*[154] it was argued that, if removal for the purposes of the Convention involved the taking of the child concerned across the frontier of the State of his habitual residence, it might be impossible for the custodial parent to show that the requirement contained in Art 3(b) was satisfied. Lord Brandon, however, took the view[155] that Art 3(b):

> '... must be construed widely as meaning that the custodial parent must be maintaining the stance and attitude of such a parent, rather than narrowly as

---

[149] [1989] 1 FLR 403.

[150] Which, as La Forest J pointed out in *Thomson v Thomson* (1995) 119 DLR (4th) 253, has 'puzzled and concerned' other Contracting States.

[151] As Hollis J pointed out in *The Ontario Court v M and M (Abduction: Children's Objections)* [1997] 1 FLR 475.

[152] *Re H (A Minor) (Abduction: Rights of Custody)* [2000] 2 AC 291, [2000] 1 FLR 374.

[153] As to the 'defence' of not actually exercising custody rights at the time or removal or retention, Wall J said in *Re W (Abduction: Procedure)* [1995] 1 FLR 878 at 888 that 'Article 13(a) refers to rights of custody which are not being actually exercised by the person who has the care of the person of the child: this contrasts with Art 3 which refers to rights of custody generally. The Art 13(a) defence in this context is thus limited to the situation in which the child's actual caretaker is not actually taking care of him. This is a much narrower situation ...'. As to the Art 13(a) 'defence', see **17.41** *et seq.*

[154] [1991] 2 AC 476, [1991] 2 FLR 262.

[155] *Ibid* at 500–501 and 272–273, respectively. Cited with approval by Lord Clarke in the Scottish decision *S v S* 2003 SLT 344 at [14].

meaning that he or she must be continuing to exercise day-to-day care and control. If the narrow meaning was adopted, it could be said that a custodial parent was not actually exercising his or her custodial rights during a period of lawful staying access with the non-custodial parent. That, as it seems to me, cannot be right.'

14.82   So a parent who consents to his child travelling or living abroad for a period of time is exercising custody rights not only when he gives permission for his child to leave his country of habitual residence, but also whilst the child is away, because his permission is regarded as a continuing exercise of custodial rights until the moment when the child is retained against his wishes.[156]

14.83   The second limb of Art 3(b), '… or would have been so exercised but for the removal or retention', operates in those cases in which the child is removed without the knowledge or consent of the other parent. But for the removal, the child would have continued to live in his State of habitual residence, and the other parent to exercise his rights of custody, including a veto on removal.[157]

---

[156]   *W v W (Child Abduction: Acquiescence)* [1993] 2 FLR 211. And see *Re W (Abduction: Procedure)* [1995] 1 FLR 878 at 887. In the same way, a parent who makes arrangements for his child to live with friends or relatives is exercising a right of custody whilst the child is living with them: see, in Australia, *Director-General, Department of Community Services v Crowe* (1996) FLC 92–717.

[157]   See *Re F (A Minor) (Abduction: Custody Rights Abroad)* [1995] Fam 224 at 230D–F, sub nom *Re F (Child Abduction: Risk if Returned)* [1995] 2 FLR 31 at 35, where Butler-Sloss LJ said that: 'I am satisfied that the father and mother both enjoyed equal and separate rights of custody by Colorado law. Equally by Colorado law in the absence of a court order to the contrary either parent could remove the child from the State and from the USA without violating any principles of Colorado law. It cannot, however, be the case that the lawful removal of the child by one parent destroys the rights of the other parent nor did any of the Colorado lawyers suggest it. The removal of the child by the mother interfered with the rights of the father in that he was prevented from actually exercising them in the USA. Such interference with rights is recognised in the Convention and Art 3 includes in its definition rights which "would have been exercised but for the removal". In my judgment the father continued to enjoy "rights of custody" subject to the effect of the orders of the Adams County Court'. Note that the fact that the removal was not unlawful did not mean that it was not 'wrongful' within the meaning of the Convention: see **14.9**.

Chapter 15

INTERNATIONAL ABDUCTIONS: HAGUE ABDUCTION CONVENTION: DECLARATORY RELIEF

DECLARATORY RELIEF UNDER THE 1980 HAGUE ABDUCTION CONVENTION

15.1 Where, prior to making a return order, there is doubt or uncertainty as to how the law of the State of the child's habitual residence applies,[1] Art 15 of the 1980 Hague Abduction Convention creates a mechanism for the judicial or administrative authorities of the requested State to ask if the removal or retention of the child was wrongful under the law of the requesting State. Article 15 provides that:

> 'The judicial or administrative authorities of a Contracting State may, prior to the making of an order for the return of the child, request that the applicant obtain from the authorities of the State of the habitual residence of the child a decision or other determination that the removal or retention was wrongful within the meaning of Article 3 of the Convention, where such a decision or determination may be obtained in that State. The Central Authorities of the Contracting States shall so far as practicable assist applicants to obtain such a decision or determination.'

15.2 So the jurisdictional requirements for making a declaration pursuant to Art 15 are that:

(i) the request originates from the judicial or administrative authorities of a State seised of a request for the return of the child; and

---

[1] See the Pérez-Vera Report, at para 120.

(ii)   the request for the declaration is made by an applicant for a return order.[2]

15.3   In her Explanatory Report, Professor Pérez-Vera noted the 'voluntary' nature of the request, in the sense that the return of the child cannot be made conditional upon a declaration being provided.[3]

DECLARATIONS OTHER THAN UNDER ARTICLE 15 OF THE 1980 HAGUE ABDUCTION CONVENTION

15.4   Article 15 may not be the only source of declaratory relief. Not only has the High Court of England and Wales an inherent jurisdiction to grant declaratory relief,[4] it has also interpreted the statutory provision relating to Art 15 as having wider effect than the narrow circumstances of the Article itself. Section 8 of the Child Abduction and Custody Act 1985 provides:

> 'The High Court or Court of Session may, on an application made for the purposes of Article 15 of the Convention by any person appearing to the court to have an interest in the matter, make a declaration or declarator that the removal of any child from, or his retention outside, the United Kingdom was wrongful within the meaning of Article 3 of the Convention.'

15.5   The High Court has taken the view that this provision enables applications for declarations to be made by any person appearing to the court to have an interest in the matter, for the purpose of satisfying, whether immediately or in the future, the judicial or administrative authorities of the requested State that the removal or retention was wrongful by the law of the requesting State. *Re J (Minor: Abduction: Ward of Court)*[5] was a case involving an application for a declaration by the father of a ward. The father had rights of access but not rights of custody, and consequently he wanted to rely on the court's rights of custody[6] in relation to its ward when his child was removed to the United States without his consent. Swinton Thomas J said:[7]

> 'To my mind those provisions [ie those in Art 15] apply to particular circumstances, and to particular circumstances only, that is to say when a contracting state to which the child has been taken wishes to obtain information from the authorities of the state of the habitual residence of the child. That is not the position here. The position in this case is that the father and his advisers have not arrived at that situation. They wish to provide the Lord Chancellor's Department, and not the judicial or administrative authorities of a contracting

---

2   See *Re J (Minor: Abduction: Ward of Court)* [1989] Fam 85, [1990] 1 FLR 276.
3   Paragraph 120.
4   See RSC 1965, Ord 15, r 16 (still applicable in family proceedings) and CPR 1998, rr 40.7 and 40.20. As to declaratory relief generally, see *Re F (Sterilisation: Mental Patient)* [1989] 2 FLR 376. In view of the wide interpretation of the Child Abduction and Custody Act 1985, s 8, it should not be necessary to have resort to the inherent powers of the High Court.
5   [1989] Fam 85, [1990] 1 FLR 276.
6   See **14.75**.
7   [1989] Fam 85 at 94, [1990] 1 FLR 276 at 285.

state, with the information that the removal of the child was wrongful. Section 8 of the 1985 Act is, in my judgment, permissive and not restrictive, permitting the courts to make declarations in the particular circumstances envisaged by the section and Art 3 but the section does not in any way preclude the court from making a declaration in the circumstances which arise here. It was suggested that I should deal with this problem by making a finding of fact and not making a declaration. That seems to me to be a distinction without a difference. I have no doubt that the court is empowered to make the declaration sought.'

15.6 This wide interpretation of s 8 was examined by the Court of Appeal in *Re P (Abduction: Declaration)*,[8] a case involving an application for a declaration made by a father to the English High Court at the suggestion of the Central Authority for England and Wales (the Lord Chancellor). Butler-Sloss LJ said:[9]

'I agree with the decision arrived at by Swinton Thomas J but disagree with his view that it was based upon the inherent jurisdiction. In my judgment in *Re J*, as in the present case, s 8 was the basis for the jurisdiction and the declaration could properly be granted without recourse to the inherent jurisdiction of the High Court.'

THE NATURE AND EFFECT OF DECLARATORY RELIEF

15.7 Declarations are discretionary remedies, and may be refused if they can make no contribution towards, or might delay or otherwise impede, the application for the return order.[10]

15.8 Of necessity, when considering an application for a declaration, the requesting State will have to consider matters which may be contested in the proceedings in the requested State, one of which might be whether the child was habitually resident in the requesting State at the time of removal. In *Re P (Abduction: Declaration)*[11] Butler-Sloss LJ said in the Court of Appeal:

'In the general run of cases on such a request made before there is a decision or assumption by the requested State as to where is the habitual residence of the child, it would be preferable for the English court, if the facts permit, to make a declaration upon the assumption that the habitual residence is in England, rather

---

8   [1995] 1 FLR 831, CA.
9   And see the judgment of Millett LJ who said: 'But it is not a pre-condition of the exercise of the jurisdiction conferred by s 8 of the 1985 Act that the procedure laid down by Art 15 of the Convention has been followed. Section 8 speaks of an application "for the purposes of Art 15" not of an application "made in accordance with the provisions of Art 15", and in my view the choice of words is deliberate' (at 839).
10 *Re P (Diplomatic Immunity: Jurisdiction)* [1998] 1 FLR 1026 (declaration refused when it could make no contribution to proceedings in the United States in which the issue was whether the children should live in the United States with the American father or in Germany with the German mother).
11 [1995] 1 FLR 831, CA.

than making a specific finding on an issue still in dispute in the other State. The issue properly to be the concern of the English court under the Convention is whether an applicant parent had rights of custody according to English law at the time of the removal. In order to make a declaration, however, under s 8 that the removal or retention was wrongful, the English court would also have to make a provisional decision about breach, although that too is a matter within the jurisdiction of the other State. The request for a declaration makes it inevitable that the English court will have to consider, however provisionally, issues which are to be decided in another place, unless the English court always declines to make a declaration which Parliament has given jurisdiction to the court to make. In my view as a question of policy the English court should not debar itself from its power to grant a declaration at the request of another signatory to the Convention. In my view the approach of the Lord Chancellor's Department, or more particularly the Official Solicitor on their behalf, to the problems of English law faced by the Central Authority of the USA in this case was helpful and the advice to seek a declaration sensible. The judge on the application was justified in granting the declaration.

The only question which remains is whether he should have made findings as to habitual residence. On the particular facts of this case with the existence of the 1992 order the judge, on being asked to make a declaration, had no alternative but to grasp the nettle and make his findings on habitual residence. If he did not on the facts of this case, he could not make a declaration nor assist the requested State.'

15.9   Accordingly, a declaration made under Art 15 can be no more than persuasive, and cannot bind the parties or the authorities of the requested State, who will accept as much or as little of the judgment as they choose.[12]

MATTERS TO BE CONSIDERED ON AN APPLICATION FOR A DECLARATION

15.10   In deciding whether to grant a declaration, the court has to consider four issues: whether the children were habitually resident in the requesting State immediately before their removal or retention; whether the applicant had rights of custody at that date; whether the applicant exercised his rights of custody at that date; and whether the children were removed from the jurisdiction in breach of those rights.[13]

---

[12]   *Re L (Children) (Abduction: Declaration)* [2001] 2 FCR 1. In *Re J (A Minor) (Abduction: Custody Rights)* [1990] 2 AC 562, at 578A, sub nom *C v S (A Minor) (Abduction)* [1990] 2 FLR 442 at 453D, Lord Brandon said of the declaration made by the Australian court after the removal of the child: 'I pay to his [Anderson J's] decision the respect which comity requires, but the courts of the UK are not bound by it and for the reasons which I have given I do not consider that it was rightly made'.

[13]   *Re L (Children) (Abduction: Declaration)* (above).

APPLICATIONS WITHOUT NOTICE

15.11   In *B v H (Habitual Residence: Wardship)*,[14] the originating summons did not include an application for declaratory relief, but Charles J was asked to make declarations about the habitual residence of the children. He declined to do so, saying:

> 'In my judgment it is not necessary, or appropriate, for me to do so because: (i) justice to the mother (and the children) can be met by a recital as to habitual residence and jurisdiction; and (ii) to do so might prejudice the father having regard to his participation in these proceedings even though I accept that as he was served and given a full opportunity to take part therein I could have made a declaration if it had been necessary. In reaching this conclusion I have had regard to *Wallersteiner v Moir; Moir v Wallersteiner and Others* [1974] 1 WLR 991 in particular at 1028H–1029D and 1030C–G.'

15.12   It is clear from the authorities that making a declaration is a judicial act, and as such ought not to be made on admissions or by consent.[15] However, those authorities are not cases under either Art 15 of the 1980 Hague Abduction Convention or s 8 of the Child Abduction and Custody Act 1985, and in the appropriate circumstances (given the *sui generis* nature of the Convention,[16] the summary nature of both Convention and non-Convention proceedings and the need for speed), courts will be prepared to grant declarations in the absence of the respondent to an application for a return order, or even without the respondent being notified of the application, especially if a declaration were necessary to engage the authorities of the requested State in searching for the child. In *Re G (Abduction: Rights of Custody)*,[17] a court in South Africa agreed to stay adoption proceedings[18] pending the outcome of Hague Convention proceedings, part of which was an application for a declaration. The defendant mother knew of the application but did not attend or instruct lawyers to appear on her behalf. However, the Official Solicitor instructed counsel to appear as Advocate to the court.[19]

---

[14]   [2002] 1 FLR 388 at [151]. See **4.47**.
[15]   See the footnotes to RSC 1965, Ord 15, r 16 in the *Supreme Court Practice*, Vol 1. And see *Wallersteiner v Moir; Moir v Wallersteiner and Others* [1974] 1 WLR 991 (declarations about fraud disapproved).
[16]   See **21.78**.
[17]   [2002] 2 FLR 703.
[18]   See Art 16.
[19]   Formerly *amicus curiae*: see **21.36**. As to the judgment in *Re G (Abduction: Rights of Custody)* as it relates to rights of custody, see **14.55**.

Chapter 16

INTERNATIONAL ABDUCTIONS: HAGUE ABDUCTION CONVENTION: THE OBLIGATION TO RETURN

ARTICLE 12(1)

16.1 Article 12(1) sets out the normal rule:[1] where a child has been wrongfully removed or retained in terms of Art 3[2] and, at the date of commencement[3] of the proceedings before the judicial or administrative authorities of the State where the child is, a period of less than one year has elapsed from the date of the wrongful removal or retention, the authority concerned must, subject to the exceptions in Art 13,[4] order the return of the child forthwith.

To return 'forthwith'

16.2 In England and Wales, the High Court recognises that the obligation is to return 'forthwith'. It does not permit much delay between order and return. The Preamble to the Convention draws attention to the need for speedy return: it refers to the 'States signatory to the present Convention ... desiring to protect children internationally from the harmful effects of their wrongful removal or retention and to establish procedures to ensure their prompt return to the state of their habitual residence ...' (emphasis added).[5] In England, the

---

[1] What the Pérez-Vera Report, at para 27, refers to as the 'basic principle of the Convention'.
[2] As to Art 3, see **14.4** *et seq*.
[3] See **17.9**.
[4] See **17.36** *et seq*.
[5] *Re O (Child Abduction: Re-abduction)* [1997] 2 FLR 702 at 719.

procedure is summary and intended expeditiously to give effect to the Convention. In *Re M (Minors) (Abductions: Undertakings),*[6] Butler-Sloss LJ said that '[b]y Art 11 of the Convention, speed is of the essence', and that delays in hearing applications should be avoided. Article 2 places an obligation on the States signatory to use the most expeditious procedures available.

16.3   Other jurisdictions also give effect to what is one of the objects of the Convention set out in Art 1(a), namely to secure the prompt return of children wrongly removed or retained. For example, the United States Court of Appeals for the 6th Circuit in *March v Levine*[7] affirmed the district court's order that the children be 'immediately returned to their father in Mexico' and, because the children had been separated from their father for almost one year, the Court of Appeals further ordered that their mandate issue forthwith,[8] and that the district court 'take appropriate action to ensure that the children are reunited with their father with all due speed'.

16.4   The Convention states in Art 18 that the provisions of Art 12 and the other Articles in Chapter III of the Convention[9] do not limit the power of the judicial or administrative authorities to order a return at any time. The meaning of this Article is discussed below in the context of the exceptions to the obligation to return.[10]

Where or to whom the child should be returned

16.5   The Convention does not state expressly where or to whom the child is to be returned. In 1987, less than 2 years after the Convention came into force in the United Kingdom, the English Court of Appeal in *Re A (A Minor) (Abduction)*[11] held that the return contemplated is a return to the country of the child's habitual residence, rather than to the custody of the primary custodial parent. However, the court appears not to have had cited to it Pérez-Vera's Explanatory Report, which points out[12] that the Convention did not accept a proposal to the effect that the return of the child should always be to the State of the child's habitual residence. Admittedly, one of the underlying reasons for requiring return is the desire to prevent the most natural forum for resolving welfare disputes, namely the State of the child's habitual residence, being evaded. However, it was thought that to include such a proposal would have made the Convention too inflexible. Thus 'the Convention's silence on this matter must therefore be understood as allowing the authorities of the State of refuge to return the child directly to the applicant, regardless of the latter's

---

[6]   [1995] 1 WLR 1021, [1995] 1 FLR 1021, CA.

[7]   6th Cir, No 00–6326/6551, 19 April 2001.

[8]   Pursuant to Fed R App P 41(a).

[9]   Viz Arts 8–20.

[10]   See **17.2–17.4**.

[11]   [1988] 1 FLR 365, 373B–C. See also *Re H (Abduction: Grave Risk)* [2003] EWCA Civ 355, [2003] 2 FLR 141 at [33], per Dame Elizabeth Butler-Sloss P.

[12]   At para 110.

present place of residence'.[13] The example given by Professor Pérez-Vera is of a situation where a child is removed from a country where he has been living with his parent, but by the time the court comes to make the order for return, that parent is no longer habitually resident there; an inflexible requirement to return to the country where he had been living would cause 'practical problems which would be difficult to resolve'.

16.6 Since 1987, the almost universal practice in England and Wales has been to order return to the State of the child's habitual residence before the removal or retention. It is suggested that such a practice is correct: such a course will almost always appropriately provide for the orderly and efficacious resolution of disputes concerning child welfare. However, it is also suggested that flexibility to depart from this practice in an exceptional case should be retained and the reasons for the deliberate silence of the Convention on this matter recognised.

The date of removal or retention

16.7 Given the serious consequences flowing from the time limit in Art 12(1), it is important to establish the date of removal or retention. As we have discussed above,[14] the House of Lords established in *Re H (Minors) (Abduction: Custody Rights)*[15] that 'removal' and 'retention' are events occurring on a specific occasion, and are not continuing states of affairs. Otherwise it would be impossible to measure the period of one year from their occurrence for the purposes of Art 12(1).

When does a wrongful removal or retention come to an end?

16.8 However, a question arises whether a return to the State of habitual residence always brings to an end the wrongful removal or retention. In *Re H (Minors) (Abduction: Acquiescence)*,[16] the House of Lords did not regard the father's request that the children be returned temporarily to Israel for Passover as being fatally inconsistent with an intention to pursue his remedies under the Convention; it did not consider whether such a return would have brought the wrongful removal to an end. In *Re S (Child Abduction: Delay)*,[17] unusually the child was returned by the mother voluntarily and temporarily to the State of habitual residence but wrongfully removed by her for a second time after 3 days. Proceedings under the Convention were commenced within one year of the second removal but not the first removal. The English High Court held that the wrongful removal for the purpose of the time limit in Art 12(1) was the second removal; on the facts, the second removal was a 'wrongful removal'

---

[13] The Pérez-Vera Report, at para 110.

[14] See **14.8**.

[15] [1991] 2 AC 476 at 499G, [1991] 2 FLR 262 at 271H. This decision was in accordance with the earlier first instance Scottish decision of *Kilgour v Kilgour* 1987 SLT 568.

[16] [1998] AC 72, [1997] 1 FLR 872, HL.

[17] [1998] 1 FLR 651.

within the meaning of Art 3, and the father was entitled to rely on that removal.

16.9 Sometimes a child is abducted from country A to country B, and then further abducted to country C where a request (or further request) under the Hague Abduction Convention is made. In *Re O (Child Abduction: Re-Abduction)*,[18] the children were abducted by the mother to Sweden from the United States; the Swedish court refused the father's application for the return of the children under the Convention; while the father's appeal was pending in Sweden he re-abducted the children to England and then applied for an order under the Convention for their return to the United States based on the mother's wrongful removal of the children from the United States. Holman J declined to entertain the father's Convention application and, having decided that the children's welfare in the short term required their return to Sweden, ordered that the children be returned to Sweden under the inherent jurisdiction of the High Court. In *Re L (Abduction: Pending Criminal Proceedings)*,[19] the children had been abducted by the mother from Florida to Denmark where an order was made for the return of the children to Florida under the Convention; the mother then abducted the children to England where she and the children remained undetected for about 10 months; on application under the Convention in England, Wilson J held that the children had been wrongfully removed from Florida and ordered that the children be returned to Florida under the Convention.

ARTICLE 12(3)

16.10 Where the judicial or administrative authority has reason to believe that the child has been taken to another State, it may stay or dismiss the proceedings.[20] If the other State is another Contracting State, the Central Authority must directly and without delay transmit the application for return to the Central Authority of the State to which the child has been taken and must inform the applicant or requesting Central Authority that it has done so.[21]

---

[18]   [1997] 2 FLR 712.
[19]   [1999] 1 FLR 433. For the leading German decision on re-abduction, see *Tiemann* BVerfG 99, 145 (FRG), discussed at **12.11**.
[20]   Article 12(3).
[21]   Article 9.

Chapter 17

INTERNATIONAL ABDUCTIONS: HAGUE ABDUCTION CONVENTION: THE EXCEPTIONS TO THE OBLIGATION TO RETURN

INTRODUCTION

17.1 Notwithstanding the basic enjoinder under Art 12[1] upon judicial and administrative authorities of Contracting States to order the immediate return of children who have been wrongfully removed from or retained outside the State of their habitual residence, the Convention itself provides exceptions to the obligation. Not surprisingly, given that judicial involvement is almost exclusively concerned with these provisions, the application of these exceptions has generated considerable attention and voluminous case-law. Nevertheless it should be stressed that a refusal to return should be regarded

---

[1]   Which the Pérez-Vera Report, at para 27, refers to as the 'basic principle' of the Convention. Note that under the revised Brussels II Regulation, as between Member States, courts when applying Arts 12 and 13 will be required to ensure that the child is given the opportunity to be heard (unless it appears inappropriate having regard to the child's age or degree of maturity). Additionally, a court will not be able to refuse to return a child unless the applicant has been given an opportunity to be heard

as the exception rather than the rule. According to the findings of the 1999 Statistical Survey conducted by Cardiff University in collaboration with the Permanent Bureau of the Hague Conference,[2] of all applications made in 1999, 11% of applications for return ended in a judicial refusal, and of those that were concluded in court, 74% ended in an order for return and 26% in a refusal to return.

17.2 Even where an exception to the obligation to return the child under Art 12(1) has been established, the court generally retains a discretion to order the child's return. The precise source of this discretionary power is not unproblematic. On the one hand, Art 13 itself clearly provides a discretion by stating at the outset that a court 'is not bound to order the return' if one of the exceptions under it is established. On the other hand, Art 18 provides:

> 'The provisions of this Chapter do not limit the power of a judicial or administrative authority to order the return of the child at any time.'

Article 18 admits of two possible interpretations: it can be regarded either as conferring a general discretion under the Convention to order a return or as preserving the application of any domestic powers outside the Convention to order a return. This distinction is important in two respects. First, it may determine whether a court has a discretion to return notwithstanding the establishment of the exception under Art 12(2).[3] Secondly, it may determine what weight should be placed on the child's welfare when exercising the discretion to return.

17.3 The English authorities, such as they are, lean to the view that Art 18 provides a general discretion to order a return under the Convention,[4] although whether this is what the drafters of the Convention intended may be open to doubt. Although the earlier history of the provision[5] points more clearly to it being intended to preserve any domestic powers, the Pérez-Vera Report is less clear but tends to support the view that Art 18 is intended to preserve domestic power to order returns. It refers[6] to the Article as underlining:

> '… the non-exhaustive, and complementary nature of the Convention. In fact it authorises the competent authorities to order the return of the child by invoking other provisions more favourable to the attainment of this end.'

---

[2]   Lowe, Armstrong and Mathias, 'A Statistical Analysis of Applications made in 1999 under the Hague Convention of 25 October 1980 on the Civil Aspects of International Child Abduction', Preliminary Document No 3 (Revised Version, November 2001) available on the Hague Conference website at http://www.hcch.net/e/conventions/reports28e.html (hereinafter referred to as 'the 1999 Statistical Survey').

[3]   See **17.5** *et seq*.

[4]   See, eg, *Re S (A Minor) (Abduction)* [1991] 2 FLR 1, CA; *Re N (Minors) (Abduction)* [1991] 1 FLR 413; and *Re L (Abduction Pending Criminal Proceedings)* [1999] 1 FLR 433.

[5]   See the Report of the Special Commission (prepared by Pérez-Vera) at para 92 on what was then Art 15.

[6]   At para 112.

17.4 Be that as it may, there seems to be general agreement that when exercising the discretion to order a child's return (ie after the establishment of an exception), whether pursuant to Art 13 or Art 18, while a court can take the child's welfare into account it is not bound to treat those interests as paramount but must instead balance them against the fundamental purpose of the Convention, namely, to order the child's return.[7] Even where there is clearly a discretion under the Convention, as there is where any exception under Art 13 is established, it remains an interesting point as to whether the exercise of discretion should be exercised differently according to which exception has been proved.[8] There is New Zealand authority[9] for saying that the establishment of more than one exception may have a cumulative effect that will weigh more heavily in favour of declining to order a return.

THE ARTICLE 12 EXCEPTION

17.5 The second paragraph of Art 12 provides:

'The judicial or administrative authority, even where the proceedings have been commenced after the expiration of the period of one year referred to in the preceding paragraph, shall also order the return of the child, unless it is demonstrated that the child is now settled in its new environment.'

Background to the exception

17.6 This provision, often referred to as Art 12(2),[10] and to which for convenience we will also so refer, is a recognition that the restoration of the *status quo ante* might no longer be possible or desirable once a child has spent a considerable time in a new environment and ought not to be ordered without an examination of the merits of doing so.[11] The potential adverse effects on a child's welfare of moving him from his settled home environment are well known and were one of the prime reasons for introducing the 1980 Hague Abduction Convention in the first place. Furthermore to return a child after he has spent a considerable period away from his country of habitual residence is very different from the classic case of a summary return in the immediate aftermath of an abduction. As Thorpe LJ said in *Re C (Abduction: Grave Risk of*

---

[7] See *Re A (Minors) (Abduction: Custody Rights) (No 2)* [1993] Fam 1, [1993] 1 All ER 272, sub nom *Re A (Minors) (Abduction: Acquiescence) (No 2)* [1993] 1 FLR 396, CA. See also *Re L (Abduction: Pending Criminal Proceedings)* [1999] 1 FLR 433. A similar interpretation is applied in Australia, see eg *Central Authority v Reissner* (1999) 25 Fam 330, and in New Zealand, see eg *Armstrong v Evans* [2000] NZ FLR 984 and *Hollins v Crozier* [2000] NZ FLR 775.

[8] See the arguments discussed in *Re D (Abduction: Discretionary Return)* [2000] 1 FLR 24 at 36.

[9] *U v R* [1998] NZFLR 385, referred to by Caldwell in 'Child welfare defences in child abduction cases' [2001] CFLQ 121 at 135.

[10] See, for example, INCADAT.

[11] See the Pérez-Vera Report, at para 107.

Psychological Harm),[12] the Convention remedy is designed to be one of hot pursuit.

17.7   It is helpful for an understanding of Art 12(2) to consider briefly the background. During early discussions on the drafting of the Convention,[13] a dual time limit was proposed. The proposal was that where the location of the child is known, there should be a mandatory return if the application is made within 6 months;[14] where the location of the child is not known, there should be a return if the application is made within 12 months. However, a single time limit was favoured[15] and in due course a consensus emerged for the 12-month limit. What became Art 12(2) was introduced so as not to exclude the possibility of a return even after 12-month limit had elapsed; the power to order a return, provided that the child has not become settled, is, on its face, indefinite in time.

17.8   Although, compared with other exceptions, there is relatively little jurisprudence on the meaning and application of Art 12(2),[16] according to the statistical survey of applications made in 1999,[17] globally 11 refusals (amounting to 11% of all refusals) were based solely on this exception[18] with a further two relying on this ground in conjunction with another.

The timescale

17.9   Since Bracewell J's decision in *Re N (Minors) (Abduction)*,[19] decided in 1990, the English courts have consistently held that the date for judging whether the child is settled is the date of commencement of the proceedings as distinct from the date of hearing; otherwise delay in hearing the case might affect the outcome. In fact, whether 'now' referred to the date of commencement of proceedings or the date of the hearing was not necessary for the decision in *Re N*, because Bracewell J expressly stated that whichever of the dates was chosen made no difference to the outcome of the particular case before her. The approach taken in *Re N* has since been doubted in the Australian decision, *Director General, Department of Community Services v*

---

12   [1999] 2 FLR 478, at 488.
13   The Pérez-Vera Report, paras 108–110 provide a summary of these discussions and the reasons for the final wording of Art 12.
14   Cf the 1980 European Custody Convention, where a distinction is drawn between the case of an application for recognition brought within 6 months of 'an improper removal' (Arts 8 and 9) and the case of an application for recognition brought after that time (Art 10). For discussion of the 1980 European Custody Convention, see Chapter 19.
15   One reason for rejecting a dual time limit was that such a system would lead to difficulties in proving the problems encountered in finding the child: the Pérez-Vera Report, para 108.
16   At the time of writing there were 29 references to this exception recorded on INCADAT.
17   *Op cit*, n 2.
18   Two of these refusals were by English courts.
19   [1991] 1 FLR 413.

M and C.[20] In that case, the Full Court of the Family Court of Australia departed from earlier authorities[21] on the correct interpretation of Art 12(2) and held that the relevant date is either at the time of the commencement of the proceedings or at the time of the hearing, depending on the context of the particular case.

17.10 The choice, by the drafters of the Convention, of the commencement of the proceedings as the cut-off date for the 12-month limit was to avoid prejudice to an applicant which might flow from delay in the judicial process.[22] The words 'commencement of the proceedings' have caused no difficulty of interpretation in England and Wales or in Scotland: this means the issuing of the originating process.[23] In jurisdictions where the Convention has been incorporated indirectly through domestic legislation, the wording of the domestic legislation may make the cut-off date clear; for example, in Australia it is 'the day on which the application is filed'.[24]

17.11 But prejudice to the applicant can arise if, after a request is made within 12 months to the Central Authority, there is delay unconnected with the applicant such that the proceedings before the judicial authorities are commenced outside the 12-month limit. Article 12(2) makes no allowance for this. In *Wojcik v Wojcik*,[25] it was unsuccessfully argued that the proceedings began when the request was made to the US Central Authority.

17.12 In England, delay in prosecuting Convention proceedings may be a ground for striking out the application without the court even considering whether Art 12(2) applies. In *Re G (Abduction: Striking Out Application)*,[26] the Convention proceedings were commenced 18 months after the wrongful retention of the child in England; thereafter the applicant parent, in disregard of the procedure,[27] did not prosecute them for another 10 months; the judge struck them out at the request of the abducting parent.

---

[20]   [1998] 24 Fam LR 168 at [91].

[21]   *In the Marriage of Graziano* (1991) 14 Fam LR 697. Note that the word 'now' does not appear in the Australian incorporating legislation, the Family Law (Child Abduction Convention) Regulations 1986 (Cth).

[22]   See the Pérez-Vera Report, para 108: '… so that potential delays in acting on the part of the competent authorities will not harm the interests of the parties protected by the Convention'.

[23]   *Re M (Abduction: Acquiescence)* [1996] 1 FLR 315 at 320 (originating summons); *Perrin v Perrin* 1994 SC 45 at 47, 1995 SLT 81 at 82 (presentation of petition).

[24]   Family Law (Child Abduction Convention) Regulations 1986 (Cth), reg 16(1)(b).

[25]   959 F Supp 413 (ED Mich 1997), United States District Court for the Eastern District of Michigan.

[26]   [1995] 2 FLR 410.

[27]   Family Proceedings Rules 1991, r 6.10. For procedure, see generally Chapter 21.

'Settled in its new environment'[28]

17.13   What is meant by the words 'settled in its new environment' has given rise to some judicial divergence. In *Re N (Minors) (Abduction)*,[29] Bracewell J held that 'settled' should be given its ordinary natural meaning; this, she held, involved two constituent elements: first, 'a physical element of relating to, being established in, a community and an environment'; and secondly 'it has an emotional constituent denoting security and stability'.[30] Bracewell J added that the 'new environment' encompasses 'place, home, school, people, friends, activities and opportunities but not, per se, the relationship with the mother [the parent], which has always existed in a close, loving attachment. That can only be relevant insofar as it impinges on the new surroundings'. The analysis in *Re N* of two constituent elements has been followed in England and Wales; in *Re M (Abduction: Acquiescence)*,[31] Thorpe J said that any survey of the degree of settlement of the child must give weight to emotional and psychological settlement as well as to physical settlement; thus the 4-year-old child's 15 months spent in England in care of the mother with the support of her wider family had led to the child becoming settled for the purposes of Art 12(2). The approach in *Re N* has also been adopted in Scotland in cases such as *Soucie v Soucie*[32] and *Perrin v Perrin*.[33]

17.14   The Full Court of the Family Court of Australia has held in *Director General, Department of Community Services v M and C*[34] that 'the test, and only test to be applied, is whether the children have settled in their new environment', and disapproved the statement in *In the Marriage of Graziano*[35] that the test was more than that the child is happy, secure and adjusted to his new surroundings. The Full Court disapproved the two constituent elements analysis as being potentially misleading. The test now applied in Australia is less restrictive than in England and Wales and in Scotland.

17.15   In *Re N* it was also said that Art 12(2) refers to 'a long-term settled position', as opposed to something which is 'transient'; and that it required 'a demonstration by a projection into the future, that the present position imports stability when looking to the future and is permanent insofar as anything in life can be said to be permanent'. The reference to the 'long-term settled position' had first been made in the English Court of Appeal in

---

28   See also the analysis by Caldwell, 'Child welfare defences in child abduction cases – some recent developments' [2001] CFLQ 121 at 133–134.

29   [1991] 1 FLR 413.

30   The US Court of Appeals for the 11th Circuit in *Lops v Lops* 140 F 3d 927 (11th Cir 1998) held that '"well-settled" means more than having a comfortable material existence'.

31   [1996] 1 FLR 315 at 321A–B.

32   1995 SC 134, 1995 SLT 413.

33   1994 SC 45, 1995 SLT 81.

34   (1999)] 24 Fam LR 168. This decision has been followed in *Townsend v Director General, Department of Families, Youth and Community Care* (1999) 24 Fam LR 495.

35   (1991) 14 Fam LR 697.

Re S (A Minor) (Abduction).[36] It has been suggested that it is going too far to insist that the settlement should be 'permanent insofar as anything in life can be said to be permanent'.[37]

17.16   Although the Family Court of Australia at first[38] followed *Re N*, the Full Court of the Family Court of Australia in *Director General, Department of Community Services v M and C*[39] has stated that there is no warrant for importing the words 'long term' in Art 12(2) and that Bracewell J's dictum in *Re N* does not represent the law so far as Australia is concerned. However, it is of note that in *M and C* the Full Court left open the question whether the fact that a child's temporary immigration status might mean that he would be required to leave the country would make it impossible to be settled in that country.

17.17   Nevertheless, *Re N* continues to be followed in England and Wales and in Scotland. In *P v S and A and West Lothian Council*,[40] the Inner House of the Court of Session disagreed with the reasoning in *Director General, Department of Community Services v M and C* and followed *Re N*. It stated that '[e]ven if, like all other terms, the expression "long term" is not ideal, we are in no doubt that in judging the present situation, and asking whether a child is settled at the present time, a projection as to what is liable to happen in the future is an inherent element in the word "settled", and reference to the intentions of others, and in particular the abducting parent, very likely to be essential'.[41]

17.18   In this context, it could be argued that it is easier for a child to become habitually resident in a country than for the child to become settled in his new environment. The former requires, in the words of Lord Scarman,[42] that the child reside in the country voluntarily and for settled purposes as part of the regular order of his life for the time being whether of short or long duration. It does not require an intention to stay in the country indefinitely; indeed, the purpose, while settled, may be for a limited period.[43]

17.19   In *P v S and A and West Lothian Council* at first instance,[44] it was said that the new environment is a wider concept than the immediate environs in which a child is living at a particular time. In that case, the trial judge held that

---

[36]   [1991] 2 FLR 1, CA. However, Art 12(2) was not the main focus of the argument or judgments in *Re S*.

[37]   *Dicey and Morris on the Conflict of Laws*, 13th edn (Sweet and Maxwell, 2000), para 19–096.

[38]   See eg *In the Marriage of Graziano* (1991) 14 Fam LR 697.

[39]   [1999] 24 Fam LR 168. This decision has been followed in *Director-General, Department of Families, Youth and Community Care v Moore* (1999) 24 Fam LR 475 and *Townsend v Director-General, Department of Families, Youth and Community Care* (1999) 24 Fam LR 495.

[40]   2002 Fam LR 2, Inner House, Court of Session (Lords Prosser, Milligan, Caplan), 2 June 2000.

[41]   *Ibid* at [45].

[42]   *R v London Borough of Barnet ex parte Khan* [1983] 2 AC 309, HL.

[43]   *Ibid.* See also *Al-Habtoor v Fotheringham* [2001] EWCA Civ 186, [2001] 1 FLR 951. For habitual residence, see generally Chapter 2.

[44]   2002 Fam LR 2, Outer House, Court of Session (Lord Bonomy).

the physical 'environment' should not be limited to the local town in Scotland where the child was residing but should be considered 'Scotland' as the child had come to know it (with its pastimes, its customs, food and icons and the people he had come to know). While the question of settlement has to be determined objectively, an important consideration is the perception which others have, and indeed the child himself has, of the child's place in the new environment. The trial judge was upheld on appeal.[45] The Full Court of the Family Court of Australia in *Director General, Department of Community Services v M and C*[46] has observed that a child can be settled in an environment and still experience severe problems; the trial judge had found that the children needed counselling and assistance to overcome the severe abuse which they had suffered. In *Rodriguez v Bucholzer*,[47] an Austrian Supreme Court refused to return a 3-year-old child to Spain some 2 years after her abduction, there being evidence that the child spoke no Spanish and was living comfortably and happily with her mother and maternal grandparents on an Austrian farm. In the United States, in *Wojcik v Wojcik*,[48] it was found that the children aged 5 and 8 were settled in Michigan after 18 months away from France.

17.20   In *Re N*, Bracewell J emphasised the requirement that the child be settled in an environment that was 'new'. In that case, the children and mother had resided with their English grandmother for 11 months and had only lived in their own accommodation for under 3 months; an order for return was made.[49] Thus, although the child may have been away from his habitual residence for some time, he may have been living in the requested State, or the part of that State, for too short a period to become settled. In *State Central Authority v Ayob*,[50] Kay J declined to find settlement where the child who had been removed from Arkansas had spent a long period in Malaysia before arriving in Australia.[51]

17.21   In Scotland, the Inner House, in *P v S and A and West Lothian Council*,[52] drew attention to the fact that Art 12(2) does not raise the question of whether the abducting *parent* is settled.[53] But where a young and dependent child is living with the abducting parent, he or she will necessarily be tied to the abducting parent in many ways, not least emotionally, and the Inner House said that it is unrealistic, and wrong, to ignore the parent's circumstances and

---

45   *P v S and A and West Lothian Council* 2002 Fam LR 2, Inner House, Court of Session.
46   [1998] 24 Fam LR 168 at [65].
47   7 Ob 573/90.
48   959 F Supp 413 (ED Mich 1997), United States District Court for the Eastern District of Michigan.
49   See also *Perrin v Perrin* 1994 SC 45, 1995 SLT 81.
50   (1997) 21 Fam LR 567, Kay J.
51   See also *In re the petition for Coffield* (1994 Ohio Court of Appeal) 96 Ohio App 3d 52, 644 NE 2d 662 (3 years between abduction and the commencement of proceedings, but only 10 months' residence in Ohio).
52   2002 Fam LR 2 at 12 (Lords Prosser, Milligan, Caplan).
53   See also *Perrin v Perrin* (above); *Re N (Minors) (Abduction)* [1991] 1 FLR 413.

intentions upon which the child's degree of settlement is dependent. Thus, where the mother's future intentions showed that she was not settled in Scotland, the trial judge was justified in finding that the child was not settled. Because of the greater dependence of a small child, the primary caretaker may take on greater weight as part of the total environment while, as children grow older and gain more mobility and independence, their friends and schools as part of the human environment take on more weight, as may also the natural environment.[54] In the Australian decision, *Secretary, Attorney General's Department v TS*,[55] Nicholson CJ held that, in the case of a very young child, such as the child in the case before him, it may be that his environment is more constrained than that of an older child. But Nicholson CJ considered that his home environment is likely to be correspondingly more important to him; and that if he is settled in it, then this would appear to be the very situation that the Convention envisages where he should not be returned having regard to the passage of time. The environment that the court must consider is the environment of the child the subject of the application and not some theoretical environment.[56]

17.22   The words of the French text of the Convention provide some further enlightenment as to the meaning of Art 12(2). The French text uses the words '... s'est intégré dans son nouveau milieu' which translates as 'is *integrated* in his new environment' (emphasis added).

17.23   The degree of settlement required in practice under Art 12(2) is great. In *Soucie v Soucie*,[57] it was said that the proper question is whether the child is so settled in his new environment that the court would be justified in disregarding an otherwise mandatory requirement to return the child, thus overriding the clear duty to order a return.

Concealment

17.24   As we have seen, one of the reasons for introducing, at a late stage in the negotiations on the Convention, the power to order the return of the child after the expiry of the 12-month period was to prevent an abductor evading the effect of the Convention by concealing the whereabouts of the child until

---

54   The Checklist of Issues to be considered at the Third Meeting of the Special Commission to Review the Operation of the Hague Convention on the Civil Aspects of International Child Abduction (1997), para 83, drawn up by Adair Dyer.

55   [2000] Fam CA 1692.

56   Cf the suggestion in *Re David S v Zamira S*, 151 Misc 2d 630 at 636, 574 NYS 2d 429 at 433 (1991) that a very young child cannot be said to be settled in its environment (where it was held that children of 3½ years old 'are not yet involved in school, extracurricular, community, religious or social activities which children of an older age would be. The children have not yet formed meaningful friendships'), which was cited with approval in *Re Robinson v Robinson* (2d Co 1997) 983 Fed Supp 1339.

57   1995 SC 134, 1995 SLT 144.

the period for mandatory return has expired.[58] One solution to this problem might be for the court, in calculating the 12-month time limit, to disregard periods during which the child is concealed. Such a solution has not been adopted in reported cases. The US Court of Appeals for the 11th Circuit in *Lops v Lops*[59] left open the question whether 'equitable tolling' ('some tolling, interruption or suspension') could apply to the 12-month time limit in cases where unlawful concealment prevents the initiation of the running of the time limit.

17.25   Rather, the courts have confronted the threat to the effectiveness of the Convention by being reluctant to find that the child is settled in its new environment where it has in fact been in hiding. Thus, in *Lops v Lops*, there was a finding that the children were not settled in a new environment because steps were taken to conceal their whereabouts during a period in excess of 2 years despite the children having been living in one location. In *Re L (Abduction: Pending Criminal Proceedings)*,[60] the Danish mother removed the children from the United States to Denmark but then fled again to England where she went into hiding. The trial judge doubted that a Danish mother who had been present with children in England for a year only because it had been a good hiding-place and who faced likely extradition proceedings could demonstrate that the children were settled in England. In *Re H (Abduction: Child of 16)*,[61] Bracewell J said that 'time in hiding cannot go to establish settlement'.

17.26   However, it is suggested that there is a distinction between those cases where the abductor and child are truly 'on the run' in the sense that it is shown that if the abductor were to be in danger of being found he would flee to another country (as in *Re L*) and those cases where the abductor (who is often the primary carer/custodial carer) is returning home after the breakdown of the marriage or relationship and would not move on if he or she were found. A finding of fact that the child is not settled in the new environment may be more problematic in such cases.

Burden of proof

17.27   As an 'exception' to the mandatory requirement to order a return, the format of Art 12(2) is different from that of Art 13. There is no express reference to the burden of proof. Article 12(2) provides for a return 'unless it is demonstrated' that the child is relevantly settled. On the other hand, Art 13 expressly provides that it is for the person, institution or other body which opposes the return to establish the matters under Art 13(a) and (b). This causes no problem in England where the burden in practice is on the party

---

[58]   See Anton, 'The Hague Convention on International Child Abduction' (1980) 30 ICLQ 537 at 549.
[59]   140 F 3d 927 (11 Cir 1998).
[60]   [1999] 1 FLR 433.
[61]   [2000] 2 FLR 51. See also Judge Green in *U v R* [1998] NZFLR 385.

opposing the return, as under Art 13(a) and (b).[62] The Family Court of Australia has held that the burden lies on the party opposing the return on this ground.[63]

17.28 It is arguable that the nature of the judicial investigation should be more detailed where the application is made more than 12 months from the date of removal or retention. Where the application is made within 12 months, the proceedings are summary in nature in order to ensure a speedy return, and the applicant enjoys an advantage in practice. The position is different when at least 12 months have elapsed since the removal or retention. The case is generally not an emergency. As was said by Hale J (as she then was) in *Re HB (Abduction: Children's Objections) (No 2)*:[64]

> 'Once the time for a speedy return has passed, it must be questioned whether it is indeed in the best interests of a child for there to be a summary return after the very limited inquiry into the merits which is involved in these cases.'

In some cases, there may necessarily be more investigation involved in demonstrating (and rebutting) the settlement of the child. As the Pérez-Vera Report says:[65]

> 'the proof or verification of a child's establishment in a new environment opens up the possibility of longer proceedings than those envisaged in the first paragraph.

Indeed, the language of Art 12 suggests a more detailed enquiry under Art 12(2): the obligation in Art 12(2) is to return, not to return 'forthwith'.[66] Nevertheless, in practice in England and Wales where Art 12(2) is invoked, proceedings retain their summary nature.

17.29 Adair Dyer, as Deputy Secretary General of the Hague Conference, has written that the consequence of the return required under Art 12(2) not being 'forthwith' is that a return may be phased; 'a period of mutual access may be needed in order to renew the child's familiarity with the bereft parent and avoid the disruption of another overly abrupt change'.[67]

---

[62] Eg *Re N (Minors) (Abduction)* [1991] 1 FLR 413. The Pérez-Vera Report envisaged that the burden would fall in this way (para 109).

[63] *In the Marriage of Graziano* (1991) 14 Fam LR 697; *Director-General of the Department of Community Services v Apostolakis* (1996) FLC 92–718.

[64] [1998] 1 FLR 564 at 568.

[65] At para 109.

[66] The Pérez-Vera Report, at para 109. See also the tension at para 108.

[67] The Checklist of Issues to be considered at the Third Meeting of the Special Commission to Review the Operation of the Hague Convention on the Civil Aspects of International Child Abduction (1997), para 82, drawn up by Adair Dyer.

The discretion to order return where it is demonstrated that the child is settled

Is there a discretion?

17.30 If it is demonstrated that 'the child is now settled in its new environment', the question arises as to whether the court has a discretion to order a return and, if there is such a discretion, how it should be exercised. The English and Scottish appellate courts have recognised the existence of such a discretion. In *Re S*,[68] the English Court of Appeal said that where settlement was demonstrated 'there is no longer an obligation to return the child forthwith but, subject to the overall discretion in Art 18,[69] the court may or may not order a return'. In *Soucie v Soucie*,[70] the Inner House of the Court of Session observed that the court has a discretionary power under Art 18 of the Convention to order the return of the child even if settlement has been demonstrated. It seems that in neither case was there prolonged argument on whether such discretion existed under the Convention. In the later English High Court case of *Re L (Abduction: Pending Criminal Proceedings)*,[71] Wilson J wondered whether Art 18 was referring to a power arising outside the Convention, for example derived from the High Court's inherent jurisdiction over children,[72] in which the child's welfare would be the court's paramount consideration. However, both counsel agreed, and the judge was satisfied, that the power referred to in Art 18, 'focused as it is upon the return of children who have been wrongfully removed or retained, is a power arising within the Convention'.

17.31 The existence of such a discretion has been left open in the appellate courts of Australia since *In the Marriage of Graziano* in 1991.[73] At first instance there are conflicting views. In the Family Court of Australia in *State Central Authority v Ayob*,[74] Kay J doubted the existence of a residual discretion arising under the Convention if settlement is demonstrated under Art 12(2), commenting: '... In my view, the Convention and regulations have no further application in respect of such a child'. But Moss J in *Director-General of the Department of Community Services v Apostolakis*[75] and Lindenmayer J in

---

[68]   *Re S (A Minor) (Abduction)* [1991] 2 FLR 1 at 24.

[69]   Article 18 provides: 'The provisions of this chapter do not limit the power of a judicial or administrative authority to order the return of the child at any time'. As to the application of Art 18, see generally **17.2** *et seq.*

[70]   1995 SC 134.

[71]   [1999] 1 FLR 433.

[72]   Or presumably under the Children Act 1989.

[73]   (1991) 14 Fam LR 697.

[74]   (1997) 21 Fam LR 567.

[75]   (1996) FLC 92–718 (Family Court of Australia). However, it is to be noted that, in saying that 'I am no longer *bound* to order a return of these children' (emphasis as in judgment), Moss J was using the language of Art 13 not Art 12(2).

Director-General, Department of Families, Youth and Community Care v Thorpe[76] accepted the existence of the discretion. The Full Court of the Family Court of Australia, without hearing full argument and without purporting to decide the point, stated in *Director-General, Department of Community Services v M and C*,[77] that it was 'not necessarily persuaded that Kay J's view is correct'. In *Director-General, Department of Families, Youth and Community Care v Moore*,[78] the Full Court noted 'the very great importance of the question' but preferred to await a case with full argument and in which the issue squarely arose before reaching a concluded view.

17.32 It is suggested with respect that there is much force in Kay J's observations in *Ayob* and Wilson J's initial reaction in *Re L*. Indeed, Professor Pérez-Vera seems to express a clear view in her Explanatory Report:[79]

'... [i]t is clear that after a child has become settled in its new environment, its return should take place only after an examination of the merits of the custody rights exercised over it – something which is outside the scope of the Convention.'

17.33 It is of note that the wording of Art 13 (the court 'is not bound to order the return'), which unquestionably gives rise to a discretion to order a return, is different to that in Art 12(2), which makes no express provision for an order for return in the event of settlement being demonstrated.

The exercise of the discretion

17.34 Notwithstanding the earlier arguments against there being a discretion, in England and Scotland, where it has been demonstrated that the child is settled in its new environment, the court exercises its discretion in a manner analogous to that arising when one of the matters under Art 13 is established.[80] As Wilson J put it in *Re L*,[81] the discretion must be exercised 'in the context of the approach of the Convention'.[82] Welfare is not paramount but is a factor; and it is hard to conceive that, if established, the settlement of the child could ever be unimportant. This highlights an important distinction between the

---

[76] (1997) FLC 92–785 (Family Court of Australia).
[77] (1999) 24 Fam LR 168.
[78] (1999) 24 Fam LR 475.
[79] At para 107, cited in *In the Marriage of Graziano* (1991) 14 Fam LR 697. The earlier history of Art 18 is clearer still (see **17.3**) that this provision was intended to preserve domestic powers rather than confer additional discretion. However, Professor Paul Lagarde in his Explanatory Report (at para 49b) on the Hague Convention on Jurisdiction, Applicable Law, Recognition, Enforcement and Co-operation in respect of Parental Responsibility and Measures for the Protection of Children of 19 October 1996 seems to assume that a discretion exists if settlement is demonstrated under Art 12(2).
[80] See *Soucie v Soucie* 1995 SC 134, 1995 SLT 413.
[81] *Re L (Abduction: Pending Criminal Proceedings)* [1999] 1 FLR 433.
[82] Words taken from *Re A (Minors) (Abduction: Custody Rights)* [1992] Fam 106 at 122E, sub nom *Re A (Minors) (Abduction: Acquiescence)* [1992] 2 FLR 14 at 28–29.

Art 12(2) discretion and that arising under Art 13. In the former case (assuming the existence of the discretion), the power to order a return exists for an indefinite period after the 12-month period; and manifestly the longer a child has been settled in the new environment the stronger becomes the argument for not uprooting him from that environment. In *Re L*, Wilson J said that the policy of the Convention would have outweighed the other factors in the exercise of his discretion: the mother had gone into hiding in England for 10 months and the children had no other connection with England.

17.35   In *Director-General of the Department of Community Services v Apostolakis*,[83] Moss J found that the children were settled, which he described as having a 'direct and fundamental relevance to the situation of the children'. He declined to order their return to Crete where their life was very different to that in Australia: to do so would undo all they had achieved in Australia and would sever, or at least severely loosen, family ties. In *Director-General, Department of Families, Youth and Community Care v Moore*,[84] the Full Court (assuming for this purpose the existence of a discretion) said that it was appropriate to have regard to the purpose of the Convention in exercising the discretion. It made the important observation that it is not the Convention's policy that, in all circumstances, children must be returned; the exceptions are inserted to permit the circumstances of the child to be taken into account in particular situations. Thus, it upheld the refusal to order a return.

THE ARTICLE 13(a) EXCEPTIONS

17.36   Article 13 provides:

> '… the judicial or administrative authority of the requested State is not bound to order the return of the child, if the person, institution or other body which opposes its return establishes that—
>
> (a)   the person, institution or other body having the care of the person of the child was not actually exercising the custody rights at the time of the removal or retention, or had consented to or subsequently acquiesced in the removal or retention.'

17.37   Article 13(a) provides three separate 'exceptions', namely, the non-exercise of rights of custody, consent to and acquiescence in the child's removal or retention. As the Pérez-Vera Report states,[85] the situations envisaged by Art 13(a):

> '… are those in which either the conditions prevailing prior to the removal of the child do not contain one of the elements essential to those relationships which the Convention seeks to protect (that of the actual exercise of custody rights), or

---

[83]   (1996) FLC 92–718 (Family Court of Australia).
[84]   (1999) 24 Fam LR 475.
[85]   At para 28.

else the subsequent behaviour of the dispossessed parent shows his acceptance of the new situation thus brought about, which makes it more difficult for him to challenge.'

In other words, these exceptions 'arise out of the fact that the conduct of the person claiming to be the guardian of the child raises doubts as to whether a wrongful removal or retention, in terms of the Convention, has taken place'.[86]

The non-exercise of rights of custody

17.38   Although, globally, it is not unknown for a refusal to return to be based on this ground (according to the 1999 Statistical Survey,[87] there were three cases in which a refusal was based solely on the non-exercise of rights of custody, with one further case in which this ground was relied upon in conjunction with another), there is no reported English example of a refusal being so based. Indeed, unusually, the English courts have passed little comment on this part of Art 13.[88] No doubt one of the reasons for this lack of use is that the non-exercise of custody rights tends to be pleaded under Art 3 in an attempt to establish that the removal or retention was not 'wrongful'.[89] In that context, Lord Brandon has helpfully observed[90] that 'exercising rights of custody':

'... must be construed widely as meaning that the custodial parent must be maintaining the stance and attitude of such a parent, rather than narrowly as meaning that he or she must be continuing to exercise day-to-day care and control.'

17.39   Applying this dictum, Waite J subsequently held in *W v W (Child Abduction: Acquiescence)*[91] that a father could not be said to have stopped exercising parental rights when he agreed to his child leaving the jurisdiction for a holiday with the mother and maternal grandparents. In *Re W (Abduction: Procedure)*,[92] Wall J considered that a similar approach had to be applied to Art 13(a). In his view, the distinction between Art 13(a) and Art 3 is that:

'Article 13(a) refers to rights of custody which are not being actually exercised by the person who has the care of the person of the child: this contrasts with Art 3 which refers to rights of custody generally. The Art 13(a) defence in this context

---

86   The Pérez-Vera Report, at para 115.
87   *Op cit*, n 2.
88   At the time of writing there were only eight references to this exception recorded on INCADAT.
89   See the discussion at **14.81**.
90   In *Re H, Re S (Minors) (Abduction: Custody Rights)* [1991] 2 AC 476 at 500, [1991] 2 FLR 262 at 272. This interpretation is in line with the domestic position of English law which allows holders of parental responsibility to delegate responsibility without being deemed to have abandoned it, see s 2(9) of the Children Act 1989.
91   [1993] 2 FLR 211.
92   [1995] 1 FLR 878 at 888.

is thus limited to the situation in which the child's actual care-taker is not actually taking care of him. This is a much narrower situation ...'

In other words the exception will only apply if it can be shown that the applicant had effectively abandoned his care-taking role. In the leading Scottish decision, *S v S*[93] it was held, having regard to the spirit and purpose of the Convention, that it would be wrong to hold that a person who was in hospital and left the children in the custody of relatives during that time, should be regarded as not exercising rights of custody.

17.40   To the extent that delegating day-to-day care of a child will not be deemed to amount to ceasing to exercise rights of custody, the English approach is reflected in other jurisdictions such as Australia,[94] Switzerland[95] and the United States.[96]

Consent

Background to the provision

17.41   The inclusion of both the consent and acquiescence exceptions was decided upon relatively late in the drafting process and followed the unanimous acceptance of a French proposal.[97]

17.42   Although there is extensive jurisprudence on the meaning and application of 'consent' under Art 13(a),[98] in practice it is not often successfully invoked, at any rate as a sole ground for refusing a return. According to the 1999 Statistical Survey,[99] globally, only four refusals (amounting to 4% of all refusals) were based solely on consent although a further eight refusals relied on this ground in conjunction with another. According to the same survey, no refusal of an application made in 1999 in England and Wales was based on consent.

---

[93]   2003 SLT 344 Outer House, Court of Session.

[94]   See eg *Director General, Department of Community Services Central Authority v Crowe* (1996) FLC 92–717: a mother requesting the paternal grandparents to look after her daughter (the grandparents subsequently removed the child to Australia) was held still to be exercising rights of custody.

[95]   See Cour d'appel du canton de Berne, 27 January 1998, INCADAT cite: HC/E/CH 433.

[96]   *Friedrich v Friedrich* 78 F 3rd 1060 (6th Cir 1996).

[97]   Their Working Document No 41 was unanimously adopted at Procès-verbal No 8 (at 298) which was similar to earlier UK and Dutch proposals: see respectively Documents No 3 (at 256), No 21 (at 274) and No 32 (at 281), but which referred to 'condoning' rather than 'consenting'. The final version of Art 13(a) was agreed at Procès-verbal No 4 (at 409) of the Séance Plénière. Prior to that, the exception, under what was then Art 12 of the Preliminary Draft, referred to the lack of good faith, which, although wider, was probably a more problematic concept than either consent or acquiescence.

[98]   At the time of writing there were, for example, 93 decisions referring to this exception reported on INCADAT, in 24 of which the exception formed the basis of the decision.

[99]   *Op cit*, n 2.

General construction issues

The distinction between 'consent' and 'acquiescence'

17.43 Although often pleaded in the alternative, consent and acquiescence are mutually exclusive. As Lord Donaldson MR put it in *Re A (Minors) (Abduction: Custody Rights)*,[100] the difference between the two 'is simply one of timing. Consent, if it occurs, precedes the wrongful taking or retention. Acquiescence, if it occurs, follows it'. This standpoint is further underpinned by Holman J's observation[101] that 'the word "subsequently" in Art 13(a) only qualifies the word "acquiesced" and that the words "had consented to" clearly refer to a consent before the act of removal or retention'.

The inter-relationship between consent and wrongful removal or retention

17.44 As Holman J pointed out in *Re C (Abduction: Consent)*,[102] it can plausibly be said that a removal or retention cannot be 'wrongful' if it is done with the consent of the other party and therefore falls outside Art 3.[103] In his view, however, such an argument cannot be made under the Hague Abduction Convention, since the issue of consent is specifically dealt with under Art 13(a) as providing an exception to the obligation to order the child's return. In *Re O (Abduction: Consent and Acquiescence)*,[104] Bennett J disagreed with Holman J insofar as he was implying that the issue of consent must always be dealt with under Art 13(a). In this view, whether consent comes within Art 3 or Art 13(a) depends on the facts. As he put it:[105]

> 'If the "non-removing" parent asserts or effectively has to concede that on the face of it he gave his consent, but asserts that it is vitiated by deceit or threats or some other vitiating factor, which he must raise in order to establish that his consent was no true consent, then the matter falls to be dealt with under Art 3. If, on the other hand, the very fact of consent is in issue, as it was in *Re C*, then the matter comes within Art 13(a) and the burden falls upon the person who asserts consent to prove it.'

In *T v T (Abduction: Consent)*,[106] however, Charles J commented *obiter* that, had it been necessary, he would have declined to follow Bennett J's 'ingenious reasoning', preferring instead Holman J's analysis. In Charles J's view, the proper construction of the Hague Abduction Convention is that all issues concerning consent should be dealt with under Art 13(a).

---

[100] [1992] Fam 106 at 123, sub nom *Re A (Minors) (Abduction: Acquiescence)* [1992] 1 FLR 14 at 29.

[101] In *Re C (Abduction: Consent)* [1996] 1 FLR 414 at 417. See also Wall J's concurring view in *Re M (Abduction) (Consent: Acquiescence)* [1999] 1 FLR 171 at 173.

[102] [1996] 1 FLR 414 at 417.

[103] Article 3 is discussed above at **14.5** *et seq*.

[104] [1997] 1 FLR 924.

[105] *Ibid* at 940.

[106] [1999] 2 FLR 912 at 918–919. See also *Re D (Abduction: Discretionary Return)* [2000] 1 FLR 24 at 26, per Wilson J.

17.45   This latter analysis is surely to be preferred.[107] Not only does it avoid the complexities inherent in the approach advocated by Bennett J, namely, having first to determine whether it is an Art 3 or an Art 13 case, which has the not insignificant consequence both of determining who has the burden of proof (viz, the applicant, if Art 3 applies, to prove that the removal or retention was wrongful; the defendant, if Art 13 applies, to show that the applicant had consented to the removal), and whether or not there is a discretion under the Convention nevertheless to order a return (which there is under Art 13 but not under Art 3), but it also seems to be what the Convention intended. According to the Pérez-Vera Report,[108] the exceptions contained in Art 13(a) 'arise out of the fact that the conduct of the person claiming to be the guardian of the child *"raises doubts as to whether a wrongful removal or retention, in terms of the Convention, has taken place"'* (emphasis added), which comment points to consent being envisaged to be pleaded under Art 13 rather than Art 3.

The meaning of consent

To what must there be consent?

17.46   The consent must be to either the child's permanent removal or permanent retention. It is not sufficient, for example, that the applicant agreed to the child being removed for a holiday.[109]

Must not be based on fraud or misunderstanding

17.47   Neither the Convention nor the Pérez-Vera Report give any assistance as to the meaning of 'consent'. According to Waite LJ in *Re B (A Minor) (Abduction)*,[110] the question of whether a purported consent to the child's removal is true consent has to be determined according to the circumstances of each case:

> 'The only starting-point that can be stated with reasonable certainty is that the courts of the requested State are unlikely to regard as valid a consent that has been obtained through a calculated and deliberate fraud on the part of the absconding parent.'

In that case a father who had agreed to his child leaving Australia for a maximum period of 6 months (and had documents to that effect drawn up and signed by the mother) was held not to have consented to the child's permanent removal. Similarly, the plea of consent failed in *T v T (Abduction: Consent)*,[111] in which a mother led the father to believe that if he consented to

---

[107] Bennett J's analysis has been rejected by the Irish Supreme Court – see *B v B (Child Abduction)* [1998] 1 IR 299 at 312–313, per Denham J.

[108] At para 115.

[109] See eg *Re B (A Minor) (Abduction)* [1994] 2 FLR 249, CA (discussed below), and *Baxley v Bull* 12 April 1994 (Full Court of the Family Court of Australia at Perth, available on INCADAT).

[110] [1994] 2 FLR 249 at 261.

[111] [1999] 2 FLR 912.

her removing the child to England there would be a chance of reconciliation between them. What she did not tell the father was that she was cohabiting with another man in England. It was held that this failure to tell the father vitiated any apparent consent.

Needs to be real and unequivocal but can be inferred

17.48 The generally accepted test applied by the English courts is that consent must be real and unequivocal and must not be based on a misunderstanding or non-disclosure.[112] It is also sometimes said that the consent needs to be 'positive'[113] but insofar as this might be taken to mean that it must be express it is misleading, since it now seems to be accepted[114] that if the evidence demonstrates a course of conduct from which consent can clearly be inferred, the fact that a parent has not made any positive or unequivocal statement of his agreement with what is proposed by the other parent does not prevent the court from finding that he has consented to the child's removal.[115] As Holman J said in *Re C (Abduction: Consent)*:[116]

> 'If it is clear, viewing a parent's words and actions as a whole and his state of knowledge of what is planned by the other parent, that he does consent to what is planned, then in my judgment that is sufficient to satisfy the requirements of Art 13. It is not necessary that there is an express statement that "I consent".'

17.49 An example of an inference of consent is *Re M (Abduction) (Consent: Acquiescence)*,[117] in which the father knew that the mother intended the move from Greece to England to be permanent. His attitude was one of 'go if you want'. This, combined with his conduct in standing by while she openly made preparations to leave, and a conversation with a friend that his wife could leave if she wished but that he did not think she would survive long on her own, was sufficient evidence from which consent could be inferred.

---

[112] See *T v T (Abduction: Consent)* [1999] 2 FLR 912 at 917, per Charles J.

[113] See eg *P v P (Abduction: Acquiescence)* [1998] 1 FLR 630 at 633, per Hale J. But note the Australian decision, *Baxley v Bull* 12 April 1994 (available on INCADAT), in which the Full Court of the Family Court of Australia held that a father's consent to his wife taking the children to Australia to visit her family was 'withdrawn' as soon as she notified him that she did not intend to return to the United States. Similarly, in *H v H (Child Abduction: Stay of Domestic Proceedings)* [1994] 1 FLR 530, Thorpe J considered that a similar position obtained upon the unilateral abandonment of an agreement to be in England for an unspecified period.

[114] Cf *Re W (Abduction: Procedure)* [1995] 1 FLR 878 at 888, in which Wall J thought it was difficult to envisage circumstances in which consent could be passive. However, his Lordship later retracted this proposition in *Re M (Abduction) (Consent: Acquiescence)* [1999] 1 FLR 171 at 187.

[115] See *Re K (Abduction: Consent)* [1997] 2 FLR 212 at 217, per Hale J, and *P v P* (above) at 633, also per Hale J.

[116] [1996] 1 FLR 414 at 419.

[117] [1999] 1 FLR 171.

17.50   According to Wall J in *Re M*,[118] consent for the purposes of Art 13(a) does not have to be accompanied by each party being content with the outcome agreed. A parent may have the gravest reservations about the child being taken to live in another country, but may nevertheless consent.

Contemporaneous or open-ended?

17.51   In *Re K (Abduction: Consent)*,[119] Hale J held that a father's consent to his daughter's removal to England was 'not taken away by [him] subsequently thinking better of it' and that the mother was entitled to rely upon it in making up her mind and keeping the child in England. In other words, *Re K* supports the proposition that once given, and acted upon, consent cannot then be withdrawn.[120] However, the full extent of this proposition has yet to be explored, at any rate by the English courts. In *Re K* itself, the father was found to have consented both to his wife coming to England to sort out her feelings (with only a 50/50 chance of her returning to her husband in the United States) and to her taking their daughter and, in the event of her deciding to remain in England, of keeping the daughter there. But suppose the mother and daughter had returned to the United States, could the father be taken to have consented to a subsequent return to England or would his consent have been 'spent' upon the mother and daughter's return to the United States? In other words, once it has been given, can consent be treated as being open-ended in the sense of covering future removals or retentions?[121] Although this issue has not been discussed by the English courts it has been further explored in the Scottish decision, *Zenel v Haddow*.[122]

17.52   In *Zenel*, an unmarried mother agreed to move from Scotland to Australia in an attempt to effect a reconciliation with the father. The parents and child lived together for about 15 months, after which the mother removed the child clandestinely from Australia and returned to Scotland. At first instance, Lord Marnoch, the Lord Ordinary, found as a fact that the father had agreed that if the attempted reconciliation failed the mother could return with the child to Scotland. The question was, however, whether that agreement could still be thought to be in existence, given the lengthy period of cohabitation in Australia during which it was accepted that the child had

---

118   [1999] 1 FLR 171 at 188.
119   [1997] 2 FLR 212 at 218.
120   Cf the similar position for acquiescence, discussed below at **17.79** *et seq.*
121   Cf where the parties have come to an open-ended arrangement about the child's location but without agreeing upon a permanent location, which, according to Hale J in *Re HB (Abduction: Children's Objections)* [1997] 1 FLR 392 at 396, was not sufficient to establish consent. This decision has been criticised by Beaumont and McEleavy, *The Hague Convention on International Child Abduction* (OUP, 1999) at 129, as being out of line with case-law on acquiescence (viz *Re AZ (A Minor) (Abduction: Acquiescence)* [1993] 1 FLR 682, CA, discussed further at **17.74**) which establishes that it does not have to be acceptance of an unchangeable state of affairs. Whether this criticism is justified can be debated.
122   1993 SC 612, 1993 SLT 975, on which see Maher, 'Consent to Wrongful Child Abduction under the Hague Convention' (1993) SLT (News) 281.

become habitually resident there. Lord Marnoch, whilst accepting that such an agreement could not continue indefinitely and would have ended had the parties become 'wholly reconciled', thought nevertheless that that stage had not been reached, so that the agreement was still in place. Accordingly, he held that the father had consented to the child's removal. His decision was upheld by a majority ruling in the Inner House. The majority accepted that consent could properly be given to an act occurring at an undetermined time in the future. In this regard, Lord Allanbridge cited the example of a parent agreeing to a child's removal as and when the child came out of hospital and was fit enough to travel. Both in his and Lord Mayfield's view, there was nothing in Art 13(a) that compelled the conclusion that consent has to be contemporaneous with the act of removal. In contrast, the dissenting Lord Morton powerfully observed:[123]

> 'To hold that a consent to subsequent removal can be given before habitual residence has begun, and remain in force throughout the period of habitual residence, and, so far as I could understand from the submissions of counsel, could not be withdrawn by the petitioner, seems to me clearly not the type of consent which was contemplated in Art 13(a).'

17.53   Although critics[124] have tended to prefer Lord Morton's stance, the majority was surely right to hold that consent does not have to be contemporaneous with the act of removal (the hospital example seems a good one). Rather, the crucial test is that the consent should be to the actual removal or retention. Whether this was so in *Zenel* itself may be doubted, and there is much to be said for the view that the clandestine removal to Scotland some 15 months after living with the father in Australia was not the act consented to by him.

Proving consent

The burden of proof

17.54   As with all the exceptions, the burden of proof lies on the person who asserts that the removal or retention was consensual. Nevertheless it has been said that it should only be an exceptional case where the onus of proof is a factor in, or determinative of, the issue of consent.[125]

The standard of proof

17.55   As the House of Lords' ruling in *Re H and Others (Minors) (Sexual Abuse: Standard of Proof)*[126] makes clear, the sole standard of proof is that of the balance of probabilities. Nevertheless, as Lord Nicholls accepted in that

---

[123]   At 629 and 986 respectively.

[124]   Viz Maher, *op cit*, n 122, at 282 and Beaumont and McEleavy, *op cit*, n 121, at 130.

[125]   Per Charles J in *T v T (Abduction: Consent)* [1999] 2 FLR 912 at 918, with whom Holman J agreed in *Re H (Abduction: Habitual Residence: Consent)* [2000] 2 FLR 294 at 301.

[126]   [1996] AC 563, sub nom *Re H and R (Child Sexual Abuse: Standard of Proof)* [1996] 1 FLR 80.

case,[127] 'the more serious the allegation the more cogent is the evidence required to overcome the unlikelihood of what is alleged and thus to prove it'. In the context of the consent exception, it has long been accepted that the evidence needs to be clear and cogent, but this has to be understood in the light of the position taken by the House of Lords in *Re H and Others*. As Holman J explained in *Re H (Abduction: Habitual Residence: Consent)*:[128]

> 'On the facts of a particular case a court may consider that evidence of consent needs to be cogent before it can overcome the degree of improbability of consent having been given on those particular facts. But in the end there is only one question, namely has consent been established? And only one standard, namely the balance of probabilities.'

In *Re H*, Holman J was at pains to refute any suggestion inherent in earlier statements he had made that there were any additional hurdles or that the test implied one of 'certainty'.[129]

Satisfying the standard of proof

17.56   Although there is only one standard of proof, the question remains as to how that standard might be satisfied. One issue is whether the consent needs to be in writing, which was at the heart of the debate as to whether consent has to be express or whether it can be inferred.[130] In *Re W (Abduction: Procedure)*,[131] Wall J said that in 'normal circumstances, such consent will need to be in writing or at the very least evidenced by documentary material'. However, in *Re C (Abduction: Consent)*,[132] Holman J took issue with Wall J. As he pointed out: 'Art 13 does not use the words "in writing", and parents do not necessarily expect to reduce their agreements and understandings about their children to writing, even at the time of marital breakdown'. In *Re K (Abduction: Consent)*,[133] Hale J agreed with Holman J that consent did not have to be written and has reiterated this view on subsequent occasions.[134]

---

[127]   At 584 and 96, respectively, adopting the point originally made by Ungoed-Thomas J in *Re Dellow's Will Trust, Lloyd's Bank v Institute of Cancer Research* [1964] 1 All ER 771 at 773.

[128]   [2000] 2 FLR 294 at 301.

[129]   See, in particular, *Re C (Abduction: Consent)* [1996] 1 FLR 414 at 419, in which he said '[Consent] needs to be proved on the balance of probabilities, but the evidence in support of it needs to be clear and cogent. *If the court is left uncertain, then the "defence" under Art 13(a) fails*' (emphasis added). In *Re H* (above) at 301, Holman J accepted, prompted by Charles J's observation in *T v T (Abduction: Consent)* [1999] 2 FLR 912 at 918, that the words emphasised were 'ill-chosen', and that insofar as this might be taken to suggest that the standard of proof was one of 'certainty', it was wrong.

[130]   Discussed above at **17.48** *et seq*.

[131]   [1995] 1 FLR 878 at 888.

[132]   [1996] 1 FLR 414 at 418.

[133]   [1997] 2 FLR 213 at 217.

[134]   Viz in *P v P (Abduction: Acquiescence)* [1998] 1 FLR 630 at 633 (not commented upon on appeal at [1998] 2 FLR 835, CA) and in *Re R (Abduction: Consent)* [1999] 1 FLR 828 at 830. See also *T v T (Abduction: Consent)* [1999] 2 FLR 912 at 917, in which Charles J considered the 'Holman position' to be the preferred view.

Faced with this opposition and recognising the undesirability of a difference of judicial opinion on such an important point, Wall J has now reconsidered his position and in *Re M (Abduction) (Consent: Acquiescence)*[135] has said that he had gone too far in suggesting (albeit *obiter*) that 'a parent who was unable to demonstrate consent on the documentation before the court by means of unequivocal written material would fail to establish the defence of consent'.

17.57   Accordingly, it now seems accepted by the English courts[136] that consent does not have to be given or evidenced in writing and implicit in this is that, in cases of irreconcilable conflict of evidence on the face of the documentation, the courts will permit oral evidence to be adduced.[137]

17.58   Notwithstanding the above, as Wall J said in *Re M*,[138] 'most people who wish to retain or remove a child would be well advised to get written consent before they do so to place the matter beyond argument'.[139]

Exercising the discretion to return

17.59   As with all the Art 13 exceptions, the establishment of consent does not automatically mean that the court will refuse to return the child. As Holman J said in *Re C (Abduction: Consent)*,[140] the effect of establishing consent under Art 13(a) is merely to 'open the door' to the exercise of a discretion whether or not to order the child's immediate return. Nevertheless once consent is established it will be relatively difficult to persuade the court to order a return. As Hale J observed in *Re K (Abduction: Consent)*,[141] while generally in exercising the discretion the court is required to balance the purpose of the Convention with a finding that an Art 13 exception has been established, 'if it has been agreed between the parents that a mother bring her child to another country and, if she so chooses, remain here with the child, then frustrating those ... proposes ... *scarcely comes into question*' (emphasis

---

[135]   [1999] 1 FLR 171 at 187.

[136]   It might be noted that, in *Re H (Abduction: Habitual Residence: Consent)* [2000] 2 FLR 294 at 301, Holman J took it as established that 'there is no requirement that consent be given or evidenced in writing'. For the position in Scotland, see *inter alia C v C* 2003 SLT 793.

[137]   See Wall J in *Re M (Abduction) (Consent: Acquiescence)* (above) at 188. See also *T v T (Abduction: Consent)* [1999] 2 FLR 912 at 917, per Charles J, in which extensive oral evidence was taken by the court, but note the criticism of this by Bridge at [1999] Fam Law 522–523. Cf Hale J's more cautious approach to the admission of oral evidence in *Re R (Abduction: Consent)* [1999] 1 FLR 828 at 830. See also **21.80**.

[138]   At 188, echoing a similar statement made by Hale J in *Re K (Abduction: Consent)* [1997] 2 FLR 212 at 217.

[139]   But note that the existence of written evidence does not necessarily solve all problems. In *Re R (Minors) (Abduction)* [1994] 1 FLR 190, the plea of consent failed notwithstanding a letter apparently agreeing to the child's removal because the court of the child's habitual residence ruled that there had been no consent to the removal.

[140]   [1996] 1 FLR 414 at 423.

[141]   [1997] 2 FLR 212 at 220.

added). In *Re D (Abduction: Discretionary Return)*,[142] Wilson J agreed that it could be said that:

> 'where there has been consent to the removal, then, in effect, the abduction is not wrongful, with the result, that the spirit of the Convention [is] less potent a factor in favour of return than in other cases under Art 13.'[143]

17.60   *Re D*, however, provides an outstanding example of a return being ordered notwithstanding the establishment of consent.[144] The case concerned two children born and raised in France. After their parents' divorce, a French court made a residence order in favour of the mother with holiday contact to the father, who had since moved to England. Subsequently, following a contact visit, the children did not return to France and it was found that the mother had consented to the children living permanently with the father in England. However, Wilson J was persuaded by a number of telling arguments to order their return to France, namely, that it was better for these French children to have their future decided by a French court[145] and, crucially, that were this not to be ordered, the children might never have been able to visit France to see their mother because of the father's fear that the French custody order in favour of the mother would be enforced.

Acquiescence

Introduction

17.61   As with consent, while there is extensive jurisprudence, particularly in England and Wales, on the meaning of 'acquiescence',[146] in practice the exception is hard to establish. According to the 1999 Statistical Survey,[147] globally, only four refusals (amounting to 4% of all refusals) were based solely on this ground, with a further two cases in which the refusal was based on this ground in conjunction with another.

17.62   As previously discussed, the crucial difference between acquiescence and consent lies in the timing of the alleged act or behaviour, namely, that it must follow the abduction rather than precede it.[148] Although in essence

---

[142]   [2000] 1 FLR 24 at 36.

[143]   One could argue further that if consent means that the removal is not 'wrongful', the court should dismiss the Hague Abduction Convention application and exercise any discretion to return under domestic law.

[144]   Note also *Re R (Minors) (Abduction)* [1994] 1 FLR 190, in which Thorpe J said that had consent been established he would have exercised his discretion to order the children's return.

[145]   The family, all French speakers, had little connection with England. An added factor was that there was no difficulty about the children accepting an order that they should go back to France.

[146]   Of the 59 cases based on this exception reported by INCADAT, 34 decisions were of English courts, with a further eight made by the Scottish courts.

[147]   *Op cit*, n 2.

[148]   See **17.43**.

acquiescence amounts to an acceptance by the left-behind parent of the situation created by the abduction, it has proved to be a more challenging concept requiring, so far as English law is concerned, a House of Lords' ruling,[149] to determine its proper scope.

The abandonment of active and passive acquiescence – the Re H test

17.63 In the past, the English Court of Appeal had drawn a distinction between 'active' and 'inactive' (or 'passive') acquiescence. In the former case, acquiescence was judged objectively on the basis of the evidence of the conduct in question. In these cases, the uncommunicated subjective intention of the wronged person was normally irrelevant. In contrast, with passive acquiescence, regard could be had to the wronged person's subjective intentions.[150] In *Re H (Minors) (Abduction: Acquiescence)*,[151] however, the House of Lords condemned these peculiarly English distinctions[152] which were not to be found in the Convention itself and stressed instead the importance of applying the same meaning in all Contracting States. Accordingly, a new test, to be applied in all cases, was established. It was summarised by Lord Browne-Wilkinson in these terms:[153]

'(1) For the purposes of Art 13 of the Convention, the question whether the wronged parent has "acquiesced" in the removal or retention of the child depends upon his actual state of mind. As Neill LJ said in [*Re S (Minors) (Abduction: Acquiescence)* [1994] 1 FLR 819 at 838]: "the court is primarily concerned, not with the question of the other parent's perception of the applicant's conduct, but with the question whether the applicant acquiesced in fact".

(2) The subjective intention of the wronged parent is a question of fact for the trial judge to determine in all the circumstances of the case, the burden of proof being on the abducting parent.

(3) The trial judge, in reaching his decision on that question of fact, will no doubt be inclined to attach more weight to the contemporaneous words and actions of the wronged parent than to his bare assertions in evidence of his intention. But that is a question of the weight to be attached to evidence and is not a question of law.

(4) There is only one exception. Where the words or actions of the wronged parent clearly and unequivocally show and have led the other parent to

---

[149] *Re H (Minors) (Abduction: Acquiescence)* [1998] AC 72, [1997] 2 WLR 563, [1997] 1 FLR 872.

[150] See *Re A (Minors) (Abduction: Custody Rights)* [1992] Fam 106, [1992] 2 WLR 536, sub nom *Re A (Minors) (Abduction: Acquiescence)* [1992] 2 FLR 14 (Balcombe LJ powerfully dissenting), *Re AZ (Minor) (Abduction: Acquiescence)* [1993] 1 FLR 682 and *Re S (Minors) (Abduction: Acquiescence)* [1994] 1 FLR 819. This approach was followed in Scotland, see *Soucie v Soucie* 1995 SLT 414, and in Ireland, see *P v B* [1995] 1 ILRM 201, per Denham J.

[151] [1998] AC 72, [1997] 2 WLR 563, [1997] 1 FLR 872, and on which see the excellent notes by McLean, 'International child abduction – some recent trends' [1997] CFLQ 387 and Bailey-Harris, 'Acquiescence under the Hague Convention on International Child Abduction' (1997) 113 LQR 529.

[152] Drawn from other areas of law, notably, waiver, election, laches and estoppel.

[153] At 90, 575–576 and 884 respectively.

believe that the wronged parent clearly is not asserting or going to assert his right to the summary return of the child and are inconsistent with such return, justice requires that the wronged parent be held to have acquiesced.'

17.64 In other words, unless the defendant can prove to the court's satisfaction that the applicant clearly acquiesced, the defence can succeed only if it falls within the 'exceptional' category. In laying emphasis upon the subjective intentions of the wronged person, Lord Browne-Wilkinson said that he was encouraged to find that this view was reflected in other jurisdictions.[154] *Re H* has since been expressly applied in Ireland.[155]

The relevance of knowledge of the Convention

17.65 Another issue of general relevance in establishing acquiescence either in the non-exceptional or exceptional category is the extent to which the wronged party needs to know of his or her Convention rights. This in turn is often coupled with the wronged party receiving erroneous legal advice.

17.66 The overall current position was well summarised by Butler-Sloss LJ in *Re S (Abduction: Acquiescence)*[156] when she observed:

'Knowledge of the facts and that the act of removal or retention is wrongful will normally usually be necessary. But to expect the applicant necessarily to have knowledge of the rights which can be enforced under the Convention is to set too high a standard. The degree of knowledge as a relevant factor will, of course, depend on the facts of each case.'

17.67 In that case it was accepted that, in the light of incorrect legal advice initially given to the father (in which no reference was made to the Hague Abduction Convention at all), it was difficult to treat his attempts to seek agreement on contact and his sending to the mother her belongings as acquiescence. However, his continuing actions to seek contact and not to seek the child's summary return, after receiving fresh realistic advice that while he might be successful under the Convention he was unlikely to be able to retain the child in his home country, were held to amount to acquiescence even though the father had not been fully informed of his rights under the Convention.

---

[154] Viz the French Cour de Cassation decision *Horlander v Horlander* (1992) 16 July, *Bulletin Civil* No 228; the District Court of Massachusetts' decision *Wanniger v Wanniger* (1994) 850 F Supp 78; and the US Court of Appeals of the Sixth Circuit's decision *Friedrich v Friedrich* (1996) 78 F 3rd 1060. But note the trenchant criticism of this 'far from impressive' authority by McLean, *op cit*, n 151 above, at 396–398. In any event, there was no overall unanimity: see eg the position then taken in Ireland where, following *P v B* [1995] 1 ILRM 201, the courts applied an objective test. But see now *K v K* (1998), reported on INCADAT (HC/E/IE/285), which applied an approach similar to *Re H*.

[155] See *K v K* (above). For review of the position in Scotland, see *S v S* 2003 SLT 344 at para [17], per Lord Clarke.

[156] [1998] 2 FLR 115 at 122, CA, applying, *inter alia*, *Re A (Minors) (Abduction: Custody Rights)* [1992] Fam 106, sub nom *Re A (Minors) (Abduction: Acquiescence)* [1992] 2 FLR 14, CA.

17.68 Whether a distinction can be drawn between the non-exceptional and exceptional category cases can be debated, but it is noticeable that in the latter type of cases the courts have been more ready to hold that ignorance of the Convention does not negate acquiescence. In *Re D (Abduction: Acquiescence)*,[157] for example, a father, who was legally represented, agreed to a residence order being made in Swansea County Court following the wrongful retention of the child by the wife. He had informed his wife that he would have no objection to her having residence if he could have the contact that he wanted. On his return to Australia, the father had second thoughts and sought to invoke the Convention. He maintained that it was only on his return that he became aware of the Convention rights. This ignorance, however, was held not to negate his acquiescence, which had been clearly demonstrated not only by his agreement to the court order but also by his indication to his wife that he would return to live in Wales.

Proving acquiescence

17.69 Following *Re H (Minors) (Abduction: Acquiescence)*,[158] the court must first determine whether the wronged person has actually acquiesced, but if not, it must then determine whether the application falls into the exceptional category.

17.70 As with all the exceptions, the burden of proof to establish acquiescence lies on the defendant. The court will clearly take into account the written evidence as to the parties' intentions,[159] but as Lord Browne-Wilkinson said in *Re H*:[160]

> '… as a matter of ordinary judicial common sense, [the judge] is likely to attach more weight to the express words or conduct of the wronged parent than to his subsequent evidence as to his state of mind.'

So far as written statements are concerned, it is well established that they must be expressed in clear and unambiguous terms.[161] Extracting a single and ambiguous sentence from a four-page letter, for example, will not be enough to establish acquiescence.[162] Furthermore, in Lord Browne-Wilkinson's view,[163] the clear and unequivocal conduct that brings the case within the exceptional

---

[157] [1998] 1 FLR 686. See also *Re B (Abduction: Acquiescence)* [1999] 2 FLR 818, and *Re AZ (A Minor) (Abduction: Acquiescence)* [1993] 1 FLR 682 (although note Sir Donald Nicholls V-C's reservation in that case), both discussed further below at **17.74–17.75**.

[158] [1988] AC 72, [1997] 2 WLR 563, [1997] 1 FLR 872.

[159] The court will hear oral evidence from the parties only when a *prima facie* case of acquiescence is raised. As to when oral evidence will be permitted, see generally **21.80**.

[160] At 88, 572 and 882 respectively.

[161] See eg *Re A (Minors) (Abduction: Custody Rights)* [1992] Fam 106, sub nom *Re A (Minors) (Abduction: Acquiescence)* [1992] 1 All ER 929, CA; and *Re S (Child Abduction and Acquiescence)* [1998] 2 FLR 893. Indeed, such clear statements can come within Lord Browne-Wilkinson's 'exceptional category'.

[162] Per Millett LJ in *Re R (Child Abduction: Acquiescence)* [1995] 1 FLR 716 at 773.

[163] At 89, 575 and 883–884 respectively.

category 'is not to be found in passing remarks or letters written by a parent who has recently suffered the trauma of the removal of his children'.

The normal case

17.71 Following *Re H*, the first question a court must settle is whether, looking at the subjective mind of the wronged person after the child's removal, he or she had in fact acquiesced or had 'gone along' with that removal. In *Re M (Abduction) (Consent: Acquiescence)*,[164] for example, it was found that a father who knew that his wife intended a permanent removal, whose attitude prior to departure was that she could do as she wished (he assumed that she would not manage on her own in England and would therefore return to Greece) and whose attitude did not change significantly after the removal in July (he came to England in November for contact) until he changed his mind the following February, was held to have acquiesced. Similarly, in *Re D (Abduction: Acquiescence)*,[165] the court had no difficulty in finding acquiescence where the applicant had genuinely agreed to the making of a residence order in favour of the abducting parent and intended to return permanently to Wales to live near to the children.

17.72 Each case has to be assessed on its own facts but, while absence of court action does not necessarily indicate acquiescence,[166] delay, particularly unexplained delay,[167] in taking any action can be indicative of acquiescence.[168] Conversely, the fact that the applicant has applied for custody in the State of the child's habitual residence is a strong indication that there has been no acquiescence,[169] although there is nothing necessarily inconsistent with acquiescing in a current state of affairs and applying for the child's care and control at a later date.[170]

The exceptional case

17.73 According to *Re H*, in rare or exceptional circumstances, courts may find that, notwithstanding that the wronged parent has not in fact done so, he

---

[164] [1999] 1 FLR 171.

[165] [1998] 2 FLR 335, CA. Cf *Re B (Minors) (Abduction)* [1993] 1 FLR 988: merely entering an appearance in the abductor's application for a residence order was held not in itself to amount to acquiescence.

[166] *Re F (A Minor) (Child Abduction)* [1992] 1 FLR 548, CA. See also *Re R (Minors) (Abduction)* [1994] 1 FLR 190: delay, *inter alia*, because of legal advice to await the outcome of domestic proceedings in France and because of the subsequent 'deplorable' delay in the French Central Authority's communication with the English Central Authority; and *Re S (Minors) (Abduction: Acquiescence)* [1994] 1 FLR 819, CA: delay due to erroneous legal advice.

[167] Cf *Soucie v Soucie* 1995 SLT 414, Court of Session, Scotland.

[168] See eg *W v W (Child Abduction: Acquiescence)* [1993] 2 FLR 211: father's inactivity for some 10 months after learning of his wife's decision not to return held to amount to acquiescence; and *Re D (Abduction: Acquiescence)* [1999] 1 FLR 36: mother who took no legal advice for almost a year and was only prompted to do so upon learning that the father had been imprisoned was held to have acquiesced.

[169] *Re A (Minors: Abduction)* [1991] 2 FLR 241, CA.

[170] *Re AZ (A Minor) (Abduction: Acquiescence)* [1993] 1 FLR 682, CA.

should be taken to have acquiesced on account of his words or actions. In formulating this test, Lord Browne-Wilkinson was alive to the argument that by so doing there was a danger that the discredited distinction between 'active' and 'passive' acquiescence would simply re-emerge in the more subtle form of that between non-exceptional and exceptional cases.[171] In his view, however, the two approaches are quite different and it was important to emphasise:

> '... that the wronged parent who has in fact never acquiesced is not to lose his right to the summary return of his children except by words or actions which unequivocally demonstrate that he was not insisting on the summary return of the child.'

17.74 In *Re H*, Lord Browne-Wilkinson mentioned two types of conduct that would fall into this exceptional category, namely, the signing of a formal agreement that the child is to remain in the country to which he has been abducted, and the active participation in proceedings in the country to which the child has been abducted to determine the child's long-term future. More specifically, he referred to *Re AZ (A Minor) (Abduction: Acquiescence)*,[172] in which a mother, with the father's consent, took their child from Germany (where the father was stationed with the US Air Force) to England to stay with her family. Once there the mother decided not to return. She left her son with her sister, and the father asked her to look after the child until he could come to England a little later. However, before his arrival, the aunt applied for residence and prohibited steps orders. The father was served with the papers after his arrival in England but, having indicated that he would not contest the application, he later told the family for the first time that he intended to take the boy back to Germany, although it was not for another 6 weeks that he finally initiated Convention proceedings. The Court of Appeal held that the father had 'acquiesced'. In Lord Browne-Wilkinson's view,[173] *Re AZ* was what he expected to be a rare example of a case falling into the exceptional category where the wronged parent's conduct is so clear as not to require proof of his subjective intention; that is, it was a case:

> '... in which the wronged parent, knowing of his rights, has so conducted himself vis-à-vis the other parent and the children that he cannot be heard to go back on what he has done and seek to persuade the judge that, all along, he has secretly intended to claim the summary return of the children.'

17.75 Another example is *Re B (Abduction: Acquiescence)*[174] where, following his wife's removal of their child to England, the father at first negotiated with

---

171 [1998] AC 72 at 90, [1999] 2 WLR 563 at 572, [1997] 1 FLR 872 at 884. His Lordship also observed that the exceptional category was not to be seen as importing the English rules of estoppel into the Convention, but rather a 'general principle to be found in all developed systems of law'.

172 [1993] 1 FLR 682, CA.

173 [1998] AC 72 at 89F, [1997] 2 WLR 563 at 574H–575A, [1997] 1 FLR 872 at 883G.

174 [1999] 2 FLR 818. See also *Re D (Abduction: Acquiescence)* [1998] 1 FLR 686, and *Re S (A Child: Abduction)* [2002] EWCA Civ 1941, [2003] 1 FLR 1008.

her, suggesting he would not oppose her move if the reconciliation he was proposing failed, and subsequently decided to settle in England and seek contact in the English courts. It was held that, notwithstanding his ignorance of the Convention (neither his American nor his English lawyers apparently mentioned it to him), his conduct overall[175] amounted to acquiescence.

17.76   In contrast to the above two cases, in *Re H* itself it was held that the father's recourse to the Beth Din (where he was told initially not to take part in the English proceedings) did not fall into the exceptional category, for there was nothing inconsistent in a wronged parent pursuing remedies in the court of habitual residence (whether religious or civil) and the subsequent recourse to the Convention for the children's summary return.

17.77   On the other hand, as was held in *P v P (Abduction: Acquiescence)*,[176] merely seeking to compromise a situation by allowing the abducting parent to remain in the country to which he or she has gone, provided that the wronged parent is satisfied as to other matters in issue between them, will not be regarded as 'acquiescence'. In this case, after the mother had left the father in Cyprus and taken the child to England, the father sought, through his lawyer in Cyprus, to negotiate a settlement under which the child would reside with his mother in England but have extensive staying contact with him in Cyprus. When these negotiations failed, the father issued Hague Convention proceedings. It was held that, in the absence of a concluded agreement, the father could not be said to have 'acquiesced' within the meaning of Lord Browne-Wilkinson's 'clear and unequivocal' conduct category. Indeed, Ward LJ agreed[177] with Hale J's observation at first instance[178] that:

> '... it would be most unfortunate if parents ... were deterred from seeking to make sensible arrangements, in consequence of what is usually an acknowledged breakdown in the relationship between them, for fear that the mere fact that they are able to contemplate that the child should remain where he has been taken will count against them in these proceedings. Such negotiations are, if anything, to be encouraged.'

17.78   The decision in *P v P* is in line with Lord Browne-Wilkinson's 'suggestion' in *Re H* that 'judges should be slow to infer an intention to acquiesce from attempts by the wronged parent to effect a reconciliation or to reach an agreed voluntary return of the abducted child'. As his Lordship

---

[175]   Note that his statements made during the negotiations were not of themselves held to be probative of acquiescence.

[176]   [1998] 2 FLR 835, CA. See also *Re I (Abduction: Acquiescence)* [1999] 1 FLR 778, in which Hogg J said 'negotiating was not acquiescing' and that therefore in seeking help and advice from the mother's solicitor the father could not be said to have acquiesced.

[177]   [1998] 2 FLR 835 at 840.

[178]   [1998] 1 FLR 630 at 635.

pointed out,[179] the Convention itself[180] places weight on the desirability of a negotiated or voluntary return or to bring about an amicable resolution of the issues. This is an important ruling and gives efficacy to mediation schemes such as the one being piloted by Reunite.[181] However, negotiation between the parents with a view to reaching a settlement will need to be concluded by the time that the case is heard in court, since a withdrawal of a Hague Convention application might prevent the wronged parent from being able to reinstate the application in the absence of any new developments.[182]

The effect of acquiescence

Acquiescence cannot subsequently be withdrawn

17.79 English case-law establishes that, since acquiescence is not a continuing state of affairs, once given it cannot be withdrawn.[183] However, as Lord Donaldson MR commented in *Re A (Minors) (Abduction: Custody Rights)*:[184]

> '... an apparent acquiescence, followed immediately by a withdrawal, may lead the court to question whether the apparent acquiescence was real, or whether it was the product of emotional turmoil which could not reasonably be interpreted as real acquiescence. That apart, the only relevance of time which elapses between acquiescence and a purported withdrawal of the acquiescence is in the context of the exercise of a discretion whether to return the child ...'

17.80 Although at first sight it may seem harsh not to permit withdrawals of acquiescence, given that its establishment still leaves the court with discretion whether or not to return (see below), the standpoint is not as draconian as it might appear.

Exercising the discretion to return

17.81 As with all the Art 13 exceptions, the establishment of acquiescence still leaves the court with a discretion whether or not to order the child's return. The English position is that, in exercising that discretion, as *Re A (Minors) (Abduction: Acquiescence) (No 2)*[185] establishes, the court is entitled to take the child's interests into account but it is not bound to treat those interests as the paramount consideration, rather it must balance them against

---

[179] See [1998] AC 72 at 88, [1997] 2 WLR 563 at 574, [1997] 1 FLR 872 at 882. See also *X v X*, Case No 228 of 16 July 1992, *Bulletin des Arrets de la Cour de Cassation Chambres Civiles*, p 151, in which the French Cour de Cassation took a similar approach.

[180] See Arts 7(c) and 10.

[181] For further discussion of which, see **13.33**.

[182] See the observation of Holman J in *Re O (Child Abduction: Re-Abduction)* [1997] 2 FLR 712 at 719. In practice, the court is likely to grant an adjournment to facilitate any imminent settlement.

[183] Per Butler-Sloss LJ in *Re S (Abduction: Acquiescence)* [1998] 2 FLR 115 at 122, CA, applying *Re A (Minors) (Abduction: Custody Rights)* [1992] Fam 106, [1992] 2 WLR 536, sub nom *Re A (Minors) (Abduction: Acquiescence)* [1992] 2 FLR 14, CA.

[184] [1992] Fam 106 at 123–124, [1992] 2 WLR 536 at 551, and [1992] 2 FLR 14 at 30, respectively.

[185] [1993] Fam 1, [1993] 2 FLR 396.

the fundamental purpose of the Convention, namely to order the child's return. In this case, the Court of Appeal upheld Booth J's refusal to order a return. In *H v H (Abduction: Acquiescence)*,[186] Waite LJ, relying on his previous decision, *W v W (Child Abduction: Acquiescence)*,[187] suggested that the following factors are relevant to the exercise of such a discretion, namely:

'(a)   the comparative suitability of the forum in the competing jurisdictions to determine the child's future in the substantive proceedings;

(b)   the likely outcome (in whichever forum they be heard) of the substantive proceedings;

(c)   the consequences of the acquiescence, with particular reference to the extent to which a child may have become settled in the requested State;

(d)   the situation which would await the absconding parent and the child if compelled to return to the requesting jurisdiction;

(e)   the anticipated emotional effect upon the child of an immediate return order (a factor which is to be treated as significant but not as paramount);

(f)   the extent to which the purpose and underlying philosophy of the Hague Convention would be at risk of frustration if a return order were to be refused.'

17.82   However, as was held in *W v W*, these criteria should not be assessed in a rigid, mathematical manner, but rather the decision should be made on the overall impression gained from the evidence. In any event, they might not be the only factors that should be taken into account. There is authority,[188] for example, for saying that the applicant's delay in pursuing his Convention remedy is also relevant. It is perhaps a moot point as to whether the discretion should be exercised differently according to whether acquiescence falls into the non-exceptional or the exceptional category.

17.83   A similar position with regard to the exercise of the discretion is taken in Australia. Indeed, that jurisdiction provides in *Townsend v Director-General, Department of Families, Youth and Community*[189] a rare example of a decision to order a return notwithstanding the establishment of acquiescence.

THE ARTICLE 13(b) EXCEPTION

17.84   Article 13 provides:

'... that the judicial or administrative authority of the requested State is not bound to order the return of the child if the person, institution or other body which opposes its return establishes that:

---

[186] [1996] 2 FLR 570 at 574–575, CA, not overruled on this point by the House of Lords, which held that there was no acquiescence: see **17.63**.

[187] [1993] 2 FLR 211.

[188] See *Re M (Abduction) (Consent: Acquiescence)* [1999] 1 FLR 171 at 191, per Wall J, relying on his earlier decision in *Re S (Child Abduction: Delay)* [1998] 1 FLR 651.

[189] (1999) 24 Fam LR 495 (Full Ct of the Family Court of Australia, Appellate Court); see also *Central Authority v Reissner* (1999) 25 Fam 330 at 346, per Lindenmayer J.

...

(b)   there is a grave risk that his or her return would expose the child to physical or psychological harm or otherwise place the child in an intolerable situation.'

Background to the provision

17.85 As the Pérez-Vera Report comments,[190] whereas the Art 13(a) exceptions are based on the wronged parent's conduct, Art 13(b) clearly derives from a consideration of the interests of the child inasmuch as 'the interest of the child in not being removed from its habitual residence ... gives way before the primary interest of any person in not being exposed to physical or psychological danger or being placed in an intolerable situation'. The limited ambit of the exception should be noted, and in particular that it is not intended simply as a child welfare defence. As the Pérez-Vera Report states,[191] each of the terms used in Art 13(b) was 'the result of a fragile compromise reached during the deliberation of the Special Commission' and it was not to be inferred 'that the exceptions are to receive a wide interpretation'.[192] Indeed, the requirement to prove a 'grave' risk was deliberately introduced as a more 'intensive qualifier' than the previously proposed epithet 'substantial'.[193] Nevertheless, be that as it may, the application of Art 13(b) is critical to the operation of the Convention for, as the Report of the Third Meeting of the Special Commission[194] agreed, this exception is a sensitive one which, if misused, could destroy the effectiveness of the Convention.

17.86 Not surprisingly, Art 13(b) is the most litigated of all the exceptions[195] and, notwithstanding a generally strict interpretation adopted in most jurisdictions (although there are signs of some relaxation),[196] it is the one most often successfully invoked. According to the 1999 Statistical Survey,[197] globally, over a fifth of all judicial refusals were based on this ground.

---

[190] At para 29, and see also para 116.

[191] At para 116.

[192] In particular, the Report states that no inference is to be drawn from the rejection of the proposal (by the American delegation) that the exception could not be invoked on the basis that a return might harm the child's economic or educational prospects.

[193] See the discussion in Procès-verbal No 15 at p 362. It might be noted in passing that the United Kingdom voted against this change.

[194] Report of the Third Meeting of the Special Commission to review the operation of the Hague Convention on the Civil Aspects of International Child Abduction (17–21 March 1997) (Hague Conference on Private International Law).

[195] At the time of writing there were, for example, 214 references to this exception reported on INCADAT.

[196] See below at **17.93**.

[197] *Op cit*, n 2.

The proper approach to Article 13(b)

Heavy burden to discharge

17.87 As with all exceptions, the burden of satisfying the court that Art 13(b) applies lies on the defendant and, in keeping with the spirit of the Convention, it is a stringent burden to discharge. As Ward LJ said in *Re C (Abduction: Grave Risk of Psychological Harm)*,[198] so far as the English courts are concerned there is:

'... an established line of authority that the court should require clear and compelling evidence of the grave risk of harm or other intolerability which must be measured as substantial, not trivial, and of a severity which is much more than is inherent in the inevitable disruption, uncertainty and anxiety which follows an unwelcome return to the jurisdiction of the court of habitual residence.'

17.88 This strict interpretation was first adopted by the Court of Appeal in *Re A (A Minor) (Abduction)*,[199] in which it was held that the risk of physical harm had to be more than an ordinary one, indeed not only had it to be weighty but also substantial and not trivial. This approach was followed in *Re C (A Minor) (Abduction)*,[200] in which Lord Donaldson MR, having pointed out that some psychological harm to the child is inherent in these type of cases whatever their outcome, referred to 'the severe degree of psychological harm which the Convention has in mind'. Similarly, in *B v B (Child Abduction: Custody Rights)*,[201] Sir Stephen Brown P referred to 'a very high degree of intolerability [which] must be established in order to bring into operation Art 13(b)', Indeed, such was the strictness of their approach that, some 8 years after the Convention had been in operation in England and Wales, Butler-Sloss LJ felt able to say in *Re M (Abduction: Undertakings)*:[202]

'It is, however, important to recognise, to my knowledge at least, no English court has yet found circumstances to meet the stringent requirements under Art 13(b), nor do I believe they have been met in the Convention countries with

---

[198] [1999] 1 FLR 1145 at 1154, CA. See also *TB v JB (Abduction: Grave Risk of Harm)* [2001] 2 FLR 515 at [39], in which Hale LJ commented: 'The policy of the Convention is that disputes about children should be determined in the courts of the country of their habitual residence. Children should not be uprooted and placed beyond their jurisdiction. It is for them to determine where the best interests of the children lie. Article 13(b) is the one exception to this. No requested country can be expected to return children to a situation where they will be at serious risk, but this must not be turned into a substitute for the welfare test, usurping the function of the courts of the home country'.

[199] [1988] 1 FLR 365 at 372, per Nourse LJ.

[200] [1989] 1 FLR 403 at 413.

[201] [1993] Fam 32 at 42, sub nom *B v B (Abduction)* [1993] 1 FLR 238 at 247.

[202] [1995] 1 FLR 1021 at 1026, CA (decided in July 1994). In point of fact, her Ladyship was wrong in thinking there had been no English decision upholding an Art 13(b) exception: see *B v K (Child Abduction)* [1993] 1 FCR 382, [1993] Fam Law 17, per Johnson J, discussed below at **17.105**. Note also the Scottish decision, *MacMillan v MacMillan* 1989 SLT 350 (on which see McClean, 'Return of Internationally Abducted Children' (1990) 106 LQR 375) in which the exception had also succeeded: see further **17.111** below.

which we principally are concerned, such as the USA, Canada, Australia and New Zealand.'

17.89   However, as Ward LJ put it in *Re C (Abduction: Grave Risk of Psychological Harm)*,[203] that 'high watermark was reached for the first time' in *Re F (A Minor) (Abduction: Custody Rights Abroad)*,[204] where the Court of Appeal found that Art 13 was established. Even in that case, however, Sir Christopher Slade was at pains to point out:

> '... that the courts of this country are only in rare cases willing to hold that the conditions of fact, which give rise to the courts' discretion under Art 13(b), are satisfied. They are in my view quite right to be cautious and to apply a stringent test. The invocation of Art 13(b), with scant justification, is all too likely to be the last resort for parents who have wrongfully removed their child to another jurisdiction.'

17.90   This strict approach of the English courts is reflected in the extensive jurisprudence in most of the other major jurisdictions. The Scottish courts, for example, have long adopted a restrictive approach, beginning with *Viola v Viola*,[205] in which a plea that there was a *prima facie* case for saying that if the child was returned she might be placed in an intolerable situation was dismissed out of hand. More recently, in *Re Q Petitioner*,[206] the Court of Session expressly applied the principles set out in the English and American authorities. The Irish courts too have applied a restrictive approach. For example, in the Irish Supreme Court decision, *AS v PS*,[207] Denham J commented:

> 'The exception to this fundamental concept [ie the requirement to return children to their habitual residence] carries a heavy burden, the test is a high one ... . It is a question of enforcing the Hague Convention which has at its core the paramount interest of the child that it should not be wrongfully removed or retained across State borders.'

17.91   In the United States, where, in any event, it is statutorily required[208] that there be 'clear and convincing evidence', in the leading and internationally influential decision, *Friedrich v Friedrich*,[209] the Sixth Circuit of the US Federal

---

203   [1999] 1 FLR 1145 at 1153.

204   [1995] Fam 224, sub nom *Re F (Child Abduction: Risk if Returned)* [1995] 2 FLR 31, CA, discussed at **17.108**. Cited by Ward LJ in *Re S (Abduction: Custody Rights)* [2002] EWCA Civ 908, [2002] 2 FLR 815 at [45].

205   1988 SLT 7.

206   2001 SLT 243, although in that case a return was in fact refused: see **17.116**. See also *Starr v Starr* 1999 SLT 335.

207   [1998] 2 IR 244. See also *CK v CK* [1994] 1 IR 250 and *P v B (No 1)* [1995] ILRM 201.

208   By s 11603(e)(2)(A) of the International Child Abduction Remedies Act of 1968. This provision also applies to Art 20 of the 1980 Hague Abduction Convention.

209   78 F 3d 1060 (6th Cir 1996), on which see Boggs, 'Remarks on the 1980 Hague Convention on the Civil Aspects of International Child Abduction' (2000) 33 New York Jo of Intl Law and Politics 43. According to Kelsey and Hartwell, 'International Custody: Two Approaches to the International Shuttling of Children' (1999) 13 American Jo of Family Law 188 at 192,

Court of Appeals espoused a particularly restrictive view of the application of Art 13(b), acknowledging 'that courts in the abducted-from country are as ready and able as we are to protect children'. Its interpretation of the 'grave risk of harm' was especially narrow, believing it to exist in only two situations; namely:

> 'First, there is a grave risk of harm when return of the child puts the child in imminent danger prior to the resolution of the custody dispute – eg returning the child to a zone of war, famine, or disease. Second, there is a grave risk of harm in cases of serious abuse or neglect, or extraordinary emotional dependence, when the court in the country of habitual residence, for whatever reason, may be incapable or unwilling to give the child adequate protection.'

17.92 In Canada and New Zealand, too, Art 13(b) has been restrictively interpreted.[210] Nor is this restrictive approach confined to common law jurisdictions. There are similarly narrow interpretations, for example, in German, French and Swiss law.[211]

17.93 Until recently, Australian law took a similar position[212] but in *DP v Commonwealth Central Authority; JLM v Director-General NSW Department of Community Services,*[213] by a majority decision, the Australian High Court has

---

there had been no American refusals based on Art 13(b) before 1999. For a discussion of American (and other jurisdictions') case-law before *Friedrich*, see Silberman, 'Hague International Child Abduction Convention: A Progress Report' (1994) 57 *Law and Contemporary Problems* 210 at 235 *et seq*. Note also *Nunez-Escudero v Tice-Menley* 58 F 3d 374 (8th Cir 1995). For a detailed discussion of the American cases, see Garbolino, *International Child Custody Cases: Handling Hague Convention Cases in US Courts*, 3rd edn (The National Judicial College, 2000) at p 169 *et seq*; Weiner, 'International Child Abduction and the Escape from Violence' (2000) 69 *Fordham Law Review* 593 at 651 *et seq*; and Weiner, 'Navigating the Road Between Uniformity and Progress: The Need for Purposive Analysis of the Hague Convention on the Civil Aspects of International Child Abduction' (2002) 33 Columbia HRLR 276, particularly at 337 *et seq*. The *Friedrich* interpretation of Art 13(b) was adopted by the NZ Court of Appeal in *A v Central Authority for New Zealand* [1996] 2 NZFLR 517.

[210] See, in Canada, *Thomson v Thomson* [1994] 3 SCR 551, (1995) 119 DLR (4th) 253 (Can Sup Ct) and the authorities cited by Bailey in 'Canada's Implementation of the 1980 Hague Convention on the Civil Aspects of International Child Abduction' [2000] 33 New York Jo of Intl Law and Politics 17 at 34 *et seq*. For New Zealand, see *A v A* [1996] NZFLR 529, *S v S* [1999] NZLR 625, *KS v LS* (unreported, 11 June 2003, CIV 2002-404-73), appeal dismissed on 16 July 2003 (CA 128/03), and the cases cited by Caldwell, 'Child welfare defences in child abduction cases – some recent developments' [2001] CFLQ 121 at 126 *et seq*.

[211] In Germany, see eg 2 B v R 982/95 and 983/95, Order of 10 October 1995, 2 B v R Order of 15 February 1996 and 2 B v R 1075, Order of 15 August 1996, but note the discussion by Siehr, 'The 1980 Hague Convention on the Civil Aspects of International Child Abduction: Failure and Successes in German Practice' (2000) 33 New York Jo of Intl Law and Politics 207 at 215–216. For a discussion of some of the French and Swiss jurisdictions, see Silberman, *op cit*, n 209, at 237 *et seq*.

[212] See eg *Murray v Director, Family Services ACT* (1993) FLC 92–416 and *Gsponer and Director General Community Services* (Vic) (1988) 12 Fam LR 755.

[213] (2001) 180 ALR 402, [2001] HCA 39, reported by Hall in *The Judge's Newsletter* (vol 3, Autumn 2001 at pp 38–41) and commented upon by McEleavy at [2002] IFL 91.

taken a markedly different line, with Gaudron, Gummow and Hayne JJ going so far as to say[214] that there is no warrant for:

> '[the] conclusion that reg 16(3)(b) [which implements Art 13b of the Convention] is to be given a "narrow" rather than a "broad" construction. There is, in these circumstances, no evident choice to be made between a "narrow"and "broad" construction of the regulation. If that is what is meant by saying that it is to be given a "narrow construction" it must be rejected. The exception is to be given the meaning its words require.'

The majority did, however, add:

> 'That is not to say, however, that reg 16(3)(b) will find frequent application. It is well nigh inevitable that a child, taken from one country to another without the agreement of one parent, will suffer disruption, uncertainty and anxiety. That disruption, uncertainty and anxiety will recur, and may well be magnified, by having to return to the country of habitual residence. Regulation 16(3)(b) and Art 13(b) of the Convention intend to refer to more than this kind of result when they speak of a grave risk to the child of exposure to physical or psychological harm on return.'

17.94   Whether this in itself signals a broader approach to Art 13(b) (which, if so, is difficult to square with what was intended) remains to be seen. However, as already intimated, even within those jurisdictions where an undoubtedly restrictive interpretation operates, there is some evidence to suggest that courts may be becoming more ready to consider that the defence is made out,[215] although in the light of the decision in *TB v JB (Abduction: Grave Risk of Harm)*,[216] it is evident that, before the English courts at any rate, it remains an extremely difficult exception to establish, and indeed in *Re S (Abduction: Custody Rights)*,[217] the Court of Appeal has now expressly distanced itself from the Australian decision in this regard.

---

[214] (2001) 180 ALR 402, [2001] HCA 39 at paras [44] and [45]. In fact, this standpoint reflects the High Court's consistently held view that the Regulation be given its 'ordinary' and not an 'international' meaning, see eg *De L v Director-General, NSW Department of Community Services* (1996) FLC 92-706. This 'narrow' view of the application of the Regulations is one of the adverse consequences of effectively re-enacting the Convention in domestic legislation.

[215] See the arguments by Caldwell, 'Child welfare defences in child abduction cases – some recent developments' [2001] CFLQ 121 at 125 *et seq*. See also, in the United States, *Blondin v Dubois* 238 F 3d 153 (2d Cir 2001), discussed by Weiner, 'Navigating the Road Between Uniformity and Progress: The Need for Purposive Analysis of the Hague Convention on the Civil Aspects of International Child Abduction' (2002) 33 Columbia HRLR 276 at 339 *et seq*. According to the 1999 Statistical Survey, *op cit*, n 2, there were four refusals in England and Wales, four in Sweden (which constituted all their refusals), three in Austria, three in Germany and two in New Zealand in that year solely based on Art 13(b).

[216] [2001] 2 FLR 515, CA, and see also *Re H (Abduction: Grave Risk)* [2003] EWCA Civ 355, [2003] 2 FLR 141, both discussed at **17.110**.

[217] [2002] EWCA Civ 908, [2002] 2 FLR 815, at [45], per Ward LJ.

'Grave risk'

17.95   As already discussed,[218] the epithet 'grave' is and was intended to be an 'intensive qualifier'. It is important to appreciate, however, that 'grave' qualifies the risk and not the ensuing harm. As Balcombe LJ observed in *Re E (A Minor) (Abduction)*,[219] the defendant 'does not have to prove that the return of the child would place him in an intolerable situation [nor *mutatis mutandi* 'exposing the child to physical or psychological harm'], but that there is a grave risk that his return would place him in an intolerable situation'.

17.96   There is some authority for saying that the time for assessing what amounts to a grave risk is the time that the application is being heard,[220] by which is meant that such a risk cannot be attributed to some hypothetical future event,[221] nor, conversely, that the court should unduly delay a decision to see if appropriate measures can be taken to obviate the risk to the child upon its return.[222] On the other hand, both the English and Scottish courts[223] have surely correctly rejected the argument that, when considering Art 13(b), they cannot take into account what would happen to the child if returned. In other words, as one commentator has put it,[224] 'any assessment of the degree of risk involved [cannot] be blinkered against sight of the practical consequences of return'. However, as Lord Prosser observed in the Scottish decision, *McCarthy v McCarthy*,[225] under Art 13(b) the court 'is concerned with exposure to harm as a consequence of return, and not an exposure to harm which might emerge at a future time, if after return an unsatisfactory situation is allowed to persist without alteration'. Consequently, the court should only be concerned with the situation following upon return as viewed in the relative short term. It may be added that in assessing the risk the court is entitled to

---

[218] See **17.85**.
[219] [1989] 1 FLR 135 at 143.
[220] See the Scottish decisions *MacMillan v MacMillan* 1989 SLT 350 at 355 and *McCarthy v McCarthy* 1994 SLT 743 at 746.
[221] See, for example, *Re S (Minors) (Child Abduction: Wrongful Removal)* [1994] Fam 70, [1994] 1 FLR 82, where the alleged risk related to the instability of life in Israel coupled with the fact that the children (aged 5 years and 15 months respectively) would have to serve in the Israeli Army which Wall J held 'did not even make a case under Art 13(b)'. See also the US decision, *Nunez-Escudero v Tice-Menley* 58 F 3d 374 (8th Cir, 1995), where an unsubstantiated claim that child would be institutionalised during the pendency of custody proceedings if returned to Mexico was held insufficient to establish an Art 13(b) 'defence', and the French decision, *Chatelard c Yan Guo*, 23 October 1990, 80 Rev crit 1991, 407, in which an Art 13(b) plea on the basis of a hypothetical future trip to China and Japan (to which the father alleged the children had returned against his wishes on an earlier occasion) was rejected.
[222] *MacMillan v MacMillan* (above) at 355. But note that this needs to be treated with caution since it is common practice for the courts to enquire about the child's protection on his return. See further **17.97** below.
[223] *Re A (A Minor) (Abduction)* [1988] 1 FLR 365, CA, and *MacMillan v MacMillan* (above).
[224] McClean, 'Return of Internationally Abducted Children' (1990) 106 LQR 375 at 377.
[225] 1994 SLT 743 at 747.

weigh the risk of harm of a return against the risk of harm of refusing a return.[226]

17.97   In judging risk, it is well established that courts should accept that, unless the contrary is proved, the administrative, judicial and social service authorities of the requesting State are equally adept in protecting children as they are in the requested State.[227] Furthermore, it is widely accepted that it is proper for courts nevertheless concerned for the safety of the child to put in place a variety of protective measures, such as the acceptance of undertakings by the applicant,[228] the making of mirror or safe harbour orders by courts of the requesting State,[229] and accepting assurances from judges of the requesting State that the matter be dealt with in a particular way.[230] These developments, together with the idea that abducting parents should not be able to rely upon the risk of harm that they themselves have created,[231] when coupled with the heavy burden of proof make it extremely difficult to establish the Art 13(b) exception.

Exposing the child to physical or psychological harm or otherwise placing the child in an intolerable situation

17.98   Although the 'grave risk' relates to the separate components, namely, physical harm, psychological harm and placing the child in an intolerable situation, in practice they are rarely pleaded or treated as distinct exceptions. In any event, it will often be the case, as one commentator has said,[232] that the 'intolerable situation' will relate to a risk of harm. In *Re S (Abduction: Custody Rights)*,[233] Ward LJ concluded, after reviewing both English and overseas authority,[234] that there is:

---

[226]   See *Re A (A Minor) (Abduction)* [1988] 1 FLR 365 at 372, CA.

[227]   See eg *Re H (Abduction: Grave Risk)* [2003] EWCA Civ 355, [2003] 2 FLR 141, *Re M (Abduction: Intolerable Situation)* [2000] 1 FLR 930 and *Re L (Abduction: Pending Criminal Proceedings)* [1999] 1 FLR 433. As Lady Paton put it, in the Scottish decision, *Re Q Petitioner* 2001 SLT 243 at 249: '(3) Prima facie, one Hague Convention country court can assume that another Hague Convention country court will be able and willing to provide adequate protection, whether interim or final. (4) In [the] normal course, therefore, there is no reason to assume that the courts of the other Hague Convention country will not have either the ability or willingness to provide adequate protection. Indeed, so to assume would be "presumptuous and offensive".' See also the Australian cases, *Cooper v Casey* [1995] FLC 92–575 and *Murray v Director, Family Services, ACT* [1993] FLC 92–416.

[228]   See **17.123** *et seq* below.

[229]   *Ibid*.

[230]   See eg *Re M and J (Abduction: International Judicial Collaboration)* [2000] 1 FLR 803.

[231]   See, in particular, *C v C (Minor: Abduction: Rights of Custody)* [1989] 1 WLR 654, sub nom *Re C (A Minor) (Abduction)* [1989] 1 FLR 403, CA, discussed at **17.101**.

[232]   Caldwell, 'Child welfare defences in child abduction cases' [2001] CFLQ 121 at 124.

[233]   [2002] EWCA Civ 908, [2002] 2 FLR 815 at [410].

[234]   Viz *Re A (A Minor) (Abduction)* [1998] 1 FLR 365 at 372, per Nourse LJ; *C v C (Minor: Abduction: Rights of Custody)* (above), per Lord Donaldson MR; *Thomson v Thomson* [1994] 6 RFL (4th) 290, (1995) 119 DLR (4th) 253, Canadian Sup Ct; and *DP v Commonwealth Central*

'... considerable international support for the view that there is a link between the limbs of Art 13(b). In our judgment, the proper approach for the court considering a defence alleging a grave risk of exposure to physical or psychological harm should be to consider the grave risk of that harm as a discrete question but then stand back and test the conclusion by looking at the Article in the round reflecting whether the risk of harm is established to an extent which would lead one to say that the child will be placed in an intolerable situation if returned.'

Whether this now means that it is no longer possible for the factors to be argued in the alternative remains to be seen, although there seems no reason to doubt an earlier decision[235] that it is possible for a number of factors only when taken together as opposed to being considered separately to satisfy the intolerability test.[236]

17.99 There is Australian authority[237] for the view that the harm or intolerable situation should arise out of the return to the child's State of habitual residence and not out of fear of returning to the complaining parent. But whether this view would be accepted by the English courts may be doubted.[238] However, there is common agreement that if the requesting State has adequate procedures for protecting the child, the chances of the abducting parent successfully opposing a return order are slim.[239]

The specific application of Article 13(b)

17.100   As already intimated, the Art 13(b) exception is difficult to establish. It is also difficult to predict which cases are likely to be successful since they are dependent upon their own facts. Nevertheless, there are some common themes which the courts regard as being of importance in reaching their decision:

(1)   the extent to which it is possible to protect the abductor (primarily the mother) and the children from the risks they allegedly face in the State of habitual residence. If the court is satisfied that the requesting State has effective mechanisms (and there is a general presumption that there

---

Authority; *JLM v Director-General NSW Department of Community Services* (2001) 180 ALR 402, [2001] HCA 39, Aust High Court.

[235]   Viz *E v E (Child Abduction: Intolerable Situation)* [1998] 2 FLR 980.

[236]   But, as Hughes J held in *E v E* (above), if the factors fail cumulatively to establish an Art 13(b) exception, they cannot succeed individually.

[237]   See *Gsponer and Director General Community Services (Vic)* (1998) 12 Fam LR 755 and *In the Marriage of Murray and Tam* (1993) 16 Fam LR 982. But cf *Laing v Central Authority* (1999) 24 Fam LR 555 at 562–563, per Nicholson CJ.

[238]   See **17.149** *et seq* for discussion of the analogous issue in relation to the child's objections to a return.

[239]   See, for example, *Re M (Abduction: Intolerable Situation)* [2000] 1 FLR 930, discussed at **17.107**, and *Re S (Abduction: Return to Care)* [1999] 1 FLR 843, discussed at **17.114**.

are)[240] to provide protection from domestic violence and/or to supervise contact in cases of alleged violence and sexual abuse, it is likely that the children will be returned;

(2) whether or not the applicant (primarily the father) is willing to make undertakings to safeguard the interests of the other parent and children. Where, for example, the father is prepared to give undertakings to provide the mother with her own accommodation so that she does not have to cohabit with him, and sufficient financial support, agrees not to pursue a criminal prosecution of the mother and undertakes not to remove the children from her care until after the courts of the State of habitual residence have ruled on the issue of custody, it will be difficult for the mother to make good her case under Art 13(b);

(3) the link the abductor has with the requested State. Of particular importance is whether the abductor is 'coming home'. Abducting parents who have little connection with the requested State are likely to find themselves swiftly being sent back to the State of habitual residence; and

(4) the court will examine whether the applicant is seeking custody or joint access in the State of habitual residence and, particularly in the case of a father, whether he is able to look after the children if the mother refuses to return. If the father cannot provide care, and the children are young, a return may not be a practical possibility, and a grave risk of harm may be established.

Separation of the child from the primary care-giver

17.101 In general, English courts have set their face against the plea that the child will suffer a grave risk of harm because the care-giver (usually the mother) refuses to return with child to the State of habitual residence. As Butler-Sloss LJ explained in *C v C (Minor: Abduction: Rights of Custody)*,[241] in such cases:

---

[240] See **17.97**. Note that under the revised Brussels II Regulation as between Member States, a court will not be able to refuse a return under Art 13(b) 'if it is established that adequate arrangements have been made to secure the protection of the child after his or her return'.

[241] [1989] 1 WLR 654, sub nom *Re C (A Minor) (Abduction)* [1989] 1 FLR 403, CA. This decision has been expressly endorsed in Australia in *Director-General, Department of Community Services Central Authority v Crowe* (1996) FLC 92–717. See also *Department of Health and Community Services v Karide* (unreported), 23 May 1996, discussed by Kaye, 'The Hague Convention and the Flight from Domestic Violence: How Women and Children are being Returned by Coach and Four' (1999) 13 Int Jo of Law, Policy and the Family 191 at 197. See also *Re C (Abduction: Grave Risk of Psychological Harm)* [1999] 1 FLR 1145, CA, in which a return order was made, notwithstanding that, because of allegations made against him, the stepfather (the children were living with the mother, stepfather and half-sister in England) would not be permitted to enter the United States. This order effectively split up the family. For a discussion of the similar position in Spain in this respect, see Beilfuss, 'International Child Abduction in Spain' (2001) 15 Int Jo of Law, Policy and the Family 327 at 338. But cf the French decision, *Re Shamee* Trib gr inst de Colmar 2d, referred to by Silberman, 'Hague International Child Abduction Convention: A Progress Report' (1994) 57 *Law and Contemporary Problems* 210 at 239.

'The grave risk of harm arises not from the return of the child, but the refusal of the mother to accompany him ... Is a parent to create the psychological situation, and then rely upon it? If the grave risk of psychological harm to a child is to be inflicted by the conduct of the parents who abducted him, then it would be relied upon by every mother of a young child who removed him out of the jurisdiction and refused to return. It would drive a coach and four through the Convention ...'

17.102 A harsh application of a court not allowing a defendant to rely upon her own wrongdoing is *Re C (Abduction: Grave Risk of Physical or Psychological Harm)*.[242] In that case the mother wrongfully removed her 6-year-old son together with his 14-year-old half-sister (who was not the subject of proceedings) from Cyprus. There was evidence that the girl had been unhappy in Cyprus, that she was well settled in England and that she would refuse to return. The mother pleaded that returning the boy to Cyprus would mean splitting the family, forcing her to choose whether to stay in England with her daughter or go back to Cyprus with her son. At first instance, it was held that if the boy was ordered to return to Cyprus he would lose his sister and possibly his mother which, in the judge's view, put the boy at grave risk of psychological harm. This was overruled on appeal, the Court of Appeal holding that the trial judge had given too much weight to the position of the girl and to the dilemma created by the mother. The court pointed out that Art 13(b) provided an exceptional remedy intended to deal with unusual cases which were outside the normal provisions of the Convention. Thorpe LJ commented:[243]

'In many cases, a balanced analysis of the assertion that an order for return would expose the child to the risk of grave psychological harm leads to the conclusion that the respondent is in reality relying upon her own wrongdoing in order to build up the statutory defence. In testing the validity of an Art 13(b) defence, trial judges should usefully ask themselves what were the intolerable features of the child's family life immediately prior to the wrongful abduction. If the answer be scant or non-existent then the circumstances in which the Art 13(b) defence would be upheld are difficult to hypothesise. In my opinion Art 13(b) is given its proper construction if ordinarily confined to meet the case where the mother's motivation for flight is to remove the child from a family situation that is damaging the child's development.'

17.103 The foregoing should not be taken to mean that the refusal of a mother to accompany her child back to the State of habitual residence can never be considered to give rise to a grave risk of harm to the child if returned.[244] Conversely, it cannot be assumed that, because the abducting

---

[242] [1999] 2 FLR 478, CA.

[243] *Ibid* at 487–488.

[244] Cf *D v D (Child Abduction: Non-Convention Country)* [1994] 1 FLR 137, in which, applying Hague Convention principles, it was held that a grave risk of harm within the contemplation of Art 13(b) had been established, *inter alia*, because the mother could not return with her two children (aged 3 and 7) because of her pregnancy. See also the NZ cases, *Hollins v Crozier* [2000] NZFLR 775 at 787, per Judge Doogue, and *S v S* [1999] NZFLR 625, and the

parent agrees to accompany the child if a return is ordered, an Art 13(b) plea will inevitably fail. For example, in *Re G (Abduction: Psychological Harm)*,[245] a return was refused on the basis that if the mother were to return with the children, as she would have done had the order been made, there was a grave risk that the children would have been exposed to physical or psychological harm because their mother's mental health would seriously deteriorate.

17.104 Separation from the primary care-giver can also be caused by returning with the child, particularly if that person is liable to criminal proceedings. However, in *Re L (Abduction: Pending Criminal Proceedings)*,[246] it was held that neither the possibility of criminal proceedings being brought nor even the possibility of the mother being arrested at the airport on her return was enough to establish a grave risk of harm to the children. It was also held in *Re C (Abduction: Grave Risk of Psychological Harm)*[247] that the possibility that the father would change his mind and bring criminal proceedings against the mother if she returned to the United States, combined with the potential splitting up of the family as the stepfather (whom the mother married after abducting the children) would not be permitted to enter the United States, was not sufficient to establish the exception under Art 13(b). Similarly, in *Re K (Abduction: Psychological Harm)*,[248] a mother who contended that, as she had no immigration status, she would be unable to support herself and would not therefore exercise any possession rights as defined by a Texan court, failed to convince the court that the child would be placed in an intolerable position if ordered to be returned to the United States. In contrast, in *The Ontario Court v M and M (Abduction: Children's Objections)*,[249] Hollis J considered the concern of a 14-year-old that she would be returned to the country of her grandmother (who had obtained in Canada a sole custody order following the abduction by both parents) whom she disliked and feared, which would thus intrude into her happy family life with her parents (her adoptive father had been deported from Canada and could not therefore return) would place her in an intolerable situation, within the meaning of Art 13(b).

Canadian decisions, *Mahler v Mahler* (2000) 3 RFL (5th) 428 at 438, per Little J, and *Thomson v Thomson* (1994) 6 RFL (4th) 290, 328, (1995) 119 DLR (4th) 253, 286, per La Forest J, discussed by Caldwell, in 'Child welfare defences in child abduction cases – some recent developments' [2001] CFLQ 121 at 128.

[245] [1995] 1 FLR 64, discussed further at **17.118**.

[246] [1999] 1 FLR 433. Note, however, that US rules have been eased through the use of 'Significant Public Benefit Parole' to facilitate the return of an abductor who might otherwise have no right of entry to the United States. See also *Re M and J (Abduction; International Judicial Collaboration)* [2000] 1 FLR 803, where, following discussion with a Californian judge, the warrant for the mother's arrest was recalled and quashed.

[247] [1999] 1 FLR 1145, CA. Note that in that case there was also evidence of the father's past violence towards the children but, as the first instance judge had concluded, there was no grave risk of harm to the children given that the father was to be supervised by the US court.

[248] [1995] 2 FLR 550, CA. See also, in Scotland, *C v C* 2003 SLT 793.

[249] [1997] 1 FLR 475.

Separating siblings

17.105 In those cases where the court refuses to return older siblings, for example, because of their objections (discussed below),[250] it can be argued that returning a younger sibling and thus separating them would cause grave harm within the meaning of Art 13(b). This argument succeeded in *B v K (Child Abduction)*,[251] where, having held that two older siblings should not be returned because of their objections, Johnson J ruled that a return order should also be refused in respect of a third child since, if he were returned and his two siblings were not, he would be exposed to psychological harm and placed in an intolerable position within the meaning of Art 13(b). In *Re T (Abduction: Child's Objections to Return)*,[252] the Court of Appeal came to a similar conclusion, albeit reluctantly, in relation to a 6-year-old (who was too young and immature for his views to be taken into account) whose 11-year-old sister on whom he was dependent (at times she was his 'little mother') had successfully objected to being returned to her mother in Spain, notwithstanding a Spanish court's assessment that whatever the mother's past failing she was currently capable of discharging her responsibilities properly.

Domestic violence[253]

17.106 Research evidence suggests that domestic violence is a common background to international child abduction.[254] As the Convention provides no specific 'defence' of domestic violence, the plea for non-return in such cases inevitably focuses on the application of Art 13(b). In this respect, it is important to appreciate that violence *per se* is insufficient to found an Art 13(b) exception, rather, from the court's point of view, the vital consideration is whether the child and abducting parent will have sufficient protection if they return to the State of habitual residence. In assessing this, the court looks at all the circumstances, including the requesting State's ability to give adequate protection and any undertakings the left-behind parent is prepared to give

---

[250] See **17.141** *et seq.*

[251] [1993] 1 FCR 382, [1993] Fam Law 17. But note that Johnson J's approach to the question of the children's objections has since been disapproved: see **17.151**, n 369.

[252] [2000] 2 FLR 192 at 212–219, per Ward LJ, and at 221–222, per Sedley LJ.

[253] For excellent overviews of both the law and the literature on this issue, see Weiner, 'International Child Abduction and the Escape from Domestic Violence' (2000) 69 *Fordham Law Review* 593, and Kaye, 'The Hague Convention and the Flight from Domestic Violence: How Women and Children are being Returned by Coach and Four' (1999) 13 Int Jo of Law, Policy and the Family 191.

[254] See Greif and Hegar, *When Parents Kidnap* (Free Press, 1993) who estimated that, in their American study of 368 left-behind parents, violence was present in 54% of the relationships. See also Girdner, Chiancone and Johnson, 'International Child Abductors: Profile of the Abductors Most Likely to Succeed' (1997) Presentation to the 2nd World Congress on Family Law and the Rights of Children and Youths in San Francisco, whose research indicates that in relation to those families that experience international child abduction, 'Family violence is a characteristic of most of these families'.

(particularly providing separate accommodation) to ensure the protection of the returning parent and child.

The English cases

17.107   The English courts, in line with other jurisdictions,[255] have generally been reluctant to base refusals to return on allegations of violence. For example, in *Re M (Abduction: Intolerable Situation)*,[256] a return order was made notwithstanding the mother's genuine fear of physical harm by her husband who, having been imprisoned for murdering someone whom he believed to be having an affair with the mother, was due to be released. The court considered that the mother would be adequately protected by the Norwegian authorities to whom mirror undertakings had been given. Similarly, in *Re M (Abduction: Acquiescence)*,[257] where there was evidence that the father had physically abused the child some 4 years previously, Thorpe J concluded that, as the child had since been properly protected by his mother, *inter alia*, by ensuring that contact with the father had always been in her presence, 'it seems to me that such risk as there may be of physical injury or psychological injury ... would be the consequence of unsupervised exposure to [the] father rather than of return to the father's homeland'. In his view, on the evidence before him, Art 13(b) had not been satisfied.[258]

17.108   A rare example of a parent successfully opposing a return order on the basis of violence is *Re F (A Minor) (Abduction: Custody Rights Abroad)*,[259] which was the first English decision where the grave harm exception succeeded. In this case there was uncontroverted evidence that the father had been violent both to the child (who was aged 4 and was asthmatic) and the mother and grandmother. He had thrown the mother and child out of the house and made threats to kill them both. Even after the mother had obtained a restraining order against him, the father had engaged in a campaign of intimidation and harassment. This violence had a serious effect upon the child who began both to suffer nightmares and bedwetting and to become unusually aggressive at his child care centre and at home. Since leaving his

---

[255]   See **17.111** *et seq.*

[256]   [2000] 1 FLR 930.

[257]   [1996] 1 FLR 315. See also *Re B (Minors)* (1997) 14 October (unreported), in which a mother, having removed the child from Portugal to England via the United States, alleged that the father had been violent to both her and the eldest child. However, following undertakings given by the father both as to finances and, crucially, separate accommodation for the mother and children, it was held that a grave risk of harm could not be found. For a not dissimilar case, see *K v K (Child Abduction)* [1998] 3 FCR 207. See also *Re C (Abduction: Grave Risk of Psychological Harm)* [1999] 1 FLR 1145, CA, in which, notwithstanding charges of serious harm, the court was satisfied that the Californian authorities could adequately protect both the child's physical and psychological well-being.

[258]   In fact, the court refused to order a return on the basis that the initial removal had not been wrongful.

[259]   [1995] Fam 224, [1995] 3 WLR 339, sub nom *Re F (Child Abduction: Risk of Return)* [1995] 2 FLR 31, CA.

home State, his behaviour improved and his nightmares and bedwetting ceased, but he regressed again upon learning he might have to return home. It was held that to return the child would be to place him back in the same situation[260] which had caused him so much distress and would present too great a risk. In the court's view, therefore, a grave risk of harm had been established and a return order was refused.

17.109   *Re F* was an extreme case. Not only was the violence severe, but the father made no attempt to refute the allegations. Moreover, it was apparent that court orders could not guarantee the child's protection. This lack of assurance as to protection may also help to explain the decision not to return the child in *Re M (Abduction: Leave to Appeal)*.[261] In that case, an English mother had wrongfully removed her 2-year-old son from South Africa where she and his father, a South African Zulu, were habitually resident. Graphic evidence was presented of considerable violence between the father and the mother,[262] which was corroborated by independent witnesses, including a social worker.[263] At first instance, Sir Stephen Brown P was satisfied that the child was not himself at risk of violence but he found the child to be wholly dependent upon the mother and could not be parted from her. Regard was also evidently[264] had to the father having a position of considerable influence in the country and to the consequent inverse power structure between him and the mother (ie there seemed concerns about whether the mother could be adequately protected on her return to South Africa). It was accordingly held that the child was at grave risk of psychological harm, and a return order was refused. On appeal, Butler-Sloss LJ commented that on the papers she would, on balance, have returned the child, but given the oral evidence that had unusually been admitted and as she had not seen the witnesses and heard that evidence, she was reluctant to overturn the decision.

17.110   Notwithstanding the above two decisions, it is evident that the English courts continue to be reluctant to base refusals on violence. At any rate, the plea failed in *TB v JB (Abduction: Grave Risk of Harm)*.[265] This case was unusual in that the source of the alleged risk to the children in question was not their father, the mother's first husband, but the mother's second husband, the father of her youngest child, who was not the subject of the proceedings. The mother, who indisputably had wrongfully removed the three children by

---

[260]   It was accepted by the court that if the mother were to return home she would have to go back to the matrimonial home.

[261]   [1999] 2 FLR 550, CA.

[262]   Photographs, adduced by the mother and taken soon after the violence, showed 'quite horrifying marks on the back of the mother'.

[263]   The President, Sir Stephen Brown had, unusually, heard oral evidence from both the father and the mother and from a consultant psychiatrist.

[264]   The report is rather brief on this: see 551F.

[265]   [2001] 2 FLR 515, CA.

her first husband[266] (plus her child by her second husband) from New Zealand to England, claimed that her primary motivation for leaving was to get away from her second husband (against whom there were allegations of maltreatment both of the mother and of the children and of bizarre behaviour) and that she was too frightened to return. The first husband applied for the return of the three older children, but at first instance this was refused under Art 13(b) on the basis of expert evidence that the mother was seriously vulnerable to the anxieties created by the second husband and that she was suffering from mild to moderate depression which would be exacerbated by a return. Accordingly, it was held that the children (who were each found to be troubled and upset)[267] would be exposed to a grave risk of harm because the mother would face the same risks as previously and may cease to cope with the pressure that could be placed on her. On appeal, however, by a majority this decision was overruled. In Laws LJ's view, Art 13(b) could only be satisfied in truly exceptional cases, of which this was not one. Arden LJ accepted that a deterioration of the mother's condition and consequently in her ability to care for her children could be sufficient to satisfy Art 13(b), but she considered that, in evaluating such a risk, the court was entitled to expect that the mother would make all appropriate use of orders of the New Zealand courts for her own and her children's protection. In her Ladyship's view, given the New Zealand court's powers to protect the mother and her children, a 'grave risk' could not be said to have been made out. Dissenting, Hale LJ recognised the vulnerability of victims of domestic abuse and did not believe that, on these facts, the New Zealand courts could realistically protect the mother and therefore the children, so that the Art 13(b) exception had been made out.[268] The court took a similarly hard line in *Re H (Abduction: Grave Risk),*[269] rejecting a mother's Art 13(b) plea based on her husband's violence (triggered by incessant and excessive drinking) both to her and to the children. Overruling a first instance decision not to return, the Court of Appeal was satisfied that the Belgian authorities were capable of managing the problem.

The position in other jurisdictions

17.111 The English reluctance to refuse a return for reasons of domestic violence is shared by other jurisdictions, notably Australia,[270]

---

[266] With whom there was a joint custody agreement.

[267] Indeed, the oldest child (aged 14), who had not seen her father since 1990, objected to returning.

[268] It may be noted that subsequent to this decision, the mother sought to set the order aside on the twin bases of fresh evidence as to her emotional state and the impracticality of enforcing the order, but this attempt failed: *Re B (Children) (Abduction: New Evidence)* [2001] EWCA Civ 625, [2001] 2 FCR 531. However, the children strongly resisted being taken to the airport, and a stay was placed on the return order.

[269] [2003] EWCA Civ 355, [2003] 2 FLR 141.

[270] See eg *Gsponer v Johnstone* (1989) FLC 92–001, *Gollogly and Owen* (1989) 13 Fam LR 622, *Murray v Director, Family Services, ACT* (1993) FLC 92–416 and *Cooper v Casey* (1995) FLC 92–416.

Canada,[271] Ireland,[272] New Zealand,[273] Scotland,[274] and the United States.[275] Nevertheless, as in England and Wales, there are now instances in each of those jurisdictions where violence has led to a refusal based on Art 13(b). In Scotland, for example, in one of the first cases to succeed under Art 13(b), *MacMillan v MacMillan*,[276] a return was refused on the basis of a grave risk of harm on account of the father's long-term depression, alcoholism and his violence towards the mother and child. Similarly, in the Canadian decision, *Pollastro v Pollastro*,[277] it was held that a return order should be refused. In that case the violence was directed against the mother, but the court reasoned that returning the 6-month-old child to a violent, volatile environment would place her in an inherently intolerable situation because of the possible harm both to the child and to the mother on whom the child was totally dependent. A not dissimilar reasoning led to a refusal to return in the New Zealand decision, *Mok v Cornelisson*.[278]

17.112   In the United States, Art 13(b) was found to be established both in *Walsh v Walsh*[279] and in *Blondin v Dubois (Blondin IV)*.[280] In the former case, the appellate court held that the district court had erred by ignoring the violence, which the children had witnessed, perpetrated by one spouse on the other. As the court pointed out, it was accepted both by State and Federal law that 'children are at increased risk of physical and psychological injury themselves when they are in contact with a spousal abuser'. In the latter, the father was physically violent both to the mother (hitting her with a belt) and to the child (including twisting some cord around her neck and threatening to kill both her

---

271   See eg *Finizio v Scoppio-Finizio* (2000) 1 RFL (5th) 222 and *Mahler v Mahler* (2000) 3 RFL (5th) 428, discussed by Caldwell, 'Child welfare defences in child abduction cases – some recent developments' [2001] CFLQ 121 at 129, and Bailey, 'Canada's Implementation of the 1980 Hague Convention on the Civil Aspects of International Child Abduction' [2000] 33 New York Jo of Intl Law and Politics 17 at 36–37.

272   See the general position as stated by *AS v PS* [1998] 2 IR 244.

273   See *A v A* [1996] NZFLR 529 and *S v S* [1999] NZFLR 625, discussed by Caldwell, *op cit*, n 271 above, at 126.

274   See the discussion eg in *Starr v Starr* 1999 SLT 335.

275   See eg *Tabacchi v Harrison* No 99C4130, 2000 WL (ND 111 10 February 2000) and *Nunez-Escudero v Tice-Menley* 58 F 3d 374 (8th Cir 1995), discussed by Weiner in 'International Child Abduction and the Escape from Domestic Violence' (2000) 69 *Fordham Law Review* 593 at 654 *et seq*.

276   1989 SLT 350, on which see McClean (1990) 106 LQR 375.

277   (1999) 171 DLR (4th) 32, Ontario CA; discussed by Caldwell, *op cit*, n 271 above, at 128–129 and Weiner, *op cit*, n 275 above, at 652–653.

278   [2000] NZFLR 582, discussed by Caldwell, *op cit*, n 271 above, at 128, and Weiner, 'Navigating the Road Between Uniformity and Progress: The Need for Purposive Analysis of the Hague Convention on the Civil Aspects of International Child Abduction' (2002) 33 Columbia HRLR 275 at 338. For examples of refusals in Ireland based on violence, see eg *MA v PR* [1993] 2 Fam LJ 52, *DC v VLC* (unreported) January 1995 (High Court), and *M v D* (unreported) 20 January 1999 (High Court).

279   221 F 3d 204 (1st Cir 2000), discussed by Weiner, *op cit*, n 271 above, at 653.

280   238 F 3d 153 (2nd Cir 2001), discussed by Weiner, *op cit*, n 280 above, at 339 *et seq*. See also *Rodrigues v Rodrigues* 33 F Supp 2d 456 (D Md 1999), discussed by Weiner, *ibid*, at 358–359.

and her mother). The abuse continued even after the parties temporarily reconciled before the mother wrongfully brought the child to the United States. After hearing testimony from Dr AJ Solnit (the world-famous expert in child psychiatry and psychology) to the effect that a return would trigger a recurrence of the post-traumatic stress disorder that the child had suffered before arrival in the United States, it was held that, notwithstanding the French ability and willingness to protect the mother and children from the father's violence, Art 13(b) had been satisfied and a return should be refused.

17.113 Although the appalling behaviour of the father in *Blondin* would seem to justify a finding of grave harm, the decision has been criticised[281] in particular for relying too heavily on the expert evidence, since that smacked of a best interests merits enquiry.

Sexual abuse

17.114 As with allegations of violence, allegations of sexual abuse of the child by the wronged parent are not in themselves sufficient to establish a grave risk of harm. The central issue is whether the child will be adequately protected if he or she is returned to the State of habitual residence. A good illustration is *Re S (Abduction: Return to Care)*[282] in which a father wrongfully refused to return his 9-year-old daughter to the mother in Sweden, following the child's allegation that the mother's cohabitant had sexually abused her. The Swedish authorities took the allegations seriously when informed and asked the mother to undertake a residential assessment, which she agreed to do. They also informed her that if she had refused, the child would have been taken into care. Sir Stephen Brown P held that in view of these arrangements the child's return to Sweden would not expose her to grave harm or place her in an intolerable position and that, accordingly, the Art 13(b) plea failed.

17.115 A similar result obtained in *N v N (Abduction: Article 13 Defence)*[283] where, notwithstanding that an allegation of sexual abuse against the applicant's father was made by the mother, the child was ordered to be returned.

17.116 These cases may be contrasted with the Scottish decision, *Re Q Petitioner*,[284] in which a return was refused because the Court of Session was not convinced that the French courts would adequately protect two children against the suspected abuse by the father, given their failure to do so in the past.

---

[281] See Weiner, *op cit*, n 280 above, at 344 *et seq*.
[282] [1999] 1 FLR 843.
[283] [1995] 1 FLR 107. See also, in Ireland, *AS v PS (Child Abduction)* [1998] 2 IR 244.
[284] 2001 SLT 243, Outer House, Court of Session.

Mental disorder on the part of the wronged parent

17.117   In a small number of cases, the abducting parent has sought to rely on mental illness as the foundation of an Art 13(b) exception. It would appear, however, that mental illness suffered by the wronged parent is unlikely to constitute sufficient reason to find the requisite grave risk of harm. As with domestic violence, the court's concern is with future risk and the ability of the State of habitual residence to provide sufficient protection. In *Re P (Minors)*[285] the father suffered from acute depressive reaction. The reasons for his mental illness were not clear but, following the abduction of the children and the making of an application under the Hague Abduction Convention, the father suffered a relapse and set fire to the matrimonial home with himself locked in. Medical evidence showed an uncertain prognosis dependent on whether there was likely to be a reconciliation. If there were not and there were to be protracted proceedings, it was likely that there could be further episodes and associated suicidal tendencies.[286] Oral evidence indicated that the mother would not contemplate reconciliation and that the father would continue to seek it, and was likely to use any contact to press his case. At first instance, the Art 13(b) exception was found to be established[287] but this was overturned on appeal. The medical evidence was found not to be sufficient to justify a finding of physical or psychological harm. The father was found by the court to be much recovered and weight was placed on the fact that he had been a good father before his illness.

17.118   *Re P* may be contrasted with *Re G (Abduction: Psychological Harm)*.[288] In that case, both parents were English but were habitually resident in the United States. The mother retained the children (all of whom had joint nationality) in England after a holiday but opposed their return on the basis of Art 13(b). She produced evidence from her doctor and psychiatrist that she was suffering from depression which a return to the United States would severely exacerbate. At first instance, it was found that the mother had herself caused the situation and could not establish harm to the children if they were to return, and a return order was made. On appeal, however, the mother introduced a psychiatric report which indicated that there was a considerable danger of the mother becoming psychotic and losing her reason. The case was resubmitted to the original judge for a rehearing on the basis of a finding that the children (aged 3 and twins aged 1) were both physically and emotionally

---

[285]   [1997] EWCA Civ 1886 (17 June 1997). A plea based, *inter alia*, on the applicant's mental incapability to cope with the children failed in the Scottish case, *McCarthy v McCarthy* 1994 SLT 743.

[286]   The hearing was adjourned for 2 weeks to allow for oral evidence. A report and oral evidence from a court welfare officer was also admitted in evidence.

[287]   The first instance judge believed that the children might be placed at grave risk of physical harm if the father had a further mental attack, and speculated that such a recurrence might extend beyond the suicidal to threaten the mother or the lives of the children. There was, however, no firm evidence to back this up.

[288]   [1995] 1 FLR 64.

dependent on the mother. Accordingly, if there was a degree of risk to the mother's mental health, it was impossible to say that there was not at least a case for investigation under Art 13. At that rehearing, Ewbank J concluded that the effect of an order returning the children to the United States 'would be that there would be a serious deterioration in the mother's condition and the children would be affected accordingly'. A return order was therefore refused.

17.119   *Re G* was expressly followed in the New Zealand decision, *Armstrong v Evans*,[289] in which it was found that the mother was at risk of severely impaired psychological functioning or suicide if she returned to Australia where she had endured a 12-year-long violent relationship with the applicant. The risk of suicide by the respondent's mother was also at the heart of the dispute in the Australian case, *JLM v Director-General NSW Department of Government Services*,[290] although in the event, the case was remitted for rehearing.

Lack of protection in the requesting State

17.120   Although, as has been said,[291] it is generally assumed that the authorities of the requesting State can adequately protect the child, if it can be shown that they cannot, or are incapable of or, even unwilling to, offer that protection, then an Art 13(b) case may well succeed.[292] It seems evident, however, that it is hard to establish a grave risk of harm based on speculation as opposed to proven inadequacies in the particular cases.[293] Certainly pleas as to the difficulties relating to the requesting State's legal system have so far met with little success before the English courts. Thus, in *Re O (Child Abduction: Undertakings)*,[294] while Singer J accepted that if it could be shown that under the law of the requesting State there is some fixed embargo on allowing the removal of children or precluding the removal of children by a parent who had once wrongly removed them, or that the length of time that the requesting State might take to decide issues concerning children is excessive, that could satisfy Art 13(b), he rejected all such arguments in the case before him. Similarly in *Re S (Abduction: Intolerable Situation: Beth Din)*,[295] Connell J rejected the mother's claim that she would be unable to get justice from the religious

---

[289] [2000] NZFLR 984, discussed by Caldwell, *op cit*, n 271 above, at 127.

[290] (2001) 180 ALR 402, [2001] HCA 39, Aust High Court, on which see McEleavy at [2002] IFL 91.

[291] See **17.97**.

[292] Cf *Friedrich v Friedrich* 78 F 3d 1060 (6th Cir 1996), discussed at **17.91**.

[293] Cf *Re F (A Minor) (Abduction: Custody Rights Abroad)* [1995] Fam 224, [1995] 3 WLR 339, sub nom *Re F (Child Abduction: Risk of Return)* [1995] 2 FLR 31, CA, discussed at **17.108**, where notwithstanding restraining orders made against him, the father continued his campaign of intimidation.

[294] [1994] 2 FLR 349 at 356. See also *Cameron v Cameron (No 3)* 1997 SCLR 192 at 194, where it was hinted that were it thought that the subsequent custody proceedings in the requesting State could not be dealt with quickly, that could amount to 'intolerability' within the meaning of Art 13(b).

[295] [2000] 1 FLR 454.

court in Israel, the Beth Din, and that as a woman she would be discriminated against since she would be unable to obtain a 'get' without the positive assistance and consent of the father. Similarly, lack of legal aid[296] or even legal representation[297] in the requesting State have been held not to constitute 'intolerability' for the purposes of Art 13(b). With respect to the latter, Leggatt LJ commented:[298]

> 'It appears to me that any such court such as the relevant Texan court can well see that justice is done, even if the mother proves not to be able to obtain legal representation.'

17.121   As posited in the American decision, *Friedrich v Friedrich*,[299] if it can be shown that the requesting State is inherently dangerous on account of civil unrest, war, famine or disease, that might be sufficient to satisfy Art 13(b). In this regard, a number of cases have been concerned with children being returned to Israel since the present *intifada* which began in September 2000.[300] However, until recently, courts both in England and elsewhere have rejected claims that the child was at grave risk of harm because of the security situation.[301] In the leading English case, *Re S (Abduction: Custody Rights)*,[302] the Court of Appeal refused to interfere with a decision to return a child to Israel. Whilst acknowledging that there was a risk of harm because of the worsening situation, it was not felt to be so great as to amount to a grave risk within the contemplation of Art 13(b), nor did the court accept the argument that because of her anxieties and concerns (which were considerable) the child was at a grave risk from the breakdown in the mother's health. The court accepted that *the mother* would find a return to Israel 'intolerable', but that was not the test under Art 13(b). Article 13(b) was however, held to be satisfied in the Australian decision *Genish-Grant v Director-General, Department of Community Services*.[303]

17.122   In some cases it has been argued that the child's health could be impaired by being returned. Whilst in theory this could establish a grave risk of harm, such arguments have so far met with little success. For example, in a

---

[296]   *Foster v Foster* 24 May 1993, Lexis, Northern Ireland.

[297]   *Re K (Abduction: Psychological Harm)* [1995] 2 FLR 550, CA.

[298]   *Ibid* at 554.

[299]   78 F 3d 1060 (6th Cir 1996).

[300]   See generally E Freedman, 'International Terrorism and the Grave Physical Risk Defence of the Hague Convention on International Child Abduction' [2002] IFL 60.

[301]   See eg the US decision, *Freier v Freier* 969 F Supp 436; *Cornfield v Cornfield* Superior Court of Justice Ontario, File 01-FA-10575, 30 November 2001; and *Watkins v Watkins* (Docket No IF3709/00 of 25 January 2001, District Court of Zweibrüchen, Germany), discussed by Freedman, *op cit*, n 300 above.

[302]   [2002] EWCA Civ 908, [2002] 2 FLR 815.

[303]   Judgment dated 27 May 2002. Cf *Silverman v Silverman*, 8th Cir No 02-2496 (8 May 2003, US Court of Appeals for the 8th Circuit, sitting *en banc*) ('*War Zone defence*': Israel not a zone of war). The authors would like to thank Dr Rhona Schuz for bringing these decisions to their attention.

Spanish case,[304] it was held that the fact that the child's health improved with the weather in Lanzarotti did not mean that the girl would suffer a grave risk of harm if returned to her habitual residence in Germany. On the other hand, the Australian case, *DP v Commonwealth Central Authority*,[305] in which it was argued that the child's autism, diagnosed only after arriving in Australia, could not be treated in the area of Greece where he formerly lived, was remitted by the Australian High Court for a rehearing on the basis that the lower courts had erred in relying on the availability of services somewhere in Greece. In the High Court's view, given the lack of services in the child's home locality, a finding of grave risk could have been made.

Undertakings, safe harbour orders and mirror orders

17.123 Mention has already been made of the acceptance of undertakings to alleviate what might have been an otherwise intolerable situation and thus to limit the ambit of Art 13(b).[306] This practice was first pioneered by the English courts.[307] As Butler-Sloss LJ explained in the leading case, *Re M (Abduction: Undertakings)*,[308] undertakings are accepted to make the return of children easier and to provide for their necessities such as a roof over their heads and adequate maintenance.[309] Where a party is not in a position to give extensive undertakings to the court, the court will not require them.[310]

17.124 Undertakings are not meant to provide long-term solutions; rather, they should have a short life, that is, until the court of the child's habitual residence becomes seised of the proceedings. Accordingly, the court should be careful not in any way to usurp or be thought to usurp the functions of the court of habitual residence. As Singer J put it:[311]

---

[304] See the case of 27 November 1999, referred to in Beilfuss, 'International Child Abduction in Spain' (2001) 15 Int Jo of Law, Policy and the Family 327 at 337.

[305] (2001) 180 ALR 402, [2001] HCA 39, Aust High Ct, on which see McEleavy [2002] IFL 91.

[306] See *Re O (Child Abduction: Undertakings)* [1994] 2 FLR 349, in which Singer J commented that, so far as the English courts were concerned, there was no doubt that it was permissible to accept undertakings to alleviate what would otherwise be an intolerable situation for the purposes of Art 13(b). Note also *Re R (Abduction: Child's Objections)* [1995] 1 FLR 977 (the court was entitled to have regard to whether any risk of harm could be reduced or might be extinguishable by undertakings); *Re O (Child Abduction: Undertakings) (No 2)* referred to at [1994] Fam Law 651; and *Re K (Abduction: Psychological Harm)* [1995] 2 FLR 550, CA.

[307] See *C v C (Abduction: Rights of Custody Abroad)* [1989] 1 WLR 654, sub nom *Re C (A Minor) (Abduction)* [1989] 1 FLR 403, CA, and *Re G (A Minor) (Abduction)* [1989] 2 FLR 475, CA.

[308] [1995] 1 FLR 1021, CA.

[309] In the earlier case of *C v C* (above), the English Court of Appeal accepted nine undertakings from the applicant father including securing a place at a named preparatory school, payment of medical expenses and the provision of a car. The current practice in England requires for more limited undertakings: see Chapter 21.

[310] See *Re A (Minors) (Abduction: Custody Rights)* [1992] Fam 106, [1992] 2 WLR 536, sub nom *Re A (Minors) (Abduction: Acquiescence)* [1992] 2 FLR 14, CA.

[311] In *Re M and J (Abduction: International Judicial Collaboration)* [2000] 1 FLR 803 at 808–809. See also *C v C* (above), per Lord Donaldson MR, at 660 and 413, respectively: 'It will be the

'... it is now well established ... that ... undertakings should not be accepted by the court save to the extent that they regulate affairs relating to the child up to but not beyond the door of the court of the children's habitual residence.'

Furthermore, the undertakings must not be so elaborate that their implementation might become bogged down in protracted hearings and investigations. In this latter regard, it is helpful to include in the court order realistic time limits within which undertakings must be complied with. It has been said[312] that, on directions hearings, the court should consider including a direction that the parties identify:

'(a)   any undertakings that they seek; and
(b)   any undertakings that they are prepared to give to focus the attention of the parties to proceedings on the detail of such undertakings with a view to avoiding or reducing negotiations as to undertakings during the hearing.'

17.125   This approach to the breadth of undertakings has also been taken in Canada,[313] Ireland,[314] and New Zealand,[315] among other common law countries. In *P v B*,[316] the Supreme Court of Ireland pointed out that there is a distinction between undertakings as to short-term accommodation and maintenance, which are compatible with the Convention and international law, and undertakings which address the long-term education and maintenance of the child and longer-term access to the child, which are not compatible with the Convention and trespass on the jurisdiction of the courts of the requesting State. The United States Court of Appeals has on a number of occasions reviewed the role and limitations of undertakings.[317] An express domestic basis for undertakings was provided in 1995 when the Australian implementing Regulations[318] were amended to include reg 15(1)(c), which enables a court ordering a return to include in the order 'a condition that the court considers to be appropriate to give effect to the Convention'.

17.126   The assumption behind the use of this type of undertaking is that the courts of the country to which the child is to be returned can properly take

---

concern of the court of the State to which the child is to be returned to minimise or eliminate this harm and, in the absence of compelling evidence to the contrary or evidence that is beyond the powers of those courts in the circumstances of the case, the courts of this country should assume that this will be done. Save in an exceptional case, our concern, ie the concern of these courts, should be limited to giving the child the maximum possible protection until the courts of the other country, Australia in this case, can resume their normal role in relation to the child'.

312   Per Charles J in *Re M (Abduction: Intolerable Situation)* [2000] 1 FLR 930 at 941.
313   See the majority in *Thompson v Thompson* (1994) 6 RFL (4th) 290 at 318, Sup Ct of Canada.
314   See *P v B* [1995] ILRM 201, Supreme Court of Ireland.
315   *A v Central Authority for New Zealand* [1996] 2 NZLR 517, Court of Appeal.
316   [1995] ILRM 201.
317   See *Feder v Feder-Evans* 63 Fed 3d 217 (3rd Cir 1995); *Walsh v Walsh* 221 F 3d 204 (1st Cir 2000); *Blondin v Dubois* 189 F 3d 240 (2nd Cir 1999).
318   Family Law (Child Abduction Convention) Regulations 1986.

care of the child.[319] However, there appears to be no requirement of minimum standards of the family justice system in the States which accede to the Convention,[320] although at one stage, consideration was given to setting such a proposal.

17.27 Another assumption is that the court of the requesting State will recognise the effect of the undertaking given to the court of the requested State; and that the person giving the undertaking, being aware of this, will be encouraged to comply with the undertaking for fear of the adverse consequences in the requesting State of doing so.[321]

17.128 In some cases, an undertaking to the court of the requested State is not seen as a sufficient safeguard for the returning child. In this context, it is permissible to explore whether the party giving the undertaking is likely to honour the undertaking. Singer J in *Re O*[322] had regard to the extent to which the undertakings could be enforced in Greece (the requesting State) and the likelihood of father honouring them once back in Greece. In *Re F (A Minor) (Abduction: Rights of Custody Abroad)*,[323] the English Court of Appeal allowed an appeal and refused to return a child. It was particularly concerned that the child would be returned to the 'very same surroundings and potentially the very same situation as that which has had such a serious effect on him' and noted, in particular, that 'there has to be concern as to whether the father would take any notice of future orders of the court or comply with the undertakings he has given to the judge'. The United States First Circuit Court of Appeals in *Walsh v Walsh*[324] refused to return the child, finding that 'there is every reason to believe that [the left-behind parent] will violate the undertakings he made to the district court in this case and any barring orders from the Irish court'.

17.129 While the fact that undertakings are directly enforceable in the requesting State may be relevant as to whether they will be honoured, it is not a prerequisite that those undertakings should be directly enforceable in the requesting State.[325] However, in some cases it may be appropriate to ensure that the undertaking is enforceable in the requesting State on the return of the child. It is noticeable that in the pioneering English case of *C v C (Abduction:*

---

[319] See *Re M (Abduction: Non-Convention Country)* [1995] 1 FLR 89, CA, which was expressly approved in the context of the Hague Abduction Convention in *Re M (Abduction: Undertakings)* [1995] 1 FLR 1021 at 1027, per Butler-Sloss LJ. See the similar view taken by the majority in the High Court of Australia in *De L v Director General, NSW Department of Security Services* (1996) FLC 92-706.

[320] *Re E (Child Abduction: Non-Convention Country)* [1999] 2 FLR 642, CA.

[321] See the discussion in *Re O (Child Abduction: Undertakings)* [1994] 2 FLR 349.

[322] *Ibid.*

[323] [1995] Fam 224, sub nom *Re F (Child Abduction: Risk of Returned)* [1995] 2 FLR 31, CA.

[324] 221 F 3d (204 (1st Cir 2000).

[325] *Re O (Child Abduction: Undertakings)* (above) at 368C–369B.

Rights of Custody)[326] and in *Re G (A Minor) (Abduction)*,[327] the undertakings were given to both the English court and to the Australian court. Where this can be done, this will be an added safeguard. In the non-Convention case of *Re M (Abduction: Non-Convention Country)*,[328] Waite LJ found it sufficient in the circumstances of the case that the applicant father produced to the English court a copy of a document he had produced to the Italian court confirming to that court his willingness 'to fulfil the [English] undertakings in the event of [the mother] returning to Italy'.

17.130   Sometimes it may be appropriate to require that the applicant obtain, in the court of the requesting State, an order safeguarding the welfare of the child on return before the court of the requested State will order the return. This is known as a safe harbour order. The giving of an enforceable undertaking to the court of the requesting State would be a form of safe harbour order. In *Director-General Department of Families, Youth and Hobbs*,[329] the Family Court of Australia made an order for the return of the child which would become operative 'conditional upon' the applicant father first filing specified undertakings in the South African court. The United States Department of State, the US Central Authority, has suggested in the past that 'where a safe-harbour order has been entered in the United States, there may be no reason for a foreign court even to consider entering undertakings as part of a basic return order'.[330]

17.131   Where safe harbour orders made in or undertakings given to the court of the requesting State are in similar terms or to similar effect as an order made in or an undertaking given to the court of the requested State, the order is known as a 'mirror order'. We discuss mirror orders in Chapters 3 and 8. Judicial co-operation may also be fruitful as a means of securing the protection of the child on return.[331]

Exercising the discretion to return

17.132   Although, as with all the Art 13 exceptions, establishing a grave risk of harm under Art 13(b) does not automatically mean that the court will refuse to return the child, in practice, given the generally rigorous test that is applied, a refusal is virtually inevitable. At any rate, there are no known examples of a court exercising its discretion to return notwithstanding the establishment of a grave risk.

---

[326] [1989] 1 WLR 654, sub nom *Re C (A Minor) (Abduction)* [1989] 1 FLR 403, CA.
[327] [1989] 2 FLR 475, CA.
[328] [1995] 1 FLR 89, CA. See also *Re S (Child Abduction: Acquiescence)* [1998] 2 FLR 893, per Sir Stephen Brown P.
[329] [2000] FLC 93-007.
[330] 10 August 1995, Correspondence from US Department of State, Annex B to *The Hague Convention and the United States of America: Report on Hague Convention Operations* (Lord Chancellor's Child Abduction Unit).
[331] See **16.5** *et seq*.

Commentary

17.133 Although, as the foregoing discussion has shown, there are a number of cases where Art 13(b) has been successfully relied upon to oppose a return, on the whole, courts have applied a strict approach when applying the exception. This narrow approach is in keeping both with what was originally intended[332] and with what is still thought to be the appropriate application. As the Common Law Judicial Conference on International Child Custody, held in Washington DC in September 2000, concluded:

> 'The Art 13(b) "grave risk" defense has generally been narrowly construed by member states. It is in keeping with the objections of the Hague Child Abduction Convention to construe the Art 13(b) grave risk defense narrowly.'

This conclusion was echoed by the International Judicial Seminar on the 1980 Hague Abduction Convention held in De Ruwenberg in October 2001, which added:

> 'A refusal to return a child on the basis of Art 13(b) should not be contemplated unless all the available alternative methods of protecting the child have been considered by the court and found to be inadequate.'

17.134 Notwithstanding this general agreement among the judiciary and policy makers, the strict interpretation of Art 13(b) has not escaped criticism by commentators, particularly in relation to allegations of sexual abuse and domestic violence. There are two levels of criticism, namely:

(1) courts too readily assume that children will in fact be adequately protected on their return; and

(2) since the Convention was initially drafted upon the assumption that abductions were commonly carried out by non-primary carers (mainly fathers), whereas it is now clear that 70% or more of abductions are carried out by primary carers (principally mothers), it has become outdated such that it may no longer be correct to assume that children's welfare is generally best served by being returned to their country of habitual residence.

17.135 With regard to the first level of criticism, the arguments are well marshalled by Kaye,[333] who suggests that courts are putting unrealistic faith in the power of legal systems to protect the returning mother and child. In particular, she takes issue with the commonly articulated standpoint that it is 'presumptuous and offensive' for courts in the requested State to conclude that the wife and child are not capable of being protected by the courts of the country of habitual residence, which, as she says, is particularly ironic for those

---

[332] See the Pérez-Vera Report at para 116, discussed above at **17.85**.

[333] 'The Hague Convention and the Flight from Domestic Violence: How Women and Children are being Returned by Coach and Four' (1999) 13 Int Jo of Law, Policy and the Family 191 at 198–205. See also Weiner, 'International Child Abduction and the Escape from Domestic Violence' (2000) 69 *Fordham Law Review* 593 and her masterly discussion of potential reforms at 674 *et seq*.

who have fled the jurisdiction for precisely this reason.[334] She questions whether their ability to obtain domestic protection orders is *ipso facto* sufficient protection, and she is also critical of the reliance on undertakings to protect the child. She also powerfully argues that 'the courts in Hague Convention cases sometimes appear to underestimate the risks to children from exposure to spousal violence and the harm which flows from being the child of a battered woman'.

17.136 These are important arguments, although that is not to say that the courts are unaware of them. The ability of the system to protect the children lay at the heart of the difference between the majority and the minority in the English decision in *TB v JB (Abduction: Grave Risk of Harm)*[335] and there are signs that courts are being more sympathetic to the impact upon the child of spousal violence.[336] On the other hand, the obvious danger of enquiring too closely into the system's ability to protect or the impact of violence on the child, is that the courts will rapidly become involved in assessing the merits of the case,[337] which is clearly contrary to the Convention.

17.137 In an attempt to safeguard returning children better, at the third Special Commission meeting to review the operation of the Convention, the Australian delegation proposed[338] that all States Parties to the Convention should consider whether Central Authorities should accept a wider responsibility to protect the welfare of children returned under the Convention.[339] The States Parties' delegates agreed that it was essential to

---

[334] Note, in this regard, Kaye's discussion of the Australian decision, *Murray v Director of Family Services, ACT* [1993] FLC 92–416.

[335] [2001] 2 FLR 515, CA, discussed above at **17.110**.

[336] See in particular, in Canada, *Pollastro v Pollastro* (1999) 171 DLR (4th) 32, and in New Zealand, *Mok v Cornelisson* [2000] NZFLR 582, discussed above at **17.111**.

[337] See, in this regard, the criticism of the US decision, *Blondin v Dubois* 238F 3d 152 (2nd Cir 2001), discussed at **17.112**, by Weiner, 'Navigating the Road Between Uniformity and Progress: The Need for Purposive Analysis of the Hague Convention on the Civil Aspects of International Child Abduction' (2002) 33 Columbia HRLR 276 at 344 *et seq*. As Weiner pointed out in her earlier article, (2000) 69 *Fordham Law Review* 593 at 694, similar arguments can be made against making a new defence for victims of domestic violence under the Convention.

[338] In Working Document No 3, distributed 17 March 1997, Appendix 3 to the Report of the Third Meeting of the Special Commission to Review the Operation of the Hague Convention on the Civil Aspects of Child Abduction (17–21 March 1997).

[339] The Australian Government noted that the Convention has come under scrutiny because of criticism that it fails to provide measures for the physical protection of abducting parents and children where children are returned under the Convention. In carrying out their obligations under the Convention, the Australian Central Authorities are increasingly faced with the difficulty of establishing to the satisfaction of the courts and the Australian community that parents and children returning to their countries of habitual residence will have adequate protection from violence, adequate financial support and adequate access to legal representation. See Appendix 3 to the Report of the Third Meeting of the Special Commission (above).

ensure the safety of children on their return to their country of habitual residence, in order to alleviate possible concerns and the reluctance of judges to order the return of children where issues of (alleged) abuse or violence arise. However, there was less agreement on how this might be done. The Permanent Bureau of the Hague Conference urged Central Authorities to accept that they had an obligation under Art 7(h) to ensure that appropriate child protection bodies are alerted so that they can act to protect the welfare of children upon return, until the jurisdiction of the appropriate court has been effectively invoked. However, as one commentator has noted:[340]

> 'Neither Art 7(h) nor the 1997 conclusions and recommendations explicitly imposes a responsibility on Central Authorities to respond to any protection or assistance needs of a returning parent. This gap is especially dangerous in cases where the person who unlawfully took or held on to the child alleges that family violence against her was a reason for doing so.'

17.138   The issue was discussed at the fourth Special Commission meeting which concluded and recommended as follows:[341]

> 'To the extent permitted by the powers of their Central Authority and by the legal and social welfare systems of their country, Contracting States accept that Central Authorities have an obligation under Article 7(h) to ensure appropriate child protection bodies are alerted so they may act to protect the welfare of children upon return in certain cases where their safety is at issue until the jurisdiction of the appropriate court has been effectively invoked.
>
> It is recognised that, in most cases, a consideration of the child's best interests requires that both parents have the opportunity to participate and be heard in custody proceedings. Central Authorities should therefore co-operate to the fullest extent possible to provide information in respect of legal, financial, protection and other resources in the requesting State, and facilitate timely contact with these bodies in appropriate cases.
>
> The measures which may be taken in fulfilment of the obligation under Article 7(h) to take or cause to be taken an action to protect the welfare of children may include, for example:
>
> (a)   alerting the appropriate protection agencies or judicial authorities in the requesting State of the return of a child who may be in danger;
>
> (b)   advising the requested State, upon request, of the protective measures and services available in the requesting State to secure the safe return of a particular child;
>
> (c)   encouraging the use of Article 21 of the Convention to secure the effective exercise of access or visitation rights.
>
> It is recognised that the protection of the child may also sometimes require steps to be taken to protect an accompanying parent.'

---

[340]   Sandor, 'Review of the Hague Child Abduction Convention: protecting both children and adults until and upon return?' (2001) 15 Australian Jo of Family Law 1 at 6.

[341]   Paragraph 1.13 of the Conclusions and Recommendations of the Fourth Meeting of the Special Commission to Review the Operation of the Hague Convention of 25 October 1980 on the Civil Aspects of International Child Abduction (22–28 March 2001).

It remains to be seen, what, if any, action will be taken by Contracting States.

17.139 The second level of criticism is more fundamental and indeed challenges the basic assumption upon which the whole Convention is predicated, namely, that it is in children's interests generally to be returned to their home jurisdiction. One commentator[342] has gone so far as to ask:

> '... can it be stated now with confidence that even the best interests of children *generally* are being protected, when the face of abduction has changed so significantly that children are being returned *from* their primary carers? Does this not represent a reversal of the prior situation, so that now the Convention works in the best interests of individual children, those few who are still being abducted by their non-custodial parents – rather than children generally – those who are being abducted by their primary carer parent? The Convention cannot have it both ways – purport to be acting in the interests of children generally and yet give no consideration to the general situation, which is that it is usually primary carers who abduct their children and, at the same time, deny individual children a full consideration of their welfare interests ...'

17.140 Although the general pattern of abductions does seem to have changed inasmuch as the majority of abductors are now primary care-giving mothers,[343] whereas it was assumed when drafting the Convention that the mischief to be dealt with was abductions by non-custodial parents (essentially fathers),[344] nor can it be denied that research is needed into what happens to children after they have been returned, it does not necessarily follow that the Convention has become fundamentally flawed. There surely remains an overwhelming argument that it is basically wrong for children to be uprooted from their home by the unilateral act of either parent and taken to a foreign jurisdiction and thus to be separated from the other parent. Admittedly, that argument becomes weaker if the left-at-home parent has been violent and the abducting parent is escaping to find sanctuary by returning to her family abroad. But, even then, it surely remains a strong argument that, provided the child and abducting parent can properly be protected, the best court to deal with the merits of the dispute is that of the *child's* home jurisdiction.[345] Whether Art 13(b), as it currently operates, properly draws the balance can and, no doubt, will continue to be debated.

---

[342] Freeman, 'In the Best Interests of Internationally Abducted Children? – Plural, Singular, Neither or Both?' [2002] IFL 77 at 82. See also Schuz, 'The Hague Child Abduction Convention: Family Law and Private International Law' (1995) 44 ICLQ 771.

[343] See, for example, Lowe and Perry, 'International Child Abduction – The English Experience' (1999) 48 ICLQ 127 at 133, who found that between 1981 and 1996 there was a shift in the ratio of mother to father abductors from about 1:1 in 1987 to more than 2.5:1 in 1996. According to the 1999 Statistical Survey, *op cit*, n 2, globally 69% of taking persons were female (mainly primary caring mothers), although this pattern was not universal. There were no statistics available in the 1970s: see Dyer, 'Report on International Child Abduction by One Parent ("legal kidnapping")', Preliminary Document No 1 of August 1978 ('the Dyer Report').

[344] See the Dyer Report, at p 19.

[345] Although note the comments to the contrary by Schuz, *op cit*, n 342 above, at 782.

CHILD'S OBJECTIONS[346]

17.141   Article 13 provides that:

> 'The judicial or administrative authority may also refuse to order the return of the child if it finds that the child objects to being returned and has attained an age and degree of maturity at which it is appropriate to take account of its views.'

Background to the provision

17.142   As part of the compromise to allow some limited defences to a return application, it was finally agreed at the Fourteenth Session, although not without debate, to vest a discretion not to order the return of a wrongfully removed or retained child based upon the child's own objections. One argument in favour of allowing such a defence was that forcible repatriation of those just below the age of 16 would have a detrimental effect on the Convention. As the Pérez-Vera Report put it,[347] 'the fact must be acknowledged that it would be very difficult to accept that a child of, for example, 15 years of age, should be returned against its will'. On the other hand, there was the obvious fear, well expressed by the American delegation,[348] that allowing the child's objection to block the return would make the child the ultimate judge of the abduction's success or failure, and that '[e]valuations of the child's views would inevitably entail a consideration of the merits of the custody question contrary to the basic objectives of the Convention'. Moreover, there was a widely held concern that, as the American delegation put it,[349] the exception places an 'inordinate burden of responsibility to make vital decisions on young children which they are not psychologically equipped

---

[346]   For an excellent analysis of the relevant UK, NZ and Australian case-law on the application of this exception, see Caldwell, 'Child welfare defences in child abduction cases – some recent developments' [2001] CFLQ 121 at 130–133. For a discussion of US case-law and practice, see Garbolino, *International Child Custody Cases: Handling Hague Convention Cases in US Courts*, 3rd edn (The National Judicial College, 2000), p 198 *et seq*; Weiner in her *Fordham Law Review* article, *op cit*, n 333 above, at 662–664 and in her Columbia HRLR article, *op cit*, n 337 above, at fn 21. For a discussion of the practice in Spain, see Beilfuss, 'International Child Abduction in Spain' (2001) 15 Int Jo of Law, Policy and the Family 327 at 339. For a recent overall critique, see Freeman, 'In the Best Interests of Internationally Abducted Children? – Plural, Singular, Neither or Both?' [2002] IFL 77 at 78–80. Note the requirement under the revised Brussels II Regulation to afford a mature child the opportunity to be heard in the proceedings: see n 1 above.

[347]   At para 30.

[348]   See Vol III of the Discussions of the Fourteenth Session, at p 243. At this stage, the inclusion of this independent exception was said to be 'seriously objectionable to the United States'. Even as late as 1997 the third meeting of the Special Commission to review the Convention found that some countries felt that the Convention 'gives too much weight to the opinion of the child, considering that what is involved is just a matter of determining the forum': see text of the Report at http://www.hcch.net.

[349]   *Ibid*. See also the Canadian delegation's comments, *ibid*, at 243.

to handle'. This concern is also adverted to in the Pérez-Vera Report, which comments:[350]

> '... this provision could prove dangerous if it were applied by means of the direct questioning of young people who may admittedly have a clear grasp of the situation but who may also suffer serious psychological harm if they think they are being forced to choose between two parents.'

These fears are further compounded by the fact that the defence lays the child open to pressure by the person in control (normally the abductor) or by other family members who live in the country to which the child has been abducted.

17.143   To address these concerns there had been certain other proposals.[351] For example, one was to lower the age of children covered by the Convention to 12 years and to exclude the defence based on the child's objections. An alternative proposal was to retain the age of 16 but to allow the child's views only to be taken into account if the child was aged between 12 and 16.

17.144   In the event, both these and other suggestions were rejected,[352] it being eventually agreed not formally to restrict the defence but instead, as the Pérez-Vera Report puts it,[353] to leave its application 'to the discretion of the competent authorities'.

17.145   Although there is extensive jurisprudence on the application of the child's objection defence,[354] the fear that it would provide a serious escape mechanism to the obligation to return has largely proved unfounded, although from time to time certain national courts have been criticised for making excessive use of this defence.[355] According to the 1999 Statistical Survey,[356]

---

[350] At para 30.

[351] Well summarised by the Canadian delegation, in Vol III of the Discussions of the Fourteenth Session, at p 243.

[352] For example, including it as a reservation, making it mandatory not to return a child where fixed reasons were given by the child aged between 10 and 12 or older, and not to apply the defence where, by the relevant law, the child under the age of 16 had the right to choose his own place of residence. It might also be noted that the proposal that the views of a child aged 12 or above should *have* to be addressed was also rejected.

[353] At para 30.

[354] At the time of writing there were, for example, 94 decisions on this exception reported on INCADAT.

[355] Germany, in particular, was singled out in this respect particularly in the mid 1990s: see eg Lowe and Perry, 'The Operation of the Hague and European Convention on International Child Abduction between England and Germany, Part II' [1998] Int FL 52. Even in 2000, both the United States and Australia have complained about the German courts' excessive consideration of the child's view and entering into the merits of the dispute: see the US Central Authority's 'Report on the Compliance with the Hague Convention of the Civil Aspects of International Child Abduction' presented to Congress in November 2000, and 'International Child Abduction – A guide for parents and practitioners' (Australian Commonwealth Attorney-General's Department, June 2000). However, the 1999 Statistical Survey, *op cit*, n 2, found that only one of the 13 judicial refusals made by the German courts was based upon the child's objections.

[356] *Op cit*, n 2.

globally, the child's objections were relied upon as the sole ground in only 10 out of 107 refusals. However, such objections were more frequently relied upon in conjunction with another ground. Overall, children's objections were relied upon in whole or in part in 22 of the 107 refusals, which was still less than the Art 13(b) exceptions, based on physical or psychological harm.[357]

General construction issues

Relationship with other parts of Article 13(b)

17.146   It is accepted by the English courts[358] that this part of Art 13 is quite separate from the rest of Art 13(b) and 'does not, therefore, depend on there being a grave risk of physical or psychological harm on the children being placed in an intolerable situation if their views are not respected'.[359] A similar view has been taken by the Irish Supreme Court.[360]

The meaning of 'objects'

17.147   *Re S (A Minor) (Abduction: Custody Rights)* also establishes that there is no warrant for importing a gloss on the words of Art 13. Consequently, the word 'objects' should be interpreted literally and not, as suggested earlier by Bracewell J in *Re R (A Minor: Abduction)*,[361] so that it 'imports a strength of feeling which goes beyond the usual ascertainment of the wishes of the child in a custody dispute'. A similar ruling has been made in Australia,[362] New Zealand,[363] and Scotland.[364]

17.148   Although there was an understandable anxiety on Bracewell J's part to limit the exception, it seems better to do this via the court's discretion as

---

[357]   Cf Lowe and Perry's admittedly more limited analysis based on the English Child Abduction Unit's records for 1996, where they found that the child's objections was the reason most frequently relied upon both for incoming and outgoing applications from England and Wales: see 'International Child Abduction – The English Experience' (1999) 48 ICLQ 127 at 144. Interestingly, in 1999 only two judicial refusals by the English courts were based on the child's objections: see the 1999 Statistical Survey, *op cit*, n 2.

[358]   See *Re S (A Minor) (Abduction: Custody Rights)* [1993] Fam 242 at 250, sub nom *S v S (Child Abduction) (Child's Views)* [1992] 2 FLR 492 at 499, per Balcombe LJ, and repeated by Ward LJ in *Re T (Abduction: Child's Objections to Return)* [2000] 2 FLR 192 at 202.

[359]   See Hale J in *Re HB (Abduction: Children's Objections)* [1997] 1 FLR 392 at 397–398 and *Re K (Abduction: Child's Objections)* [1995] 1 FLR 977 at 990, per Wall J.

[360]   See *TMM v MD (Child Abduction: Article 13)* [2000] 1 IR 149 at 161, per Denham J.

[361]   [1992] 1 FLR 105 at 107. Bracewell J was not alone in taking a restrictive view: see for example, in Australia, *De L v Director-General, NSW Department of Community Services* [1996] FLC 92–674 by the Full Court of the Family Court of Australia but not followed on appeal to the High Court (1996) 187 CLR 640 and, in New Zealand, in *Damiano v Damiano* [1993] NZFLR 548, per Boshier J, who subsequently revised his view in *Secretary of State for Justice v Penney, ex p Calatro* [1995] NZFLR 827.

[362]   *De L v Director-General, NSW Department of Community Services* (1996) 187 CLR 640, Australian High Court.

[363]   *Ryding v Turvey* (1998) NZFLR 313 at 316.

[364]   *Urness v Minto* 1994 SLT 988, Ct of Session.

to how to weigh the child's wishes rather than effectively to limit the court's opportunity to listen to the child's view. On the other hand, her Ladyship's comment that 'objection' imports more than a 'mere preference by the child' is surely correct.[365] Indeed, in Australia, the Regulations now provide that the objections of the child must import a strength of feeling beyond the mere expression of a preference or of ordinary wishes.[366]

To what must the child object?

17.149   Not all objections, even by a child of sufficient age and maturity, will *ipso facto* trigger the application of this part of Art 13, for what is required is, in Balcombe LJ's words in *Re S (A Minor) (Abduction: Custody Rights)*,[367] that the objection be to 'that which would otherwise be ordered under Art 12, viz, an immediate return to the country from which it was wrongfully removed'. In other words, in principle at least, it is not enough that the child objects to returning to the parent who happens to live in that country. Conversely, it is not necessary to show that the child objects to a return in any circumstances. A readiness, for example, to return to see the other parent on access visits does not mean that the defence of objection thereby fails.

17.150   It has been recognised, however, that this distinction between returning to a country and returning to a parent might not be so easily distinguished by the child. Accordingly, as Ward LJ observed in *Re T (Abduction: Child's Objections to Return)*,[368] it has to be borne in mind that the objection to being returned to the country of habitual residence becomes 'so inevitably and inextricably linked with an objection to living with the other parent that the two factors cannot be separated'.

17.151   In fact, in an earlier Court of Appeal decision, *Re M (A Minor) (Child Abduction)*,[369] Butler-Sloss LJ had, perhaps questionably, gone further, holding that Art 13 'does not inhibit a court from considering the objections of a child returning to a parent'. Specifically, what her Ladyship had in mind was 'the problem' where the abducting parent decides not to return with the child, in which situation it 'would be artificial to dissociate the country from the carer

---

[365]   See further, **17.162** below.

[366]   Family Law Act 1975 (Cth), s 111B(1B), as added by the Family Law Amendment Act 2000, discussed by Freeman, *op cit*, n 342 above, at 80.

[367]   [1993] Fam 242 at 250, sub nom *S v S (Child Abduction: Child's Views)* [1992] 2 FLR 492 at 499. A similar standpoint has been taken in Australia, see *Director-General, Department of Community Services v Rowe* (1996) 21 Fam LR 159, and in New Zealand, see *S v M* [1999] NZ FLR 337.

[368]   [2000] 2 FLR 192 at 203. See also, to similar effect, *Re R (Child Abduction: Acquiescence)* [1995] 1 FLR 716 at 730, per Balcombe LJ. For a similar comment in Australia, see *Director-General, NSW Department of Community Services v De L* (1996) FLC 92–674, per Nicholson CJ, subsequently endorsed in *Director-General, Department of Community Services v Rowe* (above).

[369]   [1994] 1 FLR 390 at 395, overruling Johnson J's earlier decision on this point in *B v K (Child Abduction)* [1993] 1 FCR 382, [1993] Fam Law 17.

... and to refuse to listen to the child on so technical a ground'.[370] How far this line of reasoning will be developed, remains to be seen.[371] Suffice to say that:

(a)   the defence will clearly be stronger if the objection directly relates to returning to the country;[372] and

(b)   a mere preference to remain with the abducting parent will be insufficient to justify refusing a return for, as Balcombe LJ said in *Re S (A Minor) (Abduction: Custody Rights)*,[373] '[a]ny other approach would be to drive a coach and horses through the primary scheme of the Hague Convention'.

The inter-relationship with Article 12 of the UN Convention on the Rights of the Child

17.152   As some commentators have observed,[374] since the conclusion of the Hague Abduction Convention in 1980, the legal perception of the child has moved on inasmuch as there has been what has been well described[375] as an ebbing away from a child welfare focus to a newer emphasis on 'child rights', with the child increasingly being regarded as an independent legal subject, with autonomous rights and entitlements. Foremost among these rights is that of self-expression, which is now enshrined in Art 12 of the UN Convention on the Rights of the Child, under which:

> 'States Parties shall assure to the child who is capable of forming his or her own views the right to express those views freely in all matters affecting the child, the views of the child being given due weight in accordance with the age and maturity of the child ... . The child shall in particular be provided the opportunity to be heard in any judicial and administrative proceedings affecting the child, either directly, or through a representative or appropriate body, in a manner consistent with procedural rules of matrimonial law.'

---

[370] Her Ladyship also considered that it would be contrary to Art 12 of the UN Convention on the Rights of the Child not to listen to the child's views in such circumstances, discussed further below at **17.152** *et seq*.

[371] Interestingly in *Re R (Child Abduction: Acquiescence)* [1995] 1 FLR 716 at 730, Balcombe LJ cited *Re M* for the proposition that the two issues of return to the country and return to the parent were so inevitably and inextricably linked that they could not be separated.

[372] See, for example, *Re S (A Minor) (Abduction: Custody Rights)* [1993] Fam 242, where the child in question had difficulty in assimilating into French life, and *Re M (A Minor) (Abduction: Child's Objections)* [1994] 2 FLR 126, CA, where the child in question had lost confidence in the Irish courts to protect him.

[373] [1993] Fam 242 at 252, sub nom *S v S (Child Abduction: Child's Views)* [1992] 2 FLR 492 at 501. See also *Re M (A Minor) (Child Abduction)* [1994] 1 FLR 390 at 395, per Butler-Sloss LJ.

[374] Eg Caldwell, *op cit*, n 346 above, at 133.

[375] By Caldwell, *ibid*. Cf Lowe and Murch, 'Children's participation in the family justice system – translating principles into practice' [2001] CFLQ 137 at 138, who describe this shift in terms that 'children are no longer simply seen as passive victims of family breakdown, but increasingly as participants and actors in the family justice system. In consequence, in various family proceedings it is incumbent upon the courts to ascertain and duly take into account children's own wishes and views'.

17.153 In *Re T (Abduction: Child's Objections to Return)*,[376] Ward LJ observed that under the 1980 Hague Abduction Convention the child's 'right' was, consistently with Art 12 of the UN Convention, to have the opportunity to express his or her own views and to be heard, and not to self-determination. He considered:

> 'The sentiments in both the Convention are the same and they give strong support to the idea that the purpose of the exception to the general rule of immediate return is to defer to the wishes of the child *for Convention purposes*, even if the child's wishes may not prevail if welfare were the paramount consideration.'

However,[377] he tentatively associated himself with a view expressed by Millett LJ in *Re R (Child Abduction: Acquiescence)*[378] that the Hague Convention clearly envisages that a child of sufficient age and maturity for his views to be taken into account will not be returned against his wishes 'unless there are countervailing factors which require his wishes to be overridden'. This latter point of view might be compared with that expressed in the New Zealand decision, *Hollins v Crozier*,[379] in which it had been sought to argue that a 12-year-old's views could not be given priority over the general thrust of the Hague Convention to return children. Judge Doogue considered that to accept such an argument would be to 'elevate the remedial and normative objections of the Hague Convention unduly ahead of the defence ... and the obligations this court has in administering the principles and Articles of the United Nations Convention on the Rights of the Child'. It would, moreover, treat the child as an object of return, rather than as a person in his own right, which would be contrary to Art 12 of the UN Convention.[380]

17.154 One important difference between the two instruments is that, whereas under the UN Convention it is mandatory to allow the child (regardless of maturity) the right to express his or her views, it is by no means clear that under the Hague Convention there is a positive obligation upon judicial or administrative authorities to, as they put it, 'verify whether or not a child may object'. It is certainly not the practice of the English courts to make automatic enquiries of the child's position.[381] On the other hand, it has been said[382] that this part of Art 13 'puts the court on inquiry if the child's views are

---

[376] [2000] 2 FLR 192 at 203.

[377] *Ibid* at 212–213.

[378] [1995] 1 FLR 716 at 734.

[379] [2000] NZ FLR 775, discussed by Caldwell, *op cit*, n 346 above, at 130–131.

[380] This is reminiscent of Sir Stephen Brown P's comment in *Re M (Minors) (Abduction)* [1992] 2 FCR 608 at 614: 'Children are not articles to be sent to and fro, even though the circumstances in which they have been taken from their habitual residence are wrongful and the person taking them has clearly acted in breach of an order of a court of competent jurisdiction'.

[381] See **17.157**.

[382] Per Butler-Sloss LJ in *Re M (A Minor) (Child Abduction)* [1994] 1 FLR 390 at 394–395, disapproving of *B v K (Child Abduction)* [1993] 1 FCR 382, [1993] Fam Law 17.

brought to its attention' and that it would be contrary to Art 12 of the UN Convention not to listen to a child merely because, for example, the objection is to returning to a person rather than to the home State, as the Article seems to require.

17.155   It may finally be observed that Art 13 comes into play only where the child objects to being returned. There is no requirement under the Hague Convention to pay regard to a child's wishes to return. Indeed, as Fisher J has observed in the New Zealand decision, *S v S*:[383]

> 'It is difficult to see why more weight would be given to a mature child's wishes to remain than the same child's wish to return. Either a mature child's wishes are to be respected in Hague Convention applications or they are not.'

It can certainly be argued that Art 12 of the UN Convention requires the court to listen to such views.

17.156   In short, while it may be right to regard the two Conventions as being broadly compatible, it might be unduly sanguine to think that their inter-relationship is entirely problem free.

The proper approach to a child's objection defence

Raising the defence

17.157   As has been said, the English courts do not make automatic enquiries of the child's position. As Butler-Sloss LJ observed in *Re M (A Minor) (Child Abduction)*:[384]

> 'There is nothing in Art 13 or the Child Abduction and Custody Act 1985 (which enacts the Convention), which provides for automatic inquiry into the views of older children ...'

Furthermore, according to Waite J in *P v P (Minors) (Child Abduction)*,[385] the court is not bound to adjourn the case to inquire into the nature of the child's objection and degree of maturity merely because of an assertion, even under oath, by the abducting parent, that the child objects to return to the requesting State.[386] In other words, it is either incumbent upon the defendant to provide sufficient evidence at the outset for the court to take cognisance of the child's objections, or, exceptionally, for the court otherwise to be put on enquiry (as, for example, where the child refuses to board the flight to take him back to the

---

[383]   [1999] 3 NZLR 513 at 521.

[384]   [1994] 1 FLR 390 at 394.

[385]   [1992] 1 FLR 155. See also *Re G (A Minor) (Abduction)* [1989] 2 FLR 475 in which the Court of Appeal refused to interfere with the trial judge's (Thorpe J's) refusal to allow a 9-year-old child to be interviewed.

[386]   As Waite J put it ([1992] 1 FLR 155 at 158–159), it would be contrary to the underlying assumption and purpose of the Convention to allow the absconding parent to insist *as of right* that the mandatory procedure for the child's return be suspended while detailed investigation is made into the child's views.

requesting State in compliance with a return order[387] or where the child goes missing after the making of a return order[388]) that the child's objection is a real issue.

17.158   In Australia there has been some disagreement on this issue for in *Director-General NSW Department of Community Services v De L*,[389] whereas Muskin J considered that it was not for the court to go out looking for evidence, Nicholson CJ thought that in appropriate cases a court could investigate upon its own motion whether a child objected.

17.159   Although there is an understandable reluctance to investigate the child's views unless objections are clearly an issue, given the English experience of children subsequently refusing to co-operate with a return order,[390] there is at least a case for conducting, at any rate in the case of older children, a cursory preliminary investigation into whether the child objects to be returned. Indeed, a failure to ensure that a mature child's views are heard is surely in breach of Art 12 of the UN Convention on the Rights of the Child.

The 'gateway' findings

17.160   So far as English practice is concerned, once the child's views are thought properly to be in issue then the court must determine, first, whether the child does in fact object to being returned and, secondly, if so, whether he or she has attained an age and maturity at which it is appropriate to take account of those views.[391] Although both issues have been said[392] to be questions of fact 'peculiarly within the province of the trial judge', as Ward LJ said in *Re T (Abduction: Child's Objections to Return)*:[393]

> 'whilst the question whether the child objects to being returned is truly a matter of fact, as is the establishment of … age, it is more by an exercise of judgment, rather than by finding a fact, that the court proceeds to establish a degree of maturity at which it is appropriate to take account of the child's views.'

---

[387]   As in *Re HB (Abduction: Children's Objections)* [1998] 1 FLR 422, CA. See also *Re M (A Minor) (Child Abduction)* [1994] 1 FLR 390.

[388]   See eg *Re P (Abduction: Child's Views)* [1998] 2 FCR 825, CA.

[389]   [1996] FLC 92–674. This was not considered on appeal to the Australian High Court, see *De L v Director-General, NSW Department of Community Services* (1996) 70 ALJR 932, [1996] 20 Fam LR 390.

[390]   See eg *Re M (A Minor) (Child Abduction)* (above), *Re HB (Abduction: Children's Objections)* (above), and *TB v JB (Abduction: Grave Risk of Harm)* [2001] 2 FLR 515 – editorial note at 539.

[391]   See *Re T (Abduction: Child's Objection to Return)* [2000] 2 FLR 192 at 202, per Ward LJ, relying in turn on *Re S (A Minor) (Abduction: Custody Rights)*, [1993] Fam 242, sub nom *S v S (Child Abduction: Child's Views)* [1992] 2 FLR 492. A similar standpoint is taken in other jurisdictions, see Freeman, *op cit*, n 342 above, at 79.

[392]   Per Balcombe LJ in *Re S* (above), at 251 and 500, respectively, and quoted by Ward LJ in *Re T* (above) at 202.

[393]   At 204.

A fortiori, as Millett LJ observed in *Re R (Child Abduction: Acquiescence)*,[394] determining whether it is appropriate to take account of a mature child's objections is also a question of judgment. These distinctions are not without importance for, as Ward LJ said in *Re T*,[395] insofar as there is an appeal against a value judgment, the court should be slow to interfere unless it is satisfied that the judge is 'plainly wrong'.

17.161   Determining whether the child objects and, if so, whether he or she has attained an age and maturity at which it is appropriate to take account of those views have become known as the 'gateway' findings, for, as Waite LJ observed in *Re S (Minors) (Abduction: Acquiescence)*,[396] it is only if both are answered in the affirmative that the judge 'may go on to consider whether as a matter of discretion, the return order which would otherwise be mandatory under Art 12, ought to be refused'.

17.162   So far as the child's objections are concerned, as already discussed,[397] to trigger this part of Art 13 it must be established that the child objects to being returned primarily to the State of his habitual residence rather than to the applicant, but with leeway being given to the fact that the two factors may be so inextricably linked that they cannot be separated. Little or no weight should be placed on a child's preference to remain with the abducting parent who is unwilling to return[398] and, a fortiori, if the child is ambivalent or even quite willing to return home the defence will fall at this hurdle. The court will also normally have to find out why the child objects to being returned and then to weigh the soundness and validity of those reasons. According to Ward LJ in *Re T (Abduction: Child's Objections to Return)*,[399] in determining the strength and validity of the child's views it is necessary to examine the child's own perspective of what is in his or her own short-, medium- or long- term interests; the extent to which the reasons for objection are rooted in reality or might reasonably appear to the child to be so grounded; the extent to which those views have been 'shaped or even coloured' by undue parental pressure, direct or indirect; and the extent to which the obligations would be mollified on return and, where this is the case, upon removal from any pernicious influence from the abducting parent.

17.163   So far as age and maturity of the child is concerned, as the Pérez-Vera Report says,[400] 'all efforts to agree on a minimum age at which the views of the child could be taken into account failed, since all the ages suggested seemed artificial, even arbitrary'. Consequently the Convention itself is silent on the

---

[394]   [1995] 1 FLR 716 at 734.
[395]   [2000] 2 FLR 192 at 204.
[396]   [1994] 1 FLR 819 at 826.
[397]   See **17.149–17.151**.
[398]   See eg *Re M (A Minor) (Child Abduction)* [1994] 1 FLR 390 at 395, per Butler-Sloss LJ.
[399]   [2000] 2 FLR 192 at 204.
[400]   At para 30.

matter, although it seems fair to say that those involved in the drafting process generally had in mind older children and probably would have agreed that a child under the age of 12 would not normally be considered as possessing sufficient maturity.[401]

17.164   So far as English and Wales is concerned, as Balcombe LJ has said in *Re R (Child Abduction: Acquiescence)*,[402] 'English courts have refused to lay down any chronological threshold below which a child's objections will not be taken into account', but he added, '[t]he younger the child is the less likely is it that it will have the maturity which makes it appropriate for the court to take its objections into account'.[403]

17.165   In *Re R* itself, two boys aged 7½ and 6 years old were held to be mature enough for their objections to be considered,[404] although on the facts it was decided to order their return. The lowest age at which objections have been held to justify a refusal to return, at any rate in a reported English decision, was in *B v K (Child Abduction)*,[405] where the objection of an 8-year-old girl and a 7-year-old boy were relied upon.[406] These, however, are relatively unusual cases, and children below the age of 10 or 11 are not normally considered to be sufficiently mature. Indeed, Hale J has said[407] that she would regard the chronological age of 10½ as normally being on the borderline. Conversely, her Ladyship has also remarked[408] that it would be difficult to suggest that a 13-year-old of normal intelligence and maturity should not have his views taken into account.

---

[401]   See Nygh, 'The international abduction of children', in Doek, van Loon and Vlaardingerbroek (eds), *Children on the Move* (Martinus Nijhoff, 1996), p 29 at p 39.

[402]   [1995] 1 FLR 716 at 729.

[403]   *Ibid* at 730.

[404]   Ewbank J's first instance decision in this regard being upheld by Balcombe LJ and Sir Ralph Gibson, but with Millett LJ dissenting on this point. Cf *Re K (Abduction: Child's Objections)* [1995] 1 FLR 977, in which Wall J held on the facts that a child aged 7 years and 8 months was not of an age and maturity for her views to be taken into account, and *Re C (Abduction: Grave Risk of Psychological Harm)* [1999] 1 FLR 1145 where children aged 9 and 7 were held not to have sufficient maturity.

[405]   [1993] 1 FCR 382, [1993] Fam Law 17, per Johnson J.

[406]   Note also *Re B (Abduction: Children's Objections)* [1998] 1 FLR 667, in which the objection of boys aged 12 and 7 were relied upon; *Re M (Minors) (Abduction: Psychological Harm)* [1997] 2 FCR 690, CA, in which the views of brothers aged 9 and 8 were taken into account although 'with some hesitancy'. In both *Re S (A Minor) (Abduction: Custody Rights)* [1993] Fam 242, sub nom *S v S (Child Abduction) (Child's Views)* [1992] 2 FLR 492 and *Ontario Court v M and M (Abduction: Children's Objections)* [1997] 1 FLR 475, the objections of 9-year-olds were relied upon.

[407]   In *Re R (Abduction: Hague and European Conventions)* [1997] 1 FLR 663 at 667.

[408]   In *Re HB (Abduction: Children's Objections)* [1997] 1 FLR 392 at 398. Note also her remark that an 11-year-old was more borderline.

17.166 Although the English courts are by no means alone in refusing to lay down a chronological cut off,[409] nevertheless globally, it is unusual to base a refusal to return solely upon the objection of children under the age of 11. According to the 1999 Statistical Survey,[410] only two refusals based solely on children's objections were triggered by the objections of children aged between 8 and 10 years (and none below that age). On the other hand, where such objections were relied upon in conjunction with other grounds, there were two instances in which the objections of children under the age of 7 were relied upon, with a further six where the children were aged between 8 and 10 years.

17.167 While chronological age is not unimportant, because children vary so much in their pace of development, it cannot provide clear-cut boundaries, and regard will also need to be had to the child's developmental age. After all, an individual 10-year-old can be particularly mature, while a 14-year-old may be immature. In this regard, a psychologist's report can be helpful.[411] Understandably, the courts have been reluctant to define what is meant by 'maturity'. That is essentially a matter of judgment in each case. Nevertheless, in *Re T (Abduction: Child's Objections to Return)*,[412] Ward LJ helpfully commented:

> 'Clearly the child has to know what has happened to her and to understand that there is a range of choice. A child may be mature enough for it to be appropriate for her views to be taken into account even though she may not have gained that level of maturity that she is fully emancipated from parental dependence and can claim autonomy of decision-making.'

17.168 Further, as Waite LJ observed in *Re S (Minors) (Abduction: Acquiescence)*,[413] an investigation of the appropriateness of taking into account the child's views 'is not restricted to a generalised appraisal of the child's capacity to form and express views which bear the hallmark of maturity' but can include:

> '... specific inquiry as to whether the child has reached a stage of development at which, when asked the question "Do you object to a return to your home country?" he or she can be relied on to give an answer which does not depend

---

[409] A similar standpoint is taken in other common law jurisdictions, see Caldwell, *op cit*, n 346 above, at 132. In the United States, in *Sheikh v Cahill* 546 NYS 2D 517, it was held that the 9-year-old child had not attained a sufficient degree of maturity for her views to be taken into account, while in *Tahon v Duquette* 613 A 2d 486 it was held that Art 13 'simply does not apply to a 9-year-old child': see Weiner both in (2000) 69 *Fordham Law Review* 593 at 662–664 and in (2002) 33 Columbia HRLR 276 at fn 21. For the position in Spain, see Beilfuss, *op cit*, n 346 above, at 339. In one notorious German case, the objections of a 4-year-old were relied upon: see Lowe and Perry, 'The Operation of the Hague and European Conventions on International Child Abduction between England and Germany, Part II' [1998] Int FL 52 at 55.

[410] *Op cit*, n 2, at Tables 14 *et seq*. According to the same survey, in England and Wales, there were only two refusals based upon the child's objections and neither involved children below the age of 11.

[411] For discussion about how the child's views and maturity are elicited, see **17.169**.

[412] [2000] 2 FLR 192 at 203.

[413] [1994] 1 FLR 819 at 827.

upon instinct alone, but is influenced by the discernment which a mature child brings to the question's implications for his or her own best interests in the long and the short term.'

In deciding whether the 9-year-old child in *Re S (A Minor) (Abduction: Custody Rights)*[414] had reached the required level of maturity, the judge took into account her intellectual ability, the fact that she was able to express herself, could speak fluently, could answer questions clearly and directly and was able to say what she wanted and why.

Eliciting the child's views and ascertaining maturity

The English position

17.169   Because it was considered a question 'peculiarly within the province of the judge', the Court of Appeal in *Re S (A Minor) (Abduction: Custody Rights)*[415] refused to lay down any general guidance to be adopted in ascertaining the child's view and degree of maturity. As Balcombe LJ commented:

> 'These cases under the Hague Convention came before the very experienced judges of the Family Division, and they can be relied upon, in those cases where it may be necessary to ascertain these facts, to devise an appropriate procedure, always bearing in mind that the Hague Convention is primarily designed to secure a speedy return of the child to the country from which it has been abducted.'

17.170   The normal expectation is that, where it is appropriate to inquire into the child's views, that inquiry should be made by a CAFCASS officer (formerly a court welfare officer). As Butler-Sloss LJ said in *Re M (A Minor) (Child Abduction)*,[416] a CAFCASS officer is the obvious person to assist the court both in assessing the child's maturity and in conveying to the court the views of the child he has interviewed. Indeed, it is the ability to perform this dual role that, in Butler-Sloss LJ's view, makes it an advantage to appoint such an officer rather than ordering separate representation for the child. It may be added that, as well as enabling an investigation to be conducted by an impartial and experienced childcare professional, the court reporting service is conveniently located within the High Court and is easy to access.

17.171   Although it is also open to a judge to interview the child in private in line with general domestic practice (although contrary to the practice in many other Contracting States),[417] English judges are generally reluctant to do so in abduction cases.[418]

---

[414]   [1993] Fam 242, sub nom *S v S (Child Abduction) (Child's Views)* [1992] 2 FLR 492.

[415]   *Ibid* at 251 and 500, respectively.

[416]   [1994] 1 FLR 390 at 394.

[417]   See **17.179**.

[418]   In *S v S (Child Abduction)* [1991] 2 FLR 31 at 36, Ewbank J considered that seeing the child was 'usually an inappropriate step for a judge to take'.

17.172 As well as independent reports, affidavit evidence filed by the parties relating to the child's maturity may also be considered by the judge. In *Re S (A Minor) (Abduction)*,[419] for example, in addition to the welfare report, consideration was also given to evidence from welfare workers, a local cleric and a neighbour. It would also not be uncommon to have reports from the child's school.

17.173 It is one thing to allow a child to have a voice in the proceedings but quite another to allow him or her to participate in those proceedings and to instruct a lawyer as if an adult. Nevertheless, notwithstanding that the Family Proceedings Rules 1991, which set out the defendants to be served with a Convention application,[420] do not include the child, as Butler-Sloss LJ observed in *Re M (A Minor) (Child Abduction)*,[421] the rules 'do not preclude the court from making the child a party on the rare occasion it might be necessary'. However, the English courts are extremely reluctant to join the child as a party. As Sir Thomas Bingham MR put it in *Re M*:[422]

> 'The courts would not be true to the letter or spirit of the Convention if they allowed applications to become bogged down in protracted hearings and investigations. While I accept that there is jurisdiction to permit ... children to be joined as parties it *would very rarely be right to exercise it, and compelling grounds would be needed.*' (emphasis added)

17.174 According to Wall J in *Re S (Abduction: Children: Separate Representation)*,[423] not only must there be 'exceptional circumstances which on the facts make it inappropriate for the child's wishes and feelings to be represented either by one of the existing parties to the proceedings or by the court welfare officer' but also 'an arguable case that the discretion under Art 13 will be exercised'. Although Wall J considered it to be impossible to define 'exceptional circumstances', Butler-Sloss LJ in *Re M*[424] envisaged such circumstances as including cases where 'either the court welfare officer [now a CAFCASS officer] was unable adequately to represent the views of the child concerned (see *L v L (Minors) (Separate Representation)*[425]) or expert medical opinion was needed (which would be wholly exceptional)'.

17.175 The first reported English case where separate representation was ordered, *Re M (A Minor) (Abduction: Child's Objections)*,[426] involved a 13-year-old Irish boy who claimed to have been abused by his mother's cohabitant. Notwithstanding these allegations, a series of orders were granted in the

---

419 [1991] 2 FLR 1 at 22. See also *N v N (Abduction: Article 13 Defence)* [1995] 1 FLR 107 at 111, in which the child was also interviewed by a social worker and two doctors.

420 In r 6.5.

421 [1994] 1 FLR 390 at 394.

422 *Ibid* at 397.

423 [1997] 1 FLR 486 at 493.

424 *Re M (A Minor) (Child Abduction)* (above) at 394.

425 [1994] 1 FLR 156.

426 [1994] 2 FLR 126, CA.

mother's favour but could not be implemented because the boy continually ran away. Eventually, in response to his appeal for help, the child's father brought him to England but had him placed with a police protection team and was not caring for him. Upon the mother's application, a return order was made under the Hague Abduction Convention but, as the boy again ran away, it could not be implemented. The boy then instructed his own solicitor to appeal against the return order, and the Court of Appeal agreed that, given that the dispute was between the child and the mother and not between the parents, this was one of those rare cases where it was right to join the child as a party. As Wall J later observed,[427] there was, in effect, no one to represent the child's wishes and feelings and the father was unable to do so.

17.176   Separate representation was also granted in *Re S (Abduction: Children: Separate Representation).*[428] In that case, following lengthy litigation between the parents, two children (aged 14 and nearly 12) had been made wards of the New Zealand High Court and placed in foster care. In flagrant disregard of a court order, the mother removed the children to England. Both children objected to being returned and sought leave to be joined as parties to the Hague Abduction Convention proceedings. What made the case unusual was that, had the Convention been applied, the children would effectively have been returned to the care of the court and not of the father. Indeed, there was no immediate prospect of the children even having contact with their father. On the other hand, given her contempt and her attempts unduly to influence them, it was not considered appropriate that their mother should represent the children. Indeed, there was a perceived potential for conflict between the children and the mother, which made it all the more important for the children to have the freedom in the proceedings to take independent advice. There was also thought to be a need for expert medical evidence about the children's maturity which made it inappropriate to rely on the court welfare officer in that case.[429]

17.177   One common feature of *Re M* and *Re S* was the perceived inability of or inappropriateness for either parent to represent the children's view, and this was also true of a third case in which separate representation was permitted, *Re HB (Abduction: Children's Objections).*[430] In that case, a 12-year-old girl refused to board a plane to take her back to Denmark following an initial return order made upon her mother's application. For the next 6 months, the mother

---

[427]   In *Re S (Abduction: Children: Separate Representation)* [1997] 1 FLR 486 at 493. Note also the case referred to by Wall J, in *Re S*, in which a 15-year-old French girl had, whilst in care in France, run away to her boyfriend in England. The applicant was the French *juge des enfants*, while the defendant was the boyfriend who was not thought an appropriate person to represent the girl's views, and separate representation was ordered.

[428]   [1997] 1 FLR 486. See also *Re L (Abduction: Child's Objections to Return)* [2002] EWHC 1864 (Fam), [2002] 2 FLR 1042.

[429]   For another example of where independent medical opinion was thought to be needed, see *Re P (Abduction: Minor's Views)* [1998] 2 FLR 825, CA.

[430]   [1998] 1 FLR 422, CA.

remained silent as to her future intentions about enforcing the order but when eventually she did indicate her intentions to enforce the order, the father effectively left his daughter to run her own litigation. Although the Court of Appeal made no comment upon the child being granted leave to become a party, they did express concern at the practice of children becoming enmeshed in their parents' disputes. Butler-Sloss LJ observed[431] that in this case it was 'tragic for the girl and most unfortunate for both parents – that she is now the party conducting the litigation against her own mother. I am also worried that her father has left her to fight the battles and does not seem to have the understanding or sensitivity to perceive the unsuitability of the present arrangements in the litigation'.

17.178   Looking at the matter more broadly, Thorpe LJ commented:[432]

> 'Where parties are separated but living within the same jurisdiction, adolescent children frequently exploit the opportunity to divide and conquer. Acrimony between the parents prevents them from uniting to contain the attack. Where the separated parents live in different jurisdictions the opportunity is even greater and the prospects of successful parental response even less. It is important not only that the parents should combine to contain the children but also that the court systems in each jurisdiction should equally act in concert. Once the primary jurisdiction is established then mirror orders in the other and the effective use of the Convention gives the opportunity for collaborate judicial function. The Danish judge and the English judge should be in communication.'

The position in other jurisdictions

17.179   Practice and procedure in other parts of the United Kingdom are now broadly similar to that in England and Wales. In Northern Ireland, the normal practice is for the court to direct social services to prepare a report in respect of the child and the alleged objections to return, although it is open in appropriate cases for the judge to interview the child.[433] In Scotland, where affidavit evidence only became the accepted format in Convention cases in 1996 and oral evidence is now being accepted only 'on special cause shown',[434] the better view would seem to be that the child should be heard only in very limited circumstances. At any rate, the domestic law presumption that a child aged 12 or above has the maturity to be heard and the provisions giving separate representation for children[435] do not apply to Hague Abudction Convention proceedings.[436]

---

[431] [1998] 1 FLR 422 at 429.

[432] *Ibid* at 427–428.

[433] See Lowe, Armstrong and Mathias, *Country Report: United Kingdom* (NCMEC, 2002), at 3.5.

[434] See Rules of the Court of Session, r 70.6(5).

[435] See, respectively, Legal Capacity (Scotland) Act 1991, s 4A and Children (Scotland) Act 1995, s 11(10).

[436] See the discussion by Lowe, Armstrong and Mathias: *Country Report: United Kingdom* (NCMEC, 2002).

17.180   Other common law jurisdictions, whilst having the power either directly to interview children in proceedings or to order their separate representation, are generally reluctant to involve children directly in proceedings, preferring instead to rely upon professional reports, where appropriate.[437] In Australia, where matters are in Regulatory form, the court will usually require a report to determine the child's views,[438] but can only order separate representation in 'exceptional circumstances' which must be specified by the court when making the order.[439]

17.181   In civil law jurisdictions, children are more likely to be heard by the court. Certainly this is the position in Germany, where decisions about children's objections are normally made on the basis of a personal hearing of the child before the judge.[440] In France, the procedures used to determine if a child objects to being returned are governed by Art 388–1 of the Civil Code. Where a child wishes to be heard, the judge may hear the child alone, or in the presence of a lawyer or another person of the child's choice.[441] However, in general, French judges are reluctant to hear a child's opinion, believing children frequently to be influenced by one or both parents.[442]

Exercising discretion to return

17.182   As with all Art 13 exceptions, even if it is found that a child of sufficient maturity objects to being returned, the court nevertheless has a discretion to do so.[443] So far as the English courts are concerned, in exercising

---

[437] For the position in Canada, see Lowe, Armstrong and Mathias, *Country Report: Canada* (NCMEC, 2002), at 3.5; in Ireland, see *TMM v MD (Child Abduction: Article 13)* [2000] 1 IR 149 (interviewing child in private), Guardianship of Infants Act 1964, Part IV (as inserted by the Children Act 1997) (power to hear indirect evidence from children and to take evidence for reports), and more generally, Lowe and Armstrong, *Country Report: Ireland* (NCMEC, 2002) at 3.5; in the United States, see Garbolino, *Handling Hague Convention Cases in US Courts, op cit,* n 346, at para 5.7 (pp 198–202), and Lowe, Armstrong and Mathias, *Country Report: United States* (NCMEC, 2002) at 3.5; and in New Zealand, see *Clarke v Carson* [1996] I NZLR 349, *Secretary of State for Justice v Penney* [1995] NZFLR 827 and *Damiano v Damiano* [1993] NZFLR 548.

[438] See Family Law (Child Abduction Convention) Regulations 1986, reg 26.

[439] See Family Law Act 1975 (Cth), s 68L(2A), inserted by the Family Law Amendment Act 2000, reversing the decision on this point by the High Court in *De L v Director-General, NSW Department of Community Services* (1996) 139 ALR 417, [1996] 20 Fam LR 390. See also Lowe, Armstrong and Mathias, *Country Report: Australia* (NCMEC, 2002) at 3.5.

[440] See Lowe, Armstrong and Mathias, *County Report: Germany* (NCMEC, 2002) at 3.5. In many cases, the youth welfare service will also be asked to provide a report or, alternatively, the court will appoint a curator for the child. In exceptional cases, the expert opinion of a child psychologist can be called for by the court.

[441] If the judge believes that the person nominated by the child is not suitable, he can designate another person.

[442] See Lowe, Armstrong, Mathias and Navarro, *Country Report: France* (NCMEC, 2002) at 3.5.

[443] *Re T (Abduction: Child's Objection to Return)* [2000] 2 FLR 192 at 212.

this discretion, the child's welfare is not the paramount consideration.[444] In *Re R (Child Abduction: Acquiescence)*, Balcombe LJ said:[445]

> '... it is clear that the policy of the Convention and its faithful implementation by the courts of the countries which have adopted it, should always be a very weighty factor to be brought into the scales ...'

17.183   Put succinctly, the balance is between respecting the child's objections or enforcing the spirit of the Convention despite those objections. Whether, as was argued in *Re D (Abduction: Discretionary Return)*,[446] it is more likely that a return will be refused than, say, following the establishment of consent or acquiescence may be debated, but there is some authority for saying that, once the child's objection defence has been established, it is then incumbent upon those seeking a return to adduce countervailing reasons. As Millett LJ said in *Re R*,[447] if the child is:

> 'of sufficient age and maturity for his views to be taken into account, the Convention clearly envisages that he will *not* be returned against his wishes unless there are countervailing factors which require his wishes to be overridden.'

17.184   Whether, once it has been considered appropriate to take the child's objections into account, matters other than the policy of the Convention can then be considered in deciding how to exercise the discretion is still to be authoritatively decided. In *Re R*[448] Balcombe LJ was of the view (but without deciding the matter) that they could. This was clearly the view of Wall J who, in *Re S (Child Abduction: Delay)*,[449] held that, once the child's objection defence had been established, it was proper to take into account the applicant's delay in pursuing his or her Convention remedy. Wall J has also held[450] that the mere fact that proceedings concerning the child are continuing in the requesting State is not a reason for refusing to exercise the discretion not to order a return.

17.185   English practice is in line with that taken in other common law jurisdictions. As Garbolino comments,[451] when describing the position in the United States, the child's objections do not amount to 'a veto power' since

---

[444] See *Re A (Minors) (Abduction: Acquiescence) (No 2)* [1993] Fam 1, [1993] 1 FLR 396, CA, discussed at **17.81**.

[445] [1995] 1 FLR 716 at 730–731. See also Ward LJ in *Re T (Abduction: Child's Objection to Return)* [2000] 2 FLR 192 at 202–203, who said that notwithstanding the establishment of the defence 'it is only in exceptional cases' that an immediate return should be refused.

[446] [2000] 1 FLR 24 at 36, discussed at **17.59–17.60**.

[447] At 734, a view with which Ward LJ was 'inclined to agree' in *Re T* (above) at 213.

[448] At 731.

[449] [1998] 1 FLR 651 at 659. See also *Re M (Abduction) (Consent: Acquiescence)* [1999] 1 FLR 171 at 191, in which Wall J again took into account the applicant's delay when exercising his discretion following a finding that the father had consented to the child's removal.

[450] In *Re L (Abduction: Child's Objections to Return)* [2002] EWHC 1864 (Fam), [2002] 2 FLR 1042.

[451] In *International Child Custody Cases: Handling Hague Convention Cases in US Courts, op cit*, n 346 above, at 199.

'the court retains discretion to consider this factor along with all other factors in determining whether the child should be returned'. In exercising that discretion, as one commentator has said,[452] courts in Australia and New Zealand regard the welfare of the child as a highly relevant factor 'but the objectives of the Hague Convention may be the most significant matters that are to be taken into account'. In the latter jurisdiction, there is authority[453] for saying that it is only the objectives of the Convention and the child's welfare that should be taken into account when determining how to exercise the discretion.

THE ARTICLE 20 EXCEPTION

17.186   Article 20 provides:

> 'The return of the child under the provisions of Article 12 may be refused if this would not be permitted by the fundamental principles of the requested State relating to the protection of human rights and fundamental freedoms.'

Background to the provision

17.187   The inclusion of Art 20 in the Convention was, as the Pérez-Vera Report says,[454] debated at some length and represents a compromise between those delegations which favoured and those which opposed the inclusion of a 'public policy' clause. According to the Pérez-Vera Report:[455]

> '... this particular rule is not directed at developments which have occurred on the international level, but is concerned only with the principles accepted by the law of the requested State, either through general international law and treaty law, or through internal legislation. Consequently, so as to be able to refuse to return a child on the basis of the article, it will be necessary to show that the fundamental principles of the requested State concerning the subject matter of the Convention do not permit it; it will not be sufficient to show merely that its return would be incompatible, even manifestly incompatible, with these principles.'

The Report also points out that the provision was deliberately placed as the final Article of the Chapter so as to emphasise 'the always clearly exceptional nature of this provision's application'. In fact, Art 20 is rarely applied. According to the 1999 Statistical Survey,[456] no refusals in that survey were

---

[452]   Caldwell, *op cit*, n 346, at 134, citing the New Zealand cases *S v M* [1999] NZFLR 337 at 349, *Ryding v Turvey* [1998] NZFLR 313 and *Clarke v Carson* [1996] 1 NZLR 349 at 351, and the Australian decisions, *Central Authority v Reissner* (1999) 25 Fam 330 at 346, per Lindenmayer J, and *De L v Director-General, NSW Department of Community Services* (1996) 139 ALR 417 at 430.

[453]   *S v M* (above) at 348–349, per Panckhurst J.

[454]   At para 31.

[455]   At para 118.

[456]   *Op cit*, n 2.

based on this provision and, not surprisingly, there is little jurisprudence on its application.[457]

Article 20 not implemented by the United Kingdom

17.188 Article 20 has not been implemented by the United Kingdom. Lord Hailsham LC justified its exclusion[458] in part because of the advice that it was doubtful 'whether there is any such existing fundamental provision of UK law which is not already covered by the exceptions embodied in other Articles', in part because its meaning and scope 'would at least be uncertain', and in part because it could not 'be easily accommodated in a UK legal text'. It was, however, suggested that, nevertheless, courts could still have regard to it if an issue arose where the text was relevant. However, in the only judicial comment on its application, Leggatt LJ said in *Re K (Abduction: Psychological Harm)*:[459]

> 'So far as human rights are concerned, it seems to me that there is obvious objection to adopting such a construction of Art 20 as would have the effect of overriding, or materially altering, the scope of any of the other Articles and in particular Art 13(b). It may well be that the court, as the Lord Chancellor indicated it should, will "have regard to Art 20" in the sense of seeking to construe other Articles, such as Art 13(b), in such a way as not to infringe human rights. Further than that, however, it does not go.'

Whether the United Kingdom's subsequent incorporation of the European Convention for the Protection of Human Rights and Fundamental Freedoms by the Human Rights Act 1998 will have any impact on this position remains to be seen.

17.189 Although the United Kingdom is not alone in not implementing Art 20 (Finland, for example, has likewise not done so), since no such reservation is permitted under the Convention, it might be thought that it is a breach of its international obligations. However, the point has been well made[460] that, by reducing the number of exceptions, the United Kingdom is in fact promoting the overall object of the Convention.

Application of Article 20 outside the United Kingdom

17.190 Article 20 pleas are rarely successful, but this Article was apparently relied upon in a Spanish case[461] in which, after a removal had taken place, the father, who had brought divorce proceedings in a religious court in Israel,

---

[457] At the time of writing there were only 30 references on INCADAT.

[458] See the debate on the Child Abduction and Custody Bill in *Hansard*, HL Deb, vol 461 at col 1175.

[459] [1995] 2 FLR 550 at 557.

[460] By Beaumont and McEleavy, *op cit*, n 121, at 173.

[461] See Beilfuss, 'International Child Abduction in Spain' (2001) 15 Int Jo of Law, Policy and the Family 327 at 339.

obtained a declaration that the mother was a 'rebellious wife' *(moredet)*. The Spanish court understood that to mean that, were the child to be returned to Israel, all contact with the mother would be ended. It therefore held that, since that decision would not be based on the child's best interests but on the desire to punish the mother, a return would be contrary to the fundamental principles of Spanish law.

17.191   The above-mentioned Spanish case, however, is very much the exception. Writing in 1994, Silberman[462] was able to say that there had been no refusals to return based on Art 20. The plea failed, for example, in the Canadian case, *Parsons v Styger*,[463] in which the abducting mother's claim that a return order violated the Canadian Charter of Rights and Freedoms, which guarantees Canadian citizens the right to enter and remain in Canada, was rejected on the basis that citizens do not have a right to remain in Canada in contravention of the 1980 Hague Abduction Convention. Similarly, pleas have failed in Australia. In *Director-General, Department of Families Youth and Community Care v Rhonda May Bennett*,[464] for example, the court ruled that Art 20 was extremely narrow and should be invoked only on the rare occasion that a return would utterly shock the conscience of the court or offend all motions of due process. It therefore rejected the argument that to return a child of Aboriginal or Torres Strait Islander heritage to a foreign country was in breach of any fundamental tenet of Australian law relating to the protection of human rights and fundamental freedoms.

17.192   In Ireland, pleas based on the Irish Constitution have similarly fallen on deaf ears, it being held that the personal rights of children were fully protected by the exceptions built into the Convention.[465] In the United States where Art 20 (like Art 13(b)) has to be established by 'clear and convincing evidence' rather than on the preponderance of probabilities,[466] the child's constitutional rights to due process and equal protection, thus triggering Art 20, have also been rejected.[467]

---

[462] 'Hague International Child Abduction Convention: A Progress Report' (1994) 57 *Law and Contemporary Problems* 210 at 242. See also Weiner, *op cit*, n 333, at fn 407.

[463] (1989) 67 OR (2d) 1 (Ont Sup Ct).

[464] [2000] Fam CA 253. See also *Laing v Central Authority* (1996) FLC 92–709: no evidence to suggest that the American court system would not apply the paramountcy principle.

[465] *ACW v Ireland* [1994] 3 IR 232. See also *CK v CK* [1994] 1 IR 260 and 268. See also the South African Constitutional Court decision *S v T* 2000 INCADAT HC/E/ZA 309.

[466] Section 11603(e)(2)(A) of the International Child Abduction Remedies Act of 1988.

[467] See *Ciotola v Fiocca* 684 NE 2d 763 (1997). For other American decisions rejecting Art 20 pleas, see the discussion by Garbolino, *op cit*, n 346, at 192 *et seq*. See also the cases referred by Weiner, *op cit*, n 333, at fn 407.

Chapter 18

INTERNATIONAL ABDUCTIONS WITHIN THE EUROPEAN UNION: RECOGNITION AND ENFORCEMENT UNDER BRUSSELS II

INTRODUCTION

18.1 Where a child is wrongfully removed to or retained in a Member State of the European Union (other than Denmark)[1] away from his or her home in another Member State, it may be possible to effect a return by using the provisions of Council Regulation (EC) No 1347/2000 of 29 May 2000 on jurisdiction and the recognition and enforcement of judgments in matrimonial matters and in matters of parental responsibility for children of both spouses,[2] which is colloquially known as 'Brussels II'.

---

[1]   See n 3.
[2]   OJ No L160, 30 June 2000, p 19. The Council Regulation is set out in Appendix 1.

18.2 The Council Regulation came into force in the Member States, excluding Denmark,[3] on 1 March 2001. As a Council Regulation, it is directly applicable in each Member State without the necessity for domestic legislation.[4]

18.3 As we discuss in Chapter 2,[5] the overall inspiration for Brussels II was the 1968 Brussels Convention on Jurisdiction and Enforcement of Judgments in Civil and Commercial Matters ('Brussels I') which provides a general framework for recognition and enforcement of judgments but which expressly excludes status and rights of property arising from marriage, although it does include maintenance, and which itself has now become a Regulation.[6]

18.4 In Chapters 2 and 4, we discuss the jurisdictional rules provided by the Council Regulation. This chapter is concerned with its scope and application in the context of child abduction.

THE SCOPE OF THE REGULATION

18.5 When considering the scope of the Council Regulation, it is necessary to bear in mind both that it is modelled as far as possible on Brussels I[7] and, as the Borras Report (the Explanatory Report on the 'former' Brussels II Convention)[8] explains, identical terms in this Regulation and Brussels I must be given the same meaning, with the ECJ case-law having to be taken into account. Further aid to the proper interpretation of the Council Regulation may be sought in the Borras Report itself and in the Recital to the Council Regulation.[9]

---

[3]   Article 1(3). Eire and the United Kingdom opted into the Council Regulation; Denmark has not done so; see Recital to the Council Regulation, paras 24 and 25. For ease of reference, where the term 'Member States' is used in the context of the Council Regulation, it refers to all the EU Member States excluding Denmark.

[4]   The Council Regulation forms part of the *acquis communautaire*, which States joining the EU in future will be required to adopt.

[5]   See **2.9–2.12**.

[6]   See Council Regulation No 44/2001 of 22 December 2000 on jurisdiction and the recognition and enforcement of judgments in civil and commercial matters, OJ 2001 L12/1, which has direct effect in Member States (including the United Kingdom) except Denmark, and to that extent replaces the Brussels I Convention. The Brussels I Convention, insofar as it governs relationships with Denmark, and the Lugano Convention remain in place.

[7]   Shannon with Kennedy, in 'Jurisdictional and Recognition and Enforcement Issues in Proceedings Concerning Parental Responsibility under the Brussels II Convention' [2000] IFL 111, put it well, saying that Brussels I is 'now seen as a general convention' and Brussels II 'as a "lex specialis", which follows the principles of the earlier Convention as far as possible'.

[8]   (1998) OJ C221/27, at para 6. When consulting the Borras Report in the context of the Council Regulation, it is necessary to note that the Article numbers in the Convention and the Council Regulation do not always coincide.

[9]   See also **2.11**.

18.6   The scope of the Council Regulation is governed by Art 1, which provides that it shall apply to:

> '(a)   civil proceedings relating to divorce, legal separation or marriage annulment; and
>
> (b)   civil proceedings relating to parental responsibility for the children of both spouses on the occasion of the matrimonial proceedings referred to in (a).'

By referring to 'civil' proceedings, the Regulation excludes religious proceedings.[10] On the other hand, proceedings officially recognised in a Member State are to be regarded as the equivalent to judicial proceedings, while the term 'court' extends to all authorities having jurisdiction in these matters.[11] 'Member State' specifically excludes Denmark.[12]

18.7   It will be noted that, unlike its unlimited application to proceedings relating to divorce, separation and annulment (hereafter referred to as 'matrimonial proceedings') in relation to the parties' status,[13] the scope of Art 1(1)(b) is limited to issues relating to the parental responsibility for the children of both spouses arising in those proceedings. Accordingly, the Regulation has no application to issues arising in 'non-matrimonial proceedings'[14] nor to issues arising in matrimonial proceedings unless the children concerned are those of *both* spouses. In other words, it has no application to step-children or to non-marital children even if those children were to be regarded as 'children of the family' under domestic law in England and Wales.[15]

18.8   The phrase 'children of both spouses' is not unproblematic for, while it seems clear that it refers to both the biological and adopted children of the couple,[16] it is less clear whether it covers all children regarded by any individual Member State as the legal children of both spouses, for example those conceived as a result of donor insemination or embryo transplants or even, as in the case of English law, those covered by parental orders made under s 30 of the Human Fertilisation and Embryology Act 1990. Similarly, there may be difficulty in determining what is meant by 'parental responsibility' (which is not

---

[10]   See the Borras Report at para 20B.

[11]   Article 1(2), which was drafted bearing in mind (ironically in view of Art 1(3)) the position in Denmark and in Finland: see the Borras Report at para 20A.

[12]   Article 1(3).

[13]   But note that it does not extend to matters beyond status. In particular, the Regulation has no application to matrimonial property.

[14]   Ie to 'freestanding applications' concerning children, and note that jurisdiction under the Regulation only continues until the making of a 'final' order: see Art 3(3), discussed below at **18.26**.

[15]   Under English legislation, for example, the divorce courts have jurisdiction over children who are regarded as 'children of the family' which includes those, regardless of biological origin, who have been 'treated as children of the family': see Matrimonial Causes Act 1973, s 52. For discussion of the application of the Regulation to such children, see the Borras Report at para 25.

[16]   See the Borras Report at para 25.

defined in the Regulation)[17] and in particular as to how it extends to issues ancillary to determining with whom the child is to live and with whom the child may have contact.[18] Does it automatically include all specific issue or prohibited steps orders made by a UK court?[19] Does it extend to issues concerning name changes or prohibitions against publicity? It is for each State to decide what falls within the definition of parental responsibility but, in matters of doubt, a domestic court can, and in some circumstances must, make a reference to the ECJ in Luxembourg,[20] although the ensuing delay is hardly likely to be conducive to the child's welfare.[21]

REFERENCES

18.9   Although references are generally governed by Art 234 EC, in the case of Regulations, such as Brussels II, that are made under Title IV of the EC Treaty, Art 68 provides:

> '1.   Article 234 shall apply to this Title under the following circumstances and conditions: where a question of interpretation of this Title or on the validity or interpretation of acts of the institutions of the Community based on this Title is raised in a case pending before a court or a tribunal of a Member State against whose decisions there is no judicial remedy under national law, that court or tribunal shall, if it considers that a decision on the question is necessary to enable it to give judgment, request the Court of Justice to give a ruling thereon.
>
> ...
>
> 3.   The Council, the Commission or a Member State may request the Court of Justice to give a ruling on a question of interpretation of this Title or of acts of the institutions of the Community based on this Title. The ruling given by the Courts of Justice in response to such a request shall not apply to judgments of courts or tribunals of the Member States which have become res judicata.'

18.10   The phrase 'court or tribunal ... against whose decisions there is no judicial remedy under national law' as it appears in Art 68 has not been tested, but the same phrase in Art 234 has been held to mean the final court,[22] which, according to *Lyckeskog*,[23] *excludes* a domestic court from which there is an

---

[17]   Such difficulties are hinted at in the Borras Report at para 23.

[18]   These issues are known as residence and contact issues in the United Kingdom but may be more widely referred to as custody and access issues.

[19]   In both the English and the Scottish legislation, the power to make specific issue orders and prohibited steps orders (interdicts in Scotland) is expressly confined to dealing with 'aspects of parental responsibility': see respectively s 8(1) of the Children Act 1989 and s 11(2)(e), (f) of the Children (Scotland) Act 1995.

[20]   See **18.9** *et seq*.

[21]   Cf Shannon with Kennedy, *op cit*, n 7, who comment at 112, 'The notion that custody cases should be stayed while the matter is referred to the ECJ for a preliminary ruling is absurd'.

[22]   See, eg, P Craig and G De Búrca, *EU Law, Text, Cases and Materials*, 3rd edn (OUP, 2003), p 234 and Hartley, *The Foundations of European Community Law*, 5th edn (OUP, 2003).

[23]   Case C–99/00 (judgment given on 4 June 2002).

appeal only with permission. In other words, contrary to the normal position in which any court has a discretion to make a reference, under Brussels II only the final court may do so.[24] For the purposes of domestic family law, the 'final court' would seem to be either the House of Lords, or the Court of Appeal in cases where it refuses permission to appeal, although in practice it is difficult to see when the Court of Appeal can legitimately make a reference for it will have no power to do so once it decides to hear a case since the final power to dismiss an appeal rests with the House of Lords, and it would be odd to refuse an appeal yet at the same time make a reference.[25] In other words, since only the House of Lords can make a reference, all other courts, including the Court of Appeal, are obliged to apply the Regulation as best they can, although no doubt they should give leave to appeal in cases where a reference seems desirable.

18.11   Presumably, the obligation of the final court to refer under Art 68 will be governed by the same principles as apply to the obligation of the final courts under Art 234(3).[26] Accordingly, although the parties are free to request a reference, the obligation rests on the national court itself and, under the ruling in *CILFIT*,[27] interpretation or validity of a Regulation have to be made unless the so-called '*acte clair*' principle applies, namely, that the ECJ has already determined on the point or that the answer is so clear that no reference is required. Since Brussels II is so far untested, save on points similar to those adjudicated upon under Brussels I, there seems wide scope for references.

JURISDICTION

18.12   Articles 2 to 12 of the Council Regulation set out rules as to when the courts of a Member State have jurisdiction over matters relating to parental responsibility over a child of both spouses on the occasion of matrimonial proceedings. This has been discussed in Chapter 4.

---

[24]   According to the so-called *Foto-Frost* principle (Case 314/85, *Foto-Frost v Hauptzollamt Lübeck-Ost* [1987] ECR 4199), a national court cannot hold a Community act invalid. However, it is an interesting point whether, since lower courts cannot make a reference under Art 68, they *should* be able to disapply Community acts they consider invalid. Arnull, *The European Union and its Court of Justice* (OUP, 1999), believes such courts can. It may be noted that under the draft Constitution these special rules governing references will change.

[25]   Hartley, *op cit*, n 22, at 285–286, however, considers that, following *Lykeskog* (Case C-99/00) 'unless the House of Lords decides to grant leave it should make a reference when hearing the petition for leave to appeal'. See also *Chiron v Murex Diagnostics (No 2)* [1994] 1 CMLR 410.

[26]   On which, see Craig and De Búrca, *op cit*, n 22, chapter 11.

[27]   *Srl CILFIT and Lanificio di Gavardo SpA v Ministry of Health* (Case 283/81) [1982] ECR 3415.

RECOGNITION

18.13 Recognition and enforcement are covered in Chapter III of the Regulation. So far as recognition is concerned, Art 14(1) obliges Member States to recognise 'judgments' (even those not involving cross-border issues)[28] given in other Member States party to the Regulation 'without any special procedure being required'. In other words, recognition is automatic by operation of law. Nevertheless under Art 14(3) any interested party[29] may apply 'for a decision that the judgment be or not be recognised', although recognition proceedings may be stayed if the judgment in question is subject to an appeal.[30] 'Judgments' recognised and enforced under the Council Regulation are judgments relating to parental responsibility over a child of both spouses given on the occasion of matrimonial proceedings.[31] 'Judgment' is given a wide meaning.[32] Orders covering costs and expenses are entitled to recognition and enforcement,[33] as are agreements or other instruments made part of an order or enforceable as an order.[34]

18.14 So far as judgments relating to parental responsibility[35] are concerned, the grounds of non-recognition are set out in Art 15(2). It is important to realise that this provision sets out the sole grounds. Moreover, the courts in which recognition is sought are forbidden under Art 17 to review the jurisdiction of the court of origin and under Art 18 to refuse recognition because of a difference in applicable law.[36] Importantly, at the heart of the recognition rules is the provision that under no circumstances may a judgment be reviewed as to its substance.[37] However, this prohibition is not intended to

---

28   See the arguments of Rolf Wagner, 'Recognition and Enforcement of Judgments under the Brussels II Regulation', a paper given at the UK–German Judicial Conference on Family Law held in Edinburgh, September 2000, based on the interpretations of the parallel provision, Art 25(4) of Brussels I.

29   According to the Borras Report, at para 65, the concept of an 'interested party' should be interpreted in a broad sense and 'may include the public prosecutor or other similar bodies where permitted in the State in which the judgment is to be recognised or contested'.

30   Article 20(1).

31   Article 13(1).

32   It does not matter what the judgment is called; the term includes a decree, order or decision: see Art 13(1).

33   Article 13(2).

34   Article 13(3).

35   It should be noted that, whereas it is accepted that recognition applies only to so-called 'positive decisions' in relation to divorce, nullity or separation, under the terms of Art 13(1) it would appear that recognition should *prima facie* be accorded to all decisions relating to parental responsibility.

36   Article 18.

37   Article 19. As to the similar Article in Brussels I, see *Interdesco SA v Nullifre* [1992] 1 Lloyd's Rep 180. As to the similar Article in the 1980 European Custody Convention, namely Art 9(3), see **19.99**.

prevent a court with jurisdiction making a new order when a change in circumstances occurs at a later stage.[38]

18.15 The grounds of non-recognition provided by Art 15(2) essentially replicate those provided by Art 23(2) of the 1996 Hague Convention on the Protection of Children.[39] They are not, however, exactly the same, not least because, whereas under the Council Regulation they are mandatory rules, under the 1996 Convention they are optional in that recognition may but does not have to be refused.[40] Nevertheless, it is to be noted that, unlike under the 1980 Hague Abduction Convention or indeed Conventions of the Council of Europe where interpretation is left to the discretion of domestic courts, overall interpretation of the Regulation will be subject to the ECJ, which might not necessarily apply established domestic jurisprudence under the other Conventions.

18.16 There are six grounds set out in Art 15(2), upon any of which the judgment will not be recognised:

(1) the judgment is manifestly contrary to the public policy of the Member State in which recognition is sought *taking into account the best interests of the child* (emphasis added).[41] The words emphasised make it impossible to refuse recognition on public policy grounds alone and require that consideration be given to taking the best interests of the child into account as well. Under the analogous provision in Brussels I, the public policy defence has been very narrowly construed by the ECJ;[42]

(2) the judgment was given (except in the case of urgency) without the child being given an opportunity to be heard, in violation of the fundamental principles of procedure in that Member State.[43] As the Borras Report[44] points out, while this exception is confined to the relevant rules of the Member State in question, nevertheless those rules must take account of Art 12 of the UN Convention on the Rights of the Child;

---

[38] The Borras Report, para 78.

[39] See the discussion in the Borras Report at para 73. For discussion of the 1996 Convention, see Chapter 24, and for the exceptions, see **24.39** *et seq.*

[40] These differences are important in relation to Member States' competence to ratify the 1996 Convention – see further Chapter 24.

[41] Article 15(2)(a). See the Borras Report, para 73. Article 15(2)(a) corresponds exactly to Art 23(3)(d) of the 1996 Hague Protection of Children Convention. For Art 23(3)(d) of the 1996 Convention, see **19.43–19.44**.

[42] *Hoffman v Krieg* (Case 145/86) [1988] ECR 645 (refusal to recognise based on public policy should operate only in exceptional circumstances). Even fraud is not sufficient: see *Société d'Informatique Service Réalisation v Ampersand Software BV* (1993) 35 LS Gaz R 36, (1993) 137 Sol Jo LB 189. However, see *Maronier v Larmer* [2002] EWCA Civ 774, [2003] QB 620 (it is contrary to public policy to enforce a judgment in a Member State against a defendant who has manifestly not received a fair trial in contravention of Art 6 of the ECHR).

[43] Article 15(2)(b). For Art 23(2)(b) of the 1996 Hague Protection of Children Convention, see **24.42**.

[44] At para 73.

(3)   the judgment was given in default of appearance and the person in default was not served in sufficient time and in such a way as to enable that person to arrange for his or her defence, unless it is determined that such person has accepted the judgment unequivocally.[45] The analogous provision of Brussels I has been frequently relied upon;[46]

(4)   the judgment was given without giving an opportunity for a holder of parental responsibility to be heard;[47]

(5)   the judgment is irreconcilable[48] with a later judgment given in the State in which recognition is sought;[49]

(6)   the judgment is irreconcilable with a later judgment given in another Member State or the State of the child's habitual residence,[50] provided that the later judgment fulfils the conditions necessary for its recognition in the Member State in which recognition is sought.[51]

It remains to be seen how widely (or narrowly) these exceptions will be interpreted.

18.17   The court of the Member State in which recognition is sought may stay the recognition proceedings if an appeal has been made against the judgment[52] or (if the judgment sought to be recognised was made in the United Kingdom or Eire) if the judgment has been stayed in the State of origin pending appeal.[53]

ENFORCEMENT

18.18   Unlike matrimonial judgments for which, being matters of status, recognition is sufficient, special provision is made for the enforcement of judgments relating to parental responsibility under Arts 21 to 31.

---

45   Article 15(2)(c). For the full text of Art 15(2)(c), see Appendix 1. See also *Pellegrini v Italy* (2002) 35 EHRR 2.

46   There are two elements: service according to the rules and in time: see *Klomps v Michel* (Case 166/80) [1981] ECR 1593, and *Isabelle Lancracy v Peters and Sickert* (Case 305/88) [1990] 1 ECR 2725.

47   Article 15(2)(d).

48   As to the analogous provision of Brussels I, see *Solo Kleinmotoren Gmb H v Boch* (Case C-414/92), [1994] ECR I-2237. See also **19.106** and **19.119** *et seq* for the use of the word 'incompatible' in Arts 9(1)(c) and 10(1)(d) of the 1980 European Custody Convention.

49   Article 15(2)(e).

50   Even if the State is not a member of the European Union.

51   Article 15(2)(f).

52   Article 20(1). As to the meaning of 'appeal' under Brussels I, see *Industrial Diamond Supplies v Riva* (Case 3/77) [1977] ECR 2175. See also *Wermuth v Wermuth (No 1)* [2002] EWHC 3049 (Fam), [2003] 1 FLR 1022; *A v L (Jurisdiction: Brussels II)* [2003] 1 FLR 1042; and *Re L (A Minor) (Abduction: Jurisdiction)* [2002] EWHC 1864 (Fam), [2002] 1 WLR 3208, [2002] 2 FLR 1042.

53   Article 20.

Obtaining a declaration of enforceability

18.19   The procedure for enforcement is analogous to that under Brussels I but less complex.[54] Under Art 21(1) an enforceable judgment on the exercise of parental responsibility made in one Member State can be declared enforceable in another Member State on the application of any interested party, although within the United Kingdom, under Art 21(2), a judgment becomes enforceable when upon application it has been registered for enforcement.[55] Under Art 29 there can be partial enforcement, so it will be no objection that only parts of a judgment (for example, those relating to a child of both spouses) are enforceable under the terms of the Regulation. For these purposes, 'interested party' covers not only spouses or children but also, in some States, a relevant public authority.[56] The applicant does not have to be resident in the jurisdiction.

18.20   An application for a declaration of enforceability is submitted to a prescribed level of court in each Member State.[57] In France, for example, application should be made to the presiding judge of the *Tribunal de Grande Instance*. So far as the United Kingdom is concerned, application should be made to the appropriate court respectively of England and Wales, Scotland or Northern Ireland; in England and Wales, declarations of enforceability must be made by the High Court.[58] Article 22 also makes provision for determining the jurisdiction of the local court. Articles 23 and 24 make further provision for procedure for enforcement. Articles 33 to 35 specify the documents to be produced on an application for recognition and enforcement and the time for production.

18.21   The person against whom enforcement is sought is not entitled to make any submissions at this stage.[59] Refusals will only be justified on the grounds set out in Art 15[60] with an absolute prohibition against reviewing a judgment as to its substance.[61] Under Art 26 either party can appeal against the decision in an application for declaration.[62] At this stage the person against

---

[54]   See the Borras Report at paras 82 ff. As to Brussels I, see **18.3**.

[55]   As of August 2003, it is understood that there have been no registrations in England and Wales.

[56]   See the Borras Report at para 80.

[57]   Article 22 and Annex I. This Annex sets out the relevant court for each jurisdiction of the Member States: for example, in England and Wales, the High Court of Justice; in Scotland, the Court of Session; in Northern Ireland, the High Court of Justice; in France, the presiding judge of the *Tribunal de Grande Instance*.

[58]   Article 22 and Annex I.

[59]   Article 24.

[60]   Article 24(2).

[61]   Article 24(3), which repeats the provision in Art 19.

[62]   The appropriate court to which an appeal should be made is listed in Annex II to the Regulation. In the case of England and Wales, it is the the High Court of Justice; in Scotland, the Court of Session; in Northern Ireland, the High Court of Justice; and in France, the *Cour d'Appel*.

whom enforcement is sought is entitled to be heard.[63] The procedure at this stage is again laid down in the Council Regulation.[64]

Practical measures of enforcement

18.22 The Regulation only governs the procedure necessary to obtain declarations of enforceability – actual enforcement is left to the national law of the enforcing State. It is expected that enforcement of foreign judgments will be almost automatic[65] and, in any event, refusals to enforce will only be justified on the grounds set out in Art 15[66] with an absolute prohibition against reviewing a judgment as to its substance.[67]

England and Wales

18.23 The procedure in England and Wales for recognition and enforcement is governed by FPR 1991, rr 7.40–7.50 and is discussed in Chapter 21.[68]

INTER-RELATIONSHIP WITH OTHER INTERNATIONAL INSTRUMENTS

Generally

18.24 International agreements have brought many advantages in the field of trans-border family disputes, not least in limiting the opportunities for dispute. However, a priority for future advance in international family law must be a comprehensive regime incorporating a clear hierarchy of international instruments. Under Art 37 of the Council Regulation, the Council Regulation takes precedence over the 1996 Hague Convention on the Protection of Children, with regard to children habitually resident in a Member State.[69] However, the Regulation will not prevent use being made of the 1996 Convention insofar as it does not overlap with Brussels II (although insofar as it is sought to use the Convention as well as the Regulation it makes for a complicated inter-relationship). In Chapter 24, we discuss the 1996 Convention and the problems associated with its inter-relationship with other instruments.

---

63 Article 26(3).
64 Articles 26–28.
65 At any rate this is Shannon's view: see *op cit*, n 7, at 117.
66 Article 24(2).
67 Article 24(3), which repeats the provision in Art 19.
68 See **21.105** *et seq*.
69 It also takes precedence over the Hague Convention of 5 October 1961 concerning the Powers of Authorities and the Law Applicable in respect of the Protection of Minors.

Inter-relationship with the 1980 European Custody Convention

18.25   The Council Regulation takes precedence[70] over the 1980 European Custody Convention.[71] This means that where it is sought to enforce a custody or access decision in respect of children of both spouses made in matrimonial proceedings (but not in freestanding proceedings) in another Member State, the Council Regulation *must* be used in preference to the Convention.[72] Consequently, the applicant will not be entitled, as he would under the 1980 European Custody Convention, to channel applications through Central Authorities, nor to free legal representation regardless of means or merit,[73] nor will the court have any power to modify the access order as it can under Art 11(2) of the Convention.[74] These differences become all the more exaggerated where step-children are concerned, for the application must be made, if at all, under the European Custody Convention. In these circumstances it might also be pointed out that the grounds for refusing recognition and enforcement under Arts 9 and 10 of the Convention are not the same as under the Regulation.

Inter-relationship with the 1980 Hague Abduction Convention

18.26   The inter-relationship with the 1980 Hague Abduction Convention is potentially problematic.[75] Under Art 4 of the Council Regulation, the 1980 Hague Abduction Convention[76] takes precedence over the Council Regulation in that courts in each Member State of the EU with jurisdiction within the meaning of Art 3[77] must exercise their jurisdiction in conformity with the 1980 Hague Abduction Convention, and in particular Arts 3 and 16 of that Convention.[78] The intention is to safeguard the habitual residence as the ground of jurisdiction where, as a result of a wrongful removal or retention, there has in fact been a change in habitual residence.[79] By according

---

70   See Art 37.
71   For the 1980 European Custody Convention, see **19.69**. As to the inter-relationship with other multi-lateral and bi-lateral Conventions, see Arts 36 and 40.
72   See also **21.1**.
73   Article 30 only makes provision for legal aid according to domestic law provisions. Article 30 provides that an applicant who has benefited in the Member State of origin from complete or partial legal aid is entitled 'to benefit from the most favourable legal aid or the most extensive exemption from costs and expenses provided for by the law of the Member State addressed'.
74   See **25.52–25.54**.
75   The problems are similar to those created by the inter-relationship between the 1996 Hague Protection of Children Convention and the 1980 Hague Abduction Convention which we discuss at **24.61** *et seq*.
76   For the 1980 Hague Abduction Convention, see Chapter 13.
77   As to which, see **4.14**.
78   See *Re L (A Minor) (Abduction: Jurisdiction)* [2002] EWHC 1864 (Fam), [2002] 1 WLR 3208, , sub nom *Re L (Abduction: Child's Objections to Return)* [2002] 2 FLR 1042.
79   The Borras Report, paras 40 and 41.

precedence to the 1980 Hague Abduction Convention and, in particular, Art 16 of that Convention,[80] the courts of the State to which a child has been abducted are prevented from assuming jurisdiction under Brussels II prior to any decision on return or non-return.

18.27   However, uncertainty arises where there has been a refusal to return under the 1980 Hague Abduction Convention. There is nothing to prevent an application being made for recognition and enforcement of an order for custody or return[81] made under Brussels II. In what circumstances will recognition be refused? While there would be a strong case for refusing recognition under the public policy ground in Art 15(2)(a)[82] in certain cases (for example in a case where refusal under the 1980 Hague Abduction Convention is based on the child's objections),[83] some cases may not present such a clear solution to the possible conflict between the court of the State to which the child has been taken (which has refused to return a child) and the court of the hitherto home State whose order requires a return.[84]

REVISING BRUSSELS II

French initiative on rights of access

18.28   On 3 July 2000, France presented an initiative (originally known as Brussels IIA or II bis) on the abolition of the *exequatur* process on access orders; and it coupled this with proposals for the automatic return of children unlawfully retained after access (with exceptions to such a mandatory return strictly limited). The scope of the initiative was confined to Brussels II children (ie orders in respect of children of both spouses made on the occasion of matrimonial proceedings).[85]

The revised Brussels II Regulation

18.29   However, on 3 May 2002, the Commission presented a new Proposal for a Council Regulation concerning jurisdiction and the recognition of judgments in matrimonial matters and in matters of parental responsibility, repealing Regulation (EC) No 1347/2000 and amending Regulation (EC) No 44/2001 in matters relating to maintenance. This new proposal dealt with jurisdiction over matrimonial matters and recognition of judgments given in such matters.[86] It also dealt with jurisdiction in respect of, and recognition and

---

[80]   As to Art 16, see **12.8** and **21.39**.

[81]   The order could be made prior to or subsequent to the order refusing return.

[82]   See **18.16**.

[83]   As to which, see **17.141**.

[84]   See the discussion at **24.61** *et seq*.

[85]   See **18.8**.

[86]   The new proposal contained no changes from the existing Brussels II in the field of matrimonial proceedings. However, because it was a new proposal, in theory at least, the whole text of the new proposal was open to negotiation, although no Member State took

enforcement of judgments in, all civil proceedings concerning parental responsibility.[87] It constituted a single and all-embracing EU instrument: its scope extended to all children, not just the limited class in the existing Brussels II.

18.30 The 3 May 2002 Proposal would have made a fundamental change in respect of intra-EU child abduction. An EU regime was to apply and take precedence over the 1980 Hague Abduction Convention. The proposals in respect of intra-EU abduction were controversial and led to a marked division of opinion among the Member States.

18.31 On 29 November 2002, the Council of Ministers (Justice and Home Affairs) reached agreement on revised intra-EU abduction provisions for the revised Brussels II Regulation.[88] The agreement recognised that the 1980 Hague Abduction Convention should be retained for intra-EU cases but that it should be complemented by additional provisions, first to make certain generally accepted principles of good practice in the operation of the Convention binding on EU Member States, and secondly to cover cases where the proceedings under the Convention have concluded with the making of a non-return order under Art 13. The effect of the latter provisions is to confirm that where the 'left-behind parent' (to use the most common case) does not accept the decision not to return the child pursuant to Art 13, he or she is to be entitled to apply, as is the other parent, to the courts of the Member State of origin (that is, the State in which the child was habitually resident immediately before the wrongful removal or retention) for a determination of the issue of custody. The effect in practical terms (although not as a matter of operation of the Hague Abduction Convention) is that the courts in the State of origin will be entitled to have the final say.[89] In the event that the court of origin, having taken into account the concerns of the court which made a non-return order, makes an order on the merits of custody which requires the return of the child to the custody of the left-behind parent, then that custody order will be entitled to enforcement in any other EU State where the child is present, provided that certain procedural safeguards have been observed.[90]

18.32 The revised Brussels II Regulation reads:

---

this opportunity to revisit the rules on divorce jurisdiction in Brussels II. In addition, the new proposal also regulated jurisdiction over maintenance when ancillary to parental responsibility proceedings.

[87] It included proceedings concerning public law orders such as care orders.

[88] Council of European Union Document, JUSTCIV 202 of 20 December 2002.

[89] This is based on the principle, which underlies the approach of both the 1980 Hague Abduction Convention and the 1996 Hague Protection of Children Convention, that the court of the habitual residence of the child will usually be in the better position to decide on what is in the best interests of the child, and additionally that the court of origin would, through submissions made to it, take into account the concerns of the court which made the non-return order.

[90] These are specified in s 4 of Chapter III of the revised Brussels II Regulation.

'Article 10

Jurisdiction in cases of child abduction

In case of wrongful removal or retention of the child, the courts of the Member State where the child was habitually resident immediately before the wrongful removal or retention shall retain their jurisdiction until the child has acquired a habitual residence in another Member State and:

(a) each person, institution or other body having rights of custody has acquiesced in the removal or retention; or

(b) the child has resided in that other Member State for a period of at least one year after the person, institution or other body having rights of custody has had or should have had knowledge of the whereabouts of the child and the child is settled in his or her new environment and at least one of the following conditions is met:

    (i) within one year after the holder of rights of custody has had or should have had knowledge of the whereabouts of the child, no request for return has been lodged before the competent authorities of the Member State where the child has been removed or is being retained;

    (ii) a request for return lodged by the holder of rights of custody has been withdrawn and no new request has been lodged within the time limit set in paragraph (i);

    (iii) a case before the court in the Member State where the child was habitually resident immediately before the wrongful removal or retention has been closed pursuant to Article 11(7);

    (iv) a judgment on custody that does not entail the return of the child has been issued by the courts of the Member State where the child was habitually resident immediately before the wrongful removal or retention.

Article 11

Return of the child

(1) When a person institution or other body having rights of custody applies to the competent authorities in a Member State to deliver a judgment on the basis of the Hague Convention of 25 October 1980 on the Civil Aspects of International Child Abduction (hereinafter 'the 1980 Hague Convention'), in order to obtain the return of a child that has been wrongfully removed or retained in a Member State other than the Member State where the child was habitually resident immediately before the wrongful removal or retention, paragraphs 2 to 8 shall apply.[91]

(2) When applying Articles 12 and 13 of the 1980 Hague Convention, it shall be ensured that the child is given the opportunity to be heard during the proceedings unless this appears inappropriate having regard to his or her age or degree of maturity.[92]

---

91 The intention behind this paragraph is that the 1980 Hague Abduction Convention remains applicable in cases of child abduction between Member States.

92 A recital indicates that this paragraph is not intended to modify national procedures relating to the hearing of the child.

(3) A court to which an application for return of a child is made as mentioned in paragraph 1 shall act expeditiously in proceedings on the application, using the most expeditious procedures available in national law.

Without prejudice to the first subparagraph , the court shall, unless exceptional circumstances make this impossible, issue its judgment no later than six weeks after the application is lodged.

(4) A court cannot refuse to return a child on the basis of Article 13b of the 1980 Hague Convention if it is established that adequate arrangements have been made to secure the protection of the child after his or her return.

(5) A court cannot refuse to return a child unless the person who requested the return of the child has been given an opportunity to be heard.

(6) If a court has issued an order on non-return pursuant to Article 13 of the 1980 Hague Convention, the court must immediately either directly or through its central authority transmit a copy of the court order on non-return and of the relevant documents, in particular a transcript of the hearings before the court, to the court with jurisdiction or central authority in the Member State where the child was habitually resident immediately before the wrongful removal or retention, as determined by national law. The court shall receive all the mentioned documents within one month of the date of the non-return order.

(7) Unless the courts in the Member State where the child was habitually resident immediately before the wrongful removal or retention have already been seised by one of the parties, the court or central authority that receives the information mentioned in paragraph 6 must notify the parties and invite them to make submissions to the court, in accordance with national law, within three months of the date of the notification so that the court can examine the question of custody of the child.

Without prejudice to the rules on jurisdiction contained in this Regulation, the court shall close the case if no submissions have been received by the court within the time limit.

(8) Notwithstanding a judgment of non-return pursuant to Article 13 of the 1980 Hague Convention, any subsequent judgment which requires the return of the child issued by a court having jurisdiction under this Regulation shall be enforceable in accordance with Section 4 of Chapter III below in order to secure the return of the child.'

18.33   There are other new features to the revised Brussels II Regulation.[93] 'Parental responsibility' is defined. Provision is made for prorogation of jurisdiction (Art 12) and for a limited power to transfer on *forum conveniens* grounds (Art 15). Under Arts 53 to 58, each Member State is required to designate a Central Authority[94] to assist with the application of the revised Regulation.

18.34   The grounds of non-recognition for judgments relating to parental responsibility are similar to those under the existing Brussels II. However, a

---

[93] Proposals that a child should have a right to maintain a personal relationship and contact with both parents and a right to be heard on matters relating to parental responsibility in accordance with his age or maturity have been dropped.

[94] It is thought that the Lord Chancellor's Child Abduction Unit will be the Central Authority for England and Wales.

judgment concerning a right of access and a judgment requiring the return of the child under the intra-EU abduction Article (Art 11 as set out above) is to be recognised and enforced without any special procedure or declaration of enforceability[95] and in effect without the possibility of relying on the general grounds of non-recognition.[96]

18.35   At the time of writing, it is anticipated that the final agreement on the Regulation will be reached between the Ministers of the Member States by the end of November 2003.[97] The Regulation will fully come into force on 1 March 2005. The agreed final text of the new Regulation will be posted on the website of the Council of the European Union.[98]

---

[95]   Or (presumably) in the case of the England and Wales, registration.
[96]   Article 41.
[97]   Ie by the end of the Italian Presidency of the Council of Ministers.
[98]   http://register.consilium.eu.int/utfregister/frames/introfsEN.htm.

Chapter 19

INTERNATIONAL ABDUCTIONS: THE EUROPEAN CUSTODY CONVENTION

INTRODUCTION AND BACKGROUND TO THE CONVENTION[1]

The origins of the Convention

19.1 The European Convention on the Recognition and Enforcement of Custody of Children and on Restoration of Custody of Children 1980 had its origins at the Seventh Conference of European Ministers of Justice held at Basle in 1972, which was concerned with ways of improving co-operation in respect of guardianship and custody of children.[2] Following that conference, the European Committee on Legal Co-operation was asked[3] 'to study forms of co-operation amongst member states with a view to children being afforded increased international protection based solely on their welfare'. This task was undertaken by a committee of governmental experts. At that committee's first meeting (in 1973) it was agreed that the priority task should be to draw up a European Convention on the recognition and enforcement[4] of decisions relating to the custody of children. Subsequently, however, the Swiss experts on the committee presented draft proposals for a Convention to deal with restoration of custody of children removed from their legal custodian and taken across an international frontier. Having been authorised to examine both issues, the committee of experts resolved to harmonise the two drafts so as to have a single Convention dealing with recognition and enforcement of custody decisions and restoration of custody in the case of a child's removal to another country.

19.2 The resulting draft (as amended by the European Committee on Legal Co-operation) was adopted by the Committee of Ministers and opened for signature at the Twelfth Conference of European Ministers of Justice held at Luxembourg[5] on 20 May 1980. It was signed by 15 Member States.[6]

Aims and objectives

19.3 The aims and objectives of the European Convention are set out in the Preamble (not specifically enacted in the United Kingdom). The Preamble

---

1 See generally the Council of Europe's own Explanatory Report (reprinted in 1994) on the Convention (which is also reproduced at (1981) Cmnd 8155), and RL Jones, 'Council of Europe Convention on Recognition and Enforcement of Decisions Relating to the Custody of Children' (1981) 30 ICLQ 467 (Jones was vice-chairman of the committee of experts which completed the preparatory work).

2 The Conference deliberations centred on a report presented by the then Austrian Minister of Justice, Christian Broda.

3 See Resolution No 1 of the 1972 Conference.

4 It being noted that the 1961 Hague Convention on the Protection of Minors (discussed at **24.2–24.4**) did not provide for the enforcement of orders.

5 Hence, it is also known as 'the Luxembourg Convention'.

6 Viz Austria, Belgium, Cyprus, France, the Federal Republic of Germany, Greece, Ireland, Italy, Liechtenstein, Luxembourg, the Netherlands, Portugal, Spain, Switzerland and the United Kingdom, all of which have since ratified the Convention: see **19.29** below.

begins by referring to the recognition that in Member States of the Council of Europe 'the welfare of the child is of overriding importance in reaching decisions concerning his custody'. This recognition could be important in determining whether to accept possible accessions for, unless a State shares this view of the importance of the child's welfare, it would presumably not be accepted.

19.4 This basic recognition is further augmented by the view that 'the making of arrangements to ensure that decisions concerning the custody of the child can be more widely recognised and enforced will provide greater protection of the welfare of children'. Further, as the Preamble states, it is desirable 'to emphasise that the right of access of parents is a normal corollary to the right of custody'. Describing access as a parental right now seems dated, but it nevertheless serves to underline the basic strategy of providing for the recognition and enforceability of access orders by specifying that access issues are to be treated with the same weight as custody rights.[7]

19.5 The latter part of the Preamble deals with what would now be termed international abductions.[8] Having noted 'the increasing number of cases where children have been improperly removed across an international frontier and the difficulties of securing adequate solutions to the problems caused by such cases', it refers to the desirability of:

> 'making suitable provision to enable the custody of children which has been arbitrarily interrupted to be restored.'

This last statement masked an important disagreement between Member States, namely, the extent to which there should be a residuary discretion in the State addressed not to implement a request from another State for the child's return.[9]

19.6 Finally, the Preamble refers to the desirability of making arrangements for the above-mentioned purpose 'answering to different needs and different circumstances' and of establishing 'legal co-operation' among Member States' authorities.

---

7   For a criticism of this strategy, see Bruch, 'How to Draft a Successful Family Law Convention: Lessons from the Child Abduction Convention' in Doek, van Loon and Vlaardingerbroek (eds), *Children on the Move* (Martinus Nijhoff, 1996), p 47, at p 52, n 25.

8   At one time, the term used was the emotive one of 'child kidnapping' – a term used, for example, by Jones, *op cit*, n 1, in his informative article about the establishment of the Convention.

9   See Jones, *op cit*, n 1, at 469 and see further **19.9** below.

The basic scheme

Need for a court order

19.7 In dealing with what the Convention refers to as 'improper removals',[10] the strategy employed is not to lay down any limits on the circumstances in which a Member State may assume jurisdiction but, instead, as Jones puts it,[11] to provide that 'any decision on custody or access in a State which is a party to the Convention shall be recognised and enforced in any other State unless the State addressed chooses to avail itself of one of the specified grounds for refusal of recognition and enforcement'. This basic strategy is further underpinned by the enjoinder in Art 9(3) that '[i]n no circumstances may the foreign decision be reviewed as to its substance'.

Post-removal orders under Article 12

19.8 Although this strategy broke new ground since, traditionally, child custody judgments were ignored by international recognition of judgments agreements[12] it does mean that, unlike under the 1980 Hague Abduction Convention,[13] it is a prerequisite of applying under the European Custody Convention that applicants have a custody or access order in their favour. However, applicants do not necessarily need to have such an order at the time of the child's removal because, under Art 12, decisions relating to custody made subsequent to the removal and declaring that removal to be unlawful[14] are equally recognisable and enforceable. Article 12 is intended to protect those entitled to custody by automatic operation of law (referred to by some as '*ex-lege*' rights) rather than under a court order and who are deprived of *de facto* custody by an improper removal to another jurisdiction.[15] It also counters the otherwise obvious loophole of parents deliberately removing children before any order can be obtained.

Refusing recognition and enforcement where there has been an improper removal

19.9 There was a fundamental disagreement among Member States as to the latitude that requested States should have to refuse recognition and enforcement.[16] Some States championed the view that, since the main object of the Convention should be the deterrence of abduction, the return of those children recently abducted from a State to which they were closely connected both by nationality and habitual residence, should virtually be automatic. Other

---

[10] See Art 1(d), discussed at **19.56** *et seq*.
[11] *Op cit*, n 1, at 469.
[12] See the pertinent observations of Bruch, *op cit*, n 7, at p 50, n 11.
[13] Discussed in Chapter 12.
[14] Referred to by Bruch, *op cit*, n 7, at p 50 as a 'chasing order'.
[15] See para 61 of the Explanatory Report.
[16] See Jones, *op cit*, n 1, at 472–473, where he fully articulates the debate.

States maintained that the requested State should retain an ultimate discretion to refuse a return where this would manifestly be contrary to the child's welfare.

19.10 To accommodate both views, the Convention permits States either to opt into a mandatory type of system as provided by Art 8 in particular (discussed below) or, by taking a reservation on Arts 8 and 9,[17] to elect for a more discretionary system.

The position where Art 8 applies

19.11 Under Art 8, where there has been an 'improper removal' (that is, a removal of a child across an international frontier in breach of a custody or access order),[18] the Central Authority of the State addressed is obliged to:

> '... cause steps to be taken *forthwith* to restore the custody of the child' (emphasis added).

This obligation is subject to two important provisos. First, both the child and his parents must have the sole nationality of, and the child his habitual residence in, the State that made the decision sought to be enforced either at the time of the institution of proceedings or at the time of improper removal, if earlier. Secondly, the request for restoration of custody must be made to a Central Authority within 6 months of the improper removal.[19]

19.12 In other words, under Art 8, provided the application is brought within 6 months, it is only where the child and/or his parents have no close connection (in terms of nationality and, in the case of the child, habitual residence) with the State making the decision that the obligation to restore the custody forthwith does not arise. However, the obligation under Art 8 is qualified by Art 9 which permits, in narrowly defined circumstances (viz failure to serve notice of proceedings on the defendant, lack of competence of the court of origin and a decision being incompatible with an earlier one made before the removal),[20] refusals to recognise and enforce even where applications are brought within the 6-month time limit.

19.13 Wider grounds for refusing to recognise and enforce custody orders are provided by Art 10 (in particular under Art 10(1)(b) that 'the effects of the original decision are manifestly no longer in accordance with the welfare of the child'), but in those States where no reservation is entered, these can only be invoked where the application is made more than 6 months after the improper removal.

---

[17] As permitted by Art 17, discussed at **19.34**.

[18] See Art 1(d), discussed at **19.56**.

[19] Note also Art 8(3), which specifically provides for restoration of custody following a failure to return a child at the end of agreed period of access abroad.

[20] Discussed at **19.100** *et seq.*

The position where Art 8 does not apply

19.14 For those States, such as the United Kingdom,[21] which have made reservations on Arts 8 and 9, there is no stated obligation to restore custody forthwith even if the application is brought within 6 months of an improper removal. Furthermore, both the narrow exceptions under Art 9 and the wider ones under Art 10 can be invoked regardless of when the application is made.

19.15 Although it might appear easier to recover a child taken from the United Kingdom to a State that has not entered a reservation on Arts 8 and 9, under the terms of Art 17(2), such States may, when dealing with a child brought from a State that has made the reservation, refuse recognition and enforcement 'on any of the additional grounds referred to in that reservation'. In other words, in the spirit of full reciprocity as between two Contracting States, no advantage can be taken of the one entering and the other not entering a reservation. Accordingly, in the case of improper removals from the United Kingdom, other Member States are entitled to apply Art 10 regardless of when the application is made.

Central Authorities

19.16 As under the 1980 Hague Abduction Convention, Contracting States are enjoined to appoint a Central Authority[22] which has the pivotal role both of administering the Convention's operations and of encouraging international co-operation. So far as the latter is concerned, under Art 3(1) Central Authorities are required both to co-operate with each other and to promote co-operation between competent national authorities and 'to act with all necessary despatch'. According to the Explanatory Report:[23]

> 'The objective is that these authorities should not limit themselves to considering the national aspects of the matters submitted to them, but should also take into consideration the international elements. Such co-operation should lead to the speeding up of procedures.'

19.17 Furthermore, under Art 3(2), to facilitate the operation of the Convention, Central Authorities are obliged, upon request, to provide each other with information about their law (and any changes to it) relating to custody and to keep each other informed of any difficulties that are likely to arise in applying that Convention and as far as possible to eliminate obstacles

---

[21] Other States making similar reservations are Austria, Bulgaria, Czech Republic, Denmark, Finland, France, Germany, Greece, Iceland, Ireland, Lithuania, Malta, Norway, Poland, Spain, Sweden, and Switzerland.

[22] See Art 2. Article 2(2) permits States with more than one system of law to appoint more than one Central Authority. This Article is not specifically incorporated into English law by the Child Abduction and Custody Act 1985, but see s 14, which refers to the establishment of Central Authorities for England and Wales, Scotland and Northern Ireland.

[23] At para 22.

to its application. They are also obliged to 'secure the transmission of requests coming from competent authorities and relating to legal or factual matters concerning pending proceedings'.

19.18 So far as individual applications are concerned, the general scheme provided by Arts 4 and 5 is as follows: any person wishing to have a custody decision made in one Contracting State recognised and enforced in another Contracting State may[24] apply to any[25] Central Authority. It is the responsibility of the authority receiving the application to ensure that all the documents to be provided are complete and in due form.[26] Consequently, the authority may refuse to intervene 'where it is manifestly clear that the conditions laid down by this Convention are not satisfied'.[27] Subject to this proviso, if the Central Authority is not that of the State addressed it should send the documents 'directly and without delay to the central authority'.[28]

19.19 Unless the Central Authority of the State addressed believes the child is in another Contracting State, it is obliged to take 'without delay' all appropriate steps including, where necessary, instituting proceedings, *inter alia*, to discover the child's whereabouts, to secure the recognition and enforcement of the decision and to secure the delivery of the child to the applicant where enforcement is granted.[29]

19.20 Crucially, under Art 5(3), except for the cost of repatriation, Contracting States undertake not to claim payments for the discharge of any of the foregoing duties of the requested Central Authority, including the costs of proceedings and, where applicable, the costs incurred by the assistance of a lawyer.

19.21 As under the Hague Abduction Convention, the United Kingdom has opted to implement its obligation in this respect by giving applicants free public funding regardless of means or merits.[30] Furthermore, because it is clearly a 'Convention' obligation to recognise and enforce access decisions, unlike under the Hague Convention,[31] under the European Convention,

---

[24] Ie there is no compulsion to use a Central Authority. Applicants can apply directly to the courts of the State addressed: see para 21 of the Explanatory Report.

[25] According to the Explanatory Report at para 23, this arrangement was adopted in the applicant's interests, since he will be in the best position to know which authority to approach.

[26] See Explanatory Report, para 24.

[27] Article 4(4).

[28] Article 5(2).

[29] Article 5(1).

[30] Community Legal Service (Financial) Regulations 2000, SI 2000/516, reg 3(1)(f) (England and Wales); Civil Legal Aid (Scotland) Regulations 1996, SI 1996/2444 (S 189), reg 46 (Scotland); and Legal Aid General Regulations (Northern Ireland) 1965, reg 3A (Northern Ireland). See further **21.14** *et seq.*

[31] See **25.17** *et seq.*

applicants in England and Wales[32] will still be entitled to free legal representation (formerly legal aid) to take court proceedings over access.

Effect of recognition and enforcement

19.22 Under Art 7 decisions relating to custody made in one Contracting State must be recognised and, if enforceable in the State of origin, made enforceable in every other Contracting State. So far as the United Kingdom is concerned, to be enforceable, applications first have to be made to register the order.[33] Once the order is registered, the registering court has the same powers of enforcement as if the order had originally been made by that court, and proceedings for or with respect to the enforcement may be taken accordingly.[34]

Summary of the key differences between the European Custody Convention and the Hague Abduction Convention

19.23 The crucial difference between the two Conventions is that, whereas it is a prerequisite for invoking the European Custody Convention that the applicant has a court order relating to custody or access in his favour (albeit that under Art 12 a 'post-removal' order relating to custody is sufficient), applicants do not need a prior court order to invoke the Hague Abduction Convention (although States can require applicants for a return to obtain a court declaration that a removal was wrongful).[35] On the other hand, provided there is an enforceable order, there is no requirement under the European Custody Convention that the removal is improper, and hence that Convention can be invoked in circumstances where the 1980 Hague Abduction Convention cannot because the removal was lawful.[36]

19.24 A second difference relates to the enforcement of access. Whereas under the European Custody Convention it clearly is a Convention application to take court proceedings to enforce access, it has been held both in England and Wales and in Scotland that the Hague Abduction Convention imposes no such obligation upon the judicial authorities.[37] Accordingly, it has been said[38] that it might be easier to enforce an access decision under the European Custody Convention rather than the Hague Abduction Convention, and, so far

---

32 Cf in Scotland, where a more liberal regime applies to Hague Convention applications, discussed at **25.27** *et seq*.

33 See Child Abduction and Custody Act 1985, s 16, discussed at **19.84** *et seq*.

34 See *ibid*, s 18.

35 Under Art 15 of the Hague Abduction Convention, discussed at **15.1** *et seq*.

36 See *T v R (Abduction: Forum Conveniens)* [2002] 2 FLR 544, discussed further at **19.40**, **19.110** and **19.125**.

37 *Re G (A Minor) (Enforcement of Access Abroad)* [1993] Fam 216, [1993] 1 FLR 669, CA, discussed at **25.20** and, in Scotland, *Donofrio v Burrell* 2000 SLT 1051, 2000 SCLR 465, discussed at **25.28** *et seq*.

38 Per Hoffmann LJ in *Re G* (above) at 229 and 679–680, respectively.

as England and Wales is concerned, it is only under the former Convention that free legal representation is available to pursue a court action to enforce access.[39]

19.25 A third possible difference is that, whereas the European Custody Convention can apparently operate retrospectively,[40] the Hague Abduction Convention does not.[41]

19.26 A fourth difference relates to the grounds for refusing, in the case of the European Custody Convention, to recognise and enforce an order, and, in the case of the Hague Abduction Convention, to make a return order.[42]

19.27 A fifth difference is that the so-called 'Brussels II Regulation' takes precedence over the European Custody Convention but not over the Hague Abduction Convention, and the latter takes priority over the former.[43]

19.28 Finally, the Contracting States are different (see further below).

The Contracting States

Ratifications

19.29 Under Art 21, the European Custody Convention is open for signature by Member States of the Council of Europe, but is subject to ratification, acceptance or approval. Instruments of ratification, acceptance or approval must be deposited with the Secretary General of the Council of Europe. In accordance with Art 22(1), the Convention first came into force on 1 September 1983 following its ratification by three Member States, namely France, Luxembourg and Portugal. Following this event, Art 22(2) now operates so that ratification by any Member State comes into force 3 months after the deposit of the instrument of ratification. The United Kingdom formally ratified the Convention on 21 April 1986 and that ratification came into force on 1 August 1986 (which is when the implementing legislation, the Child Abduction and Custody Act 1985,[44] came into force). This was the eighth ratification. As at October 2003 there were 31 ratifications.[45]

---

[39] See *Re T (Minors) (Hague Convention: Access)* [1993] 2 FLR 617, discussed at **25.23**. Cf Scotland, where legal aid does seem to be available, see **25.27** *et seq.*

[40] *Re L (Child Abduction: European Convention)* [1992] 2 FLR 178, per Booth J, but note the criticisms discussed at **19.50–19.51**.

[41] *Re H (Minors) (Abduction: Custody Rights); Re S (Minors) (Abduction: Custody Rights)* [1991] 2 AC 476, [1991] 1 FLR 230, HL, discussed at **12.58**.

[42] For this reason, notwithstanding that in England and Wales Hague Abduction Convention applications have precedence over European Custody Convention applications (Child Abduction and Custody Act 1985, s 16(4)(c)), it can sometimes be worthwhile pursuing an action under both Conventions: see **19.70** below.

[43] See **19.69–19.70**.

[44] See Part II and Sch 2, which implement the European Custody Convention.

[45] Except for Liechtenstein, all States parties to the European Custody Convention are also Contracting States to the Hague Abduction Convention (although Belgium only became so in May 1999, notwithstanding that it has been a Contracting State to the European

Accessions

19.30 Article 23 permits accession by non-Member States but this can only be done at the invitation of the Committee of Ministers of the Council of Europe and provided all existing Contracting States have voted in favour. At the time of writing, there has been one accession, namely that of Serbia and Montenegro.

19.31 The net result of these provisions is that, unlike under the 1980 Hague Abduction Convention,[46] it is not possible for a new Contracting State to be accepted by some but not all existing Contracting States.

Territorial extent of ratifications etc

19.32 Articles 24 and 25 deal with the territorial extent of Contracting States' ratifications or accessions. Whereas Art 24 is concerned with the application of the Convention to territories on whose behalf a Contracting State is authorised to give an undertaking, Art 25 deals with the case where the Contracting State itself (as in the case of the United Kingdom) comprises two or more territorial units with different systems of law. In each case, the State, when signing or depositing its instrument of ratification etc, may specify the territory (or territories) or territorial unit (or units) to which the Convention will apply.[47] States are also permitted both subsequently to extend the application of the Convention to other territories or units[48] or to withdraw previously declared extensions or applications.[49]

19.33 Exercising these powers, Denmark has stated that the Convention does not apply to the Faroe Islands or Greenland; the Netherlands has only accepted the Convention for the Kingdom in Europe; whilst the United Kingdom, having initially ratified the Convention on behalf of England and

---

Convention since 1986). So far as the United Kingdom is concerned, under the terms of s 13 of the Child Abduction and Custody Act 1985, the Contracting States other than the United Kingdom are those specified by an Order in Council under this section, namely the Child Abduction and Custody (Parties to Conventions) Order 1986, SI 1986/1159, as amended. This Order is often out of date. For example, in the Child Abduction and Custody (Parties to Conventions (Amendment) Order 2003, SI 2003/1518, no reference was given to Estonia and Slovakia (both of which had ratified in September 2001), the Former Yugoslav Republic of Macedonia (which ratified in March 2003), Lithuania (which ratified in May 2003) nor to Serbia and Montenegro (which acceded in May 2003), although it did add Latvia (which ratified in August 2002).

[46] See **12.37**.

[47] Articles 24(1) and 25(1).

[48] Articles 24(2) and 25(2). Such extensions are effected by a declaration addressed to the Secretary General of the Council of Europe and come into force 6 months after its receipt by the Secretary General.

[49] Articles 24(3) and 25(3). Withdrawals are affected by a simple notification addressed to the Secretary General. They take effect 6 months after their receipt. To date no withdrawals have been made.

Wales, Scotland and Northern Ireland, has since given due notice under Art 24 that the Convention extends to the Isle of Man,[50] the Falkland Islands, the Cayman Islands, Bermuda and Montserrat.

Reservations[51]

19.34 Article 27 permits Contracting States to enter certain reservations which can be declared upon either signing or ratification or accession. Reservations can also be subsequently withdrawn either wholly or in part.[52] The key permitted reservation, as we have already seen,[53] is that pursuant to Art 17 not to implement Art 8 which severely restricts refusals of recognition and enforcement where application is made within 6 months of the improper removal. Article 18 allows a reservation to be made on the application of Art 12 (which allows recognition and enforcement of orders relating to custody made after the child's improper removal),[54] but no State has entered such a reservation.

19.35 The third permitted reservation, pursuant to Art 6(3), is for Central Authorities not to accept communications in English or French instead of their own official language or languages.[55] States opting not to accept communications in either English or French (in other words only accepting communications in their own language) are Germany, Greece, Poland and Spain. Denmark, Finland, Ireland, Malta and Norway will not accept communications made in French but will accept those made in English.

Denunciations

19.36 Article 29 allows States to 'denounce' the Convention.[56] None have yet done so.

---

[50] See Council of Europe Information document DIR/JUR (96) 13, pp 22 ff.

[51] See *ibid*, at n 48.

[52] Article 27(2). Withdrawals are effected by notification to the Secretary General and take effect immediately upon their receipt.

[53] See **19.10**.

[54] Discussed at **19.8**, and see also **19.59** *et seq*. Under Art 18, States making that reservation cannot require their own decisions to be enforced under Art 12 in other Contracting States.

[55] Under Art 6(1), subject to any special arrangements made between the Central Authorities concerned, communications must be accepted either in the official language (or one of the official languages) of the State addressed or in English or in French. As Hamilton and Standley, in *Family Law in Europe* (Butterworths, 1995) at p 574, point out, the necessity of having to translate applications into another language can obviously slow down the application and act as general deterrent to using this Convention at all. In theory, applications under the Hague Abduction Convention can always be made in English or French (see Art 24) but in practice, as Chiancone and Girdner found (*Issues in Resolving Cases of International Child Abduction: Final Report* (American Bar Association, 1998)), by no means all Central Authorities will accept applications in English or French.

[56] Denunciations are effected by a notification to the Secretary General and take effect 6 months after their receipt: Art 29(2).

Notification of communication to Member States

19.37 Under Art 30, the Secretary General of the Council of Europe has to notify all Member States and any acceding State of any signature, deposits of instruments of ratification, acceptance, approval or accession, any date of entry into face of ratifications, etc, and of any other act, notification or communication relating to the Convention.

The ratification and implementation by the United Kingdom

19.38 The United Kingdom implemented the European Convention through Part II of the Child Abduction and Custody Act 1985 ('the 1985 Act'), and Sch 2 to that Act sets out the Articles of the Convention, as directly incorporated into UK law. So far as England and Wales is concerned, the statutory provisions are supplemented by Part VI of the FPR 1991.

19.39 It remains now to consider in detail how the Convention operates in England and Wales. In this chapter, we concentrate on applications to enforce custody decisions. We discuss enforcement of access in Chapter 25.

THE APPLICATION OF THE EUROPEAN CUSTODY CONVENTION IN ENGLAND AND WALES

When the Convention applies

19.40 Although perhaps commonly perceived as an instrument for dealing primarily with child abduction (or what the Convention itself refers to as 'improper removals'),[57] it is important to appreciate that the Convention has a wider ambit, namely the recognition and enforcement of decisions relating to the custody of children under the age of 16. It is not therefore confined to cases of so-called improper removals.[58] On the other hand, both the Brussels II Regulation and the 1980 Hague Abduction Convention take precedence over the application of the European Custody Convention and, in practice, severely limit its application.

'A decision relating to custody'

19.41 According to Art 1(c):

'a "decision relating to custody" means a decision of an authority in so far as it relates to the care of the person of the child, including the right to decide on the place of his residence, or to the right of access to him.'

---

[57] For the application of the Convention to 'improper removals', see the discussion at **19.55** *et seq.*

[58] See, for example, *T v R (Abduction: Forum Conveniens)* [2002] 2 FLR 544, where the father's concession that the mother's removal of the child from Sweden at a time when she had sole custody was not an 'improper removal' was accepted for the purposes of that case. See [118], per Charles J.

19.42 By Art 1(b), 'authority' for this purpose means a judicial or an administrative authority. This provision accommodates those Member States, such as Denmark, Norway and Switzerland, where decisions on custody are not the exclusive preserve of the courts, but instead can also be made by certain administrative bodies.[59]

19.43 To come within the Convention, the decision must relate either to the care of the person of the child, including the right to decide on his place of residence, or to the right of access to him. According to the Explanatory Report,[60] the term 'care of the person of the child' should 'in principle be taken to cover physical, medical, moral and intellectual care generally including education and attendance at a particular school'. However, the term was deliberately left undefined, permitting the State addressed to decide in borderline cases whether the order concerned falls within the Convention or not. The Explanatory Report cites[61] decisions bearing only on legal representation or on the granting of consent in property matters as examples of orders falling outside the Convention.

19.44 So far as English orders are concerned, the following are within the definition,[62] namely:

– residence and contact orders under s 8 of the Children Act 1989;
– care orders made under the Children Act 1989;
– care and control and access orders made under the wardship or inherent jurisdiction;
– custody,[63] care and control, custodianship[64] and access orders made before the Children Act 1989 and still in force;
– care orders and parental rights resolutions[65] made before the Children Act 1989 and still in force.

19.45 In each of the above first three categories, it would seem that interim orders are sufficient.[66] On the other hand, orders conferring status, such as parental responsibility orders made under s 4 and guardianship orders made

---

[59] See para 14 of the Explanatory Report. It has been suggested (see *Butterworths Family Law Service*, at **5A[2258]**), that former parental rights resolutions passed by local authorities under Child Care Act 1980, s 3 will therefore fall within this definition.

[60] See para 19.

[61] At para 18.

[62] See Child Abduction and Custody Act 1985, s 27(1) and Sch 3, Part I.

[63] Although it is queried whether, in the case of so-called 'split orders', those conferring 'legal custody' where the other parent is granted care and control are within the Convention definition.

[64] Custodianship orders made under Children Act 1975, s 33(1) fall outside the definition provided in Sch 3, Part I to the Child Abduction and Custody Act 1985, but they clearly relate to the case of the person of the child as contemplated by the Convention.

[65] These resolutions also fall outside the definition provided by Sch 3, Part I to the 1985 Act.

[66] Cf *Re S (A Minor) (Custody: Habitual Residence)* [1998] AC 750, [1998] 1 FLR 122, discussed further at **19.66**.

under s 5 of the Children Act 1989,[67] and those solely dealing with specific aspects of the child's upbringing, namely, specific issue orders and prohibited steps orders under s 8 (including those dealing with the child's education) or decisions made under s 13 of the 1989 Act (ie leave to remove the child from the jurisdiction and change of name) will fall outside the Convention.[68] Similarly, family assistance and supervision orders will not be enforceable under the Convention.

19.46   It will be noted that public law care orders are included in the term 'decision relating to custody' and, indeed, the Explanatory Report expressly says:[69]

> 'For the purpose of the Convention it is immaterial whether the person to whom custody is granted or refused be a physical or legal person, an institution or an authority.'

19.47   So far as foreign orders are concerned, the English court will have to be satisfied (ie the burden is on the applicant)[70] that the order sought to be enforced falls within the definition of Art 1(c). In this respect it was mooted in *Re L (Abduction: Pending Criminal Proceedings)*[71] whether a foreign court return order made under the 1980 Hague Abduction Convention is enforceable under the European Custody Convention but, in the event, Wilson J left the point open, commenting:[72]

> 'It seems to me that opposite answers to that question might each reasonably be given, although this Explanatory Report on the Convention suggests an affirmative.'

A decision relating to custody 'given in a Contracting State and which is enforceable in such a State'

19.48   The requirement under Art 1(d) that the decision relating to custody must be 'given in a Contracting State and be enforceable in such a State' gives rise to two problems: first, what is meant by 'enforceable' for these purposes; and, secondly, whether the original order should have been made in a 'Contracting State' or whether it is sufficient that it is currently enforceable in such a State.

19.49   With regard to the first point, the Convention is silent on what is meant by 'enforceable', although in its commentary on Art 7, the Explanatory

---

[67]   In these cases, however, it might not be hard to persuade the court to make a subsequent order and declaration of wrongful removal under Art 12: see **19.59** *et seq*.

[68]   Save, possibly, decisions limited to those ordering the child's return to the place where he was before the removal.

[69]   At para 16.

[70]   See para 18 of the Explanatory Report.

[71]   [1999] 1 FLR 433. The Explanatory Report suggests that such an order can be so enforced.

[72]   *Ibid* at 442.

Report makes it clear[73] that internal remedies do not first have to be exhausted. It is submitted that all that the Convention requires is that the order is potentially enforceable. So, for example, the fact that an English High Court or county court residence order might well require a s 11(7) direction or condition as well as penal notice attached to it before it can be enforced, at any rate by a committal order,[74] does not mean that those measures must be taken before it can be registered and enforced under the Convention.[75]

19.50 The second issue arose in *Re L (Child Abduction: European Convention)*,[76] in which a father sought to enforce an Irish custody order which, though subsisting at the time of the application, had nevertheless been made before Ireland's ratification of the Convention. Booth J held that the order was registerable and enforceable under the Convention. As she put it:

> '... it matters not that the order was made prior to the ratification of the Convention by Ireland and by England. The material fact is that there is in existence at this present time an order of the Irish court which is enforceable in Ireland. It is that order which it is sought to register and enforce now, and it seems to me ... that this court has jurisdiction under the Convention ...'

19.51 In short, according to this interpretation, all the Convention requires is that at the time of the application there is a presently enforceable custody order in what has become a Contracting State. Consequently, therefore, unlike the Hague Abduction Convention,[77] the European Convention has retrospective effect. Whether Booth J's interpretation is right, however, is debatable. It was based on the premise that, as the order in question was a decision relating to custody within Art 1(c), it had to be recognised under Art 7 as it was enforceable in Ireland, and had thus to be registered and enforced under the terms of the Child Abduction and Custody Act 1985.[78] However, Art 7, which states '[a] decision relating to custody given in a Contracting State shall be recognised and, where it is enforceable in the State of origin, made enforceable in every other Contracting State', seems most naturally interpreted as requiring the decision to be made in a State that has already ratified the Convention.[79]

---

[73] See para 34.
[74] See White, Carr and Lowe, *The Children Act in Practice*, 3rd edn (Butterworths, 2002), para 5.132, and Lowe, 'Enforcing orders relating to children' (1992) 4 *Journal of Child Law* 26.
[75] Although note that, according to Hale J in *Re R (Abduction: Hague and European Conventions)* [1997] 1 FLR 663 at 672, applicants seeking enforcement should at least be able to enforce the order in the State of origin in their own right.
[76] [1992] 2 FLR 178.
[77] See *Re H (Minors) (Abduction: Custody Rights); Re S (Minors) (Abduction: Custody Rights)* [1991] 2 AC 476, [1991] 2 FLR 262, HL.
[78] See [1992] 2 FLR 178 at 181A.
[79] See also the Explanatory Report at para 17, which states that the 'decisions in question must originate in a Contracting State; this follows from Art 7 and the whole structure of the Convention'.

'Child'

19.52   For the purpose of the Convention, 'child' is defined by Art 1(a) as:

> '... a person of any nationality, so long as he is under 16 years of age and has not the right to decide on his own place of residence under the law of his habitual residence, the law of his nationality or the internal law of the State addressed ...'

19.53   The requirement that the child be under the age of 16 is the same as under the Hague Abduction Convention.[80] As the Explanatory Report states, that age was taken not on the basis of legal capacity 'but because a decision on custody could not easily be enforced against the wishes of a child over that age'.[81]

19.54   The second part of the definition, that is, that referring to the child's right to decide on his own place of residence is problematic. According to the Explanatory Report, the definition of age and the right to decide residence are 'cumulative',[82] which could be taken to mean that the age of 16 is not an absolute cut-off if the child does not, either under the law of his habitual residence, or under the law of his nationality or the internal law of the State addressed, have a right to decide his own residence. Alternatively, as canvassed elsewhere,[83] Art 1(a) could be interpreted as excluding the application of the Convention to a so-called '*Gillick*-competent' child under the age of 16 who does not wish to return to his habitual residence. In other words, it remains a moot point whether the word 'and' should be read conjunctively or disjunctively. Even if, as the Explanatory Report would suggest, it should be read conjunctively, there remains the issue of what is meant by the word 'right'.[84] In this respect, it is to be noted that the definition requires the court to examine not simply its own internal law but also that of the child's habitual residence and, if different, that of the child's nationality.

The application of the Convention to 'improper removals'

19.55   In the full text of the Convention, the concept of 'improper removal' plays a key role.[85] Article 8, for example,[86] expressly states that '[i]n the case of an improper removal' Central Authorities of the State addressed should take

---

[80]   By parity of reasoning with *Re H (Abduction: Child of 16)* [2000] 2 FLR 51, discussed at **12.20**, the Convention will cease to apply to a child upon his attaining the age of 16 even if the application was made before the child was 16. There is, however, power to deal with such a child during his minority under the High Court's inherent jurisdiction. For an example of the exercise of the inherent jurisdiction, see *T v R (Abduction: Forum Conveniens)* [2002] 2 FLR 544.

[81]   See para 13.

[82]   *Ibid.*

[83]   See *Butterworths Family Law Service* at **5A[2257]**.

[84]   Can it be said under English law that a child of 16 or 17 has a 'right' to decide his own place of residence?

[85]   See para 10 of the Explanatory Report.

[86]   See **19.11**.

steps forthwith to restore custody, while the qualification to this obligation under Art 9 again begins with the words '[i]n cases of improper removal'. However, the concept appears much less important in the Convention as enacted by the United Kingdom in Sch 2 to the 1985 Act. Although it is defined in Art 1(d), since Art 8 has not been incorporated and the words 'improper removal' are excluded from Art 9, the concept is only directly referred to again in Art 10(1)(b).[87] Nevertheless, notwithstanding its relative obscurity, it is clear that it remains a key concept even in the Convention as enacted by the 1985 Act. In particular, it is of some importance to the ability, pursuant to Art 12, to obtain declarations that past removals are 'unlawful'.[88]

Defining 'improper removal'

19.56   By Art 1(d):

'"improper removal" means the removal of a child across an international frontier in breach of a decision relating to his custody which has been given in a Contracting State and which is enforceable in such a State; improper removal also includes:

(i)   the failure to return a child across an international frontier at the end of a period of the exercise of the right of access to this child or at the end of any other temporary stay in a territory other than that where the custody is exercised;

(ii)   a removal which is subsequently declared unlawful within the meaning of Article 12.'

19.57   The requirement that the improper removal be across an international frontier means that the Convention has no application to abductions within the British Isles.[89] In other words, it is not sufficient in itself that a child is removed from one legal system to another.

19.58   Article 1(d)(i) extends the definition of 'improper removal' to include the failure to return a child across an international frontier at the end of either a period of access or any other temporary stay in a territory other than that where the custody is expressed. According to para 17 of the Explanatory Report, 'a decision limited to ordering the return of the child to the place where he was before his removal is also a decision relating to custody', but, as explained at para 62, such a limited order may only be considered sufficient for the purposes of Art 12.

---

[87]   But note that, according to s 15(3) of the 1985 Act, the references in Art 9(1)(c) (discussed at **19.106**) to the 'removal' of the child are to 'his improper removal within the meaning of the Convention'.

[88]   See eg *Re S (A Minor) (Custody: Habitual Residence)* [1998] AC 750, [1998] 1 FLR 122, discussed further at **19.66**.

[89]   Ie England and Wales, Scotland, Northern Ireland, the Isle of Man and the Channel Islands. For abductions within the British Isles, see Chapter 11.

Declarations of unlawful removal

19.59 Pursuant to the policy[90] of permitting enforceable orders to be obtained *after* the child's removal, Art 1(d)(ii) specifically defines an 'improper removal' to include 'a removal which is subsequently declared unlawful within the meaning of Art 12'.[91]

19.60 Under Art 12, courts are empowered, upon the request of any interested person, to make a decision relating to custody after the child's removal and subsequently to declare the removal unlawful for the purpose of the Convention. So far as the UK courts are concerned, this power to make subsequent declarations of wrongful removal is governed by the Child Abduction and Custody Act 1985, s 23(2). According to that provision, in *any* custody proceedings[92] in which a UK court makes 'a decision relating to a child' who has been removed from the United Kingdom, the court may also, upon application:

> '... declare the removal to have been unlawful if it is satisfied that the applicant has an interest in the matter and that the child has been taken from or sent or kept out of the United Kingdom without the consent of the person (or, if more than one, all the persons) having the right to determine the child's place of residence under the law of the part of the United Kingdom in which the child was habitually resident.'[93]

19.61 Although courts at all levels are empowered to make declarations of wrongful removal, the power is contingent upon:

(a) the court having previously made a 'decision relating to the child', which for these purposes means an order within the meaning of Art 1(c);[94] and

(b) an application having been made for that purpose.[95]

---

[90] Discussed at **19.8**.

[91] By this means, as Lord Slynn observed in *Re S (A Minor) (Custody: Habitual Residence)* [1998] AC 750 at 771, [1998] 1 FLR 122 at 135, it is clear that 'improper removal' includes *unlawful* removal.

[92] Defined by s 27(1) of and Sch 3 to the 1985 Act.

[93] Note that this provision appears to limit the jurisdiction of the courts to make declarations in custody proceedings to those cases in which the child is habitually resident in one of the parts of the United Kingdom.

[94] This is the clear intention of the statute: see s 23(3) which states that a 'decision relating to custody' has the same meaning as in the Convention (although note that s 23(2) simply refers to 'a decision relating to a child'). Article 1(c) is discussed at **19.41** *et seq*. Note that, according to the Irish decision, *C v B (Child Abduction: Unlawful Removal)* [1996] 2 IR 83, Irish Supreme Court, on the not incomparable Irish Child Abduction and Enforcement of Custody Order Act 1991, s 34(1), declarations may be made only by the court that made the custody decision. In *C v B*, since the custody order had been made by a District Court, it was held that the High Court had no power to make a declaration.

[95] Ie declarations cannot be made by courts upon their own motion.

An application for a declaration under s 23(2) is made either by summons in the custody proceedings[96] or, in the magistrates' court, orally or in writing in the course of the custody proceedings.[97]

19.62 According to Art 12, applications must be made by 'any interested person' but, under s 23(2) of the 1985 Act, the court must merely be 'satisfied that the applicant has an interest in the matter'. Under either wording, those who, prior to removal, have a residence order or care and control order in their favour or who have parental responsibility and therefore whose consent is required for the child's removal, are clearly 'interested'. In this respect, as the Explanatory Report states,[98] Art 12 covers two situations, namely: 'where a person or authority has custody under the law of the State of origin and the person [typically the unmarried father who does not have parental responsibility] who removes the child has no such rights'; and 'where two persons share the child's custody [typically a married couple] and one removes the child in breach of the other's rights'.

19.63 The Report comments that, although 'a decision relating to custody is necessary in both cases, only the first case requires a confirmation of the right of custody whereas in the second case a decision of substance may be required'. In this latter situation, however, an interim residence order is sufficient.

19.64 It has become evident, however, that the Convention has a wider ambit than that envisaged by the Explanatory Report, for it is authoritatively established that it is not a prerequisite that the applicant's consent to the child's removal was required at the time of removal. This was implicit in *Re S (Abduction) (European Convention)*[99] and was expressly held by the House of Lords in *Re S (A Minor) (Custody: Habitual Residence)*.[100]

19.65 In the former *Re S*, an unmarried father without parental responsibility and who therefore had no power of consent over the child's removal from the United Kingdom, who was habitually resident in England, had already instituted proceedings under the Children Act 1989 before the child's unilateral removal to Denmark by the mother. After the removal, the father obtained an ex parte order granting him interim residence and then sought a declaration that, for the purposes of Art 12, the child's removal by the mother was unlawful. Granting him that declaration,[101] Hollis J held that, notwithstanding that when the actual removal took place the father did not have the right to

---

[96] FPR 1991, r 6.2(2).
[97] Magistrates' Courts (Child Abduction and Custody) Rules 1986, SI 1986/1141, r 9.
[98] At para 61.
[99] [1996] 1 FLR 660.
[100] [1998] AC 750, [1998] 1 FLR 122.
[101] It is to be noted that, in making the decision, Hollis J made no mention of the fact that the interim residence order had been granted by another court. Cf n 95 above.

determine the child's place of residence, s 23(2) nevertheless now applied to cover the child's removal[102] to Denmark.

19.66 A similar result obtained in the later *Re S*, which again involved an unmarried father who was habitually resident in England at the time of his child's removal. In this case, following the mother's death, the child's grandmother and aunt removed the child to Ireland without the father's knowledge and consent.[103] On the same day as the aunt obtained a care and control order from an Irish court, the English High Court granted the father interim care and control and ordered the child's return to the jurisdiction. On the following day, wardship proceedings were begun and it was in those proceedings that the father sought a declaration of unlawful removal. The House of Lords had no difficulty in holding that the father had 'an interest in the matter', notwithstanding that he did not have parental responsibility nor therefore, at the time of the removal, a right to decide the child's place of residence. Furthermore, it was held that the court was empowered to make a declaration upon the basis that, following the granting of care and control (or at any rate upon the service of the order) to the father, the retention of the child in Ireland and the failure to return him to England constituted an 'improper removal' within the meaning of Art 1(d). Accordingly, the requirements of s 23(2), namely the father's interest, the child's habitual residence in England, the father's right to determine residence following the granting of the care and control order and the child's unlawful retention outside England without the father's consent, were satisfied.

19.67 Although the applicant in each of the above cases was an unmarried father there is no reason to think that the decisions are so confined. It is no objection that the child's initial removal was lawful, and it is presumably open to anyone who can persuade a court to grant him a residence order or care and control order after the removal to seek a subsequent declaration.[104] One important proviso in cases where the child's removal was initially lawful is that

---

[102] In the light of the subsequent House of Lords' decision in *Re S (A Minor) (Custody: Habitual Residence)* [1998] AC 750, [1998] 1 FLR 122, the better analysis is that it was the mother's continued *retention* of the child in Denmark that constituted the 'improper removal'.

[103] According to Butler-Sloss LJ (see the Court of Appeal decision at [1997] 1 FLR 958 at 969), this was the first time under either the European Custody Convention or the Hague Abduction Convention that the English courts had to deal with a removal by a person without a legal right to care for the child. She also commented that this situation had not been foreseen by the authors of the Convention. Paragraph 61 of the Explanatory Report states that Art 12 'covers all situations where custody is exercised without a previous decision, *either by one of the parents or by both parents jointly*' (emphasis added).

[104] Query whether the applicant must always have an order in his favour to invoke s 23(2)? Might not grandparents, for instance, who wish to see their grandchild have 'an interest' in having their son's or daughter's custody order enforced?

retention can only become unlawful provided notice of an order granting the applicant residence or care and control has been properly given to the defendant.[105]

19.68   So far as the form of the declaration is concerned, as the Explanatory Report explains,[106] it must cover two elements, namely, it must declare the removal to be improper, and must also indicate who had the custody rights so as to enable the child to be restored to that person. According to the Report:

> 'These elements may be covered by a single decision or by two separate decisions according to the internal law of the State of origin. However, a decision which is limited to ordering the return of the child to the place where he was before the removal may be considered as being sufficient for the application of Art 12.'

Precedence of Brussels II and of Hague Convention applications

19.69   It is expressly provided by Art 37 of the Council Regulation on jurisdiction and the recognition and enforcement of judgments in matrimonial matters and in matters of parental responsibility for children of both spouses[107] (the so-called 'Brussels II Regulation') that the Regulation takes precedence over the European Custody Convention. Accordingly, if that Regulation applies, the Convention cannot be invoked.[108] This is likely to have a significant impact on the use made of the Convention, although it must be remembered that Brussels II only applies to orders made in the course of matrimonial proceedings (ie not freestanding proceedings) in respect of children of both spouses.

19.70   Pursuant to the policy of giving priority to Hague Abduction Convention applications over those made under the European Custody Convention, s 16(4)(c) of the 1985 Act obliges the court to refuse to register a decision if a Hague Convention application is pending.[109] This embargo, however, does not mean that a European Convention application has to be dismissed, merely that consideration of it has to be postponed until the determination of the Hague Convention application.[110] Indeed, it is

---

[105]   This is suggested by Lord Slynn in *Re S (A Minor) (Custody: Habitual Residence)* [1998] AC 750, [1998] 1 FLR 122. See also the Irish decision, *SD v RS (Child Abduction)* [1996] 3 IR 524.

[106]   At para 62.

[107]   Council Regulation (EC) No 1347/2000 of 29 May 2000, discussed at **4.9** *et seq* and in Chapter 18.

[108]   See Child Abduction and Custody Act 1985, s 12(2), added by the European Communities (Matrimonial Jurisdiction and Judgments) Regulations 2001, SI 2001/310, and the European Communities (Matrimonial Jurisdiction and Judgments) (Scotland) Regulations 2001, SI 2001/36.

[109]   This provision is reinforced by s 9(b) of the 1985 Act, which prevents the court from registering or enforcing an order under the European Custody Convention while considering a Hague Abduction Convention application.

[110]   For a criticism of this mandatory postponement, see *Re D (Abduction: Discretionary Return)* [2000] 1 FLR 24 at 25, per Wilson J.

established[111] that in those (comparatively rare) cases where an application for the return of a child under the Hague Abduction Convention is refused, then those proceedings are deemed to have ended and consideration can then be given to an application under the European Custody Convention. Accordingly, given that the grounds for refusing to return a child under the Hague Abduction Convention and those for refusing to register and enforce a custody decision under the European Convention are different, it can sometimes be worthwhile pursuing applications under both Conventions.

The Convention obligations

Recognition and enforcement

19.71   The key obligation is that pursuant to Art 7, which provides:

> 'A decision relating to custody given in a Contracting State shall be recognised and, where it is enforceable in the State of origin, made enforceable in every other Contracting State.'

19.72   So far as the United Kingdom is concerned, this basic obligation must be read subject to s 15(2) of the 1985 Act. That provision provides that a relevant decision made outside the United Kingdom 'shall be recognised in each part of the United Kingdom[112] as if made by a court having jurisdiction in that part' unless an appropriate court[113] declares, upon the application of any person appearing to it to have an interest in the matter, that the order should not be recognised on the basis of one of the grounds provided by Art 9 or Art 10[114] and subject to the condition that no decision is enforceable unless registered in the appropriate court in accordance with s 16.

19.73   Although this latter requirement makes registration a *sine qua non* condition to enforcement, it is established[115] that enforcement does not automatically follow registration. Accordingly, notwithstanding registration, Arts 9 and 10 can still operate to prevent enforcement.[116]

---

[111]   See *Re R (Abduction: Hague and European Conventions)* [1997] 1 FLR 663, CA, discussed further at **19.116**.

[112]   Viz, for these purposes, England and Wales, Scotland, Northern Ireland and the Isle of Man.

[113]   Ie the High Court in England and Wales, the Court of Session in Scotland, the High Court in Northern Ireland and in the Isle of Man: s 27(2) of the 1985 Act, as extended by the Child Abduction and Custody Act 1985 (Isle of Man) Order 1994, SI 1994/2799. So far as England and Wales is concerned, application must be made by way of originating summons: FPR 1991, r 6.2; see **19.85** and **21.26**.

[114]   Discussed at **19.97** *et seq*.

[115]   *Re H (A Minor) (Foreign Custody Order: Enforcement)* [1994] Fam 105, [1994] 1 FLR 512, CA.

[116]   In *Re H* itself, in proceedings brought to enforce an order registered some 3 years earlier, the application was refused on the basis that the original decision was 'manifestly no longer in accordance with the welfare of the child' within the meaning of Art 10(1)(b). The child in question was then aged 13 and was adamant that she did not wish to have any further contact with her father.

19.74 According to Art 7 itself, it is a condition of enforceability that the decision is enforceable in the State of origin. Although as the Explanatory Report says,[117] this does not mean that internal remedies in the State of origin have first to be exhausted,[118] if the decision is 'not enforceable or is enforceable only under certain conditions, such a decision will have the same effect in the State addressed'. It is submitted that provided the original decision is clearly potentially enforceable[119] that should be sufficient to trigger Art 7. At any rate, so far as English law is concerned, additional requirements, such as the need for a penal notice, can properly be regarded as part of the enforcement process rather than determining whether an order can properly be classified as 'enforceable' in the first place.[120]

19.75 The Explanatory Report points out[121] that where a decision has not yet acquired full authority in the State of origin or is subject to pending review proceedings, the court applied to can, pursuant to Art 10(2),[122] adjourn the application to await the outcome.

Applying for recognition and enforcement

The general scheme

19.76 Article 4(1) provides that any person who has obtained in a Contracting State a decision relating to the custody of a child and who wishes to have that decision recognised or enforced in another Contracting State may submit an application for this purpose to the Central Authority in any Contracting State.[123]

19.77 The Central Authority receiving the application, if it is not the Central Authority in the State addressed, must send the application directly and without delay to that Central Authority.[124] However, the obligation is subject to the receiving authority's power to refuse to intervene where it is manifestly

---

[117] See paras 34 and 35.

[118] As the Report says, were this to be required the whole value of the obligation would be undermined, since decisions on the custody of children 'must be enforced rapidly if they are to have any practical effect'.

[119] See the discussion at **19.49**, but note Hale J's view in *Re R (Abduction: Hague and European Convention)* [1997] 1 FLR 663 at 671–672 that the applicants should be entitled under the order in question to take steps in the State of origin to enforce the order *in their own right*.

[120] But note that, if the court is of the opinion that the decision is not enforceable in the State in which it was made, then under English law it must refuse to register the decision: s 16(4) of the 1985 Act, discussed at **19.121**.

[121] At para 35.

[122] Discussed at **19.123**.

[123] But note that there is no compulsion to apply to a Central Authority. Applicants can apply directly to the Central Authority of the State addressed. Under Art 4(2), the application must be accompanied by the documents mentioned in Art 13, for which see **21.13**.

[124] Article 4(3).

clear that the conditions of the Convention are not satisfied.[125] It is also the duty of the receiving authority to keep the applicant informed without delay of the progress of his application.[126]

19.78 By Art 5(1) the Central Authority of the State addressed must:

'... take or cause to be taken without delay all steps which it considers to be appropriate, if necessary by instituting proceedings before its competent authorities, in order:

(a)   to discover the whereabouts of the child;
(b)   to avoid, in particular by any necessary provisional measures, prejudice to the interests of the child or the applicant;
(c)   to secure the recognition or enforcement of the decision;
(d)   to secure the delivery of the child to the applicant where enforcement is granted;
(e)   to inform the requesting authority of the measures taken and their results.'

19.79 Under Art 5(2), where the Central Authority in the State addressed has reason to believe that the child is in the territory of another Contracting State it must send the documents directly and without delay to the Central Authority of that State.

19.80 Crucially, Art 5(3) provides that, except for the expense of repatriation, the costs of the measures taken by the Central Authority, pursuant to the obligations under Art 5(1), including the costs of proceedings and, where applicable, the costs incurred by the assistance of a lawyer, are to be borne by the Contracting State.

Seeking recognition and enforcement of orders relating to children taken from England and Wales to another European Convention country

19.81 Although, pursuant to Art 4(1), applications for return can be made to any Central Authority, usually the most practical course is to approach the Central Authority for England and Wales (that is, the Child Abduction Unit at the Official Solicitor's Department) for assistance.

19.82 The Child Abduction Unit is empowered by s 23(1) of the 1985 Act to require a UK court to furnish to it a copy of its decision, a certificate of service or a document establishing that the decision is as required by Art 13. Furthermore, where the Unit is required by the judicial or administrative authority of a Contracting State which has been asked to recognise and enforce a decision made by a court in England and Wales to make inquiries about a child,[127] it has the power to obtain a report from a local authority or probation officer or the Department of Health and Social Services in Northern Ireland

---

[125]   See Art 4(4).
[126]   Article 4(5).
[127]   Pursuant to Art 15(1)(a).

concerning any matter relating to the child which is considered relevant or to obtain a copy of a report from any court to which a written report relating to the child has been made.

Seeking recognition and enforcement of custody orders relating to children brought to England and Wales from another European Convention country

19.83   In accordance with Art 4, applications for the recognition and enforcement of custody orders may be made either directly to the Central Authority for England and Wales or, more commonly, indirectly via the Central Authority of requesting State. Provision is also specifically made for applications to be made directly to court.[128]

19.84   The system adopted in England and Wales[129] is that, pursuant to s 16 of the 1985 Act, a person on whom any rights are conferred by a decision relating to custody made by an authority in a Contracting State other than the United Kingdom may make an application for the registration of the decision in the appropriate court (ie the High Court).[130] The Central Authority must assist such a person in making such an application if a request for such assistance is made by him or on his behalf by the Central Authority of the Contracting State in question.[131] Applications for registration or requests for assistance are treated as requests for enforcement.[132] In *Re R (Abduction: Hague and European Conventions)*,[133] Hale J speculated whether the 'rights' referred to in s 16(1) have to be substantive rights or whether merely procedural rights will suffice. Without finally deciding that point, she inclined to the view that the section refers to substantive rights but in any event she held at the very least the rights must be such that would entitle the applicants to take steps in the court of origin to enforce the order in their own right.

PROCEDURE

19.85   The procedure for applying for registration is governed by the FPR 1991, Part VI. Applications must be commenced by originating summons in the High Court.[134]

19.86   The court may dispense with service of any summons, whether originating or otherwise, in any proceedings under the Child Abduction and Custody Act 1985.[135]

---

[128]   By s 16(1) of the 1985 Act, applications can be made directly to the 'appropriate court' which, by virtue of s 27(2), means the High Court.

[129]   The same system applies to the rest of the United Kingdom and the Isle of Man.

[130]   See s 27(2) of the 1985 Act.

[131]   *Ibid*, s 16(2).

[132]   *Ibid*, s 16(3).

[133]   [1997] 1 FLR 663 at 671–672, not commented upon by the Court of Appeal.

[134]   FPR 1991, r 6.2, for details of which, see **21.26**.

[135]   *Ibid*, r 6.9.

19.87 Additionally, the summons must identify the decision relating to custody that is sought to be enforced.[136] In this regard, a decision of a judicial or administrative authority outside the United Kingdom may be proved by an authenticated copy. A copy is duly authenticated if it bears the seal of, or is signed by a judge or officer of, the judicial or administrative authority; and a document provided in accordance with Art 13 of the Convention may be accepted as sufficient evidence of anything stated in it.[137]

19.88 The defendants to the application are specified by the Rules.[138]

19.89 Although the Rules make no provision for joining children as parties, it is established that, just as there is power to do so in exceptional cases under the Hague Abduction Convention, so there is under the European Custody Convention.[139]

19.90 The time-limit for acknowledging service of an originating summons by which an application is made is 7 days after service of the originating summons (including the day of service) or, in the case of a defendant in whose favour a decision relating to custody has been made, or who appears to have a sufficient interest in the child, such further time as the court may direct.[140] If the application is to be defended, it is desirable that the specific defences should be set out in a short statement simply and concisely stating the nature of the defences and the Article or Articles relied upon.[141]

19.91 A person whose application has been submitted to the Central Authority for England and Wales and on whose behalf a solicitor has been instructed is entitled to public funding without regard to his financial resources. He does not have to satisfy the Legal Services Commission that he has reasonable grounds for making the application and he cannot be refused public funding on the ground that it is unreasonable for him to be granted representation.[142]

THE HEARING

15.92 As under the Hague Abduction Convention, applications under the European Custody Convention are heard speedily. They are heard by a High Court judge sitting in chambers unless the court otherwise directs.[143] The

---

136 FPR 1991, r 6.4(2).
137 Section 22 of the 1985 Act.
138 Viz FPR 1991, r 6.5, for details of which, see **21.31**.
139 *Re T (Abduction: Appointment of Guardian ad Litem)* [1999] 2 FLR 796. For discussion of this issue under the 1980 Hague Abduction Convention: see **17.173**. See also **21.31**.
140 FPR 1991, r 6.6.
141 See *Re W (Abduction: Procedure)* [1995] 1 FLR 878 at 892, per Wall J, delivered with approval and agreement of the President.
142 Community Legal Service (Financial) Regulations 2000, reg 3, discussed at **21.15** *et seq*.
143 FPR 1991, r 6.8.

hearing of the originating summons must not be adjourned for a period exceeding 21 days at any one time.[144] The court has power to make interim directions.[145]

19.93 On issuing the originating summons, the plaintiff may lodge affidavit evidence in support. The defendant may lodge affidavit evidence within 7 days after service of the originating summons on him; the plaintiff may within 7 days thereafter lodge a statement in reply.[146] As under the Hague Abduction Convention, parties have no right to give oral evidence, although the court has a discretion to admit it.[147] Given the summary nature of proceedings, oral evidence should be sparingly admitted.[148]

THE EFFECTS OF AN APPLICATION TO REGISTER

19.94 Provided the decision sought to be enforced was made in proceedings commenced first, an application to register it under s 16 effectively freezes other pending domestic proceedings relating to custody (including wardship) and prevents the courts from enforcing a Part I order under s 29 of the Family Law Act 1986.[149] These restrictions cease if the application for registration is refused.[150]

19.95 A party to proceedings for the registration of an order under s 16 of the 1985 Act must, where he knows that an application for a care or supervision order, a residence order or an order giving care and control within wardship is pending in a court in the United Kingdom, file in the Principal Registry of the Family Division a concise statement giving details of the proceedings; the Principal Registry must notify the court where the proceedings are pending of the proceedings under s 16; and the proper officer of the court in which the proceedings are pending must notify the parties of the s 16 application.[151]

19.96 Where simultaneous applications are brought both under the European Custody Convention and the Hague Abduction Convention, the latter has priority.[152] However, if the Hague Convention application is refused, it is then possible to proceed with the European Convention application.[153]

---

[144] FPR 1991, r 6.10.

[145] *Ibid*, r 6.13, discussed at **19.127**. See also **21.69**.

[146] FPR 1991, r 6.7.

[147] See the discussion at **21.78**.

[148] *Ibid*.

[149] Section 20 of the 1985 Act. For discussion of Part I orders and their enforcement under the Family Law Act 1986, see respectively Chapters 3 and 11.

[150] Section 20 of the 1985 Act.

[151] FPR 1991, r 6.11.

[152] Section 16(4)(c) of the 1985 Act, discussed at **19.70**.

[153] See, for example, *Re R (Abduction: Hague and European Conventions)* [1997] 1 FLR 663, CA.

Refusing registration or enforcement

19.97   Notwithstanding the general enjoinder under Art 7 to recognise and enforce custody orders, Child Abduction and Custody Act 1985, s 16(4) provides:

> 'The High Court or Court of Session shall[154] refuse to register a decision if:
>
> (a)   the court is of the opinion that on any of the grounds specified in Article 9 or 10 of the Convention the decision should not be recognised in any part of the United Kingdom;
>
> (b)   the court is of the opinion that the decision is not enforceable in the Contracting State where it was made and is not a decision to which Article 12 of the Convention applies; or
>
> (c)   an application in respect of the child under Part I of this Act [viz under the Hague Abduction Convention] is pending.'

The application of s 16(4)(c) having already been discussed,[155] it remains now to examine s 16(4)(a) and (b).

19.98   Section 16(4)(a) refers to the exceptions provided by the Convention itself. Because of the reservation taken by the United Kingdom on the application of Art 8,[156] Arts 9 and 10 can be invoked at any time regardless of whether the child's removal is 'improper'.[157]

19.99   The burden of proving one of the exceptions within Arts 8 and 9 lies on the person opposing the recognition or enforcement, and the court is expected to recognise and register the order unless it expressly finds one of the exceptions proved.[158] In no event is the court entitled to review a foreign decision as to its substance.[159]

19.100   Section 15 of the Child Abduction and Custody Act 1985 enables any interested person to apply to the High Court for a declaration on any of the

---

[154]   Notwithstanding this apparently mandatory enjoinder, it seems evident from the wording of s 16(4)(a) of the 1985 Act that, even where an exception under Art 9 or Art 10 is established, the court still has a discretion whether to register and/or to enforce an order: see *Re G (A Minor) (Child Abduction: Enforcement)* [1990] 2 FLR 325, discussed at **19.103**. It can also grant an adjournment, see *T v R (Abduction: Forum Conveniens)* [2002] 2 FLR 544 at [143], discussed at **19.125**.

[155]   See **19.70**.

[156]   Discussed at **19.10** and **19.34**.

[157]   In States where no reservation is made, Art 9 provides the only grounds for refusal in cases where applications are brought within 6 months of the child's *improper removal*, which means that in these cases Art 10 can be invoked only where applications are made more than 6 months after the removal. However, in cases where there has not been an improper removal, Art 10 can be invoked regardless of when the application is brought. See the Explanatory Report at para 46.

[158]   *Re A (Foreign Access Order: Enforcement)* [1996] 1 FLR 561, CA. But note *Re H (A Minor) (Foreign Custody Order: Enforcement)* [1994] Fam 105, [1994] 1 FLR 512, CA, discussed at **19.73**, in which it was held that an exception can properly be invoked *after* registration to prevent enforcement.

[159]   Article 9(3).

grounds specified in Art 9 or Art 10 of the 1980 European Custody Convention that a decision relating to custody[160] is not to be recognised in any part of the United Kingdom. Application is made by way of originating summons.[161]

Procedural exceptions under Art 9

19.101 The exceptions provided by Art 9 are narrow and may best be thought of as comprising procedural defects in the making of the order sought to be registered or enforced.[162] Under Art 9(1), registration or enforcement may be refused where:

'(a) in the case of a decision given in the absence of the defendant or his legal representative, the defendant was not duly served with the document which instituted the proceedings or an equivalent document in sufficient time to enable him to arrange his defence, but such a failure to effect service cannot constitute a ground for refusing recognition or enforcement where service was not effected because the defendant had concealed his whereabouts from the person who instituted the proceedings in the state of origin;

(b) in the case of a decision given in the absence of the defendant or his legal representative, the competence of the authority giving the decision was not founded:

(i) on the habitual residence of the defendant; or

(ii) on the last common habitual residence of the child's parents, at least one parent being still habitually resident there, or

(iii) on the habitual residence of the child;

(c) the decision is incompatible with a decision relating to custody which became enforceable in the state addressed before the removal of the child, unless the child has had his habitual residence in the territory of the requesting state for one year before his removal.'

19.102 Both Art 9(1)(a) and (b) are restricted to cases where the relevant decision[163] was made in the defendant's absence. As the Explanatory Report explains,[164] the purpose of the former 'is to ensure that decisions are recognised or enforced only if the person who, according to the applicable law, has to be notified of any proceedings relating to the custody of the child was in fact given a reasonable opportunity to appear'. Article 9(1)(b), on the other hand, is intended 'to cover the situation where there were no sufficient links between the authority which took the decision and the parties to justify the recognition or enforcement of the decision'.

---

[160] Article 1(c).

[161] FPR 1991, r 6.2. Cf declarations under s 23(2) of the 1985 Act which are made by summons in the custody proceedings: see **19.61**.

[162] See para 45 of the Explanatory Report.

[163] Note that, in the Irish decision, *SD v RS (Child Abduction)* [1996] 3 IR 524, it was held that the term 'decision' used in Art 9(1)(a) referred both to a residence order *and* to an Art 12 declaration of an unlawful removal.

[164] At paras 41 and 42.

19.103 On the evidence of the two reported decisions that have so far considered the provisions, Art 9(1)(a) and (b) are difficult to invoke.[165] It seems clear, for example, that lack of service of notice of the relevant proceedings may not *per se* be sufficient to persuade the court to refuse recognition and enforcement. In *Re G (A Minor) (Child Abduction: Enforcement)*,[166] Booth J accepted that a mother without fault on her part had not been served with notice of proceedings[167] and was consequently ignorant of the hearing in which a Belgian court made a custody order in favour of the father, but nevertheless held that the establishment of an Art 9(1)(a) defence merely gave the court a discretion to refuse recognition and enforcement. However, Booth J was not disposed to refuse recognition because the mother later knew of the decision and had had the opportunity to draw to the Belgian court's attention the lack of notice of the earlier proceedings and had knowingly left Belgium in breach of the decision.

19.104 In *Re S (Abduction) (European Convention)*,[168] Hollis J held that neither Art 9(1)(a) nor (b) could be invoked by a mother who, without her unmarried partner's consent, had removed the child to Denmark, notwithstanding that she had not been served with notice of the ex parte proceedings which led to a court order to return the child. It was held to be sufficient that she had been served with Children Act 1989 proceedings prior to the removal, such proceedings having been brought by the father who at all times remained habitually resident in England.

19.105 According to the Explanatory Report,[169] the person who was not duly served with notice of the proceedings need not be the person opposing recognition. In cases where custody has changed, it is still open to the new custody holder to show that the original defendant was not properly notified.

19.106 Article 9(1)(c) allows recognition and enforcement to be refused if the order in question relates to a child who has been habitually resident for less than 12 months in the requesting State and is incompatible with an earlier custody decision made in the State addressed provided that the earlier decision had become enforceable before the improper removal.[170] As the Explanatory Report explains,[171] this last proviso is designed to stop 'forum shopping' in the sense of preventing a person from obtaining a favourable decision in a State

---

[165] But cf in Ireland, *SD v RS (Child Abduction)* [1996] 3 IR 524, where an Art 9(1)(a) defence was established.

[166] [1990] 2 FLR 325.

[167] The Belgian court had apparently attempted to serve the mother with notice of the proceedings but had incorrectly addressed the notice.

[168] [1996] 1 FLR 660.

[169] At para 41.

[170] References to 'removal' in Art 9(1)(c) are to be read as referring to 'improper removal' within the meaning of Art 1(d): Child Abduction and Custody Act 1985, s 15(3).

[171] At para 43.

other than where the child is and then abducting the child to that State and subsequently seeking to use the decision as a ground for refusal.

Substantive exceptions under Art 10

19.107 In contrast to the narrow procedural exceptions provided by Art 9, rather wider substantive grounds upon which a court may refuse to recognise or enforce an order are provided by Art 10. As with Art 9, the establishment of one of these grounds probably still leaves the court with a discretion as to whether or not to recognise and enforce the order.[172] Although, commonly, Art 10 will be invoked to oppose recognition, registration and enforcement, it is established[173] that it can be invoked to prevent enforcement notwithstanding the previous registration of the order.

DECISION MANIFESTLY INCOMPATIBLE WITH THE FUNDAMENTAL PRINCIPLES OF THE STATE ADDRESSED

19.108 Under Art 10(1)(a), recognition and enforcement may be refused:

'if it is found that the effects of the decision are manifestly incompatible with the fundamental principles of the law relating to the family and children in the State addressed.'

19.109 The Explanatory Report explains[174] that Art 10(1)(a) is:

'... more restrictive than the usual clause governing refusal of *exequatur* on grounds of public policy. The welfare of the child being one of the fundamental principles of law, paragraph 1.a of this Article would enable recognition and enforcement of a decision to be refused when such enforcement would constitute a manifest violation of this fundamental principle.'

Both the Explanatory Report and case-law emphasise that the term 'manifestly' is used to indicate that the ground should not be relied upon except in the clearest case.[175]

---

[172] Some commentaries cite *Re G (A Minor) (Child Abduction: Enforcement)* [1990] 2 FLR 325 in support of this proposition, but in fact that decision only specifically held Art 9(1)(a) to vest a discretion. Nevertheless, since both Articles state that both recognition and enforcement *may* be refused and each are controlled by s 16(4)(a) of the 1985 Act, it seems reasonable to suppose that a similar interpretation should be applied to all the grounds. This certainly seems to be the intention of those drafting the Convention (see para 53 of the Explanatory Report) and was thought to be the position by Charles J in *T v R (Abduction: Forum Conveniens)* [2002] 2 FLR 544. However, it is suggested that a court may be more ready to order enforcement notwithstanding some procedural defect than it would be where one of the more substantive grounds under Art 10 has been established.

[173] *Re H (A Minor) (Foreign Custody Order: Enforcement)* [1994] Fam 105, [1994] 1 FLR 512, CA, discussed at **19.73**.

[174] Paragraph 47.

[175] See para 69 of the Explanatory Report. In the Irish decision, *RJ v MR* [1994] 1 IR 271 at 289, Finlay CJ said:

'I am satisfied that to give effect to the word "manifestly" it must be interpreted as placing upon the party objecting to the making of the order an onus to prove the incompatibility as a matter of high probability.'

19.110   An attempt to invoke Art 10(1)(a) failed in *Re G (A Minor) (Child Abduction: Enforcement)*,[176] in which a Belgian court, having attempted to serve the mother with notice of the proceedings but incorrectly addressing the notice so that she did not receive it, made an order in her absence altering the joint custody vested in both parents by vesting sole custody in the father instead. Notwithstanding this change, Booth J held that, given that the order did no more than keep the child in Belgium with access to the mother including access abroad with the father's consent, there was 'nothing incompatible in the effects of that decision with any fundamental principle of law [based on the child's welfare] in this country'. An Art 10(1)(a) plea also failed in *T v R (Abduction: Forum Conveniens)*,[177] where it was unsuccessfully argued that a change of residence to the father so as to ensure that the child would have contact with both parents was incompatible with the fundamental principles of English family law, since it was within the range of orders that could have been open to an English court.

CHANGE OF CIRCUMSTANCES

19.111   The second ground upon which recognition and enforcement may be refused is where, pursuant to Art 10(1)(b):

'... it is found that by reason of a change of circumstances, including the passage of time but not including a mere change in the residence of the child after an improper removal, the effects of the original decision are manifestly no longer in accordance with the welfare of the child.'

19.112   Before making any decision under Art 10(1)(b), the court is required by Art 15(1)(a) to ascertain the child's views 'unless this is impracticable having regard in particular to his age and understanding'.[178] However, unlike under the Hague Abduction Convention, a refusal is not permitted because of the child's objections *per se*.

19.113   As the Explanatory Report explains,[179] this provision is designed to provide 'an equitable solution in cases where the court addressed has grounds for thinking that circumstances have so changed that the decision [in issue] no longer corresponds to the child's welfare'. This change may be constituted by a new factor or, *prima facie*, by the passage of time. However, to prevent an

---

For discussion of the meaning of 'manifestly' in an entirely different context of undue influence, see *Royal Bank of Scotland plc v Etridge (No 2)* [2001] UKHL 44, [2001] 3 WLR 1021, [2001] 2 FLR 1364, HL. For the meaning of 'the effects of the original decision', see **19.113**.

[176] [1990] 2 FLR 325 at 331. The defence similarly failed in the Irish case, *RJ v MR* (above), in which it was argued that an English order granting access to an unmarried father was contrary to fundamental principles of Irish family law.

[177] [2002] 2 FLR 544 at [110]–[116].

[178] Under Art 15(1)(b), the court may request that appropriate enquiries be carried out. The cost of such enquiries must be met by the authorities of the State in which they are carried out (Art 15(2)). In exceptional cases, a child may be joined as a party and separately represented: *Re T (Abduction: Appointment of Guardian ad Litem)* [1999] 2 FLR 796.

[179] At para 48.

abductor using the change of the child's place of residence, the provision provides that a change in the child's residence after an improper removal cannot of itself constitute a sufficient change of circumstances (*aliter* if there has been no improper removal). Nevertheless, as the Explanatory Report observes,[180] where an application is made a long time after the removal, such that the child is accustomed to his environment in the new place of residence, then it can be argued that 'it is not the change of residence but the child's integration into the new environment which may justify a fresh examination'. From this point of view, the timing of the application may be a critical factor. It is established[181] that, for the purposes of both Art 10(1)(a) and (b), the phrase 'the effects of the original decision' refers to the immediate effects of the enforcement decision and not to the effects of taking steps towards its enforcement or to the return of the child to the State of origin to enable it to enforce that order, if appropriate.

19.114 In line with the spirit of the Convention, Art 10(1)(b) has been strictly interpreted by the English courts. Leggatt LJ stressed in *Re A (Foreign Access Order: Enforcement)*:[182]

> 'Unless there [has] been a change of circumstances, there [can] be no refusal of recognition and then only if such a change [has] rendered the custody order manifestly no longer in accordance with the welfare of the children.'

19.115 The burden to show that the original order is '*manifestly* no longer in accordance with the child's welfare' is a heavy one. It has been held,[183] for instance, that it is not enough to show that the child has settled well and is happy.

19.116 Notwithstanding this heavy burden, there have been cases where registration and enforcement have been refused. For example, in *F v F (Minors) (Custody: Foreign Order)*,[184] it was held that a foreign order for custody should

---

180   At para 48.
181   See *T v R (Abduction: Forum Conveniens)* [2002] 2 FLR 544 at [117] *et seq.*
182   [1996] 1 FLR 561 at 564.
183   Per Booth J in *Re G (A Minor) (Child Abduction: Enforcement)* [1990] 2 FLR 325. See also *Re L (Child Abduction: European Conventions)* [1992] 2 FLR 178 at 182, *Re K (A Minor) (Abduction)* [1990] 1 FLR 387, in which the defence failed, notwithstanding that the child (aged 7 at the date of the hearing) had been living in England for 16 months, it being found that she would adjust well if returned to her native Belgium, and *Re D (Abduction: Discretionary Return)* [2000] 1 FLR 24 at 38, in which Wilson J held that, had he been called upon to do so, he would have made a return order under the European Custody Convention on the basis that the requirement to show that it was 'manifestly' no longer in the interests of the children to be returned would have posed insuperable difficulties. He made this finding notwithstanding that under the Hague Convention application he had found that the mother had 'consented' to the children living with the father in England, thus establishing an exception under Art 13 of that Convention (discussed at **17.41** *et seq*). The defence also failed in the Irish decision, *RJ v MR* [1994] 1 IR 271, where the mother's evidence of the father's drunkenness and violence was found to be 'exaggerated'.
184   [1989] Fam 1, [1988] 3 WLR 959, sub nom *Re F (Minors) (Custody: Foreign Order)* [1989] 1 FLR 335.

not be enforced where the children had been in England for 21 months, and 12 months had elapsed between the enforcement hearing and the making of the foreign order. Similarly, in *Re R (Abduction: Hague and European Conventions)*,[185] recognition and enforcement of a Swiss order in favour of grandparents were refused on the basis that the mother had since remarried and the emotional and financial support that her new spouse provided had transformed the situation, with the child in question now thriving and happy and emphatically not wishing to return to Switzerland. The Court of Appeal upheld Hale J's conclusion that the order was manifestly no longer in accordance with the child's welfare. Article 10(1)(b) was also found to be satisfied in *T v R (Abduction: Forum Conveniens)*[186] in which a return to the father in Sweden after 4 years being with the mother in England was held to be manifestly not in the child's short-term interests.

CHILD'S LINK WITH STATE ADDRESSED IS SUBSTANTIAL

19.117   The third ground for refusal provided under Art 10, is that under Art 10(1)(c), namely:

> 'if at the time when the proceedings were instituted in the State of origin:
>
> (i)   the child was a national of the State addressed or was habitually resident there and no such connection existed with the State of origin;
>
> (ii)   the child was a national both of the State of origin and of the State addressed and was habitually resident in the State addressed.'

19.118   As the Explanatory Report says,[187] the purpose of this ground is to enable recognition and enforcement to be refused where the child's links with the State addressed are substantial but his links with the State of origin are non-existent or if the only link is that he is a dual national.[188]

DECISION INCOMPATIBLE WITH A DECISION GIVEN IN THE STATE
ADDRESSED AFTER BEING GIVEN IN A THIRD STATE

19.119   The final ground for refusal is that under Art 10(1)(d):

> 'if the decision is incompatible with a decision given in the State addressed or enforceable in that State after being given in a third State, pursuant to

---

[185] [1997] 1 FLR 663, CA. Enforcement was also refused in *Re H (A Minor) (Foreign Custody Order: Enforcement)* [1994] Fam 105, [1994] 1 FLR 512, in which a 13-year-old girl, who had been in the United Kingdom for about 5 years, was adamant that she did not wish to have any further contact with her father.

[186] [2002] 2 FLR 544, but note that in this case, Charles J adjourned the application under the European Custody Convention: see further at **19.125**.

[187] At para 50.

[188] The defence seemed to have succeeded (perhaps questionably) on this ground in *Re T (Abduction: Child's Objections To Return)* [2000] 2 FLR 192 at 220, per Ward LJ, although the judgment concentrates on the application of the Hague Abduction Convention: see **17.150** and **17.153**. Cf *Re M (Child Abduction) (European Convention)* [1994] 1 FLR 552 at 554, where the defence was held 'rightly' to have been abandoned.

proceedings begun before the submission of the request for recognition or enforcement, and if the refusal is in accordance with the welfare of the child.'

19.120 This ground overlaps with that under Art 9(1)(c) but, unlike that ground, where the previous decision must have been given before the improper removal, under Art 10(1)(d) the previous decision must have been given in pursuance of proceedings begun before the institution of the procedures for recognition and enforcement. The intention here is to prevent the person with care of the child in the State addressed seeking to avoid the effect of the foreign decision by starting proceedings in the State addressed after proceedings for recognition and enforcement have been begun.[189] The defence was successfully invoked in *Re M (Child Abduction) (European Convention)*[190] in which recognition and enforcement of an Irish custody order was refused since the enforcement proceedings were begun after an English court had made ex parte an interim residence order and, on the facts, it was in accordance with the children's welfare that they remained in the home they had enjoyed for some 18 months pending the decision as to their long-term future.

The decision is not enforceable in the Contracting State where it was made

19.121 In addition to the grounds provided by Arts 9 and 10, s 16(4)(b) of the 1985 Act allows the court to refuse recognition and enforcement if it is of the opinion that the decision is not enforceable in the Contracting State where it was made and is not a decision to which Art 12 applies. This provision has yet to be tested, but *prima facie* it does no more than reflect Art 7 which only requires an order to be made enforceable in any Contracting State where it is enforceable in the State of origin. According to the Explanatory Report[191] this does not *ipso facto* mean that decisions that have not yet acquired the authority of a final and conclusive judgment (*chose jugée*) cannot be recognised and enforced. It may be, however, that in some cases the more appropriate solution will be to adjourn proceedings in accordance with Art 10(2), which is discussed below.

The effect of a refusal

19.122 In those cases where recognition or enforcement is refused, Art 5(4) provides that the Central Authority may nevertheless comply with the request of the disappointed applicant to bring in that State proceedings concerning the substance of the case. In such cases, the Central Authority should use 'its best endeavours to secure the representation of the applicant in the proceedings under conditions no less favourable than those available to a person who is resident in and a national of that State'.

---

[189] See para 51 of the Explanatory Report.
[190] [1994] 1 FLR 552. Compare *Re K (A Minor) (Abduction)* [1990] 1 FLR 387, discussed at n 183 above.
[191] See para 54, but note para 35.

Adjourning recognition or enforcement

19.123 In addition to the grounds for refusing recognition, Art 10(2) provides the following grounds upon which recognition or enforcement may be postponed, namely:

'(a) if an ordinary form of review of the original decision has been commenced;

(b) if proceedings relating to the custody of the child, commenced before the proceedings in the State of origin were instituted, are pending in the State addressed;

(c) if another decision concerning the custody of the child is the subject of proceedings for enforcement or of any other proceedings concerning the recognition of the decision.'

19.124 According to the Explanatory Report,[192] the discretionary power vested by Art 10(2) extends to enabling a judge 'to fix a time limit within which the national proceedings must be completed, failing which proceedings for recognition or enforcement can be resumed'. It is to be noted that, unlike the grounds for refusing recognition etc, the fact that other proceedings are pending is a ground for adjournment.[193]

19.125 In *T v R (Abduction: Forum Conveniens)*,[194] it was held that if the court refuses to recognise the original order under Art 10(1), it can nevertheless adjourn the application for recognition rather than dismiss it. In that case, having found Art 10(1)(b) satisfied, Charles J, exercising his inherent jurisdiction, and upon the father undertaking not to take any steps to remove the child from the mother's care, ordered the child's return to Sweden but staying the order so as to allow the mother to institute custody proceedings in Sweden. In that way, he felt best able to promote the child's long-term interests.

Interim powers

19.126 As under the Hague Abduction Convention,[195] the court has wide powers to make interim orders pending the determination of an application for registration and enforcement under the European Custody Convention. Under s 19 of the 1985 Act, the court:

'... may at any time before the application is determined, give such interim directions as it thinks fit for the purpose of securing the welfare of the child concerned or, of preventing changes in the circumstances relevant to the determination of the application or, in the case of an application for registration, to the determination of any subsequent application for the enforcement of the decision.'

---

[192] Paragraph 58.

[193] For the reasons for making this distinction, see para 56 of the Explanatory Report.

[194] [2002] 2 FLR 544 at [143] and [172].

[195] For discussion of the comparable powers under s 5 of the 1985 Act, see **21.69**.

Applications for interim directions should normally be made by summons but, in emergencies, applications may be made ex parte on affidavit.[196]

19.127   In the case of 1980 Hague Abduction Convention applications, it has been held[197] that these interim powers can be exercised in respect of a child who has not yet arrived in the jurisdiction but is expected to do so, and there is no reason to suppose that the interim powers in respect of European Custody Convention applications should be interpreted any differently.

19.128   Again, as with 1980 Hague Abduction Conventions, these already wide powers are further supplemented by that vested by s 24A of the 1985 Act to order disclosure of the child's whereabouts.[198] However, in the case of European Custody Convention applications, r 6.16 of the FPR 1991 also provides that, at any stage of the proceedings:

> 'the court may, if it has reason to believe that any person may have relevant information about the child who is the subject of those proceedings, order that person to disclose such information and may for that purpose order that the person attend before it or file affidavit evidence.'

At any stage in the proceedings, either upon its own motion or upon application by summons by a party, the court may transfer the proceedings to Scotland, Northern Ireland or the Isle of Man.[199]

The effects of registration

19.129   Where the decision relating to custody has been registered, the court in which it is registered has the same powers for the purpose of enforcing the decision as if it had been made by that court, and proceedings for or with respect to the enforcement may be taken accordingly.[200] As Hale J observed in *Re R (Abduction: Hague and European Conventions)*:[201]

> 'It is not for the enforcing court to consider the merits of the order being enforced, merely the best way to bring about its enforcement. The main measure available to the courts in this country for the enforcement of the order is the power to commit the person who has disobeyed it to prison.'

19.130   Although it is not for the enforcing court to consider the merits of the case, it does nevertheless have the power to postpone enforcement in order that the child may better adapt to the consequences of enforcement.

---

[196]   FPR 1991, r 16.13.
[197]   *Re N (Child Abduction: Jurisdiction)* [1995] Fam 96, [1995] 2 All ER 417, sub nom *A v A (Abduction: Jurisdiction)* [1995] 1 FLR 341, discussed at **21.69**.
[198]   See *Re H (Abduction: Whereabouts Order to Solicitors)* [2000] 1 FLR 766 at 768, discussed at **10.18**, **10.19** and **21.57**.
[199]   FPR 1991, r 6.12.
[200]   Section 18 of the 1985 Act.
[201]   [1997] 1 FLR 663 at 672, not commented upon by the Court of Appeal.

This power was exercised by Booth J in *Re G (A Minor) (Child Abduction: Enforcement)*,[202] *inter alia*, to allow the child to complete the current school term.

19.131　Another effect of registration is that any care or supervision order, residence order or order giving care and control within wardship[203] relating to the child ceases to have effect.[204]

Variation and revocation of registered decisions

19.132　Section 17 of the 1985 Act makes provision for registered decisions to be varied or revoked in cases where the decision has been varied or revoked by a judicial or administrative authority in the country where the decision was originally made. Where a decision which has been registered under s 16 of the 1985 Act is varied or revoked by an authority in the Contracting State in which it was made, the person on whose behalf the application for registration of the decision was made must notify the court in which the decision is registered of the variation or revocation.[205] Where a court is notified of the revocation of a decision, it must:[206]

(a)　cancel the registration, and
(b)　notify such persons as are prescribed by the rules of court (namely the person appearing to the court to have care of the child, the person on whose behalf the application for registration was made and any other party to that application)[207] of the cancellation.

19.133　Where a court is notified of the variation of a decision, it must:[208]

(a)　notify such persons as are prescribed by the rules of court (namely the person appearing to the court to have care of the child and any party to the application for registration)[209] of the variation; and
(b)　vary the registration but only after those notified have had the opportunity to make representations.[210]

19.134　The court in which a decision is registered may also, on the application of any person appearing to the court to have an interest in the matter,[211] cancel or vary the registration if it is satisfied that the decision

---

[202] [1990] 2 FLR 325 at 333–334.
[203] Ie any 'custody order' as defined by s 27(1) of the 1985 Act.
[204] Section 25(1) of the 1985 Act.
[205] Section 17(1).
[206] Section 17(2).
[207] FPR 1991, r 6.15(2).
[208] Section 17(3).
[209] FPR 1991, r 6.15(3).
[210] Applications for these purposes should be made by summons: *ibid*, r 6.15(3).
[211] Applications should be by summons: *ibid*, r 6.15(4).

has been revoked or, as the case may be, varied by an authority in the Contracting State in which it was made.[212]

EVALUATION OF THE CONVENTION

19.135 Although the European Custody Convention has attracted, and continues to attract, a growing number of signatories,[213] it is evident that it is little used, even in relation to access disputes where it is clearly superior to the 1980 Hague Abduction Convention. In their detailed research of abduction cases handled by the Child Abduction Unit in 1996, Lowe and Perry found[214] that only 7% were European Custody Convention applications (although comprising more 'outgoing' applications, 9%, than 'incoming' applications, 5%). They also found a similarly low take-up in 10 other European countries that had ratified both Conventions.[215] So far as cases handled by the Child Abduction Unit are concerned, the pattern has remained much the same since 1996 with European Custody Convention applications accounting for 10% of all Convention applications in 1997, 9% in 1998 and 9% in 1999, but only 5% in 2002. In each year there have been slightly more European Custody Convention applications in respect of children taken from England and Wales than for those brought to the jurisdiction.[216] It seems likely that, given the precedence accorded to the Brussels II Regulation, significantly fewer applications will be made in the future.

19.136 The requirement that there must be a custody or access order concerning the child, notwithstanding that it is possible to obtain a post-abduction order under Art 12, clearly limits the scope of the European Custody Convention, but, over and above this is the perceived complexity of the Convention, particularly when compared with the Hague Abduction Convention. As Bruch has perceptively commented:[217]

---

[212] Section 17(4).

[213] There were, for example, three new ratifications in 2003, namely, Bosnia and Herzegovina, Lithuania and the Former Yugoslav Republic of Macedonia, taking the total number of Contracting States (as of October 2003) to 31. In the early days there were more ratifications of the European Custody Convention than of the 1980 Hague Abduction Convention. By the end of 1986, for example, the year in which the United Kingdom ratified both Conventions, there were nine ratifications of the European Custody Convention compared to five of the Hague Abduction Convention.

[214] Lowe and Perry, 'International Child Abduction – The English Experience' (1999) 48 ICLQ 127.

[215] *Ibid*, App 1, Fig A 3 (at 152).

[216] In 1997, 11% of outgoing applications were under the European Custody Convention, compared to 7% of those incoming. In 1998, the respective figures were 10% compared to 8% and, in 1999, 9% compared to 8%.

[217] Bruch, 'How to Draft a Successful Family Law Convention: Lessons from the Child Abduction Convention' in Doek, van Loon and Vlaardingerbroek (eds), *Children on the Move* (Martinus Nijhoff, 1996), p 47 at p 54.

'The European Convention is in some ways legally sophisticated. It extends existing doctrines that prevent re-litigation of the custody area. It also delineates quite precisely when exceptions are permitted – at one stage creating chasing orders to permit relief for what were pre-judgment wrongs and, at another, specifying exceptions to the enforcement-of-judgments rule (sometimes because there were too few connections with the country that gave the judgment, sometimes because delayed enforcement would harm the child). Paradoxically, its major shortcoming is precisely this kind of sophistication – compared to the Hague Convention, the European Convention is just too complex. The more refinements there are, the more questions there are to litigate. The more questions there are to litigate, the longer things will take. The longer things take, the more likely it is that your remedy will hurt rather than help the child. If the process has taken so long that applying the enforcement rule may hurt the child, the more likely you are to apply an exception to it, rather than the enforcement rule itself.'

Chapter 20

INTERNATIONAL ABDUCTIONS: NON-CONVENTION COUNTRIES

INTRODUCTION

20.1 In this chapter we discuss the position of children wrongfully brought to or taken from England and Wales[1] from or to a non-Convention country,

---

[1] For discussion of the position in other jurisdictions, see eg in relation to Australia, Nicholson, 'Australian Judicial Attitudes to the Convention on The Civil Aspects of International Child Abduction (The Hague Convention)', in Lowe and Douglas (eds), *Families Across Frontiers* (Kluwer, 1996), p 663 at pp 666–671, and, in relation to the United States, Apy, 'Managing Child Custody Cases Involving Non-Hague Contracting States' (1997) 14 *Journal of the American Academy of Matrimonial Lawyers* 77.

by which we mean a State that is party to neither the 1980 Hague Abduction Convention nor the 1980 European Custody Convention.[2] Although official statistics are not kept on the number of such abductions, according to records kept by Reunite,[3] of the 275 new cases (involving 385 children) brought in the United Kingdom in 2001, 26% were 'non-Hague', while 48% of the 220 new cases (involving 311 children) concerned with the prevention of abductions from the United Kingdom were 'non-Hague'. It is to be noted that the English Child Abduction Unit does not deal with abduction to or from non-Convention States. Furthermore, the advantageous provisions governing public funding[4] do not apply.

CHILDREN BROUGHT TO ENGLAND AND WALES FROM A NON-CONVENTION COUNTRY

Issues of jurisdiction

Choice of domestic jurisdiction

20.2   Children brought to England and Wales from a non-Convention country remain subject to the common law. Disputes arising in this context commonly fall to be decided in wardship proceedings[5] because the invocation of that jurisdiction offers the quickest and best safeguard against the child's further removal.[6] Ironically, it is for this reason that it is often the abducting parent who wards the child.

20.3   Protection apart, however, there is no significant difference between invoking wardship and proceedings under the Children Act 1989. In each case, jurisdiction is governed by the Family Law Act 1986, as amended by the so-called 'Brussels II Regulation',[7] while, as a matter of substantive law, the

---

2   Notwithstanding this focus, it should be noted that similar issues can arise: (a) even between Convention countries, see eg *W and W v H (Child Abduction: Surrogacy) (No 2)* [2002] 2 FLR 252, in which the question arose as to whether to return twins to the United States following their removal by the mother when pregnant (see **4.47**); and (b) as between England and Wales and the Channel Islands (see the discussion at **11.40**). See also *T v R (Abduction: Forum Conveniens)* [2002] 2 FLR 544, in which, following a refusal to recognise a custody order under the terms of Art 10 of the 1980 European Custody Convention, the court ordered the child's return under its inherent jurisdiction.

3   Carter, 'The Role of Reunite and the International Child Abduction Centre and the Importance of Prevention' – paper given at the International Child Abduction Conference held in Edinburgh, June 2002.

4   Discussed at **21.15**.

5   For a discussion of which, see **4.5** *et seq*.

6   In particular, immediately the child is warded and throughout the wardship, he or she is not permitted to leave England and Wales (subject to going to another part of the United Kingdom or the Isle of Man if habitually resident there: see Family Law Act 1986, s 38, discussed at **6.14**) without court leave.

7   Viz Council Regulation (EC) No 1347/2000 of 29 May 2000 on the jurisdiction and the recognition and enforcement of judgments in matrimonial matters and in matters of

general principle to be applied, the paramountcy of the child's welfare, is governed by s 1(1) of the Children Act 1989. A court is not precluded from ordering a child's return (if that is in the child's best interests) merely because the family is involved in asylum proceedings.[8]

Deciding how to exercise jurisdiction

20.4 Under the Family Law Act 1986, as amended, unless matrimonial proceedings are continuing elsewhere in the United Kingdom or the Isle of Man, or there are relevant proceedings in an EU State under Brussels II,[9] jurisdiction can be based on the child's habitual residence or, provided the child is not habitually resident in another part of the United Kingdom or the Isle of Man, on the child's presence.[10] Accordingly, where a child has been brought to England and Wales from a non-Convention country then, irrespective of the proceedings in which the issue is raised, the central question is not whether, but how, the court should exercise its jurisdiction. In this regard, the basic issue is whether to order the child's return to the place whence he or she was taken or to allow him or her to remain in England and Wales. In making this choice, however, the court must first decide whether it should investigate the full merits of the case or simply make a summary order for the child's return. This choice is further complicated by an issue of contemporary importance and controversy, namely, the extent to which, if at all, the foreign law in question needs to be investigated, in order for the court to be satisfied that if the child is returned, his or her welfare will continue to be treated as the paramount consideration.

The basic dilemma

20.5 In deciding whether or not to make a return order, the court is faced with a dilemma. If it refuses to make a return order that will be seen as giving an advantage to the wrongdoer (ie the abducting parent, who may, though not necessarily, deliberately flouted a foreign court order), yet while a court can hardly condone abduction both in the interests of justice and comity, a refusal may well be justified in the interests of the child, which interests the

---

parental responsibility for children of both spouses, discussed at **4.9** *et seq* and in Chapter 18.

[8] See *Re S (Child Abduction: Asylum Appeal)* [2002] EWCA Civ 843, [2002] 2 FLR 465, CA, in which it was held that s 15 of the Immigration and Asylum Act 1999 was not intended to circumscribe the duty and discretion of the judge exercising the wardship jurisdiction but was instead directed to the immigration authorities. See also *Re H (A Minor) (Child Abduction: Mother's Asylum)* (2003) The Times, 8 August.

[9] Viz proceedings concerning the parental responsibility of children both of whose parents have also instituted matrimonial proceedings in that State. Note that all EU States, save for Denmark, are parties to the Council Regulation.

[10] Note that the High Court can also take jurisdiction in emergencies on the basis of the child's presence notwithstanding that matrimonial proceedings are continuing or that the child is habitually resident in another part of the United Kingdom or the Isle of Man: see Family Law Act 1986, ss 1(1)(d) and 2(3)(b). The jurisdictional rules under the 1986 Act are discussed in Chapter 3.

courts are statutorily enjoined to secure. The problem of how such apparently conflicting interests should be reconciled has been approached in different ways at different times.

The developing response to child abduction

The historical position

The relevance of foreign court orders

20.6 One crucial factor in determining what should happen to a child brought to England and Wales from abroad is the relevance of any foreign court order. During the nineteenth century that relevance depended upon whether or not the child was a British subject. If the child was not, then the foreign order was generally regarded as binding unless, exceptionally, it was thought to amount to an abdication of jurisdiction not to interfere.[11] In *Nugent v Vetzera*,[12] for example, the court refused to interfere with the appointments made by an Austrian court with respect to Austrian children who had since been sent to England to be educated. Page Wood V-C commented:[13]

> 'It would be fraught with consequences of very serious difficulty and contrary to all principles of right and justice, if this Court were to hold that when a parent or guardian (for a guardian stands in exactly the same position as a parent) in a foreign country avails himself of the opportunity for education afforded by this country, and sends his children over here, he must do it at the risk of never being able to recall them, because this Court might be of the opinion that an English course of education is better than that adopted in the country to which they belong. I cannot conceive anything more startling than such a notion, which would involve on the other hand this result, that an English ward could not be sent to France for his holidays without the risk of his being kept there and educated in the Roman Catholic religion, with no power to the father or guardian to recall the child. Surely such a state of jurisprudence would put an end to all interchange of friendship between civilised communities.'

---

11 See Page Wood V-C in *Nugent v Vetzera* (1866) LR 2 Eq 704 at 714. One example cited by Page Wood V-C was where the foreign guardians had abandoned the children. However, as Morton J observed in *Re B's Settlement, B v B* [1940] Ch 54 at 62, it was uncertain what Page Wood V-C's view would have been had there been evidence that it would be most detrimental to the health and well-being of the children if they were removed from England and sent to Austria.

12 (1866) LR 2 Eq 704. See also *Di Savini v Lousada* (1870) 18 WR 425, and the comments in Seton's *Judgments and Orders* 7th edn (1912), Vol II at pp 953, 994 and 1000.

13 At 712. Note that the English court did not necessarily regard a Scottish court order as binding, see eg *Stuart v Marquis of Bute* (1861) 9 HL Cas 440, one of the earliest reported cases of child abduction. In *Nugent v Vetzera* (above) at 713, Page Wood V-C justified this decision on the basis that the child in question was a subject of the United Kingdom and had large property situated, *inter alia*, in England. See also the comments of Lord Simonds in *McKee v McKee* [1951] AC 352 at 365. For further discussion of the relationship of court decisions within the British Isles, and in particular between England and Wales and Scotland, see Chapter 3.

20.7   Where, however, the child was found to be a British subject, a foreign court order was not treated as binding. In *Dawson v Jay*,[14] for example, the court refused to allow a maternal aunt to have custody of a child who was a British subject so that she could take her back to the United States where the child was born and had resided for 10 years, even though she had been appointed the child's guardian by a court in New York. The principal ground for this decision was that it would amount to an abdication of its function if the court sent a ward who was a British subject to another jurisdiction over which it had no control.[15]

A change of approach

20.8   By the mid-twentieth century a fundamentally different approach was established, initially through a bold first instance decision, *Re B's Settlement, B v B*[16] and then by the leading Privy Council decision, *McKee v McKee*.[17]

20.9   In *Re B's Settlement* Morton J considered that, in accordance with what was then s 1 of the Guardianship of Infants Act 1925,[18] the court was:

> 'bound in every case, without exception, to treat the welfare of its ward as being the first and paramount consideration, whatever orders may have been made by the Courts of any other country.'

In other words, regardless of the child's nationality, the English court was not bound by a foreign order, although in deciding what order to make due weight would be given to the views of the foreign court. Morton J added[19] that any observations made, *inter alia*, in *Nugent v Vetzera*[20] stating or implying a contrary view ought not to be followed.

20.10   Applying the welfare principle in *Re B's Settlement*, Morton J granted care and control of a child born in Belgium to a British mother with whom the child had been living in England for the previous 2 years, notwithstanding that the mother had clearly acted in breach of a Belgian court order granting custody to the father who was a Belgian national living in Belgium.[21]

20.11   *Re B's Settlement* was approved in *McKee v McKee*. In that case the father had deliberately flouted a Californian court order granting custody to the mother by taking the child to Ontario in Canada without either the court's or

---

14   (1854) 3 De G, M & G 764.

15   See Lord Cranworth LC (1854) 3 De G, M & G 764 at 772. See also the comments of Page Wood V-C in *Nugent v Vetzera* (1866) LR 2 Eq 704 at 713, and of Lord Simonds in *McKee v McKee* [1951] AC 352 at 365.

16   [1940] Ch 54.

17   [1951] AC 352.

18   This was re-enacted as s 1 of the Guardianship of Minors Act 1971, which in turn was replaced by the slightly differently worded s 1(1) of the Children Act 1989.

19   [1940] Ch 54 at 64.

20   (1866) LR 2 Eq 704 and in *Di Savini v Lousada* (1870) 18 WR 425.

21   Given the subsequent outbreak of World War II it is interesting to speculate whether Morton J's decision saved the child's life.

the mother's consent. The first instance judge, notwithstanding the existence of the Californian order and the father's conduct, decided to hear the case on its merits, and, having done so, concluded that it was in the child's interests that custody be granted to the father. The Privy Council upheld both the decision to hear the case on its merits and the order giving the father custody. With regard to the status of a foreign court order, Lord Simonds said:[22]

> 'the welfare and happiness of the infant is the paramount consideration in questions of custody ... . To this paramount consideration all others yield. The order of a foreign court of competent jurisdiction is no exception. Such an order has not the force of a foreign judgment: comity demands not its enforcement, but its grave consideration ... . This distinction which has long been recognised in the courts of England and Scotland (see *Johnstone v Beattie*[23] and *Stuart v Marquis of Bute*,[24] and in the courts of Ontario (see eg *Re Ethel Davis*[25] and *Re Gay*[26]), rests on the peculiar character of the jurisdiction and on the fact that an order providing for the custody of an infant cannot in its nature be final.'

20.12 On this approach it was clear that a foreign judgment was not to be ignored but that its weight depended upon the circumstances. Indeed, both Morton J and particularly Lord Simonds left it open that there may be cases where it would be in the child's interests that the court should not look beyond the circumstances in which its jurisdiction was invoked and for that reason give effect to the foreign judgment without further inquiry.[27] In other words, it was specifically recognised that there may be circumstances where the court would be justified in making a summary order for the child's return to the jurisdiction whence he was taken. It was this power to make a summary order that next came to be developed.

Favouring a summary return

20.13 Until the 1960s the debate about whether or not a child should be returned to the country whence he or she was taken very much centred on the relevance of the foreign court order. In *Re H (Infants)*,[28] however, a significantly different approach was taken in relation to what was then termed child 'kidnapping'. In that case, a mother, in contravention of a New York Supreme Court order, and without the consent of the father, brought the children to England with the intention of permanently residing there. She subsequently made the children wards of court. It was argued that once

---

22   [1951] AC 352 at 365.

23   (1843) 10 CL & Fin 42.

24   (1861) 9 HL Cas 440, 11 ER 799.

25   (1894) 25 OR 579.

26   (1926) 59 OLR 40.

27   See [1951] AC 352 at 363, per Lord Simonds, and *Re B's Settlement, B v B* [1940] Ch 54 at 64, per Morton J. For other cases where the court did investigate the merits, see eg *Re A (an infant)* (1959) *The Times*, 25 March and *Re Kernot (An Infant)* [1965] Ch 217, [1964] 3 WLR 1210. In the latter case, an important factor was that the Italian court would have applied English law anyway.

28   [1965] 3 All ER 906 (first instance); [1966] 1 All ER 886, CA.

wardship proceedings had been launched, even by someone who had wrongfully brought children to England in defiance of the laws of the country where their home was, then, unless there were exceptional circumstances, the court was bound to investigate the full merits of the case. At first instance, Cross J disagreed, holding that the court had a discretion to investigate the full merits of a case. He considered that the appropriate order in this case was to send the children back to New York. He was satisfied that they would suffer no harm if they were sent back to the United States with their father, and that, since they were American and as the mother had behaved most reprehensibly, it was right that the court should summarily order the children's return. He commented that:[29]

> '... the sudden and unauthorised removal of children from one country to another is far too frequent nowadays, and, as it seems to me, it is the duty of all courts in all countries to do all they can to ensure that the kidnapper does not gain an advantage by his wrongdoing.'

20.14 Cross J also pointed out that if the merits were to be investigated by the English court it would cause grave injustice to the father, since in the time it would take to collect the necessary evidence the children would have become more settled in England, making it more unlikely that they would be ordered to return to the United States. In summarising the considerations relevant to a so-called 'kidnapping' case, Cross J said that the court had to weigh on the one hand the public policy aspect such as the question of comity and *forum conveniens* and the injustice done to the wronged parent and, on the other hand, the interest of the child. He held that the interest of the child was sufficiently taken into account if the court was satisfied that to send the child back would cause him no harm.

20.15 The Court of Appeal upheld both the decision to send the children back and the general approach to kidnapping at least where, as in the case before them, wardship proceedings had been brought quickly. Willmer LJ expressly approved[30] Cross J's comments (cited above) about the need to ensure that a kidnapper does not gain advantage by his wrongdoing. Similarly, Harman LJ commented:[31]

> 'One starts inevitably with the view that the mother, who had done the kidnapping, should not be allowed to reap the advantage of her wrongdoing. One has only, as Russell LJ did, to reverse the position to see what our feelings would be if the American court in reverse circumstances took the course which is urged on this court.'

---

[29] [1965] 3 All ER 906 at 912. Note also his comment (at 915) that he considered Page Wood V-C's observations in *Nugent v Vetzera* (1866) LR 2 Eq 704 still to carry 'very great weight' notwithstanding the comments in *Re B's Settlement* [1940] Ch 54 and *McKee v McKee* [1951] AC 352.

[30] [1966] 1 All ER 886 at 888–889.

[31] *Ibid* at 892.

20.16   Russell LJ himself commented:[32]

'The fact that the native state administers the same jurisdiction over infants as does the court here is a factor for consideration; indeed, it is a factor in favour of exercising the jurisdiction by directing the return of these [children]; it is not an abdication of the jurisdiction to exercise it.'

20.17   In the subsequent decision, *Re E (An Infant)*,[33] a return order was refused notwithstanding an abduction. In that case, following the death in the United States of the custodial father, his sister (who was based in England) clandestinely took his American child to England. Subsequently, the American mother obtained in the United States a temporary custody order and she eventually[34] sought the child's return in the English court. It was held that, since the only home that the child had known in the United States had been destroyed, so that her freshly acquired home in England was now her only home, it would have been disastrous to order the child's return to the United States. Notwithstanding this refusal, Cross J, with whom the Court of Appeal agreed, again took the opportunity to condemn child abduction, commenting:[35]

'To my mind, it is wrong to look at such a case solely from the point of view of the welfare of the particular child … In modern conditions it is often easy and tempting for a parent who has been deprived of custody by the court of country "A" to remove the child suddenly to country "B" and to set up home there. The courts in all countries ought, as I see it, to be careful not to do anything to encourage this tendency. The substitution of self help for due process of law in this field can only harm the interest of wards generally, and a judge should, as I see it, pay regard to the orders of the proper foreign court unless he is satisfied beyond all reasonable doubt that to do so would inflict serious harm on the child.'

20.18   Until *Re T (Infants)*,[36] so-called kidnapping cases had involved the breaking of a foreign court order but the concept was extended to include the unilateral withdrawal of children from their home by one parent without the other's consent. In upholding a first instance decision to return

---

32   [1966] 1 All ER 886 at 893.

33   [1967] Ch 287, reported as *Re E (D) (An Infant)* [1967] 1 All ER 329 (first instance); [1967] 2 All ER 881, CA.

34   It took the mother about 5 months to raise the money to come to England.

35   [1967] Ch 287 at 289, [1967] 1 All ER 329 at 330, specifically approved by Willmer LJ [1967] 2 All ER 881 at 885.

36   [1968] Ch 704, [1968] 3 All ER 411, CA. In fact, as the Court of Appeal pointed out, the return order had been made only after hearing all the evidence which the parties chose to present to the court, but both Harman and Russell LJJ considered that it had been right to treat the case as being analogous to application for a summary order.

two Canadian children to Canada following their (English-born) mother's unilateral removal of them to England, Harman LJ commented:[37]

> 'It seems to me that the removal of children from their home and surroundings by one of the parents who happens to live in or have connections with another country is a thing against which the court should set its face, and that, unless there is good reason to the contrary, it should not countenance proceedings of that kind.'

In other words, a return order should be made unless it could be shown to be harmful to the children.

20.19 At one stage it seemed that the courts might make a distinction between wrongful removals and wrongful retentions (that is, keeping the child beyond the time agreed between the parents),[38] but it became clear that the availability of a summary order did not depend upon such fine distinctions.[39]

The re-assertion of the application of the paramountcy principle

20.20 The approach developed by the Court of Appeal, particularly in *Re H* and *Re E*, meant that when faced with an abduction, and provided proceedings were brought promptly, a summary order for the child's return would only be refused if it could be shown to be against the child's interests. In other words, the interests of the individual child were taken into account only to the extent that the court had to be satisfied that the child would not be harmed by a return order. Irrespective of whether this approach could be justified upon the paramountcy principle, it seemed clear that the courts themselves did not consider the child's welfare to be their only consideration.[40] These judgments, however, predated the House of Lords' decision in *J v C*[41] which made it plain that the paramountcy principle was of universal application whenever the child's custody and upbringing was in issue. Indeed, in that case, passing reference was made to abduction cases inasmuch as their Lordships approvingly referred to *Re B's Settlement*[42] and *McKee v McKee*[43] as making it plain that the paramountcy principle applied notwithstanding the existence of a foreign court order.[44]

---

37 [1968] Ch 704, [1968] 3 All ER 411 at 715 and 413. See also his comment at 713 and 412: 'This has been described as a "kidnapping" case. And so in my view it is'. See also the same judge's comments in *Re A (Infants)* [1970] Ch 665 at 673, [1970] 3 All ER 184 at 186.

38 See *Re A (Infants)* (above), in which it was held that a father who genuinely changed his mind about returning children to Jersey after an agreed period of a one-month visit to England could not be said to have 'kidnapped' the children.

39 See *Re M-R (a Minor)* (1975) 5 Fam Law 55, CA.

40 See eg Russell LJ in *Re H (Infants)* [1966] 1 All ER 886 at 893 (cited at **20.16**) and Cross J in *Re E (D) (An Infant)* [1967] Ch 287 at 289, [1967] 1 All ER 329 at 330 (cited above at **20.17**).

41 [1970] AC 688, [1969] 1 All ER 788.

42 [1940] Ch 54, discussed at **20.9–20.10**.

43 [1951] AC 352, discussed at **20.11**.

44 See in particular Lord MacDermott [1970] AC 688 at 714, [1969] 1 All ER 788 at 824, Lord Upjohn at 720 and 828–829, respectively, and Lord Guest at 700–701 and 812, respectively.

20.21   With *J v C* in mind, in *Re L (Minors) (Wardship: Jurisdiction)*,[45] Buckley LJ once again[46] emphasised that in making *any* decision, including a summary return order, the child's welfare must always be treated as the paramount consideration. As he said:[47]

> '… judges have more than once reprobated the acts of "kidnappers" in cases of this kind. I do not in any way dissent from those strictures, but it would, in my judgment, be wrong to suppose that in making orders in relation to children in this jurisdiction the court is in any way concerned with penalising any adult for his conduct. That conduct may well be a consideration to be taken into account, but, whether the court makes a summary order or an order investigating the merits, the cardinal rule applies that the welfare of the infant must always be the paramount consideration.'

20.22   In Buckley LJ's view, where the court embarked upon a full-scale investigation of the merits there was no distinction between a so-called kidnapping case and any other case – the court is called upon to weigh the various factors of which kidnapping would be one (albeit a possibly important) factor and make a decision upon the basis of what is thought to be in the child's best interests. The decision to make a summary order without investigating the merits still had to be justified in the child's best interests, although in a different way. As Buckley LJ put it:[48]

> 'To take a child from his native land, to remove him to another country where maybe, his native tongue is not spoken, to divorce him from the social customs and contacts to which he has been accustomed, to interrupt his education in his native land and subject him to a foreign system of education, are all acts (offered here as examples and, of course, not a complete catalogue of possible relevant factors) which are likely to be psychologically disturbing to the child, particularly at a time when his family life is also disrupted. If such a case is promptly brought to the attention of a court in this country, the judge may feel that it is in the best interests of the infant that these disturbing factors should be eliminated from his life as speedily as possible. A full investigation of the merits of the case in an English court may be incompatible with achieving this … . An order that the child should be returned forthwith to the country from which he has been removed in the expectation that any dispute about his custody will be satisfactorily resolved in the courts of that country may well be regarded as being in the best interests of the child.'

20.23   In *Re L* itself, an English-born mother had, on the pretext of a holiday, brought her two children aged 11 and 9 to England from Germany where they were born and had spent all their lives, with the intention of permanently remaining there. It was held that, as the children had always been brought up in Germany and were German nationals, it was in their long-term

---

45   [1974] 1 WLR 250, [1974] 1 All ER 913, CA. Note that leave to appeal to the House of Lords was refused: see [1974] 1 WLR 266.

46   As Lord Simonds had done in *McKee v McKee* [1951] AC 325.

47   At 265 and 926, respectively.

48   At 264–265 and 925–926, respectively.

interests that they should continue to live in Germany. Accordingly, their immediate return was ordered.

20.24 Buckley LJ sought to explain earlier decisions such as *Re H* as depending upon the principle of what was in the best interests of the children concerned. However, while *Re H* could be so justified, in truth the two decisions established fundamentally different approaches. The *'Re H'* approach placed the burden on the 'kidnapper' to adduce evidence that it would be harmful to the child to be returned, whereas the *'Re L'* approach placed the burden on the 'innocent' party to show that it was in the child's best interests that a summary order be made. This conflict was considered in *Re R (Minors) (Wardship: Jurisdiction)*.[49]

20.25 A Jewish couple married in England (the wife being English, the husband an Israeli) and went immediately to live in Israel where they had three children. Divorce proceedings were later commenced in Israel in which both parents sought custody of the children. The Rabbinical court ordered the mother not to leave Israel with the children but, being advised that no custody decision would be made for some time, in breach of the order, she brought the children to England where she warded them. The Rabbinical court ordered the mother to return the children to Israel. The mother unsuccessfully appealed against the order. The father then applied in the wardship proceedings for the immediate return of the children to Israel. There followed protracted litigation in England. The matter came first before Waterhouse J who held that he should apply *Re H* but, because the father had filed no evidence, he refused to make a summary order for the children's return. In subsequent proceedings, Lincoln J applied *Re L*, but declined to make a summary order for the children's return. He held, however, that since the children had always lived in Israel, and encouraged by the father's evidence that the Rabbinical court would soon reach a decision on custody, the *forum conveniens* lay with the Israeli court.

20.26 The mother successfully appealed. Ormrod LJ emphasised that the course to be followed in every case must be determined by the best interests and welfare of the children. With regard to Waterhouse J's approach, he pointed out that the House of Lords' decision in *J v C* meant in effect that *Re H* could no longer be followed and that the correct test was laid down by Buckley LJ in *Re L*. His Lordship observed:[50]

> 'It follows that the strength of an application for a summary order for the return of the child to the country from which it has been removed, must rest not on the so-called "kidnapping" of the child, or an order of a foreign court, but on the assessment of the best interests of the child. Both, or either, are relevant considerations, but the weight to be given to either of them must be measured in terms of the interests of the child, not in terms of penalising the "kidnapper", or

---

[49] (1981) 2 FLR 416. See also *Re C (Minors) (Wardship: Jurisdiction)* [1978] Fam 105, [1978] 2 All ER 230, CA.

[50] (1981) 2 FLR 416 at 425.

of comity, or any other abstraction. "Kidnapping", like other kinds of unilateral action in relation to children, is to be strongly discouraged, but the discouragement must take the form of a swift, realistic and unsentimental assessment of the best interests of the child, leading, in proper cases, to the prompt return of the child to his or her own country, but not the sacrifice of the child's welfare to some other principle of law. It might remove some of the confusion of thought which bedevils these cases if "the kidnapper" was allowed to join "the unimpeachable parent" in forensic limbo.'

20.27 Although Ormrod LJ agreed that Lincoln J was right to dismiss the father's application for a summary order, he considered it to be wrong for him nevertheless to rule that the Israeli court was the *forum conveniens*. As he put it, such a ruling was an effective abdication of jurisdiction. Ormrod LJ emphasised that the concept of *forum conveniens* had no place in the wardship jurisdiction. In his view there was no *via media* between making a summary order and investigating the full merits of the case. He concluded that having rightly decided not to make a summary order, there was no choice but to order an investigation into the facts.

20.28 Following *Re R*, it seemed settled that in abduction cases whether to make a summary order for return or to investigate the merits of the case was governed by the paramountcy principle.[51] Furthermore, Ormrod LJ's plea to consign references to 'kidnapping' to forensic limbo seems to have been heeded with the issue thereafter being more generally referred to as 'abduction'.

The modern position

Applying the philosophy of the Hague Convention to non-Convention cases

TREATING NON-CONVENTION CASES AS QUASI-HAGUE CONVENTION CASES

20.29 Notwithstanding that the law seemed settled by *Re L* and *Re R*, the Court of Appeal began to develop the notion that the principles set out by the 1980 Hague Abduction Convention should be applied by analogy to so-called non-Convention cases. This approach was first adopted in *G v G (Minors) (Abduction)*.[52] In that case, an English mother and a father of both English and American nationality lived, married and had their two children in Kenya. Following the breakdown of their marriage, the mother initiated custody proceedings in the High Court of Kenya but, pending the full hearing, the

---

[51] See eg *Re G (A Minor) (Wardship: Jurisdiction)* [1984] FLR 268, CA; *Re B (Minors) (Wardship: Interim Care and Control)* (1983) 4 FLR 472, CA; and *Re L (A Minor) (Wardship: Jurisdiction)* (1983) 4 FLR 368.

[52] [1991] 2 FLR 506. This case was in fact decided in 1989, but because it was initially unreported many were unaware of its existence. It only came into prominence when it was relied upon in *Re F (A Minor) (Abduction: Custody Rights)* [1991] Fam 25, [1991] 1 FLR 1, CA, discussed at **20.32** *et seq* below. For an excellent analysis of these and subsequent decisions, including those in Australia, see McClean and Beevers, 'International child abduction – back to common law principles' (1995) 7 JCL 128.

mother and children came to England.[53] The father followed her and instituted wardship proceedings seeking the children's immediate return to Kenya. He alleged that the mother had a drink problem and had in the past taken drugs.

20.30 The first instance judge refused the father's application, holding that in the best interests of the children a full hearing should take place to enable him properly to evaluate the evidence. This decision, however, was overturned on appeal. Balcombe LJ commented that since *Re L* and *Re R*, a new factor had come into play, namely, the enactment of the Child Abduction and Custody Act 1985 which gave effect to the 1980 Hague Abduction Convention. In his view, the 1985 Act did not, as was argued, substitute a test which did not put the child's welfare as the paramount consideration but rather:[54]

'... the philosophy behind this Act, and indeed behind the Convention which it adopted, is that in normal circumstances it is in the interests of the children that parents or others should not abduct them from one jurisdiction to another, but that any decision relating to the custody of children is best decided in the jurisdiction in which they have hitherto normally been resident.'

Accordingly, the philosophy underlying the 1985 Act applied equally to non-Convention cases. Hence, in answering the crucial question as to whether the children's welfare requires their peremptory return to a country where any issues between father and mother can be competently dealt with, or requires those issues to be decided in the State to which they have been taken, applying the philosophy of the 1985 Act, the norm should be to order their return.

20.31 In the case before the appeal court, the first instance judge was held to have erred for not considering whether the children's welfare could best be determined by the Kenyan court or the English court. The Court of Appeal was satisfied that on the available evidence there was no reason to believe that the Kenyan court was not able properly to deal with the questions that arose in the case and ordered the children's immediate return.

20.32 *G v G* was followed in *Re F (A Minor) (Abduction: Custody Rights)*,[55] in which a father had, without the mother's knowledge, brought their child to England from Israel, which was not then a Contracting State under the Hague Abduction Convention. Following this removal, an Israeli court granted the mother custody and ordered the child's immediate return to Israel. Meanwhile the father sought a custody order in England. At first instance, taking the view that, since the child had not been removed in breach of a prior foreign court order, the facts did not indicate that the child should inevitably return to

---

53 She left a note to her husband explaining her reasons for leaving, *inter alia*, because her work permit was about to expire.

54 [1991] 2 FLR 506 at 514.

55 [1991] Fam 25, sub nom *Re F (A Minor) (Abduction: Jurisdiction)* [1991] 1 FLR 1.

Israel, the county court judge granted the father interim custody, care and control pending a full hearing. This decision was overturned on appeal.

20.33 Lord Donaldson MR commented that, had this been a Convention case, the court would have returned the child since he had been 'wrongfully removed' in breach of the mother's rights of custody and there were, as he put it, 'no contra-indications, such as those contemplated by Art 13'. The question was therefore to what extent Convention principles applied in non-Convention cases. In his Lordship's view and expressly agreeing with Balcombe LJ in *G v G* (which had not been referred to at first instance), the principles were analogous, since Parliament was not departing from the fundamental principle that the welfare of the child is paramount when enacting the Child Abduction and Custody Act 1985. So far as non-Convention cases were concerned, Lord Donaldson held:[56]

> 'The welfare of the child is indeed the paramount consideration, but it has to be considered in two different contexts. The first is the context of which court shall decide what the child's best interests require. The second context, which only arises if it has first been decided that the welfare of the child requires that the English rather than a foreign court shall decide what are the requirements of the child, is what orders as to custody, care and control and so on should be made.'

20.34 In Lord Donaldson's view, the county court judge mixed the two questions by considering the possible outcome of the proceedings whether in Israel or England. As he put it:[57]

> 'This is an error in principle. Possible outcomes have no bearing on which court should decide. Which court should decide depends on whether the other court will apply principles which are acceptable to the English courts as being appropriate, subject always to any contra-indication such as those mentioned in article 13 of the Convention, or a risk of persecution or discrimination, but prima facie the court to decide is that of the state where the child was habitually resident immediately before its removal.'

20.35 Since there was no evidence that the Israeli court would adopt a significantly different approach to the English court, nor was it a case in which the father was escaping from any form of persecution, or ethnic, sex or other discrimination, there was, in Lord Donaldson's words, 'nothing to take it out of the normal rule that abducted children should be returned to their country of habitual residence'. Agreeing with Lord Donaldson, Balcombe LJ added that the decision to apply Convention principles in non-Convention cases was consistent with the practice in Australia.[58] Accordingly, the Court of Appeal ordered the child's immediate return to Israel.

---

[56] [1991] Fam 25 at 31, [1991] 1 FLR 1 at 4.

[57] *Ibid* at 31–32 and 5, respectively.

[58] He referred in particular to *In the marriage of Barrios and Sanches* (1989) FLC 92–054. Although this was true at the time, as McClean and Beevers, *op cit*, n 52, point out, since then (as in English law – see below), the Australian High Court has retracted from this

20.36 Although in making this analogy with the Hague Convention Lord Donaldson considered that he was still applying the paramountcy principle, the resulting effect of *G v G* and *Re F* was similar to the former approach favouring summary returns, in that reasons for *not* ordering a return had to be adduced rather than showing that it was in the child's interests to be returned. Whether applying the Hague Convention by analogy can truly be said to be compatible with the application of the paramountcy principle in non-Convention cases is debatable,[59] but for a time at least that seemed to be the settled approach. In *Re S (Minors) (Abduction)*, for example, Nolan LJ began his judgment with the comment:[60]

> 'It is settled law that although Pakistan is not a signatory to the Hague Convention, we must apply the philosophy of the Convention to the case before us ...'

REFINING THE APPLICATION OF THE HAGUE CONVENTION TO NON-CONVENTION CASES

20.37 Although it seemed clear that courts should apply the general principles of the 1980 Hague Abduction Convention when considering non-Convention cases, it remained uncertain as to how closely the terms of the Convention were to be applied. In *D v D (Child Abduction: Non-Convention Country)*,[61] the Court of Appeal held that the Convention was not to be applied literally. Butler-Sloss LJ commented[62] that it was:

> '... important to remember that Articles of the Convention are not to be applied literally in the wardship jurisdiction and the court retains the discretion to consider the wider aspects of the welfare of its wards.'

---

position in *ZP v PS* (1994) 181 CLR 639, (1994) 122 ALR 1, on which see also Nicholson, 'Australian Judicial Attitudes to the Convention on Civil Aspects of International Child Abduction (The Hague Convention)', in Lowe and Douglas (eds), *Families Across Frontiers*, *op cit*, n 1, p 663, at pp 666–671.

[59] See the discussion below at **20.64**.

[60] [1994] 1 FLR 297 at 304. *Re S* is discussed in detail at **20.46** *et seq* below. Waite LJ made similar comments in *Re M (Minors) (Abduction: Non-Convention Country)* [1995] 1 FLR 89 at 90, CA (in which he said that in non-Convention cases 'in acting by analogy with the Convention the court takes account of those matters which it would be relevant to consider under Art 13'), and in *Re M (Jurisdiction: Forum Conveniens)* [1995] 2 FLR 224, CA, and *Re M (Minors) (Abduction) (Peremptory Return Order)* [1996] 1 FLR 478, CA. See also *S v S (Child Abduction: Non-Convention Country)* [1994] 2 FLR 681, per Hollis J, in which the child was returned notwithstanding that, had it been applicable, the court would not have been bound by Art 12 of the Hague Convention to make a return order since there had been no breach of custody rights; and *C v C (Abduction: Jurisdiction)* [1994] 1 FCR 6, in which Cazalet J, accepting that he should pay 'full regard to the principles of the Hague Convention', nevertheless held that a return order to Brazil should not be made because of the father's passive assent to the child remaining in England and because there was a grave risk that the child's return to Brazil would place her in an intolerable situation (ie the exceptions within Art 13 applied).

[61] [1994] 1 FLR 137, CA.

[62] *Ibid* at 140.

Similarly, Balcombe LJ said:[63]

> 'I should stress that, in a non-Convention case, the welfare of the children
> remains the paramount consideration, and the principles of the Convention are
> applicable only to the extent that they indicate what is normally in the interests
> of the children.'

20.38   In that case, which involved a mother's abduction of her children
from Greece, which was not yet then a Contracting State under the Hague
Abduction Convention, fresh evidence, admitted on appeal, concerning the
mother's pregnancy by her English lover in consequence of which she was no
longer prepared to return to Greece with her children, was held to justify
hearing the merits in England. As one commentary put it,[64] in so holding,
although Butler-Sloss LJ referred by analogy to Art 13, 'her decision, that the
existence of new evidence concerning the pregnancy of the mother, the
consequent need for re-consideration, and the inevitable resulting delay all
made it better for the child that a final decision be taken by an English court,
is plainly based on … broader welfare considerations'.

RESILING FROM THE APPLICATION OF THE HAGUE CONVENTION TO NON-
CONVENTION CASES

20.39   An even clearer return to a welfare-oriented approach is evident in
Re P (A Minor) (Child Abduction: Non-Convention Country).[65] In that case an
Indian mother, born and raised in England, married an Indian father who was
born in Madagascar. After the marriage, the parties lived in Madagascar,
although the mother gave birth to the child in question in England. The family
later moved to India but the mother was unhappy there and eventually came
back to England with the child. In wardship proceedings brought by the
mother for care and control, the father sought the child's return to India.

20.40   At first instance, Stuart-White J held that, notwithstanding that on
'pure welfare principles' he would have been minded not to order the child's
immediate return, he felt constrained by authority to apply Art 13 of the 1980
Hague Abduction Convention, and since the evidence did not establish a
grave risk of psychological harm nor of the placing the child in an intolerable
situation within the meaning of that Article, he ordered the child's return. On
appeal, this decision was overturned. After an extensive review of the
authorities, Ward LJ forthrightly commented that Stuart-White J:[66]

> '… in approaching the case in the way in which he did, expressly excluded an
> overall consideration of welfare when he was required to consider it. He literally
> applied Art 13 when what was required was to look at the spirit of the
> Convention in the context of welfare overall. To elevate Art 13 into the test

---

63   [1994] 1 FLR 137 at 155, CA.
64   McClean and Beevers, 'International child abduction – back to common law principles'
     (1995) 7 JCL 128 at 131.
65   [1997] Fam 45, [1997] 1 FLR 780, CA.
66   *Ibid* at 56 and 789, respectively.

which governs return (or rather no return) is to fly in the face of the established authority because (eg per *Re R*[67]) one does not proceed upon a basis that it is necessary to establish that the child would be in some obvious moral or physical danger if returned. That is not the criterion: welfare, wide-ranging a concept as it is, is the only criterion.'

20.41 Although Ward LJ did not go so far as to say that the Hague Convention was of no relevance to non-Convention cases, by asserting that 'welfare is the only consideration which governs the court's decision'[68] (which, as he pointed out, was in line with the position now taken in Australia[69]), he left little scope even for its direct application, save perhaps for the predisposition to return abducted children to their habitual residence. It is noticeable that in two subsequent first instance decisions in non-Convention cases, *T v T (Child Abduction: Non-Convention Country)*[70] and *Re Z (Abduction: Non-Convention Country)*,[71] both Michael Horowitz QC (sitting as a deputy High Court judge) and Charles J played up the welfare principle and said little about the relevance of the Hague Convention. In *Re Z*, for example, Charles J accepted that in non-Convention cases the child's welfare was the paramount consideration but that there was a general presumption or *prima facie* position that it was in a child's best interests for his or her needs, etc, to be determined by the court of the child's habitual residence. This presumption is not, in Charles J's words,[72] 'free-standing' nor based solely on an approach by analogy to the Hague Convention cases but reflects:

'... what the courts of this country have found generally best promotes the welfare of a child who has been removed from the jurisdiction of his, or her, habitual residence without the consent of both his, or her parents. Thus the spirit of the Hague Convention, and the purpose underlying it, is recognised in non-Convention cases as something that generally best promotes the welfare of children.'

20.42 On the other hand, he also accepted that Art 13 type exceptions, such as consent or acquiescence, should be taken into account by a court in the exercise of its discretion in a non-Convention case, although it would be wrong to lay down rules or presumptions about their effect. In his view, however, the longer the period that is allowed to pass before an application for the child's return is made, the more likely it is that the court will consider the child's medium- to long-term interests, including, therefore, the likely

---

67 Ie *Re R (Minors) (Wardship: Jurisdiction)* (1981) 2 FLR 416, discussed at **20.24** *et seq* above.

68 [1997] Fam 45, [1997] 1 FLR 780, CA, at 54 and 787, respectively.

69 Ie following the Australian High Court decision in *ZP v PS* (1994) 181 CLR 639, (1994) 122 ALR 1, discussed by McClean and Beevers, *op cit*, n 52, at 130–131 and by Nicholson, 'Australian Judicial Attitudes to the Convention on Civil Aspects of International Child Abduction (The Hague Convention)' in Lowe and Douglas (eds), *Families Across Frontiers, op cit*, n 1, p 663 at pp 666–671.

70 [1998] 2 FLR 1110.

71 [1999] 1 FLR 1270.

72 *Ibid* at 1277. See also Charles J's summary at 1284–1285.

outcome of the case before the court of habitual residence and whether a return to this jurisdiction is ultimately likely.

20.43   In other words, there is nothing to prevent a court in a non-Convention case looking at Art 13 to see if there are circumstances justifying not returning a child, but in exercising its discretion to assess the child's interests, the court is neither confined to Art 13 grounds nor bound to return a child if a ground be established, since at all times the court must regard the particular child's welfare as its paramount concern.

20.44   Whether the Court of Appeal will be content to let matters rest where they now stand remains to be seen, although past history suggests that further developments or refinements can be expected. Moreover, it has to be said that the full application of the paramountcy principle has not yet been definitively resolved. However, as we now discuss, the current debate concerns the extent to which the court needs to be satisfied that the foreign court will apply principles that are acceptable to the English court.

Being satisfied that the foreign court or legal system will apply principles acceptable to the English court[73]

Introduction

20.45   Even when it was accepted that 1980 Hague Abduction Convention principles applied by analogy to non-Convention cases, it was subject to the caveat that they only did so, in Balcombe LJ's words:[74]

> 'where there was no reason to suppose that the courts of the other jurisdiction will apply an approach to the question of the case of the child significantly different to that of the English court.'

20.46   This had not been a problem in either *G v G (Minors) (Abduction)*[75] or *Re F (A Minor) (Abduction: Custody Rights)*,[76] since it was accepted that the respective courts of Kenya and Israel applied a system akin to that applied under English law. In *Re S (Minors) (Abduction)*,[77] however, it was the central issue. The children in question had been born and brought up in Pakistan by Muslim parents, both of whom had also been born in Pakistan, although the mother had lived in England since the age of 5 and had acquired British citizenship before returning to Pakistan after her marriage. Having brought the children to England without the father's consent or knowledge, the mother sought interim residence and prohibited steps orders in Children Act 1989 proceedings. The father sought the children's return to Pakistan. Since the children had, in Balcombe LJ's words, been 'wrenched away from all they

---

73   See generally the analysis by Khaliq and Young, 'Cultural diversity, human rights and inconsistency in the English courts' (2001) 21 LS 192, particularly at 203 *et seq*.
74   In *D v D (Child Abduction: Non-Convention Country)* [1994] 1 FLR 137 at 144.
75   [1991] 2 FLR 506.
76   [1991] Fam 25, [1991] 1 FLR 1, CA.
77   [1994] 1 FLR 297, CA.

knew' in Pakistan, it was accepted that it was *prima facie* in their interests to be returned to allow the courts of their own country decide what their interests required. The issue was whether the Pakistani courts would apply principles that were acceptable to the English courts as being appropriate.

20.47   At first instance, Sir Gervase Sheldon was satisfied, after hearing expert evidence, that the law applying in Pakistan under its Guardians and Wards Act 1890 approximated to the English paramountcy test under s 1(1) of the Children Act 1989. Furthermore, he held it wrong to deny a return merely because the court would try to give effect to what was in the children's welfare from a Muslim point of view. He accordingly ordered the children's immediate return.

20.48   This decision was upheld by the Court of Appeal. Although Balcombe LJ queried whether the test applied by the Pakistani courts really 'approximated' to the paramountcy principle test under English law, he nevertheless agreed[78] that Sir Gervase Sheldon was entitled on these facts to consider it wrong to deny the Pakistani courts jurisdiction merely because they would give effect to what was in the children's welfare from the Muslim point of view. Nolan LJ similarly concluded:[79]

> 'In my judgment, Sir Gervase Sheldon was fully entitled to take the view that, for Muslim children of Muslim parents whose home hitherto has been in Pakistan, the principles of Pakistani law are appropriate by English standards.'

The need for evidence: the 'Re M' *approach*

20.49   In *Re S* the decision was made only after hearing evidence as to what the Pakistani law was. In *Re M (Abduction: Non-Convention Country)*,[80] however, Waite LJ, considering the principle of comity to apply, said:[81]

> 'It is assumed, particularly in the case of States which are fellow members of the European Union, that such facilities as rights of representation, means of collecting information through independent sources and welfare reports, and opportunities of giving evidence and of interrogating the other side, all of which are necessary to place the court in a position to determine the best interests of the child concerned, will be secured as well within one State's jurisdiction as within another.'

In other words, in such cases it is to be assumed, unless evidence is led to the contrary, that the foreign court will apply principles acceptable to the English court.

20.50   *Re M* concerned an abduction from Italy at a time when that nation had not yet become a Contracting State to the 1980 Hague Abduction Convention, but it subsequently became apparent that Waite LJ considered

---

[78]   [1994] 1 FLR 297 at 303–304.
[79]   *Ibid* at 305.
[80]   [1995] 1 FLR 89, CA.
[81]   *Ibid* at 90–91.

this approach to apply to countries outside the European Union. Thus, in *Re M (Jurisdiction: Forum Conveniens)*[82] Waite LJ rejected the argument that the first instance judge had acted precipitously in ordering the return of two Maltese children to Malta (which was then not a Contracting State to the Hague Abduction Convention) since he had insufficient knowledge of the Maltese legal system. Given that speed was of the essence, Waite LJ considered the judge's limited knowledge to be 'quite sufficient'[83] especially since the general principle of returning abducted children to the place of their habitual residence:[84]

> '... has particular force in a case like the present, where the competing jurisdictions are represented by two countries with close historical ties and closely corresponding legal systems, applying a similar approach to the difficult problems to which cases of this kind inevitably give rise.'

20.51 In *Re M (Abduction: Peremptory Return Order)*,[85] Waite LJ adopted a similar standpoint in upholding an order to return abducted children to Dubai in the United Arab Emirates. Rejecting the argument that the first instance judge should have adjourned proceedings so as to have 'something more than a one-side account that was placed before the court at the last minute from the father's lawyer', Waite LJ said:[86]

> 'Underlying the whole purpose of the peremptory return order is a principle of international comity under which judges in England will assume that facilities for a fair hearing will be provided in the court of the other jurisdiction, and that due account will be taken by overseas judges of what has been said, ordered and undertaken to be done within the English jurisdiction. That is, of course, reciprocal. It is to be presumed that judges in other countries will make similar assumptions about the workings of our own judicial system.'

The need for evidence: the 'Re JA' *approach*

20.52 The trilogy of cases just referred to quickly elevated the so-called comity approach from applying to fellow EU States to applying to countries with which the United Kingdom has close historical ties, and then to applying to courts of any State.

20.53 In *Re JA (Child Abduction: Non-Convention Country)*,[87] however, the Court of Appeal held this general approach to be wrong. Indeed Ward LJ commented that, if driven to it, he would reluctantly say that *Re M (Minors)*

---

[82]   [1995] 2 FLR 224, CA.
[83]   Although he did add, *ibid* at 228, that in an ideal world it would have been helpful if the judge had been furnished with information about the operation of the Maltese family law system.
[84]   *Ibid* at 228.
[85]   [1996] 1 FLR 478, CA.
[86]   *Ibid* at 480–481.
[87]   [1998] 1 FLR 231, CA.

(Abduction: Peremptory Return Order)[88] was decided *per incuriam*. Relying on pre-Child Abduction and Custody Act 1985 case-law,[89] which in Ward LJ's view[90] clearly established 'that it is an abdication of the responsibility and an abnegation of the duty of this court to the ward under its protection to surrender the determination of its ward's future to a foreign court whose regime may be inimical to the child's welfare', his Lordship accepted the following propositions:[91]

'(1) The duty of this court is to determine the question [ie whether to order the child's return] by the test which makes welfare the paramount, and therefore, the dominant consideration.

(2) The court cannot be satisfied that it is in the best interests of the child to return it to the court of habitual residence in order that that court may resolve the disputed question, unless this court is satisfied that the welfare test will apply in that court.

(3) Consequently, this court cannot abdicate its responsibility simply by assuming that welfare will apply.

(4) The choice of residence in the foreign country may imply the voluntary assumption of disadvantage, personal and juridical by a parent but it does not justify the court in imposing any consequential detriment on the child.

(5) Whilst it may be necessary for the applicant for the peremptory order to show this comparability when inviting this court's assistance, nevertheless, since foreign law is presumed to be the same as the English law by virtue of the established rules of private international law, the practical result is that it will be for the respondent to adduce evidence of dissimilarity.

(6) It is only when this court is satisfied that the child's welfare will be protected by the foreign court that this court can entrust the decision to that foreign court.'

20.54 Under the '*Re JA* approach', before a return order can even be considered, evidence will always need to be led as to what principles the foreign court will apply so that the English court can assess whether the foreign law accords with its notion of the welfare principle. In *Re JA* itself, the court refused to order the return of child (born to an English mother and an Emirate father) to the United Arab Emirates, the evidence being that that State's court powers were limited and that the child's welfare was not the test in that the court had no power to permit the mother to return to England with the child if the father objected, regardless of the child's welfare. In other words, once the mother and child returned to the Emirates they were effectively locked there.

---

88 [1996] 1 FLR 478, CA.

89 Viz *Nugent v Vetzera* (1866) LR 2 Eq 704; *Di Savini v Lousada* (1870) 18 WR 425; *Re B's Settlement* [1940] Ch 54; *McKee v McKee* [1951] AC 352, [1951] 1 All ER 942; *J v C* [1970] AC 668 at 714F, per Lord MacDermott; *Re L (Minors) (Wardship: Jurisdiction)* [1974] 1 WLR 250 at 264–265, [1974] 1 All ER 913 at 925–926, per Buckley LJ; and *Re R (Minors) (Wardship: Jurisdiction)* (1981) 2 FLR 416 at 426.

90 [1998] 1 FLR 231 at 243.

91 *Ibid* at 241–242.

The need for evidence: a return to the 'Re M' *approach*

20.55 In *Re E (Abduction: Non-Convention Country)*,[92] a differently constituted Court of Appeal rejected Ward LJ's suggestion that *Re M* was decided *per incuriam*. In this case, the court upheld an order for the return to Sudan of three children born to Sudanese parents and habitually resident there before being wrongfully brought to England by their mother, notwithstanding that under Sudanese law the mother, having remarried, was not permitted to obtain custody (although she was entitled to seek substantial access). In reaching this decision, Thorpe LJ observed that the number and diversity of the States that have joined 'the Hague club' already made it impossible to formulate minimum standard requirements of the other family justice system. Accordingly, he was extremely doubtful of a principle enabling a judge of this jurisdiction to criticise the standards or paramount principles applied by the family justice systems of a non-Convention State save in exceptional circumstances, such as where there was found to be persecution, or ethnic, sex or other discrimination. His Lordship considered that there was no absolute standard of the concept of paramountcy and that 'what constitutes the welfare of the child must be subject to the cultural background and expectations of the jurisdictions to achieve it'.

20.56 Although Pill LJ agreed with Thorpe LJ, his approach was different and arguably more orthodox. He observed:[93]

> 'I have no difficulty in accepting the judge's conclusion that the application of Muslim law to this Muslim family is appropriate and acceptable. It is submitted on behalf of the mother that the welfare of children, paramount in English law, must take priority over notions of international comity and respect for foreign courts in non-Convention States. In my judgment the two are not inevitably in conflict. These are Sudanese children. Their welfare may be well served by a decision in accordance with Sudanese law which may be taken to reflect the norms and values of the Sudanese society in which they live. That is a principle which the judge was entitled to take into account upon the facts of the case, thereby giving paramountcy to the welfare of the children. A solution in accordance with local law is capable of being in the best interests of the child.'

He added, however:[94]

> 'There will be cases in which the links between the children and the foreign state are less strong than they are in the present case. There may also be cases ... in which the notions of the children's upbringing in the foreign state are wholly repugnant to English notions of provision for the welfare of children.'

20.57 The view that courts should be slow to find the application of Sharia law to be so repugnant to English notions of welfare as to justify making

---

92 [1999] 2 FLR 642, CA.
93 *Ibid* at 651.
94 *Ibid* at 652.

contrary orders was strongly expressed by Thorpe LJ in *Al Habtoor v Fotheringham*:[95]

> 'The United Arab Emirates constitute a foreign jurisdiction with which this country has particularly close historical connection. Orders issued by the courts of the Emirates are entitled to the regard which we would expect the courts of the Emirates to have for our orders. In my opinion the courts of this jurisdiction should be very slow to make orders that directly conflict with pre-existing orders in any friendly foreign state. The principle of comity requires no less. Particularly is this so where the order, as in this case, is unenforceable and thus empty. The temptation to make conflicting orders arises from a contemplation of the gulf between legal systems based on a Judaeo-Christian model and legal systems applying the Sharia law. But if there is to be progress in the development of understanding and collaboration in international family law it is vital that we should attempt to build bridges over the divide rather than to issue empty challenges. Of course no court in this jurisdiction would have ordered a transfer of residence from the mother to the father on the application of the paramount welfare test. The fact that that was the outcome in Dubai, even the fact that that would have probably been the outcome in Dubai without compromise, does not mean that the welfare of the child is not the first consideration for the judge of the Sharia court. Both systems are child centred. It is the interpretation of child welfare, governed as it is by different religions, cultures and traditions, that produces such starkly different outcomes.'

20.58 The so-called *Re E* approach was followed in *Re S (Child Abduction: Asylum Appeal)*,[96] in which two children of Indian parents were ordered to be returned to India. The children had been brought to England by the mother with the father's consent for a holiday, but were subsequently kept there when the mother decided not to return. In ordering the children's return to India, Bennett J (whose judgment was upheld on appeal) rejected the submission that the children's welfare would be put at grave risk. The judge was satisfied that the Indian court would endeavour at all times to promote the children's best interests.

Commentary

20.59 Pill LJ's reasoning in *Re E* is in line with Buckley LJ's classic exposition of the relevant principles in *Re L (Minors) (Wardship: Jurisdiction)*[97] and is in contrast to Thorpe LJ's approach, the danger of which, it is submitted, is that it seems to accept that sometimes an individual child's welfare has to be sacrificed for the greater international common good.[98] With

---

[95] [2001] EWCA Civ 186, [2001] 1 FLR 951 at [44].

[96] [2002] EWHC 816 (Fam), [2002] 2 FLR 437, per Bennett J, whose judgment was upheld by the Court of Appeal: see [2002] EWCA Civ 843, [2002] 2 FLR 465. See also *B v El-B (Abduction: Sharia Law: Welfare of Child)* [2003] 1 FLR 811, in which Lebanese children were ordered to be returned to Lebanon provided the father confirmed that he would not pursue criminal allegations.

[97] [1994] 1 WLR 250, [1974] 1 All ER 913, CA, discussed at **20.21–20.24**.

[98] The authors, however, are divided on what should be the preferable approach.

respect to Thorpe LJ, it by no means follows that, because no enquiries are made of the law operated in fellow Contracting States to the 1980 Hague Abduction Convention, notwithstanding that the concept of child welfare may well be understood differently, enquiries should not be made of non-Contracting States, since whereas in the former case that decision has been taken by Parliament, in the latter, the courts are still governed by the paramountcy principle, making it incumbent on them to make such enquiries. The point has also been well made[99] that Thorpe LJ's approach pays no regard to the issues of human rights, and in particular to the mother's rights not to be discriminated against.[100]

20.60   The law cannot yet be said to be certain. In the light of the foregoing case-law, however, it seems advisable to assume that, before making a return order to a non-Convention country, English courts will require at least evidence of what principles the foreign court will apply when resolving disputes about the child's upbringing. However, particularly in the light of *Re E*, *Al Habtoor v Fotheringham* and *Re S*, it would seem that, at any rate where the children and parents all have close connection with the State in question, the court will require strong evidence that the foreign law's principles are repugnant (and not merely different) to the English notion of children's welfare before refusing to make a return order.

The need to act quickly

20.61   If it is in the child's interests to be returned to his home jurisdiction then it is in those interests for the decision to made quickly. Hence, speed is of the essence even in non-Convention cases. This means, as Waite LJ observed in *Re M (Abduction: Non-Convention Country)*:[101]

> '... that the court has no time to go into matters of detail. The case has to be viewed from the perspective of a quick appraisal of its essential features. Any risk of injustice in the interests of speed is minimised by the adoption in the Court of Appeal of a policy which, while discouraging appeals that attempt to reargue the merits, allows some relaxation of the rule in *Ladd v Marshall*.[102] That relaxation is applied to the extent necessary to enable this court to determine whether there are any matters not dealt with at first instance which might have materially affected the judge's decision had he been aware of them.'

---

[99]   By Khaliq and Young, *op cit*, n 74, at 219 *et seq*.

[100]   Khaliq and Young argue that where the return of the child could result in the woman being treated unequally in a custody hearing then that very return could be considered in breach of either Art 8 or Art 6 either on its own or in conjunction with Art 14. This is supported by *Butterworths Family Law Service* which comments at **3A[6588.1]** that 'it is doubtful that uncritical applications of the comity principle is compatible with the European Convention on Human Rights, Art 6 (right to a fair trial)'.

[101]   [1995] 1 FLR 89 at 90, CA.

[102]   [1954] 1 WLR 1489, [1954] 3 All ER 745, CA.

Summary and critique

20.62 As the foregoing discussion shows, the courts have struggled to balance the individual child's welfare and the twin needs of policy of (a) not encouraging abduction and (b) not antagonising foreign regimes lest they adopt a policy of non-return of children habitually resident in England and Wales. It will be equally apparent that at different times different approaches have been taken to tackling the problem, ranging from the 'pure welfare' approach on the one hand, to a more protectionist model of returning abducted children, save where harm can be proved, on the other.[103] Indeed, it is this very oscillation that makes the current law hard to state. Nevertheless certain propositions can be made with reasonable confidence.[104]

(1) As the House of Lords made clear in *J v C*,[105] it is incumbent upon a court, even in child abduction cases, to treat the individual child's welfare as the paramount consideration.

(2) Again, as *J v C* confirmed, regardless of the child's nationality, foreign court orders concerning the child's upbringing are not binding (although due account of the court's decision will be taken).

(3) Provided an application is made quickly there is a 'predisposition' to return children who have been abducted from the State of their habitual residence. This 'predisposition' will be stronger where all the relevant members of the family have a close connection with the foreign State in question.

(4) Notwithstanding proposition (3), children will not be returned where either the relevant foreign legal system operates principles that are thought to be repugnant to the English notion of child welfare or where the child will otherwise be harmed by the return.

Settling the principle to be applied

20.63 These last two propositions, however, mask a number of problems or uncertainties. So far as proposition (3) is concerned, it is not yet settled on what basis the 'predisposition' to return is founded. Over time, different bases have been championed. In the 1960s, the policy of return was straightforwardly adopted as a means of countering the evil of abduction or child kidnapping as it was then called. It was essentially a parent-centred approach designed to ensure that the kidnapper did not gain an advantage by his wrongdoing. It is clear that this approach is no longer sustainable.

---

[103] This oscillation is not unique to English law. Australian law, for example, has also shifted from one approach to another as *In the Marriage of Barrios and Sanchez* (1989) FLC 92–054 and *ZP v PS* (1994) 181 CLR 639, (1994) 122 ALR 1, referred to at n 58 above, illustrate.

[104] Note also the summary of the law by Charles J in *Re Z (A Minor) (Abduction: Non-Convention Country)* [1999] 1 FLR 1270 at 1284–1285.

[105] [1970] AC 688, [1969] 1 All ER 788, discussed at **20.20**.

20.64   In the 1970s and 1980s, the court favoured what might best be termed the 'pure welfare' approach. As Buckley LJ explained in *Re L*[106] and as emphatically endorsed by Ormrod LJ in *Re R*,[107] because it is psychologically damaging to a child suddenly to be removed from the surroundings, culture and language of the country in which he or she was living, it is normally in that child's interests to be returned there as soon as possible. Furthermore, as Charles J added in *Re Z (A Minor) (Abduction: Non-Convention Country)*,[108] the courts of the country from which the child has been wrongfully removed will generally be in a better position to resolve disputes about the child's medium- to long-term future.

20.65   In the late 1980s and early 1990s, this welfare approach became diluted when the courts began to treat non-Convention cases as quasi-Hague Convention cases.[109] While, of course, the Hague Abduction Convention undoubtedly aims to promote all children's interests by providing the means of ensuring their speedy return to their habitual residence when they have been wrongfully removed or retained in another State, as Ward LJ rightly said in *Re JA (Child Abduction: Non-Convention Country)*,[110] when applying the Convention, the *individual* child's welfare is *not* the paramount consideration. Furthermore, whereas in non-Convention cases evidence has to be adduced to justify the return, in Hague Convention cases evidence needs to be adduced to prevent a return.

20.66   Although it has now been made clear[111] that the Hague Abduction Convention is not to be applied literally in non-Convention cases, it cannot be said in the light of the subsequent decisions, *Re M (Abduction: Peremptory Return Order)*,[112] *Re E (Abduction: Non-Convention Country)*[113] and *Re S (Child Abduction: Asylum Appeal)*,[114] that the Court of Appeal has unreservedly embraced the pure welfare approach. Indeed, to the contrary, these latter decisions rely upon notions of comity, 'do as you would be done by'[115] for generally ordering a

---

[106] *Re L (Minors) (Wardship: Jurisdiction)* [1974] 1 WLR 250 at 264-265, [1974] 1 All ER 913 at 925–926, discussed at **20.21–20.24**.

[107] *Re R (Minors) (Wardship: Jurisdiction)* (1981) 2 FLR 416, discussed at **20.25** *et seq.*

[108] [1999] 1 FLR 1270 at 1285. He also considered it generally better for the child's future to be determined without the intervention of an act by one parent which questions the rights of the other.

[109] See *G v G (Minors) (Abduction)* [1991] 2 FLR 506 and *Re F (A Minor) (Abduction: Custody Rights)* [1991] Fam 25, [1991] 1 FLR 1, discussed at **20.29** *et seq.*

[110] [1998] 1 FLR 231 at 234.

[111] See *D v D (Child Abduction: Non-Convention Country)* [1994] 1 FLR 137 and *Re P (A Minor) (Child Abduction: Non-Convention Country)* [1997] Fam 45, [1997] 1 FLR 780, discussed at **20.37** *et seq.*

[112] [1996] 1 FLR 478, discussed at **20.51**.

[113] [1999] 2 FLR 642, discussed at **20.55**.

[114] [2002] EWCA Civ 843, [2002] 2 FLR 465, discussed at **20.58**.

[115] Indeed, this theme runs through a number of decisions beginning with Page Wood V-C's judgment in *Nugent v Vetzera* (1866) LR 2 Eq 704 at 714, quoted at **20.6**. See also *Re H (Infants)* [1966] 1 All ER 886 at 892, per Harman LJ, quoted at **20.15**. Principles of comity

return. In other words, if we expect Islamic nations, in particular, to return children wrongfully taken from England and Wales, then we must be prepared to return children to those nations.

20.67 While all the above bases are rational in themselves it is submitted that, given the universal application of the paramountcy test as laid down by the House of Lords in *J v C*, unless and until the Lords rule otherwise, the only acceptable approach as a matter of principle is the 'pure welfare' approach as established by *Re L, Re P* and *Re JA*.

Justifying a refusal to return

20.68 So far as justifying a refusal to return is concerned, there are three basic issues, namely:

(1) to what extent does evidence have to be led as to the principles and procedure the foreign court will apply;

(2) how tolerant should the English court be to legal systems that have different notions of child welfare; and

(3) on what basis can harm or detriment to the child be generally established so as to justify a refusal to return.

20.69 With regard to the first of these issues there is a dispute as to whether evidence needs to be led at all. In a trilogy of decisions by Waite LJ culminating in *Re M (Minors) (Abduction: Peremptory Return)*,[116] and apparently supported by Thorpe and Pill LJJ in *Re E (Abduction: Non-Convention Country)*,[117] unless evidence is led to the contrary, it should be presumed that judges in other countries will apply a similar law and procedure to our own. In *Re JA (Abduction: Non-Convention Country)*,[118] Ward LJ (with whom Lord Woolf and Mummery LJ agreed) castigated this approach on the basis that it was an abdication of court's duty to the child not to make enquiries. It is submitted that *Re JA* is to be preferred, since that is surely consistent with the pure welfare approach by which the courts ought on principle to be bound.

20.70 The more difficult question, however, is, assuming there are no other reasons for refusing a return, how tolerant should the English courts be of other systems that do not espouse similar notions of child welfare. This is a particular problem with regard at least to some Islamic nations.[119] There are no easy answers to this issue. Following *Re E, Al Habtoor v Fotheringham*[120] and

---

were also referred to by Waite LJ in *Re M (Minors) (Abduction: Non-Convention Country)* [1995] 1 FLR 89 and in *Re M (Jurisdiction: Forum Conveniens)* [1995] 2 FLR 224. But for a convincing critique of this reliance on comity, see Khaliq and Young, *op cit*, n 74.

[116] [1996] 1 FLR 478. See also *Re M (Minors) (Abduction: Non-Convention Country* [1995] 1 FLR 89 and *Re M (Jurisdiction: Forum Conveniens)* [1995] 1 FLR 224, discussed at **20.49–20.51**.

[117] [1999] 2 FLR 642.

[118] [1998] 1 FLR 231.

[119] However, note needs to be taken, in the case of Pakistan, of the UK–Pakistan Protocol, which is reproduced at **23.6**, and discussed at **20.82**.

[120] [2001] EWCA Civ 186, [2001] 1 FLR 951, CA.

Re S (Child Abduction: Asylum Appeal),[121] as we have said, where the parents and children have a close connection with the State in question it seems that the court will require strong evidence that the foreign law's principles are repugnant in the sense of persecution or ethnic, sex or other discrimination[122] and not merely different to the English notion of welfare principles. Whether the children's welfare was really treated as the paramount consideration in *Re E* is debatable, but on welfare principles alone there ought to be some middle line between requiring the foreign law to be repugnant (in the sense described) and not merely different.

20.71 Happily, the law on what harm or detriment to the child must be generally established to justify a refusal to return can be stated with tolerable certainty. While the contra-indications (as they have been referred to)[123] as contained in Arts 12 and 13 of the 1980 Hague Abduction Convention can certainly be considered, it is clear that the Convention provisions are not slavishly to be followed so that the court is entitled to take into account broader considerations of welfare.[124] Even where an Art 13 consideration is thought to be relevant, the judge is not bound in any strict way by how that provision has been interpreted under the Hague Convention.[125]

Conclusion – need for a House of Lords' ruling

20.72 It is clearly unsatisfactory that the law remains unsettled in so many crucial respects with swings towards and away from the pure welfare approach. In retrospect, it was unfortunate that the House of Lords refused leave to appeal in *Re L*.[126] A definitive House of Lords' ruling is required to settle once and for all how, especially in the light of the Human Rights Act 1998, the welfare principles should be applied.

---

[121] [2002] EWCA Civ 843, [2002] 2 FLR 465, CA.

[122] As suggested by Lord Donaldson MR in *Re F (A Minor) (Abduction: Custody Rights)* [1991] Fam 25 at 31, sub nom *Re F (A Minor) (Abduction: Jurisdiction)* [1991] 1 FLR 1 at 4, cited at **20.34**.

[123] Per Lord Donaldson MR in *Re F* (above).

[124] See *D v D (Child Abduction: Non-Convention Country)* [1994] 1 FLR 137 and *Re P (A Minor) (Child Abduction: Non-Convention Country)* [1997] Fam 45, [1997] 1 FLR 780.

[125] See eg *Re Z (A Minor) (Abduction: Non-Convention Country)* [1999] 1 FLR 1270, discussed at **20.41**.

[126] See [1974] 1 WLR 266. Although, of course, the outlook and understanding has changed in the subsequent 30 years.

CHILDREN TAKEN FROM ENGLAND AND WALES TO A NON-CONVENTION COUNTRY

Bringing proceedings in the foreign jurisdiction and taking other practical steps[127]

20.73 Recovering a child from a non-Convention country requires speed, determination and close co-operation between lawyers in both England and the foreign country and, quite frequently, the Foreign and Commonwealth Office and Interpol. Speed is essential to avoid the child becoming settled in the foreign country,[128] and co-operation is essential to ensure that orders made by the High Court (because all these cases should be in the High Court) are tailored to meet the needs of the foreign court and that no administrative step will be taken which could inadvertently prejudice the return of the child.

20.74 Notwithstanding this desirability of speed, securing the return of a child or even access to a child wrongfully removed to a non-Convention country is likely to be difficult, time-consuming and expensive. Although remedies obtained domestically can occasionally be useful,[129] notwithstanding the obvious practical difficulties, left-behind parents are probably best advised to institute proceedings in the country to which the child has been taken or retained. Principally, this will mean commencing appropriate civil proceedings for custody or access, although it is possible, if the country in question has an extradition treaty with the United Kingdom, to bring extradition proceedings against the abductor. These latter proceedings, however, are likely to be lengthy and technical and, in any event, are directed against the wrongdoer, so that there is no guarantee that the child will be returned.

20.75 Practical advice[130] but not legal advice can be sought from the Foreign and Commonwealth Office (FCO) Consular Directorate.[131] This advice is

---

[127] See generally Hutchinson, Roberts and Setright, *International Parental Child Abduction* (Family Law, 1998).

[128] For an example of the English approach to delay in non-Convention cases, see *Re Z (Abduction: Non-Convention Country)* [1999] 1 FLR 1270.

[129] See **20.80**.

[130] *Ibid.*

[131] *Practice Note (Minor: Removal from Jurisdiction)* [1984] 1 WLR 1216, [1984] All ER 640. However, the FCO now has a dedicated unit which handles child abduction. The FCO's Child Abduction Unit (CAU) can be contacted at: The Foreign and Commonwealth Office, Child Abduction Unit, Consular Directorate, Room G58, Old Admiralty Building, London SW1A 2PA, tel: 020 7008 3000 or 020 7008 8737. FCO desk officers in London and Consular Officers at Post will provide all proper consular assistance, although the extent to which help can be provided will vary according to the country concerned. The FCO's CAU leads on all cases involving non-Convention countries; the Lord Chancellor's Child Abduction Unit leads in abductions to and from Convention countries (ie States Parties to the 1980 Hague Abduction Convention and the 1980 European Custody Convention) and is the Central Authority for England and Wales under the Conventions: see **10.49**. For an account of the involvement of the FCO in the case of a child taken to India, see *Re KR (Abduction: Forcible Removal by Parents)* [1999] 2 FLR 542 at 545.

intended to supplement that given by the aggrieved person's legal representative. Useful and practical assistance can also be gained by contacting Reunite.[132] But, in general, the key first step is to identify lawyers in the foreign country who are competent to undertake the case. The FCO and Reunite may be able to help in identifying a suitable lawyer, but it must be borne in mind that there is not a uniform standard of expertise amongst either courts or lawyers, and in some cases it may not be possible to find a lawyer willing to take the case or competent to do so.

Consular advice

20.76 The help that Consular Officers can afford depends entirely upon local circumstances; in some countries much may be done, but in others the help that can be offered may be limited. In general, Consular Officers can:

– in the absence of an amicable settlement between the parents, advise that the only recourse may be to institute legal proceedings in the courts of the foreign country;

– provide a list of local lawyers who can correspond in English and who can advise about parental rights under local law and what, if any, local customary child care and control practices exist which might influence a court's decision in a child custody case and whether legal aid is available;

– approach the local authorities for help in tracing the child. Although the FCO may engage with the local authorities and request their assistance, Interpol has the resources and contacts to do this on a much wider level;[133]

– once the child is located, and with the other parent's consent, obtain a welfare report;

– monitor the progress of court cases and occasionally (but only where staff resources permit) arrange for a Consular Officer to attend the court. Only in very exceptional circumstances would the FCO make a request of the local court to handle a case quickly; and the FCO would never seek to interfere with the legal processes of another country;

– help to establish or to keep open lines of communication between parents and children;

– sometimes offer practical assistance by way of, for example, informal translations, finding cheap accommodation and giving contact details of helpful local officials.

20.77 At the time of writing, there is in draft a President's *Practice Direction – Liaison between the Courts in England and Wales and British Embassies and High Commissions Abroad.* It is intended that the Practice Direction will describe procedures which are to be followed when a court in England and Wales exercising family jurisdiction seeks to invoke diplomatic assistance. Carefully drawn recitals and other provisions in orders made by the courts in England

---

[132] Reunite International Child Abduction Centre, PO Box 7124, Leicester LE1 7XX.
[133] See **20.84**.

and Wales modelled upon those made in *Re KR (Abduction: Forcible Removal by Parents)*[134] have proved effective in obtaining the return of abducted children.[135] It is proposed that the Practice Direction should contain specimen recitals and provisions, derived from *Re KR* and other cases, for inclusion in orders.

20.78   Dual nationals who are victims of child abduction receive the same treatment as mono-nationals. Unless the country of second nationality complains, the FCO gives normal consular assistance in respect of dual nationals. The Consular Service cannot recover children for their parents, pay for legal services, court fees or airfares or obtain visas for entry into the foreign country.

Funding proceedings

20.79   Careful thought must be given to how the case is to be funded; public funding may be available in England and Wales to get an order the primary purpose of which is to bring an action before a foreign court, but there may be no form of legal aid or assistance, *pro bono* or otherwise, in the foreign country. If there is no possibility of the left-behind parent meeting the costs of a foreign lawyer, including the court fees and incidental expenses, of travelling to the foreign country, staying for a hearing and returning with the child, it may be better to get a domestic order reciting the wrongful nature of the abductor's actions and conferring custody on the applicant, and to try to resolve the matter through other channels rather than to engage in expensive and inconclusive litigation, which could only benefit the abductor by giving the opportunity to procrastinate. However, it may be possible to take steps in the United Kingdom to obtain funds.[136]

Domestic remedies

The advantage of domestic remedies

20.80   In the face of a wrongful removal, the aggrieved parent can seek a return order from the English courts. If there are no previous legal proceedings, the quickest method of seeking a remedy is through wardship.[137] If family proceedings are already in existence then an ex parte application should be made for a specific issue order under the Children Act 1989. Where a person seeks an order for the return to him of children about to arrive by air and he wants information to enable him to meet the plane, the judge should be asked to include in his order a direction that the airline operating the flight and, if he has the information, the immigration officer at the appropriate

---

[134]   [1999] 4 All ER 954, [1999] 2 FLR 542.
[135]   See **20.81**.
[136]   See **10.41–10.48**.
[137]   As discussed at **9.30–9.31**.

airport, should supply such information to the person.[138] If a person already has an order for the child's return but wants to obtain the above information then he should apply ex parte to a judge for such a direction.

20.81   Occasionally, a return order made by an English court (particularly the High Court) can in itself be sufficiently influential to persuade the foreign authorities to return the child.[139] But another important advantage of seeking a domestic remedy is the consequential ability to invoke the court's coercive powers once any order which has been made has been broken. As discussed elsewhere,[140] it may be possible to use the court's powers in order to enable funds to be raised to meet the costs of tracing and recovering the child.

The form of order

20.82   An order should be sought within the domestic proceedings in the form recommended by the foreign lawyers as being the best to advance the case for return before the foreign court. The wardship order should then be sent, preferably with a copy of the affidavit in support and any previous orders and documents which have been directed to accompany the order, and a transcript of the judgment, to the lawyers in the foreign country to enable them to institute proceedings to enforce it. In Pakistan, for example, this would be done by way of an application for *habeas corpus* requiring the child to be brought to court. The approach of a court in Pakistan would be much like that of the High Court dealing with a non-Convention application. Indeed, under the Protocol agreed between the United Kingdom and Islamic Republic of Pakistan,[141] it is accepted that the two States 'share a common heritage of law and a commitment to the welfare of children'. According to the terms of the Protocol, a Pakistani court will not normally exercise jurisdiction (other than to order a return) over a child habitually resident in the United Kingdom who has been removed or retained in Pakistan without the consent of the parent with a custody/residence order or a restraint/interdict order made in the United Kingdom. In other countries which apply Sharia law, there is a general presumption that, usually with the permission or consent of the father, boys will stay with their mothers until they are 7 years old, and girls until they are 11.

20.83   The order of the wardship court is of the greatest importance, since the intention will be that it should be the foundation of an application for the return of the child from the foreign country, on the basis of recognition, enforcement or comity, depending on the advice of the foreign lawyers. This is likely to be in the form of a declaration that the child has been wrongfully

---

[138]   See **10.21**.

[139]   See eg *Re KR (Abduction: Forcible Removal By Parents)* [1999] 2 FLR 542, where a return order made in wardship proceedings helped to secure the return of a child abducted by her parents to India. See **10.27**.

[140]   See **9.45**.

[141]   For details of the Protocol, see **23.6**.

removed from the care of the applicant, an order conferring care and control upon the applicant (possibly for the limited purpose of returning the child to the jurisdiction), and a request addressed to the foreign court for the return of the child to the custody of the court. The order in the case of *Re KR (Abduction: Forcible Removal by Parents)* is helpfully set out in the report of the case.[142]

Criminal proceedings

20.84　There are conflicting views about how useful criminal proceedings are in international child abduction cases. To engage substantial resources of national and international police authorities in the search for a missing child will inevitably involve an allegation of a criminal offence having been committed, but despite the fact that legislation criminalising parental child abduction is common amongst Contracting States to the Hague Abduction Convention, courts often show a marked reluctance to return an abducting mother to face criminal charges, and the High Court commonly seeks an undertaking from an applicant for a return order not to institute or support criminal proceedings against the abductor.[143] In non-Convention cases, advice should be taken at an early stage as to whether the institution of criminal proceedings[144] or the involvement of Interpol[145] are likely to advance or prejudice the return of the child.

---

[142]　[1999] 2 FLR 542 at 546. See also **20.77**.
[143]　See generally **9.20**.
[144]　See **9.4** *et seq.*
[145]　See **9.21**.

Chapter 21

INTERNATIONAL ABDUCTIONS: PRACTICE AND PROCEDURE IN ENGLAND AND WALES

INTRODUCTION

21.1 There is a choice of remedies for recovering a child who has been abducted to England and Wales. Essentially, there are three routes:

(1) recognition and enforcement of an order either under the so-called 'Brussels II Regulation' or the 1980 European Custody Convention;[1]
(2) an application for a return order under the 1980 Hague Abduction Convention; and/or
(3) an application for a return order within the High Court's inherent jurisdiction with respect to children.

---

[1] But note the discussion at **18.24** regarding the precedence of Brussels II.

21.2   If there is a 'judgment on the exercise of parental responsibility' 'on the occasion of' matrimonial proceedings in respect of a child of both parties to a marriage made in a Member State of the EU, it can be enforced under the Council Regulation[2] (commonly known as 'Brussels II').[3] Similarly, a 'decision relating to custody' given in a Contracting State to the 1980 European Custody Convention can be registered and enforced.[4] If there is no order, or no order which is recognisable and enforceable, but the child has been removed from his State of habitual residence in breach of rights of custody,[5] and the State of his habitual residence is a Contracting State to the 1980 Hague Abduction Convention, an application can be made for a return order. If the circumstances of the case fall outside the Council Regulation and the two Conventions, an application can be made within the High Court's inherent jurisdiction with respect to children (known as a 'non-Convention case').[6]

21.3   Although it might seem as if the remedy of first resort when there is a judgment on the exercise of parental responsibility or decision relating to custody would be an application for registration and enforcement, in fact there is a 'hierarchy' insofar as both the Council Regulation and the 1980 Hague Abduction Convention take precedence over the 1980 European Custody Convention.[7] As a consequence, although there is a free choice of remedies, if an application is framed in the alternative, applications under the Council Regulation or the 1980 Hague Abduction Convention must be determined before any application under the 1980 European Custody Convention. As it happens, where there is an enforceable order, it has been the long-standing practice to issue an originating summons seeking: first, a return order under the 1980 Hague Abduction Convention; secondly, registration and enforcement of the custody order;[8] and, finally, a return under the inherent jurisdiction of the High Court with respect to children.

21.4   In non-Convention cases, the application for return is traditionally made within wardship proceedings,[9] although there is no real need to confer

---

2   Council Regulation (EC) No 1347/2000 of 29 May 2000 on jurisdiction and the recognition and enforcement of judgments in matrimonial matters and in matters of parented responsibility for both spouses ('the Council Regulation'). See Chapter 23.

3   *Ibid.*

4   See Chapter 19. But note that Brussels II takes precedence *whenever* applicable.

5   Rights of custody also derive from an order. For the 1980 Hague Abduction Convention, see Chapters 12–17.

6   See generally Chapter 25.

7   Council Regulation, Art 37; Child Abduction and Custody Act 1985, s 12(3), and s 16(4)(c), which also creates a hierarchy insofar as an application for registration and enforcement under the 1980 European Custody Convention cannot be dealt with whilst an application for a return order under the 1980 Hague Abduction Convention is pending.

8   Note that there are a significantly narrower range of 'defences' under the 1980 European Custody Convention than under the 1980 Hague Abduction Convention.

9   *Al-Habtoor v Fotheringham* [2001] EWCA Civ 186, [2001] 1 FLR 951. As to wardship proceedings, see Lowe and White, *Wards of Court*, 2nd edn (Barry Rose, 1986). As to the relationship between wardship and the inherent jurisdiction, see Seymour, 'Parens Patriae

the status of ward of court on the child unless there is some good reason to do so.[10] An originating summons may simply be issued in the High Court's inherent jurisdiction with respect to children seeking the return of the child. However, if there is good reason to believe that the abductor might move the child to another country before being served with the proceedings, or before being served with an order forbidding the abductor and child to leave the jurisdiction, then the status of ward of court, which is conferred on the child on the issue of the originating summons,[11] may be helpful in engaging the authorities of the State to which the child has been taken, because the custody of wards is 'in the court'.[12] Such a removal would also be a contempt of court.[13] Alternatively, an application can be made for an order under Children Act 1989, s 8: either a residence order with leave to remove or a specific issue order.

21.5 In dealing with non-Convention cases, one should not forget extra-judicial remedies. A child may have been brought into the United Kingdom with no right to enter, or with false information being given to the immigration authorities, or with a limited right to remain which has expired. Unlawful presence may cause the immigration authorities to remove the child, or the restrictions placed on the child's presence, such as having no right to resort to public services like health or education, may mean that his continued presence in the country becomes unsustainable in the face of objections to the appropriate authorities by a parent willing to care for him in the country of his nationality and habitual residence.

INCOMING ABDUCTIONS FROM A HAGUE OR EUROPEAN CONVENTION COUNTRY OR A MEMBER STATE OF THE EUROPEAN UNION[14]

Who can apply?

The 1980 Hague Abduction Convention

21.6 'Any person, institution or other body' claiming that a child has been removed or retained in breach of custody rights[15] may apply under the 1980 Hague Abduction Convention requesting the return of a child

---

and Wardship Powers: Their Nature and Origins' (1994) 14 *Oxford Journal of Legal Studies* 159.

[10] *Re Z (A Minor) (Freedom of Publication)* [1997] Fam 1 at 12 *et seq*, [1996] 1 FLR 191, at 196 *et seq*.

[11] Supreme Court Act 1981, s 41(2); FPR 1991, r 5.3(1).

[12] See Lowe and White, *Wards of Court, op cit*, n 9, at 1–8..

[13] But not 'wrongful' within the meaning of Arts 3 and 5 of the 1980 Hague Abduction Convention because the child would not be habitually resident in England and Wales.

[14] See FPR 1991, Parts VI and VII, SI 1991/1247, as amended by the Family Proceedings (Amendment) Rules 2001, SI 2001/821.

[15] Article 8. See **12.23** and **14.19**.

wrongfully removed to, or retained in, England and Wales either by applying to the Lord Chancellor's Child Abduction Unit ('the CAU')[16] or to the Central Authority of the child's State of habitual residence or to any other Central Authority (which will transmit the request to the CAU)[17] or by making an application directly to the High Court.[18] Although the applicant is usually the person or body whose rights of custody have been breached, it is permissible for a person who has no rights of custody, but has a sufficient interest in the child, to make an application based on the breach of another's rights. In a case where there has been a breach of the rights of custody held by a court,[19] the House of Lords said in *Re H (A Minor) (Abduction: Rights of Custody)*[20] that a person who has invoked the jurisdiction of the court as a result of which the court has rights of custody[21] is entitled to apply for the return based on a breach of the court's rights of custody, and that in most cases this is more appropriate than the court itself making the application. In cases decided before *Re H*, the court itself had been the applicant in proceedings under the Hague Convention in England and Wales; in *Re S (Abduction: Children: Separate Representation)*,[22] the children were wards of the High Court of New Zealand which made the application under the Convention. However, in *The Ontario Court v M and M (Children's Objections)*,[23] Hollis J doubted whether it was appropriate for the Ontario Court (the court of the requesting State) to act as applicant in circumstances where the rights of custody of the court had been breached, but it was proposed that the children should be returned to their grandmother, whose rights had not been breached, albeit that she had instigated the proceedings in Canada. Although the general practice in England and Wales has been settled by *Re H*, in abductions from the United Kingdom, the appropriate applicant should be determined by the view taken in the requested State.

The 1980 European Custody Convention

21.7 In contrast to the position under the 1980 Hague Abduction Convention, the applicant for the registration of a decision relating to custody under the 1980 European Custody Convention must be the person on whom rights are conferred by the decision.[24]

---

16   The CAU carries out the function of the Central Authority for England and Wales on behalf of the Lord Chancellor. As to the CAU generally, see **13.9** *et seq.*
17   Article 8: see **12.25**.
18   Article 29, and Child Abduction and Custody Act 1985, s 4. Note that an application must be submitted to the CAU as the Central Authority if the applicant is to obtain legal representation free of the usual means and merits tests (see **21.15**).
19   Discussed at **14.67** *et seq.*
20   [2000] 2 AC 291, [2000] 2 WLR 33, [2000] 1 FLR 374, HL.
21   See **14.67** *et seq.*
22   [1997] 1 FLR 486.
23   [1997] 1 FLR 475.
24   Child Abduction and Custody Act 1985, s 16(1). See **19.76**.

The Council Regulation

21.8 'Any interested party' may apply for a decision that a judgment relating to parental responsibility of the spouses be or not be recognised[25] or be enforced.[26] According to the Borras Report (the Explanatory Report on the Brussels I Convention),[27] the concept of an 'interested party' should be interpreted in a broad sense, so it may include not only the parents or children, but also 'the public prosecutor or other similar bodies where permitted in the State in which the judgment is to be recognised or contested'.

The inherent jurisdiction

21.9 Any person with a sufficient interest can make an application within the High Court's inherent jurisdiction with respect to children.[28]

Applications to the Lord Chancellor's Child Abduction Unit

21.10 An application for the return of a child under the 1980 Hague Abduction Convention or for recognition and enforcement of a decision relating to custody under the 1980 European Custody Convention may be made to the Central Authority in the requesting State or to the CAU as Central Authority for England and Wales and for the United Kingdom,[29] or directly to the High Court.[30]

21.11 Although the Hague Conference has a suggested model, there is no specified form for making an application to a Central Authority under either of the two Conventions. The CAU will accept an incoming application in any form, provided that it contains sufficient information, including that set out in Art 8 of the 1980 Hague Abduction Convention or in Art 13 of the 1980 European Custody Convention, and that it is accompanied by the necessary documents.

---

[25] Article 14(3) of the Council Regulation. See **18.13** *et seq.*

[26] Article 21(1).

[27] (1998) OJ C221/27, at paras 65 and 80. See **18.6**.

[28] See Lowe and White, *Wards of Court, op cit*, n 9.

[29] The functions of the Central Authority for England and Wales and for Northern Ireland are to be discharged by the Lord Chancellor, and those for Scotland by the Secretary of State for Scotland; the Lord Chancellor may receive applications for all of the United Kingdom and he will transmit those relating to Scotland to the Secretary of State for Scotland; the Secretary of State will transmit those relating to England and Wales or Northern Ireland to the Lord Chancellor: Child Abduction and Custody Act 1985, ss 3 and 14. Any application made under either Convention by or on behalf of a person outside the United Kingdom may be addressed to the Lord Chancellor as the Central Authority in the United Kingdom: *ibid*. See generally **13.9** *et seq.*

[30] Article 29 of the 1980 Hague Abduction Convention and Art 4 of the 1980 Europeran Custody Convention, and Child Abduction and Custody Act 1985, s 16(1) and (2). In practice, because of the implications for obtaining public funding, applications should initially be made to the CAU: see **21.15**.

21.12 An application under the 1980 Hague Abduction Convention must contain:[31]

(a) information concerning the identity of the applicant, of the child and of the person alleged to have removed or retained the child;

(b) where available, the date of birth of the child;

(c) the grounds on which the applicant's claim for return of the child is based;

(d) all available information relating to the whereabouts of the child and the identity of the person with whom the child is presumed to be.

The application may be accompanied or supplemented by:

(e) an authenticated copy of any relevant decision or agreement;

(f) a certificate or an affidavit emanating from a Central Authority, or other competent authority of the State of the child's habitual residence, or from a qualified person, concerning the relevant law of that State;

(g) any other relevant document.

21.13 A request for recognition or enforcement of a decision relating to custody under the 1980 European Custody Convention must be accompanied by:[32]

(a) a document authorising the Central Authority of the State addressed to act on behalf of the applicant or to designate another representative for that purpose;

(b) a copy of the decision which satisfies the necessary conditions of authenticity;

(c) in the case of a decision given in the absence of the defendant or his legal representative, a document which establishes that the defendant was duly served with the document which instituted the proceedings or an equivalent document;

(d) if applicable, any document which establishes that, in accordance with the law of the State of origin, the decision is enforceable;

(e) if possible, a statement indicating the whereabouts or likely whereabouts of the child in the State addressed;

(f) proposals as to how the custody of the child should be restored.

21.14 One important feature of the way in which cases under the 1980 Hague Abduction Convention and the 1980 European Custody Convention (known as 'Convention cases') for the return of a child are conducted in the United Kingdom is that the Central Authority does not make the application for return itself, and nor is it a party to the proceedings.[33] The applicant in all Convention cases is represented by solicitors and counsel (barristers) in private practice, who are both paid by the Legal Services

---

[31] Article 8.

[32] Article 13.

[33] In contrast to the position in some other Contracting States, for example, Australia, discussed at **22.5**.

Commission. When the CAU receives an application for the return of a child who is in England and Wales, it checks that the application meets the criteria for eligibility[34] and then asks an experienced solicitor to take on the case. The CAU has set itself an 80% target for forwarding applications to solicitors within 24 hours of initial receipt.[35] The CAU will send the solicitor a letter giving a very brief summary of the case and current procedures, and certifying that the applicant is eligible for legal representation at public expense, free of the usual means and merits tests.[36] The solicitor is then responsible for making an application for public funding and conducting the case, with the assistance of the client, the CAU, the Central Authority of the requesting State and anyone else who may be able to assist.

Applying for public funding for the applicant

21.15 An applicant for a return order under the 1980 Hague Abduction Convention or for the registration and enforcement of a custody decision under the 1980 European Custody Convention is entitled to non-means, non-merits tested legal representation, but only if the application has been submitted to the CAU pursuant to the Child Abduction and Custody Act 1985, s 3(2) or s 14(2).[37] There is no provision for back-dating an application for public funding, so if an overseas applicant approaches English solicitors directly, it is particularly important that the application is 'addressed' to the CAU as quickly as possible so that the CAU can send out the letter to the conducting solicitor certifying the applicant's entitlement to public funding free of the usual means and merits tests.[38]

21.16 Having received the letter from the CAU, the conducting solicitor should then submit an application for legal representation to the Legal Services Commission's London Regional Office, sending by facsimile

---

[34] Ie that the child in question is under the age of 16, and that there appears to be an enforceable order or rights of custody which have been breached. The CAU will scrutinise the application and may make enquiries, but will not seek to make judgments about matters which may be in dispute.

[35] According to Wall J in *Re S (Child Abduction: Delay)* [1998] 1 FLR 651 at 660, the CAU 'invariably achieves a 100% rate' in meeting this target.

[36] See **21.16**.

[37] See Community Legal Service (Financial) Regulations 2000, SI 2000/516, reg 3(1)(f) and The Legal Services Commission's Funding Code Decision-Making Guidance, para 20.24, 'Special Cases', in *The Legal Services Manual*, Part C, para 3C–287. Note that, whereas Art 8 of the 1980 Hague Abduction Convention refers to 'Any person, institution or other body …', reg 3(1)(f) refers only to a 'person', so it seems as if a body or institution – perhaps a social services department which has the care of a child – would not be eligible for legal representation at the public expense. Note that there is no automatic extension of public funding for an appeal. The question of funding for an appeal has to be put to the Legal Services Commission, which will apply a 'merits' test. As to the issue of recoverable costs, see *Re R (Costs: Child Abduction)* [1995] 2 FLR 774, and **21.17** and **21.92** *et seq*.

[38] The conducting solicitor would have to have an appropriate contract with the Legal Services Commission, as have all the solicitors who are regularly asked by the CAU to accept cases.

transmission[39] a completed form CLSAPP6, accompanied by the letter from the CAU and a very short letter setting out boldly and clearly that the application relates to proceedings under the Child Abduction and Custody Act 1985 (specifying the Hague or the European Convention, as appropriate), that it is non-means, non-merits tested, and that, accordingly, there are no other application forms to submit. The Legal Services Commission will process the application as a matter of urgency and will usually send confirmation of the granting of legal representation by facsimile transmission within 24 hours. The public funding certificate itself will be sent out within a few days.

21.17 When the public funding certificate is received it should be checked carefully to ensure that the details are correct. Any limitation on costs should be scrutinised carefully and kept under review, bearing in mind that these proceedings can be intensive, time-consuming and may incur substantial disbursements by way of translation fees. The Legal Services Commission has a list of allowable disbursements,[40] but the fact that an item is on the list of allowable disbursements means only that it is capable of being allowed, not that it will be allowed. If, for example, an applicant is directed to attend a hearing to give oral evidence, his travelling and accommodation expenses will be allowed only in exceptional circumstances where he has insufficient funds to meet those expenses, and it would not be otherwise possible to progress the case.

Applications to the High Court

The 1980 Hague Abduction Convention

21.18 Applications for assistance in securing the return of a child may be made to either the Central Authority of the child's habitual residence or the Central Authority of any other Contracting State,[41] but an application for a return order must be made to the High Court.[42] The machinery of the Convention read as a whole envisages essentially a summary procedure to be operated once only; relitigation is not permitted. In *Re O (Child Abduction: Re-Abduction)*[43] the English court refused to permit a father to make another application for a return order when the child was brought to England after the father's Convention proceedings had been dismissed in another Contracting State.[44] However, where a re-abduction took place after successful

---

[39] In very urgent cases it may be possible to deal with an application by telephone.

[40] Paragraph 2.5 of the Funding Code Decision Making Guidance, in *The Legal Services Manual*, Part C, para 3C–009.

[41] Article 8. Note that there is no obligation to route an application through a Central Authority (Art 29), but unless an application has been 'submitted' to the CAU, the applicant will not be entitled to 'free' legal representation: see **21.15**.

[42] Child Abduction and Custody Act 1985, s 4.

[43] [1997] 2 FLR 712.

[44] No order made in Convention proceedings brought in England after dismissal of the father's Convention application in Sweden for return to the United States as the State of

Convention proceedings, the English court not only entertained a fresh application for a return to the State of habitual residence but also permitted the abductor to raise new issues in opposition which had not arisen in the original Convention proceedings.[45] If the issues had been truly identical to those already adjudicated upon, the doctrine of issue estoppel would have applied.[46]

The 1980 European Custody Convention

21.19 An application for assistance in securing the recognition and enforcement of a decision relating to custody under the European Convention may be made to the Central Authority in the requesting State or to the Central Authority for England and Wales or for the United Kingdom,[47] but an application for registration and enforcement must be made to the High Court.[48]

The Council Regulation

21.20 An application for registration and enforcement must be filed with the Principal Registry of the Family Division of the High Court.[49]

Non-Convention cases

21.21 In a non-Convention case, an application may be made for a s 8 order under the Children Act 1989,[50] but it is more usual to apply for an order for summary return within the High Court's inherent jurisdiction with respect to children. Unless there is a good reason to do so, it will not be necessary to make the child a ward of court.[51] Applications under the inherent jurisdiction of the High Court with respect to children must be made to the High Court, as should applications under Children Act 1989, s 8, because of the foreign element and the likely complexity of the case.[52]

---

the children's habitual residence; order made under the inherent jurisdiction and the Children Act 1989 for summary return to Sweden.

[45] *Re L (Abduction: Pending Criminal Proceedings)* [1999] 1 FLR 433.

[46] *Ibid*. Note that the Explanatory Report to the 1980 European Custody Convention suggests that a return order made under the 1980 Hague Abduction Convention can be enforced as a 'custody order' but the matter was left open in *Re L (Abduction: Pending Criminal Proceedings)* (above) at 442. See the discussion at **19.47**.

[47] See **21.10**.

[48] Article 4 of the 1980 European Custody Convention, and Child Abduction and Custody Act 1985, s 16(1) and (2). In practice, where recognition and enforcement of a decision relating to custody are sought, the application should be made initially to the CAU.

[49] Article 22(1), Annex 1, and FPR 1991, r 7.41. See **18.23** and **21.107**.

[50] Eg a specific issue order or residence order under Children Act 1989, s 8.

[51] But see **9.31** and **20.2**.

[52] See *Practice Direction (Family Business: Distribution of Business)* (5 June 1992) [1992] 2 FLR 87.

The nature of the proceedings

21.22   Applications for return orders under the two Conventions are heard in chambers by a judge of the Family Division.[53] Being summary in nature, speed is of the essence.[54] If no decision is reached within 6 weeks of the commencement of proceedings, the applicant or the requesting Central Authority can request a statement of the reasons for the delay.[55] In *Re C (Abduction: Grave Risk of Physical or Psychological Harm)*,[56] Thorpe LJ said:

> 'The goal for which we should strive in this jurisdiction, both at first instance and on appeal, should be six weeks from initiation to conclusion. It cannot be too strongly emphasised that this is intended to be a hot pursuit remedy and if the courts permit it to linger into anything else they aid the creation of unnecessary litigation issues.'[57]

21.23   Accordingly, where an application for the return of a child was made about 18 months after the wrongful removal or retention and thereafter was not prosecuted properly, the application was struck out as an abuse of the process of the court.[58]

The originating summons

21.24   Every application under either of the two Conventions has to be made by originating summons,[59] issued out of the Principal Registry of the Family

---

53   FPR 1991, r 6.8.

54   The 1980 Hague Abduction Convention is intended to provide for a prompt and summary return: see Arts 11 and 12, and also: *Re E (A Minor) (Abduction)* [1989] 1 FLR 135 at 139C–E, 142F–H, 144H–145A, CA; *B v B (Abduction: Custody Rights)* [1993] Fam 32 at 42E, [1993] 1 FLR 238 at 247, per Sir Stephen Brown P, CA. See also: *Re S (Minors) (Abduction: Acquiescence)* [1994] 1 FLR 819, CA (per Hoffmann LJ at 836: 'a summary remedy in the sense that the child must be returned without investigation of the merits') and *Re B (Minors) (Abduction) (No 2)* [1993] 1 FLR 993 (per Waite J at 998: '… there must be an element of peremptoriness in the court's approach to their hearing. Time does not allow for more than a quick impression gained on a panoramic view of the evidence'). As to the conduct of the hearing, see **21.76**. As to discounting the time taken to find children who have been hidden ('tolling'), see *Re L (Abduction: Pending Criminal Proceedings)* [1999] 1 FLR 433 and *Re H (Abduction: Child of 16)* [2000] 2 FLR 5, and **17.24**.

55   Article 11.

56   [1999] 2 FLR 478 at 488, CA.

57   As to the speed with which proceedings are heard and the importance of avoiding delay in hearing the summons, see *Re S (Child Abduction: Delay)* [1998] 1 FLR 651 and *Re HB (Abduction: Children's Objections)* [1998] 1 FLR 422. As to the performance of the various Contracting States to the 1980 Hague Abduction Convention, see Lowe, Armstrong and Mathias, 'A Statistical Analysis of Applications made in 1999 under the Hague Convention of 25 October 1980 on the Civil Aspects of International Child Abduction', Preliminary Document No 3 (Revised Version, November 2001), available on the Hague Conference website at http://www.hcch.net/e/conventions/reports28e.html (hereinafter referred to as 'the 1999 Statistical Survey'). Note the emphasis put on a court disposal within 6 weeks by the revised Brussels II Regulation: see **12.71**.

58   *Re G (Abduction: Striking Out Application)* [1995] 2 FLR 410.

59   FPR 1991, r 6.2. The form of the originating summons is that of Form 10 in Appendix A to the RSC 1965. As to originating summonses generally, see RSC 1965, Ords 7 and 28.

Division,[60] with the exception of an application in custody proceedings for a declaration under the 1980 European Custody Convention that a removal was unlawful, which must be by summons in the proceedings.[61]

21.25   The originating summons should be intituled with the name of the child:

> 'IN THE MATTER OF JANE JONES (a Child)'

and

> 'AND IN THE MATTER OF THE CHILD ABDUCTION AND CUSTODY ACT 1985'

(if orders are to be sought under Part I of the Family Law Act 1986,[62] the summons should be intituled with that Act). Similarly, if relief is sought under the inherent jurisdiction of the High Court with respect to children,[63] either by way of interlocutory relief or as an alternative to a return order under the Conventions, the summons should be intituled:

> 'AND IN THE MATTER OF THE INHERENT JURISDICTION WITH RESPECT TO CHILDREN'.[64]

21.26   The originating summons must include:[65]

(a)   the name and date of birth of the child in respect of whom the application is made;
(b)   the names of the child's parents or guardians;
(c)   the whereabouts or suspected whereabouts of the child;
(d)   the interest of the plaintiff in the matter and the grounds of the application; and
(e)   particulars of any proceedings (including proceedings out of the jurisdiction and concluded proceedings) relating to the child.

21.27   An application for a return order under the 1980 Hague Abduction Convention must include the identity of the person alleged to have removed or retained the child and, if different, the identity of the person with whom the child is presumed to be.[66] The 'interest of the plaintiff in the matter and the grounds of the application' will be the plaintiff's rights of custody in the

---

[60]   The words 'and issued out of the principal registry' were inserted in r 6.2(1) by Family Proceedings (Amendment No 3) Rules 1997, SI 1997/1893, r 16.

[61]   Child Abduction and Custody Act 1985, s 23(2), and FPR 1991, r 6.2(2). As to the magistrates' court, see Magistrates' Courts (Child Abduction and Custody) Rules 1986, SI 1986/1141, r 9. As to declarations, see Chapter 15.

[62]   As to tracing and recovering the child, see Chapter 10 and **21.58**.

[63]   See s 100 of the Children Act 1989.

[64]   See *Re Z (A Minor) (Identification: Restrictions on Publication)* [1997] Fam 1, [1996] 1 FLR 191. Note that proceedings under the inherent jurisdiction are 'family proceedings' as defined by Children Act 1989, s 8(3)(a), so the court can make a s 8 order if a question arises with respect to the welfare of the child: see s 10(1)(b).

[65]   FPR 1991, r 6.3.

[66]   *Ibid*, r 6.4 (1)(a).

State of the child's habitual residence and the removal in breach of those rights.[67]

21.28   If a declaration under Art 15 of the 1980 Hague Abduction Convention is sought,[68] the originating summons must identify the proceedings in which the request that such a declaration be obtained was made.[69]

21.29   Applications under the 1980 European Custody Convention must identify the decision relating to custody or rights of access which is sought to be registered or enforced or in relation to which a declaration that it is not to be recognised is sought.[70]

Attachments to the originating summons

21.30   The originating summons must be accompanied by all relevant documents, including but not limited to, the documents specified in Art 8 of the 1980 Hague Abduction Convention or Art 13 of the 1980 European Custody Convention.[71] The usual practice is to exhibit these documents to the affidavit in support of the originating summons.[72]

Defendants to the originating summons

21.31   The defendants to any application under the Child Abduction and Custody Act 1985 must be:

(a)   the person alleged to have brought into the United Kingdom the child in respect of whom an application under the Hague Convention is made;

(b)   the person with whom the child is alleged to be;

(c)   any parent or guardian of the child who is within the United Kingdom and is not otherwise a party;

(d)   the person in whose favour a decision relating to custody has been made if he is not otherwise a party; and

(e)   any other person who appears to the court to have a sufficient interest in the welfare of the child.[73]

Only in the most exceptional circumstances will the court permit the child who is the subject of the proceedings to be joined as a party.[74]

Parties under a disability

21.32   A plaintiff or defendant who is a person under disability, that is, a minor or patient,[75] has to be represented in family proceedings[76] by a next

---

[67]   Article 3. See **14.5** *et seq.*

[68]   See Chapter 15.

[69]   FPR 1991, r 6.4(1)(b).

[70]   *Ibid,* r 6.4(2).

[71]   *Ibid,* r 6.3(1).

[72]   See **21.37**. As to the admissibility of the documents, see **21.67** *et seq.*

[73]   FPR 1991, r 6.5.

[74]   See **17.173**, **19.89** and **21.85**.

friend or guardian ad litem, pursuant to the provisions of Part IX of the FPR 1991. The provisions in r 9.2A enabling competent minors to begin, prosecute or defend family proceedings apply only to proceedings under the Children Act 1989 and the inherent jurisdiction,[77] so a minor plaintiff or defendant in Convention proceedings, including a child the subject of proceedings joined as a defendant, must be represented by a next friend or guardian ad litem, regardless of his competence (that is his ability, having regard to his understanding, to give instructions in relation to the proceedings).

21.33 Rule 9.5 of the FPR 1991 contemplates the appointment of an officer of CAFCASS, the Official Solicitor or some other proper person as guardian ad litem when it appears to the court, exceptionally, that it is the best interests of a child to be made a party to proceedings. As abduction cases have a significant foreign element, the proper person to act for a child is an officer of CAFCASS Legal.[78]

21.34 Where the defendant to an application under the Child Abduction and Custody Act 1985 is an adult suffering from a mental disorder, notwithstanding the apparent conflict of interest, it may be necessary for the Official Solicitor to act as that person's guardian ad litem if there is no friend or relative able and willing to do so, as otherwise it would be impossible for the application to proceed.

---

[75] FPR 1991, r 9.1: 'person under disability' means a person who is a minor or a patient; 'patient' means a person who, by reason of mental disorder within the meaning of the Mental Health Act 1983, is incapable of managing and administering his property and affairs. A 'minor' is someone who has not reached the age of majority which in England and Wales is 18: Family Law Reform Act 1969, s 1.

[76] See FPR 1991, r 1.2, which assigns to 'family proceedings' the meaning in s 32 of the Matrimonial and Family Proceedings Act 1984, that is, proceedings which are assigned only to the Family Division of the High Court by s 61 of and Sch 1 to the Supreme Court Act 1981, which includes proceedings under the Child Abduction and Custody Act 1985 and under the inherent jurisdiction of the High Court with respect to children. Note that Part IX is disapplied to children who are the subject of specified proceedings within the meaning of Children Act 1989, s 41(6) by FPR 1991, r 9.1(2).

[77] FPR 1991, r 9.1(3).

[78] See *CAFCASS Practice Note (Officers of CAFCASS Legal Services and Special Casework: Appointment in Family Proceedings)* (March 2001) [2001] 2 FLR 151. Prior to the creation of CAFCASS Legal, it had been the practice to appoint a solicitor in private practice to represent the child on those rare occasions that the child was joined as party to Convention proceedings. This was because the appointment of the Official Solicitor, who normally represented children in the High Court, might appear to give rise to a conflict of interest, the CAU (as it still is) being situated in the Official Solicitor's office. This was the course adopted in *Re M (A Minor) (Abduction: Child's Objections)* [1994] 2 FLR 126. In such circumstances, the Official Solicitor could still accept an appointment as *amicus curiae* (now advocate to the court): see *Re HB (Abduction: Children's Objections) (No 2)* [1998] 1 FLR 564. There was no such conflict in non-Convention cases, in which the Official Solicitor often represented the child: see *Practice Statement (The Official Solicitor: Appointment in Family Proceedings)* [1999] 1 FLR 310.

Diplomatic and State immunity

21.35 When considering defendants, it should not be forgotten that certain diplomats, although within the jurisdiction, are immune from suit,[79] and if a child is removed in compliance with an order of a foreign government, the removal may be subject to State immunity, because:[80]

> '[the] agent of a foreign State will enjoy immunity in respect of his acts of a sovereign or governmental nature. Accordingly there may be cases where the diplomatic agent may enjoy both diplomatic and State immunity. These immunities will not be co-extensive.'

The advocate to the court

21.36 In some cases, usually where there is a danger of an important and difficult point of law being decided without the court hearing relevant argument, the court may appoint an advocate to the court (formerly an *amicus curiae*) to assist the court.[81] The advocate to the court represents no one. His or her function is to assist the court as to the law and its application to the facts of the case. The advocate to the court will not normally be instructed to lead evidence, cross-examine witnesses or investigate the facts. The functions and duties of, and the circumstances in which the court may seek the assistance of, an advocate to the court are set out in the 'Memorandum – Requests for the Appointment of an Advocate to the Court' dated 19 December 2001, issued by the Lord Chief Justice and the Attorney-General.[82] In most cases, an advocate to the court is appointed by the Attorney-General, but a request may be made to the Official Solicitor or CAFCASS (Legal Services and Special Casework) where the issue is one in which their expertise of representing children and adults under disability gives rise to special expertise, such as in international children's cases.[83] In cases of extreme urgency, telephone requests may be made, and in some cases the

---

[79] See the Vienna Convention on Diplomatic Relations 1961 and the Diplomatic Privileges Act 1964. Note that diplomatic immunity is not immunity from legal liability, but immunity from suit, so it may be possible to institute or continue proceedings when immunity has ceased: see *Re P (Diplomatic Immunity: Jurisdiction)* [1998] 1 FLR 1026. And, in Australia, see *In the marriage of De Andrade* (1994) 19 Fam LR 271 for an examination of the extent to which diplomatic immunity covers proceedings under the Family Law Act 1975 in the light of the provisions of the Diplomatic Privileges and Immunities Act 1967. See also **9.52**. For the impact of immigration and asylum legislation on abduction litigation, see *Re S (Child Abduction: Asylum Appeal)* [2002] EWCA Civ 843, [2002] 2 FLR 465, CA, discussed at **20.3**, n 8, and in Canada, see *Kovacs v Kovacs* (2002) 212 DLR (4th) 711, Ont Sup Ct.

[80] Per Sir Stephen Brown P, in *Re P (Diplomatic Immunity: Jurisdiction)* (above) at 1034.

[81] Eg *Re G (Abduction: Rights of Custody)* [2002] 2 FLR 703, in which the court appointed the Official Solicitor as advocate to the court in an application for a declaration based on inchoate rights of custody (see **14.49** *et seq*) in which the defendant mother was not represented. Declarations for the purposes of the 1980 Hague Abduction Convention are persuasive only (see **15.7–15.9**), and the persuasive effect of a declaration being granted on the basis of rights which might be in dispute without the abductor being represented and without contrary argument must necessarily be limited.

[82] Set out in *Counsel – The Journal of the Bar of England and Wales*, February 2002, p 30.

[83] *Ibid*, para 11. The division of responsibility between the Official Solicitor and CAFCASS Legal is outlined in the Practice Notes reported at [2001] 2 FLR 151 and [2001] 2 FLR 155.

Official Solicitor himself will be appointed as advocate to the court, and there may be directions authorising him to obtain documents, conduct investigations and enquiries, and advise the court. He may appear by counsel or an in-house advocate.

The affidavit in support

21.37 On issuing an originating summons under either of the Conventions, the plaintiff may lodge affidavit evidence in the Principal Registry of the Family Division in support of his application and serve a copy on the defendant with the originating summons.[84] In practice, an affidavit is sworn and filed by the conducting solicitor, and sets out briefly the circumstances of the case, including the source of the plaintiff's rights of custody in the requesting State, a short account of the removal of the child, any communications with the abductor and the involvement (with dates) of the Central Authorities. If any immediate or interim relief is sought,[85] the evidence to support such orders should be included. The documents accompanying the application to the CAU should be exhibited to the affidavit.[86]

Other pending proceedings

21.38 The conducting solicitor must bear in mind the duty to inform the court about any pending proceedings relating to the child. A party to proceedings under the 1980 Hague Abduction Convention who knows of an application 'relating to the merits of rights of custody'[87] pending in or before a relevant authority must file in the Principal Registry of the Family Division a concise statement of the nature of the application which is pending, including the authority before which it is pending.[88] A party to proceedings for the registration and enforcement of a custody order under the 1980 European Custody Convention must,[89] where he knows that an application in relation to 'custody proceedings' (that is, an application to make, vary or revoke a care or supervision order, a residence order or an order giving care and control within wardship)[90] is pending in a court in the United Kingdom, file in the Principal Registry a concise statement of the nature of the pending application.[91] The Principal Registry must in turn notify the court where those proceedings are pending of the application for registration and enforcement, and the proper

---

[84] FPR 1991, r 6.7(1).

[85] See **21.69**.

[86] As to the admissibility of the documents accompanying the application to the CAU, see **21.66** *et seq*. As to affidavits generally, see RSC 1965, Ord 41.

[87] Article 16.

[88] FPR 1991, r 6.11(1). As to the suspension of the court's usual powers to make custody orders, see **21.91**.

[89] Child Abduction and Custody Act 1985, ss 16 and 20.

[90] *Ibid*, ss 20(2), 27(1), and Sch 3.

[91] FPR 1991, r 6.11(2).

officer of the court in which the custody proceedings are pending must notify the parties of the application for registration and enforcement.[92]

The statutory stay

21.39 After receiving notice of a wrongful removal or retention of a child in the sense of Art 3 of the 1980 Hague Abduction Convention,[93] the courts of England and Wales are prohibited from deciding on the merits of rights of custody[94] in relation to that child, and any pending proceedings are stayed[95] until it has been determined that the child is not to be returned under the Convention, unless an application under the Convention is not lodged within a reasonable time following receipt of the notice.[96] Once a court becomes aware, expressly or by necessary inference, that there has been a wrongful removal or retention within the meaning of Art 3, it has a duty (unless there is clear evidence of acquiescence) to ensure that the parent in the State from which the child was removed is informed of his or her rights under the Convention.[97] Thereafter, unless the court finds that no application under the Convention has been made within a reasonable time of its receiving notice of the wrongful removal, it should refrain from making a residence order (or, it seems, an interim residence order).[98]

21.40 When an application has been made under the 1980 European Custody Convention for the registration of a decision relating to custody (other than a decision relating solely to rights of access) made in proceedings commenced before the pending proceedings were instituted in the United Kingdom, the powers of courts in the United Kingdom are restricted both before and after such a decision has been registered,[99] in that they may not, unless the application for registration is refused, make, vary or revoke a

---

92 FPR 1991, r 6.11(2); Magistrates' Courts (Child Abduction and Custody) Rules 1986, SI 1986/1141, r 7.

93 See **14.5**.

94 That is, the court may not make, vary or revoke a care or supervision order, a residence order, an order giving care and control within wardship or any similar orders under the pre-Children Act 1989 legislation: Child Abduction and Custody Act 1985, ss 9, 27(1) and Sch 3, paras 1–4.

95 FPR 1991, r 6.11(4).

96 Article 16.

97 *R v R (Residence Order: Child Abduction)* [1995] Fam 209, [1995] 2 FLR 625. There is also a duty to bring to the attention of the aggrieved parent his rights under the Hague Convention 'by means of directions given within those proceedings, to the effect that that parent, if he wishes to seek the return of a child to the jurisdiction from which it has been removed, should without delay seek legal advice as to his rights, if any, under the Hague Convention and should communicate with the Central Authority of his State of residence, of which he should be given the name and address': *ibid* at 223 and 637, respectively.

98 *Ibid.*

99 Child Abduction and Custody Act 1985, s 20. Restrictions on the powers of the courts in Scotland and Northern Ireland and on the powers of the Secretary of State for Scotland are also set out in s 20.

custody order[100] or supervision order,[101] or enforce a Part I order in proceedings under Family Law Act 1986, s 29.[102]

Transfer of proceedings

21.41   If a family proceedings court receives notice of a wrongful removal or retention, it should transfer the proceedings before it to a county court. If the matter appears to be clear-cut, the county court should deal with the case, as provided for in *R v R (Residence Order: Child Abduction)*.[103] In cases of difficulty, and particularly where there appear to be reasons why it would not be appropriate to take steps to see that the parent resident in the State from which the child has been removed is informed of his or her rights, the matter should be transferred to the High Court.[104]

Lifting the stay after a return order

21.42   It has been said that, in exceptional circumstances where, despite the child's habitual residence in another country, the *forum conveniens*[105] for the decision on the merits of rights of custody is England and Wales, the High Court can order a return under the 1980 Hague Abduction Convention and also order the lifting of the stay on proceedings in England and Wales.[106]

Finding the child and securing the position – the first ex parte hearing

21.43   The rules envisage that an application under either of the Conventions will proceed in much the same way as other proceedings commenced by originating summons.[107] In practice, that is not the case. In international abduction cases, speed is essential and the first, and most important, step is to secure the presence of the child within the jurisdiction. Premature notice of an application for a return order might encourage an abductor to go into hiding or to move on to another country, and so the practice has developed of making an ex parte (without notice) application to the High Court Applications Judge either immediately after having issued the originating summons or immediately before (undertaking to issue forthwith) for orders designed to secure the position until there can be an inter partes (on notice)

---

[100]   That is, a care or supervision order, a residence order, an order giving care and control within wardship or any similar orders under the pre-Children Act 1989 legislation: Child Abduction and Custody Act 1985, ss 20(2), 27(1) and Sch 3, paras 1–4.

[101]   Children Act 1989, s 31.

[102]   Child Abduction and Custody Act 1985, s 20(2)(aa).

[103]   [1995] Fam 209, [1995] 2 FLR 625.

[104]   *Ibid.*

[105]   See **1.3**.

[106]   *H v H (Child Abduction: Stay of Domestic Proceedings)* [1994] 1 FLR 530 (wrongful retention was found and the father was entitled to an order under Art 12. However, on the quite exceptional facts of the case, the father's stay on the mother's Children Act 1989 proceedings pursuant to FPR 1991, r 6.11 was removed and the matter was to be adjudicated in England); *sed quaere?*

[107]   FPR 1991, r 6.6, 6.7. As to originating summonses generally, see RSC 1965, Ords 7 and 28.

directions hearing.[108] The orders sought at that first, ex parte, hearing will depend on the circumstances of the case. It is important that the children are returned to the State from which they have been removed, but care should be taken to ensure that the process does not do more harm than good. An unnecessarily aggressive approach, especially if supported by an order made by a court in the requesting State putting a child who has never been cared for by anyone other than the abductor into the custody of the plaintiff, can be counter-productive in the longer term and may prolong the proceedings.[109] By contrast, an abduction from a primary carer needs firm and decisive handling from the start.

21.44 In the majority of modern cases, in which the abductor is the primary carer of the child and the whereabouts of the child and abductor are known, all that is necessary to secure the position is to make sure that they do not change their residential address or leave England and Wales by making injunctions and taking away their passports and travel documents. This can be achieved by asking for a 'passport order'[110] which requires the defendant to hand over to the Tipstaff[111] (the High Court's enforcement officer) every passport, identity card, ticket, travel warrant or other document which would enable the defendant or the child to leave England and Wales, and which also enjoins the defendant and anyone else served with the order from removing the child from, or changing his residence within, England and Wales.

21.45 In cases in which the whereabouts of the child are not known, or where the child is at risk, it will be necessary to ask for orders directing the Tipstaff either to find the child, or to find the child and take him from the abductor, by asking for a 'location order' or a 'collection order', both of which include powers and duties backed by a power of arrest.

---

[108] See generally Chapter 10. Sometimes firm steps are necessary to secure the position. In *DM v Director General, Department of Community Services* [1998] Fam CA 1557, (1998) FLC 92–831, the Full Court of the Family Court of Australia placed the child in the care of the relevant State Central Authority. In Australia, interim orders are usually continued after the return order and pending the actual return. Ex parte applications do not deprive the defendant of a fair trial (Art 6(1) of the 1980 European Convention for the Protection of Human Rights and Fundamental Freedoms). It is always open to a party against whom an ex parte order has been made to apply to set it aside: see *Re J (Abduction: Wrongful Removal)* [2000] 1 FLR 78. Note that by entertaining the ex parte application and making orders, the court will invest itself with 'rights of custody' for the purposes of Arts 3 and 5 of the 1980 Hague Abduction Convention: see *Re J (Declaration of Wrongful Removal)* [1999] 2 FLR 653 (reported on appeal as *Re J (Abduction: Wrongful Removal)* [2000] 1 FLR 78), and see **14.73** *et seq.*

[109] As to undertakings, including undertakings not to enforce custody orders, see **17.123** *et seq.*

[110] Form 3A (reproduced in Appendix 4).

[111] 'Tipstaff' includes his deputy or assistants, and all police constables (and all police officers are constables).

Collection and location orders[112]

21.46   If the whereabouts of the child are not known but he is believed to be with an abductor who is his primary carer,[113] it is unlikely (unless there is history of abduction) that it will be in his interests, especially if he is very young and has never been cared for by anyone other than the abductor, to be removed from the abductor's care until a decision is made as to whether or not he should be returned to his home State. In those very common circumstances, a location order should be enough to secure the position.[114] A location order is supported by a direction to the Tipstaff.[115] The actual location order (which has to be served on the defendant by the Tipstaff and may also be served on others) requires the defendant and any other person served with it to inform the Tipstaff of the whereabouts of the child or of 'all matters within his knowledge or understanding which might reasonably assist him in locating the child' and to hand over to the Tipstaff for safekeeping until the court makes a further order every passport relating to the child and the defendant, and every identity card, ticket, travel warrant or other document which would enable them to leave England and Wales. The order also prohibits the defendant or any other person served with the order from causing or permitting the child to stay overnight anywhere other than the place where he was staying when the order was served. The direction to the Tipstaff (which is a semi-private[116] communication between the judge and the Tipstaff, and so is not served on the defendant or given to the parties) requires him to locate the child as soon as practicable and to inform the plaintiff (through his solicitors) of the child's whereabouts.[117] It also authorises him to enter premises (if necessary by force) and to arrest anyone whom he has reasonable cause to believe has been served with and has disobeyed the location order and bring them before the court, and requires him to keep safely any documents handed to him pursuant to the order.

21.47   If there has been an abduction from a primary carer,[118] or the case involves a serial abductor, or there is for some other reason a real fear that the child might be hidden or moved on, possibly to a non-Convention country, a

---

[112]   Prior to 11 February 2002, these orders were known as 'seek and find' (or 'find and return') and 'seek and locate' orders. A 'seek and find' order directed the Tipstaff to find the child and deliver him to a named person; a 'seek and locate' order directed the Tipstaff to find the child.

[113]   According to the 1999 Statistical Survey, *op cit*, n 57, 69% of abductions are by mothers, most of whom are primary carers of their children, and who take them to their 'home' State after the breakdown of their relationship with the children's father.

[114]   Form 1A (reproduced in Appendix 4).

[115]   Form 1B.

[116]   The privacy traditionally afforded to such directions is debatable.

[117]   There may be circumstances, including cases in which there have been allegations of domestic violence, in which the plaintiff's solicitors may be directed not to reveal the whereabouts of the child to the plaintiff without the leave of the court, or the Tipstaff might be directed to report the whereabouts of the child only to the court.

[118]   Which might include a foreign social services authority.

collection order should generally be sought.[119] In cases in which the abductor is the primary carer of the child, a difficult and sensitive balance has to be struck. If it is a long-standing abduction, the child might have very little memory of the plaintiff, or may have been told that the plaintiff is dead. Treaty obligations and the child's medium- to long-term interests have to be weighed against the damage which might be caused to him by peremptorily removing him from his current carer in what are bound to be distressing circumstances. Like a location order, a collection order is supported by a direction to the Tipstaff. The order (which, like a location order, has to be served on the defendant by the Tipstaff and may also be served on others) directs the child to be placed in the care of the plaintiff on a temporary basis until a further hearing, which must take place within 3 clear working days after the plaintiff's care begins, and requires the defendant (or any other person on whom it is served) to deliver the child into the charge of the Tipstaff. The order also requires the defendant or any other person served with it who is not in a position to deliver the child to the Tipstaff to inform him of the child's whereabouts or of all matters within their knowledge or understanding which might reasonably assist him to find the child. In addition, the order requires the defendant and any person served with it to hand over to the Tipstaff every passport, identity card, ticket, travel warrant or other document which could enable them to leave England and Wales. The order specifically states that it, or a faxed copy of it, must be served personally on the defendant and any other person whom it is proposed to make liable under it, although if a person refuses or evades personal service, it will be considered to be validly served if its effect has been brought to that person's attention.

21.48 The plaintiff and his solicitors will be required to give undertakings to the court. The plaintiff must undertake, until further hearing, not to remove the child from England and Wales or cause or permit him to stay overnight other than at an identified address. The plaintiff's solicitors must undertake to apply for a further hearing to be fixed as soon as they are aware that the child has been placed in the plaintiff's care.

21.49 The direction to the Tipstaff (which, like the direction in support of a location order, is not for service and will not be given to the parties)[120] requires him to take charge of the child as soon as practicable and place him in the care of the plaintiff, to enter (by force if necessary) any premises in which he has reasonable cause to believe the child or the defendant to be present, to arrest anyone he has reasonable cause to believe has been served with, and has disobeyed, the location order and bring them before the court, and to keep safely any documents handed to him pursuant to the order

21.50 Although the standard form of collection order contemplates the child being placed in the care of the plaintiff, there may be cases in which the child must be found before the plaintiff can come to England, or the plaintiff might be a public body in whose care the child has been. In such cases, the

---

[119] Forms 2A (reproduced in Appendix 4) and 2B.
[120] See **21.46**.

child may have to be cared for temporarily by the local authority in whose area he is found to be until more suitable arrangements can be made.[121]

21.51   The Tipstaff will, at the request of the plaintiff's solicitors, be in attendance at the applications court, and it would be wise, before making submissions to the court, to take his advice about the precise form of order which is best suited to the circumstances of the case.

21.52   Passport, location and collection orders must only be drawn by the Family Division Associates, and there must be no alteration of the words of the orders (which are framed to ensure compliance with the Human Rights Act 1998 and to clarify the role of the Tipstaff)[122] without the approval of the judge. Before an order is made, the Associate must be given a completed form containing details of the case, and at either the start or the end of the hearing, the Tipstaff will require a separate form to be completed containing information to enable him to implement the order.

21.53   It is very important to note that passport, location and collection orders must be served *only* by the Tipstaff,[123] and they will carry an endorsement to that effect.[124] The Tipstaff will retain a record of service in the event that it becomes necessary to prove that the order has been served.

21.54   Sealed copies of the orders (but *not* the directions to the Tipstaff) will be given to the plaintiff's solicitors, but they must not serve them on the defendant or anyone else. Copies of the orders must be put into the bundle of documents which must be prepared for the later hearings.[125]

Other orders

21.55   The terms of any other order sought at the first hearing will depend on whether a passport order, a location order or a collection order has been made to secure the position.

21.56   If a collection order has been made, no further order is likely to be necessary. But if a passport order or a location order has been made, it will probably be necessary to make an order providing for a hearing at which the attendance of the defendant is required within a very short period of being served,[126] so that directions can be given for a final hearing. Service of this order must be effected by the plaintiff; it will not be served by the Tipstaff.

---

[121]   As to children being looked after by a local authority to ensure their return after an order has been made, see **21.99**.

[122]   See *Court Business*.

[123]   Or the police at the request of the Tipstaff. All constables (and all police officers are constables) are agents of the Tipstaff.

[124]   The order will carry a notice saying (in capitals): 'Note that service of this order upon the defendant and any other person is to be effected only by the Tipstaff. The copy provided to the plaintiff must not be used for service upon any person'.

[125]   See **21.70**.

[126]   Note the form of words in the precedent order which provides for the attendance of the abductor before the court after the expiry of 2 working days, to enable both the plaintiff

Searching for the child[127]

21.57 If the Tipstaff's efforts to find the child are not successful, it will be necessary to go back to the court and ask for orders requiring the disclosure of information. In Convention cases, Child Abduction and Custody Act 1985. s 24A enables the court to make an order requiring any person to disclose information to the court,[128] a statutory provision reinforced in the case of proceedings under the 1980 European Custody Convention by r 6.16 of the FPR 1991.[129] Where the proceedings are for, or relate to, a Part I order,[130] similar powers are provided by Family Law Act 1986, s 33.[131] Relatives, friends, or people with whom the child or the defendant might have stayed can be ordered to attend court and give evidence as to what they know about the whereabouts of the child. Solicitors are not immune from being required to disclose information, but the order has to be carefully framed to avoid placing them in an embarrassing position.[132] Various agencies or authorities, such as British Telecom,[133] the Department of Work and Pensions,[134] the Driver and Vehicle Licensing Agency, the Home Office Immigration and Nationality Directorate, the Office of National Statistics or a local education authority, may be able to provide information from their records which casts light on the present or recent whereabouts of the child.[135]

21.58 Sometimes it is necessary to ask the media to help in finding a child by publicising the abduction. However, it has to be borne in mind that the media need a story, and those wanting their help must be prepared to co-operate with them, and not cut off relations when the child has been found.[136]

---

and the abductor to have the advantage of the abductor being legally represented. In an appropriate case, this order might require a defendant to attend court with a notification of any defence.

[127] As to tracing and recovering a child, and possible steps to prevent further abduction, see Chapter 10.

[128] While the court has power to require witnesses to attend to give information as to the abducted child's whereabouts, there is no power to order a person to give evidence after the child has been found and surrendered to the court: *Re D (A Minor) (Child Abduction) (Note)* [1989] 1 FLR 97.

[129] 'At any stage in proceedings under the European Convention, the court may, if it has reason to believe that any person may have relevant information about the child who is the subject of those proceedings, order that person to disclose such information and may for that purpose order that the person attend before it or file affidavit evidence'. The court has power to order the attendance of a witness and to give information about the whereabouts of a child: see *Re D (A Minor) (Child Abduction) (Note)* (above).

[130] Part I of the Family Law Act 1986: see **3.2** and **10.3**.

[131] Note that s 33 can only require disclosure to the court, not to a party. An application for s 33 order is made on Form C4 and the order on Form C30. Note that there are specific provisions for ex parte applications (FPR 1991, r 6.17).

[132] See *Re H (Abduction: Whereabouts Order to Solicitors)* [2000] 1 FLR 766. See **10.18**.

[133] See **10.22**.

[134] Abductors often make an application for child benefit. See generally **10.23**.

[135] See generally **10.28**.

[136] See **10.27**.

Transfer of proceedings within the United Kingdom

21.59 At any stage in the proceedings, on application by a party or of its own motion, the court may transfer the proceedings to Scotland, Northern Ireland or the Isle of Man.[137]

The first inter partes hearing

21.60 The first inter partes (on notice) hearing, often the second hearing in the case, will take place after the abductor has been served with the first order or orders, at the time directed in those orders. A proper bundle should be prepared for this hearing by the plaintiff's solicitors.[138]

21.61 At the hearing, directions should be sought for the filing of a statement of defence by the abductor[139] within a short period of time, usually 7 days, and an affidavit within 14 days. The plaintiff should be given an opportunity to reply and to adduce any other evidence which may be necessary to deal with any issues raised by the defence – for example, evidence of the plaintiff's rights in the State of habitual residence,[140] the legality of the defendant's actions or matters contradicting any defence raised under Art 13(b). A date should be fixed for the final hearing. Rule 6.10 of the FPR 1991 restricts adjournments to a period not exceeding 21 days at any one time.[141] Where the circumstances of the case permit, the practice has evolved of providing for a hearing to comply with r 6.10, but directing that no attendance is necessary unless notice is given by either party.[142]

21.62 The order may also provide for the lodging of bundles, chronologies and skeleton arguments and may include other orders (using the court's

---

[137] FPR 1991, r 6.12.

[138] *President's Direction (Family Proceedings: Court Bundles)* (10 March 2000) [2000] 1 FLR 536.

[139] If a specific defence is going to be raised, it should be mentioned in the affidavits or in a separate notice: see *Re W (Abduction: Procedure)* [1995] 1 FLR 878 (guidance given with the approval and agreement of Sir Stephen Brown P) and *Re B (Child Abduction: Habitual Residence)* [1994] 2 FLR 915 at 917B. In an appropriate case, the first, ex parte, order might require the abductor to attend at court with a notice of any defence which is to be raised: see **21.56**.

[140] Whether those rights amount to 'rights of custody' for the purposes of the 1980 Hague Abduction Convention will be a matter for the English court: see **14.26**.

[141] It is incumbent upon an applicant to observe the spirit of this rule: *Re G (Abduction: Striking Out Application)* [1995] 2 FLR 410.

[142] See the suggested form of order in Appendix A. An alternative is:
'It is ordered that:
(1) the originating summons do stand adjourned for 21 days to the [date], not to be listed or heard upon that day unless the parties do within two days of today notify the Clerk of the Rules that a hearing is required. In the event that no such notice is given, the originating summons do stand further adjourned without a hearing for 21 days or to the final hearing date whichever be the sooner, and if necessary be further adjourned to the final hearing date upon the same basis as is provided above for the [date above];
(2) the trial of this matter be listed for hearing on a date to be fixed upon application by counsels' clerks to the Clerk of the Rules (time estimate: [   ] day(s))'.

interim powers)[143] necessary to safeguard the position of the child until the final hearing. If the plaintiff is present in England and Wales or expected to be so, the order may also make arrangements for the applicant to have contact with the child.[144]

Acting for the defendant

21.63 It is imperative to ascertain as soon as possible whether there is a realistic defence to the application. Cases are dealt with expeditiously; delay and failure to give, or act promptly on, instructions are viewed unsympathetically.[145] Usually there will be only a short time before the statement of defence is due[146] or to prepare for the final hearing, and applications to adjourn because of delays in getting public funding are not treated very sympathetically. Public funding is available to a defendant, but he or she has to satisfy both the financial criteria for public funding and the requirements set out in the Legal Services Commission's Funding Code.[147] Those requirements make it clear that public funding is likely to be granted to take or defend proceedings under the Child Abduction and Custody Act 1985 only where the client has sufficient prospects of success and the likely benefits justify the likely costs.[148] The Prospects of Success criterion[149] requires the prospects of success to be at least 'borderline'. Funding cannot be guaranteed if the prospects of success are poor. However, 'success' does not necessarily mean avoiding a return order. A successful outcome might involve an order for return, but with safeguards dealing, for example, with accommodation and maintenance for the defendant and child while the future of the child is awaiting determination in the requesting State.[150] The Funding Code makes it clear that it would be unusual for a respondent who was not the caring parent

---

[143] See **21.69**.

[144] At the third meeting of the Special Commission to discuss the operation of the 1980 Hague Abduction Convention at The Hague in March 1997, the delegates agreed that during the course of Convention proceedings the court could order interim access between the plaintiff and the child.

[145] *Re S (Child Abduction: Delay)* [1998] 1 FLR 651 and *Re L (A Minor) (Abduction: Jurisdiction)* [2002] EWHC 1864 (Fam), [2002] 1 WLR 3208, [2002] 2 FLR 1042..

[146] See **21.65**.

[147] The Legal Services Commission's Funding Code Decision Making Guidance, para 20.22, 'Special Cases', in *The Legal Services Manual,* Part C, para 3C–287.

[148] Criteria 11.11.5 and 11.11.6. Note that Cost Benefit Criteria means that legal representation will be refused unless the likely benefits to be gained from the proceedings justify the likely costs, such that a reasonable private paying client would be prepared to take or defend the proceedings in all the circumstances. If the Prospects of Success Criterion is met, then the Cost Benefit Criterion is also likely to be satisfied (The Legal Services Commission's Funding Code Decision Making Guidance, para 20.22, 'Special Cases', in *The Legal Services Manual,* Part C, para 3C–287(7)).

[149] Criterion 11.11.5.

[150] The Legal Services Commission's Funding Code Decision Making Guidance, para 20.24, 'Special Cases', in *The Legal Services Manual,* Part C, para 3C–287(5).

(the parent with whom the child was living in the country of origin) to meet the criteria for funding unless there was a strong defence under Art 13.[151]

21.64   The duty to give notice of pending proceedings must be complied with.[152] If there is a real risk that the plaintiff might try to re-abduct the child, undertakings or orders should be sought at the first inter partes hearing.[153]

The statement of defence

21.65   The statement of defence should summarise the defence, but not to the extent that it is little more than a 'tick box form'. Some proper indication of the case has to be given. Admissions (for example, that the child was habitually resident in the requesting State immediately before the removal, or even that the removal was wrongful) are perfectly proper, and will narrow the scope of the final hearing. But there is nothing wrong with putting the plaintiff to proof. It may not be easy to demonstrate what the plaintiff's rights actually consist of, or that they amount to 'rights of custody',[154] and cases have been lost because the plaintiff's advisers have failed to prepare their case properly.

Evidence

21.66   While it is sensible to give some general background in an affidavit in order to explain the reason for the removal or retention and to set the actions of the abductor in context (and in a sympathetic light insofar as that may be possible), it needs to be remembered that it is very unlikely that oral evidence will be given, and so the evidence should be focused on the real issues in the case (ie the matters which go directly to the defences and anything which might give rise to the need for the plaintiff to give undertakings, without which it would be possible to establish that a return would place the child in an intolerable situation[155] or that the circumstances in Art 10(1)(a) or Art 10(1)(b)[156] of the 1980 European Custody Convention exist). Long, irrelevant affidavits will not assist a defendant, and there is the risk that the good points will lose some of their force. Nor should a defendant adduce affidavit after affidavit to the same effect.[157]

21.67   Independent evidence going to the relevant issues is always more potent, and should be adduced if it is available.[158] An extension of time for filing the affidavit evidence should be sought if information has to be

---

[151]   The Legal Services Commission's Funding Code Decision Making Guidance, para 20.24, 'Special Cases', in *The Legal Services Manual,* Part C, para 3C–287(6).
[152]   See **21.38**.
[153]   See **21.48**.
[154]   See **14.23**.
[155]   As to Art 13(b) of the 1980 Hague Abduction Convention, see **17.84**.
[156]   As to Art 10 of the 1980 European Custody Convention, see **19.107**.
[157]   *Re C (Abduction: Consent)* [1996] 1 FLR 414.
[158]   As, for example, in *Re S (Abduction: Children: Separate Representation)* [1997] 1 FLR 486 (evidence filed from the child's doctor in New Zealand).

obtained from abroad. If it is necessary to obtain advice on foreign law, the choice of the foreign expert should be made with considerable care. If the child's views are relevant, consideration needs to be given as to whether and how those views can be ascertained most effectively and transmitted to the court.[159] A direction for the interviewing of the child by a children and family reporter or child psychiatrist should preferably be sought at the second hearing.[160]

21.68   It is rare for a defendant successfully to resist an application for return under the 1980 Hague Abduction Convention or for enforcement under the 1980 European Custody Convention.[161] The Hague Convention encourages an amicable resolution of the issues,[162] and the court will look favourably on attempts to settle future of the child, either long-term or short-term, without the necessity of a contested hearing, so where an order for return or enforcement of the foreign order seems inevitable, the main focus of the defendant's advisers should be on a voluntary return with proper safeguards for the child (and the abductor if she or he is the primary carer). Thought should be given well before the final hearing as to how the return can be arranged so as to provide maximum protection, and a 'wish list' of undertakings or conditions compiled to be put to the plaintiff.[163]

Interim powers

21.69   Although cases broadly follow the same pattern, the circumstances of the child and the parties may be very different, and in Convention cases the High Court can give interim directions to secure the welfare of a child or prevent changes in the circumstances relevant to the determination of the application or its subsequent enforcement.[164] The court may use its interim powers in respect of a child who has not yet arrived but is expected to do so.[165] Interim directions may include orders for direct or indirect contact.[166]

---

[159]   See **21.88** as to the position of the child.

[160]   *Re M (Minors) (Abduction)* [1992] 2 FCR 608, Sir Stephen Brown P; *Re S (Abduction: Children: Separate Representation)* [1997] 1 FLR 486.

[161]   See **17.1** *et seq* and **19.107** *et seq*.

[162]   See Arts 7(c) and 10 discussed at **13.31**.

[163]   See **17.123** on undertakings. Many successful applications for permanent leave to remove are made after the return of a child has been ordered, and the manner in which an abductor accedes to the return of a child may have an important bearing on the success of any subsequent application for permanent leave to remove the child from the requesting State.

[164]   In cases under the 1980 Hague Abduction Convention, see Child Abduction and Custody Act 1985, s 5, and *Re D (A Minor) (Child Abduction) (Note)* [1989] 1 FLR 97. In cases under the 1980 European Custody Convention, see Child Abduction and Custody Act 1985, s 19. The court may also use its inherent powers. As to procedure on an application for interim directions, see FPR 1991, r 6.13.

[165]   *Re N (Child Abduction: Jurisdiction)* [1995] Fam 95, sub nom *A v A (Abduction: Jurisdiction)* [1995] 1 FLR 341 (the child was on a plane flying to England; it was ordered that the child be placed in the interim care of the mother on arrival in England).

[166]   See **21.62**. Possible orders (insofar as they have not been made earlier in a passport order, location order or collection order (see **21.44** *et seq*)) are: an order requiring the abductor not to change the child's residence from the place where it was when the child was found; an

The court has power to strike out applications under the 1980 Hague Abduction Convention which are not pursued expeditiously.[167]

Preparations for the final hearing

21.70 *Re W (Abduction: Procedure)*[168] sets out the administrative procedures to be followed in applications for return orders, which reflect the recent Practice Directions for family business.[169] Indexed and paginated bundles should be produced, as should skeleton arguments.[170] Directions to provide for these should be given at the second or subsequent hearings.

The final hearing

Burden of proof

21.71 Although it has been said that proceedings under the 1980 Hague Abduction Convention are *sui generis,* being neither adversarial nor inquisitorial,[171] the burden is usually regarded as being on the plaintiff to show that the case falls within the Convention.[172] So it must be demonstrated that the child was habitually resident in a Contracting State immediately before the removal or retention,[173] that the plaintiff has 'rights of custody' within

---

order restraining the abductor from removing the child from England and Wales; an order requiring the abductor not to leave England and Wales; an order requiring the abductor to surrender the abductor's and the child's passports and other travel documents, which are then to be held by the solicitor for the abductor or for the plaintiff to the order of the court or sometimes by the Tipstaff; in the exceptional case where the court fears that the abductor will not obey the interim orders preserving the status quo and will further abduct the child, the court will order that the child be removed temporarily from the abductor and be placed in England and Wales with the plaintiff (if available) or some other person. See *B v B (Injunction: Restraint on Leaving Jurisdiction)* [1997] 3 All ER 258 at 263 (normal to order that until the hearing the defendant does not leave England and Wales and does surrender his or her passport).

167 *Re G (Abduction: Striking Out Application)* [1995] 2 FLR 410. As to the need for expedition, see also **21.22**.

168 [1995] 1 FLR 878. And see *B v B (Court Bundles: Video Evidence)* [1994] 1 FLR 323.

169 *President's Direction (Family Proceedings: Court Bundles)* (10 March 2000) [2000] 1 FLR 536.

170 Note *Practice Direction (Judgments: Form and Citation)* (11 January 2001) [2001] 1 WLR 194.

171 *Re N (Child Abduction: Habitual Residence)* [1993] 2 FLR 124, CA, per Balcombe LJ: 'This is not either adversarial or inquisitorial litigation. The litigation is sui generis'; per Mann LJ: 'The misdirection fails to appreciate that there is an obligation upon the court imposed by Art 12 in the circumstances to which it is applicable and that accordingly and consequentially there is an obligation to determine, amongst other things, habitual residence upon the evidence before the court. In making that determination I regard rules relating to the onus of proof as inapposite'.

172 *Re F (A Minor) (Child Abduction)* [1992] 1 FLR 548 at 554A, CA. As to the approach to the determination of the factual issue of habitual residence in wardship, see also *Re R (Wardship: Child Abduction)* [1992] 2 FLR 481, CA, and *Re R (Wardship: Child Abduction) (No 2)* [1993] 1 FLR 249.

173 Art 4. *Re H (Minors) (Abduction: Acquiescence)* [1998] AC 72, [1997] 2 WLR 563, [1997] 1 FLR 872, HL.

the meaning of Arts 3 and 5,[174] and that the child was removed in breach of those rights.[175]

21.72 The burden is on the defendant to establish the matters under Art 13(a)[176] or Art 13(b).[177] This burden is placed on the defendant to ensure that the underlying purpose of the Convention is carried out, that is that the child is to be summarily returned unless the abductor can prove that the other parent has consented to the removal or retention or that one of the other matters which give the court a discretion as to the decision exists.[178] The doctrine of issue estoppel may be available where there has been a prior adjudication in another country of a truly identical issue.[179]

Foreign law

21.73 Unless the defendant is prepared to make an admission, foreign law has to be proved. It is not enough simply to aver in the originating summons or the affidavit in support that the plaintiff has rights of custody or that the removal breached them. However, the 1980 Hague Abduction Convention does contain some provisions intended to simplify providing evidence of the law in the requesting State.[180] One of the duties of a Central Authority is to 'provide information of a general character as to the law of their State in connection with the application of the Convention'.[181] An application to a Central Authority may contain 'a certificate or an affidavit emanating from a Central Authority, or other competent authority of the State of the child's habitual residence, or from a qualified person, concerning the relevant law of that State',[182] and any such document appended to an application is both admissible[183] and sufficient evidence of anything stated in it.[184] More importantly, Art 14 enables the judicial or administrative authorities of the

---

[174] See **14.23**.

[175] *Re M (Abduction: Acquiescence)* [1996] 1 FLR 315 (the onus was on the father to show that the removal was in breach of his custody right; he had failed to do so and his application for return under the Convention failed); *Re C (Abduction: Consent)* [1996] 1 FLR 414.

[176] *Re H (Minors) (Abduction: Acquiescence)* (above).

[177] *Re E (A Minor) (Abduction)* [1989] 1 FLR 135 at 143, CA. As to the necessity for the plaintiff to file evidence in rebuttal, see *Re F (A Minor) (Abduction: Custody Rights Abroad)* [1995] Fam 224, sub nom *Re F (Child Abduction: Risk if Returned)* [1995] 2 FLR 31, CA (in many cases the absence of evidence from the plaintiff would cause a court to hesitate to find the Art 13(b) threshold crossed, but in this case the evidence of the abducting parent would be treated as true, since the allegations affected the child, there had been an opportunity to rebut them and the consequences for the child on the evidence were potentially very serious; appeal allowed and return refused under Art 13(b)).

[178] Per Lord Browne-Wilkinson in *Re H (Minors) (Abduction: Acquiescence)* (above). See also the Professor Pérez-Vera's Explanatory Report, paras 34 and 114.

[179] *Re L (Abduction: Pending Criminal Proceedings)* [1999] 1 FLR 433, Wilson J.

[180] The general provisions about evidence, eg Art 30 and Child Abduction and Custody Act 1985, s 7 (see below), apply equally to proof of foreign law.

[181] Article 7(e). As to the duties of Central Authorities, see **13.1** *et seq*.

[182] Article 8(e) and (f).

[183] Article 30.

[184] Child Abduction and Custody Act 1985, s 7(3).

requested State to take direct notice of the law of the State of the child's habitual residence and of judicial decisions (formally recognised or not), 'without recourse to the specific procedures for the proof of that law or for the recognition of foreign decisions which would otherwise be applicable'. In addition, Child Abduction and Custody Act 1985, s 7(1) reverses the usual burden of proof by providing that a duly authenticated copy of the decision or determination shall be deemed to be true copy unless the contrary is shown.[185]

21.74 Finally, Art 15 enables the authorities of the requested State to ask the applicant to get a declaration that the removal or retention was wrongful within the meaning of Art 3.[186]

21.75 An application for recognition and enforcement under the 1980 European Custody Convention must be accompanied by a copy of the decision which 'satisfies the necessary conditions of authenticity' and, if applicable, any document which establishes in accordance with the law of the State of origin that it is enforceable. The condition for authenticity in the United Kingdom is a duly authenticated copy (that is, a copy which bears the seal of, or is signed by the judge or officer of, the authority), which proves the decision without more.[187]

Procedure at the final hearing

21.76 The form of the final hearing in a child abduction case reflects the summary and *sui generis* nature of the proceedings and the wholly documentary evidence. 'The case has to be viewed from the perspective of a quick appraisal of its essential features.'[188] To someone used to the formal minuet of the adversarial process it will seem curt and cursory, but it has to be remembered that skeleton arguments will have been filed summarising the arguments, and that the judge and the advocates are all used to dealing with these cases on almost a daily basis. The plaintiff opens the case, identifying the documents which support the essential elements of wrongful removal or retention as described above, and (if given the chance) then goes on the deal with the defence, explaining why it should not succeed. The issues in these cases are usually narrow, if complicated, and the hearing (subject to what is said below in those cases in which oral evidence is given) is likely to move rapidly to submissions on the key points – whether, for example, the child was habitually

---

[185] For these purposes, a copy is duly authenticated if it bears the seal, or is signed by a judge or officer, of the authority in question: Child Abduction and Custody Act 1985, s 7(2).

[186] The Convention uses the words 'decision or other determination'. As to declarations, see **15.1** *et seq*.

[187] Child Abduction and Custody Act 1985, s 22.

[188] Per Waite LJ in *Re M (Minors) (Abduction: Non-Convention Country)* [1995] 1 FLR 89 at 90 (application for the return of a child to Italy, at the time not a Contracting State to the 1980 Hague Abduction Convention. Note that this case was decided at a time when Convention principles were applied by analogy to non-Convention cases). See also *Re B (Minors) (Abduction) (No 2)* 1993] 1 FLR 993, in which Waite J said at 998H, 'time does not allow for more than a quick impression gained on a panoramic view of the evidence' (oral evidence was given and had enabled court to gain insight into the personalities of the parents).

resident in the requesting State[189] at the time of removal or retention, or whether the defendant's evidence about the circumstances to which the child would be returned would cross the very high threshold set to establish an exception under Art 13(b) of the 1980 Hague Abduction Convention.[190]

Other jurisdictions[191]

21.77 The courts of other Contracting States have upheld the practice of dealing with these cases expeditiously and summarily. In so doing, they comply with the obligation under Art 2 to secure the objects of the Convention using 'the most expeditious procedures available'. The US Court of Appeals for the Sixth Circuit held in *March v Levine*[192] that the Federal District Court did not exercise its discretion wrongly when it granted the father's petition for return of the children without first allowing the defendant grandparents a chance for discovery or an evidentiary hearing in order to develop their defences. The District Court had considered voluminous written evidence, and decided that the petitioner had made out his case; it did not permit discovery or oral evidence before deciding summarily to order a return. The Court of Appeals observed that the Convention itself had a number of provisions to help ensure that applications for return are handled so that swift return is possible;[193] likewise the United States' implementing legislation, the International Child Abduction Remedies Act (ICARA),[194] repeatedly uses the word 'prompt' to describe the nature of the proceedings for return of a child wrongfully removed or retained and, like the Convention, ICARA provides a generous authentication rule. It observed that:

> 'Expeditious rulings are critical to ensure that the purpose of the treaty – prompt return of wrongfully removed or retained children – is fulfilled …'

Oral evidence

21.78 The parties have no right to call oral evidence, and the court's discretion to allow it should be used sparingly.[195] An application for oral evidence should be made at the first inter partes directions hearing. If the application is allowed, directions will be given requiring the attendance of the parties at the final hearing and limiting the issues to which the oral

---

[189] See, for example, *Re N (Abduction: Habitual Residence)* [2000] 2 FLR 899.

[190] See **17.84**.

[191] See also Chapter 22.

[192] 6th Cir, No 00–6326/6551, 19 April 2001.

[193] 'For example, the treaty sets forth generous rules regarding authentication of documents and judicial notice: Art 14. The treaty further provides rights to petitioners when a decision is not rendered within a mere six weeks of filing their petition. Hague Convention, Art 11. Importantly, the treaty also provides that a court may order return of a child at any time, notwithstanding proof of treaty defenses. Hague Convention, Art 18 ("The provisions of this Chapter [pertaining to return of children] do not limit the power of a judicial or administrative authority to order the return of the child at any time.").'

[194] 42 USC 11601; see also below at **22.37**.

[195] *Re E (A Minor) (Abduction)* [1989] 1 FLR 135; *Re F (A Minor) (Child Abduction)* [1992] 1 FLR 548; *Re K (Abduction: Child's Objections)* [1995] FLR 977.

evidence will go and the time allowed for it. But it should be made clear that whether oral evidence will be adduced at the final hearing is a matter for the trial judge. In practice,[196] when a defence of consent or acquiescence is raised under Art 13(a) of the 1980 Hague Abduction Convention, the court may well order oral evidence, limited to those issues. Oral evidence is rarely given where a defence under Art 13(b) is raised.[197]

The resolution of conflicting affidavit and other non-oral evidence

21.79 The court may have to resolve disputed affidavit and other non-oral evidence.[198] The court will look to see if there is independent extraneous evidence in support of one side or the other on the issue in question;[199] that evidence must be compelling before the sworn evidence of a deponent can be rejected. The court will also consider whether the evidence contained in the affidavit is inherently improbable and therefore sufficiently unreliable to be rejected. If there are no grounds for rejecting the written evidence on either side, the party on whom the burden lies will have failed to discharge the burden of proof on the issue.[200]

Special rules of evidence under the Hague and European Conventions

21.80 In addition to the rules about proof of foreign law, the 1980 Hague Abduction Convention and the Child Abduction and Custody Act 1985 contain provisions which apply to evidence generally, and are intended to speed up the proceedings. In ascertaining whether there has been a wrongful removal or retention within the meaning of Art 3, the judicial or administrative authorities of a requested State may take direct notice of the law of, and judicial or administrative decisions (whether or not formally recognised) in, the State of habitual residence of the child, without recourse to the specific procedures for the proof of that law or for the recognition of foreign decisions which would otherwise be applicable.[201] Any application

---

[196] This is borne out by an examination of the decided cases.

[197] See *Re M (Abduction: Leave to Appeal)* [1999] 2 FLR 550, CA (permission to appeal was refused from a decision by the trial judge after hearing oral evidence that Art 13(b) established; if there had not been oral evidence, Butler-Sloss LJ would have been inclined to give permission to appeal).

[198] *Re F (A Minor) (Child Abduction)* [1992] 1 FLR 548. See also *V v B (A Minor) (Abduction)* [1991] 1 FLR 266 at 273H–274E.

[199] *V v B* (above) (report dealing with the social background of the child in Australia to which the court had regard under Art 13 contradicted the defendant's assertions in affidavit; the defendant failed to establish 'grave risk' under Art 13(b)).

[200] *Re E (A Minor) (Abduction)* [1989] 1 FLR 135.

[201] Article 14. A decision or determination of a judicial or administrative authority outside the United Kingdom may be proved by a duly authenticated copy of the decision or determination; and any document purporting to be such a copy shall be deemed to be a true copy unless the contrary is shown; for these purposes a copy is duly authenticated if it bears the seal, or is signed by a judge or officer, of the authority in question: Child Abduction and Custody Act 1985, s 7(1), (2). Any such document as is mentioned in Art 8 of the Convention, or a certified copy of any such document, is sufficient evidence of anything stated in it: *ibid*, s 7(3). As to Art 8, see **21.12**.

submitted to the Central Authority for England and Wales or directly to the High Court in accordance with the terms of the Convention, together with documents and any other information appended thereto or provided by a Central Authority,[202] is admissible.[203] In considering the circumstances referred to in Art 13, the High Court must take into account the information relating to the social background of the child provided by the Central Authority or other competent authority of the child's habitual residence.[204]

21.81 Article 23 makes it clear that no legalisation or other formality may be required in the context of the Convention, although this does not contradict the requirement in Art 8(e) that decisions or agreements should be authenticated, a provision simply to ensure that copies correspond to the originals.[205]

21.82 In proceedings under the 1980 European Custody Convention, a decision of a judicial or administrative authority outside the United Kingdom may be proved by an authenticated copy, and a document provided in accordance with Art 13 may be accepted as sufficient evidence of anything stated in it.[206]

The child as a party to the proceedings

21.83 Family Proceedings Rules 1991, r 6.5 does not preclude the court from making the child a party, but it is rare for the child to be separately represented in Convention cases or, indeed, in non-Convention cases. In cases under the 1980 Hague Abduction Convention there must be some exceptional reason why the child's objections to a return cannot be communicated by one of the existing parties or a children and family reporter.[207] In *Re M (A Minor) (Abduction)*,[208] for example, the issue was between the child and the mother (who was represented), rather than between the mother and the father (who was not represented), and therefore the child's objections could only be effectively communicated to court through his separate representation. It

---

[202] See Art 8 and the third para of Art 13.

[203] Article 30. See also **21.73–21.75**.

[204] Third paragraph of Art 13; *V v B (A Minor) (Abduction)* [1991] 1 FLR 266.

[205] See the Pérez-Vera Report, paras 101 and 131. Note the observation that any requirement of the internal law of the authorities in question that copies or private documents be authenticated remains outside the scope of Art 23.

[206] Child Abduction and Custody Act 1985, s 22.

[207] *Re M (A Minor) (Child Abduction)* [1994] 1 FLR 390, CA (separate representation should be permitted only rarely; compelling grounds needed); *Re S (Abduction: Children: Separate Representation)* [1997] 1 FLR 486; *Re HB (Children's Objections)* [1998] 1 FLR 422, CA; *Re P (Abduction: Minor's Views)* [1998] 2 FLR 825, CA (the child given leave by Wall J to appeal against an order for return made by consent; the appeal was allowed and the application remitted for rehearing on the issue of the child's objections). For an example of the separate representation of the child in Hague Convention proceedings in Australia, see *Turner v Turner* 27 June 1988, Lambert J, Family Court of Australia. As to the child's objections, see generally **17.141** *et seq.*

[208] [1994] 2 FLR 126.

could be that, for some reason, the child's views would be inadequately conveyed by a party or by a children and family reporter, or at the hearing to decide his long-term future the child is likely to be represented, or that the child himself wishes to put forward a defence (for example, under Art 13(b)) independently to that of the abductor.[209]

21.84 The same approach applies to ascertaining the child's wishes and feelings for the purposes of Art 10(1)(b) of the 1980 European Custody Convention[210] or for the purposes of the welfare checklist in a non-Convention case.[211] There must also be an arguable case that the child's views will have an effect on the outcome of the application.[212] The child may be given leave to be joined as a party for the purpose of seeking permission to appeal and appealing.[213]

21.85 The provisions in FPR 1991, r 9.2A enabling competent minors to begin, prosecute or defend family proceedings without a next friend or guardian ad litem apply only to proceedings under the Children Act 1989 and the inherent jurisdiction;[214] therefore, a child the subject of proceedings joined as defendant must be represented by a guardian ad litem, regardless of his

---

[209] *Re S (Abduction: Children: Separate Representation)* [1997] 1 FLR 486 and *Re L (A Minor) (Abduction: Jurisdiction)* [2002] EWHC 1864 (Fam), [2002] 1 WLR 3208, [2002] 2 FLR 1042.

[210] Before reaching a decision under Art 10(1)(b), the court is required to ascertain the child's views unless this is impracticable having regard to his age and understanding: Art 15. In an application brought under the European Convention, the court applies the same test for joining a child as that laid down in the cases under the Hague Convention: see *Re T (Abduction: Appointment of Guardian ad litem)* [1999] 2 FLR 796 (notwithstanding the direction that a court welfare officer report on the girl's wishes and views, on her maturity and understanding and on her existing and proposed living arrangements, the girl aged 14½ was joined as a party and a solicitor appointed as her guardian ad litem; her mother did not know all the circumstances of the girl's life, the girl had her own perception of events and she needed her own advice). As to the child's objections generally, see **19.111**.

[211] When considering whether a summary return to his home country or a more detailed investigation of his future in England and Wales would best serve the child's welfare, the court is required to have regard to the ascertainable wishes and feelings of the child considered in the light of his age and understanding: Children Act 1989, s 1(3)(a).

[212] *Re S (Abduction: Children: Separate Representation)* [1997] 1 FLR 486.

[213] *Re HB (Abduction: Children's Objections)* [1998] 1 FLR 422, CA (order made by Hale J ([1997] 1 FLR 392) for return of 11-year-old girl to Denmark; child refused to return; mother took no steps to enforce order for 7 months; child obtained leave to be joined for purpose of appealing order for return; appeal allowed and case remitted to Hale J to exercise court's discretion whether to return; per Thorpe LJ: 'This case illustrates only too vividly the enormous price that is paid when children are permitted to litigate, particularly when, as here, the parent is effectively passing the legal aid baton onto the child who thereafter takes up the running against the other parent ... I am strongly of the view that C should be demobilised from this war to become the mother's child and not her mother's adversary'). As to the subsequent hearing remitted to Hale J, see *Re HB (Abduction: Children's Objections) (No 2)* [1998] 1 FLR 564 (Convention application dismissed and Official Solicitor appointed to act for the child in wardship proceedings).

[214] FPR 1991, r 9.1(3).

competence (that is his ability, having regard to his understanding, to give instructions in relation to the proceedings).[215]

Ascertaining the child's objections – Article 13 of the 1980 Hague Abduction Convention

21.86 The court has a discretion both as to whether the evidence presented to it appears insufficient to enable it to make a decision on the questions involved in the issue of the child's objections, and as to whether further investigations should be made; the court is not bound to investigate further merely because the issue has been raised.[216] Usually a children and family reporter[217] will be asked to ascertain the child's views and to assess his or her maturity.[218] There is an advantage in the involvement of a children and family reporter over the separate representation of the child in that he or she can perform the dual role of assessment and conveying the child's views to the court.[219] In an appropriate case, which will be rare, the court will give leave for this task to be carried out by a child psychiatrist.[220] Any application for the children to be interviewed by a children and family reporter or child psychiatrist should be made at the first inter partes directions hearing.[221] In cases of urgency, the duty family reporter may be invited by the court to perform these duties at short notice, very often on the day of the hearing itself.

The order

21.87 The 1980 Hague Abduction Convention does not expressly state where or to whom the child is to be returned, but it has been held that the return contemplated is a return to the country of the child's habitual residence before the removal or retention,[222] although it is suggested that this is too

---

215 See **21.32**.

216 *P v P (Minors) (Child Abduction)* [1992] 1 FLR 155 at 160–161; *Re M (A Minor) (Child Abduction)* [1994] 1 FLR 390, CA (dictum in *P v P* approved).

217 Formerly a court welfare officer.

218 *Re S (Minors) (Abduction: Acquiescence)* [1994] 1 FLR 819 at 836, CA (two-stage approach: (1) does the child object, and has he or she attained an age and degree of maturity at which it is appropriate to take account of his views?; and (2) if the answer is yes, consider whether as a matter of discretion to refuse to order return; the child may be questioned by a suitably skilled and independent person to discover how far the child is capable of understanding and whether he does in fact understand the implications of his objection).

219 *Re M (A Minor) (Child Abduction)* [1994] 1 FLR 390, CA.

220 *Re R (Child Abduction: Acquiescence)* [1995] 1 FLR 716, CA.

221 *Re M (Minors) (Abduction)* [1992] 2 FCR 608; *Re S (Abduction: Children: Separate Representation)* [1997] 1 FLR 486.

222 See the Preamble to the Convention: 'Desiring to protect children internationally from the harmful effects of their wrongful removal or retention and to establish procedures to ensure their prompt return to the State of their habitual residence, as well as to secure protection for rights of access', and see also *Re A (A Minor) (Abduction)* [1988] 1 FLR 365 at 373B–C, CA. See generally **16.5** *et seq.*

narrow a view.[223] In practice, the order usually requires that the child be returned forthwith to a named country, which is the country where he or she was habitually resident before the wrongful removal or retention. Although the order should provide for the return of the child 'forthwith',[224] in practice some leeway is permitted as to the date of return where the interests of the child require it, and the parties are often given the opportunity to reach agreement on the precise date. with the court setting a date in default of agreement. If such a course is adopted, care should be taken to ensure that appropriate orders and injunctions are in place to prevent the child being moved on to another State pending the implementation of the order.[225] Undertakings are regularly sought and proffered to allay any fear that the child might be at risk of harm.[226]

21.88 The extent to which the return order will contain details of how the return is to be effected will depend on the circumstances of the case. Some orders may be very precise, setting out specific travel arrangements, including itineraries and flight times, so as to avoid any question of frustration, delay or further abduction. In Australia, where the regulations provide that a return order can contain directions as to how the return is to be effected,[227] the following typical examples of problems raised by abductors have been identified: refusing to hand over documentation to enable the child to leave Australia and re-enter the requesting State; refusing to share information about the arrangements for return to, or for the child in, the requesting State; insisting on a long return date for the abductor's own convenience; and 'disagreeing with every conceivable aspect of the mechanics of the return

---

[223] Paragraph 110 of the Pérez Vera Report states that the Convention's silence on this matter is to be understood as allowing the court to order a return directly to the applicant regardless of the latter's present place of residence. See also *Re L (Abduction: Pending Criminal Proceedings)* [1999] 1 FLR 433.

[224] See Appendix 4.

[225] Specific provision should be made to avoid any possibility that earlier orders made in support of the originating summons might be regarded as having been automatically discharged on its determination. Note that a removal of a child after the making of a return order might well not constitute a 'wrongful removal' within the meaning of Arts 3 and 5, because the child would probably not be regarded as being habitually resident in the United Kingdom.

[226] See **17.123**.

[227] Family Law (Child Abduction Convention) Regulations 1986, reg 15(1)(b). In *DM v Director-General, Department of Community Services* [1998] Fam CA 1557, (1998) FLC 92–831, the Full Court of the Family Court of Australia emphasised the importance of making appropriate orders to secure the child following an order for return. In other cases, the Family Court of Australia has made, as part of the return order, an order that the child attend a counselling session with a family court counsellor so that the reasons for the decision could be explained: see *Director-General, Department of Families, Youth and Community Care v Newham* (unreported) 5 December 1997, and *Director-General, Department of Families, Youth and Community Care v McCartney* (unreported) 8 June 1997. As to practice in Australia, see generally **22.1**.

proposed by the Central Authority ...'.[228] To address these problems, orders which might be made include: the passports of the child and the abductor (if returning with the child) being retained by the plaintiff's solicitors and only being handed to the abductor at the point of, and very shortly before, departure; requiring the abductor to contact the police or the Tipstaff on a regular basis pending return; and continuing existing injunctions restraining removal pending departure or making fresh injunctions.[229]

21.89 Voluntary returns whilst proceedings are in progress are not uncommon, and orders should not be drafted so that the possibility of a voluntary return is excluded, especially if a foreign court has made an order requiring the return of the child.[230]

Effect of Convention orders

21.90 Where an order is made for return of a child under the 1980 Hague Abduction Convention, any custody order[231] relating to him ceases to have effect.[232]

21.91 Where a decision with respect to a child (other than a decision relating to rights of access) is registered under the 1980 European Custody Convention,[233] any care or supervision order, residence order or order giving care and control within wardship[234] relating to him ceases to have effect.[235]

---

[228] From 'Issues Surrounding Safe Return of the Child (and the Custodial Parent)', a paper by the Delegation from the Commonwealth of Australia, A Common Law Judicial Conference on International Child Custody, Washington DC, 18–21 September 2000.

[229] Australian suggestions, *op cit* at n 227 above, include an order requiring the abductor to sign all necessary documentation to allow the child to leave the requested State and re-enter the requesting State (together with a provision enabling the Registrar to sign the documents if the abductor refuses to do so) and an order requiring the abductor to enter into a recognisance or bond forfeitable if the child is not returned in accordance with the terms of the order.

[230] An appropriate form of words might be: 'Nothing in paragraph [ ] above precludes the father/mother from complying, pursuant to arrangements which may have been made in advance between the solicitors for the parties, with the order for the return of the child to [place] made in the [court] on [date]'. In contrast to the English practice of ordering a return to the requesting State, and not to a particular place or person, an order enabling compliance with an order made in the requesting State could provide for either.

[231] Ie a care or supervision order, a residence order, an order giving care and control within wardship or any similar orders under the pre-Children Act 1989 legislation: Child Abduction and Custody Act 1985, s 27(1) and Sch 1, paras 1–4.

[232] Child Abduction and Custody Act 1985, s 25(1)(a).

[233] *Ibid*, s 16.

[234] Ie a 'custody order', as defined in Child Abduction and Custody Act 1985, s 27.

[235] *Ibid*, s 25(1).

Costs

21.92   In family proceedings governed by the FPR 1991[236] and proceedings in the Family Division, the powers of the court in relation to orders for costs and the procedure for determining the amount of any costs payable are governed by Parts 43, 44 (except rr 44.9 to 44.12), 47 and 48 of the Civil Procedure Rules 1998 and the Practice Direction about Costs which supplements those Parts. However, the general rule that the unsuccessful party will be ordered to pay the costs of the successful party[237] does not apply in such proceedings, either at first instance[238] or on appeal.[239]

21.93   It is unusual to order costs in a children case, and the general rule is that where both parties have been reasonable in their approach to the dispute there should be no order as to costs.[240] Nevertheless, exceptions are made, and an order for costs may well be made against a party when, for example, his or her conduct has been reprehensible, or his or her stance in the proceedings has been unreasonable, or there is a marked disparity in wealth.[241] The circumstances of a child abduction case may well bring it within the 'exceptional' category so far as the conduct of the abductor is concerned.[242] However, often, orders for costs are not made in circumstances where they probably should be, particularly where the abductor is in receipt of public funding or has few financial resources and an order for costs would only add to the difficulties to be faced by the abductor (and child, where the abductor is the primary carer) on return to the child's home country. It is unlikely that an applicant whose application was made through a Central Authority would be regarded as behaving or conducting the litigation in a manner such as would justify an order for costs being made against him.

21.94   Upon ordering the return of a child or issuing an order concerning rights of access under the 1980 Hague Abduction Convention, the court may, where appropriate, direct the person who removed or retained the child, or who prevented the exercise of rights of access, to pay necessary expenses incurred by or on behalf of the plaintiff, including travel expenses, any costs incurred or payments made for locating the child, the costs of legal

---

[236] That is, proceedings for which rules are made under s 40 of the Matrimonial and Family Proceedings Act 1984 which include proceedings under the Child Abduction and Custody Act 1985.

[237] CPR 1998, r 44.3(2).

[238] *Practice Direction (Family Division: Allocation of Cases: Costs)* (22 April 1999) [1999] 1 WLR 1128, [1999] 1 FLR 1295.

[239] CPR 1998, r 44.3(3).

[240] *Gojkovic v Gojkovic (No 2)* [1992] Fam 40 at 57C and 60C, CA, per Butler-Sloss LJ; *Keller v Keller and Legal Aid Board* [1998] 1 FLR 259, CA.

[241] *Keller v Keller and Legal Aid Board* (above); *R v R (Children Cases: Costs)* [1997] 2 FLR 95, CA; *Re B (Costs)* [1999] 2 FLR 221, CA; *Re G (Costs: Child Case)* [1999] 2 FLR 250, CA.

[242] For an example of the abductor being ordered to pay the costs, see *Re D (A Minor) (Child Abduction)* [1989] 1 FLR 97 (the child's whereabouts were kept hidden for 8 months by the abductor).

representation of the applicant, and those of returning the child.[243] So a party who abducts a child can be ordered to pay the costs of returning the child, even though he or she might be in receipt of public funding and would not otherwise face an order for the costs of the proceedings.[244]

Child abduction and the confidentiality of proceedings

21.95 Abduction proceedings occasionally raise an awkward tension between confidentiality and publicity. When a child is abducted and his whereabouts are unknown, the left-behind parent will try any means possible to find out where he is. This might include not only investigations by the police and Interpol, but also appeals to the public for information, using such diverse means as posters and notices on milk cartons and publicity in the mass media. Media appeals are often successful, and if they are, the newspapers and television companies will want to follow through the story.[245] So it is when the proceedings for the return of the child start that the difficulties arise, because the media will almost certainly want to publish information about them, and in England and Wales the extent to which they can do so is not entirely clear. This is a difficulty which can be exacerbated if there is extensive publicity in the country from which the child has been taken, and to which he may well be returned.

21.96 Non-Convention proceedings for the return of a child, under either the inherent jurisdiction or the Children Act 1989, are subject to the statutory restraints on the publication of information relating to such proceedings imposed by Administration of Justice Act 1960, s 12, Children Act 1989, s 97,[246] and FPR 1991, r 4.23. The scope of the restriction imposed by the Administration of Justice Act 1960 is quite narrow; unless the court makes an order to the contrary, it is not a breach of s 12, and therefore not a contempt, to publish the name of the child, the names and addresses of the parties and the witnesses or the text or summary of an order.[247] However, publishing such information might well be a criminal offence under Children Act 1989, s 97. Nevertheless, it has not been the practice to ask for injunctions restraining the

---

[243] Third paragraph of Art 26.

[244] *V v B (A Minor) (Abduction)* [1991] 1 FLR 266, per Sir Stephen Brown P; *Re D (A Minor) (Child Abduction)* [1989] 1 FLR 97. As to the automatic entitlement of an applicant to public funding in the form of legal representation in proceedings under the 1980 Hague Abduction and European Custody Conventions, see **21.15**.

[245] See **21.58**.

[246] As amended by Access to Justice Act 1999, s 72, which extended the scope of s 97(2)(a) to include the High Court and county courts. Proceedings under the inherent jurisdiction are 'family proceedings' in which the court can make orders under Children Act 1989, s 8, even if no application is made for such an order, so within its inherent jurisdiction the High Court may be able to exercise a power under the Children Act 1989 for the purposes of s 97: see Children Act 1989, ss 8(3) and 10(1)(b).

[247] Administration of Justice Act 1960, s 12(2); FPR 1991, r 4.23(1); *Re W and Others (Wards) (Publication of Information)* [1989] 1 FLR 246; *Re M and N (Minors) (Wardship: Publication of Information)* [1990] Fam 211, [1990] 1 FLR 149; and also the summary in *X v Dempster* [1999] 1 FLR 894 at 897 *et seq*, per Wilson J.

publication of the identity of the child who is the subject of non-Convention proceedings, although the court could make such an order in the exercise of its inherent jurisdiction.[248]

21.97 There does not seem to be any statutory restraint on the publication of information about proceedings under the Child Abduction and Custody Act 1985. Although such proceedings are heard in chambers,[249] that of itself is not sufficient to impose a restriction on publicising an account of the proceedings.[250] They are not mentioned in Administration of Justice Act 1960, s 12, which relates only to proceedings under the Children Act 1989, the inherent jurisdiction and proceedings which '(iii) otherwise relate wholly or mainly to the maintenance or upbringing of a minor'. It is doubtful if proceedings under the Child Abduction and Custody Act 1985 could be regarded as relating to the upbringing of the child in question.[251] However, this lack of a statutory confidentiality has not caused any real difficulty in abduction cases, because children's cases have always been regarded as being both private and confidential: 'The public is almost always excluded from children proceedings which almost invariably remain confidential, subject to judgments, made suitably anonymous in cases of wider interest, being given in public or made available for publication'.[252] In addition, in any case in which it was thought that some specific restraint was necessary, the High Court could exercise its inherent jurisdiction to make an appropriate order.[253]

Appeals

21.98 A decision to return a child made on an application under the 1980 Hague Abduction Convention is a final order not capable of variation save as to implementation; an application to set aside such an order should be by way of appeal to the Court of Appeal.[254] Since 1 January 1999, permission

---

248   *Re M and N (Minors) (Wardship: Publication of Information)* [1990] Fam 211, [1990] 1 FLR 149. It is the practice of the Court of Appeal (which sits in public) to make its 'usual direction' in children's cases restraining the publication of any information likely to identify the child who is the subject of the appeal.

249   FPR 1991, r 6.8.

250   For a summary of the law of confidentiality as it relates to proceedings in chambers, see *Clibbery v Allan and Another* [2001] 2 FLR 819, and *Clibbery v Allan* [2002] EWCA Civ 45, [2002] 1 FLR 565.

251   In *Re Z (A Minor) (Freedom of Publication)* [1997] Fam 1, [1996] 1 FLR 191, it was said that a question of upbringing is determined whenever the central issue before the court is one which relates to how the child is being reared, and in *Re S (Residence Order: Forum Conveniens)* [1995] 1 FLR 314, Thorpe J held that the choice between international forums is not a question with respect to the upbringing.

252   Per Butler-Sloss P in *Clibbery v Allen* (above) at [24].

253   Note that proceedings under the Child Abduction and Custody Act 1985 are not 'family proceedings' for the purposes of Children Act 1989, s 10: see s 8(3). So it would not be possible to make a prohibited steps order. And note that Part VI of the FPR 1991 contains no equivalent to r 4.23, which prohibits disclosure of documents held by the court and relating to proceedings under the Children Act 1989 (other than the record of an order).

254   See *Re M (A Minor) (Child Abduction)* [1994] 1 FLR 390, CA, and *Re M (Abduction: Undertakings)* [1995] 1 FLR 1021, CA. The same would seem to apply to orders enforcing a

to appeal has been required in cases involving child abduction.[255] In cases under the 1980 Hague Abduction Convention, the requirements of *Ladd v Marshall*[256] as to the admission of fresh evidence on appeal are usually relaxed.[257] Where there has been a more detailed hearing below, for example where oral evidence has been given, obtaining leave to appeal may be more difficult.[258] Applications for permission to appeal and appeals in abduction cases are heard quickly, and solicitors must ensure that the Deputy Master of Civil Appeals (responsible for Family Appeals and applications) or the Listng Manager in the Court of Appeal or, in the case of appeals to the House of Lords, the Principal Clerk or his Deputy, are told that the case involves international child abduction, so that arrangements can be made for the appeal to be expedited.[259]

The return of the child: enforcement of return orders

21.99   The order for the return of a child is expressed in terms that the child shall return 'forthwith' to the requesting State. In most cases, the return of the child causes no great difficulty. It is prudent and the common practice for the court to order that any interim orders continue in force until the child leaves the jurisdiction pursuant to the order for return.[260] If the abductor refuses to return with the child, the applicant will have to collect the child (or arrange for someone else to), unless the child can travel as an unaccompanied minor, and in the meantime, any interim restraints will remain in force or fresh orders will be made.[261] In extreme and unusual cases, where the

---

custody order under the 1980 European Custody Convention. An appeal lies to the Court of Appeal from the judgment or order of the High Court or the determination of the judge in the county court: see Supreme Court Act 1981, s 16 and County Court Act 1984, s 77. Note that there is no automatic extension of public funding for an appeal. The question of funding for an appeal has to be put to the Legal Services Commission, which will apply a 'merits' test.

[255] The position is now governed by Civil Procedure Rules 1998, Sch 1, RSC Ord 59, r 1B(1).

[256] [1954] 3 All ER 745, [1954] 1 WLR 1489.

[257] See *Re M (Abduction: Non-Convention Country)* [1995] 1 FLR 89 at 90G–H, CA (per Waite LJ: 'the relaxation is applied to the extent necessary to enable this court to determine whether there are any matters not dealt with at first instance which might have materially affected the judge's decision, had he been aware of them'); *Re M (Abduction: Undertakings)* (above). As to the admissibility of fresh evidence in the Court of Appeal in a non-Convention case, see *Re S (Minors) (Abduction)* [1993] 1 FCR 789, CA (rehearing ordered; Court of Appeal directed an investigation into the matters raised in the fresh evidence).

[258] See *Re M (Abduction: Leave to Appeal)* [1999] 2 FLR 550, CA (permission to appeal refused from decision made by trial judge after hearing oral evidence that Art 13(b) exception established; if there had not been oral evidence, Butler-Sloss LJ would have been inclined to have given permission to appeal).

[259] See **21.22** about the expectations as to time-scale, and *Re HB (Children's Objections)* [1998] 1 FLR 422, CA (per Thorpe LJ: importance of ensuring a target of 6 weeks between application and determination at first instance; in the event of appeal, a similar momentum should be achieved by the Court of Appeal).

[260] See **21.87** *et seq*.

[261] Eg requiring the (usually continuing) deposit of passports and travel documents, and forbidding the abductor from removing the child from the jurisdiction or applying for

abductor frustrates a return order, perhaps by concealing the child or by failing to comply with arrangements previously agreed, assistance in enforcing a return order may have to be sought from the Tipstaff in finding the child or otherwise helping to put the order into effect, or from the local authority in whose area the child is resident, perhaps to the extent of receiving him, possibly from the Tipstaff, and providing temporary accommodation until the child can be collected or put on a flight.

21.100 Funding the return of the child sometimes causes problems. Unusually, for a Contracting State to the 1980 Hague Abduction Convention, Australia makes public funds available for the return of children who have been wrongfully removed or retained away from its territory. If neither the wronged parent nor the abductor have the funds to meet the cost of travel, the return order will remain unexecuted, and may have to be discharged. It should be stressed, however, that whilst shortage of funds should be taken into account when considering whether to institute proceedings, it should not be a determining factor. The making of a return order may enable a parent to raise the necessary funds, by borrowing money or applying for help from charitable or other non-public funds.

21.101 In cases in which an abductor flees to another Contracting State after a return order has been made, there appears to be no mechanism within either the 1980 Hague Abduction Convention or the 1980 European Custody Convention[262] for directly enforcing an order made in another Contracting State. Fresh proceedings have to be instituted, in which the extent to which the defences can be raised will depend upon the extent to which they have been considered in the previous proceedings and the extent to which circumstances have changed.[263]

Discharge of a return order

21.102 There are occasions when it becomes impossible or undesirable to carry a return order into effect. The successful parent may not be able to fulfil the undertakings that he has given, or circumstances may change, or the child may express such a strong objection to return that it would be impossible to insist upon compliance with the order, or doing so would irreparably damage the relationship between the successful parent and the child. In such cases,

---

passports and travel documents. See **21.69**. The decision of the Court of Appeal in *Re C (A Child)* (unreported) 1 November 1999, CA, establishes that the court continues to have control over the return of the child until the implementation of the order. This control includes an ability to review the order for return (per Arden LJ in *TB v JB (Abduction: Grave Risk of Harm)* [2001] 2 FLR 515 at 542).

[262] Advice should always be taken from a local lawyer and/or the Central Authority to ascertain whether the first order can be enforced under the domestic law of the State to which the child has been further abducted.

[263] In *Re L (Abduction: Pending Criminal Proceedings)* [1999] 1 FLR 433, Wilson J said that the English High Court should apply the doctrine of issue estoppel to the prior adjudication in any other Contracting State of any issue under the 1980 Hague Abduction Convention which is truly identical.

return orders being 'final' orders, the only course is to apply to the Court of Appeal to set aside the return order, the High Court having no jurisdiction to do so.[264]

Applications for the registration or recognition of a judgment under the Council Regulation[265]

21.103 One of the most important principles of the so-called Brussels II Regulation is the automatic recognition by operation of law of judgments given in other Member States, even if those judgments do not involve cross-border issues. Judgments 'shall be recognised ... without any special procedure being required'.[266] However, 'any interested party' may apply for a decision that a judgment be or not be recognised.[267]

21.104 'Judgment' means a divorce, legal separation or marriage annulment, as well as a judgment 'relating to the parental responsibility of the spouses given on the occasion of such matrimonial proceedings'. It does not matter whether it is called a judgment, decree, order or decision, and it includes documents formally drawn up or registered (provided that they are enforceable) and enforceable settlements approved in the course of proceedings. It also includes orders dealing with costs and expenses.[268]

21.105 Whilst recognition is sufficient for judgments relating to status, enforcement of other recognisable orders made in other Member States is provided for in Art 21 of the Council Regulation; a judgment on the exercise of parental responsibility[269] which has been served and is enforceable in one

---

[264] *Re M (Minors) (Abduction: Undertakings)* [1995] 1 FLR 1021, CA. The same position would seem to apply to return orders made under the 1980 European Custody Convention. After the decision of the Court of Appeal in *TB v JB (Abduction: Grave Risk of Harm)* [2001] 2 FLR 515, attempts were made both to enforce and to set aside the order for the return of the children to New Zealand. In the event, despite the efforts of the Tipstaff and the child and family reporter, the children refused to leave the family home and the order remained unexecuted (see (2001) *The Times*, 18 May, p 4: 'Three children have defied an international Convention against child abduction by refusing to leave their British mother and board a plane to New Zealand'). And see *Re HB (Abduction: Children's Objections)* [1998] 1 FLR 422, where the child refused to board the aircraft, and *Re M (A Minor) (Child Abduction)* [1994] 1 FLR 390, in which, at the last moment, the mother refused to travel with the children who boarded the aircraft to Australia, but the elder child created a scene so violent that the captain refused to carry them.

[265] Council Regulation (EC) No 1347/2000 of 29 May 2000. See FPR 1991, Part VII, Chapter 5. As to the history of the Council Regulation and its jurisdictional rules, see **2.9**. And see Everall and Nicholls, 'Brussels I and II – the Impact on Family Law' [2002] Fam Law 674. Note that the interpretation of the Council Regulation is a matter for the ECJ: see generally Chapter 23.

[266] Article 14(1).

[267] Article 13(3). As to 'any interested party', see **18.19**.

[268] Article 13, see **18.13**.

[269] 'A judgment on the exercise of parental responsibility in respect of a child of both parties ...'. Note that the judgment must have been given on the occasion of matrimonial proceedings to fall within the definition in Art 13(1). Judgments made on other occasions are not recognisable and enforceable by way of the Council Regulation, but may fall within

Member State shall be enforced in another Member State when, on the application of 'any interested party', it has been declared enforceable there. But in the case of the United Kingdom, judgments are enforced not after a declaration of enforceability, but after they have been registered for enforcement in the appropriate part of the United Kingdom.[270]

Legal aid

21.106 Unlike applications under the 1980 Hague Abduction Convention or the 1980 European Custody Convention, applications for registration and enforcement under the Council Regulation do not qualify for legal representation at public expense, except to the extent that an applicant who benefited from complete or partial legal aid or exemption from costs or expenses in the Member State of origin shall be entitled to benefit from the most favourable legal aid or exemption from costs or expenses in the Member State in which recognition and enforcement is sought.[271]

Applications for recognition or registration

21.107 The process for applying for the recognition or registration of a 'judgment' within the meaning of Art 13[272] is set out in FPR 1991, Part VII, Chapter 5.[273] An application is made in the Principal Registry of the Family Division[274] without notice being given to any other party,[275] and must be supported by either a statement 'sworn to be true' or an affidavit stating:[276]

(i)   whether the judgment provides for the payment of a sum or sums of money;

(ii) whether interest is recoverable on the judgment or part thereof in accordance with the law of the State in which the judgment was given, and if such be the case, the rate of interest, the date from which interest is recoverable, and the date on which interest ceases to accrue,

and giving an address within the jurisdiction of the court for service of process on the party making the application and stating, so far as is known to the witness, the name and the usual or last known address or place of business

---

the provisions of the 1980 European Custody Convention. As to the proposals of the EU to extend the provisions of the Council Regulation to all orders relating to children, see **18.29** *et seq.*

[270] Article 21(2). As to registration and enforcement, see the remarks of Steyn LJ in *Re H (A Minor) (Foreign Custody Order: Enforcement)* [1994] 1 FLR 512.

[271] Article 30. Note that no security, bond or deposit may be required of an applicant for enforcement on the grounds that he is not habitually resident in the Member State in which enforcement is sought or is a foreign national or, in the case of the United Kingdom and Ireland, does not have his domicile there: Art 31.

[272] FPR 1991, r 7.40. FPR 1991, Part VII, Chapter 5 applies to authentic instruments and settlements to which Art 13(3) applies as it does to judgments, subject to any necessary modifications: see r 7.50.

[273] Inserted by SI 2001/821, and in effect from 1 April 2001.

[274] FPR 1991, r 7.41.

[275] *Ibid,* r 7.42. See Art 24.

[276] *Ibid,* r 7.43(1)(b)–(d).

of the person against whom judgment was given, and stating to the best of the information or belief of the witness:

(i) the grounds on which the right to enforce the judgment is vested in the party making the application;

(ii) as the case may require, either that at that date of the application the judgment has not been satisfied, or the part or amount in respect of which it remains unsatisfied.

21.108   The statement or affidavit must exhibit:[277]

'(i)   the judgment or a verified or certified or otherwise duly authenticated copy thereof together with such other document or documents as may be requisite to show that, according to the law of the Contracting State in which it has been given, the judgment is enforceable and has been served;

(ii)   in the case of a judgment given in default, the original or a certified true copy of the document which establishes that the party in default was served with the document instituting the proceedings or with an equivalent document;

(iii)   where it is the case, a document showing that the party making the application is in receipt of legal aid in the Contracting State in which the judgment was given;

(iv)   where the judgment or document is not in the English language, a translation thereof into English certified by a notary public or a person qualified for the purpose in one of the Contracting States or authenticated by witness statement or affidavit;

(v)   the certificate, in the form set out in Annex IV or Annex V of the Council Regulation, issued by the Contracting State in which judgment was given.'

21.109   The court does, however, have a discretion, if the applicant does not produce the documents, to fix a time within which they are to be produced, to accept equivalent documents or to dispense with their production.[278]

Applications for recognition only

21.110   In the case of applications for recognition, rather than registration, it is not necessary to produce documents which establish that, according to the law of the Contracting State in which it has been given, the judgment is enforceable and has been served or, where it is the case, a document showing that the party making the application is in receipt of legal aid in the Contracting State in which the judgment was given.[279]

Stays

21.111   Recognition proceedings may be stayed if an ordinary appeal against the judgment has been lodged.[280]

---

[277]   FPR 1991, r 7.43(1)(a).

[278]   *Ibid*, r 7.43(2).

[279]   *Ibid*, r 7.48(2).

[280]   Article 20, see **18.17**.

Grounds of non-recognition

21.112   The grounds of non-recognition are discussed in Chapter 18.[281]

The order

21.113   The order giving permission to register the judgment must be drawn by the court, and will state the period within which an appeal may be made, and that the court will not enforce the judgment until the expiry of that period (although that does not prevent the court taking protective measures in accordance with Art 12).[282]

The register of judgments

21.114   A register of judgments ordered to be registered under Art 21(2) of the Council Regulation is kept in the Principal Registry.[283] Registration serves as a decision that the judgment has been recognised for the purposes of Art 14(3).[284]

Notice of registration

21.115   Notice of the registration of a judgment must be served on the person against whom judgment was given by delivering it to him personally or by sending it to him at his usual or last-known address or place of business, or in such other manner as the court may direct. Permission is not required to serve a notice out of the jurisdiction, and FPR 1991, r 10.6 applies. The notice of the registration must state:

(a)   full particulars of the judgment registered and the order for registration;
(b)   the name of the party making the application and his or her address for service within the jurisdiction;
(c)   the right of the person against whom judgment was given to appeal against the order for registration; and
(d)   the period within which an appeal against the order for be made.[285]

Enforcing a judgment

21.116   There are no special means of enforcing a judgment. Article 23 of the Council Regulation provides that the procedure for applying for enforcement is governed by the law of the Member State in which enforcement is sought, although the applicant must give an address for service within the jurisdiction of the court applied to and provide the documents referred to in Arts 32 and 33.

---

[281]   See **18.13–18.17**.
[282]   FPR 1991, r 7.44(3).
[283]   *Ibid*, r 7.45.
[284]   *Ibid*, r 7.48(1).
[285]   *Ibid*, r 7.46.

21.117 Registered judgments may not be enforced until the time specified for appealing has expired,[286] although that does not prevent the court taking protective measures under Art 12.[287]

21.118 On an application for the enforcement of a registered judgment, the applicant must produce to the proper officer a witness statement or affidavit of service of the notice of registration of the judgment and of any order made by the court in relation to the judgment.[288]

Partial enforcement

21.119 Partial enforcement of a judgment is possible, so if a judgment deals with children some of whom are the children of both spouses and some of whom are not, that part of the judgment which relates to the children of both spouses can be enforced on request.[289]

---

[286] FPR 1991, r 7.47(1).
[287] *Ibid*, r 7.47(3). As to protective measures under Art 12, see **4.84**.
[288] *Ibid*, r 7.47(2).
[289] Article 29.

Chapter 22

INTERNATIONAL ABDUCTIONS: PRACTICE AND PROCEDURE UNDER THE HAGUE CONVENTION IN SELECTED OTHER JURISDICTIONS

AUSTRALIA[1]

22.1 Australia is a Federal nation consisting of six States and 10 Territories, and the Convention was ratified on 1 January 1987 on behalf of all six States and the two mainland Territories. Australia has accepted most acceding States to the Convention and, as of 1 August 2003, the Convention was in force between Australia and 69 other Contracting States.[2] The Convention was implemented at a Federal level through the Family Law (Child Abduction Convention) Regulations 1986[3] which rewrite the Convention. The use of Regulations to implement the Convention means that they are easier to amend and update. Important changes were made, for example, by the Family Law Amendment Act 2000. However, the fact that the Regulations do not always exactly repeat the text of the Convention is an unusual practice. Accordingly, decisions of Australian courts have to be read bearing in mind that they apply the Regulations and not the Convention.

22.2 Australia designated a Federal Central Authority known as the Commonwealth Central Authority, which is located in the International Family Law Section of the Family Branch of the Attorney General's Department in Canberra. All applications, both incoming and outgoing, are

---

[1] For further detail, see Lowe, Armstrong and Mathias, *Country Report: Australia* (NCMEC, 2002).

[2] See http://www.hcch.net/e/status/abdshte.html.

[3] Family Law (Child Abduction Convention) Regulations 1986, SR 1986 No 85, as amended.

processed by this Central Authority.[4] Additionally, there are Central Authorities in the States and relevant Territories.[5] No reservation was made to Art 24 of the Convention, and applications can therefore be received in English or French. The Commonwealth Central Authority will check that the application meets the requirements of the Convention and will then send it to the relevant Central Authority in Australia or to the foreign Central Authority if it is an outgoing application. There are a relatively high number of applications to and from Australia. In 1999, for example, there was a total of 172 applications, comprising 64 incoming return applications, 82 outgoing return applications, 14 incoming access applications and 13 outgoing access applications.[6]

22.3 Where there is an incoming application to Australia for return, the State Central Authority makes a preliminary decision as to whether it is appropriate to negotiate a voluntary return.[7] Even where it is considered appropriate to negotiate a voluntary agreement, the Central Authority may still obtain urgent ex parte restraining orders. These orders protect the Central Authority if the negotiations break down and the abducting parent tries to flee with the child. The orders may include interim orders, for example for the surrender of passports, preventing the removal of children from Australia, placing children's names on the airport 'watch list', for interim residence of the child and for the issue of warrants to apprehend children. A child may be removed from an abducting parent but only as a last resort. If a voluntary return is negotiated after obtaining these orders, the matter is resolved by consent orders for return. If it is not considered appropriate or if these measures fail, the Central Authority will forward the application to the Crown Solicitor to begin proceedings in court.[8] Under the implementing Regulations, jurisdiction to hear Convention cases is vested in both Federal and State

---

[4]   The Australian Commonwealth Central Authority makes great use of the Internet, and application forms, legislation and other information are available to view. The Central Authority also produces a booklet entitled *International Child Abduction: A Guide for Parents and Practitioners*. This can be obtained free of charge and provides information on procedures within Australia as well as other selected Contracting States.

[5]   See SR 1986 No 85, reg 8.

[6]   See Lowe, Armstrong and Mathias, 'A Statistical Analysis of Applications made in 1999 under the Hague Convention of 25 October 1980 on the Civil Aspects of International Child Abduction', Preliminary Document No 3 (Revised Version, November 2001) available on the Hague Conference website at http://www.hcch.net/e/conventions/reports28e.html (hereinafter referred to as 'the 1999 Statistical Survey'), and Lowe, Armstrong and Mathias, *Country Report: Australia* (NCMEC, 2002), at p 17 *et seq.*

[7]   In 1999, seven of the 64 incoming return applications resulted in a voluntary return, which, at 11% is below the global average of 18%. See the 1999 Statistical Survey.

[8]   According to the 1999 Statistical Survey, in 1999, 34 of the 64 return applications, representing 53%, went to court. Most of these cases, 26, resulted in an order to return the child which, at 41% of all return applications, is higher than the global average of 32%. In the remaining eight applications, return was refused which, at 13%, is also higher than the global average of 11%. Of the 14 incoming access applications, three were withdrawn, in four access was agreed, in three it was judicially granted, and in four it was judicially refused.

courts. The courts of first instance are the Family Court of Australia, the Family Court of Western Australia, the Federal Magistrates Service, and various courts of summary jurisdiction.

22.4 Generally,[9] appeals are heard by the Full Court of the Family Court of Australia, and further appeal is to the High Court of Australia. However, to appeal to the High Court, special leave is required or a certificate must be obtained from the Family Court stating that the matter involves an important question of law or of public interest.

22.5 Unusually, the Commonwealth Central Authority applies in its own name as the applicant in the proceedings. As far as the authors are aware, Australia is the only Contracting State where the Central Authority applies as the applicant. As the Central Authority is a repeat player in Convention litigation, Central Authority lawyers are able to build up expertise, and they also tend to apply only to the Family Court and the Family Court of Western Australia, thus effectively limiting the number of judges able to hear Convention cases to around 54.[10] While having the Central Authority as the applicant may in theory lead to a conflict of interests, in practice, the procedure appears to operate well. Generally, cases proceed by way of affidavit evidence, and applicants are not required to attend the hearing. The Convention obligation to act expeditiously in proceedings is reflected in reg 15(2) and (4).[11] Appeals are also expedited where possible.[12] The Regulations refer to numerous orders that the Central Authority may seek from the court with regard to enforcing the judicial decision. These include special powers to deal with contempt of court and contravention of orders. They also include the ability to seek '... any other order that the responsible Central Authority considers to be appropriate to give effect to the Convention ...'.[13]

22.6 No reservation was made to Art 26 and, consequently, where the Central Authority conducts legal proceedings, there is no charge to the applicant. In appropriate cases, costs associated with legal proceedings such as psychologist's reports, translations, and separate representation for the

---

[9] Where the first instance decision is made by a Judicial Registrar, appeal is to a single judge of the Family Court.

[10] Litigants applying directly to the courts remain free to apply to the magistrates' courts, but such applications are rare.

[11] According to the 1999 Statistical Survey, in 1999, decisions to return the child took a mean average of 91 days from initial application to conclusion. This is below the global average of 107 days. Conversely, decisions refusing return took an average of 220 days which is above the global average of 147 days.

[12] According to the 1999 Statistical Survey, in 1999, 12% of the return applications made to court were appealed, which is marginally below the global average of 14%. These cases took a mean average of 257 days to reach conclusion at final appellate level. Orders pending an appeal are commonly stayed if the status quo needs to be preserved.

[13] Regulation 14(1)(e).

child will also be covered by the Federal legal aid system.[14] Conversely, legislation permits private applications outside of the Central Authorities; however, in such cases, costs will not be covered by the State. Generally, repatriation costs for the child have to be paid by the person who has successfully sought return. However, the Central Authority may obtain an order directing that the necessary expenses incurred by or on behalf of the applicant, including travel expenses and the cost of locating the child, be paid by the respondent. The Family Law Amendment Act 2000 has strengthened the position of the applicant as regards obtaining orders for costs against the other party.[15] Legal aid is available to respondents in applications but on a means and merits test. Unusually, Australia also offers legal aid on a means and merits test to parents whose children have been removed from Australia. This may cover overseas legal fees and travel costs.

CANADA[16]

22.7 Canada is a Federal nation consisting of 10 Provinces and three Territories. It was one of the three original ratifying States, bringing the Convention into force in 1983. However, as family law comes within the constitutional jurisdiction of the Provinces and Territories, the Convention had to be implemented at a provincial level, and this process was completed throughout Canada by 1 April 1988. Canada has accepted most Contracting States who have acceded to the Convention and, as of 1 November 2003, the Convention was in force as between Canada and 68 other Contracting States.

22.8 Canada has designated a Federal Central Authority which is located in the Justice Legal Service Unit of the Department of Foreign Affairs. Additionally, there is a Central Authority in each Province and Territory. Generally, applications to Canada should be made to the Central Authority in the area where the child is believed to be. If the location of the child within Canada is not known, then the application should be sent to the Federal Central Authority. Applications are accepted in either English or French, although the Province of Quebec did make a reservation to Art 24 such that any application not already in English or French must be translated into French.[17] In 1999 Canada made and received a total of 103 applications, comprising 36 incoming return applications, 49 outgoing

---

[14] J Degeling, 'Provisions of Legal Representation in Hague Cases', presented at the Second International Forum on Parental Child Abduction, hosted by NCMEC at Alexandria, VA, United States, on 1–2 November 2000.

[15] Item 98, Sch 3 to the Family Law Amendment Act 2000.

[16] See generally Lowe, Armstrong and Mathias, *Country Report: Canada* (NCMEC, 2002).

[17] There are some useful Canadian websites which provide information to all those involved in issues relating to international child abduction, and there is a booklet available on the Internet containing detailed information on child abduction issues. See *International Child Abductions – A Manual for Parents*, available at: http://www.voyage.gc.ca/Consular-e/Publications/child_abductions-e.htm.

return applications, eight incoming access applications and 10 outgoing access applications.[18]

22.9 As the individual Provinces and Territories in Canada have implemented the Convention separately, procedure differs from one area to another. Generally, all Provinces and Territories will try to negotiate a voluntary return, either by sending a letter to the abductor, or by initiating mediation.[19] Where such negotiations fail or are inappropriate, legal proceedings will be commenced.[20] Most applicants in Canada are represented by private lawyers; however, in Manitoba and New Brunswick, Central Authority lawyers represent the applicant. Canada, with the exception of Manitoba, made a reservation to Art 26, and therefore will only assume costs so far as they are covered by its legal aid system. Conversely, in Manitoba, if the applicant is represented by the Central Authority this will be done with no charge to the applicant. Rules relating to legal aid provision differ from one Province and Territory to another. Additionally, the Royal Canadian Mountain Police's Missing Children's Registry, through its Travel Reunification Program, offers financial assistance to parents or guardians who cannot afford to have their child returned to Canada.

22.10 In many Provinces and Territories, systems are in place to expedite Convention cases.[21] However, some areas receive so few cases that such systems have not been established. Indeed in 1999, three of the Provinces and all three of the Territories received no new incoming applications.

22.11 Courts often aim to bring the left-behind parent to court so that if a child's return is ordered it can be immediately executed. There may, however, be financial problems involved in bringing the left-behind parent to the relevant Canadian court. To assist the effective enforcement of orders, the court can include a clause in the order enlisting the assistance of the police with the return of the child. Parents can also agree to undertakings, the practice of accepting of which, was endorsed by the Canadian Supreme Court

---

18   See the 1999 Statistical Survey, and *Country Report: Canada op cit*, n 16, p 19.

19   According to the 1999 Statistical Survey, in 1999, 13 of the 35 return applications resulted in a voluntary return, which, at 37%, is well above the global average of 18%.

20   According to the 1999 Statistical Survey, of the 12 return applications that went to court in 1999, eight resulted in a decision to return the child, which, at 67%, is below the global average of 74% of court cases resulting in return decisions. Altogether, 23% of applications received resulted in a judicial decision to return, which is below the global average of 32%, while four applications (11%) resulted in a decision refusing return, which is identical to the global average percentage. Of the eight incoming access applications, one was withdrawn, in two access was agreed, in three it was judicially granted and in one it was judicially refused. One case was still pending as of 30 June 2001, and in the remaining application the outcome was classified as 'other'.

21   Generally, return applications to Canada were resolved quickly, with judicial decisions to return the child taking a mean average of 84 days from initial application to final judicial decision. This compares favourably with the global average of 107 days. The applications which concluded with a voluntary return took a mean average of 90 days which is similar to the global average of 84 days. See the 1999 Statistical Survey.

in *Thomson v Thomson*.[22] Some Canadian Central Authorities include a list of possible undertakings in the information package distributed to parents or their lawyers. Undertakings that have been accepted by the courts include: the left-behind parent agreeing to pay the travel costs of the abductor and child; the left-behind parent being required to obtain housing for the abductor and child; and the left-behind parent being required not to enforce outstanding warrants for the abductor's arrest. If it is anticipated that there will be objections to return, some Central Authorities request that an applicant consider any undertakings he or she may be prepared to give.

22.12 In Quebec, as the Central Authority is always represented during Convention proceedings, judges may request the assistance of the Central Authority in enforcing return orders. The judge may authorise the Central Authority to co-ordinate the return of the child, either with the help of the police or that of the Director of Youth Protection. The Central Authority, also ensures that departures from the jurisdiction are effected without incident.[23]

22.13 In Quebec, penalties for non-compliance with a court order can include contempt of court, with a fine not exceeding $5,000 or a maximum of one year in prison.[24] Where a parent is trying to flee because he or she does not wish to return the child as decreed in the court decision it is possible to utilise criminal charges either for parental child abduction, or for breach of an order. In common law jurisdictions, the most common method of enforcement is civil contempt of court. Once a person is found to be in contempt, other orders may be made. These include imprisonment, fines or costs, stays of action, supervised access or suspension of maintenance payments and any other order deemed necessary by the judge.[25]

FRANCE[26]

22.14 The French Republic comprises the mainland (*France Metropolitaine*), the Overseas Departments (*Departments d'Outre-Mer*)[27] and the Overseas Territories (*Territoires d'Outre-Mer*).[28] The Convention came into force throughout the French Republic on 1 December 1983, following publication of the decree of ratification in the Official Journal (*Journal Officiel*). France was one of the three original ratifying States bringing the Convention into force.[29]

---

22 (1994) 6 FLR (4th) 290, (1995) 119 DLR (4th) 253.
23 Including making arrangements for the child to obtain a passport.
24 See Art 51 of the Quebec Civil Code of Procedure.
25 See J McPhail, *Enforcement Options for Custody & Access Breaches,* Manitoba Department of Justice, p 26.
26 See generally Lowe, Armstrong, Mathias and Navarro, *Country Report: France* (NCMEC, 2002).
27 Namely Martinique, Guyane, Guadeloupe, Réunion, and Saint-Pierre-et-Miquelon.
28 Namely Nouvelle-Calédonie, Wallis et Futuna and Polynésie Francaise.
29 The other two States were Canada and Portugal.

As at 1 August 2003, the Convention was in force as between France and 44 other Contracting States, France having only accepted 13 acceding States.[30]

22.15 There is one Central Authority which is responsible for all applications across the whole of the French Republic. This Central Authority is located in the *Bureau de l'entraide judiciaire en matière civile et commerciale*, which is part of the Ministry of Justice and located in Paris.[31] France made a reservation to Art 24 stating that all applications must be in French or accompanied by a translation into French. All applications to France must also include an extract (in French) of the relevant law of the Contracting State in which the application was made and an explanation of how that law may be applied. Upon receipt of an incoming application, the Central Authority will check that the relevant Convention criteria are satisfied and that appropriate documentation is attached. In 1999 the French Central Authority handled a total of 107 new applications, comprising 42 incoming return applications, 43 outgoing return applications, 15 incoming access applications, and seven outgoing access applications.[32]

22.16 The Central Authority sends applications to the *Procureur General* who forwards them to the *Procureur de la République* based in the regional court which will hear the case. Sometimes applications will be sent prior to receipt of all necessary documentation, in an attempt to speed up the system. The *Procureur de la République* will assign a *Procureur Adjoint* or a *Substitut* to represent the applicant and bring the case to court. This representation provided by the State comes at no charge to the applicant. However, applicants are often advised to appoint a separate lawyer, as the *Procureurs* are not always familiar with Convention proceedings. France made a reservation to Art 26 and, therefore, any additional representation will not be free of charge to the applicant unless he or she is eligible for legal aid. Costs of translations are also not provided. Applicants are able to bypass the Central Authority and *Procureur* procedure if they wish; however, police assistance in locating a child is not available if the *Procureur* is not used.[33]

22.17 Jurisdiction to hear Convention cases was originally vested at first instance in all the *Tribunaux de Grande Instance* (TGI) of which there are 181, the practice being that the court in the region where the child was located would hear the case.[34] However, the law of 4 March 2002 has limited the

---

30 See http://www.hcch.net/e/status/abdshte.html.

31 As of August 2002, there was no booklet or website describing the services offered under the Convention in France. However, the French Central Authority is considering both publishing a booklet and establishing a website. Additionally, the Franco-German Mediation Commission which deals with Convention cases between these States (see **22.18**) is considering creating a website which could be linked to the Central Authority site.

32 See the 1999 Statistical Survey, and *Country Report: France, op cit*, n 26, at p 13.

33 See http://www.frwebgate.access.gpo.gov.

34 According to the 1999 Statistical Survey, in 1999, 13 return applications went to court, with 10 resulting in a return order, which, at 24%, is below the global average of 32%. Similarly, just three cases ended in a refusal to return which, at 7%, is also below the global average of 11%. Of the 15 incoming access applications, five were withdrawn, in three

number of TGI able to hear Convention cases to one per appeal court region, and the number of judges able to hear cases has also been reduced.[35] It is anticipated that this concentration of jurisdiction in a smaller number of courts and judges will speed up proceedings and allow for greater expertise. Appeals lie to the *cour d'appel* of the relevant region, of which there are 36.[36] The highest court is the *cour de cassation*, which is situated in Paris and which hears only disputed points of view.

22.18   In response to the growing tension between France and Germany in relation to child abduction, the Franco-German Parliamentary Mediation Commission was set up in 1998. The Commission comprises six members, three French and three German. The Commission, which now meets regularly, is in the French view designed both to solve pending cases between the two countries through attempts at mediation and to enable conclusions to be drawn from the individual cases studied so as to prevent further abductions. As a result of recommendations made by this Commission, a permanent Family Mediation Commission (*la Mission d'aide á la Médiation pour les Familles*) has been created within the French Ministry of Justice, so as to provide, *inter alia*, mediation in individual cases.

22.19   The *Procureur* is responsible for attempting to seek voluntary resolutions.[37] Where mediation fails, the case will go to court, usually by way of an emergency procedure known as a *référé*. A *référé* is made by an *assignation en référé* which is similar to a writ of summons. Usually sessions for hearing *référé* applications are held weekly, but in cases of extreme urgency, *référé* applications can be heard immediately by filing a *référé de heure à heure*. It is not necessary for the applicant to attend proceedings or to give evidence; however, it is often desirable for the applicant to be present as this may help a return order to be executed more efficiently.[38]

22.20   The court can order temporary enforcement of decisions (*exécution provisoire ordonnée*) even where there is a claim pending before the *cour de cassation*. However, enforcement of orders which are pending appeal is often complicated. Judgments cannot be enforced until an authenticated copy of the judgment containing the enforcement procedure is delivered to the

---

cases, access was agreed and in one it was judicially granted. Three cases were still pending as of 30 June 2001, and in the remaining three applications the outcome was described as 'other'. See also *Country Report: France, op cit*, n 26, at p 16.

[35]   See Arts 20 and 21 of the Law of 4 March 2002.

[36]   According to the 1999 Statistical Survey, in 1999, 12% of the return applications going to court resulted in decisions at appellate level, which is marginally below the global average of 14%.

[37]   According to the 1999 Statistical Survey, in 1999, 11 of the 42 return applications received resulted in a voluntary return. At 26% this is higher than the global average of 18%.

[38]   The mean average number of days between the application and the decision to return the child was 126 days, which was slower than the global average of 107 days. Altogether, the system appears to operate slowly, although the reforms in the number of courts and judges empowered to hear Convention cases may have a positive effect in this area. Conversely, the voluntary returns took an average of 56 days, which is below the global average of 84 days. Figures taken from the 1999 Statistical Survey.

successful party. This will specifically require all *huissiers de justice* (bailiffs), Public Prosecutors and police officers to lend their assistance when it is requested.[39] Most orders for return are complied with; there are no contempt procedures for the enforcement of civil judgments in French law but penal measures may be used to aid enforcement. In civil cases, the judge may attach an *astrainte* to an order, which is a pecuniary penalty payable to the applicant on a daily basis until the order is complied with.[40]

22.21 Although the French Central Authority helps to facilitate enforcement of orders, the *Procureur* is responsible for overseeing the execution of orders made on French territory. The local *Procureur's* office may take the decision to invoke criminal proceedings to aid enforcement. The *Procureur* can organise meetings with a view to obtaining execution by force, and to this end may use the intervention of a *huissier*.

GERMANY[41]

22.22 Germany is a Federal State comprising 16 constituent regional States (*Länder*). The Convention was implemented at a Federal level and entered into force on 1 December 1990. Implementation was by way of legislation, the short title for which is *SorgeRÜbkAG*.[42] This applies throughout the Federal Republic of Germany and therefore equally to the former West and East Germany, which became united after the legislation was enacted but before it came into force. As at August 2003, the Convention was in force as between Germany and 65 other Contracting States.

22.23 The Federal Prosecutor General at the Federal Court of Justice is responsible for carrying out the duties of the Central Authority.[43] The office which conducts these duties is located in Bonn. The Central Authority checks incoming applications to ensure that the Convention criteria are fulfilled.[44] Following procedural reforms in October 2000, enquiries at this stage are limited to the most essential issues in an attempt to speed up procedure.

---

[39] See http://frwebgate.gpo.gov/cgi-bin/getdoc.gci?dbname=106_cong_co....:70663.wai.

[40] In practice, this order is rarely used: see *Country Report: France, op cit*, n 26, at 3.7.

[41] See generally Lowe, Armstrong and Mathias, *Country Report: Germany* (NCMEC, 2002).

[42] The full name of the legislation is Gesetz zur Ausführung des Haager Übereinkommens vom 25 Oktober 1980 über die zivilrechtlichen Aspekte internationaler Kindesentführung und des Europäischen Übereinkommens vom 20 Mai 1980 über die Anerkennung und Vollstreckung von Entscheidungen über das Sorgerecht für Kinder und die Wiederherstellung des Sorgeverhältnisses (Artikel 1 des Gesetzes zur Ausführung von Sorgerechtsübereinkommen und zur Änderung des Gesetzes über die Angelegenheiten der freiwilligen Gerichtsbarkeit sowie anderer Gesetze).

[43] See s 1 of the 1990 Implementing Act.

[44] The German Central Authority has drawn up an information booklet, currently only available in German although it is planned to produce an English version. The booklet contains the relevant application forms and information and advice. There is also a website containing the forms and other relevant information, see www.bundeszentralregister.de link HKU/ESU. At present it is only available in German.

Unusually, where the Central Authority rejects an application, this decision is open to challenge by the higher regional court in whose district the Federal Prosecutor General's main office is located (the *Oberlandesgericht* at Karlsruhe).[45] No official reservation was made to Art 24; however, it is assumed by the German authorities that it is implicit in the first paragraph of the Article that applications be accompanied by a German translation.[46] In 1999 the German Central Authority handled a total of 210 new applications, comprising 70 incoming return applications, 103 outgoing return applications, 24 incoming access applications and 13 outgoing access applications.[47]

22.24 In appropriate cases, the Central Authority writes to the respondent in an attempt to negotiate a voluntary settlement. Since reforms introduced in October 2000, the Central Authority may also simultaneously institute court proceedings without waiting for a period of time to elapse after sending the letter. This is an attempt to speed up procedure where negotiation fails and to give added weight to the letter seeking voluntary settlement. If a voluntary return is negotiated, the court proceedings are halted and no costs are incurred.[48]

22.25 The 1990 Implementing Act limited jurisdiction in Convention cases to two levels of court.[49] At first instance, the local courts (*Amtsgerichte*) are empowered to hear cases, and appeal lies to the regional appeal courts (*Oberlandesgerichte*). All the *Amtsgerichte* have specialised Family Courts attached to them. An Act of 1999 amending the 1990 Act limited jurisdiction to just 24 *Oberlandesgerichte* and 24 *Amtsgerichte*. This has since been further reduced to 22 *Amtsgerichte* and 22 *Oberlandesgerichte*. This reform has substantially reduced the number of judges competent to hear cases to around 200, although in practice most competent courts put the responsibility for hearing Hague Convention cases on judges who are specialists in the field. As discussed above,[50] Germany is a party to the Franco-German Parliamentary Mediation Commission. Unlike the French, the German part deals only with mediation. It is also noteworthy that only two of the 39 cases so far handled by the Commission were brought by Germany.

22.26 The Central Authority institutes judicial proceedings and commissions a lawyer, usually drawn from a list of 400, to file the application. The applicant is officially represented by the Central Authority, who in turn is sub-represented by the chosen lawyer. A reservation was made to Art 26 of the Convention, and therefore applicants must pay for representation. However, both applicants and respondents are entitled to seek legal aid

---

[45] According to the 1999 Statistical Survey, in 1999, out of 70 return applications received, 14% were rejected, which is marginally higher than the global average of 11%.
[46] See s 2 of the 1990 Implementing Act.
[47] See the 1999 Statistical Survey, and *Country Report: Germany*, *op cit*, n 41, at p 17.
[48] According to the 1999 Statistical Survey, in 1999, 11 of the 70 return applications resulted in a voluntary return which, at 16%, is below the global average of 18%.
[49] See s 8(2) of the 1990 Implementing Act.
[50] See **22.18** above.

(*prozesskostenhilfe*), eligibility for which is available on a means and merits test on the same basis as for any domestic litigant.[51] Prior to the reforms of October 2000, court proceedings would not commence until eligibility for legal aid was established. There is now no longer a requirement to resolve the legal aid issue first, although it is essential that legal aid applications are submitted or an advance on costs (□ 1100) is paid before the Central Authority will take action before the court.[52]

22.27 The right to appeal from a first instance decision is subject to strict time limits[53] which have been known to present problems in relation to the requirement to pay a fresh advance of □ 500 for paying litigants.[54]

22.28 In common with other continental European systems, enforcement of decisions in Germany can be problematic. The enforcement of a return order is governed by s 33 of the Act of Non-Contentious Matters. There is some confusion about which courts are entitled to enforce orders; some courts are of the opinion that enforcement powers vest exclusively in the court of first instance (which means an order for return made by an *Oberlandesgericht* can only be enforced by the *Amtsgericht* judge who first heard the case). Alternatively, some *Oberlandesgerichte* argue that it is up to them to enforce orders made by them, and not the *Amtsgericht*. Unfortunately, the wording of s 33 leaves the question unanswered.

22.29 Section 8(1), sentence 1 of the 1990 Implementation Act states that enforcement measures can be put in place only where the decision is final. However, according to s 8(2), sentence 2, *Amtsgerichte* can order the immediate enforcement of a return decision, even where an appeal has been lodged. The normal practice, however, is for orders to be stayed pending an appeal. An appeal lies against such immediate enforcement of orders.

---

[51] See s 13 of the 1990 Implementing Act.

[52] According to the 1999 Statistical Survey, in 1999, of the 70 return applications received, 26 went to court, of which 50% resulted in a decision to return the child. This figure is below the global average of 74% of court cases resulting in a decision to return. Globally 32% of all return applications received ended in judicial return, and 11% ended in judicial refusal to return, while in Germany, the percentage of applications resulting in each outcome was 19%. Of the 24 access applications, 11 were withdrawn and two were rejected. In two cases, access was agreed and in a further four it was judicially granted and in two judicially refused. Two cases were still pending as of 30 June 2001, and in the remaining application the outcome was classified as 'other'. See also *Country Report: Germany*, *op cit*, n 41, at p 20.

[53] Viz a written complaint must be received by the *Oberlandesgericht* within 2 weeks of service of the first instance order: see s 8(2) of the 1990 Implementing Act.

[54] According to the 1999 Statistical Survey, of the return applications received in 1999, four of the 26 court decisions were appealed. At 15% this is marginally above the global average of 14%. The mean average time taken from application to conclusion of the court decisions was 122 days for decisions to return the child and 164 days for decisions refusing to return. These figures are marginally slower than the global averages of 107 days and 147 days respectively. However, the number of days taken to reach voluntary return was 64 which is quicker than the global average of 84 days.

22.30   The sanctions that can be imposed[55] for non-compliance are the imposition of a coercive fine, provided it has been preceded by a formal warning; the imposition of coercive detention for up to 6 months, provided it has been preceded by a formal warning (s 33(1), (3) of the Non-Contentious Matters Act); the assistance of the court bailiff to assert with force, if necessary, the entitlement to have the child returned, and in the event of the bailiff being resisted, the assistance of the police (s 33(2)).

IRELAND[56]

22.31   Ireland ratified the 1980 Hague Abduction Convention on 1 October 1991 when the Child Abduction and Enforcement of Custody Orders Act 1991 came into force. With this implementing legislation, Ireland also ratified the 1980 European Custody Convention. Where proceedings are invoked under both Conventions, the Hague Convention takes precedence.[57] At 1 August 2003, the Hague Convention was in force as between Ireland and 66 other Contracting States.

22.32   There is one Central Authority in Ireland based in the Department of Justice, Equality and Law Reform under the management of the Civil Law Reform Division of that Department. The Central Authority also deals with applications under the 1980 European Custody Convention and the New York Maintenance Convention. On receiving an application, the Irish Central Authority examines it to ensure that it comes within the scope of the Convention. In all cases, the Central Authority will verify the child's location through the use of the National Police (*An Garda Síochána*). Ireland made no reservation to Art 24; however, in practice, all applications are received in English. Where translation of relevant documents is required, this will be arranged by the Central Authority at no cost to the applicant. The Irish Central Authority will also arrange for the translation of documents for outgoing applications from Ireland, at no cost to the applicant.[58] In 1999 the Irish Central Authority handled a total of 60 new applications, comprising 38 incoming return applications, 21 outgoing return applications, one incoming access application and no outgoing access applications.[59]

22.33   The Irish Central Authority forwards applications to the Legal Aid Board who represent the applicant at no charge, having made no reservation

---

[55]   These enforcement measures have nothing in common with the contempt of court system in some common law countries and are not to be confused with this different approach to enforcing court orders.

[56]   See generally Lowe and Armstrong, *Country Report: Ireland* (NCMEC, 2002).

[57]   See Child Abduction and Enforcement of Custody Orders Act 1991, s 28(2).

[58]   The Irish Central Authority maintains some web pages on the Irish Government website: see http://www.irlgov.ie. This site contains information on the scope of the Convention and the role of the Central Authority, including statistical information. It also details relevant legislation.

[59]   See the 1999 Statistical Survey, and *Country Report: Ireland, op cit*, n 56, at p 11.

to Art 26. Usually, the application is forwarded to this body within 24 hours of receipt. Family law in Ireland expressly encourages voluntary agreements and mediation, and the Legal Aid Board solicitors may attempt to seek a voluntary settlement.[60] Where a case does progress to court, evidence is generally heard on the basis of affidavits, and Rules of Court[61] have been made to ensure that the proceedings are expedited.[62]

22.34 The 1991 Act confers jurisdiction at first instance in Convention cases on the High Court. This is the highest court of first instance in Ireland. District Courts and Circuit Courts, which are able to hear guardianship matters, are not empowered to hear Convention cases. Appeal is to the Supreme Court. There is a statutory maximum of 28 judges able to hear cases in the High Court, and eight judges in the Supreme Court. In practice, not all of these judges hear Convention cases. The limited number of judges empowered to hear cases enables expertise to develop. Similarly, the use of Legal Aid Board solicitors means that there are a limited number of practitioners involved in cases which also means that there is a degree of expertise.

22.35 Where the Irish court orders that the child must remain in the jurisdiction, for example pending the hearing, an order may be directed to the airport or port officials and other necessary parties to prevent the child's removal from Ireland. Orders are generally enforced through contempt of court proceedings. The main enforcement agency in Ireland is *An Garda Síochána*. To date, the Irish Central Authority is not aware of any case where the necessity has arisen for anyone to be committed to prison for contempt in Convention proceedings.

22.36 The Irish courts have a wide discretion either to order immediate execution of an order, or to defer execution. They may also make interim orders where they consider it appropriate. Both High Court and Supreme Court orders are enforced in the same way. In dealing with penalties for non-compliance, judges in both courts have a wide discretion.

---

[60] According to the 1999 Statistical Survey, in 1999, seven of the 38 return applications received by Ireland resulted in a voluntary return which, at 18%, is identical to the global average.

[61] SI 94/2001, as allowed under the implementing legislation: see s 38 (2) of the 1991 Act.

[62] According to the 1999 Statistical Survey, there were 20 cases which went to court in 1999, 16 of which (80%) resulted in a return order, which is above the global average of 74%. In total, 42% of return applications resulted in a judicial order to return, which is well above the global average of 32%, and 11% of applications resulted in a judicial order refusing return, which is identical to the global average. All applications were handled relatively expeditiously with voluntary returns taking a mean average of 23 days from application to conclusion, and judicial decisions taking a mean average of 115 and 151 days for returns and refusals respectively. These figures all compare favourably with the global averages of 84, 107 and 147 days.

THE UNITED STATES[63]

22.37 The United States ratified the Convention on 1 July 1988 when the International Child Abduction Remedies Act of 1988 (ICARA) came into force.[64] The United States was the tenth Contracting State. As at 1 August 2003, the Convention was in force as between the United States and 53 other Contracting States, the United States not having accepted any accessions since accepting South Africa on 1 November 1997.[65]

22.38 Despite being a Federal nation, the United States has, by means of an Executive Order,[66] designated a single Central Authority, the State Department's Office of Consular Affairs, more specifically, the Office of Children's Issues. However, in 1995, a Co-operative Agreement[67] was signed between the US Central Authority and a private, non-profit making organisation, the National Center for Missing and Exploited Children (NCMEC), which has expertise in locating missing children within the United States. This Agreement allowed NCMEC to process all 'incoming' applications (ie applications seeking return of children from the United States), the State Department retaining responsibility for handling 'outgoing' applications.[68] The United States seems to be the only Contracting State to have split the responsibility for incoming and outgoing applications between two separate bodies. While, on the one hand, this split of responsibility allows greater expertise through the use of a specialist organisation, it may be difficult for foreign Central Authorities to build up relationships with the two different organisations which may require differing amounts of information, etc, in order to process applications. In 1999, a total of 466 new applications were handled by the US Central Authority, comprising 210 incoming applications for return, 183 outgoing applications for return, 44 incoming applications for access and 29 outgoing applications for access.[69] Predictably, the United States handled more Hague Convention applications than any other country.

22.39 The United States made a reservation to Art 24[70] of the Convention stating that all applications must be accompanied by a translation into English.

---

[63] See generally Lowe, Armstrong and Mathias, *Country Report: United States* (NCMEC, 2002).

[64] ICARA P.L. 100–300, 42 USC § 11601–11610.

[65] See http://www.hcch.net/e/status/abdshte.html.

[66] ICARA § 11606(a) requires the President to designate a Federal agency as the Central Authority for administration of the Treaty provisions within the United States. This was achieved by Executive Order No 12648, 11 August 1988.

[67] This Agreement came into force on 5 September 1995.

[68] There are useful websites (see http://www.ncmec.org and http://travel.state.gov/abduct.html) and information documents including helpful hints on how to prevent abductions and what to do if a child is abducted. See *Family Abduction: Prevention and Response*, produced by co-operation between NCMEC and the ABA Center on Children and the Law – A program of the Young Lawyers Division American Bar Association (2002). Additionally, there are country fliers explaining procedures in various foreign States.

[69] See the 1999 Statistical Survey, and *Country Report – United States, op cit*, n 63.

[70] See http://www.hcch.net/e/status/stat28e.html#us.

The United States does not provide any funding to assist with costs of translation. On receipt of a valid incoming application, and assuming the child has been located, NCMEC will write to the abductor explaining that an application has been made and requesting the abductor to return the child voluntarily. Usually, the abductor is given 10 days to respond to this letter, although where there is a danger of further abduction or possible harm being caused to the child, a letter will not be sent. Where the abductor is agreeable to a voluntary resolution, the parents, NCMEC and relevant lawyers will make the necessary arrangements.[71]

22.40 Where there is a negative response to the letter or no response at all, the application will proceed into the court system. NCMEC does not take the case to court, rather it acts as a source of information and explains procedure to the parties, lawyers and judges. After 6 weeks, NCMEC will routinely request an update on the progress of the case.[72] The United States has not concentrated jurisdiction in Convention cases to any particular courts and, under the implementing legislation, applications may be filed in Federal or State courts.[73] Consequently, there are around 30,850 judges able to hear Convention applications in the US courts, about 2,000 of whom can hear appeal cases.[74] Generally, applicants are represented by private attorneys and will have to pay for such representation, the United States having made a reservation to Art 26[75] and therefore not being bound to assume any costs relating to Convention applications. This reservation met with criticism,[76] as there is no comprehensive system of legal aid in the United States. Consequently, the US Department of Justice agreed in 1985 to fund the American Bar Association's creation of the International Child Abduction Attorney Network (ICAAN). This network consists of a pool of attorneys who have received some training from NCMEC and are able to offer reduced fee or *pro bono* representation in incoming Convention cases. Even so, proceedings can be expensive.

22.41 In California, the Attorney-General's Office and District Attorney's Office play an important role in Convention cases. Local prosecutors handle cases, often negating the need for private attorneys. The District Attorney's Office does not represent the applicant as such but rather acts as a 'friend of the court'. The use of the District Attorney's Office allows for experience to

---

[71] According to the 1999 Statistical Survey, of the 210 return applications received by the United States in 1999 which had reached a conclusion by 30 June 2001, 59, or 28%, had been concluded by way of a voluntary return of the child. This is a high proportion compared with the global average of 18%.

[72] See Art 11(2) of the Convention.

[73] ICARA § 11603 (a).

[74] See the American response to the questionnaire concerning the practical operation of the Convention and views on possible recommendations, sent out by the Permanent Bureau of the Hague Conference prior to the Fourth Special Commission (hereafter 'the USA Response to the Hague Questionnaire').

[75] See http://www.hcch.net/e/status/stat28e.html#us.

[76] For a summary of criticisms, see *Country Report: United States, op cit*, n 63.

develop and, significantly, California will pay for cases processed via the Attorney General's Office.[77]

22.42   Court proceedings in Convention cases may proceed by way of written evidence alone, although oral evidence is sometimes required, particularly where the case is considered to be sensitive, including where Art 13(b) has been raised.[78]

22.43   Overall, the disposal rate of Convention applications is relatively slow. Certainly there are no expedited procedures in Convention cases and, as one judge has commented, '[w]hen parties appeal Convention cases, "promptness" regrettably becomes a relative term'.[79]

22.44   Orders made by US courts directing the return of a child to a country outside the United States are enforceable throughout the United States by both Federal and State law enforcement authorities. Courts may enforce court orders by contempt powers, which include fines or imprisonment. In some States, the aggrieved party may also file a *habeas corpus* or analogous motion that would request that law enforcement pick up and take the child into custody.[80]

22.45   The United States considers that undertakings can be consistent with the Hague Convention. Nevertheless, the concept of undertakings is not widely used by the US courts. To the extent that undertakings are commitments on the return of the child, it is possible that, as a result of the *Blondin*[81] case, the use of such undertakings will increase.[82]

22.46   The US Court of Appeals has recognised the need for speed in the summary disposal of these applications.[83]

---

[77]   Information taken from the USA Response to the Hague Questionnaire.

[78]   According to the 1999 Statistical Survey, 60 of the 210 return applications made in 1999 and concluded by 30 June 2001 went to court. 83% of these cases resulted in a judicial order to return the child compared with a global average of 74%. As a proportion of all applications received in 1999, the judicial return rate was 24%, which is below the global average of 32% but must be read in conjunction with a high voluntary return rate of 28%. The overall proportion of applications resulting in the return of the child was 52%, which is marginally above the global average of 50%. The proportion of cases which resulted in a judicial refusal to return the child was notably low at 5%, compared with a global average of 11%. As against this, however, it is to be noted that 25 of the 210 applications received were still pending at 30 June 2001, a proportion of 12%, which is higher than the global average of 9%.

[79]   See Hon Judge James Garbolino, *International Child Custody Cases: Handling Hague Convention Cases in the US Courts*, 3rd edn (The National Judicial College, 2000) at p 52. Of the cases from 1999 concluded by 30 June 2001, the mean average number of days to reach a disposal was 185 days for a judicial decision to return the child and 149 days for a judicial decision refusing return. Globally, the averages were 107 days and 147 days, respectively. Figures in this footnote are taken from the 1999 Statistical Survey.

[80]   The USA Response to Hague Questionnaire, *op cit*, n 74, at p 7.

[81]   *Blondin v Dubois* 189 F.3d 240 (2d Cir 1999), since appealed: see 238 F.3d (2d Cir 2001).

[82]   See USA Response to Hague Questionnaire, at p 10.

[83]   See **21.77**.

Chapter 23

INTERNATIONAL ABDUCTIONS: BI-LATERAL ARRANGEMENTS BETWEEN STATES

INTRODUCTION

23.1 A number of countries have made bi-lateral agreements with individual countries which may prove effective in obtaining the return of wrongfully removed or retained children. They may also assist in securing the exercise of access rights. Some agreements are of a general nature, others are directed specifically to trans-border issues relating to children. We do not attempt a comprehensive review of such agreements; rather, we consider proposals for bi-lateral agreements between the UK government and other States. We also consider the position in some other States.[1]

23.2 Bi-lateral agreements operate in a variety of ways. Some involve judicial co-operation, others involve consular agreement or administrative agreements. The bi-lateral agreements discussed here are those involving at least one non-Hague Convention country. However, in the Conclusions and Recommendations of the Fourth Meeting of the Special Commission, Hague Abduction Convention Central Authorities were encouraged, 'in addressing any practical problems concerning the proper functioning of the Convention, to engage in dialogue with one another'.[2] It was also suggested that 'where a

---

[1] See generally the research paper by Caroline Gosselain for the Permanent Bureau of the Hague Conference on Private International Law, 'Child Abduction and Transfrontier Access: Bi-lateral Conventions and Islamic States' (Preliminary Document No 7 of August 2002 for the Attention of the Special Commission of September 2002). The texts of a number of bi-lateral agreements are annexed to the research paper.

[2] Conclusions and Recommendations of the Fourth Meeting of the Special Commission to Review the Operation of the Hague Convention of 25 October 1980 on the Civil Aspects

group of Central Authorities share a common problem, consideration should be given to joint meetings which might in some cases be facilitated by the Hague Conference'.[3] Many Central Authorities have instigated such arrangements. Furthermore, an informal questionnaire concerning existing bi-lateral agreements has been sent by the Permanent Bureau on an exploratory basis to several Central Authorities with their agreement.

BETWEEN THE UNITED KINGDOM AND OTHER STATES

23.3 At the time of writing, the United Kingdom had only one bi-lateral agreement with a non-Convention State.[4]

23.4 The UK policy is to encourage accessions to the 1980 Hague Abduction Convention where States have legal systems compatible with the Convention, but not where legal systems are incompatible.[5] In respect of the latter, the Child Abduction and Prisoner Unit of the Foreign and Commonwealth Office, set up in April 2000, is currently exploring a number of arrangements including the use of Memorandums of Understanding with non-Convention States whose legal systems are not compatible with the Convention, with the aim of securing bi-lateral agreements. According to Reunite – the International Child Abduction Centre,[6] the leading UK charity specialising in child abduction, about 40% of abductions from the United Kingdom are to non-Convention States.

23.5 The first attempt by the United Kingdom at making a bi-lateral agreement was the proposed bi-lateral agreement between the United Kingdom[7] and Egypt which is in an early draft. It is in the form of a non-binding Memorandum of Understanding between the two States. In its draft form current at the time of writing, it will apply to children, under the age of 16, born to parents:

(a) one of whom is a British national and the other of whom is an Egyptian national; or

---

of International Child Abduction (22–28 March 2001), drawn up by the Permanent Bureau, para 2.9.

[3] Conclusions and Recommendations of the Fourth Meeting of the Special Commission to Review the Operation of the Hague Convention of 25 October 1980 on the Civil Aspects of International Child Abduction (22–28 March 2001), drawn up by the Permanent Bureau, para 2.9.

[4] This agreement, with the Islamic Republic of Pakistan, is discussed at **23.6**.

[5] See the response to the questionnaire concerning the practical operation of the Convention and views on possible recommendations, sent out by the Permanent Bureau of the Hague Conference prior to the fourth meeting of the Special Commission.

[6] Reunite receives government funding jointly from the Department of Constitutional Affairs (formerly the Lord Chancellor's Department), the Foreign and Commonwealth Office and the Home Office.

[7] This will have effect in all three jurisdictions of the United Kingdom when it enters into force.

(b)   at least one of whom has dual British/Egyptian nationality; or

(c)   one of whom is a third party national residing in either United Kingdom or Egypt and the other of whom is either a British or Egyptian national.

In its present draft, its focus is limited to recognition of judicial decisions concerning rights of access; it provides for measures to secure effective access and the return of the child following access. It is intended to focus on achievable goals, such as a right of entry to and exit from Egypt and the United Kingdom and a right of access for the left-behind parent. Each State is to have a Central Authority; for the United Kingdom, the Central Authority in England and Wales will be the Lord Chancellor's Department, in Scotland, the Scottish Ministers, and in Northern Ireland, the Northern Ireland Courts Services. However, at the time of writing, this initiative is not being progressed further.

23.6   In January 2003, the President of the Family Division of the High Court of England and Wales and the Chief Justice of the Supreme Court of Pakistan signed a record of the 'consensus' and agreement reached following their meeting in London. The exact legal status and effect of the document is unclear.[8] However, it is likely to have a strong influence on the way the judges exercise their discretion in cases involving England and Wales and Pakistan. The full text of the document is set out below.[9]

> 'The President of the Family Divison and the Hon Chief Justice of Pakistan in consultation with senior members of the family judiciary of the United Kingdom ("the UK") and the Islamic Republic of Pakistan ("Pakistan"), having met on 15 to 17 January 2003 in the Royal Courts of Justice in London, reach the following consensus:
>
> WHEREAS:
>
> (a)   Desiring to protect the children of the UK and Pakistan from the harmful effects of wrongful removal or retention from one country to the other;
>
> (b)   Mindful that the UK and Pakistan share a common heritage of law and a commitment to the welfare of children;
>
> (c)   Desirous of promoting judicial cooperation, enhanced relations and the free flow of information between the judiciaries of the UK and Pakistan; and
>
> (d)   Recognising the importance of negotiation, mediation and conciliation in the resolution of family disputes;
>
> IT IS AGREED THAT:
>
> 1.   In normal circumstances the welfare of a child is best determined by the courts of the country of the child's habitual/ordinary residence.
>
> 2.   If a child is removed from the UK to Pakistan, or from Pakistan to the UK, without the consent of the parent with a custody/residence order or a restraint/interdict order from the court of the child's

---

8   See Young, 'The Constitutional Limits of Judicial Activism: Judicial Conduct of International Relations and Child Abduction' (2003) 66 MLR 823.

9   Cases falling within the terms of this Protocol are handled, where necessary, through the Child Abduction Unit of the Foreign and Commonwealth Office (as to which, see **20.75**).

habitual/ordinary residence, the judge of the court of the country to which the child has been removed shall not ordinarily exercise jurisdiction over the child, save in so far as it is necessary for the court to order the return of the child to the country of the child's habitual/ordinary residence.

3. If a child is taken from the UK to Pakistan, or from Pakistan to the UK, by a parent with visitation/access/contact rights with the consent of the parent with a custody/residence order or a restraint/interdict order from the court of the child's habitual/ordinary residence or in consequence of an order from that court permitting the visit, and the child is retained in that country after the end of the visit without consent or in breach of the court order, the judge of the court of the country in which the child has been retained shall not ordinarily exercise jurisdiction over the child, save in so far as it is necessary for the court to order the return of the child to the country of the child's habitual/ordinary residence.

4. The above principles shall apply without regard to the nationality, culture or religion of the parents or either parent and shall apply to children of mixed marriages.

5. In cases where the habitual/ordinary residence of the child is in dispute the court to which an application is made should decide the issue of habitual/ordinary residence before making any decision on the return or on the general welfare of the child, and upon determination of the preliminary issue as to habitual/ordinary residence should then apply the general principles set out above.

6. These applications should be lodged by the applicant, listed by the court and decided expeditiously.

7. It is recommended that the respective governments of the UK and Pakistan give urgent consideration to identifying or establishing an administrative service to facilitate or oversee the resolution of child abduction cases (not covered by the 1980 Hague Convention on the Civil Aspects of International Child Abduction).

8. It is further recommended that the judiciaries, the legal practitioners and the non-governmental organisations in the UK and Pakistan use their best endeavours to advance the objects of the protocol.

9. It is agreed that the UK and Pakistan shall each nominate a judge of the superior court to work in liaison with each other to advance the objects of this protocol.'

23.7 EU Member States are exploring the possibility of arrangements with non-Convention countries, mainly those in North Africa.

BETWEEN CANADA AND OTHER STATES

23.8 Encouraging States to become parties to the 1980 Hague Abduction Convention remains Canada's preferred way of managing child abduction issues.[10] Nevertheless, it is recognised that there are certain countries, particularly those operating under Sharia law, who are unlikely to

---

[10] See the Canadian response to the questionnaire concerning the practical operation of the Convention and views on possible recommendations, sent out by the Permanent Bureau of the Hague Conference prior to the fourth meeting of the Special Commission, at p 29.

accede to the Convention. To date, Canada has negotiated two bi-lateral agreements with Arab countries, and may negotiate a further agreement with Jordan.[11] The agreements are administrative in nature and aim to facilitate, through advisory mechanisms and through recommendations, the resolution of disputes involving child abduction, trans-frontier child access and the protection of the rights of children.[12]

23.9   On 10 November 1997 Canada signed a treaty with Egypt[13] under which the two countries set up a Joint Consultative Commission to discuss cases. This came into force on 1 October 1999 and has been used as a model for a similar agreement between Australia and Egypt. Canada and Lebanon[14] signed an agreement on 13 April 2000 but as of November 2001, this agreement had not yet entered into force.

BETWEEN AUSTRALIA AND OTHER STATES

23.10   Mr Justice Fogarty of the Family Court of Australia drew attention at the LAWASIA Conference 1995 to the lack of participation in the 1980 Hague Abduction Convention among Islamic, Buddhist and Hindu nations; he suggested that bi-lateral arrangements might be the way forward. Australia now has an agreement with Egypt[15] which has been signed, but which has not entered into force as Egypt has not yet notified Australia that its administrative arrangements are in place. Australia is also involved in negotiating an agreement with Lebanon, although this has not yet been concluded.

BETWEEN FRANCE AND OTHER STATES

23.11   France was a pioneer in the field of bi-lateral agreements. Strong links unite France and Arab countries, and it is these links which have, to a certain extent encouraged France to negotiate agreements with these States. The first agreement was with the Congo[16] and came into force in 1974, and the most recent agreement was with Lebanon, coming into force in 1999. Many agreements were made prior to the coming into force of the

---

[11]   See the Canadian response to the questionnaire concerning the practical operation of the Convention and views on possible recommendations, sent out by the Permanent Bureau of the Hague Conference prior to the fourth meeting of the Special Commission, at p 29.

[12]   Gosselain, *op cit*, n 1.

[13]   Agreement between the Government of Canada and the Government of the Arab Republic of Egypt regarding Co-operation on Consular Elements of Family Matters.

[14]   Agreement between the Government of Canada and the Government of the Lebanese Republic Regarding Co-operation of a Humanitarian Nature.

[15]   Agreement between the Government of Australia and the Government of the Arab Republic of Egypt regarding Co-operation on Protecting the Welfare of Children, Cairo, 22 October 2000. It is modelled on the Canada–Egypt agreement.

[16]   Congo (Popular Republic): 1 January 1974.

1980 Hague Abduction Convention, and certain agreements are with Contracting States to the Convention, prior to the Convention entering into force as between those States and France.

23.12   France has bi-lateral arrangements with Algeria,[17] Egypt,[18] Lebanon,[19] Morocco[20] and Tunisia.[21] France has a number of other relevant bi-lateral arrangements.[22] These bi-lateral agreements are of a general nature but they can be used in cases involving children.

23.13   Overall, these aerrangements do not appear to be working well. One stumbling block is that some of the agreements do not apply unless one parent is a French national, regardless of whether they in fact live in France.[23]

BETWEEN SPAIN AND MOROCCO

23.14   Spain has a bilateral agreement with Morocco,[24] which provides for the return of children to the requesting State if the removal:

(a)   infringes a judicially approved agreement between the abductor and the applicant;

(b)   violates sole custody rights of the applicant; or

(c)   infringes a judicial decision of the requesting State,

and in each case the child and the parents only have nationality of that State. Provided the application is made within 6 months of the removal, a return

---

[17]   Franco-Algerian Exchange of Letters on Co-operation and Judicial Assistance, Algiers, 18 September 1980; followed by the Convention between the Government of the French Republic and the Government of the Algerian Democratic Republic on children of separated mixed Franco-Algerian couples, Algiers, 21 June 1988.

[18]   Convention between the Government of the French Republic and the Government of the Arab Republic of Egypt on judicial co-operation in civil, social, commercial and administrative matters, Paris, 15 March 1982.

[19]   Agreement between the Government of the French Republic and the Government of the Lebanese Republic regarding co-operation in some elements of family matters, Paris, 12 July 1999.

[20]   Convention between the Government of the French Republic and the Kingdom of Morocco on the status of persons and the family and on judicial co-operation, Rabat, 10 August 1981.

[21]   Convention between the Government of the French Republic and the Government of the Tunisian Republic on judicial co-operation in matters of custody, access and maintenance obligations, Paris, 18 March 1982.

[22]   Austria: 27 February 1979 (additional to the 1954 Hague Convention); Benin: 27 February 1975; Brazil: 28 May 1996; Canada (Quebec only): 9 September 1977; Chad: 6 March 1976; Czech Republic: 10 May 1984; Djibouti: 27 September 1986; Hungary: 31 July 1980; Niger: 19 February 1977; Portugal: 20 July 1983; Senegal: 29 March 1974; Slovakia: 10 May 1984; Togo: 23 March 1976.

[23]   See Lowe, Armstrong, Mathias and Navarro: *Country Report: France* (NCMEC, 2002).

[24]   Convenio entre el Reino de España y el Reino de Marruecos sobre asistencia judicial, reconocimiento y ejecución de resoluciones judiciales en materia de derecho de custodia y derecho de visita y devolución de menores, hecho en Madrid el 30 de mayo de 1997.

should be ordered unless either the child is only a national of the requested State and the abductor is the sole custody holder, or there is a contradictory order in the requested State.

23.15 This agreement has had little success. Indeed, no case under the agreement has come before a court either in Spain or Morocco.

THE UNITED STATES

23.16 The United States has not entered into any bi-lateral agreements with non-Hague Abduction Convention States. On 15 July 1989, the Inter-American Convention about the International Restitution of Minors was adopted in Montevideo, Uruguay, by the Organisation of American States. The United States is not a party to the Montevideo Convention.

Chapter 24

THE 1996 HAGUE CONVENTION ON THE PROTECTION OF CHILDREN

INTRODUCTION

24.1   The 1996 Hague Convention on the Protection of Children[1] is the third attempt to deal with child protection. The first, the Convention on the guardianship of minors, was drawn up and signed in 1902.[2] It was ratified by 13 States, all civil law jurisdictions.[3] It became emasculated by a ruling by the International Court of Justice in the so-called *Boll* case,[4] that it applied only to private law guardianship and did not therefore extend to public law forms of guardianship in general, and to the Swedish institution of 'protective education' in particular.

24.2   Following this ruling, it was resolved to establish a new Convention on the protection of children. This was drawn up at the Ninth Session of the Conference and became the 1961 Convention Concerning the Powers of Authorities and the Law Applicable in Respect of the Protection of Infants. It was ratified by 11 States, again all civil law jurisdictions and all from continental western Europe apart from Poland and Turkey.[5]

24.3   Although it had the laudable aim 'to establish common provisions on the powers of authorities and the law applicable in respect of the protection of infants'[6] and was quite forward-thinking inasmuch as its main ground of jurisdiction in relation to measures for the protection of minors was the child's habitual residence,[7] it nevertheless proved unattractive to both the common law and Nordic jurisdictions. This was because the 1961 Convention preserved a major role for the law and authorities of the child's nationality, for, by Art 3, nationality governed any legal relationship of authority, such as parental authority or the authority of a guardian, arising by operation of law. Further, Art 3 also permitted the authorities of the child's nationality to

---

[1]   The full title is the Convention on Jurisdiction, Applicable Law, Recognition, Enforcement and Co-operation in Respect of Parental Responsibility and Measures for the Protection of Children.

[2]   Convention of 12 June 1902. The official text is in French only. See Lipstein, 'One Hundred Years of Hague Conferences on Private International Law' (1993) 42 ICLQ 553 at 568–569, and the Dyer Report on the revision of the 1961 Hague Convention on protection of minors – Part 1 (Preliminary Document No 1 of 1994).

[3]   Viz Belgium, France, Germany, Hungary, Italy, Luxembourg, Netherlands, Poland, Portugal, Romania, Spain, Sweden and Switzerland. It remains in force between Belgium and Germany and possibly Romania: see the Explanatory Report on the 1996 Convention by Paul Lagarde (hereafter 'the Lagarde Report'), para 3, n 6. See also Nygh, 'The New Hague Child Protection Convention' (1997) 11 Int Jo of Law, Policy and the Family 344.

[4]   *Netherlands v Sweden* ICJ Reports 1958 at p 55.

[5]   The ratifying States are Austria, France, Germany, Italy (which ratified only in 1995), Luxembourg, Netherlands, Poland (which ratified in 1993), Portugal, Spain, Switzerland and Turkey. Of these, only Austria and Turkey had not ratified the 1902 Convention. Of the States that ratified the 1902 Convention, only Belgium, Hungary, Romania and Sweden have not ratified the 1961 Convention.

[6]   The original text was published only in French. An English translation was published in the United Nations *Treaty Series* (1969), pp 145 ff.

[7]   Article 1.

exercise jurisdiction in any case where they considered it to be in the interests of the child, after advising the authorities of the child's habitual residence. This reliance on both habitual residence and nationality had the obvious danger of producing conflicts of jurisdiction, which danger was further exacerbated in cases where the child had dual nationality.

24.4 Potential conflicts of jurisdiction was not the only criticism of the 1961 Convention. One could also point to the poor functioning of the co-operation provisions between the authorities, the absence of a provision on enforcement, and the lack of compatibility with the 1980 Hague Abduction Convention. However, notwithstanding these criticisms and the small number of ratifying States, it would be a mistake to consider that the 1961 Convention did not have any worthwhile effects. In Germany, for example, the Convention has been actively used, with about 450 reported decisions between 1971 (when Germany ratified) and 1995.[8] Be that as it may, as one commentator has put it,[9] 'it has obviously been an important Convention for the countries who are parties to it but it is yesterday's model'. At all events, it was resolved at the Seventeenth (Centenary) Session of the Hague Conference to revise the 1961 Convention. That revision was completed at the Eighteenth Session, with the Convention being concluded in 1996.

24.5 The 1996 Convention formally came into force on 1 January 2002. when Slovakia's ratification took effect, thus providing the third ratification (Monaco and the Czech Republic having already ratified in May 1997 and March 2000, respectively) necessary for its coming into force under Art 61(1). Morocco, Latvia and Australia have since ratified the Convention (the ratifications taking effect on 1 December 2002, 1 April 2003 and 1 August 2003, respectively) and Estonia and Ecuador have acceded (the accessions taking effect on 1 June 2003 and 1 September 2003, respectively). As of August 2003, all 15 Member States of the European Union, including therefore the United Kingdom, together with Switzerland and Poland, have signed the Convention.[10] In the case of the United Kingdom, following a favourable reaction to a consultation exercise conducted in 2000–2001, the Government announced its readiness in principle to ratify.[11] However, as we discuss later,[12] the United Kingdom's ratification, as with that of other EU

---

[8] Siehr, 'Das neue Haager Übereinkommen von 1996 über den Schutz von Kuidern' (1998) *RabelsZ* 62, ss 464, 466, and Lorenz, 'The 1961 and 1996 Hague Conventions on protection of children and their future in the light of Brussels II', a paper given at the UK–German Conference on Family Law held in Edinburgh, September 2000.

[9] Clive, 'The Hague Conventions on Children of 1961 and 1996', a paper given at the UK–German Conference on Family Law held in Edinburgh, September 2000.

[10] All these States (apart from the Netherlands and Poland), together with Australia, signed the Convention on 1 April 2003. Note also *Judge's Newsletter*, vol IV at p 82, which explains that Panama has officially informed the Permanent Bureau that it is considering acceding to the Convention.

[11] See Lowe, 'The 1996 Convention on the protection of children – a fresh appraisal' [2002] CFLQ 191 at 192.

[12] See **24.56–24.57**.

States which are parties to the so-called 'Brussels II Regulation',[13] has been problematic.

THE OBJECTIVES AND FRAMEWORK OF THE CONVENTION

24.6 The 1996 Hague Convention on the Protection of Children is more ambitious than either of its two predecessors. Its objectives are set out by Art 1, namely:

'(a) to determine the State whose authorities have jurisdiction to take measures directed to the protection of the person or property of the child;

(b) to determine which law is to be applied by such authorities in exercising their jurisdiction;

(c) to determine the law applicable to parental responsibility;

(d) to provide for the recognition and enforcement of such measures or protection in all Contracting States;

(e) to establish such co-operation between the authorities of the Contracting States as may be necessary in order to achieve the purposes of this Convention.'

In short, the Convention aims to provide for the recognition and enforcement within all Contracting States of measures directed to the protection of children's person and property and to establish the necessary co-operation between the authorities of Contracting States in order to achieve this basic purpose, the overall aim being to improve the protection of children in international situations. In line with the general tradition of private international instruments produced by the Hague Conference, the 1996 Convention seeks to attain its purposes not by setting out substantive rules but rather by reducing conflict and promoting co-operation.

24.7 Although commonly referred to as the Protection of Children Convention, its full title is the Convention on Jurisdiction, Applicable Law, Recognition, Enforcement and Co-operation in Respect of Parental Responsibility and Measures for the Protection of Children. In fact, certain delegations had wanted a shorter and more elegant title, namely, 'a Convention on the Protection of Children', but this view did not prevail, in part because 'Protection of Children' was already part of the official title of the 1993 Intercountry Adoption Convention,[14] and in part because, to quote the Lagarde Report,[15] 'it would have been ambiguous in that it might have left the impression that the Convention dealt with questions of substantive law'. Accordingly, delegates approved the long title, which in fact repeats the titles

---

[13] Ie Council Regulation (EC) No 1347/2000 of 29 May 2000 on jurisdiction and the recognition of judgments in matrimonial matters and in matters of parental responsibility for children of both spouses, discussed in Chapters 4 and 18.

[14] The full title of which is the Convention on Protection of Children and Co-operation in respect of Intercountry Adoption.

[15] At para 7.

of the four principal Chapters of the Convention and which, according to the Lagarde Report, 'does not lend itself to any confusion'. Be that as it may, it is not helpful to have such a long, involved title.[16]

24.8   The Convention comprises seven Chapters:

–   *Chapter I* deals with the scope of the Convention, setting out the objectives as already described, providing that it applies to children up to the age of 18 and giving guidance on what is meant by protective measures.

–   *Chapter II* deals with jurisdiction and provides for a common set of jurisdictional rules essentially based on the child's habitual residence[17] and thus abandoning the reliance on nationality which had made the 1961 Convention so unattractive to common law and Nordic jurisdictions.

–   *Chapter III* deals with applicable law, laying down the general principle that the authority having jurisdiction should apply its own law.

–   *Chapter IV* deals with recognition and enforcement and provides the general principle that 'protective measures' taken in one Contracting State 'should be recognised by operation of law in all other Contracting States'.[18] In other words, there is no requirement for such measures to be registered or otherwise formally processed in other Contracting States. Registration is only necessary if positive enforcement is required.

–   *Chapter V* deals with co-operation and, primarily through the tried and tested medium of Central Authorities (which must be set up by each Contracting State), makes provision, *inter alia*, for the exchange of information about a child between authorities particularly in relation to making access orders and public law orders.

–   *Chapter VI* contains general provisions. *Inter alia*, it makes provision for the issuing of international certificates of parental responsibility, the confidentiality of personal data, and the inter-relationship between the 1996 Convention and other Conventions, notably the 1980 Hague Abduction Convention.

---

16   It might further be added that the Preamble is also relatively long for a Hague Convention (although it is comparable to that of the 1993 Intercountry Adoption Convention) and, to quote the Lagarde Report, para 8, represents a 'compromise between delegations which wanted to have a short Preamble, indicating simply the object of the Convention and placing this Convention in the wake of the United Nations Convention of 20 November 1989 on the Rights of the Child and those delegations which wanted to set out explicitly in the Preamble certain broad principles appearing in the latter Convention …'. In fact, the first three paragraphs set out the objects of the Convention, the fourth refers to the best interests test which is derived from the UN Convention, the fifth refers to the need to revise the 1961 Convention, and the final paragraph refers generally to the UN Convention.

17   Some accommodation is made in Art 10 to permit courts hearing divorce or separation proceedings (in which jurisdiction is based on the *adult's* habitual residence or domicile) to make orders in relation to children. See further **24.21–24.22**.

18   See Art 23(1). Recognition can be refused on the grounds set out by Art 23(2), discussed at **24.39** *et seq*.

–   *Chapter VII* provides the normal final clauses, dealing, for example, with rights to ratify and accede.

THE SCOPE OF THE CONVENTION

The meaning of 'child'

24.9   Under Art 2, the 1996 Convention applies to 'children from the moment of their birth until they reach the age of 18 years'. Three points need to be observed about the application of Art 2:

(1)   the Convention does not apply to unborn children;[19]
(2)   the Convention applies until the child reaches the age of 18 and not 16, as in the case of the 1980 Hague Abduction Convention;[20] and
(3)   notwithstanding its application until the age of 18, the Convention does not thereby determine the age of majority for any Contracting State.[21]

The meaning of 'protection'

24.10   In general terms, 'protection' refers to both private and public law[22] measures[23] taken by judicial or administrative bodies to safeguard children. In the case of private law measures, the 1996 Convention is not limited, as is 'Brussels II',[24] to divorce or other matrimonial proceedings but extends, for example, to proceedings solely concerning children.

24.11   The types of matters covered by the Convention are set out, but not exhaustively defined, by Art 3, namely: the attribution, exercise, termination and delegation of parental responsibility; rights of custody and access;[25] guardianship, curatorship and analogous institutions; the designation and

---

[19]   A proposal to extend the Convention to unborn children was decisively rejected: see the Lagarde Report, para 15.

[20]   In this regard, the 1996 Convention takes its cue from Art 1 of the UN Convention on the Rights of the Child 1989 although, unlike the latter, the 1996 Convention continues to apply up to that age even if by the law of the Contracting State the child has reached the age of majority.

[21]   See the Lagarde Report, at para 16. Emancipation is expressly excluded from the Convention by Art 4(d).

[22]   This, in fact, reflects one of the key changes made by the 1961 Convention following the ruling by the International Court of Justice in the so-called *Boll* case, discussed at **24.1**.

[23]   According to Clive, 'The New Hague Convention on Children' (1998) 3 *Juridical Review* 169 at 171, fn 8, the word 'measure' refers to a decision by a judicial or administrative authority, which is intended to have legal effect and not therefore 'a private agreement or other juridical act which confers powers', which he says can be inferred from Art 16(2), discussed further at **24.32**.

[24]   See **4.11–4.12**.

[25]   By Art 3(b), rights of custody are defined as 'including rights relating to the care of the person of the child and, in particular, the right to determine the child's place of residence, as well as rights of access including the right to take a child for a limited period of time to a place other than the child's habitual residence', which is similar to the definition in Art 5 of the 1980 Hague Abduction Convention.

functions of any person or body having charge of the child's person or property, representing or assisting the child; placing a child in foster or institutional care or the provision of care by *Kafala* or an analogous institution; public authority supervision of the care of a child by any person having charge of the child; and, finally, the administration, conservation or disposal of the child's property.

24.12 The inclusion of *Kafala* is important because it represents a real attempt to engage with Islamic nations, and it is to be noted that Morocco has already ratified the Convention. Both *Kafala* and fostering fall outside the scope of the 1993 Intercountry Adoption Convention.

24.13 Although an improvement on the 1961 Convention which used the term 'measure of protection' without defining it, Art 3 nevertheless does not provide a complete definition but only an illustrative, albeit an extensive, list, for, as the Lagarde Report comments,[26] '[s]ince the measures vary with each legal system, the enumeration given in this article could only be given in terms of examples'. In contrast, Art 4 provides an exhaustive list of what the 1996 Convention does *not* cover, namely: establishing or contesting a parent–child relationship; adoption; names; emancipation; maintenance obligations; trusts or succession; social security, general public measures on health or education; measures taken as a result of penal offences committed by children; and the right of asylum and immigration decisions.[27] Taken together, Arts 3 and 4, notwithstanding that the former is only illustrative, do give a good idea of what is and what is not covered by the Convention.[28] One further complication, however, is the power to make reservations. Under Art 55, Contracting States may reserve: (a) jurisdiction to its own authorities to take measures directed to protect a child's property[29] situated on its territory; and (b) the right not to recognise any parental responsibility or measure insofar as it is incompatible with any measure taken by its authorities in relation to that property. It seems likely that the United Kingdom will take this reservation.

---

[26] At para 18. See also Silberman, 'The 1996 Hague Convention on the Protection of Children: Should the United States Join?' (2000) 34 *Family Law Quarterly* 239 at 245.

[27] The rationale for these exclusions are that they are matters already covered by other Conventions (eg adoption, maintenance obligations, succession and trusts) or they are not really to do with the child's protection (eg establishment of the parent–child relationship, names and emancipation) or because they are public law matters over which States would not give up control (eg education, health, immigration and measures taken following the commission of penal offences by the child).

[28] But note Clive, *op cit*, n 23, at 172 that certain other issues are *implicitly* excluded, eg *general* legal remedies such as damages for tort or contract, notwithstanding that they might in certain instances protect the child.

[29] The reservation can be restricted just to certain types of property: Art 55(2).

THE JURISDICTIONAL RULES

Pre-eminence accorded to courts of the child's habitual residence

24.14　A crucial part of the Convention is the creation of a common set of jurisdictional rules designed to avoid as far as possible conflicts of jurisdiction.[30] In line with other modern child Conventions, the primary jurisdiction, as provided for by Art 5, is vested in the authorities of the Contracting State in which the child is habitually resident. Habitual residence is not defined in the Convention and no doubt cognisance will be taken of the jurisprudence developed under the 1980 Hague Abduction Convention.[31]

Jurisdictions based on presence

24.15　Supplementing this pre-eminence rule are a number of subsidiary rules. Under Art 6, jurisdiction can be based on the child's presence in the case of: (a) refugee children and those who 'due to disturbances occurring in their country, are internationally displaced'; and (b) children whose habitual residence cannot be established. So far as the former are concerned, the Lagarde Report explains[32] that they are contemplated to be 'limited to those who have left their countries because of conditions which were arising there, and who often are not accompanied and, in any case, are temporarily or definitively deprived of their parents'.[33] Such children will often need long-term protection. For those children without an habitual residence, as the Legarde Report says,[34] '[t]he court of the place where the child is present … plays the role of a jurisdiction of necessity'.

24.16　Rules have also been devised both to cover cases of urgency and to make provisional measures. So far as the former are concerned, Art 11(1) permits jurisdiction to be taken upon the basis of either the child's presence or that of his property. Furthermore, such measures have extra-territorial effect,[35]

---

[30]　As Duncan has observed in a paper, 'The Hague Convention of 1996 on the Protection of Children', given at a conference entitled 'Convego: Verso un Diriltio Minorila Europe', in Geneva, November 1997, a particular concern of delegates drafting the Convention was to avoid, in the case of intercountry custody cases in particular, 'the unhappy prospect of jurisdiction being decided according to the speed with which competing parents could reach the door of the court in their respective countries'.

[31]　See **4.24** *et seq.*

[32]　At para 44.

[33]　Ie it does not apply to runaway or abandoned children.

[34]　At para 45.

[35]　This is implicit inasmuch as by Art 23 all measures taken by one Contracting State are automatically recognised by all other Contracting States. Cf Art 12, discussed at **24.17**, which is expressly limited to having internal effect only.

although any measures taken will lapse as soon as a Contracting State otherwise with jurisdiction under the Convention takes its own protective measures.[36]

24.17   Under Art 12, jurisdiction to take measures 'of a provisional character' can, subject to Art 7,[37] and provided they are not incompatible with measures already taken, be based on the presence of the child or his property but such measures can only have effect within the territory making the order and will lapse once a Contracting State otherwise with jurisdiction takes protective measures. Article 12 was inspired by a UK proposal[38] and is designed to permit provisional and territorially limited measures to protect children present in the jurisdiction for some temporary purpose, such as visiting a holiday camp, on an educational exchange or even an access visit, even if there is no obvious emergency. As one commentator put it,[39] '[p]revention is often better than cure and this article enables local authorities to take measures without waiting for an emergency to arise'.

Surrendering jurisdiction

24.18   Notwithstanding the pre-eminence accorded to the place of the child's habitual residence (or presence under the terms of Art 6), provision is made under Art 8 for the authority having jurisdiction in that State to decide that an authority in another Contracting State may be better placed to determine the best interests of the child. In such cases, the original authority may either request that other authority (either directly or with the assistance of its Central Authority) to assume jurisdiction or suspend consideration of the case and invite the parties to submit the request to the other authority. In any event, before a decision is made, as Art 8(3) puts it, the 'authorities concerned may proceed to an exchange of views'. Under Art 8(2), the authorities to which jurisdiction may be transferred are those of a Contracting State:[40]

(a)   of which the child is a national;
(b)   in which the child's property is situated;
(c)   whose authorities are seized of matrimonial proceedings; or
(d)   with which the child has a substantial connection.

24.19   Although Art 8 will cause little difficulty to common law countries, familiar as they are with the concept of *forum non conveniens*, it is quite alien to

---

[36]   Article 11(2). Note that, under Art 11(3), measures taken in respect of a child who is habitually resident in a non-Contracting State 'lapse in each Contracting State as soon as measures required by the situation and taken by the authorities of another State are recognised in the Contracting State in question'.

[37]   Discussed at **24.23**.

[38]   See the Lagarde Report, at para 74.

[39]   Clive, *op cit*, n 23, at 175.

[40]   Ie Art 8 does *not* facilitate the transfer of jurisdiction to an authority of a non-Contracting State.

civil law jurisdictions and, being discretionary, it remains to be seen how frequently it will be exercised by such countries.

24.20   Under Art 8, the initiative for transferring jurisdiction lies with the authority of the child's habitual residence. However, Art 9 provides exactly the same scheme so as to allow the other authority to take the initiative to displace the jurisdiction based on the child's habitual residence, but it can only take jurisdiction if the authority of the child's habitual residence agrees.[41]

Jurisdiction of authority seised of matrimonial proceedings

24.21   During the negotiations on the 1996 Convention, there was extensive debate as to whether any provision should be made to allow authorities dealing with divorces, etc, to take protective measures over children.[42] On the one hand, it was argued that it would be wrong to dilute the principle of jurisdiction being based on the child's habitual residence or presence by allowing divorce courts whose jurisdiction is based on the *parents'* position (which might of course have little or no relevance to the child's circumstances) to make child protection orders. Against this was the argument that having a so-called 'one-stop' jurisdiction to deal with all matrimonial matters (which is the solution hitherto accepted by the United Kingdom)[43] is convenient and that it was also desirable to have a single unified solution where children were residing in different countries. There was also concern that if no provision were to be made there would be too great a disparity with what has now become the so-called 'Brussels II Regulation'.[44]

24.22   In the event, a compromise was reached, with Art 10 providing for authorities seized of matrimonial proceedings[45] to take measures to protect children, if their domestic law so permits, providing that, at the time of the commencement of proceedings: (a) one of the child's parents is habitually resident in that State and one of them (but not necessarily the parent just referred to) has parental responsibility; and (b) the parents and anyone else with parental responsibility agree to such jurisdiction being so exercised and that it is in the child's best interests to do so. However, jurisdiction to take protective measures ceases as soon as the decision allowing or refusing the application for divorce, etc, has become final or when the proceedings have come to an end for another reason.[46]

---

41   See Art 9(3).
42   See the Lagarde Report, at para 61; Nygh, op cit, n 3, at 350–351, and Clive, *op cit*, n 23, at 175–177.
43   See the Family Law Act 1986, discussed in Chapter 3.
44   Council Regulation (EC) No 1347/2000 of 29 May 2000 on jurisdiction and the recognition and enforcement of judgments in matrimonial matters and in matters of parental responsibility for children of both spouses. This Regulation was originally drafted as a Convention, work having begun on it in 1995, which was completed in 1998. For a discussion of the Regulation, see **4.9** *et seq* and Chapter 18.
45   Viz divorce, legal separation and annulment of marriage: see Art 10(1).
46   See Art 10(2).

The position where the child's habitual residence changes

24.23 Further provisions deal with the position where the child's habitual residence subsequently changes. *Prima facie*, as Art 5(2) provides, where the child's habitual residence changes to another Contracting State it is the authorities of this latter State that have pre-eminent jurisdiction. However, this is subject first to Art 7 which, in cases of wrongful removal or retention,[47] provides that jurisdiction remains in the State of the child's former habitual residence unless either there has been acquiescence or the child has resided in the new Contracting State for at least one year after those having rights of custody have or should have had knowledge of the child's whereabouts and 'no request for return lodged within that period is still pending and the child is settled in his or her new environment'.[48] Neither 'acquiescence' nor 'settled in his or her new environment' are defined in the 1996 Convention, but no doubt regard will be had to the jurisprudence on those concepts developed under the 1980 Hague Abduction Convention.[49]

24.24 The second proviso to authorities of the child's new habitual residence acquiring pre-eminent jurisdiction is by Art 13, which provides that authorities of a Contracting State must abstain from exercising jurisdiction (other than emergency or temporary jurisdiction)[50] if, at the time of the commencement of proceedings, corresponding measures have been requested from the authorities of another Contracting State having due jurisdiction according to Arts 5 to 10, and those proceedings are still pending.[51] The only exception to this embargo, which is aimed at removing conflicts where there are concurrent proceedings, is where the authority first seized declines jurisdiction.[52]

24.25 Both Art 7 and Art 13 have important implications for the operation of the 1980 Hague Abduction Convention which will be examined later.[53]

---

[47] Defined by Art 7(2) as where '(a) it is in breach of rights of custody attributed to a person, an institution or any other body, either jointly or alone, under the law of the State in which the child was habitually resident immediately before the removal or retention; and (b) at the time of removal or retention those rights were actually exercised, either jointly or alone, or would have been so exercised but for the removal of retention'. This definition is in the same terms as Art 3 of the Hague Abduction Convention, discussed at **14.5** *et seq.*

[48] See Art 7(1)(a) and (b). Cf s 41 of the UK Family Law Act 1986, discussed at **4.74**, which provides that in cases of wrongful removal, etc, within the United Kingdom (see *Re S (A Child: Abduction)* [2002] EWCA Civ 1941, [2003] 1 FLR 1008, the child's habitual residence is deemed to remain for the following 12 months that of the jurisdiction from which he was removed.

[49] Discussed respectively at **17.13** and **17.61**.

[50] Under Art 11 or Art 12.

[51] This embargo applies equally to authorities assuming jurisdiction under Arts 6–10.

[52] See Art 13(2).

[53] See **24.61** *et seq.*

Commentary

24.26 By making the child's habitual residence the primary basis of jurisdiction and firmly relegating nationality to a subordinate basis (which can only be exercised with leave of an authority of the child's habitual residence), the 1996 Convention addresses a major criticism of the 1961 Convention and thereby removes an objection to ratification by the common law and Nordic jurisdictions. There is indeed every justification for vesting primary jurisdiction in the child's habitual residence, since that will be where the child has his or her home, where the child can be seen in his or her usual environment and, consequently, where it is easiest to assess the child's best interests. There were delegations, notably the United States (no doubt mindful of the Swedish Supreme Court's ruling in the *Johnson*[54] abduction case), who wanted the term 'habitual residence' defined, but while it must be conceded that it is not the sharpest of concepts (as the extensive jurisprudence under the 1980 Hague Abduction Convention testifies), it is nevertheless the connecting factor now commonly agreed upon in international Conventions and, to that extent, it is a tried and tested concept.

24.27   Similarly, there can surely be no objection to basing jurisdiction on the child's presence either in the case of internationally displaced children or those having no habitual residence. The provisions for temporary jurisdiction in cases of urgency, etc, seem both essential and sensible, although their interaction with the 1980 Hague Abduction Convention requires careful scrutiny (see further below).

24.28   The provisions under Arts 8 and 9 to forgo jurisdiction, are akin to *forum non conveniens*, which is familiar to common law countries and will not in itself cause difficulty for the United Kingdom. However, this concept is by no means so familiar to civil law jurisdictions, and one wonders to what extent such countries will be prepared voluntarily to forgo jurisdiction either under Art 8 or, more worryingly from the United Kingdom's point of view, pursuant to a request made under Art 9. On the other hand, it may be that, as Contracting States become more familiar with the concept, particularly if it can be seen to operate in common law jurisdictions, they may themselves come to operate it.

24.29   Article 10, which vests limited jurisdiction in the matrimonial courts to make child protection orders, will require the United Kingdom to amend the Family Law Act 1986. At the moment, that Act gives primary jurisdiction to a court hearing matrimonial proceedings, it hitherto never being seriously questioned that it was right to have a single court dealing with all issues arising from marital breakdown, notwithstanding that jurisdiction is based on the adults' domicile or habitual residence. The Convention brings this assumption into question, and whether the compromise of permitting jurisdiction only

---

[54]   Case No 7508 (1995), judgment given by the Swedish Supreme Administrative Court on 9 May 1996.

where all those with parental responsibility agree is enough to assuage those who believe in the single jurisdiction approach remains to be seen.

APPLICABLE LAW

The general position

24.30 The basic principle, provided for by Art 15(1), is that, in exercising their jurisdiction, the authorities of the Contracting State apply their own internal law (the *lex fori*). As the Lagarde Report puts it,[55] the principal justification for this stance is that it 'facilitates the task of the authority which has taken jurisdiction since it will thus apply the law which it knows best'. But an important supporting argument is that, given the jurisdictional rules, the authority in question will generally be the closest to the child and being the most appropriate forum it is right that it should apply its own law. Nevertheless, as Nygh points out,[56] jurisdiction can be taken on the basis of the child's presence, and to take account of this, Art 15(2) provides that insofar as the protection of the person or property of the child requires, the authority assuming jurisdiction may 'exceptionally apply or take into consideration the law of another State with which the situation has a substantial connection'. It is to be noted that that State does *not* have to be a Contracting State. Article 15(3) deals with the situation where there has been a change of the child's habitual residence. Although, by Art 14, measures previously taken by other authorities remain in effect, by Art 15(3), the law of the new habitual residence will govern from the time of the change of habitual residence 'the conditions of the application of the measures taken in the State of the former habitual residence'. To illustrate how this works, the Lagarde Report gives[57] the example of a guardian who, by the law of State of the original habitual residence, needs court permission to take certain actions. If, however, the law of the State of the new habitual residence would not impose such a new requirement, Art 15(3) operates to allow that guardian to act alone.

The position with regard to parental responsibility[58]

24.31 Many of the provisions of Chapter III are concerned with parental responsibility, which, as one commentator has said,[59] is not a protective measure at all but rather 'the recognition and continuity of existing *ex lege* relationships'.

24.32 The attribution or extinguishment of parental responsibility can be determined in three different ways, namely: by operation of law (ie without the

---

[55] At para 86.

[56] *Op cit*, n 3, at 352.

[57] At para 91.

[58] See the excellent discussion by Clive, *op cit*, n 23, at 179–182, Nygh, *op cit*, n 3, at 353–354, and Silberman, *op cit*, n 26, at 261–263.

[59] Silberman, *op cit*, n 26, at 262.

intervention of a judicial or administrative authority);[60] by agreement or unilateral act, again without intervention by the courts, as where the parents make a formal agreement or appoint someone to be a guardian; or by court order as, for example, in the domestic context, when the court makes a residence order, the effect of which is to confer responsibility on that person if he or she does not have it already. In the case of the first two circumstances, Art 16(1) and (2) respectively provide that the attribution or extinguishment of parental responsibility[61] is governed by the law of the child's habitual residence (whether or not that is the law of a non-Contracting State).[62] The third circumstance is simply governed by the normal *lex fori* rule as provided for by Art 15(1).

24.33 A problem which exercised the Special Commission preparing the Convention was what effect a change of the child's habitual residence should have on the attribution of parental responsibility. This is governed by Art 16(3) and (4). These provisions respectively provide that the parental responsibility which exists under the law of the State of the child's habitual residence will continue to exist notwithstanding a change of that residence to another State (thereby ensuring continuity and stability and avoiding the need to take fresh steps in the new country), but where the law of the State of the child's new habitual residence automatically confers parental responsibility on a person who does not already have it, it is the latter law that will prevail.[63] In other words, while a change of habitual residence cannot extinguish parental responsibility, it can confer it.

24.34 To counter the consequential risk of a third party, as the Lagarde Report puts it,[64] 'committing an error about the person or the powers of the child's legal representative', Art 19(1) provides:

> 'The validity of a transaction entered into between a third party and another person who would be entitled to act as the child's legal representative under the law of the State where the transaction was concluded cannot be contested, and the third party cannot be held liable, on the sole ground that the other person was not entitled to act as the child's legal representative under the law designated by the provisions of this Chapter, unless the third party knew or should have known that the parental responsibility was governed by the latter law.'

---

[60] In England and Wales, for example, Children Act 1989, s 2, and in Scotland, Children (Scotland) Act 1995, s 3, provide for the automatic attribution of parental responsibility to married parents and the unmarried mother.

[61] Defined by Art 1(2) as 'including parental authority or any analogous relationship of authority determining the rights, powers and responsibilities of parents, guardians or other legal representatives in relation to the person or property of the child'.

[62] See Art 20.

[63] According to Clive, *op cit*, n 23, at 181, fn 4, such a result would follow anyway from the general rule that the law of the current habitual residence decides whether parental responsibility is attributed by operation of law. In his view, Art 16(4) is unnecessary, but it does make the position clear.

[64] At para 111.

In other words, as Clive puts it,[65] third parties are 'entitled to assume that the rules of their own system apply to entitlement to act as the child's legal representative unless they know or ought to know that the rules of another system are applicable under the Convention'. In this latter regard, Art 40 provides that a person with parental responsibility can obtain, from a competent authority, a certificate indicating the capacity in which that person is entitled to act and the powers conferred on him. This protection, however, only applies 'if the transaction was entered into between persons present on the territory of the same State'.[66] In any event, it is suggested in the Lagarde Report[67] that, although Art 19(1) extends protection whatever the nature of the transaction (be it 'transactions concerned with family law, successions to estates or rights to immovables'), it might reasonably be supposed that 'the diligence required on the part of the third party in order to benefit from Art 19 ought to be in proportion to the importance of transaction'.

24.35 Although the *attribution* of parental responsibility survives a change of habitual residence, under Art 17 the *exercise* of it is governed by the law of the current habitual residence. Furthermore, under Art 18, the authorities of the State of current habitual residence can subsequently terminate or modify parental responsibility, according to the general rules of the Convention.

24.36 The inclusion of the provisions governing the attribution and exercise of parental responsibility (which, as already pointed out, are not really 'protective measures' at all) was the occasion for 'significant discussions',[68] and clearly the provision for its survival notwithstanding any change of the child's habitual residence is significant. So far as English law is concerned, it would mean that, upon becoming habitually resident in England or Wales, a child's unmarried father will continue to have automatic parental responsibility if he had it under the law of the child's previous habitual residence, as for example, that of Australia. This might look odd compared with the situation of English unmarried fathers (although equally it would mean that unmarried fathers and, prospectively, step-parents[69] who have acquired parental responsibility by means of a parental responsibility agreement or order made or granted in England will continue to have parental responsibility regardless of the law of any other Contracting State to which they have moved) but, as previously argued, its virtue is that it maintains continuity and stability in the family which thus protects the child. In any event, since Art 19 protects third parties if they make a *bona fide* assumption that English law applies to the question of entitlement to act as the child's legal representative, no one can directly be prejudiced by the provision. It might be added that definite rules about attribution of parental responsibility are helpful and, when combined with the recognition of guardianship orders, will resolve current uncertainty in English

---

65 *Op cit*, n 23, at para 182.
66 Article 19(2).
67 At para 113.
68 See the Lagarde Report, at para 93.
69 As is prospectively provided by the Adoption and Children Act 2002.

law on the issue.[70] Moreover, the fact that under Art 17 the exercise of parental responsibility and the power to end it is governed by the law of the child's current habitual residence should help to allay fears that the rules governing attribution are too extreme.

RECOGNITION AND ENFORCEMENT

The basic scheme

24.37 Recognition and enforcement is governed by Chapter IV of the 1996 Convention. This Chapter is designed to address one of the serious shortcomings of the 1961 Convention under which,[71] if enforcement measures were required, the recognising State (with either nationality or habitual residence jurisdiction) was able to modify those measures. The basic rule of the Convention is, pursuant to Art 23(1), that measures taken by the authorities of a Contracting State must be recognised by operation of law in all other Contracting States. Limited exceptions to this basic obligation are provided for by Art 23(2).[72]

24.38 Under Art 26(1), measures entitled to recognition taken in one Contracting State and enforceable there must, at the request of an interested party, be declared enforceable or registered for enforcement in another Contracting State. Such a request can only be refused on one of the grounds under Art 23(2) on which recognition may be refused.[73] Under Art 26(2), Contracting States are obliged to apply 'a simple and rapid' procedure for enforcement and, under Art 27, they are forbidden to review the merits of the measure taken. Once declared enforceable or registered for enforcement, the measure can be enforced as if it had been made by the second State. According to Art 28, enforcement takes place 'in accordance with the law of the requested State to the extent provided by such law, taking into consideration the best interests of the child'.

Refusing recognition or enforcement

24.39 Limited exceptions to the basic enjoinder both to recognise and enforce measures taken by other Contracting States are provided by Art 23(2). There are six grounds, namely:

(a) jurisdiction was not based on a Convention ground;
(b) the child was not given the opportunity to be heard in violation of fundamental principles of procedure of the requested State;

---

[70] See *Re J (Adoption: Consent of Foreign Public Authority)* [2002] EWHC 766 (Fam), [2002] 2 FLR 618; *Re AGN (Adoption: Foreign Adoption)* [2000] 2 FLR 431; *Re AMR (Adoption: Procedure)* [1999] 2 FLR 807; and *Re D (Adoption: Foreign Guardianship)* [1999] 2 FLR 865.
[71] See Art 7.
[72] Discussed below at **24.39** *et seq*.
[73] Article 26(3).

(c) a person claiming parental responsibility has not been given the opportunity to be heard;

(d) recognition would be 'manifestly contrary to public policy of the requested State, taking into account the best interests of the child';

(e) the measure is incompatible with a later measure taken in the non-Convention State of the child's habitual residence, and

(f) Art 33 has not been complied with.[74]

24.40 Before examining these grounds, the following points should be made:

(1) since the clear expectation under Arts 23(1) and 26(1) is that measures be recognised and enforced, the grounds for refusal under Art 23(2) should be regarded as exceptional, although this could have been made clearer both in the Convention and in the Lagarde Report. Presumably, as with establishing the exceptions under Arts 12 and 13 of the 1980 Hague Abduction Convention,[75] the burden of proof lies on the person seeking to invoke them;

(2) in deciding whether or not to refuse recognition or enforcement, authorities are bound by findings of fact on which the authority of the State where the measures were taken based its jurisdiction (see Art 25) and are forbidden by Art 27 to review the merits of the measure taken;

(3) Art 23(2) sets out the *only* grounds on which refusal may be based;

(4) as the Lagarde Report puts it, the establishment of an Art 23(2) ground '... authorises the refusal of recognition, but does not impose it';[76]

(5) fears about non-recognition can be allayed by obtaining what in effect is an advanced ruling by the requested State under Art 24, namely, whether or not it will recognise the measure taken in another Contracting State.[77]

24.41 Some of these grounds are to be expected, such as, for example, measures being taken on a jurisdictional basis not provided for by the Convention, and measures infringing parental responsibility without the parent having an opportunity to be heard, save in emergencies, and these call for no further comment. Two other grounds are specific to 1996 Convention, namely, where the measure is incompatible with a later measure taken in the non-Contracting State of habitual residence of the child, provided the later measure fulfils the requirement for recognition in the requested State, and if the procedure under Art 33 (consent to placement in foster care or institutional care, etc) has not been complied with. The former is designed[78] to

---

[74] Article 33 is discussed at **24.50**.

[75] See Chapter 17.

[76] At para 121. A similar stance is taken in the 1980 Hague Abduction Convention, but the 1996 Convention has no equivalent provision to Art 18 of the former Convention, for discussion of which, see **17.2** *et seq*.

[77] Applications may be made by any interested party, but it is for each Contracting State to provide a procedure for dealing with such requests.

[78] See the Lagarde Report, at para 126. But note that this means that a Contracting State is prevented from recognising a measure taken in a non-Contracting State other than that of

give preference to the later measure taken by the authority that is closer to the child and therefore in a better position to assess the child's best interests. The remaining two grounds call for more detailed comment.

24.42 Article 23(2)(b) provides that, emergencies apart, recognition or enforcement can be refused if the measure was taken 'without the child having been provided the opportunity to be heard, in violation of fundamental principles of procedure of the requested State'. This provision was inspired by Art 12(2) of the UN Convention on the Rights of the Child.[79] Although the Lagarde Report comments[80] that the Article 'does not imply that the child ought to be heard in every case' it gives the requested State some latitude for refusal.[81] Germany, for example, sets great store by making extensive provision for listening to children, and the courts there would certainly do so in cases where those in England and Wales might not. As an example, one could cite the German Constitutional Court ruling in the *Tiemann* case[82] that, even in applications under the 1980 Hague Abduction Convention, where there has been a re-abduction, it is incumbent upon the court to listen to the child either directly or through his or her representative. There must, therefore, be some concern that this difference of view could lead to non-recognition under Art 23(2)(b).

24.43 Article 23(2)(d) provides that recognition may be refused upon the basis that it 'is manifestly contrary to public policy of the requested State, taking into account the best interests of the child'.

24.44 Although the prohibition under Arts 25 and 27 against going back on findings of fact and reviewing the merits of the original decision will militate against a simple application of the welfare test, there is an obvious danger that the court could rely on fresh evidence and then essentially apply a welfare test on a forward-looking basis. Could it be doubted, for example, that if a court has refused an application for the child's return under the 1980 Hague Abduction Convention on the basis of Art 13(b) founded on the left-behind parent's violence that that will not then be taken into account in applying Art 23(2)(d) in deciding whether to recognise a pre-existing custody order? Clearly, the width of Art 23(2)(d) hangs on the interpretation of the word 'manifestly'. This word is also used (although admittedly not in relation to a public policy exception) in Art 10(1)(a) and (b) of the 1980 European Custody Convention, which allows a refusal to recognise and register an order. Both the English and Irish courts have emphasised, when applying Art 10(1)(a) and (b), that the word 'manifestly' places a heavy onus on those seeking to

---

the child's habitual residence, if it is incompatible with earlier measures taken by a Contracting State.

[79] See the Lagarde Report, at para 123.

[80] At para 123.

[81] See also the comments by Silberman, *op cit*, n 26, at 265.

[82] B Verf G of 28 October 1998, JZ 1999, 459.

establish the defence,[83] and if this approach were to be followed generally, then Art 23(2)(d) should not be regarded with too much fear. The problem, of course, is that until the provision has been tested, it is hard to predict how it will be interpreted.

Enforcement

24.45 Although the enforcement provisions are a marked improvement on those under the 1961 Convention, there must still be some concern that they do not go far enough. It is one of the concerns about the working of the 1980 Hague Abduction Convention that some countries lack either an effective or a speedy system of enforcement, although in this respect note must be taken of the European Court of Human Rights rulings in *Ignoccolo-Zenide v Romania*[84] and *Sylvester v Austria*[85] that failure to enforce a return order was in breach of Art 8 of the ECHR. Consequently, Art 26(2), which simply provides that '[e]ach Contracting State should apply to the declaration of enforceability a simple and rapid procedure', seems disappointingly vague. It would have been preferable if, as in the 1980 Hague Abduction Convention, some specific time-limit had been specified.[86]

24.46 Equally worrying is the provision in Art 28 that measures having been declared enforceable or registered for enforcement are enforceable as if made in the requested State but that such enforcement 'takes place in accordance with the law of the requested State to the extent provided by such law, *taking into consideration the best interests of the child*' (emphasis added). This reference to the child's best interests could significantly dilute the powers of enforcement and contrasts with the English position in which it has been held[87] that, when imposing sanctions for non-compliance with child orders, the child's welfare is not the paramount consideration.

24.47 The provisions dealing with recognition and enforcement are crucial to the success or failure of the Convention. Although it is the clear expectation of the Convention that measures be both recognised and enforced there must be some concern that some of the grounds set out by Art 23(2), upon which recognition and enforcement may be refused, are too loosely drawn, and while individual Contracting States might well have effective mechanisms of their own, the provisions dealing with enforcement are not prescriptive enough.

---

[83] See eg *Re G (A Minor)(Child Abduction: Enforcement)* [1990] 2 FLR 325 at 331, per Booth J; *Re A (Foreign Access Order: Enforcement)* [1996] 1 FLR 561 at 564, per Leggatt LJ; and, in Ireland, *RJ v MR* [1994] 1 IR 271 at 289, per Finlay CJ, discussed at **15.109** *et seq.*

[84] (2001) 31 EHRR 7, ECtHR.

[85] [2003] 2 FLR 211, ECtHR, and *Maire v Portugal*, Application no 48206/99, ECtHR.

[86] Article 11 of the 1980 Convention refers to a 6-week time-limit.

[87] *A v N (Committal: Refusal of Contact)* [1997] 1 FLR 533, CA.

CO-OPERATION

24.48 Chapter V contains important provisions concerning co-operation. Although some delegations preparing the Convention saw these provisions as among the most important, others were fearful that if the obligations were too onerous and expensive this would deter ratifications.[88] In the end, a reasonable compromise has been achieved with many provisions being discretionary rather than obligatory and none being unduly onerous. In any event, Art 38 allows the imposition of reasonable charges for the provision of these services.

Co-operation via Central Authorities

24.49 As with other modern child Conventions, the crucial vehicle for co-operation is the Central Authority which, under Art 29, all Contracting States are obliged to create.[89] As the Lagarde Report puts it,[90] Central Authorities have a general mission of co-operation and information. Under Art 30, they must co-operate with one another to achieve the purposes of the Convention and to this end take appropriate steps to provide information as to the laws of, and services available in, their States relating to the protection of children. Under Art 31, Central Authorities must either themselves or through public authorities or other bodies take all reasonable steps:

(a) to facilitate communication between authorities where this is needed under Arts 8 and 9 (the *forum non conveniens* provisions);

(b) to facilitate by mediation, conciliation or similar means, agreed solutions for the protection of children; and

(c) to provide assistance in discovering the whereabouts of the child.

24.50 Under Art 32, a Central Authority of the place where the child is habitually resident and present may,[91] at the request of another Central Authority with which the child has a substantial connection, provide a report on the circumstances of the child and/or request the competent authority of its State to consider the need to take measures to protect the child. This provision, as Nygh points out,[92] could be useful in the context of child abduction where the court after ordering the child's return might wish to ensure that the child will be protected in the foreign State upon his or her return. This protection is further augmented by Art 36, which provides that if the child is exposed to serious danger, the competent authorities of the State where measures for protection for that child have been taken must inform the authorities of the child's residence or presence of the dangers involved and

---

[88] See Clive, *op cit*, n 23, at 185.

[89] As under the 1980 Hague Abduction Convention, Federal States, States (such as the United Kingdom) with more than one system of law, or States having autonomous territorial units, can appoint more than one Central Authority.

[90] At para 138.

[91] Ie it has a discretion whether or not to comply.

[92] *Op cit*, n 3, at 356.

the measures taken, unless this would place the child or a member of his or her family in serious danger.[93] It might further be noted that Art 33 obliges authorities contemplating the placement of a child in foster or institutional care, or *Kafala* or an analogous institution in another Contracting State, to consult with the Central Authority or other competent authority of the latter State. As we have seen,[94] failure to comply with this obligation entitles the other State to refuse to recognise the placement under Art 23(2)(f).

Safeguarding rights of access

24.51   A particularly useful provision is Art 35 which aims to safeguard rights of access to a child in another Contracting State. Article 35(1) provides:

> 'The competent authorities of a Contracting State may request the authorities of another contracting State to assist in the implementation of measures of protection taken under this Convention, especially in securing the effective exercise of rights of access as well as of the right to maintain direct contacts on a regular basis.'

Since this provision is addressed to the 'competent authorities' of a Contracting State and not simply to Central Authorities, it is wider than that provided for under Art 7(f) of the 1980 Hague Convention.[95] It has also been observed[96] that 'rights of access as well as of the right to maintain direct contact on a regular basis', is intended to include non-physical contact such as telephone or letter contact.

24.52   Another useful provision is that under Art 35(2) which permits a parent who is seeking to obtain or maintain access, but who is living in one Contracting State while the child is habitually resident in another Contracting State, to request the competent authorities of the State in which the child is residing to 'gather information or evidence and may make a finding on the suitability of that parent to exercise access and on the conditions under which access is to be exercised'. This information is then admissible evidence in proceedings in the State of the child's habitual residence and indeed, under Art 35(3), the court may adjourn proceedings pending the outcome of such a request.

RATIFICATION AND ACCESSION ISSUES

The basic position

24.53   As is usual for Hague Conventions, States Members of the Hague Conference are entitled to ratify, and all Contracting States have to accept any

---

[93]   See Art 37.
[94]   See **24.41**.
[95]   Discussed at **17.39** *et seq*.
[96]   Nygh, *op cit*, n 3, at 356–357.

ratification.[97] For these purposes, membership is judged as at the time of the Hague Conference's Eighteenth Session.[98]

24.54 Any State not entitled to ratify can accede to the Convention. However, in line with the usual Hague practice, accessions do not have to be accepted by Contracting States. However, unlike the 1980 Hague Abduction Convention, under which accessions have to be positively accepted, under Art 58(3) of the 1996 Convention, Contracting States have positively to object.[99] Although positive objections to accessions are normally required in Hague Conventions,[100] it does seem unfortunate that the 1980 Convention precedent was not used, as it is diplomatically much more difficult to have to object expressly rather than doing so by silence, which would have been preferable.

24.55 States with two or more territorial units in which different systems of law are applicable, can declare that the ratification or accession extends to all such units or to only one or more of them.[101] Such declarations can be later modified.[102] In the absence of a declaration, the Convention extends to all the territorial units of that State.[103]

Some problems with ratifications and accessions

Possible lack of competence of individual EU States to ratify

24.56 A complication that has arisen is that, following the coming into force of the so-called 'Brussels II Regulation',[104] the United Kingdom (together with other Member States of the EU) might well have lost its individual competence to ratify the 1996 Convention. The argument centres on the impact of the so-called 'ERTA case-law'[105] under which the European Court of Justice has ruled that each time the Community exercises its internal competence by adopting provisions laying down common rules, it requires *exclusive* external competence to undertake obligations with third countries that affect those rules or alter their scope. Since the 1996 Convention rather than

---

[97] This is implicit from Art 58(3).

[98] Article 57(1).

[99] Article 58(3) also allows States when ratifying or acceding to include specific objections to particular acceding States.

[100] See eg Art 44(3) of the 1993 Hague Intercountry Adoption Convention.

[101] Article 59(1).

[102] *Ibid.*

[103] Article 59(3).

[104] Ie Council Regulation (EC) No 1347/2000 of 29 May 2000 on jurisdiction and the recognition and enforcement of judgments in matrimonial matters and in matters of parental responsibility for children of both spouses discussed at **4.9** *et seq* and in Chapter 18.

[105] See Case 22/70, *Commission v Council* [*Re European Road Transport Agreement*] [1971] ECR 263, para 17; Opinion 2/91 'ILO Convention No 170 Concerning Safety in the use of Chemicals at Work', [1993] ECR 1-1061, para 26; Opinion 1/94, 'WTO' [1994] ECR 1-5267, para 77, and Opinion 2/92 'Third Revised Decision of the OECD on National Treatment' [1995] ECR 1-521, para 31.

the Regulation would apply to children habitually resident outside the EU but in a Contracting State under the Convention, it is argued that it would therefore alter the scope of the Regulation (albeit without creating a clash), and that therefore the ERTA ruling applies.

24.57   Although the United Kingdom has not formally conceded that the ERTA ruling does so apply, there is little doubt that it presented a formidable obstacle to widespread ratification of the Convention within the EU.[106] However, most significantly, the Council of the European Union, mindful of the 'valuable contribution to the protection of children' that the 1996 Convention would make to 'institutions that transcend the boundaries of the Community'[107] has now authorised Member States signing the Convention.[108] In other words, it has given the green light for EU-wide ratification.

Possible problems posed by ratification or accessions by Islamic States

24.58   It has already been observed that, by specifically dealing with *Kafala* and analogous institutions, the Convention is likely to be supported by Islamic nations and, indeed, as previously stated, Morocco has already ratified the Convention.[109] Although in global terms it is vitally important that bridges be established between western nations and Islamic States, it cannot be gainsaid that unless countries share common fundamental legal philosophies and approach it may be difficult for those States to bind themselves to the Convention aimed, *inter alia*, at the mutual recognition and enforcement of custody and access orders. Could there, for example, be confidence that an Islamic State would recognise and enforce an order giving custody, say of a 10-year-old boy to his mother? Equally, would a western State be prepared to recognise and enforce an Islamic State order granting custody of an 8-year-old boy to the father based on the tenets of Sharia law?

24.59   Of course, there are arguments on the other side. Presumably, a State would not bind itself to the Convention if it was not prepared to recognise and enforce orders (although the Convention itself provides no guarantees on this) and, indeed, were this to be the case, the Convention could provide an

---

[106] Ireland, for example, having passed legislation to ratify, accepted that it had no unilateral power to do so.

[107] See Proposal for a Council Decision authorising the Member States to sign in the interest of the European Community the 1996 Hague Convention (Com 2001) 680 final of 20.11.2001. See also Clive, 'The 1996 Hague Convention – A Proposal For Simplification' [2002] Fam Law 131. When signing, Member States will be required to make a declaration stating, *inter alia*, that they have been authorised to accept that the Convention will take precedence over Community rules in respect of children who are not habitually resident in a Member State but who are so resident in another Contracting State. It should also state that necessary steps will be taken as soon as possible to open negotiations for a protocol to be added for the accession of the Community.

[108] A formal signing ceremony took place at The Hague on 1 April 2003 involving all EU Member States (except the Netherlands, which had already signed).

[109] Both Morocco and Egypt were entitled to ratify since each was a Member State of the Hague Conference at its Eighteenth Session.

important breakthrough with regard to some child authorities.[110] It is, of course, not open to the requested State to question the merits of the decision sought to be recognised and enforced (see Art 27) so, provided each Contracting State applies the Convention, it may not matter that they do not share the same fundamental values.[111]

24.60 It should be said that, in any event, conflicts of view or matters of concern are not confined to the different values of western and Islamic States. More generally, there may be legitimate concern about whether a particular country (irrespective of tradition) is really in a position to implement the Convention or alternatively there may be no information about a potential Contracting State's legal system on which to make a judgment. There may also be concerns, not so much about a State's readiness to recognise and enforce a decision, but about whether there is in fact an adequate system of enforcement.

THE INTER-RELATIONSHIP WITH THE 1980 HAGUE ABDUCTION CONVENTION[112]

24.61 At first sight, the inter-relationship between the two Conventions seems simple enough for, as Art 50 expressly states, the 1996 Convention 'shall not affect' the application of the 1980 Convention. In other words, the 1980 Hague Abduction Convention takes precedence over the 1996 Protection of Children Convention. On closer inspection, however, the inter-relationship is more complex. First, there are those provisions in the 1996 Convention that are designed to limit jurisdiction after an adjudication has been made under the 1980 Abduction Convention. Secondly, there are provisions that will enable courts to make protective orders following an adjudication under the 1980 Convention. Thirdly, as Art 50 also expressly states that 'nothing' precludes the invocation of the 1996 Convention 'for the purposes of obtaining the return of a child who has been wrongfully removed or retained or of organising access rights', the 1996 Convention provides a wholly independent means of dealing with abductions.

24.62 It is those provisions restricting jurisdiction which give rise to the most concern and complexity. Inspired by the American delegation,[113] Art 7, by preventing jurisdiction being acquired *ipso facto* by a wrongful removal or

---

[110] Viz those where the wrongful removal or retention was in breach of a custody or access order.

[111] This, indeed, was very much the line taken by the Court of Appeal in *Re E (Abduction: Non-Convention Country)* [1999] 2 FLR 642, in which Thorpe LJ considered that there was no absolute standard of the concept of paramountcy of the child's welfare and that 'what constitutes the welfare of the child be subject to the cultural background and exceptions of the jurisdictions to achieve it'. See also Chapter 16.

[112] See also the excellent discussion by Silberman, *op cit*, n 26, at 250–254 and 270, and De Hart, 'The Relationship Between the 1980 Child Abduction Convention and the 1996 Protection Convention' [2000] 33 NYU Jo of Intl Law and Politics 83.

[113] See Nygh, *op cit*, n 3, at 348.

retention (unless acquiesced in, or 12 months has elapsed and no request for return is outstanding and the child is settled in his or her new environment), is designed to deny the court of the requested State having refused a return application under the 1980 Convention then having primary jurisdiction to make a custody order.[114] Although at first sight this seems simple enough, the problem arises as to what should happen to the child following a refusal to return under the 1980 Convention. In this respect, it is possible to envisage at least three different situations, namely: where there is a pre-existing custody order made in the requesting State; where there is an application pending for such an order; and where there is neither an order nor pending proceedings.

24.63　In the first situation, following the refusal under the 1980 Convention there is nothing to prevent an application being made under the 1996 Convention for recognition and enforcement of the custody order. However, if, despite the custody order, a return has been refused under the 1980 Convention, then the issue will inevitably be raised as to whether recognition of the custody order should also be refused under Art 23(2) of the 1996 Convention. In this context, the provision most likely to be invoked is Art 23(2)(d) that 'recognition is manifestly contrary to public policy of the requested State, taking into account the best interests of the child'. While it remains an open question as to how Art 23(2) should and will be interpreted,[115] it seems inconceivable that if a return has been refused, say, because of the child's objections or because of the left-behind parent's violence that that will not be relevant, if not decisive, under Art 23(2). Take, for example *Re T (Abduction: Child's Objections to Return)*,[116] in which the Court of Appeal refused to order a return because of the child's 'clear and reasoned' fears of returning to Spain due to her mother's drink problem, notwithstanding that the girl's testimony had previously been fully considered by the Spanish court when making a custody order (the court considered the child to have been heavily influenced by her father). If it was thought right in these circumstances not to order a return, can it be supposed that the defence under Art 23(2)(d) would not have also been considered to have been made out?

24.64　The scenario occurring in *Re T* would be more problematic if, notwithstanding the refusal to return, the court of the requesting State subsequently made a custody order in favour of the left-behind parent. This could occur either where custody proceedings were pending at the time of the 1980 Convention application[117] or where, subsequent to that ruling, a fresh

---

[114]　But note that, as *between* EU Member States, the revised Brussels II Regulation will expressly deal with this issue: see **18.32**.

[115]　See the discussion above at **24.43–24.44**.

[116]　[2000] 2 FLR 192.

[117]　Note that where an application is pending, Art 13 comes into play, preventing even a court of the child's new habitual residence from making an order while similar matters are still under consideration.

application for custody was made in the 'home' jurisdiction which was then sought to be enforced under the 1996 Convention.[118]

24.65 Irrespective of whether there is a pre-existing order, pending proceedings, or neither, the court has power, having refused to make a return order under the 1980 Convention, to make a temporary order either under Art 11 or Art 12 of the 1996 Convention. No doubt in some cases at least, the abducting parent will be granted temporary (or interim) custody. In other words, notwithstanding the aim of the 1996 Convention to avoid conflicts of orders, it seems likely that such conflicts will be created. However, not all uses of Art 11 in particular need to be viewed negatively, for these powers can be usefully employed to help protect the child following the making of a return order. One of the fears when making a return order is that the child might not be adequately protected on return and, to this end, various devices, such as mirror orders or safe harbour orders or undertakings, have been employed. Article 11 adds to these powers by enabling the courts to make protective orders in cases of urgency, which will have extra-territorial effect until superseded by an order in the 'home' jurisdiction.[119] It might be observed, however, that such orders are limited to protecting the child and cannot therefore directly protect a parent.

24.66 The third scenario is where it is sought to use the 1996 Convention rather than the 1980 Convention to combat child abduction. This remedy would be appropriate only where there is a pre-existing custody order made in the country of the child's habitual residence. In such a case, it would be perfectly possible to seek to have the order recognised and enforced under the 1996 Convention. A possible advantage of doing this is if the Art 23(2) defences prove harder to establish than those under the 1980 Convention. However, unlike the 1980 Convention, the 1996 Convention makes no provision for costs to be borne by a Contracting State. Another possible drawback is the lack of speed, since it seems likely that a 1980 Convention application will generally be disposed of more quickly than a 1996 Convention application.

24.67 It cannot be denied that the inter-relationship between the 1980 and 1996 Conventions is potentially problematic, and, in particular, the position following a refusal to return seems uncertain.[120] On the other hand, Art 11 does seem to offer new options to protect a child following the making of a return order. Furthermore, the access provisions under Art 35 will undoubtedly be more beneficial than those under the 1980 Convention. In short, the benefits may be considered to outweigh the disadvantages.

---

[118]   As Nygh, *op cit*, n 3, at 349, points out, there is nothing to stop the left-behind parent from seeking an appropriate order in the 'home' court and seeking to enforce it under the 1996 Convention.

[119]   See Nygh, *op cit*, n 3, at 351.

[120]   Silberman, *op cit*, n 26, at 270 considers the possibility of the 1996 Convention's interference with the 1980 Convention to be a cause for alarm.

OVERALL CONCLUSION

24.68 The 1996 Convention is an important international instrument dealing with issues of increasing global relevance. In the United Kingdom, for example, the number of reported child abduction cases alone has increased by 79% during the latter half of the 1990s and, since unlawful removal of children is an extreme phenomenon, how many more children must there be who are the subjects of dispute involving an international element? As Clive has said:[121]

> 'It is clearly not in the interests of children that there should be conflicts of jurisdictions and judgments relating to their long-term welfare or doubts about the law applicable to parental responsibility.'

It might also be added that it is clearly in the interests of children that there be international co-operation in discovering their whereabouts, providing information about the child's history, family background and current situation to another court or body seeking to make private or public orders protecting the child and providing information about a State's law and available service to protect children and to facilitate agreed solutions.

24.69 More specifically there seems obvious advantage in having a global system of mutual recognition and enforcement of custody, guardianship and access orders. The 1996 Convention provides important additional control on international child abduction, and its provisions regarding access might go some way to alleviate the generally acknowledged failure of the 1980 Hague Abduction Convention to deal with it. It can surely only be helpful to have agreed international rules about the attribution and exercise of parental responsibility. Indeed, it is possible to argue that, insofar as it promotes the objectives of the UN Convention on the Rights of the Child 1989, States Parties to that Convention have an international obligation to ratify. In particular it may be pointed out that Art 11 of the UN Convention enjoins States Parties to 'promote the conclusion', *inter alia*, of multilateral agreements 'to combat the illicit transfer and non-return of children abroad'. The 1996 Convention would also help promote the principles set out in:

(a) Article 18: that both parents have joint primary responsibility for bringing up their children;
(b) Article 20: to provide special protection for children deprived of their family environment, and
(c) Article 22: to provide special protection to refugee children.

24.70 The 1996 Convention is not, however, problem free. There is, for example, potential uncertainty with the interpretation of Art 23(2), under which recognition and enforcement might be refused. It remains to be seen how effective enforcement will be. There is certainly a problematic inter-relationship with the 1980 Hague Abduction Convention. Even ratification and accessions are not without difficulties. Nevertheless, without gainsaying

---

[121] *Op cit*, n 23, at 170.

the potential problems, it is strongly suggested that the potential benefits brought about, *inter alia*, by a global system of recognition and enforcement of custody access and guardianship orders, the agreed rules about the attribution and exercise of parental responsibility, and the international co-operation in providing information about the child and to facilitate agreed solutions about their upbringing, far outweigh the disadvantages. Accordingly, it must be hoped that ratifications of the 1996 Convention will gain momentum. In this regard, the recent recognition by the Council of the European Community of the 1996 Convention's 'valuable contribution to the protection of children at the international level' and its consequential smoothing of the path for EU-wide ratification, is a most welcome one. EU-wide ratification would provide an important boost for the 1996 Convention and would, for example, put pressure on the United States to ratify.[122] Were this to happen, and there is every reason to think that in time it will, then it be anticipated that at least as many States will implement the 1996 Convention as have currently become parties to the 1980 Hague Abduction Convention.

---

[122] In this respect, the endorsement of the Convention by the American commentators, namely, Silberman, *op cit*, n 26 and De Hart, *op cit*, n 112, is encouraging.

PART IV

INTERNATIONAL ACCESS

Chapter 25

INTERNATIONAL ACCESS

INTRODUCTION

25.1 In this chapter, we discuss what the 1980 Hague Abduction Convention, the 1996 Hague Protection Convention and the 1980 European Custody Convention call 'rights of access', but what domestically is now known as 'contact' and elsewhere is also referred to as 'visitation rights'. The use of the term 'rights of access' now seems dated and belongs to an era when laws referred to 'parental authority' rather than to 'parental responsibility'.[1] Nevertheless, while it may now generally be more appropriate to refer to the rights of children to have regular contact, *inter alia*, with their parents, rather than to parents' rights of access to children,[2] the following discussion will refer to 'rights of access' as understood by these Conventions.

THE 1980 HAGUE ABDUCTION CONVENTION[3]

A basic objective to respect rights of access

25.2 Under Art 1(b) it is an objective of the Convention:[4]

---

[1] Even so, even later Conventions, notably the 1996 Hague Convention on the Protection of Children, Arts 3 and 35 (discussed at **24.60** and **24.70** *et seq*) and even the amendment of the so-called Brussels II Regulation, discussed below at **25.77**, still refer to 'rights of access'. Cf the 2003 European Convention on Contact Concerning Children, discussed at **25.83** *et seq*.

[2] See, for example, Art 9(3) of the United Nations Convention on the Rights of the Child 1989, which provides: 'States Parties shall respect the rights of the child who is separated from one or both parents to maintain personal relations and direct contact with both parents on a regular basis, except if it is contrary to the child's best interests'. See also the Explanatory Report to the 2003 European Convention Concerning Children, at para 6, discussed below at **25.83**.

[3] See generally Duncan, 'Transfrontier Access/Contact and the Hague Convention of 25 October 1980 on the Civil Aspects of International Child Abduction – Final Report', Preliminary Document No 5 of July 2002 for the Special Commission of September/October 2002 (hereafter 'the Duncan Report'); Lowe, 'Problems Relating to Access Disputes under the Hague Convention on International Child Abduction' (1994) 8 Int Jo of Law and the Family 374; Thuis, 'The Implementation of Art 21 of the Hague Convention on International Child Abduction' (unpublished PhD, 1996), and Hutchinson et al, 'Enforcement of Access and Contact Internationally and the Security and Support Provided to Minor Abducted Internationally on the Return to their State of Habitual Residence', in *Report of the Cross Border Movement of Children* (Society for Advanced Legal Studies, 1999), at p 69.

[4] Note also that the Preamble (not specifically incorporated into UK law) expressly mentions securing 'protection for rights of access'.

'to ensure that rights of ... access under the law of one Contracting State are effectively respected in the other Contracting States.'

25.3 Although many might consider this to be a secondary objective behind that of securing the child's return (and, indeed, only a minority of applications under the 1980 Hague Abduction Convention are for access[5]), in theory, at any rate, there is no hierarchy of objectives under the Convention.[6] At all events, respecting rights of access has come to be regarded as an important, if not totally successful, part of the Hague Abduction Convention.

The meaning of 'rights of access'

25.4 As the Pérez-Vera Report points out,[7] it is a long-established tradition of the 1980 Hague Abduction Convention not to define the legal concepts used by it. However, to avoid compromising the Convention's objects, Art 5 does provide some guidance on the meaning of access. Article 5(b) states:

> '"rights of access" shall include the right to take a child for a limited period of time to a place other than the child's habitual residence.'

As the Pérez-Vera Report says,[8] Art 5(b) is clearly not intended to exclude other ways of exercising access rights. All that it seeks to do is 'emphasise that access rights extend also to what is called "residential access", and that it includes the right of access across national frontiers'.

25.5 As has been seen,[9] 'rights of custody' includes a right of access but, as Hale J held in *S v H (Abduction: Access Rights)*,[10] it by no means follows that because a person has 'rights of access' he or she must necessarily also have 'rights of custody'. The Convention draws a clear distinction between the two concepts. *S v H* concerned an unmarried Italian father and an English mother. The baby was born in Italy, but apart from a short period after the birth the couple had never cohabited. Under Italian law, as it was found to be,[11] in the case of unmarried parents, parental authority lay with the person with whom the child lived. The mother had a sole custody order in her favour, and there was no embargo against her taking the child out of the country.[12] In these

---

5 According to Lowe, Armstrong and Mathias, 'A Statistical Analysis of Applications made in 1999 under the Hague Convention of 25 October 1980 on the Civil Aspects of International Child Abduction', Preliminary Document No 3 (Revised Version, November 2001) available on the Hague Conference website at http://www.hcch.net/e/conventions/reports28e.html (hereinafter referred to as 'the 1999 Statistical Survey'), only 17% of applications made under this Convention in 1999 were for access.

6 See Professor Pérez-Vera's Explanatory Report at para 18.

7 At para 83.

8 At para 85.

9 See **14.44**.

10 [1997] 1 FLR 971. See also the Scottish decision, *Donofrio v Burrell* 2000 SLT 1051, discussed below at **25.28** *et seq.*

11 There was in fact a conflict of expert evidence as to what the Italian law was on this point.

12 A previous temporary order preventing removal had been revoked, although only because it appeared that the mother could not leave Italy and indeed had expressly excluded her

circumstances it was held that, notwithstanding that he had an access order in his favour, the father could not be said to have 'rights of custody'.[13] Accordingly, although the mother's action in bringing the child to England undoubtedly denied access to the father, his application for a return order was dismissed.[14]

25.6 Whether it is necessary to have a court order to establish 'rights of access' is perhaps a moot point. In the Australian decision, *Police Commissioner of South Australia v Castell*,[15] the Full Court of the Family Court of Australia rejected an application made by the South Australian Central Authority for annual physical access and telephone and letter contact on behalf of a married English father on the basis that, for the purpose of their internal legislation[16] (Australia has implemented the Convention by way of an internal Regulation rather than by direct incorporation),[17] 'rights of access' had already to be established (either by operation of law, or as a consequence of a judicial or administrative decision, or by reason of an appropriate agreement having legal effect) in another Contracting State. In this case, it was apparently insufficient that under English law the father had parental responsibility,[18] although it also needs to be borne in mind that the father's application for access before an Australian court had been struck out.

25.7 Although *Castell* turned on an interpretation of the Australian Regulation rather than the Convention[19] and in any event has since been reversed by an amendment to those Regulations,[20] the decision nevertheless

---

    intention of doing so. Although it seemed likely that the father could have re-applied for such a prohibition, which would then have given him 'rights of custody' following *Re C (A Minor) (Abduction)* [1989] 1 FLR 403, Hale J refused to accept that this '*possibility*' was sufficient to vest the father with 'rights of custody'.

[13] It might, however, have been in breach of the *court's* 'rights of custody', since Italian law seems to require the authorisation of the 'tutelage judge' to remove such a child from Italy, but the evidence was inconclusive on that issue in this case.

[14] It would, however, have been open to the father to have pursued his rights of access remedies, such as they are, under the Convention.

[15] (1997) 138 FLR 437, (1997) 21 Fam LR 643.

[16] Viz the Family Law (Child Abduction Convention) Regulations 1986 (Cth), reg 25, which provided: 'A Central Authority may apply to a court for an order that is necessary or appropriate to organise or secure the effective exercise of rights of access to a child in Australia by a person, an institution or another body having rights of access to the child'. Cf in Scotland, in which r 70.5(2) of the Rules of the Court of Session 1994 (as amended) makes provision for access applications to be brought under the Convention, discussed at **25.27** *et seq* below.

[17] See **21.122**.

[18] The judge at first instance said: 'It is accepted law in Australia that the fact of parenthood does not give rise to a right of access (or contact). It has not been suggested to me that the husband has any right in England arising out of the Children Act 1989 or any other law'. But the Full Court did not comment upon this.

[19] Although, on the face of it, it is difficult to see why the 'rights of access' referred to in reg 25 ought to have had different meaning from that to be found in the Convention from which it derives.

[20] Viz by the Family Law Amendment Act 2000, which amends reg 25 to make it clear that rights of access 'are rights already established in another Convention country either by

points up an issue that has not hitherto been considered by the English courts.[21] How should the English courts approach the issue? If *Castell* were to be followed, it would mean that holders of parental responsibility who therefore have 'rights of custody' can, in the absence of any court order or agreement, seek a return order as a means of securing contact but would not be able to invoke the Convention provisions on contact. This would surely be contrary to the policy of the Convention, which aims[22] both to secure and organise rights of access.[23] It is therefore suggested that holders of parental responsibility or joint custody ought to be regarded, for the purposes of the Convention, as having, at any rate, a presumptive right of access, and that it is not an automatic prerequisite under the Convention that a court order be first obtained. Such a presumption could, however, be rebutted where, as in *Castell*, the applicant has been expressly denied contact by a court.[24] In other words, it is suggested that, while it might not be necessary in every case to obtain a court order to establish 'rights of access', an order denying contact should be regarded as preventing a person having such rights.

The prerequisites of applying for access

25.8   Unlike when seeking a return order, it is not necessary, when applying to organise or secure access rights, to establish a 'wrongful removal or retention' within the meaning of Art 3.[25] An argument to the contrary was expressly rejected by Waterhouse J in *B v B (Minors: Enforcement of Access Abroad)*[26] since, in his view, such an interpretation would effectively deprive most non-custodial parents of any remedy under the Convention when complaining of breach of access rights.[27]

---

operation of law, or as a consequence of a judicial or administrative decision, or by means of an appropriate agreement having legal effect'. See Lowe, Armstrong and Mathias, *Country Report – Australia* (NCMEC, 2002) at 4.2, and Degeling, 'Access Provisions and the Hague Convention – An Australian Viewpoint', a paper given at the International Child Abduction Conference in Edinburgh, June 2002.

[21]   Note that, in Scotland, r 70.5(2) of the Rules of the Court of Session 1994, as now amended, applies only where there is an access order. See **25.34**.

[22]   See Arts 7(f) and 21, discussed below at **25.14** *et seq*.

[23]   In *Castell*, the court rejected arguments based on the alleged difference in meaning between 'securing' and 'organising'.

[24]   Even if, as in *Castell*, such an order was made by a court in the jurisdiction in which the Convention application is being made.

[25]   Discussed at **14.4** *et seq*. The corollary of this proposition is that breach of access rights does not, *per se*, amount to a 'wrongful removal or retention'.

[26]   [1988] 1 WLR 526, sub nom *Re B (Minors) (Access: Jurisdiction)* [1988] 2 FLR 6 and commented upon at [1988] Fam Law 208.

[27]   To illustrate this, Waterhouse J instanced the example of a custodial parent removing a child contrary to a direction not to take the child out of the country which he considered, presumably on the basis that it did not infringe the applicant's rights, not to be 'wrongful' within the narrow confines of Art 3. Such an interpretation, however, would no longer be followed, either on the basis that a removal was in breach of the mother's own rights of custody: see *Re H (A Minor) (Abduction)* [1990] 2 FLR 439; or that it was in breach of the court's rights of custody: see *B v B (Abduction)* [1993] Fam 32, [1992] 3 WLR 865, [1993] 1

25.9   Waterhouse J similarly ruled that s 2(2) of the Child Abduction and Custody Act 1985, which states that the Convention applies only to wrongful removals or retentions occurring on or after the implementation of the Convention by the relevant Contracting State,[28] had no application to access applications.

25.10   On the other hand, it seems clear that, before the Convention can be invoked, the applicant must be able to establish a breach of his or her access rights.[29] Furthermore, under Art 4, it must also be established that the child (who must be under the age of 16) 'was habitually resident in a Contracting State immediately before any breach of … access rights'.

25.11   The precise meaning of Art 4 is not without its difficulties. According to Waterhouse J in *B v B*, the Article refers to the children's habitual residence in the Contracting State in which the access rights relied upon originally existed. However, this interpretation was overruled by the Court of Appeal in *Re G (A Minor) (Enforcement of Access Abroad)*,[30] it being held that all Art 4 required was that the child must be habitually resident in *a* Contracting State and not in *the* State in which the access rights originally accrued.[31] In so concluding, Hoffmann LJ pointed out that rights of access normally have to be enforced in the country in which the child is habitually resident and that it would be unusual for a breach of access rights to occur when the child is away from home. Hence, as his Lordship observed:

> 'It follows that if Article 21 did apply to the enforcement of a foreign access right in the country of the child's habitual residence, it would seldom achieve its object of ensuring that "rights of … access under the law of one Contracting State are effectively respected in the other Contracting States".'

25.12   The importance of this ruling is two-fold. First, it virtually eliminates arguments about where the child is habitually resident since, in the vast majority of cases, it will normally be with the 'abducting' parent or, if not, in the State of the left-behind parent, either of which will satisfy the *Re G* test.[32]

FLR 238, CA. See also *Re C (A Minor) (Abduction)* [1989] 1 FLR 403 in which a removal by a custodial mother in defiance of a court order forbidding either the father or the mother from removing the child from Australia without the consent of the other was held to be in breach of the father's rights of custody within the meaning of Art 5.

[28]   It will be noted that s 2(2) of the 1985 Act enacts in terms Art 35, which has not therefore been implemented by the United Kingdom.

[29]   See Art 4.

[30]   [1993] Fam 216, [1993] 2 WLR 824, [1993] 1 FLR 669.

[31]   In reaching this conclusion, Hoffmann LJ rejected the argument that, so interpreted, Art 21 would apply to purely domestic disputes, pointing out that the Article was confined to cases giving effect to the purpose of the Convention, namely, to ensure that *foreign* access rights are respected.

[32]   Even if, as is possible where an application is brought quickly, the child has no habitual residence (cf *Re J (A Minor) (Abduction: Custody Rights)* [1990] 2 AC 562, [1990] 3 WLR 492, sub nom *C v S (Minor: Abduction: Illegitimate Child)* [1990] 2 FLR 442, HL, discussed above at **4.32**), assuming the abducting parent intends to stay in the new jurisdiction, it will only be a short time before the child will acquire an habitual residence there.

Secondly, given that it is established that the Convention is not retrospective,[33] it enables the Convention to apply in cases where it would not otherwise have done, such as, for example, contrary to the actual ruling in *B v B*, where a child left a country which was not then a Contracting State and became habitually resident in England and Wales, the application being made when both countries were Contracting States.[34]

25.13 According to the Pérez-Vera Report,[35] since it is obvious 'by the very nature of things' that access rights can be held only by individuals, courts or other bodies cannot be applicants as they can for return orders.[36] On the other hand, a whole range of individuals and not just the parents may have access rights.

The Convention obligations

25.14 The two key provisions of the Convention are Arts 7 and 20. Under Art 7, Central Authorities are generally enjoined to co-operate with each other and to promote co-operation amongst the competent authorities in their respective States to achieve the Convention's obligations including, therefore, to ensure that rights of access are 'effectively respected' in compliance with Art 1(b). They are particularly enjoined, in Art 7(f) 'either directly or through any intermediary' to take all appropriate measures:

> 'to initiate or facilitate the institution of judicial or administrative proceedings with a view to obtaining the return of the child and, in a proper case, to make arrangements for organising or securing the effective exercise of rights of access.'

25.15 Article 21 provides:

> 'An application to make arrangements for organising or securing the effective exercise of rights of access may be presented to the Central Authorities of the Contracting States in the same way as an application for the return of a child.

> The Central Authorities are bound by the obligations of co-operation which are set forth in Article 7 to promote the peaceful enjoyment of access rights and the fulfilment of any conditions to which the exercise of those rights may be subject. The Central Authorities shall take steps to remove, as far as possible, all obstacles to the exercise of such rights.

> The Central Authorities, either directly or through intermediaries, may initiate or assist the institution of proceedings with a view to organising or protecting these rights and securing respect for the conditions to which the exercise of these rights may be subject.'

---

[33] *Re H (Minors) (Abduction: Custody Rights); Re S (Minors) (Abduction: Custody Rights)* [1991] 2 AC 476, [1991] 3 WLR 68, [1991] 2 FLR 262, HL, discussed at **12.58**.

[34] It seems clear, however, that the Convention cannot operate until both countries in question are Contracting States.

[35] At para 79. But note that if this is right, Art 29 would have to be restrictively interpreted for this purpose.

[36] See **12.23** and **21.6**.

25.16   As Art 29 makes clear, the provision under Art 21 to apply for relief via a Central Authority is without prejudice to the right of:

'any person, institution or body who claims that there has been a breach of … access rights within the meaning of Article … 21 from applying directly to the judicial or administrative authorities of a Contracting State, whether or not under the provisions of this Convention.'

Interpreting the provisions – the English position

25.17   Unlike some other jurisdictions,[37] under English law neither the Child Abduction and Custody Act 1985 nor Part VI of the Family Proceedings Rules 1991 makes any specific reference to access and, accordingly, the extent of the obligations depends entirely upon the scope of the Convention Articles. Of crucial significance is Art 21.

25.18   Article 21 has been considered in a number of cases. In the first, *B v B (Minors: Enforcement Of Access Abroad)*,[38] Waterhouse J commented *obiter* that the Convention provisions in general and Art 21 in particular imposed no direct or specific duties on the judicial authority of a Contracting State in relation to access nor did they define or limit the principles upon which a court should exercise its discretion. Accordingly, whilst a court should pay due respect to any existing foreign court access order, it was nevertheless not bound by it and the judge was free to exercise his own independent judgment to determine the merits of the application based upon the paramountcy of the child's welfare.

25.19   The matter was further considered by Bracewell J in *C v C (Minors) (Child Abduction)*.[39] In this case, following the divorce of two American parents, custody of the two children was granted to the mother with reasonable access to the father. The mother began living with an English cohabitant in the United States but, following an eviction notice (issued on the father's initiative), the mother, cohabitant and children came to England without the father's knowledge or consent. The father applied under the Convention, initially seeking the children's return to the United States but eventually seeking a declaration that the removal was wrongful and a determination of the access issue. Bracewell J had no doubt that the removal was wrongful on the basis that there was settled case-law that, under New York law, a custodial parent had no right to frustrate visitation rights by unilaterally removing the children to a distant locality. On the crucial access issue, Bracewell J held, rejecting the argument that she should invoke the

---

[37]   See eg Australia, under the Family Law (Child Abduction Convention) Regulations 1986, reg 25, and Scotland under the Rules of the Court of Session 1994, r 70.5(2), discussed at **25.6–25.7** and **25.27** *et seq*.

[38]   [1988] 1 WLR 526 at 534, sub nom *B v B (Minors) (Access: Jurisdiction)* [1988] 2 FLR 6 at 14.

[39]   [1992] 1 FLR 163. See also, to similar effect, *Re C (Minors)(Enforcing Foreign Access Order)* [1993] 1 FCR 770, per Eastham J, in which limited access was given in England to an American father who was a homosexual and who suffered from AIDS.

wardship jurisdiction,[40] that there was power under the Convention to make a determination. Such a determination, however, was on the merits of the case, applying the principle of the paramountcy of the child's welfare. In the event, Bracewell J ordered limited supervised access to take place in England and, following that, a report was required to assist the court to determine the future pattern of access.

25.20 The nature and application of the access provisions under the 1980 Hague Abduction Convention was subsequently examined by the Court of Appeal in *Re G (A Minor) (Enforcement of Access Abroad)*.[41] A Kenyan Asian father and his English wife went to live in Canada where their child was born. Following allegations of violence, the mother left the home and took the child to England without the father's knowledge. The father successfully invoked the Hague Convention to have the child returned to Canada. Subsequently, the Canadian court made a consent order under which the custody of the child was given to the mother together with an option to live in England. Detailed access arrangements were made in favour of the father. The mother and child returned to England and settled there. The father later wrote to the mother giving notice of his intention to exercise his rights of staying access and when the mother said that she would not agree, he applied under the Convention for his rights of access to be protected and implemented in accordance with the Canadian consent order.

25.21 Having held that, because immediately before the breach of access rights the child was habitually resident in a Contracting State, namely, the United Kingdom, the requirements of Art 4 were satisfied, the question remained as to how the Convention applied. In this respect, it was held that, unlike Art 12, which makes mandatory provision for the return of children wrongfully removed or retained within the meaning of Art 3, Art 21 creates no rights in private law which a parent can directly enforce in respect of a child. Indeed, Hoffmann LJ queried whether Art 21 was so vague or permissive as to create no rights at all,[42] but insofar as it might, those rights were in public law and enforceable only against the Central Authority. In other words, as Waterhouse J had said *obiter* in *B v B*, Art 21 imposes no duties on the judicial authorities but only (if at all) upon the Central Authority, and that once the matter has been brought before the court then the provisions of Art 21 are exhausted. The Convention therefore provides no independent

---

[40] The principal reason for rejecting the wardship option was the inevitable delay that would thus ensue because the applicant would have to seek what would now be a fresh public funding certificate (see **21.14**). Certificates granted under the Convention procedure, which are *not* means tested, do not extend to non-Convention applications including, therefore, wardship. Ironically, however, it is now established (see, in particular, *Re T (Minors) (Hague Convention: Access)* [1993] 2 FLR 617, discussed further at **25.23**) that access applications cannot be determined under the Convention, and that instead separate applications have to be made under the Children Act 1989, for which separate public funding applications have also to be made.

[41] [1993] Fam 216, [1993] 2 WLR 824, [1993] 1 FLR 669, CA.

[42] In particular, there appears to be no obligation for the Central Authority to initiate proceedings before a court: see further at **25.23**.

source of jurisdiction and, as a result, applications to enforce access rights have to be made under the relevant domestic jurisdiction, in the case of England and Wales, for a contact order under s 8 of the Children Act 1989. In such a case, the court would then make its own independent judgment of the merits of the case, applying the paramountcy of the child's welfare but paying due regard to any existing foreign court order. In *Re G* there could be no complaint against the Central Authority since it had done all that was required by Art 21, nor could the first instance judge be criticised for the way he exercised his discretion (although query under what jurisdiction he purported to act) in that by applying the paramountcy of the child's welfare he sought to give effect to the Canadian consent order while allowing some postponement of its operation.

25.22　Following *Re G*, the Child Abduction Unit issued a Practice Note,[43] commenting that, in that case:

> 'The Court of Appeal took the view that Article 21 conferred no jurisdiction to determine matters relating to access, or to recognise or enforce foreign access orders. It provides, however, for executive co-operation in the enforcement of such recognition as national law allows.

> Accordingly, the duty of this Central Authority is to make appropriate arrangements for the applicant by providing solicitors to act on his behalf in applying for legal aid and instituting proceedings in the High Court under s 8 of the Children Act 1989.'

25.23　The nature of the Central Authority's duty was further explored in *Re T (Minors) (Hague Convention: Access)*.[44] A mother was granted care and control of her three children and given leave to reside with them in England by the Superior Court of California. Detailed orders for contact were made in favour of the father. Subsequently, when in England, the mother obtained from the English High Court a residence order and an order directing that there be no direct contact between the father and the child except for agreed visiting or contact orders. The father applied under Art 21 for an order that the mother take all the necessary steps to facilitate access to the father in California and Mexico. Bracewell J held that, upon receiving an application for the enforcement of foreign access orders under Art 21, the Central Authority only has a duty to make appropriate arrangements to provide English solicitors to act on the applicant's behalf for the purpose of instituting proceedings for a s 8 contact order under the Children Act 1989. It was not incumbent upon the Central Authority to issue a summons under the Child Abduction and Custody Act 1985 but for the applicant to apply for an order under the Children Act 1989.[45] She further held that:

---

[43]　*Practice Note – Child Abduction Unit – Lord Chancellor's Department* (5 March 1993) [1993] 1 FLR 804.

[44]　[1993] 2 FLR 617.

[45]　It is to be noted that as proceedings under the Child Abduction and Custody Act 1985 are not 'family proceedings' within the meaning of s 8(3) of the Children Act 1989, the court

(a) the advantageous provision for automatic entitlement to legal representation for applications under the Hague Convention[46] does not apply to applications under the Children Act 1989 nor can a public funding certificate issued under the Convention be extended to Children Act proceedings;

(b) since Convention proceedings are regarded as being exhausted upon presentation to the court, no stay[47] operates against any contact proceedings under the Children Act 1989.[48] Accordingly, there is no problem about bringing concurrent proceedings under Art 21 of the Convention and s 8 of the Children Act 1989.

25.24 Whether Bracewell J's conclusions concerning legal representation are unchallengeable will be discussed later in the light of the position taken in Scotland.[49]

Summary

25.25 In summary, the current English position is as follows.

(1) To invoke the 1980 Hague Abduction Convention when complaining about breach of access, it is not necessary to show that the child's removal or retention is wrongful within the meaning of Art 3.

(2) However, under Art 4, it must be shown that the child is habitually resident in a Contracting State immediately before any breach of access rights.

(3) Article 21 imposes no duties upon judicial authorities and, unlike Art 12, creates no rights in private law which a parent can directly enforce in respect of a child.

(4) Instead, Art 21 imposes executive duties upon Central Authorities, *inter alia*, 'to promote peaceful enjoyment of access rights', and 'to take steps to remove, as far as possible, all obstacles to the exercise of such rights' and a discretion to 'initiate or assist in the institution of proceedings with a view to organising or protecting these rights' which is satisfied by making appropriate arrangements for the applicant by providing solicitors to act on his behalf.

---

has no power *of its own motion* to make any s 8 order, including a contact order, ie s 10(1)(b) of the 1989 Act does *not* apply.

46 Under what is now the Community Legal Service (Financial) Regulations 2000, reg (1)(f). It may be noted that, notwithstanding Art 26, which provides that Central Authorities 'shall not impose any charges in relation to applications submitted under this Convention', by a reservation pursuant to Art 42 and s 11 of the Child Abduction and Custody Act 1985, the United Kingdom, through (in the case of England and Wales) the Lord Chancellor's Department, is not bound to assume any costs save through legal aid. It may be noted that, since any Children Act 1989 proceedings in this context will be in the High Court, they will be relatively expensive.

47 Pursuant to FPR 1991, r 6.11(4), discussed at **21.39**. In fact, however, r 6.11 does not apply to access applications in any event.

48 Per Bracewell J in *Re T (Minors) (Hague Convention: Access)* [1993] 2 FLR 617 at 621.

49 See below at **25.27** *et seq.*

(5) Once the access issue gets to court, the Convention provides no independent source of jurisdiction so that a separate application should be made under Children Act 1989, s 8.

(6) Furthermore, because Convention proceedings under Art 21 are regarded as being exhausted upon presentation to the court, no stay operates against any contact proceedings. However, the favourable public funding provisions under the Convention do not apply to domestic contact proceedings nor can a public funding certificate be extended to such proceedings.

(7) In determining an application for contact under the 1989 Act, the judge, whilst obliged to pay due regard to any existing foreign court order, is not bound by it, but instead must apply the principle that the child's welfare is the paramount consideration.

25.26 In short, access rights *per se* cannot be enforced under the Convention and, indeed, as Hoffmann LJ intimated in *Re G*,[50] given the aforesaid difficulties, if access rights arise under an order made in a State which is also a party to the 1980 European Custody Convention, it is normally advantageous to bring proceedings under that Convention[51] rather than the 1980 Hague Abduction Convention.

The position in Scotland

25.27 Unlike in England and Wales, in Scotland, the Rules make specific provision for access applications under the 1980 Hague Abduction Convention.[52] Rule 70.5(2) of the Rules of the Court of Session 1994 provides that such applications be made by petition.[53] It also sets out a number of specific requirements in relation to averments, productions, and affidavit and documentary evidence. Rule 70.6 specifies the procedure to be followed, making provision for a period of notice of 4 days; parties on whom notice must be served; and for a first hearing within 7 days of the expiry of the period of notice. The Rule also places emphasis on affidavit evidence, with oral evidence being permitted only where special cause is shown. In summary, rr 70.5(2) and 70.6 are designed to facilitate the speedy disposal of applications.

25.28 The validity and scope of these provisions as they then stood[54] were tested in *Donofrio v Burrell*.[55] Under the terms of a Canadian (Ontario) order

---

[50]   [1993] Fam 216 at 229, [1993] 2 WLR 824 at 835, [1993] 1 FLR 669 at 679.

[51]   Discussed below at **25.42** *et seq.*

[52]   Cf in Australia where specific provision is made for a Central Authority to make an access application. See n 16 above.

[53]   Note that this procedure was designed to be expeditious and is in contrast to the normal rule obtaining in family actions, namely, to proceed by summons, pursuant to r 49.1 of the 1994 Rules.

[54]   The rule was amended with effect from 18 September 2001: see **25.34**.

[55]   2000 SLT 1051, Ct of Session (Extra Division, Inner House), upholding the first instance decision by Lord Macfadyen delivered 3 March 1999, and on which see Scott, 'Donofrio v

made in 1991, the mother had been granted custody of the parties' two children and the father specified access (viz Wednesday afternoons and alternate weekends). The father regularly exercised his rights of access until 1997, when, initially with his consent, the mother and children went to Scotland to visit her ill father. They never returned to Canada. When their non-return became apparent the father brought Convention proceedings for the children's return. That action failed, however, because the 1991 order did not (albeit as a result of an oversight) contain the usual embargo against the mother removing the children outside the jurisdiction without the father's consent and, consequently, while the father could be said to have 'rights of access', he could not be said to have 'rights of custody'. Accordingly, the father subsequently sought the court's assistance in exercising his rights of access in Canada, as provided for by Art 21. He sought in particular access for half the Easter and summer school holidays every year and for the Christmas holiday every alternate year. The petition was presented in terms both of Art 21 and of the Rules. The bringing of the petition had been facilitated by what was then the Scottish Courts Administration, now the Scottish Executive, Justice Department (which acts as the Central Authority in Scotland) and, importantly, legal aid had been afforded under the special provisions relating to Convention proceedings.[56]

25.29 The father's petition was attacked on two grounds. First, it was argued that, given that Art 21 conferred no private law rights, there was no such thing as 'an application for access to a child under the Hague Convention' and, consequently, r 70.5(2) was devoid of content. Accordingly, the proper form of the application was by summons not petition. Secondly, it was argued that even if a claim for access 'under the Convention' could be competently presented as a petition under r 70.5(2), this was not such a claim since the access sought was not the access to which the father had been found entitled by the Canadian court.

25.30 At first instance, Lord Macfadyen, the Lord Ordinary, having expressly approved the analysis of the Convention by the English Court of Appeal in *Re G (A Minor) (Enforcement of Access Abroad)*,[57] agreed that, while the Convention enables holders of rights of access to enlist the help of the Central Authority in the other Contracting State to facilitate the making of an application, once the application is before these courts, there are no additional rights or remedies attributable to the Convention. However, as he put it:

'The fact that the Convention confers no separate rights or remedies in relation to access to the children which are enforceable by judicial proceedings means

Burrell – A Scottish Approach to Access Under the Hague Convention on Civil Aspects of Child Abduction', a paper presented to the International Child Abduction Convention Conference held in Edinburgh in June 2002.
[56] Viz reg 46(2) of the Civil Legal Aid (Scotland) Regulations 1996, SI 1996/2044, under which applications have to be certified by the Secretary of State as being a Convention application. Cf, in England and Wales, the Community Legal Service (Financial) Regulations 2000, reg 3(1)(f), discussed further at **25.38**.
[57] [1993] Fam 216, [1993] 2 WLR 824, [1993] 1 FLR 669, discussed at **25.20**.

that there is a sense in which no application to the court for access to a child can be made "under the Hague Convention". But that cannot be the sense in which the phrase is used in the rule. It is not, in my view, stretching the meaning of the phrase "application for access to a child under the Hague Convention" too far to conclude that it must mean an application for access (or contact, to use the terminology now adopted in the domestic context) in which:

(i)   the parent seeking the assistance of the court holds an order for access pronounced in the courts of another Contracting State in which the child was habitually resident at the time of the order;

(ii)   the parent has sought the assistance of the Scottish Courts Administration as the Central Authority in a way contemplated in Article 21; and

(iii)   the remedy which is sought from this court is sought with a view to enabling the applicant parent to exercise access to the child to which the foreign order relates.'

25.31   On appeal, the court similarly refused to strike out the petition, although in reaching this conclusion, Lord Prosser (who gave the main judgment) found it unnecessary to consider the English decisions in any detail. In Lord Prosser's view, it was possible to interpret the Rules to cover a category of access applications which could properly be said to be 'under' the Convention, although he warned:

'It does not appear to me that the mere fact of an existing order, coupled with a request for, and perhaps the grant of, assistance from a Central Authority, means that all and any future applications for access by a party are to be seen as applications under the Hague Convention. The provisions of the Convention appear to me to be intended as provisions supportive of existing rights. And while there may be cases in which it is evident that particular details of access are merely mechanisms, expressing rather than defining an existing right of access, I am also satisfied that some orders for which application might be made would be so different from the original order that the court could only properly treat the matter as essentially a new one, the Convention no longer being really in point.'

Having effectively pronounced r 70.5(2) *intra vires*, Lord Prosser agreed with Lord Macfadyen's view that the provision was unhelpful and in need of review. In both their Lordships' view, access cases did not call for unusual expedition beyond that which is appropriate in any case concerning children.[58]

25.32   Having ruled upon the general application of r 70.5(2), there remained the issue whether, given that what the father sought was different to the terms of the Canadian order, this particular application could properly be said to be 'under the Convention'. Once the argument that the difference between the order held and the order sought was irrelevant, since what was sought to be implemented was not the specific foreign court order but the father's right of access in a general sense, had been rejected, the issue was bound to be

---

58   At first instance, Lord Macfadyen expressly rejected counsel's argument that, given (a) the existence of a foreign court order which was strong evidence that access was in the child's interests and (b) that parties living abroad would be put to inordinate expense in maintaining a normal access application, the special rule was justified – *sed quaere?*

problematic. As Lord Macfadyen observed, at first instance, the extent to which the order sought corresponds to the foreign order will vary according to the circumstances. On the one hand, it may be that what is being sought is an order in identical terms or, alternatively, an ancillary order (for example, for specific travel arrangements) so as to enable the access rights already conferred to be enjoyed. While these are more obviously 'under' the Convention, does that mean that, if there is any discrepancy between the order held and the order sought, they must be regarded as being outside the Convention? Lord Macfadyen did not think so. As he pointed out, in this case the Canadian order for weeknight and weekend access had become 'virtually incapable of being given effect according to its terms now that the children are resident in Scotland'. He recognised that, in seeking a substitute for that access in residential form, which in a sense was wholly different from the order which he held, the father was nevertheless seeking 'to rely on the fact that he holds the Canadian order as part of the basis on which he asks this court to make the substitute order'. For his part, his Lordship was not prepared to hold that the father's application in this case could not be regarded as an application for access under the Convention.

25.33 A similar decision was reached on appeal. Lord Prosser commented that whether or not a particular access application was 'under' the Convention was 'ill-suited to legalistic categorisation'. He continued:

> 'I do not think it is possible to define the extent to which departure from the original order may be legitimate, although I think it is true that in some cases one will be able to differentiate between the fundamental right granted and the details of a particular award.'[59]

Nevertheless, despite his Lordship's 'very considerable misgivings' as to whether the order sought could be regarded as being under the Convention, given that, as was common ground, the merits of the application would be decided in exactly the same way as any domestic application for contact, he was not prepared at that stage to dismiss the petition. In the event, therefore, the petition was allowed to proceed as presented, with its merits to be determined by the Lord Ordinary, applying the principles applicable to any domestic application for contact.[60]

25.34 Since this ruling in *Donofrio v Burrell*, r 70.5(2) has been amended (with effect from September 2001) and now reads:

> 'An application for organising or protecting rights of access granted by any court of a Contracting party to the Hague Convention, or for securing respect for the conditions to which exercise of such rights of access is subject shall be made by petition.'

---

[59] He ventured the view that, for the future, he could 'see no reason why there should not be a single procedure, in which a party could rely both upon Art 21 (for short-term purposes, for which there might be special procedures) and also upon the ordinary law, if and when major changes in rights are sought, effectively replacing the original foreign order'.

[60] Ie akin to those made under s 11(2)(d) of the Children (Scotland) Act 1995, on which see eg Thomson, *Family Law in Scotland*, 4th edn (Butterworths, 2002).

As can be seen, this new wording limits applications under the Convention procedure to cases where there is an existing court order, but does not materially affect the decision in *Donofrio*.

Summary

25.35 The position in Scotland can be summarised as follows.

(1)　The Hague Convention in general and Art 21 in particular does no more ˋthan permit a party possessed of rights of access to present an application for assistance to the Central Authority, and permit the Central Authority to take steps to remove obstacles to the exercise of rights of access and to initiate or assist in the institution of proceedings, *inter alia*, to organise or protect such rights. But:

　　(a)　it does *not* confer upon individuals private rights or remedies attributable to the Convention; nor

　　(b)　does it place any obligation on the judicial authorities of the requested State.

(2)　Nevertheless, notwithstanding the foregoing analysis, it is possible for an access *application* to be made 'under the Convention' and therefore to be governed by r 70.5(2), even as amended.

(3)　Where this is the case, applications can properly be made by petition, and the special provisions for legal aid applicable to Convention applications can properly be sanctioned.

(4)　Although a pre-existing order is now a necessity, the mere fact that the applicant has a foreign access order in his favour does not *ipso facto* bring a case 'under the Convention' even if the applicant is assisted by the Central Authority, although on which side of the line a particular application falls is problematic. In this respect, applicants are well advised to act quickly and to keep to the original order as closely as possible.

(5)　Even if an application is regarded as having been made 'under the Convention', the court will determine the outcome just like any other domestic application for contact, with the child's welfare being the court's paramount consideration.

The position in other jurisdictions[61]

25.36　The United States takes a broadly similar approach to that in England and Wales, with decisions such as *Bromley v Bromley*[62] and *Teijeiro Fernandez v Yeagar*[63] establishing that Art 21 does not give the courts any independent authority to enforce rights of access in respect of children. In contrast, the view is taken both in Australia[64] and in New Zealand that Art 21 can be used as a basis for court proceedings. In the latter jurisdiction, it was held in

---

[61]　See the analysis in the Duncan Report, *op cit*, n 3, at paras 25 *et seq*.

[62]　30 F Supp 2d 857 (ED Pa 1998), US District Ct for the Western District of Michigan.

[63]　121 F Supp 2d 1118 (WD Mich 2000), US District Ct for the Western District of Michigan.

[64]　See *Police Commissioner of South Australia v Castell* (1997) 138 FLR 437, (1997) 21 Fam LR 643, discussed at **25.6**.

Gumbrell v Jones,[65] where two children had moved with their mother from England to New Zealand with the permission of the English court subject to detailed arrangements concerning access, that Art 21 authorised the Central Authority to apply to the court for an access order. The court duly made an order in terms which gave effect to the English order.

Commentary

25.37 As the Duncan Report concludes, there is no uniform view among Contracting States, *inter alia*, on whether Art 21 provides a basis for petitioning a court to secure access rights or, if so, within what limits.[66] There is common agreement both in England and Wales and in Scotland that Art 21 does not confer private rights or remedies or place any obligation on judicial authorities and that, accordingly, the 1980 Hague Abduction Convention does not provide a means to enforce rights of access. Such an interpretation not only reflects the wording of the Article, but also seems in accord with the intention behind the wording. As Professor Anton, Chairman of the Conference which drafted the Convention, has written:[67]

> 'The Convention contains no mandatory provisions for the support of access rights comparable with those of its provisions which protect breaches of rights of custody. This applies even in the extreme case where a child is taken to another country by the parent with custody rights and is so taken deliberately with a view to render the further enjoyment of access rights impossible. It was felt not only that mandatory rules in the fluid field of access rights would be difficult to devise but, perhaps more importantly, that the effective exercise of access rights depends in the long run more upon the goodwill or at least the restraint, of the parties than upon the existence of formal rules.'

25.38 Notwithstanding this agreement, there remain important differences between England and Wales, and Scotland. In the latter jurisdiction, as we have seen, the Rules make special provision for access applications 'under the Convention', and these have been interpreted broadly to refer to applications for assistance by a holder of rights of access in another Contracting State. Although there are no comparable Rules in England and Wales, the phrase 'under the Convention' does appear in the Community Legal Service (Financial) Regulations 2000. Specifically, reg 3(1)(f) provides that:

> 'a person whose application *under the Hague Convention* ... has been submitted to the Central Authority in England and Wales pursuant to section 3(2) ... of the Child Abduction and Custody Act 1985' (emphasis added),

is entitled to free legal representation regardless of means. Were the 'Scottish approach' to be adopted, then, notwithstanding that Art 21 creates no private rights, reg 3(1)(f) could, contrary to the ruling of Bracewell J in *Re T (Minors)*

---

65 [2001] NZFLR 593.

66 At para 30.

67 'The Hague Convention on International Child Abduction' (1981) 30 ICLQ 537, at 554–555.

(Hague Convention: Access),[68] be interpreted as applying to applications for access, at any rate provided the order sought broadly corresponded to the order already held.[69] The advantage of this approach would be to harmonise the position within the United Kingdom, whilst at the same time addressing a real problem of high costs facing foreign litigants. In any event, it could be argued that such an interpretation is in line with Art 29 which, in permitting applicants to apply for relief directly to the courts, equates breaches of custody rights with breaches of access rights within the meaning of Art 3 or Art 21.

25.39   Considering the application to be 'under the Convention' will not mean a different approach being applied to the outcome. As in Scotland,[70] applications will still be determined just like domestic applications, with the child's welfare being the court's paramount consideration. Whether the timetabling would or should be different is more problematic. In Scotland, the application of the special rules[71] means that a more expedited procedure is made applicable, whereas in England and Wales, applications for access are treated as domestic applications for contact and are subject to the timetabling provisions under the Children Act 1989. In the Scottish decision, *Donofrio v Burrell*,[72] neither Lord Macfadyen, at first instance, nor Lord Prosser on appeal, were convinced of the need for particular expedition of proceedings 'beyond that which is appropriate in any case concerning children', but it is nevertheless one complaint made against the English jurisdiction that access applications are not accorded special priority once they are before the court and are in fact disposed of slowly. Indeed, there is research evidence supporting this view, with one finding that access disputes took six times longer to resolve than return applications.[73] It is submitted that it is right to dispose of 'Hague access applications' expeditiously and that they should be treated with a similar urgency to return applications.

25.40   Further disquiet about the operation of Art 21 has been expressed at the various reviews of the Convention, particularly at the second meeting of the Special Commission.[74] However, initial calls to modernise what one delegate described as the 'rudimentary' access provisions, even to the extent of

---

68   [1993] 2 FLR 617 at 623, discussed at **25.23**.

69   See the discussion, at **25.32–25.33**, on how close the terms sought must be, compared with the order held, to be considered 'under the Convention'.

70   See n 60 above.

71   Viz r 70.6 of the Rules of the Court of Session 1994.

72   2000 SLT 1051, Ct of Session (Extra Division, Inner House).

73   See Lowe and Perry, 'The Operation of the Hague and European Conventions on International Child Abduction between England and Germany', Part 1 [1998] 1 *International Family Law* 8 at 11. See also, by the same authors, 'International Child Abduction – The English Experience' (1999) 48 ICLQ 127. This finding was confirmed by Lowe, Armstrong and Mathias in the 1999 Statistical Survey. See also, by the same authors, *Country Report: United Kingdom* (NCMEC, 2002), para 7.1.2, where all three UK jurisdictions are analysed.

74   Report of the second Special Commission meeting to review the operation of the Hague Convention on the Civil Aspects of International Child Abduction, published by the Permanent Bureau in 1993.

adding a new Protocol, became muted. In the event, the overall conclusion of the Second Special Commission was that:[75]

> 'It would be desirable to have more information about the ultimate arrangements made for the exercise of access following the wrongful removal or retention of the child, both in cases where the child has been refused and in cases where return has been refused.'

It was, however, recorded[76] that a number of experts considered the lack of firm legal provisions to enforce access to be a major problem because Central Authorities might consequently be unwilling to act.

25.41 The matter was raised again at the fourth Special Commission meeting held in March 2001, where a detailed analysis was provided by William Duncan, the Deputy Secretary General. It was resolved at that meeting to hold a Special Commission meeting specifically to discuss access further. That meeting was held in September 2002 for which Duncan prepared an impressive Report.[77] In that report, Duncan identified a number of major shortcomings, namely:[78]

(1) the failure to have uniform rules determining jurisdiction;
(2) the absence of agreement among States on the nature and level of support for those seeking to establish or secure access;
(3) the operation in some States of procedures which are both insensitive to the special features and needs of international cases and are the cause of unnecessary delays and expense; and
(4) an inadequate level of international co-operation at both administrative and judicial levels.

The Report suggested a number of strategies to meet these shortcomings, including adding a new Protocol and producing a guide to good practice. The Special Commission resolved that it was premature to work on a new Protocol, but that a guide to good practice was a good strategy. It concluded by authorising the Bureau to investigate the issue further.[79]

---

[75] See Conclusion 5 of the Report.

[76] At p 50 of the Report. The lack of enforceability of access rights was also criticised by the Washington Forum. See Lowe, *International Forum on Parental Child Abduction: Hague Convention Action Agenda* (National Center for Missing and Exploited Children, 1999) at p 13.

[77] Viz the Duncan Report, *op cit*, n 3.

[78] At para 119.

[79] See Conclusions and Recommendations of the Special Commission of September–October 2002 on the Hague Child Abduction Convention, para 2.

THE 1980 EUROPEAN CUSTODY CONVENTION[80]

Introduction

25.42 The basic scheme provided for by the 1980 European Custody Convention is that of recognition and enforcement of decisions,[81] and 'decisions', for these purposes, includes access decisions. This is made clear[82] by Art 11(1) which provides:

> 'Decisions on rights of access and provisions of decisions relating to custody which deal with the rights of access shall be recognised and enforced subject to the same conditions as other decisions relating to custody.'

25.43 In other words, in contrast to the 1980 Hague Abduction Convention, applications can be made to the court of one Contracting State for the recognition and enforcement of an access decision made in another Contracting State. Moreover, because such applications are made 'under the Convention', applicants will qualify for free legal representation regardless of means or merits in accordance with the favourable provisions established for Convention applications.[83] On the other hand, unlike the Hague Convention, this Convention does not take precedence over the so-called 'Brussels II Regulation'.[84]

Procedure for seeking to enforce access decisions

25.44 Under Art 4, any person who has obtained a decision[85] relating to access to a child and who wishes to have that decision recognised or enforced in another Contracting State may submit an application for that purpose to a Central Authority of any Contracting State.[86] If it is not the Central Authority

---

[80] See generally the Council of Europe's own Explanatory Report (reprinted in 1994) on the Convention, which is also reproduced as Cmnd 8155 (1981), paras 59 and 60. For a discussion of the application of the Convention to custody, see Chapter 19.

[81] See Art 7, which states that 'decisions relating to [access] given in a Contracting State shall be recognised and, where it is enforceable in the State of origin, made enforceable in every other Contracting State'.

[82] Although it also seems to follow from Art 1(c) which provides that a: 'decision relating to custody' means a decision of an authority insofar as it relates to the care of the person of the child, 'including the right to decide on the place of his residence, or the right of access to him'.

[83] Viz, in England and Wales, pursuant to the Community Legal Service (Financial) Regulations 2000; in Scotland, pursuant to Civil Legal Aid (Scotland) Regulations 1996, reg 46, and in Northern Ireland, pursuant to Legal Aid (General) Regulations (Northern Ireland) 1965, reg 3A.

[84] Viz Council Regulation (EC) No 1347/2000 of 29 May 2000 on jurisdiction and the recognition and enforcement of judgments in matrimonial matters and in matters of parental responsibility for children of both spouses, Art 37. See further **4.9** *et seq* and Chapter 18. It will be noted that, under the Regulation, applicants are not entitled to free legal representation regardless of means.

[85] For the position of those without a decision, see further **25.54** *et seq*.

[86] Such applications should be accompanied by the documentation required by Art 13 (discussed at **19.76**): Art 4(2).

of the State addressed,[87] the authority receiving the application must 'send the documents directly and without delay to that central authority'.[88] Unless the Central Authority of the State addressed refuses to intervene on the basis that 'it is manifestly clear that the conditions laid down by this Convention are not satisfied' as provided for by Art 4(4), then, pursuant to Art 5(1), it must 'take or cause to be taken without delay all steps which it considers to be appropriate, if necessary by instituting proceedings before its competent authorities', *inter alia*, to secure recognition or enforcement of the decision.

25.45 So far as the United Kingdom is concerned, these Convention provisions are further augmented by the provisions of the Child Abduction and Custody Act 1985 and the accompanying rules. In the case of England and Wales, applications should be made by originating summons[89] to the High Court[90] for the recognition and enforcement of an order. Section 16 of the 1985 Act provides:

'(1) A person on whom any rights are conferred by a decision relating to custody made by an authority in a Contracting State other than the United Kingdom may make an application for the registration of the decision in an appropriate court in the United Kingdom.

(2) The Central Authority in the United Kingdom shall assist such a person in making such an application if a request for such assistance is made by him or on his behalf by the Central Authority of the Contracting State in question.

(3) An application under subsection (1) above or request under subsection (2) above shall be treated as a request for enforcement for the purposes of Arts 10 and 13 of the Convention.'

25.46 Section 18 further provides that, once a decision has been registered under s 16, then the court in which it is registered has the same powers of enforcement as if the order had been made by that court and that enforcement proceedings can be taken accordingly.

The court's powers

Granting or refusing registration

25.47 Although the basic enjoinder is that an order should be both recognised and enforced, the Convention does allow for an application to be refused on the basis of the exceptions provided for by Arts 9 and 10.[91]

---

[87]   Ie the State from which the order is sought.

[88]   Article 4(3).

[89]   FPR 1991, r 6.2. A similar position obtains in Northern Ireland: see Lowe, Armstrong and Mathias, *Country Reports: United Kingdom* (NCMEC, 2000), at p 12. In Scotland, application is made by petition, pursuant to r 70.9 of the Rules of the Court of Session 1994.

[90]   The Court of Session in Scotland.

[91]   Query whether it is possible to have partial recognitions? See further **25.57**.

Section 16(4) of the 1985 Act expressly empowers the High Court[92] to refuse to register a decision if:

> '(a)   the court is of the opinion that on any grounds specified in Article 9 and 10 of the Convention the decision should not be recognised in any part of the United Kingdom ...'

25.48   This power reflects the provision under s 15(2), namely:

> 'A decision which was made in a Contracting State other than the United Kingdom shall be recognised in each part of the United Kingdom as if made by a court having jurisdiction to make it in that part but:
>
> (a)   the appropriate court in any part of the United Kingdom may, on the application of any person appearing to it to have an interest in the matter, declare on any of the grounds specified in Article 9 or 10 of the Convention that the decision is not to be recognised in any part of the United Kingdom; and
>
> (b)   the decision shall not be enforceable in any part of the United Kingdom unless registered in the appropriate court under section 16 below.'

25.49   According to *Re A (Foreign Access Order: Enforcement)*,[93] the scheme of the Convention is plain and the task of the judge is clear, namely to recognise and register the foreign access order unless an exception under Art 9 or Art 10 is established.[94] The burden for establishing a defence lies on the party opposing registration.

25.50   In *Re A*, Bracewell J was held to have erred for not deciding explicitly whether the order in question should be recognised and registered and whether the defence raised by the mother under Art 10(1)(b)[95] had been made out to the court's satisfaction. In that case, following the separation of the parents in 1991, the father returned to France and the mother subsequently brought the two children (aged 5 and 2) to England. In 1993 the father obtained a French court order that: (a) joint parental authority be awarded to both parents; (b) the children continue to live with their mother; and (c) he should have staying access in August each year in France. The father, who could only afford to have staying access in France, attempted to exercise his rights in 1994 but the mother successfully obtained an order from the English court that the children should not be removed from the jurisdiction, but that in other respects the French order was to continue. The father again applied in 1995 but Bracewell J repeated the 1994 order, refusing to enforce the access part of the French order on the ground that the children's objection to going to France appeared to have hardened, and therefore Art 10(1)(b) was satisfied.

---

[92]   The Court of Session in Scotland.

[93]   [1996] 1 FLR 561, CA.

[94]   Since Art 9 is solely concerned with procedural defects, it is more likely that Art 10 will be pleaded. For detailed discussion of these defences, see **19.101** *et seq*.

[95]   For the unsuccessful pleading of an Art 10(1)(a) defence, namely that it was 'manifestly incompatible with the fundamental principles of the law relating to the family and children in the State addressed' to grant access to an unmarried father, see the Irish decision *RJ v MR* [1994] 1 IR 271.

On appeal, however, it was held that the evidence did not establish any change of circumstance which could be said to have caused the original decision to be 'manifestly no longer in accordance with the welfare' of the children concerned. It was further held that, while the judge was right to have ascertained the children's views,[96] the finding that their views had 'hardened' came nowhere near the change of circumstances contemplated by the Convention.

25.51   In contrast, in *Re L (Abduction: European Convention: Access)*,[97] Bennett J refused to enforce an access order made in France in favour of grandparents, because it was predicated on the basis that the children were living in France at an address close to the grandparents in circumstances in which there were no practical difficulties in the way of contact, whereas the children were now living in England with their parents. Given these new circumstances, in which contact according to the terms of the French order could have required the children (aged 7 and 3) to travel to France twice a month, Bennett J had no difficulty in holding that, since enforcement of the order was neither practical nor in the children's interest, the defence under Art 10(1)(b) that enforcement was 'manifestly no longer in accordance with the welfare of the [children]' was therefore made out.

Modifying orders pursuant to Article 11(2)

25.52   Notwithstanding the general scheme to register or refuse to register access orders, Art 11(2) empowers the competent authority addressed to 'fix the conditions for implementation and exercise of the right of access taking into account, in particular, undertakings given by the parties on this matter'. In the words of one leading commentator on the Convention:[98]

'The wording of Art 11(2) represents the outcome of extensive discussion in the Committee of Experts. It reflects the difficulty frequently encountered in practice in establishing how access is to be given when the parents fail to agree on times and places. The court or other competent authority in the State where the child is living will ordinarily be in the best position to decide such details in default of agreement, since it will have better facilities than the court in the State of origin to make the necessary enquiries and a greater knowledge of local circumstances (such as, for example, when school holidays begin and end).'

25.53   In effect, Art 11(2) enables the State addressed to modify decisions of other Contracting States to make them consistent with local practice. However, as the Court of Appeal emphasised in *Re A (Foreign Access Order:*

---

[96]   Note that when an Art 10(1)(b) defence is raised, it is, pursuant to Art 15(1)(a), incumbent upon the court to ascertain the child's views save where it is 'impracticable' having regard to the child's age and understanding, as discussed at **19.112**.

[97]   [1999] 2 FLR 1089.

[98]   Jones, 'Council of Europe Convention on Recognition and Enforcement of Decisions Relating to the Custody of Children' (1981) 30 ICLQ 467 at 472. See also the Explanatory Report, para 59.

Enforcement),[99] this power is still subject to the embargo under Art 9(3) against reviewing a foreign decision as to its substance. In *Re A*, under the terms of a French court order, the father was to have annual staying access in France during August. However, at first instance, Bracewell J had instead granted the father staying access in England, even though it was known that the father could only afford staying access in France. On appeal, this was condemned. According to Waite LJ:[100]

> 'The radical change made by the judge to the French court order by giving the father staying access in England which he cannot afford to take up, instead of staying access in France which is what the French judge had directed, could not possibly have been brought within the implementation provisions of Art 11. Such a change would have amounted, as Leggatt LJ has said, to a review of the foreign decision as to its substance, a step which is specifically prohibited by Art 9(3).'

25.54 While the decision in *Re A* is perhaps understandable, given the father's inability to afford access abroad, the question remains as to what, in general, the bar against reviewing a foreign decision 'as to its substance' means. Should *Re A* be interpreted as applying Art 9(3) to *any* changes of the terms of the original order or only to those that are fundamental? Suppose, as in the Scottish case *Donofrio v Burrell*,[101] the terms of the original order were for week night and weekend access. Given that the children are now living in another jurisdiction, these terms are virtually incapable of being given effect. Would it be 'reviewing the original decision to its substance' to grant some other form of regular staying access? It is submitted that, unless it is thought right to limit Art 11(2) to being a supplementing power (for example, to give some definition to open-ended orders such as defining school holidays or 'reasonable' access), then some flexibility has to be permitted, but even then where the line is to be drawn will be problematic in a particular case.[102]

The powers under Article 11(3)

25.55 According to Art 11(3):

> 'Where no decision on the right of access has been taken or where recognition or enforcement of the decision relating to custody is refused, the central authority of the State addressed may apply to its competent authorities for a decision on the right of access, if the person claiming a right of access so requests.'

---

99 [1996] 1 FLR 561 at 565–566 (per Leggatt LJ) and at 568 (per Waite LJ). See also *Re L (Abduction: European Convention: Access)* [1999] 2 FLR 1089, in which Bennett J also refused to exercise his powers under Art 11(2), principally because no clear proposals had been put forward on to the type of access that should take place in England.

100 *Ibid* at 568.

101 2000 SLT 1051, discussed at **25.28** *et seq.*

102 There is an obvious analogy between Art 11(2) and the phrase 'under the Convention' used in the legal aid provisions both in England and Wales, and Scotland, and in r 70.5(2) of the Rules of the Court of Session 1994 (applicable in Scotland) in relation to access applications under the 1980 Hague Abduction Convention. One possible argument against too liberal interpretation of Art 11(2) is the possibly wide application of Art 11(3): see further below.

25.56 The precise scope of this provision is unclear.[103] According to Booth J in *F v F (Minors) (Custody)*,[104] Art 11(3) 'contemplates at any rate in part an application for access within the proceedings for registration and enforcement'. In this respect, it amounts to 'nothing more than a convenient and sensible shorthand for the opening words of Art 5, that is that "the Central Authority in the State addressed shall take or cause to be taken without delay all steps which it considers to be appropriate", thus enabling an application for access to be made by those appointed to act for it'. What this seems to mean is that Art 11(3) simply provides the procedural means of getting the issue to court. In other words, it could simply be read as providing a means for those without an order in their favour, for example where the parties have made an agreement concerning access, to establish a 'right of access' which could then be subsequently enforced under the terms of the Convention just discussed. However, if this is the case, then it is hard to make sense of allowing an application to be made in the case of a refusal to recognise or enforce a 'decision relating to custody', given that that phrase also includes a decision as to a right of access.[105] It is true that one can imagine a refusal based on procedural deficiencies as provided for in Art 9 when it may well be right to regard the applicant as having a right of access. Nevertheless, it seems odd to refuse recognition on the one hand yet still make a declaration on rights of access, which can then be enforced on the other hand, since that would effectively override Art 9. However, an alternative interpretation of Art 11(3) is to say that, in absence of any decision relating to access or the refusal to recognise or enforce such a decision, applications for access on their merits can be made under the Convention.[106] It remains to be seen whether such an interpretation would be accepted, but if it were, Art 11(3) would indeed be a useful remedy.

25.57 Another issue as to the application of Art 11(3) is whether it applies to partial refusals of recognition. In *Re A (Foreign Access Order: Enforcement)*,[107] for example, had total enforcement not been held appropriate, might it not have been argued in relation to the original refusal to enforce staying access in France that Art 11(3) applied rather than Art 11(2)?

Commentary

25.58 Insofar as the 1980 European Custody Convention provides a means for enforcing access orders, it is a useful counterpart to the 1980 Hague

---

[103] It is not discussed by Jones, *op cit*, n 97, while the guidance, *European Convention on Recognition and Enforcement of Decisions Relating to the Custody of Children* Cmnd 8151 (1981), para 60, merely paraphrases the wording.

[104] [1989] Fam 1 at 17, [1988] 3 WLR 959 at 974, sub nom *Re F (Minors) (Custody: Foreign Order)* [1989] 1 FLR 355 at 349.

[105] See Art 1(c), discussed at **19.41** *et seq*.

[106] The embargo against reviewing an order as to its substance under Art 9(3) has no application to Art 11(3), given either that there is no order or that there has been a refusal to recognise or enforce an order.

[107] [1996] 1 FLR 561, CA, discussed above at **25.53**.

Abduction Convention, and empirical evidence suggests that, at any rate in the past, the former was used comparatively more often for access disputes than the latter.[108] Whether this will continue to be so given the superseding priority of Brussels II now seems unlikely.

25.59 Nevertheless, it has to be said that even this part of the Convention has not proved an outstanding success and, indeed, Art 11(2) and (3) will be superseded upon a State's ratification of the 2003 European Convention on Contact Concerning Children.[109] As just discussed, unless it is sought to enforce the exact terms of an order, the application of the Convention is problematic. In particular, it seems that the power to 'modify' a foreign access order under Art 11(2) is subject to the embargo under Art 9(3) not to review the original order as to its substance, which in turn may prevent seeking any substantive changes to the original terms.[110] It is possible, however, that Art 11(3) will allow Convention applications to be made to determine an access application on its merits, *inter alia*, where a court has refused to recognise or enforce a foreign access order. If this is the case, although a definitive ruling on the ambit of the provision has yet to be made, then in certain cases, the 1980 European Custody Convention could provide a useful remedy.

THE POTENTIAL IMPACT OF THE 1996 HAGUE CONVENTION ON THE PROTECTION OF CHILDREN

25.60 The 1996 Hague Convention on the Protection of Children,[111] which the United Kingdom has now signed[112] but has not yet ratified, contains some potentially useful provisions concerning access. As we discussed in Chapter 24, the 1996 Convention is broadly concerned to improve the protection of children's person and property in international situations. To this end, it seeks:

---

108 Lowe and Perry, 'International Child Abduction – the English Experience' (1999) 48 ICLQ 127 at 130, found that, in England and Wales in 1996, whereas only 6% of incoming Hague Convention applications were for access, the figure was 25% for European Convention applications (in 1997, the respective figures were 7% and 42%); and for outgoing applications, the figures were 17% (Hague) and 42% (European) (in 1997, the two figures were 16.5% and 30%), although in each case the actual numbers were small.

109 See **25.83** *et seq.*

110 See eg *Re A (Foreign Access Order: Enforcement)* [1996] 1 FLR 561, discussed at **25.53**.

111 The full name of the Convention is the Hague Convention on Jurisdiction, Applicable Law, Recognition, Enforcement and Co-operation in Respect of Parental Responsibility and Measures for the Protection of Children 1996. For a general discussion of the Convention, see the Explanatory Report by Paul Lagarde published by the Permanent Bureau of the Hague Conference in 1998; Clive, 'The New Hague Convention on Children' (1998) 3 *Juridical Review* 169; Nygh, 'The New Hague Child Protection Convention' (1997) 11 Int Jo of Law, Policy and the Family 334; and Lowe, 'The 1996 Hague Convention on the protection of children – a fresh appraisal' [2002] CFLQ 191.

112 See **24.5**.

(a)   to provide common jurisdictional rules;

(b)   to provide for the recognition and enforcement of such measures of protection in all Contracting States; and

(c)   to establish co-operation between the authorities of the Contracting States so as to achieve the Convention's purposes.[113]

25.61   Article 3 gives a broad definition of what ranks as 'protective measures' under the Convention, with Art 3(b) providing that such measures refer to:

> 'rights of custody, including rights relating to the care of the person of the child and, in particular, the right to determine the child's place of residence, as well as rights of access including the right to take a child for a limited period of time to a place other than the child's habitual residence.'

It is to be noted that, as this Convention applies to children 'from the moment of their birth until they reach the age of 18 years',[114] it is not therefore confined, as are the 1980 Hague Abduction and 1980 European Custody Conventions, to children under the age of 16.

25.62   Insofar as the Convention affects the enforcement or promotion of access rights,[115] it is clear that it is intended to provide further or alternative relief, and not to supplant that already provided by the existing abduction conventions. Indeed, Art 50 expressly states that the 1996 Convention shall not affect the 1980 Hague Abduction Convention, although it adds:

> 'Nothing, however, precludes provisions of this Convention from being invoked for the purposes of obtaining the return of a child who has been wrongfully removed or retained or of organising access rights.'

25.63   A similar position obtains with regard to the 1980 European Custody Convention.[116] In other words, applicants are free to invoke the 1996 Convention or the 1980 Hague Abduction Convention or the 1980 European Custody Convention as they see fit. It remains now to consider the potential impact of the 1996 Convention on access issues.

Enforcing access orders

25.64   One effect of the 1996 Convention will be to provide another means by which an access order properly made in one Contracting State[117] can be enforced in another Contracting State. The recognition and enforcement provisions are set out in Chapter IV. In particular, Art 23(1) provides:

---

[113]   See Art 1.

[114]   Article 2.

[115]   Cf the making of such orders in the first place, when the 1996 Convention might operate to restrict jurisdiction: see **25.72**.

[116]   This is implicit in Art 52(1) which, as the Lagarde Report comments, was 'the fruit of very long and difficult discussions'. See also Nygh, *op cit*, n 110, at 357.

[117]   The jurisdictional rules are set out in Chapter II to the Convention, discussed at **25.14** *et seq*.

'The measures taken by the authorities of a Contracting State shall be recognised by operation of law in all other Contracting States.'[118]

25.65   The enforcement mechanism is set out in Art 26 which states:

'(1)   If measures taken in one Contracting State and enforceable there require enforcement in another Contracting State, they shall, upon request by an interested party, be declared enforceable or registered for the purpose of enforcement in that other State according to the procedure provided in the law of the latter State.

(2)   Each Contracting State shall apply to the declaration of enforceability or registration a simple and rapid procedure.'

25.66   Although Art 27 generally bars any review of the merits of, in this context, an access order, recognition and enforcement on registration can be refused on the grounds set out in Art 23(2), including:

'(d)   if such recognition is manifestly contrary to the public policy of the requested State, taking into account the best interests of the child.'

Of course, until the implementing mechanisms are in place and in the absence of any judicial indications as to how widely or narrowly the exceptions under Art 23(2) are to be interpreted, it is difficult to make firm predictions as to how effective the Convention will be.[119] Nevertheless, the following observations may be made.

25.67   First, given that the 1980 Hague Abduction Convention does not make provision for the enforcement of access orders, the 1996 Convention does offer something new as between nations who are only Contracting States to the 1980 Convention. However, in the absence of any modifying powers under the 1996 Convention, such applications would seem appropriate only where it is sought to enforce the exact terms of the original order.

25.68   Secondly, in relation to the 1980 European Custody Convention, save in relation to 16- or 17-year-olds,[120] the recognition and enforcement powers under the 1996 Convention seem inferior. There is, for example, nothing comparable to the modifying powers under Art 11(2) of the European Convention, nor to Art 11(3) in relation to the court's powers if recognition or enforcement is refused.[121] Moreover, unlike the European Convention, no provision is made under the 1996 Convention for the State to bear the costs. Accordingly, where there is a choice, it would seem preferable to seek recognition and/or enforcement of an access order under the European Convention rather than the 1996 Convention.

---

[118]   Article 24 makes provision for an interested party to apply to the competent authorities of a Contracting State for a ruling on recognition or non-recognition.

[119]   See also the discussion at **25.39** *et seq*.

[120]   The European Convention applies only to children under the age of 16, whereas the 1996 Convention applies to children under the age of 18.

[121]   Article 11(2) and (3) is discussed at **25.53** *et seq*.

Seeking co-operation

25.69 As under the 1980 Hague Abduction and 1980 European Custody Conventions, Contracting States under the 1996 Convention must establish a Central Authority[122] whose duties, *inter alia*, are to co-operate with each other to achieve the purposes of the Convention.[123] Under Art 31(b), Central Authorities must directly or through public authorities or other bodies:

'facilitate, by mediation, conciliation or similar means, agreed solutions for the protection of the person or property of the child in situations to which the Convention applies.'

This might have particular application to access disputes.

25.70 In addition to the duties expressly imposed upon Central Authorities, further provisions designed to promote co-operation are provided by Art 35 which, in the words of one commentator,[124] 'contains innovative and potentially very useful provisions, to facilitate access to a child in another Contracting State'. Article 35(1), in particular, should prove useful. That provides:

'The competent authorities of a Contracting State may request the authorities of another Contracting State to assist in the implementation of measures of protection taken under this Convention, especially in securing the effective exercise of rights of access as well as of the right to maintain direct contacts on a regular basis.'

25.71 Another useful provision is that under Art 35(2), which permits a parent who is seeking to obtain or maintain access but who is living in one Contracting State while the child is habitually resident in another Contracting State, to request the competent authorities of the State in which that parent is residing to 'gather information or evidence and may make a finding on the suitability of that parent to exercise access and on the conditions under which access is to be exercised'. This information is then admissible evidence in proceedings in the child's habitual residence and, indeed, under Art 35(3), the court may adjourn proceedings pending the outcome of such a request.

Limiting jurisdiction to make access orders

25.72 A third potential impact of the 1996 Convention will be to limit national courts' jurisdiction to make access orders in cases where there has been a wrongful removal or retention, or where an access application is already pending in a jurisdiction where, at the time of application, the child was habitually resident. The former restriction is provided by Art 7; the latter by Art 13. These provisions are discussed in Chapter 24.[125]

---

[122] See Art 29.
[123] Article 30(1).
[124] Clive, *op cit*, n 110, at 186.
[125] At **24.23–24.24**.

THE 'BRUSSELS II REGULATION'

Introduction

25.73 Council Regulation (EC) No 1347/2000 of 29 May 2000 on jurisdiction and the recognition and enforcement of judgments in matrimonial matters and in matters of parental responsibility of both spouses, otherwise known as 'the Brussels II Regulation', has been discussed in Chapters 4 and 18, but here we consider its impact on international access or contact cases.

25.74 It will be recalled that the Brussels II Regulation applies only to cases between EU Member States (other than Denmark)[126] and, so far as children are concerned, only to 'civil proceedings relating to parental responsibility for children of both spouses on the occasion of matrimonial proceedings[127] [between the parents]'.[128] 'Parental responsibility' is not defined by the Council Regulation, but must clearly include access or contact.[129] However, because of its limited scope, the Council Regulation has no application to access issues arising in 'non-matrimonial proceedings' (ie freestanding applications) or even in matrimonial proceedings in respect of step-children or non-marital children. Furthermore, the Regulation only comes into play in court proceedings and so has no application to administrative proceedings such as, for example, seeking help from a Central Authority. On the other hand, where the Regulation bites, it provides the *exclusive* rules on jurisdiction, recognition and enforcement.[130]

The inter-relationship between Brussels II and other international instruments

25.75 Although Art 4 of the Council Regulation gives precedence to the 1980 Hague Abduction Convention, it is only in respect of courts having jurisdiction under Art 3 of that Convention (viz where there is a wrongful removal or retention in breach of rights of custody), in which case they 'shall exercise their jurisdiction in conformity with the Hague Convention of 25 October 1980 … and in particular Arts 3 and 16 thereof'. This provision does not therefore extend to access issues. On the other hand, since the Regulation only applies to court proceedings, it cannot in any event prevent applicants invoking Art 21 of the 1980 Hague Abduction Convention insofar as they are seeking help from the Central Authority 'to make arrangements for

---

[126] See Art 1(3) of the Regulation.

[127] Viz divorce, legal separation or marriage annulment: Art 1(1)(a).

[128] Article 1(1)(b).

[129] Note that, in the revised Brussels II, parental responsibility will be defined and will specifically include 'rights of access'.

[130] See respectively Art 7, which provides that spouses who are habitually resident in the territory of a Member State, or are nationals of a Member State, or in the case of the United Kingdom or Ireland, are domiciled in the territory of one of those latter States, may only be sued in another Member State in accordance with Arts 2 and 6, and Arts 9 and 11(3), which limit the jurisdiction of the courts: see **4.14** *et seq*.

organising or securing the effective exercise of rights of access'.[131] However, the Regulation, when otherwise applicable, will govern both jurisdiction to make and the subsequent obligation to recognise and enforce any access orders.

25.76 Under Art 37, the Council Regulation has precedence over both the 1980 European Custody Convention and the 1996 Hague Convention on the Protection of Children. This means that, where it is sought to enforce an access decision in respect of children of both spouses made on the occasion of matrimonial proceedings in another Member State, the Regulation *must* be used and not the 1980 European Custody Convention.[132] This has the unfortunate consequence that applicants have no right to channel applications through Central Authorities and no right, as under the European Convention, to any favourable provisions for legal aid (which in the United Kingdom means free legal representation regardless of means or merit),[133] and the court has no power to modify the access order as it may under Art 11(2) of the European Convention.[134]

The revision of Brussels II

25.77 As early as July 2000, France presented an initiative on the abolition of *exequatur* on access orders and coupled this with proposals for the automatic return of children unlawfully retained after access.[135] At first, the Council concluded[136] that work on this initiative should be pursued in parallel with the proposed extension of the scope of the Regulation, first formally tabled by the Commission in September 2001.[137] However, in May 2002, it was resolved to combine the two proposals,[138] and work on this has just been completed as we write.

---

[131] Note that, according to *Re G (A Minor) (Enforcement of Access Abroad)* [1993] Fam 216, [1993] 2 WLR 824, [1993] 1 FLR 669, discussed above at **25.20** *et seq*, *Bromley v Bromley* 30 F Supp 2d 857 (ED Pa 1998), and *Gumbrell v Jones* [2001] NZFLR 593, discussed at **25.36**, Art 21 imposes no obligations upon a court.

[132] See also **18.24** and **21.1**.

[133] See **21.25**. Under Art 30 of the Regulation, an applicant is entitled, when seeking an enforcement, 'to benefit from the most favourable legal aid or the most extensive exemption from costs and expenses provided for by the law of the Member State addressed'. This is thought to oblige States to provide legal aid according to domestic law and not Convention provisions.

[134] Discussed at **25.52** *et seq*.

[135] Initiative of the French Republic with a view to adopting a Council Regulation on the mutual enforcement of judgments on rights of access to children, OJ 2000 C234/7.

[136] Viz at its meeting on 30 November 2000.

[137] Proposal for a Council Regulation on jurisdiction and the recognition and enforcement of judgments in matters of parental responsibility, OJ No 332 of 27 November 2001, p 269. For discussion of these proposals, see **18.28** *et seq*.

[138] See the Proposal for a Council Regulation concerning jurisdiction and the recognition and enforcement of judgments in matrimonial matters and in matters of parental responsibility repealing Regulation (EC) No 1347/2000 and amending Regulation (EC) No 44/2001 in matters relating to maintenance, Brussels 3 May 2002 Com (2002) 222 Final.

25.78   The importance of combining the two proposals is that, whereas the French initiative was within the confines of Brussels II (and it was dubbed 'Brussels IIA' or 'Brussels II bis'), that is, only applying to children of both spouses involved in matrimonial proceedings, the Commission's proposal was, *inter alia*, to extend the Council Regulation to issues of parental responsibility in all court proceedings and not simply matrimonial proceedings. Furthermore, it is proposed that a Central Authority be designated in each Member State through which, *inter alia*, applications to enforce access may be made.[139] Since May 2002, negotiations have continued upon the basis that the two initiatives should be contained in a single instrument.

25.79   The revised provisions on access are contained in section 4 of Chapter III on Recognition and Enforcement.[140] Article 41 provides, without prejudice to a holder of parental responsibility seeking recognition and enforcement under sections 1 and 2 of Chapter III, that rights of access granted to one of the parents:[141]

> 'in an enforceable judgment given in a Member State shall be recognised and enforceable in another Member States without the need for a declaration of enforceability and without any possibility of opposing its recognition if the judgment has been certified in the Member State of origin ...'

25.80   The procedural requirements are that the judgment was not given in default of appearance and that the child was given an opportunity to be heard unless a hearing was considered inappropriate having regard to his or her age or degree of maturity.

25.81   As now finally drafted, the Council Regulation's application to access will be considerably extended and will leave virtually no room for the operation of the 1980 European Custody Convention as between EU Member States other than Denmark. Furthermore, although it will still be open to applicants to invoke Art 21 of the 1980 Hague Abduction Convention insofar as they wish to seek the help of Central Authorities, the need to do this will be reduced by the establishment of Central Authorities under the Regulation,[142] which will be enjoined at no cost to the applicant,[143] *inter alia*, to facilitate agreement between holders of parental responsibility through mediation or other means, and to organise cross-border co-operation to this end.[144]

25.82   The revised Brussels II Regulation will offer some considerable advantages over the current Regulation, particularly with the introduction of a Central Authority and a more general application (within the EU Member States, apart from Denmark). However, it remains the case that, unlike under

---

[139]   See further the discussion at **18.33**.
[140]   See the Proposal agreed upon at the Council's meeting of 2–3 October 2003.
[141]   Note that the revised Regulation applies both to enforceable orders and to agreements.
[142]   See Art 53.
[143]   See Art 57(3).
[144]   See Art 55(e).

the 1980 European Custody Convention, applicants, at any rate those applying in the United Kingdom, will not be entitled to public funding regardless of means or merits nor will the court have any power to modify a court order.

THE 2003 EUROPEAN CONVENTION ON CONTACT CONCERNING CHILDREN

25.83 Access, particularly trans-frontier contact, issues are notoriously complex and difficult, and it is evident that neither the 1980 Hague Abduction Convention nor the 1980 European Custody Convention is particularly successful in this regard. It is further evident, that although the 1996 Hague Convention on the Protection of Children will provide further options, it will not provide a significant improvement with regard to enforcing orders. In recognition of these limitations, the Council of Europe determined to draft a new instrument solely dealing with contact,[145] the 2003 European Convention on Contact Concerning Children, which was finally opened for signature on 3 May 2003.[146] Accompanying the Convention is a detailed Explanatory Report which is essential reading for understanding the Convention.

Objects and scope

25.84 Article 1 sets out the three objects of the Convention, namely:

'(a) to determine general principles to be applied to contact orders;
(b) to fix appropriate safeguards and guarantees to ensure the proper exercise of contact and the immediate return of children at the end of the period of contact;
(c) to establish co-operation between central authorities, judicial authorities and other bodies in order to promote and improve contact between children and their parents, and other persons having family ties with children.'

25.85 Although the second object is primarily and the third object is exclusively concerned with trans-frontier contact, the first object, which sets this Convention apart from the two 1980 Conventions, is concerned to establish general principles which domestic courts should observe when dealing with contact issues. The thinking behind this is explained in the Preamble, namely that the 'machinery set up to give effect to foreign orders relating to contact concerning children is more likely to provide satisfactory results where the principles on which these foreign orders are based are similar to the principles in the State giving effect to such foreign orders'.

---

[145] For a brief history of the decision to produce a new international instrument, see the Introduction to the Explanatory Report to the Convention (as adopted on 3 May 2003).

[146] It had been planned to open the Convention for signature in October 2002, but this was delayed to resolve a dispute over EU Member States' competence to sign and ratify it.

25.86 The Convention's reference to 'contact' rather than 'access' is a deliberate change of terminology. As the Explanatory Report says,[147] 'replacing the notion of "access to children" by the notion of "contact concerning children"' strengthens the fact that 'children are holders of certain rights ... [It] is more in line with the modern concerns such as parental responsibility or parental responsibilities'.

25.87 Contact itself is widely defined by Art 2 to include staying contact for a limited time, other forms of communication and, interestingly, the provision of information both to and about the child. The Explanatory Report refers[148] to these as being 'three levels of contact'. However, a 'contact order' is defined as a decision of a judicial authority (which means both a court and an administrative authority having equivalent powers) in respect of any level of contact. An order also includes 'an agreement concerning contact which has been confirmed by a competent judicial authority or which has been formally drawn up or registered as an authentic instrument and is enforceable'. As the Explanatory Report explains,[149] 'The inclusion of both court-approved agreements and authentic instruments ... is due to the fact that in very many cases, contact with a child results from private agreements rather than a judicial decision'. However, these must be distinguished from purely private agreements which are outside the scope of the Convention.

25.88 In contrast to the two 1980 Conventions, which apply only to children under the age of 16, but in line with the 1996 Hague Convention on the Protection of Children, the 2003 Convention applies to children under the age of 18 'in respect of which a contact order may be made or enforced in a State Party'.[150] Extending the application of the Convention to children under the age of 18 will, according to the Explanatory Report,[151] 'assist in ensuring the continuation of a contact with a child and will ensure a certain continuity, as other instruments could apply after the age of 18, in particular those dealing with protective measures concerning incapable adults'. On the other hand, the qualification that an order must be capable of being made or enforced preserves the application of those internal laws where a child under the age of 18 can attain full capacity (for example, upon marriage) or where orders cannot be made or enforced where the child is 16 or over, as for example, in Scotland. Whilst this might be an inevitable compromise, it does make for some complication,[152] particularly as the differences of application are spelt out neither in the Convention nor by the Explanatory Report.[153]

---

[147] At para 6.

[148] At para 22.

[149] At para 27.

[150] Article 2(c).

[151] At para 31.

[152] But note the application of the Family Law Act 1986 (discussed in Chapter 3) within the United Kingdom, viz for children up to the age of 16 in Scotland and 18 elsewhere.

[153] It might have been useful had States been required to spell out its application upon ratification or accession.

The general principles

25.89 The general principles are set out in Chapter II. The Convention makes a basic distinction between contact with parents[154] and contact with those whom the Convention refers to as having family ties with the child. 'Family ties' are defined by Art 2(d) as meaning 'a close relationship such as between a child and his or her grandparents or siblings, based on law or on a *de facto* family relationship'. As the Explanatory Report says,[155] those included in *de facto* relationships could be a former foster parent or a current or former step-parent.

25.90 So far as contact with parents is concerned, Art 4 provides:

> '(1) A child and his or her parents shall have the right to obtain and maintain regular contact with each other.
>
> (2) Such contact may be restricted or excluded only where necessary in the best interests of the child.
>
> (3) Where it is not in the best interests of a child to maintain unsupervised contact with one of his or her parents the possibility of supervised personal contact or other forms of contact with this parent shall be considered.'

In other words, and reflecting Art 8 of the European Convention of Human Rights[156] and Arts 9(3) and 10(2) of the UN Convention on the Rights of the Child, a child and his or her parents have the right to maintain regular contact with each other, save exceptionally where it is not in the child's interests. Even then, consideration must also be given as to whether supervised contact is appropriate.

25.91 In contrast, so far as persons other than parents but nevertheless having 'family ties' with the child are concerned, Art 5 provides that, subject to the child's best interests, contact may be established. As the Explanatory Report explains,[157] such persons:

> 'may have a right to apply for contact. However, this right is not on an equal footing with the right of a child and his or her parents to contact because there is a presumption of contact for legally recognised parents and their children and only where it is necessary in the best interests of the child the parents and the child can be deprived of their right of contact ... A child and persons, other than parents, having family ties with the child do not have a right to obtain and maintain contact but may only have a right to apply for contact subject to the best interests of the child.'

States have some room for discretion in determining which persons are to be regarded by national law as having 'family ties', but they must still be guided by human rights jurisprudence.

---

[154] Viz those who by law are recognised as parents: see para 39 of the Explanatory Report.

[155] At para 34.

[156] The relevant Convention jurisprudence is set out in some detail in paras 42 and 43 of the Explanatory Report. Paragraphs 44 and 45 provide further guidance on how Art 4 should operate.

[157] At para 49.

25.92 By way of important augmentation of these foregoing general principles, under Art 6, a child considered by internal law as having sufficient understanding is entitled to receive all relevant information, to be consulted and to express his or her views. Due weight should be given to these views and to any ascertainable wishes and feelings.[158] Furthermore, Art 7 enjoins judicial authorities when resolving disputes to take all appropriate measures:

(a) to ensure that each parent is informed of the importance both for the child and for both parents of establishing and maintaining regular contact;

(b) to encourage the reaching of amicable agreements in particular through the use of family mediation; and

(c) to ensure they have sufficient information at their disposal.

Article 8 also enjoins States to encourage those making contact agreements to comply with the foregoing general principles.

25.93 Article 10 deals with the provision of safeguards and guarantees both for the purpose of ensuring that the order is carried into effect and (importantly, in the context of trans-frontier contact) for ensuring the child's return. As the Explanatory Note says,[159] such safeguards and guarantees 'are amongst the most important steps to be taken in order to facilitate the paper exercise of the right of contact'. Article 10 contains examples of practical solutions which may be used to promote and secure the proper implementation either of national or trans-frontier contact. States are required to choose three or more categories of safeguards and guarantees from a list contained in Art 10(2).[160] But this is intended as a minimum requirement. The list is not in itself meant to be exhaustive, and States are free to offer more than three types of safeguards or guarantees.

25.94 The safeguards and guarantees for ensuring that the order is carried into effect can include:

'(a) supervision of contact;

(b) the obligation for a person to provide for the travel and accommodation expenses of the child and, as may be appropriate, of any other person accompanying the child;

(c) a security to be deposited by the person with whom the child is usually living to ensure that the person seeking contact with the child is not prevented from having such contact;

(d) a fine to be imposed on the person with whom the child is usually living, should this person refuse to comply with the contact order.'

25.95 The safeguards and guarantees for ensuring the child's return or preventing an improper removal can include:

---

[158] This provision reflects the 1996 European Convention on the Exercise of Children's Rights (ETS No 160). See further the Explanatory Report to the 2003 Convention, at paras 52–56.

[159] At para 73.

[160] Under Art 10(1), States are to communicate with the Secretary General of the Council of Europe what safeguards and guarantees are available under the national law.

'— the surrender of passports or identity documents and, where appropriate, a document indicating that the person seeking contact has notified the competent consular authority about such a surrender during the period of contact;

— financial guarantees;

— charges on property;

— undertakings or stipulations to the court;

— the obligation of the person having contact with the child to present himself or herself, with the child, regularly before a competent body such as a youth welfare authority or a police station, in the place where contact is to be exercised;

— the obligation of the person seeking contact to present a document issued by the State where contact is to take place, certifying the recognition and declaration of enforceability of a custody or a contact order or both either before a contact order is made or before contact takes place; and

— the imposition of conditions in relation to the place where contact is to be exercised and, where appropriate, the registration, in any national or transfrontier information system, of a prohibition preventing the child from leaving the State where contact is to take place.'

Promoting and improving trans-frontier contact

Central Authorities

25.96 The provisions for dealing with trans-frontier contact issues are contained in Chapter III. Article 11 obliges each State Party to establish a Central Authority[161] to discharge the functions provided for by the Convention in cases of trans-frontier contact. As the Explanatory Report says,[162] Central Authorities have become a well-established structure for co-operation between States in child protection matters. Furthermore, since the 2003 Convention is intended to complement the two 1980 Conventions as well as the 1996 Hague Convention on the Protection of Children, it seems advisable to designate the same Authority as under these Conventions.

25.97 Mirroring the 1980 European Custody Convention,[163] Art 12 of the 2003 Convention enjoins Central Authorities to 'co-operate with each other and promote co-operation between the competent authorities, including judicial authorities' and to act with all 'necessary dispatch'. Central Authorities must also: provide each other on request with information about their laws relating to parental responsibility including contact, any more detailed information about the safeguards and guarantees and their available services (including legal services, publicly funded or otherwise); take all the steps to discover the child's whereabouts; secure the transmission of requests for information about specific cases; and keep each other informed of any difficulties that are likely to arise in applying the Convention; and, as far as possible, 'eliminate obstacles to its application'.

---

[161] Under Art 11(2), States with more than one system of law or those having autonomous territorial units can appoint more than one Central Authority.

[162] At para 91.

[163] Viz Art 3(1): see **19.16** *et seq*.

International co-operation

25.98   Underlining the importance of international co-operation in these matters, Art 13 enjoins judicial authorities and 'social and other bodies' to co-operate in relation to proceedings regarding trans-frontier contact. Central Authorities are particularly required to assist judicial authorities in communicating with each other and obtaining such information and assistance as may be necessary for them to achieve the Convention's objectives; and assist children, parents and others having family ties with the child to institute proceedings regarding trans-frontier contact.

25.99   As the Explanatory Report explains,[164] the co-operation envisaged by Art 13 covers the situation before, during and after the institution of any proceedings and covers all the different steps to be taken from the beginning until the end of the period of contact. Stress is placed on judicial co-operation,[165] which the Explanatory Note says should be voluntary and without necessarily involving Central Authorities.

Recognition and enforcement of trans-frontier contact orders

25.100   As the Explanatory Report says,[166] although the 2003 Convention neither establishes rules of jurisdiction nor deals directly with issues of recognition and enforcement (these questions are dealt with by several other international instruments), provision is nevertheless needed to underline 'the obligation of States Parties to establish, where applicable, in accordance with relevant international instruments, means to facilitate the exercise of contact and custody rights in the case of transfrontier contact orders'. Article 14 accordingly states that States Parties must provide 'including where applicable in accordance with relevant international instruments':

(a)   a system for recognition and operation of law and, where appropriate, enforcement of orders made in other Contracting States concerning contact and rights of custody; and
(b)   a procedure for the advance recognition and enforcement of contact orders made in other States.

25.101   Article 14 does not require a State to enforce a trans-frontier contact order that would conflict with domestic law, for example, an order concerning a child who, according to domestic law, has attained full capacity.[167]

25.102   The provision in Art 14(1)(b) for advance recognition and enforcement is both important and innovative. As the Explanatory Report says,[168] such a provision 'is the most important guarantee to be taken in order to facilitate the normal exercise of the right of transfrontier contact'. Its main

---

[164]   At paras 98 and 99.
[165]   This mirrors a similarly growing emphasis in cases under the 1980 Hague Abduction Convention: see **9.62–9.63**.
[166]   At para 108.
[167]   See the Explanatory Report, at para 109.
[168]   At para 111.

advantage is that 'the prompt return of the child after a period of contact would be facilitated in case of any removal or retention of the child and therefore the parent not having custody of the child would be less likely to try to retain the child after a period of contact'.

Modifying orders

25.103 Under Art 15 of the 2003 Convention, the judicial authority of the State Party in which a trans-frontier contact order made in another State Party is to be implemented may, when recognising or declaring enforceable such a contact order, or at any later time:

> 'fix or adapt the conditions for its implementation, as well as any safeguards or guarantees attaching to it, if necessary for facilitating the exercise of this contact, provided that the essential elements of the order are respected and taking into account, in particular, a change of circumstances and the arrangements made by the persons concerned. In no circumstances may the foreign decision be reviewed as to its substance.'

25.104 Article 15 is modelled on Art 11(2) of the 1980 European Custody Convention, which provision it will replace.[169] It is intended that the new wording will remove the current problems of interpreting Art 11(2) of the 1980 Convention.[170] One of these problems, as previously discussed,[171] is whether the courts will be empowered to change the place of contact. Although Art 15 is wider than Art 11(2) of the 1980 Convention, it is by no means certain that this 'problem' will be solved. It will turn on whether the place of contact is regarded as 'an essential element' of the order. If it is, then any change to it will be regarded as a review of the original order as to its substance. However, for States ratifying the 2003 Convention, the new wording will at least give the courts an opportunity to reconsider the interpretation of this Article, and it may be that in any event each case will be dependent upon its own facts.

Return of the child

25.105 Article 16 deals with the crucial issue of the child's return at the end of a period of trans-frontier contact. After some debate, the final version provides:

> '1. Where a child at the end of a period of transfrontier contact based on a contact order is not returned, the competent authorities shall, upon request, ensure the child's immediate return, where applicable, by applying the relevant provisions of international instruments of internal law and by implementing, where appropriate, such safeguards and guarantees as may be provided in the contact order.
> 2. A decision on the return of the child shall be made, whenever possible, within six weeks of the date of an application for the return.'

---

[169] See Art 19, under which Art 11(3) of the 1980 Convention will also cease to apply.

[170] See the Explanatory Report, at para 117. These 'problems', however, are not articulated in the Report.

[171] See **25.53** *et seq*, and *Re A (Foreign Access Order: Enforcement)* [1996] 1 FLR 561, in particular.

25.106 As the Explanatory Report says,[172] although the 2003 Convention does not itself deal with the recognition and enforcement of contact orders, Art 16 is an important additional guarantee for the proper exercise of trans-frontier contact. It is based on the idea that, to ensure the child's return, it is first necessary to apply the relevant international instruments dealing with recognition and enforcement, and also, where appropriate, to enforce the safeguards and guarantees of the contact order.

Costs

25.107 Article 17 provides that, except in relation to the cost of repatriation, a State Party cannot claim any payment from the applicant in respect of any measures taken by the Central Authority. It should be noted, however, that unlike the two 1980 Conventions, neither the costs of court proceedings nor those of lawyers are covered by this provision.[173] This seems unfortunate and makes for a difficult inter-relationship with the 1980 European Custody Convention which, if used, would apply to recognising and enforcing an access decision, but not to modifying it, since that would be governed by Art 15 of the 2003 Convention. This means that, while court costs for recognition and enforcement will be covered by the generous provisions for legal representation, this will not be the case insofar as they relate to that part of the hearing concerned with modification.

Relationship with other international instruments

25.108 Article 20 provides that the 2003 Convention does not affect the application of the following international instruments, namely, the 1961 Hague Convention on the Protection of Minors, the 1980 European Custody Convention[174] and the 1996 Hague Convention on the Protection of Children, nor that of future instruments in this field. Furthermore, Art 20(3) requires States Parties which are members of the European Community to apply Community rules and therefore that they shall not in their mutual relations apply the Convention unless there is no Community rule governing the particular subject concerned.[175] This Article underlines the general strategy of the Convention not to prejudice the operation of existing or future Conventions containing provisions on matters governed by it, but rather to promote their application and provide assistance in their implementation.[176]

Commentary

25.109 The 2003 Convention does have a positive contribution to make towards tackling the thorny problem of access or contact. It is helpful to have agreed general principles upon which orders are made in the first place and it is advantageous to have a Convention which reflects modern thinking about

---

[172] At para 118.
[173] See the Explanatory Note, at para 123.
[174] Subject to the superseding of Art 11(2), (3), by Art 15: see Art 19 of the 2003 Convention.
[175] See para 128 of the Explanatory Report.
[176] See paras 126 and 127 of the Explanatory Report.

the issue, not least by referring to 'contact' rather than 'access' and defining it appropriately and widely. The idea that provision should be made for safeguards and guarantees to be taken concerning contact is also a good one, although whether it is sensible that States be required to provide at least three such safeguards or guarantees (a technique reminiscent of that used by the 1996 European Convention on the Exercise of Children's Rights) may be debated, particularly as that will produce insufficient uniformity.

25.110 So far as trans-frontier contact is concerned, the idea of advance recognition is a good one and, depending upon its interpretation, the powers to modify an order under Art 15 might be an improvement upon Art 11 of the 1980 European Custody Convention. The provisions concerning co-operation are well thought out, although they might be considered to be a significant addition to the existing burdens and costs of Central Authorities and perhaps do not go far enough to promoting and facilitating amicable agreements.

25.111 The difficulty with the Convention is its inter-relationship with other international instruments dealing with contact. Mention has already been made of the inter-relationship with the 1980 European Custody Convention on the issue of costs,[177] which is likely to prove problematic. Apart from this, the Convention attempts to tread the fine line between not stepping on the toes of other Conventions on questions of jurisdiction and recognition and enforcement, yet making some positive contribution to dealing with the problem. Whether there is enough in the Convention to warrant its separate ratification is perhaps open to doubt. It is, for example, difficult to see what role it can usefully play as between EU Member States, particularly when the amendments to the Brussels II Regulation concerning contact[178] come into force, nor is it clear when one would choose (assuming there is a choice) to invoke this Convention rather than the 1996 Hague Convention on the Protection of Children. One fears that, in the final analysis, this Convention might be considered by many States as an unnecessary and potentially complicating international instrument.

CONCLUSION

25.112 The number of international instruments dealing with access bears testimony to the immense difficulty of providing a satisfactory all-embracing global solution to the problems. Indeed, the very proliferation of instruments has itself contributed to the difficulties of giving sound advice. Each of the instruments that have been discussed have both advantages and disadvantages. What seems to be needed is a mechanism expressed in modern terms (ie using the concept of contact rather than access) which not only provides for prompt enforcement of properly made orders but also allows for binding

---

[177] See **25.107**.
[178] Discussed at **25.77** *et seq.*

modifications to be made in the light of changed circumstances and some limited provision to refuse recognition. At the same time, provisions for co-operation between domestic agencies and courts, and between Central Authorities, and for facilitating amicable agreements between the parties are also needed. Furthermore, some guarantees that access orders will be recognised and enforced are important. The creation of international contact centres might be worth thinking about. Most of these requirements can be found in one or other international instrument, but no single instrument has all these features. In an ideal world, it would be preferable to have a single international instrument incorporating all these features but, given the existence of the current instruments, that now seems an impossibility. Accordingly, the best that can be hoped for is that there will be agreed good practice both under the 1980 Hague Abduction Convention and the revised Brussels II Regulation.

APPENDICES

APPENDICES

Appendix Contents

Appendix 3 – PROTOCOLS AND GUIDANCE 747

Appendix 4 – PRECEDENTS FOR ENGLAND AND WALES 753

APPENDIX 1

LEGISLATION

CHILD ABDUCTION AND CUSTODY ACT 1985

(1985 c 60)

PART I
INTERNATIONAL CHILD ABDUCTION

1 The Hague Convention

(1) In this Part of this Act 'the Convention' means the Convention on the Civil Aspects of International Child Abduction which was signed at The Hague on 25th October 1980.

(2) Subject to the provisions of this Part of this Act, the provisions of that Convention set out in Schedule 1 to this Act shall have the force of law in the United Kingdom.

2 Contracting States

(1) For the purposes of the Convention as it has effect under this Part of this Act the Contracting States other than the United Kingdom shall be those for the time being specified by an Order in Council under this section.

(2) An Order in Council under this section shall specify the date of the coming into force of the Convention as between the United Kingdom and any State specified in the Order; and, except where the Order otherwise provides, the Convention shall apply as between the United Kingdom and that State only in relation to wrongful removals or retentions occurring on or after that date.

(3) Where the Convention applies, or applies only, to a particular territory or particular territories specified in a declaration made by a Contracting State under Article 39 or 40 of the Convention references to that State in subsections (1) and (2) above shall be construed as references to that territory or those territories.

3 Central Authorities

(1) Subject to subsection (2) below, the functions under the Convention of a Central Authority shall be discharged—

(a) in England and Wales and in Northern Ireland by the Lord Chancellor; and
(b) in Scotland by the Secretary of State.

(2) Any application made under the Convention by or on behalf of a person outside the United Kingdom may be addressed to the Lord Chancellor as the Central Authority in the United Kingdom.

(3) Where any such application relates to a function to be discharged under subsection (1) above by the Secretary of State it shall be transmitted by the Lord Chancellor to the Secretary of State and where such an application is addressed to the Secretary of State but relates to a function to be discharged under subsection (1) above by the Lord Chancellor the Secretary of State shall transmit it to the Lord Chancellor.

4 Judicial authorities

The courts having jurisdiction to entertain applications under this Convention shall be–

> in England and Wales or in Northern Ireland the High Court; and
> in Scotland the Court of Session.

5 Interim powers

Where an application has been made to a court in the United Kingdom under the Convention, the court may, at any time before the application is determined, give such interim directions as it thinks fit for the purpose of securing the welfare of the child concerned or of preventing changes in the circumstances relevant to the determination of the application.

6 Reports

Where the Lord Chancellor or the Secretary of State is requested to provide information relating to a child under Article 7(d) of the Convention he may–

(a) request a local authority or [an officer of the Service] to make a report to him in writing with respect to any matter which appears to him to be relevant;
(b) request the Department of Health and Social Services for Northern Ireland to arrange for a suitably qualified person to make such a report to him;
(c) request any court to which a written report relating to the child has been made to send him a copy of the report;

and such a request shall be duly complied with.

Amendments – Criminal Justice and Court Services Act 2000, s 74, Sch 7, Pt II, paras 79–80.

7 Proof of documents and evidence

(1) For the purposes of Article 14 of the Convention a decision or determination of a judicial or administrative authority outside the United Kingdom may be proved by a duly authenticated copy of the decision or determination; and any document purporting to be such a copy shall be deemed to be a true copy unless the contrary is shown.

(2) For the purposes of subsection (1) above a copy is duly authenticated if it bears the seal, or is signed by a judge or officer, of the authority in question.

(3) For the purposes of Articles 14 and 30 of the Convention any such document as is mentioned in Article 8 of the Convention, or a certified copy of any such document, shall be sufficient evidence of anything stated in it.

8 Declarations by United Kingdom courts

The High Court or Court of Session may, on an application made for the purposes of Article 15 of the Convention by any person appearing to the court to have an interest in the matter, make a declaration or declarator that the removal of any child from, or his retention outside, the United Kingdom was wrongful within the meaning of Article 3 of the Convention.

9 Suspension of court's powers in cases of wrongful removal

The reference in Article 16 of the Convention to deciding on the merits of rights of custody shall be construed as a reference to–

(a) making, varying or revoking a custody order, or a supervision order under section 31 of the Children Act 1989 or Article 50 of the Children (Northern Ireland) Order 1995;

(aa) enforcing under section 29 of the Family Law Act 1986 a custody order within the meaning of Chapter V of Part I of that Act;

(b) registering or enforcing a decision under Part II of this Act;

(c) ...

(d) making, varying or discharging an order under section 86 of the Children (Scotland) Act 1995;

(e) ...

Amendments – Family Law Act 1986, s 68(1), Sch 1, para 28; Children Act 1989, s 108(5), Sch 13, para 57(1), Sch 15; Children (Scotland) Act 1995, s 105(4), Sch 4, para 37; SI 1995/756.

10 Rules of court

(1) An authority having power to make rules of court may make such provision for giving effect to this Part of this Act as appears to that authority to be necessary or expedient.

(2) Without prejudice to the generality of subsection (1) above, rules of court may make provision–

(a) with respect to the procedure on applications for the return of a child and with respect to the documents and information to be furnished and the notices to be given in connection with any such application;

(b) for the transfer of any such application between the appropriate courts in the different parts of the United Kingdom;

(c) for the giving of notices by or to a court for the purposes of the provisions of Article 16 of the Convention and section 9 above and generally as respects proceedings to which those provisions apply;

(d) for enabling a person who wishes to make an application under the Convention in a Contracting State other than the United Kingdom to obtain from any court in the United Kingdom an authenticated copy of any decision of that court relating to the child to whom the application is to relate.

11 Cost of applications

The United Kingdom having made such a reservation as is mentioned in the third paragraph of Article 26 of the Convention, the costs mentioned in that paragraph shall not be borne by any Minister or other authority in the United Kingdom except so far as they fall to be so borne by virtue of–

(a)   the provision of any service funded by the Legal Services Commission as part of the Community Legal Service, or

(b)   the grant of legal aid or legal advice and assistance under the Legal Aid (Scotland) Act 1967, Part I of the Legal Advice and Assistance Act 1972 or the Legal Aid Advice and Assistance (Northern Ireland) Order 1981.

Amendments – Legal Aid Act 1988, s 45(1), (3), Sch 5, para 16; Access to Justice Act 1999, s 24, Sch 4, para 31.

PART II
RECOGNITION AND ENFORCEMENT OF CUSTODY DECISIONS

12   The European Convention

(1)   In this Part of this Act 'the Convention' means the European Convention on Recognition and Enforcement of Decisions concerning Custody of Children and on the Restoration of Custody of Children which was signed in Luxembourg on 20th May 1980.

(2)   Subject to the provisions of this Part of this Act, the provisions of that Convention set out in Schedule 2 to this Act (which include Articles 9 and 10 as they have effect in consequence of a reservation made by the United Kingdom under Article 17) shall have the force of law in the United Kingdom.

(3)   But those provisions of the Convention are subject to Article 37 of Council Regulation (EC) No 1347/2000 of 29th May 2000 on jurisdiction and the recognition and enforcement of judgments in matrimonial matters and in matters of parental responsibility for children of both spouses (under which the Regulation takes precedence over the Convention), and the provisions of this Part of this Act, and any rules of court made pursuant to section 24 of this Act, shall be construed accordingly.

Amendments – SI 2001/310.

13   Contracting States

(1)   For the purposes of the Convention as it has effect under this Part of this Act the Contracting States other than the United Kingdom shall be those for the time being specified by an Order in Council under this section.

(2)   An Order in Council under this section shall specify the date of the coming into force of the Convention as between the United Kingdom and any State specified in the Order.

(3)   Where the Convention applies, or applies only, to a particular territory or particular territories specified by a Contracting State under Article 24 or 25 of the Convention references to that State in subsections (1) and (2) above shall be construed as references to that territory or those territories.

14   Central Authorities

(1)   Subject to subsection (2) below, the functions under the Convention of a Central Authority shall be discharged–

(a)   in England and Wales and in Northern Ireland by the Lord Chancellor; and

(b)   in Scotland by the Secretary of State.

(2)   Any application made under the Convention by or on behalf of a person outside the United Kingdom may be addressed to the Lord Chancellor as the Central Authority in the United Kingdom.

(3)   Where any such application relates to a function to be discharged under subsection (1) above by the Secretary of State it shall be transmitted by the Lord Chancellor to the Secretary of State and where such an application is addressed to the Secretary of State but relates to a function to be discharged under subsection (1) above by the Lord Chancellor, the Secretary of State shall transmit it to the Lord Chancellor.

15   Recognition of decisions

(1)   Articles 7 and 12 of the Convention shall have effect in accordance with this section.

(2)   A decision to which either of those Articles applies which was made in a Contracting State other than the United Kingdom shall be recognised in each part of the United Kingdom as if made by a court having jurisdiction to make it in that part but—

(a)   the appropriate court in any part of the United Kingdom may, on the application of any person appearing to it to have an interest in the matter, declare on any of the grounds specified in Article 9 or 10 of the Convention that the decision is not to be recognised in any part of the United Kingdom; and

(b)   the decision shall not be enforceable in any part of the United Kingdom unless registered in the appropriate court under section 16 below.

(3)   The references in Article 9(1)(c) of the Convention to the removal of the child are to his improper removal within the meaning of the Convention.

16   Registration of decisions

(1)   A person on whom any rights are conferred by a decision relating to custody made by an authority in a Contracting State other than the United Kingdom may make an application for the registration of the decision in an appropriate court in the United Kingdom.

(2)   The Central Authority in the United Kingdom shall assist such a person in making such an application if a request for such assistance is made by him or on his behalf by the Central Authority of the Contracting State in question.

(3)   An application under subsection (1) above or a request under subsection (2) above shall be treated as a request for enforcement for the purposes of Articles 10 and 13 of the Convention.

(4)   The High Court or Court of Session shall refuse to register a decision if—

(a)   the court is of the opinion that on any of the grounds specified in Article 9 or 10 of the Convention the decision should not be recognised in any part of the United Kingdom;

(b) the court is of the opinion that the decision is not enforceable in the Contracting State where it was made and is not a decision to which Article 12 of the Convention applies; or

(c) an application in respect of the child under Part I of this Act is pending.

(5) Where the Lord Chancellor is requested to assist in making an application under this section to the Court of Session he shall transmit the request to the Secretary of State and the Secretary of State shall transmit to the Lord Chancellor any such request to assist in making an application to the High Court.

(6) In this section 'decision relating to custody' has the same meaning as in the Convention.

17 Variation and revocation of registered decisions

(1) Where a decision which has been registered under section 16 above is varied or revoked by an authority in the Contracting State in which it was made, the person on whose behalf the application for registration of the decision was made shall notify the court in which the decision is registered of the variation or revocation.

(2) Where a court is notified under subsection (1) above of the revocation of a decision, it shall—

(a) cancel the registration, and
(b) notify such persons as may be prescribed by rules of court of the cancellation.

(3) Where a court is notified under subsection (1) above of the variation of a decision, it shall—

(a) notify such persons as may be prescribed by rules of court of the variation; and
(b) subject to any conditions which may be so prescribed, vary the registration.

(4) The court in which a decision is registered under section 16 above may also, on the application of any person appearing to the court to have an interest in the matter, cancel or vary the registration if it is satisfied that the decision has been revoked or, as the case may be, varied by an authority in the Contracting State in which it was made.

18 Enforcement of decisions

Where a decision relating to custody has been registered under section 16 above, the court in which it is registered shall have the same powers for the purpose of enforcing the decision as if it had been made by that court; and proceedings for or with respect to enforcement may be taken accordingly.

19 Interim powers

Where an application has been made to a court for the registration of a decision under section 16 above or for the enforcement of such a decision, the court may, at any time before the application is determined, give such interim directions as it thinks fit for the purpose of securing the welfare of the child concerned or of preventing changes in the circumstances relevant to the determination of the application or, in the case of an application for registration, to the determination of any subsequent application for the enforcement of the decision.

20 Suspension of court's powers

(1)   Where it appears to any court in which such proceedings as are mentioned in subsection (2) below are pending in respect of a child that–

(a)   an application has been made for the registration of a decision in respect of the child under section 16 above (other than a decision mentioned in subsection (3) below) or that such a decision is registered; and

(b)   the decision was made in proceedings commenced before the proceedings which are pending,

the powers of the court with respect to the child in those proceedings shall be restricted as mentioned in subsection (2) below unless, in the case of an application for registration, the application is refused.

(2)   Where subsection (1) above applies the court shall not–

(a)   in the case of custody proceedings, make, vary or revoke any custody order, or a supervision order under section 31 of the Children Act 1989 or Article 50 of the Children (Northern Ireland) Order 1995;

(aa)   in the case of proceedings under section 29 of the Family Law Act 1986 for the enforcement of a custody order within the meaning of Chapter V of Part I of that Act, enforce that order; or

(b), (c) ...

(d)   in the case of proceedings for, or for the variation or discharge of, a parental responsibilities order under section 86 of the Children (Scotland) Act 1995, make, vary or discharge any such order;....

(e)   ...

(2A)   Where it appears to the Secretary of State–

(a)   that an application has been made for the registration of a decision in respect of a child under section 16 above (other than a decision mentioned in subsection (3) below); or

(b)   that such a decision is registered,

the Secretary of State shall not make, vary or revoke any custody order in respect of the child unless, in the case of an application for registration, the application is refused.

(3)   The decision referred to in subsection (1) or (2A) above is a decision which is only a decision relating to custody within the meaning of section 16 of this Act by virtue of being a decision relating to rights of access.

(4)   Paragraph (b) of Article 10(2) of the Convention shall be construed as referring to custody proceedings within the meaning of this Act.

(5)   This section shall apply to a children's hearing (as defined in section 93(1) of the Children (Scotland) Act 1995) as it does to a court.

Amendments – Family Law Act 1986, ss 67(2), (3), 68(1), Sch 1, para 29; Children Act 1989, s 108(5), Sch 13, para 57(1), Sch 15; Children (Scotland) Act 1995, s 105(4), Sch 4, para 37; SI 1995/756.

21 Reports

Where the Lord Chancellor or the Secretary of State is requested to make enquiries about a child under Article 15(1)(b) of the Convention he may–

(a)   request a local authority or an officer of the Service to make a report to him in writing with respect to any matter relating to the child concerned which appears to him to be relevant;

(b)   request the Department of Health and Social Services for Northern Ireland to arrange for a suitably qualified person to make such a report to him;

(c)   request any court to which a written report relating to the child has been made to send him a copy of the report;

and any such request shall be duly complied with.

Amendments – Criminal Justice and Court Services Act 2000, s 74, Sch 7, para 80.

22   Proof of documents and evidence

(1)   In any proceedings under this Part of this Act a decision of an authority outside the United Kingdom may be proved by a duly authenticated copy of the decision; and any document purporting to be such a copy shall be deemed to be a true copy unless the contrary is shown.

(2)   For the purposes of subsection (1) above a copy is duly authenticated if it bears the seal, or is signed by a judge or officer, of the authority in question.

(3)   In any proceedings under this Part of this Act any such document as is mentioned in Article 13 of the Convention, or a certified copy of any such document, shall be sufficient evidence of anything stated in it.

23   Decisions of United Kingdom courts

(1)   Where a person on whom any rights are conferred by a decision relating to custody made by a court in the United Kingdom makes an application to the Lord Chancellor or the Secretary of State under Article 4 of the Convention with a view to securing its recognition or enforcement in another Contracting State, the Lord Chancellor or the Secretary of State may require the court which made the decision to furnish him with all or any of the documents referred to in Article 13(1)(b), (c) and (d) of the Convention.

(2)   Where in any custody proceedings a court in the United Kingdom makes a decision relating to a child who has been removed from the United Kingdom, the court may also, on an application made by any person for the purposes of Article 12 of the Convention, declare the removal to have been unlawful if it is satisfied that the applicant has an interest in the matter and that the child has been taken from or sent or kept out of the United Kingdom without the consent of the person (or, if more than one, all the persons) having the right to determine the child's place of residence under the law of the part of the United Kingdom in which the child was habitually resident.

(3)   In this section 'decision relating to custody' has the same meaning as in the Convention.

24   Rules of court

(1)   An authority having power to make rules of court may make such provision for giving effect to this Part of this Act as appears to that authority to be necessary or expedient.

(2)   Without prejudice to the generality of subsection (1) above, rules of court may make provision–

(a)   with respect to the procedure on applications to a court under any provision of this Part of this Act and with respect to the documents and information to be furnished and the notices to be given in connection with any such application;
(b)   for the transfer of any such application between the appropriate courts in the different parts of the United Kingdom;
(c)   for the giving of directions requiring the disclosure of information about any child who is the subject of proceedings under this Part of this Act and for safeguarding its welfare.

PART III
SUPPLEMENTARY

24A   Power to order disclosure of child's whereabouts

(1)   Where–

(a)   in proceedings for the return of a child under Part I of this Act; or
(b)   on an application for the recognition, registration or enforcement of a decision in respect of a child under Part II of this Act,

there is not available to the court adequate information as to where the child is, the court may order any person who it has reason to believe may have relevant information to disclose it to the court.

(2)   A person shall not be excused from complying with an order under subsection (1) above by reason that to do so may incriminate him or his spouse of an offence; but a statement or admission made in compliance with such an order shall not be admissible in evidence against either of them in proceedings for any offence other than perjury.

Amendments – Inserted by Family Law Act 1986, s 67(4).

25   Termination of existing custody orders, etc

(1)   Where–

(a)   an order is made for the return of a child under Part I of this Act; or
(b)   a decision with respect to a child (other than a decision mentioned in subsection (2) below) is registered under section 16 of this Act,

any custody order relating to him shall cease to have effect.

(2)   The decision referred to in subsection (1)(b) above is a decision which is only a decision relating to custody within the meaning of section 16 of this Act by virtue of being a decision relating to rights of access.

(3)–(7)   ...

Amendments – Children Act 1989, s 108(7), Sch 15; Children (Scotland) Act 1995, s 105(4), Sch 4, para 37(1), (4); SI 1995/756.

26 Expenses

There shall be paid out of money provided by Parliament–

(a) any expenses incurred by the Lord Chancellor or the Secretary of State by virtue of this Act; and

(b) any increase attributable to this Act in the sums so payable under any other Act.

27 Interpretation

(1) In this Act 'custody order' means (unless the contrary intention appears) any such order or authorisation as is mentioned in Schedule 3 to this Act and 'custody proceedings' means proceedings in which an order within paragraphs 1, 2, 5, 6, 8 or 9 of that Schedule may be made, varied or revoked.

(2) For the purposes of this Act 'part of the United Kingdom' means England and Wales, Scotland or Northern Ireland and 'the appropriate court', in relation to England and Wales or Northern Ireland means the High Court and, in relation to Scotland, the Court of Session.

(3) In this Act 'local authority' means–

(a) in relation to England and Wales, the council of a non-metropolitan county, a metropolitan district, a London borough or the Common Council of the City of London; and

(b) in relation to Scotland, a council constituted under section 2 of the Local Government etc (Scotland) Act 1994.

(4) In this Act a decision relating to rights of access in England and Wales or Scotland or Northern Ireland means a decision as to the contact which a child may, or may not, have with any person.

(5) In this Act 'officer of the Service' has the same meaning as in the Criminal Justice and Court Services Act 2000.

Amendments – Family Law Act 1986, ss 67(5), 68(1), Sch 1, para 30; Children Act 1989, s 108(5), Sch 13, para 57(2); Local Government etc (Scotland) Act 1994, s 180(1), Sch 13, para 139; Children (Scotland) Act 1995, s 105(4), Sch 4, para 37(5); SI 1995/756; Criminal Justice and Court Services Act 2000, s 74, Sch 7, para 81.

28 Application as respects British Islands and colonies

(1) Her Majesty may by Order in Council direct that any of the provisions of this Act specified in the Order shall extend, subject to such modifications as may be specified in the Order, to–

(a) the Isle of Man,
(b) any of the Channel Islands, and
(c) any colony.

(2) Her Majesty may by Order in Council direct that this Act shall have effect in the United Kingdom as if any reference in this Act, or in any amendment made by this Act, to any order which may be made, or any proceedings which may be brought or any other thing which may be done, in, or in any part of, the United Kingdom included a reference to any corresponding order which may be made or, as the case may be, proceedings which may be brought or other thing which may be done in any of the territories mentioned in subsection (1) above.

(3)   An Order in Council under this section may make such consequential, incidental and supplementary provision as Her Majesty considers appropriate.

(4)   An Order in Council under this section shall be subject to annulment in pursuance of a resolution of either House of Parliament.

29   Short title, commencement and extent

(1)   This Act may be cited as the Child Abduction and Custody Act 1985.

(2)   This Act shall come into force on such day as may be appointed by an order made by statutory instrument by the Lord Chancellor and the Lord Advocate; and different days may be so appointed for different provisions.

(3)   This Act extends to Northern Ireland.

SCHEDULE 1 – CONVENTION ON THE CIVIL ASPECTS OF INTERNATIONAL CHILD ABDUCTION

Section 1(2)

Chapter 1
Scope of the Convention

Article 3

The removal or the retention of a child is to be considered wrongful where–

(a)   it is in breach of rights of custody attributed to a person, an institution or any other body, either jointly or alone, under the law of the State in which the child was habitually resident immediately before the removal or retention; and

(b)   at the time of removal or retention those rights were actually exercised, either jointly or alone, or would have been so exercised but for the removal or retention.

The rights of custody mentioned in sub-paragraph (a) above, may arise in particular by operation of law or by reason of a judicial or administrative decision, or by reason of an agreement having legal effect under the law of that State.

Article 4

The Convention shall apply to any child who was habitually resident in a Contracting State immediately before any breach of custody or access rights. The Convention shall cease to apply when the child attains the age of sixteen years.

Article 5

For the purposes of this Convention–

(a)   'rights of custody' shall include rights relating to the care of the person of the child and, in particular, the right to determine the child's place of residence;

(b)   'rights of access' shall include the right to take a child for a limited period of time to a place other than the child's habitual residence.

Chapter II
Central Authorities

Article 7

Central Authorities shall co-operate with each other and promote co-operation amongst the competent authorities in their respective States to secure the prompt return of children and to achieve the other objects of this Convention.

In particular, either directly or through any intermediary, they shall take all appropriate measures—

(a) to discover the whereabouts of a child who has been wrongfully removed or retained;
(b) to prevent further harm to the child or prejudice to interested parties by taking or causing to be taken provisional measures;
(c) to secure the voluntary return of the child or to bring about an amicable resolution of the issues;
(d) to exchange, where desirable, information relating to the social background of the child;
(e) to provide information of a general character as to the law of their State in connection with the application of the Convention;
(f) to initiate or facilitate the institution of judicial or administrative proceedings with a view to obtaining the return of the child and, in a proper case, to make arrangements for organizing or securing the effective exercise of rights of access;
(g) where the circumstances so require, to provide or facilitate the provision of legal aid and advice, including the participation of legal counsel and advisers;
(h) to provide such administrative arrangements as may be necessary and appropriate to secure the safe return of the child;
(i) to keep each other informed with respect to the operation of this Convention and, as far as possible, to eliminate any obstacles to its application.

Chapter III
Return of Children

Article 8

Any person, institution or other body claiming that a child has been removed or retained in breach of custody rights may apply either to the Central Authority of the child's habitual residence or to the Central Authority of any other Contracting State for assistance in securing the return of the child.

The application shall contain—

(a) information concerning the identity of the applicant, of the child and of the person alleged to have removed or retained the child;
(b) where available, the date of birth of the child;
(c) the grounds on which the applicant's claim for return of the child is based;
(d) all available information relating to the whereabouts of the child and the identity of the person with whom the child is presumed to be.

The application may be accompanied or supplemented by—

(e) an authenticated copy of any relevant decision or agreement;
(f) a certificate or an affidavit emanating from a Central Authority, or other competent authority of the State of the child's habitual residence, or from a qualified person, concerning the relevant law of that State;

(g)   any other relevant document.

Article 9

If the Central Authority which receives an application referred to in Article 8 has reason to believe that the child is in another Contracting State, it shall directly and without delay transmit the application to the Central Authority of that Contracting State and inform the requesting Central Authority, or the applicant, as the case may be.

Article 10

The Central Authority of the State where the child is shall take or cause to be taken all appropriate measures in order to obtain the voluntary return of the child.

Article 11

The judicial or administrative authorities of Contracting States shall act expeditiously in proceedings for the return of children.

If the judicial or administrative authority concerned has not reached a decision within six weeks from the date of commencement of the proceedings, the applicant or the Central Authority of the requested State, on its own initiative or if asked by the Central Authority of the requesting State, shall have the right to request a statement of the reasons for the delay. If a reply is received by the Central Authority of the requested State, that Authority shall transmit the reply to the Central Authority of the requesting State, or to the applicant, as the case may be.

Article 12

Where a child has been wrongfully removed or retained in terms of Article 3 and, at the date of the commencement of the proceedings before the judicial or administrative authority of the Contracting State where the child is, a period of less than one year has elapsed from the date of the wrongful removal or retention, the authority concerned shall order the return of the child forthwith.

The judicial or administrative authority, even where the proceedings have been commenced after the expiration of the period of one year referred to in the preceding paragraph, shall also order the return of the child, unless it is demonstrated that the child is now settled in its new environment.

Where the judicial or administrative authority in the requested state has reason to believe that the child has been taken to another State, it may stay the proceedings or dismiss the application for the return of the child.

Article 13

Notwithstanding the provisions of the preceding Article, the judicial or administrative authority of the requested State is not bound to order the return of the child if the person, institution or other body which opposes its return establishes that–

(a)   the person, institution or other body having the care of the person of the child was not actually exercising the custody rights at the time of removal or retention, or had consented to or subsequently acquiesced in the removal or retention; or

(b)   there is a grave risk that his or her return would expose the child to physical or psychological harm or otherwise place the child in an intolerable situation.

The judicial or administrative authority may also refuse to order the return of the child if it finds that the child objects to being returned and has attained an age and degree of maturity at which it is appropriate to take account of its views.

In considering the circumstances referred to in this Article, the judicial and administrative authorities shall take into account the information relating to the social background of the child provided by the Central Authority or other competent authority of the child's habitual residence.

Article 14

In ascertaining whether there has been a wrongful removal or retention within the meaning of Article 3, the judicial or administrative authorities of the requested State may take notice directly of the law of, and of judicial or administrative decisions, formally recognised or not in the State of the habitual residence of the child, without recourse to the specific procedures for the proof of that law or for the recognition of foreign decisions which would otherwise be applicable.

Article 15

The judicial or administrative authorities of a Contracting State may, prior to the making of an order for the return of the child, request that the applicant obtain from the authorities of the State of the habitual residence of the child a decision or other determination that the removal or retention was wrongful within the meaning of Article 3 of the Convention, where such a decision or determination may be obtained in that State. The Central Authorities of the Contracting States shall so far as practicable assist applicants to obtain such a decision or determination.

Article 16

After receiving notice of a wrongful removal or retention of a child in the sense of Article 3, the judicial or administrative authorities of the Contracting State to which the child has been removed or in which it has been retained shall not decide on the merits of rights of custody until it has been determined that the child is not to be returned under this Convention or unless an application under this Convention is not lodged within a reasonable time following receipt of the notice.

Article 17

The sole fact that a decision relating to custody has been given in or is entitled to recognition in the requested State shall not be a ground for refusing to return a child under this Convention, but the judicial or administrative authorities of the requested State may take account of the reasons for that decision in applying this Convention.

Article 18

The provisions of this Chapter do not limit the power of a judicial or administrative authority to order the return of the child at any time.

Article 19

A decision under this Convention concerning the return of the child shall not be taken to be a determination on the merits of any custody issue.

Chapter IV
Rights of Access

Article 21

An application to make arrangements for organising or securing the effective exercise of rights of access may be presented to the Central Authorities of the Contracting States in the same way as an application for the return of a child.

The Central Authorities are bound by the obligations of co-operation which are set forth in Article 7 to promote the peaceful enjoyment of access rights and the fulfilment of any conditions to which the exercise of those rights may be subject. The Central Authorities shall take steps to remove, as far as possible, all obstacles to the exercise of such rights. The Central Authorities, either directly or through intermediaries, may initiate or assist in the institution of proceedings with a view to organising or protecting these rights and securing respect for the conditions to which the exercise of these rights may be subject.

Chapter V
General Provisions

Article 22

No security, bond or deposit, however described, shall be required to guarantee the payment of costs and expenses in the judicial or administrative proceedings falling within the scope of this Convention.

Article 24

Any application, communication or other document sent to the Central Authority of the requested State shall be in the original language, and shall be accompanied by a translation into the official language or one of the official languages of the requested State or, where that is not feasible, a translation into French or English.

Article 26

Each Central Authority shall bear its own costs in applying this Convention.

Central Authorities and other public services of Contracting States shall not impose any charges in relation to applications submitted under this Convention. In particular, they may not require any payment from the applicant towards the costs and expenses of the proceedings or, where applicable, those arising from the participation of legal counsel or advisers. However, they may require the payment of the expenses incurred or to be incurred in implementing the return of the child.

However, a Contracting State may, by making a reservation in accordance with Article 42, declare that it shall not be bound to assume any costs referred to in the preceding paragraph resulting from the participation of legal counsel or advisers or from court proceedings, except insofar as those costs may be covered by its system of legal aid and advice.

Upon ordering the return of a child or issuing an order concerning rights of access under this Convention, the judicial or administrative authorities may, where appropriate, direct the person who removed or retained the child, or who prevented the exercise of rights of access, to pay necessary expenses incurred by or on behalf of the applicant, including travel expenses, any costs incurred or payment made for locating the child, the costs of legal representation of the applicant, and those of returning the child.

Article 27

When it is manifest that the requirements of this Convention are not fulfilled or that the application is otherwise not well founded, a Central Authority is not bound to accept the application. In that case, the Central Authority shall forthwith inform the applicant or the Central Authority through which the application was submitted, as the case may be, of its reasons.

Article 28

A Central Authority may require that the application be accompanied by a written authorisation empowering it to act on behalf of the applicant, or to designate a representative so to act.

Article 29

This Convention shall not preclude any person, institution or body who claims that there has been a breach of custody or access rights within the meaning of Article 3 or 21 from applying directly to the judicial or administrative authorities of a Contracting State, whether or not under the provisions of this Convention.

Article 30

Any application submitted to the Central Authorities or directly to the judicial or administrative authorities of a Contracting State in accordance with the terms of this Convention, together with documents and any other information appended thereto or provided by a Central Authority, shall be admissible in the courts or administrative authorities of the Contracting States.

Article 31

In relation to a State which in matters of custody of children has two or more systems of law applicable in different territorial units–

(a)   any reference to habitual residence in that State shall be construed as referring to habitual residence in a territorial unit of that State;
(b)   any reference to the law of the State of habitual residence shall be construed as referring to the law of the territorial unit in that State where the child habitually resides.

Article 32

In relation to a State which in matters of custody of children has two or more systems of law applicable to different categories of persons, any reference to the law of that State shall be construed as referring to the legal system specified by the law of that State.

SCHEDULE 2 – EUROPEAN CONVENTION ON RECOGNITION AND ENFORCEMENT OF DECISIONS CONCERNING CUSTODY OF CHILDREN

Section 12(2)

Article 1

For the purposes of this Convention:

(a)   'child' means a person of any nationality, so long as he is under 16 years of age and has not the right to decide on his own place of residence under the law of his habitual residence, the law of his nationality or the internal law of the State addressed;
(b)   'authority' means a judicial or administrative authority;
(c)   'decision relating to custody' means a decision of an authority in so far as it relates to the care of the person of the child, including the right to decide on the place of his residence, or to the right of access to him;
(d)   'improper removal' means the removal of a child across an international frontier in breach of a decision relating to his custody which has been given in a

Contracting State and which is enforceable in such a State; 'improper removal' also includes:

(i) the failure to return a child across an international frontier at the end of a period of the exercise of the right of access to this child or at the end of any other temporary stay in a territory other than that where the custody is exercised;

(ii) a removal which is subsequently declared unlawful within the meaning of Article 12.

Article 4

(1) Any person who has obtained in a Contracting State a decision relating to the custody of a child and who wishes to have that decision recognised or enforced in another Contracting State may submit an application for this purpose to the central authority in any Contracting State.

(2) The application shall be accompanied by the documents mentioned in Article 13.

(3) The central authority receiving the application, if it is not the central authority in the State addressed, shall send the document directly and without delay to that central authority.

(4) The central authority receiving the application may refuse to intervene where it is manifestly clear that the conditions laid down by this Convention are not satisfied.

(5) The central authority receiving the application shall keep the applicant informed without delay of the progress of his application.

Article 5

(1) The central authority in the State addressed shall take or cause to be taken without delay all steps which it considers to be appropriate, if necessary by instituting proceedings before its competent authorities, in order:

(a) to discover the whereabouts of the child;
(b) to avoid, in particular by any necessary provisional measures, prejudice to the interests of the child or of the applicant;
(c) to secure the recognition or enforcement of the decision;
(d) to secure the delivery of the child to the applicant where enforcement is granted;
(e) to inform the requesting authority of the measures taken and their results.

(2) Where the central authority in the State addressed has reason to believe that the child is in the territory of another Contracting State it shall send the documents directly and without delay to the central authority of that State.

(3) With the exception of the cost of repatriation, each Contracting State undertakes not to claim any payment from an applicant in respect of any measures taken under paragraph (1) of this Article by the central authority of that State on the applicant's behalf, including the costs of proceedings and, where applicable, the costs incurred by the assistance of a lawyer.

(4) If recognition or enforcement is refused, and if the central authority of the State addressed considers that it should comply with a request by the applicant to bring in that State proceedings concerning the substance of the case, that authority shall use its best endeavours to secure the representation of the applicant in the proceedings under conditions no less favourable than those available to a person who is resident in and a

national of that State and for this purpose it may, in particular, institute proceedings before its competent authorities.

Article 7

A decision relating to custody given in a Contracting State shall be recognised and, where it is enforceable in the State of origin, made enforceable in every other Contracting State.

Article 9

(1) Recognition and enforcement may be refused if:

(a) in the case of a decision given in the absence of the defendant or his legal representative, the defendant was not duly served with the document which instituted the proceedings or an equivalent document in sufficient time to enable him to arrange his defence; but such a failure to effect service cannot constitute a ground for refusing recognition or enforcement where service was not effected because the defendant had concealed his whereabouts from the person who instituted the proceedings in the State of origin;

(b) in the case of a decision given in the absence of the defendant or his legal representative, the competence of the authority giving the decision was not founded:

(i)   on the habitual residence of the defendant; or

(ii)   on the last common habitual residence of the child's parents, at least one parent being still habitually resident there, or

(iii) on the habitual residence of the child;

(c) the decision is incompatible with a decision relating to custody which became enforceable in the State addressed before the removal of the child, unless the child has had his habitual residence in the territory of the requesting State for one year before his removal.

(3) In no circumstances may the foreign decision be reviewed as to its substance.

Article 10

(1) Recognition and enforcement may also be refused on any of the following grounds:

(a) if it is found that the effects of the decision are manifestly incompatible with the fundamental principles of the law relating to the family and children in the State addressed;

(b) if it is found that by reason of a change in the circumstances including the passage of time but not including a mere change in the residence of the child after an improper removal, the effects of the original decision are manifestly no longer in accordance with the welfare of the child;

(c) if at the time when the proceedings were instituted in the State of origin:

(i)   the child was a national of the State addressed or was habitually resident there and no such connection existed with the State of origin;

(ii)   the child was a national both of the State of origin and of the State addressed and was habitually resident in the State addressed;

(d) if the decision is incompatible with a decision given in the State addressed or enforceable in that State after being given in a third State, pursuant to proceedings begun before the submission of the request for recognition or enforcement, and if the refusal is in accordance with the welfare of the child.

(2)   Proceedings for recognition or enforcement may be adjourned on any of the following grounds:

(a)   if an ordinary form of review of the original decision has been commenced;

(b)   if proceedings relating to the custody of the child, commenced before the proceedings in the State of origin were instituted, are pending in the State addressed;

(c)   if another decision concerning the custody of the child is the subject of proceedings for enforcement or of any other proceedings concerning the recognition of the decision.

Article 11

(1)   Decisions on rights of access and provisions of decisions relating to custody which deal with the rights of access shall be recognised and enforced subject to the same conditions as other decisions relating to custody.

(2)   However, the competent authority of the State addressed may fix the conditions for the implementation and exercise of the right of access taking into account, in particular, undertakings given by the parties on this matter.

(3)   Where no decision on the right of access has been taken or where recognition or enforcement of the decision relating to custody is refused, the central authority of the State addressed may apply to its competent authorities for a decision on the right of access if the person claiming a right of access so requests.

Article 12

Where, at the time of the removal of a child across an international frontier, there is no enforceable decision given in a Contracting State relating to his custody, the provisions of this Convention shall apply to any subsequent decision, relating to the custody of that child and declaring the removal to be unlawful, given in a Contracting State at the request of any interested person.

Article 13

(1)   A request for recognition or enforcement in another Contracting State of a decision relating to custody shall be accompanied by:

(a)   a document authorising the central authority of the State addressed to act on behalf of the applicant or to designate another representative for that purpose;

(b)   a copy of the decision which satisfies the necessary conditions of authenticity;

(c)   in the case of a decision given in the absence of the defendant or his legal representative, a document which establishes that the defendant was duly served with the document which instituted the proceedings or an equivalent document;

(d)   if applicable, any document which establishes that, in accordance with the law of the State of origin, the decision is enforceable;

(e)   if possible, a statement indicating the whereabouts or likely whereabouts of the child in the State addressed;

(f)   proposals as to how the custody of the child should be restored.

Article 15

(1)   Before reaching a decision under paragraph (1)(b) of Article 10, the authority concerned in the State addressed:

(a)   shall ascertain the child's views unless this is impracticable having regard in particular to his age and understanding; and

(b)   may request that any appropriate enquiries be carried out.

(2)   The cost of enquiries in any Contracting State shall be met by the authorities of the State where they are carried out.

Requests for enquiries and the results of enquiries may be sent to the authority concerned through the central authorities.

Article 26

(1)   In relation to a State which has in matters of custody two or more systems of law of territorial application:

(a)   reference to the law of a person's habitual residence or to the law of a person's nationality shall be construed as referring to the system of law determined by the rules in force in that State or, if there are no such rules, to the system of law with which the person concerned is most closely connected;

(b)   reference to the State of origin or to the State addressed shall be construed as referring, as the case may be, to the territorial unit where the decision was given or to the territorial unit where recognition or enforcement of the decision or restoration of custody is requested.

(2)   Paragraph (1)(a) of this Article also applies mutatis mutandis to States which have in matters of custody two or more systems of law of personal application.

SCHEDULE 3 – CUSTODY ORDERS

Section 27(1)

Part I
England and Wales

1   The following are the orders referred to in section 27(1) of this Act–

(a)   a care order under the Children Act 1989 (as defined by section 31(11) of that Act, read with section 105(1) and Schedule 14);

(b)   a residence order (as defined by section 8 of the Act of 1989); and

(c)   any order made by a court in England and Wales under any of the following enactments–

  (i)   section 9(1), 10(1)(a) or 11(a) of the Guardianship of Minors Act 1971;

  (ii)   section 42(1) or (2) or 43(1) of the Matrimonial Causes Act 1973;

  (iii) section 2(2)(b), (4)(b) or (5) of the Guardianship Act 1973 as applied by section 34(5) of the Children Act 1975;

  (iv)   section 8(2)(a), 10(1) or 19(1)(ii) of the Domestic Proceedings and Magistrates' Courts Act 1978;

  (v)   section 26(1)(b) of the Adoption Act 1976.

Amendments – Children Act 1989, s 108(5), Sch 13, para 57(3).

2   An order made by the High Court in the exercise of its jurisdiction relating to wardship so far as it gives the care and control of a child to any person.

3   ...

4   An authorisation given by the Secretary of State under section 26(2) of the Children and Young Persons Act 1969 (except where the relevant order, within the meaning of that section, was made by virtue of the court which made it being satisfied that the child was guilty of an offence).

Part II
Scotland

5   An order made by a court of civil jurisdiction in Scotland under any enactment or rule of law with respect to the [residence, custody, care or control of a child or contact with, or access to a child, excluding–

(i)   an order placing a child under the supervision of a local authority;
(ii)   an adoption order under section 12(1) of the Adoption (Scotland) Act 1978;
(iia) an order freeing a child for adoption made under section 18 of the Adoption (Scotland) Act 1978;
(iii) an order relating to the guardianship of a child;
(iv)   an order made under section [86 of the Children (Scotland) Act 1995;
(v)   an order made, or warrant or authorisation granted, under or by virtue of Chapter 2 or 3 of Part II of the Children (Scotland) Act 1995 to remove the child to a place of safety or to secure accommodation, to keep him at such a place or in such accommodation, or to prevent his removal from a place where he is being accommodated (or an order varying or discharging any order, warrant or authorisation so made or granted);
(vi)   an order made in proceedings under this Act.

Amendments – Family Law Act 1986, s 68(1), Sch 1, para 31; Children (Scotland) Act 1995, s 105(4), Sch 4, para 37(6)(*a*).

6   A supervision requirement made by a children's hearing under section 70 of the Children (Scotland) Act 1995 (whether or not continued under section 73 of that Act) or made by the sheriff under section 51(5)(c)(iii) of that Act and any order made by a court in England and Wales or in Northern Ireland if it is an order which, by virtue of section 33(1) of that Act, has effect as if it were such a supervision requirement.

Amendments – Substituted by Children (Scotland) Act 1995, s 105(4), Sch 4, para 37(6)(b).

7   ...

Part III
Northern Ireland

8   The following orders–

(a)   a care order under the Children (Northern Ireland) Order 1995 (as defined by Article 49(1) of that Order read with Article 2(2) and Schedule 8);
(b)   a residence order (as defined by Article 8 of that Order);
(c)   any order made by a court in Northern Ireland under any of the following enactments–

(i)   section 5 of the Guardianship of Infants Act 1886 (except so far as it relates to costs);
(ii)   section 49 of the Mental Health Act (Northern Ireland) 1961;
(iii)   Article 45(1) or (2) or 46 of the Matrimonial Causes (Northern Ireland) Order 1978;
(iv)   Article 10(2)(a), 12(1) or 20(1)(ii) of the Domestic Proceedings (Northern Ireland) Order 1980;
(v)   Article 27(1)(b) of the Adoption (Northern Ireland) Order 1987.

Amendments – Substituted by SI 1995/756.

9   An order made by the High Court in the exercise of its jurisdiction relating to wardship so far as it gives the care and control of a child to any person.

10 ...

FAMILY LAW ACT 1986, ss 1–43

(1986 c 55)

PART I
CHILD CUSTODY

CHAPTER I – PRELIMINARY

1 Orders to which Part I applies

(1) Subject to the following provisions of this section, in this Part means–

(a) a section 8 order made by a court in England and Wales under the Children Act 1989, other than an order varying or discharging such an order

(b) an order made by a court of civil jurisdiction in Scotland under any enactment or rule of law with respect to the residence, custody, care or control of a child, contact with or access to a child or the education or upbringing of a child, excluding–

   (i) an order committing the care of a child to a local authority or placing a child under the supervision of a local authority;

   (ii) an adoption order as defined in section 12(1) of the Adoption (Scotland) Act 1978;

   (iii) an order freeing a child for adoption made under section 18 of the said Act of 1978;

   (iv) an order giving parental responsibilities and parental rights in relation to a child made in the course of proceedings for the adoption of the child (other than an order made following the making of a direction under section 53(1) of the Children Act 1975);

   (v) an order made under the Education (Scotland) Act 1980;

   (vi) an order made under Part II or III of the Social Work (Scotland) Act 1968;

   (vii) an order made under the Child Abduction and Custody Act 1985;

   (viii) an order for the delivery of a child or other order for the enforcement of a Part I order;

   (ix) an order relating to the guardian of a child;

(c) an Article 8 order made by a court in Northern Ireland under the Children (Northern Ireland) Order 1995, other than an order varying or discharging such an order;

(d) an order made by a court in England and Wales in the exercise of the inherent jurisdiction of the High Court with respect to children–

   (i) so far as it gives care of a child to any person or provides for contact with, or the education of, a child; but

   (ii) excluding an order varying or revoking such an order;

(e) an order made by the High Court in Northern Ireland in the exercise of its inherent jurisdiction with respect to children–

   (i) so far as it gives care of a child to any person or provides for contact with, or the education of, a child; but

   (ii) excluding an order varying or discharging such an order;

(f) an order made by a court in a specified dependent territory corresponding to an order within paragraphs (a) to (e) above.

(2) In this Part 'Part I order' does not include–

(a)–(c) ...

(3) In this Part, 'Part I order'–

(a) includes any order which would have been a custody order by virtue of this section in any form in which it was in force at any time before its amendment by the Children Act 1989 or the Children (Northern Ireland) Order 1995, as the case may be; and

(b) (subject to sections 32 and 40 of this Act) excludes any order which would have been excluded from being a custody order by virtue of this section in any such form; and

(c) excludes any order falling within subsection (1)(f) above made before the date specified opposite the name of the territory concerned in Column 2 of Schedule 1 to the Family Law Act 1986 (Dependent Territories) Order 1991, as from time to time in force.

(6) Provision may be made by act of sederunt prescribing, in relation to orders within subsection (1)(b) above, what constitutes an application for the purposes of this Part.

Amendments – Children Act 1989, s 108, Sch 13, paras 62, 63, Sch 15; Age of Legal Capacity (Scotland) Act 1991, s 10(1), Sch 1, para 44; SI 1991/1723; Children (Scotland) Act 1995, s 105(4), Sch 4, para 41; SI 1995/756.

CHAPTER II – JURISDICTION OF COURTS IN ENGLAND AND WALES

2 Jurisdiction: general

(1) A court in England and Wales shall not have jurisdiction to make a section 1(1)(a) order with respect to a child in or in connection with matrimonial proceedings in England and Wales unless–

(a) the child concerned is a child of both parties to the matrimonial proceedings and the court has jurisdiction to entertain those proceedings by virtue of the Council Regulation, or

(b) the condition in section 2A of this Act is satisfied.

(2) A court in England and Wales shall not have jurisdiction to make a section 1(1)(a) order in a non-matrimonial case (that is to say, where the condition in section 2A of this Act is not satisfied) unless the condition in section 3 of this Act is satisfied.

(3)   A court in England and Wales shall not have jurisdiction to make a section 1(1)(d) order unless–

(a)   the condition in section 3 of this Act is satisfied, or

(b)   the child concerned is present in England and Wales on the relevant date and the court considers that the immediate exercise of its powers is necessary for his protection.

Amendments – Children Act 1989, s 108(5), Sch 13, para 64; SI 2001/310.

2A   Jurisdiction in or in connection with matrimonial proceedings

(1)   The condition referred to in section 2(1) of this Act is that the matrimonial proceedings are proceedings in respect of the marriage of the parents of the child concerned and–

(a)   the proceedings–

(i)   are proceedings for divorce or nullity of marriage, and
(ii)   are continuing;

(b)   the proceedings–

(i)   are proceedings for judicial separation,
(ii)   are continuing,

and the jurisdiction of the court is not excluded by subsection (2) below; or
(c)   the proceedings have been dismissed after the beginning of the trial but–

(i)   the section 1(1)(a) order is being made forthwith, or
(ii)   the application for the order was made on or before the dismissal.

(2)   For the purposes of subsection (1)(b) above the jurisdiction of the court is excluded if, after the grant of a decree of judicial separation, on the relevant date, proceedings for divorce or nullity in respect of the marriage are continuing in Scotland, Northern Ireland or a specified dependent territory.

(3)   Subsection (2) above shall not apply if the court in which the other proceedings there referred to are continuing has made–

(a)   an order under section 13(6) or 19A(4) of this Act (not being an order made by virtue of section 13(6)(a)(i)), or a corresponding dependent territory order, or

(b)   an order under section 14(2) or 22(2) of this Act, or a corresponding dependent territory order, which is recorded as being made for the purpose of enabling Part I proceedings to be taken in England and Wales with respect to the child concerned.

(4)   Where a court–

(a)   has jurisdiction to make a section 1(1)(a) order in or in connection with matrimonial proceedings, but

(b)   considers that it would be more appropriate for Part I matters relating to the child to be determined outside England and Wales, the court may by order direct that, while the order under this subsection is in force, no section 1(1)(a) order shall be made by any court in or in connection with those proceedings.

Amendments – Inserted by Children Act 1989, s 108(5), Sch 13, para 64; amended by SI 1991/1723; SI 1995/756.

3 Habitual residence or presence of child

(1)   The condition referred to in section 2(2) of this Act is that on the relevant date the child concerned–

(a)   is habitually resident in England and Wales, or
(b)   is present in England and Wales and is not habitually resident in any part of the United Kingdom or a specified dependent territory,

and, in either case, the jurisdiction of the court is not excluded by subsection (2) below.

(2)   For the purposes of subsection (1) above, the jurisdiction of the court is excluded if, on the relevant date, matrimonial proceedings are continuing in a court in Scotland, Northern Ireland or a specified dependent territory in respect of the marriage of the parents of the child concerned.

(3)   Subsection (2) above shall not apply if the court in which the other proceedings there referred to are continuing has made–

(a)   an order under section 13(6) or 19A(4) of this Act (not being an order made by virtue of section 13(6)(a)(i)), or a corresponding dependent territory order, or
(b)   an order under section 14(2) or 22(2) of this Act, or a corresponding dependent territory order, which is recorded as made for the purpose of enabling Part I proceedings with respect to the child concerned to be taken in England and Wales,

and that order is in force.

(4)–(6)   ...

Amendments – Children Act 1989, s 108(5), (7), Sch 13, paras 62, 65, Sch 15; SI 1991/1723; SI 1995/756.

4   ...

5 Power of court to refuse application or stay proceedings

(1)   A court in England and Wales which has jurisdiction to make a Part I order may refuse an application for the order in any case where the matter in question has already been determined in proceedings outside England and Wales.

(2)   Where, at any stage of the proceedings on an application made to a court in England and Wales for a Part I order, or for the variation of a Part I order, other than proceedings governed by the Council Regulation, it appears to the court–

(a)   that proceedings with respect to the matters to which the application relates are continuing outside England and Wales, or
(b)   that it would be more appropriate for those matters to be determined in proceedings to be taken outside England and Wales,

the court may stay the proceedings on the application.

(3)   The court may remove a stay granted in accordance with subsection (2) above if it appears to the court that there has been unreasonable delay in the taking or prosecution of the other proceedings referred to in that subsection, or that those proceedings are stayed, sisted or concluded.

(4)   Nothing in this section shall affect any power exercisable apart from this section to refuse an application or to grant or remove a stay.

Amendments – Children Act 1989, s 108(5), Sch 13, para 62; SI 2001/310.

6   Duration and variation of custody orders

(1)   If a Part I order made by a court in Scotland, Northern Ireland or a specified dependent territory (or a variation of such an order) comes into force with respect to a child at a time when a Part I order made by a court in England and Wales has effect with respect to him, the latter order shall cease to have effect so far as it makes provision for any matter for which the same or different provision is made by (or by the variation of) the order made by the court in Scotland, Northern Ireland or the territory.

(2)   Where by virtue of subsection (1) above a Part I order has ceased to have effect so far as it makes provision for any matter, a court in England or Wales shall not have jurisdiction to vary that order so as to make provision for that matter.

(3)   A court in England and Wales shall not have jurisdiction to vary a Part I order if, on the relevant date, matrimonial proceedings are continuing in [Scotland, Northern Ireland or a specified dependent territory in respect of the marriage of the parents of the child concerned.

(3A)   Subsection (3) above shall not apply if–

(a)   the Part I order was made in or in connection with proceedings for divorce or nullity in England and Wales in respect of the marriage of the parents of the child concerned; and
(b)   those proceedings are continuing.

(3B)   Subsection (3) above shall not apply if–

(a)   the Part I order was made in or in connection with proceedings for judicial separation in England and Wales;
(b)   those proceedings are continuing; and
(c)   the decree of judicial separation has not yet been granted.

(4)   Subsection (3) above shall not apply if the court in which the proceedings there referred to are continuing has made–

(a)   an order under section 13(6) or 19A(4) of this Act (not being an order made by virtue of section 13(6)(a)(i)), or a corresponding dependent territory order, or
(b)   an order under section 14(2) or 22(2) of this Act, or a corresponding dependent territory order, which is recorded as made for the purpose of enabling Part I proceedings with respect to the child concerned to be taken in England and Wales,

and that order is in force.

(5)   Subsection (3) above shall not apply in the case of a variation of a section 1(1)(d) order if the child concerned is present in England and Wales on the relevant date and the court considers that the immediate exercise of its powers is necessary for his protection.

(6)   Subsection (7) below applies where a Part I order which is—

(a)   a residence order (within the meaning of the Children Act 1989) in favour of a person with respect to a child,
(b)   an order made in the exercise of the High Court's inherent jurisdiction with respect to children by virtue of which a person has care of a child, or
(c)   an order—

    (i)   of a kind mentioned in section 1(3)(a) of this Act,
    (ii)   under which a person is entitled to the actual possession of a child,

ceases to have effect in relation to that person by virtue of subsection (1) above.

(7)   Where this subsection applies, any family assistance order made under section 16 of the Children Act 1989 with respect to the child shall also cease to have effect.

(8)   For the purposes of subsection (7) above the reference to a family assistance order under section 16 of the Children Act 1989 shall be deemed to include a reference to an order for the supervision of a child made under—

(a)   section 7(4) of the Family Law Reform Act 1969;
(b)   section 44 of the Matrimonial Causes Act 1973;
(c)   section 2(2)(a) of the Guardianship Act 1973;
(d)   section 34(5) or 36(3)(b) of the Children Act 1975; or
(e)   section 9 of the Domestic Proceedings and Magistrates' Courts Act 1978;

but this subsection shall cease to have effect once all such orders for the supervision of children have ceased to have effect in accordance with Schedule 14 to the Children Act 1989.

Amendments – Children Act 1989, s 108(5), Sch 13, paras 62, 66; SI 1991/1723; SI 1995/756.

7   Interpretation of Chapter II

In this Chapter—

(a)   'child' means a person who has not attained the age of eighteen;
(b)   'matrimonial proceedings' means proceedings for divorce, nullity of marriage or judicial separation;
(c)   'the relevant date' means, in relation to the making or variation of an order—

    (i)   where an application is made for an order to be made or varied, the date of the application (or first application, if two or more are determined together), and
    (ii)   where no such application is made, the date on which the court is considering whether to make or, as the case may be, vary the order; and

(d)   'section 1(1)(a) order' and 'section 1(1)(d) order' mean orders falling within section 1(1)(a) and (d) of this Act respectively.

Amendments – Children Act 1989, s 108(5), Sch 13, para 67.

CHAPTER III – JURISDICTION OF COURTS IN SCOTLAND

8 Jurisdiction in independent proceedings

A court in Scotland may entertain an application for a Part I order otherwise than in matrimonial proceedings only if it has jurisdiction under sections 9, 10, 12 or 15(2) of this Act.

Amendments – Children Act 1989, s 108, Sch 13, para 62.

9 Habitual residence

Subject to section 11 of this Act, an application for a Part I order otherwise than in matrimonial proceedings may be entertained by–

(a) the Court of Session if, on the date of the application, the child concerned is habitually resident in Scotland;
(b) the sheriff if, on the date of the application, the child concerned is habitually resident in the sheriffdom.

Amendments – Children Act 1989, s 108, Sch 13, para 62.

10 Presence of child

Subject to section 11 of this Act, an application for a Part I order otherwise than in matrimonial proceedings may be entertained by–

(a) the Court of Session if, on the date of the application, the child concerned–

(i) is present in Scotland; and
(ii) is not habitually resident in any part of the United Kingdom [or a specified dependent territory;

(b) the sheriff if, on the date of the application,–

(i) the child is present in Scotland;
(ii) the child is not habitually resident in any part of the United Kingdom or a specified dependent territory; and
(iii) either the pursuer or the defender in the application is habitually resident in the sheriffdom.

Amendments – Children Act 1989, s 108, Sch 13, para 62; SI 1991/1723.

11 Provisions supplementary to sections 9 and 10

(1) Subject to subsection (2) below, the jurisdiction of the court to entertain an application for a Part I order with respect to a child by virtue of section 9, 10 or 15(2) of this Act is excluded if, on the date of the application, matrimonial proceedings are continuing in a court in any part of the United Kingdom or a specified dependent territory in respect of the marriage of the parents of the child.

(2) Subsection (1) above shall not apply in relation to an application for a Part I order if the court in which the matrimonial proceedings are continuing has made one of the following orders, that is to say–

(a) an order under section 2A(4), 13(6) or 19A(4) of this Act (not being an order made by virtue of section 13(6)(a)(ii)) or a corresponding dependent territory order; or

(b)   an order under section 5(2), 14(2) or 22(2) of this Act, or a corresponding dependent territory order, which is recorded as made for the purpose of enabling Part I proceedings with respect to the child concerned to be taken in Scotland or, as the case may be, in another court in Scotland,

and that order is in force.

Amendments – Children Act 1989, s 108, Sch 13, paras 62, 68; SI 1991/1723; SI 1995/756.

12   Emergency jurisdiction

Notwithstanding that any other court, whether within or outside Scotland, has jurisdiction to entertain an application for a Part I order, the Court of Session or the sheriff shall have jurisdiction to entertain such an application if–

(a)   the child concerned is present in Scotland or, as the case may be, in the sheriffdom on the date of the application; and

(b)   the Court of Session or sheriff considers that, for the protection of the V, it is necessary to make such an order immediately.

Amendments – Children Act 1989, s 108, Sch 13, para 62.

13   Jurisdiction ancillary to matrimonial proceedings

(1)   The jurisdiction of a court in Scotland to entertain an application for a Part I order in matrimonial proceedings shall be modified by the following provisions of this section.

(2)   A court in Scotland shall not have jurisdiction, after the dismissal of matrimonial proceedings or after decree of absolvitor is granted therein, to entertain an application for a Part I order under section 9(1) of the Matrimonial Proceedings (Children) Act 1958 unless the application therefore was made on or before such dismissal or the granting of the decree of absolvitor.

(3)   Where, after a decree of separation has been granted, an application is made in the separation process for a Part I order, the court in Scotland shall not have jurisdiction to entertain that application if, on the date of the application, proceedings for divorce or nullity of marriage in respect of the marriage concerned are continuing in another court in the United Kingdom [or a specified dependent territory.

(4)   A court in Scotland shall not have jurisdiction to entertain an application for the variation of a Part I order made under section 9(1) of the Matrimonial Proceedings (Children) Act 1958 if, on the date of the application, matrimonial proceedings in respect of the marriage concerned are continuing in another court in the United Kingdom or a specified dependent territory].

(5)   Subsections (3) and (4) above shall not apply if the court in which the other proceedings there referred to are continuing has made–

(a)   an order under section 2A(4) or 19A(4) of this Act or under subsection (6) below (not being an order made by virtue of paragraph (a)(ii) of that subsection), or a corresponding dependent territory order, or

(b)   an order under section 5(2), 14(2) or 22(2) of this Act, or a corresponding dependent territory order, which is recorded as made for the purpose of enabling Part I proceedings with respect to the child concerned to be taken in Scotland or, as the case may be, in another court in Scotland,

and that order is in force.

(6)   A court in Scotland which has jurisdiction in matrimonial proceedings to entertain an application for a Part I order with respect to a child may make an order declining such jurisdiction if–

(a)   it appears to the court with respect to that child that–

    (i)   but for section 11(1) of this Act, another court in Scotland would have jurisdiction to entertain an application for a Part I order, or

    (ii)   but for section 3(2), 6(3), 20(2) or 23(3) of this Act or a corresponding dependent territory provision, a court in another part of the United Kingdom or a specified dependent territory would have jurisdiction to make a Part I order] or an order varying a Part I order; and

(b)   the court considers that it would be more appropriate for Part I matters relating to that child to be determined in that other court or part.

(7)   The court may recall an order made under subsection (6) above.

Amendments – Children Act 1989, s 108, Sch 13, paras 62, 68; SI 1991/1723; SI 1995/756.

14   Power of court to refuse application or sist proceedings

(1)   A court in Scotland which has jurisdiction to entertain an application for a Part I order may refuse the application in any case where the matter in question has already been determined in other proceedings.

(2)   Where, at any stage of the proceedings on an application made to a court in Scotland for a Part I order, it appears to the court

(a)   that proceedings with respect to the matter to which the application relates are continuing outside Scotland or in another court in Scotland; or

(b)   that it would be more appropriate for those matters to be determined in proceedings outside Scotland or in another court in Scotland and that such proceedings are likely to be taken there,

the court may sist the proceedings on that application.

Amendments – Children Act 1989, s 108, Sch 13, para 62.

15   Duration, variation and recall of orders

(1)   Where, after the making by a court in Scotland of a Part I order ('the existing order') with respect to a child–

(a)   a Part I order, or an order varying a Part I order, competently made by another court in any part of the United Kingdom or in a specified dependent territory with respect to that child; or

(b)   an order for the custody of that child which is made outside the United Kingdom and any specified dependent territory and recognised in Scotland by virtue of section 26 of this Act,

comes into force, the existing order shall cease to have effect so far as it makes provision for any matter for which the same or different provision is made by the order of the other court in the United Kingdom or in the specified dependent territory or, as the case may be, the order so recognised.

(2)   Subject to sections 11(1) and 13(3) and (4) of this Act, a court in Scotland which has made a Part I order ('the original order') may, notwithstanding that it would no longer have jurisdiction to make the original order, make an order varying or recalling the original order; but if the original order has by virtue of subsection (1) above ceased to have effect so far as it makes provision for any matter, the court shall not have power to vary that order under this subsection so as to make provision for that matter.

(3)   In subsection (2) above, an order varying an original order means any Part I order made with respect to the same child as the original order was made.

(4)   Where any person who is entitled to the custody of a child under a Part I order made by a court in Scotland ceases to be so entitled by virtue of subsection (1) above, then, if there is in force an order made by a court in Scotland ... providing for the supervision of that child by a local authority, that order shall cease to have effect.

Amendments – Children Act 1989, s 108, Sch 13, para 62; SI 1991/1723; Children (Scotland) Act 1995, s 105(5), Sch 5.

16   Tutory and curatory

(1)   Subject to subsections (2) and (3) below, an application made after the commencement of this Part for an order relating to the guardianship of a child may be entertained by–

(a)   the Court of Session if, on the date of the application, the child is habitually resident in Scotland;

(b)   the sheriff if, on the date of the application, the child is habitually resident in the sheriffdom.

(2)   Subsection (1) above shall not apply to an application for the appointment or removal of a judicial factor or of a curator bonis or any application made by such factor or curator.

(3)   Subsection (1) above is without prejudice to any other ground of jurisdiction on which the Court of Session or the sheriff may entertain an application mentioned therein.

(4)   Provision may be made by act of sederunt prescribing, in relation to orders relating to the guardianship of a child, what constitutes an application for the purposes of this Chapter.

Amendments – Age of Legal Capacity (Scotland) Act 1991, s 10, Sch 1, para 45.

17   Orders for delivery of child

(1)   An application by one parent of a child for an order for the delivery of the child from the other parent, where the order is not sought to implement a Part I order, may be entertained by the Court of Session or a sheriff if, but only if, the Court of Session or, as the case may be, the sheriff would have jurisdiction under this Chapter to make a Part I order with respect to the child concerned.

(2)   ...

(3)   Subsection (1) above shall apply to an application by one party to a marriage for an order for the delivery of the child concerned from the other party where the child is the child of one of the parties and has been accepted as one of the family by the

other party as it applies to an application by one parent of a child for an order for the delivery of the child from the other parent.

Amendments – Children Act 1989, s 108, Sch 13, para 62; Children (Scotland) Act 1995, s 105(5), Sch 5.

18 Interpretation of Chapter III

(1) In this Chapter–

'child' means a person who has not attained the age of sixteen;
'matrimonial proceedings' means proceedings for divorce, nullity of marriage or judicial separation.

(2) 'the date of the application' means, where two or more applications are pending, the date of the first of those applications; and, for the purposes of this subsection, an application is pending until a Part I order or, in the case of an application mentioned in section 16(1) of this Act, an order relating to the guardianship of a childW, has been granted in pursuance of the application or the court has refused to grant such an order.

Amendments – Children Act 1989, s 108, Sch 13, para 62; Age of Legal Capacity (Scotland) Act 1991, s 10, Sch 1, para 46.

CHAPTER IV – JURISDICTION OF COURTS IN NORTHERN IRELAND

19 Jurisdiction: general

(1) A court in Northern Ireland shall not have jurisdiction to make a section 1(1)(c) order with respect to a child in or in connection with matrimonial proceedings in Northern Ireland unless

(a) the child concerned is a child of both parties to the matrimonial proceedings and the court has jurisdiction to entertain those proceedings by virtue of the Council Regulation, or
(b) the condition in section 19A of this Act is satisfied.

(2) A court in Northern Ireland shall not have jurisdiction to make a section 1(1)(c) order in a non-matrimonial case (that is to say, where the condition in section 19A is not satisfied) unless the condition in section 20 of this Act is satisfied.

(3) A court in Northern Ireland shall not have jurisdiction to make a section 1(1)(e) order unless–

(a) the condition in section 20 of this Act is satisfied, or
(b) the child concerned is present in Northern Ireland on the relevant date and the court considers that the immediate exercise of its powers is necessary for his protection.

Amendments – Substituted by SI 1995/755; amended by SI 2001/660.

19A Jurisdiction in or in connection with matrimonial proceedings

(1) The condition referred to in section 19(1) of this Act is that the matrimonial proceedings are proceedings in respect of the marriage of the parents of the child concerned and–

(a)   the proceedings—

  (i)   are proceedings for divorce or nullity of marriage, and
  (ii)   are continuing;

(b)   the proceedings—

  (i)   are proceedings for judicial separation,
  (ii)   are continuing,

  and the jurisdiction of the court is not excluded by subsection (2) below; or

(c)   the proceedings have been dismissed after the beginning of the trial but—

  (i)   the section 1(1)(c) order is being made forthwith, or
  (ii)   the application for the order was made on or before the dismissal.

(2)   For the purposes of subsection (1)(b) above, the jurisdiction of the court is excluded if, after the grant of a decree of judicial separation, on the relevant date, proceedings for divorce or nullity in respect of the marriage are continuing in England and Wales or Scotland.

(3)   Subsection (2) above shall not apply if the court in which the other proceedings there referred to are continuing has made—

(a)   an order under section 2A(4) or 13(6) of this Act (not being an order made by virtue of section 13(6)(a)(i)), or
(b)   an order under section 5(2) or 14(2) of this Act which is recorded as being made for the purpose of enabling Part I proceedings to be taken in Northern Ireland with respect to the child concerned.

(4)   Where a court—

(a)   has jurisdiction to make a section 1(1)(c) order in or in connection with matrimonial proceedings, but
(b)   considers that it would be more appropriate for Part I matters relating to the child to be determined outside Northern Ireland,

the court may by order direct that, while the order under this subsection is in force, no section 1(1)(c) order shall be made by any court in or in connection with those proceedings.

Amendments – Inserted by SI 1995/755.

20   Habitual residence or presence of child

(1)   The condition referred to in section 19(2) of this Act is that on the relevant date the child concerned—

(a)   is habitually resident in Northern Ireland, or
(b)   is present in Northern Ireland and is not habitually resident in any part of the United Kingdom or in a specified dependent territory,

and, in either case, the jurisdiction of the court is not excluded by subsection (2) below.

(2)   For the purposes of subsection (1) above, the jurisdiction of the court is excluded if, on the relevant date, matrimonial proceedings are continuing in a court in England and Wales, Scotland or a specified dependent territory in respect of the marriage of the parents of the child concerned.

(3)   Subsection (2) above shall not apply if the court in which the other proceedings there referred to are continuing has made–

(a)   an order under section 2A(4) or 13(6) of this Act (not being an order made by virtue of section 13(6)(a)(i)), or a corresponding dependent territory order, or

(b)   an order under section 5(2) or 14(2) of this Act, or a corresponding dependent territory order, which is recorded as made for the purpose of enabling [Part I proceedings with respect to the child concerned to be taken in Northern Ireland,

and that order is in force.

(4)–(6)   ....

Amendments – Children Act 1989, s 108, Sch 13, paras 62, 68, 69; SI 1991/1723; SI 1995/755.

21   ...

22   Power of court to refuse application or stay proceedings

(1)   A court in Northern Ireland which has jurisdiction to make a Part I order may refuse an application for the order in any case where the matter in question has already been determined in proceedings outside Northern Ireland.

(2)   Where, at any stage of the proceedings on an application made to a court in Northern Ireland for a Part I order, or for the variation of a Part I order, other than proceedings governed by the Council Regulation, it appears to the court–

(a)   that proceedings with respect to the matters to which the application relates are continuing outside Northern Ireland, or

(b)   that it would be more appropriate for those matters to be determined in proceedings to be taken outside Northern Ireland,

the court may stay the proceedings on the application.

(3)   The court may remove a stay granted in accordance with subsection (2) above if it appears to the court that there has been unreasonable delay in the taking or prosecution of the other proceedings referred to in that subsection, or that those proceedings are stayed, sisted or concluded.

(4)   Nothing in this section shall affect any power exercisable apart from this section to refuse an application or to grant or remove a stay.

Amendments – Children Act 1989, s 108, Sch 13, para 62; SI 2001/660.

23   Duration and variation of custody orders

(1)   If a Part I order made by a court in England and Wales, Scotland or a specified dependent territory (or a variation of such an order) comes into force with respect to a child at a time when a Part I order made by a court in Northern Ireland has effect with respect to him, the latter order shall cease to have effect so far as it makes provision for any matter for which the same or different provision is made by (or by the variation of) the order made by the court in England and Wales, Scotland or the territory.

(2)   Where by virtue of subsection (1) above a Part I order has ceased to have effect so far as it makes provision for any matter, a court in Northern Ireland shall not have jurisdiction to vary that order so as to make provision for that matter.

(3)   A court in Northern Ireland shall not have jurisdiction to vary a Part I order, if, on the relevant date, matrimonial proceedings are continuing in England and Wales or Scotland in respect of the marriage of the parents of the child concerned.

(3A)   Subsection (3) above shall not apply if–

(a)   the Part I order was made in or in connection with proceedings for divorce or nullity in Northern Ireland in respect of the marriage of the parents of the child concerned; and
(b)   those proceedings are continuing.

(3B)   Subsection (3) above shall not apply if–

(a)   the Part I order was made in or in connection with proceedings for judicial separation in Northern Ireland; and
(b)   those proceedings are continuing; and
(c)   the decree of judicial separation has not yet been granted.

(4)   Subsection (3) above shall not apply if the court in which the proceedings there referred to are continuing has made–

(a)   an order under section 2A(4) or 13(6) of this Act (not being an order made by virtue of section 13(6)(a)(i)), or a corresponding dependent territory order, or
(b)   an order under section 5(2) or 14(2) of this Act, or a corresponding dependent territory order, which is recorded as made for the purpose of enabling Part I proceedings with respect toW the child concerned to be taken in Northern Ireland,

and that order is in force.

(5)   Subsection (3) above shall not apply in the case of a variation of a section 1(1)(e) order if the child concerned is present in Northern Ireland on the relevant date and the court considers that the immediate exercise of its powers is necessary for his protection.

(6)   Subsection (7) below applies where a Part I order which is–

(a)   a residence order (within the meaning of the Children (Northern Ireland) Order 1995) in favour of a person with respect to a child,
(b)   an order made in the exercise of the High Court's inherent jurisdiction with respect to children by virtue of which a person has care of a child, or
(c)   an order–

   (i)   of a kind mentioned in section 1(3)(a) of this Act,
   (ii)   under which a person is entitled to the actual possession of a child,

ceases to have effect in relation to that person by virtue of subsection (1) above.

(7)   Where this subsection applies, any family assistance order made under Article 16 of the Children (Northern Ireland) Order 1995 with respect to the child shall also cease to have effect.

(8)   For the purposes of subsection (7) above the reference to a family assistance order under Article 16 of the Children (Northern Ireland) Order 1995 shall be deemed to include a reference to an order for the supervision of a child made under–

(a)   Article 47 of the Matrimonial Causes (Northern Ireland) Order 1978, or
(b)   Article 11 of the Domestic Proceedings (Northern Ireland) Order 1980;

but this subsection shall cease to have effect once all such orders for the supervision of children have ceased to have effect in accordance with Schedule 8 to the Children (Northern Ireland) Order 1995.

Amendments – Children Act 1989, s 108, Sch 13, paras 62, 68, 69; SI 1991/1723; SI 1995/755.

24 Interpretation of Chapter IV

In this Chapter–

(a) 'child' means a person who has not attained the age of 18;
(b) 'matrimonial proceedings' means proceedings for divorce, nullity of marriage or judicial separation;
(c) 'the relevant date' means, in relation to the making or variation of an order–

(i) where an application is made for an order to be made or varied, the date of the application (or first application, if two or more are determined together), and

(ii) where no such application is made, the date on which the court is considering whether to make or, as the case may be, vary the order; and

(d) 'section 1(1)(c) order' and 'section 1(1)(e) order' mean orders falling within section 1(1)(c) and (e) of this Act respectively.

Amendments – Substituted by SI 1995/755.

CHAPTER V – RECOGNITION AND ENFORCEMENT

25 Recognition of Part I orders]: general

(1) Where a Part I order made by a court in any part of the United Kingdom or in a specified dependent territory is in force with respect to a child who has not attained the age of sixteen, then, subject to subsection (2) below, the order shall be recognised in any other part or, in the case of a dependent territory order, any part of the United Kingdom as having the same effect in that part as if it had been made by the appropriate court in that part and as if that court had had jurisdiction to make it.

(2) Where a Part I order includes provision as to the means by which rights conferred by the order are to be enforced, subsection (1) above shall not apply to that provision.

(3) A court in a part of the United Kingdom in which a Part I order is recognised in accordance with subsection (1) above shall not enforce the order unless it has been registered in that part of the United Kingdom under section 27 of this Act and proceedings for enforcement are taken in accordance with section 29 of this Act.

Amendments – Children Act 1989, s 108(5), Sch 13, para 62; SI 1991/1723.

26 Recognition: special Scottish rule

An order relating to parental responsibilities or parental rights in relation to a child which is made outside the United Kingdom shall be recognised in Scotland if the order was made in the country where the child was habitually resident.

Amendments – Children (Scotland) Act 1995, s 105(4), Sch 4, para 41(6).

27 Registration

(1) Any person on whom any rights are conferred by a [=Part I order may apply to the court which made it for the order to be registered in another part of the United Kingdom under this section, or in a specified dependent territory under a corresponding provision

(2) An application under this section shall be made in the prescribed manner and shall contain the prescribed information and be accompanied by such documents as may be prescribed.

(3) On receiving an application under this section the court which made the Part I order shall, unless it appears to the court that the order is no longer in force, cause the following documents to be sent to the appropriate court in the part of the United Kingdom or a dependent territory specified in the application, namely–

(a) a section 1(1)(c) order of the order, and
(b) where the order has been varied, prescribed particulars of any variation which is in force, and
(c) a copy of the application and of any accompanying documents.

(4) Where the prescribed officer of the appropriate court in any part of the United Kingdom receives a certified copy of a Part I order under subsection (3) above or under a corresponding dependent territory provision, he shall forthwith cause the order, together with particulars of any variation, to be registered in that court in the prescribed manner.

(5) An order shall not be registered under this section in respect of a child who has attained the age of sixteen, and the registration of an order in respect of a child who has not attained the age of sixteen shall cease to have effect on the attainment by the child of that age.

Amendments – Children Act 1989, s 108(5), Sch 13, para 62; SI 1991/1723.

28 Cancellation and variation of registration

(1) A court which revokes, recalls or varies an order registered under section 27 of this Act shall cause notice of the revocation, recall or variation to be given in the prescribed manner to the prescribed officer of the court in which it is registered and, on receiving the notice, the prescribed officer–

(a) in the case of the revocation or recall of the order, shall cancel the registration, and
(b) in the case of the variation of the order, shall cause particulars of the variation to be registered in the prescribed manner.

(2) Where–

(a) an order registered under section 27 of this Act ceases (in whole or in part) to have effect in the part of the United Kingdom or in a specified dependent territory] in which it was made, otherwise than because of its revocation, recall or variation, or
(b) an order registered under section 27 of this Act in Scotland ceases (in whole or in part) to have effect there as a result of the making of an order in proceedings outside the United Kingdom and any specified dependent territory,

the court in which the order is registered may, of its own motion or on the application of any person who appears to the court to have an interest in the matter, cancel the registration (or, if the order has ceased to have effect in part, cancel the registration so far as it relates to the provisions which have ceased to have effect).

Amendments – SI 1991/1723.

29 Enforcement

(1) Where a Part I order has been registered under section 27 of this Act, the court in which it is registered shall have the same powers for the purpose of enforcing the order as it would have if it had itself made the order and had jurisdiction to make it; and proceedings for or with respect to enforcement may be taken accordingly.

(2) Where an application has been made to any court for the enforcement of an order registered in that court under section 27 of this Act, the court may, at any time before the application is determined, give such interim directions as it thinks fit for the purpose of securing the welfare of the child concerned or of preventing changes in the circumstances relevant to the determination of the application.

(3) The references in subsection (1) above to a Part I order do not include references to any provision of the order as to the means by which rights conferred by the order are to be enforced.

Amendments – Children Act 1989, s 108(5), Sch 13, para 62.

30 Staying or sisting of enforcement proceedings

(1) Where in accordance with section 29 of this Act proceedings are taken in any court for the enforcement of an order registered in that court, any person who appears to the court to have an interest in the matter may apply for the proceedings to be stayed or sisted on the ground that he has taken or intends to take other proceedings (in the United Kingdom or elsewhere) as a result of which the order may cease to have effect, or may have a different effect, in the part of the United Kingdom in which it is registered.

(2) If after considering an application under subsection (1) above the court considers that the proceedings for enforcement should be stayed or sisted in order that other proceedings may be taken or concluded, it shall stay or sist the proceedings for enforcement accordingly.

(3) The court may remove a stay or recall a sist granted in accordance with subsection (2) above if it appears to the court–

(a) that there has been unreasonable delay in the taking or prosecution of the other proceedings referred to in that subsection, or
(b) that those other proceedings are concluded and that the registered order, or a relevant part of it, is still in force.

(4) Nothing in this section shall affect any power exercisable apart from this section to grant, remove or recall a stay or sist.

31 Dismissal of enforcement proceedings

(1) Where in accordance with section 29 of this Act proceedings are taken in any court for the enforcement of an order registered in that court, any person who appears to the court to have an interest in the matter may apply for those proceedings to be dismissed on the ground that the order has (in whole or in part) ceased to have

effect in the part of the United Kingdom or specified dependent territory in which it was made.

(2)   Where in accordance with section 29 of this Act proceedings are taken in the Court of Session for the enforcement of an order registered in that court, any person who appears to the court to have an interest in the matter may apply for those proceedings to be dismissed on the ground that the order has (in whole or in part) ceased to have effect in Scotland as a result of the making of an order in proceedings outside the United Kingdom and any specified dependent territory.

(3)   If, after considering an application under subsection (1) or (2) above, the court is satisfied that the registered order has ceased to have effect, it shall dismiss the proceedings for enforcement (or, if it is satisfied that the order has ceased to have effect in part, it shall dismiss the proceedings so far as they relate to the enforcement of provisions which have ceased to have effect).

Amendments – SI 1991/1723.

32   Interpretation of Chapter V

(1)   In this Chapter–

'the appropriate court', in relation to England and Wales or Northern Ireland, means the High Court and, in relation to Scotland, means the Court of Session and, in relation to a specified dependent territory, means the corresponding court in that territory;
'Part I order' includes (except where the context otherwise requires) any order within section 1(3) of this Act which, on the assumptions mentioned in subsection (3) below–
    (a)   could have been made notwithstanding the provisions of this Part or the corresponding dependent territory provisions;
    (b)   would have been a Part I order for the purposes of this Part; and
    (c)   would not have ceased to have effect by virtue of section 6, 15 or 23 of this Act.

(2)   In the application of this Chapter to Scotland, 'Part I order' also includes (except where the context otherwise requires) any order within section 1(3) of this Act which, on the assumptions mentioned in subsection (3) below–

(a)   would have been a Part I order for the purposes of this Part; and
(b)   would not have ceased to have effect by virtue of section 6 or 23 of this Act,

and which, but for the provisions of this Part, would be recognised in Scotland under any rule of law.

(3)   The said assumptions are–

(a)   that this Part or the corresponding dependent territory provisions, as the case may be, had been in force at all material times; and
(b)   that any reference in section 1 of this Act to any enactment included a reference to any corresponding enactment previously in force.

Amendments – Children Act 1989, s 108(5), Sch 13, para 62; SI 1991/1723.

CHAPTER VI – MISCELLANEOUS AND SUPPLEMENTAL

33 Power to order disclosure of child's whereabouts

(1) Where in proceedings for or relating to a Part I order in respect of a child there is not available to the court adequate information as to where the child is, the court may order any person who it has reason to believe may have relevant information to disclose it to the court.

(2) A person shall not be excused from complying with an order under subsection (1) above by reason that to do so may incriminate him or his spouse of an offence; but a statement or admission made in compliance with such an order shall not be admissible in evidence against either of them in proceedings for any offence other than perjury.

(3) A court in Scotland before which proceedings are pending for the enforcement of an order relating to parental responsibilities or parental rights in relation to a child made outside the United Kingdom and any specified dependent territory which is recognised in Scotland shall have the same powers as it would have under subsection (1) above if the order were its own.

Amendments – Children Act 1989, s 108(5), Sch 13, para 62; SI 1991/1723; Children (Scotland) Act 1995, s 105(4), Sch 4, para 41(1), (7).

34 Power to order recovery of child

(1) Where–

(a) a person is required by a Part I order, or an order for the enforcement of a Part I order, to give up a child to another person ('the person concerned'), and
(b) the court which made the order imposing the requirement is satisfied that the child has not been given up in accordance with the order,

the court may make an order authorising an officer of the court or a constable to take charge of the child and deliver him to the person concerned.

(2) The authority conferred by subsection (1) above includes authority–

(a) to enter and search any premises where the person acting in pursuance of the order has reason to believe the child may be found, and
(b) to use such force as may be necessary to give effect to the purpose of the order.

(3) Where by virtue of–

(a) section 14 of the Children Act 1989, or
(b) Article 14 (enforcement of residence orders) of the Children (Northern Ireland) Order 1995,

a Part I order (or a provision of a Part I order) may be enforced as if it were an order requiring a person to give up a child to another person, subsection (1) above shall apply as if the Part I order had included such a requirement.

(4) This section is without prejudice to any power conferred on a court by or under any other enactment or rule of law.

Amendments – Children Act 1989, s 108(5), Sch 13, paras 62, 70; SI 1995/755.

35 Powers to restrict removal of child from jurisdiction

(1) ...

(2) (*not reproduced*)

(3) A court in Scotland–

(a) at any time after the commencement of proceedings in connection with which the court would have jurisdiction to make a Part I order, or

(b) in any proceedings in which it would be competent for the court to grant an interdict prohibiting the removal of a child from its jurisdiction,

may, on an application by any of the persons mentioned in subsection (4) below, grant interdict or interim interdict prohibiting the removal of the child from the United Kingdom or any part of the United Kingdom or any specified dependent territory, or out of the control of the person in whose care the child is.

(4) The said persons are–

(a) any party to the proceedings,

(b) the guardian of the child concerned, and

(c) any other person who has or wishes to obtain the ... care of the child.

(5) In subsection (3) above 'the court' means the Court of Session or the sheriff; and for the purposes of subsection (3)(a) above, proceedings shall be held to commence–

(a) in the Court of Session, when a summons is signeted or a petition is presented;

(b) in the sheriff court, when the warrant of citation is signed.

Amendments – Children Act 1989, s 108, Sch 13, para 62, Sch 15, para 62; Children (Scotland) Act 1995, s 105(4), Sch 4, para 41, Sch 5, Age of Legal Capacity (Scotland) Act 1991, s 10, Sch 1, para 45.

36 Effect of orders restricting removal

(1) This section applies to any order made by a court in the United Kingdom or any specified dependent territory prohibiting the removal of a child from the United Kingdom or from any specified part of it or from any such territory.

(2) An order to which this section applies, made by a court in one part of the United Kingdom or in a specified dependent territory, shall have effect in each other part, or, in the case of an order made in a dependent territory, each part of the United Kingdom ... –

(a) as if it had been made by the appropriate court in that ... part, and

(b) in the case of an order which has the effect of prohibiting the child's removal to that ... part, as if it had included a prohibition on his further removal to any place except one to which he could be removed consistently with the order.

(3) The references in subsections (1) and (2) above to prohibitions on a child's removal include references to prohibitions subject to exceptions; and in a case where removal is prohibited except with the consent of the court, nothing in subsection (2) above shall be construed as affecting the identity of the court whose consent is required.

(4) In this section 'child' means a person who has not attained the age of sixteen; and this section shall cease to apply to an order relating to a child when he attains the age of sixteen.

Amendments – SI 1991/1723.

37 Surrender of passports

(1) Where there is in force an order prohibiting or otherwise restricting the removal of a child from the United Kingdom or from any specified part of it or from a specified dependent territory, the court by which the order was in fact made, or by which it is treated under section 36 of this Act as having been made, may require any person to surrender any United Kingdom passport which has been issued to, or contains particulars of, the child.

(2) In this section 'United Kingdom passport' means a current passport issued by the Government of the United Kingdom.

Amendments – SI 1991/1723.

38 Automatic restriction on removal of wards of court

(1) The rule of law which (without any order of the court) restricts the removal of a ward of court from the jurisdiction of the court shall, in a case to which this section applies, have effect subject to the modifications in subsection (3) below.

(2) This section applies in relation to a ward of court if—

(a) proceedings for divorce, nullity or judicial separation in respect of the marriage of his parents are continuing in a court in another part of the United Kingdom (that is to say, in a part of the United Kingdom outside the jurisdiction of the court of which he is a ward), or in a specified dependent territory, or

(b) he is habitually resident in another part of the United Kingdom or in a specified dependent territory,

except where that other part is Scotland and he has attained the age of sixteen.

(3) Where this section applies, the rule referred to in subsection (1) above shall not prevent—

(a) the removal of the ward of court, without the consent of any court, to the other part of the United Kingdom [or the specified dependent territory mentioned in subsection (2) above, or

(b) his removal to any other place with the consent of either the appropriate court in that other part of the United Kingdom or the court mentioned in subsection (2)(a) above.

Amendments – SI 1991/1723.

39 Duty to furnish particulars of other proceedings

Parties to proceedings for or relating to a Part I order shall, to such extent and in such manner as may be prescribed, give particulars of other proceedings known to them which relate to the child concerned (including proceedings instituted abroad and proceedings which are no longer continuing).

Amendments – Children Act 1989, s 108(5), Sch 13, para 62.

40 Interpretation of Chapter VI

(1) In this Chapter—

'the appropriate court' has the same meaning as in Chapter V;
'Part I order' includes (except where the context otherwise requires) any such order as is mentioned in section 32(1) of this Act.

(2)　In the application of this Chapter to Scotland, 'Part I order' also includes (except where the context otherwise requires) any such order as is mentioned in section 32(2) of this Act.

Amendments – Children Act 1989, s 108(5), Sch 13, para 62.

41　Habitual residence after removal without consent, etc

(1)　Where a child who–

(a)　has not attained the age of sixteen, and

(b)　is habitually resident in a part of the United Kingdom or in a specified dependent territory,

becomes habitually resident outside that part of the United Kingdom or that territory in consequence of circumstances of the kind specified in subsection (2) below, he shall be treated for the purposes of this Part as continuing to be habitually resident in that part of the United Kingdom or that territory for the period of one year beginning with the date on which those circumstances arise.

(2)　The circumstances referred to in subsection (1) above exist where the child is removed from or retained outside, or himself leaves or remains outside, the part of the United Kingdom or the territory in which he was habitually resident before his change of residence–

(a)　without the agreement of the person or all the persons having, under the law of that part of the United Kingdom or that territory, the right to determine where he is to reside, or

(b)　in contravention of an order made by a court in any part of the United Kingdom or in a specified dependent territory.

(3)　A child shall cease to be treated by virtue of subsection (1) above as habitually resident in a part of the United Kingdom or a specified dependent territory if, during the period there mentioned–

(a)　he attains the age of sixteen, or

(b)　he becomes habitually resident outside that part of the United Kingdom or that territory with the agreement of the person or persons mentioned in subsection (2)(a) above and not in contravention of an order made by a court in any part of the United Kingdom or in any specified dependent territory.

Amendments – SI 1991/1723.

42　General interpretation of Part I

(1)　In this Part–

'certified copy', in relation to an order of any court, means a copy certified by the prescribed officer of the court to be a true copy of the order or of the official record of the order;

'corresponding territory order', 'corresponding dependent territory provision' and similar expressions, in relation to a specified dependent territory, shall be construed in accordance with Schedule 3 to the Family Law Act 1986 (Dependent Territories) Order 1991 as from time to time in force;

'dependent territory' has the meaning given by section 43(2) of this Act;

'parental responsibilities' and 'parental rights' have the meanings respectively given by sections 1(3) and 2(4) of the Children (Scotland) Act 1995;

'part of the United Kingdom' means England and Wales, Scotland or Northern Ireland;

'prescribed' means prescribed by rules of court or act of sederunt;

'specified dependent territory' means a dependent territory for the time being specified in Schedule 1 to the said Order of 1991.

'the Council Regulation' means Council Regulation (EC) No 1347/2000 of 29th May 2000 on jurisdiction and the recognition and enforcement of judgments in matrimonial matters and in matters of parental responsibility for children of both spouses.

(2)   For the purposes of this Part proceedings in England and Wales, Northern Ireland or a specified dependent territory for divorce, nullity or judicial separation in respect of the marriage of the parents of a child shall, unless they have been dismissed, be treated as continuing until the child concerned attains the age of eighteen (whether or not a decree has been granted and whether or not, in the case of a decree of divorce or nullity of marriage, that decree has been made absolute).

(3)   For the purposes of this Part, matrimonial proceedings in a court in Scotland which has jurisdiction in those proceedings to make a Part I order with respect to a child shall, unless they have been dismissed or decree of absolvitor has been granted therein, be treated as continuing until the child concerned attains the age of sixteen.

(4)   Any reference in this Part to proceedings in respect of the marriage of the parents of a child shall, in relation to a child who, although not a child of both parties to the marriage, is a child of the family of those parties, be construed as a reference to proceedings in respect of that marriage; and for this purpose 'child of the family'–

(a)   if the proceedings are in England and Wales, means any child who has been treated by both parties as a child of their family, except a child who is placed with those parties as foster parents by a local authority or a voluntary organisation;

(b)   if the proceedings are in Scotland, means any child who has been treated by both parties as a child of their family, except a child who has been placed with those parties as foster parents by a local authority or a voluntary organisation;

(c)   if the proceedings are in Northern Ireland, means any child who has been treated by both parties as a child of their family, except a child who is placed with those parties as foster parents by an authority within the meaning of the Children (Northern Ireland) Order 1995;

(d)   if the proceedings are in a specified dependent territory, means any child who has been treated by both parties as a child of their family, except a child who has been placed with those parties as foster parents by a public authority in that territory.

(5) References in this Part to Part I orders include (except where the context otherwise requires) references to Part I orders as varied.

(6)   For the purposes of this Part each of the following orders shall be treated as varying the Part I order to which it relates–

(a)   an order which provides for a person to be allowed contact with or to be given access to a child who is the subject of a Part I order, or which makes provision for the education of such a child,

....

(7)   In this Part–

(a)   references to Part I proceedings in respect of a child are references to any proceedings for a Part I order or an order corresponding to a Part I order and include, in relation to proceedings outside the United Kingdom and any specified dependent territory, references to proceedings before a tribunal or other authority having power under the law having effect there to determine Part I matters; and

(b)   references to Part I matters are references to matters that might be determined by a Part I order or an order corresponding to a Part I order.

Amendments – Children Act 1989, s 108(5), (7), Sch 13, paras 62, 71, Sch 15; SI 1991/1723; Children (Scotland) Act 1995, s 105(4), Sch 4, para 41(1), (9); SI 1995/756; SI 2001/310; SI 2001/660.

43   Application of Part I to dependent territories

(1)   Her Majesty may by Order in Council make provision corresponding to or applying any of the foregoing provisions of this Part, with such modifications as appear to Her Majesty to be appropriate, for the purpose of regulating–

(a)   in any dependent territory;
(b)   as between any dependent territory and any part of the United Kingdom; or
(c)   as between any dependent territory and any other such territory,

the jurisdiction of courts to make Part I orders, or orders corresponding to Part I orders, and the recognition and enforcement of such orders.

(2)   In subsection (1) above 'dependent territory' means any of the following territories–

(a)   the Isle of Man,
(b)   any of the Channel Islands, and
(c)   any colony.

(3)   An Order in Council under subsection (1) above may contain such consequential, incidental and supplementary provisions as appear to Her Majesty to be necessary or expedient.

(4)   An Order in Council under subsection (1)(b) above which makes provision affecting the law of any part of the United Kingdom shall be subject to annulment in pursuance of a resolution of either House of Parliament.

Amendments – Children Act 1989, s 108, Sch 13, para 62.

FAMILY PROCEEDINGS RULES 1991, rr 6.1–6.13, 6.15–6.17, 7.7–7.15, 7.40–7.50

SI 1991/1247

PART VI
CHILD ABDUCTION AND CUSTODY

6.1 Interpretation

In this Part, unless the context otherwise requires –

(a) 'the Act' means the Child Abduction and Custody Act 1985 and words or expressions bear the same meaning as in that Act;

(b) 'the Hague Convention' means the convention defined in section 1(1) of the Act and 'the European Convention' means the convention defined in section 12(1) of the Act.

6.2 Mode of application

(1) Except as otherwise provided by this Part, every application under the Hague Convention and the European Convention shall be made by originating summons, which shall be in Form No 10 in Appendix A to the Rules of the Supreme Court 1965 and issued out of the principal registry.

(2) An application in custody proceedings for a declaration under section 23(2) of the Act shall be made by summons in those proceedings.

6.3 Contents of originating summons: general provisions

(1) The originating summons by which any application is made under the Hague Convention or the European Convention shall state –

(a) the name and date of birth of the child in respect of whom the application is made;

(b) the names of the child's parents or guardians;

(c) the whereabouts or suspected whereabouts of the child;

(d) the interest of the plaintiff in the matter and the grounds of the application; and

(e) particulars of any proceedings (including proceedings out of the jurisdiction and concluded proceedings) relating to the child,

and shall be accompanied by all relevant documents including but not limited to the documents specified in Article 8 of the Hague Convention or, as the case may be, Article 13 of the European Convention.

6.4   Contents of originating summons: particular provisions

(1)   In applications under the Hague Convention, in addition to the matters specified in rule 6.3 –

(a)   the originating summons under which an application is made for the purposes of Article 8 for the return of a child shall state the identity of the person alleged to have removed or retained the child and, if different, the identity of the person with whom the child is presumed to be;

(b)   the originating summons under which an application is made for the purposes of Article 15 for a declaration shall identify the proceedings in which the request that such a declaration be obtained was made.

(2)   In applications under the European Convention, in addition to the matters specified in rule 6.3, the originating summons shall identify the decision relating to custody or rights of access which is sought to be registered or enforced or in relation to which a declaration that it is not to be recognised is sought.

6.5   Defendants

The defendants to an application under the Act shall be –

(a)   the person alleged to have brought into the United Kingdom the child in respect of whom an application under the Hague Convention is made;

(b)   the person with whom the child is alleged to be;

(c)   any parent or guardian of the child who is within the United Kingdom and is not otherwise a party;

(d)   the person in whose favour a decision relating to custody has been made if he is not otherwise a party; and

(e)   any other person who appears to the court to have a sufficient interest in the welfare of the child.

6.6   Acknowledgement of service

The time limit for acknowledging service of an originating summons by which an application is made under the Hague Convention or the European Convention shall be seven days after service of the originating summons (including the day of service) or, in the case of a defendant referred to in rule 6.5(d) or (e), such further time as the Court may direct.

6.7   Evidence

(1)   The plaintiff, on issuing an originating summons under the Hague Convention or the European Convention, may lodge affidavit evidence in the principal registry in support of his application and serve a copy of the same on the defendant with the originating summons.

(2)   A defendant to an application under the Hague Convention or the European Convention may lodge affidavit evidence in the principal registry and serve a copy of the same on the plaintiff within seven days after service of the originating summons on him.

(3)   The plaintiff in an application under the Hague Convention or the European Convention may within seven days thereafter lodge in the principal registry a statement in reply and serve a copy thereof on the defendant.

6.8   Hearing

Any application under the Act (other than an application (a) to join a defendant, (b) to dispense with service or extend the time for acknowledging service, or (c) for the transfer of proceedings) shall be heard and determined by a judge and shall be dealt with in chambers unless the court otherwise directs.

6.9   Dispensing with service

The court may dispense with service of any summons (whether originating or ordinary) in any proceedings under the Act.

6.10   Adjournment of summons

The hearing of the originating summons under which an application under the Hague Convention or the European Convention is made may be adjourned for a period not exceeding 21 days at any one time.

6.11   Stay of proceedings

(1)   A party to proceedings under the Hague Convention shall, where he knows that an application relating to the merits of rights of custody is pending in or before a relevant authority, file in the principal registry a concise statement of the nature of the application which is pending, including the authority before which it is pending.

(2)   A party –

(a)   to pending proceedings under section 16 of the Act, or
(b)   to proceedings as a result of which a decision relating to custody has been registered under section 16 of the Act,

shall, where he knows that such an application as is specified in section 20(2) of the Act or section 42(2) of the Child Custody Act 1987 (an Act of Tynwald) is pending in or before a relevant authority, file a concise statement of the nature of the application which is pending.

(3)   The proper officer shall on receipt of such a statement as is mentioned in paragraph (1) or (2) notify the relevant authority in which or before whom the application is pending and shall subsequently notify it or him of the result of the proceedings.

(4)   On the court receiving notification under paragraph (3) above or equivalent notification from the Court of Session, the High Court in Northern Ireland or the High Court of Justice of the Isle of Man –

(a)   where the application relates to the merits of rights of custody, all further proceedings in the action shall be stayed unless and until the proceedings under the Hague Convention in the High Court, Court of Session, the High Court in Northern Ireland or the High Court of Justice of the Isle of Man, as the case may be, are dismissed, and the parties to the action shall be notified by the proper officer of the stay and of any such dismissal accordingly, and
(b)   where the application is such a one as is specified in section 20(2) of the Act, the proper officer shall notify the parties to the action.

(5)   In this rule 'relevant authority' includes the High Court, a county court, a magistrates' court, the Court of Session, a sheriff court, a children's hearing within the

meaning of Part III of the Social Work (Scotland) Act 1968, the High Court in Northern Ireland, a county court in Northern Ireland, a court of summary jurisdiction in Northern Ireland, the High Court of Justice of the Isle of Man, a court of summary jurisdiction in the Isle of Man or the Secretary of State.

Amendments – SI 1994/2890.

6.12 Transfer of proceedings

(1) At any stage in the proceedings under the Act the court may, of its own motion or on the application by summons of any party to the proceedings issued on two days' notice, order that the proceedings be transferred to the Court of Session, the High Court in Northern Ireland or the High Court of Justice of the Isle of Man.

(2) Where an order is made under paragraph (1) the proper officer shall send a copy of the order, which shall state the grounds therefor, together with the originating summons, the documents accompanying it and any evidence, to the Court of Session, the High Court in Northern Ireland or the High Court of Justice of the Isle of Man, as the case may be.

(3) Where proceedings are transferred to the Court of Session, the High Court in Northern Ireland or the High Court of Justice of the Isle of Man the costs of the whole proceedings both before and after the transfer shall be at the discretion of the Court to which the proceedings are transferred.

(4) Where proceedings are transferred to the High Court from the Court of Session, the High Court in Northern Ireland or the High Court of Justice of the Isle of Man the proper officer shall notify the parties of the transfer and the proceedings shall continue as if they had begun by originating summons under rule 6.2.

Amendments – SI 1994/2890.

6.13 Interim directions

An application for interim directions under section 5 or section 19 of the Act may where the case is one of urgency be made ex parte on affidavit but shall otherwise be made by summons.

6.14 ...

6.15 Revocation and variation of registered decisions

(1) This rule applies to decisions which have been registered under section 16 of the Act and are subsequently varied or revoked by an authority in the Contracting State in which they were made.

(2) The court shall, on cancelling the registration of a decision which has been revoked, notify –

(a) the person appearing to the court to have care of the child,
(b) the person on whose behalf the application for registration of the decision was made, and
(c) any other party to that application,

of the cancellation.

(3)   The court shall, on being notified of the variation of a decision, notify –

(a)   the person appearing to the court to have care of the child, and

(b)   any party to the application for registration of the decision

of the variation and any such person may apply by summons in the proceedings for the registration of the decision, for the purpose of making representations to the court before the registration is varied.

(4)   Any person appearing to the court to have an interest in the matter may apply by summons in the proceedings for the registration of a decision for the cancellation or variation of the registration.

6.16   Orders for disclosure of information

At any stage in proceedings under the European Convention the court may, if it has reason to believe that any person may have relevant information about the child who is the subject of those proceedings, order that person to disclose such information and may for that purpose order that the person attend before it or file affidavit evidence.

6.17   Applications and orders under sections 33 and 34 of the Family Law Act 1986

(1)   In this rule 'the 1986 Act' means the Family Law Act 1986.

(2)   An application under section 33 of the 1986 Act shall be in Form C4 and an order made under that section shall be in Form C30.

(3)   An application under section 34 of the 1986 Act shall be in Form C3 and an order made under that section shall be in Form C31.

(4)   An application under section 33 or section 34 of the 1986 Act may be made ex parte in which case the applicant shall file the application –

(a)   where the application is made by telephone, within 24 hours after the making of the application, or

(b)   in any other case at the time when the application is made,

and shall serve a copy of the application on each respondent 48 hours after the making of the order.

(5)   Where the court refuses to make an order on an ex parte application it may direct that the application be made inter partes.

Amendments – Inserted by SI 1994/3155.

PART VII
ENFORCEMENT OF ORDERS

CHAPTER 1 – GENERAL

7.7   Registration under Family Law Act 1986

(1)   In this Chapter, unless the context otherwise requires –

'the appropriate court' means, in relation to Scotland, the Court of Session and, in relation to Northern Ireland, the High Court and, in relation to a specified dependent territory, the corresponding court in that territory;

'the appropriate officer' means, in relation to the Court of Session, the Deputy Principal Clerk of Session, in relation to the High Court in Northern Ireland, the Master (Care and Protection) of that court and, in relation to the appropriate court in a specified dependent territory, the corresponding officer of that court;

'Part I order' means an order under Part I of the Act of 1986;

'registration' means registration under Part I of the Act of 1986, and 'register' and 'registered' shall be construed accordingly;

'specified dependent territory' means a dependent territory specified in column 1 of Schedule 1 to the Family Law Act 1986 (Specified Dependent Territories) Order 1991.

(2)   The prescribed officer for the purposes of sections 27(4) and 28(1) of the Act shall be the family proceedings department manager of the principal registry and the functions of the court under sections 27(3) and 28(1) of the Act of 1986 shall be performed by the proper officer.

Amendments – SI 1994/2890; SI 1997/1056.

7.8   Application to register English Part I order

(1)   An application under section 27 of the Act of 1986 for the registration of a Part I order made by the High Court shall be made by lodging in the principal registry or the district registry, as the case may be, a certified copy of the order, together with a copy of any order which has varied any of the terms of the original order and an affidavit by the applicant in support of his application, with a copy thereof.

(2)   An application under section 27 of the Act of 1986 for the registration of a Part I order made by a county court shall be made by filing in that court a certified copy of the order, together with a certified copy of any order which has varied any of the terms of the original order and an affidavit in support of the application, with a copy thereof.

(3)   The affidavit in support under paragraphs (1) and (2) above shall state –

(a)   the name and address of the applicant and his interest under the order;

(b)   the name and date of birth of the child in respect of whom the order was made, his whereabouts or suspected whereabouts and the name of any person with whom he is alleged to be;

(c)   the name and address of any other person who has an interest under the order and whether it has been served on him;

(d)   in which of the jurisdictions of Scotland, Northern Ireland or a specified dependent territory the order is to be registered;

(e)   that, to the best of the applicant's information and belief, the order is in force;

(f)   whether, and if so where, the order is already registered; and

(g)   details of any order known to the applicant which affects the child and is in force in the jurisdiction in which the Part I order is to be registered;

and there shall be exhibited to the affidavit any document relevant to the application.

(4)   Where the documents referred to in paragraphs (1) and (3), or (2) and (3), as the case may be are to be sent to the appropriate court, the proper officer shall –

(a) retain the original affidavit and send the other documents to the appropriate officer;

(b) record the fact of transmission in the records of the court; and

(c) file a copy of the documents.

(5) On receipt of notice of the registration of a Part I order in the appropriate court the proper officer shall record the fact of registration in the records of the court.

(6) If it appears to the proper officer that the Part I order is no longer in force or that the child has attained the age of 16, he shall refuse to send the documents to the appropriate court and shall within 14 days of such refusal give notice of it, and the reason for it, to the applicant.

(7) If the proper officer refuses to send the documents to the appropriate court, the applicant may apply to the judge in chambers for an order that the documents (or any of them) be sent to the appropriate court.

Amendments – SI 1994/2890.

7.9 Registration of orders made in Scotland, Northern Ireland or a specified dependent territory

On receipt of a certified copy of an order made in Scotland, Northern Ireland or a specified dependent territory for registration, the prescribed officer shall –

(a) record the order in the register by entering particulars of –
    (i) the name and address of the applicant and his interest under the order;
    (ii) the name and whereabouts or suspected whereabouts of the child, his date of birth, and the date on which he will attain the age of 16; and
    (iii) the terms of the order, its date and the court which made it;

(b) file the certified copy and accompanying documents; and

(c) give notice to the court which sent the certified copy and to the applicant for registration that the order has been registered.

Amendments – SI 1994/2890.

7.10 Revocation and variation of English order

(1) Where a Part I order which is registered in the appropriate court is revoked or varied, the proper officer of the court making the subsequent order shall –

(a) send a certified copy of that order to the appropriate officer, and to the court which made the Part I order, if that court is different from the court making the subsequent order, for filing by that court;

(b) record the fact of transmission in the records of the court; and

(c) file a copy of the order.

(2) On receipt of notice from the appropriate court of the amendment of its register, the proper officer in the court which made the Part I order and in the court which made the subsequent order shall each record the fact of amendment.

Amendments – SI 1994/2890.

7.11 Registration of revoked, recalled or varied orders made in Scotland, Northern Ireland or a specified dependent territory

(1) On receipt of a certified copy of an order made in Scotland, Northern Ireland or a specified dependent territory which revokes, recalls or varies a registered Part I order, the proper officer shall enter particulars of the revocation, recall or variation, as the case may be, in the register, and give notice of the entry to –

(a) the court which sent the certified copy,
(b) if different, the court which made the Part I order,
(c) the applicant for registration, and
(d) if different, the applicant for the revocation, recall or variation of the order.

(2) An application under section 28(2) of the Act of 1986 shall be made by summons and may be heard and determined by a district judge.

(3) If the applicant for the Part I order is not the applicant under section 28(2) of the Act of 1986 he shall be made a defendant to the application.

(4) Where the court cancels a registration of its own motion or on an application under paragraph (2), the proper officer shall amend the register accordingly and shall give notice of the amendment to the court which made the Part I order.

Amendments – SI 1994/2890.

7.12 Interim directions

(1) An application for interim directions under section 29 of the Act of 1986 may be heard and determined by a district judge.

(2) The parties to the proceedings for enforcement and, if he is not a party thereto, the applicant for the Part I order, shall be made parties to the application.

7.13 Staying and dismissal of enforcement proceedings

(1) An application under section 30(1) or 31(1) of the Act of 1986 may be heard and determined by a district judge.

(2) The parties to the proceedings for enforcement which are sought to be stayed and, if he is not a party thereto, the applicant for the Part I order shall be made parties to an application under either of the said sections.

(3) Where the court makes an order under section 30(2) or (3) or section 31(3) of the Act of 1986, the proper officer shall amend the register accordingly, and shall give notice of the amendment to the court which made the Part I order and to the applicants for registration, for enforcement and for the stay or dismissal of the proceedings for enforcement.

7.14 Particulars of other proceedings

A party to proceedings for or relating to a Part I order who knows of other proceedings (including proceedings out of the jurisdiction and concluded proceedings) which relate to the child concerned shall file an affidavit stating –

(a) in which jurisdiction and court the other proceedings were instituted;

(b)   the nature and current state of such proceedings and the relief claimed or granted;

(c)   the names of the parties to such proceedings and their relationship to the child; and

(d)   if applicable, and if known, the reasons why the relief claimed in the proceedings for or relating to the Part I order was not claimed in the other proceedings.

7.15   Inspection of register

The following persons, namely –

(a)   the applicant for registration of a registered Part I order,

(b)   any person who satisfies a district judge that he has an interest under the Part I order, and

(c)   any person who obtains the leave of a district judge,

may inspect any entry in the register relating to the order and may bespeak copies of the order and of any document relating thereto.

...

CHAPTER 4 – ENFORCEMENT OF MAINTENANCE ORDERS

7.40   Interpretation

In this chapter 'judgment' is to be construed in accordance with the definition in Article 13 of the Council Regulation.

Amendments – Inserted by SI 2001/821.

7.41   Filing of applications

Every application to the High Court under the Council Regulation, other than an application under rule 7.49 for a certified copy of a judgment, shall be filled with the principal registry.

Amendments – Inserted by SI 2001/821.

7.42   Application for registration

An application for registration of a judgment under Article 21(2) of the Council Regulation shall be made without notice being served on any other party.

Amendments – Inserted by SI 2001/821.

7.43   Evidence in support of application

(1)   An application for registration under Article 21(2) of the Council Regulation must be supported by a statement that is sworn to be true or an affidavit –

(a)   exhibiting –

    (i)   the judgment or a verified or certified or otherwise duly authenticated copy thereof together with such other document or documents as may be requisite to show that, according to the law of the Contracting State in which it has been given, the judgment is enforceable and has been served;

(ii) in the case of a judgment given in default, the original or a certified true copy of the document which establishes that the party in default was served with the document instituting the proceedings or with an equivalent document;

(iii) where it is the case, a document showing that the party making the application is in receipt of legal aid in the Contracting State in which the judgment was given;

(iv) where the judgment or document is not in the English language, a translation thereof into English certified by a notary public or a person qualified for the purpose in one of the Contracting States or authenticated by witness statement or affidavit;

(v) the certificate, in the form set out in Annex IV or Annex V of the Council Regulation, issued by the Contracting State in which judgment was given;

(b) stating –

(i) whether the judgment provides for the payment of a sum or sums of money;

(ii) whether interest is recoverable on the judgment or part thereof in accordance with the law of the State in which the judgment was given, and if such be the case, the rate of interest, the date from which interest is recoverable, and the date on which interest ceases to accrue;

(c) giving an address within the jurisdiction of the court for service of process on the party making the application and stating, so far as is known to the witness, the name and the usual or last known address or place of business of the person against whom judgment was given; and

(d) stating to the best of the information or belief of the witness –

(i) the grounds on which the right to enforce the judgment is vested in the party making the application;

(ii) as the case may require, either that at that date of the application the judgment has not been satisfied, or the part or amount in respect of which it remains unsatisfied.

(2) Where the party making the application does not produce the documents referred to in paragraphs (1)(a)(ii) and (iii) of this rule, the court may –

(a) fix a time within which the documents are to be produced;

(b) accept equivalent documents; or

(c) dispense with production of the documents.

Amendments – Inserted by SI 2001/821.

7.44 Order for registration

(1) An order giving permission to register a judgment under Article 21(2) of the Council Regulation must be drawn up by the court.

(2) Every such order shall state the period within which an appeal may be made against the order for registration and shall contain a notification that the court will not enforce the judgment until after the expiration of that period.

(3) The notification referred to in paragraph (2) shall not prevent any application for protective measures under Article 12 of the Council Regulation pending final determination of any issue relating to enforcement of the judgment.

Amendments – Inserted by SI 2001/821.

7.45   Register of judgments

There shall be kept in the principal registry by the proper officer a register of the judgments ordered to be registered under Article 21(2) of the Council Regulation.

Amendments – Inserted by SI 2001/821.

7.46   Notice of registration

(1)   Notice of the registration of a judgment under Article 21(2) of the Council Regulation must be served on the person against whom judgment was given by delivering it to him personally or by sending it to him at his usual or last known address or place of business or in such other manner as the court may direct.

(2)   Permission is not required to serve such a notice out of the jurisdiction and rule 10.6 shall apply in relation to such a notice.

(3)   The notice of the registration must state –

(a)   full particulars of the judgment registered and the order for registration;
(b)   the name of the party making the application and his address for service within the jurisdiction;
(c)   the right of the person against whom judgment was given to appeal against the order for registration; and
(d)   the period within which an appeal against the order for registration may be made.

Amendments – Inserted by SI 2001/821.

7.47   Enforcement of judgment

(1)   A judgment registered under Article 21(2) of the Council Regulation shall not be enforced until after the expiration of the period specified in accordance with rule 7.44(2) or, if that period has been extended by the Court, until after the expiration of the period so extended.

(2)   Any party wishing to apply for the enforcement of a judgment registered under Article 21(2) of the Council Regulation must produce to the proper officer a witness statement or affidavit of service of the notice of registration of the judgment and of any order made by the court in relation to the judgment.

(3)   Nothing in this rule shall prevent the court from granting protective measures under Article 12 of the Council Regulation pending final determination of any issue relating to enforcement of the judgment.

Amendments – Inserted by SI 2001/821.

7.48   Application for recognition

(1)   Registration of the judgment under these rules shall serve for the purposes of Article 14(3) of the Council Regulation as a decision that the judgment is recognised.

(2)   Where it is sought to apply for recognition of a judgment, the rules of this chapter shall apply to such application as they apply to an application for registration under Article 21(2) of the Council Regulation, with the exception that the applicant shall not be required to produce –

(a)   a document or documents which establish that according to the law of the Contracting State in which it has been given the judgment is enforceable and has been served, or

(b)   the document referred to in rule 7.43(1)(a)(iii).

Amendments – Inserted by SI 2001/821.

7.49   Enforcement of judgments in other Contracting States

(1)   Subject to rules 10.16(2) and 10.20, an application for a certified copy of a judgment referred to in Article 32(1) of the Council Regulation must be made to the court which made the order on a witness statement or affidavit without notice being served on any other party.

(2)   A witness statement or affidavit by which such an application is made must –

(a)   give particulars of the proceedings in which the judgment was obtained;

(b)   have annexed to it a copy of the petition or application by which the proceedings were begun, the evidence of service thereof on the respondent, copies of the pleadings and particulars, if any, and a statement of the grounds on which the judgment was based together, where appropriate, with any document showing that the applicant is entitled to legal aid or assistance by way of representation for the purposes of the proceedings;

(c)   state whether the respondent did or did not object to the jurisdiction, and, if so, on what grounds;

(d)   show that the judgment has been served in accordance with rules 4.8, 10.2, 10.3, 10.4, 10.5, 10.6, 10.16 or 10.17 and is not subject to any order for the stay of proceedings;

(e)   state that the time for appealing has expired, or, as the case may be, the date on which it will expire and in either case whether notice of appeal against the judgment has been given; and

(f)   state –

(i)   whether the judgment provides for the payment of a sum of money;

(ii)   whether interest is recoverable on the judgment or part thereof and if so, the rate of interest, the date from which interest is recoverable, and the date on which interest ceases to accrue.

(3)   The certified copy of the judgment shall be an office copy sealed with the seal of the court and signed by the district judge and there shall be issued with the copy of the judgment a certified copy of any order which has varied any of the terms of the original order.

Amendments – Inserted by SI 2001/821.

7.50   Authentic instruments and court settlements

Rules 7.40 to 7.49 (except rule 7.43(1)(a)(ii)) shall apply to an authentic instrument and a settlement to which Article 13(3) of the Council Regulation applies, as they apply to a judgment subject to any necessary modifications.

Amendments – Inserted by SI 2001/821.

HAGUE CONVENTION ON THE CIVIL ASPECTS OF INTERNATIONAL CHILD ABDUCTION

(Concluded at The Hague, 25 October 1980)

The States signatory to the present Convention,

Firmly convinced that the interests of children are of paramount importance in matters relating to their custody;

Desiring to protect children internationally from the harmful effects of their wrongful removal or retention and to establish procedures to ensure their prompt return to the State of their habitual residence, as well as to secure protection for rights of access;

Have resolved to conclude a Convention to this effect, and have agreed upon the following provisions:

CHAPTER I – SCOPE OF THE CONVENTION

Article 1

The objects of the present Convention are:

(a) to secure the prompt return of children wrongfully removed to or retained in any Contracting State; and
(b) to ensure that rights of custody and of access under the law of one Contracting State are effectively respected in the other Contracting States.

Article 2

Contracting States shall take all appropriate measures to secure within their territories the implementation of the objects of the Convention. For this purpose they shall use the most expeditious procedures available.

Article 3

The removal or the retention of a child is to be considered wrongful where:

(a) it is in breach of rights of custody attributed to a person, an institution or any other body, either jointly or alone, under the law of the State in which the child was habitually resident immediately before the removal or retention; and
(b) at the time of removal or retention those rights were actually exercised, either jointly or alone, or would have been so exercised but for the removal or retention.

The rights of custody mentioned in sub-para (a) above, may arise in particular by operation of law or by reason of a judicial or administrative decision, or by reason of an agreement having legal effect under the law of that State.

Article 4

The Convention shall apply to any child who was habitually resident in a Contracting State immediately before any breach of custody or access rights. The Convention shall cease to apply when the child attains the age of 16 years.

Article 5

For the purposes of this Convention:

(a)   'rights of custody' shall include rights relating to the care of the person of the child and, in particular, the right to determine the child's place of residence;

(b)   'rights of access' shall include the right to take a child for a limited period of time to a place other than the child's habitual residence.

CHAPTER II – CENTRAL AUTHORITIES

Article 6

A Contracting State shall designate a Central Authority to discharge the duties which are imposed by the Convention upon such authorities.

Federal States, States with more than one system of law or States having autonomous territorial organizations shall be free to appoint more than one Central Authority and to specify the territorial extent of their powers. Where a State has appointed more than one Central Authority, it shall designate the Central Authority to which applications may be addressed for transmission to the appropriate Central Authority within that State.

Article 7

Central Authorities shall co-operate with each other and promote co-operation amongst the competent authorities in their respective State to secure the prompt return of children and to achieve the other objects of this Convention.

In particular, either directly or through any intermediary, they shall take all appropriate measures:

(a)   to discover the whereabouts of a child who has been wrongfully removed or retained;

(b)   to prevent further harm to the child or prejudice to interested parties by taking or causing to be taken provisional measures;

(c)   to secure the voluntary return of the child or to bring about an amicable resolution of the issues;

(d)   to exchange, where desirable, information relating to the social background of the child;

(e)   to provide information of a general character as to the law of their State in connection with the application of the Convention;

(f)   to initiate or facilitate the institution of judicial or administrative proceedings with a view to obtaining the return of the child and, in a proper case, to make arrangements for organizing or securing the effective exercise of rights of access;

(g)   where the circumstances so require, to provide or facilitate the provision of legal aid and advice, including the participation of legal counsel and advisers;

(h)   to provide such administrative arrangements as may be necessary and appropriate to secure the safe return of the child;

(i)   to keep each other informed with respect to the operation of this Convention and, as far as possible, to eliminate any obstacles to its application.

CHAPTER III – RETURN OF CHILDREN

Article 8

Any person, institution or other body claiming that a child has been removed or retained in breach of custody rights may apply either to the Central Authority of the child's habitual residence or to the Central Authority of any other Contracting State for assistance in securing the return of the child.

The application shall contain:

(a) information concerning the identity of the applicant, of the child and of the person alleged to have removed or retained the child;

(b) where available, the date of birth of the child;

(c) the grounds on which the applicant's claim for return of the child is based;

(d) all available information relating to the whereabouts of the child and the identity of the person with whom the child is presumed to be.

The application may be accompanied or supplemented by:

(e) an authenticated copy of any relevant decision or agreement;

(f) a certificate or an affidavit emanating from a Central Authority, or other competent authority of the State of the child's habitual residence, or from a qualified person, concerning the relevant law of that State;

(g) any other relevant document.

Article 9

If the Central Authority which receives an application referred to in Art 8 has reason to believe that the child is in another Contracting State, it shall directly and without delay transmit the application to the Central Authority of that Contracting State and inform the requesting Central Authority, or the applicant, as the case may be.

Article 10

The Central Authority of the State where the child is shall take or cause to be taken all appropriate measures in order to obtain the voluntary return of the child.

Article 11

The judicial or administrative authorities of Contracting States shall act expeditiously in proceedings for the return of children.

If the judicial or administrative authority concerned has not reached a decision within six weeks from the date of commencement of the proceedings, the applicant or the Central Authority of the requested State, on its own initiative or if asked by the Central Authority of the requesting State, shall have the right to request a statement of the reasons for the delay. If a reply is received by the Central Authority of the requested State, that Authority shall transmit the reply to the Central Authority of the requesting State, or to the applicant, as the case may be.

Article 12

Where a child has been wrongfully removed or retained in terms of Art 3 and, at the date of the commencement of the proceedings before the judicial or administrative authority of the Contracting State where the child is, a period of less than one year has elapsed from the date of the wrongful removal or retention, the authority concerned shall order the return of the child forthwith.

The judicial or administrative authority, even where the proceedings have been commenced after the expiration of the period of one year referred to in the preceding paragraph, shall also order the return of the child, unless it is demonstrated that the child is now settled in its new environment.

Where the judicial or administrative authority in the requested State has reason to believe that the child has been taken to another State, it may stay the proceedings or dismiss the application for the return of the child.

Article 13

Notwithstanding the provisions of the preceding Article, the judicial or administrative authority of the requested State is not bound to order the return of the child if the person, institution or other body which opposes its return establishes that:

(a) the person, institution or other body having the care of the person of the child was not actually exercising the custody rights at the time of removal or retention, or had consented to or subsequently acquiesced in the removal or retention; or

(b) there is a grave risk that his or her return would expose the child to physical or psychological harm or otherwise place the child in an intolerable situation.

The judicial or administrative authority may also refuse to order the return of the child if it finds that the child objects to being returned and has attained an age and degree of maturity at which it is appropriate to take account of its views.

In considering the circumstances referred to in this Article, the judicial and administrative authorities shall take into account the information relating to the social background of the child provided by the Central Authority or other competent authority of the child's habitual residence.

Article 14

In ascertaining whether there has been a wrongful removal or retention within the meaning of Art 3, the judicial or administrative authorities of the requested State may take notice directly of the law of, and of judicial or administrative decisions, formally recognized or not in the State of the habitual residence of the child, without recourse to the specific procedures for the proof of that law or for the recognition of foreign decisions which would otherwise be applicable.

Article 15

The judicial or administrative authorities of a Contracting State may, prior to the making of an order for the return of the child, request that the applicant obtain from the authorities of the State of the habitual residence of the child a decision or other determination that the removal or retention was wrongful within the meaning of Art 3 of the Convention, where such a decision or determination may be obtained in that State. The Central Authorities of the Contracting States shall so far as practicable assist applicants to obtain such a decision or determination.

Article 16

After receiving notice of a wrongful removal or retention of a child in the sense of Art 3, the judicial or administrative authorities of the Contracting State to which the child has been removed or in which it has been retained shall not decide on the merits of rights of custody until it has been determined that the child is not to be returned under this Convention or unless an application under this Convention is not lodged within a reasonable time following receipt of the notice.

Article 17

The sole fact that a decision relating to custody has been given in or is entitled to recognition in the requested State shall not be a ground for refusing to return a child under this Convention, but the judicial or administrative authorities of the requested State may take account of the reasons for that decision in applying this Convention.

Article 18

The provisions of this Chapter do not limit the power of a judicial or administrative authority to order the return of the child at any time.

Article 19

A decision under this Convention concerning the return of the child shall not be taken to be a determination on the merits of any custody issue.

Article 20

The return of the child under the provisions of Art 12 may be refused if this would not be permitted by the fundamental principles of the requested State relating to the protection of human rights and fundamental freedoms.

CHAPTER IV – RIGHTS OF ACCESS

Article 21

An application to make arrangements for organizing or securing the effective exercise of rights of access may be presented to the Central Authorities of the Contracting States in the same way as an application for the return of a child.

The Central Authorities are bound by the obligations of co-operation which are set forth in Art 7 to promote the peaceful enjoyment of access rights and the fulfilment of any conditions to which the exercise of those rights may be subject. The Central Authorities shall take steps to remove, as far as possible, all obstacles to the exercise of such rights.

The Central Authorities, either directly or through intermediaries, may initiate or assist in the institution of proceedings with a view to organizing or protecting these rights and securing respect for the conditions to which the exercise of these rights may be subject.

CHAPTER V – GENERAL PROVISIONS

Article 22

No security, bond or deposit, however described, shall be required to guarantee the payment of costs and expenses in the judicial or administrative proceedings falling within the scope of this Convention.

Article 23

No legalization or similar formality may be required in the context of this Convention.

Article 24

Any application, communication or other document sent to the Central Authority of the requested State shall be in the original language, and shall be accompanied by a translation into the official language or one of the official languages of the requested State or, where that is not feasible, a translation into French or English.

However, a Contracting State may, by making a reservation in accordance with Art 42, object to the use of either French or English, but not both, in any application, communication or other document sent to its Central Authority.

Article 25

Nationals of the Contracting States and persons who are habitually resident within those States shall be entitled in matters concerned with the application of this Convention to legal aid and advice in any other Contracting State on the same conditions as if they themselves were nationals of and habitually resident in that State.

Article 26

Each Central Authority shall bear its own costs in applying this Convention.

Central Authorities and other public services of Contracting States shall not impose any charges in relation to applications submitted under this Convention. In particular, they may not require any payment from the applicant towards the costs and expenses of the proceedings or, where applicable, those arising from the participation of legal counsel or advisers. However, they may require the payment of the expenses incurred or to be incurred in implementing the return of the child.

However, a Contracting State may, by making a reservation in accordance with Art 42, declare that it shall not be bound to assume any costs referred to in the preceding paragraph resulting from the participation of legal counsel or advisers or from court proceedings, except insofar as those costs may be covered by its system of legal aid and advice.

Upon ordering the return of a child or issuing an order concerning rights of access under this Convention, the judicial or administrative authorities may, where appropriate, direct the person who removed or retained the child, or who prevented the exercise of rights of access, to pay necessary expenses incurred by or on behalf of the applicant, including travel expenses, any costs incurred or payments made for locating the child, the costs of legal representation of the applicant, and those of returning the child.

Article 27

When it is manifest that the requirements of this Convention are not fulfilled or that the application is otherwise not well founded, a Central Authority is not bound to accept the application. In that case, the Central Authority shall forthwith inform the applicant or the Central Authority through which the application was submitted, as the case may be, of its reasons.

Article 28

A Central Authority may require that the application be accompanied by a written authorization empowering it to act on behalf of the applicant, or to designate a representative so to act.

Article 29

This Convention shall not preclude any person, institution or body who claims that there has been a breach of custody or access rights within the meaning of Art 3 or 21 from applying directly to the judicial or administrative authorities of a Contracting State, whether or not under the provisions of this Convention.

Article 30

Any application submitted to the Central Authorities or directly to the judicial or administrative authorities of a Contracting State in accordance with the terms of this Convention, together with documents and any other information appended thereto or provided by a Central Authority, shall be admissible in the courts or administrative authorities of the Contracting States.

Article 31

In relation to a State which in matters of custody of children has two or more systems of law applicable in different territorial units:

(a) any reference to habitual residence in that State shall be construed as referring to habitual residence in a territorial unit of that State;
(b) any reference to the law of the State of habitual residence shall be construed as referring to the law of the territorial unit in that State where the child habitually resides.

Article 32

In relation to a State which in matters of custody of children has two or more systems of law applicable to different categories of persons, any reference to the law of that State shall be construed as referring to the legal system specified by the law of that State.

Article 33

A State within which different territorial units have their own rules of law in respect of custody of children shall not be bound to apply this Convention where a State with a unified system of law would not be bound to do so.

Article 34

This Convention shall take priority in matters within its scope over the Convention of 5 October 1961 concerning the powers of authorities and the law applicable in respect of the protection of minors, as between parties to both Conventions. Otherwise the present Convention shall not restrict the application of an international instrument in force between the State of origin and the State addressed or other law of the State addressed for the purposes of obtaining the return of a child who has been wrongfully removed or retained or of organizing access rights.

Article 35

This Convention shall apply as between Contracting States only to wrongful removals or retentions occurring after its entry into force in those States.

Where a declaration has been made under Arts 39 or 40, the reference in the preceding paragraph to a Contracting State shall be taken to refer to the territorial unit or units in relation to which this Convention applies.

Article 36

Nothing in this Convention shall prevent two or more Contracting States, in order to limit the restrictions to which the return of the child may be subject, from agreeing among themselves to derogate from any provisions of this Convention which may imply such a restriction.

CHAPTER VI – FINAL CLAUSES

Article 37

The Convention shall be open for signature by the States which were Members of the Hague Conference on Private International Law at the time of its Fourteenth Session. It shall be ratified, accepted or approved and the instruments of ratification, acceptance or approval shall be deposited with the Ministry of Foreign Affairs of the Kingdom of the Netherlands.

Article 38

Any other State may accede to the Convention.

The instrument of accession shall be deposited with the Ministry of Foreign Affairs of the Kingdom of the Netherlands.

The Convention shall enter into force for a State acceding to it on the first day of the third calendar month after the deposit of its instrument of accession.

The accession will have effect only as regards the relations between the acceding State and such Contracting States as will have declared their acceptance of the accession. Such a declaration will also have to be made by any Member State ratifying, accepting or approving the Convention after an accession. Such declaration shall be deposited at the Ministry of Foreign Affairs of the Kingdom of the Netherlands; this Ministry shall forward, through diplomatic channels, a certified copy to each of the Contracting States.

The Convention will enter into force as between the acceding State and the State that has declared its acceptance of the accession on the first day of the third calendar month after the deposit of the declaration of acceptance.

Article 39

Any State may, at the time of signature, ratification, acceptance, approval or accession, declare that the Convention shall extend to all the territories for the international relations of which it is responsible, or to one or more of them. Such a declaration shall take effect at the time the Convention enters into force for that State.

Such declaration, as well as any subsequent extension, shall be notified to the Ministry of Foreign Affairs of the Kingdom of the Netherlands.

Article 40

If a Contracting State has two or more territorial units in which different systems of law are applicable in relation to matters dealt with in this Convention, it may at the time of signature, ratification, acceptance, approval or accession declare that this Convention shall extend to all its territorial units or only to one or more of them and may modify this declaration by submitting another declaration at any time.

Any such declaration shall be notified to the Ministry of Foreign Affairs of the Kingdom of the Netherlands and shall state expressly the territorial units to which the Convention applies.

Article 41

Where a Contracting State has a system of government under which executive, judicial and legislative powers are distributed between central and other authorities within that State, its signature or ratification, acceptance or approval of, or accession to this

Convention, or its making of any declaration in terms of Art 40 shall carry no implication as to the internal distribution of powers within that State.

Article 42

Any State may, not later than the time of ratification, acceptance, approval or accession, or at the time of making a declaration in terms of Art 39 or 40, make one or both of the reservations provided for in Art 24 and Art 26, third paragraph. No other reservation shall be permitted.

Any State may at any time withdraw a reservation it has made. The withdrawal shall be notified to the Ministry of Foreign Affairs of the Kingdom of the Netherlands.

The reservation shall cease to have effect on the first day of the third calendar month after the notification referred to in the preceding paragraph.

Article 43

The Convention shall enter into force on the first day of the third calendar month after the deposit of the third instrument of ratification, acceptance, approval or accession referred to in Arts 37 and 38.

Thereafter the Convention shall enter into force:

(1) for each State ratifying, accepting, approving or acceding to it subsequently, on the first day of the third calendar month after the deposit of its instrument of ratification, acceptance, approval or accession;
(2) for any territory or territorial unit to which the Convention has been extended in conformity with Art 39 or 40, on the first day of the third calendar month after the notification referred to in that Article.

Article 44

The Convention shall remain in force for five years from the date of its entry into force in accordance with the first paragraph of Art 43 even for States which subsequently have ratified, accepted, approved it or acceded to it.

If there has been no denunciation, it shall be renewed tacitly every five years.

Any denunciation shall be notified to the Ministry of Foreign Affairs of the Kingdom of the Netherlands at least six months before the expiry of the five year period. It may be limited to certain of the territories or territorial units to which the Convention applies.

The denunciation shall have effect only as regards the State which has notified it. The Convention shall remain in force for the other Contracting States.

Article 45

The Ministry of Foreign Affairs of the Kingdom of the Netherlands shall notify the States Members of the Conference, and the States which have acceded in accordance with Art 38, of the following:

(1) the signatures and ratifications, acceptances and approvals referred to in Art 37;
(2) the accessions referred to in Art 38;
(3) the date on which the Convention enters into force in accordance with Art 43;
(4) the extensions referred to in Art 39;
(5) the declarations referred to in Arts 38 and 40;
(6) the reservations referred to in Art 24 and Art 26, third paragraph, and the withdrawals referred to in Art 42;

(7) the denunciations referred to in Art 44.

In witness whereof the undersigned, being duly authorised thereto, have signed this Convention.

Done at The Hague, on the 25th day of October, 1980, in the English and French languages, both texts being equally authentic, in a single copy which shall be deposited in the archives of the Government of the Kingdom of the Netherlands, and of which a certified copy shall be sent, through diplomatic channels, to each of the States Members of the Hague Conference on Private International Law at the date of its Fourteenth Session.

COUNCIL REGULATION (EC) NO 1347/2000 OF 29 MAY 2000 ON JURISDICTION AND THE RECOGNITION AND ENFORCEMENT OF JUDGMENTS IN MATRIMONIAL MATTERS AND IN MATTERS OF PARENTAL RESPONSIBILITY FOR CHILDREN OF BOTH SPOUSES

THE COUNCIL OF THE EUROPEAN UNION,

Having regard to the Treaty establishing the European Community, and in particular Article 61(c) and Article 67(1) thereof,

Having regard to the proposal from the Commission,

Having regard to the opinion of the European Parliament,

Having regard to the opinion of the Economic and Social Committee,

Whereas:

(1) The Member States have set themselves the objective of maintaining and developing the Union as an area of freedom, security and justice, in which the free movement of persons is assured. To establish such an area, the Community is to adopt, among others, the measures relating to judicial co-operation in civil matters needed for the proper functioning of the internal market.

(2) The proper functioning of the internal market entails the need to improve and and simplify the free movement of judgments in civil matters.

(3) This is a subject now falling within the ambit of Article 65 of the Treaty.

(4) Differences between certain national rules governing jurisdiction and enforcement hamper the free movement of persons and the sound operation of the internal market. There are accordingly grounds for enacting provisions to unify the rules of conflict of jurisdiction in matrimonial matters and in matters of parental responsibility so as to simplify the formalities for rapid and automatic recognition and enforcement of judgments.

(5) In accordance with the principles of subsidiarity and proportionality as set out in Article 5 of the Treaty, the objectives of this Regulation cannot be sufficiently achieved by the Member States and can therefore be better achieved by the Community. This Regulation does not go beyond what is necessary to achieve those objectives.

(6) The Council, by an Act dated 26 May 1997, drew up a Convention on jurisdiction and the recognition and enforcement of judgments in matrimonial matters and recommended it for adoption by the Member States in accordance with their respective constitutional rules. Continuity in the results of the negotiations for conclusion of the Convention should be ensured. The content of this Regulation is substantially taken over from the Convention, but this Regulation contains a number of new provisions not in the Convention in order to secure consistency with certain provisions of the proposed regulation on

jurisdiction and the recognition and enforcement of judgments in civil and commercial matters.

(7)   In order to attain the objective of free movement of judgments in matrimonial matters and in matters of parental responsibility within the Community, it is necessary and appropriate that the cross-border recognition of jurisdiction and judgments in relation to the dissolution of matrimonial ties and to parental responsibility for the children of both spouses be governed by a mandatory, and directly applicable, Community legal instrument.

(8)   The measures laid down in this Regulation should be consistent and uniform, to enable people to move as widely as possible. Accordingly, it should also apply to nationals of non-member States whose links with the territory of a Member State are sufficiently close, in keeping with the grounds of jurisdiction laid down in the Regulation.

(9)   The scope of this Regulation should cover civil proceedings and non-judicial proceedings in matrimonial matters in certain States, and exclude purely religious procedures. It should therefore be provided that the reference to 'courts' includes all the authorities, judicial or otherwise, with jurisdiction in matrimonial matters.

(10) This Regulation should be confined to proceedings relating to divorce, legal separation or marriage annulment. The recognition of divorce and annulment rulings affects only the dissolution of matrimonial ties; despite the fact that they may be interrelated, the Regulation does not affect issues such as the fault of the spouses, property consequences of the marriage, the maintenance obligation or any other ancillary measures.

(11) This Regulation covers parental responsibility for children of both spouses on issues that are closely linked to proceedings for divorce, legal separation or marriage annulment.

(12) The grounds of jurisdiction accepted in this Regulation are based on the rule that there must be a real link between the party concerned and the Member State exercising jurisdiction; the decision to include certain grounds corresponds to the fact that they exist in different national legal systems and are accepted by the other Member States.

(13) One of the risks to be considered in relation to the protection of the children of both spouses in a marital crisis is that one of the parents will take the child to another country. The fundamental interests of the children must therefore be protected, in accordance with, in particular, the Hague Convention of 25 October 1980 on the Civil Aspects of the International Abduction of Children. The lawful habitual residence is accordingly maintained as the grounds of jurisdiction in cases where, because the child has been moved or has not been returned without lawful reason, there has been a de facto change in the habitual residence.

(14) This Regulation does not prevent the courts of a Member State from taking provisional, including protective, measures, in urgent cases, with regard to persons or property situated in that State.

(15) The word 'judgment' refers only to decisions that lead to divorce, legal separation or marriage annulment. Those documents which have been formally drawn up or registered as authentic instruments and are enforceable in one Member State are treated as equivalent to such 'judgments'.

(16) The recognition and enforcement of judgments given in a Member State are based on the principle of mutual trust. The grounds for non-recognition are kept to the minimum required. Those proceedings should incorporate provisions to ensure observance of public policy in the State addressed and to safeguard the

rights of the defence and those of the parties, including the individual rights of any child involved, and so as to withhold recognition of irreconcilable judgments.

(17) The State addressed should review neither the jurisdiction of the State of origin nor the findings of fact.

(18) No procedures may be required for the updating of civil-status documents in one Member State on the basis of a final judgment given in another Member State.

(19) The Convention concluded by the Nordic States in 1931 should be capable of application within the limits set by this Regulation.

(20) Spain, Italy and Portugal had concluded Concordats before the matters covered by this Regulation were brought within the ambit of the Treaty: it is necessary to ensure that these States do not breach their international commitments in relation to the Holy See.

(21) The Member States should remain free to agree among themselves on practical measures for the application of the Regulation as long as no Community measures have been taken to that end.

(22) Annexes I to III relating to the courts and redress procedures should be amended by the Commission on the basis of amendments transmitted by the Member State concerned. Amendments to Annexes IV and V should be adopted in accordance with Council Decision 1999/468/EC of 28 June 1999 laying down the procedures for the exercise of implementing powers conferred on the Commission.

(23) No later than five years after the date of the entry into force of this Regulation, the Commission is to review its application and propose such amendments as may appear necessary.

(24) The United Kingdom and Ireland, in accordance with Article 3 of the Protocol on the position of the United Kingdom and Ireland annexed to the Treaty on European Union and the Treaty establishing the European Community, have given notice of their wish to take part in the adoption and application of this Regulation.

(25) Denmark, in accordance with Articles 1 and 2 of the Protocol on the position of Denmark annexed to the Treaty on European Union and the Treaty establishing the European Community, is not participating in the adoption of this Regulation, and is therefore not bound by it nor subject to its application,

HAS ADOPTED THIS REGULATION:

CHAPTER I – SCOPE

Article 1

1   This Regulation shall apply to:

(a)   civil proceedings relating to divorce, legal separation or marriage annulment;

(b)   civil proceedings relating to parental responsibility for the children of both spouses on the occasion of the matrimonial proceedings referred to in (a).

2   Other proceedings officially recognised in a Member State shall be regarded as equivalent to judicial proceedings. The term 'court' shall cover all the authorities with jurisdiction in these matters in the Member States.

3   In this Regulation, the term 'Member State' shall mean all Member States with the exception of Denmark.

CHAPTER II – JURISDICTION

SECTION 1

GENERAL PROVISIONS

Article 2   Divorce, legal separation and marriage annulment

1   In matters relating to divorce, legal separation or marriage annulment, jurisdiction shall lie with the courts of the Member State:

(a)   in whose territory:
   -   the spouses are habitually resident, or
   -   the spouses were last habitually resident, insofar as one of them still resides there, or
   -   the respondent is habitually resident, or
   -   in the event of a joint application, either of the spouses is habitually resident, or
   -   the applicant is habitually resident if he or she resided there for at least a year immediately before the application was made, or
   -   the applicant is habitually resident if he or she resided there for at least six months immediately before the application was made and is either a national of the Member State in question or, in the case of the United Kingdom and Ireland, has his 'domicile' there:
(b)   of the nationality of both spouses or, in the case of the United Kingdom and Ireland, of the 'domicile' of both spouses.

2   For the purpose of this Regulation, 'domicile' shall have the same meaning as it has under the legal systems of the United Kingdom and Ireland.

Article 3   Parental responsibility

1   The Courts of a Member State exercising jurisdiction by virtue of Article 2 on an application for divorce, legal separation or marriage annulment shall have jurisdiction in a matter relating to parental responsibility over a child of both spouses where the child is habitually resident in that Member State.

2   Where the child is not habitually resident in the Member State referred to in paragraph 1, the courts of that State shall have jurisdiction in such a matter if the child is habitually resident in one of the Member States and:

(a)   at least one of the spouses has parental responsibility in relation to the child; and
(b)   the jurisdiction of the courts has been accepted by the spouses and is in the best interests of the child.

3   The jurisdiction conferred by paragraphs 1 and 2 shall cease as soon as:

(a)   the judgment allowing or refusing the application for divorce, legal separation or marriage annulment has become final; or
(b)   in those cases where proceedings in relation to parental responsibility are still pending on the date referred to in (a), a judgment in these proceedings has become final; or

(c) the proceedings referred to in (a) and (b) have come to an end for another reason.

Article 4   Child abduction

The courts with jurisdiction within the meaning of Article 3 shall exercise their jurisdiction in conformity with the Hague Convention of 25 October 1980 on the Civil Aspects of International Child Abduction, and in particular Articles 3 and 16 thereof.

Article 5   Counterclaim

The court in which proceedings are pending on the basis of Articles 2 to 4 shall also have jurisdiction to examine a counterclaim, insofar as the latter comes within the scope of this Regulation.

Article 6   Conversion of legal separation into divorce

Without prejudice to Article 2, a court of a Member State which has given a judgment on a legal separation shall also have jurisdiction for converting that judgment into a divorce, if the law of that Member State so provides.

Article 7   Exclusive nature of jurisdiction under Articles 2 to 6

A spouse who:

(a) is habitually resident in the territory of a Member State; or
(b) is a national of a Member State, or, in the case of the United Kingdom and Ireland, has his or her 'domicile' in the territory of one of the latter Member States,

may be sued in another Member State only in accordance with Articles 2 to 6.

Article 8   Residual jurisdiction

1 Where no court of a Member State has jurisdiction pursuant to Articles 2 to 6, jurisdiction shall be determined, in each Member State, by the laws of that State.

2 As against a respondent who is not habitually resident and is not either a national of a Member State or, in the case of the United Kingdom and Ireland, does not have his 'domicile' within the territory of one of the latter Member States, any national of a Member State who is habitually resident within the territory of another Member State may, like the nationals of that State, avail himself of the rules of jurisdiction applicable in that State.

SECTION 2

EXAMINATION AS TO JURISDICTION AND ADMISSIBILITY

Article 9   Examination as to jurisdiction

Where a court of a Member State is seised of a case over which it has no jurisdiction under this Regulation and over which a court of another Member State has jurisdiction by virtue of this Regulation, it shall declare of its own motion that it has no jurisdiction.

Article 10   Examination as to admissibility

1 Where a respondent habitually resident in a State other than the Member State where the action was brought does not enter an appearance, the court with jurisdiction shall stay the proceedings so long as it is not shown that the respondent has been able to receive the document instituting the proceedings or an equivalent

document in sufficient time to enable him to arrange for his defence, or that all necessary steps have been taken to this end.

2   Article 19 of Council Regulation (EC) No 1348/2000 of 29 May 2000 on the service in the Member States of judicial and extra-judicial documents in civil or commercial matters, shall apply instead of the provisions of paragraph 1 of this Article if the document instituting the proceedings or an equivalent document had to be transmitted from one Member State to another pursuant to that Regulation.

3   Where the provisions of Council Regulation (EC) No 1348/2000 are not applicable, Article 15 of the Hague Convention of 15 November 1965 on the service abroad of judicial and extra-judicial documents in civil or commercial matters shall apply if the document instituting the proceedings or an equivalent document had to be transmitted abroad pursuant to that Convention.

SECTION 3

LIS PENDENS AND DEPENDENT ACTIONS

Article 11   Costs of service

1   Where proceedings involving the same cause of action and between the same parties are brought before courts of different Member States, the court second seised shall of its own motion stay its proceedings until such time as the jurisdiction of the court first seised is established.

2   Where proceedings for divorce, legal separation or marriage annulment not involving the same cause of action and between the same parties are brought before courts of different Member States, the court second seised shall of its own motion stay its proceedings until such time as the jurisdiction of the court first seised is established.

3   Where the jurisdiction of the court first seised is established, the court second seised shall decline jurisdiction in favour of that court.

In that case, the party who brought the relevant action before the court second seised may bring that action before the court first seised.

4   For the purposes of this Article, a court shall be deemed to be seised:

(a)   at the time when the document instituting the proceedings or an equivalent document is lodged with the court, provided that the applicant has not subsequently failed to take the steps he was required to take to have service effected on the respondent; or

(b)   if the document has to be served before being lodged with the court, at the time when it is received by the authority responsible for service, provided that the applicant has not subsequently failed to take the steps he was required to take to have the document lodged with the court.

SECTION 4

PROVISIONAL, INCLUDING PROTECTIVE, MEASURES

Article 12

In urgent cases, the provisions of this Regulation shall not prevent the courts of a Member State from taking such provisional, including protective, measures in respect of persons or assets in that State as may be available under the law of that Member State, even if, under this Regulation, the court of another Member State has jurisdiction as to the substance of the matter.

CHAPTER III – RECOGNITION AND ENFORCEMENT

Article 13   Meaning of 'judgment'

1   For the purposes of this Regulation, 'judgment' means a divorce, legal separation or marriage annulment pronounced by a court of a Member State, as well as a judgment relating to the parental responsibility of the spouses given on the occasion of such matrimonial proceedings, whatever the judgment may be called, including a decree, order or decision.

2   The provisions of this chapter shall also apply to the determination of the amount of costs and expenses of proceedings under this Regulation and to the enforcement of any order concerning such costs and expenses.

3   For the purposes of implementing this Regulation, documents which have been formally drawn up or registered as authentic instruments and are enforceable in one Member State and also settlements which have been approved by a court in the course of proceedings and are enforceable in the Member State in which they were concluded shall be recognised and declared enforceable under the same conditions as the judgments referred to in paragraph 1.

SECTION 1

RECOGNITION

Article 14   Recognition of a judgment

1   A judgment given in a Member State shall be recognised in the other Member States without any special procedure being required.

2   In particular, and without prejudice to paragraph 3, no special procedure shall be required for up-dating the civil-status records of a Member State on the basis of a judgment relating to divorce, legal separation or marriage annulment given in another Member State, and against which no further appeal lies under the law of that Member State.

3   In particular, and without prejudice to paragraph 3, no special procedure shall be required for up-dating the civil-status records of a Member State on the basis of a judgment relating to divorce, legal separation or marriage annulment given in another Member State, and against which no further appeal lies under the law of that Member State.

4   Where the recognition of a judgment is raised as an incidental question in a court of a Member State, that court may determine that issue.

Article 15   Grounds of non-recognition

1   A judgment relating to a divorce, legal separation or marriage annulment shall not be recognised:

(a)   if such recognition is manifestly contrary to the public policy of the Member State in which recognition is sought;

(b)   where it was given in default of appearance, if the respondent was not served with the document which instituted the proceedings or with an equivalent document in sufficient time and in such a way as to enable the respondent to arrange for his or her defence unless it is determined that the respondent has accepted the judgment unequivocally;

(c)   if it is irreconcilable with a judgment given in proceedings between the same parties in the Member State in which recognition is sought; or

(d)   if it is irreconcilable with an earlier judgment given in another Member State or in a non-member State between the same parties, provided that the earlier judgment fulfils the conditions necessary for its recognition in the Member State in which recognition is sought.

2   A judgment relating to the parental responsibility of the spouses given on the occasion of matrimonial proceedings as referred to in Article 13 shall not be recognised:

(a)   if such recognition is manifestly contrary to the public policy of the Member State in which recognition is sought taking into account the best interests of the child;

(b)   if it was given, except in case of urgency, without the child having been given an opportunity to be heard, in violation of fundamental principles of procedure of the Member State in which recognition is sought;

(c)   where it was given in default of appearance if the person in default was not served with the document which instituted the proceedings or with an equivalent document in sufficient time and in such a way as to enable that person to arrange for his or her defence unless it is determined that such person has accepted the judgment unequivocally;

(d)   on the request of any person claiming that the judgment infringes his or her parental responsibility, if it was given without such person having been given an opportunity to be heard;

(e)   if it is irreconcilable with a later judgment relating to parental responsibility given in the Member State in which recognition is sought; or

(f)   if it is irreconcilable with a later judgment relating to parental responsibility given in another Member State or in the non-member State of the habitual residence of the child provided that the later judgment fulfils the conditions necessary for its recognition in the Member State in which recognition is sought.

Article 16   Agreement with third States

A court of a Member State may, on the basis of an agreement on the recognition and enforcement of judgments, not recognise a judgment given in another Member State where, in cases provided for in Article 8, the judgment could only be founded on grounds of jurisdiction other than those specified in Articles 2 to 7.

Article 17   Prohibition of review of jurisdiction of court of origin

The jurisdiction of the court of the Member State of origin may not be reviewed. The test of public policy referred to in Article 15(1)(a) and (2)(a) may not be applied to the rules relating to jurisdiction set out in Articles 2 to 8.

Article 18   Differences in applicable law

The recognition of a judgment relating to a divorce, legal separation or a marriage annulment may not be refused because the law of the Member State in which such recognition is sought would not allow divorce, legal separation or marriage annulment on the same facts.

Article 19   Non-review as to substance

Under no circumstances may a judgment be reviewed as to its substance.

Article 20   Stay of proceedings

1   A court of a Member State in which recognition is sought of a judgment given in another Member State may stay the proceedings if an ordinary appeal against the judgment has been lodged.

2   A court of a Member State in which recognition is sought of a judgment given in Ireland or the United Kingdom may stay the proceedings if enforcement is suspended in the Member State of origin by reason of an appeal.

SECTION 2
ENFORCEMENT

Article 21   Enforceable judgments

1   A judgment on the exercise of parental responsibility in respect of a child of both parties given in a Member State which is enforceable in that Member State and has been served shall be enforced in another member State when, on the application of any interested party, it has been declared enforceable there.

2   However, in the United Kingdom, such a judgment shall be enforced in England and Wales, in Scotland or in Northern Ireland when, on the application of any interested party, it has been registered for enforcement in that part of the United Kingdom.

Article 22   Jurisdiction of local courts

1   An application for a declaration of enforceability shall be submitted to the court appearing in the list in Annex I.

2   The local jurisdiction shall be determined by reference to the place of the habitual residence of the person against whom enforcement is sought or by reference to the habitual residence of any child to whom the application relates.

Where neither of the places referred to in the first sub-paragraph can be found in the Member State where enforcement is sought, the local jurisdiction shall be determined by reference to the place of enforcement.

3   In relation to procedures referred to in Article 14(3), the local jurisdiction shall be determined by the internal law of the Member State in which proceedings for recognition or non-recognition are brought.

Article 23   Procedure for enforcement

1   The procedure for making the application shall be governed by the law of the Member State in which enforcement is sought.

2   The applicant must give an address for service within the area of jurisdiction of the court applied to. However, if the law of the Member State in which enforcement is sought does not provide for the furnishing of such an address, the applicant shall appoint a representative ad litem.

3   The documents referred to in Articles 32 and 33 shall be attached to the application.

Article 24 Decision of the court

1 The court applied to shall give its decision without delay. The person against whom enforcement is sought shall not at this stage of the proceedings be entitled to make any submissions on the application.

2 The application may be refused only for one of the reasons specified in Articles 15, 16 and 17.

3 Under no circumstances may a judgment be reviewed as to its substance.

Article 25 Notice of the decision

The appropriate officer of the court shall without delay bring to the notice of the applicant the decision given on the application in accordance with the procedure laid down by the law of the Member State in which enforcement is sought.

Article 26 Appeal against the enforcement decision

1 The decision on the application for a declaration of enforceability may be appealed against by either party.

2 The appeal shall be lodged with the court appearing in the list in Annex II.

3 The appeal shall be dealt with in accordance with the rules governing procedure in contradictory matters.

4 If the appeal is brought by the applicant for a declaration of enforceability, the party against whom enforcement is sought shall be summoned to appear before the appellate court. If such person fails to appear, the provisions of Article 10 shall apply.

5 An appeal against a declaration of enforceability must be lodged within one month of service thereof. If the party against whom enforcement is sought is habitually resident in a Member State other than that in which the declaration of enforceability was given, the time for appealing shall be two months and shall run from the date of service, either on him or at his residence. No extension of time may be granted on account of distance.

Article 27 Courts of appeal and means of contest

The judgment given on appeal may be contested only by the proceedings referred to in Annex III.

Article 28 Stay of proceedings

1 The court with which the appeal is lodged under Articles 26 or 27 may, on the application of the party against whom enforcement is sought, stay the proceedings if an ordinary appeal has been lodged in the Member State of origin or if the time for such appeal has not yet expired. In the latter case, the court may specify the time within which an appeal is to be lodged.

2 Where the judgment was given in Ireland or the United Kingdom, any form of appeal available in the Member State of origin shall be treated as an ordinary appeal for the purposes of paragraph 1.

Article 29 Partial enforcement

1 Where a judgment has been given in respect of several matters and enforcement cannot be authorised for all of them, the court shall authorise enforcement for one or more of them.

2 An applicant may request partial enforcement of a judgment.

Article 30 Legal aid

An applicant who, in the Member State of origin, has benefited from complete or partial legal aid or exemption from costs or expenses shall be entitled, in the procedures provided for in Articles 22 to 25, to benefit from the most favourable legal aid or the most extensive exemption from costs and expenses provided for by the law of the Member State addressed.

Article 31 Security, bond or deposit

No security, bond or deposit, however described, shall be required of a party who in one Member State applies for enforcement of a judgment given in another Member State on the following grounds:

(a) that he or she is not habitually resident in the Member State in which enforcement is sought; or

(b) that he or she is either a foreign national or, where enforcement is sought in either the United Kingdom or Ireland, does not have his or her 'domicile' in either of those Member States.

SECTION 3

COMMON PROVISIONS

Article 32 Documents

1 A party seeking or contesting recognition or applying for a declaration of enforceability shall produce:

(a) a copy of the judgment which satisfies the conditions necessary to establish its authenticity; and

(b) a certificate referred to in Article 33.

2 In addition, in the case of a judgment given in default, the party seeking recognition or applying for a declaration of enforceability shall produce:

(a) the original or certified true copy of the document which establishes that the defaulting party was served with the document instituting the proceedings or with an equivalent document; or

(b) any document indicating that the defendant has accepted the judgment unequivocally.

Article 33 Other documents

The competent court or authority of a Member State where a judgment was given shall issue, at the request of any interested party, a certificate using the standard form in Annex IV (judgments in matrimonial matters) or Annex V (judgments on parental responsibility).

Article 34 Absence of documents

1 If the documents specified in Article 32(1)(*b*) or (2) are not produced, the court may specify a time for their production, accept equivalent documents or, if it considers that it has sufficient information before it, dispense with their production.

2 If the court so requires, a translation of such documents shall be furnished. The translation shall be certified by a person qualified to do so in one of the Member States.

Article 35   Legalisation or other similar formality

No legalisation or other similar formality shall be required in respect of the documents referred to in Articles 32, 33 or 34(2) or in respect of a document appointing a representative ad litem.

CHAPTER IV – GENERAL PROVISIONS

Article 36   Relation with other instruments

1   Subject to the provisions of Articles 38, 42 and paragraph 2 of this Article, this Regulation shall, for the Member States, supersede conventions existing at the time of entry into force of this Regulation which have been concluded between two or more Member States and relate to matters governed by this Regulation.

2(a)   Finland and Sweden shall have the option of declaring that the Convention of 6 February 1931 between Denmark, Finland, Iceland, Norway and Sweden comprising international private law provisions on marriage, adoption and guardianship, together with the Final Protocol thereto, will apply, in whole or in part, in their mutual relations, in place of the rules of this Regulation. Such declarations shall be annexed to this Regulation and published in the Official Journal of the European Communities. They may be withdrawn, in whole or in part, at any moment by the said Member States.

(b)   The principle of non-discrimination on the grounds of nationality between citizens of the Union shall be respected.

(c)   The rules of jurisdiction in any future agreement to be concluded between the Member States referred to in sub-paragraph (a) which relate to matters governed by this Regulation shall be in line with those laid down in this Regulation.

(d)   Judgments handed down in any of the Nordic States which have made the declaration provided for in sub-paragraph (a) under a forum of jurisdiction corresponding to one of those laid down in Chapter II, shall be recognised and enforced in the other Member States under the rules laid down in Chapter III.

3   Member States shall send to the Commission:

(a)   a copy of the agreements and uniform laws implementing these agreements referred to in paragraphs 2(a) and (c);

(b)   any denunciations of, or amendments to, those agreements or uniform laws.

Article 37   Relations with certain multilateral conventions

In relations between Member States, this Regulation shall take precedence over the following Conventions insofar as they concern matters governed by this Regulation:

—   the Hague Convention of 5 October 1961 concerning the Powers of Authorities and the Law Applicable in respect of the Protection of Minors,

—   the Luxembourg Convention of 8 September 1967 on the Recognition of Decisions Relating to the Validity of Marriages,

—   the Hague Convention of 1 June 1970 on the Recognition of Divorces and Legal Separations,

—   the European Convention of 20 May 1980 on Recognition and Enforcement of Decisions concerning Custody of Children and on Restoration of Custody of Children,

—   the Hague Convention of 19 October 1996 on Jurisdiction, Applicable law, Recognition, Enforcement and Co-operation in Respect of Parental

Responsibility and Measures for the Protection of Children, provided that the child concerned is habitually resident in a Member State.

Article 38   Extent of effects

1   The agreements and conventions referred to in Articles 36(1) and 37 shall continue to have effect in relation to matters to which this Regulation does not apply.

2   They shall continue to have effect in respect of judgments given and documents formally drawn up or registered as authentic before the entry into force of this Regulation.

Article 39   Agreements between Member States

1   Two or more Member States may conclude agreements or arrangements to amplify this Regulation or to facilitate its application.

Member States shall send to the Commission:

(a)   a copy of the draft agreements; and
(b)   any denunciations of, or amendments to, these agreements.

2   In no circumstances may the agreements or arrangements derogate from Chapters II or III.

Article 40   Treaties with the Holy See

1   This Regulation shall apply without prejudice to the International Treaty (Concordat) between the Holy See and Portugal, signed at the Vatican City on 7 May 1940.

2   Any decision as to the invalidity of a marriage taken under the Treaty referred to in paragraph 1 shall be recognised in the Member States on the conditions laid down in Chapter III.

3   The provisions laid down in paragraphs 1 and 2 shall also apply to the following international treaties (Concordats) with the Holy See:

(a)   Concordato lateranense of 11 February 1929 between Italy and the Holy See, modified by the agreement, with additional Protocol signed in Rome on 18 February 1984;
(b)   Agreement between the Holy See and Spain on legal affairs of 3 January 1979.

4   Recognition of the decisions provided for in paragraph 2 may, in Italy or in Spain, be subject to the same procedures and the same checks as are applicable to decisions of the ecclesiastical courts handed down in accordance with the international treaties concluded with the Holy See referred to in paragraph 3.

5   Member States shall send to the Commission:

(a)   a copy of the Treaties referred to in paragraphs 1 and 3;
(b)   any denunciations of or amendments to those Treaties.

Article 41   Member States with two or more legal systems

With regard to a Member State in which two or more systems of law or sets of rules concerning matters governed by this Regulation apply in different territorial units:

(a)   any reference to habitual residence in that Member State shall refer to habitual residence in a territorial unit;
(b)   any reference to nationality, or in the case of the United Kingdom 'domicile', shall refer to the territorial unit designated by the law of that State;

(c) any reference to the authority of a Member State having received an application for divorce or legal separation or for marriage annulment shall refer to the authority of a territorial unit which has received such an application;

(d) any reference to the rules of the requested Member State shall refer to the rules of the territorial unit in which jurisdiction, recognition or enforcement is invoked.

CHAPTER V – TRANSITIONAL PROVISIONS

Article 42

1 The provisions of this Regulation shall apply only to legal proceedings instituted, to documents formally drawn up or registered as authentic instruments and to settlements which have been approved by a court in the course of proceedings after its entry into force.

2 Judgments given after the date of entry into force of this Regulation in proceedings instituted before that date shall be recognised and enforced in accordance with the provisions of Chapter III if jurisdiction was founded on rules which accorded with those provided for either in Chapter II of this Regulation or in a convention concluded between the Member State of origin and the Member State addressed which was in force when the proceedings were instituted.

CHAPTER VI – FINAL PROVISIONS

Article 43 Review

No later than 1 March 2006, and every five years thereafter, the Commission shall present to the European Parliament, the Council and the Economic and Social Committee a report on the application of this Regulation, and in particular Articles 36, 39 and 40(2) thereof. The report shall be accompanied if need be by proposals for adaptations.

Article 44 Amendment to lists of courts and redress procedures

1 Member States shall notify the Commission of the texts amending the lists of courts and redress procedures set out in Annexes I to III. The Commission shall adapt the Annexes concerned accordingly.

2 The updating or making of technical amendments to the standard forms set out in Annexes IV and V shall be adopted in accordance with the advisory procedure set out in Article 45(2).

Article 45

1 The Commission shall be assisted by a committee.

2 Where reference is made to this paragraph, Articles 3 and 7 of Decision 1999/468 EC shall apply.

3 The committee shall adopt its rules of procedure.

Article 46 Entry into force

This Regulation shall enter into force on 1 March 2001.

This Regulation shall be binding in its entirety and directly applicable in the Member States in accordance with the Treaty establishing the European Community.

Done at Brussels, 29 May 2000.

For the Council
The President
A Costa

ANNEX I

The applications provided for by Article 22 shall be submitted to the following courts:

–   in Belgium, the 'tribunal de première instance'/'rechtbank van eerste aanleg'/'erstinstanzliches Gericht',
–   in Germany:
    –   in the district of the 'Kammergericht' (Berlin), The 'Familiengericht' Pankow/Weissensee',
    –   in the districts of the remaining 'Oberlandesgerichte' to the 'Familiengericht' located at the seat of the respective 'Oberlandesgericht',
–   in Greece, the 'Μονομελές Πρωτοδικείο',
–   in Spain, the 'Juzgado de Primera Instancia',
–   in France, the presiding Judge of the 'tribunal de grande instance',
–   in Ireland, the High Court,
–   in Italy, the 'Corte d'apello',
–   in Luxembourg, the presiding Judge of the 'Tribunal d'arrondissement',
–   in the Netherlands, the presiding Judge of the 'arrondissementsrechtbank',
–   in Austria, the 'Bezirksgericht',
–   in Portugal, the 'Tribunal de Comarca' or 'Tribunal de Familia',
–   in Finland, the 'käräjäoikeus'/'tinsgrätt',
–   in Sweden, the 'Svea hovrätt',
–   in the United Kingdom:
    (a)   in England and Wales, the High Court of Justice;
    (b)   in Scotland, the Court of Session;
    (c)   in Northern Ireland, the High Court of Justice;
    (d)   in Gibraltar, the Supreme Court.

ANNEX II

The appeal provided for by Article 26 shall be lodged with the courts listed below:

–   in Belgium:
    (a)   a person applying for a declaration of enforceability may lodge an appeal with the 'cour d'appel' or the 'hof van beroep';
    (b)   the person against whom enforcement is sought may lodge opposition with the 'tribunal de première instance'/'rechtbank van eerste aanleg' /'erstinstanzliches Gericht',
–   in Germany, the 'Oberlandesgericht',
–   in Greece, the 'Εφετείο',

–   in Spain, the 'Audiencia Provincial',
–   in France, the 'Cour d'appel',
–   in Ireland, the High Court,
–   in Italy, the 'Corte d'appello',
–   in Luxembourg, the 'Cour d'appel',
–   in the Netherlands:
    (a)   if the applicant or the respondent who has appeared lodges the appeal:
          with the 'gereschtshof';
    (b)   if the respondent who has been granted leave not to appear lodges the
          appeal: with the 'arrondissementsrechtbank',
–   in Austria, the 'Bezirksgericht',
–   in Portugal, the 'Tribunal da Relação',
–   in Finland, the 'hovioikeus'/'hovrätt',
–   in Sweden, the 'Svea hovrätt',
–   in the United Kingdom:
    (a)   in England and Wales, the High Court of Justice;
    (b)   in Scotland, the Court of Session;
    (c)   in Northern Ireland, the High Court of Justice;
    (d)   in Gibraltar, the Court of Appeal.

ANNEX III

The appeals provided for Article 27 may be brought only:

–   in Belgium, Greece, Spain, France, Italy, Luxembourg and in the Netherlands, by
    an appeal in cassation,
–   in Germany, by a 'Rechtsbeschwerde',
–   in Ireland, by an appeal on a point of law to the Supreme Court,
–   in Austria, by a 'Revisionsrekurs',
–   in Portugal, by a 'recurso restrito à matéria de direito',
–   in Finland, by an appeal to 'korkein oikeus'/'högsta domstolen',
–   in Sweden, by an appeal to the 'Högsta domstolen',
–   in the United Kingdom, by a single further appeal on a point of law.

COUNCIL OF EUROPE CONVENTION ON RECOGNITION AND ENFORCEMENT OF DECISIONS CONCERNING CUSTODY OF CHILDREN AND ON RESTORATION OF CUSTODY OF CHILDREN

Luxemburg, 20.V.1980

The member States of the Council of Europe, signatory hereto,

Recognising that in the member States of the Council of Europe the welfare of the child is of overriding importance in reaching decisions concerning his custody;

Considering that the making of arrangements to ensure that decisions concerning the custody of a child can be more widely recognised and enforced will provide greater protection of the welfare of children;

Considering it desirable, with this end in view, to emphasise that the right of access of parents is a normal corollary to the right of custody;

Noting the increasing number of cases where children have been improperly removed across an international frontier and the difficulties of securing adequate solutions to the problems caused by such cases;

Desirous of making suitable provision to enable the custody of children which has been arbitrarily interrupted to be restored;

Convinced of the desirability of making arrangements for this purpose answering to different needs and different circumstances;

Desiring to establish legal co-operation between their authorities,

Have agreed as follows:

Article 1

For the purposes of this Convention:

(a) child means a person of any nationality, so long as he is under 16 years of age and has not the right to decide on his own place of residence under the law of his habitual residence, the law of his nationality or the internal law of the State addressed;

(b) authority means a judicial or administrative authority;

(c) decision relating to custody means a decision of an authority in so far as it relates to the care of the person of the child, including the right to decide on the place of his residence, or to the right of access to him;

(d) improper removal means the removal of a child across an international frontier in breach of a decision relating to his custody which has been given in a Contracting State and which is enforceable in such a State; improper removal also includes:

(i)   the failure to return a child across an international frontier at the end of a period of the exercise of the right of access to this child or at the end of any other temporary stay in a territory other than that where the custody is exercised;

(ii)   a removal which is subsequently declared unlawful within the meaning of Art 12.

PART I – CENTRAL AUTHORITIES

Article 2

1   Each Contracting State shall appoint a central authority to carry out the functions provided for by this Convention.

2   Federal States and States with more than one legal system shall be free to appoint more than one central authority and shall determine the extent of their competence.

3   The Secretary General of the Council of Europe shall be notified of any appointment under this Article.

Article 3

1   The central authorities of the Contracting States shall co-operate with each other and promote co-operation between the competent authorities in their respective countries. They shall act with all necessary despatch.

2   With a view to facilitating the operation of this Convention, the central authorities of the Contracting States:

(a)   shall secure the transmission of requests for information coming from competent authorities and relating to legal or factual matters concerning pending proceedings;

(b)   shall provide each other on request with information about their law relating to the custody of children and any changes in that law;

(c)   shall keep each other informed of any difficulties likely to arise in applying the Convention and, as far as possible, eliminate obstacles to its application.

Article 4

1   Any person who has obtained in a Contracting State a decision relating to the custody of a child and who wishes to have that decision recognised or enforced in another Contracting State may submit an application for this purpose to the central authority in any Contracting State.

2   The application shall be accompanied by the documents mentioned in Art 13.

3   The central authority receiving the application, if it is not the central authority in the State addressed, shall send the documents directly and without delay to that central authority.

4   The central authority receiving the application may refuse to intervene where it is manifestly clear that the conditions laid down by this Convention are not satisfied.

5   The central authority receiving the application shall keep the applicant informed without delay of the progress of his application.

Article 5

1 The central authority in the State addressed shall take or cause to be taken without delay all steps which it considers to be appropriate, if necessary by instituting proceedings before its competent authorities, in order:

(a) to discover the whereabouts of the child;
(b) to avoid, in particular by any necessary provisional measures, prejudice to the interests of the child or of the applicant;
(c) to secure the recognition or enforcement of the decision;
(d) to secure the delivery of the child to the applicant where enforcement is granted;
(e) to inform the requesting authority of the measures taken and their results.

2 Where the central authority in the State addressed has reason to believe that the child is in the territory of another Contracting State it shall send the documents directly and without delay to the central authority of that State.

3 With the exception of the cost of repatriation, each Contracting State undertakes not to claim any payment from an applicant in respect of any measures taken under para 1 of this Article by the central authority of that State on the applicant's behalf, including the costs of proceedings and, where applicable, the costs incurred by the assistance of a lawyer.

4 If recognition or enforcement is refused, and if the central authority of the State addressed considers that it should comply with a request by the applicant to bring in that State proceedings concerning the substance of the case, that authority shall use its best endeavours to secure the representation of the applicant in the proceedings under conditions no less favourable than those available to a person who is resident in and a national of that State and for this purpose it may, in particular, institute proceedings before its competent authorities.

Article 6

1 Subject to any special agreements made between the central authorities concerned and to the provisions of para 3 of this Article:

(a) communications to the central authority of the State addressed shall be made in the official language or in one of the official languages of that State or be accompanied by a translation into that language;
(b) the central authority of the State addressed shall nevertheless accept communications made in English or in French or accompanied by a translation into one of these languages.

2 Communications coming from the central authority of the State addressed, including the results of enquiries carried out, may be made in the official language or one of the official languages of that State or in English or French.

3 A Contracting State may exclude wholly or partly the provisions of para 1(b) of this Article. When a Contracting State has made this reservation any other Contracting State may also apply the reservation in respect of that State.

PART II – RECOGNITION AND ENFORCEMENT OF DECISIONS AND RESTORATION OF CUSTODY OF CHILDREN

Article 7

A decision relating to custody given in a Contracting State shall be recognised and, where it is enforceable in the State of origin, made enforceable in every other Contracting State.

Article 8

1   In the case of an improper removal, the central authority of the State addressed shall cause steps to be taken forthwith to restore the custody of the child where:

(a)   at the time of the institution of the proceedings in the State where the decision was given or at the time of the improper removal, if earlier, the child and his parents had as their sole nationality the nationality of that State and the child had his habitual residence in the territory of that State, and

(b)   a request for the restoration was made to a central authority within a period of six months from the date of the improper removal.

2   If, in accordance with the law of the State addressed, the requirements of para 1 of this Article cannot be complied with without recourse to a judicial authority, none of the grounds of refusal specified in this Convention shall apply to the judicial proceedings.

3   Where there is an agreement officially confirmed by a competent authority between the person having the custody of the child and another person to allow the other person a right of access, and the child, having been taken abroad, has not been restored at the end of the agreed period to the person having the custody, custody of the child shall be restored in accordance with paras 1(b) and 2 of this Article. The same shall apply in the case of a decision of the competent authority granting such a right to a person who has not the custody of the child.

Article 9

1   In cases of improper removal, other than those dealt with in Art 8, in which an application has been made to a central authority within a period of six months from the date of the removal, recognition and enforcement may be refused only if:

(a)   in the case of a decision given in the absence of the defendant or his legal representative, the defendant was not duly served with the document which instituted the proceedings or an equivalent document in sufficient time to enable him to arrange his defence; but such a failure to effect service cannot constitute a ground for refusing recognition or enforcement where service was not effected because the defendant had concealed his whereabouts from the person who instituted the proceedings in the State of origin;

(b)   in the case of a decision given in the absence of the defendant or his legal representative, the competence of the authority giving the decision was not founded:

  (i)   on the habitual residence of the defendant, or

  (ii)   on the last common habitual residence of the child's parents, at least one parent being still habitually resident there, or

  (iii)   on the habitual residence of the child;

(c)   the decision is incompatible with a decision relating to custody which became enforceable in the State addressed before the removal of the child, unless the child has had his habitual residence in the territory of the requesting State for one year before his removal.

2   Where no application has been made to a central authority, the provisions of para 1 of this Article shall apply equally, if recognition and enforcement are requested within six months from the date of the improper removal.

3   In no circumstances may the foreign decision be reviewed as to its substance.

Article 10

1   In cases other than those covered by Arts 8 and 9, recognition and enforcement may be refused not only on the grounds provided for in Art 9 but also on any of the following grounds:

(a)   if it is found that the effects of the decision are manifestly incompatible with the fundamental principles of the law relating to the family and children in the State addressed;

(b)   if it is found that by reason of a change in the circumstances including the passage of time but not including a mere change in the residence of the child after an improper removal, the effects of the original decision are manifestly no longer in accordance with the welfare of the child;

(c)   if at the time when the proceedings were instituted in the State of origin:

    (i)   the child was a national of the State addressed or was habitually resident there and no such connection existed with the State of origin;

    (ii)   he child was a national both of the State of origin and of the State addressed and was habitually resident in the State addressed;

(d)   if the decision is incompatible with a decision given in the State addressed or enforceable in that State after being given in a third State, pursuant to proceedings begun before the submission of the request for recognition or enforcement, and if the refusal is in accordance with the welfare of the child.

2   In the same cases, proceedings for recognition or enforcement may be adjourned on any of the following grounds:

(a)   if an ordinary form of review of the original decision has been commenced;

(b)   if proceedings relating to the custody of the child, commenced before the proceedings in the State of origin were instituted, are pending in the State addressed;

(c)   if another decision concerning the custody of the child is the subject of proceedings for enforcement or of any other proceedings concerning the recognition of the decision.

Article 11

1   Decisions on rights of access and provisions of decisions relating to custody which deal with the right of access shall be recognised and enforced subject to the same conditions as other decisions relating to custody.

2   However, the competent authority of the State addressed may fix the conditions for the implementation and exercise of the right of access taking into account, in particular, undertakings given by the parties on this matter.

3 Where no decision on the right of access has been taken or where recognition or enforcement of the decision relating to custody is refused, the central authority of the State addressed may apply to its competent authorities for a decision on the right of access, if the person claiming a right of access so requests.

Article 12

Where, at the time of the removal of a child across an international frontier, there is no enforceable decision given in a Contracting State relating to his custody, the provisions of this Convention shall apply to any subsequent decision, relating to the custody of that child and declaring the removal to be unlawful, given in a Contracting State at the request of any interested person.

PART III – PROCEDURE

Article 13

1 A request for recognition or enforcement in another Contracting State of a decision relating to custody shall be accompanied by:

(a) a document authorising the central authority of the State addressed to act on behalf of the applicant or to designate another representative for that purpose;
(b) a copy of the decision which satisfies the necessary conditions of authenticity;
(c) in the case of a decision given in the absence of the defendant or his legal representative, a document which establishes that the defendant was duly served with the document which instituted the proceedings or an equivalent document;
(d) if applicable, any document which establishes that, in accordance with the law of the State of origin, the decision is enforceable;
(e) if possible, a statement indicating the whereabouts or likely whereabouts of the child in the State addressed;
(f) proposals as to how the custody of the child should be restored.

2 The documents mentioned above shall, where necessary, be accompanied by a translation according to the provisions laid down in Art 6.

Article 14

Each Contracting State shall apply a simple and expeditious procedure for recognition and enforcement of decisions relating to the custody of a child. To that end it shall ensure that a request for enforcement may be lodged by simple application.

Article 15

1 Before reaching a decision under para 1(b) of Art 10, the authority concerned in the State addressed:

(a) shall ascertain the child's views unless this is impracticable having regard in particular to his age and understanding; and
(b) may request that any appropriate enquiries be carried out.

2 The cost of enquiries in any Contracting State shall be met by the authorities of the State where they are carried out.

3 Request for enquiries and the results of enquiries may be sent to the authority concerned through the central authorities.

Article 16

For the purposes of this Convention, no legalisation or any like formality may be required.

PART IV – RESERVATIONS

Article 17

1   A Contracting State may make a reservation that, in cases covered by Arts 8 and 9 or either of these Articles, recognition and enforcement of decisions relating to custody may be refused on such of the grounds provided under Art 10 as may be specified in the reservation.

2   Recognition and enforcement of decisions given in a Contracting State which has made the reservation provided for in para 1 of this Article may be refused in any other Contracting State on any of the additional grounds referred to in that reservation.

Article 18

A Contracting State may make a reservation that it shall not be bound by the provisions of Art 12. The provisions of this Convention shall not apply to decisions referred to in Art 12 which have been given in a Contracting State which has made such a reservation.

PART V – OTHER INSTRUMENTS

Article 19

This Convention shall not exclude the possibility of relying on any other international instrument in force between the State of origin and the State addressed or on any other law of the State addressed not derived from an international agreement for the purpose of obtaining recognition or enforcement of a decision.

Article 20

1   This Convention shall not affect any obligations which a Contracting State may have towards a non-Contracting State under an international instrument dealing with matters governed by this Convention.

2   When two or more Contracting States have enacted uniform laws in relation to custody of children or created a special system of recognition or enforcement of decisions in this field, or if they should do so in the future, they shall be free to apply, between themselves, those laws or that system in place of this Convention or any part of it. In order to avail themselves of this provision the State shall notify their decision to the Secretary General of the Council of Europe. Any alteration or revocation of this decision must also be notified.

PART VI – FINAL CLAUSES

Article 21

This Convention shall be open for signature by the member States of the Council of Europe. It is subject to ratification, acceptance or approval. Instruments of ratification, acceptance or approval shall be deposited with the Secretary General of the Council of Europe.

Article 22

1   This Convention shall enter into force on the first day of the month following the expiration of a period of three months after the date on which three member States of the Council of Europe have expressed their consent to be bound by the Convention in accordance with the provisions of Art 21.

2   In respect of any member State which subsequently expresses its consent to be bound by it, the Convention shall enter into force on the first day of the month following the expiration of a period of three months after the date of the deposit of the instrument of ratification, acceptance or approval.

Article 23

1   After the entry into force of this Convention, the Committee of Ministers of the Council of Europe may invite any State not a member of the Council to accede to this Convention, by a decision taken by the majority provided for by Article 20.d of the Statute and by the unanimous vote of the representatives of the Contracting States entitled to sit on the Committee.

2   In respect of any acceding State, the Convention shall enter into force on the first day of the month following the expiration of a period of three months after the date of deposit of the instrument of accession with the Secretary General of the Council of Europe.

Article 24

1   Any State may at the time of signature or when depositing its instrument of ratification, acceptance, approval or accession, specify the territory or territories to which this Convention shall apply.

2   Any State may at any later date, by a declaration addressed to the Secretary General of the Council of Europe, extend the application of this Convention to any other territory specified in the declaration. In respect of such territory, the Convention shall enter into force on the first day of the month following the expiration of a period of three months after the date of receipt by the Secretary General of such declaration.

3   Any declaration made under the two preceding paragraphs may, in respect of any territory specified in such declaration, be withdrawn by a notification addressed to the Secretary General. The withdrawal shall become effective on the first day of the month following the expiration of a period of six months after the date of receipt of such notification by the Secretary General.

Article 25

1   A State which has two or more territorial units in which different systems of law apply in matters of custody of children and of recognition and enforcement of decisions relating to custody may, at the time of signature or when depositing its instrument of ratification, acceptance, approval or accession, declare that this Convention shall apply to all its territorial units or to one or more of them.

2   Such a State may at any later date, by a declaration addressed to the Secretary General of the Council of Europe, extend the application of this Convention to any other territorial unit specified in the declaration. In respect of such territorial unit the

Convention shall enter into force on the first day of the month following the expiration of a period of three months after the date of receipt by the Secretary General of such declaration.

3   Any declaration made under the two preceding paragraphs may, in respect of any territorial unit specified in such declaration, be withdrawn by notification addressed to the Secretary General. The withdrawal shall become effective on the first day of the month following the expiration of a period of six months after the date of receipt of such notification by the Secretary General.

Article 26

1   In relation to a State which has in matters of custody two or more systems of law of territorial application:

(a)   reference to the law of a person's habitual residence or to the law of a person's nationality shall be construed as referring to the system of law determined by the rules in force in that State or, if there are no such rules, to the system of law with which the person concerned is most closely connected;

(b)   reference to the State of origin or to the State addressed shall be construed as referring, as the case may, be to the territorial unit where recognition or enforcement of the decision or restoration of custody is requested.

2   Paragraph 1(a) of this article also applies *mutatis mutandis* to States which have in matters of custody two or more systems of law of personal application.

Article 27

1   Any State may, at the time of signature or when depositing its instrument of ratification, acceptance, approval or accession, declare that it avails itself of one or more of the reservations provided for in para 3 of Art 6, Art 17 and Art 18 of this Convention. No other reservation may be made.

2   Any Contracting State which has made a reservation under the preceding paragraph may wholly or partly withdraw it by means of a notification addressed to the Secretary General of the Council of Europe. The withdrawal shall take effect on the date of receipt of such notification by the Secretary General.

Article 28

At the end of the third year following the date of the entry into force of this Convention and, on his own initiative, at any time after this date, the Secretary General of the Council of Europe shall invite the representatives of the central authorities appointed by the Contracting States to meet in order to study and to facilitate the functioning of the Convention. Any member State of the Council of Europe not being a party to the Convention may be represented by an observer. A report shall be prepared on the work of each of these meetings and forwarded to the Committee of Ministers of the Council of Europe for information.

Article 29

1   Any Party may at any time denounce this Convention by means of a notification addressed to the Secretary General of the Council of Europe.

2   Such denunciation shall become effective on the first day of the month following the expiration of a period of six months after the date of receipt of the notification by the Secretary General.

Article 30

The Secretary General of the Council of Europe shall notify the member States of the Council and any State which has acceded to this Convention, of:

(a)   any signature;
(b)   the deposit of any instrument of ratification, acceptance, approval or accession;
(c)   any date of entry into force of this Convention in accordance with Arts 22, 23, 24 and 25;
(d)   any other act, notification or communication relating to this Convention.

In witness whereof the undersigned, being duly authorised thereto, have signed this Convention.

Done at Luxembourg, the 20th day of May 1980, in English and French, both texts being equally authentic, in a single copy which shall be deposited in the archives of the Council of Europe. The Secretary General of the Council of Europe shall transmit certified copies to each member State of the Council of Europe and to any State invited to accede to this Convention.

HAGUE CONVENTION ON JURISDICTION, APPLICABLE LAW, RECOGNITION, ENFORCEMENT AND CO-OPERATION IN RESPECT OF PARENTAL RESPONSIBILITY AND MEASURES FOR THE PROTECTION OF CHILDREN

(Concluded at the Hague, 19 October 1996)

The States signatory to the present Convention;

Considering the need to improve the protection of children in international situations;

Wishing to avoid conflicts between their legal systems in respect of jurisdiction, applicable law, recognition and enforcement of measures for the protection of children;

Recalling the importance of international co-operation for the protection of children;

Confirming that the best interests of the child are to be a primary consideration;

Noting that the Convention of 5 October 1961 concerning the powers of authorities and the law applicable in respect of the protection of minors is in need of revision;

Desiring to establish common provisions to this effect, taking into account the United Nations Convention on the Rights of the Child of 20 November 1989;

Have agreed on the following provisions:

CHAPTER I – SCOPE OF THE CONVENTION

Article 1

1   The objects of the present Convention are:

(a)   to determine the State whose authorities have jurisdiction to take measures directed to the protection of the person or property of the child;
(b)   to determine which law is to be applied by such authorities in exercising their jurisdiction;
(c)   to determine the law applicable to parental responsibility;
(d)   to provide for the recognition and enforcement of such measures of protection in all Contracting States;
(e)   to establish such co-operation between the authorities of the Contracting States as may be necessary in order to achieve the purposes of this Convention.

2   For the purposes of this Convention, the term 'parental responsibility' includes parental authority, or any analogous relationship of authority determining the rights,

powers and responsibilities of parents, guardians or other legal representatives in relation to the person or the property of the child.

Article 2

The Convention applies to children from the moment of their birth until they reach the age of 18 years.

Article 3

The measures referred to in Art 1 may deal in particular with –

(a)   the attribution, exercise, termination or restriction of parental responsibility, as well as its delegation;
(b)   rights of custody, including rights relating to the care of the person of the child and, in particular, the right to determine the child's place of residence, as well as rights of access including the right to take a child for a limited period of time to a place other than the child's habitual residence;
(c)   guardianship, curatorship and analogous institutions;
(d)   the designation and functions of any person or body having charge of the child's person or property, representing or assisting the child;
(e)   the placement of the child in a foster family or in institutional care, or the provision of care by *kafala* or an analogous institution;
(f)   the supervision by a public authority of the care of a child by any person having charge of the child;
(g)   the administration, conservation or disposal of the child's property.

Article 4

The Convention does not apply to:

(a)   the establishment or contesting of a parent-child relationship;
(b)   decisions on adoption, measures preparatory to adoption, or the annulment or revocation of adoption;
(c)   the name and forenames of the child;
(d)   emancipation;
(e)   maintenance obligations;
(f)   trusts or succession;
(g)   social security;
(h)   public measures of a general nature in matters of education or health;
(i)   measures taken as a result of penal offences committed by children;
(j)   decisions on the right of asylum and on immigration.

CHAPTER II – JURISDICTION

Article 5

1   The judicial or administrative authorities of the Contracting State of the habitual residence of the child have jurisdiction to take measures directed to the protection of the child's person or property.

2   Subject to Art 7, in case of a change of the child's habitual residence to another Contracting State, the authorities of the State of the new habitual residence have jurisdiction.

Article 6

1 For refugee children and children who, due to disturbances occurring in their country, are internationally displaced, the authorities of the Contracting State on the territory of which these children are present as a result of their displacement have the jurisdiction provided for in para 1 of Art 5.

2 The provisions of the preceding paragraph also apply to children whose habitual residence cannot be established.

Article 7

1 In case of wrongful removal or retention of the child, the authorities of the Contracting State in which the child was habitually resident immediately before the removal or retention keep their jurisdiction until the child has acquired a habitual residence in another State; and

(a) each person, institution or other body having rights of custody has acquiesced in the removal or retention; or

(b) the child has resided in that other State for a period of at least one year after the person, institution or other body having rights of custody has or should have had knowledge of the whereabouts of the child, no request for return lodged within that period is still pending, and the child is settled in his or her new environment.

2 The removal or the retention of a child is to be considered wrongful where:

(a) it is in breach of rights of custody attributed to a person, an institution or any other body, either jointly or alone, under the law of the State in which the child was habitually resident immediately before the removal or retention; and

(b) at the time of removal or retention those rights were actually exercised, either jointly or alone, or would have been so exercised but for the removal or retention.

The rights of custody mentioned in sub-para (a) above, may arise in particular by operation of law or by reason of a judicial or administrative decision, or by reason of an agreement having legal effect under the law of that State.

3 So long as the authorities first mentioned in para 1 keep their jurisdiction, the authorities of the Contracting State to which the child has been removed or in which he or she has been retained can take only such urgent measures under Art 11 as are necessary for the protection of the person or property of the child.

Article 8

1 By way of exception, the authority of a Contracting State having jurisdiction under Art 5 or 6, if it considers that the authority of another Contracting State would be better placed in the particular case to assess the best interests of the child, may either

- request that other authority, directly or with the assistance of the Central Authority of its State, to assume jurisdiction to take such measures of protection as it considers to be necessary: or
- suspend consideration of the case and invite the parties to introduce such a request before the authority of that other State.

2 The Contracting States whose authorities may be addressed as provided in the preceding paragraph are:

(a) a State of which the child is a national,
(b) a State in which property of the child is located,
(c) a State whose authorities are seised of an application for divorce or legal separation of the child's parents, or for annulment of their marriage,
(d) a State with which the child has a substantial connection.

3 The authorities concerned may proceed to an exchange of views.

4 The authority addressed as provided in para 1 may assume jurisdiction, in place of the authority having jurisdiction under Art 5 or 6, if it considers that this is in the child's best interests.

Article 9

1 If the authorities of a Contracting State referred to in Art 8, para 2, consider that they are better placed in the particular case to assess the child's best interests, they may either

— request the competent authority of the Contracting State of the habitual residence of the child, directly or with the assistance of the Central Authority of that State, that they be authorised to exercise jurisdiction to take the measures of protection which they consider to be necessary, or

— invite the parties to introduce such a request before the authority of the Contracting State of the habitual residence of the child.

2 The authorities concerned may proceed to an exchange of views.

3 The authority initiating the request may exercise jurisdiction in place of the authority of the Contracting State of the habitual residence of the child only if the latter authority has accepted the request.

Article 10

1 Without prejudice to Arts 5 to 9, the authorities of a Contracting State exercising jurisdiction to decide upon an application for divorce or legal separation of the parents of a child habitually resident in another Contracting State, or for annulment of their marriage, may, if the law of their State so provides, take measures directed to the protection of the person or property of such child if

(a) at the time of commencement of the proceedings, one of his or her parents habitually resides in that State and one of them has parental responsibility in relation to the child, and

(b) the jurisdiction of these authorities to take such measures has been accepted by the parents, as well as by any other person who has parental responsibility in relation to the child, and is in the best interests of the child.

2 The jurisdiction provided for by para 1 to take measures for the protection of the child ceases as soon as the decision allowing or refusing the application for divorce, legal separation or annulment of the marriage has become final, or the proceedings have come to an end for another reason.

Article 11

1 In all cases of urgency, the authorities of any Contracting State in whose territory the child or property belonging to the child is present have jurisdiction to take any necessary measures of protection.

2   The measures taken under the preceding paragraph with regard to a child habitually resident in a Contracting State shall lapse as soon as the authorities which have jurisdiction under Arts 5 to 10 have taken the measures required by the situation.

3   The measures taken under para 1 with regard to a child who is habitually resident in a non-Contracting State shall lapse in each Contracting State as soon as measures required by the situation and taken by the authorities of another State are recognised in the Contracting State in question.

Article 12

1   Subject to Art 7, the authorities of a Contracting State in whose territory the child or property belonging to the child is present have jurisdiction to take measures of a provisional character for the protection of the person or property of the child which have a territorial effect limited to the State in question, in so far as such measures are not incompatible with measures already taken by authorities which have jurisdiction under Arts 5 to 10.

2   The measures taken under the preceding paragraph with regard to a child habitually resident in a Contracting State shall lapse as soon as the authorities which have jurisdiction under Arts 5 to 10 have taken a decision in respect of the measures of protection which may be required by the situation.

3   The measures taken under para 1 with regard to a child who is habitually resident in a non-Contracting State shall lapse in the Contracting State where the measures were taken as soon as measures required by the situation and taken by the authorities of another State are recognised in the Contracting State in question.

Article 13

1   The authorities of a Contracting State which have jurisdiction under Arts 5 to 10 to take measures for the protection of the person or property of the child must abstain from exercising this jurisdiction if, at the time of the commencement of the proceedings, corresponding measures have been requested from the authorities of another Contracting State having jurisdiction under Arts 5 to 10 at the time of the request and are still under consideration.

2   The provisions of the preceding paragraph shall not apply if the authorities before whom the request for measures was initially introduced have declined jurisdiction.

Article 14

The measures taken in application of Arts 5 to 10 remain in force according to their terms, even if a change of circumstances has eliminated the basis upon which jurisdiction was founded, so long as the authorities which have jurisdiction under the Convention have not modified, replaced or terminated such measures.

CHAPTER III – APPLICABLE LAW

Article 15

1   In exercising their jurisdiction under the provisions of Chapter II, the authorities of the Contracting States shall apply their own law.

2   However, in so far as the protection of the person or the property of the child requires, they may exceptionally apply or take into consideration the law of another State with which the situation has a substantial connection.

3   If the child's habitual residence changes to another Contracting State, the law of that other State governs, from the time of the change, the conditions of application of the measures taken in the State of the former habitual residence.

Article 16

1   The attribution or extinction of parental responsibility by operation of law, without the intervention of a judicial or administrative authority, is governed by the law of the State of the habitual residence of the child.

2   The attribution or extinction of parental responsibility by an agreement or a unilateral act, without intervention of a judicial or administrative authority, is governed by the law of the State of the child's habitual residence at the time when the agreement or unilateral act takes effect.

3   Parental responsibility which exists under the law of the State of the child's habitual residence subsists after a change of that habitual residence to another State.

4   If the child's habitual residence changes, the attribution of parental responsibility by operation of law to a person who does not already have such responsibility is governed by the law of the State of the new habitual residence.

Article 17

The exercise of parental responsibility is governed by the law of the State of the child's habitual residence. If the child's habitual residence changes, it is governed by the law of the State of the new habitual residence.

Article 18

The parental responsibility referred to in Art 16 may be terminated, or the conditions of its exercise modified, by measures taken under this Convention.

Article 19

1   The validity of a transaction entered into between a third party and another person who would be entitled to act as the child's legal representative under the law of the State where the transaction was concluded cannot be contested, and the third party cannot be held liable, on the sole ground that the other person was not entitled to act as the child's legal representative under the law designated by the provisions of this Chapter, unless the third party knew or should have known that the parental responsibility was governed by the latter law.

2   The preceding paragraph applies only if the transaction was entered into between persons present on the territory of the same State.

Article 20

The provisions of this Chapter apply even if the law designated by them is the law of a non-Contracting State.

Article 21

1   In this Chapter the term 'law' means the law in force in a State other than its choice of law rules.

2   However, if the law applicable according to Art 16 is that of a non-Contracting State and if the choice of law rules of that State designate the law of another non-Contracting State which would apply its own law, the law of the latter State applies. If that other non-Contracting State would not apply its own law, the applicable law is that designated by Art 16.

Article 22

The application of the law designated by the provisions of this Chapter can be refused only if this application would be manifestly contrary to public policy, taking into account the best interests of the child.

CHAPTER IV – RECOGNITION AND ENFORCEMENT

Article 23

1   The measures taken by the authorities of a Contracting State shall be recognised by operation of law in all other Contracting States.

2   Recognition may however be refused:

(a)   if the measure was taken by an authority whose jurisdiction was not based on one of the grounds provided for in Chapter II;

(b)   if the measure was taken, except in a case of urgency, in the context of a judicial or administrative proceeding, without the child having been provided the opportunity to be heard, in violation of fundamental principles of procedure of the requested State;

(c)   on the request of any person claiming that the measure infringes his or her parental responsibility, if such measure was taken, except in a case of urgency, without such person having been given an opportunity to be heard;

(d)   if such recognition is manifestly contrary to public policy of the requested State, taking into account the best interests of the child;

(e)   if the measure is incompatible with a later measure taken in the non-Contracting State of the habitual residence of the child, where this later measure fulfils the requirements for recognition in the requested State;

(f)   if the procedure provided in Art 33 has not been complied with.

Article 24

Without prejudice to Art 23, para 1, any interested person may request from the competent authorities of a Contracting State that they decide on the recognition or non-recognition of a measure taken in another Contracting State. The procedure is governed by the law of the requested State.

Article 25

The authority of the requested State is bound by the findings of fact on which the authority of the State where the measure was taken based its jurisdiction.

Article 26

1   If measures taken in one Contracting State and enforceable there require enforcement in another Contracting State, they shall, upon request by an interested party, be declared enforceable or registered for the purpose of enforcement in that other State according to the procedure provided in the law of the latter State.

2   Each Contracting State shall apply to the declaration of enforceability or registration a simple and rapid procedure.

3   The declaration of enforceability or registration may be refused only for one of the reasons set out in Art 23, para 2.

Article 27

Without prejudice to such review as is necessary in the application of the preceding Articles, there shall be no review of the merits of the measure taken.

Article 28

Measures taken in one Contracting State and declared enforceable, or registered for the purpose of enforcement, in another Contracting State shall be enforced in the latter State as if they had been taken by the authorities of that State. Enforcement takes place in accordance with the law of the requested State to the extent provided by such law, taking into consideration the best interests of the child.

CHAPTER V – CO-OPERATION

Article 29

1   A Contracting State shall designate a Central Authority to discharge the duties which are imposed by the Convention on such authorities.

2   Federal States, States with more than one system of law or States having autonomous territorial units shall be free to appoint more than one Central Authority and to specify the territorial or personal extent of their functions. Where a State has appointed more than one Central Authority, it shall designate the Central Authority to which any communication may be addressed for transmission to the appropriate Central Authority within that State.

Article 30

1   Central Authorities shall co-operate with each other and promote co-operation amongst the competent authorities in their States to achieve the purposes of the Convention.

2   They shall, in connection with the application of the Convention, take appropriate steps to provide information as to the laws of, and services available in, their States relating to the protection of children.

Article 31

The Central Authority of a Contracting State, either directly or through public authorities or other bodies, shall take all appropriate steps to:

(a)   facilitate the communications and offer the assistance provided for in Arts 8 and 9 and in this Chapter;

(b)   facilitate, by mediation, conciliation or similar means, agreed solutions for the protection of the person or property of the child in situations to which the Convention applies;

(c)   provide, on the request of a competent authority of another Contracting State, assistance in discovering the whereabouts of a child where it appears that the child may be present and in need of protection within the territory of the requested State.

Article 32

On a request made with supporting reasons by the Central Authority or other competent authority of any Contracting State with which the child has a substantial connection, the Central Authority of the Contracting State in which the child is habitually resident and present may, directly or through public authorities or other bodies:

(a)   provide a report on the situation of the child;

(b)   request the competent authority of its State to consider the need to take measures for the protection of the person or property of the child.

Article 33

1   If an authority having jurisdiction under Arts 5 to 10 contemplates the placement of the child in a foster family or institutional care, or the provision of care by *kafala* or an analogous institution, and if such placement or such provision of care is to take place in another Contracting State, it shall first consult with the Central Authority or other competent authority of the latter State. To that effect it shall transmit a report on the child together with the reasons for the proposed placement or provision of care.

2   The decision on the placement or provision of care may be made in the requesting State only if the Central Authority or other competent authority of the requested State has consented to the placement or provision of care, taking into account the child's best interests.

Article 34

1   Where a measure of protection is contemplated, the competent authorities under the Convention, if the situation of the child so requires, may request any authority of another Contracting State which has information relevant to the protection of the child to communicate such information.

2   A Contracting State may declare that requests under para 1 shall be communicated to its authorities only through its Central Authority.

Article 35

1   The competent authorities of a Contracting State may request the authorities of another Contracting State to assist in the implementation of measures of protection taken under this Convention, especially in securing the effective exercise of rights of access as well as of the right to maintain direct contacts on a regular basis.

2   The authorities of a Contracting State in which the child does not habitually reside may, on the request of a parent residing in that State who is seeking to obtain or to maintain access to the child, gather information or evidence and may make a finding on the suitability of that parent to exercise access and on the conditions under which access is to be exercised. An authority exercising jurisdiction under Arts 5 to 10 to determine an application concerning access to the child, shall admit and consider such information, evidence and finding before reaching its decision.

3   An authority having jurisdiction under Arts 5 to 10 to decide on access may adjourn a proceeding pending the outcome of a request made under para 2, in particular, when it is considering an application to restrict or terminate access rights granted in the State of the child's former habitual residence.

4   Nothing in this Article shall prevent an authority having jurisdiction under Arts 5 to 10 from taking provisional measures pending the outcome of the request made under para 2.

Article 36

In any case where the child is exposed to a serious danger, the competent authorities of the Contracting State where measures for the protection of the child have been taken or are under consideration, if they are informed that the child's residence has changed to, or that the child is present in another State, shall inform the authorities of that other State about the danger involved and the measures taken or under consideration.

Article 37

An authority shall not request or transmit any information under this Chapter if to do so would, in its opinion, be likely to place the child's person or property in danger, or constitute a serious threat to the liberty or life of a member of the child's family.

Article 38

1   Without prejudice to the possibility of imposing reasonable charges for the provision of services, Central Authorities and other public authorities of Contracting States shall bear their own costs in applying the provisions of this Chapter.

2   Any Contracting State may enter into agreements with one or more other Contracting States concerning the allocation of charges.

Article 39

Any Contracting State may enter into agreements with one or more other Contracting States with a view to improving the application of this Chapter in their mutual relations. The States which have concluded such an agreement shall transmit a copy to the depositary of the Convention.

CHAPTER VI – GENERAL PROVISIONS

Article 40

1   The authorities of the Contracting State of the child's habitual residence, or of the Contracting State where a measure of protection has been taken, may deliver to the person having parental responsibility or to the person entrusted with protection of the child's person or property, at his or her request, a certificate indicating the capacity in which that person is entitled to act and the powers conferred upon him or her.

2   The capacity and powers indicated in the certificate are presumed to be vested in that person, in the absence of proof to the contrary.

3   Each Contracting State shall designate the authorities competent to draw up the certificate.

Article 41

Personal data gathered or transmitted under the Convention shall be used only for the purposes for which they were gathered or transmitted.

Article 42

The authorities to whom information is transmitted shall ensure its confidentiality, in accordance with the law of their State.

Article 43

All documents forwarded or delivered under this Convention shall be exempt from legalisation or any analogous formality.

Article 44

Each Contracting State may designate the authorities to which requests under Arts 8, 9 and 33 are to be addressed.

Article 45

1 The designations referred to in Arts 29 and 44 shall be communicated to the Permanent Bureau of the Hague Conference on Private International Law.

2 The declaration referred to in Art 34, para 2, shall be made to the depositary of the Convention.

Article 46

A Contracting State in which different systems of law or sets of rules of law apply to the protection of the child and his or her property shall not be bound to apply the rules of the Convention to conflicts solely between such different systems or sets of rules of law.

Article 47

In relation to a State in which two or more systems of law or sets of rules of law with regard to any matter dealt with in this Convention apply in different territorial units:

(1) any reference to habitual residence in that State shall be construed as referring to habitual residence in a territorial unit;

(2) any reference to the presence of the child in that State shall be construed as referring to presence in a territorial unit;

(3) any reference to the location of property of the child in that State shall be construed as referring to location of property of the child in a territorial unit;

(4) any reference to the State of which the child is a national shall be construed as referring to the territorial unit designated by the law of that State or, in the absence of relevant rules, to the territorial unit with which the child has the closest connection;

(5) any reference to the State whose authorities are seised of an application for divorce or legal separation of the child's parents, or for annulment of their marriage, shall be construed as referring to the territorial unit whose authorities are seised of such application;

(6) any reference to the State with which the child has a substantial connection shall be construed as referring to the territorial unit with which the child has such connection;

(7) any reference to the State to which the child has been removed or in which he or she has been retained shall be construed as referring to the relevant territorial unit to which the child has been removed or in which he or she has been retained;

(8) any reference to bodies or authorities of that State, other than Central Authorities, shall be construed as referring to those authorised to act in the relevant territorial unit;

(9) any reference to the law or procedure or authority of the State in which a measure has been taken shall be construed as referring to the law or procedure or authority of the territorial unit in which such measure was taken;

(10) any reference to the law or procedure or authority of the requested State shall be construed as referring to the law or procedure or authority of the territorial unit in which recognition or enforcement is sought.

Article 48

For the purpose of identifying the applicable law under Chapter III, in relation to a State which comprises two or more territorial units each of which has its own system of law or set of rules of law in respect of matters covered by this Convention, the following rules apply:

(a) if there are rules in force in such a State identifying which territorial unit's law is applicable, the law of that unit applies;

(b) in the absence of such rules, the law of the relevant territorial unit as defined in Art 47 applies.

Article 49

For the purpose of identifying the applicable law under Chapter III, in relation to a State which has two or more systems of law or sets of rules of law applicable to different categories of persons in respect of matters covered by this Convention, the following rules apply:

(a) if there are rules in force in such a State identifying which among such laws applies, that law applies;

(b) in the absence of such rules, the law of the system or the set of rules of law with which the child has the closest connection applies.

Article 50

This Convention shall not affect the application of the Convention of 25 October 1980 on the Civil Aspects of International Child Abduction as between Parties to both Conventions. Nothing, however, precludes provisions of this Convention from being invoked for the purposes of obtaining the return of a child who has been wrongfully removed or retained or of organising access rights.

Article 51

In relations between the Contracting States this Convention replaces the Convention of 5 October 1961 concerning the powers of authorities and the law applicable in respect of the protection of minors, and the Convention governing the guardianship of minors, signed at The Hague 12 June 1902, without prejudice to the recognition of measures taken under the Convention of 5 October 1961 mentioned above.

Article 52

1 This Convention does not affect any international instrument to which Contracting States are Parties and which contains provisions on matters governed by the Convention, unless a contrary declaration is made by the States Parties to such instrument.

2 This Convention does not affect the possibility for one or more Contracting States to conclude agreements which contain, in respect of children habitually resident in any of the States Parties to such agreements, provisions on matters governed by this Convention.

3 Agreements to be concluded by one or more Contracting States on matters within the scope of this Convention do not affect, in the relationship of such States with other Contracting States, the application of the provisions of this Convention.

4   The preceding paragraphs also apply to uniform laws based on special ties of a regional or other nature between the States concerned.

Article 53

1   The Convention shall apply to measures only if they are taken in a State after the Convention has entered into force for that State.

2   The Convention shall apply to the recognition and enforcement of measures taken after its entry into force as between the State where the measures have been taken and the requested State.

Article 54

1   Any communication sent to the Central Authority or to another authority of a Contracting State shall be in the original language, and shall be accompanied by a translation into the official language or one of the official languages of the other State or, where that is not feasible, a translation into French or English.

2   However, a Contracting State may, by making a reservation in accordance with Art 60, object to the use of either French or English, but not both.

Article 55

1   A Contracting State may, in accordance with Art 60:

(a)   reserve the jurisdiction of its authorities to take measures directed to the protection of property of a child situated on its territory;
(b)   reserve the right not to recognise any parental responsibility or measure in so far as it is incompatible with any measure taken by its authorities in relation to that property.

2   The reservation may be restricted to certain categories of property.

Article 56

The Secretary General of the Hague Conference on Private International Law shall at regular intervals convoke a Special Commission in order to review the practical operation of the Convention.

CHAPTER VII – FINAL CLAUSES

Article 57

1   The Convention shall be open for signature by the States which were Members of the Hague Conference on Private International Law at the time of its Eighteenth Session.

2   It shall be ratified, accepted or approved and the instruments of ratification, acceptance or approval shall be deposited with the Ministry of Foreign Affairs of the Kingdom of the Netherlands, depositary of the Convention.

Article 58

1   Any other State may accede to the Convention after it has entered into force in accordance with Art 61, para 1.

2   The instrument of accession shall be deposited with the depositary.

3   Such accession shall have effect only as regards the relations between the acceding State and those Contracting States which have not raised an objection to its accession

in the six months after the receipt of the notification referred to in sub-para (b) of Art 63. Such an objection may also be raised by States at the time when they ratify, accept or approve the Convention after an accession. Any such objection shall be notified to the depositary.

Article 59

1   If a State has two or more territorial units in which different systems of law are applicable in relation to matters dealt with in this Convention, it may at the time of signature, ratification, acceptance, approval or accession declare that the Convention shall extend to all its territorial units or only to one or more of them and may modify this declaration by submitting another declaration at any time.

2   Any such declaration shall be notified to the depositary and shall state expressly the territorial units to which the Convention applies.

3   If a State makes no declaration under this Article, the Convention is to extend to all territorial units of that State.

Article 60

1   Any State may, not later than the time of ratification, acceptance, approval or accession, or at the time of making a declaration in terms of Art 59, make one or both of the reservations provided for in Arts 54, para 2, and 55. No other reservation shall be permitted.

2   Any State may at any time withdraw a reservation it has made. The withdrawal shall be notified to the depositary.

3   The reservation shall cease to have effect on the first day of the third calendar month after the notification referred to in the preceding paragraph.

Article 61

1   The Convention shall enter into force on the first day of the month following the expiration of three months after the deposit of the third instrument of ratification, acceptance or approval referred to in Art 57.

2   Thereafter the Convention shall enter into force:

(a)   for each State ratifying, accepting or approving it subsequently, on the first day of the month following the expiration of three months after the deposit of its instrument of ratification, acceptance, approval or accession;

(b)   for each State acceding, on the first day of the month following the expiration of three months after the expiration of the period of six months provided in Art 58, para 3;

(c)   for a territorial unit to which the Convention has been extended in conformity with Article 59, on the first day of the month following the expiration of three months after the notification referred to in that Article.

Article 62

1   A State Party to the Convention may denounce it by a notification in writing addressed to the depositary. The denunciation may be limited to certain territorial units to which the Convention applies.

2   The denunciation takes effect on the first day of the month following the expiration of twelve months after the notification is received by the depositary. Where a longer period for the denunciation to take effect is specified in the notification, the denunciation takes effect upon the expiration of such longer period.

Article 63

The depositary shall notify the States Members of the Hague Conference on Private International Law and the States which have acceded in accordance with Art 58 of the following:

(a) the signatures, ratifications, acceptances and approvals referred to in Art 57;
(b) the accessions and objections raised to accessions referred to in Art 58;
(c) the date on which the Convention enters into force in accordance with Art 61;
(d) the declarations referred to in Arts 34, para 2, and 59;
(e) the agreements referred to in Art 39;
(f) the reservations referred to in Arts 54, para 2, and 55 and the withdrawals referred to in Art 60, para 2;
(g) the denunciations referred to in Art 62.

In witness whereof the undersigned, being duly authorised thereto, have signed this Convention.

Done at The Hague, on the 19th day of October 1996, in the English and French languages, both texts being equally authentic, in a single copy which shall be deposited in the archives of the Government of the Kingdom of the Netherlands, and of which a certified copy shall be sent, through diplomatic channels, to each of the States Members of the Hague Conference on Private International Law at the date of its Eighteenth Session.

COUNCIL OF EUROPE CONVENTION ON CONTACT CONCERNING CHILDREN

Strasbourg, 15.V.2003

PREAMBLE

The member States of the Council of Europe and the other Signatories hereto:

Taking into account the European Convention on Recognition and Enforcement of Decisions concerning Custody of Children and on Restoration of Custody of Children of 20 May 1980 (ETS No. 105);

Taking into account the Hague Convention of 25 October 1980 on the Civil Aspects of International Child Abduction and the Hague Convention of 19 October 1996 on Jurisdiction, Applicable Law, Recognition, Enforcement and Co-operation in respect of Parental Responsibility and Measures for the Protection of Children;

Taking into account the Council Regulation (EC) No 1347/2000 of 29 May 2000 on jurisdiction and the recognition and enforcement of judgments in matrimonial matters and in matters of parental responsibility for children of both spouses;

Recognising that, as provided in the different international legal instruments of the Council of Europe as well as in Art 3 of the United Nations Convention on the Rights of the Child of 20 November 1989, the best interests of the child shall be a primary consideration;

Aware of the need for further provisions to safeguard contact between children and their parents and other persons having family ties with children, as protected by Art 8 of the Convention for the Protection of Human Rights and Fundamental Freedoms of 4 November 1950 (ETS No 5);

Taking into account Art 9 of the United Nations Convention on the Rights of the Child which provides for the right of a child, who is separated from one or both parents, to maintain personal relations and direct contact with both parents on a regular basis, except when this is contrary to the child's best interests;

Taking into account para 2 of Art 10 of the United Nations Convention on the Rights of the Child, which provides for the right of the child whose parents reside in different States to maintain on a regular basis, save in exceptional circumstances, personal relations and direct contacts with both parents;

Aware of the desirability of recognising not only parents but also children as holders of rights;

Agreeing consequently to replace the notion of 'access to children' with the notion of 'contact concerning children';

Taking into account the European Convention on the Exercise of Children's Rights (ETS No 160) and the desirability of promoting measures to assist children in matters concerning contact with parents and other persons having family ties with children;

Agreeing on the need for children to have contact not only with both parents but also with certain other persons having family ties with children and the importance for parents and those other persons to remain in contact with children, subject to the best interests of the child;

Noting the need to promote the adoption by States of common principles with respect to contact concerning children, in particular in order to facilitate the application of international instruments in this field;

Realising that machinery set up to give effect to foreign orders relating to contact concerning children is more likely to provide satisfactory results where the principles on which these foreign orders are based are similar to the principles in the State giving effect to such foreign orders;

Recognising the need, when children and parents and other persons having family ties with children live in different States, to encourage judicial authorities to make more frequent use of transfrontier contact and to increase the confidence of all persons concerned that the children will be returned at the end of such contact;

Noting that the provision of efficient safeguards and additional guarantees is likely to ensure the return of children, in particular, at the end of transfrontier contact;

Noting that an additional international instrument is necessary to provide solutions relating in particular to transfrontier contact concerning children;

Desiring to establish co-operation between all central authorities and other bodies in order to promote and improve contact between children and their parents, and other persons having family ties with such children, and in particular to promote judicial co-operation in cases concerning transfrontier contact;

Have agreed as follows:

CHAPTER I – OBJECTS OF THE CONVENTION AND DEFINITIONS

Article 1   Objects of the Convention

The objects of this Convention are:

(a)   to determine general principles to be applied to contact orders;
(b)   to fix appropriate safeguards and guarantees to ensure the proper exercise of contact and the immediate return of children at the end of the period of contact;
(c)   to establish co-operation between central authorities, judicial authorities and other bodies in order to promote and improve contact between children and their parents, and other persons having family ties with children.

Article 2   Definitions

For the purposes of this Convention:

(a)   'contact' means:

    (i)   the child staying for a limited period of time with or meeting a person mentioned in Arts 4 or 5 with whom he or she is not usually living;

  (ii) any form of communication between the child and such person;

  (iii) the provision of information to such a person about the child or to the child about such a person.

(b) 'contact order' means a decision of a judicial authority concerning contact, including an agreement concerning contact which has been confirmed by a competent judicial authority or which has been formally drawn up or registered as an authentic instrument and is enforceable;

(c) 'child' means a person under 18 years of age in respect of whom a contact order may be made or enforced in a State Party;

(d) 'family ties' means a close relationship such as between a child and his or her grandparents or siblings, based on law or on a de facto family relationship;

(e) 'judicial authority' means a court or an administrative authority having equivalent powers.

CHAPTER II – GENERAL PRINCIPLES TO BE APPLIED TO CONTACT ORDERS

Article 3 Application of principles

States Parties shall adopt such legislative and other measures as may be necessary to ensure that the principles contained in this chapter are applied by judicial authorities when making, amending, suspending or revoking contact orders.

Article 4 Contact between a child and his or her parents

1 A child and his or her parents shall have the right to obtain and maintain regular contact with each other.

2 Such contact may be restricted or excluded only where necessary in the best interests of the child.

3 Where it is not in the best interests of a child to maintain unsupervised contact with one of his or her parents the possibility of supervised personal contact or other forms of contact with this parent shall be considered.

Article 5 Contact between a child and persons other than his or her parents

1 Subject to his or her best interests, contact may be established between the child and persons other than his or her parents having family ties with the child.

2 States Parties are free to extend this provision to persons other than those mentioned in para 1, and where so extended, States may freely decide what aspects of contact, as defined in Art 2 letter (a) shall apply.

Article 6 The right of a child to be informed, consulted and to express his or her views

1 A child considered by internal law as having sufficient understanding shall have the right, unless this would be manifestly contrary to his or her best interests:

  – to receive all relevant information;

  – to be consulted;

  – to express his or her views.

2 Due weight shall be given to those views and to the ascertainable wishes and feelings of the child.

Article 7   Resolving disputes concerning contact

When resolving disputes concerning contact, the judicial authorities shall take all appropriate measures:

(a)   to ensure that both parents are informed of the importance for their child and for both of them of establishing and maintaining regular contact with their child;

(b)   to encourage parents and other persons having family ties with the child to reach amicable agreements with respect to contact, in particular through the use of family mediation and other processes for resolving disputes;

(c)   before taking a decision, to ensure that they have sufficient information at their disposal, in particular from the holders of parental responsibilities, in order to take a decision in the best interests of the child and, where necessary, obtain further information from other relevant bodies or persons.

Article 8   Contact agreements

1   States Parties shall encourage, by means they consider appropriate, parents and other persons having family ties with the child to comply with the principles laid down in Arts 4 to 7 when making or modifying agreements on contact concerning a child. These agreements should preferably be in writing.

2   Upon request, judicial authorities shall, except where internal law otherwise provides, confirm an agreement on contact concerning a child, unless it is contrary to the best interests of the child.

Article 9   The carrying into effect of contact orders

States Parties shall take all appropriate measures to ensure that contact orders are carried into effect.

Article 10   Safeguards and guarantees to be taken concerning contact

1   Each State Party shall provide for and promote the use of safeguards and guarantees. It shall communicate, through its central authorities, to the Secretary General of the Council of Europe, within three months after the entry into force of this Convention for that State Party, at least three categories of safeguards and guarantees available in its internal law in addition to the safeguards and guarantees referred to in para 3 of Art 4 and in letter (b) of para 1 of Art 14 of this Convention. Changes of available safeguards and guarantees shall be communicated as soon as possible.

2   Where the circumstances of the case so require, judicial authorities may, at any time, make a contact order subject to any safeguards and guarantees both for the purpose of ensuring that the order is carried into effect and that either the child is returned at the end of the period of contact to the place where he or she usually lives or that he or she is not improperly removed.

(a)   Safeguards and guarantees for ensuring that the order is carried into effect, may in particular include:

   –   supervision of contact;
   –   the obligation for a person to provide for the travel and accommodation expenses of the child and, as may be appropriate, of any other person accompanying the child;
   –   a security to be deposited by the person with whom the child is usually living to ensure that the person seeking contact with the child is not prevented from having such contact;

– a fine to be imposed on the person with whom the child is usually living, should this person refuse to comply with the contact order.

(b) Safeguards and guarantees for ensuring the return of the child or preventing an improper removal, may in particular include:

– the surrender of passports or identity documents and, where appropriate, a document indicating that the person seeking contact has notified the competent consular authority about such a surrender during the period of contact;

– financial guarantees;

– charges on property;

– undertakings or stipulations to the court;

– the obligation of the person having contact with the child to present himself or herself, with the child regularly before a competent body such as a youth welfare authority or a police station, in the place where contact is to be exercised;

– the obligation of the person seeking contact to present a document issued by the State where contact is to take place, certifying the recognition and declaration of enforceability of a custody or a contact order or both either before a contact order is made or before contact takes place;

– the imposition of conditions in relation to the place where contact is to be exercised and, where appropriate, the registration, in any national or transfrontier information system, of a prohibition preventing the child from leaving the State where contact is to take place.

3   Any such safeguards and guarantees shall be in writing or evidenced in writing and shall form part of the contact order or the confirmed agreement.

4   If safeguards or guarantees are to be implemented in another State Party, the judicial authority shall preferably order such safeguards or guarantees as are capable of implementation in that State Party.

CHAPTER III – MEASURES TO PROMOTE AND IMPROVE TRANSFRONTIER CONTACT

Article 11   Central authorities

1   Each State Party shall appoint a central authority to carry out the functions provided for by this Convention in cases of transfrontier contact.

2   Federal States, States with more than one system of law or States having autonomous territorial units shall be free to appoint more than one central authority and to specify the territorial or personal extent of their functions. Where a State has appointed more than one central authority, it shall designate the central authority to which any communication may be addressed for transmission to the appropriate central authority within that State.

3   The Secretary General of the Council of Europe shall be notified of any appointment under this article.

Article 12   Duties of the central authorities

The central authorities of States Parties shall:

(a)   co-operate with each other and promote co-operation between the competent authorities, including judicial authorities, in their respective countries to achieve the purposes of the Convention. They shall act with all necessary despatch;

(b)   with a view to facilitating the operation of this Convention, provide each other on request with information concerning their laws relating to parental responsibilities, including contact and any more detailed information concerning safeguards and guarantees in addition to that already provided according to para 1 of Art 10, and their available services (including legal services, publicly funded or otherwise) as well as information concerning any changes in these laws and services;

(c)   take all appropriate steps in order to discover the whereabouts of the child;

(d)   secure the transmission of requests for information coming from the competent authorities and relating to legal or factual matters concerning pending proceedings;

(e)   keep each other informed of any difficulties likely to arise in applying the Convention and, as far as possible, eliminate obstacles to its application.

Article 13   International co-operation

1   The judicial authorities, the central authorities and the social and other bodies of States Parties concerned, acting within their respective competence, shall co-operate in relation to proceedings regarding transfrontier contact.

2   In particular, the central authorities shall assist the judicial authorities of States Parties in communicating with each other and obtaining such information and assistance as may be necessary for them to achieve the objects of this Convention.

3   In transfrontier cases, the central authorities shall assist children, parents and other persons having family ties with the child, in particular, to institute proceedings regarding transfrontier contact.

Article 14   Recognition and enforcement of transfrontier contact orders

1   States Parties shall provide, including where applicable in accordance with relevant international instruments:

(a)   a system for the recognition and enforcement of orders made in other States Parties concerning contact and rights of custody;

(b)   a procedure whereby orders relating to contact and rights of custody made in other States Parties may be recognised and declared enforceable in advance of contact being exercised within the State addressed.

2   If a State Party makes recognition or enforcement or both of a foreign order conditional on the existence of a treaty or reciprocity, it may consider this Convention as such a legal basis for recognition or enforcement or both of a foreign contact order.

Article 15   Conditions for implementing transfrontier contact orders

The judicial authority of the State Party in which a transfrontier contact order made in another State Party is to be implemented may, when recognising or declaring enforceable such a contact order, or at any later time, fix or adapt the conditions for its implementation, as well as any safeguards or guarantees attaching to it, if necessary for facilitating the exercise of this contact, provided that the essential elements of the order are respected and taking into account, in particular, a change of circumstances and the arrangements made by the persons concerned. In no circumstances may the foreign decision be reviewed as to its substance.

Article 16   Return of a child

1   Where a child at the end of a period of transfrontier contact based on a contact order is not returned, the competent authorities shall, upon request, ensure the child's immediate return, where applicable, by applying the relevant provisions of international instruments, of internal law and by implementing, where appropriate, such safeguards and guarantees as may be provided in the contact order.

2   A decision on the return of the child shall be made, whenever possible, within six weeks of the date of an application for the return.

Article 17   Costs

With the exception of the cost of repatriation, each State Party undertakes not to claim any payment from an applicant in respect of any measures taken under this Convention by the central authority itself of that State on the applicant's behalf.

Article 18   Language requirement

1   Subject to any special agreements made between the central authorities concerned:

(a)   communications to the central authority of the State addressed shall be made in the official language or in one of the official languages of that State or be accompanied by a translation into that language;
(b)   the central authority of the State addressed shall nevertheless accept communications made in English or in French, or accompanied by a translation into one of these languages.

2   Communications coming from the central authority of the State addressed, including the results of enquiries carried out, may be made in the official language or one of the official languages of that State or in English or French.

3   However, a State Party may, by making a declaration addressed to the Secretary General of the Council of Europe, object to the use of either French or English under paras 1 and 2 of this article, in any application, communication or other documents sent to their central authorities.

CHAPTER IV – RELATIONSHIP WITH OTHER INSTRUMENTS

Article 19   Relationship with the European Convention on Recognition and Enforcement of Decisions concerning Custody of Children and on Restoration of Custody of Children

Paras 2 and 3 of Art 11 of the European Convention of 20 May 1980 (ETS No 105) on Recognition and Enforcement of Decisions concerning Custody of Children and on Restoration of Custody of Children shall not be applied in relations between States Parties which are also States Parties of the present Convention.

Article 20   Relationships with other instruments

1   This Convention shall not affect any international instrument to which States Parties to the present Convention are Parties or shall become Parties and which contains provisions on matters governed by this Convention. In particular, this Convention shall not prejudice the application of the following legal instruments:

(a)   the Hague Convention of 5 October 1961 on the competence of authorities and the applicable law concerning the protection of minors,

(b)   the European Convention on the recognition and enforcement of decisions concerning custody of children and on restoration of custody of children of 20 May 1980, subject to Art 19 above,

(c)   the Hague Convention of 25 October 1980 on the civil aspects of international child abduction,

(d)   the Hague Convention of 19 October 1996 on jurisdiction, applicable law, recognition, enforcement and co-operation in respect of parental responsibility and measures for the protection of children.

2   Nothing in this Convention shall prevent Parties from concluding international agreements completing or developing the provisions of this Convention or extending their field of application.

3   In their mutual relations, States Parties which are members of the European Community shall apply Community rules and shall therefore not apply the rules arising from this Convention, except in so far as there is no Community rule governing the particular subject concerned.

CHAPTER V – AMENDMENTS TO THE CONVENTION

Article 21   Amendments

1   Any proposal for an amendment to this Convention presented by a Party shall be communicated to the Secretary General of the Council of Europe and forwarded by him or her to the member States of the Council of Europe, any signatory, any State Party, the European Community, to any State invited to sign this Convention in accordance with the provisions of Art 22 and to any State invited to accede to this Convention in accordance with the provisions of Art 23.

2   Any amendment proposed by a Party shall be communicated to the European Committee on Legal Co-operation (CDCJ), which shall submit to the Committee of Ministers its opinion on that proposed amendment.

3   The Committee of Ministers shall consider the proposed amendment and the opinion submitted by the CDCJ and, following consultation of the Parties to the Convention, which are not members of the Council of Europe, may adopt the amendment.

4   The text of any amendment adopted by the Committee of Ministers in accordance with para 3 of this article shall be forwarded to the Parties for acceptance.

5   Any amendment adopted in accordance with para 3 of this article shall enter into force on the first day of the month following the expiration of a period of one month after the date on which all Parties have informed the Secretary General that they have accepted it.

CHAPTER VI – FINAL CLAUSES

Article 22   Signature and entry into force

1   This Convention shall be open for signature by the member States of the Council of Europe, the non-member States which have participated in its elaboration and the European Community.

2   This Convention is subject to ratification, acceptance or approval. Instruments of ratification, acceptance or approval shall be deposited with the Secretary General of the Council of Europe.

3   This Convention shall enter into force on the first day of the month following the expiration of a period of three months after the date on which three States, including at least two member States of the Council of Europe, have expressed their consent to be bound by the Convention in accordance with the provisions of the preceding paragraph.

4   In respect of any State mentioned in para 1 or the European Community, which subsequently expresses its consent to be bound by it, the Convention shall enter into force on the first day of the month following the expiration of a period of three months after the date of the deposit of its instrument of ratification, acceptance or approval.

Article 23   Accession to the Convention

1   After the entry into force of this Convention, the Committee of Ministers of the Council of Europe may, after consultation of the Parties, invite any non-member State of the Council of Europe, which has not participated in the elaboration of the Convention, to accede to this Convention by a decision taken by the majority provided for in Art 20 d. of the Statute of the Council of Europe, and by unanimous vote of the representatives of the Contracting States entitled to sit on the Committee of Ministers.

2   In respect of any acceding State, the Convention shall enter into force on the first day of the month following the expiration of a period of three months after the date of deposit of the instrument of accession with the Secretary General of the Council of Europe.

Article 24   Territorial application

1   Any State or the European Community may, at the time of signature or when depositing its instrument of ratification, acceptance, approval or accession, specify the territory or territories to which this Convention shall apply.

2   Any Party may, at any later date, by a declaration addressed to the Secretary General of the Council of Europe, extend the application of this Convention to any other territory specified in the declaration and for whose international relations it is responsible or on whose behalf it is authorised to give undertakings. In respect of such territory, the Convention shall enter into force on the first day of the month following the expiration of a period of three months after the date of receipt of such declaration by the Secretary General.

3   Any declaration made under the two preceding paragraphs may, in respect of any territory specified in such declaration, be withdrawn by a notification addressed to the Secretary General. The withdrawal shall become effective on the first day of the

month following the expiration of a period of three months after the date of receipt of such notification by the Secretary General.

Article 25   Reservations

No reservation may be made in respect of any provision of this Convention.

Article 26   Denunciation

1   Any Party may, at any time, denounce this Convention by means of a notification addressed to the Secretary General of the Council of Europe.

2   Such denunciation shall become effective on the first day of the month following the expiration of a period of three months after the date of receipt of the notification by the Secretary General.

Article 27   Notifications

The Secretary General of the Council of Europe shall notify the member States of the Council of Europe, any State signatory, any State Party, the European Community, to any State invited to sign this Convention in accordance with the provisions of Art 22 and to any State invited to accede to this Convention in accordance with the provisions of Art 23 of:

(a)   any signature;
(b)   the deposit of any instrument of ratification, acceptance, approval or accession;
(c)   any date of entry into force of this Convention in accordance with Arts 22 and 23;
(d)   any amendment adopted in accordance with Art 21 and the date on which such an amendment enters into force;
(e)   any declaration made under the provisions of Art 18;
(f)   any denunciation made in pursuance of the provisions of Art 26;
(g)   any other act, notification or communication, in particular relating to Arts 10 and 11 of this Convention.

In witness whereof, the undersigned, being duly authorised thereto, have signed this Convention.

Done at Strasbourg, this 15th day of May 2003, in English and in French, both texts being equally authentic, in a single copy, which shall be deposited in the archives of the Council of Europe. The Secretary General of the Council of Europe shall transmit certified copies to each member State of the Council of Europe, to the non-member States which have participated in the elaboration of this Convention, to the European Community and to any State invited to accede to this Convention.

VIENNA CONVENTION ON THE LAW OF TREATIES, Arts 31, 32 and 33

INTERPRETATION OF TREATIES

Article 31   General rule of interpretation

1   A treaty shall be interpreted in good faith in accordance with the ordinary meaning to be given to the terms of the treaty in their context and in the light of its object and purpose.

2   The context for the purpose of the interpretation of a treaty shall comprise, in addition to the text, including its preamble and annexes:

(a)   any agreement relating to the treaty which was made between all the parties in connexion with the conclusion of the treaty;

(b)   any instrument which was made by one or more parties in connexion with the conclusion of the treaty and accepted by the other parties as an instrument related to the treaty.

3   There shall be taken into account, together with the context:

(a)   any subsequent agreement between the parties regarding the interpretation of the treaty or the application of its provisions:

(b)   any subsequent practice in the application of the treaty which establishes the agreement of the parties regarding its interpretation;

(c)   any relevant rules of international law applicable in the relations between the parties.

4   A special meaning shall be given to a term if it is established that the parties so intended.

Article 32   Supplementary means of interpretation

Recourse may be had to supplementary means of interpretation, including the preparatory work of the treaty and the circumstances of its conclusion, in order to confirm the meaning resulting from the application of Article 31, or to determine the meaning when the interpretation according to Article 31:

(a)   leaves the meaning ambiguous or obscure; or
(b)   leads to a result which is manifestly absurd or unreasonable.

Article 33   Interpretation of treaties authenticated in two or more languages

1   When a treaty has been authenticated in two or more languages, the text is equally authoritative in each language, unless the treaty provides or the parties agree that, in case of divergence, a particular text shall prevail.

2   A version of the treaty in a language other than one of those in which the text was authenticated shall be considered an authentic text only if the treaty so provides or the parties so agree.

3   The terms of the treaty are presumed to have the same meaning in each authentic text.

4   Except where a particular text prevails in accordance with paragraph 1, when a comparison of the authentic texts discloses a difference of meaning which the application of Articles 31 and 32 does not remove, the meaning which best reconciles the texts, having regard to the object and purpose of the treaty, shall be adopted.

DECLARATIONS FROM THE DE RUWENBERG CONFERENCES

JUDGES' SEMINAR ON INTERNATIONAL PROTECTION OF THE CHILD

(De Ruwenberg, 22–25 June 1998)

The following conclusions were reached during the final session of the Seminar during discussion on the subject 'Towards International Judicial Co-operation':

(1) The recommendation was made that, following the example of Australia, judges attending the seminar should raise with the relevant authorities in their jurisdictions (eg court presidents or other officials, as appropriate within the different legal cultures) the potential usefulness of designating one or more members of the judiciary to act as a channel of communication and liaison with their national Central Authorities, with other judges within their own jurisdictions and with judges in other states, in respect, at least initially, of issues relevant to the operation of the Hague Convention of 25 October 1980 on the Civil Aspects of International Child Abduction.

(2) In accordance with the objectives of the Grotius programme of the European Union, a number of judges outlined their plans for passing on the information and experience gained during the seminar to judicial colleagues in their several jurisdictions.

(3) As short newsletter would be circulated on a regular basis (perhaps twice yearly) by the Permanent Bureau of the Hague Conference on Private International Law to judges attending the Seminar, with a view to the exchange of information concerning judicial co-operation in matters of international child protection. The information would include any changes in personal contact details, notes on developments concerning relevant international instruments (eg new ratifications and accessions), reference to significant national developments (eg case law, procedural or organisational changes, judicial conferences/seminars, etc), and examples of successful practice in international judicial co-operation. The network would be made available to other interested judges.

(4) There was broad support for the view that efforts should be made to ensure greater judicial participation in the work of the Hague Conference on Private International Law, both in the development of new international instruments and in the periodic reviews of their practical operation.

(5) There was agreement that the seminar had been of practical value in promoting mutual understanding and in forwarding the objective of more effective international judicial co-operation in matters of international child protection. It was recommended that further seminars of this kind be organised periodically (every three or four years).

JUDGES' SEMINAR ON INTERNATIONAL PROTECTION OF THE CHILD

(De Ruwenberg, 3–6 June 2000)

Upon the request of the French and German Ministries of Justice, the Hague Conference on Private International Law hosted a Judicial Seminar on the International Protection of Children at the Conference Centre De Ruwenberg from 3–6 June 2000. Nearly 40 Judges from France, Germany, Italy, and the Netherlands engaged in intensive discussions on the application of the international instruments concerned with the protection of children. The Seminar provided an excellent opportunity for Judges from different jurisdictions to share knowledge, concerns, and ideas regarding the Hague Convention of 25 October 1980 on the Civil Aspects of International Child Abduction. At the close of the Seminar, the Judges unanimously adopted the following conclusions:

(1) The Seminar has been an important event in establishing mutual understanding, respect and trust between the Judges from the different countries – factors which are essential to the effective operation of the international instruments concerned with the protection of children, and in particular the Hague Convention of 25 October 1980 on the Civil Aspects of International Child Abduction.

(2) The format of the Seminar, involving intensive discussions among Judges from four jurisdictions around a number of practical cases, has been a success and is a model for such seminars in the future. Differences of approach, where they exist, have been revealed and the way has been opened to greater consistency in interpretation and practice under the Conventions.

(3) The Judges participating in the Seminar will endeavour to inform their colleagues in their respective jurisdictions about the seminar and its outcome, and will in particular make available information about the International Child Abduction Database (http://www.incadat.com) and about the Special Commission on the practical operation of the Hague Convention of 25 October 1980 on the Civil Aspects of International Child Abduction, which is to be held at The Hague in March 2001.

(4) It is recognised that, in cases involving the international protection of children, considerable advantages are to be gained from a concentration of jurisdiction in a limited number of courts/tribunals. These advantages include the accumulation of experience among the Judges and practitioners concerned and the development of greater mutual confidence between legal systems.

(5) The need for more effective methods of international judicial co-operation in respect of child protection is emphasised, as well as the necessity for direct communication between Judges in different jurisdictions in certain cases. The idea of the appointment of liaison Judges in the different jurisdictions, to act as channels of communication in international cases, is supported. Further exploration of the administrative and legal aspects of this concept should be

carried out. The continued development of an international network of Judges in the field of international child protection to promote personal contacts and the exchange of information is also supported.

INTERNATIONAL JUDICIAL SEMINAR ON THE 1980 HAGUE CONVENTION ON THE CIVIL ASPECTS OF INTERNATIONAL CHILD ABDUCTION

(De Ruwenberg Conference Centre, Netherlands, 20–23 October 2001)

CONCLUSIONS AND RECOMMENDATIONS

Introduction

The international judicial seminar was an initiative of Germany and the United States of America. This was the third international judicial seminar to be held at De Ruwenberg facilitated by the Permanent Bureau of the Hague Conference on Private International Law. The seminar was attended by thirty-one judges from seven jurisdictions (England and Wales (2), France (3), Germany (15), Netherlands (2), Scotland (1), Sweden (3), United States of America (5)), thirteen experts from Central Authorities and Ministries and four members of the Permanent Bureau. (The Conclusions and Recommendations set out below, which were agreed unanimously, are those of the thirty-one judges.)

1 Concentration of jurisdiction and judicial training

The considerable advantages to be gained in Hague Convention cases by a concentration of jurisdiction within a limited number of courts is re-emphasised.

The progress in this direction already made in certain Contracting States is welcomed; so too is the consideration being given to this matter in other States.

It is particularly important that judges concerned in Hague proceedings be offered appropriate training or briefing.

2 Securing the voluntary return of the child

Measures employed to assist in securing the voluntary return of the child or to bring about an amicable resolution of the issues are encouraged but should not result in any undue delay in return proceedings.

3 Speed of Hague procedures, including appeals

The judges present endorse the Conclusions and Recommendations of the March 2001 Fourth Meeting of the Special Commission to Review the Operation of the 1980 Convention:

- underscoring the obligation (Art 11) of Contracting States to process return applications expeditiously, and that this obligation extends also to appeal procedures;
- calling upon trial and appellate courts to set and adhere to timetables that ensure the speedy determination of return applications; and
- calling for the firm management by judges, both at trial and appellate levels, of the progress of return proceedings.

4   Article 13, paragraph 1(b)

The 'grave risk' defence in Art 13 1(b) of the Convention has generally been narrowly construed. It is in keeping with the objectives of the Convention, as confirmed in the Explanatory Report by Elisa Pérez-Vera, to interpret this defence in a restrictive fashion.

A refusal to return a child on the basis of Art 13 1(b) should not be contemplated unless all the available alternative methods of protecting the child have been considered by the court and found to be inadequate.

5   Protection of the returning child

When considering measures to protect a child who is the subject of a return order (and where appropriate an accompanying parent), a court should have regard to the enforceability of those measures within the country to which the child is to be returned. In this context, attention is drawn to the value of safe-return orders (including 'mirror' orders) made in that country before the child's return.

6   Follow-up studies

More 'follow-up' research, tracking the course of events following the making of return orders would be of great value to the judiciary.

7   Interim jurisdiction to make contact/access orders

A court having jurisdiction to deal with an application for the return of a child should also have authority to consider an interim application for contact/access pending the determination of the return proceedings. In this context the potential advantages of the 1996 Hague Convention on Child Protection, as an adjunct to the 1980 Hague Convention, are recognised.

8   Liaison Judges

The growth of the network of liaison judges is noted as a significant aid to international judicial communication, collaboration and understanding.

9   INCADAT

The establishment of INCADAT and its free availability on the internet are welcomed by judges as an important contribution to the spread of knowledge about the Convention and as a means of promoting consistent interpretation of the Convention internationally. States Parties are encouraged to collaborate with the Permanent Bureau to explore possible sources of funding or material assistance to assist in the completion of INCADAT and to secure its position for the future.

10   The Judges' Newsletter on International Child Protection

The establishment of the Judges' Newsletter on International Child Protection as a biannual publication is welcomed. Liaison and other recipient judges will ensure circulation to the specialist judiciary in their respective jurisdictions.

11   Consulting the judiciary on changes in the law

Legislative processes, which concern the international protection of children, including those within the European Union, should be structured in a way, which allows for timely and appropriate consultation with those elements of the judiciary with experience in the field who will have the responsibility of applying new laws or regulations.

12   International Judicial Seminars

The De Ruwenberg seminar has offered an opportunity for judges and experts from seven jurisdictions to explain and compare the operation of the 1980 Hague Convention in their countries, to share experiences and to develop the mutual confidence necessary for the operation of international instruments of this kind. The Hague Conference is invited to facilitate more international judicial conferences of this nature. States Parties are asked to recognise the importance of such events in reinforcing the international protection of their children, and to make available the necessary funding.

13   Dissemination of the work of this seminar

Acknowledging the great value of this seminar to all delegates, each participating jurisdiction will take appropriate steps to disseminate its conclusions domestically.

De Ruwenberg
23 October 2001

RESOLUTION FROM THE COMMON LAW JUDICIAL CONFERENCE ON INTERNATIONAL PARENTAL CHILD ABDUCTION

(Washington DC, 17–21 September 2000)

From 17–21 September 2000 the U.S. State Department's Office of Children's Issues, the US Central Authority for the Hague Convention of 25 October 1980 on the Civil Aspects of International Child Abduction, hosted the Common Law Judicial Conference on International Parental Child Abduction with the aim of improving understanding and interpretation of the Convention. Judges representing six delegations (Australia, Canada, Ireland, New Zealand, the United Kingdom and the United States) made the following recommendations to improve operation of the 1980 Convention. The views expressed are those of the judicial members of the delegations, and do not necessarily reflect the official views of their countries or judiciaries.

(1) This Conference supports the conclusions adopted at the analogous Judicial Seminar on the International Protection of Children at the Conference Centre De Ruwenberg, 3–6 June 2000, and adopts parallel resolutions, as follows:

(a) Such conferences are important events in emphasising mutual understanding, respect and trust between the Judges from different countries- factors which are essential to the effective operation of international instruments concerned with the protection of children, and in particular, the Hague Child Abduction Convention.

(b) The format adopted, involving intensive discussion among Judges, administrators, academics and practitioners from six common law countries (two of which are bi-jural) around a number of selected topics, has been a success and is a model for such conferences in the future. Differences of approach, where they exist, have been revealed and the way has been opened to greater consistency in interpretation and practice under the Hague Child Abduction Convention.

(c) The Judges participating in the conference will endeavour to inform their colleagues in their respective jurisdictions about the conference and its outcome, and will in particular make available information about the International Child Abduction Database (http://www.incadat.com) and about the Special Commission on the practical operation of the Hague Child Abduction Convention, which is to be held at the Hague in March 2001.

(d) It is recognised that, in cases involving the international abduction of children, considerable advantages are to be gained from a concentration of jurisdiction in a limited number of courts/tribunals. These advantages include accumulation of experience among the Judges and practitioners concerned and the development of greater mutual confidence between legal systems.

(e) The need for more effective methods of international judicial co-operation in the field of child abduction is emphasised, as well as the necessity for direct communication between Judges in different jurisdictions in certain cases. The idea of the appointment of liaison Judges in the different jurisdictions, to act as channels of communication in international cases, is supported. Further exploration of the administrative and legal aspects of this concept should be carried out. The continued development of an international network of Judges in the field of international child abduction to promote personal contacts and the exchange of information is also supported.

(2) Prompt decision making under the Hague Child Abduction Convention serves the best interests of children. It is the responsibility of the judiciary at both the trial and appellate levels firmly to manage the progress of return cases under the Convention. Trial and appellate courts should set and adhere to timetables that ensure the expeditious determination of Hague applications.

(3) Central Authorities likewise have a responsibility to process Hague applications expeditiously. Delays in the administrative process can adversely affect judicial return proceedings.

(4) It is recommended that State parties ensure that there are simple and effective mechanisms to enforce orders for the return of children.

(5) The Art 13(1)(b) 'grave risk' defence has generally been narrowly construed by courts in member states. It is in keeping with the objectives of the Hague Child Abduction Convention to construe the Art 13(1)(b) grave risk defence narrowly.

(6) Courts in many jurisdictions regard the use of orders with varying names, eg stipulations, conditions, undertakings, as a useful tool to facilitate arrangements for return and/or alleviate Art 13(1)(b) concerns. Such orders, limited in scope and duration, addressing short-term issues and remaining in effect only until such time as a court in the country to which the child is returned takes control, are in keeping with the spirit of the Hague Child Abduction Convention.

(7) Left-behind parents who seek a child's return under the Hague Child Abduction Convention need speedy and effective access to the courts. Lack of legal representation is a significant obstacle to invoking the Convention's remedies. To overcome this obstacle, left-behind parents should be provided promptly with experienced legal representation, where possible at the expense of the requested state.

(8) It is widely agreed that the problem of enforcing access rights internationally, though intertwined with international child abduction cases, is not adequately addressed by the Hague Child Abduction Convention. Other legal and judicial solutions should be pursued, including prompt consideration of the 1996 Hague Convention on the Protection of Children (which provides, inter alia, a mechanism for handling international access cases), and court-referred mediation in appropriate cases (to help parents make their own arrangements for international access).

(9) Courts take significantly different approaches to relocation cases, which are occurring with a frequency not contemplated in 1980 when the Hague Child Abduction Convention was drafted. Courts should be aware that highly restrictive approaches to relocation can adversely affect the operation of the Hague Child Abduction Convention.

(10) Judges need to be alert to the possibility of international child abduction and can be instrumental in preventing abductions by entering and enforcing orders for appropriate safeguards.

(11) Abductions to countries which are not parties to the Hague Child Abduction Convention pose serious obstacles for left-behind parents who seek return of, or access to, their children. Those government bodies responsible for foreign affairs might usefully explore the possibilities of treaty and bilateral approaches to resolve these cases, which approaches have already met with some success.

(12) Given the vital role of Judges in the operation of the Hague Child Abduction Convention, each country participating in this conference should endeavour to have at least one Judge expert in the Convention in its delegation at the Fourth Special Commission meeting at the Hague in March 2001.

(13) The support of the activities of the Permanent Bureau of the Hague Conference on Private International Law is critical to its role in co-ordinating and disseminating information to the international community. This support should extend to special projects and services provided by the Permanent Bureau, including the International Child Abduction Database ('INCADAT') developed by the Permanent Bureau, which will be of significant assistance to the judiciary, Central Authorities, legal profession, and the parties. The Judges at this Conference recognise the importance of the Permanent Bureau being adequately funded.

APPENDIX 2

SOURCES OF FURTHER INFORMATION

INTERNATIONAL WEBSITES

Child Abduction Database	www.incadat.com
Child Abduction Unit – England and Wales	www.offsol.demon.co.uk
Council of European Union Bars and Law Societies	www.ccbe.org/UK/top.htm
Countries in which Hague and European Conventions on Child Abduction are in force	www.offsol.demon.co.uk
EU and European Court information site	www.airecentre.org
European Court of Human Rights Cases	www.echr.coe.int
European Court of Justice	www.europa.eu.int/cj/en/index.htm
European Judicial Network	www.europa.eu.int/comm/justice_home/ejn
European Union Internet Resources	www.lib.berkeley.edu/GSSI/eu.html
European Union Law	www.europa.eu.int/eur-lex
Foreign and Commonwealth Office	www.fco.gov.uk
Hague Conference Conventions	www.hcch.net/e/conventions/index.html
Hague Conference on Private International Law	www.hcch.net
International Court of Justice – The Hague	www.icj-cij.org
Reunite International Child Abduction Centre	www.reunite.org
UN Convention on the Rights of the Child	www.unicef.org/crc/

Council of Europe websites

Family Law:

www.coe.int/family (for information about the work in the field of family law including conventions and recommendations)

The Forum of children and families:

www.coe.int/T/E/Social_Cohesion/Activities_for_social_Cohesion

Education:

www.coe.int/education

Youth centre:

www.coe.int/youth

Bioethics:

www.coe.int/legalcooperation, then click on 'Bioethics'

Equality between women and men:

www.humanrights.coe.int/equality

Juvenile delinquency:

www.coe.int/legalcooperation, then click on 'Crime Prevention of juvenile delinquency'

Sexual exploitation of children:

www.coe.int/legal cooperation, then click on 'Fight against sexual exploitation of children'

Parliamentary assembly:

http://assembly.coe.int

European Ministers of Justice:

www.coe.int/legalcooperation, then click on 'Conference of European Ministers of Justice'

Legal affairs:

www.coe.int/T/E/Legal_affairs

Council of Europe

www.coe.int

For specific requests by email: cifa@coe.int (for family law) or pc-s-es@coe.int (for protection of children against sexual exploitation)

APPENDIX 3

PROTOCOLS AND GUIDANCE

PROTOCOL – COMMUNICATING WITH THE PASSPORT SERVICE IN FAMILY PROCEEDINGS

Since August 2003 a protocol has now been agreed in respect of enquiries directed to the Passport Service. The procedure is as follows:

(1) Where a request is made of or an order is made against the UK Passport Service, the judge should ask the court to draw up and immediately to provide a copy of the relevant request or order in a separate document to:

> Ms Ananda Hall
> Family Division Lawyer
> President's Chambers
> Royal Courts of Justice
> Strand
> London WC2A 2LL
>
> Tel: 020 7947 7197
> Fax: 020 7947 7274
> Ananda.Hall@courtservice.gsi.gov.uk

(2) The request or order should either state or be accompanied by a letter to the Family Division Lawyer stating the following details in respect of all parties about whom they are seeking information:

    (a)   full name including all middle names;
    (b)   full date of birth; and
    (c)   any known passport numbers.

(3) The request or order should state the time by which the information is required, where possible allowing a reasonable period for the Passport Service to search their records.

(4) The request or order should identify the information required from the Passport Service.

(5) The Family Division Lawyer will then send to disclosure of information officers the enquiry, together with a copy of any request or order made. The disclosure of information officer will be responsible for retrieving the information and forwarding this to the Family Division Lawyer.

(6) The Family Division Lawyer will follow up as required in order to ensure that the information is received by the court in time, and will receive the statement before forwarding it on as instructed by the judge or court making the request.

PROTOCOL – COMMUNICATING WITH THE HOME OFFICE

(1)   Where a request is made of or an order is made against the Home Office, the judge should ask the court to draw up and immediately to provide a copy of the relevant request or order in a separate document to:

> Ms Ananda Hall
> Family Division Lawyer
> President's Chambers
> Royal Courts of Justice
> Strand
> London WC2A 2LL
>
> Tel: 020 7947 7197
> Fax: 020 7947 7274
> Ananda.Hall@courtservice.gsi.gov.uk

(2)   The request or order should either state or be accompanied by a letter to the Family Division Lawyer stating the following details in respect of all parties about whom they are seeking information:

(a)   full name including all middle names;
(b)   nationality;
(c)   full date of birth; and
(d)   any known Home Office reference number.

(3)   The request or order should state the time by which the information is required, where possible allowing a reasonable period for the Home Office to investigate and prepare its statement to the court.

(4)   The request or order should identify the questions it wishes to be answered by the Home Office.

(5)   The request or order should be forwarded to the Family Division Lawyer together with such information as is sufficient to enable the President's Office and the Home Office to understand the nature of the case, to identify whether the case involves an adoption, and whether the immigration issues raised might relate to an asylum or non-asylum application.

(6)   The Family Division Lawyer will then send to an appropriate enquiries officer in the Home Office the enquiry, together with a copy of any request or order made. The Home Office official will be personally responsible for either:

(a)   answering the query herself, by retrieving the file and preparing a statement for the court; or
(b)   if the request is for more than mere information (eg, requiring speculation as to the possible effect of an order or the likelihood of a party being granted special leave to remain), by either obtaining information from, or passing the court's order to, the relevant official with carriage of that particular file.

(7)   The Family Division Lawyer will follow up as required in order to ensure that the information is received by the court in time, and will receive the statement before forwarding it on as instructed by the judge or court making the request.

UK–PAKISTON PROTOCOL

[The text of this bilateral agreement is set out at **23.6.***]*

APPENDIX 4

PRECEDENTS FOR ENGLAND AND WALES

Originating Summons

No

[In Proposed Proceedings]

IN THE HIGH COURT OF JUSTICE

FAMILY DIVISION

PRINCIPAL REGISTRY

IN THE MATTER OF [*name*] (a Child)

AND IN THE MATTER OF THE CHILD ABDUCTION AND CUSTODY ACT 1985

[AND IN THE MATTER OF THE INHERENT JURISDICTION OF THE HIGH COURT WITH RESPECT TO CHILDREN]

B E T W E E N

[*name*]

[Proposed] Plaintiff [Father/Mother]

and

[*name*]

[Proposed] Defendant [Father/Mother]

LET THE DEFENDANT [*name*] attend before a Judge of the Family Division sitting at the Royal Courts of Justice, Strand, London WC2A 2LL on [*day*], [*date*] at [*time*] on the hearing of an application by the Plaintiff [*name*] of [*address*] for orders:

(1) that the child [*name*] ('the child') do return to [*requesting state*] forthwith;

(2) giving directions for the:

    (i) protection of the child's welfare;

    (ii) prevention of changes in the child's circumstances relevant to the determination of the application;

    (iii) [proposed] plaintiff to have access to the child pending the determination of the application and

    (iv) the enforcement of the order at (1) above;

(3) making provision for the costs of and incidental to this application incurred by or on behalf of the plaintiff including the costs of locating and returning the child.

Further particulars of this application are that:

A the plaintiff is a national of [*state of nationality*] and is the [father/mother] of the child; the defendant is the [mother/father] of the child and is a national of [*state of nationality*]. The plaintiff is married to the defendant and has rights of custody in respect of the child for the purposes of Articles 3 and 5 of the 1980 Hague Convention on the Civil Aspects of International Child Abduction by virtue of the provisions of [*eg 'ss 61B, 61C and 111B(4)(a) of the Family Law Act 1975 of Australia'*];

B the child was born on [*date*]. [He/she] is a national of [*state of nationality*] and is habitually resident in [*requesting state*]. There are no proceedings in progress in relation to the child in any jurisdiction and no orders have been made in respect of [him/her];

C on [*date*] the defendant wrongfully removed the child from [*requesting state*] to England/Wales without the consent of the plaintiff and in breach of [his/her] rights of custody; [on [*date*] the defendant wrongfully retained the child away from [*requesting state*]];

D [the defendant and child are believed to be living at [*address*]/the whereabouts of the defendant and child are not known to the plaintiff]

AND LET THE DEFENDANT within seven days after the service of this summons upon [him/her] counting the day of service return the accompanying Acknowledgement of Service form to the Principal Registry of the Family Division, First Avenue House, High Holborn, London WC1V 6NP

DATED [*date*]

NOTE: This summons may not be served later than four calendar months beginning with the above date unless renewed by order of the court.

This summons was taken out by [*solicitors*] of [*address*], solicitors for the plaintiff whose address for service is [*address, telephone and fax. numbers, e-mail and reference*]

IMPORTANT

Directions for the acknowledgement of service are given with the accompanying form.

If the defendant does not attend personally, or by counsel or solicitors, at the time and place above mentioned above, such judgment may be given, or order made against [him/her] or in relation to [him/her], as the court may think just or expedient

Signed _____

Solicitors for the Plaintiff [*name, address, reference, telephone, fax, e-mail address*]

TO THE DEFENDANT

Location Order [Form 1A]

NOTE THAT SERVICE OF THIS ORDER UPON THE DEFENDANT AND ANY OTHER PERSON IS TO BE EFFECTED ONLY BY THE TIPSTAFF. THE COPY PROVIDED TO THE PLAINTIFF MUST NOT BE USED FOR SERVICE UPON ANY PERSON

No

IN THE HIGH COURT OF JUSTICE
FAMILY DIVISION
PRINCIPAL REGISTRY

BEFORE [MR/MRS] JUSTICE [*NAME*] in Chambers

IN PROCEEDINGS UNDER THE CHILD ABDUCTION AND CUSTODY ACT 1985 RELATING TO [*NAME*] born on [*date*]

AND/OR IN THE EXERCISE OF JURISDICTION UNDER s 19 OF THE SUPREME COURT ACT 1981

BETWEEN

[*name*]

Plaintiff

and

[*name*]

Defendant

UPON HEARING [counsel/the solicitor] for the plaintiff

AND UPON RECEIVING the evidence set out in Schedule A below

AND, at the time of making this order, UPON GIVING directions to the Tipstaff of the High Court of Justice to locate [*name*] (described below as the child) and thereupon, unless he has been notified of a proposed application for a direction that he should not do so, to inform the plaintiff, through solicitors, of the child's whereabouts

AND UPON ACCEPTING the undertaking set out in Schedule B below

THE COURT HEREBY ORDERS THAT:

(1)　[*name*] (described below as the defendant) and/or any other person served with this order must each:

　　(a)　inform the Tipstaff of the whereabouts of the child, if such are known to him or her; and

　　(b)　also in any event inform the Tipstaff of all matters within his or her knowledge or understanding which might reasonably assist him in locating the child.

(2)　The defendant and/or any other person served with this order must each hand over to the Tipstaff (for safe-keeping until the court makes a further order) as many of the following documents as are in his or her possession or control:

　　(a)　every passport relating to the child, including an adult's passport by which the child is also permitted to travel, and every identity card, ticket, travel warrant or other document which would enable the child to leave England and Wales; and

　　(b)　every passport relating to the defendant and every identity card, ticket, travel warrant or other document which would enable the defendant to leave England and Wales.

(3)　The defendant and/or any other person served with this order must not knowingly cause or permit the child:

　　(a)　to be present overnight at any place other than the place where the child was staying at the time of service of this order; or

　　(b)　to be removed from the jurisdiction of England and Wales.

(4)　This order or a faxed copy of it must be personally served upon the defendant and upon any other person whom it is proposed to make liable under it;

PROVIDED THAT, if the defendant or any other person refuses or evades personal service, the court will consider that he or she has been validly served if the effect of the order has been brought to his or her attention.

(5)　The obligations under paragraph (1) above will continue until the Tipstaff locates the child and the obligations under paragraphs (2) and (3) above will continue until the court by further order provides otherwise.

(6)　Permission is given to the defendant and to any other person served with this order to apply immediately to the court for it to be discharged or varied.

Dated [*date*]

SCHEDULE A

The court received the following evidence:

(i)   Affidavit sworn by [*name*] on [*date*]
(ii)   Affidavit sworn by [*name*] on [*date*]
(iii) Oral evidence given by [*name*]

SCHEDULE B

The court accepted the following undertaking:

Of the PLAINTIFF'S SOLICITORS, namely Messrs [*name*] (ref: [*number*], tel: [*number*]) forthwith to inform the Tipstaff in writing in the event that the plaintiff should independently of the Tipstaff discover the whereabouts of the child or that for any other reason there is no further need for the Tipstaff's services herein.

IMPORTANT NOTICE TO THE DEFENDANT
AND TO ANY OTHER PERSON SERVED WITH
THIS ORDER

(1)   LIABILITY TO BE ARRESTED

At the time of making this order the court has directed the Tipstaff to arrest any person whom he has reasonable cause to believe has been served with this order and has disobeyed any part of it. If he arrests you, the Tipstaff must explain to you the ground for your arrest, must bring you before the court as soon as practicable and in any event no later than the working day immediately following your arrest and must detain you until then.

(2)   LIABILITY TO BE COMMITTED TO PRISON

Breach of any part of this order would be a contempt of court punishable by imprisonment or fine. Accordingly, whether or not the Tipstaff arrests you, you may be summoned to attend court and, if you are found to be in breach of the order, you are liable to be committed to prison or fined.

(3)   YOUR RIGHTS

You have the following rights:

(a)   to seek legal advice and, if arrested, to be given the opportunity as soon as practicable to seek legal advice. This right does not entitle you to disobey any part of this order until you have sought legal advice;

(b)   to require the plaintiff's solicitors, namely Messrs [*name*] (ref: [*number*], tel: [*number*]), at their own expense to supply you with a copy of any affidavit and their note of any oral evidence referred to in Schedule A above;

(c)   to apply, whether by counsel or solicitor or in person, to the Judge of the High Court, Family Division, assigned to hear Urgent Applications at the Royal Courts of Justice, Strand, London WC2A 2LL, if practicable after giving notice to the plaintiff's solicitors, for an order discharging or varying any part of this order. This right does not entitle you to disobey any part of this order until your application has been heard;

(d) to apply, whether by counsel or solicitor or in person, to the Judge referred to at (c), if practicable after giving notice to the plaintiff's solicitors, for a direction that the Tipstaff should not inform the plaintiff, through solicitors, of the child's whereabouts. Such a direction will be made only on substantial grounds. Once you have notified him of a proposed application for such a direction, the Tipstaff will not inform the plaintiff's solicitors of the child's whereabouts until your application has been heard; and

(e) if you do not speak or understand English adequately, to have an interpreter present in court at public expense in order to assist you at the hearing of any application relating to this order.

(4) THE TIPSTAFF

The Tipstaff is the enforcement officer of the High Court at the Royal Courts of Justice. He has a deputy and assistants and can authorise police officers to act on his behalf. Any obligation to give information to the Tipstaff or to hand over a document to him includes an obligation to do so to his deputy or assistant or a police officer acting on his behalf.

Please address all communications for the Court to the Principal Registry of the Family Division, Family Proceedings Department, First Avenue House, 42–49 High Holborn, London WC1V 6NP quoting the number in the top right hand corner of this form. The Court Office is open between 10.00 a.m. and 4.30 p.m. on Mondays to Fridays.

Collection Order [Form 2A]

NOTE THAT SERVICE OF THIS ORDER UPON THE DEFENDANT AND ANY OTHER PERSON IS TO BE EFFECTED ONLY BY THE TIPSTAFF. THE COPY PROVIDED TO THE PLAINTIFF MUST NOT BE USED FOR SERVICE UPON ANY PERSON

No

IN THE HIGH COURT OF JUSTICE

FAMILY DIVISION

PRINCIPAL REGISTRY

BEFORE [MR/MRS] JUSTICE [*NAME*] in Chambers

IN PROCEEDINGS UNDER THE CHILD ABDUCTION AND CUSTODY ACT 1985 RELATING TO [*NAME*] born on [*date*]

AND/OR IN THE EXERCISE OF JURISDICTION UNDER s 19 OF THE SUPREME COURT ACT 1981

B E T W E E N

[*name*]

Plaintiff

and

[*name*]

Defendant

UPON HEARING [counsel/the solicitor] for the Plaintiff

AND UPON RECEIVING the evidence set out in Schedule A below

AND UPON ACCEPTING the undertakings set out in Schedule B below

AND, at the time of making this order, UPON GIVING directions to the Tipstaff of the High Court of Justice to take charge of [*name*] (described below as the child) and thereupon to place the child into the care of the plaintiff

THE COURT HEREBY ORDERS THAT:

(1)   The child must be placed into the care of the plaintiff on a temporary basis, namely until a further hearing of the court which must take place within three clear working days after the plaintiff's care of the child begins.

(2)   If [*name*] (described below as the defendant) and/or any other person served with this order is in a position to do so, he or she must each deliver the child into the charge of the Tipstaff.

(3)   If the defendant or any other person served with this order is not in a position to deliver the child into the charge of the Tipstaff, he or she must each:

   (a)   inform the Tipstaff of the whereabouts of the child, if such are known to him or her; and
   (b)   also in any event inform the Tipstaff of all matters within his or her knowledge or understanding which might reasonably assist him in locating the child.

(4)   The defendant and/or any other person served with this order must each hand over to the Tipstaff (for safe-keeping until the court makes a further order) as many of the following documents as are in his or her possession or control:

   (a)   every passport relating to the child, including an adult's passport by which the child is also permitted to travel, and every identity card, ticket, travel warrant or other document which would enable the child to leave England and Wales; and
   (b)   every passport relating to the defendant and every identity card, ticket, travel warrant or other document which would enable the defendant to leave England and Wales.

(5)   This order or a faxed copy of it must be personally served upon the defendant and upon any other person whom it is proposed to make liable under it;

PROVIDED THAT, if the defendant or any other person refuses or evades personal service, the court will consider that he or she has been validly served if the effect of the order has been brought to his or her attention.

(5)   The obligations under paragraphs (2) and (3) above will continue until the Tipstaff locates the child and the obligations under paragraph (4) above will continue until the court by further order provides otherwise.

(6)   Permission is given to the defendant and to any other person served with this order to apply immediately to the court for it to be discharged or varied.

Dated [*date*]

SCHEDULE A

The court received the following evidence:

(i)   Affidavit sworn by [*name*] on [*date*]
(ii)   Affidavit sworn by [*name*] on [*date*]
(iii)   Oral evidence given by [*name*]

SCHEDULE B

The court accepted the following undertakings:

(i)   Of the PLAINTIFF that, once the child has been placed into his or her care, he or she will not remove the child from England and Wales nor cause or permit the child to stay overnight at other than [*address*] until the conclusion of the further hearing directed in paragraph (1) of this order; and

(ii)   Of the PLAINTIFF'S SOLICITORS, namely Messrs [*name*] (ref: [*number*], tel: [*number*])

    (a)   that, as soon as they become aware that the child has been placed into the plaintiff's care, they will apply for the fixing of the date, time and place of the further hearing and will take all reasonable steps to communicate them to the defendant

    (b)   that they will forthwith inform the Tipstaff in writing in the event that the plaintiff should independently of the Tipstaff receive the child into his care or that for any other reason there is no further need for the Tipstaff's services herein.

IMPORTANT NOTICE TO THE DEFENDANT
AND TO ANY OTHER PERSON SERVED WITH
THIS ORDER

(1)   LIABILITY TO BE ARRESTED

At the time of making this order the court has directed the Tipstaff to arrest any person whom he has reasonable cause to believe has been served with this order and has disobeyed any part of it. If he arrests you, the Tipstaff must explain to you the ground for your arrest, must bring you before the court as soon as practicable and in any event no later than the working day immediately following your arrest and must detain you until then.

(2)   LIABILITY TO BE COMMITTED TO PRISON

Breach of any part of this order would be a contempt of court punishable by imprisonment or fine. Accordingly, whether or not the Tipstaff arrests you, you may be summoned to attend court and, if you are found to be in breach of the order, you are liable to be committed to prison or fined.

(3)   YOUR RIGHTS

You have the following rights:

(a)   to seek legal advice and, if arrested, to be given the opportunity as soon as practicable to seek legal advice. This right does not entitle you to disobey any part of this order until you have sought legal advice;

(b)   to require the plaintiff's solicitors, named at Schedule B above, at their own expense to supply you with a copy of any affidavit and their note of any oral evidence referred to in Schedule A above;

(c) even prior to the date of the further hearing directed in paragraph (1) of this order, to apply, whether by counsel or solicitor or in person, to the Judge of the High Court, Family Division, assigned to hear Urgent Applications at the Royal Courts of Justice, Strand, London WC2A 2LL, if practicable after giving notice to the plaintiff's solicitors, for an order discharging or varying any part of this order. This right does not entitle you to disobey any part of this order until your application has been heard; and

(d) if you do not speak or understand English adequately, to have an interpreter present in court at public expense in order to assist you at the hearing of any application relating to this order.

(4) THE TIPSTAFF

The Tipstaff is the enforcement officer of the High Court at the Royal Courts of Justice. He has a deputy and assistants and can authorise police officers to act on his behalf. Any obligation to give information to the tipstaff or to hand over a document to him includes an obligation to do so to his deputy or assistant or a police officer acting on his behalf.

Please address all communications for the Court to the Principal Registry of the Family Division, Family Proceedings Department, First Avenue House, 42-49 High Holborn, London WC1V 6NP quoting the number in the top right hand corner of this form. The Court Office is open between 10.00 a.m. and 4.30 p.m. on Mondays to Fridays.

Passport Order [Form 3A]

NOTE THAT SERVICE OF THIS ORDER UPON THE DEFENDANT AND ANY OTHER PERSON IS TO EFFECTED ONLY BY THE TIPSTAFF. THE COPY PROVIDED TO THE PLAINTIFF MUST NOT BE USED FOR SERVICE UPON ANY PERSON

No

IN THE HIGH COURT OF JUSTICE

FAMILY DIVISION

PRINCIPAL REGISTRY

BEFORE [MR/MRS] JUSTICE [*NAME*] in Chambers

IN PROCEEDINGS UNDER THE CHILD ABDUCTION AND CUSTODY ACT 1985 RELATING TO [*NAME*] born on [*date*]

AND/OR IN THE EXERCISE OF JURISDICTION UNDER s 19 OF THE SUPREME COURT ACT 1981

B E T W E E N

[*name*]

Plaintiff

and

[*name*]

Defendant

UPON HEARING [counsel/the solicitor] for the Plaintiff

AND UPON RECEIVING the evidence set out in Schedule A below

AND, at the time of making this order, UPON GIVING directions to the Tipstaff of the High Court of Justice to obtain and, until further direction of the court, to keep safely the documents referred to in paragraph (1) of this order

THE COURT HEREBY ORDERS THAT:

(1) [*name*] (described below as the Defendant) and/or any other person served with this order must each hand over to the Tipstaff (for safe-keeping until the court

makes a further order) as many of the following documents as are in his or her possession or control:-

(a) every passport relating to [*name[s]*] (described below as the [child/children]), including an adult's passport by which the [child is/children are] also permitted to travel, and every identity card, ticket, travel warrant or other document which would enable the [child/children] to leave England and Wales; and

(b) every passport relating to the Defendant and every identity card, ticket, travel warrant or other document which would enable the Defendant to leave England and Wales.

(2) The Defendant and/or any other person served with this order must not knowingly cause or permit:

(a) the place at which the [child resides/children reside] within England and Wales to be changed, and

(b) the [child/children] to be removed from the jurisdiction of England and Wales.

(3) This order or a faxed copy of it must be personally served upon the Defendant and upon any other person whom it is proposed to make liable under it;

PROVIDED THAT, if the Defendant or any other person refuses or evades personal service, the court will consider that he or she has been validly served if the effect of the order has been brought to his or her attention.

(4) The obligations under paragraph (1) and (2) above will continue until the court by further order provides otherwise.

(5) Permission is given to the Defendant and to any other person served with this order to apply immediately to the court for it to be discharged or varied.

Dated [*date*]

SCHEDULE A

The court received the following evidence:

(i) Affidavit sworn by [*name*] on [*date*]
(ii) Affidavit sworn by [*name*] on [*date*]
(iii) Oral evidence given by [*name*]

IMPORTANT NOTICE TO THE DEFENDANT
AND TO ANY OTHER PERSON SERVED WITH
THIS ORDER

(1) LIABILITY TO BE ARRESTED

At the time of making this order the court has directed the tipstaff to arrest any person whom he has reasonable cause to believe has been served with this order and has disobeyed any part of it. If he arrests you, the tipstaff must explain to you the ground for your arrest, must bring you before the court as soon as practicable and in any event no later than the working day immediately following your arrest and must detain you until then.

(2) LIABILITY TO BE COMMITTED TO PRISON

Breach of any part of this order would be a contempt of court punishable by imprisonment or fine. Accordingly, whether or not the Tipstaff arrests you, you may be summoned to attend court and, if you are found to be in breach of the order, you are liable to be committed to prison or fined.

(3) YOUR RIGHTS

You have the following rights:

(a) to seek legal advice and, if arrested, to be given the opportunity as soon as practicable to seek legal advice. This right does not entitle you to disobey any part of this order until you have sought legal advice;

(b) to require the Plaintiff's solicitors, namely Messrs [*name*], (ref: [*number*], tel: [*number*]), at their own expense to supply you with a copy of any affidavit and their note of any oral evidence referred to in Schedule A above;

(c) to apply, whether by counsel or solicitor or in person, to the Judge of the High Court, Family Division, assigned to hear Urgent Applications at the Royal Courts of Justice, Strand, London WC2A 2LL, if practicable after giving notice to the Plaintiff's solicitors, for an order discharging or varying any part of this order. This right does not entitle you to disobey any part of this order until your application has been heard;

(d) to apply, whether by counsel or solicitor or in person, to the Judge referred to at (c), if practicable after giving notice to the Plaintiff's solicitors, for a direction that the Tipstaff should not inform the Plaintiff, through solicitors, of the child's whereabouts. Such a direction will be made only on substantial grounds. Once you have notified him of a proposed application for such a direction, the Tipstaff will not inform the Plaintiff's solicitors of the child's whereabouts until your application has been heard; and

(e) if you do not speak or understand English adequately, to have an interpreter present in court at public expense in order to assist you at the hearing of any application relating to this order.

(4)   THE TIPSTAFF

The Tipstaff is the enforcement officer of the High Court at the Royal Courts of Justice. He has a deputy and assistants and can authorise police officers to act on his behalf. Any obligation to give information to the Tipstaff or to hand over a document to him includes an obligation to do so to his deputy or assistant or a police officer acting on his behalf.

Please address all communications for the Court to the Principal Registry of the Family Division, Family Proceedings Department, First Avenue House, 42-49 High Holborn, London WC1V 6NP quoting the number in the top right hand corner of this form. The Court Office is open between 10.00 a.m. and 4.30 p.m. on Mondays to Fridays.

Port Alert Notice [Form 4B]

No

IN THE HIGH COURT OF JUSTICE

FAMILY DIVISION

PRINCIPAL REGISTRY

BEFORE [MR/MRS] JUSTICE [*NAME*] in Chambers

IN THE MATTER OF

B E T W E E N

[*name*]

Petitioner/Applicant/Plaintiff

and

[*name*]

Respondent/Defendant

NOTICE

(1)   Documents such as passports and tickets have just been or are about to be taken from you.

(2)   They have been or are about to be taken from you by or on behalf of the Tipstaff, who is the enforcement officer of the High Court at the Royal Courts of Justice, Strand, London WC2. He has a deputy and assistants and can authorise police officers to act on his behalf. He has an office at the Royal Courts of Justice and his telephone number is 0207 947 6200.

(3)   The court has directed the Tipstaff to take all such documents from any person who has charge of them if he has reasonable cause to believe that a child or children would otherwise be removed from England and Wales in breach of a court order.

(4)   It is under that direction that the documents have just been or are about to be taken from you.

(5)   The Tipstaff must keep the documents safely until the court makes a direction about what should happen to them.

(6)   You can apply to the court for a direction about what should happen to the documents. You should tell the Tipstaff that you wish to make the application and he will then advise you at what time and to which court you can make it and may also suggest whom you should notify in advance of it. Or you can take legal advice about what to do.

[COURT SEAL]

Please address all communications for the Court to the Principal Registry of the Family Division, Family Proceedings Department, First Avenue House, 42-49 High Holborn, London WC1V 6NP quoting the number in the top right hand corner of this form. The Court Office is open between 10.00 a.m. and 4.30 p.m. on Mondays to Fridays.

Tipstaff's Form

TIPSTAFF'S OFFICE

INFORMATION TO BE GIVEN WHEN REQUESTING EITHER A LOCATION, COLLECTION OR SEIZURE OF PASSPORTS ORDER

CHILD ONE		ADDITIONAL CHILDREN	
SURNAME			
FORENAME			
DATE OF BIRTH			
AGE AND SEX			
HEIGHT AND BUILD			
HAIR COLOUR			
COLOUR OF EYES			
SKIN COLOUR			
SPECIAL FEATURES			
NATIONALITY			

ADDRESS WHERE CHILD/REN WAS/WERE LAST SEEN, DATE AND CIRCUMSTANCES

DETAILS OF PERSON WHO CHILD IS BELIEVED TO BE WITH	ANY RISK OF VIOLENCE KNOWN
NAME	
RELATIONSHIP TO CHILD	
DATE OF BIRTH AND AGE	
HAIR	
EYES	
HEIGHT AND BUILD	
SKIN COLOUR AND NATIONALITY	
SPECIAL FEATURES	

SOLICITORS' DETAILS	
NAME AND ADDRESS OF SOLICITORS	
NAME OF SOLICITOR	
REFERENCE	
OFFICE TELEPHONE NUMBER	
OUT OF HOURS NUMBER *	
E-MAIL ADDRESS	

* IF MOBILE NUMBERS ARE GIVEN YOU MUST ENSURE THAT THESE ARE SWITCHED ON AT ALL TIMES.

IF YOU SUPPLY AN E-MAIL ADDRESS WE WILL CONTACT YOU BY
BOTH PHONE AND E-MAIL

NAME AND ADDRESS OF WHERE CHILD IS TO BE TAKEN WHEN FOUND

ALL POSSIBLE ADDRESSES WHERE CHILD COULD BE OR ANY FRIENDS OR RELATIVES WHO MAY HAVE INFORMATION.	
1)	2)
3)	4)
5)	6)

IS A PORT ALERT REQUIRED?	
YES	NO

If port stop is requested, please state Town, City or Port of destination, if known

INFORMATION SHEET 2

ADDITIONAL CHILD		ADDITIONAL CHILD	
SURNAME			
FORENAME			
DATE OF BIRTH			
AGE AND SEX			
HEIGHT			
HAIR COLOUR			
BUILD			
EYES			
SPECIAL FEATURES			
NATIONALITY			

ANY OTHER INFORMATION

Associate's Form

This form **must** be completed before any application for a location/collection order and returned to the Associate BEFORE the hearing commences,

BLOCK CAPITALS ONLY

NUMBER OF CASE:

CHILD(REN) DETAILS

NAME(S):   DOB:

PARTIES' DETAILS

BETWEEN   PLAINTIFF

AND   DEFENDANT

SOLICITORS' DETAILS

NAME: REF:

ADDRESS: TEL:

EVIDENCE

AFFIDAVIT OF: DATED:

AFFIDAVIT OF: DATED:

AFFIDAVIT OF: DATED:

ORAL EVIDENCE OF:

ADDRESS WHERE CHILD(REN) IS/ARE TO REMAIN
(*COLLECTION ORDERS ONLY*)

First (ex parte) Order

TO [*name of defendant*]

TAKE NOTICE that if you disobey this order you may be held to be in contempt of court and liable to be committed to prison or fined

No

[In Proposed Proceedings]

IN THE HIGH COURT OF JUSTICE

FAMILY DIVISION

PRINCIPAL REGISTRY

BEFORE THE HONOURABLE [MR/MRS] JUSTICE [*NAME*] [Knight/DBE] sitting in private at the Royal Courts of Justice, Strand, London WC2A 2LL

IN THE MATTER OF [*name of child*] (a Child)

AND IN THE MATTER OF THE CHILD ABDUCTION AND CUSTODY ACT 1985

[AND IN THE MATTER OF THE INHERENT JURISDICTION OF THE HIGH COURT WITH RESPECT TO CHILDREN]

B E T W E E N

[*name*]

[Proposed] Plaintiff [Father/Mother]

and

[*name*]

[Proposed] Defendant [Father/Mother]

UPON HEARING counsel for the [father/mother], the [father/mother] being neither present nor represented

AND UPON READING the affidavit of [*name*], solicitor for the [father/mother], sworn on [*date*]

[AND UPON the undertaking of the solicitors for the [father/mother] to issue the originating summons handed into court by 4.00 pm today]

[AND FURTHER TO the [passport/location] order made today]

IT IS ORDERED THAT:

(1)   this matter be restored before the Applications Judge of the Family Division sitting at the Royal Courts of Justice, Strand, London WC2A 2LL at 10.30 am on the second weekday following the date on which this order is served on the [father/mother], and in any event the matter be listed for directions on [*date*], time estimate ½ hour;

(2)   the [father/mother] shall attend the hearing provided for in paragraph (1) of this order in person as well as, if so advised, by counsel and solicitors;

(3)   and an injunction is hereby granted until further order restraining the [father/mother] either by [himself/herself] or through anyone else from:

    (i)   applying for travel documents (including passports) in respect of the child;

[*if no passport or location order has been made, but injunctions restricting the child's movement are required:*

    (ii)   causing or permitting the child to be ordinarily resident at an address other than [*address*]
    (iii)   removing the children from England and Wales;]

[*if no passport or location order has been made, but passports need to be secured:*

(4)   the [father/mother] shall within 24 hours of being served with this order deposit [his/her] passport and the passport of the child with [his/her] solicitor who shall notify the [father's/mother's] solicitors of their having received them; failing such deposit the [father/mother] shall bring [his/her] passport and the passport of the child to the hearing provided for in paragraph (1)of this order;]

(5)   the [father/mother] has permission to apply on two hours' notice in working hours to the [father/mother] by [his/her] solicitors [*name, address, telephone and fax. number, e-mail address and reference*];

(6)   in this order:

    'the mother' means the [plaintiff/defendant], [*name*], the mother of the children;
    'the father' means the [plaintiff/defendant], [*name*], the father of the children;
    'the child' means [*name and date of birth*];

(7)   costs reserved.

DATED [*date*]

Agencies Order

No

[In Proposed Proceedings]

IN THE HIGH COURT OF JUSTICE
FAMILY DIVISION
PRINCIPAL REGISTRY

BEFORE THE HONOURABLE [MR/MRS] JUSTICE [*NAME*] [Knight/DBE] sitting in private at the Royal Courts of Justice, Strand, London WC2A 2LL

IN THE MATTER OF [*name of child*] (a Child)

AND IN THE MATTER OF THE CHILD ABDUCTION AND CUSTODY ACT 1985

[AND IN THE MATTER OF THE INHERENT JURISDICTION OF THE HIGH COURT WITH RESPECT TO CHILDREN]

B E T W E E N

[*name*]

[Proposed] Plaintiff [Father/Mother]

and

[*name*]

[Proposed] Defendant [Father/Mother]

UPON HEARING counsel for the [father/mother], the [father/mother] being neither present nor represented

AND UPON READING the affidavit of [*name*], solicitor for the [father/mother], sworn on [*date*]

[AND UPON the undertaking of the solicitors for the [father/mother] to issue the originating summons handed into court by 4.00 pm today]

[AND FURTHER TO the location order made [today/on [*date*]]]

IT IS ORDERED THAT:

(1)   the [Department of Works and Pensions/Driver and Vehicle Licensing Agency/Home Office Immigration and Nationality Department/Office of National Statistics] do forthwith provide to [the [mother's/father's] solicitors/the Tipstaff] all information within their possession, custody or control relating to the whereabouts of:

    (a)   the child;
    (b)   the [father/mother];
    (c)   [*other parties, as appropriate*];

(2)   the [Department of Works and Pensions/Driver and Vehicle Licensing Agency/Home Office Immigration and Nationality Department/Office of National Statistics] is forbidden from disclosing to the [father/mother] or to any other person named in this order the existence and terms of this order without the leave of the court;

[(3)   the [father's/mother's] solicitors are forbidden to disclose to the [father/mother] any information passed to them pursuant to this order without the leave of the court;]

(4)   in this order:

'the mother' means the [plaintiff/defendant], [*name*], the mother of the child;
'the father' means the [plaintiff/defendant], [*name*], the father of the child;
'the child' means [*name and date of birth*];
'the [father's/mother's] solicitors' means [*name, address, telephone and fax number, e-mail address and reference*];

(5)   costs reserved.

DATED [*date*]

Second (inter partes) Order

No

IN THE HIGH COURT OF JUSTICE

FAMILY DIVISION

PRINCIPAL REGISTRY

BEFORE THE HONOURABLE [MR/MRS] JUSTICE [*NAME*] [Knight/DBE] sitting in private at the Royal Courts of Justice, Strand, London WC2A 2LL

IN THE MATTER OF [*name of child*] (a Child)

AND IN THE MATTER OF THE CHILD ABDUCTION AND CUSTODY ACT 1985

[AND IN THE MATTER OF THE INHERENT JURISDICTION OF THE HIGH COURT WITH RESPECT TO CHILDREN]

B E T W E E N

[*name*]

Plaintiff [Father/Mother]

and

[*name*]

Defendant [Father/Mother]

UPON HEARING counsel for the [father/mother] and counsel for the [mother/father]

IT IS ORDERED THAT

(1) the [father/mother] is to file and serve a statement of defence by 4.00 pm on [*date*] and [his/her] affidavit evidence by 4.00 pm on [*date*];

(2) the [father/mother] is to file any evidence on which [he/she] intends to rely on at the final hearing by 4.00 pm on [*date*];

(3) this matter is adjourned to [*date not more than 21 days ahead*], but on the confirmation of both parties' solicitors to the Clerk of the Rules not to be listed or heard, but further adjourned without attendance of either party to be listed for final hearing on [*date*] at 10.30 am with a time estimate of one day (at risk);

(4)   the injunctions in paragraph (2) of the [passport/location order] herein dated [*date*] are discharged; and

(5)   an injunction is hereby granted until further order restraining the [father/mother] either by [himself/herself] or through anyone else from:

    (i)   causing or permitting the child to be ordinarily resident at an address other than [*address*];

    (ii)   removing the child from England and Wales;

    (iii)   applying for travel documents (including passports) in respect of the child;

(6)   in this order:

'the mother' means the [plaintiff/defendant], [*name*], the mother of the child;
'the father' means the [plaintiff/defendant], [*name*], the father of the child;
'the child' means [*name and date of birth*];

(7)   costs reserved.

DATED [*date*]

Final Order with Undertakings[1]

TO [parties]

TAKE NOTICE that if you disobey this order (which includes the undertakings or stipulations that you have given to the Court) you may be in contempt of Court and liable to be fined or imprisoned

No

IN THE HIGH COURT OF JUSTICE

FAMILY DIVISION

PRINCIPAL REGISTRY

BEFORE THE HONOURABLE [MR/MRS] JUSTICE [*NAME*] [Knight/DBE] sitting in private at the Royal Courts of Justice, Strand, London WC2A 2LL

IN THE MATTER OF [*NAME*] (a Child)

AND IN THE MATTER OF THE HAGUE CONVENTION ON THE CIVIL ASPECTS OF INTERNATIONAL CHILD ABDUCTION

AND IN THE MATTER OF CHILD ABDUCTION AND CUSTODY ACT 1985

B E T W E E N

[*name*]

Plaintiff [Father]

and

[*name*]

Defendant [Mother]

UPON HEARING counsel for the Father, and counsel for the Mother

AND UPON READING the documents filed herein

AND UPON THE FATHER UNDERTAKING that he will cause either this order or an order in like terms (including the undertakings or stipulations set out in the First and Second Schedules hereto) to be registered or made in the Circuit Court of [*name*]

---

[1] For ease of drafting, this precedent has been set out on the assumption that the father is the plaintiff and the mother the defendant.

such that it becomes an enforceable order of that court AND that upon the arrival of the mother and the child in the State of [*name*] in the United States of America she will carry out the obligations set out in the First Schedule to this order

AND UPON THE MOTHER UNDERTAKING that she will make the Child available for visitation by the Father in the terms set out in the Second Schedule to this order and will comply with the other provisions thereof

AND IN SUPPORT OF the obligation and power conferred on this Court under Articles 12 and 18 of the 1980 Hague Convention on the Civil Aspects of International Child Abduction ('the Convention') this Court accepts the undertakings or stipulations given to this Court by the Mother and the Father set out above and in the First and Second Schedules attached hereto and being part of this order, such undertakings or stipulations constituting binding and enforceable obligations and in consequence of such undertakings or stipulations ORDERS THAT

(1)	within seven days of the mother or her solicitors receiving a copy of the order of the Circuit Court of [*name*] incorporating this order or an order in like terms, the child shall return to the United States of America (and shall do so with the mother, unless she refuses to accompany [him/her]);

(2)	that a transcript of the judgment delivered herein today be prepared urgently at public expense and copies thereof and of this order be made available to each party by their solicitors and to the Lord Chancellor's Child Abduction Unit, being the Central Authority for England and Wales, the Office of Children's Issues, being the Central Authority for the United States of America and the Circuit Court of [*name*];

(3)	that there be leave to both the mother and the father to disclose this order, the transcript of the judgment aforesaid and any other papers filed herein to their legal advisers and any court of competent jurisdiction seised of proceedings relating to the custody of the child or criminal proceedings relating to the removal of the child from the United States of America by the mother;

(4)	that the passports of the mother and of the child be released forthwith to the mother's solicitors, [*name*], to be held by them to the order of the court and to be handed to the mother in pursuance of paragraph (1) of this order at the airport of departure immediately prior to her embarkation on the date of the child's return to the United States of America. In the event of the mother refusing to accompany the child on [his/her] return to the United States of America, the mother's solicitors shall hand the child's passport to the adult responsible for accompanying the child to the United States of America and shall thereafter within forty-eight hours deliver the mother's passport to the court;

[(5)	that there be leave for the judgment delivered herein today in chambers to be reported provided that all reasonable steps are taken to preserve the anonymity of the child in any such report;]

(6)	that there be no order for costs, including any costs reserved, save that there be detailed assessment of the publicly funded costs of the mother and father

(7)	in this order:

(a)   'the mother' means [*name*], the [defendant] in these proceedings;
(b)   'the father' means [*name*] the [plaintiff] in these proceedings;
(c)   'the child' means [*name*], born on [*date*]

DATED [*date*]

PREAMBLE TO THE FIRST AND SECOND SCHEDULES

The undertakings or stipulations (which terms shall be used interchangeably) set forth in the First and Second Schedules below have been accepted by the Court to achieve the objects of Article 12 of the Convention and for the limited purpose of returning the child to the United States of America and securing [his/her] welfare until such time as the courts of the United States of America shall exercise jurisdiction over [him/her] AND HAVE BEEN OFFERED by the mother and father having both been advised by solicitors and counsel about their nature and effect and being fully aware of their binding and enforceable nature both in England and Wales and the courts of the United States of America. The undertakings or stipulations shall have effect until such time as the Circuit Court of [*name*] or some other court of competent jurisdiction in the United States of America shall exercise jurisdiction over the child and in any event for a period of not less than twenty-eight days from the date of the child's arrival in the United States of America. Nothing in the undertakings or stipulations set forth in this order shall be construed as usurping the jurisdiction of the courts of the United States of America.

THE FIRST SCHEDULE

[*Insert plaintiff's undertakings or stipulations, eg*

The father undertakes or stipulates that:

(i)   he will support any application on the part of the mother for a visa enabling her to enter and remain in the United States of America;

(ii) he will provide one-way air tickets for the mother and the child to return to the United States of America;

(iii) he will inform the appropriate authorities concerned with the prosecution of the mother under the terms of the indictment handed down by the Grand Jury in the United States District Court, on [*date*] that, the child having returned safely to the protection of the Circuit Court of [*name*], which shall now exercise jurisdiction over them, the criminal proceedings have served their purpose, and that if as the child's father he has a voice in the continuation of those proceedings he asks that they be discontinued, or if not discontinued, that the mother should be treated as leniently as possible, both before and after the trial. In particular, he will ask that the conditions of the Mother's release before trial as suggested in the letter of the Assistant US Attorney of [*date*] should be implemented;

(iv) he will not enforce the custody order made by the Circuit Court of [*name*] on [*date*] until either that court or another court of competent jurisdiction deals with the issue of the child's custody inter partes, such hearing not to take place before the expiration of twenty-eight days from the date of the child's arrival in the United States of America;

(v)   pending such a hearing he will not seek to remove the child from the care of the mother except for periods of visitation as hereinafter defined;

(vi)   he will provide accommodation, which he will not occupy, for the exclusive use of the mother and the child AND provide for the reasonable cost of the accommodation, services and medical insurance for the mother and the child and also pay her maintenance at the rate of not less than $200 (two hundred dollars) a week;

(vii)   he will not with a view to any media publicity discuss with any person any legal proceedings relating to the removal or retention of the child from or away from the United States of America by the mother or permit photographs of the child to be taken for the purposes any publicity relating to those proceedings.]

THE SECOND SCHEDULE

[Insert defendant's undertakings or stipulations, eg

The mother undertakes or stipulates that:

(i)   she will make the child available for visitation by the father for two hours a day in the first week after their arrival in the United States of America, and for the second week and thereafter for a period of four hours a day for six days of each week; in addition, she will make the child available for visitation by the father for the days [*specify dates*] inclusive for the purposes of visiting his parents if such a visit be feasible;

(ii)   she will not with a view to any media publicity discuss with any person any legal proceedings relating to her removal or retention of the child from or away from the United States of America or permit photographs of the child to be taken for the purposes any publicity relating to those proceedings;

(iii)   she will not remove the child from the jurisdiction of England and Wales save in accordance with the terms of this order.]

Signed   _____
        Father

Solicitors for the Father

Signed _____
         Mother

Solicitors for the Mother

DATED [date]

Article 21 Application

[In Form C1, insert:]

Pursuant to my application under Article 21 of the Hague Convention on the Civil Aspects of International Child Abduction made to *[Central Authority]* on *[date]* I apply for contact to my children in the terms of the order made on *[date]* by *[court]* a copy of which is annexed to this application.

INDEX

References are to paragraph numbers.